Lecture Notes in Computer Science 2519

Edited by G. Goos, J. Hartmanis, and J. van Leeuwen

Springer-Verlag Berlin Heidelberg GmbH

Series Editors

Gerhard Goos, Karlsruhe University, Germany
Juris Hartmanis, Cornell University, NY, USA
Jan van Leeuwen, Utrecht University, The Netherlands

Volume Editors

Robert Meersman
DOA Institute
p/a Leeuwlantstraat 83, 2100 Antwerp, Belgium
E-mail: Robert.Meersman@vub.ac.be

Zahir Tari
RMIT University
School of Computer Science and IT
GPO Box 2476V, VIC 3001, Melbourne, Australia
E-mail: zahirt@cs.rmit.edu.au

Cataloging-in-Publication Data applied for

Bibliographic information published by Die Deutsche Bibliothek
Die Deutsche Bibliothek lists this publication in the Deutsche Nationalbibliografie;
detailed bibliographic data is available in the Internet at http://dnb.ddb.de

CR Subject Classification (1998): H.2, C.2, H.3, H.4, H.5, I.2, D.2.12, K.4

ISBN 978-3-540-00106-5   ISBN 978-3-540-36124-4 (eBook)
DOI 10.1007/978-3-540-36124-4

http://www.springer.de

© Springer-Verlag Berlin Heidelberg 2002
Originally published by Springer-Verlag Berlin Heidelberg New York in 2002.

Typesetting: Camera-ready by author, data conversion by PTP Berlin, Stefan Sossna
Printed on acid-free paper   SPIN 10871047   06/3142   5 4 3 2 1 0

Robert Meersman
Zahir Tari et al. (Eds.)

On the Move to Meaningful Internet Systems 2002: CoopIS, DOA, and ODBASE

Confederated International Conferences
CoopIS, DOA, and ODBASE 2002
Proceedings

 Springer

Volume Editors

Robert Meersman
Zahir Tari

CoopIS 2002

Stefano Spaccapietra
Calton Pu

DOA 2002

Rachid Guerraoui
Joe Loyall
Douglas C. Schmidt

ODBASE 2002

Karl Aberer
Ling Liu

Message from General Co-chairs

As large, complex and networked yet intelligent information systems become the focus and norm for computing, software issues covering a wide range of issues such as data and web semantics, distributed objects, web services, databases, workflow, cooperation, ubiquity, interoperability, and mobility for the development of internet- and intranet-based systems in organizations and for e-business need to be addressed in a fundamental way. This federated conference event is unique in that it provides an opportunity for researchers and practitioners to understand these recent developments within their respective as well as broader contexts. It colocated for the first time three related, complementary and successful conferences: DOA, covering infrastructure-enabling technologies, distributed objects, Internet computing, protocols, etc.; ODBASE, covering web semantics, XML databases, ontologies etc.; and, finally, CoopIS, covering interoperation, workflow systems, knowledge management, etc. Each of these conferences treats its topics along multiple axes of theory (i.e., underlying theoretical solutions), design and development (e.g., technical and conceptual solutions), and applications (e.g., case studies and industrial solutions).

The three conferences share the distributed and ubiquity aspects of modern computing systems, and the resulting application/pull created by the Internet and the so-called "Semantic Web". For DOA 02 the primary emphasis is on the distributed object infrastructure; for ODBASE 02 it is on the knowledge bases and methods required for enabling semantical use; and for CoopIS 02 it is on the interaction of such technologies and methods within an organization or network of organizations. As they must, these subject areas overlap and, in fact, the organizers specifically looked for submissions in any of the areas that also emphasized the envisaged mutual impact among relevant issues. To stimulate this "cross-pollination," a common program of representative keynote speakers, a joint tutorial program, and a common Industry Track that ran parallel to the entire event were assembled.

We received many submissions for the three conferences (293 in total: 111 for CoopIS 02, 106 for DOA 02, and 76 for ODBASE 02). Not only can we claim much success in attracting so many scientific papers, but from this harvest it was possible to compose a high-quality and representative cross-section of research worldwide in the different areas covered by the federated event. Among these submitted papers, indeed only a small number could be selected (i.e., around a 25% acceptance rate). The reviewing process was excellent and each paper was reviewed by at least three experts.

On behalf of the organization committee, we really would like to thank all the people who were directly or indirectly involved in the setup of these federated conferences and therefore made it a success. We must in particular be grateful to our seven PC co-chairs who, together with their many PC members, did an excellent job in selecting the best papers. Of course handling the submission, reviewing, and notification of such a large number of papers today is not possible without suitable software and we need to thank our CyberChair expert, Kwong Lai. We would like to thank especially Ugur Cetintemel, the Publicity Chair, who made this federated event known to a very large public. Finally, our particular thanks go to Jan Demey (who built the registration system) and Daniel Meersman (who is running the conference secretariat).

We do hope that you enjoyed this federated event and that we may see you all again next year in Europe.

August 2002

Robert Meersman
Zahir Tari
Michael Papazoglou

CoopIS 02 PC Co-chairs' Message

Welcome to the Proceedings of the Tenth International Conference on Cooperative Information Systems (CoopIS 02). This year, CoopIS was part of a federated conference in Irvine, California, jointly with the International Symposium on Distributed Objects and Applications (DOA) and the International Conference on Ontologies, Databases, and Applications of Semantics for large-scale Information Systems (ODBASE). The theme of the 2002 Federated Conference was "On the Move to Meaningful Internet Systems and Ubiquitous Computing."

We received a large number of submissions this year and we had to reject many good ones. Of the 111 papers reviewed by the program committee, 30 papers were accepted for presentation and publication. In addition, 12 submissions were accepted as poster papers in the proceedings, with a short presentation at the conference.

We are happy to report that cooperative information systems continues to be a vigorous area of research for our "core" community in databases and related areas. In addition, several "new" areas of interest (new to CoopIS) are emerging. Examples of traditional CoopIS areas of interest include query processing, interoperability, workflow, work process, and business/transactions. There are examples of increasing overlap between cooperative information systems and other areas of research in mobility, agents, data and system quality issues, peer-to-peer, and ubiquitous environments. We believe this successful "broadening" of CoopIS points to the increasing relevance of the research area as well as the corresponding growth of the community.

We would like to acknowledge a number of people who made CoopIS such a growing success. First, we want to thank the authors of all the submitted papers and conference attendees, since they are the representatives of the CoopIS community. Without a vigorous community there cannot be a successful conference. Second, we thank the PC members who reviewed the papers and provided valuable feedback to the authors. Third, we would like to thank the federated conference organizers for the professional management of the electronic paper submission and review process. In particular, we recognize the efforts of Prof. Zahir Tari and Kwong Yuen Lai of RMIT University, Australia.

Thank you and we hope you enjoyed the conference and the papers.

August 2002   Stefano Spaccapietra
                                                                          Calton Pu

DOA 02 PC Co-chairs' Message

Welcome to the Proceedings of the Fourth International Symposium on Distributed Objects and Applications (DOA). There is increasing consensus among IT researchers and practitioners about the importance and potential of distributed object computing (DOC) technologies. It's also clear that there have been significant intellectual and commercial advances in this area in recent years. DOC technologies provide capabilities for use in various application domains, including aerospace, banking, process control, telecommunications, medical systems, and many other domains. They are also now offering practical, real-life production solutions to a host of technical problems, including quality-of-service enforcement and interoperability across different software, hardware, and network platforms. DOC systems are being built according to different paradigms and architectures, such as OMG's CORBA, Sun's J2EE, Microsoft's .Net, and other request broker principles and implementations, and contingent technologies such as Sun's Java-based active objects and messaging services, to provide a basis for building complex distributed applications.

Among the 106 submissions to DOA 2002, 28 papers were selected for inclusion in the technical program of the conference and 24 papers were selected for presentation in an interactive poster session at the conference. Every paper was reviewed by at least three members of the program committee. Each paper was judged according to its technical merit, originality, presentation quality, and relevance to the conference topics. The final program spans the following topics related to DOC technologies:

- Object request broker enhancements
- Web services
- Distributed object scalability and heterogeneity
- Dependability, security, and assurance
- Reflection and reconfiguration
- Mobility
- Real-time scheduling and performance
- Component-based applications

We would like to express our deepest appreciation to the authors of the submitted papers, the program committee members for their diligence in reviewing the submissions, the attendees for their participation, and finally to the members of the organizing committee for their efforts towards making DOA 2002 a successful conference.

August 2002

Rachid Guerraoui
Joe Loyall
Douglas Schmidt

ODBASE 02 PC Co-chairs' Message

Welcome to the First International Conference on Ontologies, Databases, and Applications of Semantics for Large-Scale Information Systems (ODBASE 02). ODBASE conferences present a new forum for addressing semantic issues in large-scale networked information systems, such as internet and intranet systems. ODBASE 02 has a special interest in gathering researchers and practitioners from multiple disciplines (such as web semantics, databases, knowledge management, and ontologies) and exchanging ideas and research results on semantic issues and their roles in ubiquitous computing. As the world heads towards larger-scale repositories of structured, semistructured, and unstructured information, the need to understand, capture, and utilize the semantics of these data is of growing interest. The first ODBASE conference was dedicated towards building more meaningful internet systems.

We were pleased to present a high-quality technical program. Seventy-six papers were submitted to ODBASE this year. The submissions were from more than 10 countries. Of these, only 21 full papers were accepted as the regular research papers. We were fortunate to have 40 program committee members who assisted us by giving very detailed reviews. A key aspect of ODBASE 02 was that we brought the worlds of semantic webs, ontologies, and databases together in a single high-quality forum. In addition to the regular papers, we accepted 4 poster papers where authors were able to give brief descriptions of their research. Finally, we would like to thank Kwong Yuen Lai who did an amazing amount of work in facilitating the online PC meeting, reviews, and technical program development.

August 2002

Karl Aberer
Ling Liu

Organization Committee

CoopIS 02, DOA 02 and ODBASE 02 were organized by RMIT University (School of Computer Science and Information Technology), UCI, Vrije University of Brussels (Department of Computer Science) and the University of California at Irvine (Department of Computer and Electrical Engineering).

Executive Committee

Conference Co-chairs:	Robert Meersman (Vrije University of Brussels, Belgium), Michael Papazoglou (Tilburg University, The Netherlands), and Zahir Tari (RMIT University, Australia)
CoopIS 02 PC Co-chairs:	Calton Pu (Georgia Tech., USA) and Stefano Spaccapietra (EPFL, Switzerland)
DOA 02 PC Co-chairs:	Rachid Guerraoui (EPFL, Switzerland), Joe Loyall (BBN Technologies, USA), and Douglas Schmidt (UCI, USA)
ODBASE 02 PC Co-chairs:	Karl Aberer (EPFL, Switzerland) and Ling Liu (Georgia Tech., USA)
Organizing Chair:	Angelo Corsaro (UCI, USA)
Tutorials:	Vipul Kashyap (NIH, USA)
Publicity Chair:	Ugur Cetintemel (Brown University, USA)

CoopIS 02 Program Committee

D. Abel
C. Batini
K. Becker
M. Bowman
A. Buchmann
O. Bukhres
M.S. Chen
P. Cohen
P. Constantopoulos
U. Dayal
A. Di Leva
A. Doucet
M.C. Fauvet
T. Finin
A. Gal
L. Gong

J.L. Hainaut
A. Hofstede
M. Huhns
R. Hull
Y. Kambayashi
L. Kerschberg
M. Kitsuregawa
D. Kotz
S. Laufmann
D.L. Lee
M. Luck
S. Madnick
T. Masui
D. McLeod
C. Medeiros
J. Mylopolos

C. Neuman
S. Nishio
M. Norrie
M.E. Orlowska
M. Panti
C. Parent
B. Pernici
L. Raschid
T. Risch
M. Rusinkiewicz
F. Saltor
J. Scholtz
T. Starner
W.M.P. van der Aalst
K.Y. Wang
M. Wooldridge

J. Yang
M. Yoshikawa

DOA 02 Program Committee

S. Baker
D.E. Bakken
R. Baldoni
Z. Bellahsene
G. Blair
A. Bloesch
J. Cross
P. Eugster
C. Gokey
A. Gokhale
D. Hagimont
A. Jacobsen
R. Klefstad
J. Kienzle
R. King
B. Krämer
D. Lea
F. Manola
K. Mazouni

T.Y. Meng
P. Narasimhan
F. Pacull
D. Sharp
R. Soley
R. Schantz
E. Shokri
M. van Steen
J.-B. Stefani
G. Thaker
N. Venkatasubramanian
S. Yajnik
S. Vinoski
A. Watson
D. Wells
A. Zomaya
A. Zaslavsky
G. Zhijing

ODBASE 02 Program Committee

C. Bussler
T. Catarci
A. Chen
V. Christophides
T. Critchlow
S. Decker
T. Dillon
J. Euzenat
D. Fensel
A. Gal
J. Geller
D. Georgakopoulos
N. Guarino
K. Karlapalem
V. Kashyap
M. Koubarakis

M. Lenzerini
T.W. Ling
A. Maedche
L. Mark
L. Mazzucchelli
A. Mendelzon
M. Missikoff
J. Mylopoulos
S. Navathe
E. Neuhold
M.E. Orlowska
A. Ouksel
M. Papazoglou
Q. Li
M. Scholl
A. Sheth

K. Siau   T.C. Tang
J. Sowa   H. Weigand
K. Sycara   J. Zeleznikow

Sponsors

Boeing, USA
OntoWeb, The Netherlands
Telecordia Technologies, USA

Table of Contents

COOPIS 2002 FULL PAPERS

Interoperability

Workflow

Mobility

Agents

P2P & Ubiquitous

Work Process

Business & Transactions

Infrastructure

Query Processing

Quality Issues

COOPIS 2002 POSTERS

Agents & Middlewares

DOA 2002 FULL PAPERS

ORB Enhancements

Web Services

Distributed Object Scalability and Heterogeneity

Dependability, Security, Assurance

Reflection and Reconfiguration

Mobility

Real-Time Scheduling and Performance

Component Based Applications

ODBASE 2002 FULL PAPERS

Ontology Languages

Conceptual Modelling and Ontologies

Ontology Management

Ontology Development and Engineering

XML and Data Integration

Tools for Intelligent Web

ODBASE 2002 Posters

Developing Evolutionary Cost Models for Query Optimization in a Dynamic Multidatabase Environment⋆

Amira Rahal[1], Qiang Zhu[1], and Per-Åke Larson[2]

[1] Department of Computer and Information Science
The University of Michigan - Dearborn, MI 48128, USA
{arabi,qzhu}@umich.edu
[2] Microsoft Research
One Microsoft Way, Redmond, WA 98052, USA
palarson@microsoft.com

Abstract. Deriving local cost models for query optimization in a multidatabase system (MDBS) is a challenging issue due to local autonomy. It becomes even more difficult when dynamic environmental factors are taken into consideration. In this paper, we study how to evolve a cost model to capture a slowly-changing dynamic MDBS environment so that the cost model is kept up-to-date all the time. We propose a novel evolutionary technique, called the shifting method, to tackle this issue. The key idea is to adjust a cost model by adding the up-to-date performance information of a new sample query into and, in the meantime, removing the out-of-date information of the oldest sample query from consideration at each step. It is shown that this method is more efficient than the direct re-building approach. The relevant issues including derivation of recurrence update formulas, development of efficient algorithm, analysis of complexities as well as some aspects of implementation are studied. Our theoretical and experimental results demonstrate that the proposed shifting method is quite promising in deriving accurate evolutionary cost models for a slowly-changing dynamic MDBS environment.

1 Introduction

A multidatabase system (MDBS) integrates data from multiple component (local) databases. A major challenge, among others[4,6,7,8,14], for performing global query optimization in an MDBS is that some local information required by global query optimization, such as local cost models, may not be available at the global level. However, the global query optimizer needs such local cost information to decide how to decompose a global query into local queries and where to execute the local queries.

Several techniques to derive cost models for an autonomous local database system (DBS) at the global level in an MDBS have been proposed recently in

---

⋆ Research supported by the US National Science Foundation under Grant # IIS-9811980 and The University of Michigan under OVPR and UMD grants.

R. Meersman, Z. Tari (Eds.): CoopIS/DOA/ODBASE 2002, LNCS 2519, pp. 1–18, 2002.
© Springer-Verlag Berlin Heidelberg 2002

literature. Du *et al.* proposed a calibration method that makes use of the observed costs of some special queries run against a special synthetic calibrating database to deduce necessary local cost parameters [3]. Gardarin *et al.* extended Du *et al.*'s method so as to calibrate cost models for object-oriented local DBS in an MDBS [5]. Zhu and Larson proposed a query sampling method that develops regression cost models for local query classes based on observed costs of sample queries run against actual user databases [20,21,22]. Zhu and Larson also introduced a fuzzy method based on fuzzy set theory to derive fuzzy cost models in an MDBS [19]. Naacke *et al.* suggested an approach to combining a generic cost model with specific cost information exported by wrappers for local DBSs [9]. Adali *et al.* suggested to maintain a cost vector database to record cost information for every query issued to a local DBS [1]. Roth *et al.* introduced a framework for costing in their *Garlic* federated system [13].

All the above techniques only considered a static system environment. However, in reality, an MDBS environment may change dramatically over time. There are many dynamic factors[1] in an MDBS environment. They can be classified into three types based on their changing frequencies: (I) *frequently-changing factors*, such as CPU load, number of I/Os per second, and size of memory space being used, etc; (II) *slowly-changing factors*, such as local database management system (DBMS) configuration parameters, physical data distribution/organization on a disk, local database conceptual/physical schemas, etc; and (III) *steady factors*, such as local DBMS type, local database location, local CPU speed, etc.

Clearly, the steady factors (Type III) usually do not cause any problem for a query cost model since they rarely change. To take the frequently-changing factors (Type I) into consideration for estimating query costs, Zhu *et al.* suggested three techniques in [17,18], i.e., qualitative approach, fractional analysis approach, and probabilistic approach. The qualitative approach is suitable for estimating the cost of a small query via using a cost model with a qualitative variable indicating system contention states. The fractional analysis approach is suitable for estimating the cost of a large query via analyzing cost fractions in a dynamic environment following a prior known load curve. The probabilistic approach is suitable for estimating the cost of a large query based on Markov chain theory in a randomly-changing dynamic environment.

However, no research has been done for estimating local cost parameters in a slowly-changing dynamic environment (caused by factors of Type II). Although such an environment may not change dramatically during the execution of one query, the costs of the same query executed at different times in the environment can be significantly different. Fig. 1 shows that the cost of a query in Oracle 8.0 can change dramatically as the buffer size (a configuration parameter) is adjusted by a database administrator over time. The question now is how to obtain accurate query cost estimates at all times in such a slowly-changing environment.

---

[1] Since we concern ourselves with local cost models in an MDBS, only dynamic factors at local sites are considered. In general, there are also dynamic environmental factors for the network in an MDBS, which were considered in [16].

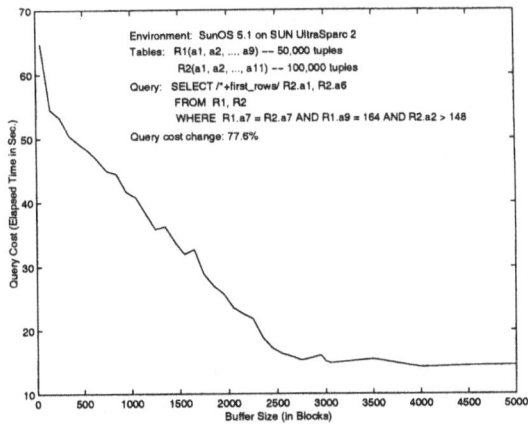

Fig. 1. Query cost affected by buffer size in Oracle 8.0

In this paper, we tackle this challenge by evolving a cost model to capture the slowly-changing environment so that the cost model is kept up-to-date all the time. One direct method is to periodically re-build the cost model by the query sampling method [20]. However, the overhead of such a re-building approach is high. To reduce the overhead, we propose a new evolutionary technique, called a shifting method. The key idea is to develop recurrence update formulas to adjust a cost model at each updating step rather than re-building the cost model from scratch every time so that some common work done previously can be saved. Evolving a cost model to capture a dynamic database environment is our novel approach, which has not been found in literature.

The rest of the paper is organized as follows. Section 2 discusses the idea of cost model evolution and the direct re-building approach. Section 3 presents the details of the shifting method. Section 4 considers some implementation issues. Section 5 shows some experimental results. Section 6 summarizes the conclusions.

2   The Re-building Approach

In the query sampling method [20,22], queries that can be performed on a local DBS are first grouped into homogeneous query classes, and a cost model is then developed for each query class based on the observed costs of sample queries drawn from the class via multiple regression analysis in statistics. Such a cost model captures the performance behavior of queries from the relevant class for a specific environment in which the sample queries were executed. If the environment has been changed dramatically since the cost model was developed, the cost model may become out-of-date. The question is how to keep the cost model up-to-date so that it always reflects the current environment.

Suppose we want to keep cost model M for a query class G up-to-date in a dynamic multidatabase environment. Let the set of significant explanatory variables determined by the query sampling method for the cost model be $\{x_1, x_2, ..., x_n\}$, e.g., the operand table size, the result table size, the operand table tuple length, etc. Cost model M is then of the following form [21]:

$$y = \beta_0 + \beta_1 x_1 + \beta_2 x_2 + \dots + \beta_n x_n . \tag{1}$$

Using the relevant value of each explanatory variable x_j $(1 \leq j \leq n)$ for query Q in G, we can estimate cost y of Q from (1).

In the rest of this paper, we adopt the following notation. A column vector is denoted by $\vec{z}$ (using a low-case letter). A row vector is denoted by the transposition of its corresponding column vector $\vec{z}^T$. A matrix is denoted by a bold-faced capital letter (e.g., $\mathbf{A}$), and the inverse of $\mathbf{A}$ is denoted by $\mathbf{A}^{-1}$. A scalar value or variable is denoted by a normal low-case letter such as b.

Let Q_i $(i = 0, 1, 2, \dots)$ be a sample query from G executed at time t_i. Let y_i be the observed cost (elapsed time) of Q_i, and x_{ij} be the observed value of j–th variable x_j $(1 \leq j \leq n)$ for Q_i. Let row vector[2] $\vec{x}_i^T = (1, x_{i1}, x_{i2}, \dots, x_{in})$. We call pair $(y_i, \vec{x}_i^T)$ as sample data point (for sample query Q_i) observed at time t_i. Hence we have a sequence of sample data points $(y_0, \vec{x}_0^T)$, $(y_1, \vec{x}_1^T)$, ...

Assume that the sample size[3] for multiple regression analysis in the query sampling method is k. At time t_{k-1}, we have k sample data points $(y_0, \vec{x}_0^T)$, $(y_1, \vec{x}_1^T)$, ..., $(y_{k-1}, \vec{x}_{k-1}^T)$. Applying the multiple regression analysis on these sample data points, we can obtain a cost model $M^{(0)}$ that reflects the system performance behavior for query class G during the time period $t_0 \sim t_{k-1}$.

As mentioned before, the system environment may change over time although we assume that it changes very slowly for our problem. If we keep using $M^{(0)}$ to estimate the costs of queries executed at time t_k, t_{k+1}, t_{k+2}, ... The estimates may become worse and worse. To get better estimates, we need to update the cost model according to sample data points observed at t_k, t_{k+1}, t_{k+2}, ... More specifically, at time t_k, when sample data point $(y_k, \vec{x}_k^T)$ is obtained, we should derive a new cost model $M^{(1)}$ based on the most recent k sample data points $(y_1, \vec{x}_1^T)$, $(y_2, \vec{x}_2^T)$, ..., $(y_k, \vec{x}_k^T)$. In other words, we should incorporate the performance information contained in the newest sample data point $(y_k, \vec{x}_k^T)$ into the cost model, since it reflects the current system environment. On the other hand, we also need to remove the oldest sample data point $(y_0, \vec{x}_0^T)$ from consideration for the cost model, since (i) it contains the least information about the performance behavior of the current system environment and (ii) keeping all old sample data points would make the sample set size grow bigger and bigger, which increases the complexity of cost model derivation.

In general, at time t_{s+k-1} $(s = 1, 2, \dots)$, when sample data point $(y_{s+k-1}, \vec{x}_{s+k-1}^T)$ is obtained, we need to derive a new cost model $M^{(s)}$ based on k sample data points $(y_s, \vec{x}_s^T)$, $(y_{s+1}, \vec{x}_{s+1}^T)$, ..., $(y_{s+k-1}, \vec{x}_{s+k-1}^T)$ (see Fig. 2). Note that although the difference between two consecutive cost models $M^{(i)}$ and $M^{(i+1)}$ $(i=0, 1, \dots)$ may be small, assuming the environment changes very slowly, the difference between two far-away cost models $M^{(i)}$ and $M^{(i+q)}$, where q is large,

---

[2] Note that the first component "1" in vector $\vec{x}_i^T$, which corresponds to the constant term in (1), is used to simplify our cost formula derivation.

[3] A commonly used rule for sampling is to sample at least 10 observations for every parameter to be estimated [11], i.e., at least $10 * (n + 2)$ sample queries in our case, where n is the number of explanatory variables in the cost model (note that the variance of error terms is also one parameter to be estimated here).

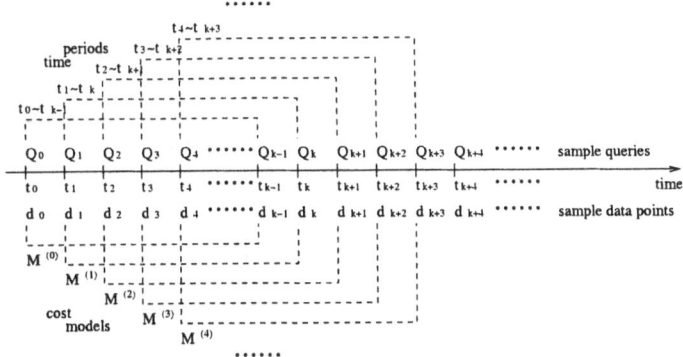

Fig. 2. Re-build up-to-date cost models

can be very significant. Using the up-to-date cost models $M^{(0)}$, $M^{(1)}$, $M^{(2)}$, ... to estimate query costs in the current system environment, we can get better cost estimates, compared with using the static cost model $M^{(0)}$ all the time.

The question is how to derive the up-to-date cost models $M^{(1)}$, $M^{(2)}$, $M^{(3)}$, ... One simple way is to re-build cost model $M^{(s)}$ from scratch at each time t_{s+k-1} ($s = 1, 2, ...$) via multiple regression analysis. In other words, we solve the following normal equations:

$$(\sum_{i=s}^{s+k-1} \vec{x}_i \vec{x}_i^T) \vec{\beta}^{(s)} - \sum_{i=s}^{s+k-1} \vec{x}_i y_i = 0 \qquad (2)$$

for the vector $[\vec{\beta}^{(s)}]^T = (\beta_0^{(s)}, \beta_1^{(s)}, ..., \beta_n^{(s)})$ of coefficients in cost model $M^{(s)}$ of form (1), which minimizes the following sum of squared error terms: $f = \sum_{i=s}^{s+k-1} (\vec{x}_i^T \vec{\beta}^{(s)} - y_i)^2$. In fact, the solution of (2) can be expressed as:

$$\vec{\beta}^{(s)} = [\mathbf{P}^{(s)}]^{-1} \sum_{i=s}^{s+k-1} \vec{x}_i y_i \; . \qquad (3)$$

where $\mathbf{P}^{(s)} = \sum_{i=s}^{s+k-1} \vec{x}_i \vec{x}_i^T$ is termed the covariance matrix of normal equations (2).

From [15], solving (2) requires

$$(k + 1)(n + 1)^2 + (k + 2)(n + 1) + (n + 1)^3 \qquad (4)$$

number of scalar multiplications[4]. Hence, the complexity for applying multiple regression p times is

$$p * ((k + 1)(n + 1)^2 + (k + 2)(n + 1) + (n + 1)^3) \; . \qquad (5)$$

When p is large, the overhead to keep the cost model updated is very significant.

A question now is if we can update the cost model more efficiently. We will present such an efficient technique in the next section.

---

[4] The number of scalar additions and/or subtraction involved is not considered here since they require less overhead.

3   The Shifting Method

Assume that we have obtained initial cost model $M^{(0)}$ (at time t_{k-1}) via multiple regression based on initial k sample data points $(y_0, \vec{x}_0^T)$, $(y_1, \vec{x}_1^T)$, ..., $(y_{k-1}, \vec{x}_{k-1}^T)$. At time t_k, when new sample data point $(y_k, \vec{x}_k^T)$ is observed, we need to get cost model $M^{(1)}$ based on k sample data points $(y_1, \vec{x}_1^T)$, $(y_2, \vec{x}_2^T)$, ..., $(y_k, \vec{x}_k^T)$. Can we avoid re-building $M^{(1)}$ from scratch? The answer is "yes".

We notice that there are $k-1$ common sample data points, i.e., $(y_1, \vec{x}_1^T)$, ..., $(y_{k-1}, \vec{x}_{k-1}^T)$, on which both cost models $M^{(1)}$ and $M^{(0)}$ are based. This fact implies that $M^{(1)}$ and $M^{(0)}$ have certain coherent relationship. Based on this observation, in this section, we develop a shifting method to obtain new cost model $M^{(1)}$ by adjusting old cost model $M^{(0)}$. The basic idea is to add the effect of the newest sample data point $(y_k, \vec{x}_k^T)$ into $M^{(0)}$ and in the meantime remove the effect of the oldest sample data point $(y_0, \vec{x}_0^T)$ from $M^{(0)}$, resulting in new cost model $M^{(1)}$. That is, $M^{(1)}$ is obtained by shifting $M^{(0)}$ one sample data point towards the new time.

Note that during the initial regression analysis for $M^{(0)}$ we can get both the coefficients vector $\vec{\beta}^{(0)}$ and the inverse covariance matrix $[\mathbf{P}^{(0)}]^{-1}$ (see (3)). In the following discussion, we assume that a cost model includes both the coefficients vector and the inverse covariance matrix. Using $\vec{\beta}^{(0)}$ and $[\mathbf{P}^{(0)}]^{-1}$ for initial cost model $M^{(0)}$ (together with $(y_0, \vec{x}_0^T)$ and $(y_k, \vec{x}_k^T)$), we can derive recurrence formulas to compute $\vec{\beta}^{(1)}$ and $[\mathbf{P}^{(1)}]^{-1}$ for new cost model $M^{(1)}$. $\vec{\beta}^{(1)}$ and $[\mathbf{P}^{(1)}]^{-1}$ can be then used to compute $\vec{\beta}^{(2)}$ and $[\mathbf{P}^{(2)}]^{-1}$ for even newer cost model $M^{(2)}$. In general, a new cost model $M^{(s)}$ ($s = 1, 2, ...$) can be obtained by adjusting the previous cost model $M^{(s-1)}$ (see Fig. 3). Hence the cost model can evolve smoothly over time with the dynamic environment in this way.

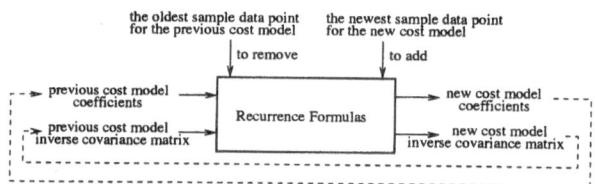

Fig. 3. The shifting method to evolve a cost model

A recurrence formula to update the cost model coefficients is given in the following theorem.

THEOREM 1 *The coefficients $\vec{\beta}^{(s)}$ of new cost model $M^{(s)}$ can be recursively updated by adjusting the coefficients $\vec{\beta}^{(s-1)}$ of previous cost model $M^{(s-1)}$ ($s = 1, 2, ...$) as follows:*

$$\vec{\beta}^{(s)} = \vec{\beta}^{(s-1)} + \vec{w}(e/(1+a)) + \vec{w}'\{e' - \vec{x}_{s-1}^T \vec{w}(e/(1+a))\}/(1+a') \qquad (6)$$

where

$$\vec{w} = [\mathbf{P}^{(s-1)}]^{-1}\vec{x}_{s+k-1} \;, \quad a = \vec{x}_{s+k-1}^T \vec{w} \;, \quad e = y_{s+k-1} - \vec{x}_{s+k-1}^T \vec{\beta}^{(s-1)} \;,$$

$$\vec{w}' = -[\mathbf{P}^{(s-1)}]^{-1}\vec{x}_{s-1} + (\vec{w}\vec{x}_{s+k-1}^T[\mathbf{P}^{(s-1)}]^{-1})\vec{x}_{s-1}/(1+a) \ , \quad a' = \vec{x}_{s-1}^T\vec{w}' \ ,$$

$$e' = y_{s-1} - \vec{x}_{s-1}^T\vec{\beta}^{(s-1)} \ .$$

PROOF. See Appendix.   □

Theorem 1 states that the coefficients $\vec{\beta}^{(s)}$ of new model $M^{(s)}$ can be obtained by adjusting the coefficients $\vec{\beta}^{(s-1)}$ of previous model $M^{(s-1)}$. The adjustments for the previous coefficients depend on the newest sample data point $((y_{s+k-1}, \vec{x}_{s+k-1}^T))$, the oldest sample data point $((y_{s-1}, \vec{x}_{s-1}^T))$, the previous inverse covariance matrix $([\mathbf{P}^{(s-1)}]^{-1})$, and the errors ($e'$ and e) of using the previous model to estimate query costs at the newest and oldest sample data points, which in turn depend on the previous coefficients ($\vec{\beta}^{(s-1)}$). Hence, the new coefficients can be obtained by using $(y_{s+k-1}, \vec{x}_{s+k-1}^T)$, $(y_{s-1}, \vec{x}_{s-1}^T)$, $[\mathbf{P}^{(s-1)}]^{-1}$ and $\vec{\beta}^{(s-1)}$. Note that $\vec{\beta}^{(s)}$ obtained from (6) is the same as the one obtained from the re-building approach in terms of accuracy.

To use (6) to update the cost model iteratively for each new sample data point, we need not only the previous coefficients but also the previous inverse covariance matrix. Thus we also need to keep the inverse covariance matrix updated at each step. The following theorem gives the recurrence formula for updating the inverse covariance matrix.

THEOREM 2 *The inverse covariance matrix* $[\mathbf{P}^{(s)}]^{-1}$ *of new cost model* $M^{(s)}$ *can be recursively updated based on the inverse covariance matrix* $[\mathbf{P}^{(s-1)}]^{-1}$ *of previous cost model* $M^{(s-1)}$ $(s = 1, 2, ...)$ *as follows:*

$$[\mathbf{P}^{(s)}]^{-1} = [\mathbf{P}^{(s-1)}]^{-1} - (\vec{w}\vec{x}_{s+k-1}^T[\mathbf{P}^{(s-1)}]^{-1})/(1+a)$$
$$- \vec{w}'\vec{x}_{s-1}^T\{[\mathbf{P}^{(s-1)}]^{-1} - (\vec{w}\vec{x}_{s+k-1}^T[\mathbf{P}^{(s-1)}]^{-1})/(1+a)\}/(1+a') \qquad (7)$$

where

$$\vec{w} = [\mathbf{P}^{(s-1)}]^{-1}\vec{x}_{s+k-1} \ , \qquad a = \vec{x}_{s+k-1}^T\vec{w} \ ,$$

$$\vec{w}' = -[\mathbf{P}^{(s-1)}]^{-1}\vec{x}_{s-1} + (\vec{w}\vec{x}_{s+k-1}^T[\mathbf{P}^{(s-1)}]^{-1})\vec{x}_{s-1}/(1+a) \ , \qquad a' = \vec{x}_{s-1}^T\vec{w}' \ .$$

PROOF. See Appendix.   □

Theorem 2 indicates that the new inverse covariance matrix $[\mathbf{P}^{(s)}]^{-1}$ can be obtained by using $(y_{s+k-1}, \vec{x}_{s+k-1}^T)$, $(y_{s-1}, \vec{x}_{s-1}^T)$, and $[\mathbf{P}^{(s-1)}]^{-1}$.

Formulas (6) and (7) share many common factors. They can be evaluated efficiently by one algorithm. To further improve performance, the following formula:

$$\vec{\beta}^{(s)} = \vec{\beta}^{(s-1)} + \vec{w}(e/(1+a))$$
$$+ \vec{w}'\{y_{s-1} - \vec{x}_{s-1}^T(\vec{\beta}^{(s-1)} + \vec{w}(e/(1+a)))\}/(1+a') \ , \qquad (8)$$

which is equivalent to (6), is adopted. The following algorithm updates the coefficients and the inverse covariance matrix of a cost model using the shifting method:

ALGORITHM 1 Cost Model Evolution Using the Shifting Method.

Input: (1) coefficients $\vec{\beta}^{(s-1)}$ of previous model $M^{(s-1)}$; (2) inverse covariance matrix $[\mathbf{P}^{(s-1)}]^{-1}$ of previous model $M^{(s-1)}$; (3) newest sample data point $(y_{s+k-1}, \vec{x}_{s+k-1}^T)$; (4) oldest sample data point $(y_{s-1}, \vec{x}_{s-1}^T)$.

Output: (1) coefficients $\vec{\beta}^{(s)}$ of new model $M^{(s)}$; (2) inverse covariance matrix $[\mathbf{P}^{(s)}]^{-1}$ of new model $M^{(s)}$.

Method:

1. Compute $\vec{w} := [\mathbf{P}^{(s-1)}]^{-1}\vec{x}_{s+k-1}$;
2. Compute $a := \vec{x}_{s+k-1}^T \vec{w}$;
3. Compute $\vec{u}^T := \vec{x}_{s+k-1}^T [\mathbf{P}^{(s-1)}]^{-1}$;
4. Compute $\mathbf{B} := \vec{w}\vec{u}^T$;
5. Compute $\mathbf{A} := \mathbf{B}/(1+a)$;
6. Compute $\mathbf{C} := [\mathbf{P}^{(s-1)}]^{-1} - \mathbf{A}$; /*1st two terms in (7)*/
7. Compute $\vec{w}' := \mathbf{C}(-\vec{x}_{s-1})$;
8. Compute $a' := \vec{x}_{s-1}^T \vec{w}'$;
9. Compute $\vec{v}^T := \vec{x}_{s-1}^T \mathbf{C}$;
10. Compute $\mathbf{D} := \vec{w}'\vec{v}^T$;
11. Compute $\mathbf{E} := \mathbf{D}/(1+a')$; /*3rd term in (7)*/
12. Compute $[\mathbf{P}^{(s)}]^{-1} := \mathbf{C} - \mathbf{E}$; /*new inverse covariance matrix*/
13. Compute $\hat{y}_{s+k-1} := \vec{x}_{s+k-1}^T \vec{\beta}^{(s-1)}$;
14. Compute $e := y_{s+k-1} - \hat{y}_{s+k-1}$;
15. Compute $h := e/(1+a)$;
16. Compute $\vec{r} := h\vec{w}$;
17. Compute $\vec{q} := \vec{\beta}^{(s-1)} + \vec{r}$; /*1st 2 terms in (8)*/
18. Compute $\hat{y}_{-1}' := \vec{x}_{s-1}^T \vec{q}$;
19. Compute $b := y_{s-1} - \hat{y}_{s-1}'$;
20. Compute $d := b/(1+a')$;
21. Compute $\vec{h} := d\vec{w}'$; /* 3rd term in (8) */
22. Compute $\vec{\beta}^{(s)} := \vec{q} + \vec{h}$; /* new coefficients*/
23. Return $\vec{\beta}^{(s)}$ and $[\mathbf{P}^{(s)}]^{-1}$.

Starting with the initial cost model $M^{(0)}$, Algorithm 1 can be repeatedly applied for each new sample data point to evolve the cost model for capturing the dynamic environment. The complexity of Algorithm 1 is given in the following corollary.

COROLLARY 1 *Algorithm 1 requires* $8(n+1)^2 + 7(n+1) + 2$ *number of scalar multiplications/divisions to calculate* $\vec{\beta}^{(s)}$ *and* $[\mathbf{P}^{(s)}]^{-1}$ *for new cost model* $M^{(s)}$ *based on* $\vec{\beta}^{(s-1)}$ *and* $[\mathbf{P}^{(s-1)}]^{-1}$ *of previous cost model* $M^{(s-1)}$, *where* n *is the number of explanatory variables in the cost model.*

PROOF. Correctness can be easily checked by counting the number of scalar multiplications/divisions required by each step in Algorithm 1. □

From Corollary 1, we can see that the asymptotic performance behavior of the shifting method for one step is $O(n^2)$ rather than $O(n^3)$ as required by the re-building approach via multiple regression for one step (see (4)).

Another very attractive advantage of the shifting method is that its complexity is independent of sample size k. To achieve a better cost model, the re-building approach has to employ a larger sample size, which implies a larger overhead, while the shifting method can obtain the same cost model without increasing any overhead. The reason for this phenomenon is that, no matter how large the sample set is, the difference between a new cost model and its previous cost model is only two sample data points, and the shifting method fully exploits the shared work for building two cost models based on the common sample data points, rather than building the new cost model from scratch.

Furthermore, based on the fact that $k \geq 10(n+2)$ (see footnote 3), we can show that the shifting method for one step is always more efficient than the re-building approach for one step for any $n \geq 0$. Clearly, the more steps the shifting method and the re-building approach are applied for, the more performance gain the shifting method will achieve. Therefore, we have the following conclusion:

COROLLARY 2 *The shifting method is more efficient than the direct re-building approach for evolving a cost model in a dynamic environment.*

Note that we have also developed another evolutionary technique, called the block-moving method. Instead of adjusting a cost model for every individual observed new sample data point, the block-moving method adjusts a cost model by adding the effect of a block (set) of new sample data points into and in the meantime removing the effect of a block of the oldest sample data points from the model every time a block of new sample data points are observed. Compared with the shifting method, this technique is usually more efficient but less accurate. Due to the space limitation of the paper, the details of the technique are discussed in a separate paper [12].

4 Evolution Procedure and Other Considerations

The shifting method for evolving cost models was developed for a multidatabase environment supported by the multidatabase prototype CORDS-MDBS [2]. Fig. 4 shows the system architecture for CORDS-MDBS. In CORDS-MDBS, the global data model is assumed to be relational and each local DBS is associated with an MDBS agent which provides a relational interface[5] if the local DBMS is non-relational. Thus the global query optimizer in the MDBS may view participating local DBMSs as relational ones.

Initially, the query sampling method in [20,22] can be employed to classify local queries and develop a cost model for each query class at a local site. The shifting method can be then applied to evolve the cost model for each query class to capture the slowly-changing dynamic environment. The cost models are kept in the multidatabase system catalog and used during global query optimization.

---

[5] In fact, the shifting method suggested in this paper does not rely on the relational data model. As long as a query class and the explanatory variables of its cost model are identified, the technique can be applied directly to evolve the cost model even if the data model is non-relational.

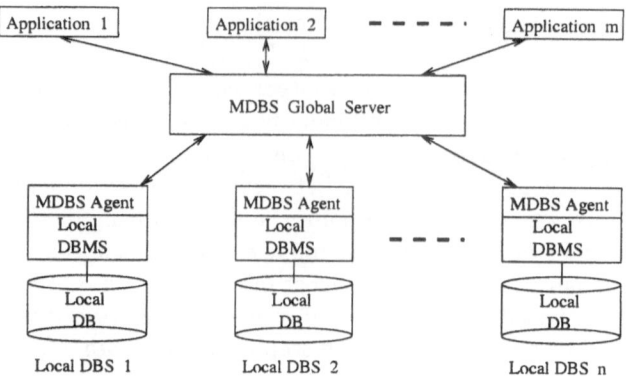

Fig. 4. A multidatabase system architecture

A question is how to obtain sample queries to update the cost model. One way is to generate artificial sample queries and run them from time to time. However, since these sample queries are extra ones run in the system, they compete for system resources with user queries. To fully utilize the work done in the system, a better way is to make use of user queries as sample queries. More specifically, when a local database system is requested to run a local user query by either the global query optimizer (due to the decomposition of a global query) or a local user, a query classifier in the MDBS agent will identify the class to which the query belongs to. This query is then used as a sample query for the corresponding query class, and its observed data are used to evolve the relevant cost model via the shifting method.

One potential problem that needs to be considered here is the starvation problem. It is possible that user queries for a particular query class are not executed as frequently as required to capture the dynamic environment. If user queries are in fact never used for a query class in an application environment, the solution is simple – we just ignore the update of the relevant cost model since we only need to maintain those cost models that are useful for practical user queries. However, if the query class is indeed needed in applications but its queries are not run as often as the environment changes, one solution in this case is to generate and run some additional artificial sample queries when necessary to supplement the user sample queries. The system makes full use of user queries and also keeps the cost model up-to-date although some extra overhead cannot be avoided in this case.

In the opposite of the starvation problem, there is an overflow problem. In other words, user queries are executed too frequently for a particular query class. In this case, the shifting method should not take every user query as a sample query to update the cost model since there might be very little change in the underlying environment. One solution to this problem is to periodically pick up a user query as a sample query to evolve the cost model. Another solution is to activate the cost model update procedure whenever an observable change in the environment is detected (e.g., the number of queries with a large error of cost estimation is beyond a threshold) and to de-activate the cost model update procedure when the cost model is up-to-date. In a practical system, the evolution procedure can also be controlled manually via some system configuration parameters or system commands.

5   Experimental Results

To test the effectiveness and efficiency of the shifting method discussed in Section 3, we conducted extensive experiments on our MDBS prototype, in which Oracle 8.0 and DB2 5.0 were used as local DBMSs running under SunOS 5.1 on SUN UltraSparc 2 workstations.

Note that conducting extensive experiments in a real slowly-changing environment is difficult since it would take too long to complete the experiments. To effectively simulate a slowly-changing dynamic environment, we artificially generate different numbers of concurrent processes with various work/sleep ratios to change the system contention level in a given environment. The cost of a small probing query is used to gage the system contention level. The higher the probing query cost is, the higher the system contention level. 49 system contention levels (with the probing query cost ranging from 3 sec. to 98 sec.) were considered in each of Oracle and DB2 environments. A slowly-changing environment is achieved by assuming that the system contention level gradually changes from the lowest level 1 to the highest level 49. Since the main purpose of our experiments is to check if the shifting method can evolve a cost model to capture a dynamic environment (no matter how the environment is changing), the above simulated environments are suitable for the experiments.

The experimental databases used in the experiments were the same as those in [17,18,20]. More specifically, each local database contains 12 tables $R_i(a_1, a_2, ..., a_j)$ ($i = 1, 2, ..., 12; j \in \{3, 5, 7, 9, 11, 13\}$) with data randomly-generated and cardinalities ranging from 3,000 $\sim$ 250,000. Each table has a number of indexed columns and various selectivities for different columns.

Note that the shifting method does not rely on any particular query class. The experimental results for all query classes are similar. In this section, we report typical experimental results for a representative query class G_{15} (defined in [20]) consisting of unary queries that have no usable indexes for their qualification conditions. To demonstrate that the technique has a similar behavior for other query classes, we also report some experimental results for another query class G_{14} consisting of unary queries that have usable (non-clustered) indexes for their qualification conditions.

The sample queries used to evolve cost models were randomly chosen from the relevant query class. 100 sample queries were executed at each system contention level on both Oracle 8.0 and DB2 5.0. Hence totally 4900 sample queries were executed in a sequence for each environment. The first 100 sample queries (i.e., sample size $k = 100$) were used to derive the initial cost model (with the number of variables $n = 6$) via the query sampling method. The shifting method was then used to evolve the cost model to capture the dynamic environment.

To examine the accuracy of the evolutionary cost models obtained from the shifting method, we also ran some test queries randomly chosen from the query class in each of Oracle and DB2 environments. The cost of each test query was estimated by using the corresponding updated cost model in the environment, and the observed and estimated costs are compared. To see accuracy gains from the evolutionary technique, the cost estimates using the initial (static) cost model were also compared.

Note that, unlike scientific computation in engineering, the accuracy of cost estimation in query optimization is not required to be very high. In our experimental analysis, the cost estimates with relative errors within 30% are considered to be very good, and the cost estimates that are within the range of one-time larger or smaller than the corresponding observed costs (e.g., 2 minutes vs. 4 minutes) are considered to be good. Only those cost estimates which are not of the same order of magnitude with the observed costs (e.g., 2 minutes vs. 3 hours) are not acceptable.

Table 1. Percentages of good cost estimates for test queries in G_{15} from experiments on Oracle 8.0 and DB2 5.0

Local DBMS	Contention level	Static: very good %	Static: good %	Evolutionary: very good %	Evolutionary: good %
	12	1 %	5 %	83 %	88 %
Oracle	25	0 %	0 %	70 %	82 %
	37	1 %	3 %	63 %	74 %
	49	0 %	1 %	70 %	87 %
	12	0 %	1 %	85 %	93 %
DB2	25	0 %	0 %	82 %	91 %
	37	0 %	0 %	65 %	88 %
	49	0 %	0 %	90 %	97 %
Average		0.25 %	1.25 %	76 %	87.50 %

Table 2. Similar experimental results obtained for test queries in G_{14} on Oracle 8.0

Local DBMS	Contention level	Static: very good %	Static: good %	Evolutionary: very good %	Evolutionary: good %
Oracle	12	0 %	1 %	82 %	93 %
	25	1 %	1 %	86 %	92 %

Table 1 shows the percentages of good and very good cost estimates for test queries in G_{15} at 4 representative contention levels (each level has 100 test queries) on Oracle 8.0 and DB2 5.0. In the table, cost estimates from the initial (static) cost model and the evolutionary cost model by the shifting method were listed. To show that the experimental results are similar for different query classes, Table 2 lists two representative sets of experimental results for another query class G_{14}.

From the experiments, we have the following observations on the effectiveness of the shifting method:

– The shifting method can derive a good evolutionary cost model to capture a slowly-changing dynamic environment. From Table 1, we can see that the

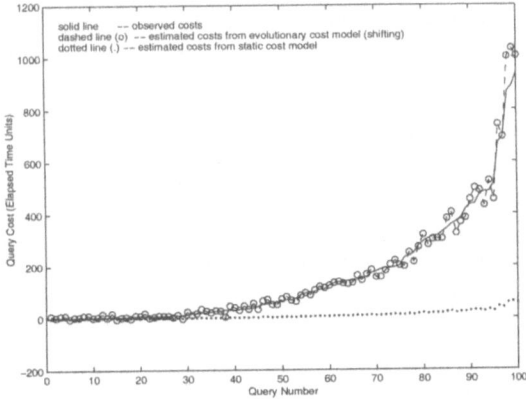

Fig. 5. Cost estimates for test queries in G_{15} from static and evolutionary models at contention level 25 on Oracle 8.0

evolutionary cost model obtained from the shifting method can give good cost estimates for most test queries (87.5% on average, including 76% very good ones). If we do not evolve the cost model and keep using the initial (static) cost model, we can only obtain 1.25% (on average) good cost estimates for the test queries in a dynamic environment. The estimation accuracy gains are dramatic. Fig.'s 5 and 6 show a typical comparison for cost estimates from the two cost models in Oracle 8.0 and DB2 5.0, respectively.

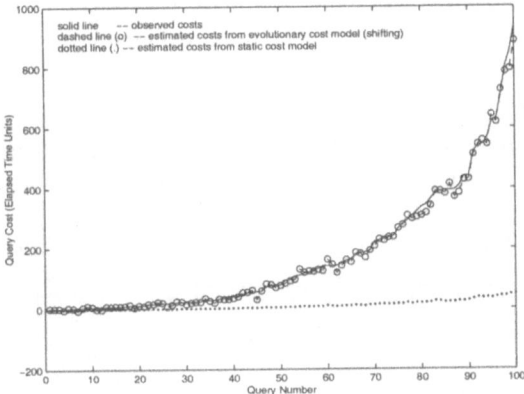

Fig. 6. Cost estimates for test queries in G_{15} from static and evolutionary models at contention level 25 on DB2 5.0

– The initial (static) cost model cannot be used in a dynamic environment. The cost models in most existing database systems currently do not cope with a dynamic environment. Our experiments demonstrate that using a static cost model can hardly give good cost estimates for queries run in a dynamic environment (see Tables 1 and 2). The situation becomes worse and worse when the environment changes farther and farther aways from the original environment. Fig. 7 shows a comparison of relative errors of cost estimation

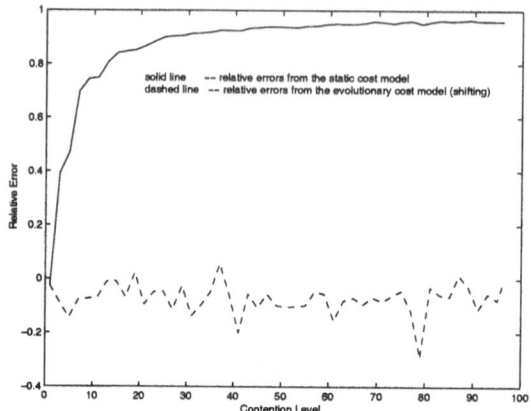

Fig. 7. Errors for cost estimates of a query executed at various contention levels from static and evolutionary cost models on Oracle 8.0

for a query run from contention level 1 to 49 in our dynamic environment by the initial (static) cost model and the evolutionary cost model obtained from the shifting method. From the figure, we can see that the relative errors become larger and larger for the static cost model as the environment is getting farther and farther away from the initial one, while the relative errors are kept within 30% by the evolutionary cost model no matter how the environment changes.

To examine the efficiency of the shifting method, we compared the execution times for the shifting method and the re-building approach for various cases. Table 3 shows the execution times of the techniques. m in the table is the number

Table 3. Execution time units for re-building and shifting methods

Repeat#/block	$m = 1$	$m = 3$	$m = 5$	$m = 10$	$m = 20$	$m = 30$	$m = 40$	...	$m = 700$	...
Re-building	0.000904	0.002678	0.004452	0.008885	0.017837	0.026902	0.035881	...	0.627712	...
Shifting	0.000110	0.000305	0.000498	0.000981	0.001947	0.002816	0.003972	...	0.068176	...

of times the relevant method is applied to update the cost model for m consecutive new sample data points. From the experiments, we can see that the shifting method is more efficient than the re-building approach. Table 3 indicates that the former can improve efficiency by about 89% for any m. The more times the shifting method is applied, the more (absolute) overhead can be saved (see Fig. 8). This observation is consistent with Corollary 2 from the theoretical analysis.

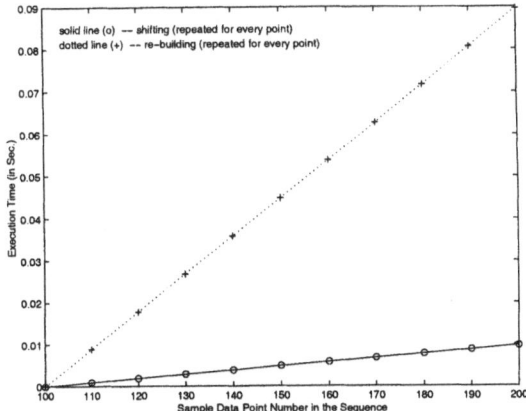

Fig. 8. Efficiency comparison for the shifting and re-building methods

6   Conclusions

A major challenge for performing global query optimization in an MDBS is that the cost models for local DBSs may not be available at the global level. Dynamic environmental factors add more difficulties to this problem. In this paper, we have suggested to evolve a cost model to capture a slowly-changing dynamic multidatabase environment so that the cost model is kept up-to-date all the time.

A direct approach to keeping a cost model up-to-date in a dynamic environment is to periodically re-build the cost model via the query sampling method [20]. However, this re-building approach incurs a high overhead. To improve the efficiency, we have proposed a new evolutionary technique (i.e., the shifting method) in this paper.

This technique employs recurrence update formulas to adjust a cost model by adding the effect of a new sample data point into and in the meantime removing the effect of the oldest sample data point from the model every time a new sample data point is observed. It is more efficient than the re-building approach since it simply adjusts the previous cost model rather than re-building the cost model from scratch using the entire set of sample data points, most of which have actually already been taken into account in the previous model. Especially when the re-building approach has to be repeatedly applied to keep the cost model updated for every new sample data point, the shifting method can save cost dramatically.

To reduce the overhead of executing sample queries, we suggest to use user queries as sample queries so that their observed information can be used to evolve a cost model. The relevant starvation problem can be solved by generating some supplemental artificial sample queries, while the relevant overflow problem can be solved by updating a cost model periodically or only when a significant change to the model has been detected.

Our experimental results are consistent with our theoretical ones, which demonstrate that the shifting method is quite promising in deriving good evolutionary cost models for a slowly-changing dynamic multidatabase environment in terms of both effectiveness and efficiency.

Acknowledgment. The authors would like to thank Yu Sun for his help with experiments for the work reported in the paper.

References

1. S. Adali, K. S. Candan, Y. Papakonstantinou and V. S. Subrahmamian . Query caching and optimization in distributed mediator systems. In *Proc. of SIGMOD*, pp 137–48, 1996.
2. G.K. Attaluri, D.P. Bradshaw, N. Coburn, P.-Å. Larson, P. Martin, A. Silberschatz, J. Slonim and Q. Zhu. The CORDS multidatabase project. *IBM Systems Journal*, 34(1):39–62, 1995.
3. W. Du, R. Krishnamurthy and M. C. Shan. Query optimization in heterogeneous DBMS. In *Proc. of VLDB*, pp 277–91, 1992.
4. W. Du, M. C. Shan and U. Dayal. Reducing multidatabase query response time by tree balancing. In *Proc. of SIGMOD*, pp 293–303, 1995.
5. G. Gardarin, F. Sha and Z.-H. Tang. Calibrating the query optimizer cost model of IRO-DB, an object-oriented federated database system. In *Proc. of VLDB*, pp 378–89, 1996.
6. C. Lee and C.-J. Chen. Query optimization in multidatabase systems considering schema conflicts. *IEEE TKDE*, 9(6):941–55, 1997.
7. W. Litwin, L. Mark and N. Roussopoulos. Interoperability of multiple autonomous databases. *ACM Comp. Surveys*, 22(3):267–93, 1990.
8. H. Lu and M.-C. Shan. On global query optimization in multidatabase systems. In *2nd Int'l workshop on Res. Issues on Data Eng.*, pp 217, Arizona, 1992.
9. H. Naacke, G. Gardarin and A. Tomasic. Leveraging mediator cost models with heterogeneous data sources. In *Proc. of ICDE*, pp 351–60, 1998.
10. J. Neter, M. Kutner and W. Wasserman. *Applied Linear Statistical Models, 3rd Ed.* Richard D. Irwin, Inc., 1990.
11. R. Pfaffenberger and James H. Patterson. *Statistical Methods for Business and Economics.* Richard D. Irwin, Inc., 1987.
12. A. Rahal, Q. Zhu and P.-Å. Larson. Evolutionary techniques for updating cost models in a dynamic multidatabase environment. *Technical Report CIS-TR-0701-02*, Dept of Comp. and Inf. Sci., The Univ. of Michigan - Dearborn, July 2002.
13. M. T. Roth, F. Ozcan and L. M. Haas. Cost models DO matter: providing cost information for diverse data sources in a federated system. In *Proc. of VLDB*, pp 599–610, 1999.
14. A. P. Sheth and J. A. Larson. Federated database systems for managing distributed, heterogeneous, and autonomous databases. *ACM Comp. Surveys*, 22(3):183–236, 1990.
15. J. Treicher and J. Richard. *Theory and Design of Adaptive Filters.* Wiley and Sons, Inc, 1987.

16. T. Urhan, M. J. Franklin and L. Amsaleg. Cost-based query scrambling for initial delays. In *Proc. of SIGMOD.*, pp 130–41, 1998.
17. Q. Zhu, Y. Sun and S. Motheramgari. Developing cost models with qualitative variables for dynamic multidatabase environments. In *Proc. of ICDE*, pp 413–24, 2000.
18. Q. Zhu, S. Motheramgari and Y. Sun. Cost estimation for large queries via fractional analysis and probabilistic approach in dynamic multidatabase environments. In *Proc. of DEXA*, pp 509–25, 2000.
19. Q. Zhu and P.-Å. Larson. A fuzzy query optimization approach for multidatabase systems. *Int'l J. of Uncertainty, Fuzziness and Knowledge-Based Sys.*, 5(6):701–22, 1997.
20. Q. Zhu and P.-Å. Larson. Solving local cost estimation problem for global query optimization in multidatabase systems. *Distributed and Parallel Databases*, 6(4): 373–420, 1998.
21. Q. Zhu and P.-Å. Larson. Building regression cost models for multidatabase systems. In *Proc. of 4th IEEE Int'l Conf. on Paral. and Distr. Inf. Syst.*, pp 220–31, 1996.
22. Q. Zhu and P.-Å. Larson. A query sampling method for estimating local cost parameters in a multidatabase system. In *Proc. of ICDE*, pp 144–53, 1994.

Appendix

In this appendix, we sketch the proofs of the main theorems in this paper. The following matrix inversion lemma from [15] is applied in the proof for Theorem 1.

LEMMA 1 *Given four matrices* $\mathbf{W}$, $\mathbf{X}$, $\mathbf{Y}$ *and* $\mathbf{Z}$, *the following equation holds:*

$$(\mathbf{W} + \mathbf{X}\mathbf{Y}\mathbf{Z})^{-1} = \mathbf{W}^{-1} - \mathbf{W}^{-1}\mathbf{X}(\mathbf{Z}\mathbf{W}^{-1}\mathbf{X} + \mathbf{Y}^{-1})^{-1}\mathbf{Z}\mathbf{W}^{-1} .$$

PROOF OF THEOREM 1:

Let $\vec{b}^{(l)} = \sum_{i=l}^{(k-1)+l} \vec{x}_i y_i$ where $l = s - 1, s$. From (3), we have

$$\vec{\beta}^{(l)} = [\mathbf{P}^{(l)}]^{-1}\vec{b}^{(l)}, \qquad l = s - 1, s . \tag{9}$$

Clearly,

$$\vec{b}^{(s)} = \vec{b}^{(s-1)} + \vec{x}_{s+k-1}y_{s+k-1} - \vec{x}_{s-1}y_{s-1} , \tag{10}$$

$$\mathbf{P}^{(s)} = \mathbf{P}^{(s-1)} + \vec{x}_{s+k-1}\vec{x}^T_{s+k-1} - \vec{x}_{s-1}\vec{x}^T_{s-1} . \tag{11}$$

Let

$$\mathbf{C}^{-1} = \mathbf{P}^{(s-1)} + \vec{x}_{s+k-1}\vec{x}^T_{s+k-1} .$$

By Lemma 1, we get

$$\mathbf{C} = [\mathbf{P}^{(s-1)}]^{-1}$$
$$\quad -[\mathbf{P}^{(s-1)}]^{-1}\vec{x}_{s+k-1}(\vec{x}^T_{s+k-1}[\mathbf{P}^{(s-1)}]^{-1}\vec{x}_{s+k-1} + 1)^{-1}\vec{x}^T_{s+k-1}[\mathbf{P}^{(s-1)}]^{-1}$$
$$\quad = [\mathbf{P}^{(s-1)}]^{-1} - (\vec{w}\vec{x}^T_{s+k-1}[\mathbf{P}^{(s-1)}]^{-1})/(1 + a) \tag{12}$$

where $\vec{w} = [\mathbf{P}^{(s-1)}]^{-1}\vec{x}_{s+k-1}$ and $a = \vec{x}_{s+k-1}^T\vec{w}$. Note that a is a scalar.

From (11) and Lemma 1, we have

$$[\mathbf{P}^{(s)}]^{-1} = (\mathbf{C}^{-1} - \vec{x}_{s-1}\vec{x}_{s-1}^T)^{-1} = \mathbf{C} - \mathbf{C}(-\vec{x}_{s-1})(\vec{x}_{s-1}^T\mathbf{C}(-\vec{x}_{s-1}) + 1)^{-1}\vec{x}_{s-1}^T\mathbf{C}$$
$$= \mathbf{C} - (\vec{w}'\vec{x}_{s-1}^T\mathbf{C})/(1 + a') \quad (13)$$

where $\vec{w}' = \mathbf{C}(-\vec{x}_{s-1})$ and $a' = \vec{x}_{s-1}^T\vec{w}'$. Note that a' is a scalar.

Let

$$\vec{q} = \mathbf{C}(\vec{b}^{(s-1)} + \vec{x}_{s+k-1}y_{s+k-1}) .$$

By (12) and (9), we get

$$\vec{q} = ([\mathbf{P}^{(s-1)}]^{-1} - (\vec{w}\vec{x}_{s+k-1}^T[\mathbf{P}^{(s-1)}]^{-1})/(1 + a))(\vec{b}^{(s-1)} + \vec{x}_{s+k-1}y_{s+k-1})$$
$$= \vec{\beta}^{(s-1)} - (\vec{w}\vec{x}_{s+k-1}^T\vec{\beta}^{(s-1)})/(1 + a) + [\mathbf{P}^{(s-1)}]^{-1}\vec{x}_{s+k-1}y_{s+k-1}$$
$$\quad - (\vec{w}\vec{x}_{s+k-1}^T[\mathbf{P}^{(s-1)}]^{-1}\vec{x}_{s+k-1}y_{s+k-1})/(1 + a)$$
$$= \vec{\beta}^{(s-1)} - (\vec{w}\vec{x}_{s+k-1}^T\vec{\beta}^{(s-1)})/(1 + a) + \vec{w}y_{s+k-1} - \vec{w}y_{s+k-1}(a/(1 + a))$$
$$= \vec{\beta}^{(s-1)} + \vec{w}(e/(1 + a)) \quad (14)$$

where $e = y_{s+k-1} - \vec{x}_{s+k-1}^T\vec{\beta}^{(s-1)}$, which is the error term for sample data point $(y_{s+k-1}, \vec{x}_{s+k-1}^T)$ using cost model $M^{(s-1)}$.

Let $\vec{b}' = \vec{b}^{(s-1)} + \vec{x}_{s+k-1}y_{s+k-1}$. From (9), (10) and (13), we have

$$\vec{\beta}^{(s)} = [\mathbf{P}^{(s)}]^{-1}\vec{b}^{(s)} = [\mathbf{P}^{(s)}]^{-1}(\vec{b}' - \vec{x}_{s-1}y_{s-1})$$
$$= (\mathbf{C} - (\vec{w}'\vec{x}_{s-1}^T\mathbf{C})/(1 + a'))(\vec{b}' - \vec{x}_{s-1}y_{s-1})$$
$$= \vec{q} - (\vec{w}'\vec{x}_{s-1}^T\vec{q})/(1 + a') + \mathbf{C}(-\vec{x}_{s-1})y_{s-1}$$
$$\quad - (\vec{w}'\vec{x}_{s-1}^T\mathbf{C})/(1 + a')(-\vec{x}_{s-1})y_{s-1}$$
$$= \vec{q} - (\vec{w}'\vec{x}_{s-1}^T\vec{q})/(1 + a') + \vec{w}'y_{s-1} - (\vec{w}'a'y_{s-1})/(1 + a')$$
$$= \vec{q} - (\vec{w}'\vec{x}_{s-1}^T\vec{q})/(1 + a') + (\vec{w}'y_{s-1})/(1 + a') .$$

From (14), we get

$$\vec{\beta}^{(s)} = \vec{q} - \vec{w}'\vec{x}_{s-1}^T\{\vec{\beta}^{(s-1)} + (e/(1 + a))\vec{w}\}/(1 + a') + (\vec{w}'y_{s-1})/(1 + a')$$
$$= \vec{q} - \vec{w}'\vec{x}_{s-1}^T\vec{\beta}^{(s-1)}/(1 + a') - (\vec{w}'\vec{x}_{s-1}^T(e/(1 + a))\vec{w})/(1 + a')$$
$$\quad + (\vec{w}'y_{s-1})/(1 + a')$$
$$= \vec{q} - (\vec{w}'\vec{x}_{s-1}^T(e/(1 + a))\vec{w})/(1 + a') + \{\vec{w}'(y_{s-1} - \vec{x}_{s-1}^T\vec{\beta}^{(s-1)})\}/(1 + a')$$
$$= \vec{q} - \vec{w}'\vec{x}_{s-1}^T(e/(1 + a))\vec{w}/(1 + a') + \vec{w}'e'/(1 + a')$$
$$= \vec{\beta}^{(s-1)} + \vec{w}(e/(1 + a)) - (\vec{w}'\vec{x}_{s-1}^T\vec{w}(e/(1 + a))/(1 + a')) + \vec{w}'e'/(1 + a')$$
$$= \vec{\beta}^{(s-1)} + \vec{w}(e/(1 + a)) + \vec{w}'\{e' - \vec{x}_{s-1}^T\vec{w}(e/(1 + a))\}/(1 + a')$$

where $e' = y_{s-1} - \vec{x}_{s-1}^T\vec{\beta}^{(s-1)}$, which is the error term for sample data point $(y_{s-1}, \vec{x}_{s-1}^T)$ using cost model $M^{(s-1)}$. □

PROOF OF THEOREM 2:

Formula (7) can be obtained by substituting (12) in (13). □

A Conceptual Markup Language That Supports Interoperability between Business Rule Modeling Systems[1]

Jan Demey, Mustafa Jarrar, and Robert Meersman[2]

VUB STARLab
Vrije Universiteit Brussel
Pleinlaan 2
1050 Brussels – Belgium
{jdemey, mjarrar, meersman}@vub.ac.be

Abstract. The Internet creates a strong demand for standardized exchange not only of data itself but especially of data semantics, as this same internet increasingly becomes the carrier of e-business activity (e.g. using web services). One way to achieve this is in the form of communicating "rich" conceptual schemas. In this paper we adopt the well-known CM technique of ORM, which has a rich complement of business rule specification, and develop ORM-ML, an XML-based markup language for ORM. Clearly domain modeling of this kind will be closely related to work on so-called ontologies and we will briefly discuss the analogies and differences, introducing methodological patterns for designing distributed business models. Since ORM schemas are typically saved as graphical files, we designed a textual representation as a marked-up document in ORM-ML so we can save these ORM schemas in a more machine exchangeable way that suits networked environments. Moreover, we can now write style sheets to convert such schemas into another syntax, e.g. pseudo natural language, a given rule engine's language, first order logic.

1 Introduction and Motivation

In an enterprise, business rules are used to represent certain aspects of a business domain (static rules) or business policy (dynamic rules). Business rules are defined in [12] as "statements that define or constrain some business aspects. They are intended to assert business or to control or influence its behavior". Modeling such rules is not an easy task since in general it is hard to arrive at the precise understandings and agreements, which they formulate; furthermore these rules may change regularly according to changes in these business aspects. Therefore business rules should be modeled separately in the logical model (i.e. not in the implementation level). They should also be modeled in a declarative manner, in order to enhance their

---

[1] An early version of this paper has been presented at the "Rule Markup Languages for Business Rules on the Semantic Web" Workshop, 2002.

[2] Author's names are in alphabetical order.

R. Meersman, Z. Tari (Eds.): CoopIS/DOA/ODBASE 2002, LNCS 2519, pp. 19–35, 2002.

maintainability and reusability [10]. Furthermore, as the volume and spread of networked business enterprises grow, especially in an open environment as the web, business rules play an important role, because agents need to exchange data and transactions according to a shared and agreed set of business rules without misunderstanding. In short, the modeling of business rules should be done at a conceptual level, and in a language that is expressive enough to capture the business complexity [22], but should also be easy and suitable for e.g. business analysts (often non-computer experts) to build and maintain.

Conceptual modeling techniques became especially well known and successful as the basis for graphical CASE tools for building information systems (IS). Many such conceptual modeling techniques exist, for example EER, ORM, the UML, by now often described in classroom textbooks [19][5][15][25]. Conceptual modeling intends to support the quality checks needed before building physical systems by aiming at the representation of data at a high level of abstraction, and therefore acquire a high degree of, often implicit, semantics. This implicitness translated in a requirement for CASE tools to interpret these conceptual specifications representing complex structures and rules (constraints) that must hold on these structures. Also queries and updates may (conceivably) become expressed at a conceptual level, requiring interaction with conceptual structures rather than their implementation (such as relational databases). NIAM [25] is based on an analysis method for natural language, the query and constraint language RIDL [24][16] was developed for this purpose; similarly for ConQuer [3] for NIAM's successor methodology ORM [15].

Using ORM for modeling business rules at a conceptual level has been proposed by e.g. [22][23][14] as a powerful and expressive approach. Indeed, ORM has critical features for this task and it has easy and expressive capabilities in its graphical notation and verbalization possibilities, as will be exploited in the system described in this paper.

In the autonomous, distributed and heterogeneous environment of the internet, there's a strong demand for the exchange of conceptual schemas to be formalized and if possible standardized, since the target application may have a different interpretation or use of a conceptual schema's "surface semantics" (e.g. an EER diagram's topology and linguistic labels, stripped of its geometrical data). Therefore it is very important that the original schema is transcribed (a) as faithfully as possible and (b) in an as standard way as possible, to allow in this way a maximum of flexibility for the target application. Examples of such target applications could be other CASE modelers (even using other meta models), verbalization tools, applications possessing and exploiting "orthogonal" semantics such as spatial, multimedia and temporal databases, or just plain defining formal "semantic" communication protocols as will be needed for the establishment of smart web Services on the so-called Semantic Web [4], [11] operating as the future literally *meaningful* infrastructure for e-commerce and e-business, both at the business to business (B2B) and at the business to customer (B2C) levels.

The format of conceptual models in an ORM CASE tool is usually proprietary and ad-hoc, therefore unsuitable to be exchanged or shared between business agents. Often ORM tools (e.g. Microsoft's VisioModeler®) only generate files for internal use that contain the graphical notation of the conceptual models. Therefore as a solution we present in this paper an XML-based ORM markup language (ORM-ML, its complete grammar defined in the XML Schema in [13]). This markup language enables exchanging ORM models *including* ORM-syntax business rules.

To facilitate validation for example, or just to provide formal —and consistent— documentation, we also developed a *verbalization style sheet* for ORM-ML documents that allows presenting the facts and the rules in pseudo natural language sentences. Related work on Markup languages for Semantic Web rules can be found in [6] and [20].

We have chosen ORM for its rich constraint vocabulary and well-defined semantics (as did e.g. [9] in an earlier paper) and to use XML Schema to define this communication "protocol" for conceptual schemas seen as XML document instances (for their syntaxes, see [26] [27]). In doing this we chose to respect the ORM structure as much as possible by *not* "collapsing" it first through the usual relational transformer that comes with most ORM-based tools (or UML, or EER tools for that matter —after all, these tools were all conceived mainly to build database schemas for in-house use...).

It is fundamental as well as illustrative of our approach to emphasize the distinction between ORM-ML —subject of this paper— and the related and interesting work that has been reported in [9] using ORM to design XML document *instances*, i.e. which contain instance data described in XML using XML Schema language. In fact, similar to the "classical" use of ORM to generate a relational database schema, in [9] a method for using ORM to design XML Schemas is described, which by definition allows any XML document which may contain such data to be validated against the generated XML Schema. In other words, the syntax of the data in the XML document is modeled using ORM, but this syntax (in this case an XML Schema) is no longer that of an ORM model.

On the other hand, in our approach ORM-ML represents ORM models textually, and the syntax of the resulting model is marked-up by XML tags' syntax (i.e. XML-based structured text document). Therefore the content of this XML document is exactly equivalent to the input ORM model, except for the geometrical information (e.g. shapes, and its positions). The latter could be considered as graphical information of an ORM *diagram*. We therefore defined an XML Schema that can act as a grammar to any ORM-ML document, see Section 3. For the benefits of doing so, see Section 2. In short, the distinction between ORM-ML, and using ORM to generate XML Schema, is that the output document in ORM-ML is a text representation of the ORM model itself, while in the earlier approach the output document is a *transformation* from ORM model to an XML Schema *instance*, which is no longer "ORM".

As a further clarification one might consider the ORM Meta schema in Section 4: its populations are ORM schemas, which our algorithm transforms into ORM-marked-up XML documents. If one would map this same meta schema through the algorithm of [9], the output XML Schema will be a close cousin to our XML Schema in [13]. Comparing the appendix with the example of [9], note also that in our approach the ORM diagram's linguistic elements (names of LOTs, NOLOTs, etc.) stay at the level of string values, emphasizing their flexible instance status while for Bird, Halpin et al. these names become XML tag names, reducing the flexibility by "freezing" them in the generated XML model.

Structure of the Paper: In § 2, we discuss modeling patterns and principles of ontologies, and differences between business rules and ontology rules. § 3 gives a bird's eye introduction to ORM, emphasizing distinguished features of ORM for business rules modeling. § 4 presents ORM-ML and includes a note about the verbalization of ORM-ML files. An algorithm to construct an ORM-ML file from an ORM schema instance (stored in the ORM Meta Schema) is presented in § 5. In § 6 we draw some conclusions including a discussion on some of the perceived advantages of a conceptual schema markup language.

2 Business Rules, Ontology Rules, and the Semantic Web

The conceptual modeling of a business' domain knowledge using entities, concepts, objects… and their associated events and governing rules has typically always been performed "individually" for the purpose of a given business' application and needs. Modeling domain knowledge "independently" of its application is the subject of the emerging theory and practice of so-called *ontologies*, but it stands to reason that some of the underlying principles and techniques must be in common. We therefore briefly clarify some of the distinctions between the modeling levels of business rules vs. ontology rules for environments like the Semantic Web [4]. An *ontology* in its most general definition is a set of (usually intensional) logical axioms that want to specify or approximate a conceptualization of a certain (e.g. business) domain. Such logical axioms are rules that therefore, typically at the type level, constrain the intended meaning (interpretation) of certain aspects of reality. By representing the semantics in a formal way, agents can share and commit to them, in order to interoperate to exchange data and transactions without misunderstanding. Note that ontologies are somewhat more "subtle" knowledge representations than an information system's data model, which always is "purely" at the type level. In particular they should be sharable, viz. IS-instance (application) independent, but may also refer to relevant "instance concepts" such as "'Euro', 'MasterCard', 'Belgium', etc. Ontologies are more than a mere taxonomy of concepts, since they may contain richer relationships such as "partOf", 'shippedVia, 'OrderedBy', etc.".

As defined in § 1, business rules are intended to constrain or represent a certain aspect of a business domain or policy, thus a similarity also appears between ontology rules and business rules. But notice that business rules will be changed according to the business policy, which changes regularly, and which mostly belongs to one or a few number of enterprises, while ontology rules are more generic and thus more stable, and are intended to be shared by a large number of applications. In short and as a methodological pattern, ontology rules represent a higher level of abstraction than business rules which themselves are on a higher level than the logical and the implementation level.

Linking a business' rules to ontology-based business rules involves aligning (referencing, linking) the concepts and the relationships involved with concepts and relationships of an existing domain ontology. By doing so, the shared understanding (*semantics*) of the business rules will be improved and thus their reusability will be enhanced as required in open environments such as the (semantic) web.

3 ORM for Modeling Business Rules

In this section we briefly present the modeling principles and capabilities of ORM in terms of modeling requirements for business rules.

ORM was originally intended for modeling and querying databases at a conceptual level where the data requirements of applications need to be represented in a readily understood manner, thus enabling non-IT professionals to assist the modeling, validating, and maintaining processes. ORM offers a number of possibilities for managers, analysts, or domain experts to be involved in the modeling of entity types, domain constraints and business rules by using their own terminology. It is perhaps worthwhile to note that ORM derives from NIAM (Natural Language Information Analysis Method), which was explicitly designed to be a stepwise methodology arriving at "semantics" of a business application's data based on this kind of natural language communication.

ORM has an extensive and powerful graphical notation for representing a domain in a declarative manner as a network of elementary facts and their constraints. Elementary facts are represented in terms of *object types* that play *roles*. This graphical representation can be fairly easily re-verbalized into statements in pseudo natural language in a structured and fixed syntax. Therefore business rule modelers could represent a business policy either graphically or textually or both, which will in general improve, simplify, help to validate, and therefore speed up the modeling process.

Modeling business rules requires an expressive modeling language in order to capture the business complexity. For this, ORM allows representing information structures in multiple ways as unary, binary, as well as n-ary facts. It has a sophisticated object type system that distinguishes between representations of lexical and non-lexical objects, and has strict "is a" relationships with "clean" multiple inheritance as in frame systems ([17]). ORM has an *a priori* given set of static and certain dynamic constraint types and derivation rules that turned out to be suitable and expressive enough to cover a significant part of the needs emerging from enterprise modeling. Such constraints and rules include classical ones such as uniqueness and mandatory roles, as well as less common ones such as subset, equality, ring, derivation and/or stored rules, etc. Rules that do not fit into one of the predetermined rule categories can be formulated using a suitable general-purpose constraint language such as RIDL ([18], [24], [16]).

ORM has well-defined semantics, and the specified facts and constraints can easily be mapped into e.g. first order logic [7]. The finiteness and selection of the set of predetermined constraint types permitted the development of formal validation and consistency analysis tools that check the correctness and the consistency of specified business rules ([8]).

Other advantages include the automated transformation of an ORM business schema into a normalized relational database schema ([8], [15]). This is partially supported by modern ORM CASE tools such as Microsoft's Visio2000 Architect, VisoModeler, and more fully by the earlier InfoModeler tool [1].

A Small Example of an ORM Schema Diagram:

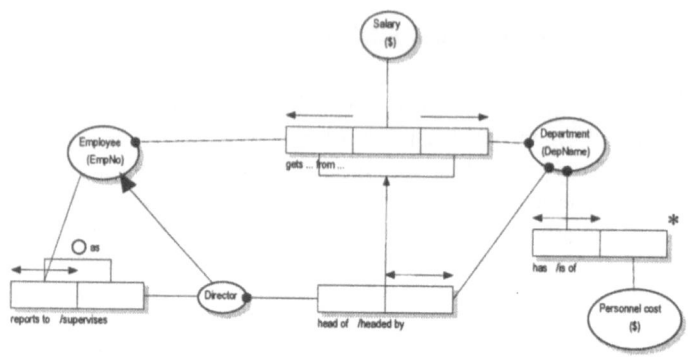

Fig. 1. Example ORM Diagram

On an ORM schema, Object types are shown as named ellipses, with their *reference schemes* in parentheses. Logical predicates (fact types) appear as named sequences of roles, where each role appears as a box. Roles are connected by line segments to the object types that "play" them.

In the Fig. 1, the object types are Employee, Department, Director, Salary and Personnel Cost. Personnel cost and Salary are referenced by an amount of $, Department by a department name (DepName), Employee by an employee number (EmpNo). The arrow connecting the object types Director and Employee denotes an is-a (strict subtype) relationship from Director to Employee. The predicates and subtype link are verbalized as follows: *Employee reports to Director and Director supervises Employee*; *Director is_a Employee*; *Employee gets Salary from Department*; *Director is head of Department and Department is headed by Director*; *Department has Personnel cost and Personnel cost is of Department*.

In what follows, we briefly name and explain the constraints occurring in the diagram, in fact by giving an (approximate) verbalization for an example occurring in Fig.1. For other types of ORM constraints, we refer to [24] or [25]; the notation and definitions in this paper will be taken from [15].

Black dots indicate a *mandatory role* constraint. Verbalization in Fig.1: *each Director is head of at least one Department*. The arrow-tipped bars above the roles are uniqueness constraints. E.g. *each Department is headed by at most one Director*. Uniqueness constraints can span more than one role, indicating that any combination that instantiates these roles should be unique. E.g. for the predicate *Employee gets Salary From Department*, there holds *each Employee gets at most one Salary from a [his] Department*. An arrow between two predicates indicates a subset constraint between the roles involved: *each Director [who] is head of a Department also works_for that Department*. A circle above a predicate indicates a *ring constraint*. In the figure the circle marked with 'as' indicates an *asymmetric* ring constraint: **if an Employee reports to a Director** (who is also an Employee), **then [his] Director must not report to this Employee**.

Finally, an asterisk beside a predicate indicates that we have a *derived fact type*. The derivation rule is then included elsewhere, linked to the schema. In Fig.1, <u>define</u> **Personnel cost for a Department** <u>as sum of all</u> **Salaries of Employees received from that [their] Department**. Instances of derived facts may be considered *stored* (i.e. pre-calculated at compile time and maintained by updates) or *interpreted* (i.e. computed on-the-fly when needed).

4 ORM-Markup Language

The ORM conceptual schema methodology is fairly comprehensive in its treatment of many "practical" or "standard" business rules and constraint types. Its detailed formal description, (we shall take ours from [15]) makes it an interesting candidate to non-trivially illustrate our XML based ORM-markup language as an exchange protocol for representing ORM conceptual models. In this section we describe the main elements of the ORM-ML grammar and demonstrate it using a few selected elementary examples. A complete formal definition of the grammar for this ORM-ML as an XML Schema instance can be found in [13]. It follows that an ORM Schema when formulated in ORM-ML must be valid according the defined XML Schema. A more complete example is provided in the appendix.

ORM-ML allows the representation of any ORM schema without loss of information or change in semantics, except for the geometry and topology (graphical layout) of the schema (e.g. location, shapes of the symbols), which we however easily may provide as a separate *graphical style sheet* to the ORM Schema (not added in this paper).

We represent the ORM document as a one node element called ORMSchema, which consists itself of two nodes: ORMMeta and ORMBody. As a header to an ORM document, and to illustrate the "ORM Schema Document" (instance) nature of the described schema, ORMMeta node includes *metadata* about the ORM *document* using the 16 well-known Dublin Core Meta Tags [RFC2431]; an example of their use appears in Table 1 below.

Table 1. Example of an ORMMeta Node in an ORM-ML File

```
...<ORMMeta>
     <dc:title>ORM-ML example</dc:title>
     <dc:creator>Jan Demey</dc:creator>
     <dc:description>A complete example of an ORM-ML file</dc:description>
     <dc:contributor>Mustafa Jarrar</dc:contributor>
     <dc:contributor>Robert Meersman</dc:contributor>
  </ORMMeta>....
```

The ORMBody node consists of at most these five different kinds of (meta-ORM) elements: Object, Subtype, Predicate, Predicate_Object and Constraint.

We adopt in the sequel the ORM modeling technique as defined in [15] except for some minor nomenclature and notation differences, argued in more detail elsewhere, which add some additional abstraction and precision. Object elements are abstract XML elements and are used to represent Object Types. They are identified by an attribute 'Name' which is the name of the Object Type in the ORM Schema (see the figure in Example 2). Objects might have some Value or ValueRange elements, which are used for *value constraints* on the Object Type (not present in Fig.2). A ValueRange element has 2 attributes: *begin* and *end*, with obvious meanings. Objects are implemented by two XML elements: LOT (Lexical Object Type, called Value Types in [15]) and NOLOT (Non-Lexical Object Type, called Entity Types in [15]). LOT elements may have a *numeric* attribute, which is a boolean and indicates whether we deal with a numeric Lexical Object Type. NOLOT elements have a boolean attribute called *independent*, which indicates whether the Non Lexical Object Type is independent (see [15] for definitions). NOLOT elements may also have a *reference* element. A reference element would indicate how this NOLOT is identified by LOTs and other NOLOTs in a given application environment. A reference element has 2 attributes: ref_name, the name of the reference and numeric, a boolean to indicate whether it is a numeric reference.

Example 2.

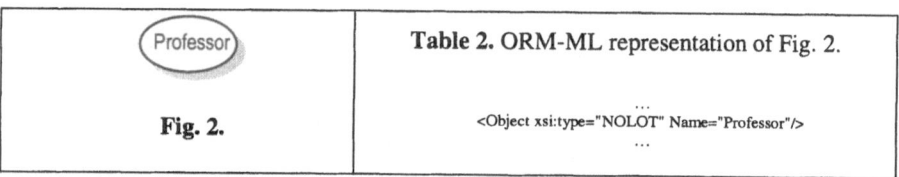

	Table 2. ORM-ML representation of Fig. 2.
(Professor) **Fig. 2.**	... <Object xsi:type="NOLOT" Name="Professor"/> ...

Subtype elements are used to represent subtype relationships between (non-lexical) object types. A subset element is required to have two attributes: parent and child, which are references to object elements (see Example 3).

Example 3.

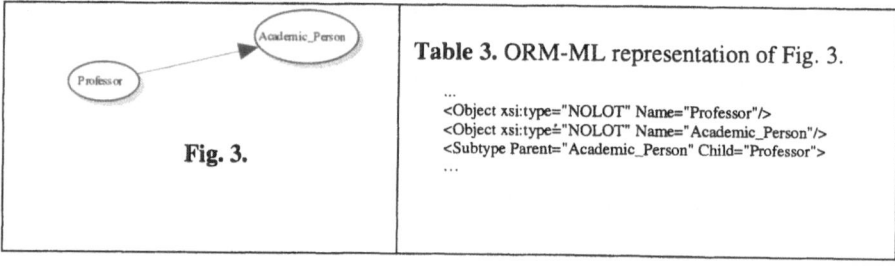

	Table 3. ORM-ML representation of Fig. 3.
(Academic_Person) (Professor) **Fig. 3.**	... <Object xsi:type="NOLOT" Name="Professor"/> <Object xsi:type="NOLOT" Name="Academic_Person"/> <Subtype Parent="Academic_Person" Child="Professor"> ...

Predicates consist of at least one Object_Role element. Such an element contains a reference to an object and may contain a role. They actually represent the rectangles in an ORM schema. Every Object_Role element needs a generated attribute 'ID' which identifies the Object_Role. By using this ID attribute, we can refer to a particular Object_Role element in the rest of the XML document, which we will need to do when e.g. we define constraints.

Predicates can have one or more rule elements. These elements can contain extra rules that are defined for the predicate.

Predicates can have one or more rule elements. These elements can contain extra rules that are defined for the predicate.

Predicates also have two boolean attributes that are optional: '*Derived*' and '*Derived_Stored*' which indicate whether a predicate respectively is derived, or derived and stored, or not.

Example 4. This example shows a simple binary predicate as in fig 4, and how it is represented in ORM-ML in Table 4.

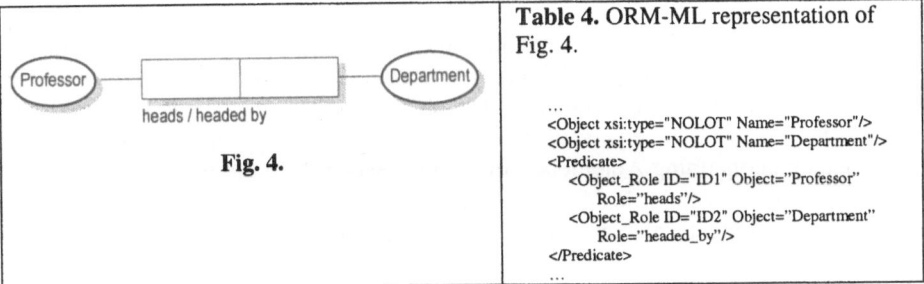

	Table 4. ORM-ML representation of Fig. 4.

heads / headed by
 	
Fig. 4.
	...
	\<Object xsi:type="NOLOT" Name="Professor"/>
	\<Object xsi:type="NOLOT" Name="Department"/>
	\<Predicate>
	   \<Object_Role ID="ID1" Object="Professor"
	      Role="heads"/>
	   \<Object_Role ID="ID2" Object="Department"
	      Role="headed_by"/>
	\</Predicate>
	...

Predicate_Objects are actually objectified predicates, which are used in nested fact types. They contain a predicate element and have an attribute called 'Predicate_Name'. So in fact they are merely a predicate that has received a (new) object type name. In building Object_Roles, the Predicate_Name can be referenced. In this way we build predicates that contain objectified predicates instead of object types. Example 5 illustrates the XML representation for nested fact types that this requires.

Example 5.

This example shows the representation of a nested fact type as in Fig. 5.

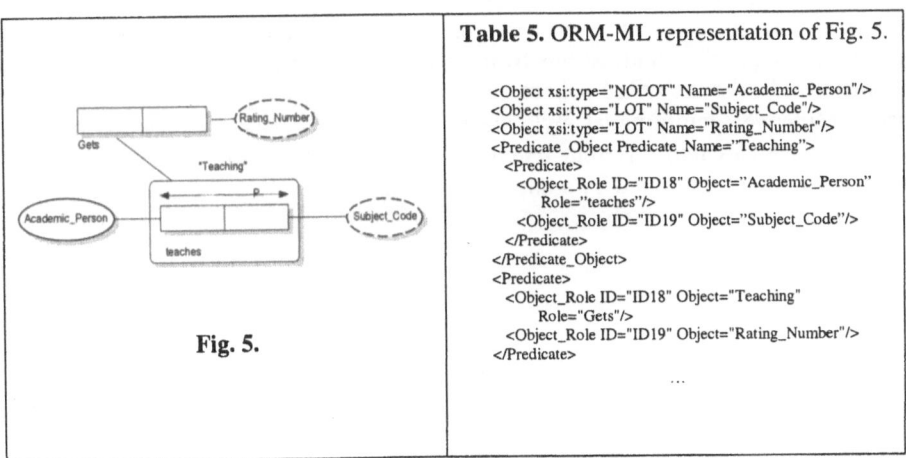

	Table 5. ORM-ML representation of Fig. 5.

Gets
"Teaching"
 	
Academic_Person
teaches
 	
Fig. 5.
	\<Object xsi:type="NOLOT" Name="Academic_Person"/>
	\<Object xsi:type="LOT" Name="Subject_Code"/>
	\<Object xsi:type="LOT" Name="Rating_Number"/>
	\<Predicate_Object Predicate_Name="Teaching">
	   \<Predicate>
	      \<Object_Role ID="ID18" Object="Academic_Person"
	         Role="teaches"/>
	      \<Object_Role ID="ID19" Object="Subject_Code"/>
	   \</Predicate>
	\</Predicate_Object>
	\<Predicate>
	   \<Object_Role ID="ID18" Object="Teaching"
	      Role="Gets"/>
	   \<Object_Role ID="ID19" Object="Rating_Number"/>
	\</Predicate>
	...

Constraint elements represent the ORM constraints. The Constraint element itself is abstract, but it is implemented by different types of constraints, viz. mandatory, use the ID-s of the Object_Role elements to define constraints (except for value constraints on an object type, because these constraints are defined in the corresponding object element).

Uniqueness and mandatory constraint elements possess only Object_Role elements (at least one). These elements are the object_roles in the ORM diagram on which the constraint is placed. In this way, there is no need to make a distinction between the ORM-ML syntax of "external" and "internal" uniqueness constraints (see [15]), or between mandatory and disjunctive mandatory constraints (see Example 6 below).

The representation for subset, equality and exclusion constraints is analogous, so we will only discuss them in general terms. Each of these latter constraints has exactly two elements that contain references to (combinations of) object_role elements. For instance, to represent an equality constraint between two predicates, we create a subset element, containing 2 elements 'First' and 'Second'. In the first element we put references to the object_roles from the first predicate, and in the second we put references to the object_roles from the second predicate (see Example 6).

Example 6.

This example shows the representation of the constraints from Fig. 6.

Finally, *ring constraint* elements simply contain references to the object_roles they are put on, and frequency constraints have two attributes: a reference to the object_role the constraint is placed on and an attribute called 'Frequency' which contains the declared frequency number.

A Note on Verbalization Style Sheets for Business Rules. Verbalization of a conceptual model is the process of writing its facts and constraints in pseudo natural language sentences, which assumedly allows non-experts to (help) check, validate, or even build conceptual schemas. The ORM modeling tool "InfoModeler" supported a built-in feature for automatic verbalization of ORM Schema or part of it. In ORM-ML, generating such verbalizations from agreed templates (i.e. "template NL" syntax) parameterized over the ORM schema is done by building separate XML-based style sheets. Moreover, multilingual style sheets[3] also become easier by translating these template sentences into different languages, its parameter values (which come from the ORM schema) translated by a human or machine.

---

[3] For ORM-ML, e.g. a multilingual verbalization style sheet was constructed in the authors' lab [ORMML], based on the XML Schema in [13], (but not discussed in this paper).

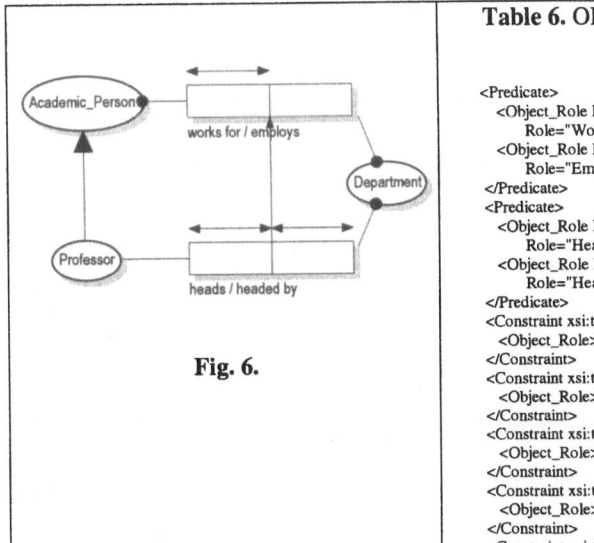

Fig. 6.

Table 6. ORM-ML representation of Fig. 6.

```
<Predicate>
  <Object_Role ID="ID8" Object="Academic_Person"
    Role="WorksFor"/>
  <Object_Role ID="ID9" Object="Department"
    Role="Employs"/>
</Predicate>
<Predicate>
  <Object_Role ID="ID12" Object="Professor"
    Role="Heads"/>
  <Object_Role ID="ID13" Object="Department"
    Role="Headed by"/>
</Predicate>
<Constraint xsi:type="Mandatory">
  <Object_Role>ID8</Object_Role>
</Constraint>
<Constraint xsi:type="Uniqueness">
  <Object_Role>ID8</Object_Role>
</Constraint>
<Constraint xsi:type="Uniqueness">
  <Object_Role>ID12</Object_Role>
</Constraint>
<Constraint xsi:type="Uniqueness">
  <Object_Role>ID13</Object_Role>
</Constraint>
<Constraint xsi:type="Mandatory">
  <Object_Role>ID9</Object_Role>
</Constraint>
<Constraint xsi:type="Mandatory">
  <Object_Role>ID13</Object_Role>
</Constraint>
<Constraint xsi:type="Subset">
  <Parent>
    <Object_Role>ID8</Object_Role>
    <Object_Role>ID9</Object_Role>
  </Parent>
  <Child>
    <Object_Role>ID12</Object_Role>
    <Object_Role>ID13</Object_Role>
  </Child> </Constraint>
```

5   Generating an ORM-ML File from an ORM Schema

XML being a computer-friendly language, it is of course not the ultimate purpose to write ORM-ML files by hand. Although it turns out relatively easy to do that, the goal must be to implement into existing conceptual modeling tools, ideally, a functionality like a "Save/Load as ORM-ML" dialog box. Because in general the repository format in which ORM (or other modeling method's) schemas are stored is proprietary or even "closed" inside the CASE tool's software, we will here just show in abstract terms the algorithm how to make the conversion, starting from a rather simplified *meta schema* for ORM given below (in ORM diagram itself, of course) in Figure 7. Remember that by the definition of Meta schema, individual ORM schema instances are considered to be stored "conceptually" in such a Meta schema in an obvious manner. After the customary application of a conceptual-to-relational transformation algorithm, its actual content is retrieved from the relational database of which the relational database tables were derived from this Meta schema (see [15], for theory and examples of this).

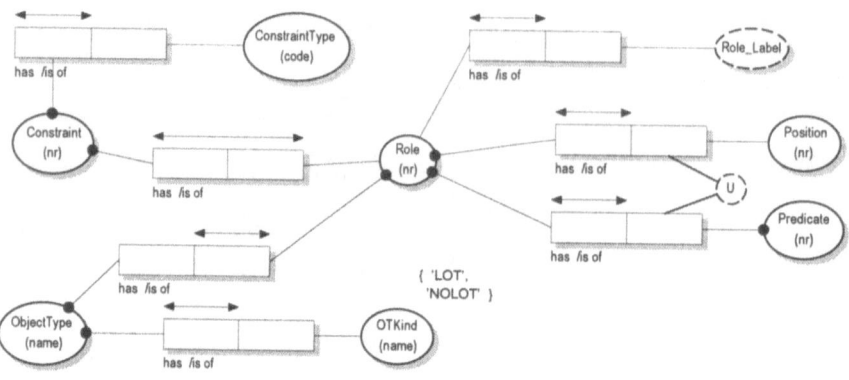

Fig. 7.

Suppose we store instances of this Meta schema in a relational database with the tables shown in figure 8.

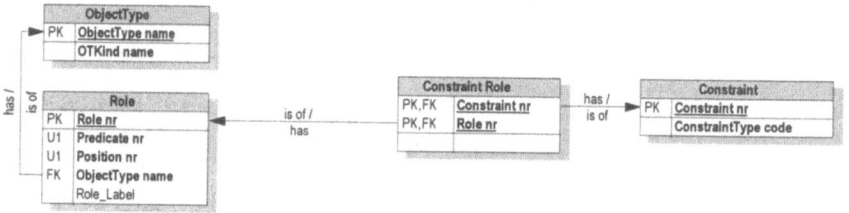

Fig. 8.

Now we easily convert its contents to ORM-ML, for instance as follows (it will be useful to consult the appendix for a detailed illustration of its result):

Sketch of ORM to ORM-ML Mapping Algorithm

(a) Obtain all *ObjectType* elements by a query **SELECT * FROM ObjectType**. Each returned row will be one ObjectType, with as name attribute ObjectType_name and as xsi:type attribute OTKind.

(b) Get predicates by issuing a query **SELECT Role_nr, Predicate_nr, Object_Type_name, Role_Label FROM Role ORDER BY Predicate_nr, Position_nr**. Start a new *predicate* element, and append an *Object_Role* element (attributes ID: Role_nr, Object: Object_Type_name, Role: Role_Label) for each row returned until the Predicate_nr changes. When the Predicate_nr changes, close the predicate element and start a new one. Repeat this until all returned rows are processed.

(c) For *Constraint* elements issue a query **SELECT C.Constraint_nr, C.ConstraintType_code, CR.Role_nr from Constraint C, Constraint_Role CR WHERE C.Constraint_nr = CR.Constraint_nr**. Open a Constraint element (attribute type: C.ConstraintType_code). Append an Object_Role element (content:

CR.Role_nr) for each row returned until C.Constraint_nr changes. When C.Constraint_nr changes, close the Constraint element and start a new one until all returned rows are processed.

Note. Naturally one could specify the above algorithm also by directly "querying" the ORM Meta Schema in Fig. 7 itself, using a suitable ORM-based query language such as RIDL [18] instead of SQL. Although this would lead to a more compact (and "conceptual" specification, we lacked the space in this paper to present the (original) RIDL language, which may be downloaded from http://www.starlab.vub.ac.be/...-> RIDL_User_Guid.zip

6 Conclusion: Some Other Advantages for ORM-ML and Future Research

In this paper we have explained how ORM could be used to design business rules. We have presented a way to save ORM schemas in an XML-based markup language. The main advantage of this markup language is that it is easy to exchange information. Like ORM-ML, any conceptual modeling approach could have a markup language, since by standardizing such a markup language several advantages are worth noting.

- *Helps schema integration and transformation.*
In information systems, it is in general easier to integrate or *align* the conceptual models of the systems than to materially integrate the logical or the physical internal representation of the system, as demonstrated by the literature on view- and schema integration (e.g. [21]). Therefore, ORM-ML as a standardized syntax for ORM models may assist interoperation tools to exchange, parse or understand the ORM schemas.
- *Interoperability for exchanging and sharing conceptual models over the Internet.*
Facilities are needed to share and exchange ORM conceptual models (not only business rules) in terms of a networked, distributed computing-driven, and collaborative environment, and to allow users to browse and edit shared domain knowledge over the Internet, intranets and other channels. A conceptual schema markup language provides a standardizable method to achieve interoperability among CASE tools that use that conceptual modeling technique.

- *Implementing a conceptual query language over the Web.*
In open and distributed environments, building queries should be possible regardless of the internal representation of the data. Query languages based on ontologies (seen as shared conceptual models) help users not only to build queries, but also make them easier, more expressive, and more understandable than corresponding queries in a language like SQL. Exchanging, reusing, or sharing such queries efficiently between agents over the web is substantially facilitated by a standardized markup language. Consequently, ORM-based query

languages (e.g. RIDL [24], [18], ConQuer [3]) would gain from ORM-ML by representing queries in such an exchangeable representation.

- *Building a standard style sheet to generate its formalizations.*

Generating verbalization style sheets for a given usage or need may require a certain kind of style sheets e.g. for first order rewriting formalisms of ORM-ML documents, or to transform the XML-based representation into another XML-based representation. Another important and strategic issue is that one could write a style sheet to generate the given ORM model instance into a given rule-engine's syntax, which allows run-time interpretation by that rule engine, for instance performing instance validation, integrity checks, etc. This also enhances the use of ORM-ML for representing and modeling ORM-based business rules at a conceptual level, making agents able to share, reuse, and exchange these rules.

Finally, it is clearly also possible to transform ORM-ML into another language's syntax. We illustrated in passing how ORM-ML may be transformed into/from (structured) pseudo natural language. Currently we are e.g. implementing and investigating mappings from ORM-inspired ontologies into languages used by a number of commercial (e.g. Haley's Authorete® [2]) and open-source rule engines.

Acknowledgments. Partial support for the reported work from the EC FP5 Thematic Network OntoWeb (IST-2000-29243) is hereby also gratefully acknowledged.

References

1. Asymetrix. InfoModeler User Manual. Asymetrix Corporation, 110-110th Avenue NE, Suite 700,Bellevue, WA 98004, Washington (1994)
2. http://www.haley.com/Authorete.html
3. Bloesch, A., Halpin, T.: Conquer: A Conceptual Query Language. In: Thalheim, B. (ed.): Conceptual Modeling - ER'96 Proceedings. LNCS, Springer Verlag (1996)
4. Berners-Lee, T. et al.: Weaving the Web: The Original Design and Ultimate Destiny of the World Wide Web by its Inventor. Harper San Francisco (1999)
5. Booch, G., Rumbaugh, J., Jacobson, I.: The UML User Guide. Addison-Wesley (1999)
6. Boley, H., Tabet, S., Wagner, G.: Design Rationale of 20: A Markup Language for Semantic Web Rules. In: International Semantic Web Working Symposium (SWWS) (2001)
7. De Troyer, O., Meersman, R.: A Logic Framework for a Semantics of Object-Oriented Data Modeling. OOER (1995) 238-249
8. De Troyer, O., Meersman, R.A., Verlinder, P.: RIDL* on the CRIS Case: a Workbench for NIAM. In: Olle, T.W., Verrijn-Stuart, A.A., Bhabuta, L. (eds.): Computerized Assistance during the Information Systems Life Cyle. Elsevier Science Publishers B.V. North-Holland (1988) 375-459
9. Bird, L., Goodchild, A., Halpin, T.A.: Object Role Modelling and XML-Schema. In: Laender, A., Liddle, S., Storey, V. (eds.): Proceedings of the 19th International Conference on Conceptual Modeling (ER'00). LNCS, Springer Verlag (1999)
10. Gottesdiener, E.: Business RULES show power, Promise. In: Issue of Application Development Trends. vol4. no3 (1997)

11. Fensel, D., Bussler, C.: The Web Service Modeling Framework WSMF. Technical Report, Vrije Universiteit Amsterdam
12. Guide Business Rules Project, 11/95, GUIDE International Corporation, available at http://www.guide.org/ap/apbrules.htm. In Business RULES show power, Promise, by E. Gottesdiener, President, EBG consulting, Issue of application Development Trends, vol4., no3, (1997)
13. http://www.starlab.vub.ac.be/ORMML/ormml.xsd
14. North, K.: Modeling, Data Semantics, and Natural Language. In: New Architect magazine (1999)
15. Halpin, T.: Information Modeling and Relational Databases. 3rd Ed., Morgan-Kaufmann (2001)
16. NN.: Terminology for the Conceptual Schema and Information System. ISO Technical Report TR9007, ISO (1990)
17. Karp, P.D.: The design space of frame knowledge representation systems, Technical Report 520, SRI International AI Center (1992)
18. Meersman, R.: Languages for the High-Level End User. In: InfoTech State of the Art Report, Pergamon Press (1981)
19. Navathe, S., Elmasri, R.: Fundamentals of Database Systems, 3rd ed., Addison-Wesley (2001)
20. http://www.dfki.uni-kl.de/20/
21. Spaccapietra, S., Parent, C.: View Integration: A Step Forward in Solving Structural Conflicts, IEEE Transactions on Data and Knowledge Engineering 6(2), IEEE (1994)
22. Halpin, T.: Business Rules and Object Role Modeling. In: Issue of Database Programming & Design, vol. 9, no. 10 (1996) 66-72
23. Halpin, T.: Modeling for Data and Business Rules. An interview with Terry Halpin conducted by Ron Ross, Editor of Database Newsletter. In: Issue of the Database Newsletter (1997)
24. Verheyen, G., van Bekkum, P.: NIAM, An Information Analysis Method. In: Olle, T.W., Sol, H., Verrijn-Stuart, A. (eds.): IFIP Conference on Comparative Review of Information Systems Methodologies, North-Holland (1982).
25. Wintraecken, J.J.V.R.: The NIAM Information Analysis Method: Theory and Practice. Kluwer Deventer Netherlands (1990)
26. http://www.w3.org/XML/
27. http://www.w3.org/XML/Schema

Appendix

A complete example of an ORM Schema with the associated ORM-ML file generated by the algorithm defined in Section 5.

```
<?xml version="1.0" encoding="UTF-8"?>
<ORMSchema xmlns:xsi=http://www.w3.org/2001/XMLSchema-instance
xsi:noNamespaceSchemaLocation=http://starlab.vub.ac.be/ORMML/ormml.xsd
xmlns:dc="http://purl.org/dc/elements/1.1/">
        <ORMMeta>
                <dc:title>ORM ML example</dc:title>
                <dc:creator>Jan Demey</dc:creator>
                <dc:description>A complete example of an ORM ML file</dc:description>
                <dc:contributor>Mustafa Jarrar</dc:contributor>
                <dc:contributor>Robert Meersman</dc:contributor>
        </ORMMeta>
        <ORMBody>
```

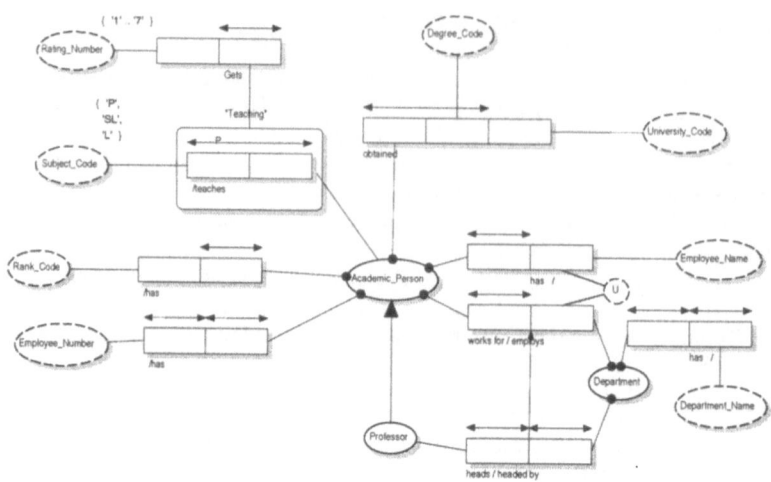

```
<Object xsi:type="NOLOT" Name="Academic_Person"/>
<Object xsi:type="LOT" Name="Employee_Number"/>
<Object xsi:type="LOT" Name="Degree_Code"/>
<Object xsi:type="LOT" Name="University_Code"/>
<Object xsi:type="LOT" Name="Employee_Name"/>
<Object xsi:type="NOLOT" Name="Professor"/>
<Object xsi:type="NOLOT" Name="Department"/>
<Object xsi:type="LOT" Name="Department_Name"/>
<Object xsi:type="LOT" Name="Rating_Number">
            <ValueRange begin="1" end="7"/>
</Object>
<Object xsi:type="LOT" Name="Subject_Code">
            <Value>P</Value>
            <Value>SL</Value>
            <Value>L</Value>
</Object>
<Object xsi:type="LOT" Name="Rank_Code"/>
<Subtype Parent="Academic_Person" Child="Professor"/>
<Predicate>
            <Object_Role ID="ID1" Object="Academic_Person" Role="Has"/>
            <Object_Role ID="ID2" Object="Employee_Number"/>
</Predicate>
<Predicate>
            <Object_Role ID="ID3" Object="Academic_Person" Role="Obtained"/>
            <Object_Role ID="ID4" Object="Degree_Code"/>
            <Object_Role ID="ID5" Object="University_Code"/>
</Predicate>
<Predicate>
            <Object_Role ID="ID6" Object="Academic_Person" Role="Has"/>
            <Object_Role ID="ID7" Object="Employee_Name"/>
</Predicate>
<Predicate>
            <Object_Role ID="ID8" Object="Academic_Person" Role="WorksFor"/>
            <Object_Role ID="ID9" Object="Department" Role="Employs"/>
</Predicate>
<Predicate>
            <Object_Role ID="ID10" Object="Department" Role="has"/>
            <Object_Role ID="ID11" Object="Department_Name"/>
</Predicate>
<Predicate>
            <Object_Role ID="ID12" Object="Professor" Role="Heads"/>
            <Object_Role ID="ID13" Object="Department" Role="Headed by"/>
</Predicate>
<Predicate>
            <Object_Role ID="ID14" Object="Academic_Person" Role="Has"/>
            <Object_Role ID="ID15" Object="Rank_Code"/>
</Predicate>
<Predicate>
            <Object_Role ID="ID18" Object="Teaching" Role="Gets"/>
            <Object_Role ID="ID19" Object="Rating_Number"/>
</Predicate>
<Predicate_Object Predicate_Name="Teaching">
            <Predicate>
                        <Object_Role ID="ID16" Object="Academic_Person" Role="Teaches"/>
                        <Object_Role ID="ID17" Object="Subject_Code"/>
            </Predicate>
</Predicate_Object>
<Constraint xsi:type="Uniqueness">
            <Object_Role>ID1</Object_Role>
</Constraint>
<Constraint xsi:type="Mandatory">
```

```
                        <Object_Role>ID1</Object_Role>
        </Constraint>
        <Constraint xsi:type="Uniqueness">
                        <Object_Role>ID2</Object_Role>
        </Constraint>
        <Constraint xsi:type="Mandatory">
                        <Object_Role>ID3</Object_Role>
        </Constraint>
        <Constraint xsi:type="Uniqueness">
                        <Object_Role>ID3</Object_Role>
                        <Object_Role>ID4</Object_Role>
        </Constraint>
        <Constraint xsi:type="Mandatory">
                        <Object_Role>ID6</Object_Role>
        </Constraint>
        <Constraint xsi:type="Uniqueness">
                        <Object_Role>ID6</Object_Role>
        </Constraint>
        <Constraint xsi:type="Mandatory">
                        <Object_Role>ID8</Object_Role>
        </Constraint>
        <Constraint xsi:type="Uniqueness">
                        <Object_Role>ID8</Object_Role>
        </Constraint>
        <Constraint xsi:type="Uniqueness">
                        <Object_Role>ID12</Object_Role>
        </Constraint>
        <Constraint xsi:type="Uniqueness">
                        <Object_Role>ID13</Object_Role>
        </Constraint>
        <Constraint xsi:type="Uniqueness">
                        <Object_Role>ID10</Object_Role>
        </Constraint>
        <Constraint xsi:type="Mandatory">
                        <Object_Role>ID10</Object_Role>
        </Constraint>
        <Constraint xsi:type="Mandatory">
                        <Object_Role>ID9</Object_Role>
        </Constraint>
        <Constraint xsi:type="Mandatory">
                        <Object_Role>ID13</Object_Role>
        </Constraint>
        <Constraint xsi:type="Uniqueness">
                        <Object_Role>ID11</Object_Role>
        </Constraint>
        <Constraint xsi:type="Uniqueness">
                        <Object_Role>ID7</Object_Role>
                        <Object_Role>ID9</Object_Role>
        </Constraint>
        <Constraint xsi:type="Subset">
                <Parent>
                                <Object_Role>ID8</Object_Role>
                                <Object_Role>ID9</Object_Role>
                </Parent>
                <Child>
                                <Object_Role>ID12</Object_Role>
                                <Object_Role>ID13</Object_Role>
                </Child>
        </Constraint>
        <Constraint xsi:type="Mandatory">
                        <Object_Role>ID14</Object_Role>
        </Constraint>
        <Constraint xsi:type="Uniqueness">
                        <Object_Role>ID14</Object_Role>
        </Constraint>
        <Constraint xsi:type="Uniqueness">
                        <Object_Role>ID16</Object_Role>
                        <Object_Role>ID17</Object_Role>
        </Constraint>
        <Constraint xsi:type="Uniqueness">
                        <Object_Role>ID18</Object_Role>
        </Constraint>
        </ORMBody>
</ORMSchema>
```

Distributed Description Logics: Directed Domain Correspondences in Federated Information Sources

Alex Borgida[1] and Luciano Serafini[2]

[1] Dept. of Computer Science
Rutgers University
New Brunswick, USA
borgida@cs.rutgers.edu
[2] ITC-IRST
Trento, Italy
serafinit@itc.it

Abstract. A central problem of co-operative information systems is the ability to integrate information from multiple sources. Although this problem has been studied for several decades, there is a need for a more refined approach in those cases where the original sources form a loose federation, each maintaining its own independent view of the world. In particular, we motivate with examples the utility of directed non-injective mappings between the individuals in the domains of multiple IS. We then extend the logical formalism of Description Logics, which has previously served successfully in IS integration and is currently being used in semantic-web ontolgies, to handle such mappings. The result is called Distributed Description Logics, and we consider some of its desirable properties, as well as some theorems concerning its computational aspects.

1 Introduction

A significant problem of modern information management is the integration of information from multiple sources. The standard version presumes a framework where users are accessing through a single interface data from several information sources (local ISs), which can include databases, web data, files, etc. The important goal here is making the users unaware of the original source of the information, thus making the interface uniform. This is usually achieved through a global (conceptual) schema that is queried by users. Local ISs are then related to this by a variety of techniques ("local as view", "global as view"), and query answering consists of identifying relevant ISs, translating the user's query into collections of queries over local ISs, and collating the answers.

A somewhat different, but related, approach is one which preserves the identity of each local IS and its user interface. However, the local system wishes to import information available in other sources, which are related to it directly

R. Meersman, Z. Tari (Eds.): CoopIS/DOA/ODBASE 2002, LNCS 2519, pp. 36–53, 2002.

through bilateral assertions. This approach is more appropriate for loosely coupled federations of information system, where the local ISs maintain a degree of autonomy. Our work is in this second paradigm.

The traditional view of database integration holds that the semantic worldviews of local IS may exhibit miss-matches (often called "conflicts" or "semantic heterogeneities") which need to be resolved in order to allow information from one source to be properly visible in the other source. Saltor and Rodriguez [19] identify three categories of such semantic heterogeneities: (i) heterogeneities between object classes, (ii) heterogeneities between class structures, and (iii) heterogeneities between object instances. The first two categories relate to the schema of the IS, and have been thoroughly studied. Some of the conflicts in the third category deal with "the facts": e.g., two IS may record the capital of China as Beijing and Peking respectively. In other situations, however, there may be more interesting systematic relationships between individuals. For example, consider the case when one IS contains personal information (e.g., from credit card purchases), while another one contains census information, which only records information about *households*. The correspondence between households and the people in it is not the identity relation, neither is it a simple functional bijection. Yet it will be important to establish and record this relationship if the two IS are to be integrated. In Section 2, we provide further examples of complex correspondences between the domains of multiple IS in a federated system.

Description Logics are formalisms for the conceptual representation of IS which have been successfully used in the past in the task of IS integration (e.g., [7,12,1,15,5,16,2]). We will therefore carry out our investigations in their context. In Section 3, we introduce Description Logics and Distributed Description Logics (DDL), provide formal semantics for them, and show how the examples are handled by the result. In Section 4, we review some desirable properties of distributed Information Systems, and discuss how DDL measure up to them. Finally, we provide a theorem which shows how DDL reasoning can often be translated into reasoning in a single, global but ordinary DL.

2 Motivating Examples

We will be considering a variety of possible correspondences between individuals in the domains of discourse of two IS, IS_1 and IS_2 say, some of which were noted already in [13].

In the simplest case of integration, the same individual (e.g., the name "Toronto"), occurs in both IS. Somewhat more complex is the situation where one needs to identify/match different representations of the same real-world individual. In the case of scaling conflicts (e.g., use of different units of measure), this relationship is quite systematic, and can be described through arithmetic equations. In other cases this needs to be achieved through the use of key attributes or heuristics (e.g., persons having the same name). Either way, the result can be thought of as a new binary relation between objects in the two IS, which happens to be a bijection.

Several complications may arise even in this situation. Consider the case when the unit of measure is currency: the conversion function Euro_to_Dollars, is not the inverse of the function Dollars_to_Euro, because banks add a surcharge to all transactions. Therefore a single conversion relation is not sufficient, and we must acknowledge the need for **directional mappings** between the domains, e.g., one from Dollars to Euro, and another from Euro to Dollars. A different complication can arise in the case when the mapping between the domains cannot be described extensionally. For example, suppose that one school assigns simple letter grades, e.g., A,B,C, while another school allows them to be qualified by plus and minus, e.g., A+. An A at the first school corresponds to one of {A+,A,A-} at the other school, but there is no way to tell which. Note however that this partial information is still important: having a grade of "A+, A or A-" is known to be better than having a grade of B!

The following examples explore further intricacies of the relationship between domain elements in different IS.

Example 21. *Suppose* BasicC, IntermC *and* AdvancedC *are 3 increasingly difficult courses on some topic. University $Univ_1$ offers* BasicC *and* AdvancedC, *while university $Univ_2$ offers* IntermC. *The universities are concerned about what classes a student has completed, in order to check the pre-requisites of other courses they are enrolling in, or to meet degree requirements. In particular, both universities allow a course x to be substituted for another course y if x is harder than y, and covers most of the material of y (say 80%). The universities also allow credits earned at one to be* transfered *to the other. $Univ_1$ may decide to accept* IntermC *as a substitute for* BasicC; *on the other hand, $Univ_2$ may only accept* AdvancedC *as a substitute for* IntermC. *Suppose that courses are modeled as concepts whose extension is the set of students who have completed them. Then we have a situation where we want the instances of* IntermC *to be included among the instances of* BasicC *according to $Univ_1$, while* IntermC *should subsume the instances of* AdvancedC *according to $Univ_2$. Despite this, $Univ_1$ may not necessarily want to view* AdvancedC *as a subclass of* BasicC, *since the courses might disagree on more than 80% of the material.*

Example 22. *Suppose IS_1 has information about married couples, while IS_2 has information about persons. We therefore need to express correspondences between individuals in the two domains, e.g., between* couple23 *in IS_1, and each of* Gianni *and* Mary, *in IS_2. But there are more general relationships between the information in the two IS. For example, we know that each couple involves exactly two persons.*

In this case, IS_1 contains information about individuals that are in some sense *abstractions* over individuals in IS_2. Similar examples arise in other situations where the so-called "materialization abstraction" [17] occurs.

Example 23. *Consider a situation where there are two IS: $IS_{Harvard}$ and IS_{MIT}, serving the needs of college libraries in some town. The libraries have* *information about* copies of books, *which can be taken by borrowers or are available on the shelf. On the other hand, $IS_{Student}$ is a database accessed by students who want to know which library they should go to if they need some book. Notice that the student does not care about which copies of a book are available, so we have once again an abstraction: the student's* Tractatus *corresponds to* TractatusCopy1,... *in* $IS_{Harvard}$, *as well as* TractatusCopy2 *in* IS_{MIT}. *Moreover, the student only wants to know about some material being located at MIT if there is a copy of it currently on the shelf at the MIT library.*

The above examples reinforce the need to consider in greater detail the role of the mapping between the domain of objects in the IS's being integrated into a federation. First, one needs a pair of general relations (not just functions) to connect each pair of IS, because information flow is "directional". Second, there are two aspects of these mappings:

- How are specific individual objects related to each other? (e.g., couple23 in IS_1 and Mary in IS_2).
- What general statements can one make about the mappings of individuals? (e.g., Couple instances in IS_1 correspond to exactly two Person instances in IS_2).

3 Formalization Using Description Logics

Description Logics (DLs) are a family of object-centered knowledge representation formalisms that have proven to be useful in the design and querying of Information Systems [3], including information integration [7,1,15,5,16,2]. They are of increasing interest, since DL-based systems such as DAML+OIL [10] are the current leading contenders for use in expressing semantic web ontologies.

3.1 Description Logics

Description logics view the world as being populated by individuals that can be grouped into classes, called *concepts*, and that can be related to each other by binary relationships, called *roles*. A specific DL provides a specific set of "constructors" for building more complex concepts and roles (much like a programming language type system provides type constructors for building complex types from simpler ones). For example, concept constructors such as conjunction (written as $A \sqcap B$) and value restriction ($\forall r.C$) can be used to describe familiar object classes such as the following necessary conditions on *Students*: $Person \sqcap \forall attends.Univeristy \sqcap \forall age.Integer$.

A typical DL, such as $\mathcal{SHIQ}^1$ [11], would start with atomic concepts A, as well as constants ANYTHING and NOTHING, denoting the universe and the empty set respectively, and then build more complex descriptions according to the syntax in the second column of Figure 1. An additional concept construc-

---

[1] This particular DL is of interest, among others, since it is the basis of the proposed DAML+OIL language for expressing web-ontologies.

Construct name	Syntax	Semantics
primitive concept	A	$A^{\mathcal{I}}$
top concept	ANYTHING	$\Delta^{\mathcal{I}}$
bottom concept	NOTHING	$\emptyset$
conjunction	$C_1 \sqcap \ldots \sqcap C_n$	$C_1^{\mathcal{I}} \cap \ldots \cap C_n^{\mathcal{I}}$
disjunction	$C_1 \sqcup \ldots \sqcup C_n$	$C_1^{\mathcal{I}} \cup \ldots \cup C_n^{\mathcal{I}}$
negation	$\neg C$	$\Delta^{\mathcal{I}} \setminus C^{\mathcal{I}}$
value restriction	$\forall R.C$	$\{d \in \Delta^{\mathcal{I}} \mid R^{\mathcal{I}}(d) \subseteq C^{\mathcal{I}}\}$
exists restriction	$\exists R.C$	$\{d \in \Delta^{\mathcal{I}} \mid R^{\mathcal{I}}(d) \cap C^{\mathcal{I}} \neq \emptyset\}$
number	$\geq n\, R$	$\{d \in \Delta^{\mathcal{I}} \mid |R^{\mathcal{I}}(d)| \geq n\}$
restrictions	$\leq n\, R$	$\{d \in \Delta^{\mathcal{I}} \mid |R^{\mathcal{I}}(d)| \leq n\}$
qualified number	$\geq n\, R.C$	$\{d \in \Delta^{\mathcal{I}} \mid |R^{\mathcal{I}}(d) \cap C^{\mathcal{I}}| \geq n\}$
restrictions	$\leq n\, R.C$	$\{d \in \Delta^{\mathcal{I}} \mid |R^{\mathcal{I}}(d) \cap C^{\mathcal{I}}| \leq n\}$
	Role	**Semantics**
primitive role	P	$P^{\mathcal{I}}$
role inverse	R^-	$\{(y,x) \mid (x,y) \in R^{\mathcal{I}}\}$

Fig. 1. Syntax and semantics of the $\mathcal{SHIQ}$ Description Logic [11]

tor that we may use, but is not available in $\mathcal{SHIQ}$, is enumeration, which describes a concept by enumerating its instances: $\{IN_1, \ldots, IN_n\}$. In addition, complex roles can also be built from simpler ones (in the case of $\mathcal{SHIQ}$, the inverse/converse), and one can sometimes add assertions about roles being more specialized (e.g., daughter is a specialization of child) or being transitive (e.g., hasSibling).

One can then make several kinds of assertions using descriptions. Most familiarly, one can claim that one description, D, **subsumes**/is more general than another one, C, written as $C \sqsubseteq D$. For example, EMPLOYEE $\sqsubseteq$ PERSON. Subsumption can be used to automatically organize sets of class descriptions into an Is-A hierarchy, and to detect if a concept C is incoherent (by checking whether $C \sqsubseteq$ NOTHING). Secondly, one can assert the membership of an *individual* in a concept, e.g., STUDENT $\sqcap \neg$MALE(Anna), or the inter-relatedness of two individuals, e.g., attends(Anna,Harvard).

Collections of subsumption assertions specify the terminology used to describe some application domain. Such a collection is called a *T-box*, and resembles the schema of an IS. Collections of assertions about individuals describe some state of world, and form an *A-box*, which resembles a database of facts in an IS. A *(DL) knowledge base* **K** will then be a pair $\langle \mathbf{T}, \mathbf{A} \rangle$, where **T** is a terminology and **A** is an A-box.

Description Logics have been quite successful at capturing the semantics of IS, either directly or as a result of algorithmic mappings from more traditional data models such as the Extended Entity Relationship model. For example, suppose we start from a typical ER relation ENROLLMENT, which relates to entity STUDENT, with cardinality upper bound 5, and to entity COURSE. Then by introducing roles who and what, one can express the ER diagram by the following subsumptions [4]:

1. ENROLLMENT $\sqsubseteq$ $\quad$ $\forall$who.STUDENT $\quad$ $\sqcap$ ($= 1$ who) $\quad$ $\sqcap \forall$what.COURSE
   $\sqcap$ ($= 1$ what)
   (* who *and* what *are functions connecting each enrollment object to a student and a course* *)

2. STUDENT $\sqsubseteq$ $\forall$who$^-$.ENROLLMENT $\sqcap$ ($\leqslant 5$ who$^-$)
   (* who *only connects enrollments to students, and a student is in at most 5 such connections; expressed using* who$^-$, *the inverse of the* who *role.* *)

3. COURSE $\sqsubseteq$ $\forall$what$^-$.ENROLLMENT
   (* what *only connects enrollments to courses* *)

A description logic has a complexity of reasoning (e.g., for computing subsumption) that depends on the set of constructors. Much of the effort in DL research has been in identifying different sets of such constructors which have at least decidable inferences, and characterizing their computational complexity. We remark on the variable-free nature of the DL formalisms, which limit their expressive power but at the same time contribute to their ability to reason efficiently even with incomplete information (see [3]).

3.2 Distributed Description Logics

Suppose I is a nonempty set of indexes, and we have a collection of information systems IS_i, for $i \in I$, each described by some (potentially different) description logic $\mathcal{DL}_i$. (The IS_i could be full DL knowledge bases $\mathbf{K}_i$, or just T-boxes $\mathbf{T}_i$.) Let us now try to express connections between them, to form a co-operative IS.

The pioneering work of Catarci and Lenzerini [7] proposed the continued use of description logics. In particular, subsumption-like assertions could relate descriptions in different knowledge bases: $GradStudent_2 \sqsubseteq_{int} Student_1$ would indicate that every graduate student in the part of the world described by IS_2 was also a student in the overlapping part of the world described by IS_1. However, the semantics in [7] implies that inter-schema assertions only have an effect on those *individuals that are shared* between the respective IS domains – i.e., the correspondence between the domain elements is identity. The reason for this is, in part, that in current DL the definition of a new concept can only retrieve a subset of the existing set of individuals, rather than create new individuals.

In order to deal with our more complex examples, we turn for inspiration to the work of Ghidini and Serafini [9] on Distributed First Order Logic. The idea is to introduce in the semantics binary relations $\mathbf{r}_{ij}$ describing the correspondences between the domains of each IS_i and IS_j, and to use so-called **bridge rules** to constrain these relationships *in an implicit manner*.

In order to support directionality, the bridge rules in a set $\mathfrak{B}_{jk}$ will be viewed as describing "flow of information" from IS_j to IS_k *from the point of view of* IS_k (i.e., IS_k "importing" information from IS_j), and hence $\mathfrak{B}_{jk}$ may be different from $\mathfrak{B}_{kj}$.

Based on studies in [9], here are some patterns of constraints on the correspondence relationships that one might like to express using bridge rules:

1. Every instance of concept A in IS_1 corresponds only to instances of concept G in IS_2.
2. All G-instances in IS_2 have a corresponding A-instance in IS_1.
3. Each A-instance has at least/at most n corresponding instances in IS_2.
4. The correspondence relation from IS_1 to IS_2 is the identity relationship.
5. The correspondence relations between IS_1 and IS_2 are converses.

In this paper we will study the first two kinds of bridge rules.

To formalize things, we begin by labeling each description E in $\mathcal{DL}_i$ with its index i (written as $i\!:\!E$). This will help disambiguate descriptions in different $\mathcal{DL}_i$. However, when talking about subsumption within a single IS_i, we will use the more readable $i\!:\!A \sqsubseteq B$, instead of the more formal $i\!:\!A \sqsubseteq i\!:\!B$.

Definition 31. *Given concepts C and E of $\mathcal{DL}_i$ and $\mathcal{DL}_j$ respectively, a bridge rule from i to j is an expression of the following two forms:*

$$i\!:\!C \xrightarrow{\sqsubseteq} j\!:\!E \ , \ called \ an \ \text{into} \ rule$$

$$i\!:\!C \xrightarrow{\sqsupseteq} j\!:\!E \ , \ called \ an \ \text{onto} \ rule$$

An into-rule specifies that C-objects in IS_i correspond only to E-objects in IS_j, while an onto-rule states that the only things that correspond to E-objects in IS_2, are C-objects in IS_1.

In Example 22, one would have the bridge rule $1\!:\!\textsf{COUPLE} \xrightarrow{\sqsubseteq} 2\!:\!\textsf{PERSON}$ to indicate that every couple has corresponding persons, but would not normally include the bridge rule $1\!:\!\textsf{COUPLE} \xrightarrow{\sqsupseteq} 2\!:\!\textsf{PERSON}$, because there may be unmarried persons, who may therefore not correspond to any couples.

In order to deal with specific correspondences between individuals, we can follow two approaches. First, if the description logic is sufficiently expressive, we can state such correspondences by using bridge rules. For example, the correspondence of couple23 to Gianni and Mary in Example 22 can be expressed by bridge rules $1\!:\!\{\textsf{couple23}\} \xrightarrow{\sqsubseteq} 2\!:\!\{\textsf{Gianni, Mary}\}$ and $1\!:\!\{\textsf{couple23}\} \xrightarrow{\sqsupseteq} 2\!:\!\{\textsf{Gianni, Mary}\}$, if the description logics support concepts formed by enumeration.

Otherwise, we need to introduce the individual-level equivalent of bridge-rules.

Definition 32. *If x is an individual in $\mathcal{DL}_i$, while $y, y_1, \dots$ are individuals of $\mathcal{DL}_j$, then a (partial) individual correspondence is an expression $i\!:\!x \mapsto j\!:\!y$, while a complete individual correspondence is an expression $i\!:\!x \xmapsto{=} j\!:\!\{y_1, y_2, \dots\}$*

The former indicates that the domain correspondence relation $\mathbf{r}_{ij}$ includes the correspondence of x and y. Note that $1\!:\!\textsf{couple23} \mapsto 2\!:\!\textsf{Gianni}$ and $1\!:\!\textsf{couple23} \mapsto 2\!:\!\textsf{Mary}$ do not capture fully the relationship between couple23, Gianni and Mary, because additional objects may still be in correspondence with couple23. Hence the need for complete correspondences: $1 : couple23 \overset{\equiv}{\mapsto} 2 : \{Gianni, Mary\}$

We are now ready to define distributed description logics.

Definition 33. *Start with a collection of description logics* $\{\mathcal{DL}_i\}_{i \in I}$.

A distributed T-box (DTB) $\mathfrak{T} = \langle \{\mathbf{T}_i\}_{i \in I}, \mathfrak{B} \rangle$ *consists of a set of T-boxes* $\{\mathbf{T}_i\}_{i \in I}$, *and a set* $\mathfrak{B} = \{\mathfrak{B}_{ij}\}$ *of bridge rules from i to j for every* $i \neq j \in I$. *For every* $k \in I$, *all descriptions in* $\mathbf{T}_k$ *must be in the corresponding language* $\mathcal{DL}_k$, *and for every bridge rule* $i : A \overset{\sqsubseteq}{\longrightarrow} j : B$ *or* $i : A \overset{\sqsupseteq}{\longrightarrow} j : B$ *in* $\mathfrak{B}_{ij}$, *the concepts A and B must be in the languages* $\mathcal{DL}_i$ *and* $\mathcal{DL}_j$ *respectively.*

A distributed A-box (DAB) $\mathfrak{A} = \langle \{\mathbf{A}_i\}_{i \in I}, \mathfrak{C} \rangle$ *consists of a set of A-boxes* $\{\mathbf{A}_i\}_{i \in I}$, *and a set* $\mathfrak{C} = \{\mathfrak{C}_{ij}\}$ *of partial and complete individual correspondences from i to j for every* $i \neq j \in I$. *For every* $k \in I$, *all descriptions in* $\mathbf{A}_k$ *must be in the corresponding language* $\mathcal{DL}_k$, *and for every correspondence rule* $i : x \mapsto j : y$ *or* $i : x \overset{\equiv}{\mapsto} \{y_1, y_2, ...\}$ *in* $\mathfrak{C}_{ij}$, *the individual name x must be in* $\mathcal{DL}_i$, *and* $y, y_1, ...$ *must be in* $\mathcal{DL}_j$.

A distributed DL knowledge base is then a pair $\langle \mathfrak{T}, \mathfrak{A} \rangle$, *consisting of a distributed T-box and a distributed A-box*

3.3 Formal Semantics of Description Logics

We present next a formal semantics for the preceding definitions, which forms the basis of the logic that we desired.

We start with an interpretation $\mathcal{I} = \langle \Delta^\mathcal{I}, \cdot^\mathcal{I} \rangle$, which assigns subsets of the domain $\Delta^\mathcal{I}$ to atomic concepts, and subsets of $\Delta^\mathcal{I} \times \Delta^\mathcal{I}$ to atomic roles, as well as distinct values of $\Delta^\mathcal{I}$ to different named individuals. The interpretation then proceeds recursively, driven by the syntax of complex concept and role constructors, as shown in column three of Figure 1.

The following notation will be used to describe satisfaction and entailment in description logic T-boxes:

$\mathcal{I} \models C \sqsubseteq D$ iff $C^\mathcal{I} \subseteq D^\mathcal{I}$.
$\mathcal{I} \models \mathbf{T}$ iff $\mathcal{I} \models A_i \sqsubseteq B_i$, for all $A_i \sqsubseteq B_i$ in $\mathbf{T}$.
$C \sqsubseteq D$ iff $\mathcal{I} \models C \sqsubseteq D$ for all possible interpretations $\mathcal{I}$.
$\mathbf{T} \models C \sqsubseteq D$ iff $\mathcal{I} \models C \sqsubseteq D$ for all interpretations $\mathcal{I}$ such that $\mathcal{I} \models \mathbf{T}$.

These definitions are extended to A-boxes according to the rules

$\mathcal{I} \models C(a)$ iff $a^\mathcal{I} \in C^\mathcal{I}$
$\mathcal{I} \models r(a, b)$ iff $(a^\mathcal{I}, b^\mathcal{I}) \in p^\mathcal{I}$.
$\mathcal{I} \models \mathbf{A}$ iff $\mathcal{I} \models \pi$ for every assertion $\pi = C(a), p(a, b)$ in $\mathbf{A}$.
$\mathbf{K} \models C(a)$ iff $\mathcal{I} \models C(a)$ for all interpretations $\mathcal{I}$ such that $\mathcal{I} \models \mathbf{K}$. Similarly for $p(a, b)$.

We provide semantics for distributed description logics by using local interpretations for the individual information systems, and connecting their domains using relations $\mathbf{r}_{ij}$.

Definition 34. *A* distributed interpretation $\mathfrak{I} = \langle \{\mathcal{I}_i\}_{i \in I}, \mathbf{r} \rangle$ *of* $\mathfrak{T}$ *consists of interpretations* $\mathcal{I}_i$ *for* $\mathcal{DL}_i$ *over domain* $\Delta^{\mathcal{I}_i}$, *and a function* $\mathbf{r}$ *associating to each* $i, j \in I$ *a binary relation* $\mathbf{r}_{ij} \subseteq \Delta^{\mathcal{I}_i} \times \Delta^{\mathcal{I}_j}$. *We use* $\mathbf{r}_{ij}(d)$ *to denote* $\{d' \in \Delta^{\mathcal{I}_j} \mid \langle d, d' \rangle \in \mathbf{r}_{ij}\}$, *and for any* $D \subseteq \Delta^{\mathcal{I}_i}$, *we use* $\mathbf{r}_{ij}(D)$ *to denote* $\bigcup_{d \in D} \mathbf{r}_{ij}(d)$.

Definition 35. *A distributed interpretation* $\mathfrak{I}$ d-satisfies *(written* $\mathfrak{I} \models_d$ *) the elements of a DTB* $\mathfrak{T} = \langle \{\mathbf{T}_i\}_{i \in I}, \{\mathfrak{B}_{ij}\} \rangle$ *according to the following clauses: For every* $i, j \in I$

1. $\mathfrak{I} \models_d i{:}B \xrightarrow{\sqsubseteq} j{:}G$, *if* $\mathbf{r}_{ij}(B^{\mathcal{I}_i}) \subseteq G^{\mathcal{I}_j}$ *(* Satisfy into-bridge rules. *)*
2. $\mathfrak{I} \models_d i{:}A \xrightarrow{\sqsupseteq} j{:}H$, *if* $\mathbf{r}_{ij}(A^{\mathcal{I}_i}) \supseteq H^{\mathcal{I}_j}$ *(* Satisfy onto-bridge rules. *)*
3. $\mathfrak{I} \models_d i{:}A \sqsubseteq B$, *if* $\mathcal{I}_i \models A \sqsubseteq B$ *(* Satisfy local subsumptions. *)*
4. $\mathfrak{I} \models_d \mathbf{T}_i$ *if* $\mathcal{I}_i \models A \sqsubseteq B$ *for all* $A \sqsubseteq B$ *in* $\mathbf{T}_i$
5. $\mathfrak{I} \models_d \mathfrak{T}$ *if, for every* $i \in I$, $\mathfrak{I} \models_d \mathbf{T}_i$, *and* $\mathfrak{I}$ *d-satisfies every bridge rule in* $\bigcup \mathfrak{B}_{ij}$.

Finally, $\mathfrak{T} \models_d i{:}C \sqsubseteq D$ *if, for every distributed interpretation* $\mathfrak{I}$, $\mathfrak{I} \models_d \mathfrak{T}$ *implies* $\mathfrak{I} \models_d i{:}C \sqsubseteq D$.

Concerning individuals, we have the following

Definition 36. *A distributed interpretation* $\mathfrak{I}$ d-satisfies *the elements of a DAB* $\mathfrak{A} = \langle \{\mathbf{A}_i\}_{i \in I}, \{\mathfrak{C}_{ij}\} \rangle$ *according to the following clauses: For every* $i, j \in I$

1. $\mathfrak{I} \models_d i{:}x \mapsto j{:}y$, *if* $y^{\mathcal{I}_j} \in \mathbf{r}_{ij}(x^{\mathcal{I}_i})$ *(* Satisfy individual correspondences *)*
2. $\mathfrak{I} \models_d i{:}x \xrightarrow{\equiv} \{y_1, y_2, ...\}$ *if* $\mathbf{r}_{ij}(x^{\mathcal{I}_i}) = \{y_1^{\mathcal{I}_j}, y_2^{\mathcal{I}_j}, ...\}$ *(* Satisfy complete correspondences *)*
3. $\mathfrak{I} \models_d i{:}C(a)$, *if* $\mathcal{I}_i \models A(a)$ *(* Satisfy local assertions. *)*
4. $\mathfrak{I} \models_d i{:}p(a, b)$, *if* $\mathcal{I}_i \models p(a, b)$
5. $\mathfrak{I} \models_d \mathbf{A}_i$ *iff* $\mathfrak{I} \models_d \pi$ *for every assertion* $\pi = C(a), p(a, b)$ *in* $\mathbf{A}_i$.
6. $\mathfrak{I} \models_d \mathfrak{A}$ *if, for every* $i \in I$, $\mathfrak{I} \models_d \mathbf{A}_i$, *and* $\mathfrak{I}$ *d-satisfies every individual correspondence in* $\bigcup \mathfrak{C}_{ij}$.

Finally, $\mathfrak{A} \models_d i{:}C(a)$ *if, for every distributed interpretation* $\mathfrak{I}$, $\mathfrak{I} \models_d \mathfrak{A}$ *implies* $\mathfrak{I} \models_d i{:}C(a)$. *Similarly for* $p(a, b)$ *replacing* $C(a)$.

3.4   Some Examples Revisited

We will now recast some of the earlier informal examples into the notation of DDLs, and briefly explore the logical consequences of the resulting theories.

To begin with, the course correspondences in Example 21 yield two bridge rules:

$$1 : \mathsf{AdvancedC} \xrightarrow{\sqsubseteq} 2 : \mathsf{IntermC}$$
$$2 : \mathsf{IntermC} \xrightarrow{\sqsubseteq} 1 : \mathsf{BasicC}$$

These allow each IS to import appropriate information from the other, but does not entail $1 : \mathsf{AdvancedC} \sqsubseteq \mathsf{BasicC}$, because the two bridge rules concern mappings in opposite directions.

Consider next Example 23, involving libraries. We have three T-boxes $\mathbf{T}_h$, $\mathbf{T}_m$ and $\mathbf{T}_s$. $\mathbf{T}_h$ and $\mathbf{T}_m$ describe the information systems of the libraries. They both have concepts BOOK, corresponding to copies of books that can be loaned, and concepts PERSON, to model the borrowers. The role taken_by is meant to record who has borrowed a book, so that the concept BOOK_ON_SHELF, in $\mathbf{T}_h$, can be defined as follows

$$\text{BOOK\_ON\_SHELF} \equiv \text{BOOK} \sqcap \neg \exists \, \text{taken\_by.PERSON}$$

The T-box $\mathbf{T}_s$, modeling the students' information system, also includes a concept called BOOK, but its meaning is different, since, as we mentioned before, these are abstractions over the libraries' copies of the book. The following bridge rules are intended to capture the fact that students see books based on copies from the respective libraries

$$h:\text{BOOK} \overset{\sqsubseteq}{\longrightarrow} s:\text{BOOK} \tag{1}$$

$$m:\text{BOOK} \overset{\sqsubseteq}{\longrightarrow} s:\text{BOOK} \tag{2}$$

Note that this does not imply that *all* books at the Harvard library can be seen in the students database (the mapping $\mathbf{r}_{hs}$ may be partial). Nor does it imply that the same book copy cannot be mapped to several books in $\text{IS}_{Student}$ – this would require a different kind of bridge rule, one expressing that the correspondence has a certain cardinality.

In addition, $\mathbf{T}_s$ has a role located_at to capture the name of the library where the student should go to get the material in question, assuming it is available there. For convenience, $\mathbf{T}_s$ contains a concept, AVAILABLE_BOOK, that lets students tell quickly if some book is available:

$$\text{AVAILABLE\_BOOK} \equiv \text{BOOK} \sqcap \exists \, \text{located\_at}$$

Since students only want to hear about material located at a library if there are some copies of it on the shelf there, we use onto bridge rules as follows[2]:

$$h:\text{BOOK\_ON\_SHELF} \overset{\sqsupseteq}{\longrightarrow} s:\exists \, \text{located\_at.}\{"\text{Harvard}"\} \tag{3}$$

$$m:\text{BOOK\_ON\_SHELF} \overset{\sqsupseteq}{\longrightarrow} s:\exists \, \text{located\_at.}\{"\text{Mit}"\} \tag{4}$$

Ignoring one of the libraries, $\mathbf{T}_m$ say, in order to simplify matters, we can then define the distributed T-box $\mathfrak{T}_{lib} = \langle \mathbf{T}_h, \mathbf{T}_s, \mathfrak{B}_{hs} \rangle$, where $\mathfrak{B}_{hs}$ contains bridge rules 1 and 3.

Figure 2 provides an example distributed interpretation $\mathfrak{I}_{lib}$ for $\mathfrak{T}_{lib}$. Bridge rule 1 is satisfied by $\mathfrak{I}_{lib}$ even though $\text{BOOK}^{\mathcal{I}_h}$ is not contained in

---

[2] Technical note: although we use enumerated concepts, such as $\{"\text{Harvard}"\}$, which are not in $\mathcal{SHIQ}$, their elements are string constants, which do not have properties of their own. It is known that such language constructs can be eliminated by using mutually exclusive primitive concepts

$$\Delta^{\mathcal{I}_h} = \{\mathsf{Tractatus}(1), \mathsf{Tractatus}(2), \mathsf{DB\_Pples}, \mathsf{Mario}\}$$
$$\mathsf{BOOK}^{\mathcal{I}_h} = \{\mathsf{Tractatus}(1), \mathsf{Tractatus}(2), \mathsf{DB\_Pples}\}$$
$$\mathsf{PERSON}^{\mathcal{I}_h} = \{\mathsf{Mario}\}$$
$$\mathsf{taken\_by}^{\mathcal{I}_h} = \{\langle \mathsf{Tractatus}(1), \mathsf{Mario}\rangle\}$$
$$\Delta^{\mathcal{I}_s} = \{\mathsf{Tractatus}, \mathsf{Philosophical\_Investigations}, "\mathsf{Harvard}", "\mathsf{Mit}"\}$$
$$\mathsf{BOOK}^{\mathcal{I}_s} = \{\mathsf{Tractatus}, \mathsf{Philosophical\_Investigations}\}$$
$$\mathsf{located\_at}^{\mathcal{I}_s} = \left\{ \begin{array}{c} \langle \mathsf{Tractatus}, "\mathsf{Harvard}"\rangle \\ \langle \mathsf{Philosophical\_Investigations}, "\mathsf{Mit}"\rangle \end{array} \right\}$$
$$\mathbf{r}_{hs} = \left\{ \begin{array}{c} \langle \mathsf{Tractatus}(1), \mathsf{Tractatus}\rangle \\ \langle \mathsf{Tractatus}(2), \mathsf{Tractatus}\rangle \end{array} \right\}$$

Fig. 2. Example of distributed interpretation for $\mathfrak{T}_{lib}$

$\mathsf{BOOK}^{\mathcal{I}_s}$; indeed, $\mathbf{r}_{hs}(\mathsf{BOOK}^{\mathcal{I}_h}) = \{\mathsf{Tractatus}\}$, is a subset of $\mathsf{BOOK}^{\mathcal{I}_s}$, which is $\{\mathsf{Tractatus}, \mathsf{Philosophical\_Investigations}\}$. $\mathfrak{I}_{lib}$ also satisfies bridge rule (3), since $\mathbf{r}_{hs}(\mathsf{BOOK\_ON\_SHELF}^{\mathcal{I}_h}) = \mathbf{r}_{hs}(\{\mathsf{Tractatus}(2), \mathsf{DB\_Pples}\}) = \{\mathsf{Tractatus}\}$, which is a superset of $(\exists \mathsf{located\_at}.\{"\mathsf{Harvard}"\})^{\mathcal{I}_s} = \{\mathsf{Tractatus}\}$.

Note that, independently of $\mathfrak{I}_{lib}$, one of the logical consequences (d-entailments) of $\mathfrak{T}_{lib}$ is

$$s : \exists \mathsf{located\_at}.\{"\mathsf{Harvard}"\} \sqsubseteq \mathsf{AVAILABLE\_BOOK}$$

This follows because the bridge rules allow us to infer in $\mathrm{IS}_{Student}$ that anything that is located at the Harvard library must be a book, and hence an instance of the concept $\mathsf{AVAILABLE\_BOOK}$ defined earlier.

The above example exhibits a common pattern of inference in our DDL:

starting from
A subsumes B in IS_1
A is mapped **into** G by a bridge rule
B is mapped **onto** H by a bridge rule
conclude that
G subsumes H in IS_2

The following is another example of this inference: suppose $\mathbf{T}_1$ contains the subsumption assertion

$$\mathsf{Villa} \sqsubseteq \mathsf{SecondResidence}$$

and there are bridge rules

$$1 : \mathsf{SecondResidence} \xrightarrow{\sqsubseteq} 2 : \mathsf{Dwelling}$$
$$1 : \mathsf{Villa} \xrightarrow{\sqsupseteq} 2 : \mathsf{Cottage}$$

One can then conclude that $2:\mathsf{Cottage} \sqsubseteq \mathsf{Dwelling}$. This inference is illustrated by the diagram in Figure 2, which should also provide some of the intuition behind it. (The horizontal arrows describe the bridge rules.)

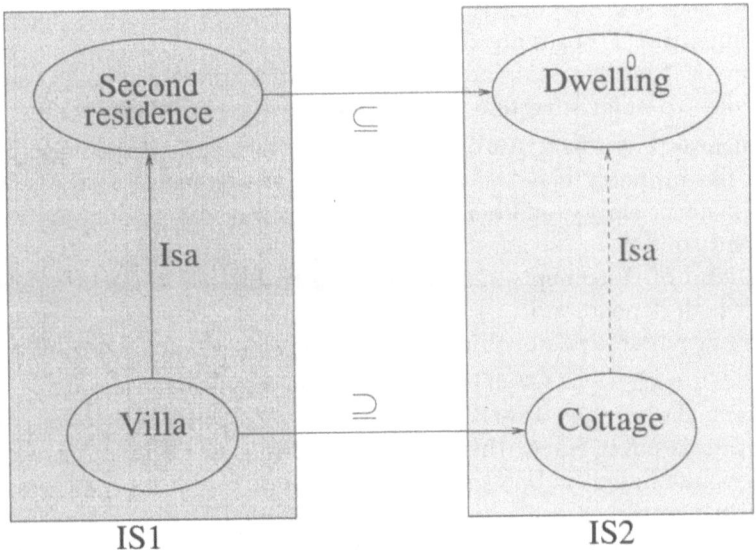

Fig. 3. Example of Inferred Subsumption Relationship (dashed line) in DDL

4   Some Properties of DDL

In this section, we will restrict our attention to the simplest kinds of DDL, namely distributed T-boxes involving only two IS, and a single set of bridge rules between them: $\mathfrak{T}_{12} = \langle \mathbf{T}_1, \mathbf{T}_2, \mathfrak{B}_{12} \rangle$.

The following is a list of intuitively desirable properties for such a system, based on our motivations:

1. When deducing things at IS_i in the distributed system, all local information should be available. (Technically, if $\mathbf{T}_i \models i : X \sqsubseteq Y$, then $\mathfrak{T}_{12} \models_d i : X \sqsubseteq Y$, for $i = 1, 2$.)
2. In the absence of bridge rules, no information should pass between the component systems. (In other words: $\langle \mathbf{T}_1, \mathbf{T}_2, \emptyset \rangle \models_d i : X \sqsubseteq Y$ if and only if $\mathbf{T}_i \models i : X \sqsubseteq Y$, for $i = 1, 2$.)
3. A DDL should exhibit "directionality", and "no backflow": we have said that $\mathfrak{B}_{12}$ contains bridge rules that are set up to provide information flow from IS_1 to IS_2. Therefore, such a set up should not affect, by itself, reasoning in IS_1. Formally, we would like to have $\mathfrak{T}_{12} \models_d 1 : A \sqsubseteq B$ iff $\mathbf{T}_1 \models A \sqsubseteq B$. This would also allow for more effective reasoning because there would be no need for a feedback loop between new inferences in IS_2 and those in IS_1.

4. A distributed system should not allow local inconsistencies to "pollute" the entire system, in the sense that if the information at IS_i is not satisfiable, then deductions at other sites should not be affected. Formally, this would mean that if $\mathbf{T}_i$ is inconsistent then $\mathfrak{T}_{12} \models_d j : X \sqsubseteq Y$ iff $\mathbf{T}_j \models X \sqsubseteq Y$ for $j = 1, 2$.

It can be easily seen that our definition of DDL does have the first two properties, if the component T-boxes are consistent.

As far as "backflow" is concerned, it is unfortunately possible to use onto bridge rules to enforce certain properties of descriptions in IS_1. For example, a rule such as $1 : A \xrightarrow{\;\sqsupseteq\;} 2 : \mathsf{ANYTHING}$ requires every distributed interpretation to have the property $\mathbf{r}_{12}(A^{\mathcal{I}_1}) \neq \emptyset$, because the extension of the $\mathsf{ANYTHING}$ concept is never empty, and hence there must always be individuals in $A^{\mathcal{I}_1}$ that correspond to it.

This kind of reasoning can sometimes be translated into new subsumptions for IS_1, which depend on IS_2. Let us introduce a role constant, $\mathsf{Universal}_{\mathsf{ROLE}}$. It relates every possible pair of objects: $\mathsf{Universal}_{\mathsf{ROLE}}^{\mathcal{I}_1} = \Delta^{\mathcal{I}_1} \times \Delta^{\mathcal{I}_1}$. Now consider the DTB $\mathfrak{T}'$, with $\mathbf{T}_2 = \{\mathsf{ANYTHING} \sqsubseteq G\}$ and one bridge rule $\{1 : A \xrightarrow{\;\sqsupseteq\;} 2 : G\}$. It d-entails the formula $1 : \mathsf{ANYTHING} \sqsubseteq \exists \mathsf{Universal}_{\mathsf{ROLE}}.A$ because, if A's interpretation is never empty then there is always some A-object to which every object can be related by $\mathsf{Universal}_{\mathsf{ROLE}}$.

Interestingly, it is possible to prove that for some DDLs such knowledge about the non-emptiness of a concept does not result in new subsumptions. For example, if the components of a DTB $\mathfrak{T}_{12}$ only involve the $\mathcal{SHIQ}$ description logic, which does not support $\mathsf{Universal}_{\mathsf{ROLE}}$, then for consistent $\mathfrak{T}_{12}$, $\mathfrak{T}_{12} \models_d 1 : A \sqsubseteq B$ iff $\mathbf{T}_1 \models A \sqsubseteq B$.

As far as inconsistency propagation, unfortunately if one of the component T-boxes is unsatisfiable then there is no interpretation satisfying the entire DTB, and therefore every possible assertion is automatically d-entailed by an unsatisfiable DTB. We must however point out that this kind of inconsistency propagation is not peculiar to DDL – it is a feature of most logic-based formal models of IS with multiple components.

Looking at the issue more closely in the context of DTBs, if $\mathbf{T}_2$ is unsatisfiable, then all conclusions of the form $1 : X \sqsubseteq Y$, for all concepts X and Y, are d-entailed by $\mathfrak{T}_{12}$. This is particularly disturbing given our desire to avoid "backflow" from IS_2 to IS_1. Of course, the inconsistency of $\mathbf{T}_1$ similarly infects reasoning in IS_2. Note that there other possible reasons for the unsatisfiability of a DTB: (i) some bridge rules may not be satisfiable (e.g., $1 : \mathsf{NOTHING} \xrightarrow{\;\sqsupseteq\;} 2 : \mathsf{ANYTHING}$); (ii) though each component on its own is satisfiable, their combination may not be so:
$$\left\langle \{A \sqsubseteq \mathsf{NOTHING}\}, \{\mathsf{ANYTHING} \sqsubseteq B\}, 1 : A \xrightarrow{\;\sqsupseteq\;} 2 : B \right\rangle.$$

One can try to modify this aspect of a logical system by using a modified semantics. The original work on Distributed First Order Logic [9] used sets of ordinary interpretations to achieve this effect. We have investigated our own simpler version of such a semantics: introducing a new, special interpretation for ordinary DL, $\mathcal{I}^\delta = \left\langle \Delta^{\mathcal{I}^\delta}, .^{\mathcal{I}^\delta} \right\rangle$. $\Delta^{\mathcal{I}^\delta}$ is any non empty set, and $.^{\mathcal{I}^\delta}$ makes the denotation of every description be the whole domain $\Delta^{\mathcal{I}^\delta}$. Intuitively $\mathcal{I}^\delta$ provides an interpretation to locally inconsistent T-boxes; indeed, in $\mathcal{I}^\delta$, every subsumption $A \sqsubseteq B$ is satisfied, including ANYTHING $\sqsubseteq$ NOTHING. Redefining d-entailment to allow $\mathcal{I}^\delta$ as one of the $\mathcal{I}_i$, produces a DDL which does limit the effect of inconsistent local T-boxes in the desired way.

5   Relating DDL and Ordinary DL

The following results provide in certain cases a connection between DDL and ordinary DLs, supplying, among others, algorithms for reasoning in the DDL.

Definition 51. *Given a family of description logics $\{\mathcal{DL}_i\}_{i \in I}$, the global description logic $\mathcal{GDL}$ is defined as follows:*

1. *The primitive concepts of $\mathcal{GDL}$ consist of $i{:}A$ for all primitive concepts or constant concepts A (such as ANYTHING) of $\mathcal{DL}_i$, for every $i \in I$.*
2. *The primitive roles of $\mathcal{GDL}$ include $i{:}p$ for all primitive or constant roles p of $\mathcal{DL}_i$, $i \in I$.*
3. *Furthermore, for any $i, j \in I$ and $i \neq j$, R_{ij} is a new role of $\mathcal{GDL}$ (intuitively, representing correspondences between domains).*
4. *There are new top and bottom concepts, ANYTHING$_g$ and NOTHING$_g$. respectively.*

Now define a mapping $\#()$ from concepts/roles of $\mathcal{DL}_i$ to $\mathcal{GDL}$, which starts from the primitive concepts, roles and individuals M of the corresponding IS_i: $\#(i{:}M) = i{:}M$. For complex concepts and roles, the function is defined by structural recursion: if ρ is a concept constructor taking k arguments, then $\#(i{:}\rho(M_1, \ldots, M_k)) = i{:}\text{ANYTHING} \sqcap \rho(\#(M_1), \ldots, \#(M_k))$. (The intersection with $i{:}$ANYTHING is needed in order to limit the effect of complement.) For example, the concept $\forall p.C$ has constructor $\forall$, and two arguments, the role and the restriction; therefore $\#(\ i{:}\forall p.C\ ) = i{:}\text{ANYTHING} \sqcap \forall(i{:}p).(i{:}\text{ANYTHING} \sqcap i{:}C)$.

Applying $\#()$ to a DTB $\mathfrak{T} = \langle\{\mathbf{T}_i\}_{i \in I}, \mathfrak{B}\rangle$, yields a T-box $\#(\mathfrak{T})$ in the language $\mathcal{GDL}$, consisting of the following:

1. (* *Copies of axioms from local T-boxes.* *)
   $\#(i{:}A) \sqsubseteq \#(i{:}B)$ for all $i{:}A \sqsubseteq B \in \mathbf{T}_i$;
2. (* *Translations of into bridge rules as value restrictions on R_{ij}.* *)
   $\#(i{:}A) \sqsubseteq \forall \mathrm{R}_{ij}.\#(j{:}G)$ for every into bridge rule $i{:}A \xrightarrow{\sqsubseteq} j{:}G \in \mathfrak{B}$;
3. (* *Translations of onto bridge rules as existential restrictions on the inverse of R_{ij}.* *)
   $\#(j{:}H) \sqsubseteq \exists \mathrm{R}_{ij}^-.\#(i{:}A)$ for every onto bridge rule $i{:}A \xrightarrow{\sqsupseteq} j{:}G \in \mathfrak{B}$;
4. (* *Restrictions on role R_{ij} so it connects only objects in $\mathbf{T}_i$ and $\mathbf{T}_j$.* *)
   ANYTHING$_g \sqsubseteq \forall \mathrm{R}_{ij}.j{:}$ANYTHING (* *the range of R_{ij} is $\Delta^{\mathcal{I}_j}$* *)
   $\neg(i{:}$ANYTHING$) \sqsubseteq \forall \mathrm{R}_{ij}.$NOTHING$_g$ (* *R_{ij} is undefined outside $\Delta^{\mathcal{I}_i}$* *)
5. (* *Restricting $i{:}$NOTHING to be the incoherent concept.* *)
   $i{:}$NOTHING $\sqsubseteq$ NOTHING$_g$

6. (* *Ensuring that* i:ANYTHING *is the proper local top of IS-A hierarchies* *)
   i:$A \sqsubseteq i$:ANYTHING, for every atomic concept A of $\mathcal{DL}_i$;
7. (* *Ensuring that every* i-*role* s *has as domain and range* i:ANYTHING *)
   i:ANYTHING $\sqsubseteq \forall(i$:$s).(i$:ANYTHING) for every role s of $\mathcal{DL}_i$ (* *the range of* i:s *is in* $\Delta^{\mathcal{I}_i}$ *);
   $\neg(i$:ANYTHING) $\sqsubseteq \forall(i$:$s)$.NOTHING$_g$ (* i:s *is undefined outside* $\Delta^{\mathcal{I}_i}$ *)

The following theorem states that d-entailment can often be reduced to ordinary DL-reasoning through the use of the above translation:

Theorem 52. *Suppose* $\mathfrak{T}$ *is a DTB, where none of the* $\mathcal{DL}_i$ *use role constants or role constructors. Then* $\#(\mathfrak{T}) \models \#(i$:$X) \sqsubseteq \#(i$:$Y)$ *if and only if* $\mathfrak{T} \models_d i$:$X \sqsubseteq Y$.

The main obstacle in generalizing the above theorem for the case when some $\mathcal{DL}_i$ has role constants or constructors is ensuring that all interpretations $\mathcal{I}^*$ of a composite i-role in $\#(\mathfrak{T})$ have as domain and range the interpretation of i:ANYTHING. This works by induction for role constructors such as conjunction, disjunction and inverse. However, it no longer holds for role complement, or constants such as the universal role. In this case, the description logic in which $\#(\mathfrak{T})$ is expressed may need to have additional, possibly more powerful, constructors such as roles defined as the product of domain and range concepts.

Using Theorem 52, we can obtain reasoners for a variety of DDL.

Proposition 53. *A DDL such that all* $\mathcal{DL}_i$ *are contained in some decidable description logic* $\mathcal{DL}_0$ *which supports (i) qualified existential restriction, and (ii) arbitrary subsumption assertions in T-boxes, can use the decision procedure of* $\mathcal{DL}_0$ *to decide unsatisfiability and d-entailment.*

This result applies even when the $\mathcal{DL}_i$ involved have role constructors such as conjunction, disjunction, inverse, composition, role hierarchies, and transitive roles. We get as corollary that DDLs with $\mathcal{DL}_i$ that are in $\mathcal{SHIQ}$ [11] can use its reasoner for determining $\models_d$.

We can extend the above translation to deal with A-boxes and individual correspondences.

1. (* *Copies of local assertions* *)
   $\#(i$:$C)(i$:$a)$ for $C(a)$ in $\mathbf{A}_i$
   $\#(i$:$p)(i$:a, i:$b)$ for $p(a, b)$ in $\mathbf{A}_i$
2. (* *Translation of correspondences* *)
   $\mathrm{R}_{ij}(i$:x, j:$y)$ for every correspondence i:$x \mapsto j$:y in $\mathfrak{C}$.
3. (* *Translation of complete correspondences* *)
   $\mathrm{R}_{ij}(i$:x, j:$y_1), \dots, \mathrm{R}_{ij}(i$:$x, j$:$y_n), (\leqslant n\, \mathrm{R}_{ij})(i$:$x)$ for every complete correspondence i:$x \overset{=}{\mapsto} j$:$\{y_1, \dots, y_n\}$ in $\mathfrak{C}$.

The key novelty is the translation of $\overset{=}{\mapsto}$, which places an upper bound on the number of values that can correspond to an individual. As a result, the DL into which translation occurs must also support number restrictions. Fortunately, $\mathcal{SHIQ}$ does have number restrictions.

We remark that the full expressive power of reasoners such as $\mathcal{SHIQ}$ may not necessarily be required in order to accommodate such translations (there are no nested existential quantifiers) so that DDL with very simple $\mathcal{DL}_i$ may have reasoners with lower complexity. Also, note that although Theorem 52 makes it seem like all $\mathbf{T}_i$ should come from the same $\mathcal{DL}$, there may be alternate ways to proceed, which make it interesting to study the use of different kinds of Description Logics, of different expressive power, in the different component T-boxes of the integrated IS.

The above results can also help focus our search for additional kinds of bridge rules to add to DDL, by trying to preserve Theorem 52. This means that the new bridge rules should be expressible as DL descriptions using the special roles R_{ij}. For example, each of the following kinds of bridge rules has the corresponding translation shown beside it:

- Every A-object has at least n corresponding G-objects: $A \sqsubseteq \geqslant n \, \mathrm{R}_{12}.G$.
- The correspondence relation from IS_1 to IS_2 is the identity: $\mathrm{R}_{12} = \mathsf{Ident}_{\mathsf{ROLE}}$.
- The correspondence relation is "injective" in the sense that different objects map to distinct images: $i : \mathsf{ANYTHING} \sqsubseteq \forall \mathrm{R}_{12}.(\leqslant 1 \, \mathrm{R}_{12}^-)$.
- The correspondence relations between IS_1 and IS_2 are converses, when directionality is not involved (e.g., scaling functions): $\mathrm{R}_{12} = \mathrm{R}_{21}^-$.

6 Summary and Related Work

The seminal work of Catarci and Lenzerini [7] on integrating ISs described by DLs, made an implicit assumption that the local ISs have the same notion of what individual objects are, and that there was only one set of (subsumption) assertions relating IS_1 and IS_2. We have argued that in cases such as federated IS, when there is no single global view, these conditions need to be relaxed, by allowing general correspondence relationships between objects in the local domains, and by having "directed" import assertions. These intuitions were formalized in DDL using the notion of bridge rules and individual correspondences.

We have identified other desirable properties of federated DL, such as "no feedback", and localizing the effect of inconsistencies so that one IS does not "infect" the reasoning of the entire system.

Among the interesting results obtained are a translation of DDL reasoning to DL reasoning, which requires only qualified existential restrictions and general theories, thus providing algorithms for reasoning in DDLs where all local ISs have $\mathcal{SHIQ}$ T-boxes.

There has been an enormous amount of work on federated/heterogeneous/multi-databases, where key questions include how to match up both schema and data-level information between multiple databases. Considerable effort has been devoted to heuristics and tools for *finding* such relationships (see [18] for a recent survey of these aspects). More relevant to the present paper is work concerned with languages for *expressing* such relationships, especially as they relate to the instance level.

Kent [13] provides an extensive list of problems that arise due to data-level mismatches between databases, recognizing the need for both domain relationships (e.g., currencies) and context-dependent use of them (e.g., salaries vs. stock prices in different currencies). He examines complex solutions that use domain mapping functions orchestrated by integrator functions, and expresses them in the Iris database programming language.

SchemaLog [14] is just one representative of the class of declarative languages for relating multi-databases that use powerful data restructuring facilities. (The paper has a fine section reviewing other similar approaches.) Its higher-order syntax allows querying the schema, as well as inter-relating schema and value identifiers. Although no special provision is made for domain conversions/correspondences, in a logic-based language such as SchemaLog, one might introduce explicit binary relations between domains (in the way in which we have done in Section 5, when simulating a DDL by translating to a global DL). These could then be used in defining views, which provide the basic mechanism for integration. This explicit invocation of conversions is cumbersome however. Similar comments apply to work on integrating heterogeneous semi-structured data sources (see [8] for a survey).

A different declarative approach to the specific problem of data mediation is illustrated in [20], where meta-attributes and rules are used to deal with complex value conversions. A desirable feature of the approach is that it introduces the notion of "contexts", which allows for the *automatic invocation* of conversion functions.

Finally, Calvanese et al [6] present another declarative mechanism for specifying data correspondences, involving conversion, as well as matching (recognizing occurrences of the same individual across different databases), and reconciling conflicting values for attributes. These correspondences are specified as Datalog-like rules for relational schemas at the "logical level". Interestingly, this work is carried out in a framework where at the "conceptual level", schema elements are related by description logic-based mechanisms. However, there is no discussion of how the concept level is affected by the domain value correspondences at the logical level.

In contrast to all the above approaches, our work on DDL extends the *reasoning* available on ordinary schemas to the case of multiple schemas connected by arbitrary binary correspondences between individuals. Such reasoning can be used for a wide variety of tasks, including query (re)formulation, and dealing with partially-specified individuals, as surveyed in [3].

References

1. Y. Arens, C.A. Knoblock, W.M. Shen. Query Reformulation for Dynamic Information Integration. *J. Intelligent Information Systems 6(2/3)*: 99-130 (1996)
2. S. Bergamaschi, S. Castano, M. Vincini, D. Beneventano. Semantic integration of heterogeneous information sources. *Data and Knowledge Engineering 36(3)*: 215–249 (2001).

3. A. Borgida. Description logics in data management. *IEEE Trans. on Knowledge and Data Engineering*, 7(5):671–682, 1995.
4. D. Calvanese, M. Lenzerini, and D. Nardi. Unifying class-based representation formalisms. *J. of Artificial Intelligence Research*, 11:199–240, 1999.
5. D. Calvanese, G. De Giacomo, M. Lenzerini, D. Nardi, and R. Rosati. Information integration: Conceptual modeling and reasoning support. *Proc. CoopIS'98*, pp.280–291, 1998.
6. D. Calvanese, G. De Giacomo, M. Lenzerini, D. Nardi, and R. Rosati. A principled approach to data integration and reconciliation in data warehousing. In *Proc. Intl. Workshop on Design and Management of Data Warehouses (DMDW'99)*, Heidelberg, Germany, 1999.
7. T. Catarci and M. Lenzerini. Representing and using interschema knowledge in cooperative information systems. *International Journal of Intelligent and Cooperative Information Systems*, 2(4):375–398, 1993.
8. D. Florescu, A. Levy, and A. Mendelzon. Database Techniques for the World-Wide Web: A Survey. *SIGMOD Record, 27(3)*:59–74, Sept. 1998.
9. C. Ghidini and L. Serafini. Distributed First Order Logics. In D. Gabbay and M. de Rijke, editors, *Frontiers Of Combining Systems 2*, Studies in Logic and Computation, pages 121–140. Research Studies Press, 1998.
10. I. Horrocks, P. Patel Schneider, and F. van Harmelen. Reviewing the design of DAML+OIL: language for the semantic web. In *Proc. AAAI'02*, 2002.
11. I. Horrocks and U. Sattler. A description logic with transitive and inverse roles and role hierarchies. *J. Logic and Computation*, 9(3):385–410, 1999.
12. V. Kashyap and A. Sheth. Semantic and Schematic Similarities Between Database Objects: A Context-Based Approach. *VLDB Journal 5(4)*: 276–304, 1996.
13. W. Kent. Solving Domain Mismatch and Schema Mismatch Problems with an Object-Oriented Database Programming Language. *Proc. VLDB'91*, pp. 147–160, 1991.
14. L. Lakshmanan, F. Sadri, and I.N. Subramanian. Logic and Algebraic Languages for Interoperability in Multi-database Systems. *Journal of Logic Programming 33(2)*:101–149, Nov. 1997.
15. A.Y. Levy, A. Rajaraman , J.J. Ordille. Query answering algorithms for information agents *Proc. AAAI'96*
16. E. Mena, V. Kashyap, A. Illarramendi and A. Sheth. Imprecise Answers on Highly Open and Distributed Environments: An Approach based on Information Loss for Multi-Ontology Based Query Processing. *Int. Journal of Cooperative Information Systems 9(4)*:403-425, December 2000.
17. A. Pirotte, E. Zimanyi, D. Massart, and T. Yakusheva. Materialization: A Powerful and Ubiquitous Abstraction Pattern. In *Proc. VLDB'94*, pp. 630–641, 1994.
18. E. Rahm, and P.A. Bernstein. A Survey of Approaches to Automatic Schema Matching. *VLDB Journal 10(4)*:334-350. Dec. 2001.
19. F. Saltor and E. Rodríguez. On Intelligent Access to Heterogeneous Information. In F. Baader, M.A. Jeusfeld & W. Nutt (eds), *Proc. KRDB'97*, Athens, Greece, August 30, 1997, pp. 15:1-15:7
20. E. Sciore, M. Siegel, and A. Rosenthal. Using semantic values to facilitate interoperability among heterogeneous information systems. *ACM TODS 19(2)*:254–290, June 1994.

Synchronization of Concurrent Workflows Using Interaction Expressions and Coordination Protocols

Christian Heinlein

Dept. of Computer Structures, University of Ulm, Germany[1]
heinlein@informatik.uni-ulm.de

Abstract. Current workflow management systems, whether they are commercial products or research prototypes, do not provide adequate means for *inter-workflow coordination* as concurrently executing workflows are considered completely independent. As this simplified view is not sufficient for many real-world application scenarios, *interaction expressions and graphs* have been developed as a simple yet powerful formalism for the specification and implementation of synchronization conditions in general and inter-workflow dependencies in particular. In this paper, different *coordination protocols* as well as an accompanying *subscription protocol* are introduced as a means to actually employ interaction expressions to efficiently synchronize concurrent workflows.

1 Introduction

Current workflow management systems (WfMS), whether they are commercial products or research prototypes, do not provide adequate means for *inter-workflow coordination* as concurrently executing workflows are considered completely independent. As this simplified view is not sufficient for many real-world application scenarios, *interaction expressions and graphs* have been developed as a simple yet powerful formalism for the specification and implementation of synchronization conditions in general and inter-workflow dependencies in particular [8, 9, 10]. As a typical example, Fig. 1 shows an interaction graph specifying a general *integrity constraint* for the activities (workflow steps) *prepare* (prepare patient p for examination x), *inform* (in-

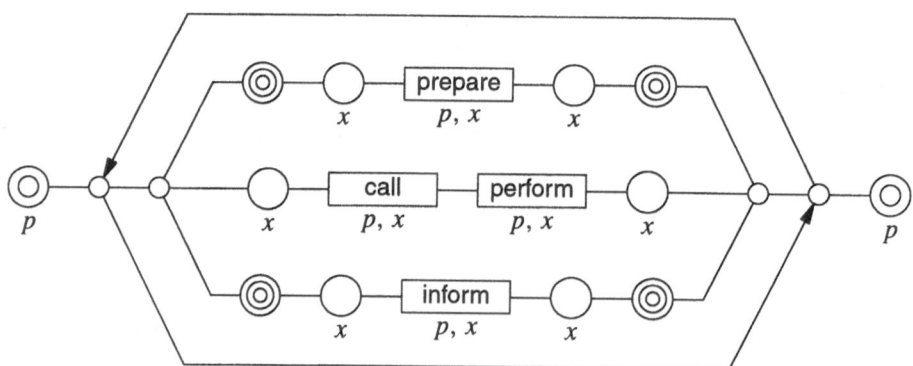

Fig. 1. Typical example of an interaction graph

---

[1] This work has been performed while the author was a member of the Dept. Databases and Information Systems at the University of Ulm.

R. Meersman, Z. Tari (Eds.): CoopIS/DOA/ODBASE 2002, LNCS 2519, pp. 54–71, 2002.
© Springer-Verlag Berlin Heidelberg 2002

form patient p about examination x), *call* (call patient p to examination x), and *perform* (perform examination x for patient p). Without needing to know in which particular workflows these activities will actually occur, the graph specifies that *for all* patients p (outermost ⊚ operators) a *mutual exclusion* of three branches (innermost ○ operators) shall be executed *repeatedly* (arrow-connected iteration operators ○): the patient might *either* pass through *exactly one* examination x (sequence call − perform, surrounded by "for some x" operators ○, in the middle branch) *or* he might be prepared for *or* informed about *several* examinations x *simultaneously* (activities prepare and inform, bracketed by ○ and "unrestricted concurrency" operators ⊚, in the upper and lower branch, respectively).[2]

For a concrete application scenario, enforcing this constraint means, for example, to forbid the execution of call and inform activities for a particular patient in all workflows, while one or more prepare activities are executed for that patient in one workflow. To prevent a user from accidentally executing such activities, they should even be removed from users' worklists (or at least tagged as currently not executable), even if they are considered executable from a single workflow's perspective.

If, for example, the two workflows depicted in Fig. 2 are executed concurrently for the same patient p, the following scenario might take place (cf. Fig. 3).

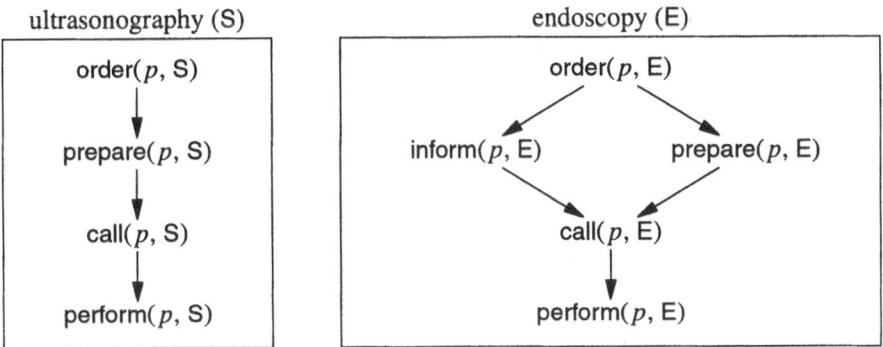

Fig. 2. Medical examination workflows

First of all, the initial activities order(p, S) and order(p, E) of both workflows can be executed independently. Afterwards, three activities are considered executable from the WfMS's perspective: prepare(p, S) and prepare(p, E), which must be performed by a nurse, and inform(p, E), which must be executed by a ward doctor. As these activities are permitted in the initial state of the interaction graph, too, they will actually appear in the corresponding worklists (cf. line 1 of Fig. 3).

If the nurse decides to start one of the prepare activities, e. g., prepare(p, S), the upper branch of the mutual exclusion is entered for that patient causing the activities of the other branches to become temporarily impermissible (for that particular patient) from the perspective of the interaction graph. Therefore, inform(p, E) must be re-

---

[2] As the focus of this paper is not the concrete formalism itself, but rather its application to *enforce* such integrity constraints or synchronization conditions, the operators shall not be explained in more detail.
The basic idea is similar to reading syntax charts: Permissible execution sequences of activities are obtained by traversing an interaction graph from left to right according to well-defined rules.

	Users' Worklists					
	Ward		Ultrasonography Department		Endoscopy Department	
	Nurse	Doctor	Med. Assist.	Physician	Med. Assist.	Physician
1	prepare(p, S) prepare(p, E)	inform(p, E)				
2	prepare(p, S) prepare(p, E)	inform(p, E)				
3	prepare(p, S) prepare(p, E)	inform(p, E)				
4		inform(p, E)	call(p, S)			
5		inform(p, E)	call(p, S)			
6			call(p, S)		call(p, E)	
7			call(p, S)		call(p, E)	
8				perform(p, S)	call(p, E)	
9				perform(p, S)	call(p, E)	
10					call(p, E)	

Fig. 3. Possible scenario

moved from the ward doctor's worklist (or at least tagged as currently not executable) despite the fact that it is still considered executable by the WfMS. Because the graph does not forbid multiple simultaneous executions of prepare for the same patient, prepare(p, E) remains permissible. The resulting situation is depicted in line 2 of Fig. 3, where currently running activities are shaded while currently impermissible ones are crossed out.

Line 3 shows the state after the nurse has also started prepare(p, E). After finishing both prepare activities, the upper branch of the mutual exclusion is completed causing a new iteration to be started for that patient where all branches are permissible again. In particular, inform(p, E) becomes permissible again and thus re-appears in the ward doctor's worklist as an executable activity. Furthermore, call(p, S) becomes executable both from the WfMS's and the interaction graph's perspective and thus appears in the worklist of a medical assistant of the ultrasonography department (line 4).

If the ward doctor decides to start inform(p, E) now, the lower branch of the mutual exclusion is entered for that patient causing call(p, S) to become temporarily impermissible. Therefore, it disappears from the medical assistant's worklist (line 5) until inform(p, E) is finished (line 6). At the same time, call(p, E) becomes executable both from the WfMS's and the interaction graph's perspective and thus appears in the worklist of a medical assistant of the endoscopy department.

Similarly, executing one of the activities call(p, S) or call(p, E) now will cause the other one to become impermissible (line 7) until the corresponding perform activity is completed (line 10), and so on.

To actually achieve the behaviour just described, three basic steps are necessary, which will be described in subsequent sections: first, a precise *operational model* of interaction graphs must be developed and implemented (Sec. 2); second, different *co-ordination protocols* as well as an accompanying *subscription protocol* constituting well-defined interfaces to this implementation must be defined and implemented (Sec. 3); and third, workflow management systems must be appropriately extended in order to be able to participate in these protocols (Sec. 4). As the primary focus of this paper are the coordination and subscription protocols, the other aspects will be described more briefly. To complete the paper, Sec. 5 discusses related work, while Sec. 6 concludes with a summary and outlook.

2 Operational Semantics and Implementation of Interaction Graphs

To implement an interaction graph like the one shown in Fig. 1, it is transformed to an equivalent *interaction expression*[3], which is in turn transformed to an operational model consisting of *states*, *state transitions*, and *state predicates*. The basic principle is similar to regular expressions and their transformation to finite state machines [11]: For each interaction expression x, there is an *initial state* $\sigma(x)$, a *state transition* function τ mapping a state s and an action[4] a to a *successor state* $\tau_a(s)$, and two *state predicates*, $\psi(s)$ and $\varphi(s)$, to determine whether a state s is *valid* or *final*, respectively. The essential difference to finite state machines is the fact that the states of an interaction expression are complex, hierarchically structured mathematical objects whose number is usually infinite. Furthermore, the distinction between valid and invalid states is not appropriate in finite state machines.

To determine whether a particular action a is *permissible* in state s of an expression x, the successor state $s' = \tau_a(s)$ is computed and checked for being valid using the state predicate $\psi(s')$. If it is invalid, the action is not permitted in state s. If a permissible action a is actually executed, the current state s, which is initialized to the initial state $\sigma(x)$, is replaced by the successor state $s' = \tau_a(s)$. The graph in Fig. 1, for example, permits in its initial state any of the activities prepare, inform, and call for any patient p and examination x. (More precisely, it permits the actions representing the *start* of these activities.) If, for instance, prepare is started for a particular patient p_1 and a particular examination x_1, i. e., a corresponding state transition is performed on the graph, the successor state will permit a matching termination action and — because of the "unrestricted concurrency" operators ◎ — additional starts of prepare for the same patient p_1 and any examination x. Due to the mutual exclusion operators, however, inform and call will no longer be permissible for that patient. Because of the outermost "for all" operators ◎, however, which specify that for each
p
patient p there is conceptually a separate repeated mutual exclusion, these activities are still permitted for all other patients.

To actually implement interaction expressions in a programming language like, e. g., C++, the mathematical definitions of $\sigma(x)$, $\tau_a(s)$, and $\varphi(s)$ are transformed to corresponding C++ functions declared as follows:

```
State init(Expr x);         // Initial state of expression x
State trans(State s, Action a); // Successor state of s and a
bool final(State s);        // Check whether s is a final state
```

The implementation of $\psi(s)$ can be conveniently integrated into trans(): Whenever the successor state is valid, it is actually returned, while otherwise a null state is returned.

---

[3] As interaction expressions and graphs are merely different representations of the same formalism, the terms will be used interchangeably in the following.

[4] *Actions* are considered discrete points in time representing either the *start* A_0 or the *termination* A_1 of an *activity* A which has a positive duration. In formal language terminology, an action corresponds to a symbol of the input alphabet.

3 Coordination and Subscription Protocols

Having introduced the basic ideas of the operational semantics and the implementation of interaction expressions derived from it, this section addresses the question how
interaction clients (i. e., programs which execute actions) can cooperate with an *interaction manager* (i. e., an implementation of interaction expressions) to actually enforce the integrity constraints specified by one or more interaction graphs.

3.1 One Phase Coordination Protocol

The simplest communication scheme between an interaction client and the interaction
manager consists of a client's *enquiry* whether a particular action is currently permissible (message type Ask) and a corresponding *answer* of the manager (message types
Accept and Reject). If the answer is Accept, it is assumed that the client will *immediately* execute the action, and therefore the manager performs the corresponding
state transition *before* transmitting the answer (cf. Fig. 4, left side). If the answer is
Reject, however, neither a state transition is performed by the manager nor must the
action be executed by the client (cf. Fig. 4, right side).[5]

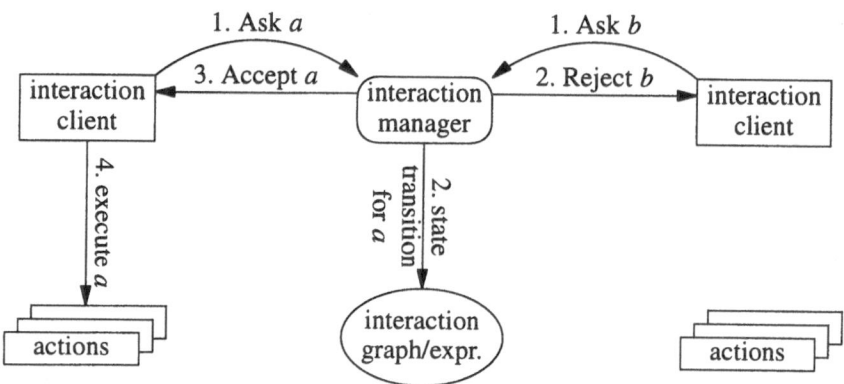

Fig. 4. One phase coordination protocol

If the exact point in time where an action is actually executed by a client is irrelevant or cannot be precisely determined, this simple form of coordination is completely
sufficient. If, for example, interaction expressions are employed to synchronize procedures of a parallel program instead of activities of parallel workflows [8, 10], the
event of starting or terminating a particular procedure cannot be observed externally.
Even if the first and last statements of a procedure produce diagnostic output messages, its actual start and termination times remain hidden. Therefore, one can assume
or assert that a procedure is started or terminated at the time the corresponding state
transition is performed by the interaction manager.

If the execution of actions is actually visible to users, however, the one phase coordination protocol is too simple, as race conditions might lead to illegal execution sequences. As a simple example, consider the expression $a - b$ (sequence of a and b). If

---

[5] There is actually a third type of answer, Unknown, which is replied if the manager does not know the en-
quired action because it does not appear in its graph. In that case, the action might be executed any time
without needing to ask the manager for permission.

a client A asks for permission to execute a and afterwards another client B asks for permission to execute b, both enquiries are answered with Accept, assuming that A will immediately execute a and afterwards B will execute b. If, however, B receives its answer before A, it might happen that b is executed before a, which is an obvious contradiction to the semantics of the expression $a - b$.[6]

3.2 Two Phase Coordination Protocol

To overcome this shortcoming of the one phase coordination protocol, it is necessary to synchronize the state transition of the interaction manager and the actual execution of the action by the client. For that purpose, the protocol is augmented with a second phase where the manager waits for a client's confirmation that it has actually executed the action (message type Exec) before performing the corresponding state transition and processing other enquiries (cf. Fig. 5, left side). By that means it is guaranteed, that actions in the real world are executed in the same order as their corresponding state transitions are performed by the manager.

If the answer to an enquiry has been Reject, however, no confirmation is expected, of course (cf. Fig. 5, right side).

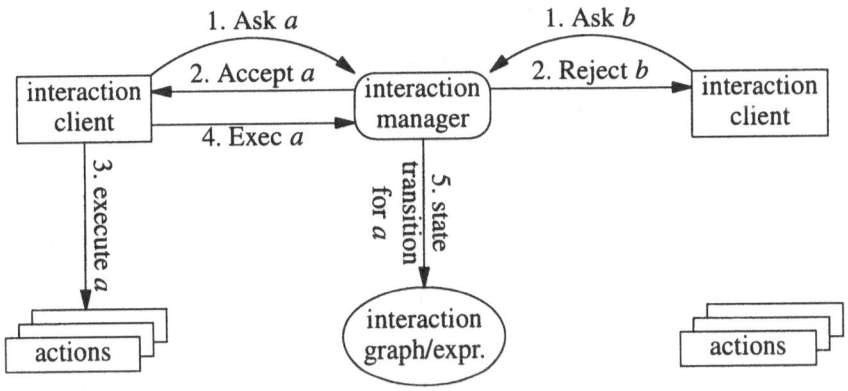

Fig. 5. Two phase coordination protocol

The structure of this two phase coordination protocol is very similar to the well-known two phase commit protocol for distributed transactions [15], where the interaction client plays the role of the commit coordinator while the interaction manager is the only regular participant: The client's enquiry (Ask) corresponds to a "prepare to commit" request causing the manager to check whether the action is currently permissible and reply either "vote commit" (Accept) or "vote abort" (Reject). In the first case (Accept), the client's confirmation (Exec) corresponds to the final "global commit" message of the coordinator, while in the latter case (Reject) no explicit "global abort" message of the coordinator (client) is necessary as the manager is the only regular participant, which has already "aborted" the transaction unilaterally.

Consequently, the two phase coordination protocol suffers from the same annoying problem as the two phase commit protocol: After replying Accept, the interaction

---

[6] In the special case, however, where only *one* client exists —and all messages are delivered and processed in the order they have been sent, which can be achieved, e. g., by using persistent message queues –, such race conditions cannot occur (cf. Sec. 4).

manager is forced to wait for the client's Exec message, no matter how long this might take. During that time, the manager must not process other client's enquiries as their actions must not be executed before the current action has definitely been executed. On the other hand, the manager cannot retract its Accept answer as the client will execute the action as soon as it receives this message. If a client dies or the connection to it breaks down before receiving its Accept or sending its Exec message, the whole system will get stuck due to the manager's inability to proceed.

Compared with the two phase commit protocol, this situation corresponds to a failure of the commit coordinator when all participants have answered "vote commit." Several approaches have been suggested in the literature to cope with such a situation, for example asking other participants about the state of the transaction or even electing a new commit coordinator. The particular problem here, however, is the fact that the interaction manager is the only regular participant and therefore there are no other participants which could be called for help.

The practical relevance of this problem depends heavily on the reliability of interaction clients. If there are only few, very reliable clients (e. g., workflow *servers*) which are critical system components themselves, the problem might be neglected as a failure of such a client would cause a system breakdown anyway. If, on the other hand, there are many, potentially unreliable clients (e. g., *worklist handlers* running on users' desktop computers which might be switched off any minute), the problem is highly relevant as a failure of such an unimportant client must under no circumstance cause a whole system to break down.

3.3 Three Phase Coordination Protocol

To solve the problem just described, it is necessary to add another phase to the coordination protocol which enables the interaction manager to "pass the buck" to the client and remain independently responsive. To achieve this goal, the semantics of the message type Accept is changed from a definite and final answer to a *preliminary* permission to execute an action which must be either confirmed (message type Commit) or retracted (message type Abort) by the interaction manager later.

For a client that means, that it must execute the action after receipt of the Accept message, send back an Exec confirmation, and then wait for the manager's final decision. If the manager does not receive the Exec message in time, it is free to retract the permission given with Accept by sending an Abort message to the client. In that case, the client is forced to *undo* the action, for example by aborting the transaction encompassing it or by some kind of semantic rollback [5] (cf. Fig. 6, right side). In the normal case, however, the manager performs the corresponding state transition after receipt of the Exec confirmation and sends back a Commit message, causing the client to finally commit the transaction encompassing the action or − if this has already been done − simply ignore the message (cf. Fig. 6, left side).

If the initial answer of the manager has been Reject, however, no additional protocol steps are necessary, of course, leading to the same reduced protocol as in Fig. 4 and 5 (right side always).

In the concrete application of workflow synchronization, executing an action means starting or terminating a workflow step (activity) − actions which are typically performed in a transaction by the WfMS. Here, Accept causes the client (WfMS) to start a corresponding transaction, put it in the "ready to commit" state, and send back an

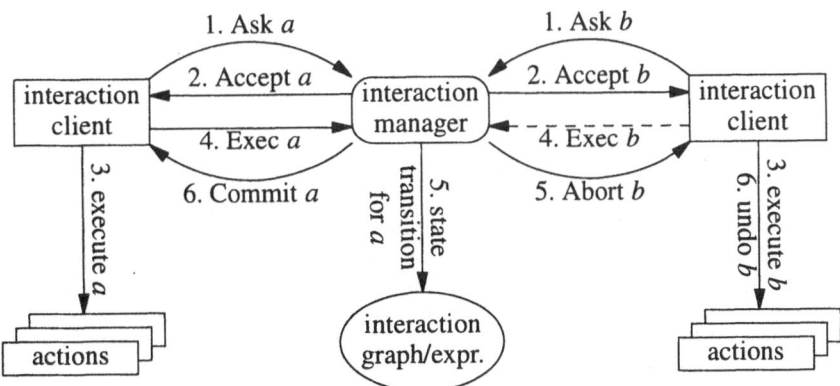

Fig. 6. Three phase coordination protocol

Exec message to the manager. Afterwards, the Commit or Abort message of the manager causes the transaction to be either committed or aborted.

Although the three phase coordination protocol might be compared with a three phase commit protocol [19, 15], it actually constitutes a two phase commit protocol with an additional "prolog" phase and exchanged roles: The enquiry message Ask of a client is not considered part of the actual commit protocol, but rather triggers the manager — which now plays the role of the commit coordinator — to initiate the commit protocol by sending an Accept message (corresponding to "prepare to commit") to the client, which is the only regular participant. The client's Exec confirmation corresponds to a "vote commit" message, while the manager's Commit or Abort message corresponds to the final "global commit" or "global abort" message of the coordinator.

By exchanging the roles of interaction manager and client, the manager becomes autonomous to avoid the danger of becoming blocked by a not responding client. On the other hand, it is of course possible that a client becomes blocked when waiting for the final Commit or Abort message of the manager. If the interaction manager or the connection to it breaks down, however, clients are unable to proceed anyway, so this blocking does not induce any additional harm in such a situation.

3.4 Multiple Interaction Managers

If multiple interaction graphs which must be enforced simultaneously are given in an application scenario, it is possible to combine them to a single graph (using a so-called *coupling operator* which is very similar to a logical *conjunction*) and process that graph with a single interaction manager. On the other hand it is possible to process each graph with a separate interaction manager if the following rules are obeyed by interaction clients:

- If an action shall be executed that does not appear in any of the graphs, no manager needs to be asked for permission; the action might be executed any time.

- If an action appears in exactly one of the graphs, exactly this manager has to be asked for permission using one of the previously described coordination protocols.

- If an action appears in several graphs, *all* corresponding managers have to be asked for permission and their state transitions must be *synchronized*.

As the two phase coordination protocol corresponds to a two phase commit protocol where an interaction *client* plays the role of the commit coordinator while the interaction manager constitutes a regular participant, this protocol can be readily used to coordinate multiple interaction managers. The only necessary extension is the addition of a message type Undo corresponding to the coordinator's "global abort" message, which will be sent by a client if one of the managers has replied Reject (corresponding to "vote abort") because the action is currently not permitted by the corresponding graph (cf. Fig. 7). If all managers have replied Accept ("vote commit"), however, the client executes the action and sends back Exec confirmations ("global commit") to all managers causing the appropriate state transition to be performed on all graphs (cf. Fig. 8).

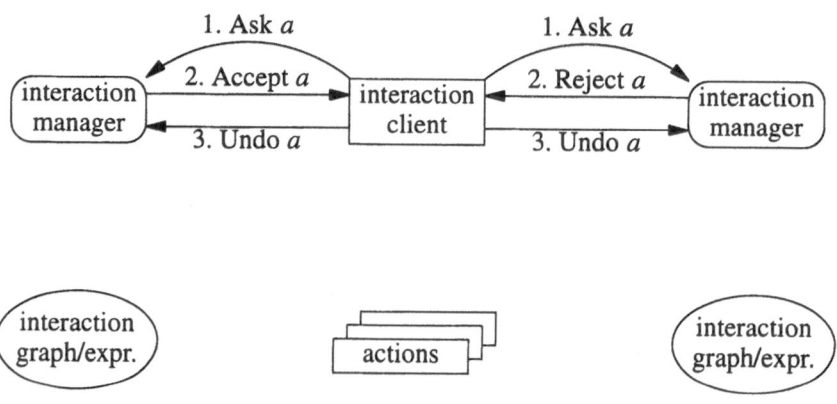

Fig. 7. Multiple interaction managers: one manager replies Reject

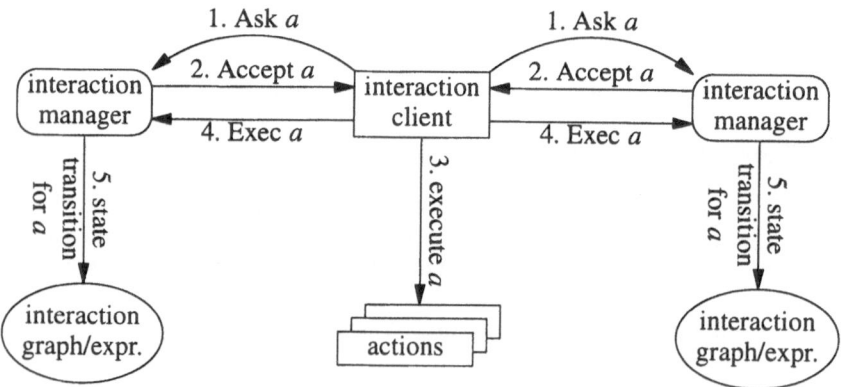

Fig. 8. Multiple interaction managers: all managers reply Accept

If the two phase coordination protocol is unsuitable, however, because interaction clients are not reliable enough, a modified three phase coordination protocol might be used, as explained in the following. If a client wants to execute a particular action, it sends corresponding Ask enquiries to all managers "knowing" this action. In addition to the action in question, each manager is informed about the other managers involved in the enquiry as it might become necessary for them to cooperate later. If all managers reply Accept, the client executes the action and sends back Exec confirmations. If all of them arrive in time, each manager performs a corresponding state transition and sends a final Commit message. If, on the other hand, one of the managers replies Reject, the client sends Undo messages to all managers causing the protocol to terminate prematurely. If one of the Exec or Undo messages is not received in time, however, the corresponding manager must *not* autonomously send an Abort message, for two reasons: First, another manager might have received the client's Exec confirmation in time and thus have sent a final Commit message; then the client would sit "between the chairs," unable to decide whether it should commit or abort the action. Second, in such a situation one of the managers would have performed a state transition for the action while another has not, causing an inconsistent global state of the graphs. To avoid such dilemmas and inconsistencies, a manager who *wants* to send an Abort message to the client must coordinate its decision with the other managers involved in the enquiry:

- If one of them has already received the client's Exec or Undo message, the other managers can react as if they have received the same message, i. e., either perform the corresponding state transition and send Commit or just terminate the protocol, respectively.

- If one of the managers has initially replied Reject, all managers can prematurely terminate the protocol, because sooner or later they will receive Undo messages from the client.

- Finally, if *all* managers have initially replied Accept, but *none* of them has received the client's Exec confirmation yet, they might agree to collectively send Abort messages to the client in order to avoid long-term blocking situations.[7]

On the one hand, these rules guarantee that a client always receives consistent answers from all managers (either only Commit or only Abort messages), and on the other hand, that state transitions are performed consistently by all managers (either all or none of the involved managers performs a state transition). Nevertheless, the interaction managers are "collectively autonomous," i. e., by working together they can break blocking situations resulting from not responding clients.[8] As interaction managers are critical system components which are assumed to be very reliable, this leads to an acceptable overall system behaviour.

Compared with distributed commit protocols, this modified three phase coordination protocol corresponds roughly to a three phase commit protocol with a simplified termination protocol in the case of a client failure.

---

[7] As the client might still decide to send Undo messages, even if all managers have initially replied Accept, the managers must *not* agree to send Commit messages in that case. The client needs this possibility because there is another "hidden" participant of the protocol, namely the WfMS which might refuse to execute an action if it has just been executed by another user (cf. Sec. 4).

[8] If *only one manager is involved* in an enquiry, the above rules lead directly to the original three phase coordination protocol described in Sec. 3.3.

3.5 Subscription Protocol

The coordination protocols presented so far are intended for situations where a client actually wants to execute a particular action. If it only wants to *know* whether a particular action is currently permissible or not (for example, to keep a user's worklist up to date), it might also ask for the corresponding execution permission by sending an Ask message to the manager, then wait for the matching Accept or Reject answer, and afterwards abort the protocol with an Undo message if the manager's answer has been Accept. As the status of an action might change any minute, this procedure must be repeated frequently in order to keep the client's information fairly up to date. This kind of misusing the coordination protocol for simple status enquiries would, however, cause a lot of network traffic as well as interaction manager workload which can be avoided by providing a more suitable *subscription protocol* for that purpose.

If a client always wants to know about the current status of a particular action, it sends a corresponding Subscribe message to the manager. Afterwards, the manager will send back matching Permit or Forbid messages whenever the status of the action changes from not permissible to permissible or vice versa, respectively. Furthermore, if the action is currently permissible, an initial Permit message is sent immediately. To terminate the protocol, the client might send a corresponding Cancel message (cf. Fig. 9).

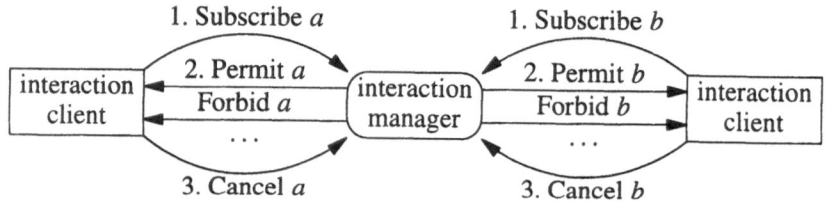

Fig. 9. Subscription protocol

The advantages of this protocol are obvious: The client's information is always up to date, while at the same time the network traffic and interaction manager workload are reduced to a minimum. To avoid misinterpretations, however, it should be emphasized that a Permit message has only informative character (the corresponding action is currently permissible) and does not represent a real execution permission. To actually execute an action, it is still necessary to pass through one of the coordination protocols described earlier. However, the receipt of a Permit message might trigger a client to initiate a coordination protocol right *now* as the chance to get an Accept answer is currently very high.

4   Integration with Workflow Management Systems

Having designed the coordination and subscription protocols, it is a rather straightforward task to implement their server (i. e., interaction manager) side. However, it remains the question how workflow management systems can actually play the corresponding client role. As a WfMS consists —very roughly spoken —of one or possibly more *workflow servers* and a set of users' *worklist handlers*, which cooperate with the workflow server(s) in executing workflow activities, there are basically two alternative ways to incorporate the coordination and subscription protocols.

The most direct approach is to include them into the workflow server, yielding the system architecture depicted in Fig. 10. Here, the workflow server is responsible for communicating with the interaction manager, while the worklist handlers remain unchanged and need not even know about the manager's existence. This approach has the advantage that the two phase coordination protocol is sufficient as a workflow server is usually as reliable as the interaction manager itself. Furthermore, the interaction manager must deal with only one (or a few) interaction clients (i. e., workflow servers), resulting in moderate network traffic and interaction manager workload.[9]

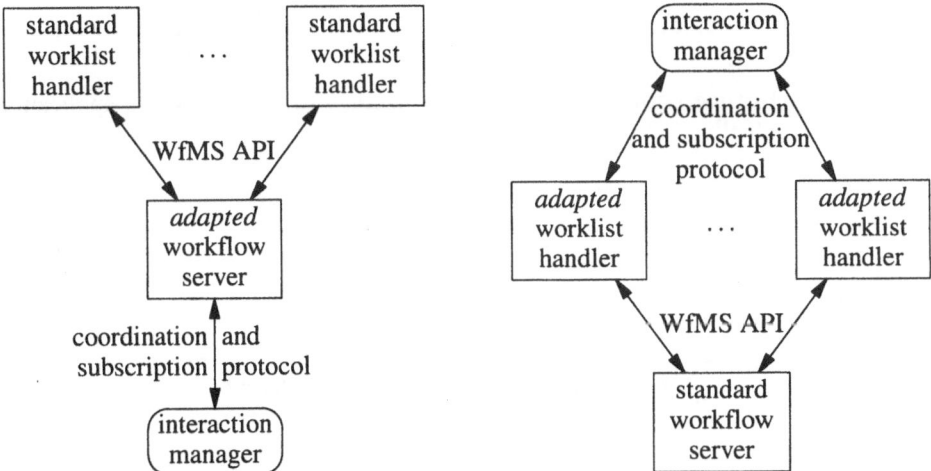

Fig. 10. Adaptation of workflow servers   **Fig. 11.** Adaptation of worklist handlers

On the other hand, it is almost impossible to implement this approach with an off-the-shelf WfMS where normally neither the source code nor appropriate documentation of the internal structure of a workflow server is available. But even for research prototypes where these "resources" are accessible, it is very difficult and expensive to modify a workflow server afterwards as it usually constitutes a very complex and extensive application. Therefore – if the integration of coordination and subscription protocols has not been planned in advance –,the second alternative depicted in Fig. 11 might be more attractive.

Here, the workflow server remains unchanged and need not even know about the interaction manager, since all necessary coordination is performed by the users' worklist handlers. If, for example, the workflow server tells a worklist handler to insert a particular activity into the user's worklist, the worklist handler will send a corresponding Subscribe message to the interaction manager and wait for a matching Permit answer before actually offering the activity to the user. Furthermore, if a Forbid message is received for one of the currently displayed activities, it is temporarily removed from the worklist – or at least tagged as currently not executable – until a corresponding Permit message is received again.

---

[9] If there is only *one* workflow server, it is even possible to employ the simple one phase coordination protocol (cf. Sec. 3.1).

Furthermore, if a user wants to execute a particular activity, the worklist handler performs the appropriate coordination protocol with the interaction manager before actually starting the activity's application program. More precisely, the steps depicted in Fig. 12 are performed by the worklist handler according to the three phase coordination protocol (which is necessary here as worklist handlers are usually rather unreliable):

- Using message type Ask, the interaction manager is asked for permission to start the activity, i. e., to execute the corresponding start action (1).

- After receipt of the corresponding Accept message (2), the workflow server is told to start the activity (3).

- When this has been confirmed (4), an Exec confirmation is sent to the interaction manager (5).

- After receipt of the corresponding Commit message (6), the activity's application program is actually started (7).

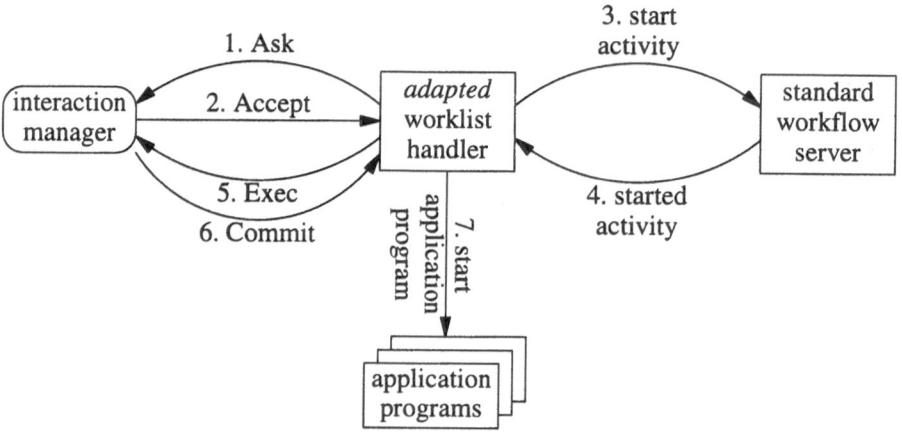

Fig. 12. Starting an activity

Of course, the following exceptions might occur while performing these steps:

- If a Reject message is received in step 2 instead of the expected Accept answer, the protocol is immediately terminated.
  This typically happens when another user has just started the activity in question or another activity which must not be executed concurrently. If the worklist handler has subscripted to the activity, a corresponding Forbid message will immediately follow causing the activity to become removed from the worklist (cf. above).

- If the workflow server does not confirm the start of the activity in step 4 (again, because another user has just started to execute it), the worklist handler terminates the coordination protocol by sending an Undo message in step 5 instead of the normal Exec message.

- If, due to unexpected timeouts, an Abort message is received in step 6 instead of the expected Commit answer, the worklist handler might repeat steps 1 to 6 (except steps 3 and 4) until it finally receives the desired Commit message. If, however, a Reject answer is received in step 2 of one of these repetitions, the workflow server must be told to abort (the transaction constituting) the execution of the activity.

The details of steps 3, 4, and 7 naturally depend strongly on the particular WfMS. The basic mechanisms should be similar for all systems, however.

Compared with the effort to integrate the coordination and subscription protocols into an existing workflow server, the implementation of an adapted worklist handler is a rather simple task. Furthermore, for many application scenarios, the standard worklist handlers provided by the WfMS are replaced by customized programs anyway, in which case the integration of the protocols requires only little additional effort.

On the other hand, it must be noted that this approach induces a much higher network traffic and interaction manager workload as the number of concurrently running worklist handlers is usually much higher than the number of workflow servers. Furthermore, as worklist handlers are rather unreliable, the more complex three phase coordination protocol must be employed.

No matter which of the integration approaches is actually chosen, it is possible to generalize it to a scenario involving multiple interaction managers as well as multiple (and even heterogeneous) workflow servers [8].

Example

If the initial part of the example of Fig. 3 (Sec. 1) is executed in a system architecture according to Fig. 11 (adapted worklist handlers), the messages shown in Fig. 13 will be exchanged between the worklist handlers of the nurse and the ward doctor, respectively, and the workflow server on the one hand and the interaction manager on the other hand.[10]

After starting both examination workflows for patient p and executing their initial activities order(p, S) and order(p, E) independently, the workflow server enables the activities prepare(p, S), prepare(p, E), and inform(p, E) and thus sends corresponding enable messages to the worklist handlers of the appropriate users, expecting them to add the activities to their worklists.[11] The worklist handlers, however, first send Subscribe messages for the starting actions $prepare_0(p, S)$, $prepare_0(p, E)$, and $inform_0(p, E)$ to the interaction manager and wait for matching Permit messages, before actually adding the activities to the users' worklists.

When the nurse decides to start prepare(p, S), her worklist handler sends an Ask message for the starting action $prepare_0(p, S)$ to the interaction manager and waits for a matching Accept message. Afterwards, the activity is actually started by sending a start message to the workflow server. After receipt of its started confirmation, the worklist handler sends an Exec confirmation to the interaction manager and waits for the corresponding Commit message before launching the activity's application program.

When performing the state transition for the action $prepare_0(p, S)$, the interaction manager detects that the action $inform_0(p, E)$ is no longer permissible in the resulting state of the interaction graph. It therefore sends a corresponding Forbid message to

---

[10] Note that there is just a *single* workflow server which has been split into two vertical time axes solely to simplify the graphical presentation.

[11] Again to simplify the presentation, the two enable messages for the prepare activities are represented by a single arrow. The same is true for subsequent Subscribe and Permit messages.

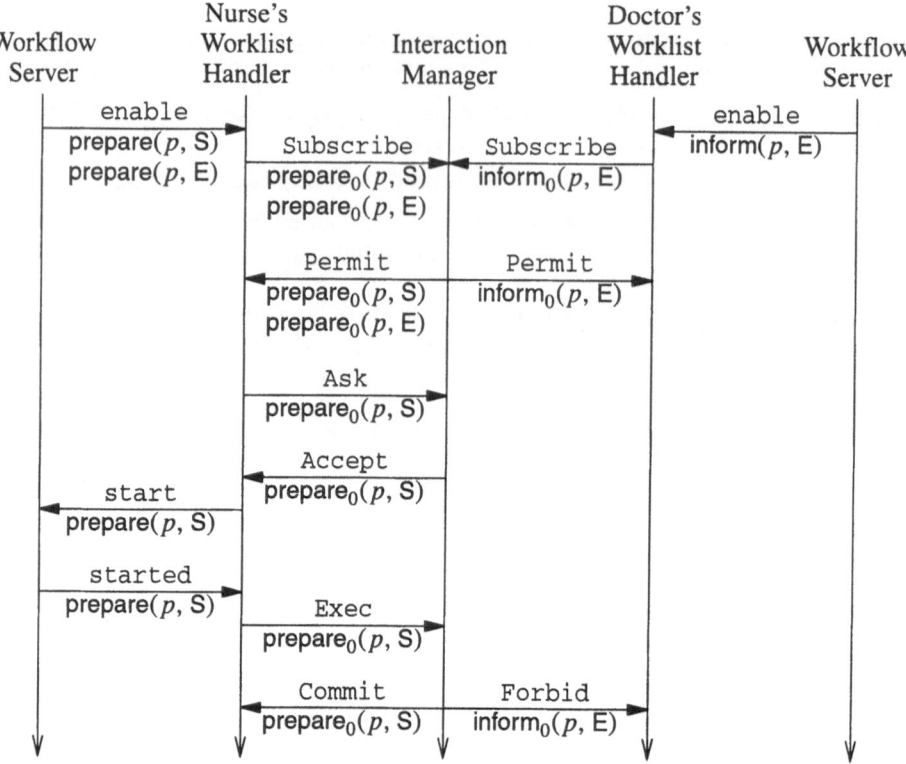

Fig. 13. Example message flow

its subscriber, i. e., to the doctor's worklist handler which in turn removes inform(p, E) from its worklist.

5 Related Work

The distributed commit protocols which inspired and influenced the design of the two and three phase coordination protocols are described in [19] as well as in textbooks on distributed database systems (e. g., [15]). Persistent message queues, which should be employed for reliable and recoverable communications between an interaction manager and its clients, are presented, e. g., in [2] and [6].

Basically similar ideas to those presented in this paper can be found in the work on *inter-task dependencies* [1, 20]. Constraints expressed using the so called *Klein primitives* [13] (corresponding to interaction expressions or graphs in our approach) are transformed to *dependency automata* (corresponding to the operational model of interaction expressions) which are enforced by a central *scheduler* (corresponding to an interaction manager). *Tasks* (corresponding to interaction clients) must ask the scheduler for permission before executing *events* (corresponding to actions). Events which are currently permissible are delegated to an *event dispatcher* which actually executes them. (With interaction expressions, they are directly executed by a client.) Events which are currently not permissible are queued by the scheduler and re-attempted to execute whenever another event has been successfully executed. (A similar feature is provided by the interaction manager implementation described in [8], but has been omitted here due to space limitations. Furthermore, the subscription protocol is usually a more adequate means to cope with currently not permissible actions.)

Despite these obvious similarities, simply adopting this approach has not been possible for several reasons: First, the formalism used to describe inter-task dependencies is hard to understand (especially for mathematically unskilled persons) and less expressive than interaction graphs. In particular, iteration operators are missing which are needed frequently in the context of inter-workflow dependencies. (They are quite irrelevant for transaction models, the primary application of the formalism.) Furthermore, the enforcement strategies suggested in [1] which rely on *forcible events* are not applicable here as an interaction manager can only forbid, but never enforce the execution of a particular action.

Transaction models employing formalisms similar to interaction expressions – regular expressions and LR(0) grammars – to specify permissible event sequences are described in [16] and [14]. While regular expressions are definitely too limited for our context, LR(0) grammars are quite expressive. Using recursive rules, it is indeed possible to specify synchronization conditions which are probably not expressible with interaction expressions.[12] On the other hand, LR(0) grammars – as well as more general context-free grammars – lack the concept of concurrency which is much more important for most applications of interaction expressions than recursion. For instance, in the graph shown in Fig. 1, the ◉ operators in the upper and lower branches of the mutual exclusion permit any number of concurrent executions of their body, i. e., the subgraph in between.

In the areas of concurrent programming and software specification, there have also been suggestions to use expression-based formalisms to specify permissible execution sequences of procedures or statements of a parallel program. However, all these formalisms are either subsumed by interaction expressions [3, 7] or possess sophisticated (and not user-friendly) operators which make them computationally complete (Turing equivalent) and thus extremely hard to implement [17, 18]. In contrast, the operational semantics of interaction expressions has been transformed to a real implementation which has been proved to process a very large and practically relevant set of expressions in a very efficient manner [8, 9].

Work dealing explicitly with inter-workflow dependencies is described, for example, in [4] and [12]. Even though these approaches address some additional topics not covered by interaction expressions (e. g., failure handling and formal properties of interacting workflows), their contributions to workflow coordination are quite limited and inflexible, however. In particular, inter-workflow dependencies must always be specified as *explicit* relationships between *particular* activities of *particular* workflows. It is not possible to specify *general* integrity constraints for activities without needing to know in which particular workflows they will occur. Therefore, it is impossible to deal with *dynamically evolving* workflow ensembles whose participants are not known in advance and might change with time, although these are frequently found in practical applications. In contrast, interaction expressions have been deliberately designed in a way which supports the specification of general integrity constraints allowing them to synchronize dynamically evolving workflow ensembles in the same way as statically defined ones.

---

[12] Currently, this is only a strong conjecture which has not been formally proved yet (cf. [8]).

6 Conclusion

Interaction expressions and graphs constitute a flexible and expressive formalism for the specification and implementation of synchronization conditions in general and inter-workflow dependencies in particular. In addition to a graph-based semi-formal interpretation, they possess a precise formal semantics, an equivalent operational semantics, and an efficient implementation of the latter whose runtime behaviour has been assessed by detailed complexity analyses [8, 9]. In this paper, different coordination protocols as well as an accompanying subscription protocol have been described as a practical way to employ interaction expressions for the synchronization of concurrent workflows. Furthermore, the basic principles to use these protocols with workflow management systems have been outlined.

Due to space limitations, several advanced topics have been mentioned only briefly or not at all (cf. [8] for details):

- Both system architectures described in Sec. 4 can be extended to the most general case where multiple interaction managers interact with multiple (and even heterogeneous) workflow servers – either directly (Fig. 10) or indirectly via adapted worklist handlers acting as mediators (Fig. 11).

- In order to fully exploit the potential of multiple interaction managers, typical interaction graphs like the one shown in Fig. 1 can be partitioned into any number of subgraphs with restricted parameter ranges which can be processed by *independent* interaction managers. This is an important property with respect to *scalability*.

- To obtain system architectures which are tolerant to network errors, persistent messages queues should be used as communication channels between interaction manager(s) and client(s) to make sure that protocol messages will arrive in order and will not get lost. Furthermore, recovery procedures have been worked out allowing an interaction manager to restore the current state of its graph (which is very important for correct system behaviour) after a crash.

In summary, all necessary ingredients are available to integrate interaction expressions into current or future workflow management systems – either by extending worklist handlers or workflow servers. Thus, it is possible to meet the requirements of many practical application scenarios where workflows – though independently modeled in order to remain comprehensible and manageable – are semantically interrelated.

References

[1] P. C. Attie, M. P. Singh, A. Sheth, M. Rusinkiewicz: "Specifying and Enforcing Intertask Dependencies." In: R. Agrawal, S. Baker, D. Bell (eds.): *Proc. 19th Int. Conf. on Very Large Data Bases (VLDB)* (Dublin, Ireland, August 1993). 1993, 134–145.

[2] P. A. Bernstein, M. Hsu, B. Mann: "Implementing Recoverable Requests Using Queues." In: *Proc. ACM SIGMOD Int. Conf. on Management of Data.* 1990, 112–122.

[3] R. H. Campbell, A. N. Habermann: "The Specification of Process Synchronization by Path Expressions." In: E. Gelenbe, C. Kaiser (eds.): *Operating Systems* (International Symposium; Rocquencourt, France, April 1974; Proceedings). Lecture Notes in Computer Science 16, Springer-Verlag, Berlin, 1974, 89–102.

[4] F. Casati, S. Ceri, B. Pernici, G. Pozzi: "Semantic WorkFlow Interoperability." In: P. Apers, M. Bouzeghoub, G. Gardarin (eds.): *Advances in Database Technology – EDBT'96* (5th Int. Conf. on Extending Database Technology; Avignon, France, March 1996; Proceedings). Lecture Notes in Computer Science 1057, Springer-Verlag, Berlin, 1996, 443–462.

[5] H. Garcia-Molina, K. Salem: "Sagas." In: U. Dayal, I. Traiger (eds.): *Proc. ACM SIGMOD Int. Conf. on Management of Data* (San Francisco, CA, May 1987), 249–259.

[6] J. Gray, A. Reuter: *Transaction Processing: Concepts and Techniques.* Morgan Kaufmann Publishers, San Mateo, CA, 1993.

[7] L. Guo, K. Salomaa, S. Yu: "On Synchronization Languages." *Fundamenta Informaticae* 25 (3+4) March 1996, 423–436.

[8] C. Heinlein: *Workflow and Process Synchronization with Interaction Expressions and Graphs.* Ph.D. Thesis (in German), Fakultät für Informatik, Universität Ulm, 2000.

[9] C. Heinlein: "Workflow and Process Synchronization with Interaction Expressions and Graphs." In: *Proc. 17th Int. Conf. on Data Engineering (ICDE)* (Heidelberg, Germany, April 2001). IEEE Computer Society, 2001, 243–252.

[10] C. Heinlein: "Advanced Thread Synchronization in Java." In: *Net.ObjectDays 2002* (Erfurt, Germany, October 2002).

[11] J. E. Hopcroft, J. D. Ullman: *Introduction to Automata Theory, Languages and Computation.* Addison-Wesley, Reading, MA, 1979.

[12] M. Kamath, K. Ramamritham: "Failure Handling and Coordinated Execution of Concurrent Workflows." In: *Proc. 14th Int. Conf. on Data Engineering (ICDE)* (Orlando, FL, February 1998). IEEE Computer Society, 1998, 334–341.

[13] J. Klein: "Advanced Rule Driven Transaction Management." (Extended Abstract). In: *Proc. 36th IEEE Computer Society Int. Conf. (COMPCON)* (San Francisco, CA, March 1991). 1991, 562–567.

[14] M. H. Nodine, S. Ramaswamy, S. B. Zdonik: "A Cooperative Transaction Model for Design Databases." In: A. K. Elmagarmid (ed.): *Database Transaction Models for Advanced Applications.* Morgan Kaufmann Publishers, San Mateo, CA, 1992, 53–85.

[15] M. T. Özsu, P. Valduriez: *Principles of Distributed Database Systems.* Prentice-Hall, Englewood Cliffs, NJ, 1991.

[16] R. Rastogi, S. Mehrotra, H. F. Korth, A. Silberschatz: "Transcending the Serializability Requirement." *IEEE Data Engineering Bulletin* 16 (2) June 1993, 8–11.

[17] W. E. Riddle: "An Approach to Software System Behavior Description." *Computer Languages* 4, 1979, 29–47.

[18] A. C. Shaw: "On the Specification of Graphics Command Languages and Their Processors." In: R. A. Guedj, P. J. W. ten Hagen, F. R. A. Hopgood, H. A. Tucker, D. A. Duce (eds.): *Methodology of Interaction* (IFIP Workshop on Methodology of Interaction; Seillac, France, May 1979). North-Holland Publishing Company, Amsterdam, 1980, 377–392.

[19] D. Skeen: "Nonblocking Commit Protocols." In: *Proc. ACM SIGMOD Int. Conf. on Management of Data* (Ann Arbor, MI, April/May 1981), 133–142.

[20] J. Tang, J. Veijalainen: "Enforcing Inter-Task Dependencies in Transactional Workflows." In: S. Laufmann, S. Spaccapietra, T. Yokoi (eds.): *Proc. 3rd Int. Conf. on Cooperative Information Systems (CoopIS)* (Vienna, Austria, May 1995). 1995, 72–86.

CPM Revisited – An Architecture Comparison

Qiming Chen and Meichun Hsu

Commerce One Labs, Commerce One Inc.
19191 Vallco Parkway, Cupertino, CA 95014
{qiming.chen; meichun.hsu}@commerceone.com

Abstract. In this report we discuss the architecture of the Collaborative Process Managers (CPMs) used to support inter-enterprise collaboration. A CPM must provide three logical functions, the *conversation management* for handling inter-enterprise document flows; *the process management* for controlling local workflows of document manipulation and other related tasks; and the *action management* for invoking local services that actually implement these tasks. Conversation models and workflow models have some similarity as well as considerable differences. The provisioning, interaction and integration of these three functions are very practical challenges faced by many organizations. Particularly, extending existing workflow engines for supporting inter-enterprise business collaboration, has become the common interest of the e-business industry. We shall first compare five different CPM architectures based on our own prototypes, and then propose the architecture characterized by interfacing a conversation manager and a process manager through *asynchronous task activation*, and by using the conversation manager as the *conversation model driven task activator* for local process management. Our experience reveals the advantages of this architecture over the others, as it allows the maximal usability of existing workflow system components, supports both conversation flow and local work flow, and provides a dynamic and simple interface between conversation management and process management. Further, by providing conversation managers under different conversation models, a CPM can support multiple inter-enterprise interaction standards.

1 Introduction

E-business is moving toward a paradigm in which enterprises interact with each other through exchanging XML documents based on well-defined protocols such as SOAP[12], WSDL[16], which enables them to interoperate their Web services in a dynamic and loosely coupled way. Further, the "conversation process" specification standards such as ebXML's BPSS (Business Process Specification Schema)[8], describe the *choreography* of document exchange as the abstract business interface, leaving the processing and provisioning of documents to local business processes or services [3,6,10]. In [2,4] we discussed the issue of inter-enterprise collaboration at the business process level, and presented a Collaborative Process Manager (CPM) proto

R. Meersman, Z. Tari (Eds.): CoopIS/DOA/ODBASE 2002, LNCS 2519, pp. 72–90, 2002.

type. In this report we shall further compare different architectures based on our own experiences, and propose an architecture that has the greatest usability, flexibility and simplicity.

1.1 Conversation Process vs. Business Process

In order for enterprises to collaborate at the business-process level, they must allow the business processes run on their local sites to interact. In order to provide abstract interfaces of business interaction distinguished from the concrete services, several Inter-enterprise Conversation Process (ICP) specification standards such as ebXML BPSS[8], WSCI (Web Service Choreography Interface) [14], WSCL (Web Service Conversation Language) [15] have been proposed. As shown in Figure 1, an ICP specifies the choreography of document exchange as the abstract interface, leaving the processing and provisioning of documents to local business processes or services. As the abstract interface, one ICP can be supported by a variety of business processes and services with different implementations.

Fig. 1. Choreographed document exchange as conversation process

An ICP (or simply a *conversation process*) is not executed on a centralized server, but carried out by multiple participating parties; each party is responsible for enforcing its peer-view of the conversation process; e.g. verifying the inbound documents and controlling the sending of outbound documents according to the ICP specification.

By conversation process, we mean the one describing conversation flow; by business process we mean the one describing work flow. To clarify, we distinguish the basic operations of conversation processes and business processes by calling them *conversation activities* and *tasks* respectively.

At one business site, conceptually a conversation process handling document exchange is coupled with a local business process handling the tasks for document processing and provisioning, and in turn, these tasks are actually performed by the concrete actions, services and other local business processes.

It is important to note the *independence* between "conversation activities" and "process tasks", and between tasks and actions; analogously,

-   for a conversation process, the conversation activities are interface level objects internal to the conversation process, and tasks for supporting the conversation activities are implementation level objects defined externally to the conversation process;

- for a business process, the tasks are interface level objects internal to the business process, and actions for performing the tasks are implementation level objects defined externally to the business process.

This implies that a CPM for supporting inter-enterprise collaboration is potentially made of three communicating components for handling conversations, local business processes and actions respectively (Figure 2).

- The Conversation Manager (CM) handles inter-enterprise business interaction based on an *ICP model* (*conversation model*). A core function of CM is to enforce the choreography of document exchange.
- The Process Manager (PM) runs local processes based on a *business process model*. A core function of PM is to enforce the rules for triggering tasks. These tasks contribute to the accomplishment of the local process, including document manipulation as required by the conversation activities.
- The Action Manager (AM) dispatches and invokes local applications, services or processes to perform process tasks. An action provides an actual implementation of document processing, provisioning or other applications. Actions may be called through local or remote invocation, based on CORBA, WSDL, etc. The invocation may be made synchronous or asynchronous.

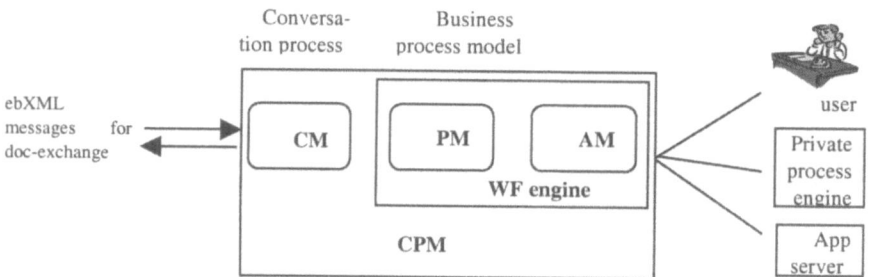

Fig. 2. CPM – conversation manager, process manager and action manager

In supporting business collaboration, CM focuses on enforcing the constraints of inter-enterprise document flow, and PM focuses on enforcing the constraints of intra-enterprise task scheduling. CM deals with choreographed document exchange; PM deals with document processing and provisioning accordingly, as well as the issues on transaction, recovery, concurrency, etc, in the context of process management [1,5,13,17].

The functions of conversation management, process management and action management may be combined in a single system, or provided by separate but communicating systems.

At a business site, a conversation process, say *C*, defining the choreography of document exchange, actually indicates the expected behavior of the coupling business process, say, *P*, for processing and producing the corresponding documents. If *P* can process and provide documents in the order that matches the order of document receiving and sending specified in *C*, we say *P* can be used to support *C*.

However, in general the conversation process and the coupling business process are based on different models. A *conversation activity* has two operations for delivering requesting and responding documents, which may map to one or more local tasks for consuming and producing the documents. The ICP models such as BPSS [8], WSCI [14], etc, are all different from the traditional workflow models such as WfMC's reference model [13]. The choreography of conversation activities and the flow of task execution are also semantically different. Since in business interactions a system at one-side cannot control the behavior of the peer-site partners, the choreography of interactions must be verified with respect to a commonly agreed conversation model.

1.2 CPM Architecture Comparison

As discussed thus far, we can see that conducting inter-enterprise collaboration requires the management for conversations, local processes and actions.

In this report we shall compare five different CPM architectures we have designed and prototyped; they fall into the following two general categories.

- A CPM is based on extending an existing workflow engine for supporting inter-enterprise conversation by embedding inter-changed documents into the payloads of process control messages. In this category we shall present the following two possible architectures:
  (1) peer process execution based on public process template;
  (2) peer process execution based on peer process template.
- A CPM is built by introducing an individual CM for handling choreographed conversation based on an ICP model. In this category we shall compare three possible architectures:
  (3) a stand-alone ICP engine constructed around the CM to support only conversation activities;
  (4) a workflow engine with the CM as its front-end for handling business conversation; and
  (5) an extended workflow engine with the CM plugged in.

In the last two architectures, we propose the mechanism called *conversation model driven asynchronous task activation* for controlling the task flow of local processes.

Most of our prototypes are based on the Business Process Manager developed at CommerceOne Inc. Our experience reveals the advantages of the last architecture over the others, as it allows the maximal usability of existing workflow system components, supports both conversation processes and local processes, and greatly simplifies the interface between CM and PM. By providing CMs under different ICP standards, a CPM can support multiple ICP languages.

1.3   Conversation Model Driven Asynchronous Task Activator as Dynamic Interface between CM and PM

Based on the comparison of several CPM prototypes, we propose the architecture for interoperating a conversation manager and a process manager based on *conversation model driven asynchronous task activation*, which allows us to make full use of existing workflow system components, to support both public conversation processes and local business processes, and to interface CM and PM dynamically.

Under the usual workflow model, conceptually a task is triggered by the satisfaction of the *"task activation conditions"*. When a process is specified with inter-linked tasks, a link from task T_p to task T actually represents an activation condition of T relating to the execution status of T_p. From this point of view, a business process may also be viewed as a set of rules for task activation, process termination, etc. The Business Process Manager developed at CommerceOne Inc, like many others, supports this model.

We distinguish two general mechanisms of task activation: *synchronous activation* and *asynchronous activation*. Given a task T,

- *synchronous activation* means an *event*, such as notifying the status of a precedent task, directly activates T;
- *asynchronous activation* means
  - ❑   an event causes the update of the base data underlying the task activation condition of T, which may potentially make the task ready to run; but
  - ❑   checking conditions and activating T is handled by a separate thread of control.

It is worth noting that activating a task may mean executing it right away or schedule it to run.

A task can be activated based on certain task-activation condition, and these conditions are checked against certain underlying data. The evolving of conversation process instance upon document exchange generates the information for updating the underlying data of task activate-conditions. Asynchronously, the task scheduler of a PM will check those conditions to schedule tasks. This is shown in Figure 3. The mapping between the information generated by CM and the base data underlying task activation condition in PM must be supported.

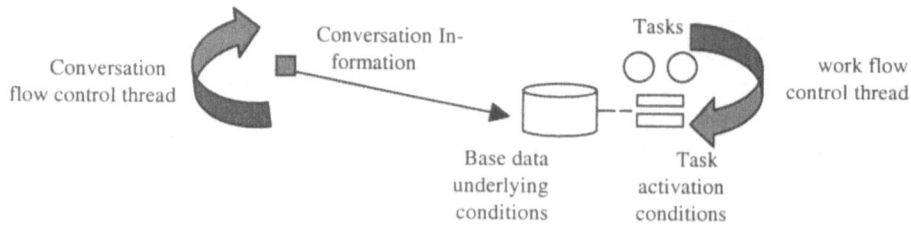

Fig. 3. Interact conversation flow and workflow asynchronously

Asynchronous task activation is important because it provides a way for separated CM and PM systems to interact. Given a conversation process, C, and the coupling local business process, P, even if the task flow of P is consistent with the order of document exchange specified in C, it is difficult to synchronize the execution paces of P and C in terms of synchronous task activation, especially when P involves other private applications and runs at a different pace from C. Asynchronous task activation provides a simple way to solve this problem, making the interface between CM and PM fairly dynamic.

1.4 Related Work

The goal of this work is to support business collaboration, with a special focus on the integration of inter-enterprise conversation process management and intra-enterprise business process management. While the former deals with interaction flow, the latter deals with work flow, and they are under different process models. From these points of view, this work, addressing peer-to-peer process interaction, differs from the centralized workflow management [13] and invocation based process decentralization [9] in general, and differs from the following related work in particular.

First, different from WSDL [16], WSFL [17], Rosetta-net [11], BPML [1], that support *point of conversation* not directly correlated at the process-level, this work focuses on *choreographed conversation*. Indeed, dealing with point of conversation can provide certain flexibility, but can hardly follow a commonly agreed conversation model standard such as ebXML BPSS [8].

Further, WSFL, BPML and WSCL [15], etc, are used to offer a *single party view* rather than the *public view*, to the collaboration. As a result, an implementation does not present a general model of peer-to-peer synchronized execution; for instance, it does not intend to specify how the partner process instances are synchronized, or made to be aware of the progress of the peer processes.

Most significantly, in this work we address the issue of how to integrate inter-enterprise collaborations with intra-enterprise business processes. This is a very practical and challenge issue faced by many organizations. We see the difference between conversation models that underlie the ICP standards and the conventional business process models that the existing workflow engines support. Most of the current efforts are characterized by adopting one kind of models, either to "simulate" conversation activities by the business process tasks, or take local processes as "point of services" to "fulfill' conversation activities. There lacks a formal execution mechanism for interacting the public conversation process execution and local business process execution at run-time.

The proposed architecture for interoperating a conversation manager and a process manager based on *conversation model driven asynchronous task activation*, allows us to make full use of existing workflow system components, to support both public conversation processes and local business processes, and to interface CM and PM dynamically. This approach also offers the potential of supporting multiple inter-enterprise interaction standards, by plugging in multiple conversation managers based on the underlying ICP models.

2   Extending Workflow System for Supporting Inter-enterprise Collaboration

Using extended workflow systems to handle both local tasks and document exchanges is a natural step from intra-enterprise business process management to inter-enterprise collaboration management. The primary consideration on this approach is relying on a PM to enable inter-business conversation without additionally introducing a CM.

To apply this approach, the following issues must be taken into account.

- A common collaboration process template must be provided and agreed by all the participating partners, and this common template must be mapped to, or represented by the local processes at the partners' sites. Such mapping may be made manually or in terms of Java or XSL tools, should the common template is specified in XML.
- The common collaboration process must specify the roles of the participants; each participant must be bound to one of these roles, and figures out its tasks based on role-matching.
- Document exchange must be synchronized with the execution of peer-processes. Especially, while sending documents is an active behavior, receiving documents is a passive behavior, how to relate receiving documents to "work flow" is an important issue of this approach.

Many efforts on extending local workflow to inter-enterprise collaboration deal with document exchange as point of conversation rather than choreographed conversation. This can be found in both platforms and languages. We solved this problem by using a typical type of process control message – the *task completion message*, to *carry interchanged documents*. This enables us to *cope document flow with peer process execution and inter-process interaction*. Below we shall compare two architectures we developed using this mechanism.

2.1   Peer Process Execution Based on Public Process Template

The starting point of this approach is the standard worlflow language PDL (Process Definition Language) and workflow architecture (let's refer to it as PDL engine). We have introduced an XML-based Collaborative PDL language, CPDL, for describing public processes, and developed a Collaborative PDL engine, CPDL-engine, to support decentralized, peer-to-peer collaboration at the business process level at HP Labs [2]. Under this approach, inter-enterprise conversation is handled by PM directly.

A CPDL public process definition is based on a commonly agreed collaboration protocol, such as the protocol for on-line purchase or auction. A public process is specified with a list of *process-roles*, indicating the logical participants. A task has a *task-role*, and that must match one of the process-roles. As each party wants to keep some process data private, but must allow some other data such as the interchanged business documents to be sharable with selected partners, the *sharing scopes* of process data objects are specified. Tasks not for generating exchanged documents can also be included in the process. Private tasks invisible to peers can be defined as private subprocesses bound to the process at run-time.

A CPDL public process is executed by multiple CPDL-engines collaboratively. Each execution of a collaborative process, or a *logical process instance*, consists of a set of *peer process instances* run by the CPDL-engines of the participating parties. A *logical identifier* for this execution must be obtained. These peer instances share the same process definition, but may have private process data and sub-processes. The CPDL-engines run these peer instances independently and collaboratively. The engine of each party is used to schedule, dispatch and control the tasks that party is responsible for, based on *role-matching*, and the engines interoperate through a messaging protocol to synchronize their progress in process execution.

As shown in Figure 4, for example, two CPDL-engines *A* and *B* collaborate on a public process for purchasing. The buyer-side engine, *A,* creates a logical instance of the purchasing process, and initiates a "buyer-side" peer instance; *A* then notifies the seller-side engine, *B,* to instantiate a "seller-side" peer instance of the purchase process. All the tasks of the process are visible to each party, but execution at a peer site is based on role match.

In the process execution at each site, a task is performed by a concrete action, and upon the completion of the action, a task-completion message is sent back to the engine for synchronizing process data and for triggering the scheduling of the next task. In this example, tasks "Order" and "Payment" are the responsibility of *A* (buyer), "Invoice" and "Shipping Notice" are the responsibility of *B* (seller). During the peer process execution at the buyer site, *A* would first execute task "Order" but later skip task "Invoice"; however, the task-completion message received by *A* will be forwarded to *B*, in order for *B* to proceed. At seller's site, *B* simply skips task "Order" and waits for the execution result from its peer. Upon receipt of the task-completion message of task "Order", *B* also marks this task as completed, and rolls forward the peer process instance to execute task "Invoice".

Under this approach, a *task completion message* contains not only the identification and status information, but also the *business documents* to be delivered to the partners. This allows us to *integrate document exchange with peer process instance synchronization*. When multiple parties are involved, a task completion message should be customized and forwarded to all the participating CPDL-engines, each forwarded message contains selected documents in its payload.

The major architecture feature of CPDL-engine is use of PM to handle conversations. Conducting document exchange at the process level through broadcasting task completion messages, rather than at action level, is the unique and significant feature of this approach. In this way the *peer-process execution synchronization* and the *business conversation* are *combined*, which provides the following advantages.

-   It requires minimal extension to existing workflow systems.
-   It allows each participating party to observe the collaborative process template, providing therefore a global view to the logical execution of the whole process.

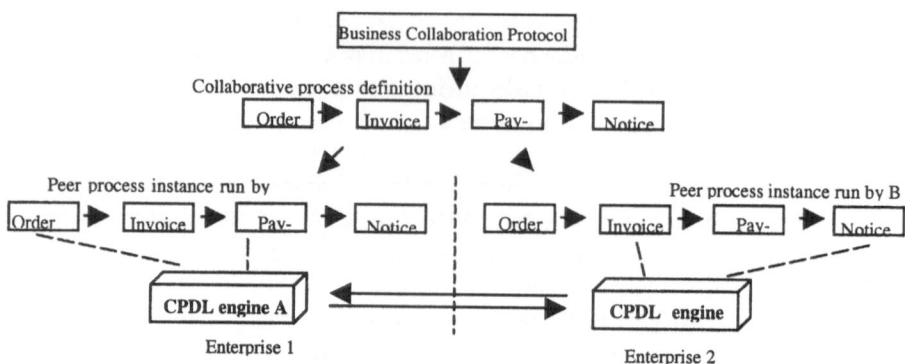

Fig. 4. Peer process execution based on public process template

- It combines document exchange with peer process execution synchronization, allowing task-flow and data-flow to be defined within a single process, and making *task flow naturally consistent with the document flow*.

  However, this approach also has the following limitations.
- Since the function of CM is actually performed by PM, it may not directly support ICP conversation models such as BPSS.
- The use of task-completion messages for peer process instance synchronization requires the use of the same workflow engines across enterprise boundaries.
- Broadcasting task-completion messages may cause message delivery mis-order problem in multi-party collaboration.

Refer to Figure 5, for example, when a logical process execution involves three peer instances run at peers *A, B* and *C*, responsible for tasks e_1, e_2 and e_3 respectively. Assume that these tasks are to be executed in the order e_1; e_2 and e_3; but the following may happen.

- Upon completion of e_1, message msg_1 was sent to *B* and *C*;
- Upon receipt of msg_1, e_2 was activated, and upon its completion, msg_2 was sent to *A* and *C* ;
- However, *C* receives msg_2 *before receiving* msg_1, then there was no ground to processing msg_2 at peer *C*.

As we mentioned in [2], complex queuing system must be added to resolve the out-of-order message delivery problem.

2.2 Peer Process Execution Based on Peer Process Template

In order to overcome the two major limitations of the architecture described above: the message delivery mis-order problem, and the lack of inter-operability of different workflow engines, we have introduced the architecture that has the following features.

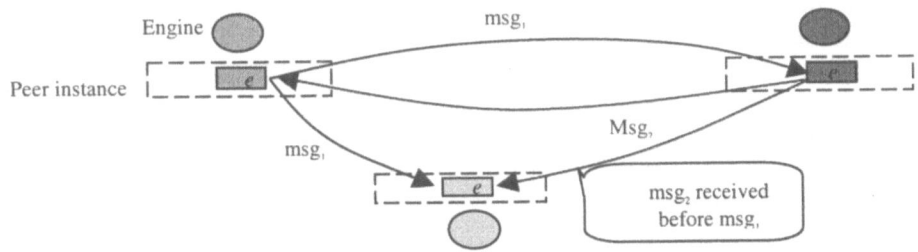

Fig. 5. Conversation messages received from pees in wrong order

- A peer process template is defined at each partner site, based on the commonly agreed business protocol or the public process template; then a peer process instance observes the peer process template rather than the public process template.
- A set of *generic workflow control messages* is abstracted, including the SYNC message corresponding to the task completion message described above. Mediated by the *generic messaging agents* for handling these messages, different kinds of workflow engines can interact.

This approach actually offers the peer view to the whole collaborative process. For each role, a role specific peer template is derived. This is analogous to generating stub/skeleton on client/server sides from a common interface specified in IDL. Accordingly, the execution of a peer-process is based on the peer template. The mapping from a public process template to peer templates may be made manually or automatically by programs. However, the resulting peer process is based on the business process model the local engine supports, rather than a conversation model. Further, the underlying peer process models may be different from one another.

As a peer process only contains the tasks belonging to the peer role, and a peer process instance only observes its own peer template, there is no need to broadcast task-completion messages. Instead, peer process instances synchronize in a peer-wise fashion, which in turn, eliminates the possibility of message delivery mis-order.

The set of generic messages for allowing different workflow engines to interoperate, are used to initiate, start and terminate processes, and to synchronize peer process executions. The payloads of the SYNC messages are the documents exchanged between peers. Generic messaging agents mediate peer-sides workflow engines conduct inter-enterprise interaction.

The generic messaging agent is provided with a list of APIs for the local workflow engine to create and dispatch generic messages. An abstract message-interpreter is defined; the local site is responsible to implement their own interpretation functions, for converting the generic messages to their system-specific messages. This interpreter can be easily plugged in the agent.

This architecture represents the following enhancement to the previous one.
- Mediated by the generic messaging agents, different workflow systems can interact to each other for conducting inter-enterprise collaboration.

- The message delivery misorder problem described in the last section can be eliminated.

    However, this architecture also has the following major limitations.

- It is still based on business process models to "simulate" conversation, as it lacks the capability of supporting an ICP conversation model.
- A peer only observes the peer process templates, lacking the global view to the overall collaboration.

3   Introducing Conversation Manager for Supporting Inter-enterprise Collaboration

The two architectures discussed above are characterized by extending workflow engines to support conversation without a specific CM and an underlying ICP model. In this section we move to the architectures including ICP model driven conversation management.

We have developed a CM system: *BPSS collaborator*, for handling choreographed conversation under the ebXML Business Process Specification Schema (BPSS) standard [8]. In this section we shall compare three possible architectures for incorporating the BPSS collaborator with a CPM:

- a CPM as a pure ICP engine for supporting conversation activities only;
- a CPM using the BPSS collaborator as the business-interaction front-end; and
- a CPM with the BPSS collaborator built-in as the conversation model driven asynchronous task activator for assisting task scheduling.

The ebXML BPSS is a standard XML language for specifying inter-enterprise conversation processes. In BPSS, a conversation process is called a collaboration. A *binary collaboration* has two *authorized-roles* and a *multi-party collaboration* has more than two *partner-roles*. The *business partners* participating in a collaboration process play these roles; they interact through a set of choreographed *conversation activities* (called business activities in BPSS). A conversation activity may represent a *business transaction* consisting of one or two predefined *business document* flows between the participating roles. Iteratively a conversation activity may also represent a nested binary collaboration. In general, the BPSS model is a conversation process model; it provides the abstract interfaces of business interaction, regardless of the concrete implementation.

Different from the usual business process specifications, a BPSS only describes the public interface between business partners, which is essentially the document exchange between them. Different from the tasks in a business process, a conversation activity in a conversation process usually represents two operations: a request and a response between the two participating roles. Moreover, different from the flat business process models, the BPSS model is hierarchically structured.

The BPSS collaborator is a CM system that we developed for handling BPSS based, peer-to-peer binary or multi-party collaboration. At a business site that participates in an inter-enterprise collaboration, the primary function of the BPSS collaborator is to enforce the "interaction-flow" constraints with its partners, based on the BPSS conversation process model. The concrete implementation of document manipulation is left to local workflow systems and services.

A collaboration specified in BPSS is in fact a process that includes multiple choreographed conversation activities rather than a single round document exchange. Thus the BPSS collaborator handles conversation activities in the way similar to that a workflow system handles process tasks. However, as mentioned before, enforcing the choreography of conversation activities at a business site must take into account not only the existence of inbound and outbound documents, but also the order and time for those documents to send or to be received. This function is not covered by the conventional workflow systems. Further, since inter-enterprise collaboration is not controlled by a single enterprise, and the behavior of other enterprises may not be trusted by default, the choreography of document exchanges must be validated.

Given the above requirements, the BPSS collaborator provides the following functions.

Support BPSS definition model. This includes the creation, maintenance and manipulation of conversation process template objects in java. These objects are created by parsing the XML specifications into DOM trees [7], and then by turning the DOM trees into the corresponding Java objects.

Support BPSS instance model at runtime. This includes creating, maintaining and evolving local-site collaboration instances step by step along with the business interactions.

Verify the choreography of conversation activities (conversation-flow). This is the core function for enforcing the document exchanges constraints in multi-party or binary collaborations that is based on the template model and the execution history of each collaboration instance. It is used for checking the consistency of document exchange with respect to the collaboration context, document types, participating roles, etc; for evolving conversation process instances consistently with respect to the inter-enterprise messages; and for ensuring peer-wise synchronization of conversation process executions. The results of the BPSS model based run-time verification is used to determine the correctness of document sending and receiving, and to generate the conditions for activating local process tasks to process inbound documents and provide outbound documents. Regarding to the interface to PM, the information returned from the BPSS collaboration verification operations are used to setup the base data for activating the local process tasks asynchronously.

Manage collaboration sessions. This includes initiating and maintaining the global conversation Id for each conversation process, and at a participant site, correlating the conversation Id with the local process that supports the corresponding conversation process.

Manage collaboration roles. Under BPSS, this includes resolving, maintaining and retrieving the authorized-roles for binary collaboration, and partner-roles for multi-party collaborations. This is essential for allowing a player to play different roles in multiple binary collaborations involved in a conversation process hierarchy or in a multi-party collaboration.

Monitor collaboration instances. A web interface is also provided for monitoring the collaboration status, documents exchanged, etc, with other partners.

The logical execution of a BPSS conversation process actually involves two or more peer-executions at the participant sites. At each site, a *peer conversation process instance* is built and evolved step by step as the document exchanges go on. For every business document, either sent or received, the BPSS collaborator will search the conversation process template to identify the conversation activity, transaction, requesting operation or responding operation that match the delivered document; and locate, update or create the corresponding instances if they are consistent with the template. Unlike a business process instance that is evolved by the workflow engine actively, a conversation process instance is evolved as the reaction to document exchanges, so in most cases it is "back-filled".

While the BPSS collaborator handles conversation activities, document consumption and production are implemented as local business processes and services. As a CM system, the BPSS collaborator can interface to either a PM or an AM; and there exist several ways to interact CM and PM. We shall compare three different CPM architectures built using the BPSS collaborator, from the following specific points of view.
- *Public interface* for dealing with inter-enterprise conversation;
- *Local interface* for coupling CM and PM;
- *Interaction with private processes*, i.e. taking a private process as a *single point of service* (POS), or having interaction points with a running private process.

3.1 Pure Conversation Process Management System

This is a CM-AM based architecture where a CPM engine similar to a workflow engine is built around the BPSS collaborator for supporting inter-enterprise conversation activities only, without dealing with the tasks for other purposes.

As shown in Figure 6, the BPSS collaborator handles the orchestration of conversation activities for enforcing the choreography of document exchange, based on the hierarchical BPSS model. It interacts with an AM system *directly* for invoking actions to consume the inbound documents and to produce the outbound documents with respect to every conversation activity. An action may be invoked synchronously or asynchronously, but only as a *single point of service* (POS). A private business process may be used to support a *single* conversation activity, e.g. processing an order document and generating the corresponding invoice document. System components for supporting business process management must be provided. A CPM system built on this architecture is similar to a full-scale workflow engine but supports conversation only.

In summary, this architecture has the following features.

Public interface. The CPM handles business interaction under the BPSS model through messages, such as ebXML messages, that bear the interchanged business documents.

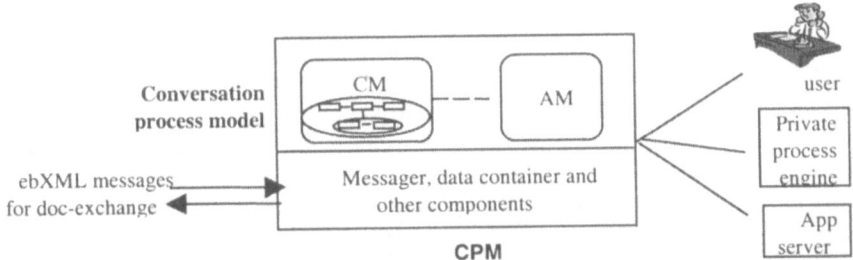

Fig. 6. A CPM built around a CM supports conversation process only

Local interface. The CM interfaces to the AM directly, and the AM only invokes POSs.

Interaction with private processes. At process level, only conversation activities, i.e. those for inter-enterprise document exchanges, are covered. A local process may be treated as a POS for processing or facilitating documents. The execution of a conversation process is not interacted with a running local business process.

The major advantage of this architecture consists in that it provides a clear separation of inter-enterprise conversation and private actions, Web services and processes; especially, it support the well- defined ICP standard - BPSS.

However, the CPM built on this architecture has the following limitations.

- It does not support processes involving the local tasks other than conversation activities; therefore it cannot accommodate the usual case that an enterprise business process is defined for conducting both public interaction and private applications.
- It does not allow a public conversation process to interact with a running local process. Further, the local services invoked by the CPM as separate POSs, are not correlated at the business process level.
- It has to deal with the scalability on its own as it cannot rely on a local workflow engine to do so. Therefore, it must be facilitated with a full spectrum of process management functions, with considerable overlap to an enterprise workflow engine.

3.2   CM as Business Interaction Front-End

This is a CM-PM-AM based architecture where the CPM is formed with the BPSS collaborator as the *front-end* CM system; it interfaces to a workflow engine that provides the PM and AM functionalities. In reality, there can be multiple conversation processes running by the BPSS collaborator, and multiple coupled local processes running by the PM.

While the BPSS collaborator manages document exchange across enterprise boundary, the PM manages the local processes for processing and generating required documents. The functions of CM and PM are clearly separated.

It is important to note that this approach is actually based on two models: the BPSS model underlying the conversation management, the workflow model underlying the local business process management. These two models are different structurally and semantically. For example, the BPSS conversation process is hierarchical and the local business process may be flat; the choreography enforcements of conversation flow and task flow also have different semantics as mentioned before.

Refer to Figure 7, the features of this architecture can be summarized as follows.

Public interface. The BPSS collaborator as the system front-end handles business interaction under the BPSS model. Both inbound and outbound documents will go through the BPSS collaborator for model-driven validation and for evolving the peer instance of the conversation process.

Local interface. The BPSS collaborator is interfaced to, either through APIs or through messages, the local PM that is responsible for managing document processing tasks and other local tasks. These tasks contribute to the accomplishment of local business processes. They are materially performed by the actions invoked through the AM. In contradistinction to the architecture presented in the last section, the CM is coupled with the PM, rather than the AM directly.

Interaction with private processes. Handled by the BPSS collaborator, a conversation process instance can interact with a running local process having *mixed tasks* for handling interchanged documents and for other private actions.

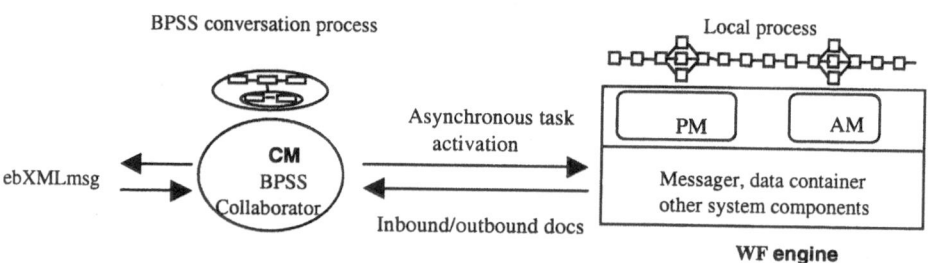

Fig. 7. CM as business interaction front-end

Asynchronous task activation mechanism best fits this architecture. Along the evolution of conversation processes, the BPSS collaborator sets up task activation conditions for the coupling local processes; a separate task scheduler of the PM is employed to schedule and queue these tasks, based on their activation conditions.

This architecture prevails over the last one for handling conversation only, for the following reasons.

- It supports both conversation processes and private processes, support both conversation activities and local tasks.
- It provides a natural interface for a conversation process to interact with a local process, based on the asynchronous task activation mechanism.
- It makes a workflow engine, i.e. the system providing PM and AM functions, reusable for a CPM, and allows the CPM to rely on the workflow engine to scale.

The major limitation of this architecture is that the BPSS collaborator needs to deal with inter-enterprise messaging, and therefore must ensure the throughput, security, etc, of message delivery. In case the backend workflow engine is facilitated with these functionalities, the BPSS collaborator should be able to reuse them, which leads to the architecture described below.

3.3 CM as Model Driven Asynchronous Task Activator

This also a CM-PM-AM based architecture, but the CM is a plug-in component of the workflow engine, rather than the front-end of it. The CM, i.e. the BPSS collaborator in our prototype, is used as the ICP based conversation model driven asynchronous task activator for assisting the PM to schedule tasks.

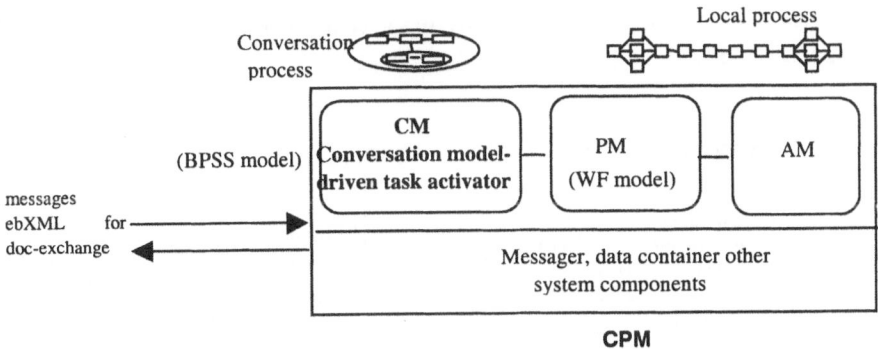

Fig. 8. CM as conversation model driven asynchronous task activator

With this architecture the functions of CM and PM are also clearly separated. While the CM is responsible for managing conversations under a conversation process model, the PM is responsible for managing the coupling local processes based on its workflow model. However, treating the BPSS collaborator as the built-in CM rather than as the front-end CM can free it from handling inter-enterprise messaging directly; allowing it to rely on the capability and scalability of the workflow engine to do so. As seen in Figure 8, in this case the CM does not act as a "message-interceptor".

Tightly coupling a CM and a PM under the *asynchronous task activation mechanism* actually represents the simplest approach to bridging a conversation model and a business process model. We see that when the BPSS collaborator verifies document exchanges, and has the verification results used to set up the task activation conditions for the local processes,

- the BPSS collaborator may be viewed as the extension of the PM's rule engine for task scheduling;
- the conversation process instance may be viewed as the extension of the "fact base" searched by the rule engine through APIs.

From this point of view, the BPSS collaborator can be considered as a *conversation model driven asynchronous task activator* that the rule based task scheduler must go through.

Asynchronous task activation, as mentioned before, is the mechanism for solving the difficulty of synchronizing a conversation process instance and the corresponding local business process instance. Refer to Figure 9, this mechanism is based on the following.

- A task can be scheduled to run based on certain task-activation conditions, and these conditions are checked against certain underlying data.
- The evolving of conversation process instance upon document exchange generates the information for updating the *"base-data"* underlying task activation-conditions.
- Asynchronously, the task scheduler of a PM will check those conditions to schedule tasks, as a separate thread of control.
- The base-data updates can be made by the CM using PM's API, or by the PM using CM's API.

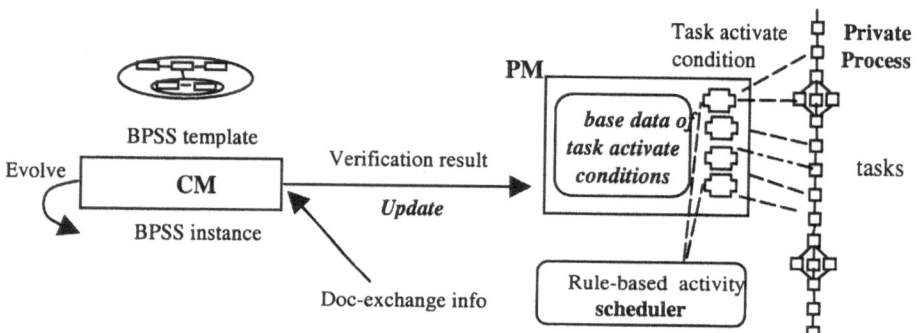

Fig. 9. CM as conversation model driven asynchronous task activator

Regarding to BPSS based conversation validation wrt document sending and receiving, the input parameters include the collaboration ID, the conversation-activity name that represents a service, the sender, receiver and document name. Based on the template and execution instance of the BPSS conversation process, when the above document exchange information is validated, at the minimum the following information will be returned; otherwise appropriate error messages will be returned.

- collaboration ID;
- conversation-activity;
- interaction-time;
- requesting player and its role;
- responding player and its role;document name;action-type ("responsing" or "requesting");
- validation status.   These resulting data may be selected to underlie task-activation conditions. It is worth noting that the mapping between the information generated by CM and the base data underlying the task activation conditions in PM must be provided. With such mapping, conversation processes and local business pro-

cesses can be defined independently. A more detailed explanation of the conversation model driven asynchronous task activation is illustrated in Figure 9.

This architecture actually turns the CM from an "active component" to a "passive component" controllable by the PM through APIs. Compared with the architecture discussed above, this one has the following features.

Public interface. The BPSS collaborator provides BPSS model based conversation management. However, it does not intercept inter-enterprise messages, instead, it obtains the information on inter-enterprise interaction from the CPM platform.

Local interface. The BPSS collaborator interfaces to the local PM through APIs, and act as the conversation model driven asynchronous task activator.

Interaction with private processes. A conversation process instance can interact with a running local process under the asynchronous task activation mechanism, the latter can have *mixed tasks* for handling interchanged documents and for other private actions.

Our experience reveals that the last architecture prevails over all the others. Overall it has the following strengths.

- It provides a clear separation of inter-enterprise conversation management and local business process management.
- It allows the maximal usability of existing workflow system components, supports both conversation processes and local processes and allows a conversation process to interact with a running local process.
- Based on the notion of *conversation model driven asynchronous task activation*, this architecture provides a clear vision for bridging the conversation model and the business process model, and supports seamless integrating of CM and PM. Multiple CM-based conversation model driven asynchronous task activators under different ICP standards can be provided which allow the CPM to support multiple ICP languages.

4 Conclusion

In order for enterprises to collaborate at the business-process level, they must allow the business processes run on their local sites to interact. Each party participating in an inter-enterprise collaboration needs to deal with two kinds of processes: the *public conversation process* specifying the "conversation-flow", and the *local business process* specifying the "work-flow" that fulfills the conversation activities. How to integrate the conversation-flow management and the workflow management, particularly, how to make full use of an existing workflow engine to support inter-enterprise collaboration, represents a common interest of the e-business industry and a major architecture challenge.

In this report we have compared five different architectures based on out prototyping experiences. We recommend the architecture for interoperating a conversation manager and a process manager based on *conversation model driven asynchro-*

nous task activation, as it allows the maximal usability of existing workflow system components, supports both conversation processes and local processes, and provides a dynamic and simple interface between conversation management and process management.

As the ICP standardization is an ongoing process, we plan to develop multiple conversation managers based on several ICP models, in order to support multiple inter-enterprise interaction standards.

References

1. BPML, "Business Process Markup Language", www.BPMI.org. 2002.
2. Qiming Chen, Meichun Hsu, "Inter-Enterprise Collaborative Business Process Management", Proc. of 17th International Conference on Data Engineering (ICDE-2001), 2001, Germany.
3. Qiming Chen, Umesh Dayal, Meichun Hsu, "Conceptual Modeling for Collaborative E-business Processes", ER-2001.
4. Qiming Chen, Meichun Hsu, Igor Kleyner, "How Agents from Different E-Commerce Enterprises Cooperate", Proc. of The Fifth International Symposium on Autonomous Decentralized Systems (ISADS'2001), 2001, USA.
5. Qiming Chen, Umeshwar Dayal, "Multi-Agent Cooperative Transactions for E-Commerce", Proc. Fifth IFCIS Conference on Cooperative Information Systems (CoopIS'2000), 2000, Israel.
6. Umesh Dayal, Meichun Hsu, Ravka ladin, "Business Process Coordination: State of the Art, Trends, and Open Issues", Presentation on VLDB 10 years best paper award, Proc. of VLDB 2001, Italy.
7. Document Object Model, http://www.w3.org/DOM/
8. EbXML.org, Business Process Specification Schema", V1.01, 2001.
9. M. Koetsier, P. Grefen, J. Vonk, "Contracts for Cross-Organizational Workflow Management", Proc. EC-Web'2000.
10. A.G. Moukas, R. H. Guttman and P. Maes, "Agent Mediated Electronic Commerce: An MIT Media Laboratory Perspective", Proc. of International Conference on Electronic Commerce, 1998.
11. Rosetta-net, www.rosettaNet.org.
12. SOAP, "Simple Object Access Protocol",
13. http://msdn.Microsoft.com/xml/general/soapspec.asp, www.w3c.org.
14. Workflow Management Coalition, www.aiim.org/wfmc/mainframe.htm.
15. WSCI, "Web Service Choreography Interface", Tech Report by Italio, SAP, BEA, Sun Microsystems. 2002.
16. WSCL, "Web Service Conversation Language", HP Submission to W3C, www.w3c.org.
17. WSDL, "Web Service Description Language", www.w3c.org.
18. WSFL, "web Service Flow Language", www-3.ibm.com/software/solutions/webservices/

Modeling Coordination and Control in Cross-Organizational Workflows

Enzo Colombo, Chiara Francalanci, and Barbara Pernici

Politecnico di Milano, Department of Electronics and Information
20133 Milano, Italy
{colombo, francala, pernici}@elet.polimi.it

Abstract. Current e-service technology paradigms require the analysis and conceptual modeling of cooperative inter-organizational workflows. Cooperation among different organizations is based on contractual agreements that coordinate production activities among cooperating companies and establish mechanisms to control the fulfillment of production goals. Existing conceptual models of workflows do not provide constructs and related methodological guidelines to support the high-level conceptual modeling of coordination and control activities. This paper presents a model that helps specifying patterns of control and coordination among different cooperating actors and associating corresponding contractual rules. Patterns are organized along a continuum between hierarchical and market control and coordination paradigms. The model is explained based on an example showing the fundamental differences between hierarchical and market coordination and control. It is also shown how operating flows change as coordination and control shift from hierarchical to market patterns, due to varying contractual rules for cooperation in executing operating activities.

1 Introduction

Workflows embed the logic of coordination among different tasks and executing actors. In the organizational literature, the very activity of organizing is defined as the design of the rules for control and coordination, which, from an information systems perspective, constitute workflow rules [9,10]. It is straightforward how coordination and control rules are unnecessary when a single individual can accomplish all the tasks needed to reach a given set of objectives. On the contrary, when tasks increase in complexity, multiple individuals or organizations need to cooperate and, hence, to coordinate with each other. Patterns of coordination and control represent a legal and social formalization of the coordinated efforts of multiple actors sharing a common set of objectives [21]. Since coordination is brought about by the need for cooperation, its primary goal is task design and allocation to different actors, either individuals or organizational units [2]. Different choices in task design and allocation translate into alternative workflow patterns.

Two fundamental control and coordination patterns are distinguished: organizational hierarchies and markets. Within organizational hierarchies, actors are organized hierarchically, ranging from top management at the highest level to

R. Meersman, Z. Tari (Eds.): CoopIS/DOA/ODBASE 2002, LNCS 2519, pp. 91–106, 2002.

operations at the lowest level. Functional specialization is usually the criterion for specialization and organizational units are built around the specific set of functional competencies that they develop, such as research, engineering, production or marketing.

Organizations can also outsource part of their production and related decision-making activities to other organizations, such as customers, suppliers, consultants or commercial partners. A relationship between distinct organizations is implemented through the execution of economic transactions, defined as exchanges of economic goods and services ruled by a price system [7,22]. This cooperation through economic transactions is referred to as market coordination and is considered an alternative to the hierarchical coordination among task executors within a single organization [13,14]. Workflows will consequently involve one or more organizations depending on what form of coordination minimizes costs, either hierarchical or market-based.

Organizational hierarchies and markets constitute the opposite ends of a continuum of coordination and control patterns [14]. Hierarchical and market coordination and control can mix and generate different workflow patterns depending on the degree of *delegation*. Within organizational hierarchies, delegation is defined as the downwards shift of decision-making responsibilities in the organizational hierarchy [21]. This reallocation of responsibilities modifies workflow patterns, since different organizational units will be involved in the execution of decision-making tasks. Delegation can be achieved only if actors within the same organization are allowed to coordinate with each other through the execution of market transactions [4,16]. Pure markets implement the maximum degree of delegation among cooperating actors. However, similar to hierarchies, markets can reduce their degree of delegation by including forms of hierarchical coordination inside their transactions.

In information systems and workflow management systems literature, the impact of the structure of the organization on process management is not considered. The emphasis is on managing the execution of activities in processes, but not on their control and coordination, other than relating a sequence of execution of activities to a given goal.

In the cooperative information system manifesto, technologies for cooperation of agents with the same goal and acting towards the fulfillment of these goals are discussed, analyzing systems, group collaboration, and organizational facets [8]. In the i* model and in subsequent work in the Tropos project, strategic relationships between actors are modeled, and are put in relationship with goals, resources, a system components [24]. However, the implications of the structure of the organization on interactions between actors and control and coordination patterns are not modeled.

In workflow literature, the structure of the organization is represented only to indicate the roles of the agents executing activities. The problem of control in WfMS is studied from the point of view of guaranteeing a correct sequence of execution of activities. Therefore the research work focuses on methodologies for modeling workflow processes [5] and on activity scheduling [23].

The goal of the present paper is to present a framework and a modeling approach to relate the structure of inter-organizational workflows to the patterns of interactions between the involved organizations. The model allow representing typical patterns of interactions, and is a basis to analyze inter-organizational workflows in terms of coherence between planned interactions and the organizational setting, and for designing workflows and interactions between workflow participants on the basis of the characteristics of a given type of interaction.

In Section 2, we present some examples which present the implications on a workflow of different cooperation settings.

In section 3, we present our model to represent organizational patterns, and in Section 4 we show how such patterns can be used to specify the interactions between organizations participating in a workflow.

2 An Example of Cross-Organizational Workflow

2.1 Cooperation Scenario 1: A Hierarchical Coordination and Control Pattern

Fig. 1 shows a cross-organizational workflow for the on-line sale of personal computers (PCs). The example involves two actors tied by a long-term contract which formalizes a tight form of cooperation that allows business partners to share information and control each other as if they were part of the same hierarchical organization which will be referred to in the following as *virtual enterprise*. The *PC seller* is responsible for administrative tasks and for the relationship with customers. Logistic, assembly and delivery tasks are instead delegated to the *Logistic Company*. PCs are delivered to a point of presence (POP) selected by the customer as part of the order procedure. The customer is notified the availability of the PC at the POP by an e-mail message from the PC seller. The customer is supposed to pay the POP when withdrawing the PC.

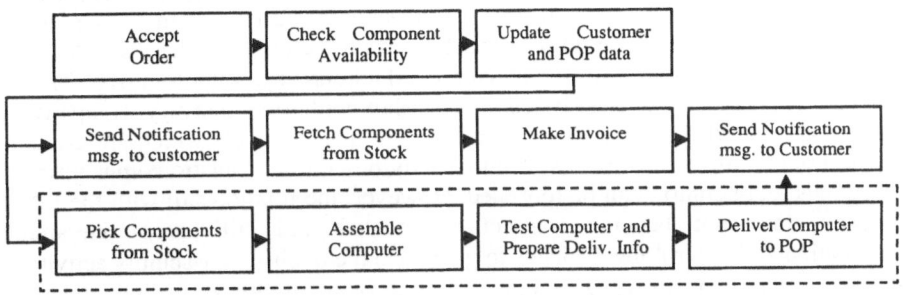

Fig. 1. Cross-organizational activity diagram of the PC sale process with outsourced logistic, assembly and delivery

In the example, the PC seller takes the order from the customer and verifies the availability of the components necessary to assembly the required computer. If all components are available in the warehouse, the PC seller sends customer and POP information to both the logistic company and the administration function. Logistic and administrative tasks can be executed in parallel, although they need to exchange coordination and control information. These information exchanges drive the degree of modeling detail. From a practical standpoint, they also highlight important information to be included in the contractual agreement between the PC seller and the logistic company.

Hence, the logistic process is decomposed into the following tasks: *pick components from stock*; *assemble computer,* which requires a technician to assemble hardware components and install system software; *test computer,* which verifies the correctness of previous tasks by means of a benchmarking application; *prepare delivery information,* which prints a form with customer and POP information; *deliver computer to POP,* which schedules and performs deliveries to POPs. The PC seller manages notification messages, that is the alert message informing the customer that the order as been received and is correct, and the notification message informing the customer of the delivery to the POP. The PC seller also manages administrative activities, that is *fetch components from stock* and *prepare invoice.*

As noted before, the PC seller has a tight form of cooperation with the logistic company. For example, at the end of the *Test computer* activity, the PC seller can check whether the computer configuration corresponds to customer requirements and/or verify the time required by different activities of the logistic process. Typically, the on-line sale process should increase the quality of service to compensate for the lack of a personal interaction with customers and possibly increase their trust. The PC seller is likely to accept only a limited error percentage on assembly and delivery tasks and will probably use the leverage from a tight cooperation with the logistic company to reduce delays. The contractual agreement among the parties may even specify monetary penalties for errors and delays.

2.2   Cooperation Scenario 2: A Multi-partner Hierarchical Coordination and Control Pattern

In the cooperation scenario 2, the logistic company is supposed not to provide a delivery service and, as a consequence, the PC seller has a long-term agreement with a *Delivery Company.* A long-term contract has been preferred by the PC seller due to the high number of PCs to be delivered which creates opportunities for scale economies. Therefore, a trust-based relationship with one delivery company can reduce costs and at the same time guarantee high quality levels which are critical to the success of on-line businesses. Control activities on the logistic company can be reduced and cooperation can be loosened. However, the relationship with the logistic company does not become transaction oriented and still needs hierarchical coordination and control mechanisms to guarantee the quality of assembly activities.

Note that when an organization interacts with multiple business partners, coordination problems can occur, typically due to the lack of parallelism among each partner's tasks and consequent interdependencies. Coordination mechanisms should address these interdependencies and control mechanisms should support the organization that is responsible for the relationship with customers to control partners during their interactions.

2.3   Cooperation Scenario 3: A Hybrid Market and Hierarchical Pattern

Here is exemplified a cooperation scenario where the PC seller outsources the delivery process to an express courier. The relationship with the courier is regulated by short-term agreements. Each delivery request is associated with a corresponding agreement. From a management perspective, this strategic choice can be motivated by a small number of PCs to be delivered and by opportunities to reduce costs by selecting the most convenient supplier at each delivery.

It can be observed that the use of an express courier for deliveries modifies the workflow. Customer and POP information does not need to be supplied to the logistic company and the *prepare delivery information* and *test computer* activities need to be synchronized before contacting the express courier. Overall, the workflow is hybrid as it is based on both hierarchical and market coordination and control mechanisms.

The next section presents a model to specify different control and coordination patterns and their consequences on workflows.

3 Modeling Control and Coordination

As highlighted in the example, the organizational structures of a virtual enterprise leverages both control and coordination of interaction modalities among an organization and its business partners and the business process flow. In the following, we define *control* as the activity performed by a participating partner to ensure that the goal is being achieved, *coordination* as the sequence of messages that allow participating actors to perform their operating activities.

Typically, the organizational structure is defined by managers while the cross-organizational workflow activity model is provided by designers. A formalized *organizational pattern* representing a) how coordination and control interactions are organized and b) a set of guidelines to model the cross-organizational workflow consistent with the specified schema can be basis for improving the quality of WF schemas being designed, reducing the traditional gap between the virtual enterprise organizational structure and the cross-organizational process descriptions.

Traditionally, the experience in system design has shown that experts working on a particular problem usually tend to capture existing, well-structured solutions for reusing best practices for their needs [3]. Our proposal of providing standardized organizational schemes as a backbone on which detailing distributed and cross-organizational workflows is consistent with this traditional trend.

In the following, first we define a model for cross-organizational workflows, and we introduce the concept of delegation. Then, in the subsequent paragraph, we discuss how cross-organizational relationships can be formalized in a contract, in which the relationship is defined on the basis of the model presented before. Finally, we model the two main types of interaction, hierarchy and market, and we represent their general schema according to the model, associating to each the typical patterns of interactions in terms of messages which are needed to control and coordinate activities.

3.1 Model's Semantics for Relationships

The goal of this section is to provide a notation encapsulating the main concepts needed to describe an organizational relationship to be able to specify (see section 3.3) a set of organizational patterns supporting the design phase. As we discussed, each design pattern defines the general characteristics of a specific organizational structure.

The notation proposed is inspired to the *i** paradigm which encapsulates the concept of actor and of organizational dependency among actors [25]. Recent literature provides an attempt to formalize organizational patterns by using the *i** paradigm for modeling Multi-Agent Systems (MAS) in the contest of early requirement analysis [6]. However, they do not formalize the implications of delegation of responsibility on control and communication interactions among organizations.

Our notation is based on the concept of goal, task and resource redefined with the purpose of modeling cross-organizational workflows. A *goal* is defined as the objective of delegating [6]. A *task* is referred to as a structured sequence of decisions and actions as a means to produce an added value transformation of inputs into outputs [21]. In our reference scenario examples of task are *assembly computer*, *test computer* and so on. Note that in this paper, for simplicity, we do not differentiate decision tasks from execution tasks.

Finally, *resources* are what an organization needs to make its business, they can be both material or immaterial and range from an organization's products and services to raw material and information. We are interested in representing cross-organizational interactions; consequently a resource is simply referred to as an information needed to execute a task and it is therefore associated with the concept of dependency. Typically, when an organization has more than one business partner, coordination problems among partners during task execution can occur due to the lack of parallelism among the activities performed by each organization. Coordination mechanisms are therefore needed to manage dependencies among the activities executed by each of the business partners. Traditionally, this type of dependencies are classified as *value dependency* and *commit dependency* [20]. From the perspective of coordination of cross-organizational activities, we deal with a value dependency when one activity performed by an organization cannot proceed in its execution until data provided by an activity performed by another organization is provided. We deal with a commit dependency instead, when we have two activities performed by two organizations of which one cannot commit unless the other commits first.

A cross-organizational process can be described by the 4-tuple $<G, T, R, \Pi>$ where $G = \{g_1..g_k\}$ is the set of goals, $T = \{t_1..t_k\}$ is the set of tasks, $R = \{r_1..r_k\}$ is the set of resources needed to execute a group of tasks and Π is the set of organizations cooperating in the virtual enterprise.

The main goal of the model is to represent dependencies among actors in terms of goals, tasks, and resources.

Dependencies among two actors π_i and π_k can therefore be expressed by using the following set of predicates:

1. *Goal dependency:* Goal(π_i, π_k, g_i) : actor π_i *delegates the goal* g_i to π_k. (π_i, $\pi_k \in \Pi$, $g_i \in G$, with i, k $\in$ N).
2. *Task dependency:* Task$(\pi_i, \pi_k, \{t_1..t_s\}, g_i)$: actor π_i *delegates the execution of tasks* $\{t_1..t_s\}$ to π_k to fulfil g_i. (π_i, $\pi_k \in \Pi$, $g_i \in G$, $\{t_1..t_s\} \subseteq T$ with i, k, s $\in$ N).
3. *Resource dependency:* Resource$(\pi_i, \pi_k, \{r_1..r_n\}, \{t_1..t_s\})$: actor π_i *requires resources* $\{r_1..r_n\}$ from π_k for the execution of tasks $\{t_1..t_s\}$. (π_i, $\pi_k \in \Pi$, $g_i \in G$, $\{t_1..t_s\} \subseteq T$, $\{r_1..r_s\} \subseteq R$ with i, k, n, s $\in$ N)

Conceptually a *goal dependency* represents a delegation of responsibility for fulfilling a goal. For instance, a situation involving a computer seller depending on a computer constructor to build PCs represents a delegation of responsibility to achieve the goal *sell computers*. *Task dependencies* are used instead when an actor is delegated the execution of a task or a set of tasks aiming to fulfill a goal. Finally, *resource dependencies* are used when an actor needs resources to execute a set of tasks.

Fig. 2 provides a graphical representation of these predicates.

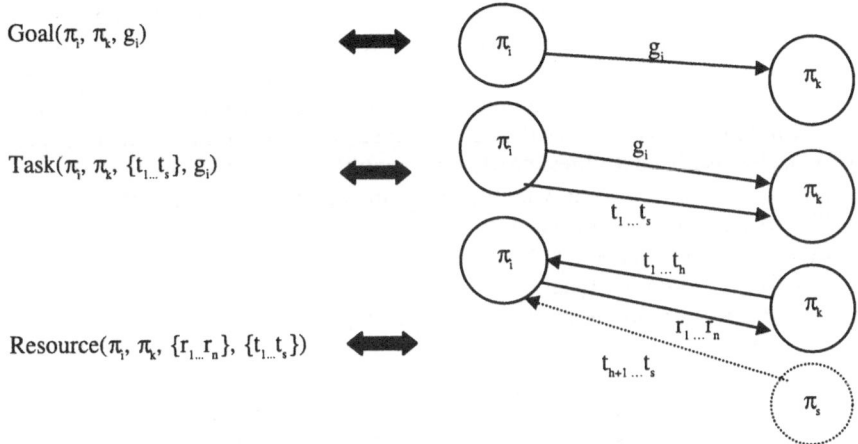

Goal(π_i, π_k, g_i)

Task(π_i, π_k, $\{t_1..t_s\}$, g_i)

Resource(π_i, π_k, $\{r_1..r_n\}$, $\{t_1..t_s\}$)

Fig. 2. Graphical representation of dependencies among actors

We define the following *consistency rules* relating the different types of dependencies:

1. *A goal dependency is always associated with at least one task dependency:* when an actor delegates a goal, it has to delegate also the set of tasks needed to fulfill it. Delegating a goal without delegating tasks is a nonsense. Note that delegating a task as a consequence of a goal delegation does not mean that the delegated actor will necessarily execute the task. In fact, the delegated actor could simply delegate the goal and consequently the set of tasks to other actors.
2. *A resource requirement always derives from a task execution* and consequently is raised by the need to fulfill a goal. Besides, a resource request could also be specified when an actor autonomously executes a task ($\{t_1..t_s\} \neq \emptyset$).

In the next section we introduce the concept of contract as the mean to represent cross-organizational agreements according to the notation provided. In fact, as we describe later in the paper, the contract is also a reference to enrich the coordination and control patterns associated with an organizational pattern by defining the content of each of the message exchanged among the counterparts.

3.2 The Contract's Structure

Typically, cross-organizational relationships among actors are often regulated by contracts among the parties and by well-defined procedures formalizing roles, tasks and consequently goals to be fulfilled [21]. In a cross-organizational workflow environment, a contract is referred to as the means to formalize short or long term agreements. Therefore, a contract includes information to be used to specify control and coordination interactions among actors.

Conceptually, a contract can be described according to a model including *general parameters*, *specific parameters* and *process variables* [1].

General parameters describe attributes that are applicable to contracts in general: the subject of the contract, which uniquely identifies the contract itself; the buyer and the seller, which uniquely identify the actor who requires one or more services and the one who performs the activities needed to supply the services to the buyer and, finally, the start and the end date which identify the contract's validity period.

Specific parameters can be used to further detail the nature of the interaction between the buyer and the seller. Specific parameters are optional and in our model they are mainly related to Quality of Service (QoS) expressed as a function of response time and exceptions allowed in providing the service (tolerance). Finally, process variables are structured according to a schedule of activities grouped by the goal to be fulfilled and a set of tasks to be performed. Grouping by goal is consistent with the semantics proposed in section 3.1. Note, that only the fulfillment of a goal as opposed to execution of a single task generates a revenue for the seller.

Besides, each contract's task is identified by a result encapsulating the type of output(s) expected, and by a set of error codes describing anomalous events that could have corrupted the task's output(s). Elementary but also complex structured output types are allowed from numerical outputs to structures encapsulating a customer's private data. Furthermore, additional information enclosed in task describes the resources needed for its correct execution and the validity time interval (star and end date) for executing and ending the task.

3.3 Structure of Organizational Patterns

In this section we provide a reference schema for organizational patterns formalized according to the model discussed in paragraph 3.1 and to the contractual specification discussed in paragraph 3.2. Each organizational pattern is described by a framework including:

1. A reference graphical schema encapsulating the semantic described in section 3.1. The reference schema highlights only the relationships among the organizations of the virtual enterprise.
2. A sequence diagram providing the *control interactions* among the organizations belonging to the same virtual enterprise.
3. A sequence diagram formalizing the *coordination interactions* among the organizations belonging to the same virtual enterprise.

We specify two patterns modeling pure hierarchical and pure market relationships among the organizations belonging to the virtual company. Since organizational theory widely discusses hierarchy and market as the basic structures to build more complex organizational structures, the choice of modeling them is justified by considering that it is a precondition for future research [14].

3.3.1 Organizational Hierarchy

Traditionally, the concept of hierarchy is based on "is chief of" relationships. If we deal with a cooperative environment involving more than one organization, the concept of hierarchy can be more correctly described by a model involving an organization outsourcing part of its activities multiple business partners. Relationships with each business partner are formalized by a long-term contract (see section 3.2). Business partners do not have direct business relationships with each other.

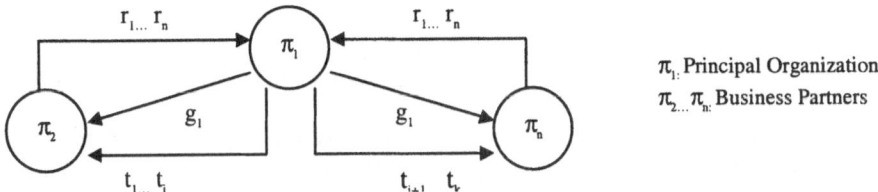

π_1: Principal Organization
$\pi_2... \pi_n$: Business Partners

Fig. 3. Graphical representation of the organizational hierarchy

Based on the semantic previously discussed (see section 3.1), Fig. 3 provides a reference graphical schema formalizing the nature of relationships among an organization and its business partners. The model specifies that a pure hierarchy is characterized by the delegation of a business goal to external business partners and consequently by the delegation of tasks to be executed to fulfill the goal.

Each business partner involved in the virtual enterprise depends on the main organization to require the resources needed to execute the outsourced tasks. Fig. 4(b) shows a typical control flow among a principal organization and its business partners. A fundamental concept is that in a hierarchy the principal organization retains a high level of control on outsourced activities. So we model interactions according to centralized control. Three phases can be identified as follow:

1. A message a business partner to the principal organization reporting the relevant information. According to our contract structure, the business partner can send information on the output of the task, on possible exceptions occurred during the execution of the task and temporal information tied to task execution.
2. A verification procedure executed by the principal organization and the subsequent update of the system status. Control activities are performed based on the information received by the business partner.
3. A response message is provided reporting the result of the verification phase.

Fig. 4(a) provides a reference model of coordination to manage resource dependencies. The graphical representation of the pattern highlights that business partners are potentially tied to the principal organization by resource dependencies. This does not mean that resource dependencies among business partners do not exist, but only that resource dependencies are mediated by the principal organization. This is consistent with the assumption that the principal organization's business partners do not have any direct business relationship with each other. So only the principal organization has the authority to require information from its partners.

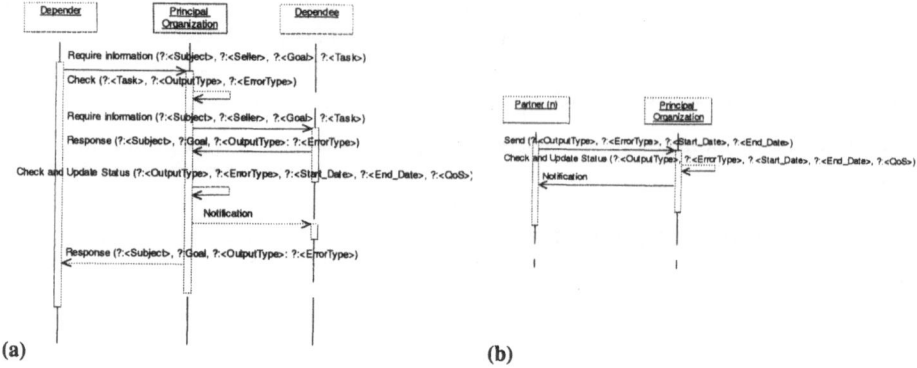

(a)   (b)

Fig. 4. Sequence diagrams of control and coordination interactions in a hierarchy

By referring to the partner needing a resource as the *depender* and to the the partner providing the resource as *dependee*, the coordination sequence can be specified by the following interaction:

1. A message encapsulating the required information is sent from the depender to the dependee. It encapsulates information identifying the contest, the goal driving the request and the task which have to provide the information.
2. The principal organization verifies whether it holds required the information. If not it requests such information from a dependee company.
3. The dependee sends the response to the principal organization. It reports identification data, the required information and possible exceptions occurred during the execution of the task which has generated the required information.

The principal organization verifies the information, and sends a notification to the dependee and responds to the depender. The verification process is performed as in the control pattern (see Fig. 4(b)).

3.3.2 Market

Fig. 5 provides a reference schema formalizing the nature of relationships among the principal organization and its business partners. Relationships with a temporary business partner are formalized by a short-term contract according to the structure discussed in section 3.2.

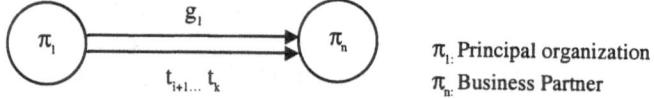

π_1: Principal organization
π_n: Business Partner

Fig. 5. Graphical representation of a market

Note that in a pure market resource dependencies are not defined. A pure market is characterized by the complete delegation (decisional + operating) of an activity to one organization providing a complete service. The service to be supplied needs only preliminary input data to be executed. Consequently, a pure market is characterized by the delegation of a business goal to an external business partner and, consequently, by the delegation of the tasks to be executed to fulfill the goal.

Due to the complete decisional and operating outsourcing of a predefined set of activities, control is completely delegated to the temporary business partner. A pure market is for definition characterized by a competition among service providers. This means that the temporary business partner desiring to gain trust of the principal organization is interested in controlling its activities.

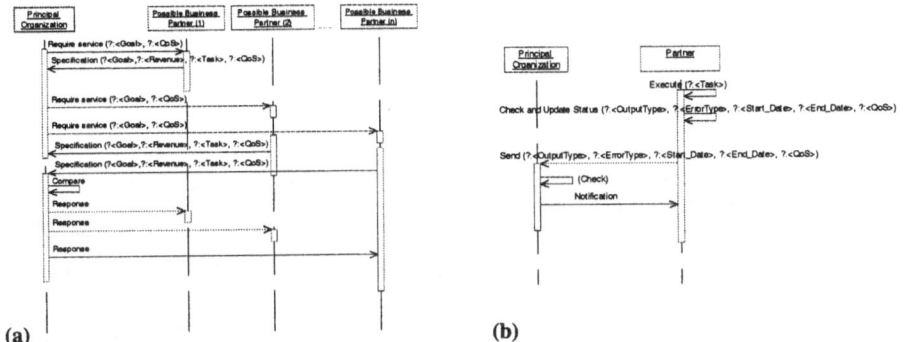

(a)   (b)

Fig. 6. Sequence diagrams of control and coordination interactions in a market

Fig. 6(b) details the control sequence among the principal organization and its temporary business partners. The verification process is applied to the task's output considering possible exceptions on temporal variables and on quality.

Since a business transaction involves only two actors (the buyer and the seller), it may appear that no coordination activities are needed when dealing with a pure market. But considering that each business transaction is preceded by a contractual phase involving more than one competitor, the problem of coordination is shifted to the choice of the business partner.

That is, a temporary partner needs to be chosen. Fig. 6(a) provides the coordination pattern managing partner selection phase. Initially, the principal organization broadcasts the goal that it wants to fulfill and QoS requirements associated with the service needed. Asynchronously, the competitors specify their economic requests and QoS corresponding levels. After comparing different offers, a response is provided by the buyer.

Note that, different from modeling an organizational hierarchy, modeling a pure market involves generic name for business partners (i.e. "delivery company" instead of the company's name).

4 Pattern Instantiation on the Reference Scenario

4.1 Instantiation of a Hierarchical Coordination and Control Pattern to Model Cooperation Scenario 1

Fig. 7(a) represents the delegation of logistic processes as a consequence of a goal dependency in cooperation scenario 1. Due to the control needs of the PC seller after the execution of the *Test computer* activity, a hierarchical control sequence should be instantiated, as shown in Fig. 7(b).

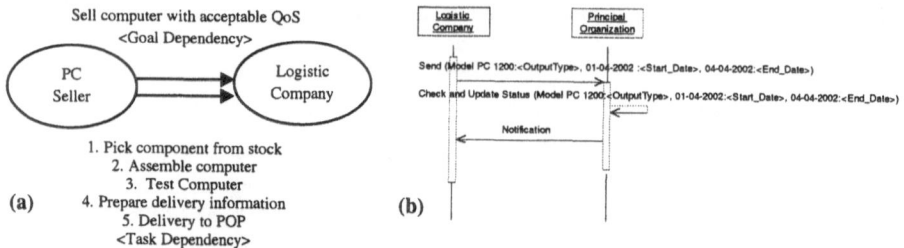

Fig. 7. (a) Hierarchical coordination and control pattern for cooperation scenario 1. (b) Sequence diagram of a centralized control interaction

The following control messages are included in the sequence diagram to account for time constraints on the logistic process:

1. A message from the logistic company after the execution of the *Test computer* activity reporting the number of days that have been required to assemble and deliver all the PCs of a customer order .
2. The PC seller controls whether the one-week time constraints on deliveries have been satisfied.
3. The PC seller communicates the result of quality verifications to the logistic company.

By assuming that QoS is tested with a one-month period, at the end of all monthly tests, the PC seller verifies the fulfillment of the "sell computer with an acceptable level of QoS" goal. The information stored during the control procedure of each order is used to determine whether the level of QoS provided by the logistic company is above the threshold of acceptability. In this case, the control sequence does not affect the flow of operating activities.

Note that if the PC seller needs to control the consistency between customers' orders and computers' configurations after testing, the control sequence does not change. The information that are exchanged represent the only variable that needs to be adapted to new control objectives. This new information can be used to modify invoices if a mismatch is found.

4.2 Instantiation of a Multi-partner Hierarchical Coordination and Control Pattern to Model Cooperation Scenario 2

Fig. 8(a) represents the delegation of logistic processes as a consequence of two goal dependencies in cooperation scenario 2. Logistic activities are fully delegated to the logistic company while delivery is delegated to the delivery company. Note that a resource dependency is also specified whose implications are discussed in the following.

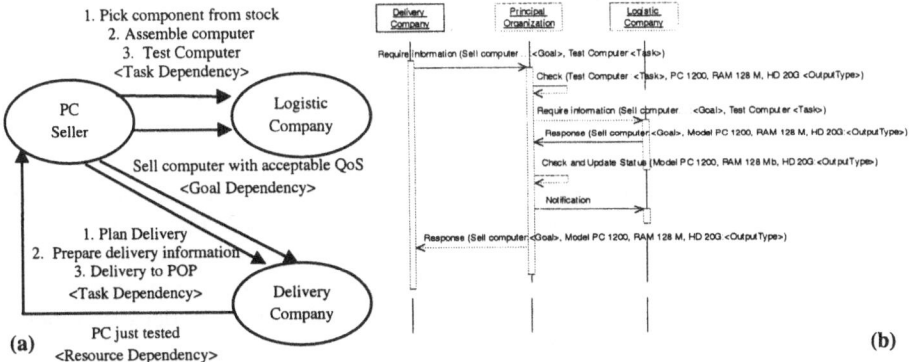

Fig. 8. (a) Hierarchical coordination and control pattern for cooperation scenario 2. (b) Sequence diagram of a multi-partner centralized control interaction

A resource dependency is defined between the *plan delivery activity* performed by the delivery company and the *test computer* activity performed by the logistic company. Let us suppose that the delivery company has to transport a set of computers and before preparing the final list of computers that will be delivered (*prepare delivery information*), if the truck is not full, it may require information about tested PCs by the logistic company to include them in the current delivery. Due to hierarchical coordination, the delivery company cannot convey a direct request of information to the logistic company. Instead, the delivery company must request the information from the PC seller which a) can provide this information if it has already received an update from the logistic company or b) conveys the request to the logistic company to obtain the information and respond to the delivery company.

Fig. 8(b) shows the corresponding sequence diagram for hierarchical control. If the PC seller holds the information required by one of its partners, the sequence diagram can be modeled according to the control pattern provided in Fig. 7(b): the delivery company requests information, the PC seller confirms that the information has been updated and returns the response. On the contrary, if the PC seller does not hold the required information, the coordination sequence should be specified as follows:

1. A request message is sent from the delivery company to the PC seller. The request should include the goal driving the request (*Sell computer with an acceptable QoS*) and the task requiring the information (*Test Computer*).
2. The PC seller verifies whether the required information is available and, if not, conveys the request to the logistic company.
3. The logistic company sends the response to the PC seller, that is the configurations of tested computers (*PC 1200, RAM 128 M, HD 20G*).
4. The PC seller verifies the response and conveys the required information to the delivery company.

A time out may also be specified, either by the PC seller or by one of its business partners. As information is valuable only if provided on time, a time out may increase the overall performance of the workflow. Note that this cooperation pattern can be designed with both a value or a commit dependency.

4.3 Instantiation of a Market and Hierarchical Pattern to Model Cooperation Scenario 3

Fig. 9(a) and Fig. 9(b) specify the sequence diagrams modeling market coordination and control, respectively. The PC seller needs information on services provided by different organizations. As a first interaction, the PC seller broadcasts its request of information by specifying its goal (*Sell computer with an acceptable QoS*) and by providing QoS constraints. Then, it receives responses, including costs and also information about QoS. After a comparison phase conducted according to subjective criteria, it communicates its choice to the winner. In our example, competitors provide services at a *$15, $10, $16* price, respectively, and with *3, 4, 10 days* delivery times.

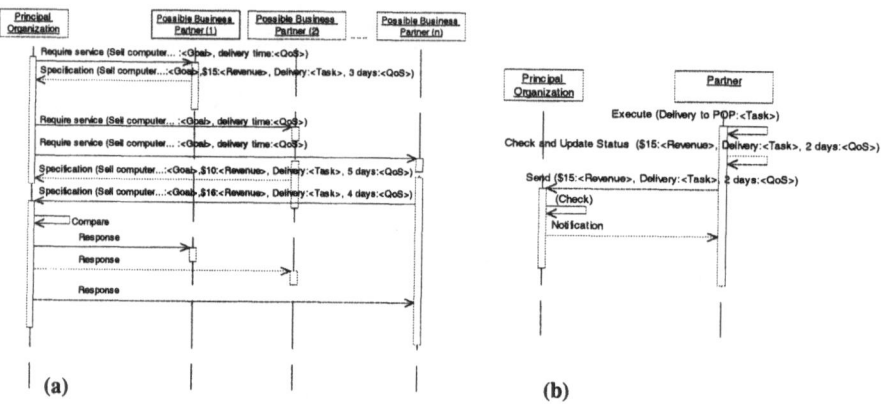

(a)   (b)

Fig. 9. Sequence diagrams of a market control and coordination interaction

Note that Fig. 9(a) presents an elementary coordination phase. A more complex specification of coordination activities can be obtained by replicating this elementary pattern for each competitor and eliminating one of them after each elementary interaction. Conceptually, a value dependency is managed, as the PC seller can start the comparison only when a sufficient number of responses is received.

The control pattern in Fig. 9(b) models the business interaction following negotiation. The main difference from hierarchical control is the delegation of control activities. The temporary business partner is interested in providing a high-quality service to gain trust and be selected for future deliveries. The control procedure is limited to the verification of the invoice and of delivery times.

5 Concluding Remarks

The paper discusses the implications of different patterns for organizational cooperation on control and coordination mechanisms. The study of cooperation patterns is the first step towards improving the quality of cross-organizational workflows and overcoming the limits of traditional intra-organizational workflow design. The concept of delegation has been introduced and defined in compliance with previous literature and its implications on cross-organizational control and coordination has been analyzed as a means to allocate the responsibility for workflow activities. Besides, a structure of contract has been discussed as a basis to formalize the control and coordination information flows associated with different workflow patterns. Three cooperation patterns have been exemplified, discussing how control and coordination mechanisms can mix organizational hierarchy or pure market patterns to build complex cooperation patterns suitable for real business cases. Future work will analyze the continuum between hierarchies and markets to complete the set of relevant variables to be included in the specification of control and coordination mechanisms and extend the model accordingly. The relationship between the structural characteristics of organizations and of the workflows in which they are involved will also be considered.

From a technological perspective, the specification of control and coordination patterns future work will focus on tools to support the conceptual specification of Web services, formalizing the messages exchanged among cooperating organizations and identifying resource and control dependencies. In turn, these conceptual characteristics of Web services will be mapped to web-services specifies using the WSDL language, associating the description of services with a corresponding control and coordination pattern. It should be noted that little effort has been made by researchers in formalizing composition and compatibility rules for services supplied by different organizations and on developing a technological architecture to enable control and coordination, which remain open issues for future work. The present work can provide a formal basis for orchestrating e-applications involving several organization, providing a coordination and control infrastructure.

References

1. Angelov, S., Grefen, P.: B2B eContract Handling – A Survey of Projects, Papers and Standards. University of Twente, The Netherlands (2001)
2. Arrow, K. J.: The limits of organization. W W Norton & Company (1974)
3. Buschmann et al.: Pattern-Oriented Software Architecture. A System of Patterns, John Wiley & Sons Ltd (1996)
4. Brynjolfsson, E., Malone, T. W., Gurbaxani, V., Kambil, A.: Does Information Technology Lead to Smaller Firms? Management Science (1994) 40(12) 1628-1645.
5. Casati F., Castano S., Fugini M., Mirbel I., Pernici B.: Using pattern to Design Rules in Workflows. IEEE Transaction on Software Engineering, (2000) 26(8) 760-785.
6. Castro J., Kolp M., Mylopoulos J.: Towards Requirement-Driven Information Systems Engineering: The Tropos Project (2002)
7. Coase, R. H.: The problem of social cost. Journal of Law and Economics (1960) 3 1-44.
8. De Michelis, G., Dubois, E., Jarke, M., Matthes, F., Mylopoulos, J., Papazoglou, M., Pohl, K., Schmidt, J., Woo, C., Yu, E. (eds.): Cooperative Information Systems: A Manifesto, Cooperative Information Systems: trends & Directions, M.P. Papazoglou, G. Schlageter, (1997)
9. Galbraith, J. R.: Designing Complex Organizations. Addison-Wesley Publishing Company, New York (NY) (1973).
10. Galbraith, J.R.: Designing Organizations. An executive briefing on strategy, structure and process. Jossey- Bass Publishers San Francisco (1995).
11. Casati F., Fugini M.G., Mirbel I., Pernici B.: WIRES, a methodology for developing workflow applications. Requirements Engineering Journal (2002)

12. Kafeza E., Chiu D., Kafeza I.: View-Based Contracts in an E-Service Cross-Organizational Workflow Environment. TES 2001, LNCS 2193, 74-88. Springer-Verlag Berlin Heidelberg (2001).
13. Malone, T. W.: Modeling Coordination in Organizations and Markets. Management Science (1987) 33(10) 1317-1332.
14. Malone, T. W., Crowston, K.: The Interdisciplinary Study of Coordination. ACM Computing Surveys (1994) 26(1), 87-119.
15. Malone, T. W.: Is Empowerment Just a Fad? Control, Decision Making and IT. Sloan Management Review (1997) 38(2), 23-35.
16. Malone, T. W., Laubacher, R. J.: The Dawn of the E-lance Economy. Harvard Business Review, (1998) 76(5), 144-152.
17. Malone, T. W., Crowston, K., Lee, J., Pentland, B.: Tools for Inventing Organizations: Towards a Handbook of Organizational Processes. Management Science (1999) 45(3), 425-443.
18. Yang J., Papazouglou M.P., van den Heuvel W.: Tackling the Challenges of Services Composition in E-Marketplaces, RIDE 2002
19. Yang J., Papazoglou M.P.: Web Component: A Substrate for Web Service Reuse and Composition. CAiSE 2002: 21-36
20. Papazouglou M., Delis A., Bouguettaya A., Haghjoo M.:. Class Library for Workflow Environments and Applications. IEEE Transactions on Computers (1997) 46 (6), 673-686.
21. Scott, W. R.: Organizations: Rational, Natural, and Open Systems. Prentice Hall, 3rd ed (1992)
22. Williamson, O. E:. Markets and hierarchies: analysis and antitrust implications. Free Press, New York (NY) (1975).
23. Workflow Management Coalition. WfMC Handbook (2001)
24. Yu, E., Du Bois, Ph., Dubois, E., Mylopoulos, J.: From organizational models to system requirements – a cooperating agents' approach. Proc. of the 3.rd International Conf. on Cooperative Information Systems (1995).
25. Yu, E., Mylopoulos, J.: Using goal, rules and methods to support reasoning in business process reengineering. International Journal of Intelligent Systems an Accounting, Finance and Management (1996) 5(1) 1-13

View Propagation and Inconsistency Detection for Cooperative Mobile Agents

Susan Weissman Lauzac[1] and Panos K. Chrysanthis[2]

[1] Dept. of Mathematics and Computer Science
University of Puget Sound
Tacoma WA 98416, USA
slauzac@ups.edu
[2] Dept. of Computer Science
University of Pittsburgh
Pittsburgh, PA 15260, USA
panos@cs.pitt.edu

Abstract. Mobile agents are autonomous programs that migrate from one machine to another within a network on behalf of a client, thus, they are ideal for mobile computing environments since tasks can be delegated to mobile agents when a mobile client is disconnected. This paper extends the traditional functionality of a mobile service agent with capabilities that facilitate asynchronous cooperation among mobile database clients. In the context of mobile client-server database applications, data cached to support disconnected operations can take the form of a materialized view. We design mobile agents to reduce computation and wireless communication costs, and use view versioning to cope with disconnected operations by allowing application sessions to access current data without invalidating work previously done. A data validation or results propagation process detects inconsistencies with newer versions of data upon reconnection. Essentially, these mobile agents will compute the period of time or *consistency window*, measured in versions, for which the results of a mobile client's application are consistent. We supply rules that govern the creation and sharing of results and show how inconsistencies can be detected to offer a higher availability of data while organizing and gracefully degrading the amount of consistency achieved between the mobile clients and the data sources.

1   Customized Query Processing for Mobile Agents

In previous work, we explored the customization and localization properties of views in the context of mobile database environments to support disconnected query processing and developed a view maintenance mechanism called the *View Holder* [8,10]. The core of the View Holder is a versioning mechanism that can adjust the currency of the data stored on the mobile client, for example, by allowing a user who was disconnected during a plane flight to later read updated derived data without necessarily discarding work performed on older data during the flight. In addition, a view holder is dynamic and stateful with respect to an

R. Meersman, Z. Tari (Eds.): CoopIS/DOA/ODBASE 2002, LNCS 2519, pp. 107–124, 2002.
© Springer-Verlag Berlin Heidelberg 2002

individual mobile client, and therefore, it can respond to a mobile client's queries for information by communicating only the differences between answers, thus reducing the cost of wireless communication. In contrast to the materialized views maintained by a large, static, and stateless data warehouse, the View Holder can be thought of as a customizable client-oriented data warehouse, and it does not require modifications to be made to the existing data sources. Delivering the results of queries in a mobile environment is different than in a traditional distributed environment due to the rapidly changing conditions of the wireless communication network, the requirements of the user in terms of the data's accuracy, and the cost the user is willing to pay for communication. Traditional query processing facilities are generally concerned with minimizing response time. By contrast, in a mobile environment, a user may want to introduce delays or change data accuracy in order to save service charges or to minimize required resources. Clearly, there is a need for devising ways by which mobile users can specify their choices for view maintenance and communication, in particular a *criteria for materialization* that describe which data changes should *invoke an update in the view holder agent.*

Instead of using a generic profile, it seems more natural to specify user preferences along with the definition of the view to be customized. Thus, we propose to extend SQL so that the **create view** statement sent within the *create view message* includes the view maintenance preferences of a cache agent (CA) residing on the mobile device. Towards this, we introduce the *ON* condition that can specify which data should be monitored by the view holder agent and how often. Essentially, the *ON* condition creates the customizable data currency, and summary required by the mobile client's application sessions (ASs).

1.1   Customized SQL Statements

The extended SQL `create view` statement offers additional but optional ([...]) clauses such as: Update On, and Maintenance.

CREATE VIEW <name of view> **AS**
  SELECT <attribute list>
  FROM <table list>
  [**WHERE** <selection and join conditions>]
  [**GROUP BY** <grouping attribute(s)>]
  [**HAVING** <group condition>]
  [**ORDERED BY** <attribute list>]
  [**UPDATE ON** logical expression of pairs:
      <condition for materialization[,Full or Partial] >]
  [**MAINTENANCE** <Recomputational or Incremental>]

The MAINTENANCE clause specifies the view maintenance strategy, either recomputational or incremental, that should be used by the view holder agent.

Finally, UPDATE-ON provides a logical expression of conditions for material-ization. This generic condition for determining materialization over data servers (DSs) and data warehouses (DWs) includes *Update ON*:

- an individual attribute at DS1: *DS1.Items.price.*
- a condition on an attribute: *DS1.Items.price > $15.*
- a maintenance transaction commits at DW:
  DW.new_transaction.
- a given amount of time has passed: *10 minutes* or *DS1 10 minutes.* This helps the CA when planning a disconnection.
- a logical combination of all the above: E.g.,
  DS1.Items.price OR DW.new_transaction;
  DS1.Items.price AND DW.new_transaction.

Although incremental view maintenance (e.g.,[12]) can be specified, the View Holder environment is different from the data warehousing environment. The amount of customized data requested by mobile clients is orders of magnitude less than what is available from a data warehouse, however, there can be many more mobile clients and their view holder agents within the fixed network. Re-computational view maintenance methods are more suitable under this scenario, since we can perform recomputation without having to capture every update performed at all the data sources because we will not be computing the Δ view during reconstruction. Natural periods of disconnection or weak connectivity allow recomputated results to be stored within the view holder agent. Recom-putational maintenance is easier to implement and incurs fewer latencies since several rounds of queries are no longer required. Since small amounts of data are requested, the storage space required for intermediate results will also be orders of magnitude smaller than what is required in data warehousing environments. Furthermore, subqueries will be requested once and only once from each data source during the recomputation. Therefore, recomputation of the view within the fixed network is more appropriate when using DBMS-agents, since these agents can travel once to each data source transporting results and reconstruct-ing a materialized view without having to backtrack and perform compensatory queries at sites already visited.

Essentially, the View Holder approach as shown in Figure 1 allows either recomputational or more complex incremental view maintenance to occur in the *fixed* network while only the Δ view (i.e., incremental maintenance) is commu-nicated across the expensive *wireless* links to the cache agent residing on the mobile device. A view holder agent computes the variations, or Δ view, between any two and possibly non-consecutive versions of a materialized view. The next section will provide an example of how the distributed query processing library routines can construct a materialization program to perform recomputational view maintenance when monitoring loops are used to evaluate the *ON* condi-tion.

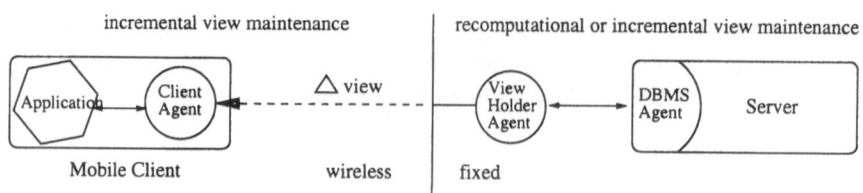

Fig. 1. View Maintenance in the Fixed and Wireless Networks

1.2   The View Holder's Materialization Program

How does the View Holder learn about relevant changes that occur at the data sources? There are three possible solutions:

- **Monitor Data:** Have the view holder agent's materialization program periodically query the relevant data sources to discover when updates or new versions have been created.
- **Monitor Catalog:** Have the materialization program query the database's catalog to determine from the last time a tuple, attribute, or table was updated if a relevant change has been made.
- **Trigger:** Build a trigger within the data warehouse and server so that the data sources notify the query processing facility of relevant changes.

Let us start by considering a query that reflects the join of data from tables r_1, r_2, r_3 of data servers $DS1, DS2, DS3$ respectively and requires monitoring at only one data source.

CREATE VIEW OneMonitor **AS**
    SELECT $DS1.a$, $DS2.b$, $DS3.c$
    FROM $DS1.r_1$, $DS2.r_2$, $DS3.r_3$
    WHERE $(DS1.r_1.b = DS2.r_2.b)$ **AND** $(DS2.r_2.c = DS3.r_3.c)$
        AND $(DS1.r_1.a < 5)$
    UPDATE ON $(DS2.r_2$, full)
    MAINTENANCE Recomputational

Table 1. Tables for Query OneMonitor

$Table\ r_1$		$Table\ r_2$		$Table\ r_3$	
A	B	B	C	C	D
1	2	-	-	3	4
7	2				

Table 1.2 shows the state of the base tables that will be used to construct a materialized view from the query OneMonitor. Once this query reaches the

view holder agent, if the MetaData maintained by the view holder agent does not contain information about the tables r_1, r_2, r_3, then this information must be obtained from the individual data sources. Once this information is gathered and stored, the query must be processed and a materialization program formed.

In this example, two DBMS-agents are necessary for the view recomputation. The *condition evaluation* DBMS-agent performs monitoring at $DS2$. The *view evaluation* DBMS-agent recomputes the view whenever a change to table r_2 occurs. To create this materialization program, a query that is expressed in a high-level query language such as SQL is represented internally as a structure known as the *query tree*. This query tree is used to create an execution strategy for accessing the data and obtaining the results. When the execution strategy is combined with a monitoring loop and condition evaluation, we call this a *materialization program strategy*. Once the execution strategy has been determined the *code generator* generates the code for executing the plan. It is this code that can be placed within a view evaluation DBMS-agent for execution at any data server.

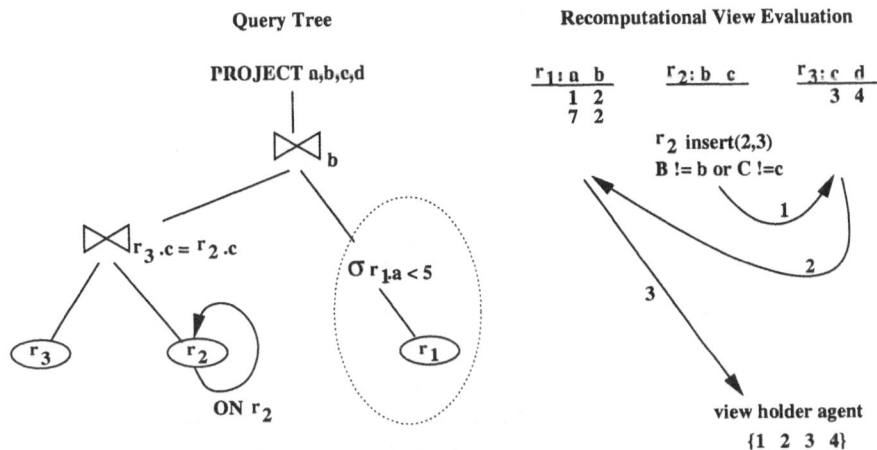

Fig. 2. Query Tree for Query OneMonitor

For our example view OneMonitor the query tree will appear as in Figure 2 (left-side). The query tree reflects the query trip plan used by the view evaluation DBMS-agent in order to perform the joins at the data servers. Once the *ON* condition is satisfied at $DS2$, the data of $DS3.r_3$ and $DS2.r_2$ will be joined (e.g., using a hash-join [2]) before this result is then later joined with the data selected from table $DS1.r_1$.

Often a query tree is built or modified to supply a more efficient strategy for executing a distributed query. One possible modification would be to know the approximate tables sizes from the MetaData maintained by the view holder agent. If the table size of $DS1.r_1 < DS3.r_3$ then the code generator would have wanted to perform the join between $DS1.r_1$ and $DS2.r_2$ first, and this strategy would have been reflected in the query tree in order to reduce the amount of data transferred across the fixed network.

Since each recomputed version of the materialized view is associated with the launching of a view evaluation DBMS-agent, we want these particular mobile agents to be processed by the data sources and view holder agent in the order they are launched. Therefore, we can associate a version number with each view evaluation DBMS-agent. At the data sources, mobile agents are buffered and executed in the order of their version number. Note that this method does not require the notion of a global time (unlike methods from [3]). since the version number is a locally maintained variable.

The condition evaluation part of the materialization program may require multiple condition evaluation DBMS-agents. For example, $cond_1$ OR $cond_2$ where $cond_1$ and $cond_2$ must be examined at separate sites, $DS1$ and $DS2$ respectively, would require a *coordinating* DBMS-agent to launch condition evaluating DBMS-agents that reside at $DS1$ and $DS2$. and supply the with the current version number.

When one of the conditions is satisfied, say at $DS1$, then the appropriate results from $DS1$ should be sent to the coordinating DBMS-agent with the current version number. The version number prevents the same materialized view version from being recomputed twice in the case where multiple condition evaluating DBMS-agents send their results to the coordinating DBMS-agent. In other words, although $cond_1$ and $cond_2$ require the use of two mobile agents, both mobile agents work toward the creation of the same view version.

Storing the results at the time the condition becomes true at $DS1$ allows the condition evaluation DBMS-agent to take a "snapshot" of the data server at a time when the *ON* condition was satisfied. For example, consider the *ON* condition $cond_1$ *AND* $cond_2$. Figure 3 shows which states of the data servers are combined to form a new state of the materialized view. Each time the condition is satisfied at a data server (for example, at $DS1$) a new version of the materialized view will be started and completed later by the coordinating DBMS-agent. However, only once the condition is also satisfied at the remaining site ($DS2$) can a new version of the materialized view be created by a view evaluation DBMS-agent. It is important to remember that there may be other remote data servers that are not part of the *ON* condition and yet are still part of the recomputation of a materialized view. The view evaluation DBMS-agent may still have other remote data servers to visit according to its query trip plan. In [9], we defined *recomputational consistency* based on the snapshots incorporated from the data sources and introduced new levels of materialized view consistency to better characterize the mobile view currency customizations available.

2   Materialized Views for a Data Processing Chain

Our data servers contain base tables regarding some sporting goods stores (Table 2). The tables shown include Items, Stores and Sales, where Sales gives

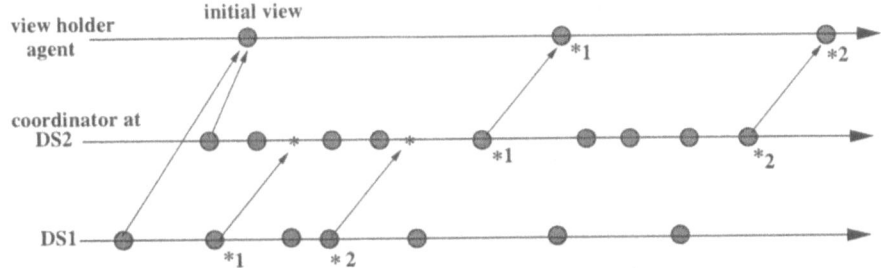

*v = ON condition satisfied at this site with version number v

Fig. 3. Evaluating the Conjunction of Two *ON* Conditions

Table 2. Tables from the Data Servers

Items			
itemid	iname	line	current_price
2	12" racquet	rqball	$30
3	instr. video	golf	$40

Stores			
sid	sname	city	manager
11	Dunham's	Pittsburgh	Ms. Crampton
12	Dunham's	Erie	Mr. Prunty
13	REI Sport	Pittsburgh	Mr. Atkins

Sales				
sid	itemid	quantity	sales_price	date
11	3	10	$40	2/5/01
12	2	20	$30	2/5/01
13	2	42	$30	2/6/01
12	2	20	$30	2/20/01
12	3	10	$40	2/20/01

individual item transaction information. Now suppose that a user are going to begin a business activity (e.g., rough calculations, contract, graph). Recall that our view holder agent will contain materialized views derived from the base tables, and maintain several separate versions of each view [10]. One materialized view, called TotalSales, periodically totals the sales by store and item:
TotalSales(tVN,sid,sname,itemid,line,Tsales)

tVN keeps the version number of the transaction that last updated this tuple. The attributes sid, city and itemid are non-updatable attributes that do not change, whereas Tsales must be periodically updated and will have a different value among the versions. We will assume that the tuples with the largest tVN numbers belong to the most *current* version of the view. Table 3 shows a possible materialization for this view where two versions are available since the *ON* condition was satisfied and either recomputational or incremental view maintenance was performed.

Table 3. View Holder's TotalSales View

tVN	sid	sname	itemid	line	Tsales
		*TotalSales*			
3	11	Dunham's	3	golf	$400
3	12	Dunham's	2	rqball	$600
3	13	REI Sport	2	rqball	$1260
4	11	Dunham's	3	golf	$400
4	12	Dunham's	2	rqball	$1200
4	12	Dunham's	3	golf	$400
4	13	REI Sport	2	rqball	$1260

Note that the view maintenance transaction that created version 3 of the view does *not* include the last two sales transactions made by the store with sid 12 on 2/20/01. Suppose a MC requested a query regarding racquetball equipment sales and the result was materialized with respect to version 3 of the TotalSales view. The MC may keep its materialization of the view for some time and may *not* receive the most current sales figures (i.e., from version 4) due to traveling or communication delays. Later, another application such as a spreadsheet and graphing tool could be started. At this point, the most recent results may be available, or communication conditions may have improved (e.g., the user is dialing up from their hotel room after work). Now, within the new application, the most recent sales figures can be incorporated into the spreadsheet. This shows how versions help cope with disconnected operations, by allowing applications to access more *current* data without invalidating work previously done.

Each *application session (AS)* running on a MC only reads view data derived from the same consistent state at the data sources. In other words, each AS is associated with one view state vs_i from the view holder agent's view state sequence, VS_{seq}. However, once the MC receives the most recent version of the data, the client will be running two ASs and accessing two separate versions (or view states) of the view *at the same time*.

3   Results in a Data Processing Chain

During disconnection and MC can execute ASs that perform work on a subset of the data cached from the view holder agent's view without having to lock data at the sources or even at the view holder agent. While working a MC can try various computations or solutions involving the data and then later, upon reconnection or improved communication conditions, it can attempt to integrate the results of the ASs within the view holder agent.

Figure 4 shows how this data processing chain works and is created within the view holder agent. Version V_3 of the materialized view was requested as input to an AS. This input was possibly combined with information from the geographical location of the mobile device in order to produce the *result data*

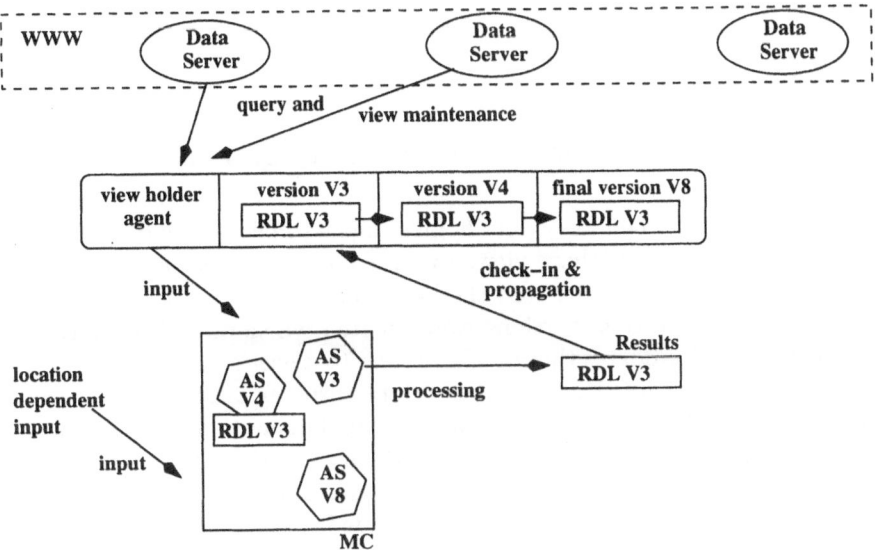

Fig. 4. Mobile Client Data Processing Chain

layer RDL_V₃. By caching the input, the mobile client was able to do this work even while disconnected. Later, during periods of quality connectivity, this RDL can be stored in the view holder and *coupled with the derived materialized data* used as input in producing these results, while additional application sessions can be started using newer versions or view states as their input.

Furthermore, the integration process will allow RDL_V_3 to *propagate* further and become associated with successive view states that are consistent with the results. An RDL is considered consistent with a successive view state, vs_i if vs_i could have been as input to create the RDL. The versions over which a result data layer can be integrated is called the *consistency window* of a RDL. Eventually these results can be sent to a results database or a results process such as a graphing tool, and then archived or stored within the remote data servers for future access.

Although we have discussed the reading of data, write transactions on base data could still originate from an AS, but these transactions are *only* performed directly with the data sources and not through the materialized views stored on the mobile client and the view holder. Changes to the base data will be inconsistent with the current version of the derived data used by an AS, therefore, an AS should write to the base sources only if these inconsistencies can be tolerated.

As stated earlier, a version of the data in the view holder agent will *not expire* even if the data sources stop maintaining it. Instead the view holder must maintain a version for as long as an AS needs it. So, the view holder agent can be seen as a *buffer*, holding versions of a specialized view for a particular AS and its results (RDLs). Therefore, even if a RDL does not propagate it can still be consistently read along with the view state used.

4   Result Propagation and Inconsistency Detection

So far, we have described how view holders agents maintain and communicate multiple versions of materialized views to overcome the limitations of MC disconnection from the data sources, and thereby, increase the concurrency of mobile client reading. In addition, versions were created whenever *ON* conditions are satisfied to prefetch updates that are of interest to a user and thus customize the currency of the AS reads. Essentially, the data currency and consistency for one AS is provided by the view holder without a MC having to stay in contact with the stateless data sources. This gives the MC more options when disconnected, for example, whenever a MC exhausts its resources, it can now suspend one or more of its active applications and reclaim needed space, then later when reconnected, these ASs can finish with the view holder's copy of the *results* stored along with the original version of the derived data used to create these results. If a new AS is started then this AS can still see the results or RDLs stored, as long as these results are consistent with the new version of the derived view being used as input to the new AS. In this way, ASs can propagate their work to new sessions. In this section, we will show how the $\Delta view$ between versions of the materialized tuples read by the MC can be used to detect inconsistencies.

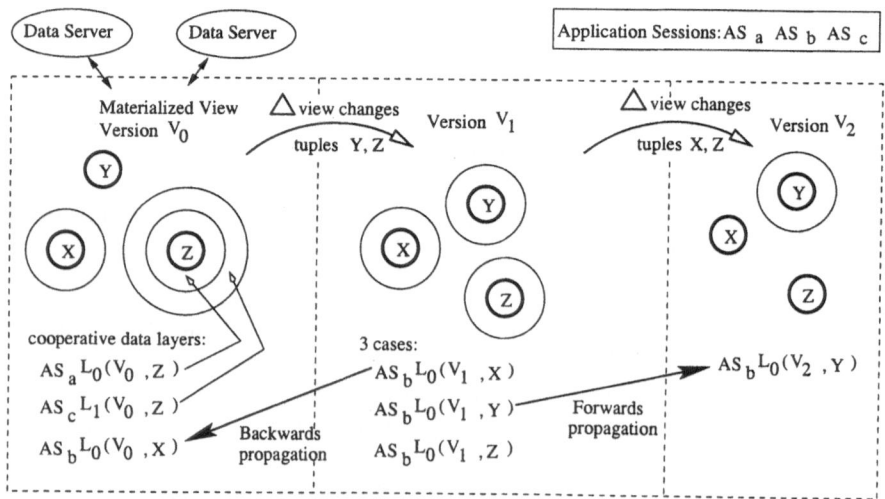

Fig. 5. The Result Data Layers

4.1   The View Holder Results Propagation Model

Figure 5 shows conceptually how the view holder agent maintains the results for a MC. When a MC begins its work it requests a specific amount of data from the sources to be maintained by the view holder agent as a materialized view. Subsets of this view can be cached, although how much data is stored depends on the storage capacity of the mobile machine. Individual ASs will read tuples from this cached subset as they perform their work, and the set of *core* tuples an AS reads from a view state of the materialized view is what we call the read set C.

In addition, each AS executing on a MC has the ability to produce results that will become part of the view state. The data one AS produces is the AS's RDL. For an AS_a operating on a MC and reading from version V_0 of the view holder agent's materialized view, we denote the RDL L_i produced as, $AS_a L_i(V_0, C)$, where C is the set of tuples read from V_0 that were used to create the AS's results. When a MC reconnects, the data layers created during disconnection are submitted for integration. A layer is integrated along with the version of data read and used to produce the layer. Whether or not these integrated results are finally committed and passed on to a results process or database is discussed in Section 4.2. We can think of a RDL as the *creation of a materialized view derived from the tuples of one version* of a view holder agent's view.

In the figure, version V_0 is created from the data sources and contains three tuples X, Y, Z. Application sessions, AS_a and AS_c operating on the MC request data from tuple Z, and create results that will be stored in the RDLs, $AS_a L_0(V_0, Z)$ and $AS_c L_1(V_0, Z)$ where AS_a integrated its results first. At this point, an *ON* condition was satisfied, and a new version of the data appears in the view holder as version V_1. The $\Delta view$ will contain the set of tuples that are different between versions V_0 and V_1. It will show what changes were made to Y and Z. AS_b can read tuples from version V_1, but what happens during integration of the results depend on the contents of the $\Delta view$ between versions. Consider the following three cases from Figure 5:

- AS_b reads X: In this case the resulting RDL exists in both version V_0 and V_1 since X is not a part of the $\Delta view$, in other words, X has not changed. We call this the *backward propagation* of data layers.
- AS_b reads Y: In this case the resulting RDL exists in version V_1 and will exist in V_2 when it is created since the tuple Y is not modified between version V_1 and version V_2. This is called *forward propagation.*
- AS_b reads Z: In this case the resulting RDL exists only for version V_1 and does not propagate because tuple Z is part of every version's $\Delta view$.

4.2   Types of Consistency Windows

Optimistic replication of data from the view holder agent to the mobile machines offers a high degree of data availability. It is this availability that becomes crucial in allowing a mobile client to work individually, especially during periods of disconnection. However, the *cost* of availability in the mobile environment comes in the form of data consistency. We can no long guarantee that work performed by a mobile client will always be consistent with later versions of a materialized view. As new data and versions of a materialized view are created, we make more current data available to the application sessions, but we do so at the expense of creating possibly even more inconsistencies.

The goal of our results propagation model is to be able to get the most we can from the results generated by a mobile client, in other words, to offer a higher availability of data while organizing and gracefully degrading the amount of consistency achieved between the results created by the mobile client and the data sources. Here, we are referring to the consistency between a version *already* constructed and stored within the view holder agent and the results produced by a mobile client. How much consistency is desirable depends on the purpose of the work performed. How well a MC may be able to achieve a desirable consistency and store its results depends on the availability and cost of the wireless network and the capabilities of the mobile client. We divide the creation of RDLs within a view holder agent into two consistency categories:

Application-specific consistency window: Work performed while disconnected on older data is still valid as long as it is consistent with a specific amount of data from within the view holder agent. This scenario is useful whenever results need to be generated over a period of time. For example, if each grouping of versions represented a month of sales figures (e.g., September, October, November), then results integrated for each month could still be used to generate earnings graphs and analysis. In this scenario, the *application's consistency window* would be the versions spanning one month of sales figures, and we would want a RDL to integrate over all versions within the window. If a RDL *cannot* be integrated over the span of the application's consistency window then it must be *aborted* and recalculated. As soon as an RDL integrates over the application's consistency window, it is considered committed.

Final version consistency window: This is the scenario where *all* RDL consistent windows must include the final version. When the mobile client has completed its individual work, it must be able to store its results as RDLs that are part of the *final* version of the view holder agent's view. As long as a MC's results can be forward propagated to the final version, it will not need to have its application session aborted or be forced to run a reconciliation procedure. Therefore, when a MC integrates its work, it does so as a *conditional commit* until the final version of the view holder agent is created. However, the further these results are able to propagate towards the final version the less reconciliation would be required. In this scenario, the consistency window for a RDL spans the initial version used by the AS to the final version stored for the MC. This is useful for any data processing chain where data computed at a mobile location can be integrated at the view holder agent, and if found to be valid used for final processing and storage.

4.3 Rules for Result Propagation

Given our results propagation model, we will now provide four rules for sharing, and propagating the RDLs created by the mobile client's ASs. Since the results can be considered a materialized view derived from a view holder agent's tuples, the granularity for detecting inconsistencies happens at the tuple level, so first we must define the set of tuples from which the results are derived. This set of tuples for a RDL is called the *core dependency set:*

Definition 1. Core Dependency Set: *An AS can read: (1) a set C of core tuples from version V_j of the view holder agent and/or, (2) a set of result data layers, where each layer L_i is derived from a core tuple set C_i of version V_j. Therefore, the set of core tuples that an AS's results or RDL are derived from is the set*
$$CoreD = C \ \cup \ \bigcup C_i.$$

- **1. Forward Propagation:** Suppose an AS's results are derived from the set $CoreD$ from version V_j of the view holder agent. The RDL produced by the AS can be forward propagated to version V_k $(k > j)$ if for all versions i, where $k > i \geq j$, $CoreD() \cap \Delta view_i = \emptyset$.
- **2. Backward Propagation:** Suppose an AS's results are derived from the set $CoreD(V_j)$ of the view holder agent. The RDL produced by the AS can be backward propagated to version V_k $(j > k)$ if for all versions i, where $j > i \geq k$, $CoreD() \cap \Delta view_i = \emptyset$.

Now we need two additional rules for integrating a RDL:

- **3. Integration:** When a new RDL is integrated, there should be an attempt to forward and backward propagate this layer to all other versions of the view.
- **4. New View Version:** When a new version V_k is created, there should be an attempt to forward propagate all RDLs associated with V_{k-1} to V_k.

What happens when a new RDL can *not* forward propagate to the latest version of the view depends on what kind of work is being done and what type of consistency window is required:

- **Application-Specific Commit Rule:** A RDL commits if it successfully forward and backward propagated over the application's consistency window, otherwise it must abort or be reconciliated.
- **Final Version Conditional Commit Rule:** Let V_k be the final version of the view holder agent's materialized view after the mobile client has integrated its RDLs. A RDL commits if it successfully forward propagated to V_k, otherwise it must abort or be reconciliated.

4.4   LTVs and Propagation

The Logical Tuple Versions (LTVs) of a view holder agent operate at the granularity of the materialized view's tuples. Figure 6 shows the scenario where an AS has requested version 3 of the materialized view while later two additional ASs are started using the latest version 4. In order to read a version V of the materialized view, the cache agent residing on the mobile device will receive the largest version number available that is less than or equal to V for each tuple in the view holder agent.

View Holder for

VN = $\boxed{3}$

Key	Non–updatable	Updatable	Count
Dunham's itemid 2	rqball $30	3 | $600	1
REI Sport itemid 2	rqball $30	3 | $1,260	1

View Holder for

VN = $\boxed{4}$

Key	Non–updatable	Updatable	Count
Dunham's itemid 2	rqball $30	3 | $600	1
		4 | $1,200	2
REI Sport itemid 2	rqball $30	3 | $1,260	3

Fig. 6. Logical Tuple Versions (LTVs)

Storing the RDLs within the view holder agent's LTVs allows layers to be automatically propagated forwards or backwards between versions of tuples. LTVs do this by implicitly calculating from the $\Delta view$ which versions of a view's tuple are consistent with a particular AS's RDL. For example, Figure 7 shows a possible scenario for the building of RDLs from the LTVs previously shown. As shown in the LTVs for version 3, suppose a MC request this version, and its AS is started. If this application session reads the REI Sport tuple and creates some sales results, then this work, $AS_a L_0(V_3, REISport)$, will be associated with the tuple REI Sport within version 3.

Once changes have occurred at the base table in the data sources, the view holder agent will build version 4 of the view incorporating the changes to the Dunham tuple by increasing the value of Tsales from $600 to $1,200. After version 4 is created, two more ASs are started, AS_b and AS_c. However, since the tuple REI Sport was *not* part of the $\Delta view$, a MC reading version 4 of this tuple from the LTVs will actually be reading the unchanged tuple from version 3 (i.e., the largest version number less than or equal to 4 for tuple REI Sport is version 3). Conceptually, this implies that any data layers associated with the tuple REI Sport are automatically propagated forward to version 4.

From Figure 7 we see that within version 4, AS_b integrates data layer $AS_b L_0$ $(V_4, Dunham's)$, while AS_c reads the tuple Dunham's and the propagated RDL $AS_a L_0 (V_4, REISport)$ in order to produce its own result data layer, $AS_c L_0(V_4,$

{*Dunham's, REISport*}). Note that since AS_c reads from AS_a its *CoreD* set must now contain both the Dunham's and REI Sport tuples. This happens by the definition of the *Core Dependencies Set*, AS_c's results are derived from its own core set C and the core set of the RDL $AS_aL_0(V_4, REISport)$. Therefore, the set $CoreD = \{$ Dunham's $\} \cup C_{AS_aL_0}$, where $C_{AS_aL_0} = \{$ REI Sport $\}$. This ensures that if work done by AS_a does not propagate forward, then neither will AS_c's RDL.

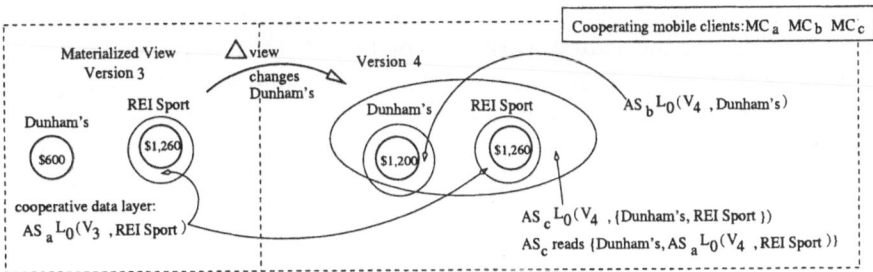

Fig. 7. Result Data Layers for Figure 6

5   Utilizing RDLs for Asynchronous Cooperation

The DVS prototype as described in [7] is a multi-tiered system architecture where the View Holders' components mediate between the data sources and the mobile clients. The **Dictionary_Vagent** keeps track of all the materialized views being maintained by the **View_Agents** and their locations. The **View_Agents** create materialized views from the various data servers, perform view maintenance, and execute queries on these views. By having a **View_Agent** also store the results created from the mobile clients utilizing a view as described in this paper, the **View_Agent** becomes a cooperative work repository and *cooperation facilitator* so that ASs executing on *different* mobile clients can share the RDLs produced.

Some asynchronous cooperative environments that have been described in the literature, such as CoAct [4] or Coda [5], employ optimistic replication strategies where each client has their own copy of the shared data they require. Later, a synchronization process allows the client's work to be integrated with the work of others while providing conflict detection and/or the reconciliation of conflicts that occurred due to concurrent accesses done to the various replicas. In the View Holder approach, the shared data is the materialized view created from the remote databases for the mobile clients. Optimistic replication happens when a mobile client requests a copy of a version of the materialized view. Once RDLs are created they can be sent to the view holder agent (i.e., **View_Agent**) in order to validate the RDLs and detect inconsistencies. If an RDL becomes integrated and coupled with version(s) of the materialized view, then another mobile client can read these results along with a version from the RDL's consistency window.

Producing Cooperative Work

Asynchronous cooperative work varies between periods of individual MC processing and periods of joint work [4]. During periods of individual work, MCs can run ASs that perform work on a subset of the data cached from the view holder agent's view without having to lock data at the sources or at the view holder. During these individual work periods, users can try out various computations or solutions involving the data, whereas during joint work the users make their results available to the other cooperative users [4].

Figure 8 shows how cooperative work is created within the view holder agent. During a period of individual work, our mobile client may cache one or more versions of a materialized view as described throughout this paper and produce results such as graph data points. Later, during periods of joint work, these results can be stored in the view holder agent *and coupled with the derived materialized data* used in producing these results (RDLs). These results can become shared among the users and eventually sent to a results database or a results process such as a graphing tool. The cooperative clients do *not* update the remote databases themselves, but perform all integration and sharing through the view holder agent.

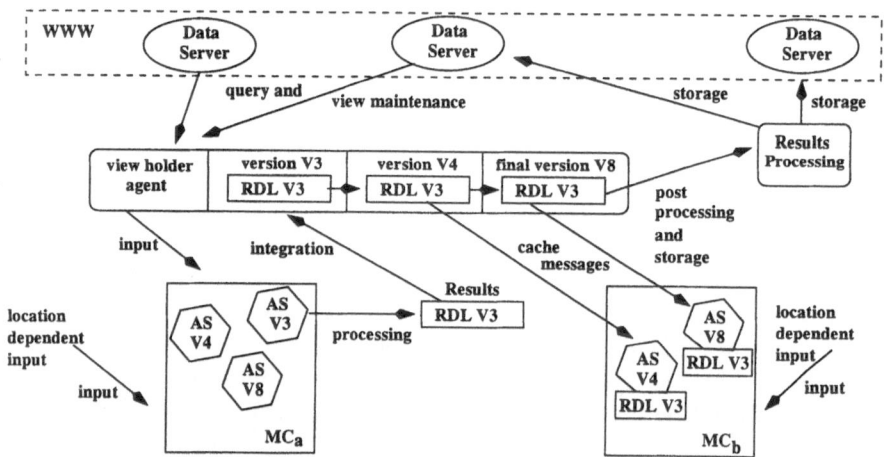

Fig. 8. Integrating and Sharing RDLs During Cooperation

View Holders maintain versions of views to allow for greater flexibility and customization in the amount of data currency and consistency achieved between the views cached on the mobile computer and the data formed within the cooperative work repository. Essentially, we extend the traditional functionality of a server-side proxy with capabilities that facilitate cooperation among the users by providing:

– **Flexible Data Currency:** The view holder agent is a mechanism where we can adjust the currency of the data stored on the mobile client, for example, so that an already working client or a new client joining the cooperative effort will be able to read newly updated derived data and results previously produced (i.e., a new version of the view and its respective RDLs). We use versioning not only to create an optimistic asynchronous cooperative strategy that allows individual work to be performed while disconnected, but also to supply changes in data currency.

– **Cooperative Work Consistency:** As individual results of the newly synthesized cooperative work are created, there is a need for providing a process that can integrate the work done by mobile clients and check for data inconsistencies. Essentially, we will be adding individual results to the cooperative work repository only if the states of the cooperative work or RDLs are consistent with the original derived version used as input, and the RDLs can propagate throughout the consistency window. Looking at our example 7 again, we can now consider AS_a, AS_b, and AS_c as application sessions executing on different MCs. The integration process within the LTVs and the rules for integration and sharing remain the same.

6   Conclusion

Within a mobile environment, we have shown how data cached can take the form of a materialized view and described a server-side agent mechanism for the fixed network or *view holder agent* that maintains versions of the views that are required by a particular mobile client's application sessions. View Holders are designed to reduce computation and wireless communication costs, and use view versioning to cope with disconnected operations, by allowing application sessions to access more *current* data without invalidating work previously done. Result propagation and inconsistency detection allow work performed during disconnection to be integrated within a view holder agent along with the original data used as input to create the results. The results are considered valid as long as they can be integrated within a consistency window of versions (i.e., view states) as required by the application. Rules were supplied that govern the creation and sharing of these result data layers among a group of application sessions possibly executing on different mobile clients and showed how inconsistencies can be detected within the LTVs of the view holder agent before sharing is allowed to proceed.

References

1. B.R. Badrinath, A. Fox, L. Kleinrock, G. Popek, P. Reiher, and M. Satyanarayanan. A Conceptual Framework for Network Adaptation. *IEEE Mobile Networks and Applications*, 5(4):221–231, 2000.
2. R. Elmasri and S. B. Navathe. Fundamentals of Database Systems. chapters 18-21, pp. 501–633. Benjamin-Cummings, 1989.
3. R. Hull and G. Zhou. A Framework for Supporting Data Integration using the Materialized and Virtual Approaches. In *the ACM SIGMOD Conf.*, pp. 481–492, Jun. 1996.

4. J. Klingemann, T. Tesch, and J. Wasch. Enabling Cooperation among Disconnected Mobile Users. In *the 1997 COOPIS Conf.*, Sept. 1997.
5. J. J. Kistler and M. Satyanarayanan. Disconnected Operation in the Coda File System. *ACM Trans. on Computer Sys.*, 10(1):3–25, Feb. 1992.
6. D. Quass and J. Widom. On-Line Warehouse View Maintenance for Batch Updates. In *the ACM SIGMOD Conf.*, pp. 393–404, May 1997.
7. C. Spyrou, G. Samaras, E. Pitoura, S. Papastavrou, and P. K. Chrysanthis. The Dynamic View System (DVS): Mobile Agents to Support Web Views. In *the 17th Int'l Conf. on Data Engineering,*pp. 30–32, 2001.
8. S. Weissman Lauzac and P. K. Chrysanthis. Programming Views for Mobile Database Clients. In *Proc. of the Nineth Int'l Workshop on Database and Expert Sys. and Applications*, pp. 408–413, 1998.
9. S. Weissman Lauzac and P. K. Chrysanthis. Personalizing Information Gathering for Mobile Database Clients. In *Proc. of the 10th ACM Symp. on Applied Computing*, Mar. 2002.
10. S. Weissman Lauzac and P. K. Chrysanthis. Utilizing Versions of Views within a Mobile Environment. *Journal of Computing and Information*, 1998.
11. Y. Zhuge, H. Garcia-Molina, J. Hammer, and J. Widom. View Maintenance in a Warehousing Environment. In *the ACM SIGMOD Conf.*, 1995.
12. Y. Zhuge, H. Garcia-Molina, and J. Wiener. Consistency Algorithms for Multi-Source Warehouse View Maintenance. *Distributed and Parallel Databases Jour.*, 4(4), 1997.

On Real-Time Top k Querying for Mobile Services

Wolf-Tilo Balke[1], Ulrich Güntzer[2], and Werner Kießling[1]

[1]Institute of Computer Science
University of Augsburg
Augsburg, Germany
{balke, kiessling}@informatik.uni-augsburg.de
[2]Institute of Computer Science
University of Tübingen
Tübingen, Germany
guentzer@informatik.uni-tuebingen.de

Abstract. Mobile services offering multi-feature query capabilities must meet tough response time requirements to gain customer acceptance. The top-k query model is a popular candidate to implement such services. We present a new algorithm SR-Combine that closely self-adapts to particular cost ratios in different environments optimizing both object accesses and query run-times. We perform a series of benchmarks to verify the superiority over existing approaches and use a psychologically founded model of response time requirements for mobile access. For a wide range of practical cases SR-Combine can already satisfy these goals. Where this isn't yet the case, we show ways to get there systematically paving the way for real-time capabilities in mobile services.

1   Introduction

Top k querying is an increasingly demanding problem in today's applications. Areas like web-based information services, enterprise information systems or content-based retrieval already make intensive use of this new paradigm. A variety of applications for ranking preferences in databases [Kie02], multi-media databases [OR+98] or recent approaches in cooperative services [DGS00] also show that top k queries are essential for advanced database retrieval.

Example 1: Business Document Repositories
Consider the case of an insurance company storing their letters and e-mails, contracts and related documents on a central server. At each damage event the person in charge needs to know about recent similar cases or some persons involved in different cases. Thus a query has to be performed like: "Give me the top cases preferably recently with most similar kinds and costs of damages and same people involved."

Here we can already identify four classifiers (kind, costs, people, time), assign scores and sort documents into lists ordered by their relevance towards these issues (what will be called a *stream* in the following). However, when it comes to real-time capabilities for combining streams, current approaches show limitations. Psychology [Pop97] teaches that users only tend to accept response times up to 3 seconds before their questions are answered. This real-time restriction can generally be applied to on-

R. Meersman, Z. Tari (Eds.): CoopIS/DOA/ODBASE 2002, LNCS 2519, pp. 125–143, 2002.
© Springer-Verlag Berlin Heidelberg 2002

line search engines and users will allow higher run-times only for very difficult tasks (e.g. in work environments). In mobile applications there are even monetary reasons involved, because the connection is often charged with respect to the usage time.

Recent approaches to top k querying were designed for special applications and tended to deteriorate in efficiency very quickly, if the application environment or score distributions for queries changed. Besides, no real-time results for algorithms in different environments have been published so far (except [BGM02] who reported hours for distributed mobile services). This is because –though optimizing the total number of object accesses– run-times will nevertheless considerably increase, if the algorithms extensively use expensive types of object accesses, cf. [WH+99]. Thus also the different costs for types of accesses and the application architecture have to be considered to build competitive algorithms. Due to the technical constraints of mobile devices in the following we focus on few streams to combine ($n < 10$), small numbers of return values ($k = 3$ to 10), and on response times of only few seconds.

2   Top k Querying for Mobile Services

2.1 Characteristics of Mobile Services

With the current developments of devices like cell phones or PDAs, pervasive access on information becomes more and more attractive. We will illustrate this by three scenarios of mobile services and discuss specific characteristics and requirements.

- **Scenario 1: Mobile access to global stock exchanges**. Typical queries are: "Get the five top performers in IT industries also involved in bio-technology." The querying is mainly attribute-based and there is virtually no difference in costs of sorted accesses and random accesses (cf. [NR99]).
- **Scenario 2: Location-based restaurant service**. Typical queries are like: "Get me the five nearest restaurants with Asian cuisine, top category and prices of about 40$ per meal." The querying often uses nearest neighbor searches. Random accesses are generally much more expensive than sorted accesses ([BGM02] determined a factor of 10 for this kind of service).
- **Scenario 3: Mobile on-line auctions**. Typical queries are like: "Get me the top five impressionist paintings, in rather brown and green colors having the lowest prices." The querying involves attribute-based parts often together with extracted multimedia features. Random accesses are more expensive than sorted accesses (tests in [WBK01] show factors of about 6).

service	complexity	updates	sources
stock market	low	often	external
location-based	medium	seldom	mixed
mobile auctions	high	seldom	central

As shown in the table above the three scenarios not only differ in the costs for object accesses, but also in characteristics like update behavior and data sources. Whereas attribute-based stock market information has update ranges of few seconds, the information for complex services involving e.g. multimedia data, is more durable. Typical update intervals range between days and weeks. This means that e.g. stock market information has to be imported directly from content providers. But durable information like multimedia data can be transferred on central servers allowing efficient storage and indexing schemes. The research area of data integration over the web [GB97, TSH01, GW00] has lead to twofold architectures for different applications:

- **Central Server Architecture (CSA):** If the service provider is also the content provider or handles mainly durable information, services are provided using a high performance server with central data repositories.
- **Distributed Sources Architecture (DSA):** If the service and content provider differ or short update ranges are necessary, services are provided using a middleware gathering information on demand from sources accessed via the Internet.

Enabling top *k* queries in mobile environments, however, poses severe problems. In [BGM02] ways to build mobile services with a DSA architecture providing direct access to various Internet sources are presented, however their tests show that the processing even for simple tasks often need hours. Thus when trying to meet real-time requirements today, we have to build all scenarios on a CSA architecture. A solution of combining Internet sources with local database servers is given by the WSQ/DSQ approach [GW00] that handles accesses to Internet sources in an asynchronous manner and caches the results for later use in virtual tables of a central database. Since the service provider can anticipate the type of queries, commonly accessed data and the update rate needed, a caching strategy with asynchronous updates is suitable.

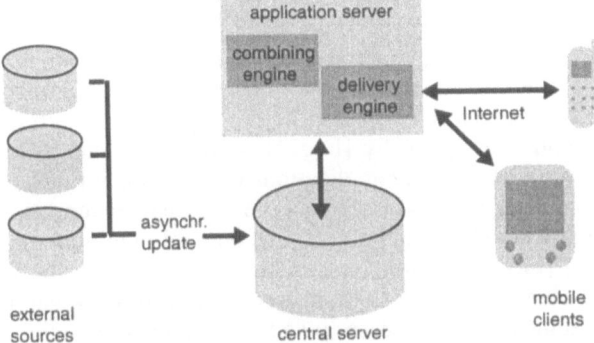

Fig. 1. Intended CSA architecture

The mobile service in Fig. 1 consists of a application server containing a combining engine which runs the *SR-Combine* algorithm. A detailed architectural study is given in [BKU02]. All the content is retrieved from a central server (updated asynchronously). As shown in [WBK01] with the example of mobile online auctions the delivery engine can automatically transform generic XML formats using XSLT to support mobile devices e.g. via WAP or i-mode gateways. Another advantage of this architecture is that data on the central server can be indexed to suit the service design. Through statistical analysis also costs for certain usage patterns can be estimated for different kinds of access personalized for each user.

2.2 Top k Querying Revisited

Since top k querying is an important feature for cooperative information systems, we will revisit some approaches that can later be used as a yard stick. Due to the nature of mobile services showing high update rates or even distributed sources, we are mainly concerned with middleware algorithms. In general those algorithms can be divided into two categories: the ones guaranteeing a correct result set and those using statistical data to get the result set more efficiently, e.g. [DR99], however with an amount of uncertainty about the correctness. Since mobile services with restricted client devices (bandwidth, display-size, etc.) demand rather small numbers of objects to be output, we will insist on a correct result set, i.e. we focus on high precision. Applications for top k querying are concerned with gathering information using a variety of classifiers. Generally speaking there are two access methods providing basic scores:

- The **sorted access** (SA) ranks database objects according to their score values (descending) with respect to a single feature and accesses objects rank by rank.
- The **random access** (RA) can be posed to a data source retrieving the score value of a single object with respect to a single stream.

Due to the CSA architecture we can rely on both kinds of accesses. Having gathered all basic score values, the total score is subsequently determined using a suitable monotonic combining function F. Both access methods can however essentially differ in their costs. The rule of thumb can be stated that the more complex the information to be queried, the more expensive random accesses will be. This leads to various applications ranging from those where random accesses are cheaper than sorted accesses [NR99], via those where random accesses are more expensive with a certain factor [WH+99], to those where random accesses are virtually impossible [Coh98].

Generally speaking algorithms for top k querying try to minimize the number of database objects that have to be accessed before being able to return a correct result set. A first algorithm was given by [Fag96] followed by improved approaches for multimedia retrieval [OR+98] and applications in fuzzy logic [NR99]. [GBK00] generalized a threshold algorithm and improved it by heuristic control flows in the Quick-Combine approach. Though it was proven to be optimal in minimizing sorted accesses for top k querying [FLN01], extensive random accesses had to be performed. Since costs for random accesses may explode in some applications, it can be far more economic to replace some random accesses by a larger number of sorted accesses.

This has lead to the development of algorithms like Stream-Combine or NRA [GKB01, FLN01] that do without random accesses. However, in practical tests those algorithms showed their limited applicability by accessing 80-90% of all database objects, if skewed data is involved, thus quickly loosing their speed-up even over the naïve approach. Extensive performance tests in [GBK00] show that Quick-Combine achieves its best results, if skewed data is involved, whereas Stream-Combine performs best in environments with uniformly distributed data. To overcome these limitations an combined algorithm called CA is given in [FLN01]. Basically CA runs NRA, but periodically performs random accesses like Quick-Combine on promising objects. However, it shows the same characteristic behavior and limitations as Quick-Combine. Thus a mere combination of known algorithms will not solve the problem, but we have to design a new paradigm to get a competitive self-adapting algorithm.

3   The *SR-Combine* Algorithm

In the following we will present the *SR-Combine* algorithm returning *k* overall best objects. We will first present a sketch of its three phases, state an adequate retrieval model and present heuristics leading to an efficient implementation of the algorithm.

Algorithm *SR-Combine*

- •**Phase 1 (Pruning Phase):** *Phase 1 gathers objects from the different streams until it can guarantee that at least one overall best object has been seen. It uses sorted accesses to see object scores in descending order in each stream and random accesses to complete the scores for objects already seen. For each object there are lower and upper bound estimations for its total score.*
- •**Phase 2 (Identifying Barriers):** *Phase 2 divides all objects seen in phase 1 into those that have no chance of being the top object and those that have, the so-called barrier objects. After phase 2 we know that the overall best object is among the barrier objects and all the non-barrier objects can be excluded in our search for the top object.*
- •**Phase 3 (Removing Barriers):** *Phase 3 successively completes scores of barrier objects. Again both sorted and random accesses are used. Whenever the information about any object is sufficient to exclude it from the barriers, the object is removed. If enough barrier objects have been removed, the algorithm can output the top object and start over to get the next best object.*

3.1   A Faster (Top *k*)* Retrieval Model

Since the correctness of the result set is guaranteed, the exact order of the best *k* matches can be neglected during the retrieval phases. As the system successively outputs objects, any object can already be output, if we are positive that it belongs to the set of *k* best matches, no matter what its exact rank or score in the final result set will be. Thus, our (top *k*)* retrieval model outputs the *k* best objects, but does not initially determine whether an object will be the first ranked or the *k*-th ranked object. Though this retrieval model will need the same total time to deliver all *k* results, it essentially improves the time needed before some first objects can be output. This is important for psychological reasons and allows an efficient use of bandwidths. Besides users get an idea of the result set and can decide, if the results are already satisfying and the algorithm can be terminated early or if a query has to be refined.

In our case the implementation of this retrieval model is the assertion that we can already output the first object, if there are only (*k*-1) barrier objects left, i.e. only (*k*-1) objects have a chance of being more relevant than our object. Inductively we can conclude, that if two objects should be output, there may at most be (*k*-2) barriers, for three objects (*k*-3) barriers, and so on. This leads to the observation, that when removing barriers for the output of a first object, we may focus on a set of only *k* objects and only need to consider the remaining barriers whenever one of our *k* barriers is removed. Inductively this again leads to a restriction to a set of (*k* - (number of objects returned)) objects, that have to be updated regularly during the removing of barriers.

3.2   The Pruning Phase

For an efficient pruning phase we now state a few heuristics and prove its correctness.

Heuristic 1: Taking the Environment into Account

The costs for sorted and random accesses may strongly differ depending on the environment [NR99, WH+99, Coh98]. Thus strategies like optimizing the total number of accesses, however using an expensive kind of access will fail. Thus the ratio between sorted and random access costs has to be taken into account. Since some sorted accesses are necessary to see new objects, during the entire algorithm our control flow takes care, that –based on the cost-ratio– for each sorted access only as many random accesses are performed, that total runtime costs may at most double, though the total number of objects accesses is still optimized. Thus the trade-off between minimizing total object accesses and ruining the runtime by using more cost expensive accesses is bounded. This technique can also be adapted to the removing barriers phase.   ∎

Heuristic 2: Using the Data Distribution

The data distribution in each stream may severely differ. There may be streams with quickly decreasing scores (skewed data), streams with uniformly distributed score values or even streams that provide similar scores for all objects. Of course the evaluation of *quickly decreasing* streams should be preferred, because they discriminate well. A second important factor to estimate a stream's influence is its weighting in the combining function. *Highly weighted* streams should be preferred. [GBK00] proposes an indicator technique that uses the relative decrease of a stream's score distribution together with a partial derivative of the combining function for the stream (if the derivative exists, otherwise - e.g. in the case of max as combining function - this part can be set to $1/n$). For the relative decrease in each stream we use the difference between the score of the last seen object (o_{last}) and the score of the p-th last seen object ($o_{p\text{-th } last}$), where p can be any number. Indicators for each stream are given by:

$$\Delta_j := |\partial F / \partial x_j| \cdot (s_j(o_{last}) - s_j(o_{p\text{-th } last})) \quad (1 \le j \le n) \tag{1}$$

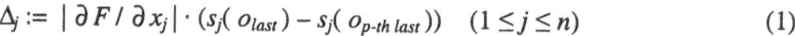

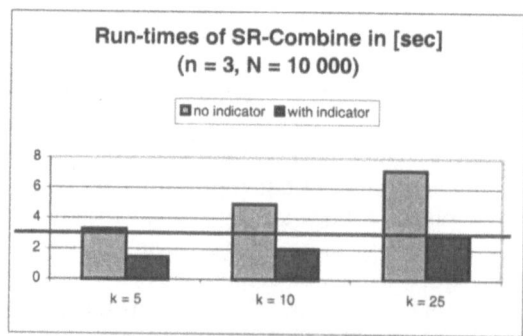

Fig. 2. Effect of indicators on run-times

Always choosing the right stream for sorted accesses leads to an important improvement factor for the algorithm's real time capabilities. Theoretically at most a factor of *n* can be reached over classical strategies. Since practical tests (cf. fig. 2) show that even in the case of only three streams involved our indicator gains a factor of 2 (in run-times and object accesses), we adapted this indicator for our algorithm. The line in our real-time diagrams marks the 3 seconds requirement (cf. section 4).

However, SR-Combine's indicators perform another important task. Since experiments show that algorithms relying on extensive random accesses tend to deteriorate in cases where uniformly distributed data prevails, in SR-Combine indicators are used for compensation. If not at least one stream is detected showing a skewed data distribution, no random accesses are granted in-spite of the cost-ratio for the performed sorted accesses. An indicator is said to show a skew, if it is larger than the expected decrease in the uniformly distributed case. For instance in the case of an arithmetical mean as combining function, an indicator that uses the distance between the last and the *p*-th last object and *N* databases objects, the expected uniformly distributed decrease in each stream is (p-1 / N). This simple heuristic takes care that SR-Combine does not deteriorate, even in cases with uniformly distributed streams only. ∎

Heuristic 3: Accessing the Most Promising Objects

Having seen some objects by sorted access the algorithm can spend random accesses granted according to the cost-ratio. However, there will not be enough random accesses to analyze objects thoroughly. Thus we have to spend our random accesses wisely for the most promising objects only. This is implemented by performing random accesses on those objects having the maximum lower bound estimation *max_low* first. Knowing the score for these objects helps to increase *max_low* quickly, which propels an early termination of the pruning phase. And the less objects we access during the pruning phase, the less barriers we have to cope with afterwards. If all objects with maximum lower bound are completely known, we will use our random accesses on those objects having the maximum upper bound estimation. Since we don't want to keep a list of the current upper bounds (that may change for most objects after each sorted access), we will use a simple heuristic and access objects in the order, they first have been seen. ∎

Theorem 1: Correct Termination of the Pruning Phase

If there is at least one object o_x whose lower bound estimation (*max_low*) is larger or equals the threshold calculated using the minimum score values of each stream as input for the monotonic combining function *F*, no object that has not been seen, can be better than all seen objects, i.e. an overall best object has already been seen.

Proof:

It is obvious that if an object's lower bound for its aggregated score is greater or equal any other object's upper bound, it has to be the overall best object. Thus, what has to be shown is that an overall best object has already been seen as the algorithm terminates the pruning phase. We know that at least one object o_x has been seen, whose lower bound is larger or equals the threshold. Due to the sorting of the streams we also know that each score of an unseen object o is smaller or equal the minimum of score values $s_i(o_i)$ seen in each stream so far. Thus the aggregated score of o is limited by the score of o_x:

$$F(s_i(o),\dots,s_n(o)) \leq F(\min(s_i(o_1)),\dots,\min(s_n(o_n))) =: thres$$
$$\leq low(o_x) \leq F(s_i(o_x),\dots,s_n(o_x))$$

(2)

∎

Now we present the complete algorithm for our pruning phase. Please note, that no expensive updates of all seen objects' upper bounds are necessary during our phase 1.

The Pruning Phase (Phase1)

While (*thres* > *max_low*) do
1. Get a new pair $(o_{new}, s_i(o_{new}))$ by sorted access on stream *i* and calculate a new indicator Δ_i
2. If there is at least one indicator showing a skew, set *random := random + co-stratio*.
3. Update $\min(s_i(o))$ with $s_i(o_{new}))$ and calculate the threshold *thres* using the minimum score values of each stream as input for *F*.
4. If o_{new} has already occurred in the index then
   4.1. Update its score entry $s_i(o_{new}))$ and recalculate its lower bound $low(o_{new})$.
5. else
   5.1. Initialize a record for o_{new} in the index, initialize its score $s_i(o_{new}))$ and calculate its lower bound $low(o_{new})$.
6. If $max\_low < low(o_{new})$ set $max\_low := low(o_{new})$.
7. While *random* ≥ 1 and (*thres* > *max_low*) do
   7.1. If the score of any object *o* having $low(o) = max\_low$ is not already entirely known, perform a random access on object *o*, set *random := random −1* and (if necessary) update $low(o)$ and *max_low*.
8. While *random* ≥ 1 and (*thres* > *max_low*) do
   8.1. Perform a random access on the object *o* that was the earliest object seen by sorted access and whose score is not already entirely known, set *random :=* *random −1* and (if necessary) update $low(o)$ and *max_low*.
9. Set $i := m$, with $\Delta_m = \max\{\Delta_j \mid 1 \leq j \leq n\}$

3.3   Identifying the Barriers

After we can guarantee the existence of at least one correct result object, we will identify all barriers. For an improved output behavior we rely on the following heuristic and state a theorem helping to distinguish between barriers and non-barrier objects.

Heuristic 4: Using the (Top k)* Retrieval Model
In the following, we will implement the (Top k)* strategy from 2.1 by choosing a subset of barriers, called the working barriers. Working barriers will be chosen as those object having the highest upper bound estimations. Only upper and lower bounds of the barriers in the working barriers set will be updated regularly. Whenever

during phase 3 an object is removed from working barriers, one of the remaining barriers is chosen as replacement.   ■

Theorem 2: Correctness of Identified Barriers
Only objects having an higher upper bound than *max_low* can have a better aggregated score, than the objects with maximum lower bound *max_low*, i.e. only those objects are barriers. (**Proof** obvious due to construction).   ■

The Identifying Barriers Phase (Phase 2)

1. Iterate the index of seen objects and update for each object *o* the upper bound for its aggregated score *upp(o)* using its known score values or –if $s_i(o)$ is unknown for any *i*– the minimum score seen by sorted access in stream *i* as input for *F*.
2. Consider the object o_{top} having the maximum lower bound *max_low*. If more such objects exist, choose one having a highest upper bound.
3. Initialize a list *barriers*, in which all the objects having an upper bound higher than *max_low* (excluding o_{top}) are contained with *oid*.
4. Choose a list *working_barriers* containing those (*k – returned*) objects from barriers that have highest upper bounds. Remove the chosen objects from *barriers*.

3.4   Removing the Barriers and Output of Objects

For the last phase we use again our heuristics from phases 1 and 2. If we remove enough barriers we can output an object guaranteed to belong to the top *k* objects:

Theorem 3: Correctness of Output Objects
Let *returned* be the number of objects already returned. If there are less than (*k – returned*) barriers left in *working_barriers* (i.e. phase 3 terminates), the object o_{top} having the maximum lower bound *max_low* is among the *k* overall best objects.

Proof:
If any object is removed from *working_barriers*, in step 3 of phase 3 the list is filled periodically by using suitable objects from the list *barriers*. If phase 3 has terminated, there must be less than (*k – returned*) objects in *working_barriers* and no more objects in *barriers*. Thus only those objects in *working_barriers* and all objects that have already been output can possibly have a better score than o_{top}. Hence there are at most ((*k – returned –1*) + *returned*) = (*k–1*) objects that can have a better score and we can safely output o_{top} as one of *k* best objects.

It remains to be shown, that phase 3 terminates at all. But since *max_low* monotonically increases and the objects' upper bounds in *barriers* and *working_barriers* monotonically decrease, the number of objects in *working_barriers* and *barriers* is steadily decreasing during phase 3. At the latest all lists would definitely be cleared, if all seen objects would have been completely determined by sorted/random access. ■

During phase 3 we will successively remove barriers by sorted or random access. We will again chose most promising candidates for random access. If no random accesses are available, we use sorted accesses and grant some more random accesses according to our cost-ratio. If the lower bound of any object gets larger than the maximum lower bound *max_low*, this object becomes our new top object and *max_low* is updated. For all updates we will only focus on the *working_barriers* subset and remove all objects whose upper bound sinks below *max_low*. Whenever objects are removed from *working_barriers*, new barriers are inserted from *barriers*, until *barriers* is empty.

The Removing Barriers Phase (Phase 3)

While the number of objects in *working_barriers* is (k – *returned*) do
1. If (*random* $\geq$ 1) then
    1.1. Perform a random access with respect to any missing stream on any object o in the list *working_barriers* having the highest upper bound. Set *random* := *random* –1.
    1.2. Recalculate the upper and lower bound for object o in the index.
    1.3. If the new upper bound of o becomes smaller than or equals *max_low*, remove o from *working_barriers*.
    1.4. If the new lower bound of o becomes larger than *max_low*, update *max_low* and o_{top}. Remove all objects from *working_barriers* whose upper bound is smaller or equals *max_low*.
2. else
    2.1. Get a new pair (o_{new}, $s_i(o_{new})$) by sorted access on stream i. Update o_{new} and its lower bound *low*(o_{new}) in the index as shown in phase 1. Recalculate the indicator for stream i.
    2.2. If there is at least one indicator showing a skew, set *random* := *random* + *costratio*.
    2.3. If *low*(o_{new}) > *max_low* then
        2.3.1. If *upp*(o_{top}) > *max_low*, insert o_{top} in *barriers*.
        2.3.2. If o_{new} is in *working_barriers* then remove o_{new} from *working_barriers*, else remove o_{new} from *barriers*.
        2.3.3. Update *max_low* and o_{top} with *low*(o_{new}) and o_{new}.
        2.3.4. Remove all those objects from *working_barriers*, whose upper bound is smaller or equals *max_low*.
    2.4. Recalculate the upper bounds *upp*(o) of all objects o in *working_barriers* (like in phase 2). If *upp*(o) $\leq$ *max_low*, remove o from *working_barriers*.
3. While the number of objects in *working_barriers* is less than (k – *returned*) and there are still objects in *barriers* do
    3.1. Choose any object from *barriers* and update its upper bound (like in phase 2 step 4).
    3.2. If the object's upper bound is larger than *max_low* move it from *barriers* to *working_barriers*, else remove it from *barriers*.

3.5 The *SR-Combine* Algorithm

Now we are ready to present the complete *SR-Combine* algorithm. This algorithm adapts closely to any application and chooses wisely how many sorted and random accesses should be performed to optimize the run-time characteristics. It is also interesting that our algorithm contains previous approaches as special cases:

Proposition 1: (proof omitted)
With *N* as number of database objects and *n* as number of streams we can state:
1. By choosing the cost-ratio as $(n-1)$ *SR-Combine* simulates the Quick-Combine approach (without heuristic 4).
2. By choosing the cost-ratio less than $1/(n\cdot N)$ the *SR-Combine* algorithm behaves like Stream-Combine.   ∎

For initialization. we take the input parameters *n*, *k* and the monotonic combining function *F* from the user's query (SR-Combine is designed for any monotonic combining function) and get the cost-ratio from the service provider (cf. section 4.1). Since information about all objects seen by sorted access has to be maintained, we intialize an adequate index structure (e.g. hash-table) to manage oids and score values ordered by oids. For each new oid the structure contains a record of an array of length *n* for its single score values, its aggregated score's upper bound and the lower bound. We initialize variables *thres* $\in$ [0,1] with 1, *max_low* $\in$ [0,1] with 0 and integer $i := 1$, counters for the number of possible random accesses *random* := 0 and the number of objects already returned *returned* := 0. We create an array of length *n* to hold the current minimum scores for each stream and initialize $\min(s_i(o)) := 1$ $(1 \leq i \leq n)$.

Algorithm *SR-Combine* (F, n, k, cost-ratio)

   While less than *k* objects have already been returned, i.e. *returned* < *k*, do
1. If the index is not empty, iterate the index and get the best lower bound, i.e. *max_low* := max(low(oid)).
2. Compute the threshold *thres* by using the minimum score values of each stream as input for *F*.
3. Perform the "**Pruning Phase**".
4. Perform the "**Identifying Barriers Phase**".
5. Perform the "**Removing Barriers Phase**".
6. Output o_{top} as one of the *k* best objects, increase *returned* by one, mark o_{top} in the index as finished (it must not be accessed again).

4   Performance Benchmarks

4.1 Determining the Cost-Ratio

An important factor to run *SR-Combine* is the cost-ratio. It determines the ratio between average costs for sorted and random accesses for the specific application. Of course costs depend on various influences, like the speed and average workload of the central server, network latencies, external data sources involved and last, but not least the specific query. Most of these influences have to be determined by the service provider. Since services are designed for a specific application, user interaction can generally be anticipated. Statistical analysis thus provides a set of typical cost-ratios.

Generally speaking, different streams may be provided by different sources or subsystems. Some of them might not allow random accesses, others probably forbid sorted accesses and even those, who admit both types may do this at different costs (in terms of money and/or time). Hence it is worthwhile to consider costs separately for each stream and calculate n specific cost-ratios. Though it is not really complicated to refine our algorithm along these lines (n different counters for sorted and random access have to be updated), we will assume an average cost-ratio to simplify matters. In the following for the average cost-ratio we will use the experimentally determined factor of 6 SA=1 RA from our scenario 3 in all experiments for comparability reasons. However, we also tried different variations of the cost-ratio leading to very similar results (cf. section 4.4).

4.2 Test Environment

For our tests we will focus on both *indirect measures* given by the number of necessary object accesses and *direct measures* concerning the real-time capabilities of our algorithm in practical applications. But first we have to look for some suitable algorithms as a benchmark. Of course one candidate is the naïve approach that shows its advantages especially in small databases due to low CPU costs. Performance tests in our experimental environment show that algorithms of the Quick-Combine or CA type perform best in environments with skewed data. However, they tend to deteriorate in efficiency, if large amounts of uniformly distributed data is involved (for n=5, k=25 CA and QC are already four times worse than the naïve approach!). Another algorithm is given by the Stream-Combine or NRA type which behave in the opposite way and are useful for uniformly distributed data only.

We will exemplify this behavior for three streams to combine and different numbers of objects to return (see diagrams in fig. 3 and 4), but the results even get worse for higher numbers of streams. Though all algorithms gain their highest performance only in special cases, we will accept the challenge and benchmark *SR-Combine* with Quick-Combine and CA for skewed data and the naïve approach and Stream-Combine for uniformly distributed data. In the diagrams we focus on run-times (in seconds) and object accesses (sorted and random accesses cumulated). On the left-hand side of the diagrams, the results for uniform distributions are given, on the right-hand side results for skewed data. Please note that though in the uniformly distributed case CA and Quick-Combine use even less accesses than Stream-Combine, the run-times are worse, due to their extensive use of expensive random accesses.

Our following tests have been performed using a Java middleware running on a 600 MHz PentiumII PC with 256 MB RAM as application server connected via a 100 MBit LAN to an IBM DB2 V7.2 Database Server for random and sorted accesses. We used JDBC for all accesses, sorted accesses are performed via Java result sets, random accesses with use of temporary tables (which allowed to change to cost-ratio for tests in section 4.4). The statistically independent data sets for our experiments contain $N =$ 10000 database objects; their scores are generated synthetically according to different practical distributions [GBK00]. The cost-ratio between random and sorted accesses was determined statistically to 6 SA=1 RA with 1 SA≈1 msec (i.e. 1 RA≈ 6 msec).

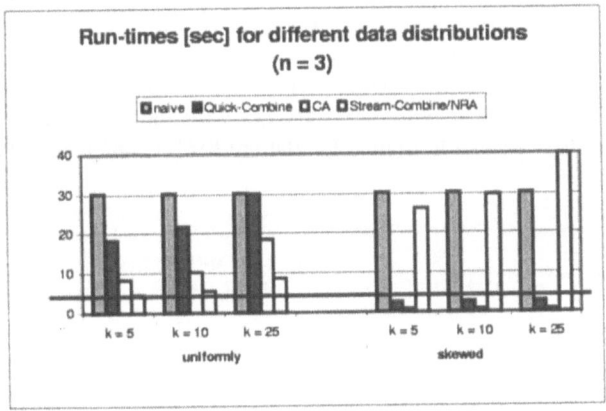

Fig. 3. Deteriorating efficiency in different environments

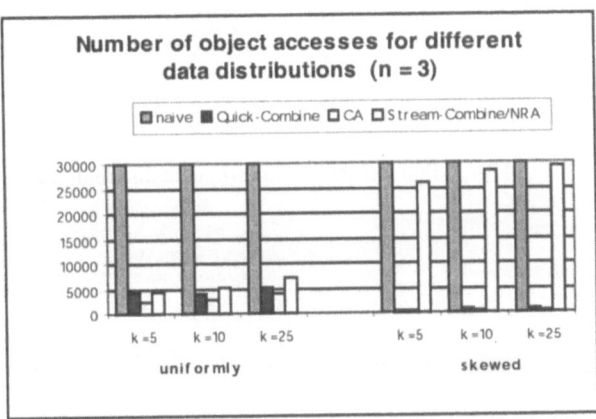

Fig. 4. Object accesses for run-times in fig. 3

4.3 *SR-Combine* vs. **Others**

Having set up the benchmark environment we performed several experiments. The diagrams show statistical averages of the experimentally determined run-times and total numbers of object accesses (SA+RA). We have set up scenarios focussing on uniformly distributed data and scenarios involving skewed data. In all scenarios we tested the algorithms in the case of three streams combined (left-hand side) and five streams combined (right-hand side) for practical values of k ($k = 5$, 10, 25). Again the horizontal line shows our target of up to 3 seconds run-time.

Fig. 5 and 6 show that in the case of uniformly distributed data the *SR-Combine* algorithm performs always much better than the naïve approach and even always better than Stream-Combine the best algorithm known in this environment. For the tests on skewed data, we left out the naïve approach, because the scale would be affected (respective runtimes for the naïve approach are 30 and 50 seconds). Fig. 7 and 8 show that also in the case involving skewed data, *SR-Combine* beats both state-of-the-art algorithms. Please note that the *SR-Combine* algorithm has been run in all of these tests (uniform *and* skewed data) always with the *same* set of input parameters (F, n, k, cost-ratio). It has automatically adapted itself to the respective situation.

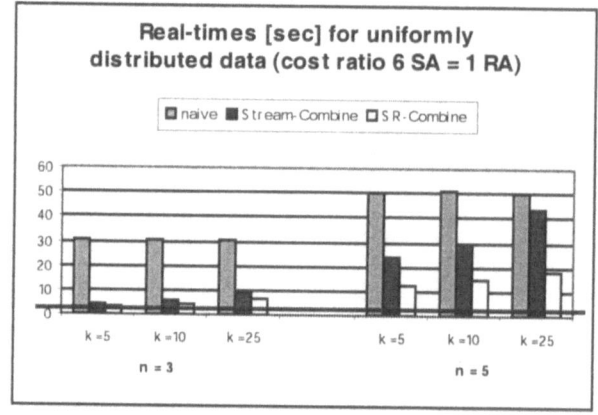

Fig. 5. Benchmark for uniform data distributions

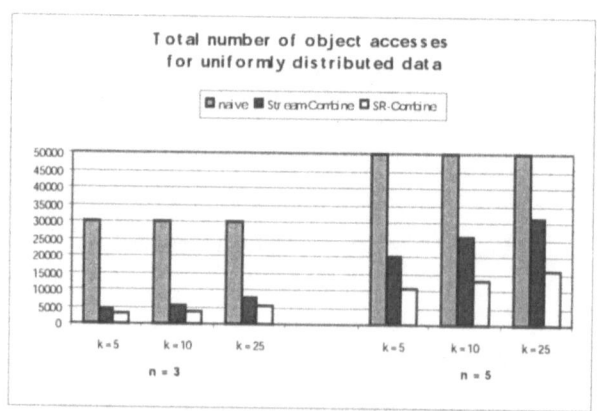

Fig. 6. Object accesses for the benchmark in fig. 5

SR-Combine in both scenarios obviously not only essentially improves the run-times, but also optimizes the total object accesses by wisely choosing the suitable kind of access. The improvement factor grows with the number of streams to combine and increasing numbers of objects to return. It also scales with the size of the database. In the case of skewed distributions our indicator-based heuristic even improves Quick-Combine and CA, that minimize the number of objects accessed.

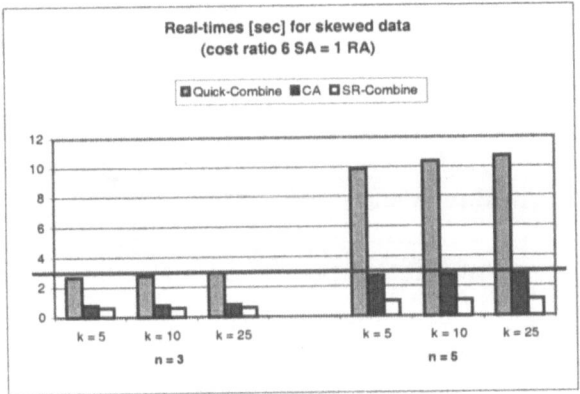

Fig. 7. Benchmark for skewed data

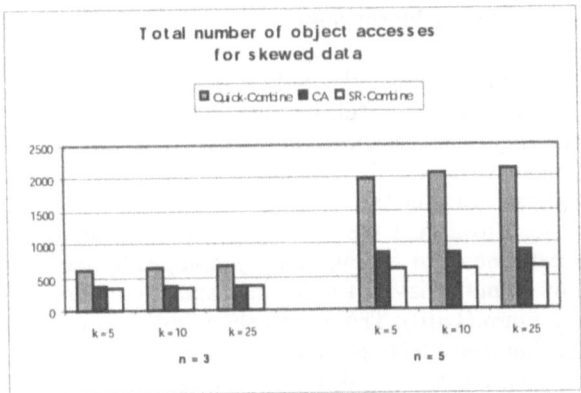

Fig. 8. Object accesses for the benchmark in fig. 7

4.4 Adaptability and Scalability

We already explained the use of cost-ratios. However, what influence have different cost-rations on the *SR-Combine* algorithm? The basic idea is that our algorithm replaces random accesses with some more sorted accesses in applications where random accesses are expensive. The following diagram shows run-times for various database sizes with different cost-ratios applied (using delays to slow or speed up accesses). We tested all different cost-ratios from our three application scenarios. Obviously SR-Combine adapts well to different applications, thus the total run-time changes only slightly for different cost-ratios (cf. fig. 9). Besides the algorithm scales well with growing database sizes. (For space reasons we only present the skewed case. However, the uniform case shows a very similar behavior).

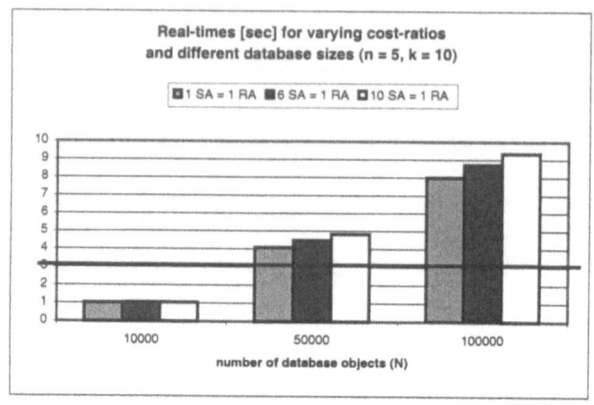

Fig. 9. Variations of cost-ratios and database sizes

4.5 Mobile Real-Time Considerations

The (top k)* retrieval model allows the earliest possible output of objects. Especially in mobile environments this is useful, because the available bandwidth can be used efficiently. But needing response times up to 3 seconds, we have seen that in environments involving skewed data, *SR-Combine* can meet these requirements, but fails if scores show uniform distributions. However, if an object is delivered every couple of seconds, users tend to accept the waiting period until all objects have been returned. Thus the real-time requirements can psychologically still be met. The diagram in fig. 10 shows the output behavior for different skews combining five streams (n=5) with ten objects to return (k=10). The graphs show how many objects are output during each 3 second time-span. Though only very skewed distributions meets the hard real-time requirements, please note that even for uniform distributions (with a total run-time of 18 seconds) *SR-Combine* delivers some first results early. Thus the subjective waiting time is improved leading to at least acceptable cases.

4.6 Lessons Learned for Mobile Applications

- Algorithms for (mobile) top k querying have to focus on both access costs and CPU costs. Choosing right streams for access will also improve average run-times.
- Run-times can be improved by balancing sorted and random accesses. A competitive algorithm has to adapt to applications characterized by different access costs.
- Psychologically the acceptable response time is about 3 seconds, but delivering already parts of the result every 3 seconds improves subjective waiting times.

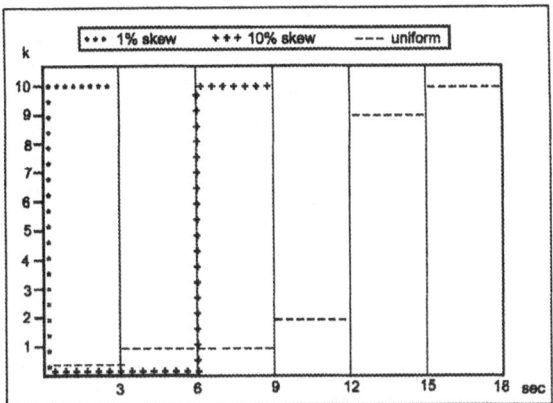

Fig. 10. Output behavior for different distributions

Our benchmark results show that *SR-Combine* already delivers results within acceptable 3 seconds for medium database sizes, if skewed data is involved and the average cost for a sorted access is about 1 msec. We also pointed out that the retrieval model psychologically helps to satisfy users. But what can be done to further improve the real-time performance in cases where the requirements are not yet met?

The access costs and the cost-ratios between sorted and random access strongly depend on the kind of service and the system environment. Thus either the hardware can be improved, or techniques can be applied to essentially speed up database accesses e.g. using multi-dimensional indexes like [CB+00, BM+01]. We have shown that *SR-Combine* essentially reduces the object accesses and copes with a wide range of service-dependent cost-ratios. Thus, if a specific service is projected and its cost parameters are known, a custom-made hardware/software selection can be designed to fit the requirements of service provider (low hardware costs, high flexibility/extensibility, etc.) and users (low service costs, waiting times, etc.).

5 Summary and Outlook

We presented a new self-adapting algorithm *SR-Combine* for top *k* retrieval and focused on its necessary real-time requirements for mobile services. We investigated different scenarios with typical environment variables and a reference central server architecture. Since *SR-Combine* flexibly adapts to various access costs, a migration to distributed service architectures is straightforward, if real-time constraints are supported by higher bandwidths or faster networks (e.g. using UMTS). We presented benchmarks with current middleware combining algorithms and showed scalability and adaptability for SR-Combine. It outperforms all current algorithms in both object accesses and real-time capabilities that are crucial for the acceptance of mobile services. Though the hard psychological real-time constraint of at most 3 seconds response time was not always meet, the algorithm has proven to be robust against changes of access costs and using an advanced retrieval model even allows to deliver objects successively. This is psychologically important, because users get at least some first objects within the expected response time reducing subjective waiting times.

Our future work will transfer efficient top k querying with *SR-Combine* into practical environments like our implementation of [WBK01]. Besides, we focus on the implementation of a mobile traffic planning service with real-time performance evaluating user preferences on travel expenses, road conditions and traffic jam awareness in a personalized manner. A first prototype is presented in [BKU02].

References

[BGM02]   N. Bruno, L. Gravano, A. Marian: Evaluating Top-k Queries over Web-Accessible Databases. *Intern. Conf. on Data Engineering (ICDE'02)*, San Jose, CA, USA, 2002.

[BKU02]   W-T. Balke, W. Kießling, C. Unbehend: A situation-aware mobile traffic information prototype. Tech. Report 2002-14, Institute of Computer Science, University of Augsburg, Germany, 2002   (submitted for publication)

[BM+01]   K. Böhm, M. Mlivoncic, H-J. Schek, R. Weber: Fast Evaluation Techniques for Complex Similarity Queries. *Intern. Conf. on Very Large Databases (VLDB'01)*, Rome, Italy, 2001

[CB+00]   Y.Chang, L. Bergman, V. Castelli, C. Li, M. Lo, J. Smith: The onion technique: indexing for linear optimization queries. *Intern. Conf. on Management of Data (SIGMOD'00)*, Dallas, USA, 2000.

[Coh98]   W. Cohen: Integration of Heterogeneous Databases Without Common Domains Using Queries Based on Textual Similarity. *Intern. Conf. on Management of Data (SIGMOD'98)*, Seattle, USA, 1998.

[DGS00]   J. Ding, L. Gravano, N. Shivakumar: Computing Geographical Scopes of Web Resources. *Intern. Conf. on Very Large Databases (VLDB'00)*, Cairo, Egypt, 2000.

[DR99]   D. Donjerkovic and R. Ramakrishnan: Probabilistic optimization of top k queries. *Intern. Conf. on Very Large Databases (VLDB'99)*, Edinburgh, Great Britain, 1999.

[Fag96]   R. Fagin. Combining fuzzy information from multiple systems. *Symposium on Principles of Database Systems (PODS'96)*, Montreal, Canada, 1996.

[FLN01]   R. Fagin, A. Lotem, and M. Naor. Optimal aggregation algorithms for middleware. *Symposium on Principles of Database Systems(PODS'01)*, Santa Barbara, CA, USA, 2001.

[GB97]   S. Gribble and E. Brewer. System design issues for internet middleware services: deductions from a large client trace. *USENIX Symposium on Internet Technologies and Systems*, Monterey, CA, USA, 1997.

[GBK00]   U. Güntzer, W-T. Balke, and W. Kießling: Optimizing multi-feature queries for image databases. *Intern. Conf. on Very Large Databases (VLDB'00)*, Cairo, Egypt, 2000.

[GBK01]   U. Güntzer, W-T. Balke, and W. Kießling: Towards efficient multi-feature queries in heterogeneous environments. *Inter. Conf. on Information Technology: Coding and Computing (ITCC'01)*, Las Vegas, USA, 2001.

[GW00]   R. Goldman, J. Widom: WSQ/DSQ: A practical approach for combined querying of databases and the web. *Intern. Conf. on Management of Data (SIGMOD'00)*, Dallas, USA, 2000.

[Kie02]   W. Kießling: Foundations of preferences in database systems. *Intern. Conf. on Very Large Databases (VLDB'02)*, Hong Kong, China, 2002.

[NR99]   S. Nepal and M. Ramakrishna: Query processing issues in image (multimedia) databases. *Intern. Conf. on Data Engineering (ICDE'99)*, Sydney, Australia, 1999.

[OR+98]   M. Ortega, Y. Rui, K. Chakrabarti, K. Porkaew, S. Mehrotra, and T. S. Huang: Supporting ranked boolean similarity queries in MARS. *IEEE Transactions on Knowledge and Data Engineering (TKDE)*, Vol. 10 (6), 1998.

[Pop97]   E. Pöppel, A hierachical model of temporal perception. *Journal of Trends in Cognitive Science*, Vol. 1, Elsevier, 1997

[TSH01]   M. Tork Roth, P. Schwarz, L. Haas: An Architecture for Transparent Access to Diverse Data Sources. *Compontent Database Systems*, Morgan Kaufmann, 2001.

[WBK01]   M. Wagner, W-T. Balke, and W. Kießling: An XML-based Multimedia Middleware for Mobile Online Auctions. *Enterprise Information Systems III*, Kluwer, 2002.

[WH+99]   E. Wimmers, L. Haas, M. Tork Roth, C. Braendli: Using Fagin's Algorithm for Merging Ranked Results in Multimedia Middleware. *Intern. Conf. on Cooperative Information Systems (CoopIS'99)*, Edinburgh, Great Britain, 1999.

Mobile Agents in Mobile Data Access Systems[1]

Yu Jiao and Ali R. Hurson

Computer Science and Engineering Department
Pennsylvania State University
220 Pond Laboratory, State College, PA 16802, U.S.A
{yjiao, Hurson}@cse.psu.edu

Abstract. The heterogeneity and geographical distribution of data sources in the presence of autonomy make it a very difficult task to provide global information sharing. When adding mobility and wireless medium to this mix (Mobile Data Access System), the constraints on bandwidth, connectivity, and resources worsen the problem. Application of mobile agent technology in a global information-sharing environment releases the global mobile users from the constraints imposed by the wireless medium and mobile devices.

This work applies the Mobile Agent technology in a Mobile Data Access System framework (MAMDAS) using the Summary Schemas Model as the underlying multidatabase platform. This approach provides better performance by reducing the network traffic and higher degree of autonomy by allowing agents to execute without the owners interference. As witnessed by our experimental results, the MAMDAS exhibits the following advantages compared to the first SSM prototype:

- It is about 6 times faster.
- It supports larger number of concurrent queries.
- It demonstrates greater scalability, portability, and robustness.

Keywords: Mobile agent, mulitdatabase, information retrieval, heterogeneous data sources, mobile device, wireless communication

1 Introduction

In a distributed heterogeneous database environment, to overcome the obstacles brought by the heterogeneity of local data sources, the literature has studied two possible solutions:

- Redesign the existing databases to form a homogeneous information sharing system, and
- Lay a global system on top of the heterogeneous local databases to provide a uniform information access method (multidatabase system).

High cost associated with the first choice prevents it from becoming a feasible solution in many cases. On the other hand, the concept of multidatabase system offers a more practical solution to share information globally. Many multidatabase

---

[1] The Office of the Naval Support under the contract N00014-02-1-0282 in part has supported this work.

R. Meersman, Z. Tari (Eds.): CoopIS/DOA/ODBASE 2002, LNCS 2519, pp. 144–162, 2002.

systems maintain a global meta-data that contains the local schema information, called global schema. Unfortunately, as the size and number of local databases grow, the global schema may become too large to manage and maintain.

The Summary Schemas Model (SSM) [3] was intended to alleviate problems associated with global-schema multidatabase approaches through abstracting the semantic of schemas. Instead of creating a global schema, the SSM relies on a hierarchical meta-data in which a parent node maintains an abstract form of its children's schema, namely a summary schema. The hierarchical structure and the schema abstraction significantly improve the robustness and provide dynamic expansion capability to the system. Using an on-line thesaurus, the SSM also supports imprecise queries. The Information Broker (IB) system, discussed later, is the first prototype of the SSM. It proves that the SSM is a practical and efficient concept to model multidatabase systems. The benefits and characteristics of the SSM are briefly addressed in section 2.

As mobile communication technology advances and the price of mobile devices decreases, mobile users become an important population among global information system users. The Mobile Data Access System (MDAS) is an information-sharing system that allows anywhere, any time access to information. However, this flexibility comes at the expense of more complicated solutions to database issues due to the limitation imposed by wireless communication and mobile devices.

The client-server paradigm is a dominant computation model in today's distributed application design. Normally, clients communicate with servers via sockets or remote procedure call (RPC). However, both of these communication methods are not suitable for the MDAS because they require network connectivity throughout a session, which cannot be guaranteed in the wireless environment. Fortunately, the agent-based programming paradigm can release this restriction.

Agents are software entities that can move from one host to another over the network, based on a certain itinerary setup, and execute designated tasks on their owners' behalf. When mobile agents are introduced into the system, mobile users only need to maintain the communication connection during the agent submission and retraction. Therefore, the use of mobile agents relaxes requirements on mobile users' critical resources such as connectivity, bandwidth and power, etc. Moreover, reduced communication would also improve the system performance. In [13], the authors showed that the performance improvement by introducing agent technology into the IB system was as high as 63.3%.

A decision was made to use Mobile Agent technology in Mobile Data Access System platform (MAMDAS) enhanced by the summary schemas model. This decision was based on the following expectations:

- Achieve higher performance compared to previous SSM prototypes by reducing the network traffic,
- Support anywhere anytime access under the constrained imposed by mobility and wireless communication, and
- Provide higher system scalability.

It should be noted that, it is not the intention of this paper to enumerate the advantages and characteristics of the SSM. The intention is to briefly outline the initial SSM prototypes and the experiences learned from these prototypes. We then focus on the application of mobile agent technology to remedy the experienced shortcomings. The rest of the paper is organized as follows: The necessary background information is briefly covered in section 2. The related work is discussed in section 3. Section 4 gives the details of the MAMDAS system. Section 5 addresses and analyzes our experimental results. Finally, we conclude our work and point out some future research plan in section 6.

2   Background

2.1   The Summary Schemas Model for Multidatabase Systems

Database systems serve critical functions in government, business applications, and academic research. In many cases, application domains are required to perform disjoint functions on shared distributed information sources using different computational platforms and/or different Database Management Systems (DBMS). Multidatabase technology has been proposed to provide a transparent uniform access method to heterogeneous data sources with minimum cost.

The literature is abounded with solutions to multidatabase system design [3]. Terms such as multidatabase language systems, global schema multidatabases, federated databases, and interoperable systems have been frequently discussed in the literature. Within the scope of multidatabase technology, the Summary Schemas Model (SSM) [3] is an attempt to provide a transparent and uniform access to heterogeneous data sources while preserving the local autonomy. It is designed to support the identification of semantically similar/dissimilar data entities. The model maintains a hierarchical meta-data based on access terms exported from underlying local databases. This meta-data is used to intelligently resolve name differences using word relationships defined in a standard dictionary such as Roget's Thesaurus. Users can submit imprecise queries at any site without knowing the location of requested access terms and/or the local access terms. Based on the data semantics, the SSM maps imprecise query terms with precise access terms found at local databases.

Figure 1 depicts the organization of the SSM model. A schema at each local node is a list of access terms. Mapping access terms of lower level nodes to their hypernyms and resolving semantic similarities among the hypernyms forms a summary schema. As one can conclude, each summary schema is smaller and more abstract than the union of its lower level schemas. The SSM model was simulated and its performance was evaluated under various schema distributions, query complexity and network topology [3]. The simulation results showed that both precise and imprecise queries incur comparable cost, and hence have comparable performance. In certain cases, the SSM imprecise query processing even outperforms a precise query processing. In general, relative to other approaches of multidatabase implementation, the SSM is a robust approach that preserves local autonomy, and offers higher performance and scalability.

2.2   The Mobile Agent Technology

Advances in wireless communication provide great convenience for mobile users to access information resources anywhere, at any time. However, wireless communication and mobility also brings some obstacles to access information. This work mainly addresses issues related to mobile users who connect to the information system through low quality, low bandwidth wireless networks.

The most common distributed application design model is the client-server model. Many client-server based applications apply one of the two communication mechanisms: *Socket* (essentially message passing) or *Remote Procedure Call* (RPC). The socket allows two programs (the client and server) to communicate through a file descriptor (a socket). The RPC hides the underlying distributed system. Programmers treat all the operations as local operations while in fact the system may perform part of the work on other machines. Unfortunately, within the domain of mobile computing, the client-server model exhibits several disadvantages:

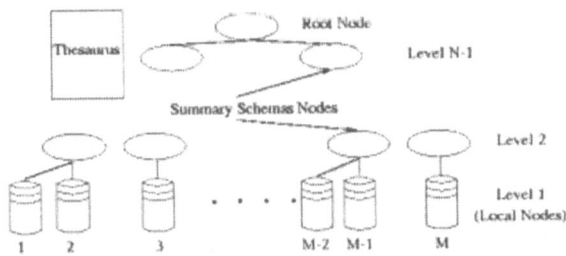

Fig. 1. A Summary Schemas Model with M local nodes and N levels.

- The physical connection between the client and the server must be maintained throughout the session. In case of disconnection, the whole communication procedure needs to be started over again. In MDAS this is not acceptable due to the limited power source at the mobile unit and low communication bandwidth of wireless medium.
- Congested network traffic since retransmissions might be necessary to compensate for disconnected session.

Based on these considerations, we concluded that the client-server paradigm is not an ideal solution for applications in a mobile environment. The use of mobile agents alleviates the problems imposed by wireless communication such as instability (frequent disconnections) and unreliability (message losses). Clients can disconnect from the network after submitting their mobile agents. Mobile agents can roam the network and fulfill their tasks such as information retrieval from a multidatabase and negotiation with other agents. Mobile agents also have the ability to make decisions based on different situations on their owner's behalf. Thus, the owner only needs to maintain the physical connection during the agent submission and retraction.

Contemporary mobile agent system implementations fall into two main groups: Java-based and non-Java-based. Systems such as IBM Aglet Workbench [9], Odyssey [16], Concordia [4], and Voyager [15] choose Java as the implementation language. Some other companies developed mobile agent systems using different languages, such as Tcl, Scheme, and python. Several examples are TACOM [15], Ara [1], and Agent Tcl [8]. We argue that Java-based agent systems are better choice for mobile agent application design in that the Java language's platform independent feature makes it ideal for distributed application designs. Thus, we chose the IBM Aglet Workbench SDK 2.0 as our implementation tool.

3   Related Work

3.1   The Information Broker System

3.1.1   System Overview

The Applied Research Lab (ARL) of Pennsylvania State University proposed the Information Broker (IB) system as a solution for remote electronic-mechanical equipment maintenance, diagnosis, and prognosis. It is the first prototype of the SSM. The IB system attempts to achieve three objectives: preserve the autonomy of all data resources, offer a uniform data search interface hiding the differences of underlying databases, and support imprecise queries and release the requirement for users' knowledge of databases.

The IB system adopts the conventional client-server computation model. The system consists of three servers: a *Thesaurus Server*, a *SSM Administration Server*, and a *Query Server*. Each server has a *Graphical User Interface* (GUI) that eases the use of the server. Local nodes and summary-schemas nodes run on a set of hosts connected through a network. The administrator can start and stop a node (either summary-schemas node or local node) by sending commands to the Daemon program residing on each host. In this system, clients communicate with the servers via datagram sockets. Figure 2 illustrates the architecture of the IB system.

The system administrator can construct the summary-schemas hierarchy through the SSM Admin GUI. Users submit queries through the Data Search GUI. In order to form a query, the user needs to supply the following information: the category preference (to narrow down the search scope), the node to start the search with, the keyword, and a preferred semantic distance (loose match or close match). The valid Data Search GUI is then submitted to the Query Server. After receiving a query, the Query Server initiates query resolution process from the originating node as designated by the user. When presenting the results, the Query Server displays all the terms satisfying the user's preferred semantic distance.

3.1.2   Observations

The first SSM prototype (the IB system) as anticipated, allows novice users to submit imprecise queries without any knowledge of the location and/or the structure of the local data sources while preserving the local database autonomy. This demonstrated the feasibility and practicality of the SSM as a tool to model multidatabase systems. In addition, the IB system also allowed us to observe several shortcomings; some due to the way the IB system was implemented:

- **Lack of portability**: This was due to the mix of C and Java languages used to build the prototype system. The server and node programs were mainly implemented in **C**, while the GUIs were written in Java. This resulted in a system with poor portability due to the **C**'s strong architectural-dependence.

- **Lack of stability**: As mentioned before, the IB system used datagram sockets to handle the communication. The datagram socket applies the User Datagram Protocol (UDP) as the transport layer protocol which does not guarantee an error-free and in-order transmission. It leaves the responsibility of ensuring a correct transmission to the application. As a result, the IB system demonstrated an unpredictable behavior in the presence of incorrect transmissions.
- **Network connectivity**: Continuous network connectivity during a complete session is one of the requirements of the socket communication mechanism. Consequently, the IB system inherited this disadvantage.

3.2   The Enhanced IB System

To overcome the deficiencies of the IB system, a decision was made to extend the scope of our prototype utilizing agent technology [13]. As a result, the client-server computation model was replaced by the agent-based paradigm. The extended system under the same experimental conditions, on the average, showed a query resolution process nearly 3 times faster than the original system [13].

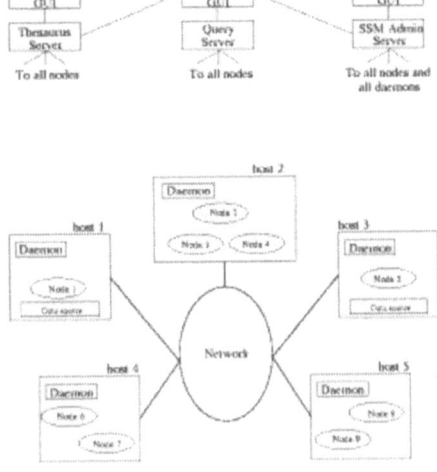

Fig. 2. An overview of the IB system architecture.

3.2.1   System Overview
Figure 3 gives an overview of the enhanced IB system. Compared to the original design (Figure 2) the new system made the following major changes:

- Three types of mobile agents were introduced: the CategorySearcher agent, the HierarchicalSearcher agent, and the QueryResolution agent. In addition, the new design completely eliminated the Query Server module.

- The enhanced IB system authorizes the QueryResolution agent to start and stop nodes when necessary. Thus, the Daemon programs were not necessary any longer. This by default reduced the overhead on individual computing resources.

The aforementioned enhances also modified to operational flow of the system. Initiation of the Data Search GUI by the user launches a CategorySearcher agent and a HierarchicalSearcher agent. These two agents migrate to the Thesaurus Server and the SSM Admin Server, respectively. The CategorySearcher agent brings back the thesaurus category information and concurrently, the HierarchicalSearcher returns with the summary-schemas hierarchy information to complete the data search GUI. At this stage, the user fills in the search term(s), chooses desired search category, starting node, semantic distance, and launches the QueryResolution agent (master) destined to the user-designated starting node. Upon arrival at the destination, the agent first activates the node and then performs the search. If there is no resolution, the agent will recursively migrate to the parent of the current node and conduct the same operation. Query resolution at a summary-schemas node allows the QueryResolution agent (master) to create its clone(s) (slave) and direct them to the proper child node(s). The clones then roam to the designated destination and try to resolve the query, while the master agent stays at the current node and waits for responses from them. After all responses from the clones, the QueryResolution agent (master) integrates and fuses the collected information, disposes all the clones, and returns to the originating node to display the result.

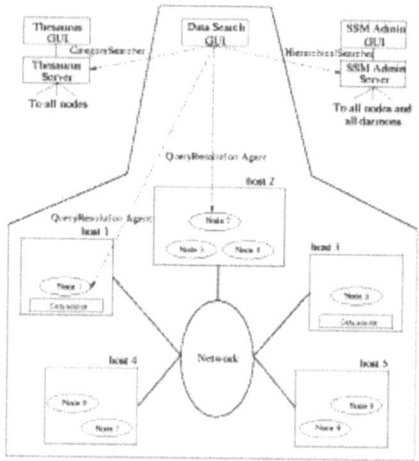

Fig. 3. An overview of the enhanced IB system architecture.

3.2.2   Lessons Learned from the Enhanced IB System

The improvement introduced by using mobile agent technology is three-fold [13].

- The enhanced IB system provided another layer of user authentication. The agent servers authenticate agents before allowing them to execute.
- The enhanced system demonstrated better performance. The simulation results indicated that the enhanced system could resolve queries nearly 3 times faster than the original system.

- The enhanced system achieved higher resource utilization. By eliminating the Daemon programs, the enhanced system frees machine resources such as CPU time, memory, ports, etc.

These advantages came, however, at the expense of local autonomy violation. Allowing a user to start and stop a node leaves the operational nodes dangerously under the user's control. As an example, if a local database is temporarily unavailable, say for maintenance, in the original prototype, it was the duty of the system administrator module to temporarily stop and remove the node from the summary-schemas hierarchy. However, in the enhanced system, a malicious user could start this node without even informing the system administrator module. In addition, each node program needs a unique port number on the local machine for its execution. If the port number is already occupied, other execution attempts of the same node program will fail. Consequently, if an intruder starts a node and never stops it, no one else can perform search on that node.

4   An Application of Mobile Agent Technology in Mobile Data Access System Design (MAMDAS)

4.1   Design Methodology

We chose Gaia, a general agent-oriented analysis and design methodology proposed by Wooldrige et al. [14], as the MAMDAS design methodology. Gaia divides the whole design process into two phases: the analysis phase (conceptual design) and the design phase (concrete design). Each phase of the Gaia method leads the developer one step further toward the final implementation. This top-down design keeps the system clean (no redundant entities) and well organized while guaranteeing to satisfy all user requirements.

During the analysis phase, two conceptual models are derived from the requirement statement: the roles model and the interactions model. The roles model identifies the key roles in the system and specifies the responsibilities and permissions associated with them. The interactions model defines a set of protocols that describe the interaction between each pair of roles.

Three concrete low-level models that can be directly implemented are generated at the design phase using the information obtained during the analysis phase: the agent model, the services model, and the acquaintance model. The agent model documents different agent types that will make up the system and estimates the number of instances of each agent type that will occur at run time. The service model briefly describes the services associated with each agent type. The acquaintance model captures the communication relationship among various agent types by directed graphs.

4.2   Designing MAMDAS

As the result of applying the Gaia methodology, we obtained the agent model, the service model, and the acquaintance model of MAMDAS. Tables 1 and 2 show the agent model and the service model. Figure 4 captures the acquaintance relation among agents in MAMDAS (arrows represent the communication direction).

4.3   System Overview

Based on the three concrete models obtained from the design process, we implemented the MAMDAS using IBM Aglet Workbench SDK 2.0. The MAMDAS consists of four major logical components: the host, the administrator, the thesaurus, and the user. Figure 5 illustrates the overall architecture of the MAMDAS. In order to avoid complication, we only demonstrate the most important agent types in this figure. Some assisting agents are not shown.

The MAMDAS can accommodate arbitrary number of hosts. A *HostMaster* agent resides on each host. A host can maintain any number and any type of nodes (local nodes or summary-schemas nodes) based on its resource availability. Each *NodeManager* agent monitors and manipulates a node. The HostMaster agent is in charge of all the NodeManagers on that host. Nodes are logically organized into a summary-schemas hierarchy. The system administrators have full control over the structure of the hierarchy. They can construct the structure by using the graphical tools provided by the *AdminMaster* agent. In Figure 5, the solid lines depict a possible summary-schemas hierarchy with the arrows indicating the hierarchical relation. The *ThesMaster* agent acts as an interface between the thesaurus server and other agents. The dashed lines with arrows indicate the communication between the agents. The *DataSearchMaster* agent provides a query interface, the data search window, to the user. It generates a *DataSearchWorker* agent for each query. The three dashed-dot-dot lines depict the scenario that three DataSearchWorkers are dispatched to different hosts and work concurrently.

Table 1. The agent model of MAMDAS.
(n=number of hosts in the system, m=number of nodes on a specific host).

Agent Name (Role Name)	Agent Mobility	Agent Instance Qualifier
HostMaster	Stationary	Occur n times
NodeManager	Stationary	Occur m times
NodeSynchronizer	Stationary	Occur n times
HostMessageHandler	Stationary	Occur one or more times
NodeMessenger	Mobile	Occur one or more times
AdminMaster	Stationary	Occur once
AdminMessenger	Mobile	Occur n times
ThesMaster	Stationary	Occur once
DataSearchMaster	Stationary	Occur zero or more times
DataSearchWorker	Mobile	Occur zero or more times
UserMessenger	Mobile	Occur zero or more times

Table 2. The service model of MAMDAS.

Service	Accept users queries
Inputs	Keyword, preferred semantic distance, category, starting node
Outputs	Query result
Pre-condition	The AdminMaster is ready, the ThesMaster is ready, and the summary-schemas hierarchy is ready.
Post-condition	True

The summary-schemas hierarchy building process in MAMDAS is very similar to the IB system and the enhanced IB system. Once the administrator decides the summary-schemas hierarchy, commands will be sent out to each involved NodeManager to build the structure. NodeManagers at the lower levels export their schemas to their parents. Parent nodes contact the thesaurus and generate an abstract version of their children's schemas. When this process reaches the root, the MAMDAS is ready to accept queries.

Fig. 4. The acquaintance model of MAMDAS.

The user can initiate a query by launching the DataSearchMaster agent on his/her own device, which can be a computer attached to the network or a mobile device. The DataSearchMaster sends out two *UserMessenger* agents (not shown in the figure) to the AdminMaster and the ThesMaster, respectively. The UserMessengers will return to the DataSearchMaster with the summary-schemas hierarchy and the category information. The DataSearchMaster then creates a data search window that shows the user the summary-schemas hierarchy and the tree structure of the category. The user then enters the keyword (s), specifies the preferred semantic distance, chooses a category, and selects a node to start the search. After the user clicks on the "Submit" button, the DataSearchMaster packs the inputs, creates a DataSearchWorker agent, and passes the inputs to it as parameters. Since the DataSearchMaster creates a DataSearchWorker to handle each query, the user can submit multiple queries concurrently.

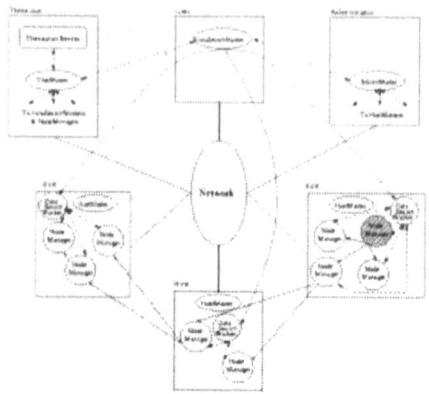

Fig. 5. An overview of the MAMDAS system architecture.

DataSearchWorkers carry the search algorithm and can migrate from host to host. Its first stop is the node designated by the user. Once dispatched, the DataSearchWorker can intelligently and independently accomplish the search task by making local decisions without the owner's interference. The search process can be described as follows:

- The DataSearchWorker contacts the NodeManager to obtain its schema, and children and parent information.
- The DataSearchWorker performs the search algorithm with the help of the ThesMaster. Note that this is the step that involves the most communication among agents.
- If there is no resolution on the current node, based on the principle of the SSM, the DataSearchWorker will conclude that there is no resolution down this sub-tree. Thus, if the current node is the root, the DataSearchWorker will return to its home (where it is created) and display "no result". If the current node is not the root, the worker agent will recursively migrate to the current node's parent and conduct the same search algorithm until it reaches the root or finds a result (assume that the DataSearchWorker does not find a solution on the current node). Another possibility is that the current node does indicate potential results. If the current node is a leaf-node, the DataSearchWorker will get all the local terms that satisfy the semantic distance and go home to display the results. In the case that the current node is a non-leaf-node, the DataSearchWorker will generate its clone for each node that may have results. To clarify the difference between the DataSearchWorker and its clones, we name the clones DataSearchSlaves even though they are essentially the same. The cloning process will happen recursively till the slaves finally reach the leaf nodes. Slaves perform the search algorithm on their destinations in parallel. To reduce unnecessary network traffic, the slaves only report the results to its originator and then die on the local host.
- When the final report reaches the DataSearchWorker, it knows that the task is done and then returns to home and display the results. After the user click on the "ok"

button or close the result display window, the DataSearchWorker will dispose itself and release all the resource it occupies.

Comparing Figure 5 with Figures 2 and 3, one can conclude that the agent-based system greatly simplifies the system architecture. It makes the system easy to maintain and use. Moreover, we expect that the reduced communication will significantly improve the average response time. Thanks to the agent's independent decision-making capability and execution autonomy, MAMDAS provides mobile users a flexible and reliable data access environment.

4.4   Optimizing the SSM Search Algorithm

According to the SSM search algorithm implemented in the IB system and the enhanced IB system, when a DataSearchWorker searches a node, it must compare each global term in the node's schema with the keyword. If the node is a local node, the user-specified semantic distance is used as the criterion to determine whether the term is of interest. If the node is a summary-schemas node, other criteria depending on the implementation can be applied to determine whether a global term indicates potential resolution or not.

Several characteristics of the SSM have drawn our attention. Observe the following facts:

- When searching a local node, the DataSearchWorker must compare each global term in the node's local-global schema in order to obtain all local terms that satisfy the user-specified semantic distance.
- When searching a summary-schemas node, the DataSearchWorker can stop as soon as it finds that all the children of the current node contains potential resolution.
- If the search on summary-schemas node A indicates that there is no resolution in this subtree, then the DataSearchWorker move to A's parent node, if a global term only exists on A (there is an entry which looks like "global term: <summary-schemas node A>"), this global term does not need to be checked. The reason is that we already know that there is no resolution on A. When the administrator organizes the summary-schemas hierarchy, naturally, he/she could prefer to cluster nodes based on their data semantics (connect nodes that contain similar contents to the same parent). Consequently, as we search down the tree, it is likely that all the children of a node have terms that are of our interest.

Based on these observations, we were able to optimize the SSM search algorithm.

- We represented the node's summary schema as a two-dimensional array with node names as row indices and global terms as column indices. If a global term's hyponym exists on a child node (as noted earlier, a summary schema's global terms are hypernyms of lower-level schemas' global terms), the corresponding array element is set to 1. Otherwise, it is set to 0. Table 3 shows an example of such array.
- By re-organizing the terms, we move the columns that have more 1's to the left. This allows us to examine more populated semantically similar data elements first. Table 4 shows the re-organization of Table 3.

As a result the search algorithm was modified as depicted in Figure 6.

Table 3. The array representation of a summary schema.

	Term$_1$	Term$_2$	Term$_3$	Term$_4$	Term$_5$	Term$_6$	Term$_7$	Term$_8$
Child$_1$	1	0	1	0	1	1	0	1
Child$_2$	0	1	0	1	0	0	0	1
Child$_3$	1	0	0	1	1	0	1	0

Assume that Term$_1$ and Term$_4$ in Table 4 indicate potential results in the subtree rooted at the current node, the DataSearchWorker only needs to make two comparisons before it proceeds to other nodes: "Term$_1$, keyword" and "Term$_4$, keyword". In contrast, the search algorithm used in the IB and the enhanced IB systems will incur 8 comparisons.

The network traffic reduction of the algorithm depends on factors such as: the structure of the summary-schemas hierarchy, the thesaurus implementation, the query distribution, etc. Thus, a quantitative measurement of the reduction is difficult. However, one thing clear is that the worst-case performance of the optimized algorithm is the same as the original search algorithm used in the other two SSM prototypes: compare every summary schema's global term with the keyword.

Table 4. Re-organization of Table 3.

	Term$_1$	Term$_4$	Term$_3$	Term$_8$	Term$_2$	Term$_5$	Term$_6$	Term$_7$
Child$_1$	1	0	1	1	0	1	1	0
Child$_2$	0	1	0	1	1	0	0	0
Child$_3$	1	1	1	0	0	0	0	1

5 Experimental Results

The MAMDAS was evaluated based on four parameters: the average response time, scalability, robustness, and portability.

5.1 Experimental Environment

We performed most of our experiments on Sun Ultra 5 workstations running Solaris 8. The machines are connected through a fast Ethernet network that supports up to 100Mbps. Some of our experiments were carried out on PCs with various processors running different versions of the Windows operating system. In general, the MAMDAS can be set up on any collection of machines that satisfy the following requirements:

1	Set all child node to be unmarked;
2	While (there exists an unexamined terms)
3	If (term is of interest)
4	Mark all the child nodes that have its hyponym term;
5	Else
6	Continue;
7	If (all the child nodes are marked)
8	break;
9	End If
10	End While
11	If (no marked child node)
12	Go to the parent node of the current node and perform the same search algorithm (if a summary schema term of the parent node only exists on the current node, we can skip this term);
13	Else
14	Create a data search slave for each marked child node;
15	Dispatch the slaves to the destinations and perform the same search algorithm;
16	End If

Fig. 6. Optimized search algorithm.

5.2 Average Response Time

We anticipate that the MAMDAS improves the average response time due to the reduced communication, application of optimized search algorithm, and its ability to exploit parallelism. Earlier research showed that the application of mobile agents improves the query response time of the IB system by a factor of 3 [13]. To demonstrate the effectiveness of the MAMDAS, we constructed the same summary-schema hierarchy as reported in [13] and conducted the same queries. Figure 7 plots the average response time of the three SSM prototypes. The result clearly shows that on the average, the MAMDAS is twice as fast as the improved IB system and 6 times faster than the IB system.

5.3 Impact of the SSM Configuration

The query response time highly depends on the SSM configuration. Therefore, how to organize the summary-schemas hierarchy should be of interest to the global DBA. Intuitively, the global DBA may apply the following configuration strategies:

- The Semantic-Aware Configuration: cluster the local databases based on their semantic contents and assign semantically similar data sources to the same entry-level summary-schemas node.

- Non-Semantic-Aware Configuration: based on the physical connectivity of the network, assign local data sources to the nearest entry-level summary-schemas nodes. As a result, there is a potential that the semantically similar data sources be distributed across the summary-schemas hierarchy.

The first strategy reduces contention at higher-level summary-schemas nodes at the expense of creating bottleneck at certain hot nodes in the network. The second approach distributes the workload among nodes and minimizes the communication distance between nodes on adjacent levels at the cost of longer search time at higher-level nodes and possible longer search path. It is a difficult task to form a well-balanced summary-schemas hierarchy and optimize the performance. The purpose of this experiment was to compare effects of the two configuration strategies and identify critical factors that affect the overall performance. The result can server as a hint to help DBAs to make configuration decisions.

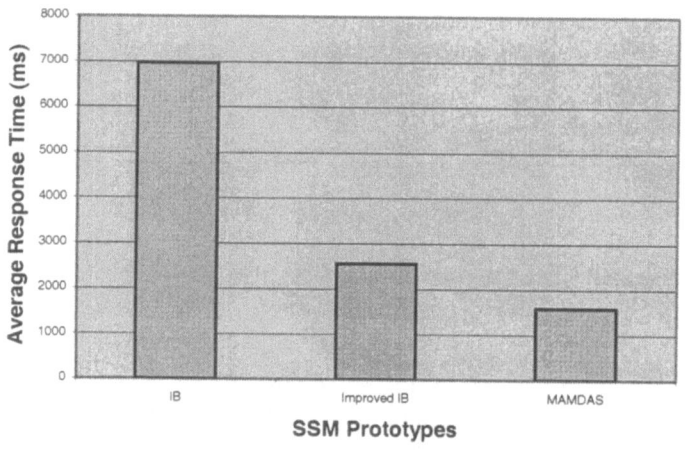

Fig. 7. Comparative response time of three SSM prototypes.

5.3.1   Semantic-Aware Configuration vs. Non-semantic-Aware Configuration

To demonstrate the impact of the aforementioned strategies, we designed two extreme cases of the two configurations: The system was composed of 1 to 7 local nodes with identical semantic contents. By manipulating the local-global schemas, we ensured that the search result exists in all local nodes but one for each simulation run and the query is always submitted to the node that does not resolve the query. The purpose is to force the agent to travel in order to find resolutions. Different SSM configurations will result in different agent travel paths. Consequently, the average response time will be different.

The Semantic-Aware Configuration assigns all nodes to the same entry-level summary-schemas node because they all have similar semantic content. The Non-Semantic-Aware Configuration creates a new path starting at the root for each newly added local node. Figure 8 illustrates structures of both configurations when the number of local nodes is 3.

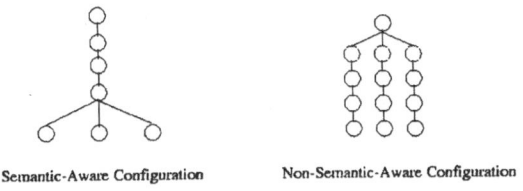

Semantic-Aware Configuration   Non-Semantic-Aware Configuration

Fig. 8. An example of Semantic-Aware and Non-Semantic-Aware configurations.

Note that when no resolution is found at the first node (we forced a search miss), in the Semantic-Aware configuration, the agent only needs to go up one level in order to find other possible resolutions. In contrast, when the Non-Semantic-Aware configuration is applied, the agent has to go all the way up to the root before it can find any other potential resolutions. After potential resolutions are identified, both configurations conduct searches in parallel. Intuitively, we anticipate that a shorter search path will demonstrate better performance. Figure 9 shows the experimental results.

As expected, the Semantic-Aware configuration outperforms the Non-Semantic-Aware configuration. However, after a closer examination of this experimental result, we noticed performance degradation when the number of local nodes searched in parallel reaches 5 (the total number of local nodes is 7). This phenomenon raises a question: from the performance point of view, is it a good idea to build wide summary-schemas hierarchy? In order to answer this question, we conducted the following experiment.

5.3.2   Scalability of Parallel Searches

From the search algorithm introduced in section 3.4 one could conclude that the query response time mainly depends on two factors, the thesaurus response time, and agent creation and migration overhead. To identify the contribution of each factor, we designed an experiment to separate the thesaurus response time from the system response time. In this experiment, the Semantic-Aware configuration was applied and the number of nodes searched in parallel ranged from 1 to 9. We also set the result to be found on every local node. All queries in this experiment are submitted to the root. Figure 10 depicts the result.

Figure 10 shows the scalability of parallel searches: for configurations with local nodes less than seven, the average response time is almost the same, regardless of the number of local nodes (note that the local nodes have the same semantic contents). A sudden increase in the response time occurs when the number of local databases grows greater than seven. The thesaurus server makes the major contribution to this performance degradation. Although the thesaurus server supports multithreading, the number of concurrent clients it can support without performance degradation is still limited. When the number reaches a certain threshold (7 in this case), the server's performance degrades dramatically. Further analysis indicates that agent cloning introduces nearly a fixed amount of overhead when agent instances increases from 1 to 10. The reason is that most part of the agent migration and execution time

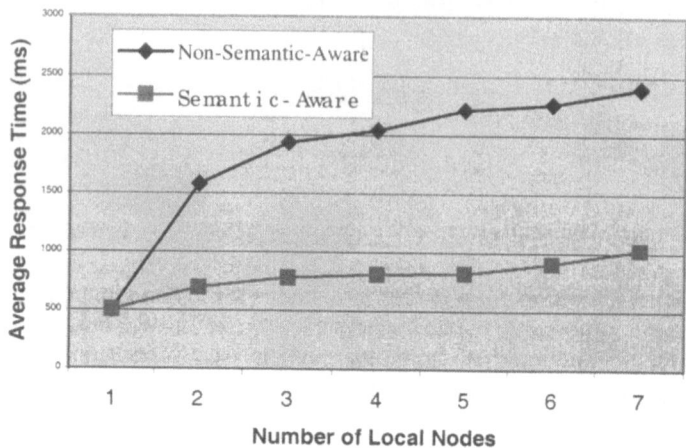

Fig. 9. Impact of SSM configurations.

is overlapped. These results suggest that, based on the present MAMDAS implementation, a fan out in the range of 3 to 5 results in a desirable summary-schemas hierarchy.

Figure 10 also implies that the optimization of the thesaurus server's performance is very important, since it contributes to almost 80% of the execution time. We will summarize the possible improvements of its performance in section 5.

5.4 Robustness and Portability

As noted before, the IB system is vulnerable to message losses and exceptions. Thus, the system is not stable and difficult to debug. The MAMDAS is much more stable than the IB system for several reasons due to the robustness of agents, the reduced communication, and good exception handling mechanism. During the course of our evaluation, we did not experience any crashes or stalls.

We intended to apply MAMDAS in a distributed environment and provide special services to mobile users. In such an environment, physical heterogeneity of the computing devices becomes a challenging issue. Thanks to the Java language's platform independent feature, our system was easily ported to any machine available to us that supported the JVM version 1.3. We successfully tested the system on PCs that run different versions of the Windows operating system without any modification.

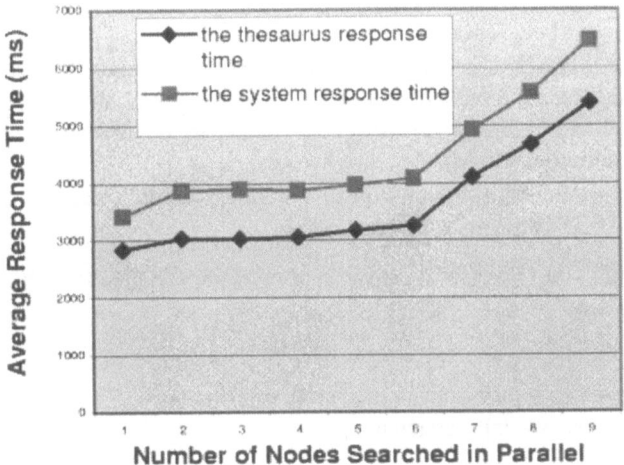

Fig. 10. The scalability of parallel searches.

6   Conclusion and Future Work

The goal of our study was to address issues in multidatabase information retrieval while providing special support for mobile users. By applying the Gaia agent-based application design methodology [14], we successfully devised and implemented the MAMDAS system – an application of Mobile Agent technology in Mobile Data Access System design. The MAMDAS chooses the SSM as its multidatabase organization model and the Java-based IBM Aglet Workbench SDK 2.0 as its implementation tool.

Our experimental results showed that MAMDAS significantly improves the average response time compared to the previous SSM prototypes. It is six times faster than the original prototype and twice as fast as the enhanced prototype. The MAMDAS demonstrated system scalability. The experimental results suggested that a reasonable width of the SSM hierarchy ranges from 3 to 5. Moreover, MAMDAS' platform-independent nature makes it an ideal choice for a distributed information retrieval system.

The scope of this research can be extended in many directions. We are intended to investigate the following issues in the future:

- The thesaurus's algorithm needs to be improved. Currently, it compares one pair of terms at a time, which means a high degree of network traffic. Naturally, the performance can be improved if the number of communications between the ThesMaster and other agents can be reduced by handling a list of query terms at a time instead of a pair of terms at a time.

- The MAMDAS uses a centralized thesaurus server. This could become a source of a bottleneck. It is possible to replicate the thesaurus and/or distribute it across the SSM. This change will significantly reduce the network traffic and hence reduces the average response time of the thesaurus. Consequently, the overall average response time will decrease.

- The current MAMDAS implementation does not take security issues into consideration. Because security is critical in a distributed environment, such issues within the scope of the software agents needs to be investigated in depth and incorporated into the MAMDAS.
- The issue of frequent disconnection in a wireless communication medium and its effect on MAMDAS needs further study.

References

1. Ara. http://wwwagss.informatik.uni-kl.de/Projekte/Ara/index_e.html
2. Beej's Guide to Network Programming.
    http://www.ecst.csuchico.edu/~beej/guide/net/html/
3. Bright, M. W., Hurson, A. R., and Pakzad, S. H. Automated resolution of semantic heterogeneity in multidatabases. *ACM Transactions on Databases Systems*, 19(2), 1994. Concordia – Mobile Agents White Paper.
4. http://www.meitca.com/HSL/Projects/Concordia/MobileAgentsWhitePaper.html
5. Crystaliz Inc, General Magic Inc., GMD FOKUS, IBM, TOG: OMG Joint Submission "Mobile Agent System Interoperability Facility", November, 1997.
6. Date, C. J. Relational Databases. Addison-Wesley, Reading, Maryland, 1986.
7. D'Atri, A. and Tarantino, L. From Browsing to Querying. *Data Engineering* 12, pp. 46-53, 1989.
8. Kotz D., Gray R., Nog S., Rus D., Chawla S., and Cybenko G. Agent tcl: Targetting the needs of mobile computing. *IEEE Internet Computing*, pages 58-67, July/August 1997.
9. IBM. *Aglets Workbench*. http://www.trl.ibm.co.jp/aglets/index.html.
10. Jiao, Y. Multidatabase Information Retrieval Using Mobile Agents. Master of Science Thesis. Department of Computer Science and Engineering, The Pennsylvania State University 2002.
11. Lange D., Oshima M. Programming and Developing Java Mobile Agents with Aglets. Addison Wesley Longman, Inc. Reading, Massachusetts, 1998.
12. Mobile Agents Bibliography. http://www.zurich.ibm.com/~spl/BibAgents.html
13. Montero G. A Mobile Agent System within the Summary Schemas Model Multidatabase. Master of Engineering paper. Department of Computer Science and Engineering, The Pennsylvania State University 2000.
14. Wooldridge M., Jennings N. R., and Kinny D. The Gaia methodology for agent-oriented analysis and design. *Journal of Autonomous Agents and Multi-Agent Systems*, 2000.
15. ObjectSpace. Voyager: ORB 3.0 Developer Guide, 1999.
    http://www.objectspace.com.
16. Odyssey Research Associates. http://www.atc-nycorp.com.

Using Agent Control and Communication in a Distributed Workflow Information System

M. Brian Blake

Department of Computer Science, Georgetown University, 234 Reiss Science Building,
Washington, DC 20057
blakeb@cs.georgetown.edu

Abstract. Agent communication has developed widely over the past decade for various types of multiple agent environments. Originally, most of this research surrounded simulation systems and inference systems. Subsequently, agents are expected to adapt to, dynamically create, and understand evolving conversation policies. This concept of agent communication is not completely necessary in some domains, especially in domains where the policy of interaction is essentially static. One such domain is that of distributed workflow management with implications into Electronic Commerce. In this domain, agents are "middle-agents" that represent the distributed components that implement each individual workflow step. By representing the component-based services of each step, multiple distributed agents can essentially manage a workflow or supply chain that spans several on-line businesses (B2B). The WARP (Workflow-Automation through Agent-Based Reflective Processes) architecture is a multi-agent architecture developed to support distributed workflow management environments where distributed components are used to implement each of the workflow steps. This paper describes a software engineering process for integrating new component-based services into a static workflow-based ontology. Furthermore, the interaction protocol and supporting implementation based on the Knowledge Query and Manipulation Language (KQML) are presented. This agent communication architecture is implemented with the latest in Sun MicroSystems' Jini technology.

Keywords. Object-oriented Ontology, Agent Communication, Workflow Management

1 Introduction

Electronic markets are becoming increasingly popular with higher expectations in the future. Many business interactions occurring over the Internet follow either workflow or supply chain models. Moreover, some on-line businesses are adopting the use of components to implement their services. Currently, components are being designed and developed with greater modularity. Independent components can fulfill substantial tasks in these on-line environments. On-line transactions occur both across distributed servers within a single company's intranet as well as across multiple companies via the Internet (sometimes considered business-to-business or B2B [1]).

R. Meersman, Z. Tari (Eds.): CoopIS/DOA/ODBASE 2002, LNCS 2519, pp. 163–178, 2002.

Subsequently, transactions are no longer the interaction of human-controlled business modules, these transactions are defined more by the configuration and coordination of independent components, regardless of where they are housed. When these transactions interact using workflow or supply chain paradigms, there must first be some way to designate policy information and secondly some architecture to sequentially invoke the independent components as dictated by that policy.

The WARP architecture was conceptualized to operate in this environment specifically where on-line workflow enactment consists of the coordination distributed components [2, 4]. The WARP architecture uses a two-phased approach. In the first phase, the WARP architecture has semi-automated functionality where humans interact with workflow manager agents in the process of designing a workflow schema. In the second phase *relevant to this paper*, multiple agents collaborate to manage a workflow of on-line distributed components. Essentially, this is an approach that uses an agent-based middleware layer to coordinate internet-based workflow. One example might be an on-line stock purchasing scenario that requires the workflow coordination of an on-line broker, an on-line trader, and an on-line banker. Each of these on-line businesses may have independent components to perform such tasks as collection of customer requests, stock trade, and payment services, respectively. WARP role agents can act as proxies for the components located at the distributed sites of the independent companies. These agents collaborate on the pre-determined workflow schema to manage the interaction among the components. A high-level architecture in context of the on-line stock-purchasing domain is shown in Figure 1.1.

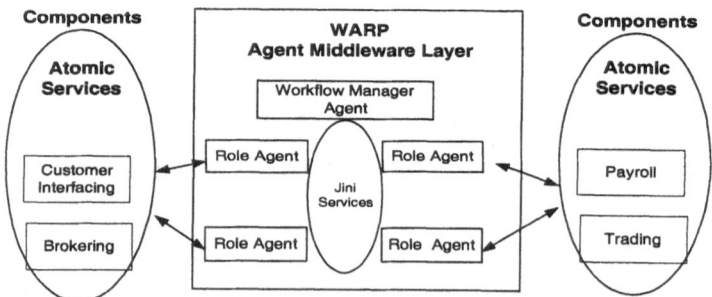

Fig. 1.1. The Agent Middleware Phase: WARP Architecture

The main focus of this paper is the communication among the role agents as a component of the workflow coordination of the distributed component-based services. This research uses a "tuple-spaces" (as first seen in the Linda project [10]) approach to communication among a group of agents. The implementation makes use of Sun Microsystem's implementation of tuple-spaces, Java Spaces. This implementation also uses the reflective capabilities in the Java programming language. The architecture is built on JavaBean component-based services. Hereafter this approach to agent communication will be referred to as KOJAC (KQML over Jini for Agent

Communication). To clarify, WARP is the overall agent architecture for the workflow enactment, while KOJAC is the protocol and software underlying WARP that handles agent communication and interaction. This paper continues in the subsequent sections with a brief background of agent communication. Next there is a brief overview of the WARP architecture. The following sections discuss the ontology and software engineering approach to KOJAC that provides communication within the WARP system. The final sections discuss the actual agent communication architecture and results.

2   Agent Communication and Electronic Commerce

This approach to agent communication gets its origins from KQML. This section gives an introduction of that part of KQML and other agent communication efforts that are pertinent to this work.

2.1 Correlation with KQML

The motivation for KQML [15, 16] was to formalize a method by which agents can communicate effectively and efficiently. The message format supplies the agent with knowledge of which agent it is communicating to, a protocol for establishing dialogue, the language by which agents are communicating, terms by which other agents will interpret expressions, and exception handling. It is not within the scope of this paper to cover the KQML specification in entirety but to introduce the portions of the protocol that may assist later interpretations

KQML is separated into 3 layers, content, message and communication layers. The content layer allows agents to communicate which language is going to be used in a particular message. The message layer contains the message to be communicated in the form of content messages and declaration messages. The final layer is the communication layer, which exchanges packages to specify communication attributes. The message layer is of importance to us. The message layer, more specifically in content messages, is what is emulated in this work. Performatives are specialized KQML message types. The specification of a performative can increase system-wide transactions and functionality. In later sections, the KOJAC approach presented in this paper will be used to implement a subset of the common reserved performatives [15] as in Table 2.1.

Table 2.1. A Subset of Reserved Performatives

Category	*Name*
Basic query	ask-one, ask-all
Generic Informational	tell-one, tell-all
Capability-definition	advertise, subscribe, monitor
Networking	register

2.2 Other Relevant Agent Communication Efforts

Over the last decade, there have been several efforts to create a data format that is acceptable to all software environments. The most notable effort is the work developing the Extensible Markup Language (XML). Currently, XML is the best choice for a language for representing data across multiple platforms. As described in the previous section, KQML has been used to represent data in agent communication. However, KQML uses a Lisp-based text representation that is not widely accepted for business transactions. If agents are to be used in electronic commerce, there is a need for a consolidation of the accepted industry-based representations like XML and the languages that the agents can understand. The latest research trends in agent communication have taken it one step further. Currently there has been the creation of an *Agent Communication Markup Language (ACML)*, which combines the traditional agent communication concepts of KQML with the industry acceptable universal format of XML [12]. Underlying the ACML is the Business Rule Markup Language (BRML). BRML is the B2B-specific content language [13].

The Foundation of Physical Agents (FIPA) has specifications for interaction protocols, communicative acts, and content messages for agent communication [8]. KQML is a subset of both the complexity and completeness of these specifications. Early in the project, we decided that the interaction protocols of KQML presented enough functionality to support this workflow-based communication. In future efforts, there is a plan to further evaluate the benefits of the evolving FIPA standards. Moreover, this research is toward implementation-level approaches to agent communication. The goal is toward the connection of agent implementation practices and those currently accepted in industry. This work has set the foundation for upcoming work that unites KOJAC with ACML-type approaches. In our most recent research, XML-based schema formats are translated into the object ontology and vice versa. Furthermore, software objects can be constructed based on individual XML documents by which agents can use for communication. The goal of this research is toward the consolidation of agents and electronic market software systems development.

3 Background of WARP

The approach to automated compositional configuration is called Workflow Automation through Agent-Based Reflective Processes (WARP). This approach is based on the use of an agent-based middleware architecture here after called the WARP architecture. This WARP architecture consists of software agents that can be configured to control the workflow operation of distributed services. The WARP architecture is divided into two layers. These layers are the application coordination layer and the automated configuration layer.

The application coordination layer is the level in which the workflow instances are instantiated and the actual workflow execution occurs. The application coordination layer consists of two agents, the Role Manager Agent (RMA) and the Workflow Manager Agent (WMA). The RMAs have knowledge of a specific workflow role. The WMA has knowledge of the workflow policy and applicable roles. When a new process is configured, the workflow policy is saved in a centralized database. The RMA plays a role in the workflow execution by fulfilling one or more services as defined by the workflow policy in the centralized database. The RMA registers for workflow step-level events in the event server based on its predefined role. When an initiation event is written into the event server, the RMA is notified. Subsequently based on its localized knowledge of services and its workflow role, the RMA invokes the correct service. The WMA has similar functionality, but instead registers for overall workflow level events (i.e. workflow initiation and nonfunctional concerns). The WMA does not control the workflow execution, but in some cases it adds events to bring about non-functional changes to the execution of the entire workflow.

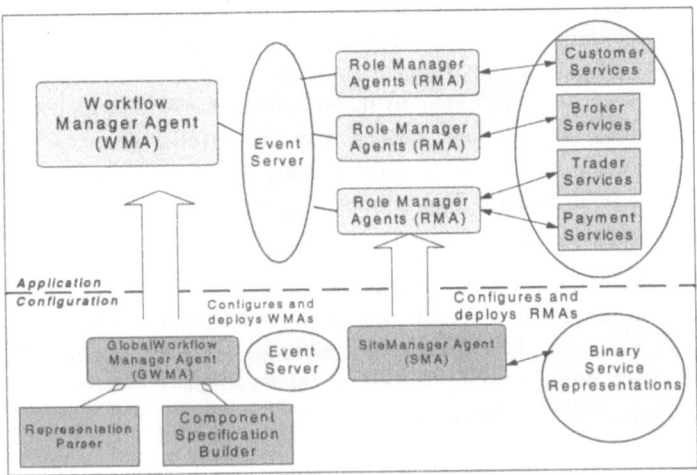

Fig. 3.1. The WARP Architecture.

At the automated configuration layer, agents accept new process specifications and deploy application coordination layer agents with the new corresponding policy. This layer consists of the Site Manager Agents (SMA) and the Global Workflow Manager Agent (GWMA). The GWMA accepts workflow representations from a workflow designer as input. The SMAs discover available services and provides service representations to the GWMAs. The GWMAs accept both of these inputs and writes the workflow policy to the centralized database. The GWMA then configures and deploys WMAs to play certain aspect-oriented roles. At the completion of workflow-level configuration, the SMA configures and deploys RMAs to play each of the roles specified in the workflow database. A general view of the WARP process is shown in Figure 3.1.

The application coordination layer is where the agent communication occurs (pertinent to this paper). To consider this operational environment, again let's use the on-line stock-purchasing domain (Figure 1.1.). A configured WARP system would have a Role Manager Agent (RMA) for each of the roles. RMAs act as middle agents [6] for components. The RMAs obtain system aspects of the component through introspection and are able to invoke component functions through the process of reflection. The three roles are the Customer Interface Role, the Broker Role, and Trading Role. There is a RMA for each role. There is one Workflow Manager Agent (WMA) that helps in the coordination of the entire workflow. Each RMA would subscribe for service completion events prior to their affiliated services. For example, the Broker (Portfolio Management) Role would monitor for the completion event of a getTradeRequest service. Suppose a customer invokes the getTradeRequest service. The Customer Interface RMA would receive a completion event from the component (actor) and would broadcast the pertinent data for this service completion. The RMA for the Broker Role would be notified of this completion. First it would check to see if this service is pertinent to any of its workflow policy responsibilities. If so, the RMA for Broker Role would wait for the ready event to be written to the server by the WMA. The WMA would have also been monitoring and notified of the getTradeRequest service completion. The WMA would post any amendments to the workflow based on nonfunctional concerns at the process level. Subsequently, the WMA would publish a ready event to the pertinent RMA. Through reflection, the RMA would invoke the proper service (searchPortfolio service) for this step (reflection) in the workflow policy. Subsequently the output data, and the service completion would be broadcast. This process sequence is shown in Figure 3.2 for the stock purchase process.

KOJAC is the approach to agent communication needed to manage the sequence of actions described in Figure 3.2. Agents must be able to understand service completions in addition to have the knowledge of resulting actions. Agents also need to communicate other nonfunctional workflow management concerns like exception-handling, atomicity, and performance.

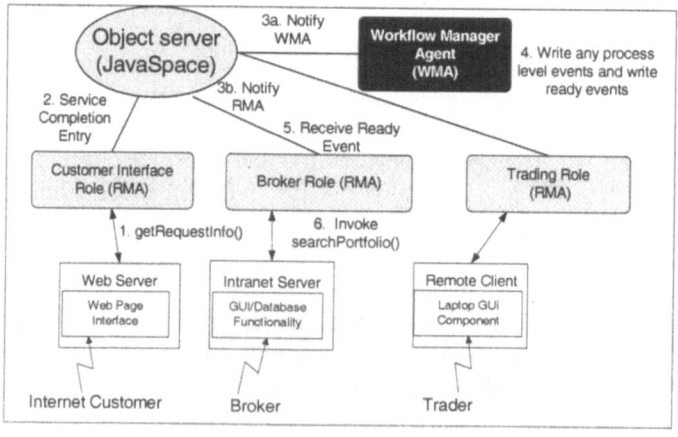

Fig. 3.2. WARP Operational Environment

4   The Static Workflow-Oriented Ontology

The agent communication in this domain relies very heavily on the concepts of workflow management. In fact, the communication protocols used in the approach are built on a workflow-based ontology. In the following section, the pertinent workflow terminology is defined. Subsequently, there are technical details of the workflow-based object-oriented ontology.

4.1 Workflow Terminology

The workflow language here follows mainstream workflow terminology used presently by researchers [17]. In order to set the nomenclature for further discussion, the following set of definitions are adhered to throughout this paper.

- A *task* is the atomic work item that is a part of a process.
- A task is implemented with a *service.*
- An *actor* or resource is a person or machine that performs a task by fulfilling a service.
- A *role* abstracts a set of tasks into a logical grouping.
- A *process* is a customer-defined business process represented as a list of tasks.
- A *workflow* (instance) is a process that is bound to particular resources that fulfill the process.

4.2 The Workflow-Based Object-Oriented Ontology

The object-oriented ontology is a shared knowledge-based among agents. This solution is practical in the context of object-oriented domain analysis [11], since agents reason about a particular domain when they communicate. E-market designers can use traditional object-oriented analysis and design techniques to construct a domain model using object-oriented structural diagrams [14]. This domain model later translates into a physical set of classes. Objects from these domain classes are later specialized to particular types of Jini/JavaSpace entry objects. This is discussed in greater detail in the operational semantics of KOJAC in 6.2.

The first implementation of KOJAC is for the WARP agents. WARP agents communicate based on a domain that considers workflow policy, roles, services, and data flow. This business process-based ontology is reusable across most Emarket domains that implement a workflow of distributed components. The static view of the workflow-based ontology is illustrated in Figure 4.1. The workflow policy is the heart of this ontology. Agents that coordinate component-based services first need to know the workflow policy. Each step in the workflow policy correlates to a role and the completion of a specific service. Each service has one or more parameters (pre-conditions) or return values (post-conditions). The workflow policy further defines the subset of parameter and returns that are populated between each individual step as a dataflow. The reason for defining data flow is because one service may return more information than the subsequent service requires. Also, multiple concurrent services may proceed a single service. In this case, a combination of returns from multiple services would precede the subsequent service.

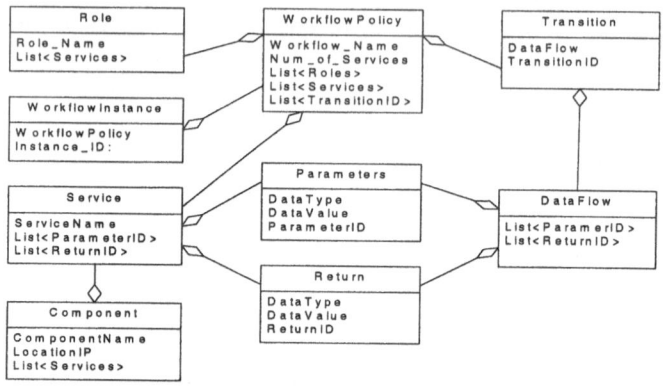

Fig. 4.1. Workflow-based Object-Oriented Ontology

5 A Software Engineering Development Approach

A common second step in object-oriented analysis and design is translating the object-oriented domain model into a software design model. In this translation, implementation classes (classes that only pertain to the software implementation domain) are added to the model such as servers, queues, stacks, etc. Also, some domain classes are translated into "proxy" classes (i.e. software classes that represent domain entities). Furthermore, some domain classes are directly transferred to the software design model. The software design model is the basis for the software implementation and development.

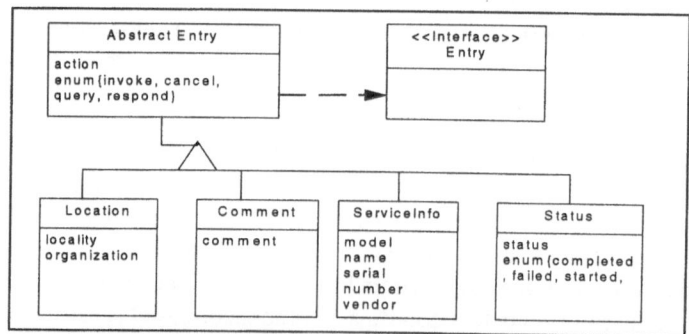

Fig. 5.1. Hierarchy of KOJAC-specific Jini Classes

KOJAC specifically isolates the original domain and proxy class implementations. The agents use the software implementations of these classes for communication. In order to facilitate this process, the software designer needs to specialize these classes to the specific set of abstract classes that adds additional communication based information. These set of abstract classes, we take from the set of classes defined in the Jini API that support JavaSpace functionality. JavaSpace communication relies heavily on the instantiation and use of objects that either implement *Entry* interfaces or subclass the *AbstractEntry* class. These objects can be written, taken, read or notified in the JavaSpace server. Jini further specializes these Entry classes. These derived classes are *Address, Comment, Location, Name, ServiceInfo, ServiceType,* and *Status*. The structural view of the Entry classes is shown in Figure 5.1. In some cases, the KOJAC approach adds another layer of specialization to include some functionality that was not included in Jini's set of specializations. For example, the native AbstractEntry class does not have an action attribute. So, this attribute was added so this class would be more consistent with the WARP workflow environment. As this idea of agent communication expands into other domains, other additions may have to be made to the native Jini classes.

In order to incorporate the domain and proxy classes with KOJAC, the designer must specialize those classes with the pertinent Entry class. If the software development process incorporates the use of Rational Rose, these specializations can be easily made with a few keystrokes. Finally, these agent communication-specific set of classes with the new specializations are compiled into a Java package. This package acts as the shared ontology for the agents. In the run-time environment, agents will reflectively access this ontology using introspection and reflection as defined in the Java development environment. The KOJAC-specific steps as they relate to a typical software development life-cycle is illustrated in Figure 5.2.

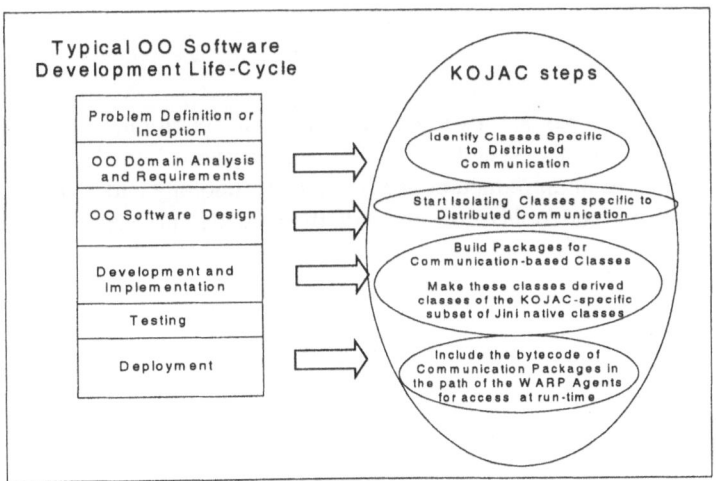

Fig. 5.2. KOJAC Steps Integrated with the Software Life-Cycle

KOJAC in the WARP Environment
In order for KOJAC to work in the WARP environment, the classes in Figure 4.1 were used as the distributed communication based classes. These workflow-oriented

classes should derive from the native Jini classes illustrated in 5.1. The WARP approach translates the domain classes illustrated in Figure 4.1 to be derived of Jini classes. In Figure 5.3, we use stereotype notation (i.e. << >>) to show from which of Jini-based classes that each of the workflow-oriented classed are derived. The Service, Parameter, Return, DataFlow, and Transition are all Status Entry classes that get passed among the RMAs and WMAs. The Component class is a Location Entry class because it reveals the location of the components that the RMAs will be invoking. Roles, WorkflowPolicy, and WorkflowInstance classes are ServiceInfo Entry classes. Interpretations of the type of Entry Classes will vary from domain to domain. Later discussions of the JavaSpace will show how sub-classing the domain classes is important for object matching.

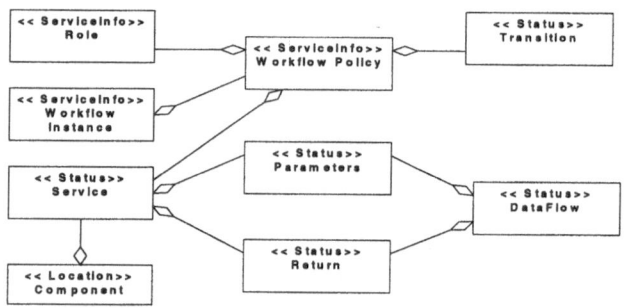

Fig. 5.3. Entry Class Specializations for the WARP Ontology

6   KOJAC

The KOJAC approach has a set of semantics and an operational environment that extensively incorporates the operations of Sun Microsystems' JavaSpace technology [5]. This section gives an introduction of JavaSpace technology and then describes the operational semantics and tools associated with the KOJAC approach.

6.1 Using Jini / JavaSpace Technology

Jini technology is a suite of services developed by Sun Microsystems that provide a simple substrate for distributed computing [7]. Jini supports most common principles surrounding distributed coordination (i.e. remote objects, leasing, transactions, and distributed events). It is not in the scope of this paper to give an in-depth description of Jini but to describe those services that are used for agent communication, specifically JavaSpaces [9]. JavaSpace technology is based on "TupleSpaces". Tuplespaces, first introduced in the context of the "Linda" project in 1982, allows distributed software processes to communicate autonomously. The tuplespace emulates a data storage server. The server receives entries from independent components and stores them for retrieval. Exterior components can be notified when an entry of a certain pattern or tuple is entered. Components can also read and take matching entries based on a tuple-based pattern they submit. Though JavaSpaces technology was motivated by tuplespace, it is slightly different. JavaSpaces is an "object" storing service. It supports read, write, take, and notify on actual software objects. A few basic JavaSpaces interactions are illustrated in Figure 6.1. Distributed components can register to a JavaSpaces server. Distributed component A can request notification when a test object is inserted into the server as in step 1. When that test object is written into the server by component B, component A will receive an event notification. Component C can read the test object and receive a copy, while component D takes the test object and removes it from the server.

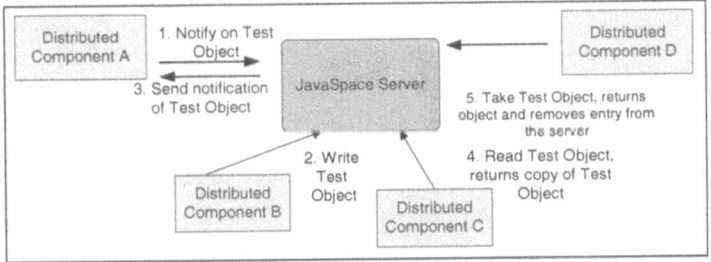

Fig. 6.1. Basic JavaSpace Functions

6.2 KOJAC:Operational Semantics

KOJAC's interaction protocols are based on a subset of the reserved KQML performatives from Table 2.1 using the WARP environment as an example. It is not the intent to detail all possible interactions but more to show how typical interactions would occur.

Let's consider the scenario when an agent registers its interest. An agent can *register and subscribe* by connecting (Line 1) to the JavaSpace server and setting notify commands for all entries that it is interested in. For example, a Broker (Portfolio Management) RMA as in Figure 3.2 would first connect to the JavaSpace server, then it would set notifications for Status entries (Service Class) on services that it can perform. This will enable notifications to be sent to that agent when there are status messages pertinent to its services. Also, the Broker RMA would set notifications for ServiceInfo entries (Workflow Instance Class) that include services that it encapsulates (Line 8,9,14, and 15). Therefore, when an WMA distributes new workflow instances that contains a service that can be fulfilled by the Broker RMA, then that agent is notified. The Java-based syntax to register is detailed in Figure 6.2. This code shows hard-coded service names for demonstration only, however in operational environments this information is dynamically imported from a relational database.

An agent can *tell-all* or *broadcast* a message with the JavaSpace write command. All agents interested in certain information would have naturally subscribed to that type of message as above. After an agent issues the write command all interested agents would be notified by the JavaSpace server. These are just a few performatives that were implemented using Jini/Javaspace technology.

```
[1] // Get reference to Javaspace Server
[2] JavaSpace SpaceWARP = (JavaSpace)rh.proxy();

[3] //Instantiate Status Entry
[4] this_Service = new Service();
[5] Service.ServiceName = "searchPortfolioInfo";
[6] // Other fields are set to null (WILDCARDS)
[7] // Instantiate ServiceInfo
[8] this_WFInstance = new WorkflowInstance();
[9] this_WFInstance.Service = "searchPortfolioInfo";

[10] // Notify on Service
[11] EventRegistration thisReg =
[12] SpaceWARP.notify(thisService, null, null,Lease.ANY, null);

[13] // Notify on WFInstance
[14] EventRegistration thisReg =
[15] SpaceWARP.notify(thisWFInstance, null, null,Lease.ANY,null);
```

Fig. 6.2. Java-based Syntax that Implements KOJAC's JavaSpace Functionality

6.3 KOJAC Components

KOJAC consists of a set of object-oriented tools that can be integrated with the Java-based agents to assist in using the JavaSpace and Jini's Entry classes. This toolkit can be incorporated into the agent communication functionality or it can be called remotely through Java Remote Method Invocation (RMI). The component diagram for the KOJAC tools is detailed in Figure 6.3.

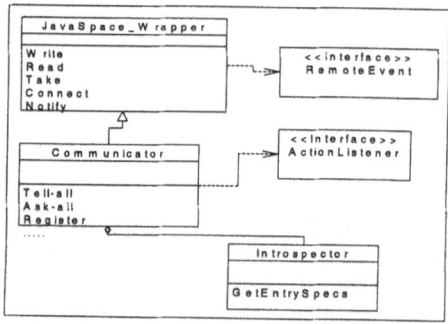

Fig. 6.3. KOJAC Component Diagram

The KOJAC architecture consists of a Communicator class The KOJAC architecture consists of a Communicator class that inherits function ality from a JavaSpace_wrapper. The JavaSpace_wrapper class implements all of the native JavaSpace commands. The Introspector class looks into the ontology-based package to construct entries used by the Communicator class. The Communicator class also brokers events between the JavaSpace server and the agents.

When a component completes a service, it fires a completion event. The completion event is captured by the RMA. Since the WARP agents are workflow-based, they contain internal intelligence mapping workflow-based events to agent communication actions. This mapping would be different in different domains and would have to be incorporated in the agents of that domain. The RMA classifies the event as a completion. The RMA invokes the Tell-all method from within the Communicator class as in Figure 6.2. Communicator incorporates the Introspector class within its Tell-all functionality. The Introspector searches the ontology-based package (Java bytecode) for an entry class that has the same name as the completed service. The introspected class is returned and the action field is populated as a completion. Finally, the inherited write function (from JavaSpace_wrapper parent class) is called with introspected class as a parameter.

7   KOJAC Prototype

A prototype of the WARP architecture was implemented using 3 Dell workstations [1]. One workstation containing the WMA was contained on a Dell Workstation running Windows NT Server 4.0. This workstation was running Apache's Tomcat webserver and contained an Oracle 8i relational database. This workstation also contained Sun Microsystems' JavaSpace server. Two other Dell Workstations, running Windows 98 were connected as peers to the initial workstation. The peer workstations each contained RMAs. This environment was used to simulate the workflow coordination of distributed components. Each peer-level workstation contained several JavaBean components that acted as the underlying services in this prototypical workflow management scenario. The aforementioned operational environment is illustrated in Figure 7.1. Early results from the WARP architecture showed that there is a high degree of overhead when reflectively invoking the component-based services, specifically with large numbers of concurrent workflow instances. The WARP architecture dynamically accesses and invokes JavaBean components that are available on Java's RMI registry. Major overhead is associated with the introspection of components that are registered on that registry as opposed to components that are on the local disk. However, since the bytecode for the communication-based ontology is local to the WARP agents, the communication classes do not have to be registered on the registry and reflection occurs locally. These interactions do not cause a great deal of overhead even with a large number of concurrent workflow instances being executed. However, a future expectation is to distribute the agent communication knowledge to prevent maintaining multiple copies. This would entail including the agent communication byte code on the registry, which is clearly a potential problem

176   M.B. Blake

for future research in addition to being a problem widely known in the area of distributed object management.

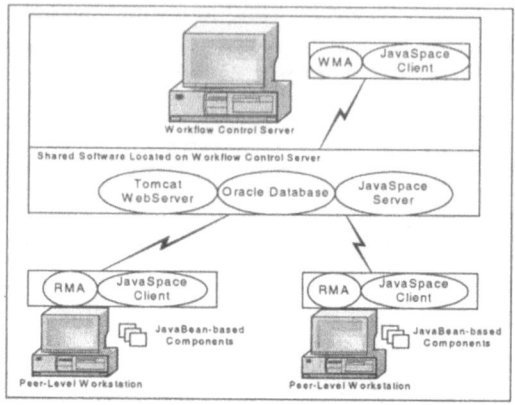

Fig. 7.1. KOJAC/WARP Prototype Environment

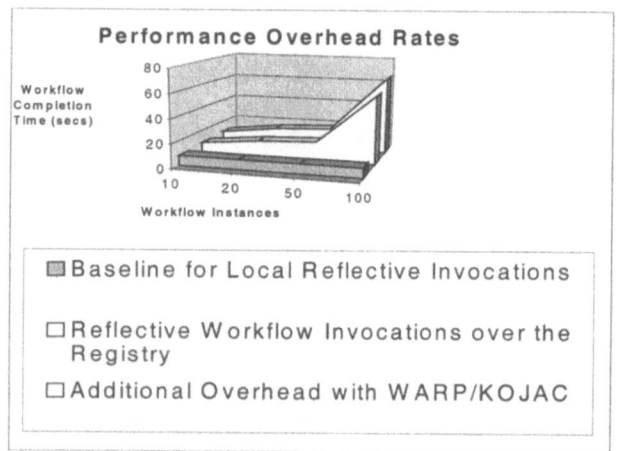

Fig. 7.2. Performance Overhead Rates

Three important performance measurements are shown in Figure 7.2. The first measurement baselines the performance when a workflow of components (10 JavaBean components) are invoked locally through reflection (this is without WARP/KOJAC). This performance can be measured with differing numbers of concurrent workflows (i.e. workflow instances are initiated instantaneously). The workflow completion time in this case was almost consistently ~8.5 seconds. The second performance measurement shows the same circumstances as the first, however the components are invoked reflectively from a registry. This added substantial overhead as mentioned above. Finally, the final measurements contain all of the dynamic management ability of the WARP/KOJAC architecture as a workflow of components are reflectively invoked over a registry. Outside of the overhead associated with reflection, WARP/KOJAC only adds an additional 15%. This 15% rate is consistent as workflow instances vary from 10 to 100.

8   Discussion and Future Work

This paper suggests an approach to agent communication that implements KQML semantics using Jini services. Two main focuses in specifying an implementation for agent communication languages are developing a standard suite of APIs that support message transfer and an infrastructure of services that support basic facilitation services [16]. The problem with this currently is that there are many different implementations that tend to deviate from the semantics. KOJAC standardizes an implementation by integrating a standard ACL into a known set of tools and services. By using the primitive structures and functions, other agent-based developers using Java-based technologies can incorporate the same semantics. By using Jini services, agent communication inherits common distributed programming features by default. This use also enforces the standardization of the agent communication semantics.

This approach integrates well with current software development lifecycles as the Rational Unified Process (RUP) [14]. In fact, tools implementing RUP can automatically generate the source code that is used as the agent communication ontology. Using bytecode as a method for storing agent communication knowledge makes a useful connection between software development processes and agent integration. In addition, this approach fits seamlessly with current distributed event-based development tools like Jini. However, this research has proven that with the distribution of this bytecode across networks and among separate networks, there is a huge amount of performance overhead. This overhead may even suggest that this approach may be impractical when large numbers of components are distributed among multiple networks.

Consequently, performance results in this work have opened avenues for future research. Initially, we plan to investigate other architectures that may efficiently support this approach to agent communication. Another area of research is storing the ontology in XML schema or even ACML schema. This research would be promising in making a connection to other relevant agent communication efforts. The best connection would be the translation of the agent ontology from the KOJAC software design steps illustrated in Figure 4.3 directly to XML/ACML-based semantics. Finally, communicative acts should be modeled using FIPA-ACL semantics.

References

[1]   Blake, M.B. " B2B Electronic Commerce: Where do Agents Fit In? ", Proceedings at the AAAI-2002 Workshop on Agent Technologies for B2B E-Commerce/AAAI Press, Edmonton, Alberta, Canada, July 28, 2002

[2]   Blake, M.B. "WARP: Workflow Automation through Agent-Based Reflective Processes", *Proceedings at the 5th International Conference on Autonomous Agents*, Montreal, Canada, May 2001 (software demonstration)

[3]   Blake, M.B. Rule-Driven Coordination Agents: A Self-Configurable Architecture, *Proceedings of the 5th International Symposium on Autonomous Decentralized Systems (ISADS2001)*, Dallas, TX, IEEE Computer Society Press, March 2001

[4]   Blake, M.B. WARP: An Agent-Based Process and Architecture for Workflow-Oriented Distributed Component Configuration. *Proceedings of the 2000 International Conference of Artificial Intelligence*, Las Vegas, NV, June 2000

[5]   Blake, M.B., KOJAC: Implementing KQML with Jini to Support Agent-Based Communications in Emarkets, AAAI-2000 Workshop on Knowledge-based Electronic Markets (KBEM2000) (AAAI Press, Technical Report WS-00-04) Austin, TX, August 2000

[6]   Decker, K., Sycara, K., and Williamson, M. Middle Agents for the Internet, *In the Proceedings of the 15th International Joint Conference on Artificial Intelligence*, Nagoya, Japan.

[7]   Edwards, K. *Core Jini*. Upper Saddle River, N.J.: Prentice Hall 1999

[8]   FIPA Interaction Protocol Specification(2002), http:// www.fipa.org/repository/ips.html

[9]   Freeman, E., Hupfer, S., and Arnold, K. JavaSpaces Principles, Patterns, and Practice, Reading, MA.:Addison Wesley 1999

[10] Gelernter, D. Generative Communication in Linda. *ACM Transactions on Programming Languages and Systems*, Vol. 7, No. 1, pp. 80-112 1985

[11] Gomaa H and Kerschberg, L. An Evolutionary Domain Life Cycle Model for Domain Modeling and Target System Generation, *In Proceedings of the Workshop on Domain Modeling for Software Engineering, International Conference on Software Engineering,* Austin, TX 1997

[12] Grosof, B. and Labrou, Y., An Approach to using XML and a Rule-based Content Language with an Agent Communication Language, IJCAI-99 Workshop on Agent Communication Languages, Stockholm, Germany 1999

[13] Grosof, B., Labrou,Y. and Chan, H. "A Declarative Approach to Business Rules in Contracts: Courteous Logic Programs in XML. Proceedings of the 1st ACM Conference on Electronic Commerce (EC-99) Denver, Colorado: ACM Press, 1999.

[14] Krutchen, P. The Rational Unified Process: An Introduction (2nd Ed.). Prentice Hall, 2000

[15] Labrou, Y. and Finin,T. A semantics approach for KQML – a general purpose communication language for software agents. *Proceedings of the Third International Conference on Information and Knowledge Management (CIKM-94)*, Gaithersburg, MD 1994

[16] Labrou, Y., Finin, T. and Peng, Y. "The current landscape of Agent Communication Languages", *Intelligent Systems*, 14(2): IEEE Computer Society 1999

[17] Lei, K. and Singh, M. A Comparison of Workflow Metamodels, Proceedings of the ER-97 Workshop on Behavioral Modeling and Design Transformations: Issues and Opportunities in Conceptual Modeling, Los Angeles, CA 1995

An Extended Alternating-Offers Bargaining Protocol for Automated Negotiation in Multi-agent Systems

Pinata Winoto, Gordon McCalla, and Julita Vassileva

Dept. of Computer Science, University of Saskatchewan
Saskatoon, SK, S7N 1L7, Canada
piw410@mail.usask.ca, {mccalla, jiv}@cs.usask.ca

Abstract. This paper focuses on the study of bilateral bargaining protocol for competitive agents within the context of automated negotiation. Some modifications are proposed to improve the classical alternating-offers bargaining model and corresponding experimentation is designed to study the advantages/ disadvantages of this modified bargaining.

1 Introduction

Negotiation in multi-agent system (MAS) is one of the most active research areas in MAS. For instance, approximately 19% of the full papers accepted in the AAMAS 2002 conference, which is the most prestigious conference in MAS, are related to negotiation. And 7 out of 16 agent-related papers in the AAAI/IAAI 2000 conference and 13 out of 27 agent-related papers in IJCAI 2001 are also related to negotiation in MAS. This is a relatively fast growing research area since it only accounted for 6% of all agent-related papers indexed in BibTeX up to 1997. In the early 1990s, the role of negotiation in MAS was to solve conflicts of interest among agents during task allocation in distributed problem solving and resource allocation among agents. However, with the birth of e-commerce in the mid 1990s, the study of negotiation became broader, especially the study of open electronic marketplaces where humans can delegate their agents to negotiate with other agents. This paper will focus on one of the negotiation mechanisms used in e-commerce: bargaining.

Bargaining is among the oldest negotiation mechanisms in human history, even before the emergence of market or money as a means of finding a resolution among interested parties in the presence of conflicts of interest (cooperative behavior in a competitive situation). Basically, there are three elements as a prerequisite for bargaining: bargainers, conflict(s) and protocol. The protocol will tell the bargainers about how they can resolve the conflict, such as when the bargaining start or end, who move first and next, what kind of information allowed in exchange, etc. However, there is no guarantee for the existence of solution(s). In section 2, after some brief description of automated negotiation mechanisms the conditions for the existence of solution(s) will be studied. Some modifications to the standard alternating-offer bargaining protocol (and their advantages) are described in section 3. Finally, some conclusions will be derived in section 4.

R. Meersman, Z. Tari (Eds.): CoopIS/DOA/ODBASE 2002, LNCS 2519, pp. 179–194, 2002.
© Springer-Verlag Berlin Heidelberg 2002

2   Automated Negotiation

2.1   Negotiation Mechanisms

A negotiation can be classified in many ways, based on the items being negotiated, the character of the negotiators, the negotiation protocol, the characteristics of information (completeness and symmetry), the negotiation period (continuous, one-step, multiple stage), and other factors (openness, with penalty, etc). Based on the negotiated items, negotiation could be differentiated into negotiation of single-attribute items or multiple-attribute items. An example of a multiple-attribute item is when negotiators consider price, quantity, quality, delivery time, and payment methods as a bundle. Moreover, negotiation can be categorized into one-to-one, one-to-many, or many-to-many negotiations. An English auction for antiques is a one-to-many negotiation (one auctioneer and many bidders), for example. Generally, a negotiator represents an individual/groups of individuals with specific/common goal(s). If a group of individuals is considered, it should take a single collective action or decision at any time and the negotiation results apply to all members of group. For example, the result of collective bargaining between workers and a company would apply to all workers.

Based on the character of the negotiators, a negotiation can be classified as cooperative or competitive. Cooperative negotiation is characterized by aiming for mutual social benefit (maximizing joint utility) for the negotiators. And competitive negotiation is characterized by seeking individual benefit for the negotiators (maximizing individual utility). Negotiation among agents in distributed problem solving usually falls into the former category, while negotiation in e-commerce falls into the latter. With the growth of various services in e-commerce, the trade of services among unknown problem solvers becomes possible. For instance, our agent might pay $10 to an agent from the US for estimating the NASDAQ stock index next week, and pay another $10 to another agent from Hong Kong for estimating the Hangseng stock index next week, and so on, in order to help in financial planning.

Depending on the protocol type, a negotiation can be categorized as an auction, a contract-net protocol, voting or bargaining. Some examples of well-known auction types in MAS are English auction, Dutch auction, double auction, first-price sealed-bid auction and Vickrey auction. English auction, Dutch auction and double auction are characterized by sequential decision making and open-bid. First-price sealed-bid auction and Vickrey auction are characterized by simultaneous decision and sealed-bid. One of the advantages of the auction mechanism lies in its high efficiency, i.e., in terms of the trading surplus extracted and the computational cost of the strategy used by bidders. Moreover, the best strategy of bidders in an English auction (usually used in auctions for antiques) is to increase the bid from zero until their private valuation. A bidder's valuation here means her/his minimum or maximum acceptable price depending on whether her/his position is as a seller or a buyer. For example, Tom is willing to accept $5000 for his car; thus any price above $5000 (his minimum acceptable price as a seller) generates a surplus for him. And Pat is willing to buy a sculpture for at most $1000 (her maximum acceptable price as a buyer); therefore her best strategy in an English auction is to compete with others up to at most $1000. Moreover, the best strategy of bidders in a Vickrey auction (second price sealed bid auction: the winner is the one with highest bid but pays the second highest bid) is to bid their true valuation, e.g. Pat bids $1000 [24]. The simplicity of these strategies can save computational costs.

If the auction mechanism is good, why is bargaining still important? The answers are:

1. Most auctions only allow negotiation for price, not other attributes (delivery time, payment method, etc.).
2. In some cases, feedback from negotiators is important. For instance, a buyer may disagree with the delivery method and thus does not participate in the auction, while the auctioneer can solve this problem trivially.
3. Auctions usually are scheduled in advance and with time restrictions, e.g. some online auctions range from 1 hour to 1 week. Intrinsically, auctions need multiple buyers or sellers in order to work well, therefore needing some time for gathering participants. Some buyers/sellers may not want to wait until an auction opens or finalizes.
4. In some circumstances, non-attribute factors are important, e.g., trusteeships, friendships, etc. Auctions cannot accommodate these factors.
5. Most auctions extract the surplus for the benefit of the auctioneer. For instance, in the Vickrey auction if the difference between the highest and second highest valuation is small (as usually happens if there is a significant number of bidders), the auctioneer can extract the most bidder surplus.[1] This could be considered as unfair and thus restrict the participation of bidders.

Considering these limitations, bargaining still plays an important role in automated negotiations in e-commerce.

Another approach, the Contract-net protocol [15, 16, 17, 21], on the other hand, provides a simple but powerful negotiation mechanism for solving a complex task by means of distributed problem solving. The underlying mechanism of a contract-net system is to decompose a task into sub-tasks and assign them to other agents. An agent will accept a contract if its marginal cost is less than its marginal benefit [15, 16, 17]. For example, if an agent already has many tasks to do, then any additional task will generate high marginal cost (e.g., cause slower computation). Moreover, every agent can sub-contract/re-contract its (previous) tasks to others who are willing to accept them. But usually it is assumed that each agent does not know the marginal cost of these tasks for other agents. This is true especially if we consider an open MAS where our agent will assign a task to another agent (e.g. as in our previous example of estimating the NASDAQ index). The common way to assign a task is to open an auction/bargaining and assign the task to the winner. Using this self-organizing mechanism, the system would perform optimal task allocation, which is pareto optimal. "Pareto optimum" is defined to be the situation where we cannot make anyone better off without making other(s) worst of. The following example illustrates this concept. Assume there are two agents A and B who can solve two

---

[1] Consider 100 bidders with their valuations randomly generated from $\{1, 2, .., 100\}$; then the winner, who has highest valuation $x, will bid $x and very likely pays $(x-1), thus getting $1 surplus. However, if there are only 10 bidders in a similar situation, then the winner, who has valuation $y, very likely pays $(y-10), thus getting $10 surplus.

disjoint tasks a and b with cost vector $CostA$ = ($8 $10) and $CostB$ = ($10 $8), where the value of x and y in vector (x y) represents the cost for solving task a and b respectively. That is, A is good at solving a and B is good at solving b. So, if someone pays $20 to A to solve both a and b, then the best action of A is to solve a and sub-contract b to B, which generates total cost equals to $8 + $8 = $16, which is pareto optimum. But$A$ might not know $CostB$. In this two agents situation, A will announce simultaneously several options to B, such as (task a, pay $7), (task b, pay $9), or (task a and b, pay $16). And B will counter propose with its proposals. However, if the number of agents is large, conducting bargaining will be inefficient.

Another approach to resolving conflicts is voting. Voting is a social choice mechanism in selecting social preferences over a set of alternatives. One of the applications of voting in MAS is resource allocation by means of majority voting. For example, in order to use a common resource (e.g. a supercomputer), an agent can broadcast a request to all other agents to collect access keys from these agents. If two agents compete to use the same resource, then the first who gets the majority votes (>50% of access keys) will be able to access the resource. This mechanism is considered less effective than auctions for at least two reasons:

- Voting cannot accommodate the urgency of access. For example, if an agent A who very urgently needs a resource comes later than agent B, who has collected 50% of votes, then A will lose although it needs the resource more. Modification by using a multi-priorities mechanism (e.g. veto) can solve this problem but with the overhead of lower efficiency. However, in auctions urgency can be represented by private valuation. Thus, the resource will be allocated to whoever needs it most (bids highest).
- Even agents who are not concerned to use the resource reply to any request made by agents needing the resource, which increases the communication cost. But in auctions, only those who need the resource will participate.

In summary, auctions are efficient if the number of agents is large.

2.2 Bargaining

Basically, we can divide bargaining theory into two main categories: axiomatic bargaining theory and strategic bargaining theory [12, 17].

Axiomatic bargaining first sets several axioms (such as all bargainers are individually rational, the solution is invariant to independent changes of utilities, the solution is pareto optimal, bargainers are symmetric and independent of irrelevant alternatives).It then finds unique bargaining solution(s) based on these axioms.

Some of the well-known axiomatic bargaining solutions are the egalitarian solution, the utilitarian solution, the Nash solution, and the Kalai-Smorodinsky solution [8, 10, 14]. The Egalitarian solution solves the bargaining problem by splitting the surplus equally among all bargainers. The Utilitarian solution solves the bargaining problem by finding the maximum sum of bargainers' utility. For example, if a seller needs money for medication for her child while a buyer does not need money, the utilitarian solution will give the entire bargaining surplus to the seller, i.e. the buyer pays as much as his valuation to the seller. One of the applications of axiomatic bargaining is in labor arbitration, where union and company submit their proposals to an arbitrator who decides the final result.

In contrast, strategic bargaining theory does not assume a centralized decision maker (arbitrator), but allows the bargainers to solve the dispute by offer and counter-offer proposals. In this model, a bargainer A starts the negotiation by sending a proposal to his opponent B, who chooses either to accept or reject the proposal. If B accepts it, then the negotiation terminates. If B rejects it, then she must send back a counter-proposal to specify her preferences to A. Now A will evaluate the proposal and choose either to accept or reject it. The process continues until agreement is reached. Strategic bargaining uses, primarily, assumptions and techniques from game theory, such as backward induction. Currently, there are many variants of this model, such as a model with a time deadline, with various information levels (complete /incomplete, symmetric/ asymmetric), with risk of breakdown (one party walks out before negotiation ends), with risk-averse agents, etc. Most of the theoretical foundations of these various models have been studied by game theorists [2, 3, 4, 5, 12, 13]. One of the seminal works in strategic bargaining theory is Rubinstein's dividing pie problem [12, 13], where two agents offer and counter-offer proposals about how to divide a pie in the presence of the waiting cost.[2] Rubinstein uses backward induction to solve the problem and shows that the bargaining process only takes one step, i.e., an agent will send only one proposal that is accepted immediately by another agent. The outcome is based on some strict assumptions such as every agent is perfectly rational and has perfect foresight.

Generally, the bargaining model in MAS adopts the classical alternating-offers model. However, some important limitations of the game-theoretic approach come from its strict assumptions such as:

- All agents are perfectly rational, which means every agent has a preference order over available choices and always seeks the best choice (utility maximizer).
  Objection: In order to provide a complete preference order to an agent, clients/owners might need to rank all available choices, which might be very complicated, and then tell it to their agents. Do clients really care if their agent buys a book for $42 instead of $41.99? Therefore, it is not necessary for an agent in e-commerce to get her client's complete preference order and solve the bargaining problem in such a strict way. Instead, an agent needs to be *bounded rational*: able to rank some important choices and seek the best one [20].
- All agents know the payoffs of each action and can predict their opponents' actions perfectly (perfect foresight).
  Objection: This assumption is implausible in an open MAS. Even where each agent can learn from past experience, by detecting and memorizing all attributes of his/her opponents, there is no guarantee that his/her opponents will be consistent with their actions over time.
- All agents can search for the solution in exhaustive fashion. For instance, they are able to consider all possible states of a game. In other words, they are computationally unlimited.
  Objection: Computationally limited agents are characteristic of MAS.

---

[2] Some people use a melting (ice cream) cake rather than a pie to illustrate the waiting cost. Longer bargaining time causes a smaller final cake, thus forcing all bargainers to act fast.

- If there are game theoretic equilibrium strategies, such as the Nash equilibrium strategy or the dominant strategy, then all agents will choose one of them.
  Objection: This is a controversial issue in social science, especially in the Prisoner's Dilemma game where the dominant strategy for both players is to confess. However, "confess" is not the pareto solution while "not confess" is. But from the MAS perspective, only pareto solutions are favorable.
- Agents do not recall past experiences, and therefore no learning mechanism is involved.
  Objection: One of the advantages of agents is their ability to memorize important things, which in turn can reduce computation. (e.g. case-based reasoning).

Considering the limitations of computational power and the existence of imperfect information in the real world, many heuristic techniques from AI have been adopted to develop new models called heuristic-based negotiation models. Most of them are characterized by learning mechanisms such as Bayesian learning, influence diagrams, genetic programming, etc. [9, 18, 23, 25]. Using this model, the negotiators can make decisions faster to find a good solution instead of the best one. However, game theory is still used as a benchmark (comparison) in the evaluation process; for instance, we could measure the effectiveness of a heuristic method by comparing its result to the theoretical result derived from game theory. In addition to these two approaches, some researchers have proposed another model namely an argumentation-based model that focuses more on natural language-like negotiation [6, 7, 19, 22]. The spirit of this work is to provide more flexibility in the negotiation process, such as to allow a negotiator to persuade their opponents to change their perceptions about them or the world states.

In general, in order to produce a bargaining solution, the valuations of seller and buyer should intercept or overlap (create a feasible set). Figure 1 shows a feasible set in the bargaining of two continuous attributes: unit price and quality. In figure 1, the seller's private valuation is a straight line representing the minimum selling price at different quality. An upward sloping of that line means the minimum acceptable price increases as the quality increases. The "seller's acceptable set" is all acceptable bargaining points from the seller's view, in which higher point (higher price for the same quality) is strictly preferred. Conversely, the buyer's private valuation is the buyer's maximum buying price at different qualities. And the buyer's acceptable set is all acceptable bargaining points from the buyer's view, in which a lower point is strictly preferred. Conclusively, any point in the acceptable set farther from private valuation line is strictly preferred. The intersection between two acceptable sets is a feasible set. Intuitively, the result of bargaining will fall in the feasible set, where both buyer and seller make a surplus.

Formally, assume there are only two agents $i \in \{1, 2\}$ bargaining over N-attributes. An alternative region A is defined as all possible points in the bargaining space of N-dimensional attributes. And both agents have their own preference order $\succsim_i$ over A ($\succsim_i$

is complete, reflexive and transitive in the bounded rationality sense)[3] and private valuation set $V_i \subseteq A$, where $\forall v_m, v_n \in V_i \Rightarrow v_m \sim_i v_n$ (agent i is indifferent over all her valuations). Then, for any agent i, if an alternative $a \succ_i V_i$, then a generates a positive surplus for her, denoted by $Sur_i(a) \geq 0$ or $Sur_i(a)^+$. In figure 1, N equals to 2, A is the rectangle area, V is the straight line representing seller's or buyer's private valuation, v is a point in the straight line, a is a point in A, and $Sur_i(a)^+$ occurs if point a falls in the i's acceptable set. Now we are ready with some definitions,

Definition 1. An *acceptable set* $Acc_i \subseteq A$ for agent i is a set such that $\forall a \in Acc_i \Rightarrow Sur_i(a)^+$.

Definition 2. A *feasible set* $S \subseteq A$ is a compact set (closed and bounded) such that $\forall s \in S \Rightarrow Sur_1(s)^+ \wedge Sur_2(s)^+$.

Definition 3. A *disagreement set* is $D = A \backslash S$.

In figure 1, the disagreement set is all points outside the feasible set.

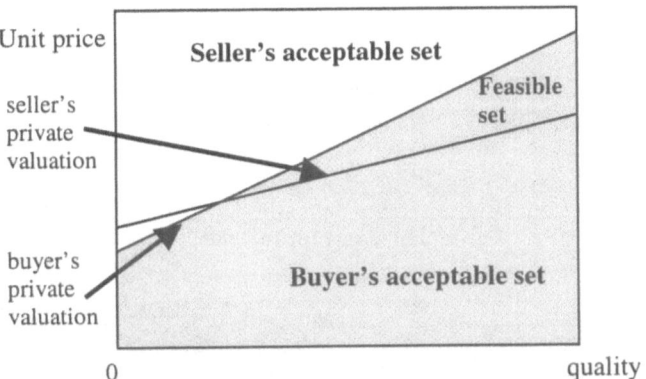

Fig. 1. Bargaining solution

In the alternating-offers bargaining between two bounded rational agents[4], the bargaining process can be illustrated (see figure 2) as picking some initial pairs of alternative points (e.g. four points in the buyer's acceptable set and four other points in the seller's acceptable set) and then repeatedly changing those points such that they become closer until one or more of them reaches a solution, as shown by the direction of the arrows. In the bargaining of multiple-attribute items, a proposal may consist of a set of alternatives (e.g., four in figure 2) and the bargained variable could be one

---

[3] Throughout this paper, the binary operator $\geq$ refers to weak preference "at least as good as", and $\prec$ refers to strict preference "strictly preferred than", and $\sim$ refers to indifference relation "as preferred as".

[4] In the rest of this paper, we will use the term *rational* instead of *bounded rational* and use *agent* and *bargainer* interchangeably.

dimensional or multi-dimensional. Figure 2 shows multi-attribute-one-dimensional bargaining, and figure 3 shows multi-attribute-multi-dimensional bargaining.

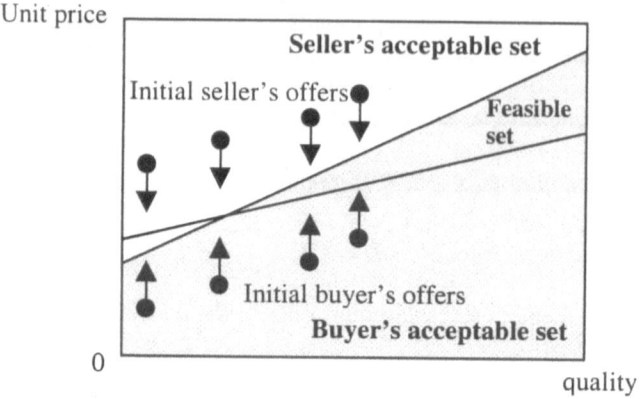

Fig. 2. Two-attribute bargaining process

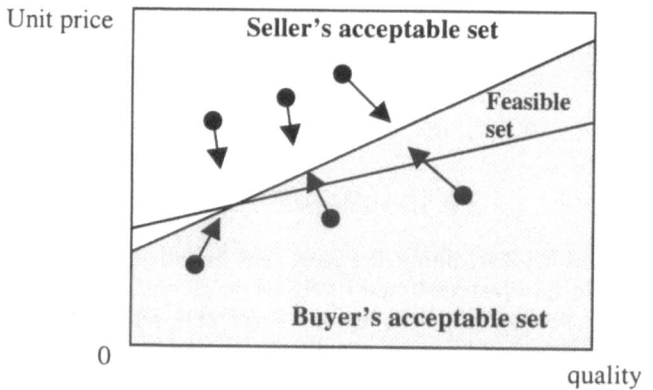

Fig. 3. Multi-dimensional bargaining

In figure 2, the bargained variable is the unit price (one-dimension vertical arrows). For example, in a bargaining of chemical goods a seller might say "Ok, I will give you more discounts; a 5% discount for goods with purity 90%, and a 10% discount for goods with purity 85%. But no discount for goods with purity 95%." In other words, the seller only changes the price of each different good (different quality). In figure 3, the dimension of the bargaining is both the unit price and the quality (two-dimension arrows). For example, a buyer may say "I am willing to increase my offer by $1 if you could increase the purity to 99.5%." Where the new offer is both increasing the price and the quality. Or in the foods industry, a seller might say, "Ok,

I will give you 0.5% more discount but half of them will expire by March 2003 and the rest will expire by December 2003." Where the new offer is both decreasing the price and the quality.

The *convergence direction* (arrows' direction in figures 2 and 3) of the multiple-attribute bargaining informs us of two things:
1. The important of each attribute. For instance, the example in figure 2 tells us that the bargainers prefer to choose a specific quality of goods and bargain around it using price adjustment.
2. The strategic maneuvering of the bargainers. For instance, a bargainer might say $100 for 85% purity and then say $95 for 80% where both may be the same for him.

Beside the convergence direction shown in figure 2 and 3, another important factor in bargaining is the *convergence rate*. The *convergence rate* of the bargaining indicates the character of the bargainers. In order to understand the convergence rate of the bargaining, the following assumptions are needed:

Assumption 1. A rational agent will choose an alternative that yields the highest *expected* value, i.e., $Max_a(\text{prob}(a) \times Sur_i(a)^+)$, where prob($a$) refers to the subjective probability that alternative a will be accepted by her opponent.

Assumption 2. A learning agent will revise her belief of the subjective value of prob(a) according to her experiences. If a is rejected, then she will reduce her subjective prob(a') $\forall a' \in Acc$. However, the reduction may not be the same for all a', i.e., the reduction monotonically increases as the alternative becomes farther from her own private valuation (less likely to be accepted by her opponent).

The following example illustrates our assumptions. Assume that two agents are bargaining for a car, and the buyer's valuation is $2500 and the seller's valuation is $2000. The seller opens the bargaining by offering $3000. After thinking for a while, the buyer makes some predictions: prob($1800)=0.2, prob($2000)=0.5, prob ($2200)=0.7 and prob($2500) =1. From these predictions the expected surpluses of each alternative are $140, $250, $210 and $0 respectively (by assumption 1). Therefore, the buyer asks for $2000, which maximizes her expected surplus. If the seller does not accept the offer after a certain time (either insists on $3000 or makes a counter offer of x > $2500), then the learning buyer will conclude that she may not get the car for $2000. So she will revise her prediction. Assume that her revision follows this rule: reduce all prob(x) by 0.4 if x is less than or equals the current offer, or reduce by 0.1 otherwise. Thus, from the example above: prob($1800) = 0.2 - 0.4 = -0.2 = 0, prob($2000) = 0.5 - 0.4 = 0.1, prob($2200) = 0.7 - 0.1 = 0.6 and prob($2500) = 1 - 0.1 = 0.9. Now, the expected surpluses are $0, $50, $180 and $0 respectively. And the buyer will ask for $2200 now.

Corollary 1. Due to the asymmetric reductions as stated in *assumption 2*, the offers/asks made by seller/buyer are monotonically decreasing/increasing (closer to their private valuation).

Proof. If agent i is rational, then by *assumption 1*, $a_x \succsim_i a_y$ iff prob(a_x) $\times Sur_i(a_x)^+ \geq$ prob(a_y) $\times Sur_i(a_y)^+$. Assume a_x is chosen, that is the expected surplus of a_x (= prob(a_x) $\times Sur_i(a_x)^+$) is the highest. Assume a_x is rejected, then all prob(a) will be reduced by y, where y monotonically increases as a goes farther from the agent's private valuation. Thus the reduction of corresponding expected surplus also monotonically increases as a goes farther from the private valuation. Consequently, if after the reduction the expected surplus of a_x is still the highest one, then a_x is retained, but if there exists a_y such that its expected surplus is greater than the expected surplus of a_x, then a_y is closer to the private valuation.   Q.E.D.

Proposition 1. If both agents are rational and able to learn, then their proposals converge as bargaining time $t \to \infty$, unless a solution is found or both proposals equal their private valuation (thus generating zero surplus).

Proof. In the initial bargaining $t=0$, both agent 1 and 2 will propose their favorite proposal, a^1 and a^2 respectively. If $a^1 = a^2$ then the solution is found and the bargaining ends. Otherwise, after waiting for Δt both agents will realize that prob(a^1) and prob(a^2) are lower than what they believed, thus a^1 and a^2 are no longer their favorite proposals. Following the corollary above, a new a closer to a^2 will be chosen by agent 1, unless $a^1 \in V_1$. And a similar thing applies to agent 2, thus the bargaining converges. Q.E.D.

In static bargaining for a single-attribute item, where the feasible set S does not change over time, if the feasible set $S \neq \varnothing$ and agents are rational, then the existence of a bargaining solution is guaranteed. However, in static bargaining for a multiple-attribute item, rationality and non-emptiness of the feasible set do not guarantee the existence of a bargaining solution. The following two propositions state these intuitions.

Proposition 2. In the static framework when the feasible set S does not change over time, the bargaining solution of single-attribute item is guaranteed *if* agents are rational and the feasible set $S \neq \varnothing$.

Proof. Assume that both agents start the bargaining with two proposals not belonging to the feasible set. Then by *proposition 1* both proposals will move closer until a solution is found or both agents will be stuck in their own valuation set. Assume that both agents are stuck in their own valuation set. Then any agent will have incentive to accept the other's proposal because it generates positive surplus, which is better than not to accept (surplus = 0). Thus the bargaining solution is guaranteed.   Q.E.D.

Proposition 3. In the static framework when the feasible set S does not change over time, the rationality and non-emptiness of the feasible set do not guarantee the existence of the bargaining solution over a multiple-attribute item.

Proof (sketch). Assume that both agents start the bargaining with two proposals not belonging to the feasible set, and each proposal only consists one alternative as shown in the left-most pair of alternatives in figure 2. Then by *proposition 1*, both alternatives will converge and get stuck on the private valuation set. Thus, no bargaining solution will be found.   Q.E.D.

Corollary 2. In the static framework when the feasible set S does not change over time, the bargaining solution of a multi-attribute item is guaranteed *if* agents are rational and their private valuation set $V_1 \subseteq Acc_2$ and $V_2 \subseteq Acc_1$.

Proof (sketch). Since $V_1 \subseteq Acc_2$ and $V_2 \subseteq Acc_1$, then there is at least one dimension where the mapping of any pair of alternatives into that dimension produces a one-dimensional bargaining with guaranteed solution. Then by *proposition 1* if the solution of any pairs is guaranteed, the collective solutions of them are also guaranteed.   Q.E.D.

Proposition 4. In a dynamic framework when the feasible set S moves dynamically during the bargaining process (e.g., due to changes of private valuations), then the existence of a single-attribute bargaining solution is guaranteed if agents are rational, $S \neq \varnothing$ and $\Delta S/\Delta t <$ convergence rate.

Proof (sketch). Since the convergence rate $> \Delta S/\Delta t$, then the distances between the alternatives proposed with the feasible set is decreasing over time. Thus, the alternatives proposed eventually enter the feasible set, and the bargaining solution is guaranteed.   Q.E.D.

3 Extended Bargaining Protocol

As described before, many modifications of the classical alternating-offer model have been suggested in order to improve the bargaining model. This project is motivated by the same spirit, i.e., relaxing the classical alternating-offer model and then studying the new model's advantages/disadvantages. This approach is adapted directly from the open economy view: create as many bargaining variations as possible and let nature select the best one. In particular this research proposes the following modifications to the classical alternating-offer protocol:

1. Allowing bargaining without revealing the negotiators' preferences to each other. For example in the bargaining between seller S and buyer B, the following negotiations would be allowed:

   S: I offer you $500 per unit.
   B: your price is too high, give me a lower price.
   Or
   S: I will not sell for less than $500.
   B: I cannot afford more than $400.

   In the first case, S sets the upper bound, and B asks for a reduction without revealing its minimum willingness to pay. In the second case, neither side reveals their exact valuations, but a range of them. Therefore, the first step of negotiation is to find an agreement on the range, and then proceed to the exact amount.

2. Allowing negotiation using strategic delay [1, 4]. A strategic delay is especially important at the beginning of the bargaining since it could serve as a signal of the negotiators' valuation. The less expected gain a negotiator anticipated from the bargaining, the more patient he is [4].

3. Allowing any revisions of the proposal before agreement is reached. In almost all the literature, it is assumed that the sequence of proposals monotonically converges to the agreement. For instance, the sequence of seller A and buyer B may look like <A offers $500, B asks $400, A offers $450, B asks $425, A accepts>. It is common that A will not revise its offer to be higher than the last offer. However, this convergence of values is not always true in an open system, because during the negotiation A may revise its valuation dynamically (e.g. the average price increases, or the demand for the same good increases, etc.). Consequently, allowing such properties will increase the complexity of the bargaining strategy (cf. proposition 2 and proposition 4).

4. Allowing negotiators to try to stimulate changes in each other's beliefs. In almost all the literature, it is assumed that the bargaining is only for the price. However, many real bargaining situations do not involve price, and in fact often implicitly or explicitly involve changing attitudes.

3.1   Issues in the Design of New Protocols

Rosenschein and Zlotkin [11] point out some important properties of a negotiation protocol:
1. efficiency: the result should be either pareto optimal or global optimal.
2. stability: there should be no incentive for all agents to deviate from agreed-upon strategies.
3. simplicity: there should be as little computational and communication cost as possible.
4. distribution: there should be no central decision-maker (a potential point of failure).
5. symmetry: the protocol should be the same for all similar agents. For instance, none of the agents is treated differently by the protocol.

Sandholm [17] extends this list by adding other possible properties such as guaranteed success and individual rationality. However, none of the properties above guarantee that the system will attract users' participation, especially in an open electronic marketplace. Therefore, we may add another property to be considered: attractiveness, i.e., the protocol should be able to attract users' (agents or human) participation. Due to the nature of the problem raised, the design of the protocol in this project only considers efficiency, simplicity, distribution, symmetry, and attractiveness. A proposed protocol should encourage agents to use various strategies. And some agents may deviate from the best strategy due to internal factors (such as not knowing the best strategy or making an error in computation) or external factors (such as being interrupted by other agents/owner or finding a better deal). Thus, individual rationality is excluded.

3.2   Design an Experimental Study

In order to evaluate the performance of the new protocols, we should test them against the classical alternating-offer protocol. The experiments will consist of 2 sessions: experiment with a classical alternating-offer protocol (control) and a modified protocol designed using some or all of the modifications described earlier. There are three criteria used in the measurement of the protocol's efficiency: percentage of failure, length of bargaining, and computational cost. And there are also two metrics to find the protocol's effectiveness: fairness and participation rate.

The measurement of these five criteria is as follows:
- Percentage of failure = number of failures (walkout)/ number of bargaining sessions.
- Length of bargaining = number of alternations until negotiation concluded.
- Computational costs = time needed for each decision.
- Fairness = % difference between buyer and seller surplus.
- Participation rate = proportion of participants in extended alternating-offer bargaining compared to participants in classical alternating-offer bargaining.

In order to measure these five criteria, the agents used in the experiments should be bounded rational and learning agents, as stated in assumptions 1 and 2. Moreover, the bargaining systems chosen are static-single-attribute bargaining and dynamic-single-attribute bargaining. The dynamics appear through changes of agents' perceptions toward their goal. From proposition 4, the existence of the bargaining solution is guaranteed only if the dynamics change slower than the convergence rate. Therefore, a controllable change is introduced into the bargaining system by the change of market price at each period. Basically, each agent has a negotiation deadline.

The computation models of each bargainer are now discussed. The buyer will maximize her utility U_B, as follows:

A buyer has private valuation: v_B, time deadline: τ_B, belief about market price: M_B^T, belief about seller's time deadline: τ_B^s, belief about the probability of seller to walkout: p_B^{Sout}. Let p_B^M be the buyer's perceived probability that there are sellers who are willing to sell at market price M. P^{BO} is the price offered/counter offered by the buyer. P^{SO} is the price offered/counter offered by the seller. P_B^{SAcc} is the buyer's perceived probability that the seller will accept P^{BO}. δ is the kroneker delta, equaling 1 if $t \leq \tau_B$ or zero otherwise. ω is the weight (importance) assigned to the market price. And the buyer's belief about the trustworthiness of the seller's statement is $trust_B^s$.

Buyer's Expected Utilities:

If the buyer chooses to reject the offer and walkout (WO), then her utility for walk out is:

$$U_B^{WO} = \delta_{t+1} p_B^M \left(v_B - M_B^\tau\right) \tag{1}$$

By choosing walkout, the buyer's expected utility depends on the probability to find a seller who is willing to sell the goods at market price M_B^T such that the buyer could make surplus $v_B - M_B^T$ before the deadline arrives (multiplied by the kroneker delta).

If the buyer chooses to accept (Acc) the offer then her utility is:

$$U_B^{Acc} = \left(v_B - P^{SO}\right) + \omega\left(M_B^\tau - P^{SO}\right) \tag{2}$$

where the first term is the surplus she got at price P^{SO} (the price offered by the seller), and the second term is the surplus she 'feels' will come from the market. However, her feeling about the difference between her bargained price and the market price may not be the same over time. For example, if Pat is driving in a desert and suddenly finds a grocery which sells ice cream for \$5, will she consider how much is the market price? If not at all, then assign $\omega = 0$. If she cares a lot, assign it = 1. Note: here we don't need δ_{t+1} because she will get the utility immediately after she accepts.

If the buyer chooses to counter offer/re-offer (CO) then her expected utility is:

$$U_B^{CO} = \delta_{t+1}\left[p_B^{SAcc}\left[\left(v_B - P^{BO}\right) + \omega\left(M_B^\tau - P^{BO}\right)\right] + p_B^{SOut}U_B^{WO}\right] \tag{3}$$

where

$$p_B^{SAcc} = (1 - p_B^{SOut})p_B(SAcc \mid \sim SOut) \tag{4}$$

Or P_B^{SAcc} is the buyer's perceived probability that the seller will accept her offer P^{BO}. Thus, the expected utility is the sum of the expected surplus made if seller accepts the buyer's offer and the expected utility if the seller walks out.

The utility of choosing to strategically delay (SD) is:

$$U_B^{SD} = \delta_{t+1} \left[p_B^{SAcc} \left[\left(v_B - P^{CO} \right) + \omega \left(M_B^\tau - P^{CO} \right) \right] + p_B^{SOut} U_B^{WO} \right]$$ (5)

The utility function above equals the utility of not re-offering or insisting on a previous offer. Generally, the purpose of strategic delay is broader than just calculating utility function. For example, strategic delay by agent i could be

- a signal of her unwillingness to accept an offer by her opponent, indirectly telling her opponent to revise his subjective probability prob(a);
- a signal of her insistence to stick to her previous offer;
- a signal of her patience that she can wait for a longer time, which also reveals the importance of the bargained item to her.

Therefore, strategic delay is selected if

- it is effective to let the opponent revise their perceived value of the agent's acceptance;
- it is better not to re-offer any value other than the previous offer;
- it is effective to let the opponent revise their perceived values of the agent's discount rate and valuation;
- simultaneously any combinations of the three situations above are true.

The utility to make an argument (Arg) is:

$$U_B^{Arg} = \delta_{t+1} \left[p_{BNEW}^{SAcc} \left[\left(v_B - P^{CO} \right) + \omega \left(M_B^\tau - P^{CO} \right) \right] + p_{BNEW}^{SOut} U_B^{WO} \right]$$ (6)

By making an argument, the agent tries to change the opponent's perception about the current world state. At this point, the argument tries to persuade the opponent to revise their perceived market price. For example, by indicating that the market price will be very low in the near future, a buyer can persuade a seller to sell with a lower price today, since if the buyer walks out, the seller will get less from the market.

Seller's Expected Utilities:
The seller's expected utilities are almost the same as the buyer's expected utilities, except that some calculations come from the seller's perspective. For example, the seller's expected surplus (profit) is calculated as the offered price minus valuation, instead of valuation minus the offered price in the buyer's case.

Reject and walkout (WO):

$$U_S^{WO} = \delta_{t+1} p_S^M \left(M_S^\tau - v_S \right)$$ (7)

Accept (Acc):

$$U_S^{Acc} = \left(P^{BO} - v_S \right) + \omega \left(P^{BO} - M_S^\tau \right)$$ (8)

Offer/Counter offer/Re-offer (CO):

$$U_S^{CO} = \delta_{t+1} \left[p_S^{BAcc} \left[\left(P^{SO} - v_S \right) + \omega \left(P^{SO} - M_S^\tau \right) \right] + P_S^{BOut} U_S^{WO} \right]$$ (9)

where

$$p_S^{BAcc} = (1 - p_S^{BOut}) p_S (BAcc \mid \sim BOut)$$ (10)

Strategic Delay (SD):

$$U_s^{SD} = \delta_{t+1}\left[p_s^{BAcc}\left[\left(P^{CO} - v_s\right) + \omega\left(P^{CO} - M_s^\tau\right)\right] + p_s^{BOut}U_s^{WO}\right] \tag{11}$$

Argumentation (Arg):

$$U_s^{Arg} = \delta_{t+1}\left[p_{SNEW}^{BAcc}\left[\left(P^{CO} - v_s\right) + \omega\left(P^{CO} - M_s^\tau\right)\right] + p_{SNEW}^{BOut}U_s^{WO}\right] \tag{12}$$

Based on the utility functions above, both buyer and seller make their choice consecutively, i.e., they choose the decision that generates highest utility from their point of view.

4 Conclusion

The goal of this paper is to prepare the basic framework in the design of a new alternating-offers bargaining protocol. Up to now, there are three contributions of this paper towards this end:

- The characteristics of the bargaining protocols have been analytically studied to find the answer to some basic questions: such as, can the bargaining always converge? in what conditions do bargaining solutions exist? what happens if two agents use different criteria to update their beliefs? Some of the simple questions have been answered in this paper. Nevertheless, there are many other questions waiting deeper study.
- The paper has explored the usefulness of trying to improve alternating-offers bargaining, in particular to apply it to e-commerce applications. So far, most of the work in negotiation in MAS concentrates on auctions. This paper tries to highlight the importance of bargaining in negotiation. One of the future challenges is to build not only an agent-agent bargaining system, but also a human-agent bargaining system, or human-agent-agent-human bargaining system.
- The paper has set the groundwork for an agent-based simulation, which could serve as a test-bed of the protocol design. Currently, several mechanisms for an agent's decision making have been identified. However, there are still many unsolved problems, such as what kind of learning mechanism is appropriate? should an agent trust the arguments made by her opponent? should every agent maintain the history and a model of other agents?

Our future research aims to implement the design, run experiment and find better protocol, which can accommodate more sophisticated bargaining strategy.

References

1. Admati, A. R. and Perry, M. (1987) "Strategic Delay in Bargaining" *Review of Economic Studies*, 54, 345-364.
2. Cho, I. (1990) "Uncertainty and Delay in Bargaining" *Review of Economic Studies*, 57, 575-596.
3. Cramton, P. C. (1984) "Bargaining with Incomplete Information: An Infinite-Horizon Model with Continuous Uncertainty" *Review of Economic Studies*, 51, 579-593.
4. Cramton, P. C. (1992) "Strategic Delay in Bargaining with Two-Sided Uncertainty" *Review of Economic Studies*, 59(1), 205-225.

5. Fudenberg, D. and Tirole, J. (1983) "Sequential Bargaining with Incomplete Information" *Review of Economic Studies*, 2, 221-247.
6. Jennings, N. R., Faratin, P., Lomuscio, A. R., Parsons, S., Sierra, C. and Wooldridge, M. (2001) "Automated negotiation: prospects, methods and challenges" *Int. J. of Group Decision and Negotiation*, 10 (2) 199-215.
7. Kraus, S., Sycara, K. and Evenchik, A. (1998) "Reaching Agreements through Argumentation: A Logical Model and Implementation." *Artificial Intelligence*, 104(1-2), 1-69.
8. Mas-Colell, A., Whinston, M.D. and Green, J.R. (1995) *Microeconomic Theory*. Oxford University Press, New York.
9. Mudgal, C. and Vassileva, J. (2000) "Bilateral Negotiation with Incomplete and Uncertain Information: A Decision-Theoretic Approach Using a Model of the Opponent." In Klusch and Kerschberg (Eds.) *Cooperative Information Agents IV*, LNAI volume 1860, 107-118, Springer-Verlag.
10. Nash, J. F. (1950) "The Bargaining Problem." *Econometrica*, 18(2), 155-162.
11. Rosenschein, J. S. and Zlotkin, G. (1994) *Rules of Encounter*. MIT Press.
12. Rubinstein, A. (1982) "Perfect Equilibrium in a Bargaining Model." *Econometrica*, 50(1), 97-110.
13. Rubinstein, A. (1985) "A Bargaining Model with Incomplete Information about Time Preferences." *Econometrica*, 53, 1151-1172.
14. Rubinstein, A., Safra, Z. and Thompson, W. (1992) "On the Interpretation of the Nash Bargaining Solution and Its Extension to Non-Expected Utility Preferences." *Econometrica*, 60(5), 1171-1186.
15. Sandholm, T. W. (1993) "An implementation of the contract net protocol based on marginal cost calculations." In *Proc. 11th National Conference on AI* (AAAI-93).
16. Sandholm, T. W. and Lesser, V. (1995) "Issues in Automated Negotiation and Electronic Commerce: Extending the Contract Net Framework." In *Proc. First International Conference on Multiagent Systems* (ICMAS-95), San Francisco, 328-335.
17. Sandholm, T. W. (1999) "Distributed Rational Decision Making" In Weiss, G. (ed.) *Multiagent Systems*, MIT Press, 201-258.
18. Sandholm, T. W. and Vulkan, N. (1999) "Bargaining with Deadlines." In *Proc. National Conference on Artificial Intelligence* (AAAI-99), 44-51, Orlando, FL.
19. Sierra, C., Jennings, N. R., Noriega, P., Parsons, S. (1997) "A Framework for Argumentation-Based Negotiation" In *Proc. 4th Int. Workshop on Agent Theories, Architectures and Languages*, Rode Island, USA, 177-192.
20. Simon, H. A. (1982) *Models of bounded rationality*. MIT Press, Cambridge.
21. Smith, R. G. (1980) "The Contract Net Protocol: High-level Communication and Control in a Distributed Problem Solver." *IEEE Transaction on Computers*, C-29(12), 1104-1113.
22. Sycara, K. (1989) "Argumentation: Planning other Agents' Plans" In *Proc. 11th IJCAI*, 517-523.
23. van Bragt, D.D.B., Gerding, E.H., and La Poutre, J.A. (2000) "Equilibrium Selection in Alternating-Offers Bargaining Models: The Evolutionary Computing Approach" *CWI Technical Report* available at http://www.cwi.nl/projects/ASTA/2000Q3.html
24. Vickrey, W. (1961) "Counterspeculation, Auction, and Competitive Sealed Tenders." *Journal of Finance*, 16, 8-37.
25. Zeng, D. and Sycara, K. (1998) "Bayesian Learning in Negotiation." *Int. Journal Human-Computer Studies*, 48, 125-141.

A Human Based Perception Model for Cooperative Intelligent Virtual Agents

Pilar Herrero and Angélica de Antonio

Facultad de Informática. Universidad Politécnica de Madrid. Campus de Montegancedo
S/N. 28.660 Boadilla del Monte. Madrid. Spain
{pherrero,angelica}@fi.upm.es

Abstract. Interactive virtual worlds provide a powerful medium for
experimental learning and entertainment. Nowadays, virtual environments often
incorporate human-like embodied virtual agents with varying degrees of
intelligence, getting what we call Intelligent Virtual Agents (IVAs). Collaboration between agents can be very important to reach aware of what is
surrounding each agent each and every moment. This paper tries to find how to
endow IVAs with a human perceptual model based on the reinterpretation of
one of the more successful awareness models for Computer Supported Cooperative Work (CSCW).

1 Introduction

The Interactive virtual worlds or virtual environments provide a powerful medium for
experimental learning and entertainment, being almost unlimited the range of worlds
that people can explore, periods of time – past, present or future –, situations that the
user can live – from factual to fantasy –, and interactivity that the user can
experiment.

In fact, what makes virtual environments distinct from all other human-computer
interfaces is that the user feels the illusion of being completely surrounded by spatial
information. In this case, the user is aware of other users that might be connected, and
the feeling of immersion, shared presence and the degree of interactivity (with objects
and other participants) is very high.

As a consequence of this high feeling of immersion, when a user is navigating
through a virtual environment, conscious or unconsciously, he is expecting to have
the chance of living there any kind of situation. The user is not prepared to *distinguish*
what kind of situation is possible to be lived in a virtual environment from the ones
that are only possible to be lived in a real environment.

In the attempt to simulate the appearance and the functions of life, it is inevitable
to come to the point of simulating humans. Nowadays, virtual environments often
incorporate human-like embodied virtual agents with varying degrees of intelligence,
getting what we call Intelligent Virtual Agents (IVAs). An IVA is an autonomous
embodied agent in an interactive graphical environment, usually 3D, which draws on
AI and ALife technology so as to interact intelligently with its environment and with
human users.

R. Meersman, Z. Tari (Eds.): CoopIS/DOA/ODBASE 2002, LNCS 2519, pp. 195–212, 2002.
© Springer-Verlag Berlin Heidelberg 2002

The field of Intelligent Virtual Agents (IVAs) is a new emerging and multidisciplinary area. It is making rapid progress, owing to its inherent attractiveness to diverse fields, such as education, entertainment computer games or communication.

Strongly related to VEs is the field of Multi-Agent Systems (MAS). MAS contain autonomous and distributed agents that may be co-operative or self-interested. But, the agents in a MAS do not need to be embodied. They can be pure software agents.

The scope of our research is what we call mIVA-VE systems (VEs populated by multiple IVAs). An IVA-VE is particular type of MAS in which both users and agents are embodied and may interact with each other.

Virtual humans [2] or synthetic actors [27], as IVAs are also called, must have autonomous behaviours, look real and be able to interact with each other in virtual scenes representing the real world. One of the most important characteristics of IVAs must be the ability to be aware of the current situation of the environment where they reside and operate. Therefore, they may require from lower-level vision activities to high-level cognition, going through understanding, reasoning, and decision making.

MIVA-VE systems can be used to simulate real life from any point of view. One of the most typical uses are the war simulations, where risky situations are simulated by this kind of systems and soldiers are trained for living them. In these kind of scenarios the realism is very important. The more realistic is the simulation the better training the soldiers will have.

Many works in mIVA-VEs have the goal to provide agents with a higher degree of realism, and realism has often been sought providing human-like appearance or behaviour. However, the realism of perception has been ignored for a long time ago.

The result of an IVA perceiving an object/agent is its becoming aware of this object/agent. The research that we present in this paper is precisely oriented towards the endowment of IVAs with perception mechanisms that allow them to be "realistically" aware of their surroundings. We propose a perception model, which seeks to introduce more coherence between IVA's perception and human being perception. In this way, the psychological "*coherence*" between the real life and the virtual environment experience will be incremented.

Drawing from the idea of an IVA "being aware", we found that the concept of awareness is a familiar one in the context of CSCW. In fact, there are some abstract models of awareness, such as the "Spatial Model of Interaction" [4], which have been tested with successful results in CSCW multi-user environments. Having in mind that the physical perception can be understood as the first level of an "awareness model" [31] [12] [13], the first goal for our research was to provide a reinterpretation of a CSCW awareness model to be used as a perception model for applying it to IVAs. The Spatial Model of Interaction was our reference awareness model.

Before we discuss our definition of "awareness", we will describe how the term has been used and defined in CSCW literature. Probably the best-known definition for awareness in CSCW literature was given by Dourish and Bellotti [11] in their seminal paper on awareness and coordination in shared workspaces. They define wareness as "an understanding of the activities of others which provides a context for your own activity".

From this definition we can take out that the term "awareness" naturally implies a broader meaning than actually intended by most publications in CSCW literature. What is usually meant here is "group awareness" or "co-operation awareness", being knowledge about the state of a co-operative effort of a group of people.

A number of different physical environments have been developed to support the public nature of work and to promote co-ordination. When the environment is a 3D distributed virtual environment, within which the user feels a high degree of immersion, it is usually called Collaborative Virtual Environment (CVE). A definition for CVE is given by Greenhalgh as "distributed multi-user virtual environment that supports co-operative work and play".

The Spatial Model of Interaction was first proposed as a way of managing awareness in CVEs through the mechanisms of focus, nimbus, aura, awareness and adapters [4], [5].

This model was initially demonstrated in the DIVE system and then first fully implemented as the MASSIVE system [14]. MASSIVE has since been used to hold many virtual meetings and several papers have emerged from these experiences including studies of interaction. Parallel to these studies, other models have been proposed for awareness in CVEs. In all these models, CVEs are inhabited by users represented by avatars. It is important to note that in all these models of awareness, the one who is aware is the "user" of the environment, not the virtual humans that may be populating it.

The aim of our research is not just to extend the Spatial Model of Interaction to mIVA-VEs, but also to make it more realistic introducing some concepts typical in human-like perception.

2 Agent Perception

Agents can be inhabiting a variety of environments, depending on the application purpose which it was developed for. Some of these environments are just based on text and the flow of information that is passing through the environment, and has to be perceived, *is not sensorial.*

However, interactive virtual worlds combined with agents offer an exciting new tool for entertainment, education and training. In the last few years, this new technology has experimented an exciting progress but virtual agents still have a limited range of capabilities. Agent perception in mIVA-VEs is *sensorial*, and has to provide the agent with knowledge about its "physical" surroundings.

A general definition of perception is given by Chenney [8]. He defines the perception of autonomous agents as a process of interaction with the environment to collect and exchange information about the environment and the agent itself, and classifies the perception as:

- *Active Sensing*: Information is continuously being provided, regardless of the agent being explicitly looking for it.
- *Passive Sensing*: "Passive sense data is only generated when required" Passive sensing is generally implemented as a query procedure. Almost all the implemented agent architectures support passive sensing. For example, SodaJack queries a sensing system to determine if goals have been achieved or are achievable. Tu and Terzopoulos [39] use a *focusser*, which is essentially a selective filter, to perform passive sensing.
- *Feedback Sensing*: "Feedback sensing may be considered a special case of passive sensing; however it differs in that it is generally not integrated with the

general sensing system. Rather, it is coupled to the motor controllers that require the feedback"

In sensory systems, the agent (human or artificial) not only sees and feels but looks and touches, i.e. perception is an active process of seeking information from the environment [39], [32]. This idea finds its origins in human psychology, especially as formulated by Gibson, although it was introduced as active perception some years later.

Tu and Terzopoulos [39] introduced a vision-based perception for fishes. In [33] Terzopoulos and Rabie propose a new paradigm for active vision research. Their software prescribes artificial animals, situated in physics-based virtual worlds as autonomous virtual robots possessing active perception systems. The animals autonomously control their eyes and muscle-actuated body, applying computer vision algorithms to continuously analyse the retinal image streams acquired by its eyes in order to locomote purposefully through their world. By emulating the appearance, motion and behaviour of real fishes these animals are capable of building spatial non uniform retinal images, stabilising retinal image, recognising colour object, and navigating perceptually-guided. The authors make an effort to re-model biological vision systems, based on 2D image processing, in order to make their results useful for robotics.

Another example of artificial perception is the ALIVE system, created by Blumberg [6], where an autonomous animated dog was endowed with synthetic sensors (eyes, ears) in order to interact with its environment.

Noser [27] uses the hardware Z-buffer of the IRIS graphics system for fast calculation, approaching the visual perception by the Z-buffer of the vision image. The Z-buffer algorithm, which is a simple method for hidden surface removal, consists of an array containing the depth value for each pixel of the image to be displayed. The algorithm uses these Z-buffer values for efficient rendering of 3D scenes. Nowadays, Z-buffer algorithms are generally implemented on graphics terminals which offer the corresponding technology. Noser [27] simulates vision more on the functional level than on the biological level. An special application of the principle of synthetic vision is presented using Z-buffer techniques and colour coding in the estimation of light in simulation of plant development. He renders the tree from the point of view of the light source. As each leaf is colour coded and identified, a colour histogram of the rendered image can be used to calculate the amount of light "seen" by each leaf. Then, this information can be employed for the further development of each leaf.

Although some years ago the aim of agent's perception was just to seek basic information about the environment, the requirements have changed and, currently, a wide range of realistic simulation applications have been developed, mainly for training purposes, requiring a relatively high fidelity model of perception. Development of these realistic models has been identified as very important for Computer Generated Forces (CGFs) and a greater emphasis must be placed on developing realistic and human-like models of perception, cognition and motor behaviour [20]. Pew [28] recommends as a top short-term goal to improve situation awareness modelling: *"include explicitly in human behaviour representation a perceptual "front end" serving as the interface between the outside world and the internal processing of the human behaviour representation."* Situation awareness plays a central role in cognition, which comprises the entire spectrum of cognitive activities from perception, such as lower-level vision activities, to high-level cognition, such as understanding, reasoning, and decision making.

Various performance models have been developed to account for human perception and motor actions. The Model Human Processor (MHP) [7] is probably the most referenced model of human information processing. It provides a theory of the perception and motor mechanisms with specific delays and decay of perceived data. Several systems were subsequently developed. EPIC (Executive Process-Interactive Control) [23] is an executable model of human performance that has been used to predict performance in multi-modal high-performance tasks. This system requires a specific simulation environment that can be programmed to reproduce the specific layout of a user interface, being able to handle very low level sensory information.

In most CGF, the modeller can focus the application development effort on object representations and cognitive processes specification. An example of this is the cognitive agent COGNET, based on Rasmussen's integrated theory of human information processing. In COGNET [10], the role of the perception mechanism is to transfer the data obtained from the external world to the cognitive processor. In the initial version of COGNET, this role was played by model components designated as 'demons,' which basically converted the input data into the symbolic format used by the cognitive model, paying little attention to modelling the human perception mechanisms. In subsequent versions of COGNET the perception layer was different from EPIC and MHP. This new approach, called "simulator-centric", is the perspective of most human perception models. Information in this world is represented as objects (in the sense of Object Oriented design) that contain the appropriate numerical or symbolic values. Unlike MHP or EPIC models, here perceptual images may be stored in extended working memory. A sensory resource (visual or auditory) can query all the objects in its range, compare the result to expectations and interference, in order to determine which of them are likely to reach the extended working memory on any perceptual cycle. A working memory moderator accounts for the limited perceptual bandwidths and the decay of perceptions. By acting on the working memory, providing a forgetting mechanism, this memory moderator can impose constraints on the number of elements that can be stored in specified parts of the working memory. The memory moderator may not reproduce exactly the same perception bandwidth mechanisms of MHP. It provides a specific theory of perception for the visual, auditory, or tactile sensory channels, and proposes a generic architecture that lets the programmer implement the desired level of abstraction. The perceived objects are stored in dedicated portions of extended working memory (the blackboard), and then used in cognitive processing by the cognitive tasks. Modelling of sensory distortion and limited sensory resources are handled by some perception functions, which determine the delays of perceptions.

Today, through special interfaces, a user can even interactively participate in a virtual scene, having the possibility to experiment with primitive autonomous creatures in virtual environments simulated on powerful computers.

IVAs are programmed with some behavioural rules and endowed with synthetic vision, reacting to their environment and taking decisions based on perception systems, memory and reasoning. The computer renders from the actor's point of view the virtual environment in a window corresponding to the actor's vision image.

IVAs perceive information from the environment through virtual sensors: visual, tactile and auditory sensors [27], [37]. An IVA may simply evolve in his environment or he may interact with this environment or even communicate with other IVAs.

IVAs have been developed with very varied aims and features, and, for this reason, perception in those agents has been modelled in diverse ways, depending on what they were designed for. This perception can be focussed on implementing the processing of sensory inputs or the cognitive process.

The implementation of sensory inputs can be done in different ways. Some people use virtual sensors, like visual, tactile and auditory sensors. These sensors have been used as basic factors for implementing everyday human behaviour [37], [36] such as visually directed locomotion, handling objects, and responding to sounds or images. Relying on a set of onboard virtual sensors to gather information about the dynamic environment, it is possible be aware of the world, but in order to achieve natural sensorimotor behaviours, it is necessary to model not only the abilities but also the limitations of animal perception systems, as for example the attention mechanism [35]. A biomimetic approach to perception based on computational vision was developed by Tamer Rabie at the University of Toronto [34].

Another instance are the virtual pilots described in 1999 by Hill [20], [21], which didn't have a head or body; rather, their perception was modelled as a set of visual sensors without being concerned about the appearance or control of the body. In this way, the Soar Virtual Pilot application [21] implements visual perception via look-ahead sensors that perceive the terrain as sample points along the flight path for their altitude, and the pilot adjusts the flight parameters accordingly. In this case, the system simulated the visual capabilities of a human-like eye sensor without worrying about gaze control.

As for the implementation of the cognitive process of perception, it can be focused on implementing just a factor (as i.e. attention) or a part of the cognitive process (as i.e. recognition or learning) or, even, proposing a cognitive modelling architecture as COGNET [10] (above detailed). In this way, some approaches employed for implementing the cognitive process of perception are:

- Using techniques for learning and then recognising the shapes and behaviours of objects within a scene.
- Using a cognitive mapping technique. An example of this is the cognitive mapping technique implemented by Hill et al. [17] [19]. Their implementation is based on a computational framework proposed by Yeap and Jefferies [41] that represents a local environment as a structure called an Absolute Space Representation (ASR). Building an ASR involves perceiving the environment and building up a mental model of the space. The area perceived is not just the local where the virtual human is but also the local surroundings, the area immediately visible to the viewer, and computing the boundaries - that prohibit movement through the space – and exits – gaps in the boundaries that permit the agents to leave this space. Taking this framework Hill has applied a theoretical computational framework of cognitive mapping to a training application that includes virtual humans in a virtual environment. The cognitive mapping algorithms used are an extension of those presented by Yeap and Jefferies [41]. Cognitive mapping is not limited to places that have been physically explored. Virtual humans build cognitive maps in anticipation of the next space they will enter. To get it, agents perceive through the exits in the local environment and construct the new ASRs before the areas are visited. Hill has also used neural networks to recognise and predict patterns of behaviour [18] with specific applications, for example, to direct the virtual helicopter pilot's gaze when

searching for a target to be reacquired [18]. In this example, the neural network functioned in concert with the perceptual model already implemented in the virtual pilot [42], [21], having a hybrid system that combined neural networks with the perceptual model, and the symbolic reasoning capabilities of a Soar agent [20].

- Providing a model of visual attention for virtual humans [9], [21]. Chopra is based on human psychological research, specifies the types of visual attention that are required for a variety of basic tasks (e.g., locomotion, object manipulation, and visual search), as well as the mechanisms for dividing attention among multiple such tasks. In the Soar Virtual Pilot, Hill is also focused on providing a model of perceptual attention for virtual humans in synthetic battlefield [21]. The goal of this application is to develop individual combatants where virtual pilots are implemented in a distributed, interactive simulation called ModSAF. In this application, the virtual helicopter pilot's gaze plays an important role, much more when the pilot is searching for a target.

Another way of implementing perception, different to those we have presented in this section, and connected with Chenney classification above mentioned, is used by Rickel et al. in Steve. Steve is a pedagogical agent (Soar Training Expert for Virtual Environments) that supports the learning process for training and education [29].

Steve consists of three main modules: perception, cognition, and motor control. All of these modules communicate with each other by message passing (via the message dispatcher). The perception module monitors messages from the message dispatcher and identifies events that are relevant to Steve, such as actions taken in the virtual world by people and agents and changes in the state of the virtual world, regardless of his current location or state of attention. The cognition module interprets the input it receives from the perception module, chooses appropriate goals, constructs and executes plans to achieve those goals, and sends out motor commands to control the agent's body. The cognition module sends a message to the perception module when it is ready for an update on the state of the virtual world; the perception module responds with a snapshot of the state of the world and a set of important events that occurred since the last snapshot it sent (e.g. actions taken by people and agents).

3   The Spatial Model of Interaction

Perhaps the most well-known awareness model for multi-user CSCW environments is the Spatial Model of Interaction. This model was developed between 1991 and 1993 by Professor Steve Benford at the *School of Computer Science and Information Technology*, in the Nottingham University, Lennart E. Fahlén at *The Swedish Institute of Computer Science (SICS)* and John Bowers at *The Royal Institute of Technology (KTH)* in Stockholm (Sweden).

The spatial model, as its name suggests, uses the properties of space as the basis for mediating interaction. It was proposed as a way to control the flow of information of the environment in CVEs (Collaborative Virtual Environments). It allows objects in a virtual world to govern their interaction through some key concepts: medium, aura, awareness, focus, nimbus, adaptors and boundaries [4].

Simultaneous interaction between all objects is not computationally manageable, in any large-scale environment. For this reason, it is important to determine which objects are capable of interacting with which others at a given time. A prerequisite for useful communication is that two objects have a compatible *medium* in which both objects can communicate.

Aura as the sub-space which effectively bounds the presence of an object within a given medium and which acts as an enabler of potential interaction. Once aura has been used to determine the potential for object interactions, the objects themselves are subsequently responsible for controlling these interactions. "When two auras collide, interaction between the objects in the medium becomes a possibility" [4].

In each particular medium, it is possible to delimit the observing object's interest. This idea was called *focus* and it was defined by S. Benford in 1993 as "The more an object is within your focus the more aware you are of it" [4].

In the same way, it is possible to represent the observed object's projection in a particular medium. This area is called *nimbus*: "The more an object is within your nimbus the more aware it is of you" [4].

The main concept involved in controlling interaction between objects is *"awareness"*. One object's awareness of another object quantifies the subjective importance or relevance of that object.

The awareness relationship between every pair of objects is achieved on the basis of quantifiable *levels* of awareness between them and it is unidirectional and specific to each medium [4].

Awareness between objects in a given medium is manipulated via *focus* and *nimbus*. Moreover, an object's aura, focus, nimbus, and hence awareness, can be modified through some artefacts called *adaptors* [4], such as, a microphone, a megaphone, a speaker or a podium in order to address a large audience.

Finally, aura, focus and nimbus may be manipulated through *boundaries* in space. Boundaries have more importance in structuring social interaction.

Between 1994 and 1996, the University of Nottingham continued to work on this topic. Some of the concepts above mentioned were studied and redefined, for example, the boundary concept. More specifically, boundaries were classified as having different kinds of effects, which can be: *obstructive, non-obstructive, conditionally obstructive* and *transforming*.

A lot of researches have been carried out starting from this model. Rodden developed a new model of awareness for *Cooperative Applications* [30], and Greenhalgh [9] introduced *"Third Party Objects"* and developed *MASSIVE-2*, a distributed virtual reality system, which aimed to support very large numbers of participants [9] and to experiment with the third party objects extension to the spatial model.

4   Human Factors in Awareness Functions

All of the current awareness models are (deliberately) quite abstract in their evaluation of awareness and they don't have in mind human being factors. However, for some applications, e.g. human-like embodied agents, it would be valuable to have more 'realistic' (i.e. physically and physiologically based) models of awareness across a range of media. In order to improve such models, we are going to introduce a set of new concepts.

Our main work hypothesis is that the knowledge of a human-like virtual agent about its surroundings should depend on and be limited by its perception, and its perceptual capabilities should faithfully resemble those of a human being. In human perception [16]:

- Each sense has a specific ability to resolve fine details that is called "**Sense Acuity**" [15]. The most well known is the Visual Acuity, which is a measure of the eye's ability to resolve fine detail and is dependent upon the person itself, the accommodative state of the eye, the illumination level and the contrast between target and background [22]. By implementing this human factor within the agent's perceptual system, an agent will be able to determine if it can see an object by taking into account its visual acuity, and calculating the distance object-agent, the object's size, the illumination and contrast. If the agent's perceptual system realises that the object is too far to be perceived, the agent will not be aware of it. In this paper we are going to focus on the visual perception process.

- The clarity of perception is gradual, so it is possible to find an interval in the space between the perfect and the null perception. In this region, called "**Sense Transition Region**" (STR) the perception is not clear but it is possible to make out something. Virtual agents should exhibit this characteristic to avoid anomalous behaviours, as for example, those that will happen if an agent is not aware of and can not interact with another agent which is inside the STR but out of the focus.

- Individual differences affect the perception process. The process of perception selects from an extensive area, which may contain a lot of objects, only those that we are interested in. By introducing "**Internal Filters**" in agent perception, agents should be able to make their own process of selection within their focus, paying attention only to those objects they are interested in.

5   An Architecture for the Agent's Perception

We have selected a *vertical layering* agent architecture, like the Triple Tower Model of Nilsson [26], as the starting point for our architecture because of its simplicity and flexibility.

This architecture has three main blocks (figure 1), representing the agent's perception, the agent's central processing and the agent's actions, but we are going to concentrate our attention just on the agent's perception block. This component is concerned with modelling the agent's unique perception of their environment.

The perception block, or perception engine, operates concurrently with the central processing block, and some of the interpretations of the perceived data or some of the parameters of the agent's internal model can in turn modify the perception process.

The perception engine will deal with the interaction with the environment and it will be composed by the following four modules (figure 2): *Sensitive Perception, Attenuation and Internal Filtering.*

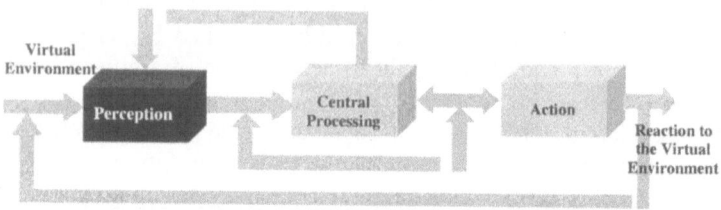

Fig. 1. Agent's Architecture

The sensitive perception module simulates the typical process by which organisms receive sensations from the environment. Sensation usually refers to the immediate, relatively unprocessed result of stimulation of sensory receptors in the eyes, ears, nose, tongue, or skin. Sensitive perception depends on some relevant sensorial concepts as (figure 3): *Sense Acuity, Object Factors, Sense Transition Region, and Adaptors* [16].

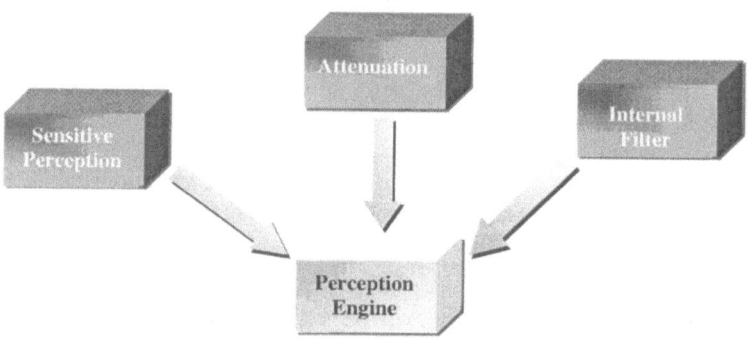

Fig. 2. Perception Engine

Once an object's nimbus is inside the agent's focus the sensitive perception module will calculate the *clarity of perception* for this object.

Perceptual sensations are subjectively attenuated with time. The attenuation module will introduce a reduction experienced by the signal coming from the sensitive perception]. On the other hand, the selection of the most relevant objects within the focus will be done by the Internal Filtering module.

The combined action of these modules will provide the virtual agents with a perceptual system which is more coherent with that of the human beings, thus allowing them to exhibit a more realistic behaviour, according to the expectations of the users of this kind of environments.

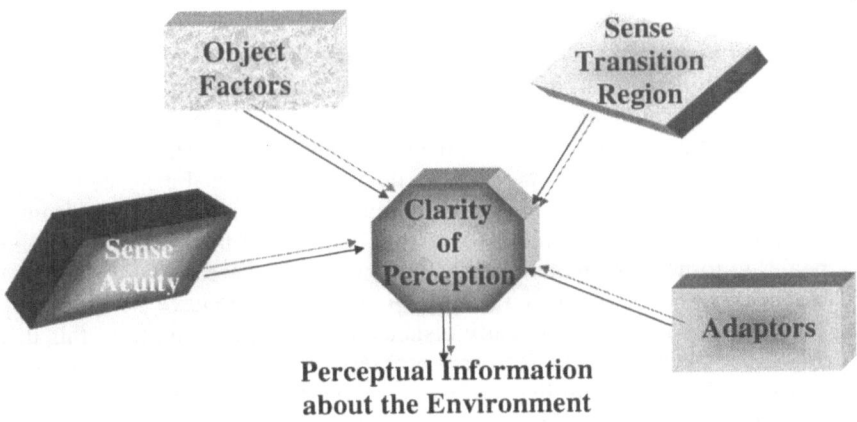

Fig. 3. Sensitive Perception

6   The Clarity of Perception

Our approach to modelling the human perception is modelling the ability to clearly distinguish what kind of object is being perceived, inside the agent's focus.

In general, as it was showed in the figure 3, the clarity of perception should depend on the following human factors: Sense Acuity, Object Factors (such as size or colour), Sense Transition Region, Adaptors and the distance between the object and the position of the agent's eye ($d_{eye-object}$). This distance can be smaller, bigger or equal to the visual acuity distance (Dm), which, by definition, is the maximum distance to resolve the fine details of an object of a given size. The eye-object distance, and clarity of perception, in general, should be considered a key concept in agent's perception because it introduces more realism, believability and efficiency. For example, it will be necessary to check its value to know if an agent can read a cartel at a fixed distance. Moreover, making awareness dependent on this factor is totally new, no other model had it in mind before.

The process of human visual perception is continuous and the size of the image on the retina will continuously depend on the distance between the eye and the object to be perceived. Therefore, from the sensorial point of view, if the clarity of perception denotes the ability to distinguish what kind of object is being perceived, then it should depend on the object's image that we have on the retina. Moreover, if the retinal image decreases continuously with the eye-object distance then the clarity of perception should decrease continuously with this distance as well. But we are having in mind the size constancy phenomenon, by which object's size tends to appear constant in spite of it changing with the distance. This factor will imply that the clarity of perception will fall still more smoothly. For this reason, and following the studies of Levi et. al [24], we propose a Gaussian function to describe the variation that the clarity of perception has with the eye-object distance (figure 4) for a fixed object's size.

To analyse the proposed clarity of perception function, it will be necessary to consider the following key points:

1.- There is a minimum distance (d_1) necessary to have a clear perception of an object, starting from which the object can be perceived. Usually, this distance is known as the *minimum distance for distinct vision* or *near point*. Under this distance the perception is blurred, the more beneath this distance an object is, the worse the human eye will perceive its details. The optimal distance for vision in a person with normal vision is, approximately, 25cm horizontally in front of the eye (and this will be our reference value). Any closer than that and the observer begins to lose focus (in other words, he can no longer see it clearly)..

2.- On the other hand, , there is a maximum distance (d_2) to have a clear perception. This distance is the visual acuity distance ($d_2 = D_m$). Starting from this distance the object's level of detail decreases progressively in the forward direction.

3.- When the level of detail that can be perceived from an object starts decreasing, there is a region (interval between d_2 and d_3) yet, where it is possible to perceive an important part of detail although not the whole detail. Starting from this distance, it will be difficult to perceive the object's details, though some of them, those which appeal more to the observer's attention, can still been perceived (between d_3 and d_4). The value of the distance d_3 depends on the target size and distance [24].

4.- There is a point (d_4) starting from which the human eye can not perceive almost any detail from any object. This furthest point at which the eye can see clearly is known as the *far point* in optics. A normal near point is 25 cm, while the normal far point is at infinity.

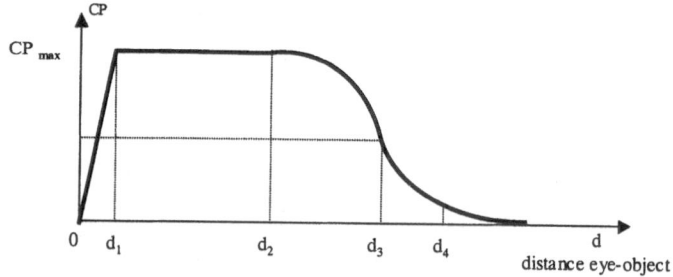

Fig. 4. Clarity of perception relative to distance inside the focus foreground region

The maximum value for this function (CP_{max}) will be 1.0, and this will mean that the observer can perceive the whole of the details. The minimum value for this function will be 0.0, and it will be assigned when the observer can't perceive any detail from the object. But the clarity of perception function is continuous, which means that the CP(d) value is limited by 1.0 (maximum value) and 0.0 (minimum value), although it is possible to find any value between them ($0.0 \leq CP(d) \leq 1.0$) in which the observer will be able to perceive some details from the object, being the level of detail dependent on the distance. The value 1.0 is obtained when the object is placed between d_1 and d_2.

On the other hand, the clarity of perception that we can have for an object placed at a distance $d \leq d_1$ is very low; in fact, if the object is placed very close to the origin (d≈0), the perception will be blurred (CP(0) ≈0). On the contrary, if the object's position is d, being $d \geq d_4$, the clarity of perception will be very low, almost null. Finally, if d is between d_2 and d_4, it will be possible to perceive the object with some detail (the degree of detail will be decreasing as d is closer to d_4).

Mathematically, the clarity of perception will be described by the following function:

$$
\begin{aligned}
0.0 \leq d \leq d_1 \quad & CP(d) = \lambda d \\
d_1 \leq d \leq d_2 \quad & CP(d) = CP_{max} \\
d \geq d_2 \quad & CP(d) = \frac{1}{\sigma * \sqrt{2 * \pi}} * \exp\left\{-\frac{(d - d_2)^2}{2 * \sigma^2}\right\}
\end{aligned}
$$

(Eq. 1)

The clarity of perception function can be determined as the function above mentioned in the focus forward direction, when we see things with a kind of mild tunnel vision or 'foveal' vision, where we are very focused on one thing and ignore everything else around. This situation happens very often, for example, when you watch TV and you don't really notice the rest of the room, or using a computer when you concentrate your vision on the screen, or reading or writing, where we only really see the page. Even talking to people, we tend to focus on their eyes and faces and ignore the rest of them.

The clarity of perception function in the transition region has to have in mind the presence of peripheral vision. Peripheral vision, as it was mentioned above, is paying attention to what's happening at the periphery of your field of vision. In this area you may become aware of movement, but you may be less aware of colour and contrast distinctions.

In the retina we have two types of light receptor cells – cone cells, which detect colour, and rod cells, which detect movement. The cone cells are grouped towards the middle of the retina, while rod cells predominate around the edges. Moreover, the receptors density depends on the eccentricity of the eye (figure 3), and it decreases at the same time that the eccentricity increases from the fovea to the nasal area. This is why we notice movement rather than colour and details at the periphery of our vision. This means that, if the object is within the transition region, the user's resources to perceive it are lower than if the object is inside the focus foreground region and the level of detail that we can get from that object is lower as well. Starting from this theory the clarity of perception in STR will have a different meaning because in this area we are not perceiving object's details but we are perceiving object's movements.

In the peripheral region, detection acuity in peripheral vision is limited by retinal image quality, contrast-transfer properties of the eye's optical system, and resolution acuity is limited by the ambiguity introduced by the photoreceptors [40], [38]. Although in foveal region critical distances depend on the target's size, in peripheral vision they depend on eye eccentricity [25]. Human acuity declines more rapidly in peripheral vision than in foveal vision [3]. This acuity is measured following models of eccentricity scaling of contrast sensitivity and the scaling law $F = 1 + E/E_2$. Where F is the scaling factor indicating how a spatial property or performance varies, E is the retinal eccentricity, and E_2 is the eccentricity for which performance doubles with respect to the foveal value. For example, following some experiments realised by

Anderson [1] over a user subject (RSA) who has 30 deg eccentricity with a long-stroke letter E (which is the traditional tumbling E stimulus used clinically), and $E_2=0.98$ the MAR value is 0.49. For this reason, and following the researches realised by Levi et. al [25], we propose a Gaussian function to describe the variation that the clarity of perception has with the distance eye-object (figure 5) for a fixed object's size.

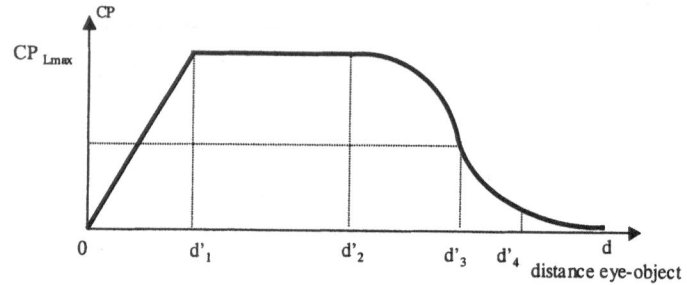

Fig. 5. Clarity of perception relative to distance inside the focus transition region

Where:

$$0.0 < CP_{L\max} < CP_{\max}$$
$$d'_1 > d_1 \quad d'_2 < d_2 \quad d'_3 > d_3 \quad d'_4 \approx d_4$$

(Eq. 2)

The density of visual receptors is continuous along the eccentricity of the human eye. So, the clarity of perception that a human being has of an object placed in the focus foreground region is given by the equation 3 (figure 4) while that if the object is placed in the focus transition region it will be given by the equation 4 (figure 5), being the transition between both continuous.

7   Some Scenarios for Human Like Perception

In order to prove the usefulness of the proposed perception model, consider that, as it was previously mentioned, mIVA-VE systems can be used to simulate risky situations, as for example, a world-wide war, where the soldiers training plays a very important role. In this kind of systems, soldiers can be trained for living and surviving the worse real-life situations. To get a useful training, it is important to endow soldier agents with a human-like perception model. Moreover, collaboration between agents can be very important to reach awareness of what is surrounding each soldier each and every moment. Different scenarios and situations can be raised where human-like perception plays a very important role. In this section we are going to describe a couple of them.

Lets imagine that a soldier agent is perceiving a plane but it has not enough visual acuity as to recognise neither the model of the plane nor its coat of arms. So, this soldier can make a mistake and confuse the coming plane with a friendly plane instead of recognising it as the hostile plane that it really is. But perhaps there is another soldier agent close to him that can alert him and, finally, both of them can escape from the enemy attack. As it is possible to appreciate here, an agent with a perfect vision would not faithfully simulate real life,

Now, lets imagine the following situation, where a soldier agent (A) is walking through a forest looking for the enemy, and while the soldier A is passing close to a tree, an enemy soldier (B) tries to throw towards the soldier A's neck with the aim of killing him. In this moment, the soldier A can not be aware of the soldier B's presence because B is not inside it's A's field of vision and, consequently, the soldier A can not react to the soldier B's attack. This is an example of how boundaries should limit the agent's perception in order to achieve more realism.

A similar situation to the last one would happen if the soldier B is inside the soldier A's field of vision but placed on its peripheral area of vision. The soldier A would have been able to detect the soldier B's movement but it wouldn't have been able to detect if it was an enemy because in the peripheral area one can perceive the object's movement but not any detail of it. In this case, the focus concept, as it was considered by the Spatial Model of Interaction, would not have been enough.

8   Conclusion

The field of Intelligent Virtual Agents (IVAs) is a new emerging and multidisciplinary area. It is making rapid progress, owing to its inherent attractiveness to diverse fields, such as education, entertainment computer games or communication.

This paper describe the work that is been done at the Universidad Politécnica de Madrid, in a close collaboration with the University of Nottingham, with the aim of endowing Intelligent Virtual Agents (IVAs) with a human-like perception model. This physical perception model can be understood as the first level of an "awareness model", with a broader interpretation of the term "awareness" than that used in CSCW. Among all the exiting awareness models we have chosen the "Spatial Model of Interaction" for this propose.

In this paper, we propose to introduce the "Spatial Model of Interaction" as a part of the perception, in order to endow the agent with "knowledge" (an "awareness") about its surroundings. If this happens and the agent will be able to experiment, in real-time, any virtual simulated environment, having knowledge about its surroundings. Moreover, the agent will behave and respond to stimuli of their environment, which have previously been perceived, having then the possibility of interacting and communicating with humans rather naturally.

Acknowledgments. The work presented in this paper has been supported by the Communication Research Group (CRG), led by Steve Benford and Chris Greenhalgh at the School of Computer Science and Information Technology in the University of Nottingham.

References

1. Anderson, R. Thibos, L. The Relationship Between Acuity for Gratings and for Tumbling-E Letters inPeripheral Vision.
2. http://research.opt.indiana.edu/Library/acuitytumbling/acuitytumbling.html. Consulted in 2002
3. Balcisoy, S. Kallmann, M. Torre, R. Fua, P. Thalmann, D. Interaction Techniques with Virtual Humans in Mixed Environments. In International Symposium on Mixed Reality, Tokyo, Japan, 2001 (extended version to be publishedin Presence, MIT Press).
4. Beckmann, P. J. Legge G. E. Effects of Preneural Factors on Letter Acuity in Central and Peripheral Vision. http://vision.psych.umn.edu/www/ARVO/PJB98.html. Consulted in 2002
5. Benford, S.D., and Fahlén, L.E. A spatial model of interaction in large virtual environments, in Proc. Third European Conference on Computer Supported Cooperative Work (ECSCW'93), Milano, Italy. Kluwer Academic Publishers, 1993, pp. 109-124..
6. Benford, S. et al. User Embodiment in Collaborative Virtual Environments Proc. ACM CHI95. 1995.
7. Blumberg, B. Go with the Flow: Synthetic Vision for Autonomous Animated Creatures. Proceedings of the First International Conference on Autonomous Agents (Agents'97), Marina del Rey, CA, 1997.
8. Card, S., Moran, T., & Newell, A. The Psychology of Human-Computer Interaction. N.J., Erlbaum. 1983.
9. Chenney Stevephen Sensing for Autonomous Agents in Virtual Environments,1996. http://www.cs.berkeley.edu/~schenney/autonomous/sensing.html
10. Chopra-Khullar, S. and Badler, N. "Where to look? Automating attending behaviors of virtual human characters," Autonomous Agents and Multi-agent Systems 4(1/2), 2001, pp. 9-23.
11. Das, S. K. Grecu, D. L. COGENT: cognitive agent to amplify human perception and cognition. . Proceedings of the Fourth International Conference on Autonomous Agents, June 5-7, 2000, Barcelona, Spain.
12. Dourish, P., Bellotti, V.: "Awareness and Coordination in Shared Workspaces", in: Proceedings of the 4th ACM Conference on CSCW. Toronto / Canada, Oktober 1992.
13. Endsley. M., Design and evaluation for situation awareness enhancement. In Proceedings of Human Factors Society and Annual Meeting, volume 1, 1988.
14. Endsley. M. Towards a theory of situation awareness. Technical report, Texas Technical University, Department of Industrial Engineering, 1993.
15. Greenhalgh, C., Large Scale Collaborative Virtual Environments, Doctoral Thesis. University of Nottingham. October 1997
16. Herrero P., De Antonio A., Segovia J. Is the Awareness of Avatars in a Virtual World Different from Human Awareness? Workshop on the Future of Cves: "Voltage in the Milky Night: The Future of CVE's" The Third International Conference on Collaborative Virtual Environments. ACM Collaborative Virtual Environments 2000. San Francisco (California). USA. September 2000.
17. Herrero P., De Antonio A., Benford S., Greenhalgh C., Increasing the Coherence between Human Beings and Virtual Agents Proceedings of the First International Joint Conference on Autonomous Agents and Multiagent Systems, Bologna, Italy, July, 2002.
18. Hill, R. Han, C. van Lent, M. Perceptually Driven Cognitive Mapping of Urban Environments. Proceedings of the First International Joint Conference on Autonomous Agents and Multiagent Systems, Bologna, Italy, July, 2002.
19. Hill, R. Kim, Y. van Lent. M. Anticipating Where to Look: Predicting the Movements of Mobile Agents in Complex Terrain. Proceedings of the First International Joint Conference on Autonomous Agents and Multiagent Systems, Bologna, Italy, July, 2002.

20. Hill, R. Han, C. van Lent, M. Applying Perceptually Driven Cognitive Mapping To Virtual Urban Environments. Conference on Innovative Applications of Artificial Intelligence (IAAI-2002) in Edmonton, Canada.2002.
21. Hill R. Soar: An Architecture for Human Behavior Representation. Invited Panel Member and Presentatio at the Workshop on Human Behavioral Representation, Conference on Modeling and Simulation, American Institute for Aeronautics and Astronautics (AIAA), August 9-11, Portland, Oregon , 1999.
22. Hill, R. Modeling Perceptual Attention in Virtual Humans. Proceedings of the 8th Conference on Computer Generated Forces and Behavioral Representation, Orlando, FL, May 1999.
23. Howarth, P. A. and Costello P.J., Contemporary Ergonomics 1997, Ed. S.A.Robertson, Taylor and Francis London, 1997, pp 109-116.
24. Kieras, D. E. & Meyer, D. E. The EPIC architecture for modelling human information-processing and performance: a brief introduction. Technical Report TR-94/ONR-EPIC-1,University of Michigan. 1994.
25. Levi, D.M., Klein, S.A. & Hariharan, S. Suppressive and Facilitatory Spatial Interactions in Foveal Vision: Foveal Crowding is simple contrast masking. Journal of Vision, 2, 140-166. 2002. http://journalofvision.org/2/2/2/
26. Levi, D.M., Hariharan, S. & Klein, S.A. Suppressive and Facilitatory Spatial Interactions in Peripheral Vision: Peripheral Crowding is neither size invariant nor simple contrast masking. Journal of Vision, 2, 167-177.2002. http://www.journalofvision.org/2/2/3/
27. Nilsson, N. Teleo-Reactive Programs and the Triple-Tower Architecture. Electronic Transactions on Artificial Intelligence, Vol. 5, Section B, pp. 99-110. 2001.
28. Noser, H., A Behavioral Animation System Based on L-systems and Synthetic Sensors for Actors. PhD Thesis. École Polytechnique Fédérale De Lausanne. 1997
29. Pew R.W. and Mavor, A.S. editors. Modelling Human and Organizational Behaviour: Application to Military Simulations. National Academy Press, Wash., D.C. 1998.
30. Rickel, J. Gratch, J. Hill, R. Marsella, S. and Swartout, W. "Steve Goes to Bosnia: Towards a New Generation of Virtual Humans for Interactive Experiences." In AAAI Spring Symposium on Artificial Intelligence and Interactive Entertainment, Stanford University, CA, March 20, 2001.
31. Rodden, Tom, Populating the Application: A Model of Awareness for Cooperative Applications, in Proc. ACM 1996 Conference on Computer Supported Cooperative Work (CSCW'96), November 16-20, 1996, Boston, Massachusetts, USA, ACM Press, pp. 87-96.
32. Shively, R. J., Brickner, M., Silbiger J., A Computational Model of Situational Awareness Instantiated in MIDAS 1997
33. Terzopoulos D., Tu X. and Grzeszczuk, R. Artificial fishes: Autonomous locomotion, perception, behavior, and learning in a simulated physical world. Journal of Artificial Life, 1, 4, 1994.
34. Terzopoulos D., Rabie T. F., Animat Vision: Active Vision in Artificial Animals, Proc. of the Fifth Int. Conf. on Computer Vision (ICCV'95), Cambridge, MA, USA, June, 1995.
35. Terzopoulos D. and Rabie, T.F. Animat Vision: Active Vision in Artificial Animals. Published in Videre: Journal of Computer Vision Research, 1(1):2-19, 1997.
36. Terzopoulos D. Biological and Evolutionary Models give life to self-animating graphical characters with bodies,brains, behavior, perception, learning, and cognition. Artificial Life for Computer Graphics. Communications of the ACM August 1999/Vol. 42, No. 8
37. Thalmann, D. The Foundations to Build a Virtual Human Society, Proc. Intelligent Virtual Actors (IVA) 2001, Madrid, Spain
38. Thalmann, D. ANewGeneration of Synthetic Actors: the Interactive Perceptive Actors Proc.Pacific Graphics 96 Taipeh, Taiwan, August 1996.
39. http://research.opt.indiana.edu/Researchers/Thibos/sum89-94.html. Consulted in 2002.
40. Tu X. and Terzopoulos D., Artificial Fishes: Physics, Locomotion, Perception, Behaviour. Computer Graphics Proceedings of SIGGRAPH 94, pp 43-50, 1994.

41. Wang, Y. Thibos, L. Bradley, A. Effects of Refractive Error on Detection Acuity and Resolution Acuity in Peripheral Vision Investigative Ophthalmology & Visual Science, 38, 2134-2143.2002.
42. Yeap, W.K. and Jefferies, M.E. 1999. Computing a representation of the local environment. Artificial Intelligence 107:265-301.
43. Zhang W. and Hill, R. A Template-Based and Pattern-Driven Approach to Situation Awareness and Assessment in Virtual Humans. Proceedings of the Fourth International Conference on Autonomous Agents, June 5-7, 2000, Barcelona, Spain.

A Decentralized Algorithm for Coordinating Independent Peers: An Initial Examination

Girish Suryanarayana and Richard Taylor

Institute of Software Research, University of California, Irvine
{sgirish, taylor}@ics.uci.edu

Abstract. Peer-to-peer (P2P) applications are composed of a distributed collection of peers that cooperate in order to perform some common task. Though P2P applications have attracted the attention of researchers, there has been little exploration of the deep issues; rather initial attention has been on widely known but technically shallow applications such as found in Napster and Gnutella. One particularly rich domain for examining the utility of P2P applications is distributed, decentralized crisis response. This paper studies the applicability of a peer-to-peer approach in such an emergency response situation. We have developed a prototype peer-to-peer infrastructure that models a group of firefighters who communicate with each other while fighting fires. Each firefighter (peer) runs a novel distributed "k-server" algorithm that makes local autonomous decisions based on the information received from other firefighters. While this study was limited in that it used a simulation to study the algorithm, the emergent behavior observed suggests that further, more detailed investigations are warranted.

1 Introduction

Communication, completeness, and accuracy of information and decision-making are the most important characteristics of applications that belong to an emergency response domain. Typically, in such situations, a centralized authority gathers information about the system from workers in the field and makes decisions regarding their placement. Accordingly, workers are distributed across the system, with each one carrying out his tasks. This central control can be a bottleneck and can cause disastrous delays. Further, in an emergency situation there is not enough time and resources to set up a centralized authority and follow a command structure.

Peer-to-peer (P2P) applications are composed of a distributed collection of entities (called peers) that cooperate in order to perform some common task. The enormous success of systems like Napster [2], Gnutella [3], Magi [5] etc. has given a major boost to the P2P paradigm. Consequently, there has been an increase in the awareness of the potential utility of the P2P approach. However, decentralized emergency response applications have been largely unexplored. As stated above, in an emergency response application, setting up a centralized solution is often not practical given short

R. Meersman, Z. Tari (Eds.): CoopIS/DOA/ODBASE 2002, LNCS 2519, pp. 213–229, 2002.

time frames or physical constraints. P2P applications, however, can operate without a central infrastructure and are self-organizing thereby reducing set up time and resource costs.

In this paper, we describe our approach of applying P2P techniques to an emergency response application. We first present a model of the system, mapping elements from the emergency response domain to P2P concepts. A set of parameters is associated with every peer and request that determines their characteristics.

Then, we present a distributed algorithm that is run on every peer in the system. Our algorithm is a variant of distributed solutions to the "k-server" problem [24]. In the k-server problem, servers are placed in a virtual 'space' and can move within the space to serve requests. Over time, requests arrive at points in the space. As soon as a request comes in, a server must be moved in order to serve the request. The act of movement incurs some cost. The goal is to decide which servers to move so that a sequence of requests can be served with a cost as small as possible [21].

To evaluate the algorithm we built a simulator that simulates a group of firefighters trying to extinguish brush fires. We refined the algorithm gradually by experimenting with various input parameters and observing the resultant system behavior. Evaluation results primarily show that though no firefighter has complete knowledge of the system and is unaware of the state of other firefighters, the universal system goal is nonetheless achieved, thus exhibiting an emergent behavior.

Our approach draws from a large number of computer-related disciplines including networking, distributed algorithms, wireless communications, and graphical real-time simulations. This paper contributes a novel distributed k-server algorithm that is executed on every peer and a P2P infrastructure that allows extensive experimentation to evaluate P2P approaches and techniques. The paper also represents a significant data point in the feasibility and utility of P2P approaches.

2 Motivation

Consider the scenario where groups of firefighters are battling a large brush fire that is spread over many square miles. It is essential that a firefighter be able to communicate to the rest of the firefighters various kinds of information, for example, the intensity of the fires, the direction in which the fires are spreading, the direction of winds etc. This communication is necessary because critical decisions need to be made based on the information that each of the firefighters provide, for instance, which fires should be tackled first and by whom. Since a wrong decision can result in a disaster, it is imperative that the information provided be complete and correct so that correct decisions can be made by the system. Moreover, a firefighter should also be able to call for assistance in fighting a fire and be able to provide information regarding the status of the fire he is fighting. Thus, it is vital that all the firefighters in the system stay connected as much as possible.

The demands on communication, completeness and accuracy of information and decision-making are not limited to a fire-fighting scenario. There are several other scenarios where a similar solution is required. These include other emergency situations that arise during natural disasters like earthquakes, floods, and storms. Sensor devices in an exploratory mission, robots in hazardous situations and soldiers in a hostile territory are other cases where a group of entities work autonomously to attain a common system goal.

The US Department of Labor states "In national forests and parks, forest fire inspectors and prevention specialists spot fires from watchtowers and report their findings to headquarters by telephone or radio. When fires break out, crews of firefighters are brought in to suppress the blaze using heavy equipment, hand-tools, and water hoses." [1] In a typical scenario, if the necessary infrastructure to coordinate firefighting exists and is in place, the firefighters will first evaluate the fires and inform the central controller at a distant location about the intensity and capacity of each fire. Based on such information received from various firefighters, the central controller will then make decisions about the importance of each fire and the allocation of firefighters among the fires. Each firefighter will accept directions from the controller and move towards the fire that he has been assigned to deal with. However, this central authority is, in fact, a bottleneck: commands are sent out in a sequential manner introducing arbitrary delays and the possibility of a system failure at the command post. Moreover, one cannot know the locations of fires that will occur in the future and accordingly cannot set up a system in advance to fight the fires. When an actual fire occurs, response will be slowed because of the requirement to utilize the centralized control. Furthermore, communication is limited because of distance and terrain, so in some circumstances the centralized control structure may break down completely.

3 Background

3.1 Peer-to-Peer Applications

In a peer-to-peer architecture, each of the peers can act both as a client and a server. When a peer requests a service, it acts like a client, and when it fulfills a request from another peer, it adopts the role of a server. Requests for service are called peer-to-peer *events*.

Peer-to-peer (P2P) applications came to the fore primarily due to Napster [2], which was an immensely popular system for exchanging music files. Napster allows a user to first search for a file using a keyword and returns a list of all peers who have the file. The user then connects directly to a peer and downloads the file without involving any intermediate server in the process. However, since Napster uses a central server to keep track of all the clients that are connected to it and which files they are sharing, it is not considered as a pure P2P application by many. However Clay Shirky in [7] claims Napster is a P2P application because it allows for variable connectivity by having the addresses of Napster nodes bypass DNS and gives peers at the edges of the network significant autonomy by moving control of file transfers to them.

In contrast, an application that implements the Gnutella protocol [3] does not rely on a central authority to manage the network or to broker transactions. A peer connects to a Gnutella host and uses a ping-pong message sequence to locate other peers nearby [8]. When a peer needs a file, it queries the peers it is connected to. The peers search on their system for the requested file and also pass the request onto other peers to whom they are connected. The results are returned to the querying peer who can then select a peer and download the file directly from that peer.

Though P2P rose to the forefront primarily due to music sharing, it has also been used in collaborative tools such as Groove [4]. Groove is a decentralized Internet-based platform for secure collaboration. Groove users make immediate and direct connections with other users for a wide variety of activities including: working on a project, sharing drafts, coordinating schedules and discussing issues etc. Groove also offers communication tools like instant messaging and threaded discussions as well as content-sharing tools like shared files and shared contacts. It also permits other features like co-browsing and co-editing of Microsoft Word documents. Activity in Groove occurs in a "shared space"—a secure space in which group members carry on conversations. A copy of the Groove shared space is stored locally on the computers of each of the members of the space. When one member adds something new to the space, that change is reflected on everyone's machine – thus every member of the space gets a single consistent view of the project's data [9].

Micro-Apache Generic Interface (Magi) is an open architecture framework that facilitates messaging and deployment across a broad range of computing platforms [6]. Magi is a general-purpose, peer-to-peer infrastructure for both embedded and enterprise applications. It offers an end-user application for installation on desktops, laptops and even PDA devices and allows secure collaborative applications to run on these machines. It also offers features like building work team communities, file sharing, chat and messaging Each Magi peer provides a set of core services that can be extended to create modules for each peer based on the services it provides and the capabilities of the platform on which it is installed [5].

The aforesaid developments in the P2P world have brought this field to prominence. This has led to awareness of the potential of the peer-to-peer approach among the research community.

3.2 Mobile Ad-hoc Networks

A mobile ad-hoc network (MANET) is a collection of mobile wireless nodes that form a temporary network without the aid of a centralized administration or standard support services that are regularly available on conventional networks [10]. Such a collection of mobile hosts that enables communication between users without an infrastructure is called an "ad-hoc" network. It can be deployed rapidly because it needs no infrastructure. In a mobile ad-hoc network different hosts communicate over wireless links and messages may traverse multiple wireless links before reaching their destination. Since mobile nodes tend to "wander around" changing their location, ad-hoc networks must deal with frequent changes in topology as well as one-way connectivity and transient connectivity. Consequently, research on mobile ad-hoc networks has concentrated primarily on routing protocols that are necessary to facilitate the exchange of packets between two hosts that may not be able to communicate directly [12][14].

In the algorithm that we have developed, firefighters communicate using message broadcast. Research results in mobile ad-hoc communication have shown that message broadcast communication tends to consume excessive network bandwidth [16]. However, the MANET community has developed routing algorithms that enable efficient message distribution that could be leveraged in the implementation of our algorithm [11] [13].

3.3   Control Algorithms

A considerable amount of effort has gone into research on the online "k-server" problem in algorithm literature [20] [22]. In the k-server problem, first defined in [21], initially each server is positioned at some point of the metric space. A metric space can be considered as an edge-weighted graph over n vertices with edge weights corresponding to distances between the endpoints. Requests arrive for service at points of the space. When a request comes in at some point of the space, a server must be moved to that point (if none is there) in order to serve the request. Besides the server that moves to the point of request, the other servers are also free to move so that they can position themselves favorably for handling subsequent requests. When a server moves, a cost equal to the distance it covers is incurred. The cost of a request is equal to the sum of the costs incurred by all servers during the service of that request. The cost of a sequence of requests is equal to the sum of the costs of all requests in the sequence.

The goal of researchers has been to design algorithms that will decide which servers to move when a request arrives so that any sequence of requests can be served with a cost as small as possible. Whereas in an off-line problem the complete input is known and the goal is to search for a time-efficient algorithm, in the case of an online problem the input is not known beforehand but is revealed only during the execution of the algorithm. We deal only with the on-line k-server problem because, for us, the sequence of requests for service is not known in advance, but revealed request by request [19].

The algorithm research community has mostly concentrated on centralized solutions to the "k-server" problem [22] [23]. Such a typical solution consists of a global-control algorithm that gets the requests and governs the motion of the servers with no cost incurred for acquiring the knowledge about all the requests and for transmitting motion instructions to the servers.

A distributed k-server algorithm [24] has to deal not only with the problems of lack of knowledge of future requests but also with incomplete information about previous requests. While a centralized solution to the "k-server" problem incurs cost only when a server moves from one location to another, in the case of a distributed algorithm additional cost is incurred because of the transmission of messages among the servers.

We map the "k-server" problem to our firefighters application. Fires are the points of space that require service. Each firefighter acts like a server that moves to a fire to service it and the cost incurred is the energy that is expended by a firefighter to do certain tasks.

Though the distributed k-server problem is the basis of our problem, our domain introduces significant differences from the traditional k-server problem. Each point of request (fire) may require more than one server (firefighter) to service it. A firefighter may provide service only when his energy level is above a certain threshold. When a firefighter moves from one location to another, he spends energy that depends on the distance he moves. While a server does not incur costs while servicing a request in an ideal distributed "k-server" setting, a firefighter exhausts most of his energy in fighting fires. The problem is thus to find a satisfactory solution that will decide which firefighters to move towards which fire so that all the fires are extinguished in as little time as possible with minimum energy expenditure.

4 Approach

To address this issue we first modeled the system, mapping elements from the firefighting domain such as fires and firefighters to P2P concepts such as work requests and peers, respectively. After examining the problem, we developed an algorithm that is a variant of the distributed "k-server" algorithm specifically to address the firefighter problem.

4.1 "Firefighter" Model

In the firefighter model each firefighter takes the role of a peer that communicates with other peers to exchange information. Every firefighter is assumed to have a device (like a Personal Digital Assistant) that not only enables communication but also permits information storage and computing. Each firefighter has four salient properties: his position (expressed as an (x, y) coordinate in a two-dimensional plane), his maximum energy capacity (expressed as an integer), his energy level (expressed as an integer) and his current task (resting, looking for fires, moving towards a fire or fighting fires). Energy is consumed when a firefighter moves towards a fire and when he fights the fire. A firefighter gains energy when he is resting or looking for new fires. Associated with each firefighter is an attribute reflecting how much energy he expends running and fighting fires. The energy level of a firefighter dictates his behavior. There are three energy thresholds: critical energy threshold, minimum energy threshold and the maximum energy threshold. If a firefighter is currently *en route* to a fire and his energy level drops to the minimum energy threshold he must stop and rest. However, if he is fighting a fire when this happens, he continues fighting until either the fire is extinguished or his energy level reaches the critical energy threshold. When his energy level goes below the critical energy threshold, he must stop and rest irrespective of his current task. A firefighter who has completed work on a fire will rest until his energy capacity has reached the maximum energy threshold. We have defined a firefighter's maximum energy threshold to be 80%, the minimum energy threshold to be 20% and the critical energy threshold to be 1% of his maximum energy capacity. The algorithm, explained later, determines a firefighter's status and current task.

In this model we associate "hot spots" of the fire with P2P events. These events are passive objects that are manipulated by firefighters. Each fire is created requiring a certain amount of effort to be extinguished. In this model, the amount of effort required to extinguish a fire does not increase over time and only decreases by the actions of working firefighters.

Similar to other pure peer-to-peer applications, the communication among firefighters occurs without the intervention of any central routing authority. A firefighter peer does not need to know about the existence of other firefighters in the system. We limit communications and information exchange exclusively to radio and visual proximity to an event. This implies that any two firefighters that are not in radio range cannot communicate directly; however, if an intermediate is available he can act as a proxy and can forward the messages he received to other firefighters within his range. Because of the scale of the environment the impact of other forms of communications such as verbal and visual gestures can be ignored without loss of expressive power. We also assume that the digital communication system follows a probabilistic model of delivery; that is, message delivery is not guaranteed. In reality, digital communications normally have a sharp drop-off point at a fixed distance; however, various obstructions can cause significant signal attenuation resulting in decay. The radio model is simplified to facilitate implementation. In our model, as in a typical radio system, the strength of the signal is inversely proportional to the square of the distance from the transmitter (inverse square law). The likelihood of the message being received is directly proportional to the signal strength. The messaging model used is broadcasting, with a static hop-count. Each receiver will automatically rebroadcast a received message (with a decremented hop-count) if its hop-count is greater than zero.

4.2 System Architecture

Fig. 1 is a simple illustration of the architecture of the "Firefighters" model. Firefighters communicate with each other through the universal radio band that acts as a connector bus. Any message that is sent to the radio band is forwarded to all other firefighters *provided they are within radio range of the sender*. Thus the radio band also acts like a "distance filter" since it filters messages based on the distance from the sender.

An alternative view of the architecture can be seen in Fig 2. In this diagram, the radio band has been divided to illustrate the distance-limited communication among firefighters. RB1 and RB2 are two parts of the universal radio band. F1, F2 and F3 are all within communication range of each other and so they are connected to RB1. However, F4 is within range of only F3 and so F3 and F4 are connected to RB 2. However, this view of the architecture is not constant since the position of firefighters is not fixed. The architecture is dynamic and may change as the firefighters move to new locations.

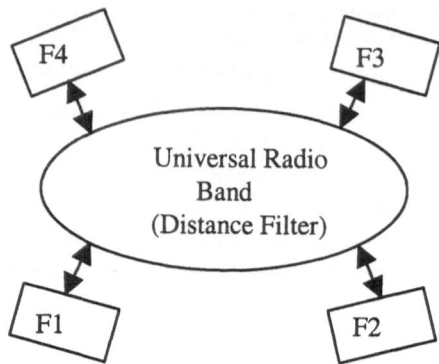

Fig. 1. Conceptual Model of the system architecture. *F* refers to firemen

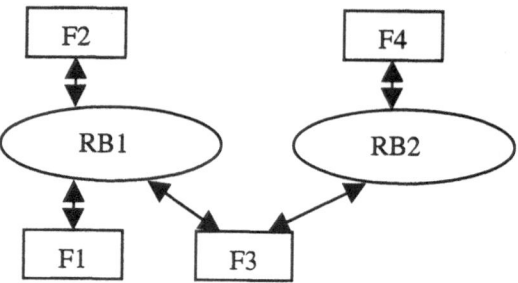

Fig. 2. Distance-limited Model of the system architecture. *RB* refers to radio band

4.3 Algorithm

For our firefighters application, we execute a decentralized "*k*-server" algorithm on each of the firefighter peers. When a firefighter discovers a fire he sends out a message with information about the fire. If he has no other destination, he moves toward the fire. When a firefighter without a current destination receives a message informing him about the occurrence of a fire, he replies with information about his current energy level and location. He then begins moving toward the fire. The first firefighter to arrive at a fire is elected that fire's leader. He is responsible for determining how much effort the fire requires and calculates the number of firefighters required to fight the fire based upon its size. The leader's PDA device extracts energy level and location information from all the messages that it received from the firefighters in response to the initial message. It evaluates the energies of all the firefighters headed towards the fire and selects the most suitable amongst them. It then notifies those firefighters approaching the event if they are needed or not.

We conservatively tell only those firefighters who are not needed to stop coming; in the event of lost messages, extra firefighters arrive rather than insufficient firefighters. While this may not be the optimal allocation of effort, it is "safe" in the sense that at least the required number of firefighters will arrive, providing they are available. Firefighters continue to fight the fire until either it is extinguished or their energy level drops below the critical energy level.

If a firefighter is free and has no knowledge of any new fire or existing fires requiring more firefighters, he assists other firefighters in fighting fires even though he is not required. This helps to extinguish all the fires in the system faster. This also avoids the extreme fatigue of certain firefighters who fight fires that require few firefighters but more effort. If a fire event has only a fraction of the necessary firefighters it can still be extinguished although it will take a longer amount of time. Following is the pseudo-code for our distributed algorithm.

```
Algorithm {

  updatePossibleDestinations();

   if destination is not null {

     if firefighter is at destination

         fightFire();

     else

         moveToDestination();

   }

   if destination is null {

     if firefighter has sufficient energy

     {

        setNewDestination();

        if destination is still null

          lookForNewFires();

        else if he has a destination

          moveToDestination();
```

```
        }

    else if firefighter is exhausted relax();

  }

updatePossibleDestinations() {

Get a list of all visible fires and add to it a list of
known fires that are not directly visible.

Remove from this list fires that do not need more fire-
fighters and fires that have been extinguished;

Send "AssistRequestMessage" for all visible fires.

}

fightFire() {

  currentStatus is "Fighting";

  if firefighter is assigned to the fire        {

    destination.workEffort();

Decrease the energy level of the firefighter by a fixed
amount;

If he is the leader selectFiremen();

If the energy level is below the critical energy level,
remove self from fire and rest;

  }

else destination of firefighter is set to null;

}

selectFiremen() {

Sort through a list of messages received, on the basis
of energy levels of firefighters approaching fire;

Tell firefighters that are not needed to choose other
destinations by sending "AbortMoveMessage"
```

```
}

moveToDestination() {

  currentStatus = "Moving to fire";

  Increment position of the firefighter;

  Decrease energy level by fixed amount  and if it goes
  below the minimum threshold set the destination to
  null;

}

setNewDestination() {

Select the nearest fire from the list of possible des-
tinations;

}

lookForNewFires() {

  Increment position of the firefighter;

  currentStatus is "Looking for Fires";

Increase energy level by a fixed amount only as long as
it is below the maximum energy capacity;

}

relax() {

  currentStatus is "Resting"

Increment energy level by fixed amount only as long as
it is below the maximum energy capacity;

}
```

There are four types of messages that are used by firefighters to communicate in our algorithm, namely, *AssistRequest*, *ResourceStatus*, *AbortMove* and *FireOut*. Each message consists of a unique identifier and a hop-count and contains information about the originator and the sender of the message. A firefighter rebroadcasts a message only if the hop-count is greater than zero. Every time the message is re-broadcast, the hop-count is decremented by one.

When a firefighter discovers a fire he broadcasts an *AssistRequest* message to other firefighters. When another firefighter receives an *AssistRequest* message, he puts the location of the event in his possible list of destinations. If the firefighter has no destination (i.e. is wandering and searching for fires), he sets his destination to that of the new fire and broadcasts a *ResourceStatus* message. This message contains information regarding the current energy level of the firefighter and his current location. On receiving these *ResourceStatus* messages, the leader firefighter's PDA evaluates the energy levels of each of the firefighters moving towards the fire. He then generates an *AbortMove* message, which is addressed only to those firefighters who are not needed. On receiving an *AbortMove* message addressed to him, the firefighter either starts moving towards another fire or continues searching for new fires. When a fire is extinguished, a *FireOut* message is sent by the leader firefighter.

Since most messages hold *some* interest for the receivers, the broadcast model is deemed necessary for the system to function properly. Only one message sent has an explicit receiver (*AbortMove*), and that is used only to request additional actions on that unit's part; our assumption that messages may be dropped and our use of rebroadcasting proxies further illuminates the need for broadcasting even in situations where messages have a specific destination. For best performance, all the firefighters need to receive all the messages. Firefighters who receive only a subset of messages will not perform as well as those who do. Hence the broadcasting communication model best suits the "firefighters" application.

5 Evaluation

This section describes techniques and tools that were used to evaluate the P2P infrastructure and the algorithms that we developed.

5.1 Simulator

We built a multi-threaded asynchronous application in Java to simulate the Firefighter problem. To preserve autonomy among the firefighters, we model them as individual threads. This prevents any form of implicit synchronization between their interactions. No explicit synchronization is performed except when transmitting and receiving messages, since a radio frequency can only accommodate one message at a time. Fires are generated at random locations. An independent thread known as an *EventManager* creates random events (fires) at random times.

An annotated screenshot of our simulator is shown in Figure 3. Each numbered black dot represents a firefighter and the black squares represent fires. The big circles around each dot represent the range of sight of the firefighters.

5.2 Algorithm Evaluation

Using the simulator, we evaluated the algorithm on the basis of the time required to extinguish all the fires and the exhaustion level of the firefighters. Input parameters were identified and the behavior of the system was studied as we varied the parameters. The feedback obtained was then used to refine the algorithm.

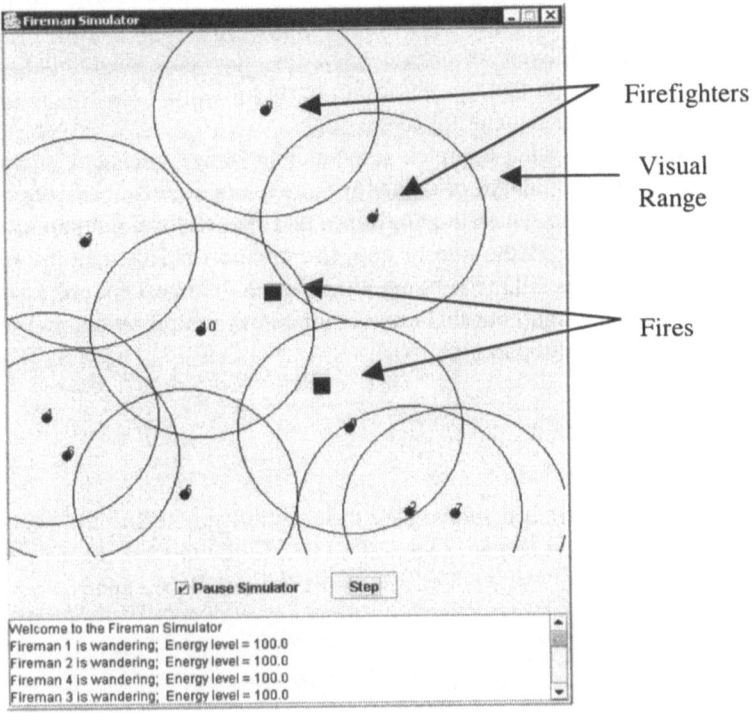

Fig. 3. Simulator Screenshot with two fires and ten firemen

We first experimented with varying hop-counts for re-broadcasting and discovered that if the message hop count was too high, it resulted in packet flooding. With 5 firefighters and maximum of 10 concurrent fires, we found that a static hop count of 5 was most favorable for our application. The next parameter we studied was the number of firefighters in the system. We varied the number of firefighters, keeping the maximum number of concurrent fires constant. Though the time required to extinguish all the fires depends partially on the random work effort required per fire, we found over a number of simulations that the time required for extinguishing all the fires decreased noticeably when the number of firefighters was increased, indicating that our basic assumptions about the overall system behavior were correct.

Changing the threshold energy levels of the firefighters had a remarkable effect on system behavior. More specifically, when the minimum energy threshold of the firefighters was lowered, the overall resultant exhaustion of the set of firefighters as a whole decreased, as did the time required to extinguish all fires.

We dropped some messages during the simulation to model signal decay and studied the resulting behavior of the firefighters. We observed some expected inefficiencies in the system. For example, firefighters who did not receive a *FireOut* message would continue moving towards the location of the fire even though it no longer existed. To address this problem, we refined our algorithm so a firefighter will check for the existence of the fire visually once it is in range of his sight. In spite of not using a guaranteed message delivery or message acknowledgement scheme in our communication model, we noticed that our algorithm ensured that the system goal was eventually achieved even with some dropped messages.

Though no firefighter has complete knowledge of the system and is unaware of the behavior, location, and number of other firefighters, an emergent behavior is observed when each firefighter executes the algorithm and makes local autonomous decisions. We found that, as long as the rate of new fire creation is less than the rate at which firefighters put out fires, all the fires are extinguished. One exception is that fires must be discovered to be fought, but this issue is inherent in the problem and would be the case in a centralized solution as well.

6 Future Work

The firefighter application demonstrates the feasibility of using the peer-to-peer approach in an emergency response situation. The following sub-sections discuss how we plan to add new features to the existing infrastructure in the future.

6.1 Limitations

Broadcast of messages leads to inefficient utilization of network bandwidth. The number of messages that are broadcast increases exponentially with the number of firefighters in the system. Our future work will include the evaluation of routing protocols based on those developed by the MANET community [15] and the subsequent selection of routing algorithms for our P2P infrastructure. In the current application, when a firefighter broadcasts a message he does not know whether it was received by any one. A message acknowledgement scheme can be used to notify the sender of received messages. This can be used to increase the reliability of message delivery since a sender can resend his message if he does not receive any acknowledgements.

Our algorithm uses a simple leader election mechanism to choose the leader for a fire. In the future, we will consider the application of leader election algorithms developed by the MANET community for our algorithm [17] [18].

In our simulator, we assume that unattended fires do not increase in size and intensity with time. Further, when a large fire is reduced to a small fire some firefighters should be able to leave that fire and move towards other demanding fires so that they do not grow beyond control. We plan to implement these changes to our system model and refine the algorithm accordingly. In the future, we also intend to compare the performance of our algorithm with other trivial solutions that are possible for such emergency response systems.

We also plan to experiment with different "wandering" algorithms to find one that enables firefighters to discover fires more effectively. We believe that enhanced communication among firefighters about their wandering behavior will allow all firefighters (as a whole) to discover fires more quickly than with random wandering.

Currently, the application uses a simple messaging framework consisting of just four kinds of messages. Though this set of messages addresses most of the information required by firefighters, it is not complete with respect to real world situations. In the case where a firefighter needs personal help because he is in danger, he needs to communicate the nature of help required to other firefighters in the system. Having a message type to convey this is a viable option, however, this may not solve the problem completely. Therefore, it may also be necessary to prioritize messages so that the most important messages are received and addressed first. We will also concentrate on extending the message framework to support more message types and developing a priority scheme for the messages.

6.2 Infrastructure Evolution

In the future, we plan to execute our distributed algorithm on wireless PDA devices (Compaq's IPAQ) to study the behavior of the system in the "field." All devices are also equipped with a GPS (Global Positioning System) unit so that each peer can exchange positional information with other peers. Our control algorithms will be implemented on top of Magi, which will be used as the P2P infrastructure running on the devices.

7 Conclusions

This exercise supports the contention that P2P architectures have significant, novel applications, arguing for further exploration of the topic. This exercise focused primarily on the decentralized algorithm used on each peer within a fire-fighting scenario. We demonstrate that a peer-to-peer solution can be applied to an emergency response situation effectively. We have developed a novel variant of the distributed "k-server" algorithm which, when executed, leads to an emergent behavior. Provided the existence of each of the fires is known to at least one firefighter, all the fires in the system are eventually extinguished if there are an adequate number of firefighters in the system. Though none of the firefighters possess complete knowledge of the system, they make local autonomous decisions that lead to a feasible system solution.

The P2P framework that we have constructed (in the form of our simulator) is scalable, multi-threaded and asynchronous, and provides an excellent framework for further experimentation. The flexibility of our framework allows us to inject other management models so we can compare them as well.

Applying the P2P approach to the emergency response domain has also brought to the fore a set of rules and principles for handling emergency situations. Clearly, a fuller exploration of this scenario will require experimentation in which actual distributed devices are used, such that the interaction between algorithm, P2P infrastructure, ad-hoc networking, power management, and so forth can be explored.

Acknowledgements. We would like to thank Michael Goodrich and Sandra Irani for their invaluable feedback and contributions.

References

1. Firefighting Occupations - Nature of the Work http://www.bls.gov/oco/ocos158.htm
2. Napster http://www.napster.com
3. Gnutella.com http://www.gnutella.com
4. Groove Networks, Inc., Platform for inter-enterprise communication and collaboration http://www.groove.net
5. Bolcer, G., Gorlick, M., Hitomi, A., Kammer, P., Morrow, B., Oreizy, P., Taylor, R. Peer-to-Peer Architectures and the Magi Open-Source Infrastructure. Endeavors Technology, Inc. (Dec 2000) http://www.endtech.com/papers.html
6. Bolcer, G. (Endeavors Technology, Inc.) Magi: An Architecture for Mobile and Disconnected Workflow. IEEE Internet Computing special edition on Internet-Based Workflow, (May/June 2000) 46-54.
7. Shirky, C. Listening to Napster in Andy Oram, ed. Peer-to-Peer: Harnessing the Benefits of a Disruptive Technology. O'Reilly & Associates, March 2001, 21-37.
8. Kan, G. Gnutella in Andy Oram, ed. Peer-to-Peer: Harnessing the Benefits of a Disruptive Technology. Andy Oram O'Reilly & Associates, March 2001, 94-122.
9. Udell, J., Asthagiri, N., Tuvell, W. Security in *Peer-to-Peer:* Harnessing the Benefits of a Disruptive Technology. Andy Oram O'Reilly & Associates, March 2001, 354-380.
10. Johnson, D. Routing in Ad Hoc Networks of Mobile Hosts. Proceedings of the IEEE Workshop on Mobile Computing Systems and Applications (Dec 1994)
11. Perkins, C., Bhagwat, P. Highly dynamic Destination-Sequenced Distance Vector Routing (DSDV) for Mobile Computers. Proceedings of the SIGCOMM '94 Conference on Communications, Architectures, Protocols and Applications (Aug 1994), 234-244.
12. Johnson, D. Dynamic Source Routing in Ad Hoc Wireless Networks, Mobile Computing, Kluwer Academic Publishers, 1996.
13. Park, V., Corson, S. A Highly Adaptive Distributed Routing Algorithm for Mobile Wireless Networks. Proceedings of IEEE INFOCOM (April 1997).
14. Garcia-Luna-Aceves, J.J., Madruga, E.L. The Core Assisted Mesh Protocol. IEEE Journal on Selected Areas in Communications, Special Issue on Ad-Hoc Networks, Vol. 17, No. 8, (Aug 1999) 1380-1394.
15. Royer, E., Toh, C-K. A Review of Current Routing Protocols for Ad-Hoc Mobile Wireless Networks. IEEE Personal Communications Magazine (Apr 1999) 46-55.

16. Basagni, S., Chlamtac, I. Broadcast in Peer-to-Peer Networks. Proceedings of the Second IASTED International Conference European Parallel and Distributed Systems (Vienna, Austria July 1998) 117-122.
17. Malpani, N., Welch, J., Vaidya, N. Leader Election Algorithms for Mobile Ad Hoc Networks. Proceedings of the 4th International Workshop on Discrete Algorithms and Methods for Mobile Computing and Communications (DIAL M for Mobility) (Aug 2000) 96-103.
18. Hatzis, K., Pentaris, G., Spirakis, P., Tampakas, V., Tan, R. Fundamental Control Algorithms in Mobile Networks. Proceedings of the Eleventh Annual ACM Symposium on Parallel Algorithms and Architectures (Saint-Malo, France June 1999) 251-260.
19. Borodin, A., Linial, N., Saks, M. An optimal online algorithm for metrical task system. Journal of the Association for Computing Machinery, vol. 39, (no.4) (Oct 1992), 745-763.
20. Koutsoupias, E., Papadimitriou, C. On the k-server conjecture. Journal of the Association for Computing Machinery, vol.42, (no.5) ACM (Sep 1995), 971-983.
21. Manasse, M., McGeoch, L., Sleator, D. Competitive algorithms for on-line problems Proceedings of the Twentieth Annual ACM Symposium on Theory of Computing (Chicago IL, May 1988) 322-333
22. Fiat, A., Rabani, Y., Ravid, Y. Competitive k-Server Algorithms. Proceedings of the 31st Ann. IEEE Symposium on Foundations of Computer Science, (October 1990), 454-463.
23. Grove, E. The Harmonic k-Server Algorithm is Competitive. Proceedings of the 23rd Annual ACM Symposium on Theory of Computing, (May 1991), 260-266.
24. Bartal, Y., and Rosen, A. The Distributed k-Server Problem – A Competitive Distributed Translator for k-Server Algorithms. Journal of Algorithms, vol.23, (no.2), Academic Press (May 1997), 241-264.

Supporting Peer-to-Peer User Communities

Julita Vassileva

Computer Science Department
University of Saskatchewan
57 Campus Drive
Saskatoon, Saskatchewan, S7N 5A9 Canada
jiv@cs.usask.ca

Abstract. The paper describes a design of a peer-to-peer system which is being developed currently to support file and service (help, advise) sharing in research groups and groups of learners. The design addresses some non-technical problems in the deployment of P2P systems, such as coping with free riders, creating closely-knit groups of users sharing common interests and trust. It describes a user modelling approach for servents and presents several approaches for motivating users to participate and contribute to the community.

1 Introduction

In our experience in designing and deploying on a large scale a multi-agent system for peer help called "I-Help" [18], we encountered many issues that are important in the design and practical usage of Peer-to-Peer (P2P) systems. Instead of file sharing, I-Help allows exchange of help and advice services, or "peer-help" among the students. A student needing help related to assignment in a class can request it through her agent who finds other students who are currently on-line and have expertise in the area related to the question. Thus, the help request can be considered as an analogue to a search query in a P2P system and locating an appropriate helper can be considered equivalent to a "hit". In I-Help, agents act on behalf of the users instead of servents, and there is a centralized matchmaker service, which maintains models of the user's competences and matches them to the help-requests. Thus, the I-Help architecture is similar to Napster, which is generally considered a P2P system [12]. The actual service (peer-help) is provided through a chat session, which is recorded. If both users have evaluated it positively and agree to make it public, the recorded session becomes a resource that is available to other students in the system, who come with the same or a similar question. I-Help has been deployed for two years in most undergraduate classes at the University of Saskatchewan and has taught us a lot of lessons [7,18] that are relevant to peer-to-peer systems in general.

Most of these lessons concern non-technical problems in the deployment of P2P systems, such as coping with free riders, creating feelings of trust in the users and motivation to participate and contribute to the community. One major lesson we learned is that the success of such a system requires a "critical mass" of users to participate at each given time. To achieve this it is necessary to know more about the

R. Meersman, Z. Tari (Eds.): CoopIS/DOA/ODBASE 2002, LNCS 2519, pp. 230–247, 2002.
© Springer-Verlag Berlin Heidelberg 2002

users, i.e. to create models of the users and of their emerging social relationships with other users in the system. We also learned some important lessons about different ways to motivate participation and contribution to the community.

We are currently re-implementing I-Help as a peer-to-peer application, called COMUTELLA (Community Gnutella). The system will enable research or study groups of students to collaborate and share resources, e.g. to exchange both services and files. The goals are:

- to increase the performance, i.e. the speed and quality of search (in terms of precision / recall);
- to increase the satisfaction of the users, their participation and level of contribution.
- to provide a possibility for tightly-bound interest groups of users and to ensure fast routing of queries to the appropriate groups.

Therefore this paper does not report on a piece of finished work; it rather describes the design of a system that is being developed right now, and which draws on our previous experience and some knowledge of P2P computing. The remainder of the paper is organized as follows: section 2 presents a motivation for group formation in P2P systems, section 3 presents the user modeling that needs to be done to allow this, section 4 discusses various methods of motivating users to participate actively, section 5 explores some aspects of the global behavior of the system and section 6 presents a discussion comparing this approach with other work.

2 Intelligent Routing and User Interest Groups

Intelligent routing and network organization in Peer-to-Peer networks has been a topic or active research recently [12]. The most prominent approach for document routing, used in FreeNet involves moving data in the network and storing it at certain nodes (servents) to optimize performance. This approach ensures privacy and contributes to a very efficient routing in large, global communities. However, it causes loss of information about the application and the locality [9] and is prone to splitting the network into "islands" [12].

More recently, approaches that try to exploit the social interactions between peers have been proposed. Local search strategies introduced in [1] use well-connected servents and have costs that scale sub-linearly with the size of the network. Ramanathan et al. [13] propose to modify the approach of query broadcast in a random servent neighborhood adopted by Gnutella. They propose selecting the set of neighbors among those that have the highest number of query-related files (hits). Thus a new neighborhood of the servent will be defined for the current search, which contains the most promising at the moment neighbors. This reduces the number of query messages sent in the network by both reducing the number of servents to which a query is broadcasted and the time-to-live (TTL) of each query. This approach has no "memory" of which nodes were returning many hits about a particular area in a past session. It adapts reactively to the current search, and in order to achieve a better adaptation of the neighborhood, it requires that the users make several consecutive queries in the same general area of search. The approach will not work if the user searches for a given thing just once, or if the user searches for two different things in parallel.

Another approach for semantic routing of queries was adopted in NeuroGrid [8]. It assumes that nodes / servents will store files according to the interests of their users and will persist in the network. The main idea is that each servent stores associations between keywords and other NeuroGrid servents that have returned hits for these keywords in the past. A new query is forwarded to a subset of servents that historically have shown to possess matches to the keywords in this query. This approach makes a shift towards modeling long-term characteristics in the files and nodes to facilitate search. These characteristics are the semantic of the files/resources and associating servents / nodes with particular semantics. One possible criticism is that the network is so dynamic, that there is no guarantee that the nodes with resources matching a particular keyword will be available at the time of the search. However, if they are not available, NeuroGrid can always rely on the default Gnutella neighborhood, i.e. there is no loss, but there can be win, in case these nodes are on-line. NeuroGrid makes a first step towards modeling similarity in interests of users, but this is done implicitly and neutrally, for all search queries passing through each servent. We believe that modeling the interests of users explicitly and maintaining lists of "friends" with similar interests may reap more benefits, since it allows taking into account similarities in patterns of time on-line. We propose that the servent should use a model of its user's interests and relationships in section 2.

An extension to the Gnutella protocol was proposed in [3] which allows servents to exchange reputation information. The subjective reputation is learned from their previous experience with other servents and reflects the quality of resources and service. There is no semantics associated with the reputation, i.e. "node x is good in area y". Thus modeling the servent's reputation does not benefit the search, but assists the user to decide whether to download a file from a given servent, if there are several hits available.

A further step towards facilitating search and selecting quality files/services is to provide mechanisms for servents in P2P systems to self-organize into *groups* based on similarity of interest between their users and on shared positive experiences reflecting quality of resource, speed of download or quality of service.

Many Internet communities, like newsgroups, chat-rooms, and virtual cities constitute examples of self-organizing groups of users with similar interests. Their success could be explained with the high value (or usefulness) of networks that allow group formation. Such networks are known as Group-Forming Networks (GFN). In general, the value of a network is defined [14] as the sum of different access points (users) that can be connected for a transaction for any particular access point (user) when the need arises. There are three categories of values that networks can provide: a linear value, a square value, and an exponential value. The Sarnoff's Law [15] that states that the power of a broadcasting network is linearly increasing in proportion to the number of its users. Examples of broadcasting networks are TV channels or news sites.

The Metcalfe's Law [11] that states that the value of a peer-to-peer network is proportional to the square of the number of its users. Metcalfe's law is applicable to networks such as telephony systems or P2P networks and has been used by economists as an explanation for the fast growth of the Internet.

Reed [14,15] finds that the networks that allow group affiliation are even more powerful. According to his GFN Law, the value of group-forming networks grows exponentially with the number of users. As a consequence, networks that allow group formation among its components (users or agents) are expected to bring the highest economical benefit.

We envisage a group forming mechanism for Peer-to-Peer networks, based on user's long-term interests and common patterns of behavior. We provides servents with the capability to learn not only about the user's interests, but also to establish relationships with other servents, based on the user's compatibility in interests and satisfaction from previous interactions. It allows for creating long-term relationships between users, takes into account the balance of taking / giving from the community, thus creating a "small-world" – a tightly coupled community based on shared interests, where we believe mechanisms for motivating user's participation can be successfully incorporated.

3   User Modeling

To create user groups based on interest, the servent needs to understand the interests of the user and facilitate finding and maintaining relationships with users with similar interests. In the next sections we will explain how this can be achieved.

3.1 User Model Representation

The user model contains three different parts:
– a model of the user's interests,
– a model of the user's resources (files or services),
– a model of the user's relationships.

The model of user interests is represented as a list of topics / areas in which the user is interested. An ontology representing topics and sub-areas in a given semantic area allows clustering users into groups sharing similar interests. It is important to note, that these user groups can overlap on various levels, e.g. one user can be a member of a group interested in Bulgarian folk music and in a group interested in blues. The same user can be also a member of a group interested in peer-to-peer computing and in a group interested in multi-agent systems. However, s/he may be a member of a sub-group of the multi-agent systems group interested in agent negotiation and coalition formation and not be a member of a group interested in animated avatar agents (see Figure 1).

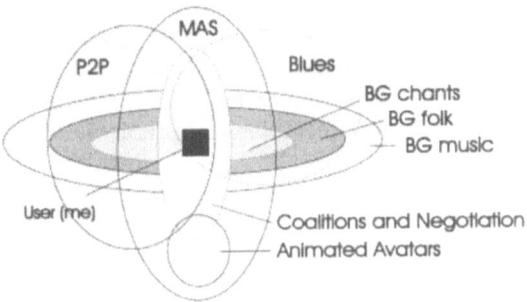

Fig. 1. User interest groups.

The model of user interests is organized hierarchically as an overlay over the domain ontology. Sub-areas in which the user has shown interest by issuing queries are represented, along with a value that indicates the strength of user interest in the area and a time stamp showing when the user made the last query in this area. The user's strength of interest in an area is calculated based on how many times the user has searched in this area, and how recently s/he has searched in this area. The user's interest in areas that are more general (higher in the ontology heterarchy) than the current area of search are also impacted, but in a much weaker way.

It is clear that in order to apply this approach, one condition is that all servents use a compatible representation of a domain ontology or ontology of services. There are various tools to developing such ontologies, e.g. DAML-S [4]. Another condition is that at two stages an association has to be made between areas/topics, keywords and resources /services: when the resource/service is introduced into the system, and when the user is making a query. The need to annotate a resource/service with respect to an area / topic and to provide keywords can be an impediment to both users bringing in resources/services from outside and to users searching, since it makes it necessary to make at least two more clicks (e.g. selecting the appropriate area /topic from a pull down menu) and entering keywords or selecting a directory to indicate the location of the file / service. To compensate for this extra effort we deploy a variety of motivation mechanisms discussed in the next section.

The model of the user's resources/services includes the files or services offered by the user (either actively, by bringing them in the system from outside, or by sharing files and services taken from others). When a new resource/service is created by the user, it has to be indexed by the user with respect to a certain area of interest and optional keywords, which are stored in an annotation file associated with the resource / service. When the user is offering a resource/service that has been taken from other users in the network, it does not need to be annotated. Each resource is associated with two measures of importance in the model – one denoting the subjective importance of the resource/service for the user, and one denoting the importance of the resource/service for the community.

The model of the user's relationships includes the users with whom the user has interacted frequently, i.e. from whom the user has downloaded files frequently and also users, who have downloaded files frequently from the user. These relationships are represented in a list where each relationship contains the unique id of the other user, the search area in the context of which the users have interacted, two numbers representing the strength and the balance of the relationship and a time-stamp showing the last time the relationship was updated. The strength is a subjective factor reflecting how often the user has used resources/services from the other users, and how satisfied the user was with the interactions, i.e. if s/he kept the downloaded file or deleted it, if she used the file frequently. The balance of the relationship denotes the direction of services / files, i.e. who of the users predominantly uses and who offers resources / services. The next section explains how these three representations are created and updated.

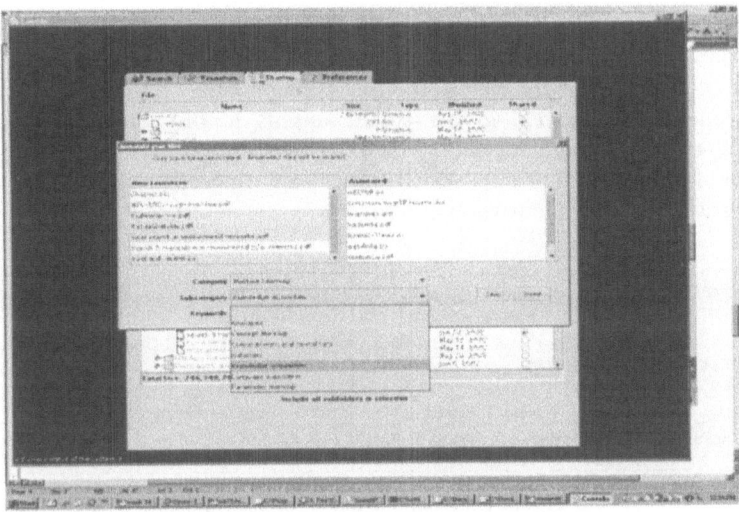

Fig. 2. The user interface for annotating a new resource. The black background visualizes the community and is replaced with a night sky image when there are other uses on-line.

3.2   Creating and Updating the User Model

The user model is updated each time the user adds a new resource or service to share, when the user searches services/resources in a particular area, when she downloads files or uses a service. There is also a possibility to update the user model by adding relationships with users who are searching for queries that are only passing through the servent, i.e. to "listen" to the traffic and thus develop awareness about who looks for what. However, we are not exploring this option here, since it will lead to developing very large user models, containing relationships in all possible areas of search, which are not likely to be useful most of the time. We keep our model focused on the areas in which the user has been searching previously expecting that the user is likely to search again in these areas.

3.2.1   Modelling User Interests
Each servent keeps track of the words / phrases entered by the user for search and adds the related areas to the model of user interests. The areas are retrieved from a lookup table reflecting the ontology of the domain. The strength of user interest S^a at time t in each sub-area a in the ontological heterarchy that is on the path leading to the sub-area related to the query is updated according to a simple reinforcement learning formula:

$$S^a(e_p, t) = i * S^a(e_{i-p}, t-1) + (1 - i) * e_t \tag{1}$$

where the new (at time t) evidence of interest $e_t \in [0, 1]$ is calculated as $e_t = 1/d$, where $d = 1 + the\ distance$ between the level of the sub-area of the query and the level of the area a in the ontology graph.

The parameter $i \in [0.5, 1]$ is an inflation rate used to model the fact that older experiences become less important over time t, while the most recent experience is the most relevant (since the user's preferences may change over time). It can be fixed at a given value, say 0.5, giving equal weights to old and new evidence. The parameter i can also be a variable, which depends on the time elapsed since the last evidence of interest in this area, which allows capturing better the current tendency in user interests. An example is shown in Figure 3.

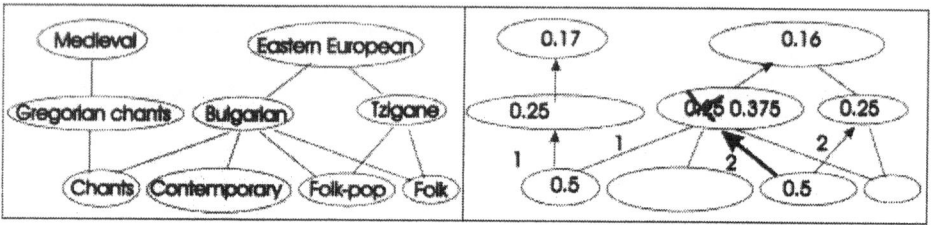

Fig. 3. Updating the model of user interests

3.2.2 Modelling the User Resources / Services

To model the resources / services of the user, the servent keeps track of the following:
- what files/service the user has downloaded/ used,
- what the user does with each downloaded file,
- what files/ services are downloaded and used from the user .

The actions of the user concerning the file / service (e.g. if s/he keeps or deletes the file, how often s/he accesses it or uses the service) are used to calculate the ranking of the file w.r.t. "subjective" importance for the user. The actions of other users concerning the file / service (e.g. how often it is requested / downloaded / used) are used to update the "objective" importance of the resource, i.e. how important is the resource for other users on a community level.

The ranking of resources is used by the servent to compute the cost of keeping a given file locally. If the servent has a strong relationship with another servent in the group and the second servent has the file, the first servent has to decide, if it is worth keeping the file and eventually, suggest the user to delete it. More about the "specialization" of servents in a group is given in section 5.

3.2.3 Modelling the User's Relationships

To model the relationships of the user, the servent keeps track of the following:
- which servents respond with relatively many hits to the user's query,
- from which servents the user chooses to download files or to request service,
- the success of each download / service,
- who issues queries that result in hits in the list of resources of the user,
- who downloads files from the user.

The servents who have returned many hits along with those from whom the user has chosen to request service or download a file are entered in the user's list of formal "relationships" with an indication of the context of the particular area of interest (request) in which the relationship was created. The success of each download or service is used to update the *strength of the relationship* between the users using a formula similar to (1). Servents who are searching for files / services that are offered by the user and who choose to download files or use the services offered by the user are also added to the list of "relationships" of the user for the particular area of interest depending on the query used for the search.

Two users can be involved in relationships in several different contexts, indicating that they share interests in different areas. As a result, such users will have a very strong relationship (it will be the sum of the strength of the relationships for the individual areas).

The relationships that the user maintains with other users in a given area of interest can be sorted with respect to their strength. From these, a subset of currently active servents can be selected as the immediate neighbors to whom to send queries at any given moment. There are various policies for forming the neighborhood, which are described below.

One possibility is to select the top relationships from the area that corresponds to the current search area. This approach would follow the spirit of Ramanathan et al. [13] where the neighborhood changes with each search. However, since it is not sure that the user is going to continue searching in the area, or if she is going to issue another query in a different area, it probably doesn't make sense to change the whole neighborhood. Probably changing only a few of the neighbors, or forming the neighborhood of the global top n (across all areas) servents that are active at a given moment would allow better flexibility for future queries.

In addition to the relationship's strength and context, the servent keeps track of the balance (reciprocity) of the relationship. The servent of user X calculates the balance of its relationship with the servent of user Y as:

$$B^{XY} = N^{X \leftarrow Y} - N^{Y \leftarrow X} \tag{2}$$

i.e. the difference between the number of times when the user X has downloaded files from Y and the number of times when user Y has downloaded files from X. If the balance is negative, the user X "owes" user Y. The servent ranks the requests coming from other servents depending on the balance and the importance of the relationship. In this way, in a download queue, priority or more bandwidth will be given to request from important servents to the user, or to servents, from who the user has downloaded often resources or whose services were often used. Another "favor" that a servent X that "owes" to another servent Y does is not to decrement the time to live (TTL) i.e. the number of hops that the query can make, of a query sent by Y. In this way, the search horizon of a user who has contributed resources to users in the group increases.

The sum of the balances of all relationships of a user defines how much s/he has contributed to the community and how much s/he has consumed. Keeping a balance of each relationship allows maintaining a model of the user's contribution to individual users, to every interest group in which s/he participates and to the network as a whole. It is used by the servent to provide an individualized motivational interface for the user, to persuade her/him to contribute to the community.

The described method for updating the user model uses an unobtrusive way of obtaining user information, posing no additional load on the user (such as requiring the user to enter ratings, or answer specific questions).

3.2.4 Sharing User Models among Servents

While not involved actively in search, servents could communicate with each other and learn about other users with the similar interests. This learning could take two forms:

− *Direct:* without explicit request from the user, the servent sends queries in a particular area to find out servents that have resources and enters them in the list of relationships of the user. The strength of relationship can be updated as in [13] by the percentage of the number of hits by this servent over the total number of hits. In this way the servent explores the network. Also the time of request and reply can be recorded, to capture the compatibility in time patterns of being on-line. This approach, however, creates a lot of additional traffic in the network, and Gnutella has proven to be vulnerable to denial of service attacks caused unwittingly by servents that try to explore the network generating too much traffic [10].

− *Indirect:* by requesting from "friend-servents" the list of their relationships in a particular area. "Friend-servents" are those with whom the servent has a strong relationship in a given area. In this way the IDs of servents that have been frequently available and have provided a good service in a given area (e.g. good resources or services, did not interrupt the connection during download) are shared among the servents.

In a P2P network that is not very dynamic, i.e. most of the servents are active at approximately the same time, indirect learning will ultimately lead to all communicating agents from one interest group having the same list of relationships, which will lead to an implicit objective measure of quality / ranking of each servent within the group. This objective ranking will be contextualized, i.e. it will make sense only in the context of one interest group / coalition, since people behave differently in different communities. Of course, this will not prevent servents who have a high rank in one group to achieve a high rank in another group too.

There are a number of open questions concerning the interpretation of information received from others. One approach is when the servent requests relationships only from its "best friend" in an area.

However, it is also possible to request data from all existing "acquaintances" and use the strength of relationship with each source to compute the strength of relationship in the new "acquaintance". This approach is similar to approaches for trust propagation among agents in multi-agent communities [22,23]. There are different possible ways how information about a given servent coming along a chain of "acquaintances" can be interpreted: by voting among the sources, by averaging the strength values along the path, or by multiplying them. It is also necessary to define a policy for resolving conflicts between different chains of sources. Another question is if one representation of relationship strength is sufficient, or if each servent should keep two separate representations of the strength of relationship: a subjective one based on the servent's own experience, and objective reputation based on information received from other servents. How can these two representations be combined and when?

We could argue against using global reputation measures in P2P systems because of the dynamics and the variety of preferences of users in the system, which can render any "objective" measures useless. For example, if user X requests a service from user Y always at 1 a.m. and never gets anything, since Y is never on-line at that time, X's strength of relationship with Y would be 0. However, Y could be a very active member of the community, providing useful files and services at other times. The strength of relationship that X has with Y reflects also the compatibility between X's and Y's preferences in the time pattern of usage, and it can not be generalized into one number without loosing valuable context information. Therefore, just averaging the strength of relationship values of many users without considering the contextual information would not be appropriate. More sophisticated techniques than the currently existing reputation techniques deployed in Multi-Agent systems are necessary to retrieve information from appropriate servents, to interpret it in a context and purpose-dependent way.

4 Motivating Users to Participate

Motivation of users to participate in the community is a crucial factor for the success for a P2P system. There is an ongoing discussion in the literature about the harm vs. benefit of free-riders for P2P systems [16]. The main argument in favor of free riding is that digital resources will never suffer from the tragedy of commons effect. They can be endlessly replicated, and each replica adds to the common (if the user who downloads the file shares it with the community). However, with free riders only the community can not create any wealth. There is a need for altruists or community-oriented users who create the resources or services once, before they start being shared and multiplied by free riders. Our experience with I-Help, a peer-to-peer system for help for over 2 years in the University of Saskatchewan shows that if the the system lacks a "critical mass" of active users, it will never be able to take off [5, 11, 12].

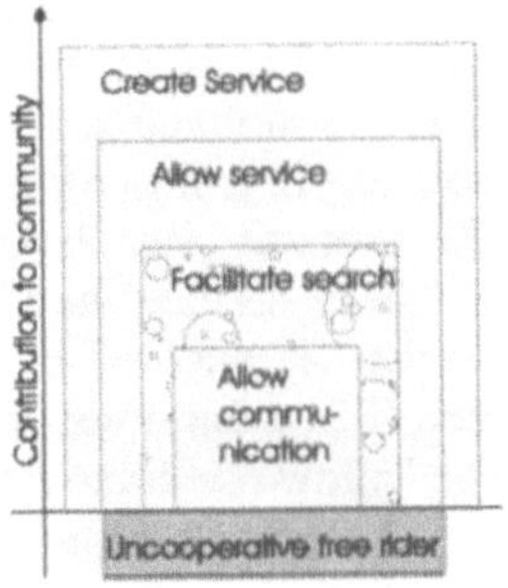

Fig. 4. Levels of user cooperativeness.

In I-Help we observed several levels of user cooperative participation (Fig.4). Below we generalize them to the case of a P2P system where the servents deploy user modeling as proposed in section 2. These levels of participation are characterized with decreasing degree of active user involvement (activeness):

- *create service*: creating new resources or services and offering them to the community,
- *allow service*: providing to the community disk space to store files for downloads or computing resources to enable a service that has been created by another participant in the community

- *facilitate search*: providing its list of relationships from the various groups in which the user participates to other users to facilitate search of files or services. This level of cooperativeness is possible if the servents model the "good" relationships with peers, as we proposed in the previous section.
- *allow communication*: forwarding ping-pong, query and hit messages, i.e. actively participating in the protocol of the network, i.e. participating in the peer infrastructure [2].
- *uncooperative free-rider*: downloading files or utilizing services when needed, but going off line immediately afterwards.

The "create service" level usually includes "allow service", "facilitate search" and "allow communication", i.e. it describes the most socially cooperative type of user behavior.

The more typical level is "allow service", describing a user who contributes passively to the community, by providing her resources and relationships, as well as the functionality of her servent to enhance the infrastructure of the community, but does not actively bring new resources or services into the system. As shown in [2], in Gnutella only a tiny minority falls into this category – 5% of the users is responsible for sharing over 70% of the files.

According to [2], the majority of users (66%) fall into the category, "allow communication" – they participate in the network infrastructure and therefore can be detected and taken into account. Unfortunately, there is no way to know at any moment how many users are "uncooperative free riders" or "creators of service" due to the lack of history in Gnutella and the anonymity, which does not allow to identify who first introduced a file into the system.

According to [20], more than 80% of the users of Mojo Nation were "1-time, 1-hour" users, and of the remaining users a significant part were "1 time, less than 24 hour" users. We observed a similar behavior of users in our I-Help system in certain classes, where the instructors failed to motivate a "critical mass" of active users in the beginning, when most of the users log-in just to try the system [18].

All popular file sharing P2P systems, like NAPSTER, Morpheus /KaZaA and LimeWire try to ensure both the "allow service" and "allow communication " levels of cooperation. Usually "allow service" is ensured by a default setting in the servent, which commands the downloaded files to be saved in a standard shared folder, so that other servents can find them. The "allow communication" level is achieved by making it hard to quit the servent. For example, a typical servent will not be quitted by clicking on the "close window" button, but will remain active on the task bar, until the user quits it again explicitly. These default settings can be changed by the user, e.g. the downloaded files can be saved in a file different from the default shared Folder, or the servent can be quit by one click, but it requires more knowledge and active involvement from the user, which is a form of "punishment" for uncooperative behaviour.

There are three principle ways of motivating users to participate in a community [17]:

- by trying to influence the user's feelings (of guilt, of belonging or owing to the group) to stimulate her altruism towards the community.
- by rewarding the user with visibility / reputation in the group depending on his/her contribution.

– by providing an economical model which ensures incentive for user contribution, (e.g. better quality of service, priority in the queues).

It is likely that choosing an appropriate way of motivation depends:

– On the personality of the user
– On the nature or the user's interest in the area.

Thus, the same user can be altruistic in one group, motivated by reputation in another group and by economic rewards in a third group.

4.1 Motivating Altruistic Users

Altruistically motivated users are devoted to a particular cause (e.g. finding extra-terrestrial intelligence, cancer research or genome sequencing). They are likely to be active participants on the highest level (create service) in an interest group dedicated to the cause, like SETI@home. Influencing people to be altruistic for a given cause is a very difficult task; it requires a very detailed and broad model of user interests and of her acquaintances in the real world (who might be involved in a interest group with a certain altruistic purpose). This is still beyond the scope of the current user models and corresponding captology [5] (persuasion) techniques deployed in intelligent computer interfaces. A much more simplistic way that could hopefully influence the user is trying to provoke a feeling of quilt for not contributing to a community from which the user has taken a lot of resources. This could be attempted by using subtle cues like running messages in the window frame, or by a face or animal figure that changes its expression with the change in the owing balance of the user to the group (see section 3.2.3). We are currently developing a simple iconic avatar that represents the user in the community, and changes gradually to reflect the level of cooperativeness of the user. This level is computed from the sum of balances of the user's relationships with the members of the community, the number of files shared by the user, the relative duration in which the user's servent is active, and the number of user actions that are deemed as uncooperative, such as removing downloaded files from the shared folder, interrupting an ongoing file transfer or a service.

For each avatar there is a set of variants that differ in the level of friendliness of expression. Depending on the user's level of participation in the community, the avatar changes from a friendly sympathetic expression to an unfriendly and even vicious ghostly expression. This is accompanied with a running message on the bottom of the window suggesting what the user can do to participate more actively in the community, depending on the current level of participation of the user. The idea is that, similar to Oscar Wilde's "The Picture of Dorian Grey" [21], the user will be cued to reflect on her social behavior and how she can possibly change it for the better.

4.2 Motivating Reputation-Aware Users

Users motivated by social reputation are more likely to be active participants in groups where they already knows some participants (even if by alias) and are known themselves. This impact on the user can be achieved through an appropriately designed interface of the servent that creates a global view of the group, visualizing in an appropriate way the servents that contribute most. We are currently developing a dynamic background image of the servent for this purpose (see Fig.2). It is inspired by the idea of a night sky where servents are represented as stars varying in size and brightness. The size denotes the amount of resources / services shared by the servent and the brightness denotes the amount of relationships that the servent has with other servents. The user can access an annotated version of the image, and by positioning the mouse on a star the user can see the name / alias of the servent. The star representing the servent of the user shines in a different color, so the user can see his/her significance in the community by the size and brightness. The image is generated / refreshed periodically to reflect changes in the group.

4.3 Rewarding Participation

Several P2P systems (most prominently, Mojo Nation [20]) rely on a economic model based on micro-payments to stimulate and reward participation. The basic assumption in the design of an economic model is that the effort and time spent bring new resources or services in the community have inherent costs. To take these costs into account, the resources/services should be made tradable. Thus the payment in a virtual currency (e-cash, mojo) may motivate a user to create new resources / services. It was shown theoretically [6] that if users/nodes are viewed as rational game-players, micro-payments for resources create a mechanism to balance the supply and demand of resources/ services.

Introducing an economy allows taking into account the different quality of resources or services provided. For example, a servent can jump to the top of the queue for a given service that is in a great demand at the moment, depending on the amount of mojo it is willing to pay for the service. In this way users who have contributed to the community and earned a lot of mojo are able to gain a better quality of service, which is a significant reward. Another way of reward with a better Quality of Service (QoS) within the system would be by protecting the user from unwanted advertisements.

A new way of providing better QoS that has not been proposed so far is to allow "richer" servents to "buy" themselves a wider search horizon by negotiating the TTL of each query. Thus users who have contributed have a better chance to find resources / files.

However, peer economies have raised a lot of criticism [16], mainly related to the fact that users prefer to pay flat rates rather than to bear the cognitive load of making decisions about micro-payment at each transaction. While this has been pointed as the reason for the failure of Mojo Nation to attract users, we believe, that the problem of the higher cognitive load can be avoided if the servent makes decisions on user behalf [19]. The user doesn't even need to be aware of the micro-payments happening in the background; what she sees is a better or worse QoS depending on the economic state of her servent, which results directly from the cooperativeness of the user. In this way, if the accumulated currency is "cashed" in better QoS, it is important to ensure a gradual improvement or decrease in the QoS depending on the level of user contribution (level of accumulated currency) and always to maintain clear cues in the interface as to what is the reason for the increase / decrease in the QoS and what the user should to in order to improve it.

Motivating users to participate is very similar to teaching them how to behave as good citizens. A basic principle of good teaching is to provide a plenty of positive feedback, i.e. it is important to reward users for good behavior and not to give them the feeling that they are "punished" for bad behavior (at least not in the beginning), since they may withdraw entirely from the system. Of course, negative feedback should be present too, in carefully selected doses depending on the user's level of participation, so that the QoS doesn't deteriorate completely even for uncooperative free riders, since there is always the hope that they may become cooperative when they find the right interest group where they feel safe and comfortable.

It is possible to reward the accumulated currency outside of the P2P system. The choice of reward depends on the type of the interest group. One possibility that was adopted in Mojo Nation is to cash the currency in gift certificates from real-world vendors (possibly using the P2P system for advertisements). Another possibility, suggested in [16] is to give the benefits for cooperation up-front, in terms of for example, 100$ off the next purchase of computer, or payment of the user's Internet service bill.

An economic model in a P2P system requires additional reasoning capabilities (utility computation and decision making) on behalf of the servents, it reduces the anonymity in the system [12] and requires centralized components to be introduced to be responsible for the currency / payment (as in Mojo Nation).

Our current implementation does not deploy an economic model. However, the advantages of such model as a motivation and regulation mechanism are significant and we will probably incorporate such a model in the future.

5 Group Evolution, Servent Specialization

To achieve a system that is able to dynamically self-organize to optimize the distribution of resources, the servents should be equipped with reasoning mechanisms that allow them to make decisions about how to optimize the amount of resources / servers kept locally and the relationships it keeps with other servents. The reasoning of the servent should be motivated by individual benefit, i.e. like a rational agent, the server should optimize its individual utility function. However, on a global level, this individual behavior should result in a self-regulation mechanism, similar to the document routing model used by FreeNet that optimizes the efficiency of search and storage management for the whole community by locating files at particular servents.

Servents can specialize in two main ways:

- Across areas, servents can either specialize in a given group (interest area) or specialize as "hubs" maintaining relationships to well connected servents in many different areas,
- Within one area, with respect to providing either resources/ services or relationships ("hub"), or both.

Some servents can specialize in particular areas of interest by keeping mainly resources/services from this area and relationships to other servents in this area. Other servents will become "hubs", maintaining many relationships with specialized servents in various areas.

It is in the best interest for all servents to be members of all possible interest groups since in this way they will have access to a maximum number of good peers and their resources. Since the servents are able to learn from each other and share relationships, as described, this is technically possible. However, it too expensive for one servent to be a member of all coalitions in terms of disk-space for storing resources and user models, bandwidth, and computing power to reason about ranking and balancing relationships. It should be preferable for a servent not to specialize in particular area, if it has a strong relationship with an agent who is specialized in this area or an agent who is well connected with various groups. The decision in which group to specialize should take into account how often the user makes requests in the area of interest, the duration the user's interest in a given area as well as how many strong relationships the servent has with other servents in this area.

An indication for a persistent user interest in a given area is what the user does with downloaded files or how s/he organizes her services. For example, if the user creates a special sub-directory for downloaded files from this area, this is evidence that s/he has a long-term interest in the area. If the user deletes all the files related to a given area, this could be evidence that the user is no longer interested. Of course, the user might also want to be uncooperative and to avoid sharing the files, if she has copied them in another directory. Therefore, a fine grain analysis of users' actions not only within the P2P application, but also on an operating systems level, especially those related to file management are relevant.

If the servent has several strong relationships in an area (denoting similarities in users' tastes and time patterns) and the user does not frequently search items in the area, it may be better not to specialize in the area but only keep the relationships, in case the user wants to search again in the area. Of course, there will be no guarantee that these relationships will be available at a later time, but it is still a better starting point than the uninformed broadcast currently deployed in Gnutella.

Finally, the decision about specialization in an area of interest should probably involve the user. If this decision is not required too often, it might be appropriate to alert the user and request indication if she is interested in the area and would like the servent to specialize in this area, thus implying that the user participates in the community of other users interested in the area.

There are two kinds of specialization that a servent can choose within a given area:
- to keep a lot of resources or services;
- to serve as a directory service or a relationship hub for the group.

If we do not consider the costs of keeping resources or services [16], the benefit in keeping a lot of resources is for servents of users who access the resources frequently themselves. The benefit of keeping many relationships is that "knowing" other servents that are either well-connected or well equipped with resources minimizes the number of hops a query will make and maximizes the likelihood that it will get a hit.

Even if we do not want to adopt an economic incentive model involving real payments (like the one used in Mojo Nation) the fact that keeping resources or services implies costs in terms of disk space and bandwidth has to be considered. Therefore, there is a motivation for the server to keep resources / services only if:
- the user frequently needs the resource herself, it can be retrieved locally.
- there is a reward that can be received for each download of the resource or usage of the service by other servents.

This reward does not need to be necessarily payment, but it can be, for example, a better quality of service. In order to measure this, some form of bookkeeping is necessary. We have argued in section 4.3 that a micro-payment computed and carried out by the servent, in a system-level economy, which the user doesn't even need to know about is necessary.

In this case, the servent first faces the question how to determine the price that it can charge other servents for the resource. The price depends on the cost of keeping the file/service (e.g. file size / hard disk space) and on the cost of providing the file for others (e.g. file size / available bandwidth). It also depends on the current demand for the resource/service, which can be measured by the number of requests queued. If the cost component of the price is too high as a result of small hard disk and/or bandwidth and there is no demand (either from the user or from other servents), and there are good relationships in the group of interest to servents that have the file, there is probably no good reason to keep the file. The servent should suggest to the user deleting the file from the shared folder. It is important to let the user make the ultimate decision because if she feels lack of control, she may distrust the servent and the whole P2P system [16].

In an economic model, users with large storage and bandwidth capacity can afford to specialize as servers. In this way they will earn currency with each download, while other users may become pariahs, i.e. go in "depth" and create very unbalanced relationships. These users will have to contribute resources or services to the community or do a lot of searching in different areas to allow their servents to build relationships and become specialized as relationship hubs.

The motivation for relationship hubs to specialize in this way in an economic model is that they can "charge" a minimum connection fee for each query passed through them that results in hit.

We are currently investigating what could be a simple and effective pricing policy for micro-payments. Our next steps will be simulating the economy to see what parameter values can be controlled to achieve an equilibrium state and implementing the decision making process for servent specialization.

6 Discussion and Conclusions

We propose that the servent keeps a user model, which allows it to know the areas in which the user has interests and who are "the friends" of the user in each area of interest. Unlike the approach proposed in [13], where the interest groups of users were highly dynamic and changed rapidly to reflect the current search performed by the user, our approach relies on the assumption that users have long-term interests and are likely to search repeatedly in the same area at different times. Therefore, it makes sense to keep track of all "interest groups" of the user, to be able to use them again when a new search happens.

In addition, our approach assumes that the topology of the network in an established active interest group does not change too rapidly. We believe that even though one of the biggest strengths of P2P systems is the ability to work in a highly dynamic environment, where servents (e.g. users) can come on-line and leave at any time, there is a pattern of behavior that can be tracked (locally, by the individual servents) and adapted to, for the benefit of the users. The strength of the relationship between two users reflects not only a certain similarity in tastes and interest, but also a compatible pattern of being on-line. Users, who are related with strong relationships, who have been able to share valuable files / services in a mutually convenient time in the past, are likely to be able to do this again in the future.

The idea of flexibly changing the horizon for search has been proposed in [13], depending on the how promising is the immediate neighbor to whom the request is sent. We extend this idea with the possibility of negotiating the search horizon between the servents considering the strength and the balance of relationship with the servent, thus giving advantage to servents who have been cooperative in the past.

We also discussed various ways to motivate users to contribute actively in the community. Unlike [2], we don't see free riders as a necessary evil, but we don't think they should be praised either (unlike [16]), since we realize that it is impossible to build a successful P2P sharing community with free riders only. In contrast with [13], where goal is to reduce network traffic, and with [6], where the goal is to pay users for sharing files, our goal is simply to ensure a better quality of service to users who contribute to the community.

Our future steps and evaluating the advantages and disadvantages of the proposed design of COMUTELLA with respect to user satisfaction and performance.

Acknowledgements. The author thanks Christopher Cox, who implemented the Comutella servent, and Helen Bretzke, who implemented the interface and developed some of the motivational strategies. Yamini Upadrashta implemented the user model. Thanks go also to Ralph Deters, John Kaufmann, Yao Wang, Chris Brooks. This work has been funded by two NSERC undergraduate summer scholarships, the CRA-Women peer mentor program and the NSERC operating research grant of the author.

References

1. Adamic (2000) The Small World Web. Technical Report, Xerox PARC.
2. Adar E., Huberman B. (2000) Free Riding on Gnutella. First Monday, vol. 5, no. 10. Also available on line at: http://www.firstmonday.dk/issues/issue5_10/adar/
3. Cornelli, F., Damiani, E., De Capitani di Vimercati, S., Paraboschi S., Samarati P. (2001). Implementing a Reputation-Aware Gnutella Servent. Proc. Int. Workshop on Peer-to-Peer Computing, collocated with Networking 2002, May 19-24, Pisa, Italy.
4. DAML Services: http://www.daml.org/services/
5. Fogg B.J. (1998) Persuasive Computing: Perspectives and Research Directions, Proceedings CHI'88, http://hci.stanford.edu/captology/Key_Concepts/Papers/papers.html
6. Golle Ph., Leyton-Brown K., Mironov I. (2001) Incentives for Sharing in Peer-to-Peer Networks. Proceedings EC'01, October 12-17, 2001, Tampa, Florida, ACM press, 264-267.
7. Greer J., McCalla G., Vassileva J., Deters R., Bull S., Kettel L. (2001) Lessons Learned in Deploying a Multi-Agent Learning Support System: The I-Help Experience, Proceedings of AI in Education AIED'2001, San Antonio, IOS Press: Amsterdam, 410-421. Available on line at: http://julita.usask.ca/homepage/public.htm
8. Joseph S. (2001) NeuroGrid: Semantically Routing Queries in Peer-to-Peer Networks. Proc. Int. Workshop on Peer-to-Peer Computing, collocated with Networking 2002, May 19-24, Pisa, Italy, available on line at: http://www.elet.polimi.it/p2p/.
9. Keleher P. Bhattacharjee S. Silaghi B. (2002) Are Virtualized Overlay Networks Too Much of a Good Thing? in Electronic Proceedings for the 1st International Workshop on Peer-to-Peer Systems (IPTPS '02) available at: http://www.cs.rice.edu/Conferences/IPTPS02/
10. Manjoo F. (2002) Gnutella Bandwidth Bandits. Salon, August 2002, available on line at: http://www.salon.com/tech/feature/2002/08/08/gnutella_developers/print.html

12. Milojicic D., Kalogeraki V., Lukose R., Nagaraja K., Pruyne J., Richard B., Rollins S., Xu Z. (2002) Peer to Peer Computing. Technical Report HPL-2002-57, HP Laboratories Palo Alto.

13. Ramanathan M. K., Kalogeraki, V. Pruyne J. (2001) Finding Good Peers in Peer-to-Peer Networks. Technical Report HPL-2001-271, HP Laboratories Palo Alto.

14. Reed D. P. (1999) That Sneaky Exponential-Beyond Metcalfe's Law to the Power of Community Building. Context magazine. Spring 1999. available on line at: http://www.contextmag.com/setFrameRedirect.asp?src=/archives/200208/0ToC.asp

15. Reed D.P. (1999) Weapon of Math Destruction, Context Magazine, Spring 1999. at: http://www.contextmag.com/setFrameRedirect.asp?src=/archives/199903/DIGITALSTRA TEGY.asp

16. Shirky C. (2000) In Praise of Freeloaders, The O'Reilly Network. Available on line at: http://www.oreillynet.com/pub/a/p2p/2000/12/01/shirky_freeloading.html

17. Vassileva J. (2002) Motivating Participation in Virtual Communities, Proceedings of the 12th International Conference of Women in Engineering and Science, ICWES'12, July 27-31, 2002, Ottawa, Canada.

18. Vassileva J., Deters R. (2001) Lessons from Deploying I-Help, in J. Whatley & M. Beers (eds.) Proceedings of the Workshop on Agents and Internet Learning, AIL'2001 at the Autonomous Agents'2001 Conference, Montreal, May 28, 2001.

19. Vassileva J., J. Greer, G. McCalla, R. Deters, D. Zapata, C. Mudgal, S. Grant (1999) A Multi-Agent Approach to the Design of Peer-Help Environments, in Proceedings of AIED'99, Le Mans, France, July, 1999, 38-45. Available on line at: http://julita.usask.ca/homepage/public.htm

20. Wilcox-O'Hearn B. (2002) Experiences Deploying a Large-Scale Emergent Network, in Electronic Proceedings for the 1st International Workshop on Peer-to-Peer Systems (IPTPS '02) available on line at: http://www.cs.rice.edu/Conferences/IPTPS02/

21. Wilde O. (1891) The Picture of Dorian Gray, available on line: http://www.bibliomania.com/0/0/57/103/frameset.html

22. Yu, B., Singh, M. (2002) An Evidential Model of Distributed Reputation Management, Proceedings of the First International Joint Conference on Autonomous Agents and Multiagent Systems: part 1, July 2002, Bologna, July 15-19, 2002.

23. Yu, B., Singh. M. (2002) Emergence of Agent-Based Referral Networks. Proceedings of the First International Joint Conference on Autonomous Agents and Multiagent Systems: part 3, July 2002, Bologna, July 15-19, 2002.

Context Spaces – Self-Structuring Distributed Networks for Contextual Messaging and Resource Discovery

Dominic Heutelbeck

University of Hagen, Department of Computer Science, 58084 Hagen, Germany
`Dominic.Heutelbeck@fernuni-hagen.de`

Abstract. Geographical addressing and resource discovery are important services in mobile context-aware computing environments. In this paper we present a protocol that maintains a self-organizing routing backbone that supports these services. Every node taking part in the protocol actively participates in the maintenance of the network. While distributing administrative tasks, the protocol takes into account the context and capabilities of the nodes. The network acts robustly with respect to massive geographical movement of the participating nodes and runs without central administration. We also introduce the concept of context spaces that act as a tool for context-awareness, information filtering, and workload distribution. Context spaces can be used to build complex context-aware systems. Based on our protocol, we also present a new approach for structuring file-sharing networks.

1 Introduction

In an environment with ubiquitous mobile computing equipment, information about the current context of the different entities is valuable information. The prime example for context data is the geographical location of an entity. This information can be gathered directly by the entities using positioning hardware like GPS-receivers, but it can also be collected by remote tracking systems via tags or image processing.

As positioning hardware and connected mobile devices are more and more available, a user may also want to collect context data about other entities in his surrounding. Based on this data, spontaneous collaborations can emerge.

When we want to create real world applications that make use of such context data, we have to face the increasing number of technologies connecting mobile devices, e.g. WLAN, Bluetooth, GPRS, UMTS etc. Also each single technology is accessed through a large number of different service providers. We do not focus on the special capabilities of a technology, but we observe that the TCP/IP protocol suite supports all considered technologies.

In the described scenario, ad-hoc routing protocols [9] can not directly be applied, as they assume a direct communication channel between nearby nodes. But in our scenario, each node is directly connected to the Internet through its

R. Meersman, Z. Tari (Eds.): CoopIS/DOA/ODBASE 2002, LNCS 2519, pp. 248–265, 2002.

own fixed provider. This results in a network, where entities in spatial proximity can be arbitrary far away from each other in terms of physical network topology.

In such a situation it is difficult to discover nearby entities. Multicast approaches are likely to fail, because this service is not available through all providers or the provider may not propagate the multicast traffic to other subnets.

This motivates to develop another kind of infrastructure to support contextual resource discovery. Similar problems arise in contextual messaging, where we want to propagate a message to all nodes residing in a spatial region. Geographical messages are again the prime example.

In this paper we present a protocol that creates a self-structuring logical network that supports these operations without the need for central administration. This is achieved by the collaboration of all participating nodes in a peer-to-peer fashion. The protocol distributes the workload in respect to the context and resources of each participating node. We also propose a new way to structure file-sharing networks, that overcomes some common problems in current file-sharing applications.

2   Related Work

Imielinski and Navas [7] propose three possible solutions for geographic addressing, routing, and resource discovery.

The *geographic routing method* proposes the installation of an infrastructure of *geographic routers*, each serving the region covered by the connected networks. These routers maintain a routing table with next-hop entries for different regions. Additionally, *GeoHosts* are installed that act as a buffer for messages that should be repeated for a given period of time.

The *geographic-multicast routing method* hierarchically maps geographical regions and additional context information to multicast groups. These groups are administered by a hierarchical connected set of nodes. Additionally, there are special multicast groups dedicated to monitor a region. The multicasting protocol has to be adjusted to the special needs of the approach.

The *domain name server solution* proposes the introduction of a new top-level domain called ".geo". Special name servers map addresses to a set of IP addresses or a temporary multicast group.

These three approaches try to integrate geographical routing into the core functionalities of the Internet and rely on the installation and administration of fixed infrastructures. They explore the same basic functions we are examining. Especially the multicast approach provides a powerful tool. The difficulty in these approaches is that the fixed infrastructures used can not be taken for granted in all situations. The multicast approach relies on the deployment of IPv6 and the availability of multicasting as a continuous service. To ensure the scalability of this solution, the multicasting protocol needs modification. Our approach only relies on minimal suppositions, we only assume that any nodes can communicate via unicast TCP/IP.

The *content-based networking* scheme proposed by Carzaniga and Wolf [3] presents a more general approach to the problem. It relies on an underlying infrastructure of routers that resembles the geographic routing method. Instead of using geographical regions more general predicates are used for addressing, similar to the use of the multicast addresses in the geographic-multicast routing method but without the limitations of an IP address space.

Another solution of the resource discovery problem is a central database. Classical databases are designed to store data that does not change rapidly; an example are the locations of mobile nodes. Harter et al. [5] from AT&T Cambridge overcome these limitations of a central database by routing frequently changing location information through dynamically loaded proxies that do not update the actual database. Other informations are still retrieved from a central database. The challenges for databases that actually store the location data are formulated by Sistla et al. [11] and lead to the "Moving Objects Spatio-Temporal data model" (MOST). The proposed databases store linear movement functions for each node to minimize the number of updates. These specifications also lead to database architectures that structurally resemble our approach, e.g. Tayeb et al. [14] use a Quadtree to store the data.

The Nexus platform presented by Hohl et al. [6] is an open platform for spatial-aware and augmented reality applications. The platform facilitates a model called *augmented areas*, arbritrary areas which contain data about objects located inside of them. These areas can be integrated into a *augmented world* model that provides uniform access to the different areas. The data of these areas are stored in different nodes of the platform that maintain databases for the different objects of the areas.

Spreitzer and Theimer from Xerox PARC designed a system [13] that supports location based information about the entities in the system, but takes into account some privacy issues. The mobile entities are registered at a central server. The entities may choose to hide their personal information and to register with their location and a network address only. If it does so, it has to implement access control itself.

Dey [4] created the Context Toolkit to support the development of context-aware applications. It uses federations of so-called *Discoverers* to support the discovery of context sensors. These sensors subscribes itself to a Discoverer. Applications query a Discoverer for sensors and can subscribe to them. Sensors inform their subscribers about changes in the context they sense.

All these projects and platforms rely on fixed infrastructures and on central administration. On the one hand, the deployment of such infrastructures and their maintenance can provide efficient systems, but on the other hand, it causes high costs and it makes the user dependent of the provider of these infrastructures. Our approach bypasses the need for these structures and gives the user the power to provide and gather context information and services on a peer-to-peer basis.

Resource discovery in highly distributed, heterogenous networks is the core functionality in file-sharing networks. They also are a good example for peer-to-peer networks bypassing central server structures to enable users to use and provide services. The Gnutella protocol [12] for example connects arbitrary nodes in a pseudo-random network. Search queries are flooded throughout the network for a limited number of hops, resulting in massive traffic. It does not guarantee that the nodes maintaining the desired file receive the queries for it.

In this paper we present an application of our approach that reduces redundant traffic and guarantees the discovery of demanded files for a special case variant of file-sharing networks. This is achieved by structuring the network based on metadata.

3   Context Spaces and Presences

Our central aim is to create a system with no central administration that supports two basic operations:

1. *Contextual messaging*: Send a message m to all mobile entities in the target region T. We call such a message a *ContextCast message*.
2. *Contextual resource discovery*: Find all mobile entities in the region T.

We divide the actual global space in local, possibly overlapping subspaces.

Definition 1.   *1. The global context space $G \subset \mathbb{Z}^n$, $n \in \mathbb{N}$ is the cross product of the bounding intervals $G_i = [l_i, u_i]$, $i \in \{0, \ldots, n-1\}$, $l_i, u_i \in \mathbb{Z}$ and $l_i \leq u_i$.*
2. A context space S is a tuple consisting of a subcube S^* of the global context space G and an unique name s. S^* is the cross product of subintervals of the bounding intervals of G.

The prime example for a global context space is the physical space surrounding earth. One can easily map GPS-coordinates to the global context space. In this case we speak about a 3-dimensional context space $G \subset \mathbb{Z}^3$. For some application it is important to have more detailed context informations available about the entities. In addition to the spatial information additional contexts like the vacancy of cabs or the heart rate of persons can be used as additional dimensions. We will demonstrate a more abstract use of n-dimensional context spaces in file-sharing in section 10.

We create individual networks for each new context space. A context space is introduced to support an interest group in a given subcube of the global context space. The interest group can be derived from the name of a context space.

If a user starts a context-aware collaborative application, e.g. a game as described by Björk et al. [2], she defines a game area and a name for the game session. With these parameters, she creates a context space which covers the game area. Other users joining the game share context information and communicate through the resulting network. They do not deal with traffic caused by other mobile nodes in spatial proximity that are unrelated to the game session. In this way, context spaces filter traffic that would stress the connection of their nodes in a single global network.

The selection of a context space also acts as a filter for the user to choose from the available context information, e.g. in the scenario outlined above the information is restricted to game region and session data. Without such a filter the connection of the device and the receptiveness of the user may become overcharged quickly.

Each context space covering a given area can be interpreted as a reality superimposing the actual physical space. A user can gather information about other entities in physical proximity, which define an alternative view of the surrounding reality. This information can for example be gathered through the proposed discovery scheme and further direct communication with the discovered entities. This information can also be used to render an augmented reality [1]. Multiple context spaces can be combined to build individual views of reality, for different users.

To create such a system without central administration, we choose a completely distributed peer-to-peer approach, where every participating node actively supports the system with its resources.

We call all mobile entities in our system *presences*. We define them as follows.

Definition 2. *1. A presence is a process running on an arbitrary host and has the following properties:*
- *a descriptive name string d,*
- *a current location $l \in G$,*
- *a maximal bandwidth α in kB/s,*
- *a measure $\beta \in \mathbb{N}$ for the mobility of the presence,*
- *a network address consisting of the IP address of the host and a port number.*
2. A presence with an actual physical representation is called physical, a presence without such a representation is called virtual.
3. A presence where the position of the host is identical to the position of the presence is called sticky, all other presences are called free.

An example of a sticky physical presence is a user with a wearable computer [1]. The user creates a presence of herself on the wearable computer, which determines the user's location and manages the network connections. The location of the host correlates to the location of the presence and the presence correlates to a physical entity. Free physical presences may be information services of sights. The the local government may create such presences to inform tourists about the historical backgrounds of the sights. These presences may offer further interactive services. In this example, the physical entity of the presence does not move. To create free physical presences of mobile entities, special tracking hardware is

Table 1. Examples for possible presences.

	sticky	free
physical	user with wearable computer	sight information system
virtual	virtual artwork	travel guide

necessary. A free virtual presence may be a virtual travel guide. Such a travel guide presence can follow and guide the movements of a user to direct her to places of interest. It can be represented by an avatar on the user's computing device. The travel guide computes a route to a destination and moves along this route in a constant distance to the user, who can follow the guide. Such travel guides can be hosted centrally. Sticky virtual presences may find their application in a virtual artwork, that resides on a host with location sensors. The artwork consists of a presence of itself at the location of its host. Even if one uses a remote host to host an artwork at the same location, the sticky variant retains more properties of a classical piece of art. It is unique and in the act of installation, it resembles its classical counterpart. Table 1 summarizes these examples.

4   Structure of a ContextCast Network

Our goal is to provide the different entities in a system with location services without using a central administration scheme. We build a distributed network of presences that only relies on a connection to the Internet without the need for the administration of further central components. Every presence has to take part in the maintenance of our network. But a presence should only have to forward messages that are relevant to it and only as many as are manageable with its resources. As the context space brings presences semantically together, a presence should only forward messages in its own context space. We assume that communication between presences in close proximity are more likely than between presences that are far apart. Therefore a presence should mostly forward messages that are targeted to regions nearby. To summarize the requirements for our system:

- It has to support contextual messaging and resource discovery.
- There should be no central administration.
- Each presence should actively support the system with its resources.
- Each presence should mainly forward locally relevant messages.
- It has to stay consistent under insertion, removal and movement of presences.
- It should support physical, virtual, sticky and free presences.

The ContextCast network is based on a recursive decomposition of the context space into a hierarchical structure of clusters. In an n-dimensional context space, each cluster is recursively decomposed into 2^n subclusters of equal size. Each cluster is a subcube of S^*.

Definition 3. *Let S be a context space, $smin(S)$ the minimal size of all bounding intervals from S^*. Let the address set A be the set of all sequences in $B_n := \{0, \ldots, 2^n - 1\}$, $A_k \subset A$ the set of all sequences of length k, $k \in \mathbb{N}_0$.*

We use sequences from A to address the subclusters of the context space. For the empty sequence a we set $S_a := S^*$ and decompose it recursively by applying the following rule:

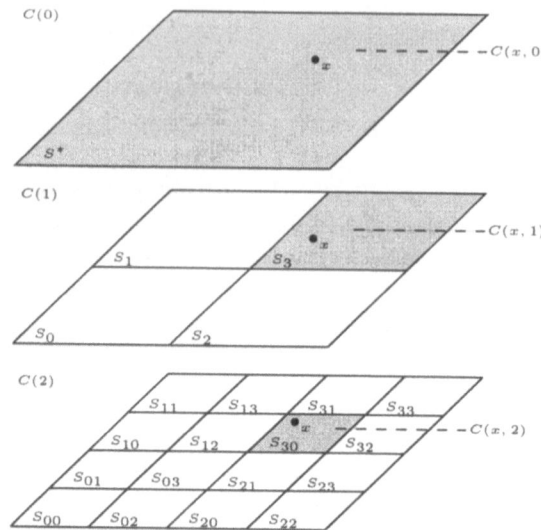

Fig. 1. The cube S^* is recursively decomposed into subclusters. The clusters on each level are a partition of S^*. For all x there exists exactly one $C(x, l)$ for each l that contains x.

A cluster S_a with the address $a = a_0, \ldots, a_{k-1} \in A_k$, is decomposed into the 2^n subclusters with the addresses from $A' = \{a_0, \ldots, a_{k-1}, a_k | a_k \in B_n\}$. These addresses are constructed from the address of S_a by appending a value from B_n. A subcluster $S_{a'}$, $a' \in A'$, is constructed from S_a by cutting the interval of each coordinate in half. For the i-th coordinate, the i-th bit of a_k defines, if the upper or lower half belongs to $S_{a'}$.

Because S^* is a finite cube, we can split it at most $d(S) := \lfloor \log(smin(S)) \rfloor$ times.

Definition 4. *Let the clusterlevel l of S_a be the length of a, $l \in \mathbb{N}_0$ and $l \leq d(S)$. Let $C(l)$ be the set of all clusters S_a with the clusterlevel l. Let $C(x, l)$ be a cluster of $C(l)$ which contains $x \in S^*$.*

It is easy to see, that $C(l)$ is a partition of S^* for all l, therefore $C(x, l)$ is unique for a fixed l. We illustrate these definitions in figure 1.

Presences take over administrational tasks for certain clusters. We call these presences *clusterheads*. We are aim to assign the administrational tasks, i.e. clusterhead roles, to presences for which this particular task is of high relevance. Therefore a presence only becomes clusterhead of clusters in which it is located, but other parameters play an important role, too. We describe further details in section 6.

A presence that creates a context space takes over the role of the clusterhead in the complete space and registers itself as a leaf in the cluster. The topology of the created network is tree shaped, and every presence is at least represented by a leaf in the tree. Each following presence has to register itself at the clusterhead,

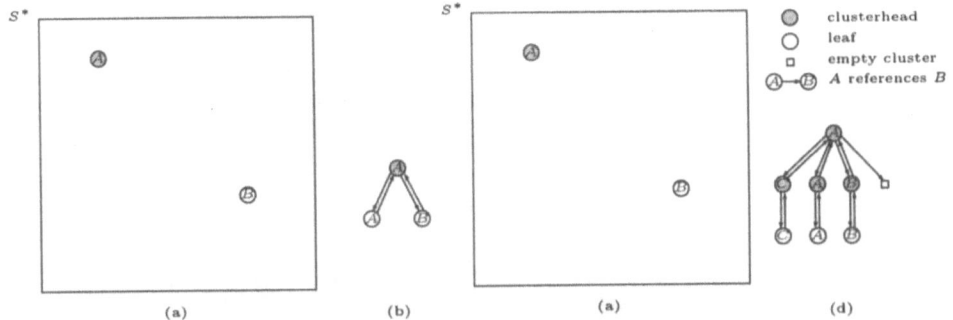

Fig. 2. (a) A context space S with two presences A and B. (b) The resulting topology of the ContextCast network. (c) S after the accedence of a third presence C. (d) The network topology after the accedence of C.

also becoming a leaf. All leaf presences inform their clusterhead when their location changes. The clusterhead forwards ContextCast messages to nodes in the target region and acts as a cache for resource discovery. When the traffic caused by these responsibilities exceeds the bandwidth of the clusterhead, the cluster is split into subclusters of equal size. The original clusterhead remains the clusterhead of the complete context space, but appoints new clusterheads for the newly created subclusters. A clusterhead is always located in the cluster it manages. Figure 2 shows a possible ContextCast network before and after a split caused by the addition of a new presence.

The splitting is continued recursively when new presences are added to the network. The clusterheads act as a routing backbone for ContextCast messages by forwarding the messages along the edges of the tree. A presence is at least a leaf in the network and may be the clusterhead of several nested clusters. To network is connected by references between the topological neighbors in the tree. These references are noted in the figures by directed edges in the graph representation. In three dimensions, this topology resembles a distributed version of an PR-Octree [10], or more exactly an approach of Matsuyama et al. [8] that uses such a tree to decompose a point space into buckets of finite capacity. The following sections describe, how the space is exactly decomposed, new clusterheads are determined, messages are passed through the network and the network is kept consistent while presences are moving.

5   Routing

If a presence F wishes to send a message to a target region T, it is propagated through the network bottom up, starting at the clusterlevel of F. The clusterlevel $level(p)$ of a presence p with location x is the level of the deepest cluster that contains x and has a clusterhead.

1. First the presence p sends the message m for the target area T to its clusterhead on the clusterlevel $level(p)$.

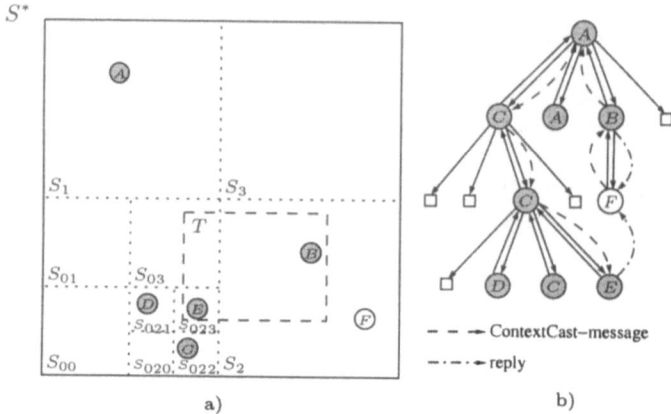

Fig. 3. a) The presence F wishes to send a message to all nodes in the region T. b) The route of the message and possible replies of the target node. Some leaf nodes are omitted for a simpler graphical representation.

2. A presence C, which receives the message m as the clusterhead of S_a on level l, now propagates the message through the network, following these steps:
   a) If level l has no subclusters, send m to all leafs in $S_a \cap T$.
   b) Otherwise, send each clusterhead of a direct subcluster $S_{a'}$ a copy of m with the new target area $T' = T \cap S_{a'}$, if $T' \neq \emptyset$.
   c) Set $T = T \setminus S_a$.
   d) If $T \neq \emptyset$, send m to the parent clusterhead of C on level $l - 1$.

Figure 3 illustrates a possible route for a ContextCast message. By adding the address of the source presence to the message, other presences may reply directly to the source presence. Contextual resource discovery can be implemented in this way. To increase the performance and reduce the traffic, clusterheads may act as a cache for their leaf presences and answer with a single message that contains a list of fitting presences.

6   Creating a Network

Since we have to keep a distributed structure consistent, we have to use safe communication also at some points we need to make assumptions about the message ordering. To keep the protocol and the implementation simple we use TCP to exchange messages. This is a trade-off for some traffic overhead. Each presence manages a single queue of incoming messages and each message is completely processed by the presence before the next is examined. Every message contains the address of the original sender.

We build one ContextCast network for each context space. A presence can join or create arbitrary ContextCast networks.

To create a ContextCast network, a presence selects a cube $S^* \subseteq G$ that contains the location of the presence. Then it chooses a new identifier s which is currently not in use for a context space with S^*. A new context space S is composed from S^* and s. Now it assumes the clusterhead role for S^* and waits for other presences to join. A presence A has to know at least one member B of an existing ContextCast network to join it. If A knows such a presence, it sends a JOIN message to it. This join message contains the location of A. When B receives the JOIN message, the message is hierarchically route to the clusterhead H of the smallest cluster S_a in the network that contains the location of A. The route of the message is selected in an analogous way to the routing of a ContextCast message.

If a clusterhead on this route notices, that no such clusterhead exists, i.e. the cluster is empty, it registers A as the new clusterhead of that cluster. Then it informs A about it by sending a SPLIT message, since the steps A has to execute are the same as if it becomes a clusterhead because of a split.

When the JOIN message reaches H, this clusterhead has to decide if its bandwidth is sufficient to handle the additional load. If yes, H sends a JOINACK message to A. Otherwise, H splits the cluster. We look at these steps of H in more detail:

1. If the bandwidth of H can handle the expected load of A, H sends a JOINACK message to A and registers A as a new leaf.
2. Else split the deepest cluster S_a, $a \in A_k$ of which H is the clusterhead.
   a) Split S_a, $a \in A_k$, into the subclusters with addresses from $A' = \{a_0, \ldots, a_{k-1}, a_k | a_k \in B_n\}$.
   b) If all presences in S_a including the joining presence are located in exactly one of these subclusters $S_{a'}$, and the maximal depth of the space has not yet been reached, repeat the previous step with $S_{a'}$.
   c) If no set of clusters is found, where at least two clusters contain a presence, do not split at all. Send a JOINACK message to A and register A as a new leaf in cluster S_a and stop.
   d) Select a new clusterhead for each subcluster.
   e) Send a SPLIT message to all new clusterheads. The message contains the new cluster and a list of leaf presences in it, excluding A.
   f) Send a SPLIT message, containing the new cluster and the clusterhead, to all other nodes, excluding A.
   g) If A does not become clusterhead of one of the clusters, forward the JOIN message from A to the new clusterhead that manages the subcluster containing the location of A.

When several presences have the same location or are close to each other, it may happen that one cannot split the cluster. In this case H has to register A as a leaf, even if this means that the performance of the network decreases, because H cannot handle the load with its bandwidth. A possible solution is to hand over the cluster to a presence with more resources. A protocol for such a handover is described in section 7.2.

If H was able to find a set of subclusters, it has to appoint new clusterheads for these clusters. The selection is based on the location, bandwidth α, and mobility β of the presences. The clusterhead has to be located in the cluster it manages, it should have enough bandwidth to handle the traffic, and it should be able to hold the clusterhead role for a long time. The mobility of the presences is a good indicator for the probability, that a presence may leave a cluster soon. Therefore, presences with a low value for mobility are good candidates for a clusterhead. Very mobile nodes change the clusters frequently and the resulting handovers of the clusterhead roles cause traffic we wish to avoid. As a simple heuristic for the selection of the clusterhead, we can define an order over the tuples (α, β) by calculating a weighted arithmetic average of α and β. We apply this heuristic and select the new clusterheads following these rules:

- A only becomes clusterhead, if it is the only presence in the subcluster, i.e. a new presence should not take over administrative tasks immediately if not necessary.
- Select the "best" presence located in each subcluster by applying the heuristic. The selected presence becomes the clusterhead of the cluster.
- H becomes clusterhead of all clusterlevels between the current and the clusterlevel of the selected subclusters.

7   Movement

Our network adheres to two invariants:

- Every presence may only be a clusterhead of clusters in which it is located.
- Every presence may only be a leaf in a cluster in which it is located.

The main difficulty in the protocol is to maintain these invariants, while the presences are moving arbitrarily. The location l of a presence is always the location under which it is registered inside the ContextCast network. The actual physical location of the presence may differ from this location. Also a constant update of the location data in the network may cause unnecessary traffic. The presence has to decide how its location should be updated, based on the jitter of its sensors (in the case of physical presences) and the needs of the application. Usually, a presence updates its location, if its physical location changes more than a given threshold. If a presence decides to update its location, it buffers the original location until the rest of the network registered the new location. If the location has to be updated before the first movement is completed, the latest location is buffered, too. After the initial movement is completed, the location is updated to the latest buffered location.

7.1   Movement inside a Cluster

A clusterhead stores the current location of its leafs to be able to send ContextCast messages to the right recipients, to act as a cache for resource discovery, and to split clusters correctly. Therefore presences have to inform their clusterhead, i.e. the clusterhead that has registered the presence as a leaf, about movement. To do so, it sends a MOVE message to its clusterhead, which replies with a MOVEACK message to acknowledge that the new location is registered. When the moving presence receives this acknowledgment, it can forget its old location. This handshake is necessary because a race condition can occur during a cluster split.

If a split happens before the movement of a cluster was registered by the clusterhead, it can happen that the moving presence ends up in a cluster that does not contain its new location. Both, the clusterhead and the moving presence can detect this situation. The clusterhead notes that it got a MOVE message with a target location outside the cluster in which its leafs reside and drops this message. The moving presence detects that it got a SPLIT message while it was waiting for the MOVEACK message. The moving presence processes the SPLIT message. Now it resides in a new cluster and restarts the movement. This movement causes the presence to leave the cluster.

7.2   Moving from One Cluster to Another

To move from one cluster to another, a presence has to leave its original cluster, handover or close all clusters it controls that do not contain the target location, and has to join the target cluster. A presence has to perform similar steps, when it leaves the network completely. In this case it does not join again.

Leaving a Cluster. When leaving a cluster, the leaving presence A has to inform its clusterhead H about it by sending a LEAVE message. Before the clusterhead receives this message, it may split the cluster or hand over the cluster to the leaving node. These situations are handled in a way analogous to the situation, when a cluster is split before a movement was confirmed and the moving presence ends up in the wrong cluster. The leaving presence processes the SPLIT- or HANDOVER messages and after completing the actions triggered by these messages it retries to leave the cluster until it is successful. When the clusterhead registers that the presence left, it acknowledges this with a LEAVEACK message. In the case that the moving presence does not have to hand over or close any further clusters, it can alter its location locally and send a JOIN message. With this message the presence requests to join a cluster containing its new location. A problem is the selection where a presence has to send the JOIN message to. The only other presence known to A is its former clusterhead H. After leaving the cluster, A is no longer informed about changes in the cluster. H may already have moved to a completely different cluster, or left the network completely. Usually movement is continuous, so it is desirable to send the JOIN message to H, since from there the path to the new cluster for A is probably short. To make sure that A can send its JOIN message to H, the clusterhead does not close or hand over the cluster until it gets a LEAVEFIN message assuring H that no JOIN message from A follows. In the case described, A sends its JOIN message followed by the LEAVEFIN message. If A does not need to send a JOIN

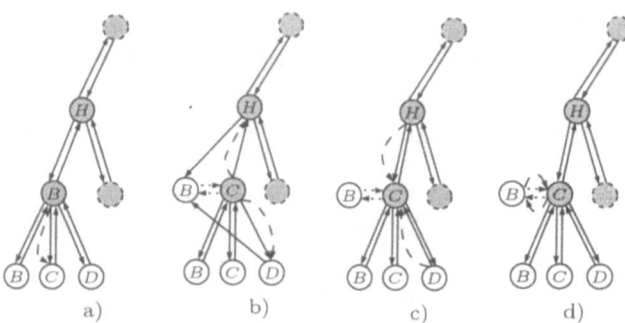

Fig. 4. Topology and message passing in a handover. Sending messages is represented by dashed lines. Dotted lines represent temporary references. a) B sends a HANDOVER message to C. b) C assumes the clusterhead role and sends NEWCLUSTERHEAD messages to the presences that still reference B as the clusterhead. c) The presences H and D register C as the new clusterhead and reply with NEWCLUSTERHEADACK messages. d) C sends a HANDOVERACK message to B, which replies with HANDOVERFIN. C successfully took over the role as the clusterhead.

message, it only sends the LEAVEFIN message and continues with the protocol if there are more clusters to hand over.

Closing a Cluster. When a presence A leaves a cluster in which it is the only presence left, i.e. is the clusterhead, it has to inform its parent clusterhead H, that the cluster is now empty. This is performed by exchanging a CLOSECLUSTER message, an acknowledgment CLOSECLUSTERACK and a finishing message CLOSECLUSTERFIN.

It may occur that H forwards a JOIN message to A, before H processes the CLOSECLUSTER message. The presence A can detect this and sends the JOIN message back to H. The parent clusterhead processes this JOIN message after the CLOSECLUSTER message and can handle it appropriately now.

Handing Over a Cluster. The most complex basic operation in the protocol is to hand over a clusterhead role to a different presence. We remember that for each clusterhead or leaf role of a presence it stores references to its neighbors in the network. To hand over a cluster, a presence has to select a new clusterhead and to make sure it assumed the clusterhead role and all neighbor presences are aware of this change.

Figure 4 illustrates how the topology of a ContextCast network changes in a handover. First the presence B that wants to hand over the cluster selects a new clusterhead C from all presences it knows that are located inside the cluster. The selection is based on the same heuristic used while splitting a cluster. Then it sends a HANDOVER message to the new clusterhead C. At this moment, B gives up the clusterhead role and forwards all messages, that reach it as the clusterhead, to C. The HANDOVER message contains all informations C needs and C assumes a clusterhead role. Now C sends a NEWCLUSTERHEAD message to all neighbor nodes, that are not yet aware of the handover, announcing its new role. These nodes register the new clusterhead and reply with an NEW-CLUSTERHEADACK message. After collecting all acknowledgments, C sends a HANDOVERACK message to B. The presence B can now be sure that it will get no more messages destined for its former clusterhead role. As in the previous operations, B may now send a JOIN message. Then B finishes the handover with a HANDOVERFIN message to C. To avoid an infinite loop of handovers when a presence leaves a cluster, it omits itself from the list of leaf nodes which it sends to the new clusterhead.

Scheduling the Handovers. To ensure that a movement does not run into an endless loop of handover operations, the sequence of operations has to be chosen carefully.

A clusterhead H can choose a new clusterhead from all presences it knows that are located inside the cluster that is going to be handed over. That are all presences that are direct children of any H-node in the subtree T rooted at the node that H wants to hand over. For example, if the presence H first hands over the highest cluster of the clusters it has to hand over, the new clusterhead H' may select H as the clusterhead of the cluster again, because it may still be known as a clusterhead in the subtree T. One has to make sure that the presence H is no longer available for the selection as a clusterhead in T. We hand over the clusters bottom up and only start one handover after the previous one has completed. This way we can be sure that a presence can never become clusterhead of a cluster below the one it already handed over. Scheduling the handovers bottom up, it still can happen that a presence that is moving becomes clusterhead of a cluster above the one it is currently handing over. If that cluster contains the target location, the presence can keep this role. If not, it continues with its handovers bottom up like described. When it reaches the level of the newly acquired cluster and the handover protocol did not finish then, the presence waits until the handover finishes, i.e. the presence gets a HANDOVERFIN message regarding that cluster. After receiving this message, it can select a new clusterhead for the cluster and hand it over.

With these basic operations we completed the description of the basic protocol.

8   Local Optimization

All clusterheads can perform local optimizations of the network topology. A cluster can regularly look for more suitable presences for the clusterhead role than itself. To see if such a node exists, it uses the same heuristic as outlined in section 6. If it finds one, it can hand over the cluster to this presence. By performing this operation regularly, one rules out the situation, that weak presence remain at important positions in the hierarchy. Such a node would cause the unnecessary early splitting of clusters. Once a cluster is split, the protocol does not offer an explicit way to merge the subclusters again if they become sparsely populated. A coordinated merger of multiple sparsely populated subclusters is a difficult operation. In the given protocol direct subclusters of a cluster merge, if they become completely empty. In this case, the last clusterhead leaving the subclusters also leaves the entire cluster and closes it at the parent clusterhead. When a new presence enters the now empty cluster, it becomes the clusterhead of the entire cluster. One can easily achieve an earlier merging of subclusters in a special case. If a presence is the clusterhead of several subsequent clusters at the bottom of the network topology and it notices that the neighbor clusters of the bottom cluster become empty, it can drop the bottom cluster and tell the leafs about the change.

9   Bootstrapping

To join a ContextCast network, a presence has to know which networks are available at its current location, and at least one presence inside the network. We propose two approaches to get this information.

In a local environment where IP multicast is available, it is convenient to let the root clusterheads of all ContextCast networks join one multicast group. A presence can then issue queries with its location to that multicast group, and clusterheads in context spaces that contain the location reply to the presence with the necessary informations about the context space and their address.

In the global Internet multicast IP is not widely available. Alternatively, a central well-known host or a set of such hosts, can manage the information about the context spaces.

Once this information is acquired, the presence can choose a context space to join or can create its own context space.

10   Enhanced File-Sharing

Resource discovery in a distributed spontaneous network is the core functionality of file-sharing networks like Gnutella. Gnutella uses a simple flood scheme and a pseudo random network topology. This strategy leads to a lot of useless traffic. It is easy to convert a ContextCast network into a file-sharing network that supports a certain class of queries. This network minimizes redundant traffic and ensures the discovery of files that match the query, if such files exist.

We interpret strings of fixed length n as n-adian numbers, where the first character is mapped to the largest factor. Numbers represented by strings with the same prefix are close to each other. Each prefix defines an interval of strings. We can use this interval as a target area for search queries. If we create one presence for each file and use its filename as its location, we can efficiently search for files with a given prefix. A more sophisticated variation of this scheme is to use a multi-dimensional ContextCast network. We create a ContextCast network for each file type. For each file type we can determine a set of d metadata fields, e.g. author, title, etc. Then we create a d-dimensional context space where each dimension is mapped to one metadata field. In the resulting network we can search for files where the metadata fits a set of prefix conditions. Currently, we have to create a presence for each single file. That is the reason why this approach is not suitable for hosts with very large collections of files. With the ContextCast approach for file-sharing we overcome a central problem of the Gnutella network. We are routing the search queries directly to where the desired data resides. The ContextCast approach minimizes redundant traffic and if a certain data is registered in the network we will find it. This is achieved by structuring the network not based on the physical network topology, but on the actual content and its distribution.

11   Future Work

In the ContextCast protocol a presence does not have a spatial expansion. We only support point spaces. There are numerous applications, where presences with a spatial expansion are practical to have. Supporting such presences requires different clustering strategies. An important application of such a network may be the management of the global context space. Each local context space would be a presence in this network.

In the current protocol we use a fixed decomposition rule for clusters, where the size and shape of the resulting clusters is independent of the location and density of the presences in the original cluster. It may be interesting to compare this with more adaptive decomposition rules.

The protocol does not include recovery strategies that recover the network integrity if a clusterhead fails or spontaneously disconnects without handing over all responsibilities. In the future we want to address this problem and for performance reasons, the current use of TCP should be reconsidered.

It should be investigated how the privacy concerns of the different presences in the network can be addressed.

We have implemented the protocol in Java. This implementation will be used for further evaluation of the protocol.

12   Conclusions

With the ContextCast protocol, we created a completely self-organizing network that supports contextual messaging and resource discovery. The protocol takes into account the context information and the capabilities of the single presences. The routing backbone created is kept consistent with the context of the presences, even when the presences are constantly moving.

We also introduced the concept of context spaces that act as tools for information filtering, workload distribution and the user's context-awareness. Context spaces can become a central concept for mobile context-aware applications.

We allow end users to offer location based services. A computer with an uplink to the Internet via an ISP is sufficient. No further supporting servers need to be installed, but the protocol is very flexible and optionally allows the installation of such a fixed supporting infrastructure by means of simple parameterization of the supporting nodes.

We presented enhanced file-sharing as an alternative application of our approach that is able to solve some shortcomings of the original systems by structuring the network based on metadata.

The core idea of the ContextCast protocol is to build a structure where the topology is not dictated by the physical connections between the nodes, but by their context. The ContextCast protocol brings semantically close presences closer together. Doing so, it makes it easy for applications to become aware of other presences in close proximity. This awareness is a tool to spawn spontaneous collaboration between presences with similar interest in a heterogenous network environment. Without a support for context information in a heterogenous network environment, one may pass up many chances for collaboration.

Table 2. An overview of the messages in the ContextCast protocol

Message	Description
JOIN p	The presence p wants to join.
JOINACK H S_a	Join acknowledgment for cluster S_a with clusterhead H.
SPLIT H S_a N	Split of a cluster. The new cluster is S_a, with clusterhead H. If applicable, the set N of leafs is sent, too.
MOVE p l	The presence p moves to its new location l.
MOVEACK	Acknowledgment for movement.
LEAVE p	The presence p wants to leave the current cluster.
LEAVEACK	Acknowledgment for the leaving of a cluster.
LEAVEFIN	Unlock the parent clusterhead for further movement.
CLOSECLUSTER S_a	Tells a clusterhead, that the subcluster S_a is now empty.
CLOSECLUSTERACK S_a	Acknowledgment for the closing of S_a.
CLOSECLUSTERFIN S_a	Unlock the parent clusterhead for further movement.
HANDOVER S_a P N	Handover of the cluster S_a to another presence, with the set N of leaf presences resp. clusterhead of the subclusters. The parent clusterhead is P.
HANDOVERACK S_a	Acknowledgment of the handover of S_a
HANDOVERFIN S_a	Unlock the new clusterhead for further movement.
NEWCLUSTERHEAD S_a H	Announces the new clusterhead H of the cluster S_a.
NEWCLUSTERHEADACK S_a	Acknowledges the registration of the new clusterhead of S_a.

References

1. Woodrow Barfield and Thomas Caudell, editors. *Fundamentals of Wearable Computers and Augmented Reality.* Lawrence Erlbaum Associates, 2001.

2. Staffan Björk, Jennica Falk, Rebecca Hansson, and Peter Ljungstrand. Pirates! using the physical world as a game board. In *Interact 2001, IFIP TC.13 Conference on Human-Computer Interaction*, 2001.
3. Antonio Carzaniga and Alexander L. Wolf. Content-based networking: A new communication infrastructure. In *NSF Workshop on an Infrastructure for Mobile and Wireless Systems*, Scottsdale, Arizona, October 2001.
4. Anind K. Dey. *Providing Architectural Support for Building Context-Aware Applications*. PhD thesis, Georgia Institute of Technology, 2000.
5. Andy Harter, Andy Hopper, Pete Steggles, Andy Ward, and Paul Webster. The anatomy of a context-aware application. In *Proceedings of the Fifth Annual ACM/IEEE International Conference on Mobile Computing and Networking, MOBICOM'99*, pages 59–68, August 1999.
6. Fritz Hohl, Uwe Kubach, Alexander Leonhardi, Kurt Rothermel, and Markus Schwehm. Next century challenges: Nexus - an open global infrastructure for spatial-aware applications. In *Proceedings of the Fifth Annual ACM/IEEE International Conference on Mobile Computing and Networking (MobiCom'99)*, pages 249–255. ACM Press, 1999.
7. Tomasz Imielinski and Julio C. Navas. Gps-based geographic addressing, routing, and resource discovery. *Communications of the ACM*, 42(4):86–92, April 1999.
8. T. Matsuyama, L. Hao, and M. Nagao. A file organization for geographic information systems based on spatial proximity. *Comput. Vision Gr. Image Process.*, 26(3):303–318, June 1984.
9. Charles Perkins, editor. *Ad Hoc Networking*. Addison Wesley, 2001.
10. Hanan Samet. The quadtree and related hierachical data structures. *Computing Surveys*, 16(2):1987–260, June 1984.
11. A. Prasad Sistla, Ouri Wolfson, Sam Chamberlain, and Son Dao. Modeling and querying moving objects. In Alex Gray and Per-Åke Larson, editors, *Proceedings of the Thirteenth International Conference on Data Engineering, April 7-11, 1997 Birmingham U.K*, pages 422–432. IEEE Computer Society, 1997.
12. Clip2 Distributed Search Solutions. The gnutella protocol specification v0.4. http://www.clip2.com/GnutellaProtocol04.pdf.
13. Mike Spreitzer and Marvin Theimer. Providing location information in a ubiquitous computing environment. In *Proceedings of the fourteenth ACM symposium on Operating systems principles*, pages 270–283. ACM Press, 1993.
14. Jamel Tayeb, Özgür Ulusoy, and Ouri Wolfson. A quadtree-based dynamic attribute indexing method. *The Computer Journal*, 41(3):185–200, 1998.

Supporting Cooperative Learning in Distributed Project Teams

Weigang Wang[1], Jörg M. Haake[2], and Martin Wessner[1]

[1] Fraunhofer Institute for Integrated Publication and Information Systems (IPSI)
Dolivostr. 15, 64293 Darmstadt
{wwang, wessner}@ipsi.fhg.de
[2] FernUniversitaet Hagen, Computer Science VI
Informatikzentrum, Universitaetsstr. 1
D-58084 Hagen, Germany
joerg.haake@fernuni-hagen.de

Abstract. The trend towards rapid development and globalization of business activities requires business teams to carry out their projects in a distributed environment. Changes in the environment as well as in the team require these teams to continuously learn and to learn new knowledge and skills and to adapt their work processes. In such a distributed working and learning setting, team members need a shared information space to interact with various information resources and to coordinate and communicate to harmonize their actions. In our approach we combine work (i.e. the definition and execution of work processes) and learning (i.e. the learning and practicing of work processes) of distributed project teams. A cooperative visual hypermedia environment has been developed which offers support for cooperative work and learning. This visual environment provides various real-time dynamic views of the underlying work processes. These views help team members to identify situations that trigger a need for cooperative learning. By combining the work and the learning processes, this environment offers new possibilities for cooperative learning in distributed project teams such as process simulation, guided tours by experts through process descriptions and best practice examples, and cooperative role-play for practicing work processes.

1 Introduction

In today's global economy, companies operate on a global scale. New forms of organizations, such as extended enterprises and virtual companies, are formed to meet the challenges of globalization. In these networked organizations, business processes require distributed teamwork. Due to changes of the environment, of the team, of the business processes themselves, teams must continuously learn and improve. This requires not only support for collaborative execution of business processes, but also demands support for continuous learning in the team. Since work and learning are interrelated activities, integrated support for working and learning together is needed. Current approaches to support joint execution of business processes focus on the flexible modeling and execution of business processes, e.g. by flexible, emergent workflow management systems (Haake & Wang 1999). However, these approaches

R. Meersman, Z. Tari (Eds.): CoopIS/DOA/ODBASE 2002, LNCS 2519, pp. 266–285, 2002.

neglect the need to support learning in the team. On the other hand, collaborative learning environments aim on supporting learning in co-located and distributed teams (Stahl 2002). However, these approaches are primarily applied in school and university settings, and they do not take into account the needs of work process execution (as is the primary goal of business activities). Consequently, current collaborative learning environments have not been applied to support work execution. Thus, the provision of an integrated working and learning environment is an open issue.

Our approach to solving this problem is to provide a cooperative visual hypermedia environment. This approach combines the description of the work process ("process to be learnt and executed") and the "learning process" (i.e. didactics) in a flexible manner. Such an environment offers new possibilities for learning in distributed teams, such as animated simulations of processes, guided tours by experts through process descriptions and best practice examples, and cooperative role-play for practicing the task. Based on its shared hypermedia workspace and process support, this environment provides support for a combination of cooperative work and cooperative learning.

The rest of the paper is organized as follows: In section 2 we identify requirements to the support of teams for cooperative work and learning, followed by a discussion of related work in section 3. Section 4 presents our approach: cooperative visual hypermedia. Section 5 describes the implementation of an environment for cooperative work and learning based on the cooperative visual hypermedia approach. Section 6 presents a use case and user experience. Section 7 concludes the paper with a summary, a comparison to related work, and plans for further work.

2 Problem Analysis

As sketched in the introductory section, collaborative execution of business processes lead to a high demand for joint learning in the team. We use a typical scenario from a software production company to illustrate the problems.

A distributed software development team consists of several software developers and a project manager and an assistant. The team was assigned a software development project for a customer. Within a given time and budget, the team must deliver the software, the documentation etc. We can view the project plan and the assignment of tasks to team members as the business process or work process executed by the team. When new team members join, obviously a need for learning (by the new member) and adapting the process (by assigning work to the new member) arises. In the company, a separate testing unit ensures the quality of the code developed in each project. When the method employed by this testing unit changes (e.g. from code review to computer generated tests), this has an impact on all projects, which may need to deliver different data to the test unit at a different schedule. Thus, a need for learning about the change and its consequences as well as necessary adaptations of the project plan arises. While doing their work, a team member might recognize a problem in the current project plan (e.g. a certain procedure cannot be applied in this case, which invalidates the whole plan). The team must now be notified about the problem. After some joint discussion, a solution is found and must be reflected in a change of the project plan and its implementation (i.e. the work process structure of the team). These changes need to be communicated, learned, tested and practiced, before the work can continue. When the solution to the problem requires adopting a completely new process (e.g. a switch from the traditional software development methodology to a new one, such a extreme programming, or a new documentation policy required by the customer or the law), the team must jointly understand and practice the new process, before they can work effectively.

Learning in the team is primarily triggered by the following two types of causes:

(1) External causes (caused from the environment):
- Changing team members: new team members need to understand the way the team works, e.g. the goals and objectives, the work processes and their decomposition and dependencies, the allocation of tasks to people, the way the team coordinates and communicates;
- Changing work processes: business processes usually depend on other business processes. If some of the "external" business processes change (e.g. the buying process of a company is changed), the "internal" business process (e.g. those business processes using the buying process, such as a production process needing to buy parts) is affected and needs to be adapted. In this case, the team needs to learn about the external changes and to develop (and learn) a new way of doing their work;

(2) Internal causes (caused/triggered within the team):
- Problems during work process execution due to inadequate processes: here, a team member might detect a problem with a task within the work process (e.g. that process is not applicable to the case at hand). In this situation, the team members who are working on dependent tasks need to jointly adapt their work process to solve the problem. The new work process, if sufficiently new and different from prior work practice, may need to be practiced and tested;
- Problems during work process execution due to unknown/new processes: here, the team members need to jointly understand and practice the new work process, before it can be successfully executed.

As a consequence of the above problem analysis, we can identify the following requirements for learning support addressing the needs of collaborative execution of business processes in distributed teams:

- Joint execution support is the basis for the team work:
    o Representing, sharing and joint execution of work processes
    o Coordination of work distribution and work performance
    o Coordination of access to shared documents used in different sub tasks
- Individual learning support:
    o Understand work process structure (goals, objectives, work decomposition, dependencies)
    o Find examples of process execution (best practice)

- Support for external process changes
    o Signal changes to members working on dependent tasks
    o Explain changes
    o Provide training for changed processes
    o Support adaptation of current tasks
- Support for joint modification of work processes
    o Support discussion of detected problems
    o Support joint adaptation of work processes
    o Support documentation of the changes
- Support joint learning and training
    o Support for jointly explore and understand a new process
    o Support for practicing a new process in the team
- Support for joint evaluation and improvement of the team's performance

3 Related Work

Related work can be primarily found in three areas: workflow management, shared workspace systems, and collaborative learning environments.

Workflow systems focus on automated process support. Usually, a workflow system supports the definition and coordinated execution of work processes, including the provision of access to information resources needed in specific tasks (Graether et al 1997). Learning about processes is usually not explicitly supported. Some workflow systems support modifications of running work processes. These ad hoc or emergent workflow systems provide more flexibility with respect to exception handling (Haake & Wang 1999). However, they do not support learning about process changes and training of redefined processes. Workflow systems in general focus on a separation of individual definition and execution phases. Thus, joint discussion of problems and joint construction or adaptation of processes are not supported. Likewise, there is no support for joint learning and training of work processes. Finally, workflow systems are good in collecting performance data. However, they neglect joint evaluation and improvement of a team's performance.

Whereas shared document systems, such as BSCW (Bentley et al 1995) enable shared viewing or shared editing of isolated documents, this work tries to exploit CSCW and hypermedia technology to facilitate rich information structures and seamless process support through the provision of shared workspaces.

Collaborative learning environments support the joint construction and acquisition of knowledge. Often, this includes also support for individual learning as a prerequisite for or as a component of collaborative learning. Process support is offered by some systems as support for specific learning methods, e.g. following the concept of scripted cooperation (Wessner et al. 1999). Work processes as the subject of learning are usually not explicitly supported. Some collaborative learning systems support role-play, which can be used to practice work processes in the team. Often performance data is logged and used by collaborative learning systems in order to provide information on the participation and its distribution in a team. Some systems support one or a limited set of (well structured) learning situations where conflicts in the learning process can be detected automatically (Mühlenbrock & Hoppe 1999).

While workflow systems support the definition and coordinated execution of work processes and collaborative learning systems support the joint construction and acquisition of knowledge, there is no system which fulfills the requirements for learning support addressing the needs of collaborative execution of distributed business processes as identified above.

4   The Cooperative Visual Hypermedia Approach

In the following subsections, we first outline the cooperative visual hypermedia approach to integrating cooperative learning support into cooperative work settings. Then, the concept cooperative visual hypermedia is presented and related to other hypertext domains. After that, the approach is detailed with respect to the support for work processes and the support for change management. The implementation of an environment based on this approach will be provided in section 5.

4.1   The Approach in a Nutshell

Our approach is based on cooperative visual hypermedia technology, which provides a shared hypermedia information space with the following key features:

- An extensible set of visual hypermedia object types that can represent not only shared information objects and structures (e.g. the content to work on or to learn from) but also cooperative processes (i.e. the working or learning processes). These include object types representing
  - Content structures (i.e., information resources) composed of object types such as graphical and textual types for sketching ideas (e.g., scribble and text), types for presenting a domain-specific hypertext structure, and types for referring to external documents.
  - Process structures composed of object types such as types for presenting tasks, nested composite tasks, and types for representing dependency relationships.
  - Team structures (i.e., organization structures) composed of object types such as types for team, role, and person, types representing the relationships within team structures, and
  - Types for relationships across content, team, and process structures.
- Flexible process support
  - For process enactment, which allows both automatic process execution and interactive execution (especially when a problem arises).
  - For cooperative process modeling and for the joint modification of a running process and its resources.
  - For cooperative process animation (animated simulation) and role-play.
- Change management support for identifying and handling changes caused by both internal and external reasons.   This is supported by using three kinds of dynamic views on the same hypermedia model in the shared workspace:
  - A tree view which provides an overview across multiple process structures run by different projects and teams,
  - A nested view which provides a detailed local view at each level of a process structure, and

o   A swim lane view that provides a filtered flat view of a running process with ordered tasks in individual lanes for each respective team member.

Other features, which are not discussed in detail due to space reasons, include the session management, the integration of communication and cooperation tools, document handling, and the integration with the Web:

o   Session management enables the users to meet in a virtual place (in the shared information space).

o   Cooperative visual hypermedia environments foster communication and cooperation also by the integration of textual and audio/video communication, application sharing, and document handling capabilities.

o   Document handling capabilities allow external documents be linked into the process structure for accessing, manipulating, and managing them in a process context.

o   The tight integration with the Web enables wide accessibility of the environment, reuse of existing documents, dealing with firewall problems etc.

4.2   Cooperative Visual Hypermedia

The cooperative visual hypermedia presented in this paper combines features found in the several hypertext domains and in many object-oriented drawing systems.

Hypertext and hypertext domains. The classical hypertext is a graph-based navigational hypertext, which distinguishes information components (nodes) and relationships (links) between these components (Halasz & Schwartz 1994). Using links, linear as well as nonlinear network structures can be formed. In addition to the basic notion of nodes and links, one can introduce types of nodes and types of links. These types can be used to capture application or domain semantics, e.g., by determining allowed types of nodes as link end points of specific types of links. In addition to simple nodes, many hypertext systems introduced composite nodes (composites) that can contain other nodes and links. Composite nodes can be used to form aggregated subnets within a hyperdocument, which lead to the possibility of layered graphs or networks. Navigational hypertext is normally presented to users as a content page with highlight embedded links (e.g. a Web page).   Navigational hypertext structures may also be presented visually as hypertext maps, in which labeled square or icons represented nodes and arrow lines between them represent links. In addition to navigational hypertext, there are also several other hypertext flavors (or domains), such as set-based taxonomy hypertext (Parnuak & Van Dyke 1991), layout-based spatial hypertext (Marshal & Shipman III 1997), and automaton-based workflow hypertext (Furuta & Stotts 1994):

-    Set-based hypertext uses containment relationship exclusively, e.g. to represent taxonomy hierarchies. Set-based hypertext is presented as unfoldable indented hierarchies or nested graphical areas.

-    Spatial hypertext uses spatial layout and some visual characteristics to represent relationship. For instances, similar information objects are placed near to each other.

- Workflow hypertext is hypertext with application domain specific computational semantics, for instance, browsing semantics or control flow and data flow semantics along links.

Two other extensions of the hypertext concept are hypermedia and collaborative hypermedia: Hypermedia allows text as well as any kind of multimedia information to be the content of a node. Collaborative hypermedia or groupware hypermedia adds to the hypermedia concept the possibility of sharing a hypermedia workspace among many people.

Visual hypermedia. Visual hypermedia combines various features found in the above-mentioned hypertext domains and in many object-oriented drawing systems. In addition to explicit links, such a system can make use of various visual properties found in drawing systems for the expressing relationship among various visual artifacts. These visual properties include the (foreground and background) colors, patterns, images, the label text, the size, the orientation, the position, the shape, and the Z-ordering of the visual components. For instance, similar things may be placed near to each other and visualized in similar color or image patterns. What differs from a drawing system is that all these visual components are hypermedia objects that can be re-organized into different sets or nested structures, be linked to or referred to each other, and linked to external documents.

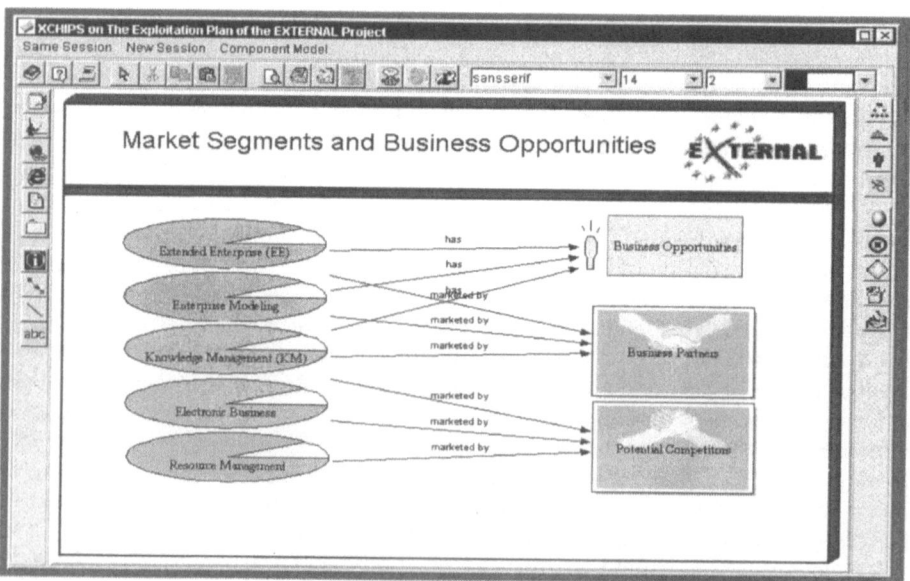

Fig. 1. Visual hypermedia: a mixture of multiple hypertext flavors

Figure 1 shows an example of the visual content captured in a learning session on market analysis. In this example, the graphical representations of spatial and navigational hypermedia co-exist in the content pane. A list of pie chart images are placed together representing Market Segments. The Business Partner (as an image of shaking hands) and the Business Competitor (as an image of wrestling hands) are placed near to each other and both of them use a similar background image pattern. Explicit links (represented as arrow lines) are used to indicate that some of the market segments are in the scope of the business partners and that others are in the scope of the business competitors. Here the navigational (semantic network map) metaphor is used together with the spatial and visual metaphors to enrich the expressiveness of a visual hypermedia.

Visual hypermedia can be used to represent the content of a cooperation, the cooperating team, and the cooperation process itself. Moving from individual to cooperative visual hypermedia and based on the workflow hypertext functionality, these processes can also be defined and executed jointly.

4.3 Flexible Process Support

A process structure can be described as a directed graph consisting of a coordination structure among the steps. Such a graph can be modeled as a typed hypermedia structure (see also (Haake & Wang 1999)). In our approach, the process structure is represented by a set of pre-defined hypermedia object types:

- Task nodes, which may carry a description of the task and other information objects (such as embedded links to external documents) as its contents, and which can be related to other resources via specific explicit links, such as a "assign" link from a role (or position). When a task node contains other task nodes connected with process links, it becomes a composite task node that presents a process or a sub process. Thus, processes can be nested and may form a layered graph. This nesting allows for representing the decomposition of work procedures into smaller parts. Task nodes have process-specific attributes, such as state, scheduled starting time, and duration. They have also process-specific behaviors, such as state transitions and activation of certain actions,
- Process links, which represent precedence relationship between task nodes. Process links have control flow and data flow behaviors. For example, instances of the process link type "precede" can be used to link tasks and processes into sequences or parallel structures, where each precede link specifies under which condition the successor node can be activated and which documents will then flow from the predecessor node to the successor node,
- Role (or position) nodes, which specify the responsibility in a process or an organization,
- Assignment links, which assign a role to a task.
- Person nodes, placeholders that present actual individuals,
- Filled-by links, which specify which Roles are assumed by which Persons, and
- Any other nodes or links for additional information, such as information about the goals and objectives of the work process, background information, and resources.

Thus, in such a typed hypermedia environment, a process can be represented as graphs consisting of typed hypermedia objects, together with additional information related to the process.

For a clear overview of the state of a process, the state information of task nodes is color-coded in their views (white for inactive, yellow for enabled, green for active and brown for completed). Tasks can be performed by menu operations activated on the task nodes. Selecting "enable" and then "activate" menu operations on the root composite task node of a process structure can start the process execution. When a composite task node is "activated", the starting tasks of the process structure nested in the composite task node are "enabled". The "enabled" tasks can then be "activated" automatically (if they are automatic tasks) or manually (if they are manual tasks). When the work of a task is finished, its actor can select the "complete" menu operation on the task node (if the task is an automatic task, the "complete" operation will be automatically triggered when the action defined in the automatic task is finished). When all the predecessors of a task are completed, the task is "enabled". A process is completed when all its subtasks are completed.

As a process structure in our approach is represented by shared hypermedia objects, it can be created or modified asynchronously or synchronously in a joint cooperative session by team members (see following sections). Our approach also allows the modification of a running process. This is made possible by visualizing monitoring the same process structure as both a process definition and as a running instance when execution starts. The execution of a process can be started by the person manages the process and the enactment of individual tasks can be done by the team members who are assigned to the tasks according to the roles they are taking. The cooperative process animation (animated simulation) and role-play is supported by cloning and enacting the process clone or by running a process in a testing mode (for either testing or learning purposes).

4.4 Change Management Support

In order to deal with changes in the work process caused by internal and external reasons the hypermedia model can be presented in a number of dynamically generated views. Here, three cooperative visual hypermedia views are defined for change management: the tree view, the nested view, and the flat view of the underlying hypermedia models.

Tree view for an overview. A tree view provides an overview of the task (process) break down structure of a single process or multiple processes. It also shows all the resources related to the tasks. A browser for this view is a hierarchical structure navigator, which can fold and unfold a hierarchy to show all the sub tasks and all the resources (such as roles, persons, and information objects) associated with the sub tasks (See Figure 2). The tree view may help team members to go up and down a process hierarchy of a single process or a set of processes, so as to identify a task in an overall context and find all the sub tasks and all the resources relating to the task. With such a clear view about a task, when there is anything wrong with it and needs a change, team members could easily see the scope of its impact and learn changed process structure.

Nested view for local details. A nested view presents the details at each level of the task break down structure (i.e. sub process structures). A co-operative hypermedia model browser for this view allows team members to navigate in the nested structure and to create and modify a project plan (i.e., a process structure and its related resources) co-operatively. A browser for this view (see Figure 3) provides functionality of an object-oriented drawing tool: Pre-defined visual hypermedia object types can be placed in the hypermedia workspace. These object types include object types for process modeling and object types for creating information objects. There are also a general node type and a general link type that can be used to derive new

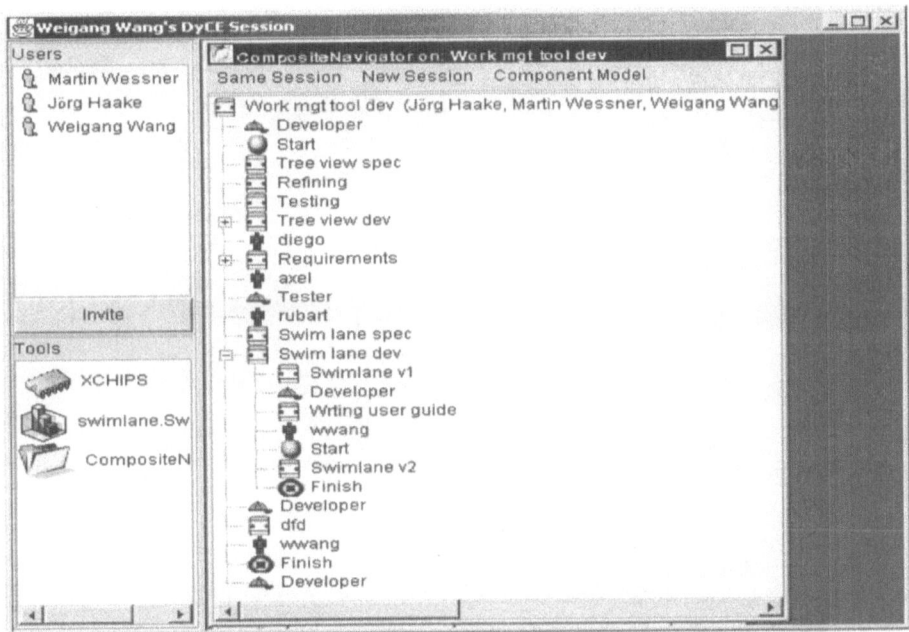

Fig. 2. Tree view browser

node and link types. The appearance of a new node type can be defined by modifying a newly created general node, for instance, to change its foreground and background colors or patterns, the label text, the size, the orientation, the shape, or to load an image (if it is node). Any visual object in the content pane can be used as a prototype for creating new instances of the same type. The whole nested structure of a composite node can be cloned in one operation.

Flat swim lane view.
The swim lane view is a flat view: all tasks are presented on the same surface no matter which nesting levels they are. A swim lane view presents multiple ordered task list in lanes for each task performer (See Figure 4). Filtering criteria is supported to generate many kinds of task lists, such as to-do lists and overdue lists. This view supports dynamic task planning and resource assignment at any time, especially for last minute or just-past-execution changes. They are also used as a work list handler for task execution and as a task control panel for monitoring the task execution. Colors are used to show the state of a task: The red outline indicates overdue tasks. The blue outline indicates delayed tasks. The white background color is for not ready tasks. The green background color is for ongoing tasks and the yellow is for to do tasks. A variety of filtering and ordering criteria can be used to tailor the view. Unlike a to-do list in most workflow systems, such swim lane view allows team members to get an overview of various task lists of all the team members. With such a browser, team members can identify delays, actor backlogs, and bottleneck tasks that require changes of re-scheduling, resource re-assignment, and process structure modification.

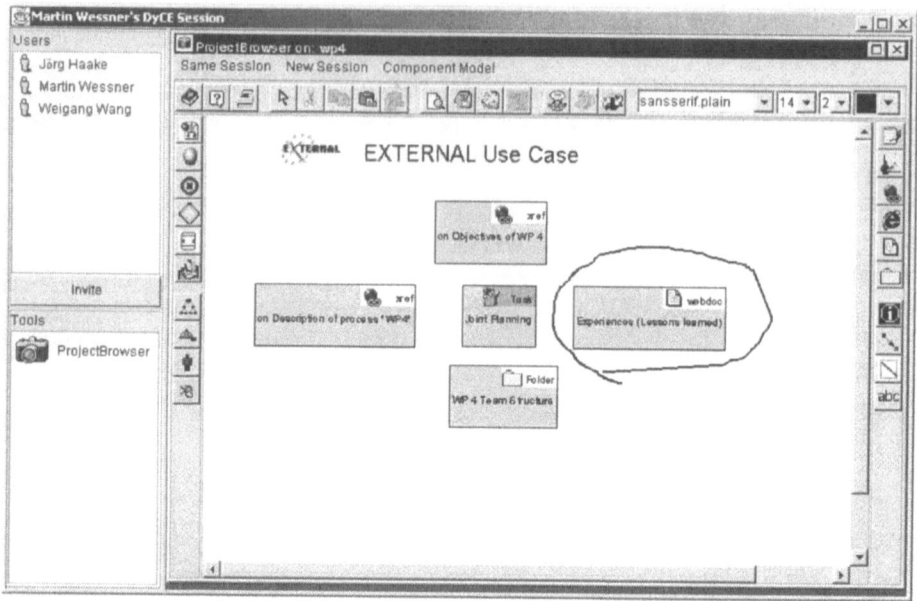

Fig. 3. The nested view browser

4.5 Cooperative Sessions

Distributed cooperative work and learning usually happen in a series of distributed meetings. A meeting is normally organized into one or more sessions. A session is also a meeting, which may involve all or part of meeting participants. In the following, we do not differentiate between meeting and session. In our approach, a session is made up of a collection of people, groupware components, and shared objects. To provide a sense of virtual place, each session is visualized as a separated session window. Each window lists the names of the on-line participants of the meeting (see Figure 2). Groupware tools used in the session will be opened in the session window. All participants of a session have a synchronous instance of the session window. Working with one browser on a view in a session, other groupware components invoked from the browser user interface or from the shared objects in its content pane can be activated. Other components can be opened either in the same session window (thus becoming accessible to all users within this session) or in a new session window (providing a simple transition to individual work or a subgroup meeting in a new session). Meeting organizers can invite other users to join their working session. Users can also use a query tool to search for all the active meeting sessions and request to join selected sessions.

Communication and cooperation in the session is supported by the integration of a chat, audio/video communication, and application sharing for all on-line participants in the session.

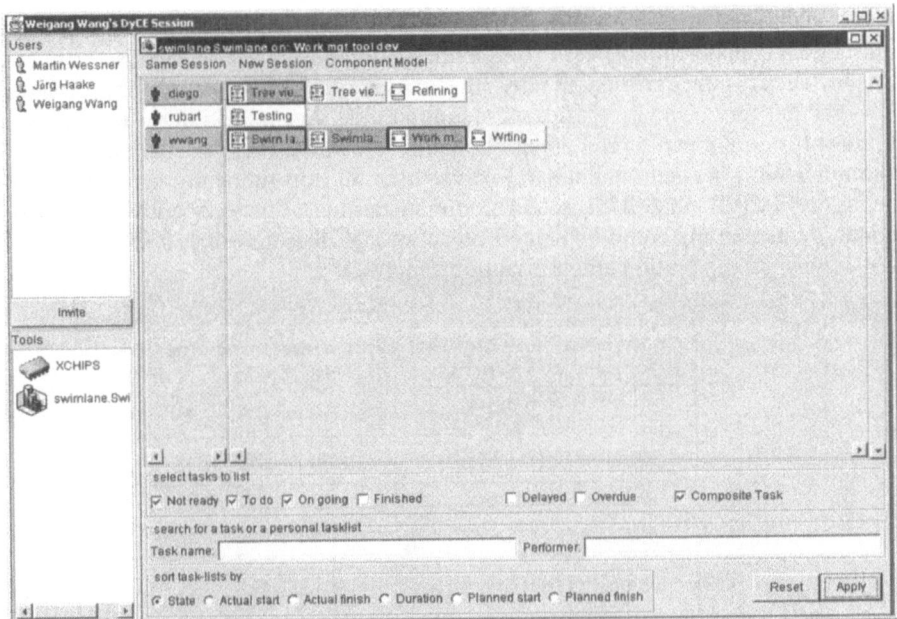

Fig. 4. Swim lane browser

5 Implementation Techniques

The cooperative visual hypermedia approach to support collaborative learning in distributed project teams presented in the last section has been implemented in the XCHIPS system. Throughout the preceding section screenshots form XCHIPS have been used to illustrate the approach. XCHIPS stands for eXtensible Cooperative Hypermedia Integrated with Process Support. It is a Java-based follow-up system of the Smalltalk-based CHIPS system (Haake & Wang 1999). Its process enactment support, role-based access control, and example based schema definition techniques have been published in (Haake & Wang 1999, Wang 1999, Wang & Haake 2000). For space reasons we focus on two key technologies in this section: the Java and DyCE (Tietze & Steinmetz 2000) based cooperative hypermedia system architecture and the tight integration of XCHIPS with the web. DyCE is a Java-based Dynamic Cooperation Environment. It provides dynamically replicated-shared data as well as transactional support for access to and modification of this shared data. In addition, it supports dynamic extension of the working environment by enabling users to add new mobile UI components at runtime.

5.1 System Architecture

XCHIPS adopts a Web-based system architecture (See Figure 5). It Web server includes services for shared object management, groupware component management, and some infrastructure services (such as those for naming and locking). The shared object management service provides dynamically replicated-shared data as well as transactional support for access to and modification of this shared data, so as to ensure the persistency and consistency of the shared data. The groupware component management service and the Web server support the dynamic addition and removal of groupware components and their dynamic download at the client side. The communication between clients and server uses an http tunneling service to replace the direct TCP/IP and RMI based communication. The cooperative hypermedia model is built on the common shared object model, therefore it has all the capability of the dynamic replication and transaction support.

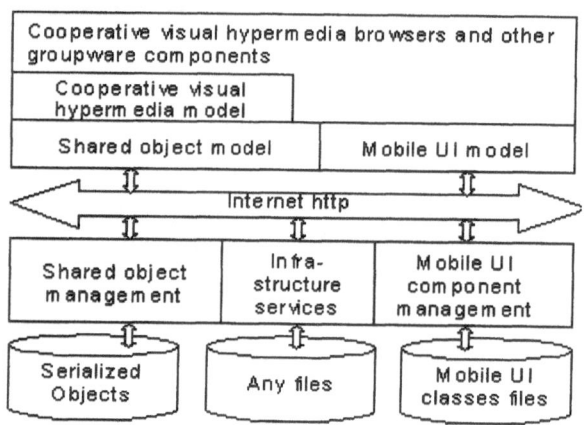

Fig. 5. System Architecture

In the DyCE framework, a groupware component consists of a shared data object and mobile UI component. The mobile UI component defines the view and controller (i.e., the user interface) of the shared data object. The mobile UI model provides a framework for creating new mobile UI components. The framework supports event-based notification for dynamic UI update when any interested aspects of the shared data changes. The XCHIPS browser is also a mobile UI component. Its shared data model is a composite object that may contain other hypermedia objects to be visualized in the browser. The relationship between a shared object type and a mobile UI component class is defined by a UIClass-service-dataClass triple declared in the mobile UI class. One data object may have more than one UI component. Their binding is decided at run time. When a user opens a node in the XCHIPS browsers, all the triple UIClass-service-dataClass objects will be searched to find the candidate UI components (classes) that may work on the shared data object (which may be the node itself or referred by the node). In XCHIPS, session and user objects are also managed as shared objects.

5.2 Integration with the Web

Based on the Web-based architecture, XCHIPS is integrated with the web in order to re-use, import and export documents and in order to ease the accessibility and execution of the system. The tight Web integration is implemented in the following ways:

- Integrated document handling into the shared visual hypermedia space. In order to integrate documents on the web into the shared visual hypermedia space and the process structures, two types of nodes are defined: The *href* node refers to a Web address (a URL). When it is opened, its corresponding information resource will be presented in the Web browser (or in a plug-in application). The node can also be opened for all participants in a session by using the *open for all* menu operation. The *Webdoc* node refers to a URL. When it is opened, the URL resource is locked, downloaded, and opened in a corresponding application, e.g. a Word document in MS Word. As a kind of group awareness information, the user name will appear on the node view. After editing, the document can be upload (back) to the document repository and unlocked. The *href* and *Webdoc* node types are implemented using a Java-COM bridge.
- Implemented XML import and export utilities based on a common type definition DTD developed in the EXTERNAL project [EXTERNAL paper], so as to allow the system to work on models created by other systems (e.g., in a joint review meeting).
- Using Java Web Start technique to deploy, update, and launch the system from a Web portal. As Java Web Start can automatically update a deployed system before launch it, it greatly simplifies the deployment and upgrade process.
- Using http tunneling to replace direct TCP/IP and RMI communication between XCHIPS server and clients, so as to solve the firewall problems.
- Implemented an http-based API, so that the shared hypermedia objects (i.e., the distributed object ids) can be embedded in Web pages for invoking XCHIPS on specific objects. These objects can be root objects of meeting processes or business processes a team is working on.

In this way, XCHIPS (and its visual hypermedia) can be accessed through standard Web browsers. Further more, by using pre-defined (visual) hypermedia types, the document handling and process support can be extended to a wide range of information resources on the Web.

By doing so, the collaborative hypermedia-based process support can be tightly integrated with Web-based information resources to extend the scope of the shared hypermedia workspace beyond what is available in XCHIPS itself. Using such extensions, background material for process learning or reference material for the context of the shared hypermedia workspace can be included in the collaborative process, the jointly created shared workspace contents can serve as meta-structure for HTML or XML pages.

6 Use Cases and User Experience

In this section, we present a typical use case scenario and show how our approach is used to support it. Then we summarize our initial user experience.

6.1 A Typical User Scenario

In section 2 we introduced a typical scenario from a software production company to illustrate the need for and problems of cooperative learning during teamwork. In the following, we show how our approach was used to support such a scenario by real users. Our usage experience comes from the EXTERNAL IST-1999-10091 project funded by the European Union. EXTERNAL develops an infrastructure, tools and a methodology for supporting the formation and operation of extended enterprises. Within the EXTERNAL project, our approach is currently used to support cooperative project planning and cooperative work execution.

The EXTERNAL team consists of members from five companies located in three countries. Work has been split into 9 work packages each lead by a work package manager and staffed by members from several companies. A project manager coordinates the overall project, i.e. the proper execution of the overall project plan and the continuous adaptation of the project plan. The project plan can be interpreted as the core business process, which the team is performing. It is, of course, tightly interwoven with the business processes of the partner companies. We will now have a closer look how our approach addresses the cooperative learning needs in EXTERNAL:

Changing team members: During the 2.5 years of EXTERNAL, there has been some constant change of team members, ranging from developers to work package managers to even the project manager. New team members need to understand the way the team works, e.g. the goals and objectives, the work processes and their decomposition and dependencies, the allocation of tasks to people, the way the team coordinates and communicates. This is supported by the shared hypermedia workspace to provide access to all critical information resources through a single portal (see figure 3): the goals and objectives, the organizational structures (people and their roles) as well as the project plan and all information objects used/produced in the different tasks. When a new member joins the project, she is registered in the system and given access to all information. After reading the overall goals and objectives, she looks up all the task assigned to her. In the XCHIPS Tree View browser (see figure 2), she can explore her current tasks and check how they are related to other tasks. In order to understand how this task contributes to the overall project, she checks how it developed in the past and how its results will be used in the future. She quickly finds out who else is working on related tasks by looking at the staffing of dependent tasks and by looking at people working on documents shared by several tasks. Since the project plan is a live document, i.e. it is used to perform the project work and reflects its current status, she can quickly learn how formal communication and coordination works in the project. In addition, her predecessor kept annotations in the work plan, which indicate when, why and with what results he (informally) communicated with other colleagues. So far, our approach supported some individual learning of the new team member. The system enables to discuss questions or work plans with colleagues (a form of collaborative learning). In addition, this approach helps newcomers to gain access to information, which would have not been so easy in the distributed setting of the EXTERNAL project.

Changing work processes: In EXTERNAL, many interdependencies exist between work packages. Results from one work package are needed in another. If one work package is delayed, this may have consequences for others. Often, problems appear in one work package, which lead to changes in that work package. If those changes influence the results needed by others (e.g. the functional specification of a software module is changed due to implementation or resource problems) we must resolve these inconsistencies as early as possible. In EXTERNAL, the execution status of tasks are marked by color-coding of the task nodes in the shared workplan (see the swim-lane view in Figure 4). When a task is changed, it is easy to compute and show (in a tree view) all other tasks potentially affected by the change (e.g. all tasks which import a software module or document, or tasks which now have to wait for a delayed task). Likewise, when the work plan of a task is changed, all dependent tasks (e.g. those sharing the same resources, results, or a timing dependency) can be shown and then manually checked for any inconsistencies. For this purpose, a separate joint project planning work process was established in EXTERNAL (see figure 2). It guides how work package and project managers perform the periodic progress reporting and planning, and supports the detection and correction of inconsistent work plans. Furthermore, notifications can be sent by the system to people involved in tasks affected by potential inconsistencies or by changed task descriptions. These people can then use the system to look at the changes and to learn about how their work should be adapted.

Problems during work process execution due to inadequate processes: In EXTERNAL, team members frequently detect problems with various tasks within the work process (e.g. a certain approach does not work as planned). In this situation, the team members who are working on dependent tasks need to jointly adapt their work process so as to solve the problem. This is supported by allowing all members to jointly browse the problematic parts of the project plan and to discuss the required changes. This can be done asynchronously (via annotations and mail) or synchronuously (in a virtual meeting where people use chat and audio conference facilities together with joint editing of the shared workspace). Here, the visual hypermedia approach shows one of its strenghts: people can scribble, draw and annotate the work plan and gradually shift towards a more formal solution (i.e. the new workplan). Communication and construction of the solution is performed in the same medium. Our experience indicates that for small groups of affected team members (e.g. three workpackage managers solving a conflict, or four developers resolving an integration problem) this approach works well. As a benefit of the more formal work plan in the shared hypermedia workspace, team members affected by these changes can be notified and can use the system to learn about the changes. If needed, they can also practice the new work process (see below).

Problems during work process execution due to unknown/new processes: As mentioned above, team members may need to jointly understand and practice new work processes, before they can be successfully executed. Examples in EXTERNAL include the introduction of a new project reporting and planning policy. This new procedure was described in the system as a new task with a complex, nested work plan consisting of approximately 45 (small) sub tasks. The 9 workpackage managers and the project manager used the system to first individually explore the new task and then they met in a synchronous virtual meeting where all participants jointly browsed and discuss the new proposed work process. They used the animated simulation feature to see and discuss how the process would work, and resolved several potential problems by adapting the proposed work process to their needs. Eventually, the new work process for joint reporting and planning was accepted and then execution started in the environment. Though execution was largely done asynchronously, some synchronous virtual meetings happened in the shared hypermedia workspace. These were either pre-planned coordination and conflict resolution meetings, or spontaneous meetings between workpackage managers who detected mutual conflicts between their work plans. After all, participants liked the support for exploring and practicing new work processes together, and they emphasized the usefulness of learning team processes together.

6.2   User Experience

So far, we have used three versions of our system in the EXTERNAL project for the last 9 months.   Initial evaluation results indicate that the visual cooperative hypermedia approach supported can meet many challenges of supporting integrated cooperative working and learning:

- The visual hypermedia models capture a rich set of relationships between the organizations, people, processes and resources of the virtual enterprise. Through analysis and activation, the models become applied as sources of knowledge, providing the basis for knowledge exchange and learning.
- Different forms of learning (individual and collaborative, ranging from joint exploration to discussions to group simulation and practicing) can successfully be supported. For small groups (2-8 people), synchronous discussions and joint browsing/editing facilitate collaborative learning. For larger groups, asynchronous exploration, annotation and discussion were regarded more helpful.
- *Planning*, the joint construction of the current work plan by the participants is well supported.
- *Communication* is supported through the visual expressiveness of the shared hypermedia workspace, the infrastructure, and the terminology of the modeling language used for describing the shared work plan. The joint modeling of the workplan facilitates common understanding, and the extensibility of the modeling language enables local shared understanding to be expressed and utilized.
- Flexibility is ensured through *interactive model interpretation*, combining the capabilities of the system to automate predefined parts of the work processes and the users to handle incompletely specified parts of the work plan.

Users liked the color-coding of the task nodes and various content types accessible from the task node. As this allows them to see (particularly for the late comers of a meeting) what has been performed, what is on-going, and what are the next tasks.

A major benefit of a persistent shared hypermedia workspace was also seen in the capture of discussion results. When used for virtual conflict resolution meetings, other team members who are not able to attend the meeting can navigate the meeting process structure (i.e. the content of the meeting task object) to learn what happened in the meeting and to find and understand the decisions made in its original meeting context. Users also liked the ability to write, scribble, post visual artifacts, and to reorganize them for on-line discussions. The handling of MS documents and its integration into a process structure were considered a useful and practical solution, as all the user organizations of the use case partners of the project have MS Office suite and Windows operating system used in their daily working environment.

7 Conclusions and Future Work

Computer support for cooperative work and for cooperative learning are both hot research topics. Cooperative work and cooperative learning also happen more and more often in project teams. However, these have been separated areas in both research and practice. Learning systems in most cases cannot handle real working situations; while working systems have rarely addressed the needs for cooperative learning.

In this paper, we described an approach that supports cooperative learning in distributed project teams by providing a shared hypermedia information space with

- A rich set of visual hypermedia objects that people can use to sketch ideas in group discussion and that can represent not only learning materials (i.e. the content to work on and to learn from) but also working and learning processes (i.e. the coordination and learning strategies),
- Flexible process support for process modeling, process execution, process animation, and process adaptation.
- Three kind of related dynamic views of a process centric project model. With the flexible process support and visual hypermedia browsers for these views, changes caused by both internal and external reasons can be handled.
- Session management for team members to meet in a virtual place and use a set of cooperative tools for jointing editing and navigation,
- Integrated support for textual and audio/video communication, application sharing, and document handling,
- Integration with the Web for wide accessibility.

In this approach, the cooperation environment is used as a medium for cooperative work and learning. Such a cooperative environment offers new possibilities for learning in distributed teams, such as animated simulations of processes, guided tours by experts through process descriptions and best practice examples, and cooperative role-play for practicing the task.

Furthermore, this approach combines the description of the "learning process" (i.e. didactics) and the "process to be learnt" (i.e. the content of learning) in a flexible manner. Based on the shared hypermedia workspace and the process support, this approach provides support for a combination of work and learning. Here, learning smoothly turns into working (e.g. by adapting process structures to the task at hand) and vice versa (e.g. when a problem occurs during process execution and the team has to learn how to fix it, and to document it for future learners).

As a sample implementation of our approach, we described the XCHIPS system, which provides cooperative visual hypermedia-based process definition and enactment support for modeling, disseminating, and evolving process knowledge. A use case showed how it can be used for supporting cooperative learning needs arising in working situations. In this work, we extended our component-based cooperative hypermedia system XCHIPS [7, 22, 23] with visual hypertext artifacts, their higher-level dynamic views, and synchronous session support for virtual learning teams.

The XCHIPS system is one of the tools we developed in the EXTERNAL project (IST1999-10091) funded by the CEC. EXTERNAL focuses on the engineering and operation of networked organizations, and the management and learning of process knowledge. Next, we will broaden and apply our approach to process knowledge management, and evaluate this approach in three real-world use cases.

Acknowledgments. Thanks due to all the team members of the EXTERNAL project partners for their cooperation and feedback.

References

(Bentley et al 1995) Bentley, R., Horstmann, T., Sikkel, K., and Trevor J. Supporting Collaborative Information Sharing with the World Wide Web: The BSCW Shared Workspace System. *Proc. of the 4th Int. WWW Conference*, Issue 1, O'Reilly, Dec. 1995, pp. 63-74.

(Desanctis et al 2001) Desanctis, G, Wright, M and Jiang, Lu, Building a global learning community. *Comm. of the ACM*, vol. 44, December 2001, pp. 80-82.

(Furuta & Stotts 1994) R. Furuta, and D. Stotts, Interpreted collaboration protocols and their use in groupware prototyping. *Proc. of ACM CSCW'94*, pp. 121-313.

(Graether et al 1997) Wolfgang Graether, Wolfgang Prinz and Sabine Kolvenbach Gräther, Enhancing Workflows by Web Technology. *Proc. of ACM Group '97*, pp. 271-280.

(Haake & Wang 1999) Joerg Haake and Weigang Wang (1999) Flexible Support for Business Processes: Extending Cooperative Hypermedia with Process Support. *Information and Software Technology* (41) 6, 1999, pp. 355-366.

(Halasz & Schwartz 1994) Halasz, F., and Schwartz, M. The Dexter hypertext reference model. K. Grønbæk and R. Trigg, (Eds.) *Comm. of the ACM* 37, 2, 1994, pp. 30-39.

(Marshal & Shipman III 1997) Marshal, Catherine C and Shipman III, Frank M.: Spatial Hypertext and the Practice of Information Triage. *Proc. of ACM Hypertext '97*, pp. 124-133.

(Mühlenbrock & Hoppe 1999) M. Muehlenbrock & H.U. Hoppe (1999). Computer supported interaction analysis of group problem solving. In J. Roschelle & C. Hoadley (Eds), *Proc. of the Conference on Computer Supported Collaborative Learning CSCL-99*, 1999, pp. 398-405.

(Parnuak & Van Dyke 1991) Parunak, H. Van Dyke: Don't Link Me In: Set Based Hypermedia for Taxonomic Reasoning. *Proc. of ACM Hypertext '91*, pp.233-242.

(Stahl 2002) G. Stahl (Ed.). Computer Support for Collaborative Learning. Foundations for a CSCL Community. *Proc. of CSCL 2002*, January 7-11, 2002, Boulder, CO, USA. Lawrence Erlbaum: Hillsdale NJ, USA.

(Tietze & Steinmetz 2000) Daniel A. Tietze, Ralf Steinmetz Ein Framework zur Entwicklung komponentenbasierter Groupware. *Proc. D-CSCW 2000*, pp 49-62.

(Wang & Haake 2000) Weigang Wang and Joerg M. Haake (2000) Tailoring Groupware: The Cooperative Hypermedia Approach. Special Issue on Tailorable Systems and Cooperative Work, *Computer Supported Cooperative Work: The Journal of Collaborative Computing*, Kluwer, 9(1), pp. 123-146.

(Wang 1999) Weigang Wang, Team-and-Role-based Organizational Context and Access Control for Cooperative Hypermedia Environments, *Proc. of ACM Hypertext'99*, pp 37-46.
(Wessner et al. 1999) M. Wessner, H. Pfister, Y. Miao, Using Learning Protocols to Structure Computer-Supported Cooperative Learning. *Proc. of the ED-MEDIA 1999*, pp. 471-476.

Discovering Emergent Virtual Work Processes in Collaborative Systems

Simeon J. Simoff[1] and Robert P. Biuk-Aghai[2]

[1] Faculty of Information Technology, University of Technology, Sydney
Broadway, NSW 2007, Australia
simeon@it.uts.edu.au
[2] Faculty of Science and Technology, University of Macau
P.O. Box 3001, Macau, S.A.R. China
fst.robert@umac.mo

Abstract. The design of virtual workplaces that can support virtual work processes has traditionally been either ad-hoc, or has been influenced by the top-down approaches, such as 'virtual architecture' and requirements identification and analysis. There are several problems with the top-down approaches. We still lack knowledge about how people collaborate in distributed computer-mediated information environments, hence, the requirements in the top-down approach are usually derived from the expectation of how the business process will run in a face-to-face environment. Another problem with existing groupware support for such environments is the difficulty in obtaining, and subsequently retaining and reusing, ready-made configurations of collaborative work processes. Such configurations naturally occur during the actual use of collaborative system when conducting projects. These configurations reflect the actual dynamics of the process, adapting the environment to support emerging work processes. Can we learn more about the actual collaboration in a virtual environment (rather than the one derived from the face-to-face expectations)? Can we reuse this knowledge for better support of computer-mediated collaborative projects? Can we predict some elements of the evolution of a new collaborative process, based on similarities and analogies with processes formalised and supported before? Can we predict possible emergent processes and cater for them? Can we capture and utilise the evolutionary component in the workspace design process, so that we can provide better support to the developers of collaborative workspaces? The paper presents the latest developments of a new approach for supporting the design and redesign of collaborative virtual workplaces, based on combining data mining techniques for refining lower level models with a reverse engineering cycle to create upper level models. The methodology utilises an apriori knowledge about the data models in the systems and a visual language for formal process representation.

1 Introduction

Supporting collaboration among a distributed group of users can be complex and time-consuming. One of the key components in setting up virtual collaboration is the design of the *virtual workspace*—the information environment that unites the

R. Meersman, Z. Tari (Eds.): CoopIS/DOA/ODBASE 2002, LNCS 2519, pp. 286–303, 2002.
© Springer-Verlag Berlin Heidelberg 2002

networked computers in a coherent medium to support the activities involved in collaborative project development. During the recent years, an alternative approach has been to *design* collaborative virtual *workplaces* (CVWs), using and integrating existing underlying groupware technologies. These technologies provide virtual environments, workspaces, or virtual places for collaboration, and can be populated with people, items and tools required for collaboration. We refer to the various kinds of groupware technologies collectively as collaborative virtual environments (CVEs). The goal of the design of a virtual workplace is to meet some needs (requirements) of the collaborators (usually geographically dispersed), whether this be an educational, research or business collaboration. Such requirements are usually expressed in terms of activities (see [12, 13] for examples of how the notion of activities is used in design, and how a design ontology can be refined, respectively) and their attributes (e.g. people who are executing those activities, objects involved in the activities, etc). Thus, the design can be viewed as an ordering and definition of a semantic information space and types of objects that inhabit that space. Virtual architecture and requirements engineering (see Fig. 1) are the two most common approaches to systematic design of collaborative virtual workplaces. In virtual architecture, the left half of Fig. 1, the emphasis in the design is in reflecting some social and cultural needs and values in particular forms [1] and their semantics. An established method in virtual architecture is to start with the development of ontology of the virtual place. The ontology usually operates with architectural terms. For example, the ontology of a building as a collection of rooms and their content is popular among the designers of virtual environments independently of the underlying technology [5, 14]. An example of the application of virtual architecture to the design of virtual design workplaces is presented in [9]. Procedurally, virtual architecture begins with the analysis of the design brief, followed by a conceptual design, and then, by the detailed design of the workplace. In general, this is a top-down process, which in practice has a number of loops between the different stages.

Design Concepts for CVW

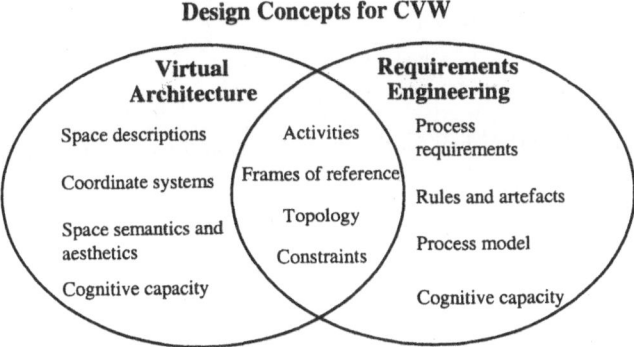

Fig. 1. Design concepts in virtual architecture and requirements engineering

The right-hand part of Fig. 1 presents another top-down approach towards the design of virtual workplaces, based on the requirements engineering methodologies. This approach assumes that sufficient knowledge about the collaboration process is available to make it possible to model it. Knowledge-intensive activities, such as product innovation or collaborative design, usually follow only general process structures, with details of the process emerging during execution. Processes of this type need a greater degree of flexibility. Environments that are based on the notion of virtual workspace, incorporating features of document management, inter-personal and group communication, notification, and a configurable governance structure provide a more adequate form of support [2].

One approach to deal with the human factor in the requirements engineering approach is based on the soft systems methodology [11]. An instance of such a modeling methodology that addresses the requirements of collaborative processes has been proposed in [8]. The methodology consists of four modeling steps (see Fig. 2): (1) System analysis: develop an understanding of the current system, which is documented in an analysis model using a modified form of rich pictures, accompanied by so-called transition diagrams; (2) Requirements analysis: develop a requirements model, describing required changes to the existing system; (3) Broad design: prepare a design model, which describes the modified collaboration process, incorporating the requirements identified in the previous step, and which is again represented by a modified rich picture notation and transition diagrams and; (4) Detailed design: produce a specification model which shows the detailed setup of collaboration spaces needed to support the new design, using a notation called MOO diagrams.

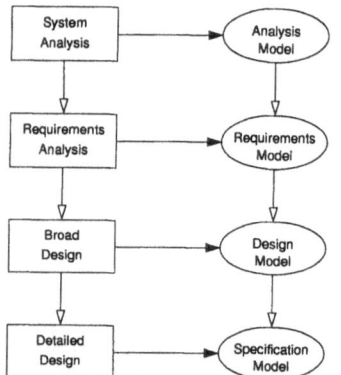

Fig. 2. Analysis and design method for developing support for virtual work processes (adapted from [8])

As an overall approach of conceptual modeling, this is an *activity-centered* approach. We illustrate the main modeling steps and notations by applying them to the formalisation of a manuscript preparation process. Fig. 3 shows a rich picture that conveys high-level properties of the process. The figure reveals the main *activities* (shown as clouds), the *roles*, or main *actors* (shown as stick figures) that are engaged in these activities, and the main *artefacts* (shown as boxes) that are used and produced by these activities. The transition diagram in Fig. 4 shows the sequence in which the activities of this process are carried out. It can be seen that two of the activities, Chapter acquisition and Reviewing, may be performed iteratively.

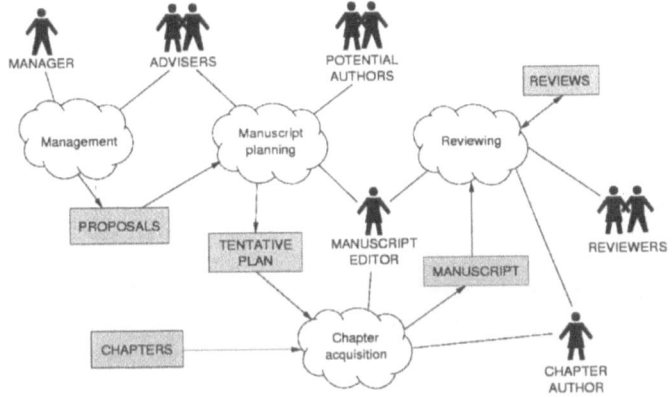

Fig. 3. Rich picture of a manuscript preparation process

Fig. 4. Transition diagram of a manuscript preparation process

For each activity in the rich picture, a separate MOO diagram shows details of required support from a collaboration space (see Fig. 5 for the MOO diagram for the Reviewing activity). It shows which roles (ovals) have which kind of access (directionality of arrows) to which artefacts (boxes with rounded corners), and which discussion forums (hexagons) they are assigned to. The example illustrates the double blind review process where communications between authors and reviewers are mediated through a separate entity, here the manuscript editor.

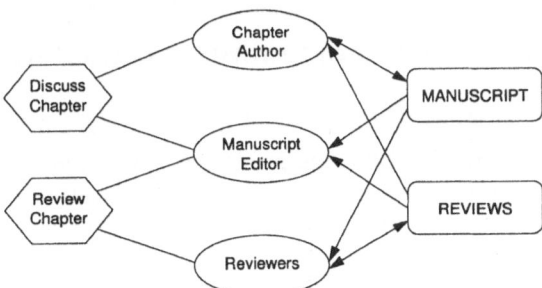

Fig. 5. MOO diagram of the Reviewing activity

For each MOO diagram, a collaboration space with the corresponding features needs to be created. This is where the requirements engineering top-down approach ends. The example in Fig. 6a illustrates this idea—the formalised process is the actual design.

However, the initial configuration of collaboration spaces and their features are meant to represent only a general structure, a starting point for the collaboration process. During the process, the initial configuration will be modified and tailored by the collaborators according to the evolving needs of the collaboration. The example in Fig. 6b illustrates this idea—it constitutes an evolution of the original process and thus contains more workspaces than were initially identified and created.

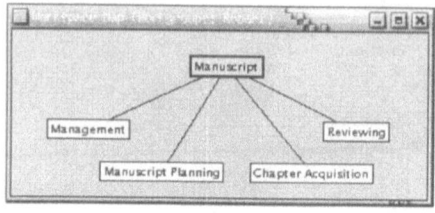 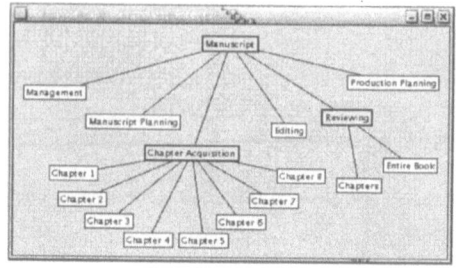

a. Network of collaborative workspaces at the end of a requirements engineering cycle

b. Network of collaborative workspaces that has evolved as a result of the evolution of the process

Fig. 6. Examples of resulting workspaces in the requirements engineering approach

Can we predict some elements of the evolution of a new collaborative process, based on similarities and analogies with processes formalised and supported before? Can we capture and utilise in the workspace design process the evolutionary component, so that we can provide better support to the developers of collaborative workspaces? The rest of the paper presents a new approach for supporting design and redesign of virtual environments, based on combining data mining techniques for refining the lower level models with a reverse engineering cycle to create upper level models.

2   Principles of the Approach towards Process Reverse Engineering

Our approach is based on the following principles: (1) *Availability of a schema* is a prerequisite for the development of effective reverse engineering methods in CVEs. If a well-defined methodology is used to design the virtual workplace (e.g. similar to the one presented in Section 1.2), then some kind of schema (ontology), which preserves the design semantics, is applied during the workplace design process; (2) *Collaboration data*, collected during the evolution of the virtual workplace, is the source for the reverse engineering discoveries, and; (3) *Data mining and knowledge discovery methods* applied to the collaboration data need to take into account the schema (ontology) of the design methodology used for the initial development of the workplace.

Reverse engineering of processes from CVEs is possible through the analysis of collaboration data, which includes structural and behavioural data. Structural data captures static aspects of collaboration, such as the configuration of a collaboration space (e.g., structural data can capture the variety of roles and artefacts in each workspace, and the links between the workspaces). Behavioural data captures dynamic aspects of collaboration, such as the actions performed by a virtual team in a collaboration space. The assumption is that such data reflects the types of activities supported in the environment, the corresponding topology of the collaboration space and the corresponding underlying technological representation.

When analysing such data, the ontology of the environment where it has been collected provides most of the semantic information needed for understanding and designing the data collection. A framework that embeds knowledge discovery in the design and use of CVEs has been presented in [4], and is shown in Fig. 7. This framework suggests (1) how to obtain process knowledge from CVEs, and (2) how to feed discovered process knowledge back into the ongoing use of CVEs.

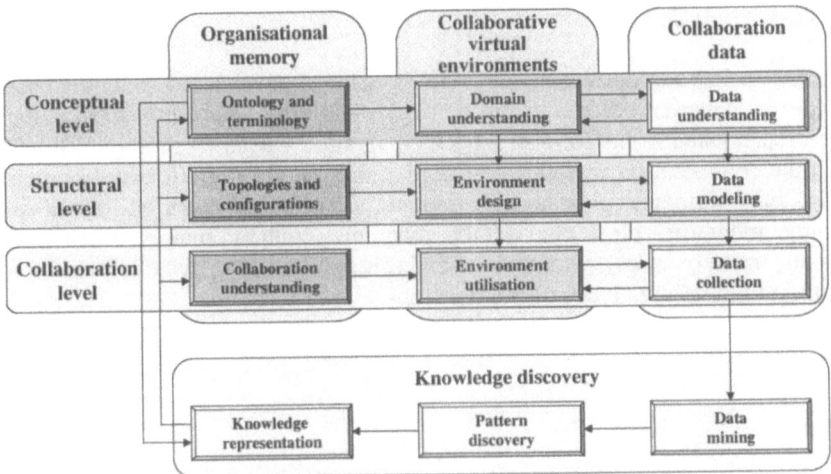

Fig. 7. Framework for extracting and feeding back process knowledge in collaborative virtual environments

The framework consists of four inter-woven components: collaborative virtual environments, collaboration data, knowledge discovery and organizational memory. The three components appearing in the upper part of the figure consist of three parts, at different levels of abstraction: conceptual, structural and collaboration levels. Collaborative virtual environments are seen as central in this framework. This is where processes supporting collaboration are designed and later enacted. This occurs in three steps: initially, understanding of the concepts of the domain to be supported is achieved, followed by the design of the collaboration environment according to requirements of the process to be supported (e.g. following the methodology discussed in Section 1.2), and lastly the utilisation of the environment to carry out the process. The knowledge discovery component of the framework is a slight departure from the classical schema [6] in that the selection and data pre-processing stages are implicitly embedded in the data design. The reader is referred to [4] for more details about the framework components. The following section discusses how process patterns can be obtained through the analysis of collaboration data, using this framework.

3 Method for Reverse Engineering of Processes

The reverse engineering method presented here aims to recover, or discover, the design of a collaborative process, and express it using the modeling notations introduced in the introduction, i.e. rich pictures, transition diagrams, and MOO diagrams. Rich pictures are used for representing entire processes, transition diagrams for showing task sequences, and MOO diagrams for showing individual task detail. The method proceeds in the reverse order of Hawryszkiewycz's methodology: first individual task models are obtained, then these are combined to a process model, and finally a model of task sequences is obtained, as illustrated in Fig. 8.

3.1 Task Analysis

Individual collaboration spaces are seen as being equivalent to individual tasks (or *activities* in Hawryszkiewycz's terminology). Analysing a task aims to produce a task model, represented in the form of a MOO diagram. Depending on the CVE system in which the collaboration was carried out, this may be a straightforward mapping that can be fully automated, or it may require a manual process of identifying and mapping modeling elements. MOO diagrams contain mainly three modeling elements, namely roles, artefacts, and discussion forums, which may be related through certain defined types of relationships.

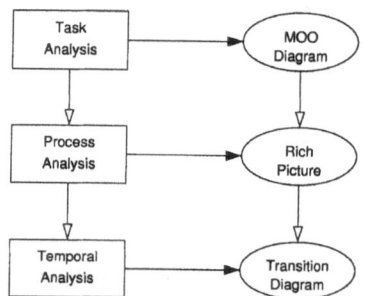

Fig. 8. Method for reverse engineering of processes

3.2 Process Analysis

Once task models have been produced, relationships between tasks need to be analysed in order to discover which tasks belong to the same process. A number of methods are available to aid in this analysis.

One method is to analyse shared task elements, such as artefacts, discussion forums, roles, users, etc. The higher the proportion of shared elements between a pair of collaboration spaces, the greater the likelihood that the tasks in the two spaces are related and are part of the same process.

Another method of analysis is to examine traversal patterns between collaboration spaces. This can reveal a network of spaces among which their users traverse back and forth. Such networks are a good indication of related tasks that are part of the same process.

A further method is to look for so-called "handover points", where objects are passed from one collaboration space to another. Such handovers occur when an object, such as an artefact, is produced by one task as its output, and is received by another task as its input. A handover point usually is a good indicator that two tasks are part of the same process.

To produce the final set of tasks belonging to the same process, each of the above methods is applied to every pair of collaboration spaces, producing an *individual process predictor* value. Next, all of these values are summed together, to yield the *total process predictor* value. The tasks are considered to belong to the same process if their total process predictor value exceeds a given threshold, which is empirically defined. Pairs of tasks are linked together into a task network in such a way that each pair of connected nodes in the network is represented in the set of pairs of tasks remaining from the previous elimination step. The final output of this step is a process model, expressed as a rich picture.

3.3 Temporal Analysis

Once a process model has been obtained, further analysis can be performed to derive a task sequence model. This analysis takes the temporal relationship of actions in different collaboration spaces into account. Actions that occur in different spaces can be related to each other in time in different ways. Looking at all the actions occurring in a collaboration space in their entirety, fundamentally there are only two temporal relationship types: either actions in one space precede actions in another space, or actions in two spaces occur in parallel. Usually a combination of these relationship types exists in a given pair of collaboration spaces, e.g. partially overlapping actions, interleaved actions, etc.

To determine task sequences, an analysis of temporal action relationships is performed on a pair of tasks taken from the process model. This analysis is based on *action levels*, which refers to the temporal clustering of actions in a given task, i.e. task intensity. For each collaboration space, action levels over the entire recorded history of the space are obtained, broken down per unit of time (e.g. day, week). Next, based on the observed distribution of action levels, a threshold is established above which activity in the collaboration space is considered to represent task activity. Using this threshold, a temporal sequencing of actions in collaboration spaces, and thus of corresponding tasks, is now possible. It also makes it possible to identify parallel or interleaved tasks, where after the handover from one task to another, the previous task resumes activity. When this is followed by a switch back to the successor task, an iteration, or loop, is identified. Once all task sequences have been identified, a task sequence model can be produced, represented in the form of a transition diagram.

At the end of the reverse engineering cycle, a set of models is available which reflect certain essential process features, expressed in terms of the ontology of the CVE from which they were obtained. These can be deposited in an organizational memory as expressions of how collaboration has occurred, i.e. as procedural memory, complementing other information on the outcomes of the collaboration. Such process models thus become available for future retrieval and reuse, adding to the tool chest of the designers of collaboration environments.

4   Example of Reverse Engineering of Processes in a CVE System

In this section we present an example of the application of our methodology for reverse engineering of processes. The CVE system in our example is LiveNet, a virtual collaboration system prototype developed at the University of Technology, Sydney [7]. It supports mainly asynchronous collaboration of distributed groups of people, i.e. different-time, different-place interactions, most commonly through a Web interface (as illustrated in Fig. 9a). The environment is built around a particular ontology, which is one of the premises for the application of our method. A simplified ontology of the LiveNet CVE is shown in Fig. 9b. In terms of the ontology, workspaces contain roles, occupied by participants (i.e. actual people), who perform actions. Some actions may operate on document artefacts, others may be interactions with other workspace participants through discussions. Most workspace elements such as documents, discussions and participants may be shared between workspaces.

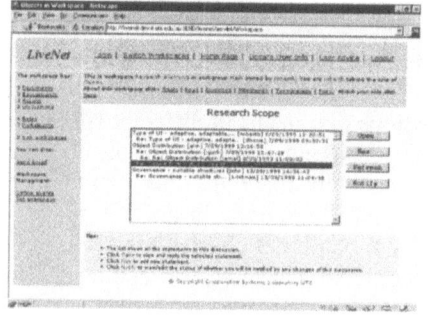
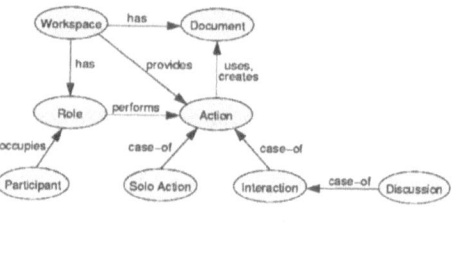

a. Web interface to LiveNet   b. Simplified ontology of LiveNet

Fig. 9. LiveNet underlying model and interface.

LiveNet workspaces are not just stand-alone entities, but nodes in a network of inter-connected collaboration spaces. Neither are structures of workspaces in LiveNet static—once created, a workspace can be dynamically adapted to evolve together with the collaboration carried out in it.

4.1   Reverse Engineering of Processes in the LiveNet CVE System

The presented reverse engineering method for process extraction was applied to data collected from the LiveNet collaboration system. The data originated from 513 student and staff users at the University of Technology, Sydney who used LiveNet for a number of purposes. The collaboration data spans a three-month period in the second half of 2000, during which time a total of 721 workspaces were created. Reverse engineering focused on a set of workspaces that were set up by students learning to use collaboration technology, in this case to support a construction management task. The following describes one instance of reverse engineering of a process designed to support construction management.

4.1.1 Task analysis. Initially, information visualization aided the identification of potential candidates for reverse engineering. A specialized tool, the workspace visualizer, developed by us for the visualization of instances of workspaces, was used for this purpose [3]. An example of a so-called *inter-workspace map*, displaying relationships between workspaces, is shown in Fig. 10.

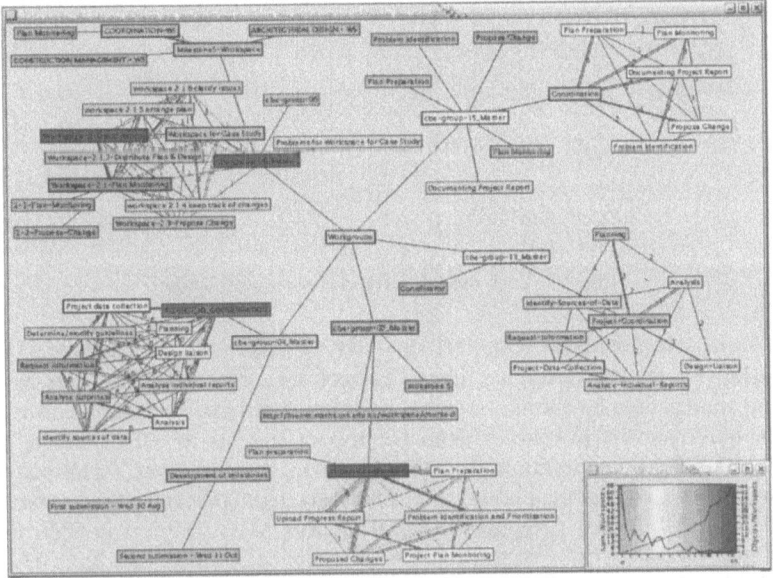

Fig. 10. Map of LiveNet workspaces

This map reveals a number of *clusters* of workspaces that appear to be closely related and could be part of the same work process. Later, process analysis will show whether this assumption can be supported. Firstly, task analysis is performed for all workspaces. To illustrate this, Fig. 11a shows an *intra-workspace* map (also produced by our visualisation tool), displaying the relationships among the elements internal to a workspace, such as roles, documents, and discussion forums. Fig. 11b shows the MOO diagram that has been derived from this intra-workspace map. Both figures show that almost all assignments of documents and discussion forums to roles in the workspace are identical. The only differences exist in the creation/modification of the Problem and Proposed Change documents (arrow pointing from the role to the document), which may only be performed by the Client and Coordinator roles, respectively. Coupled with the presence of the discussion forums for commenting on the design and discussing changes, this indicates a participatory work process: all roles may read all documents and join in the discussions, while changes to documents are coordinated by having only one role in charge of making such changes.

Given an ontology of the CVE and a set of rules, the task analysis and derivation of a MOO diagram can be performed automatically. The task analysis is performed for all workspaces under consideration. In the example of the inter-workspace map shown in Fig. 10, this is done for 65 workspaces (out of the total of 721).

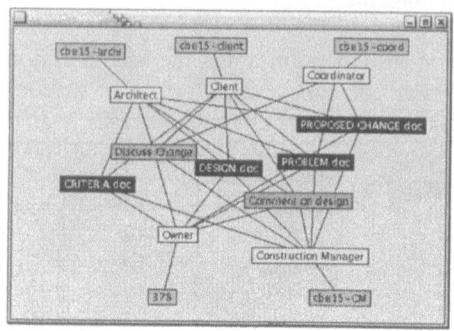

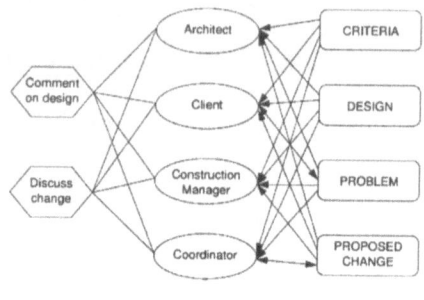

a. Intra-workspace map of the "Propose Change" workspace

b. Corresponding MOO diagram capturing essential aspects of the "Propose Change" workspace

Fig. 11. Task model derived from a workspace

4.1.2 Process analysis. Following task analysis, process analysis attempts to discover which tasks (i.e. workspaces) are likely part of the same process. This begins by examining shared task elements, traversal patterns, and handover points, as discussed earlier. Table 1 shows an extract from the top of the list of all candidate pairs of workspaces under consideration, together with their individual and total process predictor values. The table shows, for example, that the two workspaces "Plan Preparation" and "Propose Change", listed at the top, have 10 items in common, were involved in traversals from one to the other workspace 3 times, and have 1 item that serves as a handover point, i.e. constitutes the outcome of one task and the input of the next, yielding a total process predictor value of 14.

Following the derivation of these process predictor values, those pairs of workspaces for which the value is below the defined threshold are eliminated from further consideration. In this case the threshold was set at 3, below which predictors were insignificant in predicting process membership. This left 13 pairs of workspaces, which next were linked together into a task network according to the established relationship. By adding shared roles and artefacts, this network was augmented to produce a process rich picture. Fig. 12b shows the resulting rich picture, corresponding to the cluster of workspaces shown in Fig. 12a. Both of these figures reveal the greatly inter-connected nature of the tasks in this process: most of the tasks (i.e. workspaces) share a majority of both artefacts and roles, and every task has some relationship to every other task. This is typical of collaborative and knowledge-intensive work processes, which have been described as resulting in "disconnected and parallel work that must nevertheless be guided to a common goal" [7].

Table 1. Process predictor values for candidate workspace pairs (extract)

Workspace 1	Workspace 2	Shared Elements	Traversals	Handover Points	Total Process Predictor Value
Plan Preparation	Propose Change	10	3	1	14
Coordination	Plan Preparation	9	1	2	12
Plan Monitoring	Plan Preparation	5	7	0	12
Plan Monitoring	Problem Identification	7	4	1	12
⋮	⋮	⋮	⋮	⋮	⋮

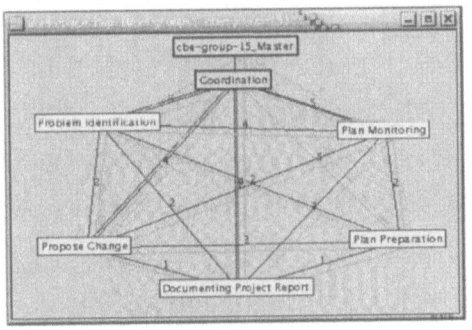

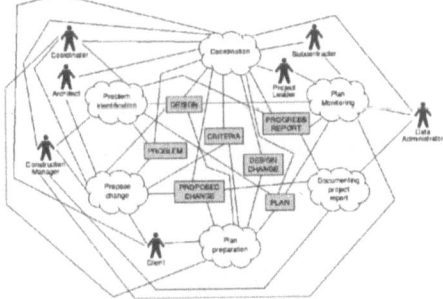

a. Inter-workspace map showing a cluster of workspaces

b. Rich picture of the corresponding tasks of the workspace cluster

Fig. 12. Process model derived from a collection of workspaces

4.1.3 Temporal Analysis. The final step of reverse engineering consists of performing temporal analysis on the actions in the workspaces of the derived process model in order to obtain a task sequence model. First, the history of actions in the workspaces is broken down into chunks, in this case at the level of days. Based on the distribution of action levels per day, which ranged from a minimum of 1 to a maximum of 120, with the majority of workspaces having action levels in the 10-20 range on most days, a threshold of 5 was set to distinguish tasks. Below this value, an excessive number of task switches resulted, often incurred only for such "tasks" as entering another workspace to look up a document or discussion item.

Temporal analysis then obtained sequences of task switches, which were consolidated into the task sequence model shown in Fig. 13. The temporal analysis revealed that tasks in this process were tightly integrated: not only was work interleaved, with frequent switching between tasks, but also was it often parallel. Nonetheless, the transition diagram in Fig. 13 does reveal definite patterns of task switching. For example, there is only uni-directional switching in five cases (such as from Plan monitoring to Problem identification), and bi-directional switching in four cases (such as between Plan monitoring and Coordination). Certain potential paths don't exist at all (for example, there is no switch between Plan preparation and Problem identification). This indicates to us that even in such relatively poorly structured processes—as compared to workflow processes—certain patterns of work emerge, which are reflected in the collected collaboration data and subsequently the derived process models.

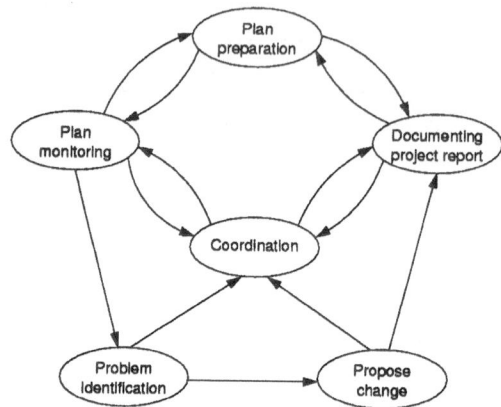

Fig. 13. Task sequence model derived from observed actions in a network of workspaces

5   Example of Integrating Collaboration Knowledge in a CVE System

Collaboration data in LiveNet consists of two parts: a database contains the internal data of the CVE, maintaining the current state of all workspace elements (documents, roles, participants, etc.). The second part is a set of log files that are external to the system itself and which record all user actions carried out in the system over time. The log records captured by the LiveNet server are on a semantically much higher level than those in the corresponding web access log. The LiveNet log records include the name of the workspace and its owner, the name of the participant carrying out the action, his/her role name, the LiveNet server command requested, etc. This allows analysis to exploit metadata available in the application and to capture higher-level actions than a mere web log does. The analysis we carried out focused primarily on the log of collaboration actions, and to a lesser extent on the workspace database. It involved pre-processing of the log, visualization of workspace data, and actual data mining. The pre-processing step normalizes session numbers, aggregates lower-level events into higher-level actions, and calculates session summaries. In this context, a session is the sequence of actions carried out by a user from login to logout time. Data pre-processing is considered part of collaboration data collection and is usually automatically performed. The data used originated from students and instructors of a number of courses at the University of Technology, Sydney, who used the LiveNet system both to coordinate their work, and to set up workspaces as part of the students' assignments. The data covers a three month period, with a total of 571,319 log records, They were aggregated into 178,488 higher-level actions in a total of 24,628 sessions involving 721 workspaces and 513 users.

5.1   Workspace Structuring

During knowledge discovery, using visualisation certain of the relationships existing within and between workspaces can be discovered. This particularly aids exploratory analysis, when the purpose is to get an understanding of the structure of, and patterns in, the data. We selected data originating from students of one course who used LiveNet during the mentioned period. There were a total of 187 student users, organized into 50 mostly 3-5 person groups, whose use accounted for about 20% of the above-mentioned log data. Initial visualization focused on networks of workspaces, to discover how individual student groups partitioned their work in terms of distinct workspaces, and to what extent these workspaces were linked to one another. This exploratory analysis revealed two distinct patterns: the majority of users preferred to use just one workspace to organize all their course work (such as posting drafts of assignment documents, discussing work distribution and problems, etc.). This workspace tended to contain many objects—or have a high *absolute workspace density*. We term such groups *centralizers*. To a certain extent, this mode corresponds to the single-task collaboration mentioned earlier. On the other hand, a few groups tended to partition their work across a collection of connected workspaces, usually with a separate workspace for each major course assignment. These workspaces tended to contain fewer objects (having a lower absolute workspace density) than the ones of the centralizers. We term these groups *partitioners*. Their collaboration style corresponds to the multi-task collaboration. Fig. 14 shows a map of LiveNet workspaces with colours highlighting absolute workspace density—lighter colour indicating lower density, darker colour indicating higher density. Branching out from the central node at the top are networks of workspaces for three groups. Nodes represent workspaces, edges represent hierarchical relationships between workspaces. What the map reveals is that the group on the right, Team40, has a very high density in the workspace used for facilitating its work (the workspace Team40_Master). Moreover, it uses only one workspace for this purpose. Thus the right group is a typical example of a centralizer. On the other hand, workspaces in the group at the centre have a much lower density. Out of the 8 workspaces in this group, six are used for facilitating aspects of the group's work. This is indicative of a partitioner group.

There are plausible explanations for both the centralizer and partitioner cases. Both approaches have their own advantages: in the centralizer case, it is convenience in not having to create multiple workspaces, to switch between them, and in addition to have everything available to all participants in a single location. In the partitioner case, the advantage is increased clarity, structuring according to task, and consequently reduced cognitive load in the case of multi-task collaboration. Furthermore, some groups may bring certain preferences as to the way to organize their work into workspaces and enact these preferences in the way they structure their virtual working environment. When such preferences are recognized during knowledge discovery, and deposited in the organizational memory, they can feed back into the design of new virtual collaboration environments, thus helping to offer more adequate support to cooperative groups with diverse working styles.

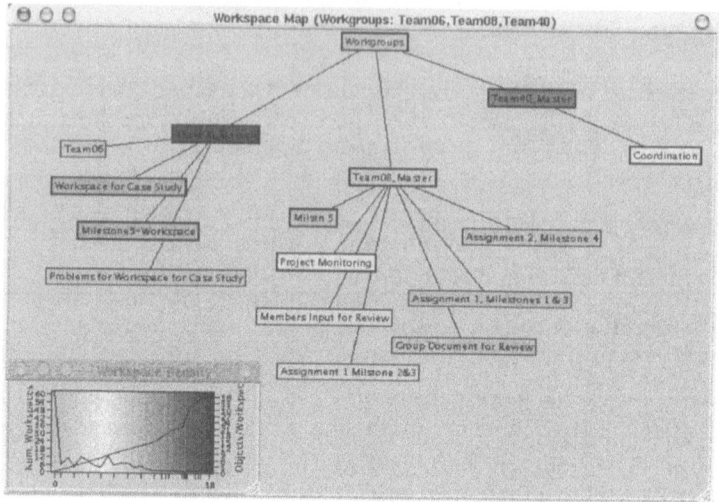

Fig. 14. Workspace densities of three different groups

5.2 Feasible Actions

A further area we investigated was focused on identifying which actions different groups mainly carried out within LiveNet. All in all, 80 different actions are available in LiveNet. The majority of student groups used only about half of these. The major actions carried out are related to the main LiveNet conceptual elements: workspaces, roles, participants, documents, and discussions. A taxonomy of these actions is presented in Fig. 15. While all groups had been given the same task—to prepare a number of assignments and to set up a collection of workspaces to support a given process—the way they implemented this task varied markedly. This was evident in a number of aspects of their use of the LiveNet system, such as intensity of use, number of workspaces created, number and length of sessions, number of actions per session, etc. One area of our analysis focused on the proportional distribution of main actions. This revealed that strong differences existed among different groups. To illustrate two examples, Fig. 16 shows action distributions among the major high-level actions of the taxonomy of Fig. 15 for one group whose distribution of actions was fairly even across categories (with the exception of the participant category): the five major action categories did not vary greatly, none of them exceeding 0.29 of the total (circle size signifies proportion out of the total). Fig. 17, on the other hand, shows a highly uneven distribution of actions in another group, where one action category (role) strongly dominates with 0.56 of the total, and two other action categories (document and discussion) barely register.

This difference may be explained when considering that group 1 (Fig. 16) had a total of 627 sessions consisting of a total of 7446 actions, while group 50 (Fig. 17) had only 36 sessions and 633 actions. Not only did group 1 use LiveNet much more intensively, but they also made much greater use of the system to facilitate their own

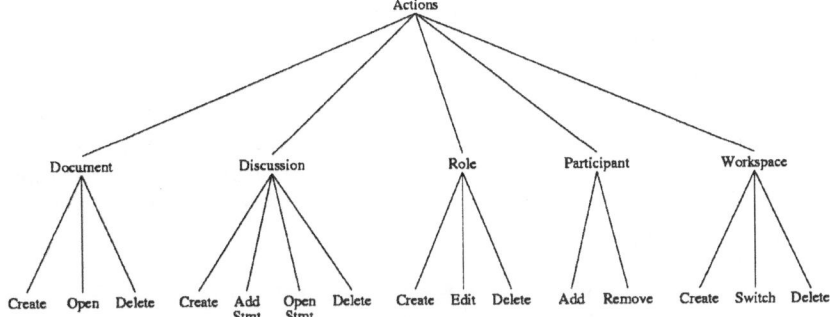

Fig. 15. Taxonomy of major high-level LiveNet actions

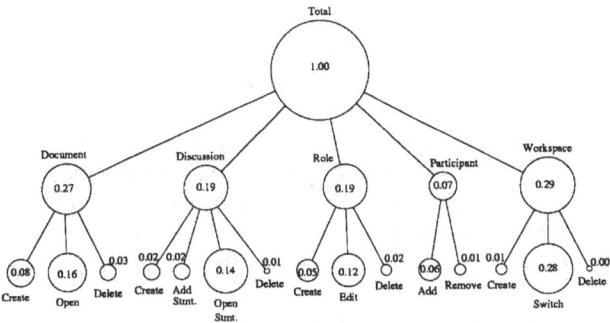

Fig. 16. Relatively even distribution of actions in group 1

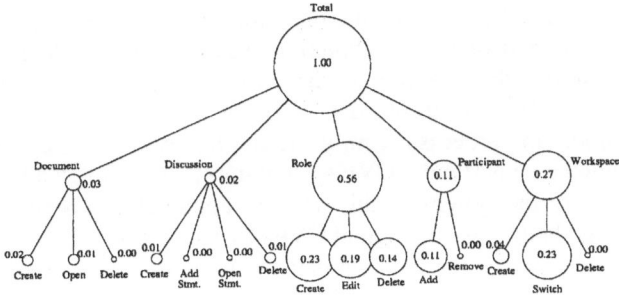

Fig. 17. Highly uneven distribution of actions in group 50

work (as manifested in the solid proportion of actions in the document and discussion categories). Thus the skew in action distribution towards role-related actions on the part of group 50 is caused by the under-utilization of other LiveNet features, not by an absolute high number of actions related to roles (in absolute terms, group 1 carried out 431 role-related actions, while group 50 carried out only 142 such actions). The choice of these two groups for illustration was not coincidental: group 1 was the best-performing group in the course, while group 50 was the worst-performing group, as measured in the marks obtained for their assignments in the course. The situation was comparable in other similarly scoring groups.

When such cases are identified and included in the organizational memory as part of a record of collaboration, they can be of use in evaluating virtual work. This can be particularly useful with virtual teams that never meet face-to-face, where conventional management methods for project monitoring and control are severely limited or absent. The organizational memory thus takes on the additional role of a managment instrument.

6 Conclusions

While business process (re-)engineering has received much attention in the past years, very little, if any, work has been performed on reverse engineering of work processes, particularly in the realm of virtual collaboration. This paper has presented a novel methodology for reverse engineering of virtual work processes performed through collaborative virtual environments. It produces design models at micro (task) and macro (process) levels of these processes using notations from a (forward engineering) design methodology intended for virtual collaboration. Presented methodology allows tracing the evolution of processes from an initial design and discovering of ad-hoc and emergent processes for which no such initial design was prepared. In both cases, processes obtained through reverse engineering can be retained in a library of reusable process templates.

The presented methodology is independent of the underlying CVE system employed, and only requires knowledge of its schema, i.e. ontology. Only the concrete implementation of the data mining methods used needs to be adapted to the given CVE system so as to capture different CVE elements needed in the calculation of process predictors. Likewise, the interpretation of discovered patterns will need to be framed in the context of the collaboration system utilised. When combined with the framework presented in Section 2, the proposed approach has the potential to influence the way CVEs are designed or redesigned. Insights obtained through the analysis of collaboration processes can, for example, reveal deficiencies in the levels of support provided by a particular CVE system implementation, leading to a redesign of a future version of the system. In this way, the approach can become the backbone of a new design methodology—design of CVEs by adaptation.

Finally, the illustrated combination of data mining and reverse engineering, and the availability of a rich source of data on actual collaborative practices, can lead to a better understanding of the influence of computer mediation on collaborative processes. The development of CVEs that support the reverse engineering cycle, and the data mining of the internal structures of such environments, are areas for further research to focus on.

Acknowledgments. The support by the Australian Research Council, the University of Technology, Sydney, and the University of Macau, which has made this research possible, is gratefully acknowledged.

References

1. P. Anders, *Envisioning cyberspace: Designing 3-D electronic spaces*. New York: McGraw-Hill, 1999.
2. R. P. Biuk-Aghai, "Virtual Workspaces for Web-Based Emergent Processes," in *Fourth Pacific Asia Conference on Information Systems: Electronic Commerce and Web-Based Information Systems*. Hong Kong, China, 2000, pp. 864-880.
3. R. P. Biuk-Aghai, "Visualization of Web-Based Workspace Structures," in *Proceedings of the 1st International Conference on Web Information Systems Engineering*, vol. 1, Q. Li, Z. M. Ozsoyoglu, R. Wagner, Y. Kambayashi, and Y. Zhang, Eds. Hong Kong, China: IEEE Computer Society, 2000, pp. 302-309.
4. R. P. Biuk-Aghai and S. J. Simoff, "An Integrative Framework for Knowledge Extraction in Collaborative Virtual Environments," in *Proceedings of the ACM 2001 International Conference on Supporting Group Work*. Boulder, CO, USA: ACM Press, 2001.
5. T. L. Fanderclai, "MUDs in education: new environments, new pedagogies," *Computer Mediated Communication Magazine*, vol. 2, 1995.
6. U. M. Fayyad, G. Piatetsky-Shapiro, and P. Smyth, "From data mining to knowledge discovery: An overview," in *Advances in Knowledge Discovery and Data Mining*, U. M. Fayyad, G. Piatetsky-Shapiro, P. Smyth, and R. Uthurusamy, Eds. Menlo Park, CA, USA: AAAI Press/MIT Press, 1996.
7. I. T. Hawryszkiewycz, "Workspace Networks for Knowledge Sharing," in *Proceedings of AusWeb99, the Fifth Australian World Wide Web Conference*, R. Debrency and A. Ellis, Eds. Ballina, Australia, 1999, pp. 219-227.
8. I. T. Hawryszkiewycz, "Analysis for Cooperative Business Processes," in *Proceedings of the Fifth Australian Workshop on Requirements Engineering*, D. Zowghi, Ed. Brisbane, Australia, 2000, pp. 3-11.
9. M. L. Maher, S. Simoff, N. Gu, and K. H. Lau, "Two Approaches to a Virtual Design Office," *International Journal of Design Computing*, vol. 2, 2000.
10. C. Moorman and A. S. Miner, "Organizational Improvisation and Organizational Memory," *Academy of Management Review*, vol. 23, pp. 698-723, 1998.
11. D. Patching, *Practical Soft Systems Analysis*. London: Pitman, 1990.
12. D. Richards and S. J. Simoff, "Design ontology in context - A situated cognition approach to conceptual modeling," *AI in Engineering*, vol. 15, 2001.
13. S. Simoff and M. L. Maher, "Designing with the activity/space ontology," in *Artificial Intelligence in Design 98*, J. S. Gero and F. Sudweeks, Eds. Dordrecht: Kluwer Academic, 1998, pp. 23-44.
14. S J. Simoff and M. L. Maher, "Loosely-integrated open virtual environments as places," *IEEE Learning Technology*, vol. 3, 2001.

Flexible Merging for Asynchronous Collaborative Systems

Haifeng Shen and Chengzheng Sun

School of Computing and Information Technology
Griffith University
Brisbane, Qld 4111, Australia
{Hf.Shen, C.Sun}@cit.gu.edu.au

Abstract. Version control systems are widely used asynchronous collaborative systems in team-working environments, where document merging is a key function. However most existing systems only support limited semantic merging, and techniques for supporting semantic merging are strictly bound up with the merging algorithms that do syntactic merging. In this paper, we propose a flexible merging framework in which semantic merging policies are separated from the syntactic merging mechanism for asynchronous collaborative systems. In this framework, semantic merging policies are not restricted by the merging algorithms used in the syntactic merging mechanism, and the syntactic merging mechanism is flexible to support a wide range of semantic merging policies. This framework can be used to describe and compare a range of existing merging policies and mechanisms, and to guide the design of new merging policies and mechanisms. The proposed framework has been applied to the design of a flexible merging component in *FORCE* (Flexible Operation-based Revision Control Environment) prototype, which uses a single syntactic merging mechanism to support a range of semantic merging policies.

Keywords: Collaborative system, version control system, document merging, operational transformation

1 Introduction

It is very common that multiple developers are involved in developing a large software project. These developers may be dispersed in different offices or even scattered geographically over the world, but they need to simultaneously modify the code of the shared project. Version control systems are therefore widely used nowadays to facilitate collaborative work in team-working environments. The configuration of a version control system can be illustrated by Figure 1: a repository server maintains all evolving versions of a software project and developers have network connections with the repository server. A version control system is a typical asynchronous collaborative system, which works in the manner of *Copy-Modify-Merge* [5]: each developer checks out a separate *working copy* of

R. Meersman, Z. Tari (Eds.): CoopIS/DOA/ODBASE 2002, LNCS 2519, pp. 304–321, 2002.
© Springer-Verlag Berlin Heidelberg 2002

the original copy from the repository; then modifies her/his working copy independently; and finally merges her/his working copy with other copies. *Merging is the process of integrating multiple documents to generate a new document,* which is an essential function in asynchronous collaborative systems. As shown

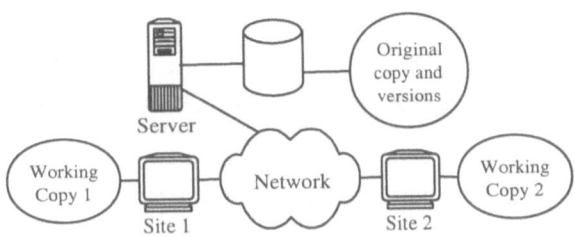

Fig. 1. The configuration of a version control system

in Figure 2, merging may happen at two stages. One is at the *committing stage* when a working copy (W_m^1) is committed into the repository to form a new version $R_1 = W_m^1$. At this stage, updates made between W_0^1 and W_m^1 are merged into its original copy R_0 in the repository. The other is at the *updating stage* when a working copy W_n^2 is updated by a committed working copy (or version) R_1 from the repository. At this stage, updates made between R_0 and R_1 are merged into W_n^2 to generate a new document state W_{n+1}^2.

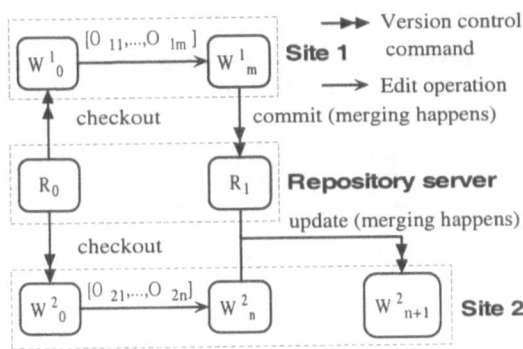

Fig. 2. Merging may happen at two stages

Merging at the committing stage can be easily achieved by re-applying those updates made in the working copy (i.e., updates made between W_0^1 and W_m^1) to its original copy R_0 in the repository because $R_0 = W_0^1$ on which those updates were generated. In contrast, merging at the updating stage is far more difficult. Updates made in a committed working copy (i.e., updates made between R_0

and R_1) cannot be simply re-applied in W_n^2 because $W_n^2 \neq R_0$ on which those updates were generated.

Because of the difficulties involved in merging at the updating stage, most existing systems only support limited *semantic merging* (i.e., semantically merging two documents), and techniques for supporting semantic merging are strictly bound up with the merging algorithms that do *syntactic merging* ((i.e., syntactically merging two documents). Those systems usually adopt ad hoc techniques to glue semantic merging and syntactic merging together. For example, in *RCS* (Revision Control System) [14] and *CVS* (Concurrent Versions System) [3], the semantic merging policy defines that concurrent updates made within the same line are semantically conflicting while concurrent updates made in different lines are not. This policy, although simple, is very restrictive. On one hand, concurrent updates made within the same line do not necessarily imply they must conflict. For example, suppose a document contains a line *"You are student"*. A user inserts an article *"a"* between *"are"* and *"student"* to fix a grammar error while another user appends a full stop mark *"."* to the line to make it a complete sentence. Although these two updates are made within the same line, they are not semantically conflicting at all.

On the other hand, concurrent updates made in different lines do not necessarily imply they would not be conflicting either. For example, suppose a document contains two lines: *"You are"* and *"student."*. A user appends an article *"a"* to the first line while another user inserts character *"s"* between *"t"* and *"."* in the second line to make *"student"* plural. Although these two updates are made in different lines, they are semantically conflicting. The main reason for adopting this kind of semantic merging policy is due to the limitation of the syntactic merging algorithm *diff3* [9], which is unable to merge concurrent updates made within the same line.

In this paper, we propose a flexible merging framework in which semantic merging policies are separated from the syntactic merging mechanism for asynchronous collaborative systems. In this framework, semantic merging policies are not restricted by the merging algorithms used in the syntactic merging mechanism, and the syntactic merging mechanism is flexible to support a wide range of semantic merging policies. This framework can be used to describe and compare a range of existing merging policies and mechanisms, and to guide the design of new merging policies and mechanisms. We will show how to apply the proposed framework to the design of a flexible merging component in *FORCE* (Flexible Operation-based Revision Control Environment) prototype, which uses a single syntactic merging mechanism to support a range of semantic merging policies.

The rest of the paper is organized as follows. After the introduction, a flexible merging framework is described. Then the next two sections systematically present a flexible merging component for a version control system, which uses a single syntactic merging mechanism to support multiple semantic merging policies. Finally the paper is concluded with a summary of our major contributions and future work.

2   A Flexible Merging Framework

As shown in Figure 3, in the proposed merging framework, semantic merging and syntactic merging are separated in two components: *Policy* component and *Mechanism* component.

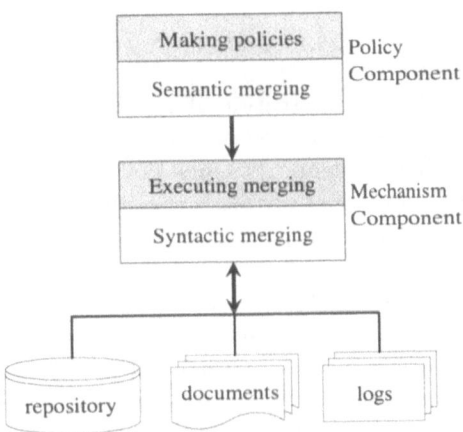

Fig. 3. A flexible merging framework

2.1   The Policy Component

The policy component makes various semantic merging policies. These policies are application-dependent. For example, if the shared document is an article, the semantic merging policies could specify a set of spell and grammar checking rules, and possibly the roles of participants. If the shared document is a computer program, the semantic policies could specify the programming language's syntax parsing rules, and possibly how the work is divided among those participants. Our observation is if the work is properly divided among participants in the way that different participants play different roles, it is possible that their concurrent updates made to the shared document do not semantically conflict with each other, and therefore a new document could be generated to integrate all updates made by different participants. For example, two authors are jointly revising a scientific paper, one correcting spell/grammar errors while the other adding references. Their concurrent updates made to the paper could be as close as within the same line. But these updates would not cause any semantic conflict.

A semantic merging policy is specified as a set of Semantic Merging Rules (*SMR*) with which a function *Semantic-Conflict* (*SMR*, O_r, O_l, *CT*) determines whether two concurrent updates O_r and O_l are semantically conflicting according to the context *CT* on which they were generated. On one extreme, the function could automatically return *true/false* without human intervention if the *SMR* has been well formulated. For instance, O_r and O_l were made concurrently by two users, both aiming to make the sentence *"You are student."* grammatically correct. O_r inserted an article *"a"* between *"are"* and *"student"* while O_l made *"student"* plural by appending character *"s"* between *"t"* and *"."*. If the *SMR* specifies the grammar checking rules, *Semantic-Conflict* $(SMR, O_r, O_l,$ *"You are student."*$)$ can automatically return *true* because reapplying O_r/O_l to the other copy leads to the result *"You are a students."*, which is incorrect according to the *SMR*. Automatic detection of conflicts is the most desirable way. However, it is not easy to achieve.

On the other extreme, the detection of conflicts could be completely manual if the *SMR* is unable to be formulated in any way. As a result, it is completely up to the user to determine what updates made by another user should be merged into her/his working copy, possibly with consultation with that user. Manual detection of conflicts is the most general way for all applications, although it is the lest desirable way. In most cases, the detection of conflicts is the combination of automatic and manual detections. In other words, some conflicts can be automatically detected while others have to be detected by human.

The formulation of the *SMR* is non-trivial, particularly for those semantic rich applications. Therefore the formulation of the *SMR* itself deserves a lot of research on it. In the *FORCE* (Flexible Operation-based Revision Control Environment) prototype, some simple semantic merging policies based on which the *SMR* is easy to be formulated are used just for demonstrating the feasibility of separating semantic and syntactic merging. Our focus in this paper is to devise a generic and flexible syntactic merging mechanism, which is able to support a range of semantic merging policies provided the *SMR* has been formulated and the *Semantic-Conflict* function has been defined.

2.2   The Mechanism Component

The mechanism component executes syntactic merging according to the *SMR* specified in the policy component. A remote update will be applied to a local working copy only if it does not semantically conflict with any update performed by the local user according to the specified *SMR*. The mechanism component also includes some data structures: repository for storing versions, logs for storing updates, and documents of working copies. These data structures are needed for the mechanism component to execute syntactic merging.

What semantic merging policies can be supported by the syntactic merging mechanism strictly relies on how the syntactic merging mechanism is designed. As explained before, if the syntactic merging mechanism is unable to merge concurrent updates made within the same line, the semantic merging policy cannot support integrating concurrent updates made within the same line. Most existing asynchronous collaborative systems, such as *RCS* [14], *CVS* [3], *ClearCase* [1], and *Subversion* [4] adopt the *state-based merging* approach as the syntactic merging mechanism.

State-based merging [8], as the name implies, is performed by comparing different documents to generate *deltas* against the *base* document (one of those documents), and then applying the deltas on the *base* document to generate a new document. State-based merging is mainly used to merge text documents. A representative is the *diff3* [9] merging algorithm, which is used to merge updates made between the original copy and a developed working copy into another concurrently developed working copy. However, the merging algorithm may not be able to merge all updates made in one developed working copy into another although there is no semantic conflict at all. The main reason is derived deltas are coarse-grained.

Deltas are coarse-grained in the sense that they are line-based, which means if there is a single update in a line, the entire line is regarded as updated. Consequently the deltas would be the deletion of the old line, and then the insertion of the new line. Deltas could even be block-based, which means if every line in a block (i.e., several consecutive lines) contains an update, the deltas would be the deletion of the old block, and then the insertion of the new block. We refer to the block as an *edit block*, which contains a single line or several consecutive lines in a document. As a result, the *effect region* of a delta must start at the beginning of a line and contain one or several consecutive lines. In state-based merging, if an edit block in a working copy is overlapping with an edit block in another copy, updates in the edit block made in that copy are not able to be merged into the other copy. An typical example is an update made within a line in one working copy cannot be merged into another working copy in which an concurrent update has been made within the same line.

As an alternative to state-based merging, *operation-based merging* [8], saves operations (updates) on a document into a log as the deltas between the current state and the initial state of that document. Operation-based merging is done by re-executing operations performed in one working copy on another copy. For example, consider the configuration in Figure 2. If $R_0 = W_0^1 = W_0^2$ contains *"You are student"*. *Site 1* performs an operation O_{11} to insert a space and an article *"a"* between *"are"* and *"student"*, and then $W_1^1 = $ *"You are a student"*. Therefore the delta between W_1^1 and W_0^1 is O_{11}. *Site 2* performs an operation O_{21} to append a full stop mark to the line, and then $W_1^2 = $ *"You are student."*. Therefore the delta between W_1^2 and W_0^2 is O_{21}. To merge the update made at *Site 1* into *Site 2*'s working copy whose current document state is W_1^2, simply re-executing O_{11} on W_1^2 would do, and the new document state of *Site 2* 's working copy would become $W_2^2 = $ *"You are a student."*, which has integrated the effects of both O_{11} and O_{21}.

Operations are far more fine-grained than the deltas generated in state-based merging because the effect region of an operation could start at any position and contain arbitrary number of characters in a document. There are two types of primitive editing operations *insert* and *delete*. The basic notation of an editing operation is $ins/del[P, L, S]$, representing inserting/deleting string S whose length is L at position P in a document. The fine-granularity of operations makes operation-based merging capable of syntactically merging all concurrent updates made to a shared document by different users. We therefore adopt operation-based merging as the syntactic merging mechanism for the proposed merging framework. Moreover, operation-based merging could support more document types in addition to text documents. For example, operation-based merging was used in the *GINA* application framework [2] to merge command objects performed in an multi-user application at one site into another. The *Bayou* infrastructure [6] used operation-based merging to merge operations performed in one copy of a shared database into another.

2.3   Issues of Operation-Based Merging

Operation-based merging has its own challenging issues. One major issue is how to control the size of logs that store saved operations. In a distributed teamworking environment, each participant works independently on his own working copy and her/his independent work tends to be very long. With executed operations accumulated in a log, the log could grow very huge, resulting in a poor system response because the larger a log is, the longer transferring it over the network plus executing operations within it takes.

This issue was raised in [6,10], but few solutions were proposed. We have devised the technique of operational merging [11] by which operations whose effect regions are overlapping or adjacent can be merged. As a result, a log can be compressed in the way that its size and the number of operations within it are reduced. With the proposed *CALOM* (Compress A Log by Operational Merging) control algorithm [11], a log can be fully compressed in the sense that given any two operations in the log, their effect regions are neither overlapping nor adjacent. Moreover, the compressed log is equivalent to its original log in the sense that the compressed log has the exact effect as the original one, which guarantees the correctness of the compression.

Our focus in this paper is to tackle another challenging issue, that is how to devise operation-based merging protocols and algorithms for the syntactic merging mechanism, which is able to support a range of semantic merging policies. As explained in the previous section, merging at the committing stage is easy. The problem is merging at the updating stage. Firstly, some operations performed in one working copy may not be able to be re-executed in another due to semantic conflicts. Secondly, if an operation can be re-executed, it may not be able to be re-executed as is because the current document state of a working copy is different from the one on which it was defined. For example, suppose a document contains a line *"You are student"*. A user performs an operation $O_1 = ins[7, 2, $ " a "$]$ to insert a space and an article *"a"* at position 7 (i.e., between *"are"* and *"student"*) while another user performs an operation $O_2 = ins[15, 1, $ "."$]$ to insert a full stop mark *"."* after *"student"*. O_1 and O_2 are not semantically conflicting, but re-executing O_2 in the other copy would produce the result *"You are a stude.nt"*, which is obviously wrong. Finally, as shown in Figure 2, operations $O_{11}, \cdots, O_{1m}$ represent the deltas between W_m^1 and its original copy R_0 while operations $O_{21}, \cdots, O_{2n}$ represent the deltas between W_n^2 and its original copy R_0. When *Site 2* updates her/his working copy with version R_1 to generate a new document state W_{n+1}^2, what are the deltas between W_{n+1}^2 and its original copy R_1?

It is non-trivial to solve these issues. The IceCube approach [7] attempted to find an ordering of operations when doing merging to minimize conflicts in terms of application semantics and user intentions. The Bayou infrastructure [6] tried to achieve correct merging with a set of ordering and closure constraints on the propagation of the operations made to a shared and replicated database. These solutions are ad hoc and strictly glue semantic merging and syntactic merging together. Therefore they are unsuitable to be adopted as the syntactic merging mechanism to support a range of semantic merging policies. In the following section, we will systematically address these issues and present merging protocols that have been implemented in the *FORCE* (Flexible Operation-based Revision Control Environment) prototype.

3   Merging Protocols and Algorithms

At the very beginning, the full state of a document is imported into the repository and marked as the initial version *V.0*. To collaboratively edit the document, every participant needs to check out a separate copy of *V.0* as her/his *working copy*, and the version number 0 as her/his *base version* number. The *checkout* protocol will be presented later in this section. Then s/he starts editing her/his own working copy with editing operations continuously accumulated in a log sequentially.

3.1   Commit a Working Copy

To commit a working copy into the repository, the *OMCS* (Operation-based Merging at the Committing Stage) protocol is devised as follows.

Protocol 1. OMCS

Suppose the user at *Site k* whose base version number is bv and log is LL, wants to commit her/his working copy into the repository:

1. *Site k* sends a committing request to the repository server, containing the base version number bv.
2. Upon receiving the request, if the repository has been locked because someone is updating it, the repository server puts the request into the waiting queue. When the lock is released and it is time to respond *Site k*'s committing request:
   - If the *latest version V.lv* in the repository is *V.bv*, the repository server locks the repository and sends a consentient reply to *Site k*.
   - Otherwise, the repository sends a rejective reply to *Site k*.
3. Upon receiving the reply from the repository server, if it is rejective, *Site k* warns the user to update her/his working copy before committing. If it is consentient:
   - *Site k* sends all operations in LL to the repository server, and then empties the log LL.
   - *Site k* updates the base version number to $bv+1$.

4. Upon receiving operations from *Site k*, the repository server executes these operations sequentially on *V.bv* to generate the full state of the latest version *V.lt* = *V.bv+1*, and *V.bv* is then replaced with those operations, which are the deltas between *V.bv+1* and *V.bv*. After then, the lock on the repository is released.

3.2 Update a Working Copy

Suppose two users *User 1* and *User 2* have concurrently developed their own working copies from the same base version. To merge updates made in one working copy into the other, some essential issues need to be discussed.

Firstly, some operations performed by *User 1* may not be able to be re-executed in *User 2*'s working copy because they are semantically conflicting with some operations performed by *User 2*. As explained in previous section, the *Semantic-Conflict*(*SMR*, O_r, O_l, *CT*) function can determine whether O_r and O_l are semantically conflicting according to the *SMR*. A precondition for the function to return the correct judgement is O_r and O_l must be defined on the same context *CT*. In other words, O_r and O_l must refer to the same context so that their parameters are directly comparable. The following concepts can help clarify this issue.

Definition 1. *Operation context*
Given an operation O, its *context*, denoted as CT_O, is the document state on which O's parameters are defined.

Given an initial document state S_0 and a list of operations in $L = [O_1, \cdots, O_n]$ performed on S_0. The current document state is denoted as $S_0 \circ L = S_0 \circ [O_1, \cdots, O_n]$. So $CT_{O_1} = S_0$, $CT_{O_i} = CT_{O_{i-1}} \circ [O_{i-1}]$ $(1 < i \leq n)$. Apparently the deltas between the current document state and S_0 is the list of operations $[O_1, \cdots, O_n]$.

Definition 2. *Context equivalent relation* " $\sqcup$ "
Given two operation O_a and O_b, O_a is context equivalent O_b, denoted as $O_a \sqcup O_b$, iff $CT_{O_b} = CT_{O_a}$.

So the precondition of the *Semantic-Conflict*(*SMR*, O_r, O_l, *CT*) function is $O_r \sqcup O_l$ with $CT_{O_r} = CT_{O_l} = CT$. An example is given below to show how the function returns a wrong judgement when the precondition is violated. Consider a document contains one line "*abcd*". *User 1* performs an operation O_{11} to delete the character located at position 2 in line 1, that is character "*c*". *User 2* performs two operations O_{21} and O_{22} sequentially. O_{21} inserts a *newline* character "\n" at position 2 in line 1, that is between character "*b*" and "*c*". After then the document contains two lines: "*ab*" and "*cd*". Then O_{22} deletes the character at position 1 in line 2, that is character "*d*". If the *SMR* specifies that operations performed within the same line are semantically conflicting, then *Semantic-Conflict* function would return *false* because it detects O_{11} and O_{22} were performed in different lines. This judgement is obviously wrong because O_{11} and O_{22} are actually targeting at the same line that contains characters "*c*" and "d". The root of the problem is it does not hold that $O_{11} \sqcup O_{22}$. O_{11} was defined when the document contains only one line "abcd" while O_{22} was defined when the document contains two lines "ab" and "cd". As a result, their line parameters are not directly comparable. However, given two lists of operations $L_1 = [O_1^1, \cdots, O_m^1]$ and $L_2 = [O_1^2, \cdots, O_n^2]$ performed on the same base version, $O_1^1 \sqcup O_1^2$, but it does not hold that $O_i^1 \sqcup O_j^2$ ($1 < i \le m$, $1 \le j \le m$).

The next definition helps derive the second issue.

Definition 3. *Context preceding relation* " $\mapsto$ "

Given two operation O_a and O_b, O_a is context preceding O_b, denoted as $O_a \mapsto O_b$, *iff* $CT_{O_b} = CT_{O_a} \circ [O_a]$.

Given a log $L = [O_1, \cdots, O_n]$, it must be $O_{i-1} \mapsto O_i$ ($1 < i \le n$). Suppose an operation O_k ($1 < k < n$) cannot be re-executed, O_k cannot be simply omitted by executing O_{k+1} right after O_{k-1} because O_{k+1} was defined on the document state after the execution of O_k and cannot be executed as is on the document state before the execution of O_k. So the second issue is that in order to omit O_k, operations $O_{k+1}, \cdots, O_n$ must be changed to achieve $O_{k-1} \mapsto O_{k+1}$, and $O_j \mapsto O_{j+1}$ ($k+1 \le j < n$) so that operations $O_{k+1}, \cdots, O_n$ can be correctly re-executed.

Thirdly, if an operation performed by *User 1* does not semantically conflict with any operation performed by *User 2*, that operation should be re-executed in *User 2*'s working copy. But as explained in previous section, that operation may not be able to be executed as is because the current document state of *User 2*'s working copy is different from the one of *User 1*'s working copy on which that operation was originally defined. When we investigated this problem, we found it is the same in nature as the intention violation problem [13] in real-time distributed collaborative editing systems. Therefore operational transformation technique [12] proposed for solving the intention violation problem in real-time distributed collaborative editing systems can be used to tackle this problem. Some background knowledge about the operational transformation technology, which is related to our solution, is briefly introduced as follows.

There are two types of primitive transformation functions [12]: one is the *Inclusion Transformation* function – $IT(O_a, O_b)$, which transforms operation O_a against operation O_b in such a way that the impact of O_b is effectively included in the parameters of the output operation O_a' if $O_a \sqcup O_b$; and the other is the *Exclusion Transformation* function – $ET(O_a, O_b)$, which transforms O_a against O_b in such a way that the impact of O_b is effectively excluded from the parameters of the output operation O_a' if $O_a \mapsto O_b$.

For the example given in previous section, the document initially contains a line "You are student". Operation $O_1 = ins[7, 2, " a"]$ performed by *User 1* is to insert a space and an article "a" between "are" and "student", and operation $O_2 = ins[15, 1, "."]$ performed by *User 2* is to insert a full stop mark "." after "student". When O_2 is to be re-executed on the current document state of *User 1*'s working copy, its execution form at *Site 1*, denoted as EO_2, should be achieved by inclusively transforming O_2 against the concurrent operation O_1 at this site to take into account O_1's effect. In other words, $EO_2 = IT (O_2,$

$O_1) = ins[17, 1, \text{"."}]$. After the execution of EO_2, O_2 would have been correctly merged into *Site 1*'s working copy to produce a new document state *"You are a student."*. The first issue re-emerges here, that is, to ensure $IT(O_r, O_l)$ returns a correct result, the precondition is $O_r \sqcup O_l$ so that the parameters of O_r and O_l are directly comparable [12].

The operational transformation technology can also be used to help solve the second issue. A procedure *Transpose* (O_a, O_b) is defined to transpose O_a and O_b where $O_a \mapsto O_b$ to achieve $O_b \mapsto O_a$. Therefore, if $O_{k-1} \mapsto O_k \mapsto O_{k+1}$, after *Transpose* (O_k, O_{k+1}), it becomes $O_{k-1} \mapsto O_{k+1} \mapsto O_k$. As a result, O_{k+1} can be executed right after O_{k-1}.

Procedure 1. *Transpose*(O_a, O_b)

```
{      O := ET(Ob, Oa);
       Ob := IT(Oa, O);
       Oa := O;
}
```

An important issue is the $ET(O_b, O_a)$ function used in *Transpose* may not succeed if the effects of O_a and O_b are overlapping [11]. For example, consider a document initially contains string *"abc"*. Two operations O_1 and O_2 have been executed sequentially. $O_1 = ins[3, 3, \text{"123"}]$ to insert string *"123"* after *"c"* and $O_2 = del[2, 3, \text{"c12"}]$ to delete string *"c12"*. Then $ET(O_2, O_1)$ would not succeed because it is impossible to exclude O_1's effect from O_2 since the definition of O_2 relies on the characters *"12"* inserted by O_1. The operational merging technique [11] can be used to make their effects disjointed [11], thus making ET transformation successful. In this example, O_1 and O_2 should be merged as two disjointed operations $O_1' = ins[3, 1, \text{"3"}]$ and $O_2' = del[2, 1, \text{"c"}]$. So *Transpose* $(O_1', O_2') = (O_2'', O_1'')$ where $O_2'' = ET(O_2', O_1') = del[2, 1, \text{"c"}]$ and $O_1'' = IT(O_1', O_2') = ins[2, 1, \text{"3"}]$.

Suppose *User 1* and *User 2* have concurrently developed their working copies from the same base version $V.bv_1 = V.bv_2 = V.0$. *User 1*'s log $L_1 = [O_{11}]$ and s/he committed her/his working copy as $V.1$. *User 2*'s log $L_2 = [O_{21}]$ and s/he wants to update her/his working copy with $V.1$. On one hand, if O_{11} can be re-executed in *User 2*'s working copy, its execution form EO_{11} should be $IT(O_{11}, O_{21})$. After the execution of EO_{11}, bv_2 should be update to 1. The last issue is O_{21} is not able to represent the delta between the current document state after the execution of EO_{11} and the base version $V.1$ because O_{21} represents the delta between the document state before the execution of EO_{11} and base version $V.0$. The delta between the current document state after the execution of EO_{11} and $V.1$ should be $O_{21}' = IT(O_{21}, O_{11})$. The reasoning is as follows. The current document state $CDS = V.0 \circ [O_{21}, EO_{11}] = V.0 \circ [O_{11}, O_{21}']$ (where $O_{21}' = IT(O_{21}, O_{11})$, derived from the Transformation Property 1 [12]) $= V.0 \circ O_{11} \circ [O_{21}'] = V.1 \circ [O_{21}']$. As a result, the delta between CDS and $V.1$ is O_{21}'.

Because O_{11} and O_{21} need to be inclusively transformed against each other, the $SIT(O_a, O_b)$ (Symmetric Inclusive Transformation) procedure is defined to inclusively transform operations O_a and O_b symmetrically.

Procedure 2. $SIT(O_a, O_b)$

```
{    O'_a := IT (O_a, O_b);
     O'_b := IT (O_b, O_a);
     O_a := O'_a;
     O_b := O'_b;
}
```

On the other hand, if O_{11} cannot be re-executed in *User 2*'s working copy, the deltas between the current document state and *V.1* should be the list of operations $[\overline{O_{11}}, O_{21}]$ where $\overline{O_{11}}$ is the inverse of O_{11}. The inverse of an operation reverses the effect of that operation. For instance, if an operation deletes a string at some place in a document, then its inverse would be to insert that string at that place into the document. The *makeInverse* (O) function has been defined to make operation O's inverse operation $\overline{O}$, which has the same parameters as O's except its operation type is opposite to O's. The reasoning is as follows. The current document state $CDS = V.0 \circ [O_{21}] = V.0 \circ [I, O_{21}]$ (where I is an *identity* or a *null* operation) $- V.0 \circ [O_{11}, \overline{O_{11}}, O_{21}]$ $(O_{11} \circ \overline{O_{11}} - I) - V.0 \circ O_{11} \circ [\overline{O_{11}}, O_{21}] = V.1 \circ [\overline{O_{11}}, O_{21}]$. As a result, the deltas between the current document state and *V.1* are the list of operations $[\overline{O_{11}}, O_{21}]$.

In sum, the *Merge-Control (RL, LL, V.bv)* function is defined with inputs: *RL* - a list of operations that represent the deltas between the version *V.bv* and the latest version *V.lt* in the repository; and *LL* - a list of operations that represent the deltas between the base version *V.bv* and current document state *CDS* at a site. The output are two lists of operations *ERL* and *TLL* where the *ERL* stores a list of operations that should be executed sequentially on the current document state of the working copy to be updated, and *TLL* stores a list of operations that represent the deltas between the new base version and the new current document state of the working copy that has been updated by the execution of operations in the *ERL*.

Function 1. *Merge-Control(RL, LL, V.bv): (ERL, TLL)*

```
{    RCT := V.bv; //initial remote context
     for (i = 1; i ≤ |RL|; i++)
     {   //make copies of RO[i]'s and LL's current states
         CRL_i := makeCopy (RL[i]);
         CLL := makeCopy (LL);
         LCT := RCT; //initial local context
         for (j = 1; j ≤ |LL|; j++)
         {   if Semantic-Conflict (SMR, RL[i], LL[j], LCT)
             {   //Recover RO[i]'s and LL's states
                 RL[i] := CRL_i;
                 LL := CLL;
                 //Remove RL[i] from RL
                 O := Remove-Operation (i, RL);
                 i := i-1;
                 //Append Ō to TLL
                 Append-To (makeInverse(O), TLL);
```

```
                    //Exit the loop since a conflict occurs
                    break;
                } else
                    //update local context
                    LCT := execute LL[j] on LCT;
                    //Transform RL[i] and LL[j] against each other
                    SIT (RL[i], LL[j]);
                }
                //If RL[i] is not conflicting with any
                //operation in LL, append it to ERL
                if (j > |LL|)
                { Append-To (RL[i], ERL);
                  //update remote context
                  RCT := execute CRL_i on RCT;
                }
            }
        }
        //All transformed operations in LL are appended to TLL
        Append-To (LL, TLL);

        return ERL, TLL;
}
```

The *Remove-Operation* (k, L) function is defined to remove the kth operation O_k in the list L, and return O_k on the current context. In other words, after the removal of O_k, L would become $[O_1, \cdots, O_{k-1}, O_{k+1}, \cdots, O_{|L|}]$ where $O_i \mapsto O_{i+1}$ $(1 \leq i < k\text{-}1)$, $O_{k-1} \mapsto O_{k+1}$, $O_j \mapsto O_{j+1}$ $(k\text{+}1 \leq j < |L|)$, and $O_{|L|} \mapsto O_k$.

Function 2. *Remove-Operation(k, L): O_k*

```
{       for (i = k; i < |L|; i++)
            Transpose (L[i], L[i+1]);
        O_k := L[i];
        Remove (L[i]);
        return O_k;
}
```

The *OMUS* (Operation-based Merging at the Updating Stage) protocol is devised as follows.

Protocol 2. OMUS

Suppose the user at *Site k* whose base version number is *bv* and log is *LL*, wants to update her/his working copy with concurrent changes made by other users, which have been committed into the repository:

1. *Site k* sends a updating request to the repository server, containing the base version number *bv*.
2. Upon receiving the request, if the repository is locked, the repository server puts the request into the waiting queue. When the lock is released and it is time to respond *Site k*'s updating request:

- If the latest version in the repository is $V.bv$, the repository server sends a reply to *Site k*, telling no update available.
- Otherwise, the repository server sends a list of operations to *Site k*, which are the deltas between version $V.bv$ and the latest version $V.lt$.

3. Upon receiving the operations from the repository, *Site k* puts them in a list RL with early committed operations on the left and later committed operation on the right, and executes *Merge-Control* $(RL, LL, V.bv) = (ERL, TLL)$. After then,

   a) *Site k* executes operations in the ERL sequentially on the current document state.
   b) *Site k* updates its base version number from bv to lt.
   c) *Site k* substitutes TLL for its log LL.

3.3 Checkout a Working Copy

The *checkout* process does not involve document merging. However it is essential to merging because base versions, which are indispensable for merging, are retrieved from the repository only by means of the *checkout* process. The *checkout* process is closely related to how versions are stored in the repository. Statistics shows that checking out the latest version is far more frequent than checking out old versions [14]. So in the repository, the latest version of a document is stored as the full state while other versions are represented as deltas.

In state-base merging, an old version is represented as reverse deltas [14] from the latest version to that version. As a result, an old version can be retrieved by executing all reverse deltas on the latest version in the repository. In operation-based merging, an old version is represented as deltas from that version to the latest version. As a result, an old version should be retrieved by undoing all operations in the deltas between that version and the latest version in the repository. There are three reasons why reverse deltas are not used. First, the *Merge-Control* function for the *OMUS* protocol requires operations in RL are deltas not reverse deltas. Second, operations used for representing deltas are able to represent reverse deltas as well by using their inverse operations. Last, updating a working copy is far more frequent than checking out a new working copy. Therefore it is more efficient to store deltas instead of reverse deltas in the repository.

To checkout a new working copy from the repository, the *COCO* (Control Operation-based Check Out) protocol is devised as follows.

Protocol 3. COCO

Suppose the user at *Site k* wants to checkout version $V.vn$ from the repository as her/his working copy:

1. *Site k* sends a checkout request to the repository server, containing the version number vn. If the version number is omitted, the latest version would be checked out.

2. Upon receiving the request, if the repository is locked, the repository server puts the request into the waiting queue. When the lock is released and it is time to respond *Site k*'s checkout request:
   - If *vn* is omitted, or $vn = lt$ where *lt* is the latest version number in the repository, the repository server sends the full state of *V.lt* to *Site k*.
   - If $vn > lt$, the repository server sends a rejective reply to *Site k*.
   - If $vn < lt$, the repository server generates the full state of *V.vn* by executing the inverses of operations in *V.lt-1* from the right to the left, then the inverses of operations in *V.lt-2* from the right to the left, until the inverses of operations in *V.vn* from the right to the left on version *V.lt*, and then sends the full state of *V.vn* to *Site k*. For example, if $V.lt\text{-}1 = [O_1^{lt-1}, \cdots, O_m^{lt-1}]$ and $V.vn = [O_1^{vn}, \cdots, O_n^{vn}]$, the execution sequence would be $\overline{O_m^{lt-1}}, \cdots, \overline{O_1^{lt-1}}, \cdots, \overline{O_n^{vn}}, \cdots, \overline{O_1^{vn}}$.

3. Upon receiving the reply from the repository server, if it is rejective, *Site k* warns the user of the invalid version number. If it is a file, *Site k* makes it as the working copy and marks the base version number $bv = vn$.

4   An Example

In this section, we use a concrete example to illustrate the proposed merging protocols and algorithms presented in the previous section. As shown in Figure 4, a document initially contains a line *"You are student"*, which has been imported into the repository as the initial version *V.0*. Two users *User 1* and *User 2* want to collaboratively edit the document, so they *checkout* (at *step 1*) separate working copies of *V.0* from the repository. Initially, their working copies have the same document state $CDS_1 = CDS_2 =$ *"You are student"* and their base version numbers have the same value $bv_1 = bv_2 = 0$. *User 1* performed two operations O_{11} and O_{12} sequentially where $O_{11} = ins[15, 1, "s"]$ to insert character *"s"* after *"student"* and $O_{12} = ins[8, 5, "good\ "]$ to insert *"good"* between *"are"* and *"student"*. After then its current document state CDS_1 becomes *"You are good students"*, and its log $LL_1 = [O_{11}, O_{12}]$. At the same time, *User 2* also performed two operations O_{21} and O_{22} sequentially where $O_{21} = ins[15, 1, "."]$ to insert a full stop mark *"."* after *"student"* and $O_{22} = ins[7, 2, "\ a"]$ to insert a space and an article *"a"* between *"are"* and *"student"*. After then its current document state CDS_2 becomes *"You are a student."*, and its log $LL_2 = [O_{21}, O_{22}]$.

At this moment, *User 1* and *User 2* both want to commit [3] their working copies into the repository. Suppose *User 1* gets access to the repository first, then *User 2*'s commit request would be blocked. At *step 2*, because $lt = bv_1 = 0$, operations in $LL_1 = [O_{11}, O_{12}]$ would be sent to the repository server and re-executed on $V.lt = V.0 =$ *"You are student"*. After then, a new version $V.lt = V.1 =$ *"You are good students"* is generated, and *V.0* is replaced with the list of operations O_{11} and O_{12}. At *User 1*'s site, bv_1 is updated to 1, and LL_1 is emptied. Then *User 2* gets access to the repository, because $(lt=1) > (bv_2=0)$, *User 1* would be warned to update her/his working copy.

At *step 3*, the deltas between $V.bv_2 = V.0$ and the latest version $V.lt = V.1$, O_{11} and O_{12}, would be transferred to *User 2*'s site and stored in a list RL. Then

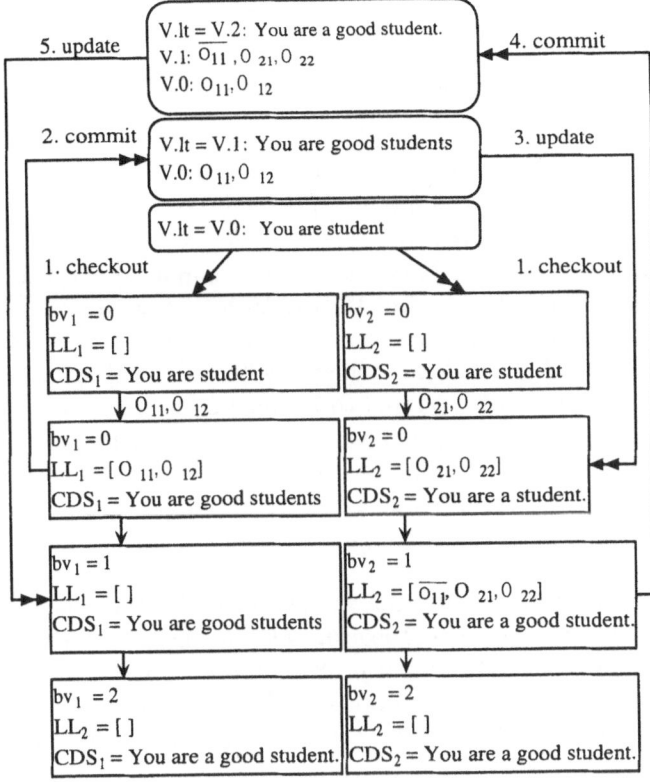

Fig. 4. An example of operation-based merging

Merge-Control(RL, LL_2, $V.0$) is executed as follows. Suppose the *SMR* specifies grammar checking rules.

1. $CRL_1 = makeCopy\,(O_{11}) = ins[15, 1, \text{"s"}]$ and $CLL_2 = makeCopy\,(LL_2)$
   $= [O_{21}, O_{22}]$ where $O_{21} = ins[15, 1, \text{"."}]$ and $O_{21} = ins[7, 2, \text{" a"}]$.
   a) *Semantic-Conflict (SMR, O_{11}, O_{21}, "You are student")* $= false$, so after
      $SIT\,(O_{11}, O_{21})$, $O_{11} = ins[15, 1, \text{"s"}]$ and $O_{21} = ins[16, 1, \text{"."}]$.
   b) *Semantic-Conflict (SMR, O_{11}, O_{22}, "You are student.")* $= true$, so O_{11} is
      recovered with $CRL_1 = ins[15, 1, \text{"s"}]$ and LL_2 is recovered with CLL_2
      $= [O_{21}, O_{22}]$ where $O_{21} = ins[15, 1, \text{"."}]$ and $O_{21} = ins[7, 2, \text{" a"}]$. Then
      after *Remove-Operation (1, RL)*, $O_{11} = ins[20, 1, \text{"s"}]$, and $RL = [O_{12}]$
      where $O_{12} = ins[8, 5, \text{"good "}]$. Finally $\overline{O_{11}} = del[20, 1, \text{"s"}]$ is put into
      TLL.
2. $CRL_1 = makeCopy\,(O_{12}) = ins[8, 5, \text{"good "}]$ and $CLL_2 = makeCopy\,(LL_2)$
   $= [O_{21}, O_{22}]$ where $O_{21} = ins[15, 1, \text{"."}]$ and $O_{22} = ins[7, 2, \text{" a"}]$.
   a) *Semantic-Conflict (SMR, O_{12}, O_{21}, "You are students")* $= false$. Then
      after *SIT (O_{12}, O_{21})*, $O_{12} = ins[8, 5, \text{"good "}]$ and $O_{21} = ins[20, 1, \text{"."}]$.
   b) *Semantic-Conflict (SMR, O_{12}, O_{22}, "You are students.")* $= false$. Then
      after *SIT (O_{12}, O_{22})*, $O_{12} = ins[10, 5, \text{"good "}]$ and $O_{22} = ins[7, 2, \text{" a"}]$.

c) $O_{12} = ins[10, 5,$ "good "$]$ is put into ERL.

3. Finally O_{21} and O_{22} are put into TLL. Then $TLL = [\overline{O_{11}}, O_{21}, O_{22}]$ where $\overline{O_{11}} = ins[20, 1,$ "s"$]$, $O_{21} = ins[20, 1,$ "."$]$, and $O_{22} = ins[7, 2,$ " a"$]$. $ERL = [O_{12}]$ where $ins[10, 5,$ "good "$]$.

By executing operation $O_{12} = ins[10, 5,$ "good "$]$ in ERL on the current document state $CDS_2 = $ "You are a student.", CDS_2 becomes "You are a good student.". Then bv_2 is updated to $lt = 1$, and LL_2 is replaced with $TLL = [\overline{O_{11}}, O_{21}, O_{22}]$. Now $bv_2 = lt = 1$, User 2 is able to commit [3] her/his working copy into the repository. At step 4, after the executions of operations $\overline{O_{11}}, O_{21}, O_{22}$ on $V.1 = $ "You are good students", a new version $V.lt = V.2 = $ "You are a good student." is generated. Then $V.1$ is replaced with the list of operations $\overline{O_{11}}, O_{21}, O_{22}$. At User 2's site, bv_2 is updated to 2, and LL_2 is emptied.

Finally in step 5, when User 1 wants to update [3] her/his working copy, because LL_1 is empty, operations $\overline{O_{11}}, O_{21}, O_{22}$ from the repository would be executed as is on the current document state $CDS_1 = $ "You are good students" to generate a new document state $CDS_1 = $ "You are a good student.". Then bv_1 is updated to 2.

At this time, if another user User 3 wants to checkout $V.0$ as her/his working copy, the repository server would execute $\overline{O_{22}} = ins[7, 2,$ " a"$]$, $\overline{O_{21}} = ins[20, 1,$ "."$]$, $O_{11} = ins[20, 1,$ "s"$]$, $\overline{O_{12}} = del[8, 5,$ "good "$]$, and $\overline{O_{11}} = del[15, 1,$ "s"$]$ sequentially on $V.lt = V.2 = $ "You are a good student." to recover $V.0$, and send the full state of $V.0 = $ "You are student" to User 3. Then $bv_3 = 0$ and $CDS_3 = $ "You are student".

5   Conclusions and Future Work

In this paper, we contribute a flexible merging framework in which semantic merging policies and the syntactic merging mechanism are separated. The policy component makes various application-dependent semantic merging policies by formulating semantic merging rules (SMR). The mechanism component performs syntactic merging according to the SMR specified by the policy component. We have applied the proposed framework to the design of a flexible syntactic merging component for a version control system, which uses a single syntactic merging mechanism to support a range of semantic merging policies. We devised operation-based merging protocols: $OMCS$ for operation-based merging at the committing stage and $OMUS$ for operation-based merging at the updating stage. We also devised the operation-based checkout protocol $COCO$ for checking out new working copies as base versions. In addition, we devised a merging algorithm $Merge\text{-}Control$ and some auxiliary algorithms to do syntactic merging at the updating stage. These protocols and algorithms have been implemented in $FORCE$, a testbed for demonstrating the proposed merging framework.

In the future, we will continue validating and evaluating the proposed merging framework. We will also investigate possible issues involved in adopting distributed repositories in the framework.

Acknowledgments. The work reported in this paper has been partially supported by an ARC (Australian Research Council) Large Grant (000-00711). The authors also wish to thank David Chen, Aguido Horatio Davis, and Jingzhi Guo for their valuable comments.

References

1. L. Allen, G. Fernandez, K. Kane, D. Leblang, D. Minard, and J. Posner. Clearcase multisite:supporting geographically -distributed software development. *Software Configuration Management: Selected Papers of the ICSE SCM-4 and SCM-5 Workshops*, (number 1005 in LNCS):194–214, 1995.
2. T. Berlage and A. Genau. A framework for shared applications with a replicated architecure. In *Proc. of ACM Symposium on User Interface Software and Technology*, pages 249–257, 1993.
3. B. Berliner. Cvs ii:parallelizing software development. In *Proc. of 1990 Winter USENIX*, pages 341–352, 1990.
4. B. Collins-Sussman. The subversion project: buiding a better cvs. *Linux Journal*, Volume 2002(Issue 94), 2002.
5. W. Courington. The network software environment. In *Technical Report FE197-0, Sun Microsystems*, 1989.
6. W. K. Edwards, E. D. Mynatt, K. Petersen, M. J. Spreitzer, D. B. Terry, and M. M. Theimer. Designing and implementing asynchronous collaborative applications with bayou. In *Proc. of ACM Sympisium on User Interface Software anf Technology*, pages 119–128, 1997.
7. A. M. Kermarrec and P. Druschel. The icecube approach to the reconciliation of divergent replicas. In *Proc. of ACM Symposium on Principles of Distributed Computing*, pages 210 – 218, 2001.
8. E. Lippe and N. van Oosterom. Operation-based merging. In *Proc. of the Fifth ACM SIGSOFT Symposium on Software development environments*, pages 78 – 87, 1992.
9. W. Miller and E. W. Myers. A file comparison program. *Software - Practice and Experience*, 15(1):1025–1040, 1990.
10. J. P. Munson and P. Dewan. A flexible object merging framework. In *Proc. of ACM conference on Computer Supported Cooperative Work*, pages 231 – 242, 1994.
11. H. Shen and C. Sun. A log compression algorithm for operation-based version control systems. In *Proc. of the 26th IEEE Annual International Computer Software and Application Conference*, to appear.
12. C. Sun and C. A. Ellis. Operational transformation in real-time group editors: issues, algorithms, and achievements. In *Proc. of ACM conference on Computer Supported Cooperative Work*, pages 59–68, 1998.
13. C. Sun, X. Jia, Y. Zhang, Y. Yang, and D. Chen. Achieving convergence, causality-preservation, and intention-preservation in real-time cooperative editing systems. *ACM Transaction on Computer Human Interaction*, 5(1):63–108, 1998.
14. W. F. Ticky. Rcs – a system for version control. *Software Practice and Experience*, 15(7):637–654, 1985.

A Multi-version Transaction Model to Improve Data Availability in Mobile Computing

Sanjay Kumar Madria[1], Mohammed Baseer[1], and Sourav S. Bhowmick[2]

[1]Department of Computer Science, University of Missouri-Rolla, Rolla, MO 65401
{madrias, mohammed}@umr.edu,
[2]School of Computer Engineering, Nanyang Technological University, Singapore
assourav@ntu.edu.sg

Abstract. In this paper, we present a multi-version transaction model, which exploits versions to increase availability in a mobile database environment. Each transaction in our model is either in start, committed or terminated state. A transaction can start and commit at mobile host (MH) but terminates only at mobile service station (MSS). We first present a two-version model, where each data object can have two versions, one committed and the other is terminated. A read transaction is never blocked, as it is always made available either a committed or a terminated version. We have extended the model to handle multiversions.

1 Introduction

Wireless computing suggests that there will be more competition for shared data since it provides user with ability to access information and services through wireless connections that can be retained even while the user is moving. Further, mobile users will have to share their data with others independent of their physical location. The task of ensuring consistency of shared data becomes more difficult in mobile computing because of limitations of wireless communication channels and restrictions imposed due to mobility and portability. Some of the problems involved in supporting transaction services and distributed data management in a mobile environment have been identified in [MBMB]. The access to the information systems through mobile computers will be performed with the help of mobile transactions. However, a transaction in this environment is different than the transactions in the centralized or distributed databases in the following ways.

- The mobile transactions are long-lived due to the mobility of both the data and users, and due to the frequent disconnection.
- The mobile transactions might have to split their computations into sets of operations, some of which execute on mobile host (MH) while others on MSS. A mobile transaction shares their states and partial results with other transactions due to disconnection and mobility.
- The mobile transactions require computations and communications to be supported by mobile service stations (MSS).
- As the mobile hosts move from one cell to another, the states of transaction, states of accessed data objects, and the location information also move.

R. Meersman, Z. Tari (Eds.): CoopIS/DOA/ODBASE 2002, LNCS 2519, pp. 322–338, 2002.

- The mobile transactions should support and handle concurrency, recovery, disconnection and mutual consistency of the replicated data objects.

In general to support mobile computing, the transaction processing models should accommodate the limitations of mobile computing such as unreliable communication, limited battery life, low bandwidth communication and reduced storage capacity. Mobile computations should minimize transaction aborts due to disconnection. Operations on shared data must ensure correctness of transactions executed on both stationary hosts and mobile hosts. The blocking of a transaction's execution on either the stationary or mobile hosts must be minimized to reduce communication cost and to increase concurrency. Proper support for mobile transactions must provide for local autonomy to allow transactions to be processed and committed on the mobile host despite temporary disconnection.

Many concurrency control protocols [BHG] are based on the notion of locks where a data object in the database can be accessed only after a lock on that object has been acquired for the duration of the read or writes. After acquiring the lock, the transaction executes its operation and then may release the locks. Since read operations do not conflict, many read transactions may share the read-lock on an object but sharing is not permitted if one of the locks is a write-lock. The above design is more suitable for database management systems that support short-duration transactions that read and write data objects for a short period of time. However, in case of long-duration transactions such as in mobile computing, the concurrency control algorithms based on above protocols suffer from performance degradation. Due to isolation requirements, the data items held by long transactions at mobile service station cannot be released until the transaction commits. Therefore, once the transaction acquires a write-lock at mobile service station, the other transactions at mobile host may have to wait for very long before they get the lock. Thus, if short-duration transactions at mobile host want to read some data items held by a long-lived transaction at mobile service station, it will end up waiting for the long-lived transaction to commit. Also, if a transaction is considered as a basic unit of work, a significant amount of work may be lost in case of a failure. Therefore, it is desirable to make the response of a system fast particularly for read-only transactions. Also, the system should not delay short-duration transactions at mobile host due to the presence of long transactions at mobile service station.

Multiversions of data have been used for historical purposes as well as for issues related to the transaction management. Versions can substantially impact the level of concurrency. Many multiversion concurrency control algorithms [BHG,GBM] use bounded number of versions for the data items to improve the performance of transaction processing. The mixed multiversions [CFL+,W,AS,BC] have two types of transactions, i.e., the read-only transaction and update transaction. The read only transactions read the old but consistent versions while update transactions manipulate only "current" version via two phase locking. However, the increase in the size and frequency of the updates limits the performance of the systems in case only "current" versions are available for their synchronization. Also, read-only transactions always read out-of-date data. These schemes may work well in mobile scenario if one allows reads to occur at mobile host only and writes to be executed at mobile service stations. Moreover, reads are also allowed to return out-of-date data, which however may not be accepted in many applications. Multiversion schemes using two phase locking [KSI,BHG] utilizes the versions to allow the concurrent execution of the conflicting transactions. Since the concurrent access of the conflicting read-write actions is allowed on different versions of a data item in unrestricted fashion, the execution of a transaction must be validated before it can commit. In this case, the effort in executing the transaction that fails validation is wasted. This situation is undesirable in mobile computing as transactions are long. These multiversions are optimistic concurrency control schemes and aborts due to failed validation grows rapidly and therefore, performance becomes more prominent in mobile computing as the size of transaction grows.

With the given mobile computing constraints, a mobile transaction model has to be balanced to cope with limited resources but at the same time enhance availability. At the same time, we also want to maintain the autonomy of the mobile host with respect to read and write operations and follow the two phase locking algorithms and the classical serializability [P].

In this paper, we present a multi-version transaction scheme to increase data availability in a mobile environment. Each transaction in our model is either in start, committed or terminated state. A transaction can start and commit at mobile host (MH) but terminates only at mobile service station (MSS). Our scheme can synchronize the read and write lock request on different versions of a data item in a constrained manner. The constraints are specified in terms of timestamps on the lock requested and on the lock held for the data item. The correctness of the transaction execution is guaranteed if the transaction can announce its commit by submitting its commit action to the MSS. No separate validation phase for validating the transaction execution is required. The model supports concurrent read and write operations without blocking. Read actions always get the last committed or terminated versions and are never blocked.

Our mobile transaction model increases data availability at MH and MSS. More specifically, our model supports both short and long transactions without blocking or aborting short-transactions. We use timestamps to avoid deadlocks in the scheme, which are not desirable and are expensive in mobile computing. Our concurrency control protocols use locks but produces no cascading aborts. We have introduced one more type of lock (verified-lock) other than usual read- and write-locks. A write-lock is converted to verified-lock after the commit of the transaction. We have discussed two versions case and later extended to handle more than two versions.

A read request is completed by using the Read rule similar to the multiversion timestamp ordering (MVTO) read rule in [BG]. The action taken by the scheduler on the lock request that fails to satisfy the constraints is either rejected to avoid conflicts are blocked otherwise. Since no lock request gets blocked for indefinite periods of time, the conflicting transactions never deadlock on a lock request.

2   Mobile Architecture

In a mobile computing environment, the network consists of stationary and mobile hosts. A mobile host or unit (MH or MU) changes its location and network connections while computations are being processed. While in motion, a mobile host retains its network connections through the support of stationary hosts with wireless connections. These stationary hosts are called mobile support stations (MSS), also called Base station (BS). Each MSS is responsible for all the mobile hosts within a given small geographical area, known as a cell. At any given instant, a MH communicates only with MSS responsible for its cell. When a MH leaves a cell serviced by a MSS, a hand-off protocol is used to transfer the responsibility of mobile transaction and data support to MSS of the new cell. A typical architecture for this environment is as follows:

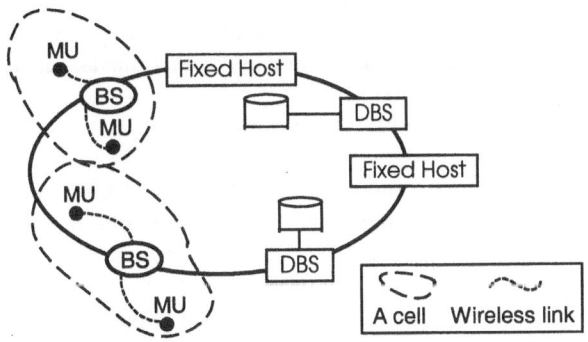

Fig. 1. Mobile Architecture

The mobile transaction execution is different from the normal centralized transaction in the way that, in the mobile transaction we need to consider various other factors like the disconnection of mobile host, the weak connection, the low battery power of MH and so on. There are different possible ways in which a mobile transaction can be executed: First, MH submits the complete transaction to MSS and waits for the result from MSS. MSS informs MH whether the transaction is successfully completed or aborted. Second, MH can execute the transactions at the mobile host itself (Obtaining the characteristic of a database server). Third, MH executes some operations of the transaction and MSS executes some operations. In this scenario, the transaction is not executed at one place but rather executed at different places. It is divided into two parts. One part of the transaction is executed on the mobile host (in disconnected mode) and the other part is executed at the mobile support station (MSS) that is connected to the fixed network.

We maintain a database of all available data items at Database server (DBS) as it is on the fixed, reliable network. MSS maintains copies of versions data items used by the active transactions currently running on MSS. The data items present on MSS are consistent with the data items present at DBS (since they are connected through fixed network) and hence are reliable. Since MH is weakly connected and is more error-prone, the values of the data items at MH are inconsistent and hence unreliable. MSS is responsible for granting locks to different mobile transactions belonging to different MH, successfully updating the data item values at DBS and terminating the mobile transactions. MSS is responsible for maintaining serializable execution of transactions in consultation with DBS. It is also responsible for the correctness of the data item values written by any transaction that can be committed.

2.1 Review of Research Techniques in Mobile Transaction Processing

The mobile transaction processing is an active area of research [MBMB]. We outline some of the existing ideas as follows.

- Semantic based transaction processing models [BK,RC] have been extended for mobile computing in [WC] to increase concurrency by exploiting commutative operations. These techniques require caching large portion of the database or maintain multiple copies of many data items. In [WC], fragmentability of data objects has been used to facilitate semantic based transaction processing in mobile databases. The scheme fragments data objects. Each fragmented data object has to be cached independently and manipulated synchronously. This scheme works in the situations where the data objects can be fragmented like sets, aggregates, stacks and queues.

- In optimistic concurrency control based schemes [KS], cached objects on mobile hosts can be updated without any co-ordination but the updates need to be propagated and validated at the database servers for the commitment of transactions. This scheme leads to aborts of mobile transactions unless the conflicts are rare. Since mobile transactions are expected to be long-lived due to disconnection and long network delays, the conflicts will be more in mobile computing environment.

- In pessimistic schemes, cached objects can be locked exclusively and mobile transactions can be committed locally. The pessimistic schemes lead to unnecessary transaction blocking since mobile hosts can not release any cached objects while it is disconnected. Existing caching methods attempt to cache the entire data objects or in some case the complete file. Caching of these potentially large objects over low bandwidth communication channels can result in wireless network congestion and high communication cost. The limited memory size of the MH allows only a small number of objects to be cached at any given time.

- Dynamic object clustering has been proposed in mobile computing in [PB] using *weak-read*, *weak-write*, *strict-read* and *strict-write*. Strict-read and strict-write have the same semantics as normal read and write operations invoked by transactions satisfying ACID properties [BHG]. A weak-read returns the value of a locally cached object written by a strict-write or a weak-write. A weak-write operation only updates a locally cached object, which might become permanent on cluster merging if the weak-write does not conflict with any strict-read or strict-write operation. The weak transactions use local and global commits. The "local commit" is same as our "pre-commit" and "global commit" is same as our "final commit" (see Section 3). However, a weak transaction after local commit can abort and is compensated. In our model, a pre-committed transaction does not abort and hence, requires no undo or compensation. A weak transaction's updates are visible to other weak transactions whereas prewrites are visible to all transactions. [LS] presents a new transaction model using isolation-only transactions (IOT). IOTs do not provide failure atomicity and are similar to weak transactions of [PB].

- An open nested transaction model has been proposed in [C] for modeling mobile transactions as a set of subtransactions. The model allows transactions to be executed on disconnection. It supports unilateral commitment of subtransactions and compensating transactions. However, not all the operations are compensated [C], and compensation is costly in mobile computing.

- A kangaroo transaction (KT) model was given in [EH]. It incorporates the property that transactions in a mobile computing hop from a base station to another as the mobile unit moves. The mobility of the transaction model is captured by the use of split transaction [PKH]. A split transaction divides an on going transaction into serializable subtransactions. Earlier created subtransaction may commit and the second subtransaction can continue its execution. The mobile transaction splits when a hop occurs. The model captures the data behavior of the mobile transaction using global and local transactions. The model also relies on compensating transaction in case a transaction aborts. Unlike KT, our model does not need any compensatory transaction.

- Transaction models for mobile computing that perform updates at mobile computers have been developed in [C,PBa]. These efforts propose a new correctness criterion [C] that is weaker than the serializability. They can cope more efficiently with the restrictions of mobile and wireless communications. Our motivation is to increase availability and at the same time our model should remain within the correctness as defined by the classical serializability theory.

- In [MB], a prewrite operation before a write operation is used in a mobile transaction to improve data availability. A prewrite operation does not update the state of a data object but only makes visible the future value that the data object will have after the final commit of the transaction. Once a transaction reads all the values and declares all the prewrites, it can pre-commit at mobile host (MH) (i.e., computer connected to unreliable mobile communication network). The remaining part of a transaction's execution is shifted to MSS. Writes on database consume time and resources at stationary host and are therefore, delayed. A pre-committed transaction's prewrite value is made visible both at mobile and stationary hosts before the final commit of the transaction. Thus, increases data availability during frequent disconnection common in mobile computing.

3   Mobile Transaction Model

A transaction is a partial order of some read and writes performed on different data items. Mobile transactions are no exception. In our model, a transaction arrives at MH and is executed partially at MH and rest of transaction execution is shifted to MSS. We consider the following scenario: A transaction can arrive at MSS from any MH within its cell of control and at the same time some other transaction can start at MSS initiated by some other host connected via fixed network.

In our model, a mobile transaction consists of three states of execution. They are: (i) Start state, (ii) Commit State and (iii) Termination State.

The start of the transaction is the state at which MH starts a new transaction. The commitment of the transaction is initiated at MH but it always terminates at MSS only. The commitment of the transaction is the logical completion of the transaction. A transaction that can be committed successfully is assured of successful termination. MH sends the data items written by it (if any) to MSS after the commit of transaction at MH. Termination of transaction is the state at which MSS revokes all the locks assigned to the transaction and the data item values written by the transaction are successfully updated into the database at DBS.

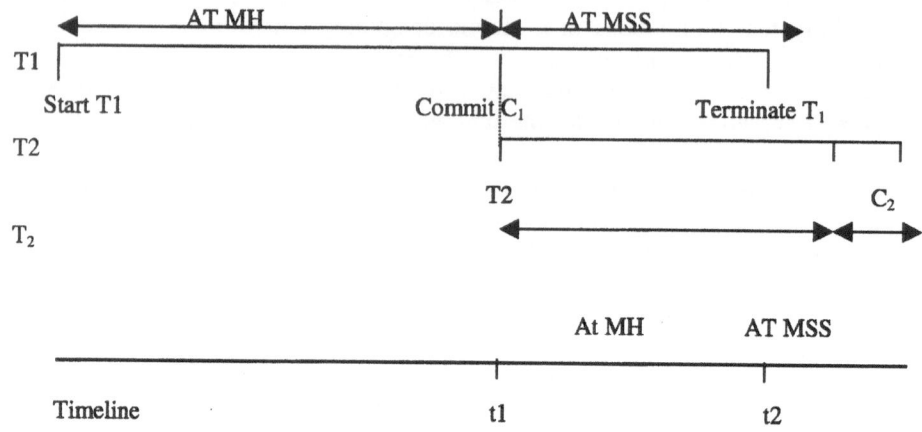

Fig. 2. Concurrent Transaction Execution.

Formally, any mobile transaction T_i, consists of read and writes operations, commit 'C_i' of transaction and terminate 't_i' of transaction. The read-write operations and commit 'C_i' operation are performed at MH. The terminate 't_i' operation is performed at MSS. The actions performed at the commit 'C_i' of the transaction and termination 't_i' of the transaction are discussed in detail later in the paper.

Example: Consider two transactions T1 and T2 being executed at two MHs controlled by the same MSS (see Figure 2). In the Figure 2, the transaction T2 starts as soon as the transaction T1 executes commit operation, C_1, but before it terminates. T2 does not wait for the transaction T1 to terminate in order to start its operations, thus increases concurrency. If a transaction is allowed to commit at MH, the data item values that are written by the mobile transaction at MH, are send to MSS, which are then available to other transactions.

Application: In banking application, once a check is deposited, the balance gets updated (commit) but the check-deposit transaction terminates only next day when the deposited money can be withdrawn. However, the account balance is available for reading after the commit of the check-deposit transaction.

3.1 Multi-versions of Data Items

In order to develop the proposed transaction model, we exploit the concept of multi-versions of data items. We maintain a maximum of two versions of the data item at any particular instance. Both the versions of data items are available at MSS at any instance. MH requests for a data item and is assigned one of the two versions depending upon specified constraints (to be discussed later in the section). We represent a version of data item as $X^i_{ts(i)}$, where 'X' is the data item; 'i' is the timestamp of the mobile transaction T_i that has written the version of the data item. 'ts(i)' stands for the current timestamp of data item version $X^i_{ts(i)}$ used in version selection to process a read action on data item 'X'. It also represents that the transaction T_i, which has written the data item, has been successfully committed at MH but is yet to be terminated at MSS. MSS assigns timestamps to the data objects when a transaction accesses them.

Formally, the two versions of a data item 'X' maintained at MSS are:

1. X^j_0.
2. $X^k_{ts(k)}$.

X^j_0 is the data version written by the mobile transaction T_j, which has been terminated successfully at MSS. The subscript 'zero' indicates successful commitment of T_j at MH and its successful termination at MSS. $X^k_{ts(k)}$, as said earlier, is the new version of data item written or created by the mobile transaction T_k that has committed the values written, but is yet to be terminated by MSS. We discuss two cases depending on the existence of versions of data items at MSS (DBS) and MH.

Case 1: Concurrent Read-Write Access to Increase Availability

In this case, we discuss how two versions, committed and terminated, are used to increase concurrency among read and write operations. In Figure 3, we see that MSS has one version of data item 'X' and two versions of data item 'Z'. The versions of data items, X^i_0 and Z^i_0, represent that a transaction T_i which updated X and Z has been most recently terminated at MSS. The version $Z^k_{ts(k)}$, represents that there is a transaction T_k that is committed but is yet to be terminated by MSS. The data item versions present at MH represents that an earlier transaction T_j executed at MH has requested a read operation on data item 'Z' and a write operation on data item 'X'. MSS assigned the most up-to-date version of data items to the read operation. Hence, T_j read data committed version $Z^k_{ts(k)}$ and X^i_0 (terminated version) available at MSS. After obtaining write permission (write-lock) on data item 'X', it writes its version $X^j_{ts(j)}$. The data item version $Z^k_{ts(k)}$ at MSS represents that there existed a transaction T_k that has committed at MH but yet to be terminated at MSS. In the proposed model, in order to maintain exactly two versions of a data items, we do not assign write permission on a data item to any transaction if there exists another transaction that holds the write permission on the data item. Concurrent write operations on a data item conflict with each other. Also, if a transaction aborts after acquiring write permission it might result in cascading aborts. It is also possible that both the transactions can simultaneously commit themselves at MH resulting in the existence of more than one committed version of data item. Therefore, MH cannot obtain a write permission and write its version of 'Z' but can only read the version $Z^k_{ts(k)}$.

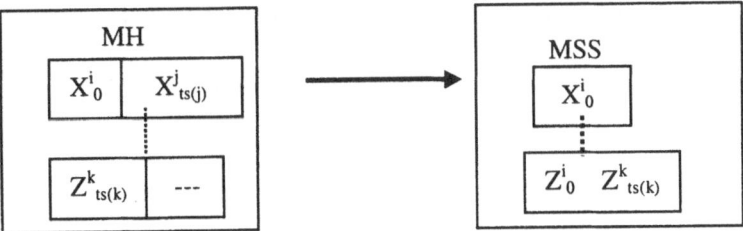

Fig. 3. Case1: Data Versions at MH and MSS

Case 2: Concurrent Write-Write Access to Increase Availability

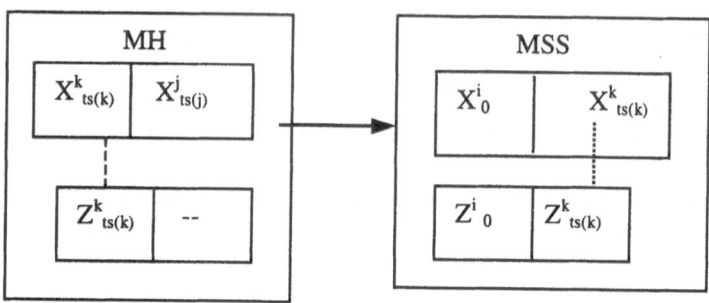

Fig. 4. Case2: Data Versions at MH and MSS, before T_j commits at MH

In Figure 4, we see that there exist two versions of both the data items 'X' and 'Z' at MSS. As discussed in the earlier case, the data items $X^k_{ts(k)}$ and $Z^k_{ts(k)}$ represent that there exists a committed but yet to be terminated transaction T_k at MSS. The data items X^i_0 and Z^i_0 represent a transaction T_i that is most recently terminated at MSS. We see that the transaction T_j being executed on MH reads the version $X^k_{ts(k)}$ at MH. Here, we have relaxed the condition that: "There cannot exist more than one committed version of data item at MSS". That is, MSS assigns the write permission to transaction T_j at MH on data item 'X' even though there exists a committed but yet to be terminated transaction T_k at MSS that has written a committed version $X^k_{ts(k)}$ present at the MSS. This is possible because the transaction T_k is committed and therefore assured of successful termination at MSS. The version of data item written by such transaction is reliable and most up-to-date and can be used by another transaction. Since all the transactions can be terminated only at MSS, MSS can keep track of the order in which the transactions need to be terminated after their commit so that the execution of transactions is serializable. Thus, MSS can give write permission on data item when there exists some other transaction that is committed on the same data item but yet to be terminated.[1] Hence, T_j at MH is assigned the write permission on data item 'X' with version $X^k_{ts(k)}$. It then writes its own version of data item, $X^j_{ts(j)}$. The transaction T_j then commits at MH and sends the version $X^j_{ts(j)}$ to MSS in order to terminate.

In general, we can see that there can be more than one committed version of data items present at MSS resulting from transactions that have written newer versions of data item 'X' and are successfully committed at MH but yet to be terminated at MSS (see Figure 4.1). MSS terminates them in the order in which they have been committed earlier. In Figure 4.1, T_k terminates first and T_j is terminated next and so

---

[1] The committed transaction T_k at MSS holds verified lock (vl[x]) on $X^k_{ts(k)}$ but not the write lock and hence transaction T_j requesting write lock is assigned the lock on x by MSS. Refer to figure 6, the lock compatibility matrix for details.

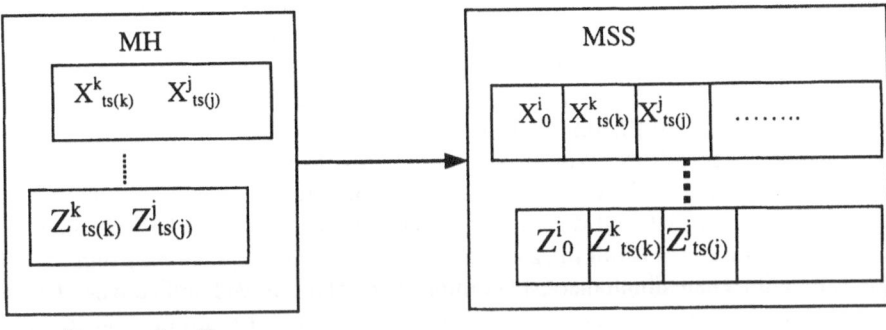

Transaction T_j

Fig. 4.1. Data versions at MSS and MH (case 2) after T_j commits at MH

on. Thus, MSS improves the concurrency of transaction executions. Note that if a new transaction T_1 arrives at MSS requesting for read or write lock on the data item 'x' when T_j holds the write lock, it is blocked until T_j commits and converts its write lock into verified lock. The actual lock-acquiring scenario is discussed in the next section where we introduce the locking protocol and read & write rule constraints.

4   Locking Protocol

In this section, we discuss locking protocols to control all the concurrent execution of transactions discussed in case-1 and case-2.

Locking Rules for Case 1: MSS assigns the locks to the requesting transactions. These transactions can be initiated at MH or at MSS. There are two kinds of read locks: $rl^{=0}(X)$ and $rl^{\neq 0}(X)$. Two different read-locks differentiate two different versions of data items read, $rl^{=0}(x)$ for version x^i_0 and $rl^{\neq 0}(X)$ for version $X^k_{ts(k)}$ respectively. We have write lock $wl(X)$ for write operation and an another lock called verified lock $vl(X)$. The verified lock shows the transition from 'Commit State' of mobile transaction at MH to 'Termination State' of mobile transaction at MSS.

Lock Holding at MSS

T_i Holding at MSS

		Readlock(rl)	Writelock(wl)	Verifiedlock(vl)
T_j requesting lock at MH	Readlock(rl)	√	√	√
	Writelock(wl)	√	X	X
	Verifiedlock(vl)	√	X	X

Fig. 5. Lock Compatibility Matrix (case1)

In the proposed model, a mobile transaction at MH should acquire the required locks on the data items before performing any read or write operation. MSS assigns MH the appropriate version of the data item to the read operation.[2] The requested locks on a data item are assigned in such a manner that there does not exist any other transaction holding conflicting locks on the data items. The read locks do not conflict with any of the read lock, write lock or the verified lock. The write lock conflict with the write lock and verified locks because a transaction can be aborted after it has acquired the write lock and if some other transaction is assigned the write lock on the same data item, it can result in cascade of transaction aborts. One may think that both the transactions can simultaneously commit themselves at MH and convert their write locks to verified locks which may result in the existence of more than one committed version of data item (possible only when the other transaction holding write lock has already committed as discussed earlier in case2, figure 4.3). This situation may occur when both the transactions try to obtain the verified locks, which results in violation of the condition that: "there exists at the most two versions of data item at any instance of time at MSS. One of which is a terminated version and the other is committed but yet to be terminated version of data item". The conflicts between different locks is given in the compatibility matrix shown in Figure 5.

There are two constraints that need to be satisfied by any transaction for obtaining the locks. MSS does the constraint checking before assigning locks. MSS assign verified lock to a transaction when it has completed all it's read and write operations and it executes the commit 'C_i'. The actions that are performed when MH executes the commit command are:

1. The new versions of data items (if any) are sent to MSS.
2. The write locks held by mobile transaction are converted into verified locks at MSS.
3. The committed version of data items written by transaction, $X^i_{ts(i)}$, is available for other transactions.

MSS later executes terminate 't_i' command to end the transaction execution. The different actions performed at the execution of terminate command at MSS are:

1. All the transactions holding read locks $rl^{\neq 0}(X)$ on data item version $X^i_{ts(i)}$ are converted to $rl^{=0}(X)$.
2. The previous committed and terminated version of data item X^j_0 is deleted and data version $X^i_{ts(i)}$ is converted to X^i_0.
3. All the verified locks are revoked and so are the read and the write locks assigned to transaction T_i.
4. Once the locks are revoked and the version of the data item being updated at MSS (DBS), MSS completes the transaction.

Due to the conflicts between the write and verified locks we have only two versions of a data item available at MSS. From the compatibility matrix we can see that no two transactions can have write locks on the same data item simultaneously.

---

[2] MSS first obtains the data items from the DBS and then provides them to MH. The time taken for this process is negligible as both DBS and MSS are on fixed, reliable network with bandwidth of the order of Gbps.

T$_i$ holding lock at MSS

	Readlock(rl)	Writelock(wl)	Verifiedlock (vl)
Readlock (rl)	√	√	√
Writelock(wl)	√	X	√(T$_i$-Committed)
Verifiedlock(vl)	√	X	√(T$_i$- Committed)

T$_j$ requesting lock at MH

Fig. 6. Lock Compatibility Matrix (case2)

Locking Rules for Case 2: We relax the condition that *at the most only two versions of data item at any instance of time* are available to improve concurrency of transaction execution in this case. The compatibility matrix for this case is shown in Figure 6 and the data versions scenario at MSS and MH is shown in Figure 4.1. In Figure 6, if a transaction holding the verified lock on the data item is committed but is still to be terminated at MSS then MSS can assign the conflicting write lock or verified lock to another transaction requesting the lock at MH. It can do that by maintaining the order in which the transactions need to be terminated, as discussed earlier in case 2(Figure 4.1). This is possible because MSS can only assign locks to MH and also MSS finally terminates a transaction. Thus, when a transaction T$_j$ at MH requests MSS a write or a verified lock on data item 'x', MSS can assign the write lock or verified lock to T$_j$ provided the current lock held by transaction T$_i$ on MSS is the verified lock. After assigning the lock to T$_j$, MSS records the order of verified locks and when transaction T$_j$ commits and comes to MSS to be terminated, MSS performs termination in the order in which it has assigned the verified locks, i.e., T$_i$ first and then T$_j$. In case T$_i$ cannot be terminated, the transaction T$_j$ is also held from termination until T$_i$ is terminated. Note that by doing so, MSS preserves the correct serial order of transaction execution. Also, the value read by transaction T$_j$ is a correct value written by T$_i$ since T$_j$ gets the write lock only after T$_i$ is committed but is yet to be terminated.

5   Read and Write Rule Constraints

In our model, a read request is completed at MSS using Read rule similar to the multi-version timestamp ordering (MVTO) read rule [CC]. Whenever a transaction requests for a data item to be read: *The committed version of the data item with the largest timestamp less than or equal to the timestamp of the data item with the read request is selected.* That is, if there exists both the versions: X^1_0 and $X^2_{ts(2)}$ at MSS and there is transaction T3 at MH or at MSS requesting data item X having a timestamp ts(T3)>ts(2), then T3 is given $X^2_{ts(2)}$ and otherwise X^1_0. A read action R$_i$[X] on a data item X in transaction T$_i$ (either local on MSS or a remote one initiated by MH) follows the locking protocol as follows:

- T$_i$ requests a read lock on the data item X.
- MSS grants the $rl^0_i(X)$ or $rl^{\neq 0}_i(X)$ read lock corresponding to whether the version X^j_0 or version $X^k_{ts(k)}$ (if it exists and is committed) is selected in accordance with the read rule; and the read lock version satisfies the

specified constraints (which specify the conditions for selection of appropriate version and correspondingly appropriate read lock among the two different locks present).

- Transaction T_i reads the selected version of X after obtaining the corresponding read lock version.

The write action $w_i(X)$ on data item X in transaction T_i at MH follows the following locking protocol:

- T_i requests a write lock on data item X.
- MSS grants the $wl_i(X)$, the write lock on data item X, if there are no conflicts (according to any of the two compatibility matrices of Fig 5 and Fig 6) and the lock request satisfies the specified constraints.
- T_i creates a new version $X^i_{ts(i)}$ for data item X.

The *constraints satisfaction* is done at MSS each time a MH request for a read or writes lock on a data item. They are to be satisfied by the transactions in order to fulfill the read and write requests successfully before obtaining the respective locks. The constraints to be checked by MSS are:

Constraint 1:

The read lock request on data item X by the transaction T_i (at MH or at MSS) must satisfy: *"If there is any other transaction T_j at MSS holding $wl_j(X)$ lock, then timestamp(T_j) > timestamp (T_i)"*. This condition checks for the situation that no read request is processed violating the Read rule, that is, if the transaction T_j that is holding a write lock on the data item has a timestamp less than the transaction T_i that is requesting a read lock then, granting a read lock might result in violation of serializability and also might result in cascade of aborts. This constraint satisfaction results automatically in maintaining serializability of transaction execution at MSS.

Constraint 2:

The write lock request $wl_i(X)$ or verified lock request $vl_i(X)$ for transaction T_i (at MH or at MSS) must satisfy:

a) There does not exist any transaction at MSS holding $wl(X)$ or $vl(X)$ (verified lock); and for all transaction T_j at MH that holds $rl^0_j(X)$, the timestamp(T_i) $\geq$ timestamp(T_j).

b) If there is any other transaction T_k at MSS holding $vl_k(X)$ lock, then timestamp(T_k) < timestamp (T_i), where T_i is a requesting verified or write-lock on X

This constraint ensures that the transactions at MSS, already having the read locks on previous version of data items are not made void by assigning a write lock or verified lock to another transaction that comes after these transactions, thus avoiding transaction aborts.

Rule for Terminating a Transaction: It must be noted that the terminate action for transaction T_i may not be invoked immediately after T_i commits. The following rules must be observed for correct execution of transactions:

- A transaction T_i at MH will precede a transaction T_j at MSS in commit order if the transaction T_i has read a previous version of a data item for which T_j has created a new version or T_j has read the committed version of the data item written by T_i. This is because if T_i reads previous version of a data object, which has later been updated by T_j then if T_j commits before T_i then it should read the updated version. Note that a read-only transaction also needs to send the commit information to MSS. Other alternative is that such read-only transaction can be switched back in the transaction history for serialization purposes. In the second possibility, if T_j has read the committed version written by T_i then T_i should come before T_j in the serialization order.

- T_j can not terminate at MSS until each transaction T_i at MH that has either read version X^k_0 (for some k) or written a committed version $X^i_{ts(i)}$ that has been read by T_j, has been terminated. This is because a transaction may be reading two data items, for one it may get a data version written by the last terminated transaction and other data item version it may read, is written by the committed transaction. Thus, there is no equivalent serial order as read-only transaction read one version of data object at initial state and updated version for the second object.

- T_i executed at MH cannot terminate at MSS until the transaction T_j that has committed before T_j terminates at MSS.

Blocking Transactions. Deadlocks and subsequent aborts could be costlier in mobile environment. Also, wireless connection from MH to MSS is costlier, therefore, we would like to avoid MH contacting MSS as far possible. In some situations when a lock cannot be granted, a transaction can be blocked rather than aborted and when the lock is available it can be broadcasted.

Consider the constraint-1 discussed above. A read transaction initiated by MH which does not satisfy this constraint, can be blocked at MSS rather aborting the transaction. When the transaction's holding the write-lock on the data object at MSS is converted into the verified-lock (until the transaction commits), the read transaction blocked at MH can read the committed version. MSS can broadcast this message and MH needs not contacted MSS again.

Deadlock Avoidance. The following rule can be used to avoid deadlocks between conflicting write-lock and verified-lock.

Rule – If a transaction T_i holds a write- or verified-lock lock on data object X then the write-lock request on X by other transaction T_j is rejected if timestamp(T_i)> timestamp(T_j); and is blocked otherwise.

Above rule along with the write-lock requests that fail the constraint-2 can make the execution deadlock free. Since the lock requests are blocked only in asymmetric fashion; only transaction with higher timestamp may be blocked by a lock held by a transaction with a lower timestamp, there will be no deadlocks.

5.1 Read-Only Transaction

In this case MH requests for only read locks on the data items. MSS checks for the non-existence of conflicts with the requesting locks on the data items by checking the constraint satisfaction described before. If it can grant all the requested locks, it sends the respective versions of data items to MH. Here, we should note that if there is some other mobile transaction, which is not a read-only transaction, and requests conflicting locks on the same data items, MSS can grant locks to the other transaction. In such cases, read-only transaction reads the terminated version according to constraint 1, so that the other transaction can write the committed value. However, if a read-only transaction gets the committed version, then it can finally terminate before the write transaction terminates at MSS. Note that a read-only transaction can commit and terminate at MH whether it gets the terminated or committed values, since a committed transaction never aborts and in serialization order, terminate orders at MSS can be switched.

Example:
Consider two mobile transactions belonging to two MH controlled by the same MSS:

T1	T2
Read (X)	Read(X)
Read(Y)	Write(X)
Read(Z)	

These two mobile transactions T1 and T2 arrive at MSS requesting locks on the respective data items. Consider the mobile transaction T1 arrives before the mobile transaction T2. Assume there is no other transaction holding read locks on these data items. MSS assigns these locks to T1 subject to the constraint satisfaction (constraint 1). MSS sends a copy of data items 'X', 'Y' and 'Z' to MH (assume all terminated versions). MH can terminate the transaction immediately after receiving the data items from MSS, since there are no new versions of data items to be written by MH. MSS assigns the read locks to the second mobile transaction T2 and doesn't wait for the mobile transaction T1 to commit or terminate. Lets assume other case where T2 arrives first and is committed but not terminated. In such case also, T1 can read the committed version of X and terminates at MH without waiting for T2's termination. Since T2 does not abort being committed, it does not create any inconsistency. Note that constraint1 avoids the situation when T1 arrives after T2 but is assigned the previous version of X but not the committed version of X written by T2. Since ts(T1)>ts(T2) either T1 is blocked or it is rejected thus avoiding the violation of serializability.

6   Comparison with Constrained Shared Locking Model

The lock acquisition in our proposed model has some similarity with the constrained shared locking model in [CSL]. The Lock Acquisition rule in constrained shared locking model states that: In an history H, for any two operations $p_i[x]$ and $q_j[x]$ such that $pl_i[x] \Rightarrow ql_j[x]$ is permitted, if T_i acquires $pl_i[x]$ before T_j acquires $ql_j[x]$, then execution of $p_i[x]$ must precede the execution of $q_j[x]$. In our proposed model, according to Property$_{2a}$: For any two transactions T_i and T_j at MSS, if $c_i < c_j$ then $vl_i(x) < vl_j(x)$ and $t_i < t_j$, we state that the transactions obtain verified locks at MSS and also terminate in the order they commit. That is, for two transactions T_i and T_j if there exists an ordering $c_i(x) \Rightarrow c_j(x)$ then

1.   they obtain verified locks in the same order of the form $vl_i(x) \Rightarrow vl_j(x)$ and
2.   the corresponding termination operations have ordering of the form $t_i \Rightarrow t_j$.

There is an ordering for obtaining conflicting write locks and verified locks given a condition that one of the two transactions is a committed transaction at MSS. That is for a transaction T_i which is committed at MSS and holding $vl_i(x)$ lock, if there is another transaction T_j requesting a write-lock on x, it is assigned the write lock by maintaining an order between $vl_i(x)$ and $wl_j(x)$. Therefore if $vl_i(x) \Rightarrow wl_j(x)$ then $vl_i(x) \Rightarrow vl_j(x)$ and $t_i \Rightarrow t_j$. The compatibility matrix shown in figure 6 is redrawn below depicting the above-discussed cases where there is a similarity between the proposed model and the constrained shared locking model of [CSL].

T_i holding lock at MSS

	Readlock(rl)	Writelock(wl)	Verifiedlock (vl)
Readlock (rl)	√	√	√
Writelock(wl)	√	X	$\Rightarrow (T_i\text{-Committed})$
Verifiedlock(vl)	√	X	$\Rightarrow (T_i\text{- Committed})$

T_j requesting at MH

7   Conclusions

In this paper, we have presented a multiversion transaction model, which increases availability in mobile computing environment. We have first discussed the model that handles two versions and later extended it to handle multiversions. We have discussed the locking algorithms to control the concurrent executions under both scenarios. We have omitted details proof of correctness due to space constraints. Currently, we are developing a simulation model to evaluate its performance. We are extending the model to handle multiversion transaction management using broadcasting.

References

[AS]   Agrawal, D. and Sengupta, S., Modular Synchronization in Multiversion Databases: Version Control and Concurrency Control. In ACM Proceedings of SIGMOD, pp.408-417, New York, May 1989.

[BC]   Bober, Paul and Carey, Michael J., On Mixing Queries and Transactions via Multiversion Locking. Technical report, Computer Science Department, University of Wisconsin-Madison, Nov 1991.

[BG]   Philip A. Bernstein and N. Goodman. Multiversion Concurrency Control - Theory and Algorithms. ACM TODS, 8(4):465-483, December 1983.

[BHG]   Bernstein P., Hadzilacos, V. and Goodman, N., Concurrency Control and Recovery in Database Systems. Addison-Wesley Publishing Co.,1987.

[BK]   Barghouti, N. and Kaiser G., Concurrency Control in Advanced Database Applications. ACM Computing Surveys, 23(3):269-317,1991.

[C]   Chrysanthis, P.K., Transaction Processing in a Mobile Computing Environment. In Proceedings of IEEE workshop on Advances in Parallel and Distributed Systems, pp.77-82, Oct.1993.

[CSL]   D.Agrawal amd A.El Abbadi , Constrained shared locks for increasing concurrency in databases, Journal of Computer and System Sciences, Vol. 51, pp. 53-63, 1995.

[CFL⁺]   Chan, A., Fox, S., Lin, W., Nori, A. and Ries, D., The Implementation of an Integrated Concurrency Control and Recovery Scheme. In *ACM Proceedings of SIGMOD*, pp. 184-191. ACM Press, New York, 1982.

[EH]   Eich, M. H. and Helal, A., A Mobile Transaction Model That Captures Both Data and Movement Behavior. ACM/Baltzer Journal on Special Topics on Mobile Networks and Applications, 1997.

[GBM]   Goel, S., Bhargava, B. and Madria, S.K., An Adaptable Constrained Locking Protocol for High Data Contention Environments. In Proceedings of IEEE for 6th Intl. Conference on Database Systems for Advanced Applications (DASFAA,99), April 1999, Taiwan.

[KS]   Kisler J. and Satyanarayanan, M., Disconnected Operation in the Coda File System. ACM Transactions on Computer Systems, 10(1), 1992.

[KSI]   Kataoka, R., Satoh, T. and Inoue, U., A multiversion Concurrency Control Algorithm for Concurrent Execution of Partial Update and Bulk Retrieval Transactions. In Proceedings 10th Intl. Phoenix Conference on Computers and Communications, pages 130-136. IEEE Computer Society Press, New Jersey, 1991.

[LS]   Lu Q. and Satyanaraynan, M., Improving Data Consistency in Mobile Computing Using Isolation-Only Transactions. In proceedings of the fifth Workshop on Hot Topics in Operating Systems, Washington, May 1995.

[MB]   Madria, S.K. and Bhargava, B., A Transaction Model to Improve Availability in Mobile Computing Environment, Distributed and Parallel Database Systems Journal, Sept. 2001.

[MBMB]   Madria, S.K., Bhargava, B. Mohania, M. and Bhowmick, S. Data and Transaction Management in a Mobile Environment. To appear as a book chapter in Mobile Computing: Implementing Pervasive Information and Communication Technologies, Kluwer Academic Publishers, Dec 2001.

[P]   Papadimitriou, C. H., The Serializability of Concurrent Database Updates. Journal of ACM, 26:4, pp.631-653, 1979.

[PB]   Pitoura E. and B. Bhargava, Maintaining Consistency of Data in Mobile Computing Environments. In proceedings of 15th International Conference on Distributed Computing Systems, June, 1995. Extended version has appeared in IEEE TKDE, 2000.

[PKH]   Pu C., Kaiser G. and Hutchinson, Split-transactions for Open-ended Activities. In Proceedings of the 14th VLDB Conference, 1988.

[RC]   Ramamritham K. and Chrysanthis, P.K., A Taxonomy of Correctness Criterion in Database Applications. Journal of Very Large Databases, 4(1), Jan.1996.

[W]   Weihl, W.E., Distributed Version Management for Read-Only Actions. IEEE Transactions Software Engineering, 13(1), 55-64, January 1987.

[WC]   Walborn, G. D. and Chrysanthis, P.K., Supporting Semantics-Based Transaction Processing in Mobile Database Applications. In Proceedings of 14th IEEE Symposium on Reliable Distributed Systems, pp.31-40, Sept.1995.

Finding Trading Partners to Establish Ad-hoc Business Processes*

Andreas Wombacher and Bendick Mahleko

Fraunhofer Gesellschaft, Integrated Publication and Information Systems Institute,
64293 Darmstadt, Germany
{Andreas.Wombacher,Bendick.Mahleko}@ipsi.fhg.de
http://ipsi.fhg.de/oasys/

Abstract. Enabling technology for realizing ad-hoc business processes currently is becoming more and more popular, like for example web services. Ad-hoc business processes are semantically characterized by a description of the exchanged messages and by the potential message sequences. These semantic meta-data are required to enable efficient and precise searching and finding of potential trading partners. Based on the experience of current web technology, manual maintenance of meta-data is neglected by most editors, therefore the meta-data must be generated automatically. Within this paper, we propose a method to derive a specification of potential message sequences based on a private workflow model. Further, we describe an algorithm for matchmaking of message sequence specifications as part of a search engine for ad-hoc business processes.

1 Introduction

Electronic data interchange is nearly explicitly used in long lasting B-2-B relationships, because high investments are needed for setting up cross-organizational processes by using for example EDIFACT. More flexible business relationships and especially B-2-C process coupling is either done without EDI or proprietarily implemented. Due to the fact of increasing speed of innovation resulting in shortened product life cycles there is a need for optimization of business processes and cost reduction resulting in establishing EDI on a more flexible or ad-hoc basis.

Ad-hoc business processes provide the flexibility of selecting appropriate business partners and establishing cross-organizational business processes dynamically. Exemplary arising technologies are ebXML mainly applied in the domain of B-2-B relationships or Web services targeting all types of business relationships. One of the main problems of ad-hoc business processes is to find appropriate trading partners, which are using the same messages in a similar way; that is to be able to process the same potential message sequences.

---

* This work has been partially funded by the European Comission under contract IST-1999-11060 (eBroker) as part of the Information Technology Society program.

R. Meersman, Z. Tari (Eds.): CoopIS/DOA/ODBASE 2002, LNCS 2519, pp. 339–355, 2002.

1.1 Motivation

Finding appropriate trading partners to establish an ad-hoc business process requires that both parties are using the same messages and support the same business scenarios instantiated in the same potential message sequences. In the following, we name the potential message sequences supported by a trading partner an *interaction pattern*.

Potential trading parties must support the *same messages*, if they want to interact. This requirement can easily be understood, because two persons not talking the same language will not understand each other and therefore can not interact.

Potential trading parties must support the *same interaction patterns*, if they want to set up an ad-hoc business process. We assume, the trading partners support the same messages (language). In addition, it is required that they have a common understanding how to interact. If, for example, two human beings want to do a phone call, both parties must be familiar on how to do it. In particular, the communication is initiated by the caller dialing the number, while the called person says hello, continued by the caller telling his name and the matter of his call. After this initialisation, they start a discussion and follow their specific common protocol how to finish the phone call. If one of the two persons is not familiar with the protocol or interaction pattern of a phone call, communication becomes difficult and will result in several misunderstandings. While human beings may be able to resolve the misunderstandings automized ad-hoc business processes typically will not. Therefore, trading partners in an ad-hoc business process must support similar interaction patterns.

Thus, to be able to find a potential trading partner, the matchmaking must take both dimensions into account.

- comparing the semantics of the messages used by the business processes, and
- comparing the process interaction patterns specified by the business processes, i.e. the containment of all potential message sequences required by the user and supported by the provider.

While the first type of comparison is based on flat key word comparison the second one is dealing with structured specifications, which is not supported by current search engines. Using both types of comparison within the matchmaking increases the quality of the searching result, that is precision and re-call improve.

The above mentioned type of matchmaking requires the availability of meta-data specifying the interaction patterns. Generation of meta-data is an additional time-consuming task, which has to be automized to increase usability and to avoid meta-data inconsistency.

In accordance with this approach we propose within this paper a concept for automatic generation of interaction patterns for bilateral ad-hoc business processes and their usage within the searching and matchmaking process.

1.2 Example

The example depicted in Fig. 1 describes two different business models provided by the vendor resulting in different interaction patterns. The first business model (depicted on the left hand side of the Figure) involves a customer A and the vendor himself. It specifies

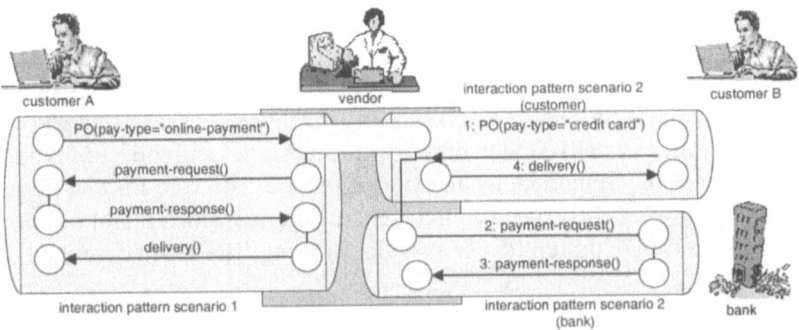

Fig. 1. Scenario

a purchase using an online-payment, where the customer sends a purchase order (PO) containing the payment type to the vendor, who requests and receives the payment from the customer using an online-payment and afterwards delivering the content. The second business model (depicted on the right hand side of the Figure) involves a customer B and a bank. It specifies a credit card purchase, where the customer sends a purchase order (PO) containing the payment type and the credit card details to the vendor, who requests and receives the payment from a bank and finally delivers the content to the customer.

In both cases, the vendor receives a PO first and continues afterwards with different sequences depending on a parameter represented in the PO. Observing the interaction of the vendor with the customer, it turns out that the required message types as well as the sequencing differs within the scenarios.

Within the first scenario the vendor communicates exclusively with customer A, so if a customer wants to purchase a good from the vendor using online payment, he must be able to handle the specified process, that is must support this interaction pattern. The second scenario contains a bank and a customer in addition to the vendor. The depicted communication results in two interaction patterns, because the bank is not involved in interactions between the vendor and the customer and vice versa.

We assume the vendor has specified the provided interaction patterns and made these accessible by a search engine. We now consider a customer willing to do a purchase. Because of the limitation of his internal workflow he is capable to perform credit card payment only. To specify the query for searching an appropriate vendor the customer must specify a description of supported messages and interaction patterns. Based on this description the search engine is able to determine a qualified list of vendors, which might be used to establish an ad-hoc business process.

1.3 Application Domain: Web Services

Currently, the application domain of web services is facing the problem described above. There are language proposals available to describe complex, hierarchical workflows (like Web Service Flow Language (WSFL) [1] or XLANG [2]) used to represent and enact internal processes of a single party as well as representing global views for interactions among parties. Further, the Web Service Definition Language (WSDL) [3] proposes a specification language of message types providing extension capabilities, like for example the specification of Quality of Service aspects using Web Service Endpoint Language (WSEL) [1]. While WSFL and XLANG specify the internal process of a party (interactions among parties as well), WSDL describes the messages and collections of messages exported, respectively imported, by an external service. The Web Service Communication Language (WSCL [4]) specifies interaction patterns, which might be added as an extension to the WSDL description of a service offering. The above described problems still remain:

- There are tools available for specifying an internal workflow, providing workflow and WSDL descriptions, but not supporting automated generation of interaction pattern descriptions.
- Within web service architecture there is no matchmaking of interaction patterns specified.

This paper aims at addressing the problems highlighted above. Section 2 presents two things, which are (i) a way how to generate views of a business process to allow only parts relevant to intended collaboration to be made public and (ii) a way how to find if a business process of a service requestor is compatible with the stored process of a service provider (i.e., business process matching). Section 3 is on related work and Section 4 is summary and future work.

2   Approach

In this paper we propose a novel approach for generating business process views and matching of business processes for bilateral collaborations. We will build on the example given in the above section, where two parties play complementary roles i.e., that of a service provider and a service requestor. We will assume in our model that parties involved in collaborations use standard vocabulary, e.g., EDI standard terms.

Fig. 2 shows a typical application scenario. We imagine a situation were a service provider (e.g. the seller of the example above) has a complex workflow depicting the various types of interactions that are needed for his business. Since business processes are regarded as assets by most organizations, the service provider will publish only those parts of his business process that are needed for interaction with outside organizations. This implies that the service provider must generate a view of his business process that is relevant to potential business partners. Multiple views of the same business process can be generated, depending on who the service provider intends to interact with. There might be a view for interacting with buyers, shipping companies, financial service providers etc. An automated way to perform such an operation is desirable, but unfortunately, traditional Web Service technologies do not offer it.

We imagine also that a service requestor (e.g. customer of the example above) wants to search for a service provider whose business process is compatible with his, i.e., a service requestor already has a business process, and he wants to find a provider with a matching business process, e.g., so that he does not have to alter any of his processes. The service requestor will generate a service provider's view of his business process to

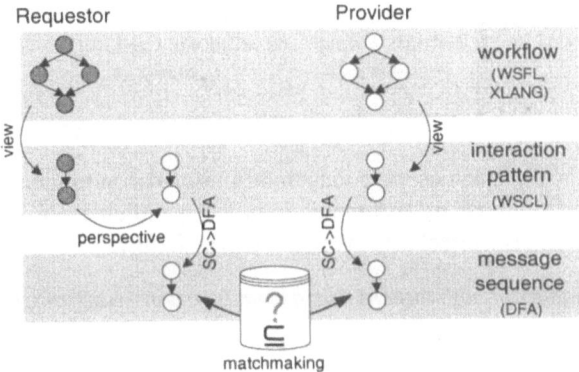

Legend
DFA : Deterministic Finite Automata
SC : Statechart

Fig. 2. Overview

remain with only those parts of his business process that are relevant to the interaction with a service provider. So again, like the service provider, the service requestor will generate a provider's view of his business process.

To be able to check if the business process of the service requestor matches with that of the service provider stored in the repository, we compute the perspective of the provider on the requestors process. By computing the perspective, we mean we derive a flow model from an existing business process by observing the pattern of incoming and outgoing messages and the changes in state that take place. The derived model represents a business process that is compatible with the stored service provider process model. Not all potential partners will utilize all the interaction functionalities offered by the generated model. This is because the generated process model must capture a wide range of interaction possibilities, but for some potential partners, not all of them might be necessary. Therefore, it is enough if the generated process is a subset of the process of a service provider. So, to check if the process of a service requestor matches with that of a provider we have to prove that his process is a subset of the generated process. Fig. 2 gives a high-level view of the needed steps.

In this paper, statecharts are the used business modeling technique for a number of reasons [5]. We agree with the findings of Benyoucef and Keller that statecharts are adequate to model e-negotiations [5]. Statecharts are also used in SELF-SERV to model services that are to be composed in a peer-to-peer environment [6]. The simplicity of the formalism and the availability of tool-support makes them appealing for business process modeling [7]. The UML standard also supports statecharts, making them (statecharts) readily available in commercial tools that are based on UML. In addition, off-the-shelf simulation and analysis tools e.g., STATEMATE [8], are readily available which can be used to validate statechart models. We also believe that conversion to other commercial tools will not be a problem due to the wide popularity of statecharts (e.g., it is supported by UML). The next section gives a basic introduction to statecharts.

2.1 Statecharts

Statecharts can be regarded as an extension of finite state automata with constructs for hierarchy of states, broadcast communication and parallelism of execution [7,9]. We extend the definition of statecharts given in [10], as follows:

Definition 1 (Statechart) *A statechart is a structure consisting of* $\langle \Pi, S, T, r, V, F, R \rangle$, *where*

- Π *is a set of primitive events.*
- S *is a non-empty finite set of states.*
- $T \subseteq S \times \Pi \times \Pi \times S$, *is a non-empty finite set of transitions.*
- $r \in S$ *is the root state.*
- V *is a set of variables.*
- $F \subseteq S$ *is a finite set of terminal states.*
- R *is a finite set of roles.*

The extension of statecharts definition made in this paper makes extensive use of the concept of a *role*. A role refers to the *type* of a trading partner without referring to concrete instances. The set of roles might comprise *buyer* and *seller* roles which means the types of partners needed to fulfill a given business activity.

There are three functions which define structural relations between states:

- The function $children : S \longrightarrow 2^S$ defines the immediate substates subsumed by each state. A state s is called *basic* if $children(s) = \emptyset$; otherwise it is *composite*. If a state $s_2 \in chilren(s_1)$, s_1 is a *parent* of s_2, and s_2 is a *child* of s_1. There exists a unique state $r \in S$ which has no parent, i.e., $\forall s \in S, r \notin children(s)$. This state is called the *root* of the statechart.
- The function $type : S \longrightarrow \{and, or\}$ is a partial function that assigns to each *composite* state its type, and identifies it as either an *or-state* or an *and-state*.
- The function $default : S \longrightarrow S$ identifies for each *or-state* s, one of its children $default(s) \in children(s)$ as its initial state. This has the same meaning as the *start state* in finite state automata.

Several functions that identify parameters of transitions have been defined in [10]. We briefly introduce them below:

- $source(t), t \in T$: identifies a non-empty set of source states from which a transition departs.
- $target(t), t \in T$: identifies the set of target states.
- $arena(t), t \in T$: identifies an *or-state* which contains both $source(t)$ and $target(t)$.
- $trigger(t), t \in T$: consists of a set of literals $\ell_1 \ldots \ell_k, k \geq 0$, each of which is a primitive event $e \in \Pi$ that trigger a transition t. In this paper, we will deviate from the semantics of [10] by disallowing negation of events.

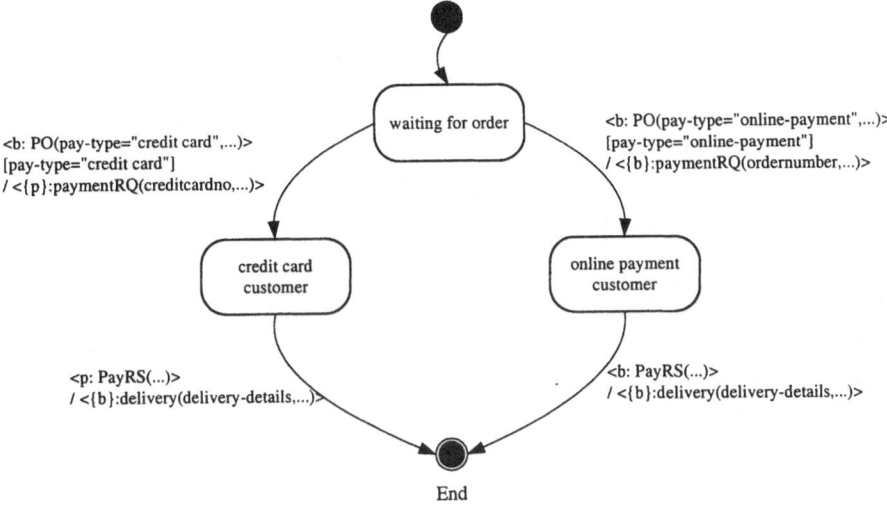

Fig. 3. Vendor Business Process as a Statechart, b is a customer, p is a payment processor

- $triggered(E), E \subseteq \Pi$: a transition t is triggered by E if $\forall e, e \in E, e \in trigger(t)$.
- $actions(t), t \in T$: is a set of events $g_1, \ldots, g_m$, where $g_i \in \Pi$, for $i = 1, \ldots, m$ that is generated when transition t is taken.
- $generated(T) = \cup_{t \in T} actions(t)$, the set of events generated when the set of events, T was taken.

Statecharts are a powerful modeling tool for concurrently communicating processes [7]. In this paper, we restrict the communication notion of statecharts to directed channel communication, where an *event* is prefixed with the sender identity and the *actions* are prefixed with the recipient identity rather than broadcast to everyone who is listening, i.e., every event e and action a takes the form $e \in R \times \Pi$ and $a \in 2^R \times \Pi$ respectively. This restricts communication to known entities, allowing us to study the behavior of such entities by examining the messages they receive (events) and send outside (actions). We will use the following notation:

Definition 2 (Event) *An event $e \in R \times \Pi$ is of the form $\langle p : \ell(x_1, \ldots, x_n) \rangle$, where $p \in R$, the sender of the event and $\ell(x_1, \ldots, x_n) \in \Pi$, the primitive event, and $x_1, \ldots, x_n$ are parameters.*

Definition 3 (Action) *An action $a \in 2^R \times \Pi$ is of the form $\langle P : g(x_1, \ldots, x_n) \rangle$ where $P \subseteq R$, the set of recipients of the action and $g(x_1, \ldots, x_n) \in \Pi$, the primitive event, and $x_1, \ldots, x_n$ are parameters.*

The business process for the vendor as depicted in Fig. 1 can be represented by a statechart in Fig. 3. The figure shows that the vendor business process stays in a *default* state, the *wait for order state* until he receives a $\langle b: PO(pay\text{-}type=\text{"credit card"},...)\rangle$ event or $\langle b:$

PO(pay-type="online-payment",...)⟩ event. On receiving one of these events, the vendor
uses his internal business rules to determine how to process it. If the requestor wants
to pay by credit card, the internal logic of the vendor will take him to the *credit card
customer state*; if the requestor wants to pay via online-payment, the internal logic of
the vendor will take him to the *online payment customer state*. If the requestor is paying
by credit card, the vendor system will automatically generate an action event that will
be sent to a payment processor to check the credit card credentials of the requestor. If
the credit card details are verified to be okay, the payment processor sends a message
to okay the transaction; on receiving the okay event from the payment processor, the
vendor sends a message to the requestor informing him that his order has been processed
along with delivery information. Different processing steps are taken if the requestor was
paying by online-payment as shown in Fig. 3. The next section discusses view generation
of a statechart to derive interaction patterns.

2.2   Generating Views

In this section we give a step by step description explaining how views are generated
from a statechart that represents a business process. A view of a statechart is a subset of
a more general statechart that pertains to a specific role, e.g., we can generate the view
of a service requestor on a service provider statechart. As explained in previous sections,
views are generated by observing the behavior of a business model which is described in
terms of *received events* and *sent actions* of the relevant statechart. We begin by giving
some definitions.

Definition 4 (Participant's View on Events) *From the statechart of a role p, if events*
$e \in \Pi$, *with form* $\langle p_1 : \ell_1(x_{1,1}, \cdots, x_{1,m}) \rangle \wedge \ldots \wedge \langle p_n : \ell_n(x_{n,1}, \cdots, x_{n,m}) \rangle$, *are given,*
the view of a complementary role p_c *on the events is,*

$$view(p_c, e) := view(p_c, \langle p_1 : \ell_1(x_{1,1}, \cdots, x_{1,m}) \rangle) \wedge \ldots \wedge$$
$$view(p_c, \langle p_n : \ell_n(x_{n,1}, \cdots, x_{n,m}) \rangle)$$

with $view(p_c, \langle p_i : \ell_i(x_{i,1}, \cdots, x_{i,m}) \rangle) := \begin{cases} \langle p_c : \ell_i(x_{i,1}, \cdots, x_{i,m}) \rangle, & if \ p_i == p_c, \\ \epsilon, & else. \end{cases}$

The definition implies that a role's p_c view on events is obtained by retaining those events
that were sent by him, and discarding those that were not sent by him.

Definition 5 (Participant's View on Actions) *From the statechart of a role p, if actions*
$a \in \Pi$, *with form* $\langle P_1 : g_1(x_{1,1}, \cdots, x_{1,m}) \rangle, \ldots, (P_n : g_n(x_{n,1}, \cdots, x_{n,m}) \rangle$, *are given,*
the view of a complementary role p_c *on the actions is,*

$$view(p_c, a) := view(p_c, \langle P_1 : g_1(x_{1,1}, \cdots, x_{1,m}) \rangle), \ldots,$$
$$view(p_c, \langle P_n : g_n(x_{n,1}, \cdots, x_{n,m}) \rangle)$$

with $view(p_c, \langle P_i : g_i(x_{i,1}, \cdots, x_{i,m}) \rangle) := \begin{cases} \langle \{p_c\} : g_i(x_{i,1}, \cdots, x_{i,m}) \rangle, & if \ p_c \in P_i, \\ \epsilon, & else. \end{cases}$

This definition implies that the view of a role *p* on a set of actions is obtained by retaining
all actions of which the recipient p_c is among the recipients, and discarding those of which
he is not among the recipients.

Definition 6 (Participant's View on Transitions) *From the statechart of a role p, if a transition t : $(source(t), trigger(t), actions(t), target(t))$ is given, the view of a complementary role p_c on t is,*
$view(p_c, t) := (source(t), view(p_c, trigger(t)), view(p_c, actions(t)), target(t))$.

The definition uses earlier definitions for views on events and actions to derive transitions, where a transition's label is changed such that it comprises only events and actions whose views are of this role.

Definition 7 (Participant's View on a Statechart) *From the statechart*
$S = \langle \Pi, S, T, r, V, F, R \rangle$ *of a role p, a complementary role p_c's view on S is a statechart*
$S_c := \langle \Pi, S, T_c, r, V, F, R \rangle$, *where*
$T_c := \{view(p_c, t) | t \in T\}$.

This definition says the view of a role p_c on a statechart is obtained by computing the views of the role p_c in question on each transition of the statechart. This makes use of the view on transitions definition.

To make things more clearer, we will use the statechart in Fig. 3 to compute the view of a requestor who is a customer in our example. *Definition 7* implies that to get the view of the given statechart, we must compute the participant's view on each transition of the given statechart. There are four transitions in the original statechart, and for convenience, we label them as shown below:

- t_1: $\big($waiting for order, $\langle b$: PO(pay-type="online-payment",...)$\rangle$,
  $\langle \{b\}$:paymentRQ(ordernumber,...)$\rangle$, online payment customer$\big)$,

- t_2: $\big($online payment customer, $\langle b$: PayRS(...)$\rangle$,
  $\langle \{b\}$:delivery(delivery-details,...)$\rangle$, End$\big)$,

- t_3: $\big($waiting for order, $\langle b$: PO(pay-type="credit card",...)$\rangle$,
  $\langle \{p\}$:paymentRQ(creditcardno,...)$\rangle$, credit card customer$\big)$,

- t_4: $\big($credit card customer, $\langle p$: PayRS(...)$\rangle$, $\langle \{b\}$:delivery(delivery-details,...)$\rangle$, End$\big)$.

By applying the view definition (which also relies on action and event definitions) on transitions, t_1, t_2, t_3, t_4 with $t_i' := view(b, t_i)$ calculates to

- transition t_1 and t_2 remain unchanged, thus $t_1' = t_1$ and $t_2' = t_2$

- t_3': $\big($waiting for order, $\langle b$: PO(pay-type="credit card",...)$\rangle$,ϵ, credit card customer$\big)$,

- t_4': $\big($credit card customer, ϵ, $\langle \{b\}$:delivery(delivery-details,...)$\rangle$, End$\big)$.

According to the definition we gave, the *default state* remains the same. Graphically, the requestor's view on the statechart of Fig. 3 is as depicted in Fig. 4).

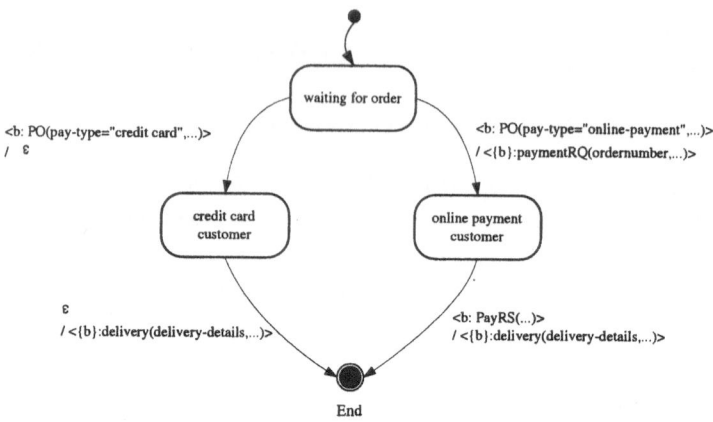

Fig. 4. Requestor's View on the Provider's Statechart

2.3 Generating Perspectives

In this section we give descriptions how to generate a participant's perspective from the statechart of another participant. The approach is to transform all events that are in the view of the involved participant and convert them to actions, with the role changing to the one that receives the action. Actions are treated in a similar way, i.e., all actions that are in the view of the participant are converted to events, with the role part changing to the one that sends the event. We give the used definitions below, and illustrate this concept with an example.

Definition 8 (Participant's Perspective on Events) *Given a statechart*
$S_c = \langle \Pi, S, T_c, r, V, F, R \rangle$ *of a role p representing the view of role p_c; p's perspective on events e of form* $\langle p_1 : \ell_1(x_{1,1}, \ldots, x_{1,m}) \rangle \wedge \ldots \wedge \langle p_n : \ell_n(x_{n,1}, \ldots, x_{n,m}) \rangle$ *is,*
$$perspective(p_c, e) := perspective(p_c, \langle p_1 : \ell_1(x_{1,1}, \ldots, x_{1,n}) \rangle), \ldots,$$
$$perspective(p_c, \langle p_n : \ell_n(x_{n,1}, \ldots, x_{n,m}) \rangle)$$
with
$perspective(p_c, \langle p_i : \ell_i(x_{i,1}, \ldots, x_{i,m}) \rangle) := \langle \{p\} : \ell_i(x_{i,1}, \ldots, x_{i,m}) \rangle$ *and*
$perspective(p_c, \epsilon) := \epsilon$

What this definition says is that an event is in the perspective of a role p_c if that role is a sender of that event, hence the role part changes to that of the source statechart. The rational for the change in role part is that this event is perceived as an action by the role whose perspective we are generating. In the definition, a set with a single element is returned because an event is changed to an action and actions are defined based on the powerset of roles (see definition of statechart).

Definition 9 (Participant's Perspective on Actions) *Given a statechart*
$S_c = \langle \Pi, S, T_c, r, V, F, R \rangle$ *of a role p representing the view of role p_c; p's perspective on actions a of form* $\langle \{p_c\} : g_1(x_{1,1}, \ldots, x_{1,m}), \ldots, \langle \{p_c\} : g_n(x_{n,1}, \ldots, x_{n,m}) \rangle$ *is,*

$$perspective(p_c, a) := perspective(p_c, \langle \{p_c\} : g_1(x_{1,1}, \ldots, x_{1,n})\rangle) \wedge \ldots \wedge$$
$$perspective(p_c, \langle \{p_c\} : g_n(x_{n,1}, \ldots, x_{n,m})\rangle)$$

with
$$perspective(p_c, \langle \{p_c\} : g_i(x_{i,1}, \ldots, x_{i,m})\rangle) := \langle p : g_i(x_{i,1}, \ldots, x_{i,m})\rangle \ and$$
$$perspective(p_c, \epsilon) := \epsilon$$

The meaning of this definition is that an action is in the perspective of a role if this role is among the recipients of the action, hence the role part of the action changes to that of the source statechart. The change of role is due to the fact that the action will be perceived as an event by the role whose perspective we are generating.

Definition 10 (Participant's Perspective on Transitions) *From the statechart*
$S_c = \langle \Pi, S, T_c, r, V, F, R\rangle$ *of a role p representing the view of role p_c, if a transition*
$t : (source(t), trigger(t), actions(t), target(t))$ *is given, we want to compute the perspective of a complementary role p on t. This is computed as follows,*
$$perspective(p_c, t) := (source(t), perspective(p_r, actions(t)),$$
$$perspective(p_c, trigger(t)), target(t)).$$

The definition means that the perspective of a role on a transition is obtained by first computing perspectives on events and actions for the role (as described in *definition 8 and 9* respectively), and swapping them, i.e., events that are in the perspective of the role become actions, and actions that were in the perspective of the role become events. The rational is that if in a source statechart, an event was sent by a given role, then in his statechart, this event must have been an action directed at the statechart we are using as source. The same explanation goes for actions, i.e., if an action is send to a role, this action will be perceived as an event coming from the statechart which is acting as the source.

Definition 11 (Participant's Perspective on a Statechart) *From the statechart*
$S = \langle \Pi, S, T, r, V, F, R\rangle$ *of a role p representing the view of role p_c, a complementary role p's perspective on S is a statechart*
$S_{c'} := \langle \Pi, S, T_{c'}, r, V, F, R\rangle$, *where*
$T_{c'} := \{perspective(p_c, t) | t \in T_c\}$.

This definition allows us to transform all transitions in a source statechart by recursively calling the perspective function on each transition of the source statechart.

Before we give an example to illustrate the definitions given above, we will describe the pre-processing needed on the source statechart before perspective rules can be applied. This is the separation of events from actions.

Definition 12 (How to Separate Events from Actions) *Given a statechart*
$S = \langle \Pi, S, T, r, V, F, R\rangle$, *separate events and actions that lie on the same transitions T as follows:*
For each transition $t \in T$, create an intermediary state s_t such that the new set of states
S' *is* $S' = S \cup \{s_t \mid t \in T\}$), *and the new transition set T' is*
$T' = \{(source(t), trigger(t), \epsilon, s_t), (s_t, \epsilon, actions(t), target(t)) \mid t \in T\}$.

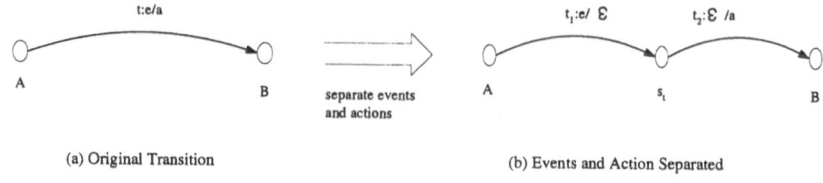

(a) Original Transition   (b) Events and Action Separated

Fig. 5. Separating Events and Actions

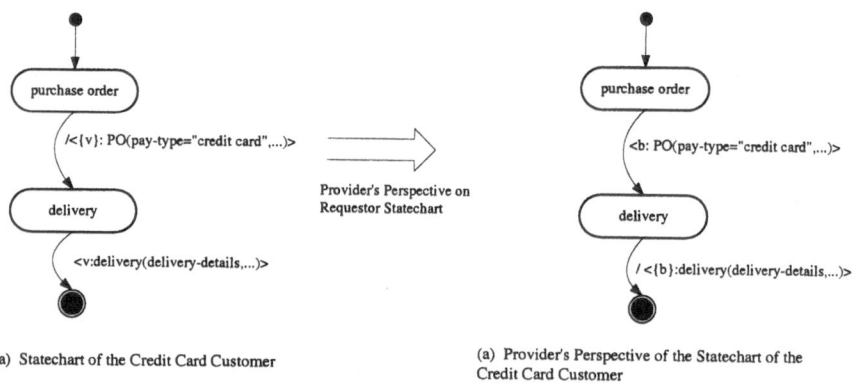

(a) Statechart of the Credit Card Customer   (a) Provider's Perspective of the Statechart of the Credit Card Customer

Fig. 6. Provider Perspective on Credit Card Customer's Statechart, v represents the vendor, b the customer

Fig. 5 illustrates how to separate events and actions. This step is needed so that when we do the transformation, we preserve the causative relationship between actions and events that lie on the same transition, i.e., events trigger actions during a transition. The statechart of the requestor (see Fig. 6(a)), however does not comprise actions and events on the transitions, so trying separate actions and events will yield the same statechart. In more complicated statecharts however, we need to.

We want to generate the perspective of the provider on the statechart of the requestor. *Definition 11* for perspective generation implies that we must compute the perspective of a given role on each transition of the source statechart. By taking each transition of Fig. 6(a), and using *definition 10*, we get Fig. 6(b). which represents the perspective of the provider on the statechart of the requestor (perspective of vendor on the statechart of the credit card customer).

2.4   Process Matching

Earlier on in this section we described the steps needed to match business processes (see Fig. 2). Here we show how each step is realized.

The first step is to generate views for both service provider and requestor. The view generated from the service provider's statechart is stored in a repository. In Fig. 4 we

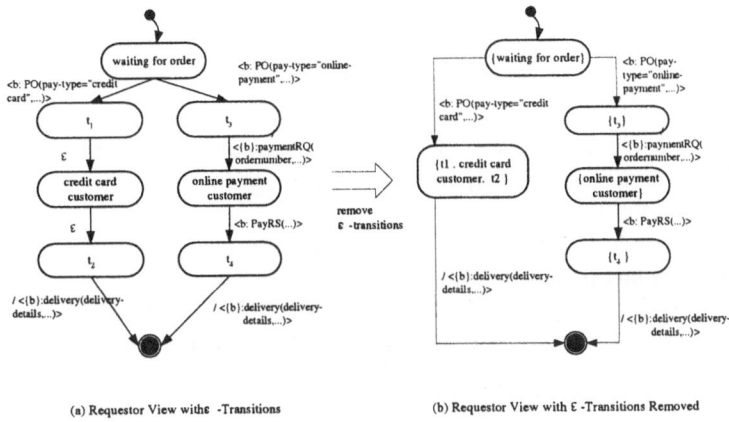

(a) Requestor View withε -Transitions   (b) Requestor View with ε -Transitions Removed

Fig. 7. Requestor's View on the Provider's Statechart with Actions and Events Separated

shown how to generate the view of a requestor on the statechart of a provider. This view represents a subset of the service provider's business process that he wants to make public. Before storing this view on a repository, we must separate events and actions using *Algorithm 12*, and then remove all ε-transitions (see [11] for algorithm to remove ε-transitions) to make the statechart simple and ease to understand. Fig. 7 shows a requestor's view on the provider's statechart with events and actions removed (Fig. 7(a)), and ε-transitions removed (Fig. 7(b)). The statechart depicted in Fig. 7(b) is stored on the repository and will be used for matching purposes.

In the next step, we compute the provider perspective on the requestor. We have already shown how to compute the perspective of a participant in the previous section. Fig. 6 shows a statechart representing a requestor that uses a credit card for buying, and the provider's perspective of it. We now give detailed descriptions of the steps to be taken.

1. Convert the provider's statechart stored in the repository to a deterministic finite state automata (DFA) S_p (see algorithm 1).
2. Convert the requestor's statechart (in Fig. 6(b)) to a deterministic finite state automata (DFA) S_r (see algorithm 1).
3. Check if $S_r \subseteq S_p$ as follows,
   if $(S_r \cap \overline{S_p} = \emptyset)$
   > then the requestor process is compatible with the provider process,
   else
   > the requestor process is not compatible with the provider process. [12]

The above steps need some explaining. Before applying the above steps, we eliminated those parts of the process models that are not relevant to the collaboration between the requestor and provider. This has been achieved by generating mutual views based on the respective statecharts of requestor and provider. Next, we computed the provider's perspective on the requestor's statechart to get Fig. 6. Like we said before, Fig. 6 must be a subset of the stored provider process if at all the requestor's process can match with the provider process. To do that we check if the generated statechart is a subset of the stored provider statechart.

Statecharts are not deterministic finite state automata (DFA), but rather an extension of them [9] so we cannot directly use a DFA subsumption algorithm without first converting the statecharts to DFA. The algorithm for converting a statechart to its equivalent DFA can be described as follows:

Given a statechart $S = \langle \Pi, S, T, r, V, F, R \rangle$, we can change S to an equivalent statechart S_a without hierarchical states as follows,

Algorithm 1 (Changing Statechart to Equivalent DFA) *The algorithm is,*

1. For each composite state $s \in S$,
      For each transition $t \in T$,
         if (target(t) == {s})
            then target(t) = {default(s)}.
         if (source(t) == {s})
            then source(t) = children(s).
2. remove all superstates.
3. make the resulting statechart deterministic using standard finite state automata algorithms, e.g., [11].

The final step is checking for subsumption. To check if the process of the requestor is compatible with that of the provider, we must prove that the DFA of the generated process (which is compatible with the process of the provider) is a subset of the DFA of the stored provider process. Below we give references how the subsumption problem is solved.

Definition 13 (DFA Subsumption) *Given two DFA, D_1 and D_2,*
to check if D_2 is subsumed by D_1, i.e., $D_2 \subseteq D_1$ we must show that $D_2 \cap \overline{D_1} = \emptyset$ [12].

Computing the complement of a DFA can be done using standard algorithms [12] and takes linear time. A liner time algorithm to test for emptiness of intersection of two DFA is also available in [12].

3   Related Work

A lot of research has been carried out to allow organizations to establish ad hoc business relationships. In the Web Service domain, a number of standards have been developed with this goal in mind. WSDL [3] which is now a W3C Note allows organizations to publish descriptions of their applications in such a way that they can be invoked over the Internet. The WSDL standard however does not give a way to describe business processes, i.e., specify the choreograph in which processes are called. Standards like WSFL [1], XLANG [2] and WSCL [4] address this problem by describing ways to model business process interactions. UDDI [13] describes an XML Schema to publish and discover services. The UDDI repository stores information that is necessary to find a service and a way how to dynamically invoke it. In a way, these Web Service technologies play complementary roles with the goal of allowing business organizations to seamlessly interoperate on a global scale irrespective of the platforms they use. What seems to be missing from this picture is how to match business processes dynamically. It is possible for example to search for a business partner in a certain category based on meta-data, but so far there is no way to search for a partner with a compatible business process. Our work is a contribution in this regard.

ebXML is an initiative by OASIS and UN/CEFACT to develop standards that allow organizations to make their business processes interoperable to facilitate trade on a global scale [14]. A number of standards have been developed, among them the *Business Process Specification Schema (BPSC)* [15] and *Collaboration-Protocol Profile and Agreement Specification* [16]. [15] provides a standard schema which organizations should use in order to facilitate interoperability among potential business partner processes. [16] on the other hand uses the schema described by [15] to create business contracts in terms of exchanged messages. The standards however do not address the problem highlighted in this paper, i.e., how to automatically find matching business processes.

Additional approaches dealing with view generation and matchmaking of services are supported by the workflow community. In [17] a method for generating local workflows based on a global one is described. The approach is based on petri-nets and addresses the problem of setting up inter-organisational workflows based on a global workflow, while our approach is based on local workflows.

Another approach is described in [18] where views are defined on behalf of a local workflow. The views are then compiled to contracts by using additional knowledge of a global workflow. It seems that the major advantage of this view is hiding mission critical information from the outside world and transformation of the interface provided by a local workflow to fit the requirements of the global one.

Within [19] the expressivnes of interaction patterns with regard to establish inter-organizational workflows is compared to global workflow defintions and the differences are stated.

The issue of matchmaking is addressed in [20], where M. Mecella, B. Pernici and P. Craca describe an algorithm for checking if two e-Services are compatible. They do this by checking if every possible trace in one flow has got a compatible one in another without describing how they perform this checking in case the traces are compatible.

In addition to the workflow community also the semantic web community [21,22] is dealing with matchmaking of services. In [23] a language is introduced describing the functional aspects as well as the messages and their parameters based on a domain specific ontology. DAML-S described in [24] uses workflow aspects as well as the functional semantic description of the service within the matchmaking. The generation of these descriptions is not elaborated in the publications and seems to be done manually.

4   Summary and Future Work

This paper has presented two things which are (i) a way how to generate views of a business process to allow only parts relevant to intended collaboration to be made public and (ii) a way how to find if a business process of a service requestor is compatible with the stored process of a service provider (i.e., business process matching). We illustrated with an example how business process view generation and matching concepts can be incorporated into the Web Service infrastructure (see Figure 2). This will extend metadata search with search based on a compatible business processes thereby making ad-hoc business relationships to be more easily established. These ideas are novel and can greatly facilitate inter-organizational business collaboration on an ad-hoc basis. Rather than companies having to rely on long-term established contracts to trade, more flexible business relationships can be established on an as needed basis, i.e., companies can quickly find partners with matching business processes and also break away from such relationships more easily.

In this paper we dealt only with business process view generation and matching for bilateral collaborations. In future work we will extend these concepts for multi-party collaborations. This is an important extension in that most of today's trading relationships are based on multi-party interactions, e.g., a long-running transaction might comprise interaction with a buyer, a supplier, a shipping company, an insurance company and a bank. Automatic checking of business process matching with all concerned parties is a non-trivial endeavor. We are also interested in investigating how to automatically enforce contracts in multi-party business process collaborations that have been deemed compatible.

References

1. F. Leymann. Web services flow language (WSFL 1.0), May 2001. http://www-3.ibm.com/software/solutions/webservices/pdf/WSFL.pdf.
2. S. Thatte. XLANG web services for business process design.
3. E. Christensen, F. Curbera, G. Meredith, and S. Weerawarana. Web services description language (WSDL) 1.1 W3C note, March 2001. http://www.w3.org/TR/wsdl.
4. A. Banerji, C. Bartolini, D. Beringer, V. Chopella, K. Govindarajan, A. Karp, H. Kuno, M. Lemon, G. Pogossiants, S. Sharma, and S. Williams. Web services conversation language (WSCL) 1.0 W3C note, March 2002. http://www.w3.org/TR/wscl10/.
5. M. Benyoucef and R. K. Keller. An evaluation of formalisms for negotiations in e-commerce. *Proceedings of the Workshop on Distributed Communities on the Web*, June 2000.
6. Q.Z. Sheng, B. Benatallah, M. Dumas, and E.O.-Y. Mak. SELF-SERV: A platform for rapid composition of web services in a peer-to-peer environment. In *Proc. of 28th VLDB Conference*, Hong Kong, China, 2002.
7. D. Harel. Statecharts: A visual formalism for complex systems. *Science of Computer Programming*, 8(3):231–274, June 1987.
8. D. Harel and A. Naamad. The STATEMATE semantics of statecharts. *ACM Transactions on Software Engineering and Methodology*, 5(4):293–333, 1996.
9. V. Hilaire, A. Koukam, P. Gruer, and J. Muller. Formal specification and prototyping of multi-agent systems. pages 114–127, 2000. http://citeseer.nj.nec.com/430779.html.
10. A. Pnueli and M. Shalev. What is in a step: On the semantics of statecharts. In T. Ito and A.R. Meyer, editors, *Theoretical Aspects of Computer Software*, pages 244–264. Springer, 1991. Lecture notes in Computer Science 526.
11. J. E. Hopcroft, R. Motwani, and J. D. Ullman. *Introduction to Automata Theory, Languages, and Computation*. Addison Wesley, 2001.
12. I. Wegener. *Theoretische Informatik*. B. G. Teubner Stuttgart, Germany, 1993.

13. Inc. Ariba, IBM Corporation, and Microsoft Corporation. Universal description, discovery and integration, September 2000. http://www.uddi.org/.
14. ebXML. ebXML standardization. http://www.ebxml.org/.
15. Business Process Team. Business process specification schema v1.01, May 2001.
16. Trading Partners Team. Collaboration-protocol profile and agreement specification v1.0, May 2001.
17. W.M.P. van der Aalst and M. Weske. The P2P approach to interorganizational workflows. In *Proc. of 13. Int. Conf. on Advanced Information Systems Engeneering (CAISE'01)*, Interlaken, Switzerland, 2001.
18. E. Kafeza, D. K. W. Chiu, and I. Kafeza. View-based contracts in an e-service cross-organizational workflow environment. In F. Casati, D. Georgakopoulos, and M. Shan, editors, *TES 2001 LNCS 2193*, pages 74–88. Springer, 2001.
19. W. v.d. Aalst. Interorganizational workflows: An approach based on message sequence charts and petri nets. *Systems Analysis - Modelling - Simulation*, 34(3):335–367, 1999.
20. M. Mecella, B. Pernici, and P. Craca. Compatibility of e-services in a cooperative multi-platform environment. In F. Casati, D. Georgakopoulos, and M. Shan, editors, *TES 2001 LNCS 2193*, pages 44–57. Springer, 2001. Lecture notes in Computer Science 2193.
21. T. Berbers-Lee, J. Hendler, and O. Lassila. The semantic web. *Scientific America*, 284(5):34–43, 2001.
22. S. McIlraith, T. Son, and H. Zeng. Semantic web services. *IEEE Intelligent Systems (Special Issue on the Semantic Web)*, April 2001.
23. K. P. Sycara, M. Klusch, S. Widoff, and J. Lu. Dynamic service matchmaking among agents in open information environments. *SIGMOD Record*, 28(1):47–53, 1999.
24. Daml-S Coalition Anupriya. DAML-S: Web serice description for the semantic web, 2002.

Regulating Work in Digital Enterprises: A Flexible Managerial Framework⋆

Takahiro Murata and Naftaly H. Minsky

Department of Computer Science
Rutgers University
Piscataway, NJ 08854, USA
{murata|minsky}@cs.rutgers.edu

Abstract. This paper demonstrates that work in digital enterprises—like work in conventional enterprises—can be carried out effectively by *autonomous agents*, subject to a regulatory regime that combines standing enterprise-wide policies with flexible managerial controls. The proposed regulatory mechanism, which is based on the concept of Law Governed Interaction (LGI), can support a wide range of enterprise policies, and a wide spectrum of managerial styles—including the procedural style underlying the so called Workflow Management System (WfMS).

1 Introduction

As information technology is embraced by the business world, a new mode of work is emerging. The presence of goods, funds, and services is represented electronically, and their handling (moving, storing, selling, buying, etc.) is carried out by acting upon such electronic representation. Moreover, it is becoming increasingly common, in such *digital enterprises*, for electronic actors, e.g., stock trading agents, auction agents, etc., to initiate such actions automatically. One consequence of these trends is that work in digital enterprises tends to be quite invisible, and be carried out in enormous speed, making such work difficult to control and to audit. There clearly is a need for new approaches for the management of this kind of work.

The currently leading approach for the management of work within digital enterprises is the, so called, Workflow Management System (WfMS). Although this concept has many variations, they are all reasonably close to the following definition in the "Workflow Reference Model" [16]:

"A Workflow Management System is one which provides *procedural automation* [emphasis is ours] of a business process by management of the sequence of work activities and the invocation of appropriate human and/or IT resources associated with the various activity steps."

⋆ Work supported in part by NSF grant No. CCR-98-03698, and by the NJ Comission on Science and Technology "excellence award"

R. Meersman, Z. Tari (Eds.): CoopIS/DOA/ODBASE 2002, LNCS 2519, pp. 356–372, 2002.

In spite of its popularity, this procedural approach to the management of business processes has its critics. One apt criticism of WfMS has been raised in [17], as follows:

> "Business processes are highly dynamic and unpredictable—it is difficult to give a complete *a priori* specification of all the activities that need to be performed and how they should be ordered. Any detailed time plans which are produced are often disrupted by unavoidable delays or unanticipated events."

As an alternative for procedural specification, these authors propose the following:

> "...the most natural way to view the business process is as a collection of *autonomous* [emphasis is ours] problem solving agents, which interact when they have interdependencies."

We too believe in the importance of autonomy for the participants in business processes, for the above mentioned reason, and for others. In particular, an autonomous agent can take "opportunity-based initiatives" [20], based on his/her[1] intimate familiarity with the operating environment, which may not be available to the manager. An attempt to communicate such information to one's manager, or to a workflow mechanism, could be impractical when fast response is required—particularly in a distributed setup, when the agent in question is geographically separated from his manager.

However, we maintain that such autonomy cannot be unlimited. Indeed, the autonomy of agents operating within a conventional enterprises is generally limited by the rules and regulations imposed on them by their environment. Let us examine the nature of such limitations.

Broadly speaking, one can distinguish between two types of regulations that govern agents operating within an enterprise: (a) *enterprise policies* and (b) *managerial controls*. By enterprise policies we mean the standing rules of the enterprise, regarding the behavior of its agents when involved in certain activities, and regarding the use of its resources. For example, an enterprise may have a policy stipulating that issuance of purchase orders must be subject to the availability of funds, and that it must be audited. Such a policy may also require that every purchase order is cosigned by somebody other than its originator (a case of *separation of duties*).

Of course, a typical enterprise is bound to be governed by a multitude of policies. They might have diverse reasons for their existence, such as: (a) the internal business practices of the enterprise; (b) product design and manufacturing constraints; (c) the auditability of the enterprise; (d) security considerations; (e) software engineering principles; and (f) government regulations. Such policies are likely to be interrelated in complex ways, forming an *ensemble* that is to govern the enterprise as a whole.

---

[1] We will henceforth use "he" when referring to a human agent, for simplicity, and we will use "it" when an agent is, or is likely to be, a software component.

By *managerial controls* we mean more timely, and usually more detailed, specifications of what is to be done, when it should be done, and by whom. Such controls can be exercised at various levels of specificity. In particular, a manager can give each of its subordinates some broadly specified tasks, providing them with appropriate resources, such as budget, space, etc.; and then let them do their work autonomously. A more hand-on manager might monitor the progress of its subordinates, and, if necessary, steer them towards a desired goal. Finally, a manager might micro-manage the task he is in charge of, by dynamically assigning a specific agent to each specific task, when it is to be carried out. This extreme mode of management, which severely curtails the autonomy of the agents, is what the workflow management systems generally employ.

Note that these two types of regulation, i.e., enterprise policies and managerial controls, are interrelated. First, because the ability of managers to manage must be grounded on some enterprise policies, which provide managers with a degree of control over their subordinates. And, second, because agents must generally conform to the enterprise policies governing them, even when following the dictates of their managers.

The purpose of this paper is to demonstrate that work in digital enterprises—like work in conventional enterprises—can be carried out effectively by *autonomous agents*, subject to a regulatory regime that combines standing enterprise-wide policies with flexible managerial controls. The proposed regulatory mechanism can support a wide range of enterprise policies, and a wide spectrum of managerial styles—including the currently popular, procedural style underlying workflow management systems.

The computational means for our regulatory mechanism are based on a generic coordination and control mechanism for distributed systems called Law Governed Interaction (LGI), first introduced, under a different name, in [21]. This mechanism provides for the explicit specification, and for the scalable enforcement, of policies governing the interaction between distributed agents.

We start in the next section with an example designed to motivate the need for flexible regulation of work in digital enterprises, and to demonstrate the nature of the required regulatory mechanism. We then provide an overview of LGI in Sect. 3, which is the basis for the regulatory mechanism being proposed here. In Sect. 4, we demonstrate how the regulatory mechanism allows for the formulation and the enforcement of the the example policy introduced earlier. Finally we discuss related research, including workflows, and we conclude.

2   Management by Regulation: A Case Study

Consider a department store that deploys teams of agents whose purpose is to supply its various departments with the merchandise they need. Each such team consists of a set of *buyers*, and a *manager*; and there is a distinguished agent called the *auditor*, whose job is to maintain the audit trail of the various purchasing activities. Let all such teams be governed by the following policy (which we call *BT*, for "buying-team"):

1. *A manager can give each buyer in his team a collection of assignments, each consisting of the identification of the merchandise to be purchased, and the deadline for the purchase to be carried out. The manager can also provide each buyer with a budget for all his purchases.*
2. *Every buyer is allowed to issue purchase orders (POs) as set forth by his current assignments, while remaining within his budget. Every PO issued by a buyer is to be monitored by the auditor.*
3. *A buyer can transfer any of his assignments to another buyer in his team, unless the assignment is marked as "exclusive."*
4. *The manager can check the status of each buyer, in terms of the progress of his assignments, and his remaining budget. He also monitors any transfer of assignments between buyers.*
5. *The manager can change the assignments and the budget of every buyer in his team. He can also mark an assignment as "exclusive," thus preventing it from being transferred to another buyer as described in Point 3 above.*
6. *The role played by all participants in this activity—both managers and buyers—needs to be certified by a specific certification authority (CA), called here* admin.

This is a reasonable policy for a traditional department store to employ (with the possible exception of Point 6 above). Later we will show how this policy can be formalized as a law under LGI, and enforced on a more digital department store.

2.1   On the Nature of This Policy

One can distinguish between two aspects of this policy: (a) its broad regulation of the activities of the otherwise autonomous buyers, and (b) the control it provides a manager over the buyers working for him.

First, buyers are provided by this policy with a carefully circumscribed autonomy. According to Point 2, each buyer can satisfy his assignments by issuing purchase orders to vendors of their choice, at arbitrary prices—within his total budget—and in arbitrary order. Moreover, according to Point 3 of this policy, a buyer can transfer to other members of his team any of his non-exclusive assignments. Such an autonomy is very important, particularly if the buyers travel around the country, or around the world, and have to make their decisions on the basis of what they find in the field. Note that such autonomy of action does not imply any loss of accountability, because this policy requires all issuance of POs to be monitored by the auditor, and all exchanges of assignments to be monitored by the manager. So, buyers cannot conduct their deals in the dark.

Second, the above mentioned autonomy of buyers can be restricted in various ways by their manager, who is given a great deal of control over them by this policy. First, by Point 1 of policy *BT*, it is the manager who can define the initial assignments of his buyers, and who can provide them with their budgets. Second, by Point 4, the manager can monitor the progress of each of his buyers, and by Point 5, he can steer the activities of his team of buyers dynamically, by changing their assignments and their budgets, at will.

A good manager is likely to use his ability to control his buyers sparingly. But a manager does have it in his power, under policy BT, to force his team of buyers to operate as a kind of workflow. That is, he can give a specific assignment, and a suitable budget, to a specific buyer, when he wants this particular buyer to carry out this assignment. And then, when this assignment is carried out, he can give the next assignment to the next buyer, and so on. This would be a very inefficient way for managing teams of buyers, in most circumstances. But it might be appropriate in some rare situations.

We would like to point out—what may already be obvious to the reader—that there is no primitive concept of a *manager* in our framework. An agent playing the role of a manager under policy BT has specific powers over members of his team, which allows him to manage his team's work as has been described above. But these powers have been defined specifically by this policy. It is quite possible to provide managers with different types of power; or to provide a single team with several managers, each with its own powers; or to have a team operate as a set of peers, with no manager to supervise them. In short, it is the policy that is fundamental in this framework, not the manager.

Finally, we point out that all but the last points of this policy can be reasonably formulated for a traditional enterprise. Point 6, however, is meaningful only for a digital enterprise. This point prescribe the manner in which all participants in the purchasing activities need to authenticate their roles—via certificates issued by a specified certification authority.

2.2   Broader Perspectives

So far we have treated BT as an isolated policy, governing purchasing activities without any regard to whatever else is going on in the enterprise in question. This is an oversimplification. As we have already pointed out, a typical enterprise is bound to be governed by a whole ensemble of interrelated policies. As a simple example, when a buyer, operating under policy BT, makes a purchase he may need to reserve transportation for it. But the agents that deal with transportation are likely to be operating under their own policy, which may require these two policies to interoperate. We will also describe later how such interoperation between policies is carried out under the proposed regulatory mechanism.

3   The Concept of Law Governed Interaction (LGI) – An Overview

As mentioned earlier, we turn to Law Governed Interaction (LGI) [21,23,3] as an underlying communication and computational mechanism of our framework. Broadly speaking, LGI is a message-exchange mechanism that allows a group of distributed agents to engage in a mode of interaction *governed* by an explicitly specified policy, called the *law* of the group. The messages thus exchanged under a given law $\mathcal{L}$ are called $\mathcal{L}$-*messages*, and the group of agents interacting via $\mathcal{L}$-messages is called an $\mathcal{L}$-*community* $\mathcal{C}_{\mathcal{L}}$ (or simply community $\mathcal{C}$). No assumptions are made about the structure and behavior of the community member agents[2], which might be software processes, or human beings.

For each agent x in a given community C_L, LGI maintains the *control-state* CS_x of this agent, in the form of a bag of terms. These control-states, which can change dynamically, subject to law $\mathcal{L}$, enable the law to make distinctions between agents, and to be sensitive to dynamic changes in their state. The semantics of control-states for a given community is defined by its law, and could represent such things as the role of an agent in this community, along with privileges and tokens it carries. For example, under the law introduced later in Sect. 4, which implements the regulation discussed in Sect. 2, the term manager in the control-state of an agent denotes that this agent plays the role of the manager in the buyers' mission.

We elaborate on several aspects of LGI below, focusing on (a) its concept of law, (b) its mechanism for law enforcement, and (c) its interoperability between communities, while additional features of LGI essential to enforcing policy BT will be explained later when the actual law is presented. For the aspects of LGI not covered here, including the treatment of *exceptions*, the expressiveness, and the deployment of LGI communities, the reader is referred to [23,29,2].

The Concept of Law: Law $\mathcal{L}$ of community C_L is defined over a certain types of events, occurring at members of C. These events subject to laws, called *regulated events*, include (among others): the *sending* and the *arrival* of an $\mathcal{L}$-message; the *coming due of an obligation* previously imposed on a given agent; and the *submission of a digital certificate*. Given a regulated event, law $\mathcal{L}$ produces its mandate called the *ruling* for that event. A ruling is made of a list of *primitive operations*, which include operations on the control-state of the agent where the event occurred (called, the "home agent"), such as insertion (+t), removal (-t), and replacement (t<-s) of terms; operations on messages, such as forward and deliver; and the imposition of an obligation on the home agent.

LGI currently supports two languages for writing laws: (a) a Prolog-like language, introduced in [21], and (b) a restricted version of Java, described in [27]. The former of these languages is employed in this paper.

Law $\mathcal{L}$ is enforceable strictly *locally* at each member of C, leading to scalability. This is due to the following: (1) $\mathcal{L}$ only regulates local events at individual agents; (2) the ruling of $\mathcal{L}$ for an event e at agent x depends only on e and the local control-state CS_x of x; (3) the ruling of $\mathcal{L}$ at x can mandate only local operations to be carried out at x. Note that we lose no expressiveness in stating policies to be enforced, by limiting ourselves to such local laws, as shown in [23].

Law-Enforcement Mechanism: The law $\mathcal{L}$ of community C is enforced by a *middleware* consisting of a set of trusted agents called *controllers* that mediate the exchange of $\mathcal{L}$-messages between members of C. Every member x of C has a

---

[2] Given the popular usages of the term "agent," it is important to point out that we do not imply by it either "intelligence" nor mobility, although neither of these is being ruled out by this model.

controller $\mathcal{T}_x$ assigned to it ($\mathcal{T}$ here stands for "trusted agent") which maintains the control-state $\mathcal{CS}_x$ of its client x. Controllers are *generic* in that it can interpret and enforce any well-formed law; they operate as independent processes anywhere in the network, and a set of active controllers is maintained by *controller-service*. (Concerning the basis for trust in this mechanism, the reader is referred to [3].)

All these controllers, which are logically placed between the members of $\mathcal{C}$ and the communications medium (as illustrated in Fig. 1) carry the *same law*[3] $\mathcal{L}$. Every exchange between a pair of agents x and y is thus mediated by *their* controllers $\mathcal{T}_x$ and $\mathcal{T}_y$, so that this enforcement is inherently decentralized. Several agents can share a single controller, if such sharing is desired. (The efficiency of this mechanism, and its scalability, are discussed in [23].)

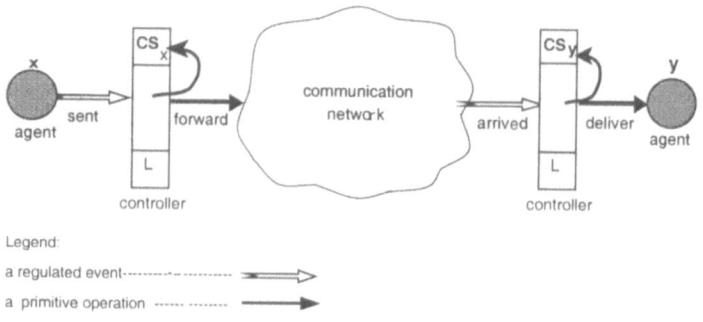

Fig. 1. Enforcement of the law

The fact that the same law is enforced at *all* agents of a community gives LGI its necessary global scope, establishing a *common* set of ground rules for all members of $\mathcal{C}$ and providing them with the ability to trust each other, in spite of the heterogeneity of the community.

Interoperability between Communities: Finally, we point out that LGI supports the ability of agents x and y operating under distinct laws $\mathcal{L}$ and $\mathcal{L}'$, respectively, to exchange messages. Such interoperation is regulated under the authorization by each law, and may cause an effect only on the recipient of a message as stipulated by the recipient's law. Consequently, interoperating parties need not be aware of the details of each other law.

To achieve such interoperability, primitive operation `export` and regulated event `imported` are provided as follows:

- `export(x,m,[y,L'])`: invoked by agent x under law $\mathcal{L}$; initiates the transmission of a message m from x to agent y operating under law $\mathcal{L}'$.

---

[3] A one-way hash [25] of the law is used for the controllers to establish the identity of laws they carry.

- `imported([x,L],m,y)`: occurs when a message m exported by x under law $\mathcal{L}$ arrives at y under $\mathcal{L}'$.

4   Establishing the *BT* Policy in a Digital Context

We will formulate here our example policy *BT* as a law $\mathcal{L}_{BT}$ under LGI, and then explain how this law is enforced. Then, we illustrate, via a very simplified example, how agents operating under this law can interoperate with agents operating under different laws in the enterprise.

Note that law $\mathcal{L}_{BT}$ is formulated under the following simplifying assumptions: (1) every purchase is made electronically; (2) any PO issued by an authorized buyer will not be rejected by the vendor chosen for that purchase; (3) the payment and the delivery for any purchase will be carried out accordingly once the PO has been sent; and (4) there is only one team of buyers (this assumption, which can be easily removed, is to avoid the need to identify the team, when buyers and their manager are authenticated under Point 6 of policy *BT*).

4.1   Law $\mathcal{L}_{BT}$ of Buying Team

Shown in Figs. 2 and 3, law $\mathcal{L}_{BT}$ implements the policy stipulated in Sect. 2, which regulates the entire interaction of the buyers' mission. In general an LGI law consists of two parts: the preamble and the rule section. The preamble of $\mathcal{L}_{BT}$ specifies the following: (1) admin as a trusted CA, identified by its public key; (2) the certification requirement on the controllers that interpret this law, with the public key of the CA to certify them (and optionally the attributes that the controllers need to be certified about), whose compliance is verified by the controllers that communicate with each other under the law, as well as each agent at the time of joining this $\mathcal{L}$-group; (3) `auditor`, with its identifier, for auditing; and (4) the initial control state given to every agent that adopts the law, in this case empty.

The rest of the law stipulates a set of rules, in a Prolog-like syntax. Most rules are followed by a comment (in italic), which, together with our discussion, should be understandable even for a reader not well versed in the LGI language for writing laws. Each rule has a *head*, up to symbol `:-`, and a *body*, the rest. Recall that the same law is interpreted though individually by the controller assigned to each agent in the community. A regulated event occurring at this agent triggers a rule that has a matching head, if any (in the order in which the rules are written when more than one match). The triggered rule proceeds to check if all the goals in its body are attained, given the context of the control-state of this agent.

In addition to the standard types of Prolog goals, the body of a rule may contain two distinguished types of goals. These are the *sensor-goals*, which allow the law to "sense" the control-state of the home agent, and the *do-goals* that contribute to the ruling of the law. A *sensor-goal* has the form t@CS, where t is any Prolog term. It attempts to unify t with each term in the control-state of

---

Preamble:
    authority(admin, publicKeyOfAdmin).
    portal(thisLaw, publicKeyOfAdmin, []).
    alias(auditor, "auditor@someDepartment.com").
    initialCS([]).

$\mathcal{R}$1. `certified([issuer(admin),subject(Self),attributes([role(R)])])`
      `:- (R=buyer ; R=manager), do(+R).`
    Every participant needs to be certified via admin *for the respective role.*

$\mathcal{R}$2. `sent(M, Msg, B) :- (Msg=addAsmt(Spec,Due,Excl); Msg=delAsmt(Spec);`
      `Msg=budget(Op,A)), manager@CS, do(forward).`
    The manager can impose some (additional) assignment on a buyer or take some off.

$\mathcal{R}$3. `arrived(M, addAsmt(Spec,Due,Excl), B) :- buyer@CS,`
      `(not(mgr(_)@CS)->do(+mgr(M)); true),`
      `do(+asmt(Spec,act,Due,Excl)),`
      `do(imposeObligation(asmtDue(Spec),Due)), do(deliver).`

$\mathcal{R}$4. `arrived(M, delAsmt(Spec), B)`
      `:- buyer@CS, do(-asmt(Spec,act,_,_)), do(deliver).`

$\mathcal{R}$5. `obligationDue(asmtDue(Spec)) :- asmt(Spec,act,Due,Excl)@CS,`
      `do(asmt(Spec,act,Due,Excl)<-asmt(Spec,unf,Due,Excl)).`
    When an assignment turns due without the merchandise purchased, it is classified as unfulfilled.

$\mathcal{R}$6. `arrived(M, budget(Op,A), B) :- buyer@CS,`
      `(Op=add->(budget(A1)@CS,A2 is A1+A,`
                       `do(budget(A1)<-budget(A2));`
            `do(+budget(A))) ;`
      `Op=del->budget(A1)@CS,A2 is A1-A,`
                      `do(budget(A1)<-budget(A2))),`
      `do(deliver).`
    The manager can add/delete some amount to/from a buyer's budget.

Fig. 2. Law $\mathcal{L}_{BT}$ of buying team

the home agent. A *do-goal*, which always succeeds, has the form do(p), where p is one of the primitive-operations, mentioned in Sect. 3. It appends the term p to the ruling of the law. Thus, a successful rule body leads to non-empty ruling if it contains do-goals. (By default, an empty ruling implies that the event in question has no consequences—such an event is effectively ignored.)

Rule $\mathcal{R}$1 implements Point 6 of policy*BT*, which regulates the status of buyers, and that of the manager. The `certified` event that triggers this rule is generated when the controller is presented with a valid certificate, i.e., duly signed by an authority declared in an `authority` clause, in this case admin.[4] The `certified` event has as its argument the following representation of the submitted certificate: `[issuer(admin), subject(Self),` `attributes([role(R)])]`. Term `issuer(admin)` tells about the issuer of the certificate, while `subject(Self)` is used to signify the subject of the certification. `Self` is an LGI built-in variable bound to the identifier (id) of the home-agent[5], which means that this rule requires a self-certificate be presented. Term `attributes` in the above argument describes what is certified about the subject, and in this case asserts that the agent should be allowed to play role R, either `buyer` or `manager`[6], which is recorded in the control-state by this rule.

Rules $\mathcal{R}2$ and $\mathcal{R}3$ allow the manager to impose an (additional) assignment to a buyer. $\mathcal{R}2$ checks if the sender has the manager status before forwarding the message, either of `asmt` or of `budget` (`Msg` is another LGI built-in variable bound to the regulated message).[7] $\mathcal{R}3$, after ensuring that the recipient is a buyer, adds a `asmt` term to the control-state, representing this assignment item, including the information regarding its deadline and whether it is exclusive (`excl`) or transferable (`trans`), bound to `Due` and `Excl`, respectively. The second argument `act` of this `asmt` term stands for this assignment item being active. In parallel, $\mathcal{R}4$, in reducing the assignment, removes the corresponding `asmt` term from the recipient's control-state. Note, when an assignment is added, LGI obligation named `asmtDue(Spec)` is imposed to manage the deadline of this assignment (whose becoming due will be explained shortly). Thus these rules implement a part of Points 1 and 5 that concerns assigning and adjusting the buyers' tasks. Similarly, the other part of these policy points for setting and adjusting the buyers' budget is implemented by rules $\mathcal{R}2$ and $\mathcal{R}6$.

By rule $\mathcal{R}7$, a buyer can issue a PO for a merchandise, assigned, but not obtained yet, within the remaining budget. This rule changes the status of this assignment from active to fulfilled, by replacing the second argument of the `asmt` term from `act` to the price of the merchandise (P). Then, the PO is delivered to the intended supplier.[8] Notice that the message content, together with the PO recipient's id, is also delivered by $\mathcal{R}7$ to `auditor` for auditing. The deadline expiry of an assignment is handled by rule $\mathcal{R}5$, which revises the status of this assignment to be unfulfilled if it is still active at this point. Thus, these rules implement Point 2.

Rules $\mathcal{R}8$ and $\mathcal{R}9$ implement Point 3 that permits buyers to coordinate by exchanging their assignment. A buyer can send a `transfer` message specifying an item to be transferred ($\mathcal{R}8$). However, notice that the specified item must be transferable; i.e., the fourth argument of the corresponding `asmt` term should be `trans` (not `excl`), which is removed from the control-state. The arrival of

---

[4] If the certificate is found invalid, then an `exception` event is triggered.

[5] An agent id is of the form: `local-name@domain-name` [2].

[6] Syntax (P;Q) in the laws should read P or Q; similarly (P->Q;R) means if P then Q else R.

[7] When the addressed recipient is absent from the group, an LGI exception is raised; again, the handling such exceptions is omitted in this paper for brevity.

[8] Sending a message via `deliver` to a non-home-agent triggers no regulated event on the recipient side (just like `deliver` to a home-agent, but unlike `forward`).

```
R7. sent(B, po(Spec,P), S)
        :- buyer@CS, budget(A)@CS, asmt(Spec,act,D,E)@CS,
           R is A-P, R>=0, do(budget(A)<-budget(R)),
           do(asmt(Spec,act,D,E)<-asmt(Spec,P,D,E)),
           do(deliver(B,Msg,S)), do(deliver(B,po(Spec,P,S),auditor)).
    A buyer can send a PO, while not exceeding his budget.


R8. sent(B, transfer(Spec), B1)
        :- buyer@CS, asmt(Spec,act,D,trans)@CS,
           do(-asmt(Spec,act,D,trans)), mgr(M)@CS,
           do(forward(B,transfer(Spec,D,M),B1)),
           do(deliver(B,monitored(Msg,to(B1)),M)).
    A buyer can transfer some assignment to another buyer unless marked "exclu-
    sive."
R9. arrived(B, transfer(Spec,D,M), B1)
        :- (not(mgr(_)@CS)->do(+mgr(M)) ; true),
           (buyer@CS -> do(+asmt(Spec,act,D,trans)),
               imposeObligation(asmtDue(Spec),D), do(deliver) ;
           do(forward(B1,notApply(transfer(Spec,D)),B))).


R10. arrived(B1, notApply(transfer(Spec,D)), B)
        :- do(+asmt(Spec,act,D,trans)), do(deliver).


R11. sent(M, checkStatus, B) :- manager@CS, do(forward).
    The manager can check the status of a buyer.
R12. arrived(M, checkStatus, B) :- buyer@CS, budget(A)@CS,
            findall(asmt(S1,P),
               (asmt(S1,P,D1,E1)@CS,number(P)), Fs),
            findall(asmt(S2,act), asmt(S2,act,D2,E2)@CS, As),
            findall(asmt(S3,unf), asmt(S3,unf,D3,E3)@CS, Us),
            do(deliver(B,status(B,
                    [active(As),filled(Fs),unfilled(Us),budget(A)]),
            M)).
```

Fig. 3. Law $\mathcal{L}_{BT}$ of buying team (cont'd)

the transfered item adds the corresponding asmt term to the control-state ($\mathcal{R}9$). Note that if the recipient is not a buyer, the transfered item is returned in a notApply message, whose arrival causes $\mathcal{R}10$ to add the asmt term back to the control-state of the original sender.

Rules $\mathcal{R}11$ and $\mathcal{R}12$ implement a part of Point 4 that permits the manager to check the status of each buyer. $\mathcal{R}12$ uses (higher-order) built-in operation findall to pick up all assignments whose corresponding asmt terms qualify the specification given as its second parameter, and to accumulate them in a list bound to its third parameter; the first, the second, and the third invocation of findall are to collect the filled assignments, the active ones, and the unfilled (expired) ones, respectively. Combined with the remaining budget, these are delivered in a **status** message back to the manager.

The rest of Point 4 that allows the manager to monitor assignment exchange among buyers is implemented by rule $\mathcal{R}8$, which delivers a notice of the occurrence of this monitored event to the manager. The manager's id in term **mgr** of the control-state should have been inserted by $\mathcal{R}3$ (or by $\mathcal{R}9$) when the buyer first received an assignment from the manager (or another buyer, resp.).

4.2   Interoperability between Policies

So far we have concentrated on a single policy; namely, one that governs the purchasing of merchandises. However it is highly likely that such an activity is conducted in association with other activities inside (or outside) the pertinent enterprise, each of which regulated by its own policy. Thus, there ought to be a means to establish interoperability between those policies, which we illustrate by building on our previous example.

Suppose, having purchased a merchandise, buyers acting under law $\mathcal{L}_{BT}$ should reserve the means of its transportation through some authorized agent. Such an agent is engaged in finding a means of transportation upon receiving a specific request from a buyer, which is regulated by law $\mathcal{L}_T$. Having located and booked a means to qualify the given request, the transportation agent notifies the requester of the booking information; failing to book any means within the deadline specified by the requester, the agent must notify the requester of the failure.

Using interoperability of laws in LGI, we achieve this interaction between two policies, one for purchasing, and the other for reserving transportation means, as follows.

In Fig. 4, we show an additional portion of law $\mathcal{L}_{BT}$ to enable this interoperation. First, it has an additional portal clause in the preamble, which identifies law $\mathcal{L}_T$, shown below, as a law to interoperate with. Note the name **transportationLaw** given to $\mathcal{L}_T$ is only local to this law, $\mathcal{L}_{BT}$, and the hash of $\mathcal{L}_T$ is used to identify it. Then, rule $\mathcal{R}13$ allows a buyer, who has purchased an assigned merchandise, to send a request message to a transportation agent, specifying the merchandise, the origin, the required arrival date, and the deadline for finding an appropriate means. Note that the rule prohibits the buyer to send more than one request while an agent is searching for a means. The message is conveyed to law $\mathcal{L}_T$ via **export** operation.

Rules $\mathcal{R}14$ and $\mathcal{R}15$ are triggered when an agent acting under $\mathcal{L}_T$ exports a **booked** message and a **notFound** message, respectively, as described below.

Figure 5 is an excerpt of law $\mathcal{L}_T$ that governs the activity of locating and reserving transportation means. (It does not show how an agent goes about making a reservation with a carrier.) Its preamble has a **portal** clause to declare reciprocally $\mathcal{L}_{BT}$ for interoperation, under local name **buyersLaw**. The entry of role **transportation** allowed by $\mathcal{R}1$, via an appropriate certificate issued by admin, is similar to $\mathcal{R}1$ of $\mathcal{L}_{BT}$.

```
Preamble:
    portal(transportationLaw, hashOfTransportationLaw).

R13. sent(B, reqTrans(Spec,Fm,By,Due), T) :- buyer@CS,
        asmt(Spec,P,_,_)@CS, number(P), not(requested(Spec)),
        do(+requested(Spec)),
        do(export(B,Msg,[T,transportationLaw])).

R14. imported([T,transportationLaw], booked(Spec,Tspec), B)
        :- do(+trans(Spec,Tspec)), do(deliver).

R15. imported([T,transportationLaw], notFound(Spec), B)
        :- do(-requested(Spec)), do(deliver).
```

Fig. 4. Law $\mathcal{L}_{\mathcal{BT}}$ of buying team (interoperability)

```
Preamble:
    authority(admin, publicKeyOfAdmin).
    portal(thisLaw, publicKeyOfAdmin, []).
    portal(buyersLaw, hashOfBuyersLaw).
    initialCS([]).

R1. certified([issuer(admin),subject(Self),
        attributes([role(transportation)])]) :- do(+transportation).

R2. imported([B,buyersLaw], reqTrans(Spec,Fm,By,Due), T)
        :- transportation@CS, do(request(Spec,B)@CS),
        do(imposeObligation(replyDue(Spec),Due)), do(deliver).

R3. sent(T,booked(Spec,Tspec),B) :- request(Spec,B)@CS,
        do(-request(Spec,B)), do(export(T,Msg,[B,buyersLaw])).

R4. obligationDue(replyDue(Spec))
        :- request(Spec,B)@CS, do(-request(Spec,B)),
        do(export(Self,notFound(Spec),[B,buyersLaw])).
```

Fig. 5. Law $\mathcal{L}_{\mathcal{T}}$ for transportation

The `imported` event generated on the receipt of a request message conveyed from $\mathcal{L}_{\mathcal{BT}}$ to $\mathcal{L}_{\mathcal{T}}$ triggers rule $\mathcal{R}2$. After making sure that the recipient is a transportation agent, and storing the request information, this rule imposes an obligation named `replyDue` to issue a failure message back to the requester ($\mathcal{R}4$), if no such means is found. Finally, rule $\mathcal{R}3$ allows a transportation agent to send the booking information for a requested means, which checks the presence of the corresponding `request` term, and verifies the destination of such a message.

As seen above, in administrating the transportation reservation, the effect of receiving a request is determined by law $\mathcal{L}_{\mathcal{T}}$ alone, while, regarding the legitimacy of such a request, the buyers' purchasing activity, regulated by law $\mathcal{L}_{BT}$, is trusted. In particular, $\mathcal{L}_T$ does not reflect under what condition a buyer can send such a request, and leaves it to the regulation under $\mathcal{L}_{BT}$. (Similarly, the legitimacy of booking information received by a buyer under $\mathcal{L}_{BT}$ derives from the fact that it originates an agent acting under $\mathcal{L}_T$, regardless of the detail of its regulation.) Such transparency is an important factor in achieving interoperability among multiple policies without incurring unnecessary administrative overhead.

5   Comparison with Related Work

We will discuss here briefly related work concerning three aspects of this paper: workflow management systems, the autonomy of workers, and enterprise-wide policies.

Workflows: Broadly speaking, a workflow [16] is a procedural specification of a sequence of tasks to be performed by participating agents. For enacting such specification, a WfMS is deployed to initiate planned tasks one by one. This general concept has many variations, generated by researchers attempting to enhance its flexibility, by such means as: handling of workflow exceptions [15,24, 10]; run-time evolution of the process models [12,9]; accommodating different degrees in the models' specificity [6]; and generating the process model at run-time [18]. Some other researchers [5,8,14,30] attempted to augment this procedural model with explicit means of communication between procedures enacted by the WfMS. All these variations can be incorporated into a community governed by a law such as $\mathcal{L}_{BT}$, by having the manager instruct each agent what to do, when; or even by adopting a WfMS as an LGI agent playing the role of the manager.

So, workflows represent just one management style, among many. In particular, they do not give any support to styles such as: (1) having no explicit managerial roles, allowing the peers to completely coordinate by themselves, under a policy that imposes certain rules of engagement; and (2) having more than one manager monitor and steer the activity, while interacting between themselves (to adjust the "territory" from time to time, say).

Moreover, there is a problem with WfMSs, even for one who likes their management style. The problem is that workflows do not have the means to ensure that all the managerial role players and participating agents conform to the given enterprise-wide policies. Granted that some workflow systems, e.g., [7], provide a language to specify constraints on assigning tasks to agents, along with an algorithm to enforce them. However, such an approach cannot ensure a policy that ranges over multiple, possibly heterogeneous WfMSs; e.g., requiring that the issuing of POs from all buying teams, each supported by a distinct WfMS of its department, be monitored by a designated auditor.

The Autonomy of Agents: Several researchers [28,20,17] consider the the autonomy of participating agents to be crucial for conducting work effectively. Each of these proposal has its own approach for such agents to collaborate harmoniously towards a common goal. Action Workflow [20], in particular, is conceptualized as a counter-theme to the workflow model, which relies on "better educated workers who combine structured work with opportunity-based initiative and individual responsibility for quality and customer satisfaction." Jennings et al. [17] view a business process as collection of autonomous problem solving agents, who negotiate the terms and conditions of the service to be provided, in order to cope with a highly dynamic, unpredictable aspect of business processes.

However, all these researchers seem to miss the need for limiting the autonomy of agents by enterprise policies and managerial controls.

Enterprise-Wide Policies: Such policies are widely considered fundamental to enterprise modeling, and their specification were the subject of several recent investigations, such as [11]. But this modeling work is interested mostly in the specification of policies, and not in their enforcement. Enforcement of enterprise-wide policies has been addressed mostly in the context of access control. Several policy enforcement mechanism have been proposed [13,4,19]. All of them rely on a centralized enforcement mechanism, however. We believe that such centralization constitute a dangerous single-point of failure and performance bottleneck, and is thus not scalable. Attempts to solve these problems through replication leads to difficulty in enforcing *stateful* policies, such as those we have described here, which are necessary for proper regulation of work in digital enterprises.

6   Conclusion

We have demonstrated in this paper that work in digital enterprises can be carried out effectively by *autonomous agents*, subject to a regulatory regime that combines standing enterprise-wide policies with flexible managerial controls. The proposed regulatory mechanism can support a wide range of enterprise policies, and a wide spectrum of managerial styles—including the procedural style underlying workflow management systems.

The regulatory mechanism described in this paper has been implemented. And it has been tested on several applications relevant to this paper. These include establishing a policy that governs the work of distributed committees [26]; establishing a policy that enforces certain broad accounting principles over the work done in a financial system [22]; and establishing an access control policy that manages dissemination of patient records in a medical center [3]. But much work remains to be done for making this technique usable in industrial context. In particular, it is necessary to support the complex ensemble of interrelated policies that governs the various activities within a typical enterprise, following preliminary work in this direction that has been published in [1]. Also, there is work in progress on allowing *hot update* of laws; namely the update of a law while the distributed community governed by it continues to operate.

References

1. X. Ao, Minsky N. H., and T. Nguyen. A hierarchical policy specification language, and enforcement mechanism, for governing digital enterprises. In *Proc. of the IEEE 3rd International Workshop on Policies for Distributed Systems and Networks Monterey California*, June 2002. (available from http://www.cs.rutgers.edu/~minsky/pubs.html).

2. X. Ao, N. Minsky, T. Nguyen, and V. Ungureanu. Law-governed communities over the internet. In *Proc. of Fourth International Conference on Coordination Models and Languages; Limassol, Cyprus; LNCS 1906*, pages 133–147, September 2000. (available from http://www.cs.rutgers.edu/~minsky/pubs.html).

3. X. Ao, N. Minsky, and V. Ungureanu. Formal treatment of certificate revocation under communal access control. In *Proc. of the 2001 IEEE Symposium on Security and Privacy, May 2001, Oakland California*, May 2001. (available from http://www.cs.rutgers.edu/~minsky/pubs.html).

4. J. Barkley, K. Beznosov, and J. Uppal. Supporting relationships in access control using role based access control. In *Proceedings of the Fourth ACM Workshop on Role-Based Access Control*, pages 55–65, October 1999.

5. J Barron. Dialogue and process design for interactive information systems using taxis. In *Proc. SIGOA Conf, on Office Information Systems*, June 1982.

6. A. Bernstein. How can cooperative work tools support dynamic group processes? Bridging the specificity frontier. In *Proceedings of ACM 2000 Conference on Computer Supported Cooperative Work*, December 2000.

7. E. Bertino, E. Ferrari, and V. Atluri. The specification and enforcement of authorization constraints in workflow management systems. *ACM Transactions on Information and System Security*, 2(1):65–104, February 1999.

8. F. Casati, S. Ceri, B. Pernici, and G. Pozzi. Semantic workflow interoperability. In *Proceedings of EDBT'96, 5th International Conference on Extending Database Technology*, pages 443–462, March 1996.

9. F. Casati, S. Ceri, B. Pernici, and G. Pozzi. Workflow evolution. *Data & Knowledge Engineering*, 24(3):211–238, January 1998.

10. D.K.W. Chiu, Q. Li, and K. Karlapalem. A meta modeling approach to workflow management systems supporting exception handling. *Information Systems*, 24(2):159–184, 1999.

11. J. Cole, Derrick J., Z. Milosevic, and K. Raymond. Policies in an enterprise specification. In Morris Sloman, editor, *Proc. of Policy Worshop, 2001, Bristol UK*, January 2001.

12. C.A. Ellis and K. Keddara. ML-DEWS: Modeling language to support dynamic evolution with workflow systems. *Computer Supported Cooperative Work*, 9(3/4):293–333, November 2000.

13. D. Ferraiolo, J. Barkley, and R. Kuhn. A role based access control model and refernce implementation within a corporate intranets. *ACM Transactions on Information and System Security*, 2(1), February 1999.

14. C. Hagen and G. Alonso. Beyond the black box: Event-based inter-process communication in process support systems. In *Proceedings of Intn'l Conf. on Distributed Computing Systems (ICDCS'99)*, May-June 1999.

15. C. Hagen and G. Alonso. Exception handling in workflow management systems. *IEEE Transactions on Software Engineering*, 26(10):943–958, October 2000.

16. D. Hollingsworth. The workflow reference model. Technical Report WFMC-TC-1003 Issue 1.1, WfMC, January 1995.

17. N.R. Jennings, P. Faratin, M.J. Johnson, P. O'Brien, and M.E. Wiegand. Using intelligent agents to manage business processes. In *Proc. of First Intn'l Conf. on The Practical Application of Intelligent Agents and Multi-Agent Technology (PAAM96)*, pages 345–360, 1996.

18. H. Jørgensen. Interaction as a framework for flexible workflow modelling. In *Proceedings of ACM 2001 Intn'l Conf. on Supporting Group Work (GROUP 2001)*, October 2001.

19. G. Karjoth. The authorization service of tivoli policy director. In *Proc. of the 17th Annual Computer Security Applications Conference (ACSAC 2001)*, December 2001. (to appear).

20. R. Medina-Mora, T. Winograd, R. Flores, and F. Flores. The action workflow approach to workflow management technology. In *Proceedings of ACM 1992 Conference on Computer Supported Cooperative Work*, pages 281–288, November 1992.

21. N.H. Minsky. The imposition of protocols over open distributed systems. *IEEE Transactions on Software Engineering*, February 1991.

22. N.H. Minsky. Establishing accounting principles as invariants of financial systems. In *Proc. of the Fourth International IFIP TC-11 WG 11.5 Conference on Integrity and Internal Control in Information Systems, Brussels, Belgium*, November 2001. (available from http://www.cs.rutgers.edu/~minsky/pubs.html).

23. N.H. Minsky and V. Ungureanu. Law-governed interaction: a coordination and control mechanism for heterogeneous distributed systems. *TOSEM, ACM Transactions on Software Engineering and Methodology*, 9(3):273–305, July 2000. (available from http://www.cs.rutgers.edu/~minsky/pubs.html).

24. T. Murata and A. Borgida. Handling of irregularities in human centered systems: A unified framework for data and processes. *IEEE Transactions on Software Engineering*, 26(10):959–977, October 2000.

25. B. Schneier. *Applied Cryptography*. John Wiley and Sons, 1996.

26. C. Serban, X. Ao, and N.H. Minsky. Establishing enterprise communities. In *Proc. of the 5th IEEE International Enterprise Distributed Object Computing Conference (EDOC 2001), Seattle, Washington*, September 2001. (available from http://www.cs.rutgers.edu/~minsky/pubs.html).

27. C. Serban and N.H. Minsky. Using java as a language for writing lgi-laws. Technical report, Rutgers University, July 2002.

28. L.A. Suchman. *Plans and Situated Actions: The Problem of Human-Machine Communication*. Cambridge University Press, 1987.

29. V. Ungureanu and N.H. Minsky. Establishing business rules for inter-enterprise electronic commerce. In *Proc. of the 14th International Symposium on DIStributed Computing (DISC 2000); Toledo, Spain; LNCS 1914*, pages 179–193, October 2000. (available from http://www.cs.rutgers.edu/~minsky/pubs.html).

30. W.M.P. van der Aalst, P. Barthelmess, C.A. Ellis, and J. Wainer. Proclets: a framework for lightweight interacting workflow processes. *International Journal of Cooperative Information Systems*, 10(4):443–481, 2001.

Collecting and Querying Distributed Traces of Composite Service Executions

Marie-Christine Fauvet[1]*, Marlon Dumas[2], and Boualem Benatallah[1]

[1] School of Computer Science & Engineering, The University of New South Wales
Sydney NSW 2052, Australia
`fauvet@imag.fr, boualem@cse.unsw.edu.au`
[2] Centre for Information Technology Innovation, Queensland University of Technology
GPO Box 2434, Brisbane QLD 4001, Australia
`m.dumas@qut.edu.au`

Abstract. The development of new Web services by composition of existing ones is becoming a widespread approach to realise business-to-business collaborations. The composite services obtained in this way are then eventually used in other compositions. Given the dynamic nature of the Web, this recursive composition of services rapidly leads to intricate dependencies between them. On the other hand, businesses need to track the executions of their composite services in order to ensure explainability in case of failure and to support decision making. This paper deals with the issue of tracing composite service executions over the Web. It describes a model and an XML representation of service execution traces, an approach for collecting and storing these traces in a distributed environment, and an approach to evaluate queries over distributed repositories of traces.

1 Introduction and Motivation

The connectivity generated by the Internet is re-shaping the way organisations architect their collaborations with other organisations, as well as their interactions with their customers. Organisations of all sizes are profiting of this connectivity to form online alliances by inter-connecting their services for the purpose of providing one-stop shops to their customers.

In this setting, the idea of developing new services by composition of existing ones is becoming the keystone of the next generation of Internet systems. A service is seen as an abstraction of a set of activities involving a number of resources (e.g., data sources, application programs, business processes), intended to fulfil a class of customer needs or business requirements. In order to satisfy complex needs, services are inter-connected among them, thereby forming *composite services*. Examples of composite services include a travel management service combining flight and accommodation booking services, or an account aggregation service that integrates banking, tax declaration, and financial services.

In order to satisfy current users and to attract new customers, organisations need to pay special attention to the quality of their services. In particular, they need to trace

---

* On leave from LSR-IMAG, University of Grenoble, France.

R. Meersman, Z. Tari (Eds.): CoopIS/DOA/ODBASE 2002, LNCS 2519, pp. 373–390, 2002.

executions of these services in order to ensure explainability in case of failure or auditing, as well as to support decision-making aimed at improving the structure and dynamics of the services. These traces of ongoing and past executions of services provide the information required to answer queries for the following purposes (among others):

Customer feedback: to explain specific failures. A query in this context would be *"Retrieve the traces of all executions that have been triggered for a given client"*.

Quality assessment: to detect services whose executions tend to fail, like for example in *"Retrieve the executions of a given service that have been stalled since more than 30 minutes"* or to make a report on past service executions as in *"Retrieve the components of a composite service whose executions take the most time on average"*.

Monitoring and control: to adapt the service to the actual requirements by identifying, in the context of a given service, some patterns of its component executions. An example would be *"In how many executions of the service S, the execution sequence of the service A, then B and finally C has been observed?"*. Also, the ongoing execution of a service could be adapted *on the fly* by analysing what has happened so far. For example, the choice of which component to trigger at a given point of an execution, could be based on information extracted from the traces of the composite service.

Audit: to conduct routine or ad-hoc checks involving the executions of a service, like for example when validating the bills issued by the providers of a service.

This paper presents a framework for the collection and management of traces about either past or ongoing executions of composite services. The proposed framework includes: (i) a generic model of traces of composite services; (ii) a concrete representation of traces in XML; (iii) an approach to collect and store these traces in a distributed environment; and (iv) a method for evaluating queries over these traces. The framework addresses the following issues:

- The traces are distributed: querying the traces of a service's executions may therefore require multiple sub-queries to be sent to the providers who have hosted the execution of the component services. This issue is different to the one addressed by classical approaches in the context of distributed query processing. These approaches typically rely on a centralised knowledge of the meta-data describing the topology of the network where the data are distributed. In contrast, the partitioning of the execution traces across service providers can only be incrementally discovered when browsing the traces themselves.

- The number of providers can be large and continuously changing: the provider of a component within a composite service may be dynamically selected based on various factors. As a result, the service providers involved in a composite service varies from one execution to another. In addition, providers of component services may join and leave a composite service at any time.

- The traces are heterogeneous: although conforming to a common generic interface, each provider will offer its own service interfaces, with a different set of states and observation points than those of other providers. This means in particular that traces must be treated as semi-structured data, which motivates the choice of XML.

The rest of the paper is organised as follows. Section 2 introduces the basic concepts of the proposed framework. Section 3 deals with the collection of traces represented in

XML. In section 4 we discuss and illustrate the evaluation of queries in a distributed environment. Finally, section 5 compares the proposal with similar or complementary ones, while section 6 concludes.

2 Design Overview

In this section we introduce the framework that we adopt for service composition and execution, and for querying traces. In order to ensure a broad applicability, this framework is intended to be independent of specific service implementation technologies (e.g., J2EE, .Net), service description languages (e.g., WSDL) and service registration and discovery infrastructures (e.g., UDDI).

2.1 Service Composition

We distinguish between *elementary* and *composite* services. Elementary services are pre-existing or native services that should be treated as black boxes from the perspective of other services or application programs. A composite service is an aggregation of other (either composite or elementary) services, which are referred to as its *component services*. At a very abstract level, a composite service is modelled as a graph whose nodes are labelled with invocations to the component services. The edges between these nodes capture data and control-flow dependencies. Control-flow dependencies determine which nodes (if any) need to be entered after the service invoked by a given node completes its execution. Control-flow dependencies also establish timing constraints, signal sending and processing, etc. Data-flow dependencies on the other hand determine the data items that must be passed from one node to another when a control-flow link is taken.

Each node in a composite service is associated to an organisational entity which is responsible for handling the service invocation associated to that node. The organisational entity associated with a node can be either an individual provider or a community of providers. In the former case, the designated provider is responsible for executing all the instances of this service. It may eventually partially or totally delegate the execution of these instances to another provider, but this delegation is hidden to the users of the composite service. On the other hand, a community of providers will systematically and transparently delegate the execution of a service to its members. This delegation is carried out by the *representative* of the community, which effectively acts as a service broker. The means by which a community's representative chooses a member to execute a request, is specified via a selection policy [1].

One way of concretely describing the control and data-flow dependencies of a composite services is to use an existing process modelling language, and especially, one of those that have proven to be suitable for workflow specification. There are numerous workflow specification languages based upon different paradigms. In fact, each commercial Workflow Management System implements its own specification language, with little effort being done to provide some degree of uniformity between products. In this respect, the Workflow Management Coalition [5] has defined a set of glossaries and notations that encompass some of the constructs used in existing workflow specification languages. Unfortunately, this standardisation effort has not yet led to a standard language for process modelling, which could be applied for the specification of control and data-flow within a composite service. Recently, WSFL[1], XLANG[2], and the ebXML Business Process Specification Schema (BPSS)[3] have been proposed as candidate languages for this purpose. At present, standardisation efforts are underway based on these proposals, but no consensus has been reached yet.

For the purpose of this paper and to keep the model general enough, we choose to specify control and data-flow dependencies using statecharts [9]: a widely used formalism in reactive systems which has been integrated into the Unified Modelling Language (UML) [17]. Statecharts offer constructs for modelling sequence, loops, branching, concurrent threads, and communication between threads based on signals. Since these are the basic concepts found in most process specification languages, we expect that our results can be adapted to other composition languages such as WSFL, XLANG, and BPSS.

The statechart in Figure 1 specifies the control-flow dependencies of a composite service S. S1 and S2 are invoked first and executed in parallel. When both finish, either S3 or S4 is executed according to the condition C. Then S5 is finally executed.

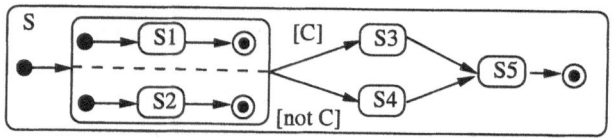

Fig. 1. Control-flow statechart of a composite service.

2.2 System Architecture

The basic entities of the framework architecture are "wrappers", "schedulers" and "multiplexers". The entities are described in turn below.

Wrappers. A provider of a service has to supply a *wrapper*. The wrapper of a service ensures that a native service can be invoked regardless of its underlying data model, message format and interaction protocol. For this purpose, a service's wrapper handles (among other things) data conversion between the data model of the service interface and that of its implementation [1]. Other issues that wrappers can address include security management and protocol heterogeneity. In our tracing model, the service wrapper is also responsible for recording facts about each execution of the wrapped service. These facts are stored locally by the wrapper in a repository of traces and made available through a query interface as discussed later in the paper.

Schedulers. The provider of a composite service hosts a *composite service scheduler* for that service. Interactions among components of a composite service are implemented by a *composite service scheduler* (a scheduler in short). A scheduler is responsible for orchestrating the executions of the composite service by triggering the executions of

[1] http://www-3.ibm.com/software/solutions/webservices/pdf/WSFL.pdf

[2] http://www.gotdotnet.com/team/xml_wsspecs/xlang-c

[3] http://www.ebxml.org

the component services according to the control-flow dependencies associated with the composite service. The scheduler is also responsible for handling and processing data according to the data-flow dependencies encoded within the statechart.

The scheduler of a composite service can be either located in a central location (the *centralised orchestration approach*) or implemented as a set of distributed processes that cooperate in a peer-to-peer manner (the *P2P orchestration approach*). In the centralised approach, the scheduler of a composite service S is implemented as a single software module as in [11], [2] and [21]. This scheduler is responsible for initiating the execution of the components of S according to the control-flow statechart associated with S. To do so, the scheduler of S invokes each of the components of S according to the control-flow dependencies of the composite service.

In the P2P approach, the scheduler is implemented as a collection of software modules communicating with each other directly as in [16], [7] and [4]. Each participant in a composite service hosts one of these software modules, that we call a *local scheduler* in the sequel. On the other hand, the provider of the composite service hosts another software module that we call the *global scheduler*. When the global scheduler receives a request to start an execution, it sends messages to the local schedulers of those participants that need to start their executions in the first place. Each of these local schedulers invokes the underlying service through its wrapper, waits until the execution resulting from this invocation is completed, and when this happens, it sends a message to the local schedulers of those participants that need to be executed next according to the control-flow dependencies of the composite service. These peer-to-peer exchanges between local schedulers continues until eventually one of the local schedulers indicates to the global scheduler that the overall composite service execution has completed. A more detailed description of this model and its implementation can be found in [1].

Query multiplexers. Each service provider hosts a software module call the *query multiplexer*, which is responsible for: (i) receiving a query from a requester and pre-processing it, (ii) identifying the eventual sub-queries and if any, (iii) dispatching them to the corresponding providers, (iv) receiving the sub-results for the providers, (v) merging local and remote results, and finally, (vi) sending back the overall result to the requester. The features of the query multiplexer are detailed and illustrated in section 4.

3 Modelling, Representing, and Collecting Traces

3.1 Modelling Traces

Simplifying assumptions. For the sake of simplicity, we assume that the wrapper and the scheduler of a composite service share a common time line. This can be achieved using well-known clock synchronisation protocols such as NTP [10]. We also assume that all temporal values (time instants, durations and intervals), are expressed at the same level of granularity (e.g., at the granularity of the minute or of the second). Under this assumption, instants and durations are unambiguously represented as integers, while an interval is represented as a pair of integers corresponding to its bounds.

Life cycle of a service instance. Throughout its life cycle, a service execution goes through a series of statuses. The following statuses are predefined by the tracing model:

enabled, *running*, *stalled*, *completed*, and *cancelled*. These predefined statuses can be specialised (or refined) by a given service provider in order to accommodate application specific semantics. For example, the provider of a service "Currency Converter" can declare that a service specialises the status "running" into 3 sub-statuses: *getting data*, *processing data*, and *displaying results*. When an execution of this service is in the "running" status, in can be in either of these three sub-statuses as well.

Every service is associated to a *life cycle statechart*[4] that models the possible statuses through which the executions of this service can go, and the possible transitions between these statuses. The transitions of this statechart are labelled with the events that fire them. These events can be internal to the service execution (e.g., the service starts running), or external (e.g., the user sends a cancellation message). In both cases, an event occurrence within an execution is processed by the wrapper of the service, which determines which transition in the life cycle statechart needs to be fired (if any), and records the new status in the trace of the service execution.

The *standard life cycle statechart* defined by the tracing model is depicted in Figure 2. When an execution of a service is started, it enters the running status. While on this status, the service can be suspended due to an external request, or stalled because a resource required for the service execution is temporarily unavailable. This is notified to the wrapper through an event *stall*. From the *stalled* status, the service instance can subsequently either move back to the running state or to the cancelled status. From the running status, it can move either to the completed status or to the cancelled one.

The states of this statechart can be refined by a given service provider in order to incorporate application-specific statuses, transitions, and events. For example, the "running" service of the standard life cycle statechart can be refined into a statechart with 3 states connected in sequence: *getting data*, *processing data*, and *displaying results*.

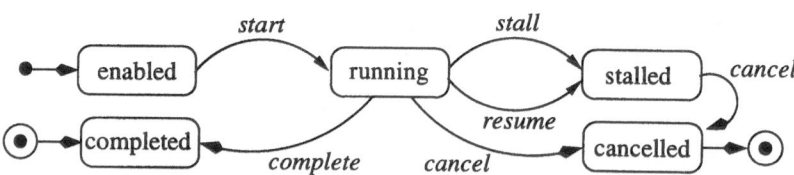

Fig. 2. A statechart modelling the life cycle of a service execution.

The tracing model does not impose any explicit relationship between the life cycle of a composite service and those of its components. For example, a composite service execution can very well be in the "running" status even if one or several of its components are in a "stalled" status. When an execution of a component service reaches a particular status, if any change of status has to be propagated to the composite service execution, a notification message is sent to the wrapper of the composite service, who determines whether a change of status at the composite service level is required.

Status history. A status history is a log of the life cycle of a service execution, that is, the statuses through which this execution went through, and the times of the transitions.

---

[4] The life cycle statechart is not to be mistaken with the control-flow statechart of a composite service (see section 2.1), which determines the order in which its components are triggered.

At an abstract level a status history is defined as a function from a set of instants to a set of status values. At a concrete level a status history is represented by an ordered set of interval-timestamped statuses. For example, the status history [<[3..3], enabled>, <[4..7], running>, <[8..8], completed>] indicates that the execution was enabled at instant 3, then it ran from instant 4 to instant 7 before being completed at instant 8.

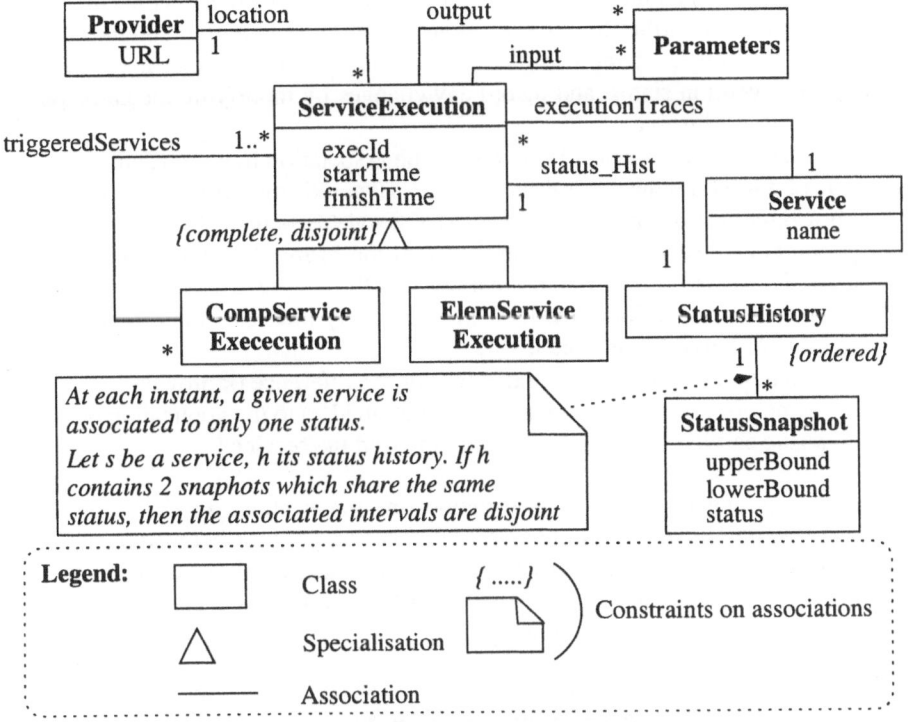

Fig. 3. UML class diagram for service execution traces.

Trace of a service execution. The trace of a service execution, whether elementary or composite, includes (i) a status history; (ii) a set of effective input and output parameters; and (iii) the location of the provider to whom the service execution was dynamically assigned. A composite service execution trace has an additional property modelling the set of other service executions that it triggered (i.e. its triggered components).

The UML class diagram in Figure 3 describes the data model for service execution traces. In this diagram, the main class is ServiceExecution, whose instances model traces of service executions. This class has two sub-classes: one for composite services and the other for elementary services. The status history associated to a service execution is modelled as a set of snapshots, each of which associates an interval (upper and lower bound) with a status.

3.2   Collecting Traces

The responsibility to trace the executions of a composite service S is distributed across the wrappers of this service (as many wrappers as actual providers for the component services). The wrapper of a service S is responsible for:

- Creating and instantiating an object of the class ServiceExecution. This involves generating an identifier for the execution, and recording the start and the end times.
- During the course of the execution, processing any events that may change the current execution status, and record any changes by modifying the corresponding object's status history.
- If S is a composite service, instantiating the association triggeredComponents: for each of the component services that are triggered, the wrapper of S must obtain a reference to an object of the class ServiceExecution from the wrapper of the component service. Such reference is of the form: <provider's url>/<service name>/<execution id> is the identifier locally assigned by the provider of the component service. The provider's URL uniquely identifies the repository where the value of the object is stored.
- At the end of the service execution, returning the reference (<provider's url>/<service name>/<execution id> where <execution id>) to the application program or composite service wrapper that initially invoked the service S.

Hence, a wrapper is responsible for collecting traces about the execution it is supervising, and passing the resulting object reference to whoever initiated the execution. The tracing model defines two alternative approaches for collecting the object references from the component service wrappers: one for the centralised orchestration model, and one for the peer-to-peer orchestration model.

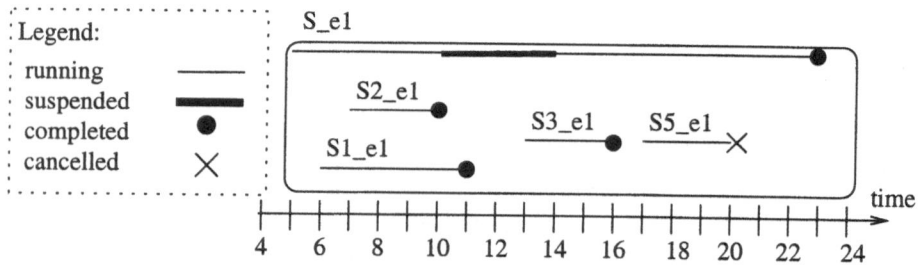

Fig. 4. An execution scenario for the service S.

To illustrate the two approaches to trace collection, let us consider again the service S depicted in Figure 1. Figure 4 describes an execution scenario where service S is executed. This execution is identified by S_e1. The execution e1 of service S started at time 5. It ran until time 10 (excluded) before being stalled from 10 to 14 (excluded). Then, the execution resumed and ran again from 14 to 23 (excluded) before being completed at time 23. The execution e1 of the component S1 was triggered at time 6; it ran until 11 (excluded) and completed at 11. We assume that S_e1 could complete even that S5_e1 has been cancelled. Such a recovery mechanism has to be implemented in S itself.

Given the execution S_e1 shown in Figure 4, Table 1 shows message passing between the central scheduler and the wrappers in the case of a centralised orchestration approach, while Table 2 shows message passings in the case of peer-to-peer orchestration approach. In both tables, the columns Sender and Recipient identify either wrappers or schedulers, while the column Message content shows information exchanged for the purpose of tracing only. A symbol of the form X_e1 (X ∈ {S1, S2, S3, S4, S5}) denotes an instance of the class ServiceExecution corresponding to an execution of service X. For example, the object X_e1 is created by the wrapper of X at the beginning of the execution e1.

Table 1. Messages between the central scheduler and the component services' wrappers during the execution of S_e1 (centralised orchestration model)

Time	Sender	Recipient	Message Content
10	S2_e1	S_e1	www.prov1.com.au/S2/e1.xml
11	S1_e1	S_e1	www.prov1.com.au/S1/e1.xml
16	S3_e1	S_e1	www.prov2.com.au/S3/e1.xml
20	S5_e1	S_e1	www.prov3.com.au/S5/e1.xml

Table 2. Messages between global and local schedulers during the execution of S_e1 (peer-to-peer orchestration model)

Time	Sender	Recipient	Message Content
10	S2_e1	S3_e1, S4_e1	{www.prov1.com.au/S2/e1.xml}
11	S1_e1	S3_e1, S4_e1	{www.prov1.com.au/S1/e1.xml}
16	S3_e1	S5_e1	{www.prov1.com.au/S2/e1.xml, www.prov1.com.au/S1/e1.xml, www.prov2.com.au/S3/e1.xml}
20	S5_e1	S_e1	{www.prov1.com.au/S2/e1.xml, www.prov1.com.au/S1/e1.xml, www.prov2.com.au/S3/e1.xml, www.prov3.com.au/S5/e1.xml}

The 1st and 2nd lines of table 2 can be read as follows. At time 10 (respectively 11) S2's wrapper (respectively S1) sends its trace identifier in the form of a reference to a repository to both S3'wrapper and S4's wrapper. Because the boolean expression [C] evaluates to true, S4 is not required to be executed, so the local scheduler of the state that labelled S4 discards the collection of references that were sent to it by the local schedulers of S1 and S2. When S3 finishes (3rd line), its wrapper sends the collection of references that it has received so far, augmented with its own reference. The wrapper of S3 on the other hand does keep these collections of references and starts the an execution of S3. When this execution competed (3rd line of table 2), the wrapper of S3 sends to the wrapper of S the collection of references that it received from S1, merged with that received from S2, and augmented with its own reference to an object of the class ServiceExecution. At the end, as shown in the 4th line, the wrapper of S (through its associated global scheduler) receives all references to repositories describing the traces for S_e1 triggered components and populates its own repository based on them. A detailed description of the trace collection method can be found in [7].

3.3   XML Representation for Traces

A trace of a service's execution trace is represented as an XML [23] document supplied by the provider who has hosted the service execution. The provider's URL combined with the document name and the service execution id is used as an URI (Universal Resource Identifier) to locate the service execution trace.

The choice of XML as a language for externally representing and exchanging traces is mainly motivated by two reasons:

- Although conforming to a common generic interface, each provider will offer its own service interfaces with a different set of states and observation points than those of other providers. XML provides mechanisms (e.g. namespaces and mixed elements) to deal with this form of controlled heterogeneity.
- The traces are intended to be exchanged between different sites both during service execution and during trace querying. The use of XML enables service providers to internally store these traces using (e.g.) relational databases, and to dynamically translate them to and from XML using well-known tools.

The structure of XML documents is directly derived from the class diagram depicted in Figure 3. Given the execution scenario depicted in Figure 4, the XML document below contains sample data collected during the execution of services that have been hosted by the provider foo.com.au:

```
<traces>
  <serviceExecution name="S" execId="e1" loc="www.foo.com.au/S/e1.xml">
    <time start="5" finish="23"/>
    <inputs> <input name="X" value="100"></input> </inputs>
    <outputs>
      <output name="Y" value="20"></output>
      <output name="Z" value="500"></output>
    </outputs>
    <triggeredComponents>
      <serviceExecution name="S1" execId="e1" loc="www.prov1.com/S1/e1.xml"/>
      <serviceExecution name="S2" execId="e1" loc="www.prov1.com/S2/e1.xml"/>
      <serviceExecution name="S3" execId="e1" loc="www.prov2.com/S3/e1.xml"/>
      <serviceExecution name="S5" execId="e1" loc="www.prov3.com/S5/e1.xml"/>
    </triggeredComponents>
    <statusHistory>
      <statusSnapshot status="running" lowerBound="5" upperBound="9"/>
      <statusSnapshot status="suspended" lowerBound="10" upperBound="13"/>
      <statusSnapshot status="running" lowerBound="14" upperBound="22"/>
      <statusSnapshot status="completed" lowerBound="23" upperBound="23"/>
    </statusHistory>
  </serviceExecution>
  <serviceExecution> ....
</traces>
```

As discussed earlier, the provider of a service has the right to specialise the predefined statuses by defining sub-statuses (e.g., defining sub-statuses of the status "running"). These sub-statuses can appear in the traces of a service execution within sub-snapshots of the snapshots involving predefined statuses. This approach is similar to the one discussed in [20]. For example, if we assume that the composite service S defines 3 sub-statuses of the status "running", namely "searching", "displaying" and "booking", then the XML elements representing snapshots involving the "running" status, can have children elements representing sub-snapshots involving these 3 sub-statuses. Hence, the italicized line in the XML code above could then be refined as follows:

```
<statusSnapshot status="running" lowerBound= 5 upperBound= 9>
    <subSnapshot substatus = "searching" lowerBound = 5 upperBound = 6/>
    <subSnapshot substatus = "displaying" lowerBound = 7 upperBound = 8/>
    <subSnapshot substatus = "booking" lowerBound = 9 upperBound = 9/>
</statusSnapshot>
```

4 Querying Traces

This section describes and illustrates a mechanism to split a query on the execution traces of a composite service into subqueries to be executed by providers of the (direct and indirect) components of the composite service. The results of these subqueries are then collected and merged in order to build the result of the initial query. Queries are expressed in Quilt query language [3] a dialect of Xquery language [25]. XPath expressions are used as means to navigate through hierarchy of nodes [26].

4.1 Towards a Query Multiplexer

The query multiplexer of a service provider is responsible for processing queries regarding all the execution traces hosted by that provider. The scope of the queries that the query multiplexer of a provider P can handle is modelled as a tree. The root of this tree contains an XML document with a sequence of elements serviceExecution, describing all the service executions hosted by the provider P (see Section 3.3). A node other than the root contains an XML document with a single element serviceExecution describing an execution hosted by another provider than P, and linked to upper nodes through the "composite service–component service" relationship. An edge of the tree therefore models the invocation of a service: an edge from a node n1 to another n2 denotes the fact that the service execution described in n2 was triggered in the context of the (composite service) execution described in node n1.

At an abstract level this tree can be seen as a single XML document that contains the data required to answer any query related to the services hosted by P, at any level of detail. This abstract representation is obtained by replacing the elements serviceExecution in the root, with the contents of the XML file referenced in the attribute loc (see section 3.3). This expansion mechanism has to be recursively carried out starting from the root node, every time that the element serviceExecution is encountered . This mechanism is similar to the one implemented by XInclude [24]. In the sequel, we call the document obtained by expansion, *traces.xml*.

From the user's point of view, queries are processed on the abstract document *traces.xml*. For efficiency reasons and given that this "abstract" document is a continuously evolving view, the document is not built a priori and stored in a central location. Instead, when a query is submitted to the multiplexer, it is locally analysed and split into multiple subqueries. The result of this analysis is an XML document that contains tags indicating for each subquery the provider responsible for its execution. Each subquery is then sent to the corresponding provider whose query multiplexer in turn processes it and returns a result. When the results of all subqueries have been received, they are merged with the main result to produce the final output. This mechanism is carried out recursively each time that a subquery involves distributed traces. Similar mechanisms have been studied in the context of distributed query processing [13]. However, classical approaches in this area rely on a centralised knowledge of the topology of the network where the data are distributed. In contrast, the partitioning of the traces across the service providers is only discovered when browsing the traces.

Our splitting and merging mechanisms are formalised below. We adopt the following notations: Q is the set of queries (expressed in Xquery), X is the set of XML documents, and P is the set of service providers. T1 $\longrightarrow$ T2 stands for the type of all functions with domain T1 and range T2. {T} denotes the type of sets of T. $\langle$ T1, T2, ... , Tn$\rangle$ designates the type of tuples whose i^{th} component is of type Ti ($1 \leq i \leq n$).

The multiplexer procedure for a query q (q $\in$ Q) on an abstract root XML document d (d $\in$ D), is captured by two functions Split^d and Merge^d defined below:

Split^d: Q $\longrightarrow$ $\langle$ {$\langle$P, Q$\rangle$}, Q $\rangle$
/* $\langle$ $\langle$ p$_n$, q$_n$ $\rangle$, main$\rangle$ $\in$ Split^d(q) $\iff$ *the provider* p$_n$ *is responsible for processing* q$_n$ *according to the document* d, *and returning the result.* main *is the XML document which contains tags indicating for each subquery the provider who is responsible for.* */

Merge^d: $\langle$ { X }, X $\rangle$ $\longrightarrow$ X
/* Merge^d (Split^d (q)) *is the XML document resulting from* q *processed on* d. */

Roughly speaking, the Split operator analyses the query given as parameter, and detects whether there is any navigation expression in this query containing the element trigerredComponents followed immediately by the element serviceExecution. If such a navigation expression is found, this means that the query must be split and executed in a distributed fashion. Accordingly, the Split operator evaluates the navigation expression up to (and including) the leftmost occurrence of the element trigerredComponents. This yields a collection of invocations to component services. The operator Split then retrieves the providers to which these invocations where assigned (through the provider attribute), and associates to each of them a query containing the rest of the navigation path (after the leftmost occurrence trigerredComponents), as well as any part of the original query involving a variable bound to the considered navigation expression.

The Merge operator on the other hand, performs embeds the query outputs that are given to it as parameter, into the output of the locally evaluated part of the query. It then applies any required aggregation function over the resulting document.

This approach is illustrated in Figure 5 and exemplified in the next sub-section.

4.2   Query Examples

The following query illustrates the situation that arises when all the data involved in the query are locally stored by the provider who has received the query request.
Q.1: Query locally processed
For each component triggered in the context of the execution e1 of S, give its name, the Id of its execution instance, and the location where the execution trace is stored.

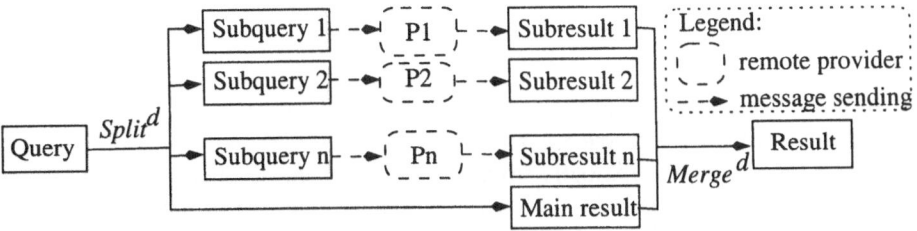

Fig. 5. Querying distributed traces: splitting, dispatching and merging sub-results.

```
For $se in document("traces.xml")/serviceExecution[@name="S" and @execId="e1"]
    /triggeredComponents/serviceExecution
return <serviceExec name=$se/@name execId=$se/@execId loc=$se/@loc/>
```

In this query, the following expressions are used:

- document("traces.xml") is the root node of the document.
- between [and] is a filter: serviceExecution[@name="S" and @execId="e1"] selects elements whose value of the attribute name is S and for the attribute execId is e1.
- / provides access to the children of the current node. Therefore, /serviceExecution locates children of the root node. The result is a set of nodes, each one is an element containing information required by the query.
- the For ... return loop iterates over the set obtained by the previous step. The variable $se denotes a serviceExecution element.
- @ locates attributes of the current node. Therefore, serviceExecution/@name denotes the attribute name for a given serviceExecution element.

The above query is locally processed since it only involves executions that have been locally hosted. According to the XML document of Section 3.3 the result is:

```
<result>
    <serviceExecution name ="S1" execId="e1" loc="www.prov1.com/S1/e1.xml"/>
    <serviceExecution name ="S2" execId="e1" loc="www.prov1.com/S2/e1.xml"/>
    <serviceExecution name ="S3" execId="e1" loc="www.prov2.com/S3/e1.xml"/>
    <serviceExecution name ="S5" execId="e1" loc="www.prov3.com/S5/e1.xml"/>
</result>
```

Q.2: Query involving multiple remote sites

For each component triggered in the context the execution e1 of S, retrieve its name, the IDs of its execution instance its duration, and details about its triggered components (name, execution identifier, and location where the trace has been stored).

```
For $se in document("traces.xml")/serviceExecution [@name="S" and @execID="e1"]
    /triggeredComponents/serviceExecution return
        <service>
            <name> $se/@name </name> <execId> $se/@execId </execId>
            <duration> $se/time/@start - $se/time/@finish </duration>
            <triggeredComponents> $se/triggeredComponents/serviceExecution
```

```
</triggeredComponents>
</service>
```

In the above query, expressions $se/time/@start, $se/time/@finish and $se/triggeredComponents/serviceExecution cannot be executed locally. The scope of this query includes XML documents remotely stored by providers prov1.com (who hosted execution e1 of S1 and e1 of S2), prov2.com (who hosted execution e1 of S3), and prov3.com (who hosted execution e1 of S5). The processing of this query is described below.

- The first step is to split the query into 4 sub-queries, and to execute the main query. This results in an XML document that contains subqueries to be executed remotely and contains for each of them, the URL of the provider who is responsible for its processing. In the sequel we detail only the part of the document dedicated to the service S1:

```
<result> <service>
  <name> S1 </name> <execId> e1 </execId>
  <query> <recipient> www.prov1.com </recipient>
    <queryText> <duration>
      document("S1/e1.xml")/serviceExecution/time/@start
      - document("S1/e1.xml")/serviceExecution/time/@finish
    </duration> </queryText>
  </query>
  <query> <recipient> www.prov1.com </recipient>
    <queryText> <triggeredComponents>
      document("S1/e1.xml")
        /serviceExecution/triggeredComponents/serviceExecution
    </triggeredComponents> </queryText>
  </query>
</service>
...
/* Subqueries related to S2, S3 and S5 are similarly described */
</result>
```

- The second step, consists in sending each subquery to the corresponding provider who executes it and returns the result:

```
Q1: <duration> document("S1/e1.xml")/serviceExecution/time/@start
    - document("S1/e1.xml")/serviceExecution/time/@finish </duration>
to prov1.com
```

whose result is (see Figure 4): <duration> 5 </duration>.

```
Q2: document("S1/e1.xml")
      /serviceExecution/triggeredComponents/serviceExecution
to prov1.com
```

whose result is: <triggeredComponents> <!– empty –> </triggeredComponents> Subqueries related to other services (respectively S2, S3 and S5) are processed similarly except they are sent respectively to prov1.com, prov2.com and prov3.com.

– Finally results received for remote subqueries are merged in order to produce the overall query result:

```
<result>
  <service>
    <name> S1 </name> <execId> e1 </execId> <duration> 5 </duration>
    <triggeredComponents> </triggeredComponents>
  </service>
  <service>
    <name> S2 </name> <execId> e1 </execId> <duration> 3 </duration>
    <triggeredComponents> </triggeredComponents>
  </service>
  <service>
    <name> S3 </name> <execId> e1 </execId> <duration> 3 </duration>
    <triggeredComponents> </triggeredComponents>
  </service>
  <service>
    <name> S5 </name> <execId> e1 </execId> <duration> 3 </duration>
    <triggeredComponents> </triggeredComponents>
  </service>
</result>
```

5 Related Work

The issue of collecting traces of Web service executions is addressed in [18]. The authors present a mechanism for tracking messages exchanged between Web services. Traces are represented as pads added to XML messages. The trace of a composite service execution goes from the first component service to be executed to the last one through all the intermediate components that incrementally enrich the traces with data describing their own execution. At the end, the overall trace is stored by the provider who was responsible for executing the initial component service. This peer-to-peer communication for trace collection is very close to the one proposed in our approach. Unlike the present proposal however, [18] does not address the issue of storing and querying traces in a distributed environment. Instead, the entire trace of a composite service execution is stored in a single site.

The issue of tracing the execution of Web services is closely related to that of work-flow tracing, which has been addressed in [15] and [12]. [15] presents an approach for tracing the execution of workflows expressed as statecharts. Specifically, the authors show that the process of tracing a workflow execution can itself be seen as a workflow. Consequently, by merging a workflow W, with the workflow dedicated to tracing the execution of W, one obtains a "self-traceable workflow". Unlike our proposal however, [15] does not discuss the issue of tracing process executions in a distributed and inter-organisational environment, which is the kind of environment where Web services are typically executed. Also, the work reported in [15] differs from ours in that it does not address the issue of querying the traces of process executions.

In [12] the authors assume that workflows are executed in a distributed environment, and that each node (in our context: each provider) maintains the history of its task executions (in our context: its service executions). Within this context, the authors present several strategies for evaluating queries such as "retrieve the history of a given process instance". In [12], the set of entities participating in the execution of a workflow is assumed to be fixed, whereas our approach caters for runtime provider selection. Our approach also differs from the above one in that we consider traces stored in XML, whereas [12] relies on an object-oriented database supporting OQL.

As discussed in the introduction of this paper, the traces of service executions can be used for different purposes: audit, monitoring, optimisation, etc. In particular, a number of research efforts in the area of workflow management have been directed towards developing techniques for predicting exceptions and preventing deadline expirations by analysing process execution traces (e.g. [8,6]). [8] studies the use of data mining techniques to analyse (centralised) workflow execution logs, in order to predict and prevent exceptions of various kinds, such as deviations from the optimal or acceptable process execution that hinder the delivery of services with the expected quality.

The above discussion is summarised in Table 3. For each approach, the column Collection states whether the trace collection is done through a central scheduler (centralised orchestration) or through peer-to-peer exchanges between the component services (P2P orchestration). The column Storage states whether the storage of the traces is centralised or distributed. The column Querying, when applicable, indicates the querying techniques used by the approach.

Table 3. Comparison of related work on tracing composite service executions

Approach	Collection	Storage	Querying
[8]	N/A	centralised	data mining
[12]	centralised	distributed	OQL
[15]	centralised	centralised	N/A
[14,18]	P2P	centralised	N/A
our approach	centralised/P2P	distributed	Xquery

6   Conclusion

The work reported in this paper addressed the issue of tracing composite services. The main contributions are:

- A data model of traces of composite service executions.
- A representation of these traces in XML.
- Two approaches for collecting execution traces: one with a central scheduler, and one based on P2P interactions.
- An approach to store these traces in a distributed environment.
- An approach to execute queries over these distributed traces.

We have implemented a prototype of the collection and querying approaches. The communications between providers are implemented in Java RMI [22]. The query engine has been built on top of Kweelt [19]: a tool that implements Quilt [3] a dialect of XQuery. The prototype supports most basic XQuery features, although it does not support advanced features such as the closure operator. Ongoing work is being dedicated to generalising the query multiplexer in order to tackle all Xquery expressions, and to design optimisation strategies aimed at minimising communication costs. An example of such optimisation is to group together all the subqueries to be sent to the same provider.

On the other hand efforts are being directed towards designing techniques for analysing traces of past executions in order to perform optimisations and self-tuning both statically and at run-time. In particular, the use of execution traces for run-time provider selection is being studied in the context of the SELF-SERV system [1].

Acknowledgments. We thank the anonymous reviewers of CoopIS'02 for their valuable feedback.

References

1. B. Benatallah, M. Dumas, Q.-Z. Sheng, and A. Ngu. Declarative composition and peer-to-peer provisioning of dynamic web services. In IEEE Computer Society, editor, *Proceedings of ICDE'02 Conference*, San Jose, California, 2002.

2. F. Casati, S. Ilnicki, L.-J. Jin, V. Krishnamoorthy, and M.-C. Shan. Adaptive and dynamic service composition in eFlow. In *Proc. of the Int. Conference on Advanced Information Systems Engineering (CAiSE)*, Stockholm, Sweden, June 2000. Springer Verlag.

3. D. Chamberlin, J. Robie, and D. Florescu. Quilt: an XML query language for heterogenous data sources. In *Proc. of the Workshop on the Web and Databases (WedDB). In conj. with SIGMOD'00*, Dallas - Texas, May 2000. Addison Wesley.

4. Q. Chen and M. Hsu. Inter-enterprise collaborative business process management. In *Proc. of the Int. Conf. on Data Engineering (ICDE)*, Heidelberg, Germany, April 2001.

5. WorkFlow Management Coalition. Terminology and glossary. Technical Report WFMS-TC-1011, Workflow Management Coalition, Brussels – Belgium, 1996.

6. J. Eder, E. Panagos, and M. Rabinovich. Time constraints in workflow systems. In *Proc. of the 11th Conference on Advanced Information Systems Engineering (CAiSE)*, Heidelberg, Germany, 1999.

7. M.-C. Fauvet, M. Dumas, B. Benatallah, and H. Paik. Peer-to-peer traced execution of composite services. In *Proceedings of the International Workshop on Technologies for E-Services (TES 2001). In cooperation with VLDB.*, Roma, Italy, 2001.

8. D. Grigori, F. Casati, U. Dayal, and M.-C. Shan. Improving business process quality through exception understanding, prediction, and prevention. In *Proc. of the 27th VLDB Conference*, Roma, Italy, 2001.

9. D. Harel and A. Naamad. The STATEMATE semantics of statecharts. *ACM Transactions on Software Engineering and Methodology*, 5(4):293–333, October 1996.

10. Internet RFC-1305. Network Time Protocol Specification Version 3. http://www.landfield.com/rfcs/rfc1305.html.

11. N.R. Jennings, T.J. Norman, P. Faratin, P. O'Brien, and B. Odgers. Autonomous agents for business process management. *Journal of Applied Artificial Intelligence*, 14(2):145–189, 2000.

12. P. Koksal, S. Arpinar, and A. Dogac. Workflow history management. *SIGMOD Record*, 27(1), 1998.

13. D. Kossman. The state of the art in distributed query processing. *ACM Computing Surveys*, 32(4), December 2000.

14. V. Machiraju and A. Sahai. A peer-to-peer service interface for manageability. Technical Report HPL-2001-61, Hewlett-Packard Laboratories, 2001. http://www.hpl.hp.com/reports/2001/HPL-2001-61.html.

15. P. Muth, J. Weissenfels, M. Gillmann, and G. Weikum. Workflow history management in virtual enterprises using a light-weight workflow management system. In *Proc. of 9th International Workshop on Research Issues in Data Engineering (RIDE)*, Sydney, Australia, March 1999.

16. P. Muth, D. Wodtke, J. Weissenfels, A.K. Dittrich, and G. Weikum. From centralized workflow specification to distributed workflow execution. *Journal of Intelligent Information Systems*, 10(2), March 1998.

17. J. Rumbaugh, I. Jacobson, and G. Booch. *The Unified Modeling Language Reference Manual*. Addison-Wesley, 1999.

18. A. Sahai, V. Machiraju, J. Ouyang, and K. Wurster. Message tracking in SOAP-based Web services. Technical Report HPL-2001-199, Hewlett-Packard Laboratories, 2001. http://www.hpl.hp.com/reports/2001/HPL-2001-199.html.

19. A. Sahuguet, L. Dupont, and T.-L. Nguyen. Kweelt. http://kweelt.sourceforge.net/.

20. H. Schuster, D. Georgakopoulos, A. Cichocki, and D. Baker. Modeling and composing service-based and reference process-based multi-enterprise processes. In *Proc. of the Int. Conference on Advanced Information Systems Engineering (CAiSE)*, Stockholm, Sweden, June 2000. Springer Verlag.

21. Hans Schuster, Donald Baker, Andrzej Cichocki, Dimitrios Georgakopoulos, and Marek Rusinkiewicz. The collaboration management infrastructure. In *Proc. of the IEEE Int. Conference on Data Engineering (ICDE)*, San Diego CA, USA, February 2000. System Demonstration.

22. Sun Microsystems Inc. Java RMI. http://java.sun.com/products/jdk/rmi.

23. W3C. Extensible Markup Language (XML). http://www.w3.org/XML/.

24. W3C. XInclude. http://www.w3.org/TR/xinclude/.

25. W3C. XML Query. http://www.w3.org/XML/Query.

26. W3C. XPath. http://www.w3.org/TR/xpath20.

An Architecture of a Web-Based Collaborative Image Search Engine

Wei-Cheng Lai[1], Gerard Sychay[2], and Edward Chang[2]

[1] VIMA Technologies, 3944 State Street, Suite #340
Santa Barbara, CA 93105, USA
wlai@vimatech.com
[2] Electrical & Computer Engineering
University of California
Santa Barbara, CA 93106, USA
gerard@cs.ucsb.edu,echang@ece.ucsb.edu

Abstract. We present a *perception-based* paradigm for image retrieval. The central component of this paradigm is a *query-concept learner*, which can learn users' subjective query concepts through an intelligent sampling process. We show that the learner can collect user feedback and use it to perform *collaborative image annotation* in addition to learning subjective query concepts. On the one hand, the improved annotation can help provide better initial keyword-search results to seed perception-based image retrieval. On the other hand, the more effective image-research results can further refine annotation quality. The users of the system collaboratively help improve search quality through the query-concept learner. Our empirical results show that an image retrieval system powered by this perception-based paradigm performs significantly better than traditional systems in search accuracy, in multimodal integration, and in capability for personalization.

Keywords: Active learning, perception-based image retrieval, relevance feedback, image annotation.

1 Introduction

The proliferation of digital cameras and the deployment of broadband infrastructure have drastically increased the multimedia content on the World Wide Web. Searching for multimedia information, however, can be much more challenging than searching for text documents. This is partly because multimedia content can be difficult to articulate, and partly because articulation can be subjective. For instance, it is difficult to describe a desired image fully by using low-level features such as color, shape, and texture, or by keywords alone. Moreover, different users may perceive the same image differently; and even if an image is perceived similarly, users may use different vocabulary (i.e., different combinations of low-level features) to depict it. It is thus necessary to build intelligent search engines

R. Meersman, Z. Tari (Eds.): CoopIS/DOA/ODBASE 2002, LNCS 2519, pp. 391–409, 2002.

that can provide the following two capabilities: *alleviating the need for users to specify complex query concepts*, and *supporting personalized searches.*

For enabling user-friendly query-concept formulation and effective personalized searches in Web-based or large-scale image libraries, this paper presents a *perception-based search paradigm*. A search engine built on such a paradigm can *learn* users' subjective query concepts quickly through an intelligent sampling process. We first present two active learning algorithms, MEGA [10] and SVM_{Active} [48], that we recently developed. We then propose a novel scheme that combines these two algorithms to learn a query concept in a small number of user iterations.

In addition to learning subjective query concepts, our learner can collect user feedback to be used for performing *collaborative image annotation*. For instance, at the end of a "flowers" query, the relevant images can be annotated by the keyword "flower." The confidence level of such a word-image association is measured by the number of users who have "voted" for that association. One advantage is that the improved annotation can help provide better initial keyword-search results to seed perception-based image retrieval. Another advantage is that the more effective image-search results can further help refine annotation quality. The users collaboratively help improve search quality through the query-concept learner.

To make concept-learning, annotation refinement, and image retrieval all effective, efficient and scalable, our architecture employs a multi-resolution image-feature extractor (Section 3.1) and a high-dimensional indexer (Section 3.3), together with some traditional search-engine components— including a crawler and a user interface. Through experimental results, we show that our system performs significantly better than traditional image search engines in search accuracy, in integrating text and perceptual features, and in capability for personalizing multimedia searches.

The rest of the paper is organized as follows: Section 2 discusses related work. In Section 3, we outline the components of our search engine. In Section 4, we describe the collaborative image annotation and refinement schemes. In Section 5, we present the learning algorithm that powers our perception-based image retrieval engine. Section 6 reports experimental results. Our concluding remarks in Section 7 summarize the innovations this research has contributed.

2   Related Work

Typical content-based image retrieval systems such as VIRAGE [29], Columbia VisualSEEk and WebSEEL [47], NEC AMORA [40], and Stanford SIMPLIcity [50] assume that users can provide a "good" example to start a query. This requirement may not be realistic, since if good examples could always be found, then the search engine would not be needed. In addition, these systems assume that similar images possess similar visual features. This restrictive assumption may not be able to model a query concept such as flowers of different kinds that have diversified visual features. Keyword-based image retrieval systems such as Google and Yahoo! suffer from low precision. For instance, a "tiger" query yields not only animals but also baseball team Detroit Tigers, and golf champion Tiger Woods. Our perception-based paradigm uses both content and text to learn query concepts much more thoroughly so that the users' needs can be understood and matched.

The core of our proposed architecture is a query concept learner, which employs intelligent sampling methods to minimize the number of samples required to train a binary classifier (one that separates the objects matching the concept from those do not match). To improve classification accuracy, some researchers have recently proposed a number of ensemble techniques such as *bagging* [4], *arcing* [5], and *boosting* [45,28]. These ensemble schemes enjoy success in improving classification accuracy through reduction in bias or variance, but they do not help reduce the number of samples required to learn a query concept. In fact, most ensemble schemes actually increase learning time because they introduce learning redundancy in an attempt to improve accuracy [20,28,39].

To reduce the number of required samples, researchers in the machine learning community have conducted several studies of active learning for classification. The *query by committee* algorithm [46,23] uses a distribution over all possible classifiers and attempts to greedily reduce the entropy of this distribution. This general-purpose algorithm has been applied in a number of domains (although, to our knowledge, not to the image retrieval domain) using classifiers (such as Naive Bayes classifiers [19,37]) for which specifying and sampling classifiers from a distribution is natural. Probabilistic models such as the Naive Bayes classifier provide interpretable models and principled ways to incorporate prior knowledge and data with missing values. However, they typically do not perform as well as discriminative methods such as SVMs [31,21].

Specifically for image retrieval, the PicHunter system [17,16,15,18] uses Bayesian prediction to infer the goal image, based upon users' input. Mathematically, the goal of PicHunter is to find a single goal point in the feature space (e.g., a particular flower image), whereas our goal is to hunt down all points that match a query concept (e.g., the entire flower category, which consists of flowers of different colors, shapes, and textures, depicted against different backgrounds). Note that the points matching a target concept can be scattered all over the feature space. To find these points quickly with few hints, our project must deal with many daunting challenges.

3 System Architecture

The goal of our image retrieval system is to offer a comprehensive image search capability. First, our system combines the strengths of content-based and text-based techniques to enable multimodal image searches on a large-scale image database. Moreover, our perception-based paradigm uses both content and text to learn individuals' subjective query concepts effectively.

To facilitate a text-based search, this system applies the collaborative image annotation and refinement scheme to assign keywords to images in semi-automatic fashion. In addition, the system supports two other options to start an image query, *query-by-example* and *query-by-nothing*. Users can start a search by providing a keyword, an image, or nothing. The system will make use of such seeding information to generate a set of sample images for user feedback. Once some images relevant to the query concept are found, our perception-based search engine can learn the query concept, search through the image database, and report the most relevant images.

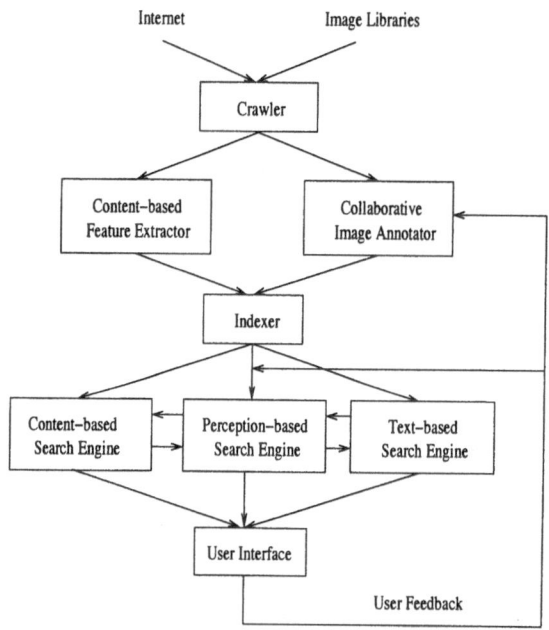

Fig. 1. System Components.

We need several system components to make perception-based image retrieval work. Figure 1 presents the architecture, which consists of eight components: *crawler, collaborative image annotator, content-based feature extractor, indexer, perception-based search engine, content-based search engine, text-based search engine*, and *user interface*.

Not all image search engines employ all eight of those components. The Web sites Google and Yahoo! presently support keyword-only image searches (they do not have the content-based and perception-based components). Some systems such as VisualSEEk [47] can support keyword and content-based image retrieval (they do not the perception-based component). In this section, we briefly describe selected components, including the content-based feature extractor, collaborative image annotator, high-dimensional indexer, perception-based search engine, and content-based search engine. (We omit discussing components that are well understood such as crawler, text-based search engine, and user interface.) In Sections 4 and 5, we will discuss in depth the two core techniques—the image annotation method that powers the image annotator, and a hybrid active learning algorithm that powers the perception-based search engine.

3.1 Content-Based Feature Extractor

Our feature extractor collects perceptual features from images. Common perceptual features include color, shape, texture, and the spatial layout of these features. Feature extraction can be performed off-line; however, since the number of images can be large, feature extraction should be both efficient and effective. In other words, we would like to extract features that can represent images well, and at the same time, keep the extraction time reasonably short.

We have two major types of features [11], color and texture. For color, we have 12 color bins for the 11 culture colors (*black, white, red, yellow, green, blue, brown, purple, pink, orange,* and *gray*) and one outlier bin. We characterize each color with color histograms, color mean (in HSV channels), color variance (in HSV channels), elongation and spreadness. Texture consists of vertical, horizontal and diagonal orientations. For each orientation, we have texture energy mean, variance, elongation and spreadness. This gives us 12 texture features. For each of these, we extract coarse, medium and fine texture features. Altogether, we have 108 color and 36 texture features [48].

3.2 Collaborative Image Annotator

Initial keywords of an image can come from many sources: the text surrounding the image, its filename, and manual annotations. Initial annotations can be incomplete and inaccurate; nevertheless, even low-precision keyword-search results can provide some relevant images to the perception-based engine to bootstrap query-concept learning.

The collaborative annotator collects user feedback during relevance feedback to provide and to refine annotations. The annotator employs the Content-based Soft Annotation (CBSA) algorithm, which annotates images in two stages. In the first stage, CBSA propagates available keywords to unlabeled images using image classifiers [27]. In the refinement stage, CBSA improves the annotation quality through relevance feedback with active learning.

Each image is annotated by CBSA with a label-vector, and each label in the vector is assigned a confidence factor. For instance, each image in a training set is initially labeled with one of K labels such as forest, tiger, sky, and so on. At the end of the CBSA process, each image is annotated with a word vector of K labels.

For instance, an image label-vector ($forest : 0.1, tiger : 0.9, sky : 0.7, \cdots$) means that the image is believed to contain semantics of *forest*, *tiger*, and *sky* with 10%, 90%, and 70% confidence, respectively. When a text-based search is initiated with keywords, images are ranked and retrieved based on their combined confidence factors in the matching labels.

In summary, CBSA consists of the following steps:

1. Manually or semi-automatically labeling a set of training images with some semantic labels. The initial set of labels could be extracted by the keyword extractor or pre-selected by users.
2. Training K classifiers [27]. Based on the labeled instances, we train an ensemble of K SVM binary classifiers. Each classifier assumes the task of determining the confidence factor for a semantic label.
3. Automatically annotating images using an ensemble scheme of the K classifiers. Each classifier assigns each image a confidence factor for the label that the classifier has the responsibility to predict. As a result, a K-nary vector consisting of K-class membership is generated for each image.
4. Refining annotation via active learning. When a keyword-based query is issued, we return some matching images as well as some that are most ambiguous in semantics with respect to the words to solicit user feedback. The feedback is used to retrain the classifier ensemble, and then the ensemble refines the annotation.

The collaborative image-annotation algorithm will be detailed in Section 4.

3.3   High-Dimensional Indexer

An indexer is essential to make both query-concept learning and image retrieval efficient. In addition, to take users' subjectivity into consideration, an indexer must support dynamic feature weighting. To deal with the "dimensionality-curse" problem and to support dynamic feature weighting, we propose an indexing scheme using clustering and classification methods for supporting *approximate similarity searches*. In many applications it is sufficient to perform an approximate search that returns many but not all nearest neighbors [1,14,13,30,34,35]. (A feature vector is often an approximate characterization of an object, so we are already dealing with approximations.) For instance, in content-based image retrieval [22,36,41,47] and document copy detection [6,12,24], it is usually acceptable to overlook a small fraction of the target objects. Thus it is not necessary to incur the high cost of an exact search.

Our indexing method [26] is a statistical approach that works in two steps. It first performs non-supervised clustering using Tree-Structured Vector Quantization (TSVQ) [25] to group similar objects together. To maximize IO efficiency, each cluster is stored in a sequential file. A similarity search is then treated as a classification problem. Our hypothesis is that if a query object's class prediction yields C probable classes, then the probability is high that its nearest neighbors can be found in these C classes. This hypothesis is analogous to looking for books in a library. If we want to look for a calculus book and we know calculus belongs in the math category, by visiting the math section we can find many calculus books. Similarly, by searching for the most probable clusters into which the query object might be classified, we can harvest most of the similar objects.

3.4 Perception-Based Search Engine

The perception-based search engine is the heart of our architecture for supporting personalized image retrieval. The engine learns users' query concepts as if learning a binary classifier that separates the images relevant to the query concept from the irrelevant ones. The learning takes place in an iterative process: The system presents examples to the users to refine the class boundary. The final class boundary is established based on users' relevance feedback.

Relevance feedback is not new. Unfortunately, traditional relevance feedback methods require a large number of training instances to converge to a target concept. In our perception-based engine, we explore several active learning algorithms, which can "grasp" a query profile with a small number of training instances. We recently proposed two active learning algorithms, MEGA (The Maximizing Expected Generalization Algorithm) [10] and SVM$_{Active}$ (Support Vector Machine Active Learning) [48] to tackle the problem effectively. In Section 5 we explain how these two active learning algorithms work, and then we propose a novel technique, which combines the strengths of MEGA and SVM$_{Active}$.

3.5 Content-Based Search Engine

The content-based search engine queries the image database using an image example selected by the user. Given the selected image, this engine finds all similar images based on some appearance criteria such as color, texture, and shape. One limitation of the query-by-example approach is that it cannot capture semantic similarity. Again, this drawback can be overcome by the perception-based search engine. A query-by-example engine is still a useful tool if users just want to find images that "appear" similar to a query image.

4 Collaborative Image Annotation

Many image annotation techniques are based on some sort of propagation. Typically, a subset of images is manually annotated. Then this annotation is propagated to the rest of the set using some machine learning or statistical methods. Picard and Minka [42] use image texture to propagate annotation. After a user labels a patch of an image, this label can be propagated to other images with similar patches of texture. Saber and Tekalp [44] propose extracting objects from an image based on color and edge detection. Their method then matches an object with a set of predefined object templates and, if a match is found, uses the template's annotation for that object. More recently, Barnard and Forsyth [2,3] suggest using statistical learning to associate image segments with words. Once some segments are annotated, an unlabeled segment's annotation can be inferred from some labeled ones.

As pointed out by [51], providing images with some reliable semantic labels and then refining these *unconfirmed* labels via relevance feedback is believed to be an effective approach. CBSA aims to initialize images with a set of semantic words using ensemble schemes such as OPC, PWC, or ECOC. Our empirical study shows that even though the initial annotation may not be perfect, CBSA assists a user to find some relevant images rapidly via a keyword search. Once some relevant images are found, active learning methods (Section 5) can be employed to zoom quickly into the user's query concept. At the same time, user feedback is collected to improve annotation quality. In the rest of this section, we first describe the classifier ensemble we use for performing annotation propagation. We then describe how CBSA refines annotation.

4.1   Content-Based Soft Annotation (CBSA)

Image classification systems work by classifying an image into one of the predefined set of categories. Usually, a confidence score is assigned to each category. The category with the highest score is chosen, and the rest are ignored. In our scheme, we are interested in the scores of *all* categories.

We define a set of N labels where each label characterizes the representative semantics of an image category. Each unannotated image is classified against the N categories using SVM-OPC, and is assigned the categories' confidence probability (converted from the SVM score). The labels of these N categories, along with their probabilities, become the annotation for this image. The probability represents the weight of a label in the overall description of an image. The rationale is that in classifying an image of, say, a landscape with clouds in the sky, the classifier will assign the highest probability to the landscape label and the second highest probability to the clouds label. This ranking can be very useful in retrieval. After an image is annotated, it is associated with an N-ary label-vector. Each element in the label-vector is a keyword, and the value for that element is the weight of the keyword. A typical vector might look like this:

$$\{(landscape, 0.5), (cloud, 0.7), ..., (tiger, 0.9)\}.$$

To convert SVM scores to probability values, we employ Platt's sigmoid fitting [43] to map the SVM outputs into posterior probabilities. Platt suggests that one possible way of fitting probabilities is to use Gaussians to form class-conditional probabilities $p(f|y = \pm 1)$. Bayes' rule can then be used to compute the posterior probability as:

$$P(y = 1|f) = \frac{p(f|y = 1)P(y = 1)}{\sum_{i=-1,1} p(f|y = i)P(y = i)}, \tag{1}$$

where $P(y = i)$ indicates prior probabilities calculated from the training set.

We can also use a parametric model to fit the posterior $P(y = 1|f)$ directly without having to estimate the class-conditional densities $p(f|y)$. According to empirical data, the class-conditional densities between SVM margins are exponential. Bayes' rule from Equation 1 on two exponentials implies that the form of the sigmoid function is

$$P(y = 1|f) = \frac{1}{1 + exp(Af + B)}. \tag{2}$$

This model assumes that the SVM outputs are proportional to the log odds of a positive example. The parameters A and B of Equation 2 are fitted using maximum likelihood estimation from a training set. A and B are obtained by minimizing the negative log likelihood of the sigmoid training data using a model-trust minimization algorithm. The target probabilities are derived from Bayes' rule. Given N_+ positive examples, the target probability for positive examples is

$$t_+ = \frac{N_+ + 1}{N_+ + 2} \tag{3}$$

and for N_- negative examples, the target probability is

$$t_- = \frac{1}{N_- + 2}. \tag{4}$$

We use a fixed sigmoid for all SVM classifiers in our scheme. This sigmoid is chosen so that a highly-confident positive SVM score (greater than 1) will be mapped to a probability value greater than 0.9, whereas a highly-confident negative score (less than -1) has a probability value less than 0.1.

4.2   Annotation Refinement

Initial annotation can be improved through user feedback. CBSA uses *active learning* to perform annotation refinement. (The details of active learning algorithms are described in Section 5.)

Unlike other relevance feedback schemes in which the pool of samples presented for the user to label is the same as the pool of results, CBSA presents two pools: one set of samples for the user to label, and one set of top query results [8,9]. The user conducts a search with one of the three seeding options: by example, by keyword, or by nothing. The search engine returns most uncertain samples via active learning for soliciting user feedback. Relevant images are marked positive; the rest are assumed to be negative. CBSA finds another batch of most uncertain images for user labeling. The process repeats until the user is satisfied with the output in the result pool.

Depending on a query's seeding option, CBSA gets keywords from four sources:

1. Query keywords. The keywords used by the user to start a query, when the query is conducted by using the query-by-keyword option.
2. Keywords associated with the query image. If the query image used in the query-by-example mode has had keywords with high confidence factors, the words can be used.
3. Keywords associated with positively labeled images. The common keywords of the positively labeled instances indicate with high probability that the query concept can be annotated by those words.
4. User input. At the end of a query session, the user can be prompted to enter keywords.

The collected keywords are used by CBSA to annotate the images in the result pool with a factor that depends on both the source confidence and the class prediction confidence. The annotation of an image is refined by the users of the system in a collaborative manner.

5   Active Learning Algorithms

We first examine two active learning algorithms: MEGA and SVM$_{Active}$. In Section 5.3, we will propose a hybrid approach that combines the strengths of MEGA and SVM$_{Active}$.

5.1   MEGA

The first challenge of query concept learning is to find some relevant objects so that the concept boundary can be fuzzily identified. Finding a relevant object can be difficult if only a small fraction of the dataset satisfies the target concept. We can improve the odds with an intelligent sampling method MEGA (The Maximizing Expected Generalization Algorithm), which finds relevant samples quickly, to initialize query-concept learning.

MEGA models query concepts in k-CNF [32], which can formulate virtually all practical query concepts[1]. MEGA uses k-DNF to bound the sampling space from which to select the most informative samples for soliciting user feedback.

Definition 1: k-**CNF**: For constant k, the representation class k-CNF consists of Boolean formulae of the form $c_1 \wedge \cdots \wedge c_\theta$, where each c_i is a disjunction

---

[1] k-CNF is more expressive than k-term DNF, and it has both polynomial sample complexity and time complexity [33,38].

of at most k literals over the Boolean variables $x_1, \ldots, x_n$. (A Boolean variable represents an image feature.) No prior bound is placed on θ.

Definition 2: k**-DNF**: For constant k, the representation class k-DNF consists of Boolean formulae of the form $d_1 \vee \cdots \vee d_\theta$, where each d_i is a conjunction of at most k literals over the Boolean variables $x_1, \ldots, x_n$. No prior bound is placed on θ.

MEGA initializes the query concept-space (QCS) as a k-CNF and the candidate concept-space (CCS) as a k-DNF. The QCS starts as the most specific concept and the CCS as the most general concept. The target concept is more general than the initial QCS and more specific than the initial CCS. The learner learns the QCS, while at the same time refining the CCS to delimit the boundary of the sampling space.

To learn a target concept, the well-known Valiant's algorithm [49] uses positive-labeled instances to refine QCS and negative-labeled instances to refine CCS. The key difference between Valiant's algorithm and MEGA lies in how training samples are selected. Valiant's algorithm employs a random sampling strategy. MEGA makes sure that each sample can be most useful, and hence reduces the number of samples needed to learn a concept by employing dual strategies.

1. Bounding the sample space: Avoid choosing useless unlabeled instances by using the CCS and QCS to delimit the sampling boundary.

2. Maximizing the usefulness of a sample: Choose an example that will remove the maximum expected number of disjunctive terms from QCS. In other words, we choose an example that can maximize the expected generalization of the concept. Even if the example is labeled negative by the user, it can be useful to remove conjunctive terms in the CCS.

It may appear that if we pick an example that has more dissimilar disjunctions (compared to the QCS), we would have a better chance of eliminating more disjunctive terms. This is, however, not true. An example must be labeled by the user as positive to be useful for refining QCS. Unfortunately, an example is less likely to be labeled positive when it has more disjunctions that are dissimilar to the target concept. Therefore, there is a tradeoff between choosing an example that has more contradictory terms and choosing one that is more likely to be labeled positive. The detailed MEGA algorithm is documented in [10].

5.2 SVM$_{Active}$

Once some relevant and some irrelevant samples are marked, we employ SVM$_{Active}$ to refine the class boundary. We add the active learning component to SVMs for selecting the most informative samples to query a user and to quickly refine a boundary that separates data objects that satisfy the user's query concept from the rest of the dataset.

For the purpose of query-concept learning, we consider SVMs in the binary classification setting. We are given training data $\{\mathbf{x}_1 \ldots \mathbf{x}_n\}$ that are vectors in some space $\mathcal{X} \subseteq \mathbb{R}^d$. We are also given their labels $\{y_1 \ldots y_n\}$ where $y_i \in \{-1, 1\}$. In their simplest form, SVMs are hyperplanes that separate the training data by a maximal margin. All vectors lying on one side of the hyperplane are labeled as -1, and all vectors lying on the other side are labeled as 1. The training instances that lie closest to the hyperplane are called *support vectors*. More generally, SVMs allow us to project the original training data in space $\mathcal{X}$ to a higher dimensional feature space $\mathcal{F}$ via a Mercer kernel operator K. In other words, we consider the set of classifiers of the form: $f(\mathbf{x}) = \sum_{i=1}^n \alpha_i K(\mathbf{x}_i, \mathbf{x})$. When $f(\mathbf{x}) \geq 0$ we classify $\mathbf{x}$ as $+1$, otherwise we classify $\mathbf{x}$ as -1.

When K satisfies Mercer's condition [7] we can write: $K(\mathbf{u}, \mathbf{v}) = \Phi(\mathbf{u}) \cdot \Phi(\mathbf{v})$ where $\Phi : \mathcal{X} \to \mathcal{F}$ and "." denotes an inner product. We can then rewrite f as:

$$f(\mathbf{x}) = \mathbf{w} \cdot \Phi(\mathbf{x}), \text{ where } \mathbf{w} = \sum_{i=1}^n \alpha_i \Phi(\mathbf{x}_i). \tag{5}$$

Thus, by using K we are implicitly projecting the training data into a different (often higher dimensional) feature space $\mathcal{F}$. The SVM then computes the α_is that correspond to the maximal margin hyperplane in $\mathcal{F}$. By choosing different kernel functions, we can implicitly project the training data from $\mathcal{X}$ into spaces $\mathcal{F}$ for which hyperplanes in $\mathcal{F}$ correspond to more complex decision boundaries in the original space $\mathcal{X}$. The detailed SVM$_{Active}$ algorithm is documented in [48].

Intuitively, SVM$_{Active}$ works by combining the following three ideas:

1. SVM$_{Active}$ regards the task of learning a target concept as one of learning an SVM binary classifier. An SVM captures the query concept by separating the relevant images from the irrelevant images with a hyperplane in a projected space, usually a very high-dimensional one. The projected points on one side of the hyperplane are considered relevant to the query concept and the rest irrelevant.

2. SVM$_{Active}$ learns the classifier quickly via active learning. The active part of SVM$_{Active}$ selects the most informative instances with which to train the SVM classifier. This step ensures fast convergence to the query concept in a small number of feedback rounds.

3. Once the classifier is trained, SVM$_{Active}$ returns the top-k most relevant images. These are the k images farthest from the hyperplane on the query concept side.

5.3   Pipeline Learning

As discussed in Section 5.2, the SVM$_{Active}$ scheme needs at least one positive and one negative example to start. MEGA is not restricted by this seeding requirement, and it is able to find relevant examples quickly by refining the sampling boundary. It is therefore logical to employ MEGA to perform the *initialization* task. Once some relevant images are found, the refinement step can be executed by either MEGA or SVM$_{Active}$. Thus, we can have three execution alternatives.

1. MEGA only. Use MEGA all the way to learn a concept.
2. SVM$_{Active}$ only. Use random sampling to find the first relevant example(s) and then use SVM$_{Active}$ to learn a concept.
3. Pipeline learning. Use MEGA to find initial relevant objects, and then switch to SVM$_{Active}$ for refining the binary classifier and ranking returned objects.

6   Experiments and Discussion

We implemented both MEGA, SVM$_{Active}$, and CBSA in C, $C++$, and tested using an Intel Pentium III^{TM} workstation running Linux. For our empirical evaluation, we used two real-world image datasets:

- *Twenty-category* set. This data set contains twenty categories where each category consisted of 200 to 300 images. Images for this dataset were collected from Corel Image CDs.
- *Web-based* set. This set consists of nearly $50,000$ images that we crawled from various sites including Yahoo!, eBay, and Google.

We separate our queries into two categories: 5% and 1% queries. The matching images for each of the more specific query concepts such as "purple flowers" and "white bears" account for about 1% of the total dataset. More general concepts such as "bears," "flowers," and "architectures" have about 5% matching images in the dataset. For each experiment, we will report results for these two categories of queries separately.

6.1   Content-Based Soft Annotation Scheme (CBSA)

In our experiments, we used the twenty-category set to evaluate the effectiveness of our content-based annotation scheme. We set up three sets of baselines for evaluating the active learning scheme. For the first set, we assumed no annotation was available, or 0% annotated. In the second set, we assumed 10% were annotated, and in the third second set, 20%. We named these three baselines 0%, 10%, and 20%, keeping them to be used for training CBSA.

We compared three methods of sampling images for labeling:

1. Select the most ambiguous images to label (*active learning*).
2. Select the *top retrieved* results (no active learning).
3. *Randomly* select images to label.

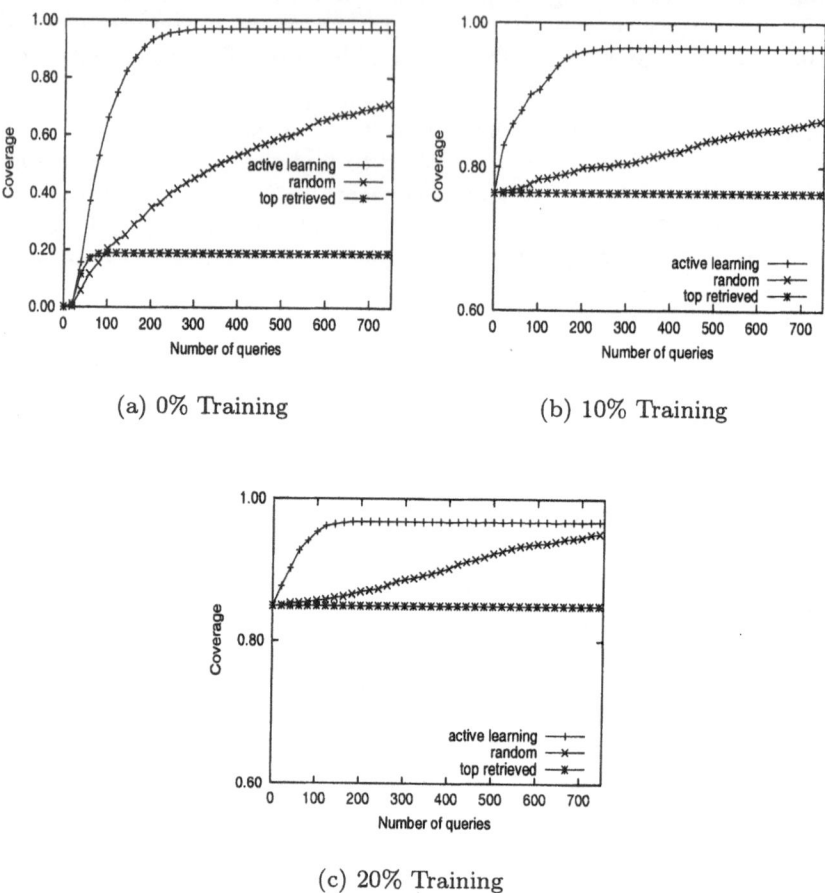

(a) 0% Training

(b) 10% Training

(c) 20% Training

Fig. 2. Annotation coverage over an image set annotated by a (a) 0%, (b) 10%, (c) 20% classifier.

For each image in the data set the category name was the ground truth keyword for that particular image. We defined a metric, *annotation coverage*, as the percentage of images in the entire data set that are correctly labeled. Good annotation coverage will provide good retrieval recall and precision.

In Figures 2 (a-c), we present the percentage of annotation coverage over a number of queries, after the data set has been initially annotated by CBSA with (a) 0%, (b) 10%, and (c) 20% training.

We observed that using active learning to improve annotation proved beneficial in all cases. Without active learning, the coverage progress was slow. With active learning, the coverage improved rapidly. In the 0% case, coverage improved from 0% to over 80% after just 200 queries.

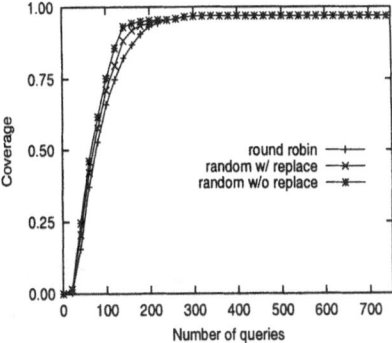

Fig. 3. Three annotation scenarios for 0% active learning. The similarity of results shows that annotation order does not matter.

We could get even better coverage by taking initial annotations from image captions or surrounding text. For example, with 10% initial annotation, we achieved 95% coverage after 200 refinement iterations. For applications that collect annotation automatically from surrounding text such as that from a Web site, the combined approach of classification (for label propagation) and active learning (for label refinement) is very attractive in CBSA.

For each sampling method, we also simulated three annotation scenarios in order to examine their respective performances:

1. Annotate one label at a time in order. We queried each of 20 keywords in a *round-robin* fashion. We did this 50 times for a total of 750 queries.
2. Annotate one label at a time randomly without replacement. We randomly queried each of the 20 keywords until all 20 were used. We did this 50 times for a total of 750 queries.
3. Annotate one label at a time randomly with replacement. We randomly selected a keyword to query, one at a time for 750 times.

Figure 3 shows coverage using active learning for 0% training. We graphed results for each annotation scenario but observed that this did not make a noticeable difference. This means that the annotation improvement is insensitive to the order in which refinement is done. Therefore, we can make the system available to the public and collect users' feedback to refine the annotation online. (Because graphs for 10% and 20% training showed similar results, they are omitted for brevity.)

6.2   MEGA, SVM$_{Active}$, and Pipelining MEGA with SVM$_{Active}$

For top-10 retrieval with 5% matching data (Figure 4(a)), SVM$_{Active}$ clearly outperforms MEGA. The major weakness of SVM$_{Active}$ is in finding the first few

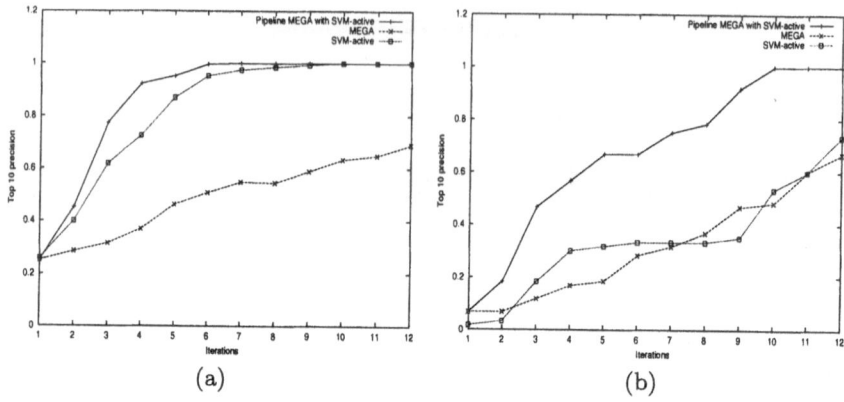

Fig. 4. Precision versus iterations for top-10 retrieval (a) 5% and (b) 1% queries.

positive samples. Such weakness does not seriously affect this experiment, since there is a high probability of finding one of the 5% positive examples through random sampling. For queries with only 1% matching data (Figure 4(b)), such a weakness becomes more significant, because it substantially degrades the performance of SVM_{Active}. Overall, the precision of MEGA and SVM_{Active} is similar for 1% queries.

The hybrid algorithm (pipelining MEGA with SVM_{Active}) clearly outperforms both SVM_{Active} and MEGA. The difference in precision is more significant for queries with 1% matching data than for those with 5% matching data. This trend indicates the strength of the hybrid algorithm in handling more specific query concepts and/or larger datasets.

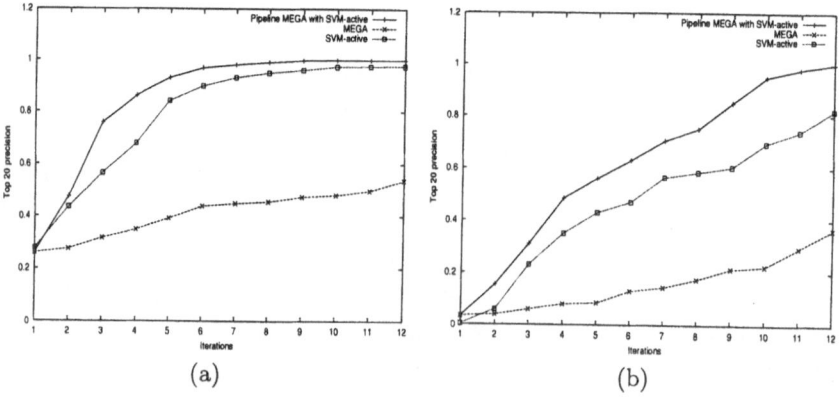

Fig. 5. Precision versus iterations for top-20 retrieval (a) 5% and (b) 1% queries.

For top-20 retrieval (Figures 5(a) and (b)), the precision of the hybrid algorithm remains the highest, followed by SVM_{Active} and MEGA. As expected, the differences in their performances are more significant for queries with 1% matching data than for those with 5% matching data.

7   Conclusion

In this paper we have proposed an image retrieval architecture that employs a perception-based search paradigm [11]. The core of the perception-based search paradigm is the active learning technique that can quickly capture complex, subjective query concepts. We proposed using MEGA followed by SVM$_{Active}$ as our perception-based search engine. Our experimental results show that this hybrid approach outperforms MEGA and SVM$_{Active}$ when they are used separately. In addition to learning query concepts effectively, this method shows that the feedback collected from active learning can be used collaboratively to refine image annotations.

In summary, our proposed architecture combines the strengths of the text-based and content-based image retrieval paradigms. The perception-based search engine provides the critical glue to integrate the two paradigms. Furthermore, it can learn a subjective query concept that cannot be conveyed with a few keywords or a couple of example-images. In addition to making searches more effective, the architecture also contains components that make the system efficient and scalable. We have demonstrated the superiority of our system over traditional systems in terms of personalization, accuracy, and efficiency, through algorithms and prototype implementation [8,9].

References

1. S. Arya, D. Mount, N. Netanyahu, R. Silverman, and A. Wu. An optimal algorithm for approximate nearest neighbor searching in fixed dimensions. *Proceedings of the 5th SODA*, pages 573–82, 1994.
2. K. Barnard and D. Forsyth. Learning the semantics of words and pictures. In *International Conference on Computer Vision*, volume 2, pages 408–415, 2000.
3. K. Barnard and D. Forsyth. Clustering art. In *CVPR*, 2001.
4. L. Breiman. Bagging predicators. *Machine Learning*, pages 123–140, 1996.
5. L. Breiman. Arcing classifiers. *The Annals of Statistics*, pages 801–849, 1998.
6. S. Brin and H. Garcia-Molina. Copy detection mechanisms for digital documents. *Proceedings of ACM SIGMOD*, May 1995.
7. C. Burges. A tutorial on support vector machines for pattern recognition. *Data Mining and Knowledge Discovery*, 2:121–167, 1998.
8. E. Chang, K.-T. Cheng, and L. Chang. PBIR — perception-based image retrieval. *ACM Sigmod (Demo)*, May 2001.
9. E. Chang, K.-T. Cheng, W.-C. Lai, C.-T. Wu, C.-W. Chang, and Y.-L. Wu. PBIR — a system that learns subjective image query concepts. *Proceedings of ACM Multimedia, http://www.mmdb.ece.ucsb.edu/~demo/corelacm/*, pages 611–614, October 2001.

10. E. Chang and B. Li. Mega — the maximizing expected generalization algorithm for learning complex query concepts (extended version). *Technical Report http://www-db.stanford.edu/~echang/mega.pdf*, November 2000.
11. E. Chang, B. Li, and C. Li. Towards perception-based image retrieval. *IEEE Content-Based Access of Image and Video Libraries*, pages 101–105, June 2000.
12. E. Chang, J. Wang, C. Li, and G. Wiederhold. RIME - a replicated image detector for the www. *Proc. of SPIE Symposium of Voice, Video, and Data Communications*, November 1998.
13. P. Ciaccia and M. Patella. Pac nearest neighbor queries: Approximate and controlled search in high-dimensional and metric spaces. *Proceedings of ICDE*, pages 244–255, 2000.
14. K. Clarkson. An algorithm for approximate closest-point queries. *Proceedings of the 10th SCG*, pages 160–64, 1994.
15. I. Cox, J. Ghosn, M. Miller, T. Papathomas, and P. Yianilos. Introduces pichunter, the bayesian framework, and describes a working system including measured user performance. hidden annotation in content based image retrieval. In *IEEE Workshop on Content-Based Access of Image & Video Libraries*, pages 76–81, June 1997.
16. I. Cox, M. Miller, S. Omohundo, and P. Yianilos. Pichunter: Bayesian relevance feedback for image retrieval. In *13th International Conference on Pattern Recognition*, pages 361–369, August 1996.
17. I. Cox, M. Miller, S. Omohundo, and P. Yianilos. Target testing and the pichunter bayesian multimedia retrieval system. In *Proceedings of the Forum on Research & Technology Advances in Digital Libraries*, pages 66–75, 1996.
18. I. J. Cox, M. L. Miller, T. P. Minka, T. V. Papathomas, and P. N. Yianilos. The bayesian image retrieval system, pichunter: Theory, implementation and psychological experiments. *IEEE Transaction on Image Processing (to appear)*, 2000.
19. I. Dagan and S. Engelson. Committee-based sampling for training probabilistic classifiers. In *Proceedings of the Twelfth International Conference on Machine Learning*, pages 150–157. Morgan Kaufmann, 1995.
20. T. Dietterich and G. Bakiri. Solving multiclass learning problems via error-correcting output codes. *Journal of Artifical Intelligence Research*, 2, 1995.
21. S. Dumais, J. Platt, D. Heckerman, and M. Sahami. Inductive learning algorithms and representations for text categorization. In *Proceedings of the Seventh International Conference on Information and Knowledge Management*. ACM Press, 1998.
22. M. Flickner, H. Sawhney, J. Ashley, Q. Huang, B. Dom, M. Gorkani, J. Hafner, D. Lee, D. Petkovic, D. Steele, and P. Yanker. Query by image and video content: the QBIC system. *IEEE Computer*, 28(9):23–32, 1995.
23. Y. Freund, H. Seung, E. Shamir, and N. Tishby. Selective sampling using the Query by Committee algorithm. *Machine Learning*, 28:133–168, 1997.
24. H. Garcia-Molina, S. Ketchpel, and N. Shivakumar. Safeguarding and charging for information on the internet. *Proceedings of ICDE*, 1998.
25. A. Gersho and R. Gray. *Vector Quantization and Signal Compression*. Kluwer Academic, 1991.
26. K. Goh and E. Chang. Indexing multimedia data in high-dimensional and dynamic weighted feature spaces. *The 6th Visual Database Conference (invited paper)*, May 2002.
27. K. Goh, E. Chang, and K. T. Cheng. Svm binary classifier ensembles for image classification. In *Proc. of ACM CIKM 2001*, Nov. 2001.
28. A. Grove and D. Schuurmans. Boosting in the limit: Maximizing the margin of learned ensembles. In *Proc. 15th National Conference on Artificial Intelligence (AAAI)*, 1998.

29. A. Gupta and R. Jain. Visual information retrieval. *Comm. of the ACM*, 40(5):69–79, 1997.
30. P. Indyk and R. Motwani. Approximate nearest neighbors: Towards removing the curse of dimensionality. *Proceedings of the 30th STOC*, pages 604–13, 1998.
31. T. Joachims. Text categorization with support vector machines. In *Proceedings of the European Conference on Machine Learning*. Springer-Verlag, 1998.
32. M. Kearns, M. Li, and L. Valiant. Learning boolean formulae. *Journal of ACM*, 41(6):1298–1328, 1994.
33. M. Kearns and U. Vazirani. *An Introduction to Computational Learning Theory*. MIT Press, 1994.
34. J. M. Kleinberg. Two algorithms for nearest-neighbor search in high dimensions. *Proceedings of the 29th STOC*, 1997.
35. E. Kushilevitz, R. Ostrovsky, and Y. Rabani. Efficient search for approximate nearest neighbor in high dimensional spaces. *Proceedings of the 30th STOC*, pages 614–23, 1998.
36. J. Li, J. Z. Wang, and G. Wiederhold. Irm: Integrated region matching for image retrieval. *Proceedings of ACM Multimedia*, October 2000.
37. A. McCallum and K. Nigam. Employing EM in pool-based active learning for text classification. In *Proceedings of the Fifteenth International Conference on Machine Learning*. Morgan Kaufmann, 1998.
38. T. Michell. *Machine Learning*. McGraw Hill, 1997.
39. M. Moreira and E. Mayoraz. Improving pairwise coupling classification with error correcting classifiers. *Proceedings of the Tenth European Conference on Machine Learning*, April 1998.
40. S. Mukherjea, K. Hirata, and Y. Hara. Amore: A world wide web image retrieval engine. *Proc. World Wide Web*, 2(3):115–132, 1999.
41. A. Natsev, R. Rastogi, and K. Shim. Walruc: A similarity retrieval algorithm for image databases. *Proceedings of ACM Sigmod*, June 1999.
42. R. W. Picard and T. P. Minka. Vision texture for annotation. *Journal of Multimedia Systems*, 3:3–14, 1995.
43. J. Platt. Probabilistic outputs for svms and comparisons to regularized likelihood methods. In *Advances in Large Margin Classifiers*. MIT Press, 1999.
44. E. Saber and A. M. Tekalp. Region-based affine shape matching for automatic image annotation and query-by-example. *Journal of Visual Communication and Image Representation*, 8(1):3–20, Mar. 1997.
45. R. Schapire, Y. Freund, P. Bartlett, and W. Lee. Boosting the margin: A new explanation for the effectiveness of voting methods. In *Proceeding of the Fourteenth International Conference on Machine Learning*. Morgan Kaufmann, 1997.
46. H. Seung, M. Opper, and H. Sompolinsky. Query by committee. In *Proceedings of the Fifth Workshop on Computational Learning Theory*, pages 287–294. Morgan Kaufmann, 1992.
47. J. R. Smith and S.-F. Chang. Visualseek: A fully automated content-based image query system. *ACM Multimedia Conference*, 1996.
48. S. Tong and E. Chang. Support vector machine active learning for image retrieval. *Proceedings of ACM International Conference on Multimedia*, pages 107–118, October 2001.
49. L. Valiant. A theory of learnable. *Proceedings of the Sixteenth Annual ACM Symposium on Theory of Computing*, pages 436–445, 1984.
50. J. Wang, J. Li, and G. Wiederhold. Simplicity: Semantics-sensitive integrated matching for picture libraries. *ACM Multimedia Conference*, 2000.
51. L. Wenyin, S. Dumais, Y. Sun, H. Zhang, M. Czerwinski, and B. Field. Semi-automatic image annotation. In *Proc. of Interact 2001: Conference on Human-Computer Interaction*, pages 326–333, July 2001.

Parallel Processing with Autonomous Databases in a Cluster System

Stéphane Gançarski[1], Hubert Naacke[1], Esther Pacitti[2], and Patrick Valduriez[1]

[1]LIP6, University Paris 6
8, rue du Cap. Scott 75015 PARIS
FirstName.LastName@lip6.fr
[2]Institut de Recherche en Informatique de Nantes
Esther.Pacitti@irin.univ-nantes.fr

Abstract. We consider the use of a cluster system for Application Service Provider (ASP). In the ASP context, hosted applications and databases can be update-intensive and must remain autonomous. In this paper, we propose a new solution for parallel processing with autonomous databases, using a replicated database organization. The main idea is to allow the system administrator to control the tradeoff between database consistency and application performance. Application requirements are captured through execution rules stored in a shared directory. They are used (at run time) to allocate cluster nodes to user requests in a way that optimizes load balancing while satisfying application consistency requirements. We also propose a new preventive replication method and a transaction load balancing architecture which can trade-off consistency for performance using execution rules. Finally, we discuss the on-going implementation at LIP6 using a Linux cluster running Oracle 8i.

1 Introduction

Clusters of PC servers now provide a cheap alternative to tightly-coupled multiprocessors such as Symmetric Multiprocessor (SMP) or Non Uniform Memory Architecture (NUMA). They make new businesses like Application Service Provider (ASP) economically viable. In the ASP model, customers' applications and databases (including data and DBMS) are hosted at the provider site and need be available, typically through the Internet, as efficiently as if they were local to the customer site. Thus, the challenge for a provider is to fully exploit the cluster's parallelism and load balancing capabilities to obtain a good cost/performance ratio. The typical solution to obtain good load balancing in cluster architectures is to replicate applications and data at different nodes so that users can be served by any of the nodes depending on the current load. This also provides high-availability since, in the event of a node failure, other nodes can still do the work. This solution has been successfully used by Web sites such as search engines using high-volume server farms (*e.g.*, Google). However, Web sites are typically read-intensive which makes it easier to exploit parallelism.

R. Meersman, Z. Tari (Eds.): CoopIS/DOA/ODBASE 2002, LNCS 2519, pp. 410–428, 2002.

In the ASP context, the problem is far more difficult. First, applications can be update-intensive. Second, applications and databases must remain autonomous so they can be subject to definition changes to accommodate customer requirements. Replicating databases at several nodes, so they can be accessed by different users through the same or different applications in parallel, can create consistency problems [15], [9]. For instance, two users at different nodes could generate conflicting updates to the same data, thereby producing an inconsistent database. This is because consistency control is done at each node through its local DBMS. There are two main solutions readily available to enforce global consistency. One is to use a transaction processing monitor to control the access to replicated data. However, this requires significant rewriting of the applications and may hurt transaction throughput. A more efficient solution is to use a parallel DBMS such as Oracle Rapid Application Cluster or DB2 Parallel Edition. Parallel DBMS typically provide a shared disk abstraction to the applications [21] so that parallelism can be automatically inferred. But this requires heavy migration to the parallel DBMS and hurts database autonomy.

Ideally, applications and databases should remain unchanged when moved to the provider site's cluster. In this paper, we propose a new solution for load balancing of autonomous applications and databases which addresses this requirement. This work is done in the context of the Leg@Net project[1] sponsored by the RNTL between LIP6, Prologue Software and ASPLine, whose objective is to demonstrate the viability of the ASP model for pharmacy applications in France. Our solution exploits a replicated database organization. The main idea is to allow the system administrator to control the database consistency/performance tradeoff when placing applications and databases onto cluster nodes. Databases and applications can be replicated at multiple nodes to obtain good load balancing. Application requirements are captured (at compile time) through execution rules stored in a shared directory used (at run time) to allocate cluster nodes to user requests. Depending on the users' requirements, we can control database consistency at the cluster level. For instance, if an application is read-only or the required consistency is weak, then it is easy to execute multiple requests in parallel at different nodes. If, instead, an application is update-intensive and requires strong consistency (*e.g.* integrity constraints satisfaction), then an extreme solution is to run it at a single node and trade performance for consistency. Or, if we want both consistency and replication (*e.g.* for high availability), another extreme solution is synchronous replication with 2 phase commit (2PC) [9] for refreshing replicas. However, 2PC is both costly in terms of messages and blocking (failure of the coordinator cannot be terminated independently by the participants).

There are cases where copy consistency can be relaxed. With optimistic replication [12], transactions are locally committed and different replicas may get different values. Replica divergence remains until reconciliation. Meanwhile, the divergence must be controlled for at least two reasons. First, since synchronization consists in producing a single history from several diverging ones, the higher the divergence is, the more difficult the reconciliation. The second reason is that read-only applications do not always require to read perfectly consistent data and may tolerate some inconsistency. In

---

[1] see www.industrie.gouv.fr/rntl/AAP2001/Fiches_Resume/LEG@NET.htm

this case, inconsistency reflects a divergence between the value actually read and the value that should have been read in ACID mode. Non-isolated queries are also useful in non replicated environments [2]. Specification of inconsistency for queries has been widely studied in the literature, and may be divided in two dimensions, temporal and spatial [19]. An example of temporal dimension is found in quasi-copies [1], where a cached (image) copy may be read-accessed according to temporal conditions, such as an allowable delay between the last update of the copy and the last update of the master copy. The spatial dimension consists of allowing a given "quantity of changes" between the values read-accessed and the effective values stored at the same time. This quantity of changes, referred to as import-limit in epsilon transactions [24], may be for instance the number of data items changed, the number of updates performed or the absolute value of the update. In the continuous consistency model [25], both temporal dimension (staleness) and spatial dimension (numerical error and order error) are controlled. Each node propagates its writes by either pull or push access to other nodes, so that each node maintains a predefined level of consistency for each dimension. Then each query can be sent to a node having a satisfying level of consistency (w.r.t. the query) in order to optimize load balancing.

In this paper, we strive to capitalize on the work on relaxing database consistency for higher performance which we apply in the context of cluster systems. We make the following contributions: **(i)** a replicated database architecture for cluster systems that does not hurt application and database autonomy, using non intrusive database techniques, *i.e.* techniques that work independently of any DBMS; **(ii)** a new preventive replication method that provides strong consistency without the overhead of synchronous replication, by exploiting the cluster's high speed network; **(iii)** a transaction load balancing architecture which can trade-off consistency for performance using optimistic replication and execution rules; **(iv)** a conflict manager architecture which exploits the database logs and execution rules to perform replica reconciliation among heterogeneous databases.

This paper is organized as follows. Section 2 introduces our cluster system architecture with database replication. Section 3 presents our replication model with both preventive and optimistic replication. Section 4 describes the way we can capture and exploit execution rules about applications. Section 5 describes our execution model which uses these rules to perform load balancing and manage global consistency. Section 6 briefly describes our on-going implementation. .Section 7 compares our approach with related work. Section 8 concludes.

2   Cluster Architecture

In this section, we introduce the architecture for processing user requests coming, for instance, from the Internet, into our cluster system and discuss our solution for placing applications, DBMS and databases in the system.

The general processing of a user request is as follows. First, the request is authenticated and authorized using a directory which captures information about users and applications. The directory is also used to route requests to nodes. If successful, the user gets a connection to the application (possibly after instantiation) at some node which can then connect to a DBMS at some, possibly different, node and issue queries for retrieving and updating database data.

We consider a cluster system with similar nodes, each having one or more processors, main memory (RAM) and disk. Similar to multiprocessors, various cluster system architectures are possible: shared-disk, shared-cache and shared-nothing [10]. Shared-disk and shared-cache require a special interconnect that provide a shared space to all nodes with provision for cache coherence using either hardware or software. Using shared disk or shared cache requires a specific DBMS implementation like Oracle Rapid Application Cluster or DB2 Parallel Edition. Shared-nothing is the only architecture that supports our autonomy requirements without the additional cost of a special interconnect. Thus, we strive to exploit a shared-nothing architecture.

There are various ways to organize the applications, DBMS and databases in our shared-nothing cluster system. We assume applications typically written in a programming language like C, C++ or Java making DBMS calls to stored procedures using a standard interface like ODBC or JDBC. Stored procedures are in SQL, PSM (SQL3's Persistent Stored Modules) or any proprietary language like Oracle's PL/SQL or Microsoft's TSQL. In [4], we presented and discussed three main organizations to obtain parallelism. The first one is *client-server DBMS* connection whereby a client application at one node connects to a remote DBMS at another node (where the same application can also run). The second organization is *peer-to-peer DBMS* connection whereby a client application at one node connects to a local DBMS which transparently accesses the same DBMS at another node using a distributed database capability. The third organization is *replicated database* whereby a database and DBMS is replicated across several nodes. These three organizations are interesting alternatives which can be combined to better control the consistency/performance trade-off of various applications and optimize load balancing. For instance, an application at one node could do client-server connection to one or more replicated databases, the choice of the replicated database being made depending on the load.

In this paper, we focus on the replicated database organization which is the most general as it provides for both application and database access parallelism. We use multimaster replication [15] whereby each (master) node can perform updates to the replica it holds. However, conflicting updates to the database from two different nodes can yield to consistency problems (*e.g.* the same data get different values in different replicas). The classical solution to this problem is optimistic and based on conflict detection and resolution. However, there is also a preventive solution which we propose and avoids conflicts at the expense of a forced waiting time for transactions. Thus, we support both replication schemes to provide a continuum from strong consistency with preventive replication to weaker consistency with optimistic replication.

Based on these choices, we propose the cluster system architecture in Figure 1 which does not hurt application and database autonomy. Applications, databases and DBMS are replicated at different nodes without any change by the cluster administrator. Besides the directory, we add 4 new modules which can be implemented at any node. The *application load balancer* simply routes user requests to application nodes using a traditional load balancing algorithm. The *transaction load balancer* intercepts DBMS procedure calls (in ODBC or JDBC) from the applications, generates a transaction execution plan (TEP), based on application and user consistency requirements obtained from the directory. For instance, it decides on the use of preventive or optimistic replication for a transaction. Finally, it triggers transaction execution (to execute stored procedures) at the best nodes, using run-time information on nodes' load. The *preventive replication manager* orders transactions at each node in a way that prevents conflicts and generates refresh transactions to update replicas. The conflict manager periodically detects conflicts introduced on replicas by transactions run in optimistic mode using the DBMS logs and solves them using information in the directory.

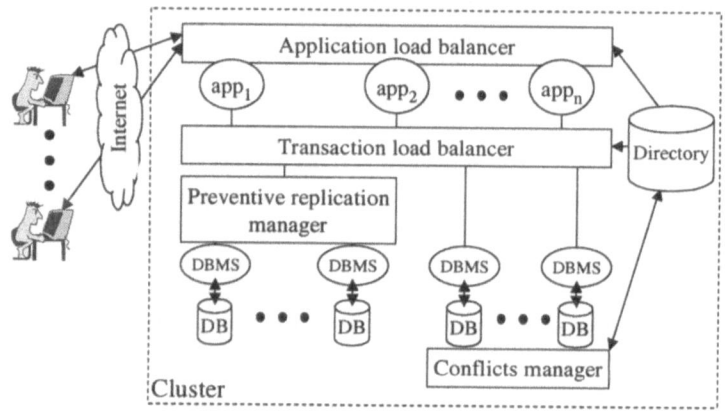

Fig. 1. Cluster system architecture

3 Replication Model

In our context, replication of data at different cluster nodes is a major way to increase parallelism. However, updates to replicated data need be propagated efficiently to all other copies. A general solution widely used in database systems is lazy replication. In this section, we discuss the value of lazy replication in cluster systems, and propose a new multi-master lazy replication scheme with conflict prevention and its architecture. Our scheme can also reduce to the classical multi-master replication scheme with conflict resolution.

3.1 Lazy Replication

With lazy replication, a transaction can commit after updating a replica at some node. After the transaction commits, the updates are propagated towards the other replicas, which are then updated in separate transactions. Unlike synchronous replication (with 2 phase commit), updating transactions need not wait that mutual copy consistency be enforced. Thus lazy replication does not block and scales up much better compared with the synchronous approach. This performance advantage has made lazy replication widely accepted in practice, *e.g.* in data warehousing and collaborative applications on the Web [12].

Following [13] [14], we characterize a lazy replication scheme using: ownership, configuration, transaction model propagation, refreshment. The *ownership* parameter defines the permissions for updating replicas. If a replica R is updateable, it is called a *primary copy*, otherwise it is called a *secondary copy*, noted r. A node M is said to be a master node if it only stores primary copies. A node S is said to be a slave node if it only stores secondary copies. In addition, if a replica copy R is updateable by several master nodes then it is said to be a *multi-owner copy*. A node MO is said to be a *multi-owner master* node if it stores only multi-owner copies. For cluster computing we only consider master, slave and multi-owner master nodes. A master node M or a multi-owner node MO is said to be a master of a slave node S iff there exists a secondary copy of r in S of a primary copy R in M or MO. We also say that S is a *slave* of M or MO.

The *transaction model* defines the properties of the transactions that access replicas at each node. Moreover, we assume that, once a transaction is submitted for execution to a local transaction manager at a node, all conflicts are handled by the local concurrency control protocol. In our framework, we fix the properties of the transactions. We focus on four types of transactions that read or write replicas: update transactions, multi-owner transactions, refresh transactions and queries. An *update transaction T* updates a set of primary copies. A refresh transaction, *RT*, is associated with an update transaction T, and is made of the sequence of write operations performed by T used to refresh secondary copies. We use the term *multi-owner transaction,* noted *MOT*, to refer to a transaction that updates a *multi-owner copy*. Finally, a *query Q*, consists of a sequence of read operations on primary or secondary copies.

The *propagation* parameter defines when the updates to a primary copy or multi-owner copy R must be *multicast* towards the slaves of R or all owners of R. The multicast protocol is assumed to be reliable and preserve the global FIFO order [17]. We focus on deferred update propagation: the sequence of operations of each refresh transaction associated with an update transaction T is multicast to the appropriate nodes within a single message M, after the commitment of T.

The refreshment parameter defines when should a *MOT* or *RT* be triggered and the commit order of these transactions. We consider the *deferred* triggering mode. With a *deferred-immediate* strategy, a *RT* or *MOT* is submitted for execution as soon as the corresponding message M is received by the node.

3.2 Managing Replica Consistency

Depending on which node is allowed user updates to a replica, several replication configurations can be obtained. The lazy master (or asymmetric) configuration allows only one node, called master node, to perform user updates on the replica; the other nodes can only perform reads. Figure 2(a) shows an example of a lazy master bowtie configuration in which there are two nodes storing primary copies R and S and their secondary copies r_1, s_1 and r_2, s_2 at the slave nodes. The multi-master (or symmetric) configuration allows all nodes storing a replica to be masters. Figure 2(b) shows an example of a multi-master configuration in which all master nodes store a primary copy of S and R. There are also hybrid configurations.

Different configurations yield different performance/consistency trade-offs. For instance a lazy master configuration such as bowtie is well suited for read intensive workloads because reading secondary copies does not conflict with any update transaction. In addition, since the updates are rare, the results of a query on a secondary copy r at time t would be, in most cases, the same as reading the corresponding primary copy R at time t. Thus, the choice of a configuration should be based on the knowledge of the transaction workload. For update-intensive workloads, the multi-master configuration seems best as the load of update transactions can be distributed among several nodes.

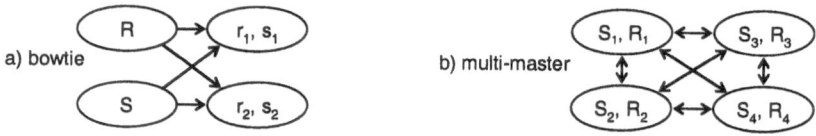

Fig. 2. Replication configurations

For all configurations, the problem is to manage data consistency. That is, any node that holds a replica should always see the same sequence of updates to this replica. Consistency management for lazy master has been addressed in [14]. The problem is more difficult with multi-master where independent transactions can update the same replica at different master nodes. A conflict arises whenever two or more transactions update the same object. The main solution used by replication products [20] is to tolerate and resolve conflicts. After the commitment of a transaction, a conflict detection mechanism checks for conflicts which are resolved by undoing and redoing transactions using a log history. During the time interval between the commitment of a transaction and conflict resolution, users may read and write inconsistent data. This solution is optimistic and works best with few conflicts. However, it may introduce inconsistencies.

We propose an alternative, new solution which prevents conflicts and thus avoids inconsistency. A detailed presentation of the preventive replication scheme and its algorithms is in [15]. With this preventive solution, each transaction T is associated with a chronological timestamp value, and a delay d is introduced before each transaction submission. This delay corresponds to the maximum amount of time to propagate a message between any two nodes. During this delay, all transactions received are ordered following the timestamp value. After the delay has expired, all transactions younger than T are guaranteed to be received. Therefore, transactions at each node are executed following the same timestamp order and consistency is assured.

This preventive approach imposes waiting a specific delay d, before the execution of multi-owner and refresh transactions. Our cluster computing context is characterized by short distance, high performance inter-process communication where error rates are typically low. Thus, d can be negligible to attain strong consistency. On the other hand, the optimistic approach avoids the waiting time d but must deal with inconsistency management. However, there are many applications that tolerate reading inconsistent data. Therefore, we decided to support both replication schemes to provide a continuum from strong consistency with preventive replication to weaker consistency with optimistic replication.

3.3 Preventive Replication Manager Architecture

This section presents the system architecture of a master, multi-master or slave node with conflict prevention. This architecture can be easily adapted to the simpler optimistic approach, with the addition of a conflict manager (see Section 5). To maintain the autonomy of each node, we assume that six components are added to a regular database system in order to support lazy replication (see Figure 3).

The *Replica Interface* manages the incoming multi-owner transaction submission. The *Receiver* and *Propagator* implement reception and propagation of messages, respectively. The *Refresher* implements a refreshment algorithm. Finally, the *Deliverer* manages the submission of multi-owner transactions and refresh transactions to the local transaction manager.

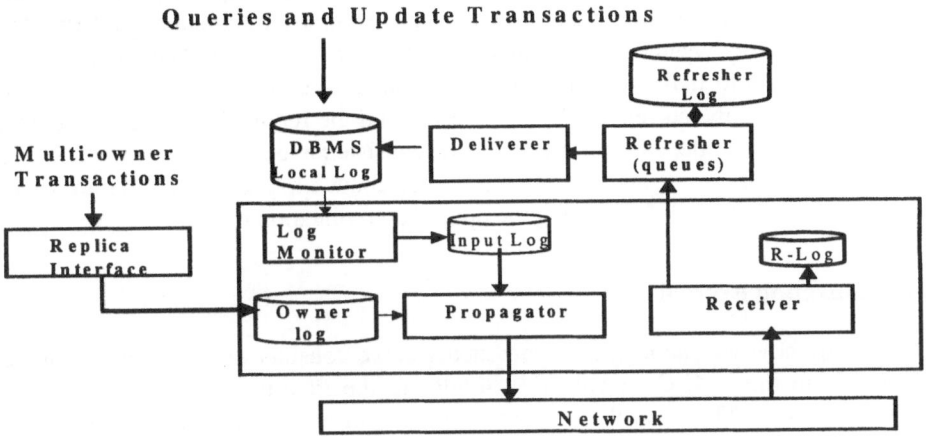

Fig. 3. Master, Multi-owner or Slave node Architecture

The *Log Monitor* uses log sniffing to extract the changes to primary copies by continuously reading the content of a local History Log (noted H). The sequence of updates of an update transaction T and its timestamp C are read from H and written to the *Input Log,* that is used by the Propagator.

Next, multi-owner transactions are submitted through the *Replica Interface*. The application program calls the *Replica Interface* passing as parameter the multi-owner transaction *MOT*. The Replica Interface then establishes a timestamp value C for *MOT*. Afterwards, the sequence of operations of *MOT* is written into the *Owner Log* followed by C. Whenever the multi-owner transaction commits, the *Deliverer* notifies the event Replica Interface. After *MOT* commitment, the replica interface ends its processing and the application program continues its next execution step.

The *Receiver* implements message reception. Messages are received and stored in a *Reception Log*. The receiver then reads messages from this log and stores each message in an appropriate *FIFO pending queue*. The content of the queues form the input to the Refresher. The *Propagator* reads continuously the contents of the *Owner* and *Input Log* and for each sequence of updates followed by *C* read, it constructs a message *M*. Messages are multicast through the network interface.

The *Refresher* implements the refreshment algorithm. It reads the contents of a set of pending queues. Based on its refreshment parameters, it submits refresh transactions and multi-owner update transactions by inserting them into the running queue. The running queue contains all ordered transactions not yet entirely executed. Finally, the *Deliverer* submits refresh and multi-owner transactions to the local transaction manager. It reads the contents of the running queue in a FIFO order and submits each write operation as part of a transaction to the local transaction manager. Whenever a multi-owner transaction is committed, it notifies the event to the *Replica Interface*.

4 Trading Consistency for Load Balancing

The replicated database organization may increase transaction parallelism. For simplicity, we focus on inter-transaction parallelism, whereby transactions updating the same database are dynamically allocated to different master nodes. There are two important decisions to make for an incoming transaction: choosing the node to run it, which depends on the current load of the cluster, and the replication mode (preventive or optimistic) which depends on the degree of consistency desired. In this section, we show how we can capture and use execution rules about applications in order to obtain transaction parallelism, by exploiting the optimistic replication mode.

4.1 Motivating Example

To illustrate how we can tolerate inconsistencies, we consider a very simple example adapted from the TPC-C benchmark[1]. Similar to the Pharmacy applications in our Leg@net project, TPC-C deals with customers that order products whose stock must be controlled by a threshold value. We focus on table Stock(item, quantity, threshold). Procedure DecreaseStock decreases the stock quantity of item *id* by *q*.

> procedure DecreaseStock(id, q) :
> UPDATE Stock SET quantity = quantity – q WHERE item = id;

Let us consider a Stock tuple [1, 30, 10] replicated at nodes N1 and N2, transaction T1 at N1 that calls DecreaseStock(1, 15) and transaction T2 at N2 that calls DecreaseStock(1, 10). If T1 and T2 are executed in parallel in optimistic mode, we get [1, 15, 10] at N1 and [1, 20, 10] at N2. Thus, the Stock replicas are inconsistent and require reconciliation. After reconciliation, the tuple value will be [1, 5, 10]. Now, assume query Q that checks for stocks to renew:

> SELECT item FROM Stock WHERE quantity < threshold

---

[1] see www.tpc.org/tpcc

Executing Q at either node N1 or N2 will not retrieve item 1. However, after reconciliation (see Section 6.2), the final value of item 1 will be [1, 5, 10]. If the application tolerates inconsistencies, it is aware that the results may have been incomplete and can either reissue Q after some time necessary to reach the next reconciliation step and produce a correct result, or execute Q at either node N1 or N2 and produce the results with a bounded inaccuracy. In our example, item 1 would not be selected, which may be acceptable for the user.

Assume now there is an integrity constraint C: (quantity > threshold*0.5) on table Stock. The final result after reconciliation clearly violates the constraint for item 1. However, this violation cannot be detected by either N1 after executing T1 or N2 after executing T2. There are two ways to solve this problem: either prevent T1 and T2 to be executed at different nodes in optimistic mode, or, at reconciliation time, validate one transaction (*e.g.* with highest priority) and compensate, if possible, the other one.

4.2 Execution Rules

Application consistency requirements are expressed in terms of *execution rules*. Examples of execution rules are data-independency between transactions, integrity constraints [1], access control rules, etc. They may be stored explicitly by the system administrator or inferred from the DBMS catalogs. They are primarily used by the system administrator to place and replicate data in the cluster, similar to parallel DBMS [12], [21]. They are also used by the system to decide at which nodes and under which conditions a transaction can be executed.

Execution rules are stored in the directory (see Figure 4) . They are expressed in a declarative language. Implicit rules refer to data already maintained by the system (*e.g.* users authorizations). Hence, they include queries sent to the database catalog to retrieve the data. Incoming transactions are managed by the policy manager. It retrieves execution rules associated with a given transaction and defines a run-time policy for the transaction. The run-time policy controls the execution of the transaction at the required level of consistency. The couple (transaction, run-time policy) is called *transaction policy* (TP) and is sent to the transaction router, which in turns computes a cost function to elaborate the *transaction execution plan* (TEP) which includes the best node among the candidates to perform the transaction with the appropriate mode.

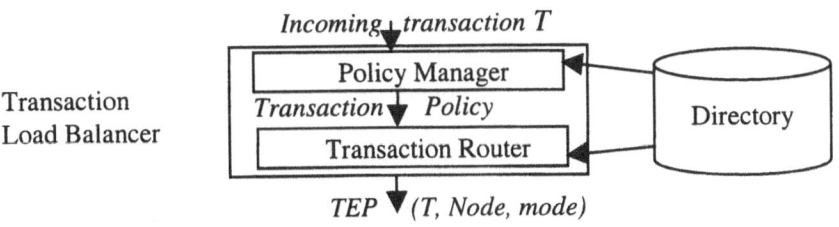

Fig. 4. Transaction load balancer architecture

4.3 Defining Execution Rules

A transaction is defined by $T = (P, param, user, add\text{-}req)$, where: P is the application program of which T is an instance with *param* as parameters,
user is the user who sends the transaction, and *add-req* are additional execution requirements for the transaction.

Execution rules use information about the transaction (the four elements above) and the data stored in the database. In order to preserve application autonomy, execution rules cannot be defined at a finer granularity than the program. Such information may be already existing in the database catalog. Otherwise, it must be explicitly specified or inferred from other information. Information related to a program includes its type (query or update), its conflict classes [16], *i.e.* the data the program may read or write, and its relative priority. If P is a query, the required precision of the results must be specified. If P is an update, the directory must capture under which conditions (parameters) T is compensatable, the compensating transaction, whether T should be retried and under which temporal conditions. For a couple (P, D), where D is a data in the write conflict class of P, the administrator may specify *max-change(P,D)* which is defined as follows. If D is an attribute, *max-change* states how much change (relative or absolute) a transaction T(P) may do to D. If D is a table, max-change states how many tuples T(P) may update. In our example, we have max-change(Decrease-Stock(id,q), Stock.quantity) = q, max-change(Decrease-Stock(id,q), Stock) = 1.

This information is used to determine the run-time policy for transaction T and a partially ordered set of candidate nodes at which the transaction may be executed. As those nodes may be master, slave or multi-owner, the run-time policy may be different for each type of node. The run-time policy is described as follows:

- *type(T)*: denotes if T is a query or a (multi-owner) transaction.
- *priority(T)*: the absolute priority level of the transaction, computed from the relative priorities of the user and the program, and the relative priority of the transaction itself (included in the add-req parameter).
- *compatible(T, T')*: for each transaction T', this vector stores whether T and T' are disjoint (resp. commutative). It is computed with compatibility information about programs, conflict classes and effective parameters of the transactions. This information is used by the load balancer to address transactions to different nodes in non-isolated mode to the replication manager. In our example, it is obvious that T1 and T2 are not disjoint but commutative.
- *query-mode(T)*: if T is a query, the query mode models the spatial and temporal dimensions of the query quality requirements. For instance, a query may tolerate an imprecision of 5% if the answer is delivered within 10 seconds, or 2% if delivered within one minute and may choose to abort if the response time is beyond 2 minutes. The query mode may include different spatial dimensions (absolute value, number of updates) and give a trade-off between the temporal and spatial dimensions (*e.g.* find the best precision within a given time or answer as soon as possible

within a given acceptable precision). In our example, we assume that Q accepts an error of at most 5 items in the results.

- *update-mode(T)*: the update mode models if a multi-owner transaction may be performed in non-isolated mode on a master copy and compensated if the conflict resolution fails, under which temporal conditions and with which compensating transaction. The update mode also models under which conditions a transaction should be automatically retried if aborted. In our example, neither T1 nor T2 are compensatable since the Decrease-Stock procedure corresponds to a real withdrawal of goods in stock.
- *IC(T)*: the set of integrity constraints T is likely to violate. In our example, IC(T1) = IC(T2) = {C}.
- *max-change(T,D)*: for each data D, the maximum of change the transaction may produce. In our example : max-change(T1, Stock.quantity) = 15, max-change(T2, Stock.quantity) = 10, max-change(T1, Stock) = max-change(T2, Stock) = 1.

In our example, the following TPs would be produced :

- (*T1*, *type* = trans., *priority* = null, *compatible* = (), *update-mode* = no-compensate, *IC* = (C), *max-change* = { (Stock.quantity, 15), (Stock, 1) });
- (*T2*, *type* = trans., *priority* = null, *compatible* = ((T1, commut.)), *update-mode* = no-compensate, *IC* = (C), *max-change* = { (Stock.quantity, 10), (Stock, 1) });
- (*Q*, *type*=query, *priority*=null, *compatible*=((T1, no-commut), (T2, no-commut)), query-mode = ((imprecision= 5 unit), (time-bound = no), (priority = time)).

5 Execution Model

In this section, we present the execution model for our cluster system. The objective is to increase load balancing based on execution rules. The problem can be reduced as follows: given the cluster's state (nodes load, running transactions, etc.), the cluster's data placement, and a transaction T with a number of consistency requirements, choose one optimal node and execute T at that node. Choosing the optimal node requires to first choose the replication mode, and then choose the candidate nodes where to execute T with that replication mode. This yields a set of TEPs (one TEP per candidate node) among which the best one can be selected based on a cost function. In the rest of this section, we present the algorithm to produce candidates TEPs and the way to select the best TEP and execute it. Finally, we illustrate the transaction routing process on our running example.

5.1 Algorithm for Choosing Candidate TEPs

A TEP must specify whether preventive or optimistic replication is to be used. Preventive replication always preserves data consistency but may increase contention as the degree of concurrency increases. On the other hand, optimistic replication performs replica synchronization after the transaction commitment at specified times. If a conflict occurs during synchronization, since the transaction has been committed, the only solutions are to either compensate the transaction or notify the user or administrator. Thus, optimistic replication is best when T is disjoint from all the transactions that accessed data in optimistic replication mode since the last synchronization point, and when the chance of conflict is low.

The algorithm to choose the candidate TEPs proceeds as follows. The input is a transaction policy consisting of transaction T, conflict description (*i.e.* which transactions commute or not with T), required precision (*Imp* value), and update description (*maxChange* property). The output is a set of candidate TEPs, each specifying a node N for executing T and how. The algorithm has two steps. First, it finds the candidate TEPs with preventive replication to prevent the occurrence of non resolvable conflicts. This involves assessing the probability of conflict between T and all the committed transactions that have accessed data in optimistic mode since the last synchronization point. In case of potential conflict at a node, a TEP with preventive replication is built.

In case of non-conflicting transaction T (second step), the algorithm finds the candidate nodes with optimistic replication for data accessed by T. If the execution of T requires accessing consistent data not available at a node, the algorithm adds the necessary synchronization before processing T as follows. For each node N and each data D, it computes the imprecision *Imax(D,N)* of processing T at N. Imax is the sum of the maximum changes of all transactions t such that (**i**) updates of t and T are not disjoint, (**ii**) t was processed at a node M $\neq$ N, (**iii**) t updates are not yet propagated to N. If N can process T with the required consistency (*i.e.* Imax(D,N) < Imp(N) for all D accessed by T) then a TEP (T,N) is built. Otherwise, the minimal synchronization for N is specified and added to the TEP.

5.2 Choice of Optimal Node and Transaction Execution

Choosing the optimal node is an optimization problem with the objective of minimizing response time. The cost of a given TEP(T, N, sync) includes the synchronization cost (for propagating all updates to N) and the processing cost of T at N. After an optimal node is selected, the transaction router triggers execution as follows. First, it performs synchronization if necessary. If preventive replication has been selected, it sends the transaction to the receiver module of the replication manager. Otherwise, it sends the transaction directly to the DBMS. By default, the transaction router checks precision requirements of T before processing it, assuming that they are still valid at the end of T. This is not always true if a concurrent update occurs during the processing of T. To ensure that the precision requirements of T are met at the end of T, a solution is to process T by iteration until the precision requirements are reached. If the precision requirements cannot be reached, T must be aborted. Otherwise, T can be committed. Another solution is to forbid the execution of concurrent transactions that would prevent T from reaching its consistency requirements.

Replica synchronization is delegated to the conflict manager which must also perform conflict detection and resolution. To have detailed information about the current state of replicas, the conflict manager reads the DBMS log (which keeps the history of update operations) of all the nodes that have executed transactions since the last synchronization point. Then, it resolves the conflicts based on priority, timestamps, or user-defined reconciliation rules. If automatic conflict resolution is not possible, the conflict manager sends a notification alert to the user or the administrator with details about the conflicting operations.

5.3 Example of Transaction Routing

Let us now illustrate the previous algorithms on the transactions of the example of Section 4.1 and show how TEPs are produced from the TP sent by the policy manager. We assume that the TPs are received in order (T1, T2, Q), that data at nodes N1 and N2 is accessed in optimistic mode and that no other transaction is running and conflicting with T1, T2 or Q. We first consider a case where integrity constraint C is not taken into account. Then we show how C influences transaction routing.

Case 1: No Integrity Constraint
Upon receiving TP (*T1, type* = trans., *priority* = null, *compatible* = (), *update-mode* = no-compensate, *IC* = (C), *max-change* = {(Stock.quantity, 15), (Stock, 1)}), the transaction router does the following: (**i**) computes the set of candidate nodes {N1, N2}; (**ii**) detects that T1 is not conflicting with any running transaction, thus the candidate nodes are {N1, N2}; (**iii**) sends T1 to the least loaded node (say N1) with T1 as synchronization, which means that N1 must send T1 to the other node as a synchronizing transaction; (**iv**) infers Imax(Stock, N1)=1, which means that at most one tuple can be modified at N1 before synchronization.
Upon receiving TP (*T2, type* = trans., *priority* = null, *compatible* = ((T1, commut.)), *update-mode* = no-compensate, *IC* = (C), *max-change* = {(Stock.quantity, 10), (Stock, 1)}), the transaction router does the following : (**i**) computes the set of candidate nodes {N1, N2}; (**ii**) detects that T2 is conflicting with T1 but commutes with it; (**iii**) sends T2 to the least loaded node (assume N2) with T2 as synchronization. As T1 and T2 are commutable, the order in which they will be executed at N1 (resp. N2) does not matter; (**iv**) infers Imax(Stock, N2) = 1.
Upon receiving TP (*Q, type*=query., *priority*=null, *compatible*=((T1, no-commut.), (T2, no-commut.)), query-mode=((imprecision = 5 unit), (time-bound=no), (priority = time))), the transaction router does the following: (**i**) computes the set of candidate nodes {N1, N2}; (**ii**) detects that Q is conflicting with both T1 and T2; (**iii**) from the current values of Imax(Stock, N1) and Imax(Stock, N2), it computes that executing Q at either N1 or N2 would yield a result with an imprecision of at most one unit. As the query mode imposes an imprecision of at most 5 units, Q is sent to the least loaded node (say N1). In the case the query mode of Q was not allowing any imprecision, the router would have waited for the next synchronization of N1 and N2 to send Q.

Case 2: With Integrity Constraint
The transaction router would detect that both T1 and T2 are likely to violate C and are not compensatable. Sending T1 and T2 to different nodes could lead to the situation

where C is not violated at either N1 or N2, but is violated during synchronization. Since T1 and T2 are not compensatable, this situation is not acceptable and T2 must be sent to the same node as T1. Then we have Imax(Stock, N1) = 0 and Imax(Stock, N2) = 2. Upon receiving Q, the transaction router may still choose the least loaded node to execute it. Since the priority is given to time in the query mode, the least loaded node is chosen: N2. Had the priority been given to precision, N1 would have been selected by the transaction router.

6 Implementation

In this section, we briefly describe our current implementation on a cluster of PCs under Linux. We plan to first experiment our approach with the Oracle DBMS. However, we use standards like LDAP and JDBC, so the main part of our prototype is independent of the target environment.

6.1 Transaction Load Balancer

The transaction load balancer is implemented in Java. It acts as a JDBC server for the application, preserving the application autonomy through the JDBC standard interface. Inter-process communication between the application and the load balancer uses Remote Method Invocation. To reduce contention, the load balancer takes advantage of the multi-threading capabilities of Java based on the Linux's native threads. For each incoming transaction, the load balancer delegates transaction policy management and transaction routing to a distinct thread. The transaction router sends transactions for execution to DBMS nodes through JDBC drivers provided by the DBMS vendors. To reduce latency when executing transactions, the transaction router maintains a pool of JDBC connections to all cluster nodes.

6.2 Conflict Manager

The conflict manager is composed of three modules: (i) Log analyzer : reads the DBMS log to capture the updates made by the local transactions; (ii) Conflict solver : analyzes updates made on each node in order to detect and solve conflicts; (iii) Synchronizer : manages synchronization processes.

At each node, the log manager runs as an independent process and reads the log to detect updates performed by the local transactions. Those updates are sent to the conflict solver through time-stamped messages. The Oracle LogMiner tool can be used to implement this module, and messages can be managed with the Advanced Queuing tool. To illustrate the log analysis on our running example, the Stock update made by transaction T1 is detected by the following query on the LogMiner schema:

```
SELECT scn, sql_redo, sql_undo
FROM v$logmnr_contents
WHERE seg_name='STOCK';
```

The conflict solver receives messages from the log analyzer, analyzes them to detect conflicting writes (*e.g.* update/update or update/delete) on a same data. It then computes how conflicts can be solved. In the best case, the conflict is solved by propagating updates from one node to the other ones. In the worst case, the conflict is solved by choosing a transaction (the one with less priority) to be compensated. In both cases, synchronizing transactions (propagation or compensation) are sent to the corresponding nodes.

The synchronizer receives synchronizing transactions from the conflict solver. It may execute them either periodically or upon receiving an order from the transaction load balancer for an immediate synchronization.

The preventive replication manager is implemented as an enhanced version of a preceding implementation [11]. To implement reliable message broadcast, we plan to use Ensemble [6], a group communication software package from Cornell University.

6.3 Directory

All information used for load balancing (execution rules, data placement, replication mode, cluster load) is stored in an LDAP compliant directory. The directory is accessed through Java Directory Naming Interface (JDNI) which provides an LDAP client implementation. Dynamic parameters measuring the cluster activity (load, resource usage) are stored in the directory. They are used for transaction routing. Values are updated periodically at each node. To measure DBMS node activity (*e.g.* CPU usage and I/O made by all running transactions), we take advantage of dynamic views maintained by Oracle.

6.4 Planned Experimentations

The experimental cluster is composed of 5 nodes: 4 DBMS nodes + 1 application node. At each DBMS node, there is a TPC-C database (500MB to 2GB) and TPC-C stored procedures. The application node sends the transactional workload to the transaction load balancer through TPC-C stored procedures. The cluster data placement and replication (optimistic and preventive) may be configured depending on the experiment goal. We plan to first measure the cluster performance (transactional throughput) when the database is replicated on the 4 nodes and accessed in either preventive or optimistic replication mode, by varying the update rates and the probability of conflict. We also plan to measure the scalability of our approach. We will simply implement a logical 16 node cluster where each node runs 4 DBMS instances to behave like a 4 node cluster. Based on the actual performance numbers with 4 nodes, this will yield confident results.

7 Comparison with Related Work

The main work related to ours is replication in either large-scale distributed systems or cluster systems and advanced transaction models that trade consistency for improved performance. In synchronous replication, 2PC can be used to update replicas. However 2PC is blocking and the number of messages exchanged to control transaction commitment is significant. It cannot scale up to cluster configurations to large numbers of nodes. [7] addresses the replica consistency problem for synchronous replication. The number of messages exchanged is reduced compared to 2PC but the solution is still blocking and it is not clear whether it scales up. In addition, synchronous solutions cannot perform load balancing as we do. The common point with our preventive approach is that we both consider the use of communication services to guarantee that messages are delivered at each node in a specific order. [14] proposes a refreshment algorithm that assures correctness for lazy-master configurations, but does not consider multi-master configurations as we do here. Multi-master asynchronous replication [20] has been successfully implemented in commercial systems such as Oracle and Sybase. However, only the optimistic approach with conflict detection and conciliation is supported.

There are interesting projects for replicated data management in cluster architectures. The PowerDB project at ETH Zurich deals with the coordination of the cluster nodes in order to provide a uniform and consistent view to the clients. Its solution fits well for some kinds of applications, such as XML document management [5] or read-intensive OLAP queries [18]. However, it does not address the problem of seamless integration of legacy applications. The GMS project [22] uses global information to optimize page replacement and prefetching decisions over the cluster. However, it mainly addresses system-level or Internet applications (such as the Porcupine mail server). Other projects are developed in the context of wide-area networks. The Trapp project at Stanford University [8] addresses the problem of precision/performance trade-off. However, the focus is on numeric computation of aggregation queries and minimizing communication costs. The TACT middleware layer [25] implements the continuous consistency model. Despite the fact that additional messages are used to limit divergence, a substantial gain in performance may be obtained if users accept a rather small error rate. However, read and write operations are mediated individually: an operation is blocked until consistency requirements can be guaranteed. This implies monitoring at the server level, and it is not clear if it allows installation of a legacy application in an ASP cluster. In the quasi-copy caching approach [1], four consistency conditions are defined. Quasi-copies can be seen as materialized views with limited inconsistency. However, they only accept single master replication, which is not adapted to our multi-master replication in a cluster system. Finally, epsilon transactions [24] provide a nice theoretical framework for dealing with divergence control. As in the continuous consistency model [25], it allows different consistency metrics to give answers to queries with bounded imprecision. However, it requires to significantly alter the concurrency control, since each lock request must read or write an additional counter to decide whether the lock is compatible with the required level of consistency. In summary, none of the existing approaches addresses the problems of leaving databases and applications autonomous and unchanged as in our work.

8 Conclusion

In this paper, we proposed a new solution for parallel processing with autonomous databases in a cluster system for ASP, using a replicated database organization. The main idea is to allow the system administrator to control the consistency/performance tradeoff when placing applications and databases onto cluster nodes. Application requirements are captured through execution rules stored in a shared directory. They are used at configuration time to choose the best organization for applications and databases. They are also used at run-time to either prevent or tolerate copy inconsistency in order to optimize load balancing.

Capitalizing on the work on relaxing database consistency for higher performance, this paper makes several contributions in the context of cluster systems. First, we defined a replicated database architecture for clusters systems that does not hurt application and database autonomy. We use non intrusive techniques by intercepting DBMS transaction calls or exploiting DBMS's log interfaces.

Second, we proposed a new preventive replication method that provides strong consistency without the overhead of synchronous replication by exploiting the cluster's high speed network. The preventive replication architecture maintains DBMS's autonomy and can support optimistic replication as well, with the addition of a conflict manager.

Third, we proposed a transaction load balancing architecture which can trade-off consistency for performance using optimistic replication and execution rules. Support for both preventive and optimistic replication provides a continuum from strong consistency to weaker consistency with different cost/performance. Execution rules can be defined at different levels of granularity (program or transaction, table or attribute or tuple) to express application semantics. The distinction between Transaction Policy (what we want) and Transaction Execution Plan (how we optimize it) eases the system's evolution (by changing rules) and load balancing decisions.

Finally, we presented an execution model to execute Transaction Execution Plans in a way that optimizes load balancing. The optimal node is selected based on the replication mode that should be used and a cost function which estimates nodes's load. We also proposed a conflict manager architecture which exploits the database logs and execution rules to perform replica reconciliation among heterogeneous databases.

We have started to implement the proposed solution on LIP6's cluster architecture running Linux and Oracle 8i. We are experimenting with the TPC-C benchmark to assess the cost/performance of preventive replication and optimistic replication (with relaxed consistency) under various workloads. We will also develop a simulation model, calibrated with our implementation, to study how our solution scales up to very large cluster configurations.

References

[1]   R. Alonso, D. Barbará, H. Garcia-Molina. Data Caching Issues in an Information Retrieval System. ACM Transactions on Database Systems (TODS), 15(3), 1990.

[2]   H. Berenson, P. Bernstein, J. Gray, J. Melton, E. O'Neil, P. O'Neil. A Critique of ANSI SQL Isolation Levels. In ACM SIGMOD Int. Conf. on Management of Data, 1995.

[3]   A. Doucet, S. Gançarski, C. León, M. Rukoz. Checking Integrity Constraints in Multi-database Systems with Nested Transactions. In Int. Conf. On Cooperative Information Systems (CoopIS), 2001.

[4]   S. Gançarski, H. Naacke, P. Valduriez. Load Balancing of Autonomous Applications and Databases in a Cluster System. In 4th Workshop on Distributed Data and Structure (WDAS), 2002.

[5]   T. Grabs, K. Böhm, H.-J. Schek. Scalable Distributed Query and Update Service Implementations for XML Document Elements. In IEEE RIDE Int. Workshop on Document Management for Data Intensive Business and Scientific Applications, 2001.

[6]   M. Hayden. The Ensemble System. Technical Report, Departement of Computer Science, Cornell University, TR-98-1662, 1998.

[7]   B. Kemme, G. Alonso. Don't be lazy be consistent : Postgres-R, A new way to implement Database Replication. In Int. Conf on Very Large Databases (VLDB), 2000.

[8]   C. Olston, J. Widom. Offering a Precision-Performance Tradeoff for Aggregation Queries over Replicated Data. In Int. Conf. on Very Large Databases (VLDB), 2000.

[9]   T. Özsu, P. Valduriez. Principles of Distributed Database Systems. Prentice Hall, 2nd edition, 1999.

[10]   T. Özsu, P. Valduriez. Distributed and Parallel Database Systems - Technology and current state-of-the-art. ACM Computing Surveys, 28(1), 1996.

[11]   E. Pacitti. Improving Data Freshness in Replicated Databases. PhD Thesis, INRIA-RR 3617, 1999.

[12]   E. Pacitti, O. Dedieu. Algorithms for Optimistic Replication on the Web. Journal of the Brazilian Computing Society, 2002, to appear.

[13]   E. Pacitti, P. Minet, E. Simon. Fast Algorithms for Maintaining Replica Consistency in Lazy Master Replicated Databases. In Int. Conf. on Very Large Databases (VLDB), 1999.

[14]   E. Pacitti, P. Minet, E. Simon. Replica Consistency in Lazy Master Replicated Databases. Distributed and Parallel Databases, 9(3), 2001.

[15]   E. Pacitti. Preventive Lazy Replication in Cluster Systems. Technical Report RR-2002-01, CRIP5, University Paris 5, 2002.

[16]   M. Patiño-Martínez, R. Jiménez-Peris, B. Kemme, G. Alonso. Scalable Replication in Database Clusters. In Int. Conf. on Distributed Computing (DISC), 2000.

[17]   D. Powel et al. Group communication (special issue). Communication of the ACM, 39(4), 1996.

[18]   U. Röhm, K. Böhm, H.-J. Schek. Cache-Aware Query Routing in a Cluster of Databases. Int. Conf. on Data Engineering (ICDE), 2001.

[19]   A. Sheth, M. Rusinkiewicz. Management of Interdependent Data: Specifying Dependency and Consistency Requirements. Workshop on the Management of Replicated Data, 1990.

[20]   D. Stacey. Replication: DB2, Oracle, or Sybase. Database Programming & Design. 7(12), 1994.

[21]   P. Valduriez. Parallel Database Systems: open problems and new issues. Int. Journal on Distributed and Parallel Databases, 1(2), 1993.

[22]   G. Voelker et al. Implementing Cooperative Prefetching and Caching in a Global Memory System. In ACM Sigmetrics Conf. on Performance Measurement, Modeling, and Evaluation, 1998.

[23]   G. Weikum. Principles and Realization Strategies of Multilevel Transaction Management. ACM Transactions on Database Systems (TODS), 16(1), 1991.

[24]   K. L. Wu, P. S Yu, C. Pu. Divergence Control for Epsilon-Serializability. In 8th Int. Conf. on Data Engineering (ICDE), 1992.

[25]   H. Yu, A. Vahdat. Efficient Numerical Error Bounding for Replicated Network Services. In Int. Conf. On Very Large Databases (VLDB), 2000.

Querying XML Sources Using an Ontology-Based Mediator

Bernd Amann[1], Catriel Beeri[*2], Irini Fundulaki[1], and Michel Scholl[1]

[1] Cedric-CNAM Paris and INRIA-Futurs, France
{amann,fundulak,scholl}@cnam.fr
[2] The Hebrew University, Jerusalem, Israel
beeri@cs.huji.ac.il

Abstract. In this paper we propose a mediator architecture for the querying and integration of Web-accessible XML data sources. Our contributions are (i) the definition of a simple but expressive mapping language, following the *local as view* approach and describing XML resources as local views of some global schema, and (ii) efficient algorithms for rewriting user queries according to existing source descriptions. The approach has been validated by the $ST_\gamma X$ prototype.

1 Introduction

During the last decade, there has been a significant focus on data integration. In a nutshell, data integration can be described as follows: given *heterogeneous* and *autonomous* information sources in a *specific domain of interest*, the goal is to enable users to *query* the data as if it resides in a *single source*, with a *single schema*. To achieve this goal, a *global schema* of the data is defined, and related to the schemas of the individual sources. Queries are formulated in terms of this global schema. Since the actual data resides in the sources, queries are rewritten into queries over the source schemas, which are then evaluated at the sources. The answers returned from the sources are combined, transformed to be compatible with the global schema, and presented to the user. The integration facilities, namely the global schema, the query translation and query processing algorithms, are performed by a *mediator*, whose main task is to provide users with a unique interface for querying the data. The fact that the sources concern a *restricted domain of interest*, is crucial for the successful deployment of integration systems.

Well-known projects that deal with data integration include Information Manifold [12], Tsimmis [14], Picsel [10], Agora [13] and MIX [3]. As the goal of integration is to support declarative querying and automatic query and result transformations, a number of data integration systems use the well-established tools available for such purposes in the relational model, such as query and transformation languages.

Recently, XML [1] has emerged as the *de-facto* standard for *publishing* and *exchanging* data on the Web. Many data sources export XML data, and publish their contents using DTD's or XML schemas. Thus, independently of whether the data is actually stored in XML native mode or in a relational store, the view presented to the users is XML-based. The use of XML as a data representation and exchange standard raises

---

* Research supported by grant 018-019 by the Israeli Ministry of Science.

R. Meersman, Z. Tari (Eds.): CoopIS/DOA/ODBASE 2002, LNCS 2519, pp. 429–448, 2002.

new issues for data integration. A significant issue, as argued in [2], is the inadequacy of XML to serve as a global integration schema.

In this paper we describe an approach to the integration of XML sources, based on the *local-as view* [11] approach to data integration. Our main contributions are as follows: (i) the use of *ontologies* for the global schema; (ii) the definition of a simple but expressive language for *describing* XML resources as *views* of the global schema; (iii) an approach to *query processing*, that includes query *rewriting* from the terms of the global schema into one or more XML queries over the local sources, and (iv) the generation of *query execution plans* that may decompose a single query into queries over multiple sources. The approach has been validated by the ST_YX prototype [9].

The paper is organized as follows : in Section 2 we illustrate the main ideas of the approach by an example. Section 3 presents the *integration data model*, and the *mapping language* for the description of XML resources as views over the global schema. The *query language*, and the *query processing* algorithms are given in Section 4. The ST_YX prototype is sketched in Section 5. Related work is presented in Section 6, and Section 7 presents our conclusions.

2   System Overview

We illustrate our approach via an example dealing with the integration of XML-based information sources on *art and culture*. Formal definitions and technical details are deferred to subsequent sections.

2.1   XML Resources

Source S_1, located at *http://www.paintings.com* is an XML resource about painters and their paintings; its XML DTD is illustrated in Fig. 1.

```
<!ELEMENT Painter  (Painting+)>
<!ATTLIST Painter  name CDATA #REQUIRED>
<!ELEMENT Painting EMPTY>
<!ATTLIST Painting title CDATA #IMPLIED
                   year  CDATA #IMPLIED>
```

Fig. 1. XML DTD for source S_1, located at URL *http://www.paintings.com*

The XML DTD for the second source S_2, located at URL *http://www.art.com*, is described in Fig. 2.

As is common in data integration scenarios, a single source may provide only *part* of the information available on a subject. Furthermore, sources differ not only in terms of contents, but also in terms of structure and terminology. Given the hierarchical structure of XML, such differences of structure may be more significant that those that exist in relational sources. For an example of a difference of contents, note that source S_2 might record information on the location of paintings, which is absent in source S_1. As for structure, note that in source S_2 paintings are organized by museums, not by their

```
<!ELEMENT Museum (MuseumName, City, Painting+)>
<!ELEMENT Painting (Title)>
<!ELEMENT MuseumName #PCDATA>
<!ELEMENT City #PCDATA>
<!ELEMENT Title #PCDATA>
```

Fig. 2. XML DTD for source S_2, located at *http://www.art.com*

painters as in source S_1. Consequently, while in the hierarchy of S_1 a painting occurs *below* its painter, in source S_2, if the source were interested in adding the painter for each painting, the painter would occur *below* the painting.

2.2   The Global Schema

The main task of an integration mediator is to provide users with a unique interface for querying the data, independently of its actual organization and location. In our approach, this interface, or global schema, is described as an *ontology*. As used here, an *ontology* denotes a light-weight conceptual model and not a hierarchy of terms or a hierarchy of concepts.

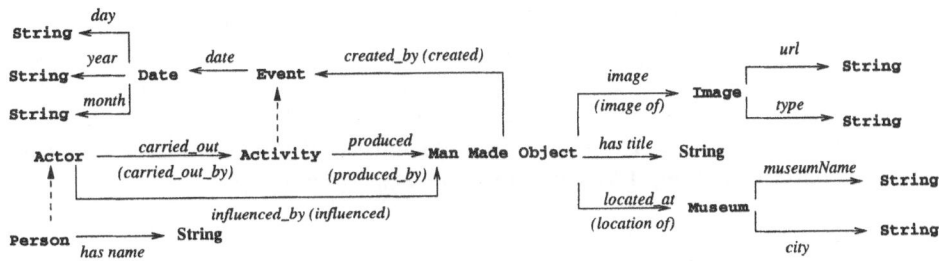

Fig. 3. An Ontology for Cultural Artifacts

Fig. 3 illustrates (part of) a global schema for cultural artifacts inspired by the ICOM/CIDOC Reference Model[1], an international standard for museum documentation. The schema is represented as a *labeled graph*. In this graph, the nodes correspond to *concepts* and *value types*, and the edges depict *roles*, *attributes*, and simple *inheritance* (i.e., *isa*) links. Roles are binary relations between concepts; attributes connect concepts to value types. Both are depicted by solid arcs. Inheritance (*isa*) links connect concepts and are depicted by dashed arcs. Each role has an *inverse* depicted in Fig. 3 within parentheses.

The concepts in this schema include Actor, its subconcept Person, and Man Made_ _Object. An actor (instance of concept Actor) carries out an activity (instance of concept

---

[1] http://cidoc.ics.forth.gr/crm_intro.html

Activity) to produce a man made object (instance of concept **Man_Made_Object**). These relationships are represented by roles *carried_out* and *produced*, respectively. The name of a person (instance of concept **Person**) is represented by the attribute *has_name*.

The global schema can be viewed as a simple object-oriented data model. Hence, a global schema can be viewed as defining a database of objects, connected by roles, with the concept extents related by subset relationships as per the *isa* links in the schema. Since it is an integration schema, this is a virtual database. The actual materialization exists in the sources.

Roles can be composed, provided they satisfy certain compatibility constraints. Such compositions are *derived roles*. For example, *carried_out.produced* is a derived role that connects **Actor** to **Man_Made_Object**. Combining concepts with (simple or derived) roles induces *derived concepts*. For example, **Actor**.*carried_out.produced* can be viewed as the sub-concept of **Man_Made_Object** made of those objects that are reachable from some actor by an instance of this derived role. Both derived roles and derived concepts are referred to as *schema paths*.

The augmentation of the given schema with the derived roles and concepts gives a *derived schema*. It is significant for the integration, since it provides an interpretation for the *mapping rules* (see the following) that describe the sources in terms of schema paths, hence for query processing, as discussed next.

2.3 Mapping Rules

Our integration approach describes XML sources as *local views* on the global schema. Among the different possibilities listed in [7] for defining such mappings, we have chosen the *path-to-path approach*. The description of a source consists of *mapping rules* that associate paths in the source DTD, expressed in *XPath* [6], with paths in the global schema (schema paths). For example, the rules illustrated in Fig. 4 map paths in the source S_1 described in Fig. 1 to paths in the global schema of Fig. 3.

R_1: `http://www.paintings.com/Painter` as u_1 → Person
R_2: u_1/`@name` as u_2 → has_name
R_3: u_1/`Painting` as u_3 → carried_out.produced
R_4: u_3/`@title` as u_4 → has_title
R_5: u_3/`@year` as u_5 → created_by.date.year

Fig. 4. Set of Mapping Rules for source *http://www.paintings.com*

A rule consists of a name, a left hand side (LHS) and a right hand side (RHS). The LHS contains an *XPath pattern* [6] that starts at a context which is either a concrete URL, as in rule R_1 or a variable, as in rule R_2. The XPath pattern is called the *location path* of the rule. The LHS of a rule also contains a variable declaration (the use of variables will be explained later). The RHS of a mapping rule is a path in the global schema, called the *schema path* of the rule.

Mapping rules define instances of concepts and relationships between them. As an example for the first case, consider the rule R_1 in Fig. 4. It states that the elements of type

`Painter`, children of the root elements of the XML documents in S_1 are (descriptions of) instances of concept **Person**. As an example for the second case, rule R_2 specifies that the value obtained by evaluating XPath pattern @name on some XML element x returned by rule R_1, corresponds to a value of attribute *has_name* of x (x is an instance of concept **Person**). In the same way, rule R_3 connects all instances obtained by rule R_1 to all instances of concept **Man_Made_Object** obtained by following the path *carried_out-.produced*.

This view of mapping rules allows us to define the semantics of XML fragments and their structural relationships in terms of the global derived schema. Thus, R_1 defines a subset of the extent of concept **Person**, while rule R_3 relates elements in this subset by the derived role *carried_out.produced* to a subset of the extent of **Man_Made_Object**.

2.4   Query Processing

Users formulate queries on the global schema using a simplified variant of OQL, the standard for querying object databases. For example, here is a query Q_1 that asks for *"titles of the man made objects created by Van Gogh"* :

Q_1: **select** c
 from   Person a, a.has_name b,
      a.carried_out.produced.has_title c
 where $b =$ "Van Gogh"

We now discuss the options available for answering such a query, given a set of sources S and mapping rules that relate them to the global schema.

The first, simple, solution is to evaluate this query over each source in S. This means that, given a source $s \in S$, we need to *rewrite* it into an XML query that s can answer. The idea behind this rewriting is the following: Each variable in the query is bound to some schema path. We search for mapping rules or concatenations of mapping rules, that can be used to translate these schema paths to local paths in the source DTD. This is done by *matching* the *schema paths* in the query against the *schema paths* of the mapping rules. A successful matching associates a query variable with a rule, or a concatenation of rules. A *binding* is a vector of such associations for query variables. A *full binding* associates each variable in the query to some rule or concatenation of rules. It can be used to rewrite the query into a query to be evaluated by the XML source.

For example for Q_1 above and for source S_1 we see that instances for variable a are found by rule R_1, for variable b by R_2 and for variable c by the *concatenation* of rule R_3 with rule R_4. The resulting binding is $[a \rightarrow R_1, b \rightarrow R_2, c \rightarrow R_3.R_4]$. By substituting the schema path of each query variable with the location path (LHS) of the corresponding rule, we obtain query $Q_1(a)$:

$Q_1(a)$: **select** c
    from `http://www.paintings.com/Painter` a,
        a./@name b, a./Painting/@title c,
    where $b =$ "Van Gogh"

Query $Q_1(a)$ can be easily translated into the XQuery expression $Q_1(b)$:

$Q_1(b)$: **FOR** $a **IN** document('http://www.paintings.com')/Painter,
                  $b **IN** $a/@name,
                  $c **IN** $a/Painting/@title
          WHERE $b = "Van Gogh"
          RETURN $c

Such a matching/rewriting process should be attempted for each source. Then the answers are gathered and returned to the user.

In some cases, however, we cannot obtain a full binding for a given source. Then a second solution for query evaluation is to *decompose* the query into several queries that are evaluated against different sources. Consider the following query Q_2, which asks for *"titles of objects created by Van Gogh, as well as the name and the city of the museum where they are exposed"* :

Q_2: **select** d, f, g
       from   Person a, a.has_name b,
                  a.carried_out.produced c, c.has_title d,
                  c.located_at e, e.museumName f, e.city g
       where b = "Van Gogh"

Source S_1 cannot provide information about the locations of objects, hence there is no mapping rule whose schema path (RHS) matches the schema path *located_at* of query variable e. Thus, we can only obtain a *partial answer* from this source, by evaluating the query $Q_2(a)$ illustrated in Fig. 5. To obtain a full answer we have to join partial answers from different sources.

For the example, the missing information is represented by subquery $Q_2(b)$ illustrated also in Fig. 5, that involves the variables c, e, f, g. The variable c is included in $Q_2(b)$ since it is the *join* variable between the two queries. Thus, we have *decomposed* the initial query into two subqueries $Q_2(a)$ and $Q_2(b)$. Assuming the latter query is successfully evaluated over some source (e.g., source S_2), the results of the two queries are *joined* on c to provide a complete answer to the original query. If such a decomposition cannot be found, the best we can do is to present to the user only the partial results from $Q_2(a)$ evaluated against the first source.

Note that to join two fragments from different sources requires to decide whether the two fragments represent identical objects. *Keys* are introduced to identify objects. In particular, results of queries $Q_2(a)$ over a source S_1 and of $Q_2(b)$ over a source S_2 can be joined only if the same key for man made objects can be provided by these two sources. This implies the use of keys, both in the *global schema* and in the *sources* (the DTD's in Fig. 1 and Fig. 2 do not define such keys). We introduce keys and their usage in Section 3.2.

3   Integration Model

This section is devoted to the detailed presentation of our integration model. Due to space limitations we leave out a detailed discussion concerning the choices of the integration method, and the choice of having a light weight conceptual schema for the mediator schema instead of an XML-based model. A detailed presentation of these choices is

$Q_2(a)$: **select** d
    from   Person a, a.has_name b
            a.carried_out.produced c,
            c.has_title d
    where b = "Van Gogh"

$Q_2(b)$: **select** f, g
    from   Man_Made_Object c,
            c.located_at e,
            e.museumName f, e.city g

Fig. 5. Queries $Q_2(a)$ and $Q_2(b)$

given in [2]. We first provide a formal definition of the global schema and introduce the notion of derived schema. Mapping rules are described afterwards and we finish this section with a short discussion on keys.

Global Schemas

A global schema is a 6-tuple $\mathcal{S} = (C, R, A, isa, source, target)$, where: (i) C is a set of concepts, (ii) R is a set of typed binary roles connecting concepts in C, (iii) A is a set of attributes of type String[2], (iv) isa is a *binary relationship* between concepts in C, (v) $source$ and $target$ are two typing functions returning for each role/attribute its domain concept and its range concept/type respectively.

A global schema can be represented as a graph of concepts connected by roles. The semantics of a schema is defined by the set of databases that *conform to it*. Each such database contains a set of objects (instances) for each concept in C. These objects are related to each other by instances of roles in R, and to values by instances of attributes in A. Instances of roles and attributes satisfy the typing constraints implied by $source$ and $target$. Roles and attributes are multi-valued and optional. The isa relationship defines a partial order in $\mathcal{S}$, namely a directed acyclic graph. It carries subset semantics and supports role and attribute inheritance. Namely, if $c\ isa\ c'$, then the set of objects of c is a subset of the set of objects of c' and all roles/attributes defined in c' are also defined in c (and its subconcepts). However, if c is not a subconcept of c' such that $source(r) = c'$ for a role r or $source(a) = c'$ for an attribute a, then no object o' of c is related by an instance of r or a to any object, or value respectively. We say that c, c' are *isa-related* if either $c = c'$, $c\ isa\ c'$ or $c'\ isa\ c$.

Finally, we consider schema graphs to be *symmetric* : each role $r \in R$ has an inverse role, denoted r^-, in R. Obviously, $target(r^-) = source(r)$, and $source(r^-) = target(r)$. This is useful for modelling the contents of XML resources as well as for query formulation and, hence, beneficial to have in a conceptual schema.

Schema Paths and Derived Schemas.
We distinguish two kinds of paths in a schema :

- A *role path* is a sequence of roles $r = r_1 \ldots r_n$, where for all roles r_i ($1 \leq i \leq n-1$), $target(r_i)\ isa\ source(r_{i+1})$. Given a role path $r = r_1 \ldots r_n$, we define its *inverse role path* $r^- = r_n^- \ldots r_1^-$ where r_i^- is the inverse role of r_i

---

[2] Wlg. we assume that all attributes are of type string; an extension to the types proposed by the XPath model or XML schema should be straightforward.

- A *concept path* p is either of the form c, or a sequence $c.r$, where c is a concept and r is a role path, such that $c \, isa \, source(r)$. The source of p is c and its $target$ is c in the first case, and $target(r)$ in the second case.

The composition of a concept path p and a role path r, denoted $p \circ r$, is well-defined provided that $target(p) \, isa \, source(r)$.

A concept path $p = c.r$ can be viewed as a *derived concept* (denoted by $conc(p)$), standing for *"the instances of $target(p)$ that can be reached from instances of $source(p)$ by following the roles in p, in order"*. Obviously, every concept is also a derived concept.

In the same way, a role path $r = r_1 \ldots r_n$ can be viewed as a *derived role* (denoted by $role(r)$) connecting instances of concept $source(r_1)$ to instances of concept $target(r_n)$. Similarly to derived roles, we can define *derived attributes*, by a role path followed by an attribute. Like attributes, these do not have inverses. Clearly, every role (attribute) is also a derived role (attribute).

Let $p = c.r$ be a concept path, q be a prefix of r, and $q \setminus r$ denote r with q removed. If c' is either $target(c.q)$ or a superconcept thereof but a subconcept of $source(q \setminus r)$, then $c'.(q \setminus r)$ is called a *suffix* of $c.r$. Obviously, $target(p)$ is a suffix of p.

Given DB, a database of S, we can associate extents with derived concepts in a straightforward manner. We note the following facts concerning these extents. First, the extent of $conc(p)$ is a subset of the extent of $target(p)$, hence also of its superconcepts in S. Second, the extent of $conc(p)$ is a subset of the extent of each of its suffixes. For example, it is easy to see that $p'=$Activity.*produced* is a suffix of $p=$Person.*carried_out-.produced* and all instances of p (objects produced by an activity carried out by a person) are instances of p' (objects produced by activities).

Given a global schema S, the *derived schema* (or *extended schema*) $S_\chi = (C_\chi, R_\chi, A_\chi, source, target, isa_\chi)$ is defined as follows : (i) C_χ is the set of all derived concepts, defined by the concept paths definable in S; (ii) $R_\chi(A_\chi)$ is the set of all the derived roles (attributes) defined by the role (attribute) paths definable in S, and $source$ and $target$ are defined as above; (iii) the isa_χ relation contains the isa relations from S, and additionally each pair c, c', where c is a derived concept defined by a concept path p in S, and c' is the derived concept defined by a suffix of p.

Our interest in the derived schema is motivated by the fact that some sources may provide data only for derived concepts. The isa relationships in the derived schema enable us to use these sources to provide answers in terms of the original concepts. For example, even if a source provides only information about Person.*carried_out.produced*, this allows us to obtain some instances of Man_Made_Object, although not necessarily all. Note that answers obtained from sources in the *local as view* approach are partial answers in any case.

3.1 Mapping Rules

A source is integrated to the system, by providing a set of *mapping rules* that describe the relationships between the source schema and the global schema. There exist different ways for defining such views varying in terms of size and preciseness of the definition but also in the complexity of the query rewriting algorithm [7]. We have chosen essentially the same approach as in [7], namely to associate paths in the global schema with paths in the source schemas. This allows us to both associate concepts with XML nodes in the sources, and to associate relationships among concepts (expressed as roles or derived roles in the global schema) with XPath *location paths* in the XML sources.

Paths in a source are described in terms of XPath [6] location paths. We assume familiarity with the XPath language. Described in a nutshell, an XPath location path is composed of a sequence of location steps. Location steps have three parts: (i) an *axis* specifies the relationship (child, descendant, ancestor, attribute etc.) between the nodes selected by the location step and the context node, (ii) a *node test* specifies a node's XML type (element, attribute, and so on) and possibly its name, and (iii) *optional predicates* which use XPath expressions to further refine the set of selected nodes.

Let V be a set of variables, and U be a set of URLs. A *mapping rule* is an expression of the form $R : u/q \ as \ v \rightarrow p$, where : (i) R is the rule's *label*; (ii) $u \in V \cup U$, the rule's *root*, is either a variable or a URL (u is called the root of R); (iii) q is an XPath *location path*, called the *location path* of the rule; (iv) *as v* is a *binding* of v (R is called the binding rule of v), where $v \in V$ is a variable; (v) p is a *schema path*. More precisely, it is a role path if u is a variable and a concept path otherwise. A rule R is called a *relative mapping rule* if its root is a variable u, and an *absolute mapping rule* otherwise. In the first case, u is the *root variable* of R, and this occurrence of u is a *use* of the variable. Let $lp(R)$, $sp(R)$ denote R's *location path* and *schema path*, respectively.

Given a set of mapping rules for a source s, we define *reachability* (in s) for rules and variables, as follows : (1) each rule whose root is a URL (the URL of s) is reachable; (2) each variable bound by a reachable rule is reachable; (3) finally, each rule whose root is a reachable variable is reachable. The set of mapping rules is *cyclic* if this definition of reachability leads to a cycle. The simplest case of a cycle is a rule whose left-hand-side contains $v/A \ as \ v$ (provided that v can be reached from a URL by other rules). In this work we consider only acyclic mappings.

A *mapping* M over $\mathcal{S_X}$ and for a source s is a set of mapping rules such that 1) labels are unique (that is, no two rules have the same label), 2) all rules and variables are reachable in M, 3) the concepts, roles and attributes used in its rules occur in $\mathcal{S_X}$ and 4) it contains no cycles.

The concatenation of mapping rules is defined as follows : two rules $R_1 : a/q_1 \ as \ v_1 \rightarrow p_1$, $R_2 : v_1/q_2 \ as \ v_2 \rightarrow p_2$, can be *concatenated*, if the composition of their schema paths, $p_1 \circ p_2$ is well defined[3]. Note the constraint that the root of R_2 is bound in R_1 and that concatenation is possible only if p_2 is a role path. The result of the concatenation is the rule $R_1.R_2 : a/q_1/q_2 \ as \ v_2 \rightarrow p_1 \circ p_2$.

Given a mapping M, its *closure* is the set of all rules that can be obtained from M by repeated concatenation. It is denoted by M^*. Its *expansion*, denoted $\hat{M}$, is the set of absolute rules in M^* ($\hat{M} \subseteq M^*$) and can be computed by a bottom-up fixpoint computation (since we only consider acyclic mappings, we are sure that a finite fixpoint exists).

Given a global schema $\mathcal{S}$, a mapping M over $\mathcal{S}$ can naturally be interpreted in the derived schema $\mathcal{S_X}$. Each absolute rule in $\hat{M}$ defines a derived concept, and each relative rule in M^* defines a derived role (attribute). Let us denote by $\mathcal{S}_M$ the restriction of $\mathcal{S_X}$ to the derived concepts, roles and attributes of M^*.

---

[3] We do not define any restriction on the concatenation of the rules' location paths.

For example, rule $R_1.R_3$ defines a derived concept, *conc(Person.carried_out.-produced)* subconcept of Man_Made_Object, and rule R_3 defines a derived role, *role(carried_out.produced)*, between concept Person and concept Man Made Object. Rule $R_3.R_4$ defines a derived attribute *attr(carried_out.produced.has_title)* of concept Person.

A mapping M for a source s associated with URL u, allows us to view a collection of XML fragments reachable from u as a database that conforms to $\mathcal{S}_M$. To define this database, the population of each derived concept, *conc(p)*, is defined as the union of the set of fragments returned by all absolute rules R in $\hat{M}$ where $sp(R) = p$ or p is a suffix of $sp(R)$.

The set of fragments X_R returned by some absolute rule R in $\hat{M}$ is defined as follows. The root of an absolute rule R is the URL u. Hence X_R is assigned the set of XML fragments that can be obtained by applying the location path $lp(R)$ to the XML document identified by u. The set X_R can be computed by a simple fixpoint computation, using rules in M. Since M^* is finite, alternatively the rules of $\hat{M}$ can be used directly.

Similarly, the relative rules of M^* are interpreted as roles (or attributes) of $\mathcal{S}_M$ in this database of XML fragments, represented by location paths.

Before leaving this subject, we note that according to the LAV approach, XML extents defined as above for the concepts are viewed as subsets of the real (but unknown) extents. Indeed, as sources are added, and rules are added to a mapping, the extents grow. In the LAV approach, any set of answers returned for a query is assumed to be a subset of the full (but unknown) answer.

3.2 Keys

As illustrated in Section 2, *keys* are essential to decide whether two XML fragments describe the same concept. We assume that sources are heterogeneous and autonomous, and we do not expect that they provide us with persistent object identifiers that are valid for all sources. The ID/IDREF XML attribute mechanisms are used for internal references, but cannot serve for a key mechanism to perform joins between objects that originate from different sources. Sources might specify meaningful keys in terms of XML elements/attributes as proposed in [4,8,16], but one cannot expect different autonomous sources to always use the same keys. For example a painting might be identified by its title in one source, by its title and the year of creation in another source.

A way to overcome this problem is to define *global keys* for *concepts* in the global schema. A *key* for a concept c is defined as a list of *derived attributes* (called *key paths*) that originate from concept c and is denoted by $key(c) = \{a_1, a_2, \ldots a_n\}$. W.l.g we assume in this paper that a concept is associated with at most one key, and all its subconcepts (including the derived ones) share the same key.

In our global schema, we could state for example, that an instance of concept Person is identified by attribute *has_name*: $key(\text{Person})=\{has\_name\}$. Instances of concept Man_Made_Object are identifiable by their title and their year of creation: $key(\text{Man\_Made\_Object})= \{has\_title, created\_by.date.year\}$. Images have no key, i.e. $key(\text{Image})=\emptyset$.

4 Query Processing

Our query processing approach is presented in this section. We first introduce the user query language (section 4.1). Two query processing strategies are then discussed. In the first approach (section 4.2), the solution to a query is the union of the complete answers from individual sources. If no complete answer can be obtained from a source, then the source is abandoned. In contrast, the second approach (section 4.3) allows also for incomplete answers from a given source. If a source s can only partially answer a query, then the query is decomposed in two parts one to be fully answered by s and the other part being sent to the other sources. The partial results from different sources are then joined by the mediator using *global keys*.

4.1 Query Language

The users query the virtual database as presented via the global schema, using simple *tree queries*, based on **select-from-where** clauses following an OQL-like syntax. Queries are of the form:

$$Q: \textbf{select} \ \ x_i, x_j, ...$$
$$\textbf{from} \ \ \ \ p_1 \ x_1,$$
$$x_{j_2}.p_2 \ x_2, ...$$
$$x_{j_i}.p_i \ x_i, ...$$
$$\textbf{where} \ \ c_0 \ \textbf{and} \ c_1 \ \textbf{and} \ ...$$

The x_i's are *query variables* and each p_i in the **from** clause is a path in the global schema (schema path), called the *binding path* of x_i and denoted $bp(x_i)$. The first variable x_1 is the *root variable* of the query, and its binding path p_1 is a concept path. For each $i > 1$, there is a single clause $x_{j_i}.p_i \ x_i$, and p_i is a role path. We call x_{j_i} the *parent* of x_i. We assume the parenthood relation between variables forms a tree, with x_1 as its root. x_1 ranges over the extent of the derived concept $conc(p_1)$, and $x_i, i > 1$, ranges over the instances defined by traversing instances of the derived role p_i from the instances of its parent.

We assume queries satisfy the following restrictions. First, no restructuring is allowed in the **select** clause. Although this may add expressive power to the language, we feel it is not strictly needed for our application. Certainly, it is orthogonal to the issue of retrieving data from sources, addressed in this paper.   Second, the **where** clause is a conjunction of simple predicates, where a simple predicate is of the form $x_i \theta d$ in which $\theta \in \{=, <, >, \le, \ge\}$ and d is an atomic value. Thus, it is not possible to express joins by equalities between variables, i.e., by predicates of the form $x_i = x_j$. This restricts the expressive power of the query language but simplifies the rewriting and evaluation of queries. Third, schema paths occur in the **from** clause, but not in the **select** clause or the **where** clause of a query. It is easy to show that a query with schema paths in the **select** and the **where** clause can be rewritten into an equivalent query in which they appear only in the **from** clause. Last, the language has no quantifiers, aggregates, or subqueries. However, a variable x_j present in the **from** clause is implicitly existentially quantified. Thus, queries with certain kinds of existential quantification can be expressed in the above form.

Since no joins are allowed in the **where** clause, a query whose variables form a forest can be decomposed into a cross product of several tree queries: the restriction to tree rather than forest queries results in no loss of expressive power.

The result of a such a query is a *set of tuples* of the form $\{[a_i, a_j, \ldots a_k]\}$ where $a_i, a_j, \ldots a_k$ are instances of the variables in the query's **select** clause and can be either atomic values, or XML fragments.

In the sequel, the following representation of tree queries is used. A tree query Q is represented as a labeled tree, $T(Q) = (X, par, bp, ops)$ where X is the set of query variables (tree nodes), par is the parent binary relation between nodes defined above, $bp(x)$ is the binding path of x and ops is a set of operations associated with variable x, defined as follows : for a variable x in the **select** clause $\pi \in ops(x)$, and for each condition $x\theta d$ in the **where** clause, $\sigma_{x\theta d} \in ops(x)$.

4.2   Variable to Rules Bindings

We now proceed to the details of query processing. We first present a simple approach in which a source contributes to the answer only if it can fully answer the query.

To evaluate a query, we need to *rewrite* it into an XML query that some sources can answer. Obviously, in general only some of the sources contain the data requested in the query. Each such source returns a subset of the possible answers; the union of the answers from all relevant sources is presented to the user (see Section 5).

For this rewriting, we use the mapping rules. For a query Q and a source s, we define a *variable to rule binding*, or shortly *variable binding*, as a mapping β from a set of query variables to M^*. We consider only bindings such that $dom(\beta)$ is either empty or is the set of nodes of some prefix[4] of $T(Q)$. The empty binding is denoted by $\beta_{\emptyset}$. If β binds all variables in Q then it is called a *full binding*, otherwise it is a *partial binding*.

The properties of a binding β are the following : if $dom(\beta)$ is not empty, then β associates each variable in it with a rule of M^*, such that the following hold:

1. if x is the root of query Q, then $\beta(x)$ is an absolute mapping rule such that $conc(sp(\beta(x)))$ isa_M $conc(bp(x))$, i.e., the derived concept defined by $sp(\beta(x))$ is a subconcept of the derived concept defined by the binding path $bp(x)$ in S_M,
2. else, let $par(x) = x'$, then $\beta(x)$ is a relative rule, and
   - the root variable of rule $\beta(x)$ is bound in rule $\beta(x')$,
   - the role path (RHS) of the rule $\beta(x)$ is equal to the binding path $bp(x)$,
   - and finally, the concatenation of the two rules $\beta(x')$ and $\beta(x)$ is well-defined.

In the first case, x is the root of Q and bound to some (possibly derived) concept by its binding path $bp(x)$ that has the form c or $c.r$. An absolute rule R can provide instances for this concept if its concept path (RHS) $sp(R)$, viewed as a derived concept, is a sub-concept of $bp(x)$ (i.e. if the latter is a suffix of $sp(R)$ or it defines a superconcept thereof). Note that we use here both derived concepts and the isa relationship between them. Thus, the derived schema defined in Section 3 is essential for our approach to query processing.

---

[4] A tree T' is a prefix of a tree T if it is a subtree of T and its root is the same as that of T.

In the second case, the assumption that if β is defined on x then it is defined on the parent of x follows from the requirement that its domain is a prefix of $T(Q)$. In this case, the declaration of x in Q has the form $x'.q\ x$, and $bp(x) = q$. Answers for x can be obtained from answers for x', by following the binding path q of x.

A partial binding β is called *maximal* if there does not exist a binding β' such that $dom(\beta) \subset dom(\beta')$ and $\beta(x) = \beta'(x)$ for all x in $dom(\beta)$. It is evident that a full binding is a maximal binding.

Variable Binding Algorithm. We will now describe a *variable binding* algorithm $\mathcal{B}(Q, s)$ which takes as an input a query Q and a mapping M for a source s and returns a set of maximal bindings. A binding β is represented as a vector of associations of variables to rules, $[x_1 \mapsto R_1, \ldots x_n \mapsto R_n]$. The algorithm is illustrated in more detail in Fig. 6. First, the variables of the query tree are arranged in pre-order: the root is first, and every other node occurs after its parent. The algorithm starts from the empty binding, and once a set of partial bindings have been constructed, it tries to extend each one, using the ordering of the variables. The extension of a partial binding β by $[x \mapsto R]$ is denoted $\beta \times [x \mapsto R]$.

In the first step, we extend $\beta_\emptyset$ to the root variable x_1. For each absolute rule R in M^* such that the derived concept defined by $sp(R)$ is a subconcept of the derived concept defined by the concept path $bp(x_1)$ in $\mathcal{S}_M$, we create the binding $[x_1 \mapsto R]$ and add it to the set of bindings for x_1. If no absolute rule is found such that the above conditions hold, then the algorithm stops, and returns the empty set. Then, we iterate through the sequence of variables, from the left. Let the current, not yet treated, variable be x_i, and let y be its parent. For each binding β constructed so far, if $y \notin dom(\beta)$ then β cannot be extended to x_i (recall that a binding is always defined on a prefix of $T(Q)$). Else, let binding β associate rule R' with y. Then, for each relative rule R of M^*, such that $bp(x_i) = sp(R)$, if R and R' can be concatenated (i.e, R' binds the variable that is the root of R, and their schema paths can be composed), we extend β by $[x_i \mapsto R]$. In this case, β can be dropped, since the new binding extends it. Note that the edge from y to x_i is *traversed in this step, and only in this step*.

$\mathcal{B}(Q, s)$ finds the *maximal* bindings for a query Q and a mapping M on source s. The proof is straightforward. Consider a binding β in the result set of $\mathcal{B}(Q, s)$. If there exists a variable x that we could add in $dom(\beta)$, this means that there exists some rule R such that $\beta(parent(x)).R$ is well-defined, then by the algorithm x would already be in $dom(\beta)$ which is a contradiction, from the above assumption.

Let us illustrate the algorithm with query Q_2 presented earlier, and the mapping rules for source S_1 illustrated in Fig. 4. Rule R_1 returns answers for variable a. The rule's schema path is **Person** which is equal to a's binding path (**Person**). Rule R_2 returns answers for b, since (1) its schema path *has_name* is equal to the variable's binding path, (2) its root variable u_1 is bound in rule R_1, and (3) the composition of the schema paths of rules R_1 and R_2 is well defined, since attribute *has_name* is defined in concept **Person**. In a similar manner, we find that variable c is bound to rule R_3 and variable d to rule R_4. For variable e, we do not find a mapping rule whose schema path is equal to the variable's binding path (*located_at*). The result $\mathcal{B}(Q_2, S_1)$ is the singleton $\{\beta_1\} = \{[a \mapsto R_1, b \mapsto R_2, c \mapsto R_3, d \mapsto R_4]\}$.

Input :   the sequence of variables of query Q, in pre-order: $x_1, \ldots, x_n$;
                     the closure of mapping rules M^* of some mapping M for source s;
Output :   the set B of maximal bindings for Q and M
Algorithm : $B := \emptyset$;
                     for each absolute rule $R \in \hat{M}$
                         if concept path $bp(x_1)$ is equal to or is a suffix of path $sp(R)$
                             /* $conc(sp(R))$ *is a subconcept of* $conc(bp(x_1))$ */
                             add $[x_1 \mapsto R]$ to B;
                     for $i = 2, \ldots, n$ {
                         /* $Temp$ *contains all maximal bindings up to* x_{i-1} */
                         $Temp := B$;
                         $y :=$ parent of x_i;
                         for each binding $\beta \in Temp$ where $y \in dom(\beta)$ {
                             for each rule R in M^* where $sp(R) = bp(x_i)$
                                 if the composition of $\beta(y).R$ is well defined
                                     /* β *is extended to* x_i *and added to* B */
                                     add $\beta \times [x_i \mapsto R]$ to B;
                             if β was extended to x_i
                                 remove β from B;
                         }
                     }
                     return B;

Fig. 6. Variable binding Algorithm $\mathcal{B}(Q, s)$

4.3   Query Decomposition

Let S be the set of sources mapped to the global schema. Algorithm $\mathcal{B}(Q, s)$ returns for each source s in S the set of maximal bindings. Each such binding β is either full, i.e. $dom(\beta)$ contains all variables in Q (then s can answer the query using β), or *partial*. In the latter case, β provides us with partial answers, i.e. does not provide answers for all variables in the query. To complete these partial answers, we *decompose* the query Q into (i) a *prefix query* that source s can answer using binding β, denoted $Q_p(\beta)$, and (ii) a set of *suffix queries*, denoted $\mathcal{QS}(\beta)$.

As an example, take the result of algorithm $\mathcal{B}(Q_2, S_1)$ calculated for query Q_2, and source S_1 published by the mapping rules illustrated in Fig. 4. It contains a *partial* binding β_1 defined on a proper subset of the variables in the initial query : for an instance of variable c we miss instances for variable e (and its descendants).

To obtain the complete answer, we define (1) a *prefix query* that source S_1 can answer using β (query $Q_p(\beta_1) = Q_2(a)$ illustrated in Fig. 5) and one *suffix* query (query $Q_2(b)$ illustrated in Fig. 5). The prefix query $Q_p(\beta)$ is a prefix of $T(Q)$ and is defined on the set of variables in $dom(\beta)$.   The suffix queries of a prefix $Q_p(\beta)$ in Q are defined as follows. Let N be the set of variables in $Q_p(\beta)$ which contain at least one child in Q but not in $Q_p(\beta)$ (we call N the *boundary* of $Q_p(\beta)$). Then we define a suffix query for each variable x in N as the subtree of Q rooted at x and containing all descendants of x not in $Q_p(\beta)$. It is easy to see that query $Q_2(b)$ illustrated in Fig. 5 is a suffix query of

$Q_2(a)$ in Q_2. Observe that for a given prefix query there might exist zero, one or more suffix queries.

Joining the results. The results of the prefix query and the suffix queries must be joined. In order to perform the join between a prefix and a suffix query the following two conditions must hold : (1) the concept to which the root of a suffix query is bound, should have a key, and (2) the sources on which the join is performed should provide complete values for this key.

The *key values* of an instance of a concept c are obtained by considering $key(c)$ as a query ranging over all **key paths** in it. The result of a key query is of the form $\{[x_1, x_2, .., x_n]\}$, where the $x_i's$ are instances of the variables to which the key paths are bound in the key query. For example, the query illustrated below returns the key values for an instance x of concept **Man_Made_Object**:

$key(Man\_Made\_Object)$: **select** t, y
    from Man_Made_Object x,
        x.has_title t, x.created_by.date.year y

Given a (prefix or suffix) query Q whose result is of the form $\{[a_1, a_2, \ldots a_n]\}$ where the $a_i's$ are instances of the variables in the query's **select** clause and a key query $key(c)$, where c is the concept on which the join will be performed, Q is extended to Q' so as to get, as well as the a_i's, the key values for the fragments, instances of concept c, accessed by Q. The result of Q' is of the form $\{[a_1, a_2, \ldots a_n, x_1, x_2, \ldots , x_p]\}$ where the x_j's are instances of the key query variables (variables bound to the key paths in $key(c)$). For example, the prefix query obtained after extending query $Q_2(a)$ of Fig. 5 by the key of concept **Man_Made_Object** is given below[5].

$ext(Q_2(a))$: **select** d, t, y
        from   Person a, a.has_name b,
            a.carried_out.produced c, c.has_title d,
            c.has_title t, c.created_by.date.year y
        where $b = $ "Van Gogh"

Query Execution Plans. Let Q be a query and S be a set of sources. A *decomposition* of Q w.r.t. some maximal binding β is a couple $\mathcal{D}(Q, \beta) = [Q_p(\beta), \mathcal{QS}(\beta)]$ such that $Q_p(\beta)$ is a prefix query of Q on source s in S and $\mathcal{QS}(\beta)$ is the set of suffix queries of $Q_p(\beta)$ in Q. For example, $\mathcal{D}(Q, \beta_1) = [Q_2(a), \{Q_2(b)\}]$ is a decomposition for query Q_2 and the maximal binding β_1 defined on source S_1. Observe that $\mathcal{QS}(\beta)$ is empty if β is a full binding for Q.

Let $\mathcal{D}(Q, \beta) = [Q_p(\beta), \mathcal{QS}(\beta)]$ be a decomposition of Q. Then $Q_p(\beta)$ can be translated into a source query using binding β. For each suffix query in $\mathcal{QS}(\beta)$ either a full binding is found or the suffix query has still to be decomposed. Let Q_i be a suffix query in $\mathcal{QS}(\beta)$ and $k_i = [x_1, \ldots x_p]$ denote the *key* query variables bound to the key paths of concept c_j associated to the root variable of Q_i. Then $Q_p(\beta) \boxtimes_{k_i} Q_i$ denotes the *join* operation between $Q_p(\beta)$ and Q_i (we assume that both queries are extended by

---

[5] This query can be optimized by keeping the variables that are common to the key query and the prefix query (the case of variables d and t in the example above).

the appropriate key queries). A *prefix query rewriting* $\mathcal{LR}(Q, \beta)$ for a decomposition $\mathcal{D}(Q, \beta)$ is defined as the join between a prefix query and all suffix queries $Q_i, 1 \leq i \leq n$, in $\mathcal{QS}(\beta)$ (if β is a full binding for Q then $\mathcal{QS}(\beta)$ is empty and $\mathcal{LR}(Q, \beta) = Q_p(\beta)$):

$$\mathcal{LR}(Q, \beta) = Q_p(\beta) \bowtie_{k_1} \mathcal{GR}(Q_1, S) \bowtie_{k_2} \ldots \bowtie_{k_n} \mathcal{GR}(Q_n, S))$$

Then the initial query Q can be rewritten as $\mathcal{GR}$(Q,S) defined as the union of all prefix rewritings for sources in S:

$$\mathcal{GR}(Q, S) = \bigcup_{s \in S} \bigcup_{\beta \in \mathcal{B}(Q, s)} \mathcal{LR}(Q, \beta)$$

Let a *query execution plan* (QEP) be defined as follows : (1) a query q that can be answered by a single source (that is a query for which there exists a full binding) is a(n atomic) QEP; (2) the union of two QEP's is a QEP [6]; (3) the join of two QEP's is a QEP [7]. Basically, sources answer atomic queries in a QEP and the mediator performs joins and unions. A QEP can involve several atomic queries sent to a given source. It might be interesting to combine such queries in a single query. This implies the reorganization using classical properties such as distributivity of union w.r.t. join. Such properties and reorganizations as well as other optimizations are beyond the scope of this paper.

Given a set of sources S and a query Q, the algorithm P(Q) shown in Fig. 7 computes a query execution plan for Q. For each source s and maximal binding $\beta \in \mathcal{B}(Q, s)$, a QEP $P(\beta)$ of the prefix rewriting $\mathcal{LR}(Q, \beta)$ is computed : if β is a full binding (i.e. complete answers are obtained), the result is query Q. Else, if β is a partial binding, then query Q is decomposed into a prefix query $Q_p(\beta)$ and a set of suffix queries $\mathcal{QS}(\beta)$ (these queries are also extended by the key queries as shown before). The query execution plan of Q against source s is obtained by joining $Q_p(\beta)$ with the query execution plan for each suffix query $Q' \in \mathcal{QS}(\beta)$ (variable k' denotes the key query variables of Q'). To calculate the query execution plan of a suffix query Q' the algorithm is called recursively. Finally the obtained plan is added to the existing plan by union.

Observe that there are two reasons to interrupt the calculation of a query execution plan for a given source s and binding β. The most trivial case is that there exists no maximal binding for Q in s. The second reason is that there exists at least one suffix query which cannot be satisfied (empty query execution plan).

5   System Architecture

In this section we sketch the architecture of the prototype ST_YX [9] (Fig. 8) that implements the data integration approach described previously. XML Web resources can

---

[6] Remember that union is heterogeneous, that is two sets of tuples answering the same query but resulting from different sources might have different structures for the i-th component.

[7] We restrict join to the non commutative aforementioned definition of join: the root of the second QEP should belong to the boundary of the first QEP and each of them should correspond to a concept for which a key has been defined.

Input: a query Q and a set of sources S
Output: a query execution plan for Q;
Algorithm: $QEP(Q, S) = \emptyset$;
                    for all sources $s \in S$ {
                        if $\mathcal{B}(Q, s) \neq \emptyset$ {
                            /* there exists at least one maximal binding for Q in s */
                            for all bindings $\beta \in \mathcal{B}(Q, s)$ {
                                if β is a full binding $P(\beta) := Q$;
                                else { $P(\beta) := Q_p(\beta)$;
                                    for all suffix queries $Q' \in \mathcal{QS}(\beta)$
                                        if $P(\beta) \neq \emptyset$
                                            /* there exists a non-empty query plan */
                                            /* for all subqueries up to Q' */
                                            if $QEP(Q', S) \neq \emptyset$
                                                /* there exists a query plan of Q' */
                                                $P(\beta) := P(\beta) \boxtimes_{k'} QEP(Q', S)$;
                                            else $P(\beta) := \emptyset$;
                                }
                                $QEP(Q, S) = QEP(Q, S) \cup P(\beta)$
                            }
                        }
                    }
                    return $QEP(Q, S)$;

Fig. 7. Query Execution Plans Generation

be published on the fly by creating/modifying/deleting mapping rules between source fragments and the global schema using the *Source Publication Interface*. The global schema can be consulted through the *Schema Manager* which is also responsible for its loading in a ST_YX portal. The mapping rules are first validated by the *Rules Manager* which is also responsible for their storage. The publication of a resource also consists in providing an XSLT transformation program[8] that can be used for formatting source data in the query result[9]. *Query processing* is done in several steps: first *user queries* can be formulated using a standard Web browser. They are either created by a generic *Query Interface*, or simply stored in the form of a hypertext link (URL). The *Query Interface* communicates with the *Schema Manager* allowing the user to browse the global schema for the formulation of a query. The *Query Interface* forwards the query to the *Query Parser* which performs a syntactical analysis of the query with some type-checking w.r.t. the global schema and produces a language neutral intermediate representation of it. The query is then forwarded to the *Query Execution Plans Generator*, which creates the query execution plan. The *Integration Module* rewrites the queries into Quilt Queries

---

[8] XSL Transformations (XSLT : http://www.w3.org/TR/xslt)
[9] If the query result contains XML fragments from a source, then those are transformed using the source's XSL Stylesheet.

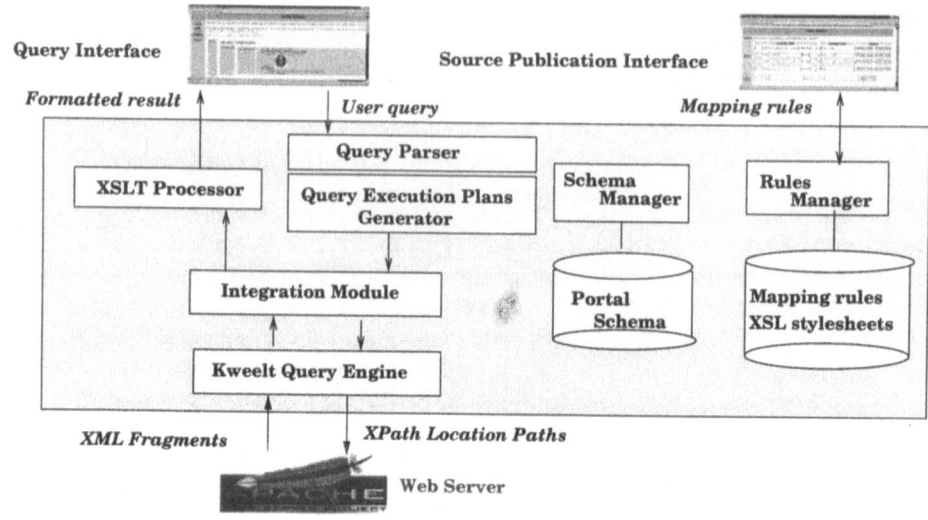

Fig. 8. ST_YX Portal Architecture

and sends them to the *Kweelt Query Engine*[10] for evaluation[11]. The resulting XML fragments are sent to the *Integration Module* that combines the results. This module, based on the query and the mapping rules, inserts schema specific tags, and then the *XSLT Processor* (Cocoon[12]) finally transforms the result into an HTML document which is displayed to the browser of the user.

The ST_YX prototype was implemented in Java JDK 1.2. XML technologies such as XSLT, XPath and the Xalan XML Stylesheet processor[13] were used.

6   Related Work

Data integration has become an important issue during the past years and a large number of integration systems have been proposed. These systems can be classified according to the architectures used for query processing : *data warehouse* systems materialize all source data before query processing, whereas *mediators* propose a virtual database and push queries to the source level based on sophisticated query rewriting algorithms. Our approach clearly belongs to the second category.

Mediator systems are classified according to the way sources are described to the mediator and queries are evaluated [11]. Tsimmis [14], MIX [3], YAT [5] and Picsel [10] follow the *global as view* approach and are not directly comparable to ours. On the other hand, Information Manifold [12] follows the *local as view* approach. In this system the

---

[10] Kweelt Query Engine : http://db.cis.upenn.edu/Kweelt/.
[11] The Kweelt query engine can evaluate the subset of XQuery expressions presented in this paper.
[12] http://xml.apache.org/cocoon
[13] http://xml.apache.org/xalan-j/index.html

global schema is a flat relational schema, and Description Logics is used to represent hierarchies of classes. The sources are expressed as *relational views* over this schema. Query rewriting is done by the *Bucket* algorithm which rewrites a *conjunctive query* expressed in terms of the global schema using the source views. It examines independently each of the query subgoals and tries to find rewritings but loses some by considering the subgoals in isolation. The *MiniCon* algorithm [15] improves the Bucket algorithm by exploiting the input/output dependencies between the query subgoals for reducing the search space of possible rewritings. Algorithm $\mathcal{B}(Q, S)$ presented in this paper resembles to MiniCon since it exploits the *parent/child* dependencies of query variables for query decomposition.

The Agora [13] system, offers an XML view for relational and XML data and user queries are XQuery expressions. Although XML is used as the global data model, an extended use of the relational model is made : the XML view is translated into a generic relational schema, XML resources are described as relational views over this schema and XQuery expressions are translated to standard SQL queries which are then decomposed, optimized and evaluated. Our system and query rewriting algorithm extensively exploit the tree structure of XML data which is described as local views of a more powerful conceptual schema with inheritance.

Last, the Xyleme [7] system is based on a data-warehouse solution for the integration of XML data ("all XML data of the Web"). However, it can be considered as a mediator system, since source data is stored without transformation and users can query this data via different views. Each view is described by a DTD, called *abstract DTD*, and source data is mapped to one or several DTDs using path-to-path mapping rules. These rules are similar to our mapping rules with the difference that they map absolute source paths (starting from the document root) to absolute paths in the abstract DTD (starting from the DTD root element).

7   Conclusions

We proposed in this paper an alternate approach for integrating XML sources following the LAV approach. Instead of choosing for the global view, a relational or XML schema, we advocated the use of an ontology-based mediation. The global schema is close to an object-oriented schema on a terminology describing a common domain of interest and users issue queries on this global schema. Our contributions are (i) a view definition language, (ii) a rewriting algorithm, (iii) an algorithm for generating execution plans, and (iv) a prototype validating the approach.

We are currently working on several extensions concerning our integration model. First, we try to extend the query language by allowing explicit joins in the **where** clause of a query. This does not change the binding algorithm, but increases the complexity of query processing. A second issue we are looking at concerns the usage of *maximal* bindings for query decomposition. In fact, the current version of the rewriting algorithm generates query execution plans which favor information stored locally in the same document. For example, if some source s provides a single full binding for some query Q, the algorithm will return the result of Q in s, but will not try to join s with some other source s'. This restriction can be removed by allowing also partial bindings that are not maximal, but will increase the number of possible decompositions significantly.

References

1. S. Abiteboul, P. Buneman, and D. Suciu. *Data On the Web: From Relations to Semistructured Data and XML*. Morgan Kaufmann, October 1999.
2. B. Amann, C. Beeri, I. Fundulaki, and M. Scholl. Ontology-Based Integration of XML Web Resources. In *International Semantic Web Conference (ISWC)*, Sardinia, Italy, 2002.
3. C. Baru, A. Gupta, B. Ludäscher, R. Marciano, Y. Papakonstantinou, P. Velikhov, and V. Chu. XML-based information mediation with MIX. In *Demonstrations, ACM/SIGMOD*, pages 597–599, 1999.
4. P. Buneman, S. B. Davidson, W. Fan, C. S. Hara, and W. C. Tan. Keys for XML. In *Proc. WWW10*, pages 201–210, 2001.
5. V. Christophides, S. Cluet, and J. Simeon. On Wrapping Query Languages and Efficient XML Integration. In *Proc. of ACM SIGMOD*, Dallas, USA, May 2000.
6. J. Clark and S. DeRose (eds.). XML Path Language (XPath) Version 1.0. W3C Recommendation, November 1999. http://www.w3c.org/TR/xpath.
7. S. Cluet, P. Veltri, and D. Vodislav. Views in a Large Scale XML Repository. In *Proc. VLDB*, Rome, Italy, September 2001.
8. W. Fan, G. Kooper, and J. Simeon. A Unified Constraint Model for XML. In *Proc. WWW10*, Hong-Kong, China, May 2001.
9. I. Fundulaki, B. Amann, C. Beeri, and M. Scholl. STYX : Connecting the XML World to the World of Semantics. In *Proceedings of EDBT*, Prague, Czech Republic, March 2002. (Demonstration).
10. F. Goasdoué, V. Lattés, and M-C. Rousset. The use of CARIN language and algorithms for information integration: The PICSEL System. *International Journal on Cooperative Information Systems*, 2000.
11. A. Halevy. Theory of answering queries using views. *SIGMOD Record*, 29(4):40–47, 2000.
12. A. Levy, A. Rajaraman, and J. Ordille. Querying Heterogeneous Information Sources Using Source Descriptions. In *Proc. VLDB*, pages 251–262, Mumbai (Bombay), India, September 1996.
13. I. Manolescu, D. Florescu, and D. Kossmann. Answering XML Queries over Hterogeneous Data Sources. In *Proc. VLDB*, Rome, Italy, September 2001.
14. Y. Papakonstantinou, H. Garcia-Molina, and J. Widom. Object Exchange Across Heterogeneous Information Sources. In *Proc. ICDE*, pages 251–260, Taipei, Taiwan, March 1995.
15. R. Pottinger and A. Levy. A Scalable Algorithm for Answering Queries Using Views. In *Proc. VLDB*, pages 484–495, Cairo, Egypt, September 2000.
16. H. Thompson, D. Beech, M. Maloney, and N. Mendelsohn. XML Schema Part 1: Structures. W3C Recommendation, May 2001. http://www.w3.org/TR/XML-schema-1.

Handling Partial Matches in Semistructured Data with Cooperative Query Answering Techniques

Antonio Badia[1] and Sanjay Kumar Madria[2]

[1] Computer Engineering and Computer Science department,
University of Louisville, Louisville KY 40292
abadia@louisville.edu
[2] Computer Science department,
University of Missouri-Rolla, Rolla, M), 65409
madria@umr.edu

Abstract. We describe for the first time in the literature the application of Cooperative Query Answering techniques to semistructured data. In particular, we develop methods to deal with partial matching of path expressions when querying data in a graph-based model. We identify different types of mismatch and offer heuristics to handle them. We also describe a preliminary implementation.

1 Introduction

Semistructured data is a new paradigm in database research which studies collections of heterogeneous, irregularly structured data ([Abi97,Bun97,Suc97]). Querying semistructured data poses some particular challenges. Since semistructured data is accessed by many kinds of users, including casual (non expert) users, the chances of formulating a query incorrectly are higher than in traditional databases. The lack of a completely regular structure also increases the likelihood of making a mistake when writing a query. Finally, query languages for semistructured data still share the notion of exact answer with more traditional query languages. Thus, they are as inflexible in that they require exact matches between the query specification and the data in the database, and are unable to point out closely related information to the user. Therefore, systems that store semistructured data could benefit from cooperative behavior ([Abi97]).

Cooperative behavior in query answering has been studied under the label of Cooperative Query Answering (CQA). CQA may be described as the set of theory, tools and techniques that allow information systems to extend the traditional notion of answer in such a way that the system meets the expectations of intelligent, cooperating agents who try to maximize meaningful information transfer ([GGM92]). Most techniques for CQA have been developed in the context of traditional databases, usually relational or Datalog databases ([ID94]).

In this paper we define new methods to achieve cooperative query answering in the context of semistructured data. In particular, we relax the condition that

R. Meersman, Z. Tari (Eds.): CoopIS/DOA/ODBASE 2002, LNCS 2519, pp. 449–467, 2002.
© Springer-Verlag Berlin Heidelberg 2002

data must match exactly the query specification in order to qualify for an answer, and describe methods by which to find data that is reasonably close to what was asked for. We focus on partial matches in *path expressions*, which is an integral mechanism of most query languages for semistructured data.

In the next section, we introduce some background, including the basic ideas from (traditional) cooperative query answering, as well as some related research. In section 3, we introduce the mechanisms by which to handle the problem we focus on in this paper: partial matches. We first give some basic definitions for the problem, then show heuristics to solve it and finally discuss an initial implementation. We conclude by sketching some future work.

2   Background and Related Research

In this section we briefly describe cooperative query answering concepts in its standard setting, relational and logical databases. We also mention research which is along the lines of the work presented here.

Semistructured data is assumed not to have a strict type, but to posses irregular, partial organization ([Abi97,Bun97]). Because, in addition, the data may evolve rapidly, the schema for such data is usually large, dynamic, and is not strictly respected. Data models have been proposed that try to adapt to those characteristics. Several of them have in common that they can be thought of as directed, labeled graphs (for many applications, the graph is actually a tree)([Suc97]). The schema information is maintained in the *labels* of the graph which describe the data (i.e. they correspond to the attribute names of a relational schema). Because of the labels, the data is considered *self-describing* (we note that, since the graph also contains the data elements, this blurs the distinction between *schema* and data in traditional databases). Nodes in the graph contain the data; they are seen as *objects* in more traditional object-oriented databases. Nodes with no outgoing edges (or leaves on a tree) are seen as atomic objects, while nodes with outgoing edges correspond to complex objects. The value of an atomic object is simply a string labeling the node; the value of a complex object is the subgraph that has the complex object as root. The objects contained in such a value are *subobjects* of the root object. Given an object or node o, `attributes(o)` is the set of labels in outgoing edges of o, and `roles(o)` is the set of labels in ingoing edges of o (if o denotes an atomic object, `attributes(o)` = $\emptyset$). For instance, objects in the *Object Exchange Model* (OEM) ([PGMW95]) are defined, formally, as 4-tuples *(label, type, value, oid)*, where *label* is a string, identifying the object (in the sense of denoting it, a label is *not* a key); *type* refers to the data type, and can be either *atomic* or *complex* (in the latter case, it is either a set or a list); the *value* of an atomic object is drawn from one of the basic atomic types (integer, real, string, gif,...), while the value of a complex object is a set or list of atomic values or oids; and *oid* is a unique identifier. By allowing oids to appear in the value field (i.e. in a set or list of oids), we obtain nesting and complex object structure. Note that OEM is *self-describing* in the sense that each object carries its own label. OEM can also be considered *schema-less*, given its lack of constraints on the allowed structures. Figure 1 shows an example of an OEM database, drawn as a graph; object identifiers are not shown for simplicity.

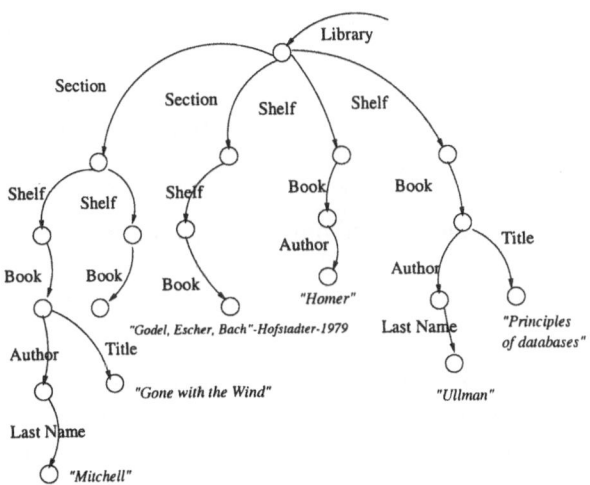

Fig. 1. An OEM database

Query languages for semistructured data models combine techniques from database query languages, navigation interfaces (like Web browsers) and information retrieval. Since data can be seen as a graph, navigating the data is seen as moving through the graph, starting at certain nodes considered *entry points* (usually the *root* in the case of a tree). Vertical traveling of the graph (going down from the entry point) is usually done through *path expressions*. Paths expressions are strings of labels that indicate a path in the data. Usually *regular expressions* are allowed to specify paths. Pattern matching is used to determine which paths in the data are indicated by path expressions in a query. The paths in the data are said to be *realizations* of the path expression. Several query languages have been proposed. In this paper we will use Lore for our examples, but the techniques mentioned are not dependent on this particular language. Lore ([MAG+97]) is similar to OQL ([Cat94]) in that it extends SQL-like SELECT ... FROM ... WHERE syntax by allowing subqueries anywhere, and having the ability to return complex (and heterogeneous) types in an answer (the FROM clause is omitted in many Lore examples as it is not necessary -or convenient)

We will use the Library (see figure 1), Guide and Movie databases for our examples. They contain a collection of entries for books, restaurants and movies, respectively. Queries expressed in English are written in *emphasis* font and queries expressed in Lore are written in typewriter font. As an example, consider the query

```
Select R.LastName from Library.*.Author R where R.address.zipcode = 92310
```

which obtains author's names in a given zipcode. The zipcode may be represented as an integer (as the query does) or as a string. The Lore system ignores these differences in type, and automatically tries to convert between types (a feature called *coercion*) to make the query syntactically correct. Some authors may have several zipcodes (or even several addresses!), some may have no zipcode at all. Again, the Lore system ignores these differences. This is achieved by assuming all properties are set-valued. Then the empty set (not zipcodes) and the singleton (only one address) are just special cases. As a consequence, authors without zipcodes do not cause an error. As another example, the query

```
Select R.LastName from Library.Section.Shelf.Book.Author R
```

would retrieve, when applied to the database of Figure 1, the value *"Mitchell"*. We note that only the leftmost path in Figure 1 would match such a query, despite the obvious similarities of other paths with the one in the query. Thus, *partial matches* in query paths are not considered.

The field of Cooperative Query Answering is very diverse; for an old but excellent overview see [GGM92]. The conferences ([ACL98,LKZ^{+}00]) give a more up-to-date view of the field. Most of the work in CQA has been done in the context of the relational or logical data models ([Ull89]). CQA may be composed of one or more of the following: query intent analysis; query rewriting; answer transformation; and answer explanation ([HHC96]). The first part covers modeling user goals, beliefs, expectations and intentions; the third part covers intensional answers and dealing with presuppositions and assumptions ([CMG87], [GM88],[Bad99]). *Answer explanation* covers creating justifications for answers, that is, explanations of why certain items are (not) part of the answer set, including listing whatever facts and rules were used in constructing the answer set ([Mot89]). We will not address these issues here, concentrating instead on query rewriting. This part covers transforming the query based on information about the contents of the database. Most commonly, the techniques in this area are based on deduction using *constraints*, especially integrity constraints (ICs). Relaxation and generalization are two primary examples of these techniques; in relaxation, the original query is *weakened* so that it admits information that was not originally asked for but is closely related to the information requested. It is usually extremely complex to determine what is the proper way to relax a query, and the analysis mentioned previously about users' goals is used to provide some guidance. Generalization can be seen as a type of relaxation in which weakening is achieved by moving from the concrete to the general in some kind of hierarchy. For instance, assume that the query `Select Book Where Library.*.Book.Theme = graph-algorithms` returns an empty answer. Assuming a hierarchy of `themes` where `graph-algorithms` is a subtype of `algorithms` and `graph-theory`, we could try to rephrase the query as `Select Book Where Library.*.Book.theme = graph-theory or algorithms`, hoping the additional information is useful to the user. A framework which uses hierarchies to support query relaxation and generalization is presented in [CC94]; an application of this approach is the

CO-BASE system [CCML96], where domain hierarchies are used to guide the manipulation of the query. Another approach to relaxation is that of [Gaa97].

Related research is very limited since this is a nascent field. Recently, some efforts have been made in the direction of similarity-based, approximate queries in XML environment ([Sch01,TW00]). In [Sch01], an approximate pattern matching language ApproXQL is proposed to handle queries which are not exact. The approach is to formulate queries as conjunctive query in the form of a tree and perform a tree matching to retrieve results. However, the query returns exact matches in the sense that all labels of the query occur in the result and the parent-child relationships are preserved. In [TW00], a language called XXL is presented where similarity operators have been introduced and are applied to element names and to text sequence. The query processor searches for matches similar to the names or text specified and assign probabilities to matches. Another language, ELIXIL ([TK01]) is comparable to XXL but additionally supports similarity joins. However, neither language allows for partial structural matches. Finally, we note that [KNS99] and [KS01] have proposed ways to model *incomplete answers* (i.e. answers where not all variables have been bound) in the context of semistructured data.

3   Techniques for Semistructured Data

Query languages developed for semistructured data allow querying data with irregular structure (missing or set-valued attributes) and with heterogeneity (different attributes and/or attribute types); However, precisely because of this flexibility it is even more important that when the query fails to produce an answer, the system is able to react appropriately. New techniques are needed for this functionality in the context of the new data models and query languages, e.g. working with path expressions. As pointed out in previous examples, systems like Lore do not consider *partial matches* in query paths. This idea is novel in that what is relaxed is *structure*, while in more traditional (relational, Datalog) settings, relaxation usually means relaxation of *values*. While this is certainly possible in semistructured data (by allowing substitution of some labels by other (related) labels, for instance), in this paper we develop the idea of allowing changes in structure, since it is the structural flexibility which is a trademark of semistructured data.

3.1   Paths Expressions, Realizations, and Partial Matches

The main technique for specifying queries in semistructured data is the use of paths and path expressions. A path is said to be *realized* in the database if there is any object in that database that contains a matching path. Misconceptions about the data structure will result in paths that are not realized. By concentrating on *partial matches* and assuming that they result from incomplete or erroneous knowledge about the database objects, we can provide the users with useful feedback or try to coerce database objects that are close to the description to fit in the answer.

To explain the techniques, we need some basic definitions first. For simplicity, we consider a given database as fixed. We take for granted the usual definitions of a path as a sequence of labels[1]. We use $p_1, \ldots, p_n, p_1', \ldots$ as variables for labels and denote paths as a concatenation of labels with the dot operator (for instance, $p_1.p_2.p_3$). To avoid confusion, we may enclose in parenthesis paths with only one label (for example, (p_1)); when we do not wish to specify all labels in a path we use *underscores* (_) to denote an arbitrary sequence of labels. Thus $p_1.\_.p_n$ denotes a path where only the first and last node in the sequence are specified. p_1 is called the *root node* of p (in symbols $root(p)$) and p_n is called the *ending node* of p (in symbols, $end(p)$). We use $p, p', p'', \ldots$ as variables over paths. The labels in any path will be labels from the database or the special labels '?' or '*', which are assumed not to occur in the database. Two paths $p = p_1.\_.p_n$ and $p' = p_1'.\_.p_n'$ are *equivalent* iff $p_i = p_i'$ for $1 \le i \le n$. A *subpath* of a path p is another path p' such that all labels in p' appear in p and *respect the order* of p (ie. p_i appears before p_j in p' iff p_i appears before p_j in p). An *infix* is a subpath with the further property that two labels are adjacent in the infix iff they are adjacent in the path. Thus $p_2.p_4$ is a subpath of $p_1.p_2.p_3.p_4$, but not an infix; $p_2.p_3$ is an infix. We reserve the words subpath and infix for paths that are *not* equivalent to the given one (i.e. a proper subpath or infix). An infix that contains the root node of p is called a *prefix* of p; an infix that contains the end node of p is called a *suffix* of p. A path is called *grounded* if it does not contain the labels '?' and '*'. Otherwise the path is called *regular*. Note that only grounded paths occur in the database. For a given database, we say that a path $p_1.\_.p_n$ *leads to object o* if the path exists in the database and following it one ends up in node (object) o. Abusing the notation a bit, we will sometimes identify a path with the object it leads to, when there is no risk of confusion. Given database DB, a *full* path in DB is a path that occurs in DB and which is not a prefix of another path occurring in DB. In other words, a full path leads to a node with no outgoing edges (atomic object). For a given object o, we define $out(o)$ as the set of outgoing edges of o. The objects that elements of $out(o)$ lead to are called the *attributes* of o (in symbols, $attr(o)$). Also, $in(o)$ is the set of incoming edges of o. The set of labels in edges of $in(o)$ are called the *roles* of o.

Matching of two paths is also defined in the usual way. Thus, two grounded paths match only if they are equivalent. The symbols '?' and '*' are interpreted with their usual meaning in regular expressions: '?' means matching one label, the symbol '*' means matching one or more labels (i.e. an infix).

Definition 31 A path p *has a realization* in the database if there is a path in the database that matches p. We say that p is *realized*, and define $match(p)$ as the set of all paths in the database that match p.

The reader is directed to note the difference between *equivalence* and *sameness* in paths: in figure 2 we have two graphs, each graph containing two paths.

---

[1] In what follows we restrict ourselves to non empty, finite sequences.

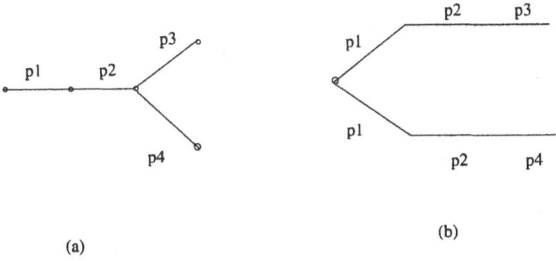

Fig. 2. Two different graphs

In (a), the two paths *share* a common prefix, while in (b) the two paths *have the same* prefix. Thus, we say that in (a) the prefix is *part of* both paths, while in (b) it is not.

Intuitively, we want to capture the notion of a path that is only partially matched by some path in the database. This may happen because of several possibilities, which are considered in the next definition.

Definition 32 A path p in a query is *overspecified (as a prefix, as a suffix, as an infix, as a subpath)* in the database if p is *not* realized in the database but there exists a full path p' in the database that matches a prefix (suffix, infix, subpath) of p, as far as the prefix (suffix, infix, subpath) is not one of (?), (*).

Definition 33 A path p in a query is *underspecified (as a prefix, as a suffix, as an infix, as a subpath)* in the database if p is *not* realized in the database but there exists a full path p' in the database such that a prefix (suffix, infix, subpath) of p' matches p.

Note that if p is realized in the database, there are paths in the database that match prefixes, suffixes, infixes and subpaths of p (the prefixes, suffixes, infixes and subpaths of any path in $match(p)$, respectively). Thus, we restrict ourselves to consider paths that do not have realizations in the database. Note also the final restriction for overspecified paths: since paths in the queries may contain regular expressions, we have to be careful with the paths that we consider for matching. For example, (*) is an infix of $p_1.*.p_2$, and it is matched by any path, which makes it uninteresting. The restriction to full paths is a simplification of the approach; further work will remove this limitation.

Example 1. The path p = Section.Shelf.Book has three realizations in the database of Figure 1, i.e. there are three elements in match(p) (two of them share a common prefix). This implies that prefixes (like Section.Shelf), suffixes (like Shelf.Book) and infixes (like Shelf) of p also have realizations in the database (at the very least, those coming from elements in match(p)).

The above definitions leave us with eight possibilities. One of them is partially handled by current systems: when path p in a query is underspecified as a prefix (i.e. p has no match but there exists a path p' in the database with a prefix that matches p) the system simply returns any object reachable by that prefix of p' as part of the answer (remember that nodes in the graph represent objects. The fact that p' is an extension of p just means that such a node is a complex object[2]). However, when there is a condition on such a path, equaling its value to an atomic value, the system cannot handle it.

Example 2. Let $p = Library.Section.Shelf.Book$ be a path in the WHERE clause of a query. If there is a path $p' = Library.Section.Shelf.Book.Author.LastName$ in the database, the (complex) object that the prefix of p' Library.Section.Shelf. Book leads to will be returned as part of the answer by systems like Lore. However, if the query had a condition like Library.Section.Shelf.Book = "Lost Horizons", the path p' would fail to provide an answer.

Definition 34 If p is overspecified as a prefix, $stem(p)$ is the set of paths in the database that match a prefix of p. If p is overspecified as a suffix, $term(p)$ is the set of paths in the database that match a suffix of p. If p is overspecified as an infix, $part(p)$ is the set of paths in the database that match an infix of p. If p is overspecified as a subpath, $sub(p)$ is the set of paths in the database that match a subpath of p.

Note that if a path p is overspecified, there may be in general several partial matches, some more complete than others. We will only be interested in *maximal* elements, defined next.

Definition 35 Given a set of paths S, an element p is *maximal* in S iff there is no path p' in S such that p is a prefix, suffix or subpath of p'. $Max(S)$ is defined as the set of maximal elements in S.

Example 3. Let $p = Library.Section.Shelf.Book.Author.LastName$ be a path. If there is no path matching p in the database, then

- *If there is a path $p' = Library.Section.Shelf.Book$ in the database, p is overspecified as a prefix, and $p' \in stem(p)$. However, every prefix of p' is also an element of $stem(p)$; p' itself is a maximal element for all of them. Whether p' is in $Max(stem(p))$ or not depends on the presence or absence in $stem(p)$ of another path of which p' is a prefix, suffix, or infix. The same is true for the other cases of this example.*
- *If there is a path $p' = Shelf.Book.Author.LastName$ in the database, p is overspecified as a suffix, and $p' \in term(p)$. However, every suffix of p' is also an element of $term(p)$; p' itself is a maximal element for all of them.*
- *If there is a path $p' = Shelf.Book.Author$ in the database, p is overspecified as an infix, and $p' \in part(p)$. However, every prefix, suffix and infix of p' is also an element of $part(p)$; p' itself is a maximal element for all of them.*

---

[2] By slightly abusing the notation, we will refer to the object as a node or as the subgraph rooted at that node.

– If there is a path $p' = Section.Shelf.Author$ in the database, p is overspecified as a subpath, and $p' \in sub(p)$. However, every prefix, suffix, infix and subpath of p' is also an element of $sub(p)$; p' itself is a maximal element for all of them.

Note that a path may be overspecified as a prefix, as a suffix, as an infix and as a subpath at the same time, or any combination thereof.

Example 4. The previous path was grounded, and therefore only identical paths in the database would match it. With a path like $p'' = Library.Section. *$ $.LastName$, the system could come up with very different partial matchings. It is also possible for p'' to be overspecified, underspecified and semispecified at the same time. Note that the use of the wildcard '*' does not help the problem that we are describing; i.e. neither one of the paths p' in the previous example matches p''. Again, note that the infix $(*)$ will not be considered as a target for matching.

3.2   Constructing Answers

For simplicity we will consider queries containing only one path condition. Combinations of path conditions are also possible and can be dealt similarly, but have not been explained here for simplicity. Note that once a set of objects has been retrieved by manipulating path expressions, the query may enforce further conditions on the objects. Here we limit ourselves to giving a *candidate set* of objects for the final answer.

As stated above, given a query with path p, it is possible that the path is either overspecified (as a prefix, suffix, infix or subpath) or underspecified (as a prefix, suffix, infix or subpath). It is also possible that it both overspecified and underspecified or a combination of all at the same time. It is also possible that a path finds matchings in a database and at the same time also finds partial matchings which are not *trivial* (i.e. not part of a matching path). We will thus relax our original definition as follows:

Definition 36 A path p is *overspecified* (*as a prefix, as a suffix, as an infix, as a subpath*) in the database if there exists a path p' in the database that matches a prefix (suffix, infix, subpath) of p, as far as the prefix (suffix, infix, subpath) is not one of (?), (*), and p' is not *part of* some path in $match(p)$.

The definition of *underspecified* is relaxed similarly.
  We now have several cases to examine:

– $match(p) \neq \emptyset$. Obviously $match(p)$ constitutes a solution and should be offered to the user. If, furthermore, $Max(stem(p)) = Max(term(p)) = Max(part(p)) = Max(sub(p)) = \emptyset$, $match(p)$ is the only possible answer. In this case, we say that p is *categorical* in the database. However, if any one of $Max(stem(p))$, $Max(term(p))$, $Max(part(p))$ or $Max(sub(p))$ is not empty, then we have a *potential answer set*, which *may* be offered to the user.

- $match(p) = \emptyset$. This means that the user did not find *any* answers to his/her query *as posed*. Again, there are two possibilities. If $Max(stem(p)) = Max(term(p)) = Max(part(p)) = Max(sub(p)) = \emptyset$, there is no possible alternative. In this case, we say that p is *negative categorical* in the database. The user should probably be invited to query the *schema* of the database. However, if any one of $Max(stem(p))$, $Max(term(p))$, $Max(part(p))$ or $Max(sub(p))$ is not empty, then the potential answer set should probably be offered to the user.

The intuitive idea is that, while a negative categorical path reveals a deep user misconception about the schema or contents of the database, an overspecified (underspecified) path p reveals a *partial* misconception or lack of knowledge. In this case, we may consider the paths in $Max(stem(p))$, $Max(term(p))$, $Max(part(p))$ or $Max(sub(p))$ as candidates for the answer.

We next discuss a technique to generate approximate answers by transforming the candidate paths to become part of the answer. We will implicitly assume that only one of $Max(stem(p))$, $Max(term(p))$, $Max(part(p))$ or $Max(sub(p))$ is non empty. When more than one set is not empty, the partial matches could be combined; however, this complicates the approach. Thus, developing techniques for combining paths is left for future research. The following example motivates the approach.

Example 5. Assume that some Author *objects in the data repository contain the attribute* Address. *Consider the query which retrieves authors living in Palo Alto:*

`Select Author.*.LastName where Author.*.Address.City = ''Palo Alto''.`
In some object o_1, Address *may be an atomic object, with value of type string ("15000 El Camino Real Palo Alto"), while in another object o_2* Address *may be a complex object, with subobjects* City, zip, Street *and* Number. *In this case, the object o_2 may contribute to the answer, but o_1 will not. This is a problem of overspecified paths.*

Note that the query has to overspecify the path in order to introduce the constraint that the city in the address is Palo Alto. In order to realize that o_1 is part of the answer, we need to be able to coerce between atomic and complex values[3].

The following technique covers the cases where the path in the query is overspecified as a prefix (infix or subpath) by *expanding* the terminal node (root node, root and terminal node, respectively) of a partially matching path in the database, and the case where the path in the query is underspecified as a prefix (suffix, infix) by *collapsing* the terminal node (root node, root and terminal node, respectively) of a partially matching path in the database. Thus, the basic

---

[3] The reason to limit ourselves to full paths becomes now clear: we want to be able to manipulate paths with no restrictions; if the path under consideration is an infix of another path, some of the proposed transformation may yield unintuitive results. To deal with them, one must admit the possibility that a complex object can be expanded in more than one way, which results in a high degree of complexity

procedure will be to transform the paths in the database by manipulation, we will either *expand* a path, which means taking the (atomic) object that the path leads to and converting it into a complex object by adding outgoing edges to it, or *collapse* a path, which means taking a (complex) object in the path (except the terminal node) and making it atomic, thus converting it to terminal node. Hence, we can transform atomic objects into complex object and complex objects into atomic ones.

For expanding, the idea is to infer some structure from an atomic object o to create a complex object. Thus, the value assigned to atomic object is expanded into several parts, and each part is *tagged*. This way, a graph rooted at o can be created, with one edge for each subpart, labeled by the tag, and pointing to a node that contains a part of the original value. In the example above, we have an atomic object (o_1) with a value of type string and would like to transform it into a complex object with each sub-object with its own value. The problem here is to come up with a meaningful division of the value and assigning them to some meaningful tags. In general, this problem requires some knowledge about the domain. Two strategies seem possible:

— When the (regular) answer to a query is not empty, use as guidance other objects in the database which match the query. In the example above, object o_2 provides a possible division for an atomic object. However, note that the value of the atomic object may not contain all the information to support such a division; heuristics as to which part is more important or likely to appear are needed. Also, there may be several object qualifying for the answer which have different structure, and therefore offer more than one possible division. Again, heuristics are necessary in order to make a good choice. The technique we propose to deal with this problem is called the *preference table*. Given paths in the database p and p', with p a proper prefix of p', for the object at the end of p, o, there is another object o' in p' such that o and o' have the same labels, o is atomic and o' is complex. We consider the class of all objects o' which are in this relationship to o (called $sim(o)$), and build an entry for o in the preference table. The entry keeps a list of any sub-object of any $o' \in sim(o)$, and for each sub-object, the *minimum* number of appearances (which can be 0 if the sub-object does not appear in some $o' \in sim(o)$), the *maximum* number of appearances, and the percentage of times the sub-object appears at least once. As an example, assume that for some object o, $sim(o) = \{o_1, o_2, o_3\}$, and that o_1 has a sub-object o_s, while o_2 does not have such a sub-object and o_3 has two subobjects with that label. Then the minimum of o_s is 0 (as it does not appear in o_2), the maximum is 2 (as it appears twice in o_3), and its percentage is 2/3 (as it appears at least one in o_1 and o_3, two objects out of 3). The preference table indicates, for a label o, possible ways to expand an atomic value into parts, by using the following rules:
   • subobjects that have a minimum of 1 are *required* subparts, therefore very likely to be present;
   • subobjects that have a maximum of 1 are present only once;
   • subobjects with larger percentages are more likely to be present.

Note that objects with a minimum of 1 will have a 100% percentages; the information is useful in trying to decide whether to use a sub-object which is not required but still present often (say in 9 out of 10 objects). Note also that this information can be extracted from the database automatically and, if kept incrementally, be calculated in a very efficient way.

- Use heuristics based on some metadata information or concept hierarchies. If the fact that an **address** usually has parts named **house number** (with a string value), **street** (with a string value), **city** (with a string value), **zip** (with a string of 6 characters in US/Canada)is available on a metadata repository, we could divide an atomic value using such metadata as guidance. The fact that each data includes its data type and other information will help divide the atomic value. For instance, in this example we will not confuse a street name with a zip code (although we may confuse the street name and the city name).

The idea behind collapsing is to be able to integrate several values into a single one. The following example shows its application.

Example 6. Assume that some **Author** *objects have the attribute* **Address** *which in turn is a complex object with attribute* **City**. *Consider the query asking for authors where* *.**Address** = ''Palo Alto''. *In some object* o_3, **Address** *has attribute* **City** *with value the string "Palo Alto" (o_3 may have other attributes). In this case, o_3 does not contribute to the answer because of an underspecified path in the query.*

There is a general procedure to manipulate all *printable* values, i.e. all values for which an alphanumeric representation exists (printable types include many computer-supported types -string, integer, real, boolean-, but audiovisual types -jpeg images, video streams- cannot be transformed so simply). We can obtain the atomic value from the complex one, by concatenating (with whitespaces in between) all the values of the subobjects in their printable form. Let o be any object, *wconc* a method that concatenates an arbitrary number of strings into one (adding whitespaces between arguments) and *toAlpha(type, value)* a method that transforms value *value* of type *type* into a string. Then we can define a method *toStr* which will convert any object (atomic or complex) into an atomic, string-valued object (we ignore the issue of generating an oid for the new object and creating an appropriate node and edge):

$$toStr(o) = \begin{cases} o & \text{if } o \text{ is atomic and of type string} \\ toAlpha(t, v) & \text{if } o \text{ is atomic, of type } t \text{ and value } v \\ wconc(toStr(o_1), \ldots, toStr(o_n)) & \text{if } o \text{ is complex and } attr(o) = \{o_1, \ldots, o_n\} \end{cases}$$

Note that once we have the complex value as a string we still need to determine the behavior of equality, i.e. whether particular constants or expressions match. Thus, in the example above, the object o_3 is made atomic by combining the values of all its subobjects into a single string which becomes the value of o_3. Such a string will contain the substring ''Palo Alto'', but the condition in the query must be changed from equality to substring inclusion, in order for o_3

to quality for the answer. Note also that the outgoing edges of a node are not, in the general case, ordered, and therefore one would need to specify an order in which to combine all values (or accept all possible orders)[4]. In order to deal with this problem, we propose a technique called *unordered matching*. In this technique, we match *parts* of a string. Note that our concatenation algorithm keeps whitespaces between components. Thus, an object like o_2 in example 5 can be collapsed to an atomic value by concatenating values from `City`, `Zip`, `Street` and `Number`, to "Palo_Alto 90040 El_Camino_Real 15000". However, the user may have specified the address as "15000 El Camino Real Palo Alto 90040". A literal match of both strings will fail. In unordered matching, we match parts of the string one by one and declare a matching as successful if all parts find a match. Thus, we would look for substring "Palo Alto" in "15000 El Camino Real Palo Alto 90040" first, and find it. Then we would continue and look for "90040", and so on. When all parts matched, we would declare the two strings as successfully matched.

4   Implementation

In order to evaluate our ideas in an experimental setting, some of the procedures sketched above have been implemented. Our system finds partial matches (both for over- and under-specified queries, in any situation) and uses additional tables to expand and collapse paths. The automatic creation of preference tables and the unordered match idea are not implemented yet. Our current implementation works in main memory; it assumes that the whole database and any auxiliary data are present in memory. While this is a simplification of the problem, our intention was to separate the issues of partial matching (how to detect partial matches, heuristics for path transformation) from issues of efficiency (indexing issues, etc.). This strategy is based on the fact that even though both kinds of issues are related (and both need to be addressed and solved), each one of them raises enough challenges to warrant its study in isolation. Presently, we are concentrating in developing and testing robust heuristics to deal with partial matches. In the future, we plan to study indexing structures which may help in making our approach scalable. The OEM database is represented as a sequence of objects (nodes). Additional information is expressed in the form of look-up tables. The database of figure 3 was used, together with some additional hand coded information, as input to the algorithm. Examples of queries that our system can handle and would not be answerable in current systems are:

1. Overspecified queries. As stated above, a path in the query may be over-specified. Note that because of the flexibility of most XML query languages, the overspecified path may appear in the `where` `select` or `from` clause, or in several clauses.

---

[4] It is interesting that a proposal to extend OEM to deal with XML has added, among other features, an ordering among the attributes of a given node ([PGMW95]).

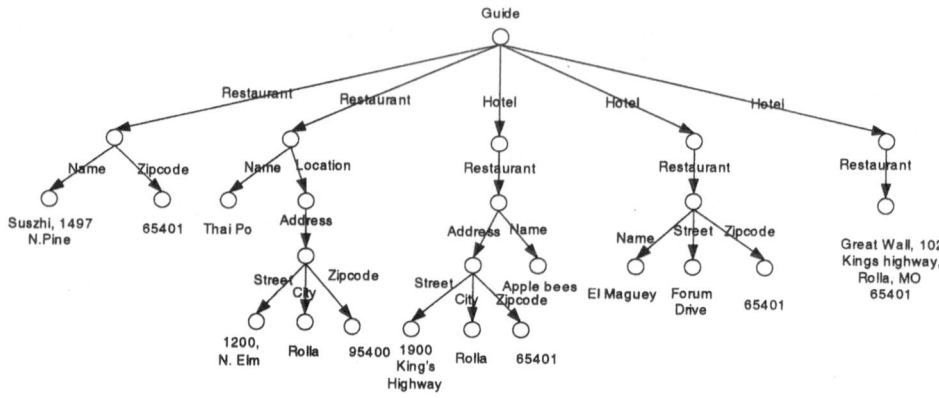

Fig. 3. OEM database for the example

a) Overspecified as a prefix: consider the path
p = guide.hotel.restaurant.address.zipcode in the query and path
p1 = guide.hotel.restaurant.address in the database. This is over-specified as a prefix, as p1 is a prefix of p.

b) Overspecified as a suffix: consider the path
p = hotel.restaurant.address.zipcode in the query and path p1 = restaurant.address.zipcode in the database. This is overspecified as a suffix, as p1 is a suffix of p.

c) Overspecified as a infix: consider the path
p = hotel.restaurant.address.zipcode in the query and path p1 = restaurant.address in the database This is overspecified as a infix, as p1 is a infix of p.

d) Overspecified as a sub path: consider the path
p = hotel.restaurant.location.address.zipcode in the query and path p1 = restaurant.address in the database This is overspecified as a sub path, as p1 is a sub path of p.

2. Underspecified queries. Again, there are various ways in which paths can be under specified, and such paths may appear in several clauses in the query.

a) Underspecified as prefix: consider
p = hotel.restaurant.location.address.zipcode in the database and p1 = restaurant.address in the query. This is underspecified as prefix because p1 is a prefix to p

b) Underspecified as suffix: consider
p = hotel.restaurant.address.zipcode in the database and p1 = restaurant.address.zipcode in the query. This is underspecified as a suffix, as p1 is a suffix of p.

c) Under specified as a infix: consider path
p = hotel.restaurant.address.zipcode in the database and path p1 = restaurant.address in the query. This is underspecified as a infix, as p1 is a infix of p.

The algorithm has been tested on the examples given above. We describe the behavior of the algorithm in some of these examples. Let 'P' be the query expression, and 'Q' be the set of paths in the OEM data model.

1. For underspecified path: let P= `guide.restaurant.location=` "65400" be the path in the query. For branch 2, i.e. i=2
   Q[i] = `guide.restaurant.location.address.zipcode`. Match(P, Q[i]) will be null initially, atomic(P, Q [i]) will return P, i.e., on one to one comparison between P and Q[i] we reach P's atomic object first. This makes it an under-specified path. In this case finalP = `location` and finalQ = `zipcode`. We find parentQ of finalQ till we get finalQ = finalP(i.e., `location`). Simultaneously we convert street, city and zipcode into strings and concatenate them. For example, consider one non-atomic node like address which has many atomic nodes like street, zipcode and city (the data types of these nodes may be different; zipcode may be of integer type, whereas street and city of string type). We than can do bottom-up traversal by converting street, zipcode and city into strings and concatenate them to form one string for the parent node address. Tostring () function can be used to convert them into string and Concat(string1,string2) function can be used to combine different strings to one string. This continues until the finalQ=location. At this point we parse finalQ for the value of location and give the result if it is realized.

2. For overspecified as a prefix: let P = `guide.hotel.restaurant.zipcode=` "65409" be the path in the query. For branch 5, i.e. i=5,
   Q[i] = `guide.hotel.restaurant.` match(P, Q[i]) will be null initially, atomic(P, Q [i]) will return Q[i], i.e., on one to one comparison between P and Q[i] we reach Q[i]'s atomic object first. This makes P a path overspec-ified as a prefix. In this case finalP= `zipcode` and finalQ = `restaurant`. We find parentP equal to parent of `zipcode` in P which is `restaurant`. We find max(stem(P)) by using function path(P, finalQ) Parse finalQ for "65409" on the basis of delimiters (",", or whitespace) and give the result.

3. For overspecified as a suffix: let P = `guide.restaurant.zipcode=65401` be the path of the query. Let Q = `restaurant.zipcode` be a path in the OEM database. Match(P, Q) is null, so this does not return a value. Atomic(P,Q) returns an exception, we assign suffixP to P, i.e. `guide.restaurant.zipcode`, then rootP = `guide` and rootQ = `restaurant`. We remove rootP from suffixP until term(rootP)=Q or atomic (suffix,Q) re-turns some value. If match(term(P),Q) is not null we query; in this case term (P)= `restaurant.zipcode`, which is equal to Q so this is used to return an answer.

4. For overspecified as subpath: for a particular query, if none of the above steps in the algorithm yield any match then the query can be classified as overspecified as a subpath. This can be explained with an example: let P = `guide.restaurant.location.address=` "65400", and
   Q = `restaurant.address`. In this example, the path P will be searched for some important nodes (we assume that as explained previously, OEM can define some nodes which are mandatory to be present in the query before it

can be processed). In this example, "restaurant" is one such node. The next step is to match the path from root to the important node . For this example, P will be overspecified as suffix. Then the paths P and Q are matched for the leaf node "address". The next step is to parse Q and generate results. By applying the algorithm for overspecified and underspecified paths when and where required, the path which is overspecified as a subpath can be realized.

We now explain how the two tables given below can be used as metadata information. For any query Q and any path P in the OEM Table 1 contains terminal node of Q as first column and the non terminal nodes where terminal node of Q can occur in the second column. This makes the search easier and faster for the nodes in Q in P. Consider the query path
$Q = $ guide.restaurant.zipcode='65401'. We can find the terminal node of Q i.e. 'zipcode' and for 'zipcode' we find the non terminal in any path of the OEM where it can be present from Table1. These nodes are searched in the same order as they appear in the table. For 'zipcode', we start searching in the order of 'address', 'location', 'restaurant' and then 'hotel'. This makes the search faster; we do not have to search for terminal nodes in all the complex nodes.

It may happen that an terminal node in the query Q may not have the same node name as in the OEM path P and may be hidden in the terminal nodes in the same path P. In this case we may have to decipher terminal node of the query from the terminal node we are searching in the OEM. In these cases, Table 2 may be helpful. From this table we can find the order in which the nodes of the query can occur in the terminal nodes of the OEM if not specifically given. The terminal node of Q is in the first column, its corresponding terminal node of P is in second column and the order of occurrence is in the third column. The order starts from 0 to the probable number of nodes present. 0 means that after parsing the terminal node in the OEM the first token can be atomic node of the query and so on. For example, consider the query path which has terminal node 'zipcode'. If 'zipcode' is not present in a particular OEM path and if the terminal node of the path in OEM is 'city' then the corresponding Order is 1. This order indicates the token in which zipcode can be present after parsing of terminal node 'city' in the OEM path. Hence, after parsing 'city' we search for zipcode in the second token. Again there is no strict rule that this token has to be zipcode. The disadvantage of this is that the use of metadata makes the solution more specific for a particular OEM.

Table 1.

Zip code	Address Location Restaurant Hotel
City	Address Location Restaurant Hotel
Street	Address Location Restaurant Hotel
Name	Restaurant Hotel
Address	Location Restaurant Hotel
Location	Restaurant Hotel

Table 2.

Zip code	Zip code City Street Name	0 1 2 3
City	City Street Name	0 1 2
Street	Street Name	0 1
Name	Name	0

One important issue that must be dealt with is the degree to which mismatch is allowed. That is, how far are we willing to go in changing paths to force a match? If one introduces radical changes in a path, in order to make it match a path expression, there is a risk that irrelevant, unrelated data may be included in the query answer. Our approach to this problem is twofold. First, since what we are proposing are heuristics, data obtained by transformation must clearly indicate to the user that it was obtained by indirect methods. Seconds, answers must be *ranked* so that the user has an idea of the degree with which they were transformed (which in turn is an indication of the degree with which they matched the original query). This way, the user can choose a cut point at which answers are deemed no longer relevant. We have developed some techniques to measure the degree of difference between the path in the query and the path in the database returned by approximate matching. The measure takes into account not only the number of matching (and non-matching label) but also the position of the matches (the distance between matching labels). The measure is normalized as a ratio of the total length of the path, and it can take weights if the user wishes to give some labels more importance then others. This work is not described here in detail due to lack of space.

5   Conclusion and Further Research

We have introduced some of the basic concepts of cooperative query answering (CQA) in the semistructured data environment. We have argued that CQA is very relevant for semistructured data, and have shown examples of new CQA techniques developed to deal with the characteristics of semistructured data. As far as the authors are aware, this paper is the first attempt in the literature to apply CQA techniques to semistructured data. This paper presents ongoing research on a new area; therefore there are many issues that deserve further development. In particular, some that have already been pointed out include dealing with queries using multiple conditions on multiple paths, and implementing algorithms to rank partial matches and return only the best ones. Also, developing indexing structures which help find partial matches efficiently is a necessary step to carry the implementation presented here to a realistic scale.

References

[Abi97]   S. Abiteboul. Querying semistructured data. In *Proceedings of ICDT*, 1997.

[ACL98]   T. Andreasen, H. Christiansen, and H.L. Larsen, editors. *Flexible Query Answering Systems, Third International Conference (FQAS'98)*, volume 1495 of *Lecture Notes in Computer Science*. Springer-Verlag, 1998.

[Bad99]   A. Badia. Cooperative query answering with generalized quantifiers. *Journal of Intelligent Information Systems*, 12:75–97, 1999.

[Bun97]   P. Buneman. Tutorial: Semistructured data. In *Proceedings of PODS*, 1997.

[Cat94]   R. G. Catell. *Object Data Management*. Addison-Wesley, 1994.

[CC94]   W. Chu and Q. Chen. A structured approach for cooperative query answering. *IEEE Transactions on Knowledge and Data Engineering*, 1994.

[CCML96]   W. Chu, K. Chiang, M. Minock, and C. Larson. Cobase: A scalable and extendible cooperative information system. *Journal of Intelligent Information Systems*, 6, 1996.

[CMG87]   U. Chakravarthy, J. Minker, and J. Grant. Semantic query optimization: Additional constraints and control strategies. In L. Kerschberg, editor, *Proceedings from the First International Conference in Expert Database Systems*. 1987.

[Gaa97]   T. Gaasterland. Cooperative answering through controlled query relaxation. *IEEE Expert*, 12(5), September/October 1997.

[GGM92]   T. Gaasterland, P. Godfrey, and J. Minker. An overview of cooperative answering. *Journal of Inteligent Information Systems*, 1, 1992.

[GM88]   A. Gal and J. Minker. Informative and cooperative answers in databases using integrity constraints. In V. Dahl and P. Saint-Dizier, editors, *Natural Language Understanding and Logic Programming*. 1988.

[HHC96]   J. Han, Y. Huang, and N. Cercone. Intelligent query answering by knowledge discovery techniques. *IEEE Transactions on Knowledge and Data Engineering*, 8, 1996.

[ID94]   T. Imielinski and R. Demolombe. *Nonstandard Queries and nonstandard answers*. Oxford University Press, 1994.

[KNS99]   Y. Kanza, W. Nutt, and Y. Sagiv. Queries with incomplete answers over semistructured data. In *Proceedings of ACM PODS*, 1999.

[KS01]   Y. Kanza and Y. Sagiv. Flexible queries over semistructured data. In *Proceedings of ACM PODS*, 2001.

[LKZ+00]   H.L. Larsen, J. Kacprzyk, S. Zadrozny, T. Andreasen, and H. Christiansen, editors. *Flexible Query Answering Systems, Recent Advances, Proceedings of the Fourth International Conference on Flexible Query Answering Systems (FQAS 2000)*. Springer-Verlag, 2000.

[MAG+97]   J. McHugh, S. Abiteboul, R. Goldman, D. Quass, and J. Widom. Lore: A database management system for semistructured data. *SIGMOD Record*, 26, 1997.

[Mot89]   A. Motro. Using constraints to provide intensional answers to relational queries. In *Proceedings of VLDB*, 1989.

[PGMW95]   Y. Papakonstantinou, H. Garcia-Molina, and J. Widom. Object exchange across heterogeneous information sources. In *Proceedings of the 11th ICDE*, 1995.

[Sch01]   T. Schlieder. Approxql: Design and implementation of an approximate pattern matching language for xml. Technical Report Technical Report B 01-02,, Freie Universit t Berlin, May 2001.

[Suc97]   D. Suciu. Semistructured data in the real world: XML. Technical report, AT&T Labs, 1997.

[TK01]   Chinenyanga T.T. and N. Kushmerick. Expressive and efficient ranked queries for xml data. In *Proceedings of the 4th International Workshop on the Web and Databases (WebDB'01)*, pages 1–6, 2001.

[TW00]   A. Theobald and G. Weikum. Adding relevance to xml. In *International Workshop on Web and Databases (WebDB)*, 2000.

[Ull89]   J.D. Ullman. *Principles of Database and Knowledge-Base Systems*, volume I. Computer Science Press, 1989.

Efficient Querying of Distributed Resources in Mediator Systems

Ioana Manolescu[1], Luc Bouganim[1, 2], Françoise Fabret[1], and Eric Simon[1]

[1] INRIA Rocquencourt, France.
< Firstname.Lastname >@inria.fr

[2] PRISM Laboratory, 78035 Versailles – France.
<Firstname.Lastname>@prism.uvsq.fr

Abstract. This work investigates the integration of heterogeneous resources, such as data and programs, in a fully distributed peer-to-peer mediation architecture. The challenge in making such a system succeed at a large scale is twofold. First, we need a simple concept for modeling resources. Second, we need efficient operators for distributed query execution, capable of handling well costly computations and large data transfers. To model heterogeneous resources, we use the model of table with binding patterns. To exploit a resource with restricted binding patterns, we propose an efficient BindJoin operator, optimized for minimizing large data transfers and costly computations. Furthermore, the proposed BindJoin operator delivers most of its output in the early stages of the execution, which is an important asset in a system meant for human interaction. Our experimental evaluation validates the proposed BindJoin algorithm on queries involving expensive programs.

1 Introduction

There is a growing interest in the scientific community to allow disparate groups of users (a.k.a. virtual organizations) to share resources consisting of both data collections and programs. This vision is best reflected by recent initiatives such as the "Grid Computing" infrastructure, that aims at constructing a "meta computer": a large scale, distributed computing environment, providing transparent access to highly heterogeneous resources. A frequent domain of applications is that of international scientific cooperation, where remote laboratories share their data and programs.

LeSelect [18] is a mediator system developed at INRIA, which allows the users to publish their resources (data and functions – corresponding to programs) so they can be transparently accessed. In LeSelect, several distributed mediators (a.k.a. servers) cooperate in a peer-to-peer fashion to allow large-scale integration of data and functions. LeSelect is currently used in many earth-science cooperation projects like Thetis (coastal zone management) [7], Decair (air quality models) [7] and SIMBio (bio-corrosion monitoring) [8].

As an example of such projects, consider the following distributed scientific application. On site S_1, satellite images have been processed into a map of the ozone cover of the French territory. On site S_2, a survey of the traffic in the same area resulted in a set of records corresponding to the days when traffic was particularly

R. Meersman, Z. Tari (Eds.): CoopIS/DOA/ODBASE 2002, LNCS 2519, pp. 468–485, 2002.

intense. On site S_3, a function *OzoneLevels* →*{level}* computes the set of distinct ozone density levels found in an ozone cover image. If a user on site S_4 wants to match heavy traffic data from S_2 with the days with low ozone levels in images found on S_1, the OzoneLevels function on S_3 needs to be invoked on images from S_1. In this example, answering the user query will *necessitate manipulation of large data* (e.g., images) and potentially *expensive function invocations*.

This work investigates data and program integration in a fully distributed peer-to-peer mediation architecture. The challenge in making such a system succeed at a large scale is twofold: First, a publication model needs to be chosen for representing the published data (e.g. satellite images and high traffic data), and functions (e.g. *OzoneLevels*). This model should be simple, since the publisher is not supposed to be a computer scientist. Second, we need efficient operators for distributed query execution, capable of handling costly computations and/or large data transfers. *Costly computations* arise with (i) expensive functions [3], [5], [14], [15] like *OzoneLevels*, reflecting a domain-specific knowledge, and performing complex mathematic computations, (ii) Web accesses [11], and (iii) correlated subqueries [14]. *Large data transfers* (e.g. satellite images) are necessary when functions only run on their native site, and cannot be shipped through the network. This is the case of the major part of scientific applications, in which the programs were written in isolation (without concern for their future integration in a larger setting) [3].

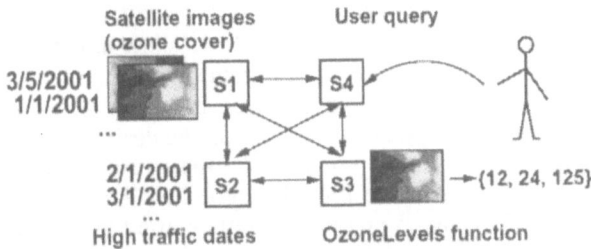

Fig. 1. Sample configuration and query on distributed data and functions.

Our general objective is to minimize the publisher task while providing the best performance for queries involving expensive functions or large data. Our approach can be summarized in three points:

1. We base the modeling of our resources on the concept of table with binding patterns (introduced in [21] for a different purpose), and the associated logical BindJoin operator. The logical *BindJoin* operator is a variant of the relational join operator to access tables with binding patterns. Binding patterns can naturally be used to model functions. We propose to use the same modelization for table with large binary objects (thereafter called *blobs*).

2. We analyze the impact of expensive functions and blobs on the design of the BindJoin operator and on its integration in the query execution plan (*QEP*). First, the *total work* (TW) and *response time* (RT) of queries including blob transfers and expensive function calls must be reduced, by employing caching and asynchronism techniques. Second, we show the importance of the *early tuple output rate* (ER), that is, we are interested by a QEP that returns as much results as possible *early on* during query execution. Indeed, in a data integration setting like the one above, queries are asked by human users that wait for the result in

front of their stations. Moreover, in many cases, several exploratory queries are asked before the user identifies the data segments he/she is really interested in. Therefore, users typically want to see at least part of the result as soon as possible; the same query pattern also appears in online decisional applications. *We therefore identify a good ER as an important performance requirement for the execution of distributed queries like the one in our example.*

3. We propose to include every optimization (caching, asynchronism and ER specific optimizations) in the BindJoin operator. While this approach complicates significantly the design and implementation of the BindJoin operator, it reduces to the minimum the publisher task. The publisher must only provide a call-based interface of the form *callFunction(arguments)* for functions and *readBlob(blobName)* for accessing blobs.

Our contribution, following our objectives of publisher task minimization and performance maximization, is twofold:

*   First, we show how the model of tables with binding patterns can be used to uniformly model data sources including functions as well as blobs and explain why that modelization provides benefits similar to those of semi-joins, without their drawbacks.
*   Second, we propose, implement and assess the performance of a highly efficient BindJoin operator, improving over the state-of-the-art algorithms by having much better ER properties.

This paper is organized as follows. In section 2, we show how the paradigm of tables with binding patterns can be used to describe data (including blobs) and functions and present the associated logical BindJoin operator. In section 3, we analyze the impact of expensive functions and large binary objects on the design of the BindJoin operator and on its integration in the QEP. We describe the optimizations that our BindJoin operator should include in order to provide a good ER behavior. Section 4 presents the associated physical operators and the algorithms used in case of limited memory. Section 5 demonstrates the good ER of our BindJoin operator through a series of experiments. Related work is presented in section 6. We conclude in section 7.

2 Modeling and Querying Resources

In this section, we first describe the concept of table with binding patterns and the associated BindJoin and BindAccess operators. Then we explain how we use these concepts to model several classes of resources. Finally, we compare our approach with the classical semi-join technique.

2.1 The Concept of Table with Binding Patterns

Binding patterns [21] can be attached to a relational table to describe the restrictions that we encounter in accessing it. These restrictions may stem from confidentiality or performance reasons, or simply reflect the restricted nature of the resource: for example, web sources can be represented as virtual tables with a binding pattern where input parameters have to be provided in order to obtain the results.

A binding pattern *bp* for a table $R(X_1, X_2 ... X_n)$, is a partial mapping from $\{X_1, X_2 ... X_n\}$ to the alphabet $\{b, f\}$. The meaning of a binding pattern is the following: those X_i mapped to b are *bound*, i.e., their values must be supplied in order to obtain information from R, while values of attributes mapped to f are *free* and can be obtained from the data source, as soon as values for all b attributes are supplied. If a binding pattern maps all attributes of R to f, then tuples of R can be obtained without any restriction (just like a usual Scan). For example, if it was possible to obtain the full data contained in a web Yellow Pages source of the form *YP(name, address, phoneNo)*, this would be indicated by a $YP(name^f address^f phoneNo^f)$ binding pattern. On the contrary, $YP(name^b address^f phoneNo^f)$ specifies that the values of the name attribute have to be supplied in order to obtain addresses and phone numbers from *YP*.

2.2 The BindJoin and BindAccess Operators

The presence of access restrictions, formalized using binding patterns, makes the regular set of relational operators insufficient in order to answer queries.

The BindJoin operator: The standard relational join operator does not capture well the semantics of combining two tables, if at least one has a restricted access pattern. To illustrate, consider a QEP fragment that joins the $YP(name^b address^f phoneNo^f)$ with an $Employee(name^f salary^f)$ table on their *name* field. Due to the commutativity of the standard join operator, we might try to write this fragment as $Employee \bowtie_{name} YP$, or as $YP \bowtie_{name} Employee$.

However, the first variant is valid, while the second one is not: as described by the binding pattern of *YP*, we cannot start by accessing it, before supplying some bindings for its *name* field. Thus, we adopt a variant of the relational join operator, the BindJoin logical operator (denoted $\bowtie$ and used, e.g., in [9], [11], also known as dependent join, theta semi-join, functional join etc.) to capture this asymmetric behavior: the right-hand child of a BindJoin operator cannot be executed on its own, since it depends on the join values passed across the BindJoin operator.

The BindAccess operator: Due to the semantics of the binding pattern $YP(name^b phoneNo^f)$, we cannot perform a scan on the *YP* table. Instead, we have to supply some values for the *name* attribute in order to get *YP* tuples. Furthermore, the set of tuples that we can extract from *YP*, following this binding pattern, depends on the values that we supply for *name* (in contrast, the result of a Scan is always the same). To capture the special semantics of a restricted access, we use a special *BindAccess* operator. As an intuition, think of the BindAccess as being a "parameterized Scan", where the parameters are the values supplied for the bound attributes.

The formal semantics of BindAccess and BindJoin can be specified as follows. Consider two tables $R(X, Y)$ and $S(U, V)$, where X, Y, U and V are pairwise disjoint sets of variables. Let $R(X^b Y^f)$ and $S(U^b V^f)$ be binding patterns of R and S, and X be a set of values for X. Then, denoting the BindAccess by BA, we have: $BA(R(X^b Y^f), X) = \sigma_{X \in X} R(X, Y, Z)$.

Furthermore, the BindJoin of $Scan(S(U^f V^f))$ and $BA(R(X^b Y^f))$ has the following semantics: $Scan(S(U^f V^f)) \bowtie_{U=X} BA(R(X^b Y^f)) = \{(u,v,x,y) \mid (u,v) \in S \wedge (x,y) \in R \wedge u=x\}$

While this formula shows that the set of tuples returned by a BindJoin is similar to the one returned by a regular join, keep in mind that the similarity stops here. Indeed, neither the optimization techniques for join queries nor the join operator algorithms can be directly reused for two distinct reasons: First, the asymmetric character of the BindJoin greatly impacts the optimizer's search space [9]. Second, BindJoins often involve costly computations, which have deep implications on the operator algorithm.

2.3 Modeling Resources Using Tables with Binding Patterns

A function is naturally represented as a table, whose binding pattern distinguishes the attributes that correspond to function arguments (which need to be supplied in the query) from the function results. For example, the binding pattern of the *OzoneLevels* function is $OzoneLevels(img^b\ level^f)$.

We propose a specific modeling for data resources involving blobs in order to optimize their transfer through the network. This modeling imposes some requirements on the publication of a table with blobs: for every blob attribute B of table R, R must also contain a small-sized attribute Bid that determines the value of B, i.e., such that the functional dependency $Bid \rightarrow B$ holds. Furthermore, among the binding patterns of R, we require the presence of $R(Bid^b\ B^f)$. As an example, assume that the *id* field in the *SatImg* table determines the *img* field. Then, the binding pattern set for *SatImg* must at least contain $SatImg(id^b\ img^f)$. BlobIDs are system-generated in the case of published data residing in a DBMS. In a simpler setting, a blob is usually stored in a separate file, whose complete name (i.e. host/path) is used as a blobID.

The purpose of requiring a blob identifier is to reduce the blob transfers to a minimum. First, we transfer identifiers instead of blobs, whenever the blobs themselves are not needed; blob identifiers enable us to transport *only once only the necessary* blobs, as follows. First, when a set of blob transfers are necessary, by comparing the identifiers of two blobs, we can decide whether or not they are the same, and if yes, make the transfer only once. Second, if in a given QEP several selections and/or joins apply on the tuples containing blob identifiers, we avoid transferring blobs (for some further processing) once we know that some of them were not necessary (eliminated by joins or selections).

At this point, the similarity between calling a function and getting a blob becomes evident. Both are modeled by an access to a resource following a restricted binding pattern. Both are expensive operations, suggesting the usage of a cache for function results and blobs. Thus, in the following, we will no longer make the distinction between the two: they are accessed using the same operators (section 3), and the same techniques apply.

In the table below, at left, we show the tables with binding patterns and the user query corresponding to the scientific data integration scenario that we presented:

S_1:	SatImg(id, date, img); SatImg(id^f $date^f$), SatImg(id^b img^f)	Select	i.img, i.date, h.date, ol(i.img)
S_2:	HighTraffic(date); HighTraffic($date^f$)	From	S_1:SatImg i, S_2:HighTraffic h, S_3:OzoneLevels ol
S_3:	OzoneLevels(img, level); OzoneLevels(img^b $level^f$)	Where	(i.date>=h.date) and (i.date< h.date+3) and (ol(i.img) < 45)

Figure 2 shows one possible QEP for evaluating this query; we circled together operators successively executed on the same site, while blob transfer edges are shown in thick lines. The bottom join operator correlates the dates from the *SatImg* and

HighTraffic sources. The join may pair some tuples from *SatImg* with several tuples from *HighTraffic*; other *SatImg* tuples are eliminated by the join.

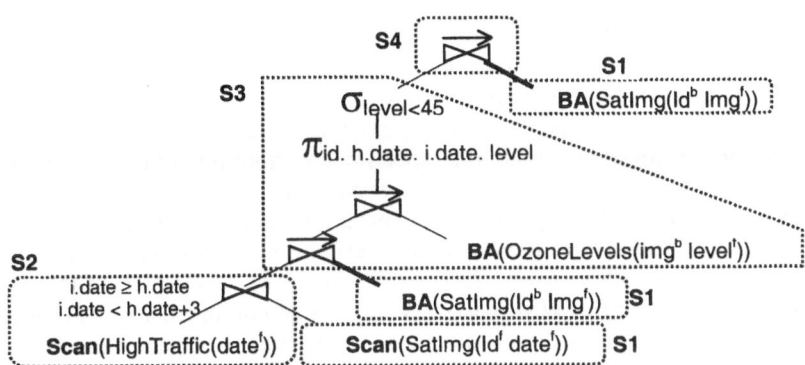

Fig. 2. QEP for our sample query, using BindJoins.

Then, images that survived the join predicate are fetched (and cached locally) on site S_3 by a BindJoin, and a second BindJoin invokes *OzoneLevels* on them. We then project out the images, and apply the selection on the result of the *OzoneLevels* function; this selection eliminates part of the tuples, and thus some image identifiers. The last BindJoin retrieves on site S_4 only the images corresponding to identifiers that survived both the join and selection predicate. Note that we perform two BindJoins with the table *SatImg(id^{f}blob^f)*, corresponding to the two unavoidable transfers: from S_1 to S_3, and from S_1 to S_4. In both cases, we only transfer the images that are actually needed on the destination sites.

A well-known method for achieving the performance gains of the QEP in figure 2 consists of optimizing with semi-joins, introduced in [2]. A QEP using semi-joins equivalent, in terms of blob transfers and function calls, to the one in figure 2, is presented in [19]. Such a QEP, and in general, a semi-join based solution, may incur a high processing overhead, and hinder pipelined execution (see section 3). Finally, optimization with semi-joins is quite complex. Instead, we adopted a lighter approach: assuming only that our BindJoin operator uses a cache, our modeling provides the advantages of semi-joins, without their drawbacks, for the specific redundant operations that we consider.

3   Designing an Efficient BindJoin Operator

In this section, we describe a physical BindJoin providing for efficient execution of distributed queries involving blobs and/or expensive functions.

Traditionally, query processing performance is assessed using three measures [17]: *total work* (TW), including all processing and data transfer costs, *response time* (RT), measuring the time elapsed until the query result has been completely received on the query site, and *time to the first tuple* (FT), accounting only for the time elapsed until the result starts arriving. Note that in fact, the FT metric typically accounts for the early tuple output rate (also called "low latency" in [16]): the property of a QEP to produce as much results as possible early on during query execution. Rather than FT, we use the more expressive *"early output rate"* (ER) term to designate this property. As mentioned in section 1, ER is an important performance goal in the context that we consider and is thus more detailed in the next sections.

We propose a new physical BindJoin that helps reduce the TW and RT of distributed queries with blobs and expensive functions; the main innovation of this operator is its good ER, significantly improved over the state-of-the-art algorithms (as we show in section 5). However, an efficient operator must integrate well with, and take advantage of, standard query execution and optimization techniques.

This section demonstrates both our specific contribution in the design of the operator and its good integration with the existing techniques. We first introduce some simple notations to support our exposition. We then discuss both *local optimizations* (i.e., applying at the operator level) and *global optimizations* (i.e., that must be decided at the QEP level). Sections 3.1 and 3.2 show which of the existing optimizations for reducing TW respectively RT can be combined with our BindJoin. Section 3.3 is specific to our contribution, as it presents the special techniques we employ to provide our BindJoin operator a good ER behavior (local optimization).

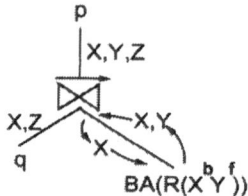

Fig. 3. The BindJoin and BindAccess operators.

We use capital letters, e.g., *X, Y,...* , for attribute names, and corresponding lower case letters, like *x, y,...* for attribute values. We consider a BindJoin operator which receives from its left-hand child operator, denoted *q* in figure 3, tuples of the form *(X, Z)*, and uses the *X* arguments to access the resource *R*, following its binding pattern $R(X^b Y^f)$. The BindAccess operator returns *(x, y)* tuples for each *x*, and the BindJoin concatenates these tuples with the *z* attribute, not needed to access R (figure 3).

3.1 Reducing Total Work (TW)

Local optimization: Reducing total work at the level of the BindJoin operator can be done by using *caching techniques* as suggested in [14]. Caching is profitable for function evaluation and blob transfers as soon as (i) retrieving a function result, respectively blob from the cache is less expensive that computing the results, respectively transferring the blob and (ii) there are duplicate values in the input table. Consider a tuple *(x,z)* coming from *q*. If the y values associated with *x* are stored in a cache, the tuple enriched with *y* can be output directly, short-circuiting the BindAccess operator. Otherwise, a (potentially expensive) access to the restricted resource *R* is made with *x* as an argument. *We decide therefore to include a cache in our BindJoin operator.* Several caching techniques have been proposed in, e.g., [14]
Global optimization: Global optimization of queries with expensive functions has been extensively studied [6, 7, 17, 22, 26]. Due to our modeling based on binding

patterns, these results apply for function calls as well as for blob transfers. Query optimization in the context of tables with binding patterns is addressed in [9].

3.2 Reducing Response Time (RT)

Running several tasks in parallel may reduce response time as soon as that tasks consume distinct resources. This simple principle applies at the local level, i.e. intra-operator parallelism, and at the global level, i.e. inter-operator parallelism.

Local optimization: Our interest in *intra-operator parallelism* is restricted to the costlier operations, namely function invocation and blob transfer. Performing in parallel several function calls or blob transfers allows to fully exploit the query processing - respectively the network transfer – capacity [11]. This could be useful when several processors are available in order to compute a function, or when the same blobs exist in several source sites. Our physical BindJoin operator is designed to include such intra-operator parallelism; due to space limitations, this aspect is relegated to the extended version of this article [19].

Global optimization: Inter-operator parallelism is interesting in a distributed QEP where BindJoins run on distinct sites, but also within a single site if the BindJoins consume different resources. Depending on whether a producer-consumer dependency exists between two BindJoins, they run in pipeline, respectively, independent parallelism. *De-synchronizing the BindJoin from its neighbor operators* (p and q in figure 3) allows such inter-operator parallelism. As a consequence, during the execution, a BindJoin may accumulate tuples waiting to be processed, if q outputs tuples faster than the BindJoin can consume them. Conversely, it may also accumulate result tuples, input for a slower parent operator.

3.3 Improving ER Behavior

The BindJoin informally described so far is pipelined, and treats tuples from q in the order of their arrival. At the beginning of the execution of a query, the cache is empty, and most tuples take a long time to get through the BindJoin, corresponding to an access to the restricted resource. During the execution, the cache is progressively filled, and probably tuples are output at a faster rate towards the end. The early tuple output rate is likely to be small, and most tuples are output in the last stages of the execution.

Local optimization: If the operator denoted q in figure 3 has a good ER behavior, several tuples output by q may accumulate in the BindJoin, waiting to be processed. These waiting tuples can be split in two categories: those for which the result has already been computed and is in the cache; and those for which we need to access the restricted resource in order to get the result. If waiting tuples are processed in the arrival order, a tuple τ from the first category can only be output after processing all tuples ρ from the second category, such that ρ arrived before τ. However, tuples like τ and ρ could very well be processed in parallel, since they have distinct requirements: to output τ it is enough to access the cache, while for ρ we need to access the restricted resource.

Finally, when selecting the next x value to be processed, we may choose the most advantageous x value with respect to the ER behavior: the x value corresponding to the currently largest number of (x, z) tuples waiting to be processed (we term this value the *most frequent*). The advantage of choosing the most frequent x value is obvious: when the restricted access to R using x is finished, a large number of (x, y, z) tuples corresponding to x can be sent simultaneously to the output, improving even more the ER of the BindJoin.

Global optimization: With respect to the global ER of a QEP, we make the following remarks. (i) The delay incurred by a single blocking operator in a QEP is a direct loss for the QEP's ER; therefore, when ER is a concern, pipelined operators are required. (ii) The ER of an operator is a measure relative to the rate of its input operators: of course, if the child of operator *op* is blocking and does not output any tuple in the first minute of query execution, there is little that *op* can do to improve the query's ER. As a consequence, *op* has good ER behavior if its ER is *as good as it can be* with respect to the ER of its input operators. (iii) The good ER behavior of several operators in a QEP re-enforce each other: if a leaf operator (e.g. Scan) has an important ER, and if its parent is able to exploit it, then ER of the QEP rooted at the parent is important, too. Thus, *an important early tuple rate propagates upward in the QEP*, up to the topmost operator, whose ER directly benefits the user. In this paper we propose a BindJoin operator optimized for ER; relational operators for reordering [22], join [13], [16], [26] or online aggregation [13] with good ER behavior have already been described, and should be used together with our BindJoin.

While a global optimization strategy [6], [7], [9], [15], [20], [24] will order BindJoins after selections (to reduce the number of tuples on which an expensive operation is performed), it may place BindJoins *after join operators*, as soon as a *cache* is used in the BindJoin. Indeed, joins can produce many tuples but *will never produce new values,* and in particular, values for the BindJoin's inputs. This remark increases the interest of the ER optimizations we propose, since duplicates are more likely to appear in the input of a BindJoin as a consequence of a join operator.

Finally, one should note that ER optimization may also reduce response time by absorbing synchronization problems between several BindJoins (see section 5.3).

4   Operator Implementation

This section describes the physical operators that implement the BindJoin and BindAccess operators. The internal data structure used for these optimizations is depicted in section 4.2. Section 4.3 explains how our BindJoin algorithm deals with limited memory execution environments.

4.1   Physical Operators for BindJoin and BindAccess

We now describe the physical operators for the BindJoin and BindAccess, implemented as iterators, following [12]. The API of an iterator consists of an initialization *open()* method, a *next()* method producing one tuple at a time, and a *close()* method to release resources and terminate.

Figure 4 depicts our proposed decomposition of the logical BindJoin and BindAccess operators into physical operators, implementing the techniques described in the previous section. A single data structure, belonging to the BindJoin, is used to hold (a) tuples waiting to be processed, (b) a result cache and (c) processed tuples waiting to be output.

Physical operators for the BindJoin: We decompose the BindJoin in four physical operators, termed *BJStore, BJCompute, BJGetBindings* and *BJGet* in figure 4.

1. BJStore retrieves *(x, z)* tuples from *q* and checks *x* against the cache. If *x* is present in the cache, then BJStore inserts the tuple in the set of processed tuples; otherwise, in the set of waiting tuples.
2. On a *next* call from the BindAccess, BJGetBindings chooses the next *x* value to be processed and returns it.
3. BJCompute retrieves *(x, y)* tuples from the BindAccess, and updates the cache and the set of processed tuples accordingly.
4. Finally, BJGet answers *next()* calls from *p*, the operator above the BindJoin in the QEP, returning an *(x,y,z)* tuple to *p*. This tuple is erased from the set of tuples waiting to be output.

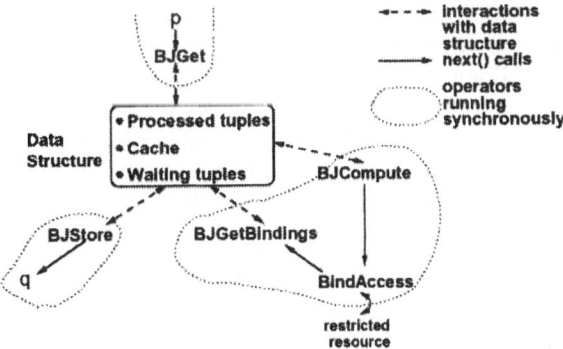

Fig. 4. Physical operators for a BindJoin and a BindAccess on the same site

Physical BindAccess operator: We use a single physical BindAccess operator, as shown in figure 4, to implement the logical BindAccess. This operator obtains *x* values from BJGetBindings, and performs a call to the restricted resource providing *x* as argument. On a *next()* call from BJCompute, BindAccess returns a *(x,y)* tuple. Thus, the access to the resource is encapsulated within BindAccess; this operator is generic and can be provided by the integration system, making the publication process easy for the resource owner. The only thing required to "plug" a BindAccess on a given restricted resource is a call interface to that resource (e.g. *callFunction(arg₁,arg₂,...,argₖ)* for functions and *readBlob(blobID, startOffset, endOffset, memBuffer)* for accessing blobs).

Operator synchronization: In figure 4, we represented the case when the BindJoin and the BindAccess operators run on the same site. In this case, BJCompute, BindAccess and BJGetBindings run synchronously, since there is no gain in parallelizing these operators within a single site. However, note that in parallel with these three operators run, on one hand, *p* and BJGet, and on the other hand, *q* and BJStore. Decoupling in such a way the execution of the BindJoin-BindAccess pair from the rest of the QEP allows for inter-operator parallelism.

4.2 Organization of the BindJoin's Internal Data Structure

The data structure holding the data internal to the BindJoin is basically organized as a hash table. Every hash bucket contains a set of cells; one cell corresponds to a given value for x, the argument value for accessing the restricted resource. Within one bucket, cells are organized in a linked list. Two extra data structures are maintained among the cells in the hash table. First, a doubly-linked frequency list connects cells corresponding to x values not yet in the cache, in the order of their frequency. Second, we also keep a processed tuple set, containing the cells for which x is already in the cache, and besides, there currently are some (x,y,z) tuples produced and not output yet. More details on the data structure and its API are provided in [19].

4.3 BindJoin Behavior in the Presence of Limited Memory

The techniques presented so far assume that the data structure holds in memory, which may not be the case. Note that if X, Y or Z are blobs, their storage is delegated to a special BlobManager component [19], which flushes them to disk; in this case, the data structure will contain the blobID, not the blob. Since blob transfers are achieved by BindJoins (with cache*), a blob is never transmitted twice by the same operator*, and thus will not be repeatedly loaded in memory and flushed to disk.

There is, however, a risk of overflow even if X, Y and X are not blob attributes. In this case, our goal is to conserve as much as possible its good ER properties. To that purpose, we attempt to keep in memory all (X,Y) pairs, so that we can process in parallel tuples with new values and those for which the results are in the cache.

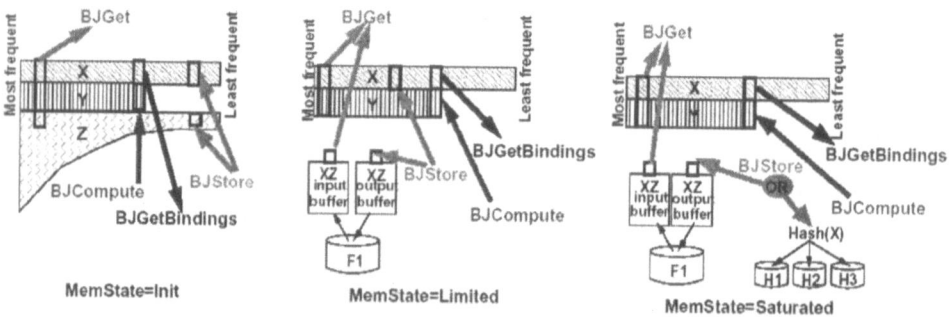

Fig. 5. The BindJoin behavior in the presence of memory limitations.

The BindJoin's memory consumption due to the internal data structure has a continuously increasing component, the (X,Y) cache, and a variable component, due to (X,Z) tuples waiting to be processed, or (X,Y,Z) tuples waiting to be output. We distinguish four execution phases, corresponding to four memory states. (i) In the Init phase, there is enough memory for all the data structure. (ii) In the Limited phase, all the (X,Y) pairs produced so far still hold in memory, but there is no place to store the Z values. (iii) In the Saturated phase, there is no place left to produce new (X,Y) pairs, so some data has to be temporarily stored to disk. (iv) Finally, during the Cleanup phase, data previously flushed to disk is processed.

The data structure and the behavior of the BindJoin's physical operators are depicted in figure 5. We represent the three types of information stored in the data structure (X, Y, and Z values) in separate areas. Graphically, the Y and Z values appearing "under" a given X value are associated to it, in the sense that (X,Z) tuples corresponding to these values were received from q and Y is the value obtained by accessing the resource with the argument X. From left to right in the data structure, there are less and less Z values for a given X value. The thick arrows designate the tuples inserted/extracted by the physical operators from the data structure.

The Init phase: At the beginning of the execution, BJStore inserts (X,Z) tuples, BJGetBindings picks the most frequent X not yet processed. BJCompute inserts in the data structure the Y results (when they are available) for this X, while BJGet extracts (X,Y,Z) tuples. When memory runs out, we enter the Limited phase.

The Limited phase: In this phase, we first flush to disk all (X,Z) pairs obtained so far (whether Y has been computed or not), in the decreasing order of X frequency. Whenever it obtains a new (X,Z) tuple, BJStore inserts X in the data structure, and sends (X,Z) to the "XZ output buffer", to be written to the temporary FIFO file F_l. Note that we need to store (X,Z) pairs, not just Z values, in order to be able to re-compute the tuples. BJGet outputs tuples from a buffer of data sequentially read from F_l; the first such buffer to be brought in memory corresponds to the most frequent X value, for which the result has probably already been computed. For each (X,Z) tuple read, if the result is already in the memory cache, BJGet outputs the (X,Y,Z) tuple; otherwise, its waits for the result to become available. When the available memory is insufficient for storing the (X,Y) pairs, we enter the Saturated phase.

The Saturated phase: In this phase, whenever BJStore obtains a new (X,Z) tuple, if X is already in memory, its corresponding frequency counter is updated, and (X,Z) is sent to F_l. Otherwise, we apply the hashing function $H(X)$ to distribute the (X,Z) tuple in the disk buckets noted H_l, H_2 and H_3 in figure 5 at right. This phase ends when BJStore encounters *EOF*.

The Cleanup phase: At this point, BJGetBindings reads F_l page by page, the corresponding Y results are taken from the cache or computed, and the (X,Y,Z) tuples output. When F_l is finished, the current (X,Y) cache can be completely discarded, since no tuple on disk has an X value among those in the cache. Then, the partitions made by the function H are loaded in memory one by one, and their tuples are processed as in the Init phase. To that purpose, the function H is chosen so that each partition fits in memory, by a technique similar to the one proposed in [14].

The BindJoin's behavior in the case of limited memory incurs a minimal overhead; indeed, no tuple is written to disk more than once during the processing.

5   Experimental Evaluation of the BindJoin ER

This section compares the ER of our BindJoin operator with that provided by the state-of-the-art algorithms for handling expensive functions.

5.1   Experimental Platform

We experimented with several algorithms, QEPs, data distribution parameters, data delivery rate and tuple orderings. For space reasons, we only include here the most significant ones, and comment on some others. More results are described in [19].

BindJoin algorithms: We compare our BindJoin physical operator (denoted ERBJ) with two algorithms previously proposed for handling expensive functions [5], [14]. The simplest one uses a *hash-based (memoization) cache* and will be denoted HBBJ.

The second one is *sort-based* (SBBJ): before accessing an expensive resource, the arguments are materialized and sorted, and thus a cache of just one value is sufficient. To ensure a fair comparison, HBBJ is de-synchronized from its parent and child operators through the standard Exchange operator [12].

QEPs tested: We study the tuple output rate from the following three QEPs:

- QEP1: $q(X, Z) \bowtie_x BA(f(X^b Y^f))$

- QEP2: $q(X, Z) \bowtie_x BA(f(X^b Y^f)) \bowtie_z BA(g(Z^b T^f))$

- QEP3: $\sigma_s (q(X, Z) \bowtie_x BA(f(X^b Y^f))) \bowtie_z BA(g(Z^b T^f))$

X, Y, Z and T are integer attributes, q is a given QEP producing tuples of the form *(X,Z)*, and s is a selection condition on the result of function f. While very simple, such QEPs are very general, as the subplan q may be arbitrarily complex. Indeed, as mentioned in section 3.3, global optimization techniques [6], [15], [24] would order relational operator *before* expensive BindJoins. QEP3 is represen[tative of plans with restrictions on the function results.

Characteristics of the tuples produced by q: We use a data generator which constructs the set of *(X,Z)* tuples output by q according to a set of parameters: (i) the number of tuples; (ii) the number of distinct values for each attribute; (iii) the distribution law, assuming that the distributions of the attributes are mutually independent; and (iv) the rate at which tuples can be obtained from q. This rate is important, since an ERBJ can only accumulate tuples if the tuple input rate is larger than its processing rate. Finally, we are able to deliver the tuples in specific orders. When generating X and Z according to a uniform data distribution, we did not enforce perfect uniformity; rather, we used a uniformly distributed random variable to draw 10,000 values out of 2,500 possible, yielding 2450 values. For Zipfian distributions, we used a low zipf factor ($\alpha = 0.2$) representative of real-life databases distributions delivering a total of 1,450 distinct values in 10,000 tuples.

Graphs: Each graph presented in the sequel shows the number of result tuples as a function of the running time. Thus, the response time is indicated by the width of the curve while the good ER behavior is shown by the convexity of the curve.

5.2 ER Behavior of the BindJoin on Simple Query Plans

Our first four experiments study the ER behavior of QEP1 and QEP2, in which all BindJoins are implemented using as HBBJ, SBBJ, and ERBJ, when q's output follows a uniform, respectively Zipfian input data distribution (see figure 6-10). In this section, we assume that all tuples output by q have been transmitted towards its parent operator before the BindJoins start to run. This assumption will be lifted in the next sections; however, it is quite realistic if q consists only of regular relational operations, while the accesses to f and g are much more expensive (this configuration is also considered in [3], [6], [11]).

In experiments 1-4, HBBJ delivers few tuples at the beginning, since most X values that f (or g) processes are new; f (or g) must be computed. As the cache gets filled, toward the end of the execution, the output rate increases. With a Zipfian distribution, the ER behavior is slightly improved since some values are very frequent.

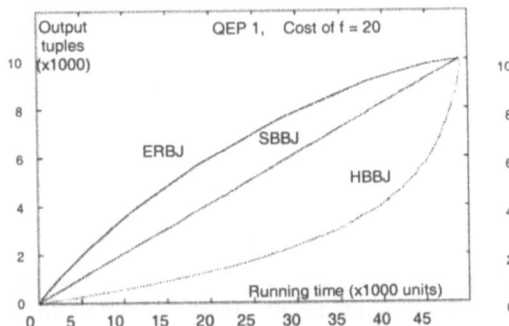

Fig. 6. Exp.1: one BindJoin, uniform dist.   **Fig. 7.** Exp. 2: one BindJoin, Zipfian dist.

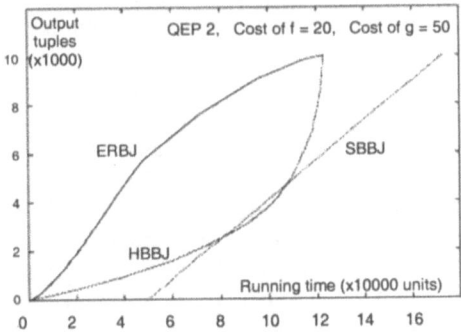 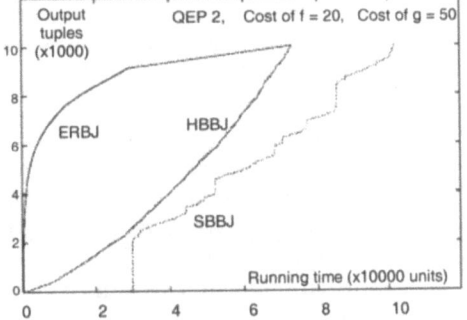

Fig. 8. Exp.3: two BindJoins, uniform dist.   **Fig. 9.** Exp.4: two BindJoins, Zipfian dist.

In experiment 1 (figure 6), the curve for SBBJ is almost a straight line: after each processed value, SBBJ outputs in average 4 tuples (2.450 distinct values in 10.000 tuples). With the Zipfian distribution, in experiment 2 (figure 7), SBBJ outputs bursts of tuples corresponding to the groups of tuples sharing the same X value. Unfortunately, SBBJ is not able to exploit the most frequent values, since it is encountered somewhere in the middle of the value range. In the case of QEP2 (figures 8 and 9), the SBBJ output is delayed until the first BindJoin has finished, since the tuples have to be re-sorted on Z before the second BindJoin can start. The overall ER of the plan using SBBJ is poor.

In figure 6, ERBJ does slightly better than SBBJ, since it chooses the most frequent values first, even if there is only a very small frequency variation in uniform distributions (in our randomly generated distribution the frequency varies from 3 to 6 with an average of 4). With Zipfian distributions (figures 7 and 9), ERBJ exploits the presence of the few very popular values (characteristic to Zipf) by a very large pack of tuples output right at the beginning of the execution.

Conclusions: HBBJ has a bad ER behavior since tuples for which the result was already in the cache have to wait for their turn before being output. However, HBBJ is non-blocking and works in pipeline. SBBJ does not take advantage of the most frequent values, since it sorts in a *value based* data order in which most frequent values do not necessarily come first. But the main disadvantage of SBBJ is its blocking aspect, which leads to very poor ER and increased response time. Our proposed *ERBJ* consistently outperforms the others. Like HBBJ, it is non-blocking;

like SBBJ, it outputs simultaneously several tuples sharing an argument value, when the result for this value is available. All three algorithms use a cache, and therefore are useful if there are duplicates in their input. However, the advantage of the ERBJ over the two others is increased by the presence of skewed distributions, since it processes first the more popular values to improve its output rate.

5.3 ER Behavior and Response Time with More Complex Plans

In experiment 5 (figure 10), we study the output rate of QEP_1 when q only provides one tuple every time unit (since, e.g., it retrieves input data from a remote site or performs a complex subplan). For comparison, we also plotted the curve for ERBJ when there is no input limitation (the same as in figure 7). The curve corresponding to ERBJ with delay between inputs has an almost linear aspect for the first *10,000* running time units; then, it joins the curve of ERBJ without delays. The join occurs after 10,000 time units; thus, even with tuple buffer limited by the slow input, the ERBJ has been able to choose frequent values to process (otherwise, it would have met the non-restricted curve even later). The ERBJ curve is quite close to the absolute optimum in the presence of restrictions, which would be to output 1 tuple every time unit (as soon as it arrives). Note, however, this optimum is not achievable, since new values require processing. The ERBJ is so good because the most frequent values are scattered uniformly over a data set following a Zipf distribution. It would not be the case with larger delays and a very bad data order (e.g. the most frequent values last), since the ERBJ could not see (and choose) frequent values early. HBBJ is not affected by the delay between inputs since it is de-synchronized from q. Obviously, with a larger delay, idle time may occur. Finally, as expected, SBBJ has to wait 10,000 time units before it can sort them and proceed.

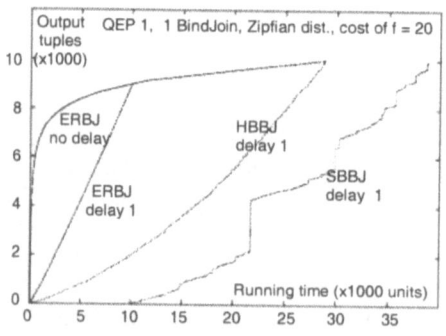

Fig. 10. Exp.5: effect of delays

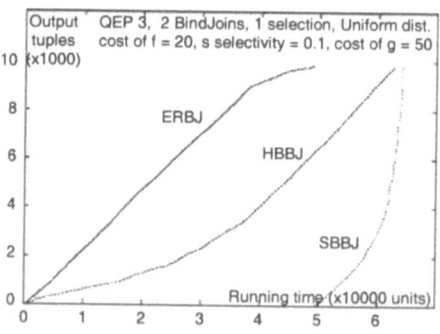

Fig. 11. Exp.6: selection with 2 BindJoins

Experiment 6 (figure 11) studies the output of QEP_3, when the selection σ_s eliminates nine (X,Y,Z) tuples out of ten. HBBJ not only has a worse ER than the ERBJ, but also a longer response time. At the beginning of the execution, the first HBBJ outputs few tuples, of which very few survive the selection. The second HBBJ is therefore often idle. Towards the end of the execution, as the cache of the first BindJoin fills, it generates tuples at a faster rate, and the second BindJoin, even after the selection, becomes overloaded with new values. This behavior (first idle, then overloaded) translates into the increased running time. The same synchronization problem can arise in a variety of settings – for example, if we replace σ_s by a regular join, a mixture of joins and selections etc. The same holds for QEP_2, if g is significantly more expensive than f [19]. By contrast, when using ERBJs, the large early output rate of the first one, even if trimmed by the selection, means that the second one is always busy. Therefore, the pipeline between the two is perfect (in figure 11, the total running time is that of the first BindJoin). The curve corresponding to sort-based BindJoins is delayed by the running time of the first BindJoin.

5.4 Other Experiments and Conclusion

We summarize here the results of some other measures that we performed but do not present here (see the extended version of this paper [19]).

A BindJoin's input data can come in various orders, resulting from the processing of the subplan q. The ERBJ and the SBBJ are not sensitive to such orders, since they perform their own re-ordering (unless delays proscribe it). In contrast, the HBBJ is very sensitive to the order.

We have performed experiments on QEPs with up to four BindJoins. We have noticed that as the number of BindJoin increases, if they have different costs, produce several output tuples per input tuple, or if there are interspersed selections, the probability of synchronization problems for hash-based BindJoins (as in figure 10) increases. The explanation is that some BindJoins are successively idle then overloaded. Therefore, the advantage of ERBJ over hash-based BindJoins is more important.

In conclusion, ERBJ provides always a significantly better ER than the state-of-the-art algorithms for accessing restricted resources, This advantage depends on the presence of duplicates in the input, and increases with the non-uniform distribution of input values. It is remarkably stable with variations in the input order, delays between two successive input tuples, and synchronization problems in the QEP. Furthermore, its excellent ER properties may improve the overall RT of complex queries.

6   Related Optimization and Execution Techniques

Significant work has been done on online and adaptive query processing; see, e.g., [1], [13], [16], [22], [25]. These works do not address the specific BindJoin operator but are however complementary. Indeed, as mentioned in section 3.3, the ER behavior of a QEP is the result of the good ER behavior of all its query operators.

The ObjectGlobe [4] project uses Java user-defined operators, loadable from external code repositories. Mocha [23] addresses query optimization for user-defined functions that may be shipped across the network. When possible, this technique is very profitable, since it avoids data transfer, however, its application is limited, as restricted resources depend on a particular environment, or cannot be copied.

In [5], the sort-based BindJoin algorithm, with which we compared in section 5, is presented. In [14], the authors propose a *hybrid cache* algorithm that degrades gracefully if the cache outgrows the available memory. Compared with [5], [14], our BindJoin exploits duplicates and parallelism to improve its ER; also, we use it for avoiding duplicate blob transfers. We have shown in section 4.3 how our ERBJ deals with memory limitations: thus, it has the good properties of the hybrid cache algorithm, plus an improved ER behavior.

[20] studies query execution in a client-server context, with expensive UDFs. They recognized that UDF can be executed as joins, and that existing work on distributed join processing, and semi-joins, could be reused. Our techniques have a broader scope, since they apply for *any* restricted resource access, and improve ER.

Two approaches for modeling expensive functions exist, and therefore two classes of optimization algorithms. LDL [7] models a function as a table. While this requires little modification to a regular optimizer, the number of functions is reflected exponentially in the size of the search space, just like the number of regular tables. This drawback is avoided by the second approach, in which expensive functions are assimilated with selections. Optimization methods based on *predicate ranking* have been proposed in, e.g., [15], [6]; in a distributed setting, they are no longer optimal, due to data transfer costs [20]. In [24], efficient optimization algorithms improve over predicate ranking by considering interesting data orders, and bushy QEPs.

Our modeling is closer to LDL, for the following reason. In general, a restricted, expensive resource is *not* a function or a predicate. It may be a full-parameterized sub-query, optimized as a complex operator tree QEP (caching for sub-query results has been suggested in [14]). Ignoring such parameterized sub-plans may lead to loss of optimality [9]. To combine a sub-plan, providing bindings, with another parameterized sub-plan requiring them, we need a *binary* BindJoin operator, not a selection one. Query optimization algorithms for tables with binding patterns, using joins and BindJoins, are provided in [9], which shows that in practical cases, the presence of access restrictions drastically limits the size of the search space.

7 Conclusion

In this paper, we investigate the publication model and algorithms for resource sharing in a fully distributed peer-to-peer mediation architecture. We showed how binding patterns can be used to uniformly model data sources including functions as well as blobs, providing an attractive alternative to semi-joins. We analyzed the impact of expensive functions and blobs on the design of the BindJoin operator and on its integration in the query execution plan. We considered three performance goals: (i) total work; (ii) response time; and (iii), the more specific early tuple output rate. The main specificity of our BindJoin is that it exploits the presence of duplicates in its input to provide an important early tuple output rate, so that the user obtains most of the query results fast. Since our BindJoin operator includes all the optimizations, the publisher task is significantly reduced, while providing good query performance.

References

[1]   R. Avnur and J. Hellerstein. Eddies: Continuously adaptive query processing. *IN PROC. OF ACM SIGMOD CONF.*, 2000.
[2]   P. Bernstein and D W. Chiu. Using semi-joins to solve relational queries. *Journal of the ACM*, 1981.
[3]   L. Bouganim, F. Fabret, F. Porto, and P. Valduriez. Processing queries with expensive functions and large objects in distributed mediator systems. *ICDE* 2001.

[4]   R. Braumandl, M. Keidl, A. Kemper, and D. Kossmann et al. ObjectGlobe: Ubiquitous query processing on the internet. In *Workshop on Technologies for E-Services*, 2000.

[5]   S. Chaudhuri and K. Shim. Query optimization in the presence of foreign functions. In *Proc. of the VLDB Conf.*, 1993.

[6]   S. Chaudhuri and K. Shim. Optimization of queries with user-defined predicates. *ACM Transaction on database system (TODS)*, 2(24), 1999.

[7]   The Decair and Thetis projects. Available at http://www-caravel.inria.fr/Econtrats.html.

[8]   The Ecobase Team. The Ecobase project: Database and web technologies for environmental information systems. *SIGMOD Record*, 30(3), 2001.

[9]   D. Florescu, A. Levy, I. Manolescu, and D. Suciu Query optimization in the presence of limited access patterns. *In Proc. of ACM SIGMOD Conf.*, 1999.

[10] S. Ganguly, W. Hassan, and R. Krishnamurthy. Query optimization for parallel execution. *In Proc. of ACM SIGMOD Conf.*, 1992.

[11] R. Goldman and J. Widom. WSQ/DSQ: A practical approach for combined querying of databases and the web. *In Proc. of ACM SIGMOD Conf.*, 2000.

[12] G. Graefe. Query evaluation techniques for large databases. *ACM Computing Surveys*, 25(2), June 1993.

[13] P. Haas and J. Hellerstein. Ripple joins for online aggregation. *SIGMOD Conf.*, 1999.

[14] J. Hellerstein and J. Naughton. Query execution techniques for caching expensive methods. *In Proc. of ACM SIGMOD Conf.*, 1996.

[15] J. Hellerstein and M. Stonebraker. Predicate migration: Optimizing queries with expensive predicates. *In Proc. of ACM SIGMOD Conf.*, 1993.

[16] Z. Ives, D. Florescu, M. Friedman, D. Weld, and A. Levy. An adaptive query execution system for data integration. *In Proc. of ACM SIGMOD Conf.*, 1999.

[17] D. Kossmann. The state of the art in distributed query processing. *ACM Computing Surveys*, 2000.

[18] The LeSelect Project. Available at http://www-caravel.inria.fr/LeSelect.

[19] I. Manolescu, L. Bouganim, F. Fabret, and E. Simon. Efficient data and program integration using binding patterns. Tech. Report no. 4239, INRIA. Extended version available at: www-rocq.inria.fr/~manolesc/BJ-extended.ps

[20] T. Mayr and P. Seshadri. Client-site query extensions. *In Proc. of ACM SIGMOD.*, 1999.

[21] A. Rajaraman, Y. Sagiv, and J. Ullman. Answering queries using templates with binding patterns. In *Proc. of the ACM PODS*, San Jose, CA, 1995.

[22] A. Raman, B. Raman, and J. Hellerstein. Online dynamic reordering for interactive data processing. In *Proc. of the VLDB Conf.*, 1999.

[23] M. Rodriguez-Martinez and N. Roussopoulos. MOCHA: A self-extensible database middleware system for distributed data sources. In *Proc. of ACM SIGMOD Conf*, 2000.

[24] W. Scheufele and G. Moerkotte. Efficient dynamic programming algorithms for ordering expensive joins and selections. In *Proc. of the EDBT Conf.*, 1998.

[25] T. Urhan and M. Franklin. XJoin: a reactively scheduled pipelined join operator. In *IEEE Data Engineering Bulletin*, 2000.

[26] A.N. Wilschut and P.M.G. Apers. Dataflow query execution in a parallel main-memory environment. In *Proc. of the PDIS Conf.*, 1991.

Managing Data Quality in Cooperative Information Systems

Massimo Mecella[1], Monica Scannapieco[1,2], Antonino Virgillito[1],
Roberto Baldoni[1], Tiziana Catarci[1], and Carlo Batini[3]

[1] Università di Roma "La Sapienza", DIS
{mecella,monscan,virgi,baldoni,catarci}@dis.uniroma1.it
[2] Consiglio Nazionale delle Ricerche, IASI
[3] Università di Milano "Bicocca", DISCo
batini@disco.unimib.it

Abstract. Current approaches to the development of cooperative information systems are based on services to be offered by cooperating organizations, and on the opportunity of building coordinators and brokers on top of such services. The quality of data exchanged and provided by different services hampers such approaches, as data of low quality can spread all over the cooperative system. At the same time, improvement can be based on comparing data, correcting them and disseminating high quality data. In this paper, a service-based framework for managing data quality in cooperative information systems is presented. An XML-based model for data and quality data is proposed, and the design of a broker, which selects the best available data from different services, is presented. Such a broker also supports the improvement of data based on feedbacks to source services.

1 Introduction

A *Cooperative Information System (CIS)* is a large scale information system that interconnects various systems of different and autonomous organizations, geographically distributed and sharing common objectives. Among the different resources that are shared by organizations, data are fundamental; in real world scenarios, an organization A may not request data from an organization B if it does not "trust" B data, i.e., if A does not know that the quality of the data that B can provide is high. As an example, in an *e*-Government scenario in which public administrations cooperate in order to fulfill service requests from citizens and enterprises [1], administrations very often prefer asking citizens for data, rather than other administrations that have stored the same data, because the quality of such data is not known. Therefore, lack of cooperation may occur due to lack of quality certification.

Uncertified quality can also cause a deterioration of the data quality inside single organizations. If organizations exchange data without knowing their actual quality, it may happen that data of low quality spread all over the CIS.

R. Meersman, Z. Tari (Eds.): CoopIS/DOA/ODBASE 2002, LNCS 2519, pp. 486–502, 2002.

On the other hand, CIS's are characterized by high data replication, i.e., different copies of the same data are stored by different organizations. From a data quality perspective this is a great opportunity: improvement actions can be carried out on the basis of comparisons among different copies, in order either to select the most appropriate one or to reconcile available copies, thus producing a new improved copy to be notified to all involved organizations.

CIS's designed according to a service-based approach [2] consider cooperation among different organizations to be obtained by sharing and integrating services across networks; such services, commonly referred to as e-Services and Web-Services [3], are exported by different organizations as well defined operations that allow users and applications to access and perform tasks offered by back-end business applications.

In this paper, we propose a service-based framework and an overall architecture for managing data quality in CIS's. The architecture aims at avoiding dissemination of low qualified data through the CIS, by providing a support for data quality diffusion and improvement. At the best of our knowledge, this is a novel contribution in the information quality area, that aims at integrating, in the specific context of CIS, both modeling and architectural issues. To enforce this vision, our work, beside presenting the general architecture, focuses on two specific elements of the problem, that we consider of primary importance. More specifically:

❒ we first face the problem of lack of quality certification by proposing a model for each organization to export data with associated quality information. The model is XML-based in order to address interoperability issues existing in cooperative information systems;

❒ then, we present the distributed design of a single architectural service, based on the model cited above, namely the Data Quality Broker, which allows each organization involved in the CIS to retrieve data specifying their quality requirements. The service offers only data that satisfies the given requirements and notifies organizations about the highest quality values found within the CIS. The design of the distributed service takes into account reliable communication issues and shows the feasibility of our approach in practical scenarios.

The structure of the paper is as follows. In Section 2, related research work is discussed. In Section 3, a service-based framework for Cooperative Information Systems is proposed. On the basis of such a framework, in Section 4, an architecture specifically addressing quality related issues is described. In Section 5, a model for both the exchanged data and their quality is presented. In Section 6, the distributed design of the Data Quality Broker service is described. Finally, Section 7 concludes the paper by drawing future work.

2   Related Work

Data Quality has been traditionally investigated in the context of single information systems; only recently, a methodological framework for data quality in cooperative systems has been proposed, consisting of five phases (i.e., definition, measurement, exchange, analysis and improvement) [4].

In cooperative scenarios, the main data quality issues regard: *(i)* assessment of the quality of the data owned by each organization; *(ii)* methods and techniques for exchanging quality information; *(iii)* improvement of quality within each cooperating organization; and *(iv)* heterogeneity, due to the presence of different organizations, in general with different data semantics.

For the assessment *(i)* and the heterogeneity *(iv)* issues, some of the results already achieved for traditional systems can be borrowed, e.g., [5,6]. Methods and techniques for exchanging quality information *(ii)* have been only partially addressed in the literature. When considering the issue of exchanging data and the associated quality, a model to export data and quality data needs to be defined. Some conceptual models to associate quality information to data have been proposed: an extension of the Entity-Relationship model [7], and a data warehouse conceptual model with quality features described through the Description Logic formalism [6]. Both models are thought for a specific purpose: the former to introduce quality elements in relational database design; the latter to introduce quality elements in the data warehouse design. Whereas, in the present paper the aim is to enable quality exchanging in a generic CIS, independently of the specific data model and system architecture.

In [8], the problem of the quality of web-available information has been faced in order to select data with high quality coming from distinct sources: every source has to evaluate some pre-defined data quality parameters, and to make their values available through the exposition of meta-data. Our proposal is different as we propose an ad-hoc service that brokers data requests and replies on the basis of data quality information. Moreover, we also take into account improvement features *(iii)* that are not considered in [8].

3   The Framework

In current business scenarios, organizations need to cooperate in order to offer services to their customers and partners. Organizations that cooperate have business links (i.e., relationships, exchanged documents, resources, knowledge, etc.) connecting each other. Specifically, organizations exploit business services (e.g., they exchange data or require services to be carried out) on the basis of business links, and therefore the network of organizations and business links constitutes a cooperative business system.

As an example, a supply chain, in which some enterprises offer basic products and some others assemble them in order to deliver final products to customers, is a cooperative business system. As another example, a set of public administrations which need to exchange information about citizens and their health state in order to provide social aids, is a cooperative business system derived from the Italian *e*-Government scenario [1].

A cooperative business system exists independently of the presence of a software infrastructure supporting electronic data exchange and service provisioning.

Indeed cooperative information systems are software systems supporting cooperative business systems; in the remaining of this paper, the following definition of CIS is considered:

A cooperative information system is formed by a set of organizations *{ Org_1, ..., Org_n } which cooperate through a communication software infrastructure $\mathbb{N}$, which may provide software services, referred to as infrastructure services (IS's), to organizations as wells as reliable connectivity. Each organization Org_i is connected to $\mathbb{N}$ through a gateway G_i, on which application services (AS's) offered by Org_i to other organizations are deployed. We denote as $\mathcal{AS}_{j,i}$ the j-th application service offered by Org_i.*

The difference between application and infrastructure services is that the latter can be designed independently of organizations. Application services can perform different operations, such as initiating complex transactions on back-end systems, providing access to data, etc. In the present work we only consider *read-only access* services, that is application services returning application data stored inside organizations without modifying them. We will assume the following definition of application service:

A generic application service $\mathcal{AS}_{j,i}$ offered by a cooperating organization Org_i is a set of operations $\{s_1, ..., s_n\}$, each one specified by a signature of the following form:

$$s_i(p_1, ..., p_n) \rightarrow \{\mathcal{O}_1, ..., \mathcal{O}_n\}$$

where $p_1, ..., p_n$ is the list of parameters and $\{\mathcal{O}_1, ..., \mathcal{O}_n\}$ is the set of data items returned by s_i.

The $\mathcal{O}_i$'s returned by application services are expressed as XML documents that convey not only application data items, but also data about the quality of such data items (see Section 5).

4   An Architecture for Data Quality

A typical feature of CIS's is the high degree of data replicated in different organizations. As an example, in an *e*-Government scenario, the personal data of a citizen are stored by almost all the administrations. On the basis of the proposed definition of CIS, more than one organization can implement the same application service. Therefore, according to our assumption of considering only access data services, several organizations can provide the same data though with different quality levels. Any requester of data may want to have the data with the highest quality level, among the provided ones. Thus only the highest quality data are returned to the requester, limiting the dissemination of low quality data. Moreover, the comparison of the gathered data values can be used to enforce a general improvement of data quality in all the organizations.

In the context of the DaQuinCIS project[1], we propose an architecture for the management of data quality in CIS's; such an architecture allows the diffusion of data and related quality and exploits data replication to improve the overall quality of cooperative data. According to the logical model of a CIS presented in the previous section, we need to define both a model for the organizations to exchange data and data quality data and a set of infrastructure services that realize quality management functions.

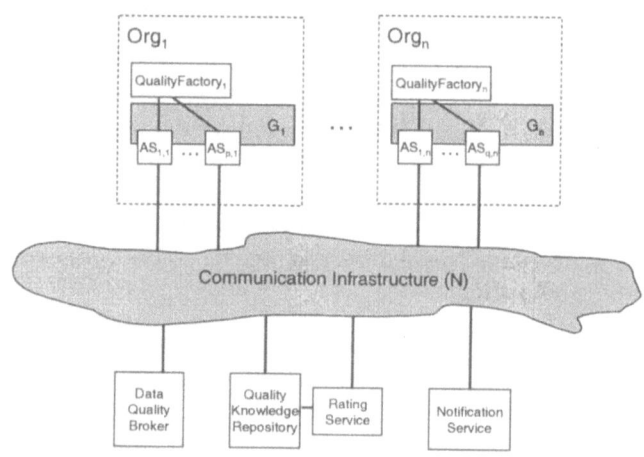

Fig. 1. An architecture for data quality diffusion and improvement

The model for data quality we propose in this paper is called *Data and Data Quality (D^2Q) model*. It includes the definitions of *(i)* constructs to represent data, *(ii)* a common set of data quality properties, *(iii)* constructs to represent them and *(iv)* the association between data and quality data. The D^2Q model is described in Section 5.

In order to produce data and quality data according to the D^2Q model, each organization holds a **Quality Factory** that is responsible for evaluating the quality of its own data. The overall architecture is depicted in Figure 1. In the following we give a description of each element:

◻ **Data Quality Broker**: it is the core of the architecture. It performs, on behalf of a requesting organization, a data request on all the AS's, also specifying a set of quality requirements that the desired data have to satisfy (*quality brokering function*). Different copies of the same data received as responses to the request are reconciled and a best-quality value is selected

---

[1] "DaQuinCIS - Methodologies and Tools for Data Quality in Cooperative Information Systems" is an Italian research project carried out by Università di Roma "La Sapienza", Università di Milano "Bicocca" and Politecnico di Milano (http://www.dis.uniroma1.it/~dq/).

and proposed to organizations, that can choose to discard their data and adopt higher quality ones (*quality improvement function*). Quality brokering and improvement are described in Section 6. If the requirements specified in the request cannot be satisfied, then the broker initiates a negotiation with the requester that can optionally weaken the constraints on the desired data.

❏ **Quality Knowledge Repository**: it consists of a knowledge base used by the other components in order to perform their functions. For example, it maintains *(i)* the interschema knowledge representing the relationships among schemas that allow to determine intensional and extensional equivalence of data in different organizations [10], and *(ii)* historical quality knowledge, including statistics related to data quality ensured by organizations in the past, that is also used to realize a rating service for source reliability.

❏ **Notification Service**: it is a publish/subscribe engine used as a general message bus between components and/or organizations. More specifically, it allows quality-based subscriptions for organizations to be notified for quality changes in data. For example, an organization may want to be notified if the quality of a data it uses degrades below a certain acceptable threshold, or when high quality data are available.

❏ **Rating Service**: it associates trust values to each data source in the CIS. These are used by the Data Quality Broker to determine the reliability of the quality evaluation made by organizations. Trust values are dynamically updated from the statistics from the Quality Knowledge Repository and take also into account the current availability of the data source.

The detailed design of such components is currently under investigation [9, 11]; in this paper, we only focus on the architectural design of the data quality broker, which is detailed in Section 6.

5   The D^2Q Model

All cooperating organizations export their application data and quality data (i.e., data quality dimension values evaluated for the application data) according to a specific data model. Exported data and quality data can be accessed by other organizations by means of application service operations that each cooperating organization makes available to the others. The model for exporting data and quality data is referred to as *Data and Data Quality (D^2Q) model*. In this section, we first introduce the data quality dimensions used in this paper (Section 5.1), then we describe the D^2Q model with respect to the data features (Section 5.2) and the quality features (Section 5.3).

5.1   Data Quality Dimensions

Data quality dimensions are properties of data such as correctness or degree of updating. The data quality dimensions used in this work concern only data values; instead, they do not deal with aspects concerning quality of logical schema and data format [12].

In this section, we propose and outline some data quality dimensions to be used in CIS's, stemming from real requirements of CIS's scenarios that we experienced [1]. The reader should refer to [9] for complete definitions, examples and possible evaluation methods related to each of them.

In the following, the general concept of *schema element* is used, corresponding, for instance, to an entity in an Entity-Relationship schema or to a class in a Unified Modeling Language diagram. We define:

☐ **Accuracy**. It is the distance between v and v', being v' the value considered as correct.
☐ **Completeness**. It is the degree to which values of a schema element are present in the schema element instance.
☐ **Currency**. The currency dimension refers only to data values that may vary in time; as an example, values of `Address` may vary in time, whereas `DateOfBirth` can be considered invariant. Therefore, currency can be defined as the "age" of a value. Namely, currency is the distance between the instant when a value changes in the real world and the instant when the value itself is modified in the information system.
☐ **Internal Consistency**. Consistency implies that two or more values do not conflict each other. Internal consistency means that all values being compared in order to evaluate consistency are within a specific instance of a schema element. A semantic rule is a constraint that must hold among values of attributes of a schema element, depending on the application domain modeled by the schema element. Then, internal consistency can be defined as the degree to which the values of the attributes of an instance of a schema element satisfy the specific set of semantic rules defined on the schema element.

5.2   Data Model

The D^2Q model is inspired by the data model underlying XML-QL [13]. A database view of XML is adopted: an XML Document is a set of data items, and a Document Type Definition (DTD) is the schema of such data items, consisting of *data* and *quality classes*. In particular, a D^2Q XML document contains both application data, in the form of a D^2Q *data graph*, and the related data quality values, in the form of four D^2Q *quality graphs*, one for each quality dimension introduced in Section 5.1. Specifically, nodes of the D^2Q data graph are linked to the corresponding ones of the D^2Q quality graphs through links, as shown in Figure 2. Operations offered by the application services return D^2Q *XML documents* as outputs.

A D^2Q XML document corresponds to a set of conceptual data items, which are instances of conceptual schema elements; schema elements are data and quality classes, and instances are data and quality objects. Data classes and objects are straightforwardly represented as D^2Q data graphs, as detailed in the following of this section, and quality classes and objects are represented as D^2Q quality graphs, as detailed in Section 5.3.

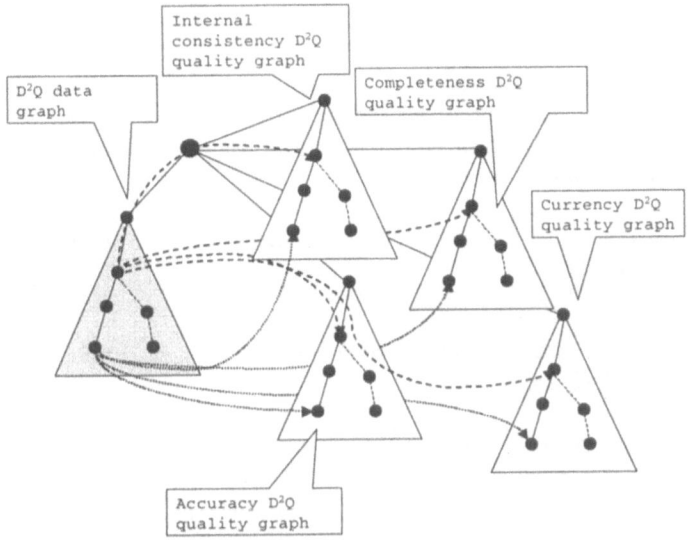

Fig. 2. The generic structure of a D^2Q XML document, returned as result by a service operation

In order to clarify our definition of data class in XML, we preliminary recall a typical definition of data class from ODMG [14].

A data class δ $(\pi_1, \ldots, \pi_n)$ consists of:

☐ *a name δ;*
☐ *a set of properties π_i = $< name_i : type_i >$, $i = 1 \ldots n$, $n \geq 1$, where $name_i$ is the name of the property π_i and $type_i$ can be:*
   – *either a basic type^2;*
   – *or a data class;*
   – *or a type* set-of $< X >$, *where* $< X >$ *can be either a basic type or a data class.*

We define a D^2Q *data graph* as follows:

A D^2Q data graph $\mathbb{G}$ is a graph with the following features:

☐ *a set of nodes $\mathcal{N}$; each node (i) is identified by an object identifier and (ii) is the source of 4 different links to quality objects, each one for a different quality dimension. A link is a pair attribute-value, in which attribute represents the specific quality dimension for the element tag and value is an IDREF link^3;*

---

^{2} Basic types are the ones provided by the most common programming languages and SQL, that is `Integer`, `Real`, `Boolean`, `String`, `Date`, `Time`, `Interval`, `Currency`, `Any`.
^{3} The use of links will be further explained in Section 5.3, when quality graphs are introduced.

□ *a set of edges* $\mathcal{E} \subset \mathcal{N} \times \mathcal{N}$; *each edge is labeled by a string, which represents an element tag of an XML document;*

□ *a single root node* $\mathcal{R}$;

□ *a set of leaves; leaves are nodes that* (i) *are not identified and* (ii) *are labeled by strings, which represent element tag values, i.e., the values of the element tags labeling edges to them.*

Data class instances can be represented as D^2Q data graphs, according to the following rules.

Let δ $(\pi_1, \ldots, \pi_n)$ *be a data class with n properties, and let* $\mathcal{O}$ *be a data object, i.e., an instance of the data class. Such an instance is represented by a* D^2Q *data graph* $\mathbb{G}$ *as follows:*

□ *The root* $\mathcal{R}$ *of* $\mathbb{G}$ *is labeled with the object identifier of the instance* $\mathcal{O}$.

□ *For each* $\pi_i = <name_i : type_i>$ *the following rules hold:*
  - *if* $type_i$ *is a basic type, then* $\mathcal{R}$ *is connected to a leaf* lv_i *by the edge* $<\mathcal{R}, lv_i>$; *the edge is labeled with* $name_i$ *and the leaf* lv_i *is labeled with the property value* $\mathcal{O}.name_i$;
  - *if* $type_i$ *is a data class, then* $\mathcal{R}$ *is connected to the* D^2Q *data graph which represents the property value* $\mathcal{O}' = \mathcal{O}.name_i$ *by an edge labeled with* $name_i$;
  - *if* $type_i$ *is a* set-of $<X>$, *then:*
    * *let C be the cardinality of* $\mathcal{O}.name_i$; $\mathcal{R}$ *is connected to C elements as it follows: if* (i) $<X>$ *is a basic type, then the elements are leaves (each of them labeled with a property value of the set); otherwise if* (ii) $<X>$ *is a data class, then the elements are* D^2Q *data graphs, each of them representing a data object of the set;*
    * *edges connecting the root to the elements are all labeled with* $name_i$.

In Figure 3(a), a D^2Q data graph is shown: an object instance **Maria Rossi** of the data class **Citizen** is considered. The data class has **Name** and **Surname** as properties of basic types, a property of type **set-of** $<$ **TelephoneNumber** $>$ and another property of data class type **ResidenceAddress**; the data class **ResidenceAddress** has all properties of basic types.

5.3   Quality Model

So far the data portion of the D^2Q model has been described. However, organizations export XML documents containing not only data objects, but also quality data concerning the four dimensions introduced in Section 5.1.

Quality data are represented as graphs, too; they correspond to a set of conceptual quality data items, which are instances of conceptual quality schema elements; quality schema elements are referred to as *quality classes* and instances as *quality objects*. A quality class models a specific quality dimension for a specific data class: the property values of a quality object represent the quality dimension values of the property values of a data object. Therefore, each data object (i.e.,

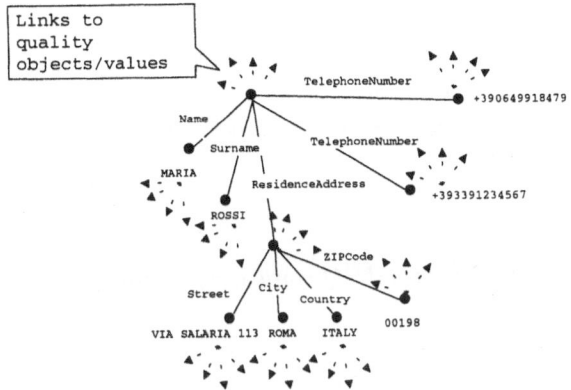

(a) D^2Q data graph

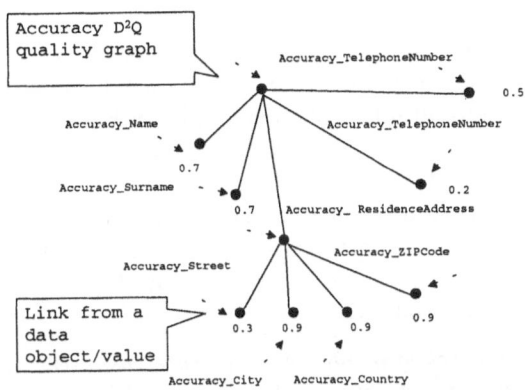

(b) Accuracy D^2Q quality graph

Fig. 3. An example

node) and value (i.e., leaf) of a D^2Q data graph is linked to respectively four quality objects and values.

Let $\delta\ (\pi_1,\ \ldots,\ \pi_n)$ be a data class. A quality class $\delta^D\ (\pi_1^D,\ \ldots,\ \pi_n^D)$ consists of:

☐ a name δ^D, with $D\ \in\ \{$ Accuracy, Completeness, Currency, InternalConsistency $\}$;

☐ a set of tuples $\pi_i^D\ =\ <\ name_i^D\ :\ type_i^D\ >,\ i = 1\ldots n,\ n \geq 1,$

where:

❑ δ^D *is associated to* δ *by a one-to-one relationship and corresponds to the quality dimension* D *evaluated for* δ;

❑ π_i^D *is associated to* π_i *of* δ *by a one-to-one relationship, and corresponds to the quality dimension* D *evaluated for* π_i;

❑ $type_i^D$ *is either a basic type or a quality class or a* set-of *type, according to the structure of the data class* δ.

In order to represent quality objects, we define a D^2Q *quality graph* as follows:

A D^2Q *quality graph* $\mathbb{G}^D$ *is a* D^2Q *data graph with the following additional features:*

❑ *no node nor leaf is linked to any other element;*

❑ *labels of edges are strings of the form* D_name *(e.g.,* Accuracy_Citizen*);*

❑ *labels of leaves are strings representing quality values;*

❑ *leaves are identified by object identifiers.*

A quality class instance can be straightforwardly represented as a D^2Q quality graph, on the basis on rules analogous to the ones previously presented for data objects and D^2Q data graphs. As an example, in Figure 3(b), a D^2Q quality graph concerning accuracy is shown, and links are highlighted; for instance, the accuracy of Maria is 0.7.

Service operations return a result document which consists of D^2Q graphs. Specifically, for each data class instance there is a D^2Q data graph linked to four D^2Q quality graphs, expressing the quality of the data objects for each dimension introduced in Section 5.1.

Let $\{\ \mathcal{O}_1, \ldots,\ \mathcal{O}_m\ \}$ *be a set of* m *objects which are instances of the same data class* δ; *a* D^2Q *XML document is a graph consisting of:*

❑ *a root node* $\mathcal{ROOT}$;

❑ m D^2Q *data graph* $\mathcal{G}_i$, $i = 1 \ldots m$, *each of them representing the data objects* $\mathcal{O}_i$;

❑ $4 * m$ D^2Q *quality graph* $\mathcal{G}_i^D$, $i = 1 \ldots m$, *each of them representing the quality graph related to* $\mathcal{O}_i$ *concerning the quality dimension* D;

❑ $\mathcal{ROOT}$ *is connected to the* m D^2Q *data graphs by edges labeled with the name of the data class, i.e.,* δ;

❑ *for each quality dimension* D, $\mathcal{ROOT}$ *is connected to the* m D^2Q *quality graph* $\mathcal{G}_i^D$ *by edges labeled with the name of the quality class, i.e.,* δ^D.

The model proposed in this work adopts several graphs instead of embedding metadata within the data graph. Such a decision increases the document size, but on the other hand allows a modular and "fit-for-all" design: *(i)* extending the model to new dimensions is straightforward, as it requires to define the new dimension quality graph, and *(ii)* specific applications, requiring only some dimension values, will adopt only the appropriate subset of the graphs.

6   The Data Quality Broker

In this section, we present a distributed implementation of the Data Quality Broker component (DQB). For some issues concerning the high level design of this component, as well as examples of its possible usage in real scenarios, the reader should also refer to [15].

As mentioned in Section 4, the DQB service provides the following features:

❏ **Quality brokering function:** an organization can invoke DQB specifying a data request constrained by a set of data quality requirements. The data request is performed by invoking an operation s. DQB discovers (through the Quality Knowledge Repository) all application services in the CIS offering s or operations equivalent to s^4, invokes them, gathers all responses and then returns only data items satisfying the requirements.

❏ **Quality improvement function:** DQB notifies organizations with low quality data and proposes them the highest quality value obtained in the previous step. Organizations may choose to adopt such a highest quality data.

The idea behind the brokering function is that DQB filters the normal interaction that a client has with organizations in the CIS, adding the possibility to discover and invoke equivalent services in different organizations and to execute a quality-based filtering of the results obtained. The improvement function is a feedback mechanism that uses the results of the brokering to propagate highest quality data.

The design of DQB is presented by specifying how the above functions are provided to organizations by each copy of the service and implemented through distributed protocols. A distributed service is inherently more scalable and robust than a service implemented as a centralized component, since request load is automatically shared among all the components implementing DQB and the fault of a single component does not impact on the availability of the whole service. These features make this choice more appropriate in the CIS context.

Details on how to perform quality comparison and how to determine the highest quality value are abstracted in this context, since we assume they are provided from other architectural components.

6.1   Preliminary Assumptions

In order to model the communication environment of the CIS we make the following assumptions:

❏ both application and infrastructure services are implemented by one or more software components. Such software components can fail by *crashing*, thus causing the *down* of the service;

---

^{4} In the context of this paper, we simply consider an intuitive definition of operational equivalence, i.e., two operations are equivalent if they return equivalent data, as defined in the Quality Knowledge Repository.

❏ the communication infrastructure ℕ is abstracted as an *asynchronous distributed system* [16]: communication links provided by ℕ are reliable (i.e., each message sent by a non-down component is eventually delivered to a non-down recipient) but message transfer delay is unpredictable. Moreover, a service can be arbitrarily slow down due to unpredictable service workload.

On the basis of such assumptions, it is impossible to distinguish a down service from one that is up but extremely slow [17]; therefore, in order to guarantee service termination, an additional assumption is required: only a minority of DQB software components can crash at the same time.

6.2   Service Design

Some preliminary definitions are required before specifying the service. We define a quality requirement as a constraint on the value of a specific dimension over a property of a data object, represented as a D^2Q data graph:

A data quality requirement is a set qr $=$ { p, D, op, v }, where p is the name of a property, D is a data quality dimension defined in the D^2Q model, op can be =, <, >, ≤ or ≥, and v is a value defined in the domain of the data quality dimension D.

If $eval(D, \mathcal{O})$ is a function that assesses the quality of D for the data object $\mathcal{O}$, we say that a data object $\mathcal{O}$ *satisfies* a data quality requirement $qr = \{ p, D, op, v \}$ if $\mathcal{O}$ "contains" a property that corresponds to p and $eval(D, \mathcal{O})$ op v is true.

The input to the primitive *read*, which will be defined in the following, is a set of quality requirements $\mathcal{QR} = \{ qr_1, \ldots, qr_n \}$; $\mathcal{O}$ satisfies $\mathcal{QR}$ when it satisfies each $qr_i \in \mathcal{QR}$.

The functions of DQB are provided by two primitives:

❏ $read(s, \mathcal{QR})$: it invokes the operation s upon all the AS's that implement it or an equivalent operation, and returns only the data that satisfy the set of quality requirements $\mathcal{QR}$. It represents the way a software system belonging to an organization can access the DQB service;
❏ $propose(\mathcal{O})$: it proposes the data object $\mathcal{O}$ to organizations. It is the mechanism that DQB uses in order to provide organizations with quality feedbacks.

The DQB service is invoked by a software system inside an organization Org_i by making a call to the *read* primitive. *read* will return to its caller all (and only) the data objects satisfying all the requirements. Among all the obtained objects, one will be chosen to be proposed to each organization, through the *propose* primitive; the *propose* is used by the DQB service to give a non-invasive feedback upon the quality of a data object, allowing an organization to improve the quality of its data while maintaining its autonomy in the decision.

The implementation of the service relies on a function abstracted as a further primitive realized in cooperation with other architectural components:

❐ *compare*($\{\mathcal{O}_1, \ldots, \mathcal{O}_n\}, \mathcal{QD}$): it returns the data object with the highest quality in the set $\{\mathcal{O}_1, \ldots, \mathcal{O}_n\}$, with respect to the set of quality dimensions $\mathcal{QD}$.

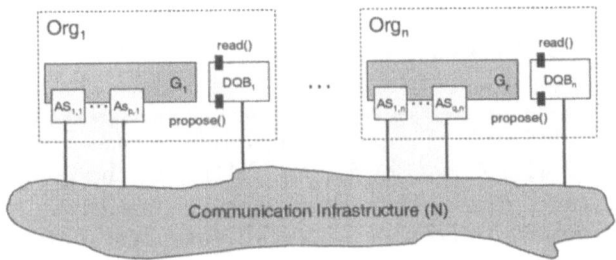

Fig. 4. Deployment of the Data Quality Broker service

The *compare* primitive abstracts the execution of a quality comparison among a set of data instances. The comparison is possible only if the two data objects are instance of equivalent classes, otherwise the returned result is not determined. Here we do not specify the mechanisms and the criteria used for the comparison. These issues are beyond the scope of this paper. We just point out that the comparison have to take into account the trust values provided by the Rating Service, in order to avoid that erroneous evaluations from mistrusted organizations let low quality data propagate.

6.3 DQB Protocols

The DQB service is implemented by a set of identical software components $\{DQB_1, .., DQB_n\}$, where each DQB_i is deployed inside a different organization Org_i and is executed independently of the others (see Figure 4).

Each DQB_i locally implements the primitives defined in the previous section. Moreover, it has access to a *reliable multicast* primitive [18], denoted $RM(m)$, used to send a message m to other DQB_i with specific delivery guarantees. Informally, reliable multicast ensures that each non-crashed component eventually delivers the same set of messages sent by other components. The primitive can be implemented in an asynchronous distributed system with simple deterministic algorithms [18].

We describe in the following the steps of the protocol executed by DQB components when a $read(s, \mathcal{QR})$ is invoked on a DQB_i. For the sake of simplicity, we assume the same operation s as implemented by more than one organization. Real-world cases present equivalent operations returning equivalent data, discovered through the Quality Knowledge Repository. The protocol works as follows (an example of the run of the protocol is depicted in Figure 5):

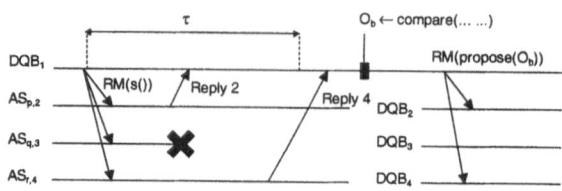

Fig. 5. An example of the Data Quality Broker execution

1. Let Org_i be the invoking organization, DQB_i invokes s on each application service $AS_{j,\ell}$ with $\ell \neq i$, by issuing $RM(s)$ to the group of application services implementing s. Then DQB_i starts a timeout τ.
2. Each $AS_{j,\ell}$ returns to DBQ_i a D^2Q XML document containing objects and their quality.
3. If the timeout τ expires before all the application services have replied, DQB_i further waits only till the majority is reached. This condition eventually will occur as previously supposed.
4. After gathering the replies, DQB_i will return to its caller a D^2Q XML document $\mathcal{Y}$ including the data objects that satisfy the quality requirements.
5. DQB_i applies the *compare* primitive in order to obtain the highest quality data object $\mathcal{O}_b$ among the ones in $\mathcal{Y}$.
6. DQB_i invokes *propose*$(\mathcal{O}_b)$ on each DQB component by issuing $RM($ *propose*$(\mathcal{O}_b)$).

Intuitively, the protocol always terminates, exploiting the preliminary condition that at least a majority of components will reply. The reliable multicast primitive, which is used for the communication, also ensures that all the non-crashed DQB components receive the proposal. Note that in order to ensure termination, the service can guarantee only a best-effort semantic, i.e., it might not return all the data which satisfy the requirements. In this case a negotiation can start between DQB and the requester, that can choose to relax the conditions both for quality of data and for protocol parameters, for example specifying less strict quality requirements or a higher timeout value.

7   Conclusions and Future Work

Managing data quality in CIS's merges issues from many research areas of computer science such as databases, software engineering, distributed computing, security, and information systems. This implies that the proposal of integrated solutions is very challenging. In this paper, an overall framework to support data quality management in CIS's has been proposed. Specifically, this framework includes *(i)* a model for data and quality data exported by cooperating organizations and *(ii)* the design of an infrastructure service for brokering and improving quality data.

The complete development of a complex framework for data quality management in CIS's requires the solution of further issues, such as:

❏ Application services considered in the work are simple read-only data access services, that export data with the associated quality. More general application services (i.e., encapsulating business logic, able to make updates, etc.) will be considered; the impact of such extensions on the quality of the data they "manage" will be considered.

❏ Algorithms for data quality improvement in distributed settings will be also investigated. Given multiple copies of the same data, there are two ways according to which it is possible to engage improvement actions: *(i)* a *reconciliation approach*, consisting of reconciling the differences among the multiple copies into a single representation; *(ii)* a *selecting approach*, that implies the choice of the copy of data with the best quality. Both these approaches have been widely considered in the literature, but in our framework we have the further opportunity to rely on the available quality data in adopting each of them.

❏ The "reliability" of cooperating organizations and more generally trust issues also need to be taken into account; as an example, by considering what happens if an organization provides data with a low quality but certifies a high quality for them.

Acknowledgments. This work is supported by MIUR, COFIN 2001 Project "DaQuinCIS – Methodologies and Tools for Data Quality in Cooperative Information Systems" (http://www.dis.uniroma1.it/~dq/).

References

1. C. Batini and M. Mecella, "Enabling Italian e-Government Through a Cooperative Architecture," *IEEE Computer*, vol. 34, no. 2, 2001.

2. U. Dayal, M. Hsu, and R. Ladin, "Business Process Coordination: State of the Art, Trends and Open Issues," in *Proceedings of the 27th Very Large Databases Conference (VLDB 2001)*, Roma, Italy, 2001.

3. F. Casati, D. Georgakopoulos, and M.C. Shan, Eds., *Proceedings of the 2nd VLDB International Workshop on Technologies for e-Services (VLDB-TES 2001)*, Rome, Italy, 2001.

4. P. Bertolazzi and M. Scannapieco, "Introducing Data Quality in a Cooperative Context," in *Proceedings of the 6th International Conference on Information Quality (IQ'01)*, Boston, MA, USA, 2001.

5. H. Galhardas, D. Florescu, D. Shasha, and E. Simon, "An Extensible Framework for Data Cleaning," in *Proceedings of the 16th International Conference on Data Engineering (ICDE 2000)*, San Diego, CA, USA, 2000.

6. M. Jarke, M. Lenzerini, Y. Vassiliou, and Panos Vassiliadis, Eds., *Fundamentals of Data Warehouses*, Springer Verlag, 1999.

7. H.B. Kon, R.Y. Wang and S.E. Madnick, "Data Quality Requirements: Analysis and Modeling," in *Proceedings of the 9th International Conference on Data Engineering (ICDE '93)*, Vienna, Austria, 1993.

8. G. Mihaila, L. Raschid, and M. Vidal, "Querying Quality of Data Metadata," in *Proceedings of the 6th International Conference on Extending Database Technology (EDBT'98)*, Valencia, Spain, 1998.

9. M. Mecella, M. Scannapieco, A. Virgillito, R. Baldoni, T. Catarci, and C. Batini, "Architectural Support for Data Quality in Cooperative Information Systems," Technical report of the DaQuinCIS project, Dipartimento di Informatica e Sistemistica, Università di Roma "La Sapienza", Roma, Italy, 2002.

10. T. Catarci and M. Lenzerini, "Representing and Using Interschema Knowledge in Cooperative Information Systems," *Journal of Intelligent and Cooperative Information Systems*, vol. 2, no. 4, 1993.

11. M. Scannapieco, "Data Quality in Cooperative Information Systems," Doctoral Poster at the 28th Very Large Databases Conference (VLDB 2002), Hong Kong, 2002.

12. T.C. Redman, *Data Quality for the Information Age*, Artech House, 1996.

13. A. Deutsch, M. Fernandez, D. Florescu, A. Levy, and D. Suciu, "XML-QL: A Query Language for XML," in *Proceedings of the 8th International World Wide Web Conference (WWW8)*, Toronto, Canada, 1999.

14. R.G.G. Cattell and D.K. Barry, Eds., *The Object Database Standard: ODMG 2.0*, Morgan Kaufmann Publishers, 1997.

15. M. Scannapieco, V. Mirabella, M. Mecella, and C. Batini, "Data Quality in e-Business," in *Proceedings of the Workshop on Web Services, e-Business, and the Semantic Web: Foundations, Models, Architecture, Engineering and Applications, in conjunction with CAiSE 2002*, Toronto, Ontario, Canada, 2002.

16. F.B. Schneider, "What Goods are Models and What Models are Good?," in *Distributed Systems*, S. Mullender, Ed. ACM Press, 1994.

17. M.J. Fischer, N.A. Lynch, and M.S. Paterson, "Impossibility of Distributed Consensus with One Faulty Process," *Journal of the ACM*, vol. 32, no. 2, 1985.

18. V. Hadzilacos and S. Toueg, "Fault-Tolerant Broadcasts and Related Problems," in *Distributed Systems*, S. Mullender, Ed. ACM Press, 1994.

Adaptive Fault Tolerant Hospital Resource Scheduling*

Umesh Deshpande, Arobinda Gupta, and Anupam Basu

Department of Computer Science and Engineering
IIT, Kharagpur-721302, India
{uad, agupta, anupam}@cse.iitkgp.ernet.in

Abstract. In a distributed hospital system, different hospitals should collaborate among themselves for sharing their resources to provide better and faster service to the patients. We address the distributed hospital resource scheduling problem and apply the Generalized Partial Global Planning (GPGP) approach used for multiagent systems for the same. An adaptive coordination mechanism based on the contract net protocol is proposed to support inter-hospital collaboration. We have performed simulation studies and the experimental results show that our coordination mechanism performs better than commonly used schemes. Fault handling mechanisms are presented so that the system continues to provide service even in the presence of faults. The proposed approach is applicable in contexts other than the distributed hospital system as well.

Keywords: Collaborative Computing, Multi-agent systems, Contract Net Protocol, Fault Tolerance, Real-time Scheduling.

1 Introduction

The organization of real hospitals indicates that hospital resource scheduling is inherently a distributed problem. It has been pointed out in [7] that coordination mechanisms are necessary for addressing this problem since the current medical procedures are complex and that there are different kinds of relationships between the associated tests and treatments. The mechanisms have to be designed keeping in mind that the hospital departments, nursing units, and ancillary units should be able to retain maximum autonomy in their functioning.

In a realistic scenario, it is often the case that any single hospital may not have all the required resources or capabilities. We refer to capabilities as a special category of resources that can be migrated and thus can be requested by one hospital from another. For example, a hospital H_1 may have a CAT scanner but may not have an expert dental surgeon. Some other hospital H_2 may have an

---

* This work is supported by the Ministry of Human Resources and Development, Govt. of India grant for the project entitled "Collaborative Computing Using Intelligent Agents".

R. Meersman, Z. Tari (Eds.): CoopIS/DOA/ODBASE 2002, LNCS 2519, pp. 503–520, 2002.

expert dental surgeon but may not have a CAT scanner. A CAT scanner may be thought of as a resource present at hospital H_1 while the expert dental surgeon could be thought of as a capability of hospital H_2. In such a scenario, the hospitals need to share their resources and capabilities (we will henceforth use the common term 'entity' for a resource or a capability). In order to provide better service to the patients, hospitals must collaborate with one another. Autonomy preserving coordination mechanisms assume all the more importance here because the hospitals may be distantly located and have to act independently of one another.

We address the problem of resource coordination in a distributed hospital system. In the case of the absence of an entity from a hospital, any request for the same needs to be migrated to some other hospital. The load on the remote hospitals, and the quality and cost of the entities at the remote hospitals are important in making the migration decision. We apply the Generalized Partial Global Planning (GPGP) [1] approach and propose an adaptive resource coordination mechanism using the contract net protocol for the migration decision. Our work generalises the distributed problem solving approach for hospital scheduling proposed in [2] by providing inter-hospital collaboration.

A distributed hospital system has inherent redundancy since some of the entities are present at multiple nodes which can lead to increased availability of the system. Hence, in the presence of faults, the system should adapt by incorporating fault handling mechanisms to provide service to the patients, maybe with some performance degradation. In this paper, we consider two types of faults - permanent faults, in which the fault repair time is not known a-priori (e.g. x-ray machine failure) and transient faults in which the fault repair time is known a-priori (e.g. a technician is on a short leave and his date of joining back is known). We present fault handling techniques required to tolerate the above two kinds of faults.

Although the focus of this paper is on the distributed hospital system itself, the approach presented is general enough and could be used in any application domain where distributed resource coordination is required. The usage of the proposed techniques in another application of an e-University system are currently under investigation [4].

The following are the main contributions of the paper.

1. An architecture of a typical hospital and a model of a distributed hospital system is presented.
2. A mechanism for the coordination across hospitals is proposed. If a required non-local entity is present at multiple hospitals, then the decision process for selecting one of them is discussed.
3. Simulation studies and comparison with commonly used inter-hospital coordination schemes have been performed. We present the performance evaluation results. The results show that our scheme performs better than other commonly used schemes.
4. Fault tolerance techniques for providing graceful degradation of service in the presence of faults are presented.

The paper is organised as follows. In section 2, we present an overview of the GPGP approach and the TAEMS task modeling language. We introduce the hospital resource scheduling problem, propose an architecture of a hospital, and present a model for a distributed hospital system in section 3. The coordination mechanism is explained in section 4. In section 5 we present the scheduler. Simulation studies and experimental results are presented in section 6. Fault handling mechanisms are discussed in section 7. Section 8 concludes the paper.

2   Generalized Partial Global Planning

Generalized Partial Global Planning (GPGP) is a task environment centered approach to coordination. The basic idea in GPGP is that each agent constructs its own local view of the structure and relationships of its intended tasks. This view may then be augmented by information from other agents, and it may change in other ways dynamically over time. The GPGP approach uses a set of individual coordination mechanisms to help construct these partial views, and to recognize and respond to particular task structure relationships by making commitments to other agents. These commitments result in more coherent and coordinated behaviour. Several architectural assumptions are made on the agents involved. Most important of these is that the agent represents its current set of intended tasks using the TAEMS (Task Analysis Environment Modeling and Simulation) task structure representation language [1]. TAEMS task structures are abstraction hierarchies whose leaf nodes are instantiated basic actions or "executable methods". It allows the specification of dynamically changing and uncertain task characteristics that effect an agent's preferences (utility) for some state of the world, including tasks with hard or soft deadlines. A TAEMS specification also indicates relationships between local and non-local tasks or resources that effect these agent preference characteristics. In utility theory, agents have preferences over possible final states (action or plan outcomes), and preference-relevant features of an outcome are called attributes. In GPGP, only attributes that are considered are quality, cost and duration.

A TAEMS action (or executable method) represents the smallest unit of analysis. A task (or subtask) represents a set of related subtasks or actions joined by a common quality accumulation function. If the function is min (AND) then it indicates that all subtasks must be accomplished to achieve the parent task. If the function is max (OR) then it indicates that the quality accumulated by the parent task is the maximum of those achieved by any of the subtasks. Any TAEMS action/method or a task T containing such a method, may potentially affect some other method M through a non-local effect (NLE). Three of the NLEs: *enables, facilitates, and mutex* are relevant to our work and will be used in future discussion. If a task T *enables* action M then a rational method would not execute M before T is completed. One task T_1 may provide results to another task that *facilitates (inhibits)* the second task T_2 by decreasing (increasing) the duration or increasing (decreasing) the quality of its partial result. *Mutex* relationships for a resource R between a set of methods M indicate that at any

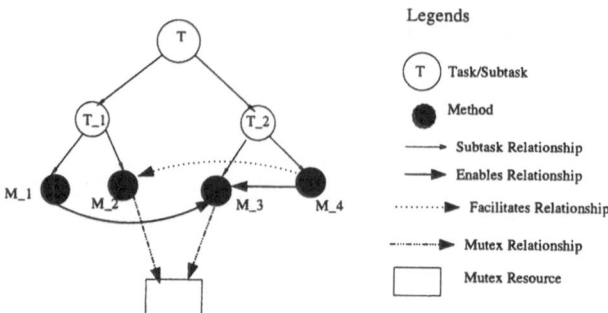

Fig. 1. A TAEMS task

point of time only one of the methods in M could be executing actions for the resource R. Figure 1 shows an example of a task defined using TAEMS.

An agent using the GPGP approach provides a planner to create task structures that attempt to achieve agent goals, and a scheduler that attempts to maximize the utility via choice, serialization and absolute temporal location of basic actions in the task structure. Each GPGP mechanism examines the changing task relationship, and responds by making local and non-local commitments to tasks, possibly creating new communication actions to transmit commitments of partial task structure information to other agents. The types of commitments are the *DO, DONT, Deadline and Earliest Start Time* commitments. Initially, GPGP defined the following five coordination mechanisms based on [5] - *Updating non-local viewpoints, Communicate results, Handling simple redundancy, Handling hard relationships and Handling soft relationships.*

3   The Hospital Resource Scheduling Problem

We introduce the problem with a case study drawn from an actual hospital scenario [7].

Patients in General Hospital reside in units that are organised by branches of medicine, such as orthopedics or neurosurgery. Each day, physicians request certain tests and/or therapy to be performed as a part of the diagnosis and treatment of a patient. Tests are performed by separate, independent and distantly located ancillary departments in the hospital.

Each test/therapy may interact with other tests in different kinds of relationships. A few examples of such relationships could be *enables, requires-delay* (the second task should be executed with some delay after the first one) and *facilitates.* As discussed in [2], the task structure representing the hospital scheduling problem has the following specific features:

– Tasks execution have no redundancy. Each test can only be done by a single ancillary department.

- Since all the tests need to be done, the quality accumulation function of the non-executable tasks is always min.
- In our work, a test can be in either of the two states - done or not done. We assume that the tests are carried out in a non pre-emptive manner.
- In the hospital scheduling problem, since all the tests/therapies need to be done, there is no redundant task and hence the coordination mechanism of handling redundancy is not needed.
- Some tests/therapies may require the presence of the patient. Hence the patient becomes a mutually exclusive resource.

In [2], a coordination mechanism has been proposed to handle mutex relationships. When several agents try to use the same non-sharable resource at overlapping times, only one agent can actually get the resource and execute its task. The idea behind the resource constraint mechanism is that when an agent intends to execute a resource-constrained task, it sends a directed bid of the time interval it needs and the local priority. After a communication delay, the agent knows all the bids given by other agents for the same time interval. Since all the agents who bid have the same information, they can use the commonly accepted rule (highest priority first) to decide the winner at this round of negotiation. The agent who won, will execute the task and all other agents will mark this time interval with a DONT commitment. They all will bid again in the next round.

3.1   A Proposed Architecture of a Hospital

When all the hospitals do not have all possible resources, they have to cooperate and coordinate with one another. We identify a Liaison Unit present in each hospital that is responsible for the coordination. Figure 2 shows the proposed architecture of a typical hospital. It is a hierarchical organization with the nursing units (NU) at the top, the departments (D) and sub-departments (SD) at the middle and the functional units (FU) at the bottom. It is to be noted that the communication across hospitals takes place through the Liaison Unit (LU) only.

In the architecture, a patient(task) enters any of the nursing units. We assume that every NU, D, SD, FU and the LU has an agent present in it that defines the functioning of the unit. A functional unit FU_i controls the entity R_i. We assume that the duration of usage of an entity which is the amount of time an entity requires to perform a job is constant. We say that a FU is active if it can perform the task given to it (i.e. the resource is available) otherwise it is passive. A FU can become passive in two cases, either some fault has occurred in the entity it is controlling, or it is controlling a capability and the capability has migrated.

When a patient enters a hospital's nursing unit, a set of tests/therapies required for the patient is prescribed. This can be described as a task group T using TAEMS. An appropriate deadline may be mentioned depending on the case. If it recognises that a subtask T_i of T needs an entity that is not present

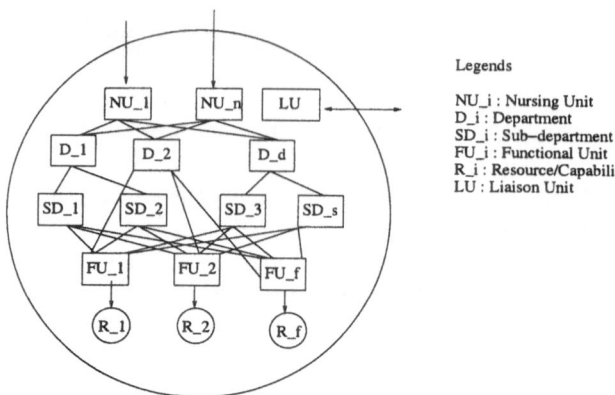

Fig. 2. A Hospital Architecture

locally, it sends a request to the Liaison unit. The Liaison unit decides the appropriate remote hospital where T_i could be migrated. One of the following three possible migrations would be required to realise T_i.

- Case 1 - Migration of Data: This may be sufficient for performing certain kinds of tests. For example, a blood report could be passed and analysed at the remote hospital.
- Case 2 - Migration of Patient (and Computation): For certain tests or therapies the patient needs to be moved along with the required tasks. For example, CAT Scan, surgery, etc. would require the presence of the patient.
- Case 3 - Migration of Capability: An expert from a remote hospital may be requested to visit and provide some necessary service required using the locally available resources.

3.2   Modeling of the Distributed Hospital System

In this section, we explain the model of the distributed hospital system. We present the system model followed by the model of the agents at the departments, sub-departments, nursing units, functional units and the Liaison Unit of each hospital.

The System Model. There are n nodes, $H_1, H_2, \ldots, H_n$ in the distributed hospital system which communicate only through messages. The architecture of every node is the one that is presented in section 3.1. A task specified in the TAEMS model can be submitted to any node. The nodes are logically completely connected. It is assumed that the communication delay for sending/receiving messages between any two nodes H_i and H_j can be estimated and is a constant c_{ij}.

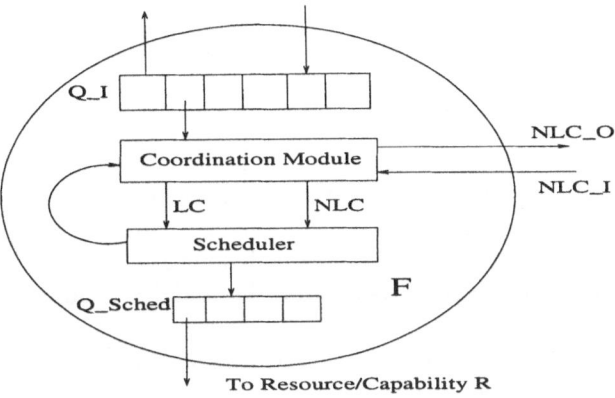

Fig. 3. Agent F at the Functional Unit

Modeling of the Middle Agents and the Nursing Units. We refer to Middle Agents as the agents at the departments or the sub-departments. Each middle agent M consists of an input queue Q_I where the tasks coming from agents that are higher up in the organizational hierarchy are kept, and an output queue Q_O where the subtasks given to agents down are kept. When the agents down finish the subtask, they return the completion time to M. After the entire task is finished, M passes the completion time to an agent up, from which it received the task. The agents at the Nursing Units are similar to the Middle Agents except for the following additional functionality. For each task T input, they have to find out the entities that are not present at the node. Requests for these entities have to be sent to the Liaison Unit.

Modeling of the agents at the Functional Units. Let us assume that the agent F (as shown in figure 3) at the functional unit FU_i controls the entity R which has a duration of usage Δ. F consists of an input queue Q_I that is similar to the one present in the middle agents, a coordination module and a scheduler that work together to prepare schedules for the input tasks, and a schedule queue Q_{Sched} which contains the dispatch times of the tasks input to F. The agents at the different functional units coordinate with one another using commitments. The local commitments (LC) for F are those which the coordination module of F passes on to the local scheduler of F. The nonlocal commitments (NLC) for F are those which the coordination module of F exchanges with the coordination module of an agent of some other functional unit. We refer to NLC_I as the set of commitments that are input from other agents to F and NLC_O as the set of output commitments passed on to other agents by F. The set NLC_O is generated by the coordination module looking at the outgoing relationships of a subtask T_{ij} of task T_i. The coordination module invokes the local scheduler in the query mode for obtaining these. The scheduler looks at the LC and the NLC_I sets to generate schedules, which it inserts in Q_{Sched}.

Modeling of the agent at the Liaison Unit. The agent at the Liaison Unit LU consists of five queues. The queues and the corresponding actions are described below.

1. $Q_{Wait\text{-}Local}$: The requests from the local node for entities that are not locally present queue up here. These requests arise either for any entity that is not present locally or when faults occur. Along with a request, *priority* is passed. It is a measure calculated for a sub-task depending on the number of outgoing relationships it has with other sub-tasks and its deadline. The more the number of relationships, and the earlier the deadline the more the priority. In general, *priority* = f(no-of-outgoing relationships, *deadline*) where f is some function with the above mentioned characteristics. The input to $Q_{Wait\text{-}Local}$ is normally from the NU after it analyses the input task structure and finds an entity that is not present locally. $Q_{Wait\text{-}Local}$ is operated on as a priority queue.

2. $Q_{Processing}$: The tasks for whom the decision of the destination of migration is being arrived at are kept here. The requests are sent to different nodes where the required entity is present. The *fitness-value* is reported by the destination node for every task. It is a measure of goodness with which the task would be serviced at that node.

3. $Q_{Task\text{-}Sent}$: After getting and evaluating all the fitness-values for a task, it is sent for migration to a node chosen based on the coordination algorithm. The tasks that are sent to the remote nodes are kept in this queue.

4. $Q_{Wait\text{-}Nonlocal}$: The requests from the remote nodes queue up here. For each request, the fitness-value is queried from the FU that handles the requested entity.

5. $Q_{Task\text{-}Recd}$: The tasks received from remote nodes are kept here. After a task is received, it is sent to the FU handling the entity. After getting the results, the same are sent to the requesting remote node.

4   A Mechanism for Coordination across Hospitals

A coordination mechanism is proposed in this paper, with which different hospitals would coordinate with one another to provide better service to the patients. In the discussion that follows, we would use the terms hospital and node interchangeably.

The basic idea of the mechanism is based on the contract net protocol [8], [9]. When a node requires an entity, that is not present locally, it tries to find out if there exists a node, called the focused addressing node, where the request for the service of that entity is most likely to be satisfied. In addition to this node, it also asks for bids from a subset of the nodes present in the network. If the request can be satisfied at the focused addressing node, all the bids by other nodes are ignored. Otherwise, the node with the best bid is chosen and the migration is done.

4.1   The Liaison Unit: Data Structures and Algorithms

The Liaison Unit on each node H_i maintains the following two tables.

Local Entity Table - This has the following format.

Name	Duration	Surplus Time	List of previous requesters

- *Name* is the name of the entity, say e_k, present locally at the node H_i.
- *Duration* is the duration of usage of e_k.
- *Surplus Time* is the amount of time e_k was not used in a past window of length WL_k. It is an indication of the load on e_k. The window length is chosen appropriately depending on the *duration* of e_k. The surplus time is sent periodically to the other nodes as well as piggybacked with message exchanges.
- A *list of previous l requesters* is kept so that the surplus time can be sent to the nodes that are likely to make a request in the near future for e_k (l is a system-wide parameter).

Remote Entity Table - This table keeps information about the entities present at other nodes in the network. It has the following format.

Name	Id	Duration	Surplus Time	Delay Estimate

- *Id* is the identifier of the node where the mentioned entity, say e_k, with name *Name* is present.
- *Duration* is the duration for the usage of e_k at that node. This may be different for different nodes.
- *Surplus Time* is the one that was most recently obtained from the remote node with the id *Id*. For each entity, the entries are ordered in the decreasing order of the surplus. If the surplus is the same for two entries, then the ordering is done according to the duration (the lesser duration one comes earlier).
- The *Delay Estimate* is explained next. Let us say that a remote node H_j promised a bid for time t_0 but the actual finish time of the service of the required entity e_k is t_1. The difference $t_1 - t_0$ is referred to as the delay. This delay can be estimated for every entity present at each remote hospital depending on its previous history. *Delay estimate* is a measure of the same.

The *delay estimate*, τ_n, for the nth request for an entity e_k requested by a source node s and serviced at a destination node d is computed using exponential smoothening as follows.

$$\tau_n = \alpha_{kd} * t_{n-1} + (1 - \alpha_{kd}) * \tau_{n-1}$$

where
τ_{n-1} is the estimated delay for the $(n-1)^{th}$ request ($\tau_0 = 0$),
t_{n-1} is the difference between the actual finish time (the task result arrival time) and the bid promised for the $(n-1)^{th}$ request, and
α_{kd} is a value ($0 \leq \alpha_{kd} \leq 1$) chosen appropriately for the $< e_k, d >$ pair. It can be a constant or can be a function learned over time.

4.2   The Bid Process

An agent N at the Nursing unit of node H_i sends a request to the agent at the Liaison unit if an entity e_k, required by a subtask T is not available locally. Along with the request, it also sends the *Expected Worst Case Time (EWCT)*. EWCT for T is the latest time by which T must be serviced otherwise the task would miss its deadline. EWCT is computed by the local scheduler which is explained in section 5.

The first entry from the Remote Entity Table, with *id* say H_j, for the requested entity is picked up. Note that H_j would have the maximum surplus. If *surplus* $> \Theta_k$ *and current time* $+ 4 * c_{ij} + delay\ estimate < EWCT$ then the node is chosen for focused addressing. Θ_k is a constant threshold chosen depending on the entity e_k. The multiplication by 4 is used since there would be atleast four communications between H_i and H_j (first for requesting the bid by H_i, second for sending the bid by H_j, third for sending the task by H_i and the last for sending the results by H_j). When a focused addressing node is found, the request for bid is sent to it.

In addition, the following steps are done in parallel.

> *For the next $x - 1$ entries*
> */*x is a system wide parameter and is used to minimize the communication overhead. */*
> *begin*
> > *Let the node chosen be H_h.*
> > *If the $4 * c_{ih} + current\ time + estimated\ delay > EWCT$*
> > > *stop the bid process for T.*
> > *Else send a request for bid to the node.*
> *end*

When a focused addressing node receives a bid, it invokes the local scheduler of the required FU to find if it can guarantee the request. It sends such a message to the requester. The requester will ignore all other bids if the focused addressing node answered yes. If the answer is no, the requester would wait for bids from other nodes and would select the best bidder. When a node (not the focused one), say H_h, receives a request for bid message, it checks if it can satisfy the request. If the request can be guaranteed, it sends the *earliest possible finish time (EFT)*. The best bidder is the one that returns the least value of $2 * c_{ih} + EFT$. The multiplication factor is 2 here since only the last two communications of the four mentioned above would be required after a bid is obtained. If no favourable bids are available till that time, then the LU could choose to send T randomly to any node where e_k is present.

The coordination mechanism uses the *surplus time* and the *delay estimate* parameters for bidding. Both these are dynamic and change as tasks arrive in the system and as remote requests are serviced by nodes. Hence, the coordination mechanism is adaptive since it also makes changes in the migration decision based on these parameters. The EWCT, EFT and the guarantee routine required by the mechanism are provided by the scheduler which is explained in section 5. In the model proposed in section 3.2, the *fitness-value* for a task T is its EFT.

5 The Local Scheduler

The local scheduler used at each FU is a simplified version of the heuristic Design-to-Time Scheduler proposed by Garvey and Lesser [6]. In our domain model of hospital scheduling all the tests/therapies must be performed(the quality accumulation function is always min). In such a case, a simpler polynomial time scheduler algorithm may be designed which would not have the scaling problems that are present in [6]. In this section we give a brief overview of the scheduler present at a FU F which controls an entity R that has a duration of usage Δ. The full details are presented in [4].

At each invocation, the scheduler first finds out all the enabled tasks from Q_I. The enabled tasks are those whose all earliest start times for the incoming enabling relationships are known. The enabling time for a task is the maximum of the earliest start times. If there are no incoming enabling relationships, the enabling time is assumed to be the current time. The expected worst case times (EWCT is explained in section 5.1) of all the enabled tasks are computed. The tasks are rated according to heuristics that increase the rating of tasks that have more outgoing *facilitates* relationships, decrease the rating of those which have more incoming *facilitates* relationships and increase the rating of tasks proportional to the earliness of their EWCT. The scheduler prepares a set of tasks $Q_{Enabled}$ in which tasks are kept in the decreasing order of their ratings. The following algorithm explains the scheduler functioning. Recall that the queue Q_{Sched} contains the the dispatch times of tasks at F.

For each task T in $Q_{Enabled}$ do
begin

1. *Find the set* Overlap *for T which contains all the tasks whose execution intervals overlap with T. The execution interval of T is [enabling time, EWCT]. Find the best-time for scheduling T such that T can be introduced in Q_{Sched} without disturbing other tasks already in it.*
2. *If the mutex resource is not required, insert T in Q_{Sched} with the dispatch time being the best-time.*
3. *Else invoke the mutex resource coordination algorithm of Decker and Li [2] with the bidding time as the best-time. If the bid is won, insert T in Q_{Sched} else repeat from step 1 by finding a best-time later than that won at this round.*

end.

5.1 Expected Worst Case Time (EWCT) Computation

EWCT of a subtask T' of a task T is an approximate measure of the time by which a subtask T' should be executed at F otherwise T might miss its deadline. For an exact computation of the EWCT, we have to explore all the possible paths of the *enables* relationships in the task tree generated. Hence, the exact computation is intractable. An approximation of the measure is computed as explained below.

Let $M = \{T_{m_1}, T_{m_2}, \ldots, T_{m_m}\}$ be the set of subtasks present in T that require the mutex resource, have a lower priority than T' and who have not yet won a bid. Identify a set of tasks $E = \{T_{e_1}, T_{e_2}, \ldots, T_{e_e}\}$ present in T such that T_{e_1} is enabled by T' and has the maximum duration among those tasks that T' enables. Similarly each subsequent task $T_{e_{k+1}}$ is enabled by T_{e_k} and $T_{e_{k+1}}$ has the maximum duration amongst those tasks that T_{e_k} enables. Note that the two sets M and E may have common entries. We find the union of the two sets $W = M \cup E$. Let $W = \{T_{w_1}, T_{w_2}, \ldots, T_{w_w}\}$. We define $\Delta_w = \Sigma_{i=1}^{w} duration(T_{w_i})$. The EWCT of T' is approximated as $D - \Delta_w - \Delta$ where D is the deadline of T.

It is to be noted that if the subtask T' is to be chosen for migration, the computation of EWCT would be done by the NU where T arrives.

5.2 The Guarantee Routine

The scheduler is invoked in the query mode to check if a remote subtask T' could be guaranteed at this node. The EWCT for T' is also sent by the remote node. The arrival time A'_T of the task is optimistically assumed to be the time at which the request for bid was received $+2 * c_{sd}$, where s is the source node and d is the destination node. The multiplication by 2 is there since atleast two communications are required between s and d before T' arrives - one for sending the bid by d and the other for sending T' by s. Hence, the interval for execution of T' becomes $[A'_T, \text{EWCT}]$. The *best-time* for T' is found out as before. If it is less than EWCT, then the task can be guaranteed otherwise not.

5.3 Earliest Possible Finish Time (EFT) Computation

The scheduler at F computes the EFT for a remote subtask T' when it is invoked in the query mode. This is sent as the bid for T'. As before, the *best-time* for T' is found which is its EFT.

6 Evaluation of the Coordination Mechanism

We have simulated a network of six hospitals (nodes). The resources/capabilities (entities) are distributed across the nodes. To simulate a hospital resource scheduling problem, we first create a task template that represents all the possible nursing units, departments, sub-departments, entities and inter-relationships. In our case, we have 3 nursing units, 4 departments, 9 sub-departments and 43 entities. Then, we identify a set of tasks for each patient. This is a subset of the task template previously defined. The probability of the presence of a relationship is chosen randomly. We use the *average task waiting time (W)* and the *guarantee ratio (G = number of tasks that finish within the deadline / total number of tasks)* as the performance measures. The task waiting time is an indication of the latency of the system and the guarantee ratio indicates how the system gives importance to the criticality of patient care. The patient arrival at the hospitals is modeled as a Poisson process. The arrival rate at each node may be different leading to differences in the node loads. Let us define the term *system wide arrival rate - R* as the sum of arrival rates of all the nodes. We conduct experiments on the following three groups of agents.

- Group 1: These agents select a node randomly when a required entity is not present locally and perform one of the three possible migrations. We call this as the *random case*.
- Group 2: In this case, for each entity that is not available locally, these agents select a closest node in the network where the entity is available. We call this case as the *nearest case*. This is a more informed decision than the random node case as it takes into account the travel times.
- Group 3: Here the agents use the coordination mechanisms proposed in section 4 to select a node if a entity is not available locally. We call this case as the *cnp case*.

It should be noted that the random case and the nearest case represent the commonly used practices for interaction across hospitals. We define G_c, G_r and G_n as the guarantee ratios in cnp, random and nearest cases respectively. Also, W_c, W_r and W_n are the average waiting times in cnp, random and nearest cases respectively. Each of the following experiments was conducted for a total of 10000 time units for every arrival rate R. We note the G and W values in all the three cases with R varying from 1 to 8. Figures 4 to 6 show the results. From the observations the following conclusions can be drawn.

1. The *cnp case* performs better than the random and the nearest cases in all the scenarios. This is because the coordination mechanism takes into account both the loads at the different nodes and the travel time required for migration. At best, the *cnp case* performs 18% better than the nearest case and 20% better than the random case as regards the G values are concerned. It performs 38% better than the nearest case and 45% better than the random case as regards the W values are concerned.
2. When there are more lightly loaded nodes in the system than heavily loaded nodes (figure 5), the nearest case performs better than the random case and its performance is close to the performance of the *cnp case*. This observation complies with the fact that for low arrival rates and the total system load being low (more lightly loaded nodes), the travel times play a significant role.
3. When the system load is almost equally distributed across all the nodes and when the arrival rate is high (figure 6), all the three cases perform equally well with the *cnp case* being slightly better. In such a case there is very little to choose between two nodes. The coordination mechanism does not have much gains since it spends time in the bidding process itself. Still, the *cnp case* performs 6% better than nearest case and 8% better than random case as regards the G values are concerned. It performs 5% better than nearest case and 6% better than random case as regards the W values are concerned.

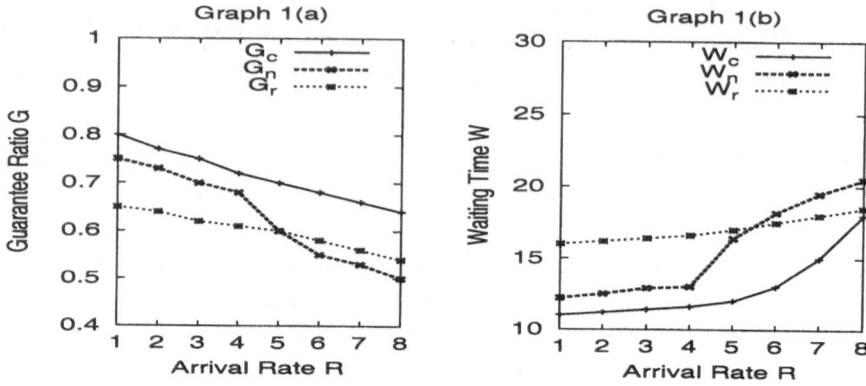

Fig. 4. G and W values with four heavily and two lightly loaded nodes

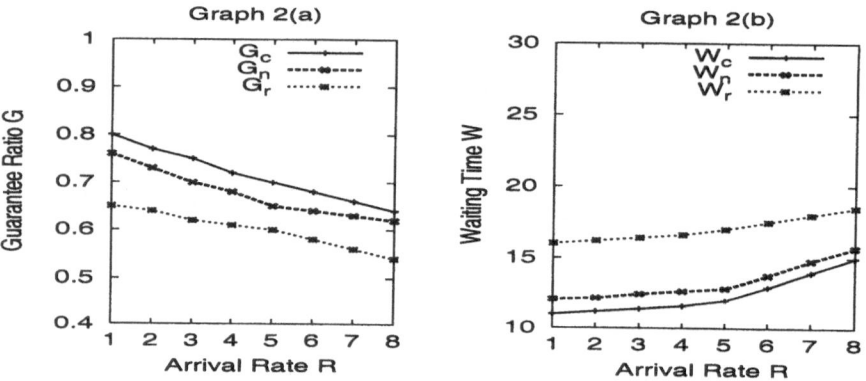

Fig. 5. G and W values with two heavily and four lightly loaded nodes

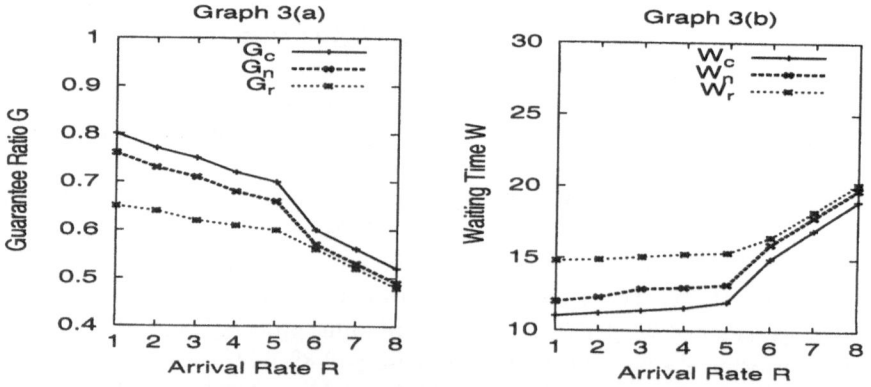

Fig. 6. G and W values with three heavily and three lightly loaded nodes

7   Adaptation in the Presence of Faults

In this paper, we consider two types of faults of an entity. The first, which we call as a permanent fault, is one where the entity has crashed leading to failure in providing service for tasks requiring the entity. Also, the time at which the entity would recover from the fault is not known a-priori. Examples of a permanent fault are cases when a X-ray machine fails or when an expert dealing with cardiac problems has resigned from the job. The time at which the X-ray machine would be repaired or a new cardiac expert would join is not known a-priori. The second type of fault, which we call as a transient fault, is similar to the first one but in this case the time at which the entity would recover from the fault is known a-priori. We call this time as the repair time of the entity. Examples of a transient fault are cases when a technician is on a short leave and the time of his joining duty back is known or when a vaccine is out of stock and the time when the stocks arrive is known. The implication of the a-priori knowledge of the repair time in the case of a transient fault of an entity R at a node N is that *not all* tasks that were already admitted at N and requiring R need to be migrated. Only those which would miss their deadlines should be identified and considered for migration.

When a fault is eventually repaired, the system should be reconfigured. The normal functioning of a node N which had encountered the fault of entity R should be resumed. Any newly arriving tasks that require R should now be serviced at N. Any task which was chosen for migration because of the fault, but has not been actually migrated has to be identified. Then it should be checked whether the task could be serviced earlier at N itself. If that is so, the task should not be migrated.

7.1   Actions in Case of a Permanent Fault

Let us say that at a node N an entity R has a permanent fault. In this case, all the tasks which require R have to be migrated to some other nodes where the FU with R is active. In the discussion that follows, we describe the actions performed by the various agents present at the node N.

Actions of the FU F where R had encountered a fault

- Pass on any tasks received by F to the LU. First the tasks in Q_{Sched}, then those from the input queue Q_I and then any newly arriving tasks are sent with the *priority* calculation as explained in section 3.2.
- After the results are available they are passed to the agent which had submitted the task to F (this could either be a department or a sub-department).

Actions of the Middle Agents and the Nursing Unit

- Identify all tasks that require R and send them to the LU.
- Pass on the tasks down as in the case of normal operation with an indication that they have been passed to the LU already (so that they are not resent to LU).

- The NUs mark that R is not locally available so that the newly arriving tasks requiring R would be handled directly by NUs as if R never existed.

Actions of all other FUs and LU remain unchanged.

7.2   Actions in Case of a Transient Fault

Let us say that an entity R at the node N has a transient fault and the repair-time is U_R^t. In this case only those tasks whose deadlines cannot be met at this node and which may be satisfied at some other node need to be identified and migrated. In the discussion that follows we describe the actions performed by the various agents present at the node N.

Actions of the FU F where R encountered a fault

- The tasks that should be migrated are found using the following algorithm.

  Consider a task T with deadline D. Let duration of usage of R be Δ. Let T have outgoing *enables* relationships with y tasks $T_1, \ldots, T_y$ with deadlines $D_1, \ldots, D_y$, and the durations of usage of the FUs where these tasks would be executed be $\Delta_1, \ldots, \Delta_y$ respectively. T can be sent to the LU for considering possible migration if $U_R^t > D - \Delta$. We calculate $D' = min(D, min(\forall_{i:1..y}(D_i - \Delta_i)))$. The deadline of T is modified to D'. If the best *fitness-value* returned by the LU is less than D', then T should be migrated to a node chosen by the LU using the coordination mechanism. Otherwise the *fitness-value* for the task T is queried from F. If this value is worse than the one which LU has got, then T should be migrated otherwise not.
- The tasks in Q_{Sched} are considered for migration first in FIFO (first in first out) order and then those from Q_I are considered in EDF (earliest deadline first) order.
- The tasks which are migrated are kept in a special queue $Q_{Migrated}$ at F and deleted from Q_{Sched} or Q_I. The queue $Q_{Migrated}$ is deleted after U_R^t.
- The results obtained from LU are passed up to the agent that had submitted the task to F.
- All further incoming tasks received before U_R^t are handled in the same manner.
- The normal operation is resumed after U_R^t.

Actions performed by the Middle agents and the NUs are similar. Actions of all other FUs and LU remain unchanged.

7.3   Reconfiguration of the System after Fault Repair

In this section we explain the actions performed when an entity R at a node N is repaired from a fault. In this case the normal functioning should be resumed. The tasks in LU requiring R that can be serviced earlier at N itself should be identified and sent back to the functional unit F handling R.

- F sends a message up the hierarchy and to LU that it now can service requests for R.
- The middle agents, the other FUs and the NUs resume their normal operations. In addition the NUs delete the entry saying that R is unavailable at N.
- **Actions performed by LU**

  - For every task T present in $Q_{Processing}$ the following steps are carried out. If $B_T + 2 * c_{max} < U_R^t$ then T remains in $Q_{Processing}$ and would be migrated. B_T is the best *fitness-value* received for the task T and c_{max} is the maximum communication delay between any two nodes in the network. The multiplication by 2 is required since atmost two communications would be required after getting the *fitness-values* - one for migrating the task and the other for receiving the results.
  - All the remaining tasks are sent to F in the order of their priority.

8   Conclusions

We have addressed the problem for resource coordination in a distributed hospital system. We have extended the GPGP approach for multiagent systems to support inter-hospital collaboration. Such a collaboration is necessary since all the hospitals may not have all the possible resources or capabilities (entities). A coordination mechanism is proposed that would decide where a task should be migrated if the entities required for the accomplishment of the task are not available locally at a hospital. This mechanism is adaptive since it uses the dynamic information about the loads at other hospitals and previous requests made in order to arrive at this decision. Simulation studies have been performed to compare our mechanism with the techniques currently used in practice. It is observed that our mechanism performs better than those under all circumstances.

We have presented mechanisms for handling two kinds of faults - permanent and transient. These mechanisms are also adaptive since they in turn make use of the adaptive coordination mechanism. The mechanisms allow for continued functioning with graceful degradation in the performance in the presence of faults. On-line reconfiguration of the system after a fault is repaired is also discussed.

As a part of future work, we are incorporating user defined preferences (at the time of submission of a task) for multiple criteria like quality, duration and cost. This would give rise to a multi-objective decision making process. We also propose to identify learning techniques so that performance improvement could be achieved. The approach presented is general enough and can be used in any application where distributed resource coordination is required. We are currently investigating, the usage of the techniques proposed in a different application - that of an e-University system.

References

1. K.S. Decker: Environment Centered Analysis and Design of Coordination Mechanisms. *Ph.D. thesis*, University of Massachusetts. (1995)
2. K.S. Decker, J. Li: Coordinating Mutually Exclusive Resources Using GPGP. *Autonomous Agents and Multi-Agent Systems.* **3** (2000) 1–27
3. K.S. Decker, V.R. Lesser: Designing a Family of Coordination Algorithms. *In Proceedings of the First International Conference on Multi-Agent Systems, San Francisco.* (June 1995) 73–80
4. U. Deshpande, A. Gupta, A. Basu: Collaboration in a Distributed Hospital Environment. *Technical Report No. IITKGP/CSE/AB/2002/1, Department of Computer Science and Engineering, IIT-Kharagpur, India.* (July 2002)
5. E.H. Durfee, V.R. Lesser: Using Partial Global Plans to Coordinate Distributed Problem Solvers. *In Proceedings of the Tenth International Joint Conference on Artificial Intelligence.* (August 1987)
6. A.Garvey, V.Lesser: Design-to-time Real-Time Scheduling. *IEEE Transactions on Systems, Man and Cybernetics.* **23(6)** (1993) 1491–1502
7. A. Kumar, P.S. Ow: A Study of Distributed Problem Solving for Patient Scheduling. *In Proc. ORSA/TIMS*, Washington, D.C. (1988)
8. K. Ramamritham, J. Stankovic, W. Zhao: Distributed Scheduling of Tasks with Deadlines and Resource Requirements. *IEEE Transactions on Computers.* **38(8)** (August 1989) 1110–1123
9. R.G. Smith: The Contract Net Protocol: High Level Communication and Control in a Distributed Problem Solver. *IEEE Transactions on Computers.* **29(12)** (Dec. 1980) 1104–1113

Mining 'Living' Data – Providing Context Information to a Negotiation Process

Simeon J. Simoff

Faculty of IT, University of Technology, Sydney
NSW 2007, Australia
simeon@it.uts.edu.au

Negotiation is the process whereby two (or more) individual agents with conflicting interests reach a mutually beneficial agreement on a set of issues. In negotiation the exchange of information is as important as the exchange of offers. During a negotiation, an agent may actively acquire contextual information that it may, or may not, choose to place on the negotiation table. This work presents a multi-agent framework for negotiation support and discusses on more details a framework for on-line data mining that supports the identification of contextual information and providing it on negotiator's demand. The smart data mining agents that support the negotiation agent, are expected to operate under time-constraints and over dynamically changing corpus of information. They need to determine the sources of information, the confidence and validity of these sources and a way of combining extracted information. All transactions, including complex requests for information and combination of results, are managed as business processes. There are a number of challenges that the smart data mining architecture is addressing, including critical pieces of information being held in different repositories; non-standard nomenclatures; radically different data types and models; possible duplicative, inconsistent and erroneous data; and possible high rate of change of the models representing data content. The mining and discovery procedures include: (i) mining the opponent's profile information (this is a broad group of methodologies in which adapt and further develop: user-centric and site-centric data mining methods, methods for mining social networks in electronic communities for information about opponents reputation, text data mining methods, including discovering unexpected information about the opponent from competitors sources, methods for topic detection in communication transcripts); (ii) mining deal profiles information — these methods analyse the preconditions of negotiations, and the dynamics of change in negotiation issues; (iii) event sequence mining — will extract behaviour patterns of negotiating parties from the 'utterances', sequences of key events that can change negotiation (based on past experiences and current situation on the 'negotiation table'). The complete integration of contextual support into the negotiation process is a novel addition to negotiation systems.

R. Meersman, Z. Tari (Eds.): CoopIS/DOA/ODBASE 2002, LNCS 2519, p. 521, 2002.
© Springer-Verlag Berlin Heidelberg 2002

The Neem Platform: An Evolvable Framework for Perceptual Collaborative Applications

P. Barthelmess and C.A. Ellis

Department of Computer Science, University of Colorado at Boulder, Campus Box 430,
Boulder, CO 80309-0430, USA.
{barthelm,skip}@colorado.edu

Abstract. Project Neem targets real-time distributed multipoint perceptual collaborative applications, focusing on the dynamic aspects that characterize human-
to-human group interaction. Neem adopts a Perceptual Interface paradigm – applications can make use of multiple communication channels (voice, facial expressions, gestures) to both capture context and for presentation through *virtual
participants* that take part in group conversations. To facilitate the development
of these applications, an evolvable component-based platform has been built, that
provides plug-in extensibility and embedded support for Wizard of Oz experiments.

Project Neem at University of Colorado is concerned with the development of socially
and culturally aware collaborative systems. Neem's focus is on the dynamic aspects
that characterize group interaction. The goal is to build applications that mediate group
human-to-human interactions, by extracting context and reacting in real-time in context-
appropriate ways, e.g., by suggesting different courses of action based on what participants are doing (which tools they are operating and how), what they are saying to each
other, the expressions of their faces, and the kinds of gestures they are making. The
paradigm that is adopted is therefore a Perceptual Interface one where applications have
access to multimodal human communication channels both for capturing context and
for presenting themselves as *virtual participants* that take part in group conversations.

Applications are based on real-time, distributed, multipoint perceptual collaboration. Applications of this kind are characterized by the need for flexible support for
heterogeneous distributed process creation and communication, session management,
consistency control, data distribution and access control. The perceptual paradigm introduces in addition the need for user actions capture, reasoning, and reaction, exploring
multiple input and output modalities such as voice, facial expressions and gesture.

The burden of dealing with the above mentioned aspects is taken from the applications
by an evolvable development platform. Applications are then free to concentrate on
domain specific issues. The development cycle is thus potentially reduced, becoming
roughly equivalent to the effort required to develop single-user applications (singleware).

The platform provides more than a closed set of pre-existing behaviors - the platform
itself is designed to be extensible and adaptable, and its functionality is expected to
follow an evolutive cycle alongside applications. The distinction between application
development and platform refinement is thus blurred. Further details can be found in [1].

R. Meersman, Z. Tari (Eds.): CoopIS/DOA/ODBASE 2002, LNCS 2519, pp. 522–523, 2002.
© Springer-Verlag Berlin Heidelberg 2002

References

1. P. Barthelmess and C.A. Ellis. The neem platform: an evolvable framework for perceptual collaborative applications. Technical Report CU-CS-936-02, University of Colorado at Boulder, Computer Science Department, 2002.

A Model for Process Service Interaction

Karim Baïna, Samir Tata, and Khalid Benali

LORIA – INRIA – CNRS (UMR 7503)
BP 239, F-54506 Vandœuvre-lès-Nancy Cedex, France
{baina,tata,benali}@loria.fr

Due to business process automation development, process interconnection becomes an important matter. Actually, if a wide spectrum of business process management systems (BPMS) exist (e.g. workflows, shared agendas, project managers, to do lists, etc.), they have been mainly developed to suit the internal needs of enterprises. Moreover, if we focus particularly on workflow management systems (WFMS), existing interconnection solutions are mostly static, proprietary, and depend on specific business process definition languages, specific WFMS platforms, private data exchange formats, etc. To improve generic process interconnection support within existing WFMS, related interconnection models deal with awareness and dataflow formalisation between two interleaving processes (i.e. shared dataspace models, message passing mechanisms, event subscription/notification paradigms, remote object invocation, transfer protocol extension, ...), or with interleaving process control (i.e. transactional protocols, ...). In our opinion, the more promising and the more generic approach for interconnecting processes is a service oriented approach. Our purpose is to conceive a model for enterprise processes interconnection through process service interaction. A process service can represent either the description of a task that an enterprise may wish to outsource (e.g. because of time lack, cost reducing, or skill needs) or a specific task that an entreprise is known to be skilled to accomplish. This task may be managed by an automatic, a semi-automatic, or a manual process. It may be performable by a unique "provider" (atomic process service), or may need cooperation of several providers (composite process service) for example because it needs several skills not necessary within the scope of a single provider. A "requester" can compose the needed process services by using process services supplied by several providers. Existing process management systems often consider process instance as a black box (process method calls, execution events, and intermediate data are not visible from outside). This approach does not suit process cooperation needs. One of the aim of our process service interaction model is to allow processes to cooperate through partial visibility of their resources (e.g. data sharing, group awareness) by permitting access to a set of their own methods and events.

The interaction model we propose focuses on process service coordination by data sharing and control flow management. We define our process service interaction model as 5 sets : (1) a set of access contracts on shared data, (2) a set of visible method execution contracts, (3) a set of visible event reception contracts, (4) a set of coordination contracts based on shared data states, and (5) a set of coordination contracts based on process service states.

R. Meersman, Z. Tari (Eds.): CoopIS/DOA/ODBASE 2002, LNCS 2519, p. 524, 2002.

Leveraging Dynamic Inheritance in Complex Ontology Representation

Hasan M. Jamil and Giovanni A. Modica

Department of Computer Science, Mississippi State University, USA

Real life ontologies for web based systems, such as B2B, P2P, and B2C applications, are usually complex and large, and generally contain numerous intricate rules, exceptions and integrity constraints. Representing such ontologies in a concise but effective manner warrants sophisticated and higher level abstractions. In this paper we present an object-oriented approach to ontology representation and show that inheritance can be exploited to model and represent complex ontologies. For this purpose, we extend XML to include inheritance and methods, and demonstrate that such an extended XML actually help design and represent better ontologies that are modular, concise and low in maintenance overhead. The figure below shows an example of a complex ontology represented using our proposed XML extension. A complete discussion on XML++ and and its use in ontology representation may be found in an extended version of this paper in [1].

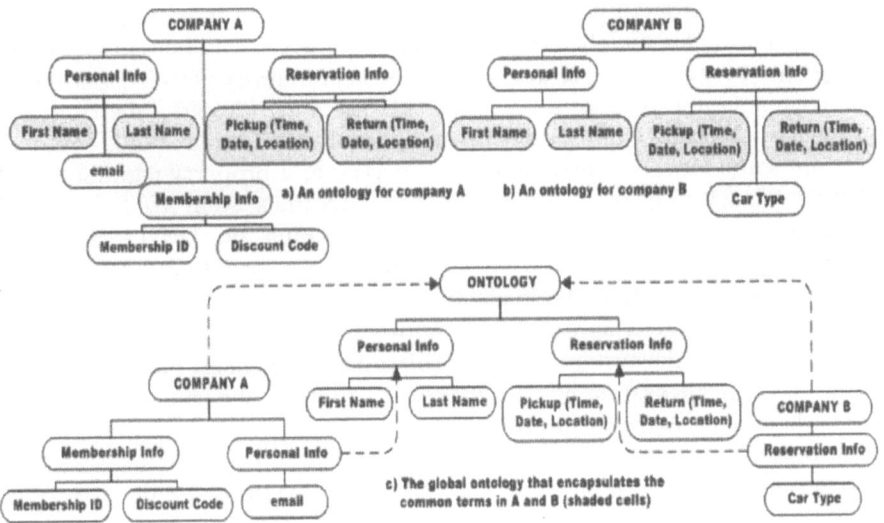

References

1. Jamil, H.M., Modica, G.A.: What object-orientation can do for XML. Technical Report TR-IDB-2002-06, Computer Science Department, Mississippi State University (2002)

R. Meersman, Z. Tari (Eds.): CoopIS/DOA/ODBASE 2002, LNCS 2519, p. 525, 2002.
© Springer-Verlag Berlin Heidelberg 2002

A Database Approach to Global Document Spaces: Replacing Files with Shared, Connected Objects

G. Rivera and M.C. Norrie

Institute for Information Systems
ETH Zurich, CH-8092 Zurich, Switzerland

User interaction with computers is centred on the file system and most user information is organised, retrieved, managed and shared via files. While the last two decades have seen major changes in tools to visualise and navigate file systems, the fundamental concepts in terms of structure and purpose have remained unchanged: Basically, file systems are *still* single-user, single-location and single-structure.

Alternative models for document systems have been proposed in several projects such as Lifestreams, Presto and SHORE. Either they replace the traditional hierarchical model with other models (Lifestreams) or they abandon any form of structured document space, and replace it with a concept of *placeless documents* with attached properties (Presto), or merge object-oriented database system and file system technologies (SHORE). In all of these approaches, a satisfactory model for a global document space supporting remote access to shared documents, and cooperative working within a community of users, is still missing. Lifestreams is not appropriate for multiple users working in a distributed environment with large, complex document space. Presto requires user communities to adopt some form of convention for properties and property naming. SHORE's limitation is actually the modelling of the UNIX file system itself: The resulting restrictions imposed by the application programming interface (API) mean that it is not possible to introduce to new, higher-level concepts into the file system.

While the motivation and goals of our work are similar to other projects, we have taken a different approach in that we essentially consider the design and development of a file system as an information management problem. Our vision is an extended file system which supports the notion of a shared, personalisable global document space. A file system of the next generation should satisfy three basic requirements in terms of constructs, namely: The existing notion of file should be replaced with one of typed persistent, distributed objects; the system should provide a mechanism for classifying files in various ways and independently from their types; the system should provide a mechanism for specifying dependencies and associations between files.

Therefore, we first defined a metamodel that incorporates the concepts of users, documents, document collections and document associations. The result is a two-level model that is able to distinguish between the classification and typing of documents and hence provide a flexible means of organising the document space into possibly overlapping, heterogeneous collections. We have demon-

R. Meersman, Z. Tari (Eds.): CoopIS/DOA/ODBASE 2002, LNCS 2519, pp. 526–527, 2002.

strated the approach by developing the file system OMX-FS in the context of the Oberon system. OMX-FS provides a suitable platform to support the development of cooperative working environments, greatly simplifying the coding effort since persistence, distribution and multi-user support are already supplied within the system. (Details available at
`http://www.globis.ethz.ch/reports/omx-fs.pdf`)

PROLOG/RDBMS Integration in the NED Intelligent Information System

F. Maier[1], D. Nute[1], W.D. Potter[1], J. Wang[1], M. Twery[2], H.M. Rauscher[3],
P. Knopp[2], S. Thomasma[2], M. Dass[1], and H. Uchiyama[1]

[1] Artificial Intelligence Center, The University of Georgia, Athens, GA, USA
[2] Northeastern Research Station, USDA Forest Service, Burlington, VT, USA
[3] Southern Research Station, USDA Forest Service, Asheville, NC, USA

NED-2 is a software system in development by the USDA Forest Service to facilitate ecosystem management. Using PROLOG knowledge bases and inference engines, NED-2 evaluates forest inventories to determine the degree to which they satisfy a set of predefined goals. By integrating third-party simulation and visualization packages, NED-2 allows the user to plan, predict, and assess forest treatment scenarios.

NED-2 is a blackboard based system with agents implemented in PROLOG. The blackboard itself is a composition of PROLOG clauses and relational databases which may be queried as if they were a single source. In order to achieve this uniform appearance, a language was created especially for NED allowing queries to be posed from within PROLOG without specifying the source or location of the information. The appropriate source of information is determined dynamically using metadata about each source stored as PROLOG clauses. Queries to be answered by a relational database system are translated into SQL. The metadata about each source is also used to automatically create join constraints, thereby simplifying the original query and reducing the risk of ill formed questions. When multiple sources are capable of providing solutions, the system can backtrack in usual PROLOG fashion to produce them.

This approach offers advantages over the usual method of querying a relational database from PROLOG—that of treating relation tuples as PROLOG facts to be retrieved a one at a time (this is sometimes called *relational access*). The most significant advantage is that this approach makes full use of a database system's capabilities and is thereby much more efficient than relational access. It is generally much faster to pose complex queries to a database system and let it do the work in solving a problem rather than making many simple queries and combining the results. This approach also does not require full knowledge of database schemas, nor even that the schemas remain fixed. This means that alterations made to the databases do not require sweeping changes to be made to the rest of the system. It is thought that this querying technique provides an efficient, simple, and robust means of gathering information from heterogeneous data sources.

Further information on the NED project and on the integration of PROLOG and database systems in NED-2 can be obtained at the following addresses:
`http://www.cs.uga.edu/~potter/dendrite/index.html`, and
`http://www.fs.us/ne/burlington/ned/`.

R. Meersman, Z. Tari (Eds.): CoopIS/DOA/ODBASE 2002, LNCS 2519, p. 528, 2002.
© Springer-Verlag Berlin Heidelberg 2002

New Location Management for Reducing HLR Overhead Traffic in Mobile Networks

Dong Chun Lee[1], Hyun Cheul Shin[2], and Jeom Goo Kim[3]

[1] Dept. of Computer Science Howon Univ., Korea
[2] Dept. of Computer Information Cheonan College of Foreign Studies, Korea
[3] Dept. of Computer Science Namseoul Univ., Korea.

1 Introduction and Leaving Trace Scheme

IS-41 and GSM have a structural drawback : as the number of users increase, home location register(HLR) becomes the bottleneck problem. We propose a new mobility management method, Leaving Trace (LT) scheme, which effectively reduces mobility management cost in mobile network. The basic idea is that putting the VLR ID of the registration area where the terminal currently resides into the registration-cancellation message, the trace of terminals is left in the VLRs visited so that querying to the VLRs rather than to the HLR when the terminal-terminated-call occurs may connect a call. The LT scheme distributes messages to VLRs. The location registration process is performed as follows: 1. The terminal stores the ID of the new VLR into the tail of its queue. If the number of IDs stored in the queue exceeds the terminal K, the terminal deletes the VLR ID stored in the head of the queue in order to keep the trace length of the terminal K and generates a pointer cancellation (POCANC) message which will be sent to the VLR whose ID is just deleted from the queue. 2. The routing request (REGREQ) message and the POCANC message (if exists) are sent to the new VLR. 3. The new VLR checks whether the terminal is already registered. If not, it sends the registration notification message to the HLR and the POCANC message to the new VLR to the old VLR. 4. The HLR sends a registration cancellation message including the ID of the new VLR to the old VLR. 5. The old VLR generates a pointer composed of the terminal ID and the ID of the new VLR. Also, the call delivery process is performed as follows: 1.The VLR of the caller is queried and a pointer to the callee is found. The VLR sends a ROUTREQ message including its ID to the pointed VLR. 2.The VLR which received the ROUTREQ message sends this message to the next VLR until the pointer ends. 3.If the callee is found in the VLR where it currently resides, a temporary local directory numbers (TLDN) is assigned to the callee and sent to the VLR of the caller by using the VLR ID included in the ROUTREQ message. 4.The call is established between caller and callee using the TLDN.

R. Meersman, Z. Tari (Eds.): CoopIS/DOA/ODBASE 2002, LNCS 2519, pp. 529–530, 2002.
© Springer-Verlag Berlin Heidelberg 2002

2   Analytic Model and Conclusion

To estimate overall mobility management cost, the simulation model is based on the Jackson's network. Considering the delay times both in HLR and VLR, and considering both location registration cost and call delivery cost, the proposed LT scheme performs better than IS-41 because it efficiently utilizes the characteristics of the third generation network.

A Filter Object Framework for MICO

Pranav S. Nabar[1], Amit L. Padalkar[1], and Rushikesh K. Joshi[2]

[1] K. R. School of Information Technology,
Indian Institute of Technology Bombay, Mumbai, INDIA.
{pranav, amitp}@it.iitb.ac.in,
[2] Department of Computer Science and Engineering,
Indian Institute of Technology Bombay, Mumbai, INDIA.
rkj@cse.iitb.ac.in

Abstract. Filtered delivery model of message passing in an object-oriented distributed computing environment facilitates separation of message control from message processing in a transparent manner. In this model, special objects called *filter objects* have the ability to filter messages in transit and perform intermediate actions. We present the design and implementation of the message filtering model for transparent dynamically pluggable filter objects for MICO, an open-source CORBA implementation. For implementing the filtering framework, enhancements to the MICO implementation model are proposed. A process for development of filter objects with related tool support has also been outlined.

Keywords: CORBA, filter objects, MICO, pluggable filters, transparency.

1 Introduction

Distributed object-oriented systems are built using collaborating objects on a distributed platform. These distributed objects collaborate by passing messages. In some cases, applications may require to change their message control policies dynamically. For example, an application might need to check message contents for validity or against security concerns. In such cases, message control cannot be abstracted out without breaking its transparency. In applications like these, interceptors[8] or filtering models models such as Composition Filters[1], Filter Objects[6] and Encapsulators[9] achieve separation between message processing and message control. In the filter object model, messages sent to the destination objects can be intercepted by first class filter objects. While filter objects intercept messages, the calling semantics of the source object do not change. This behavior of filter objects can be employed to change the system behavior by transparently intercepting calls and controlling or modifying the invocation requests coming from clients. In this paper, an implementation of a filter object framework for MICO[12], an open source implementation of CORBA[12] is described.

R. Meersman, Z. Tari (Eds.): CoopIS/DOA/ODBASE 2002, LNCS 2519, pp. 531–548, 2002.

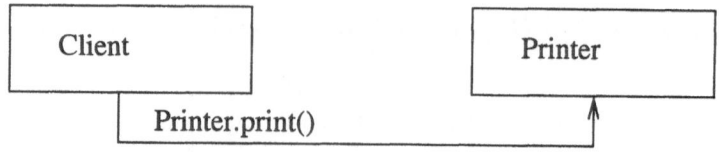

Fig. 1. Direct delivery model

1.1 Filter Objects

Figure 1 shows the conventional direct delivery message passing model. A
Client object on a network sends a print() message to a Printer object. The message is delivered directly to the destination object, which in
this case is Printer. As a result, the corresponding operation is invoked
at the destination object. This implies that any intermediate message control cannot be decoupled from the operation without sacrificing its transparency.

For example, after a period of time, it may be found that one Printer is
insufficient to fulfill the needs of increasing number of clients, and more printers
need to be added to the system for load balancing. But it may not possible to
dynamically introduce this solution without making considerable changes to the
Printer object code.

Filter objects provide an elegant, modular solution to the above problem.
Removal, addition and replacement of filter objects do not require any modification of code, either at the source object or at the destination object. Figure 2
shows how load balancing can be introduced through the filtered delivery model.
Here a LoadBalancer object, which maintains a list of additional Printer
objects, is plugged to original Printer object. It intercepts all the incoming
print() requests to original Printer object, and redirects them to one of the
Printer objects to achieve load-balancing.

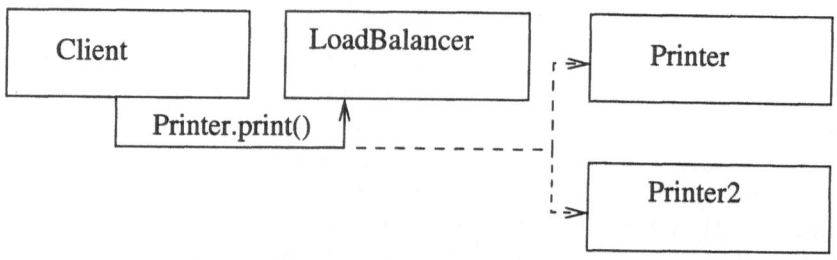

Fig. 2. Filtered delivery model

CORBA implementations such as Visibroker[2] and Orbix[3] provide interceptors. Visibroker provides various kinds of client and server interception points such as bind interception, client request interception, POA create/destroy interception, server request interception etc. Orbix provides filters in per-process and per object categories. Various kinds of filtering points may be specified such as pre-marshaling and post-marshaling filter points per process and pre-invocation and per-invocation filter points per object are supported.

Filter objects[6] on the other hand are first class dynamically pluggable objects, which are provided in the current implementation as full fledged CORBA objects. Apart from their filtering capabilities, they may also provide public interfaces. Filter objects have been implemented for Java[7] and C++[6], and in distributed environment at user level for MICO[11] and on an AspectJ based environment[5]. The current work enhances the MICO kernel to support a kernel level implementation of first class filter objects such that the ORB becomes *filter-aware*.

1.2   Filter Object Framework for MICO

MICO[12] is a CORBA 2.3 compliant open-source implementation of the OMG-CORBA standard. We have designed and implemented a filter object framework in MICO version 2.3.4. This involved several system-level enhancements to the MICO kernel. In our framework, filter objects are full-fledged CORBA objects. Filter objects can be plugged and unplugged onto server objects transparently. The framework is based on the *message filtering model*[6] for filter objects. This paper introduces the filtering framework to a considerable detail.

We, first discuss the design and implementation of the framework in subsequent sections. The static and dynamic models are elaborated. Further, the development process, tool support and applications of filter objects are also discussed. Finally performance indices are provided for the implementation running on a Linux cluster.

2   Design of the Filter Object Framework

We begin our discussion by documenting the design requirements and subsequently discuss various design alternatives.

2.1   Design Issues and Requirements

Besides seamlessly fitting into the existing MICO framework, the filter design has to meet the following requirements.

- Support basic filtering actions like pass and bounce.
- Support extended filter object properties, like layering and grouping.
- Filter objects need to be transparent to clients as well as servers.
- Evolution of the system using filter objects should involve minimal change (ideally *no* change) in the existing system code.

- Development process of a system using filter objects should not be radically different from the existing object-oriented development processes.
- Addition of filtering framework into the system should not substantially increase the overheads on the system.
- Granularity of control over filtering actions is also a design issue.
- We assume filters are plugged and unplugged by trusted hosts. Security issues are not considered.

The design alternatives were largely based on two major considerations, the location where the mappings between the server and the filter objects would be held and the point in the actual invocation interaction where the call would be intercepted. On detailed analysis of the implementation model, it was found that the second consideration was dependent on where the mappings would be located. This meant, we only needed to evaluate the choices for locating the mappings between server objects and the filter objects plugged onto them. An analysis led us to three main design alternatives discussed below.

- **Choice 1:** *A CORBA object/service stores the mappings:* In this alternative, a service is used to maintain the mappings between server and filter objects. The CORBA object providing this service has a standard interface. This makes it similar to other standard CORBA services. Applications use plug() and unplug() interfaces on this service to plug and unplug filters onto the server objects. Whenever the server receives an invocation, it uses a reference to the mapping service to check for attached filters and take appropriate action. This design results in high timing overloads during method invocations.
- **Choice 2:** *Mappings maintained in micod:* In this case, we store the filter-server mappings in the micod daemon. Local plug and unplug calls are forwarded to micod for plugging and unplugging filters. Whenever client makes a method invocation, it has to pass through micod, which checks for the filters plugged to servers and forwards the call accordingly. This leads to an overhead during method invocation in the case of normal invocation, when no filters are plugged.
- **Choice 3:** *Mappings maintained at the server-side:* Here the mappings are maintained in an object in the server-side library. During method invocation, the presence of plugged filters is checked at the server-side and appropriate action is taken. Overheads on *normal* method invocation are localized.

2.2 Evaluation of Design Choices

The comparison between the design alternatives can be abstracted in a feature matrix. Choice 1, 2 and 3 refer to position of *server-filter* mappings in separate CORBA object providing a mapping service, in BOA daemon (micod) and in server object respectively as described in the previous section.

We observe that all three choices are capable of supporting both essential and extended properties of filter objects. Hence the distinguishing factor between

Table 1. Feature matrix

Overheads	Design Choices 1 2 3
Plug/Unplug	High Low High
Method invocation without filters	High High Low
Method invocation with filters	High High High

these choices is overheads incurred by each of them. We have considered two main types of overheads viz. plug/unplug overhead and method invocation overhead, with and without plugged filters. These form the basis of comparison aided by feature matrix shown in Table 1.

In choice 1, where client-filter mappings are stored in a mapping service, both the overheads are high. In this case, every plug/unplug beta message and method invocation has to consult the mapping service resulting in higher overheads. In the case of choice 2, mappings are maintained in the BOA daemon micod. This choice reduces plug/unplug overhead since these beta messages are sent to the daemon instead of a mapping service. However the method invocation overhead increases even for normal method calls. Whenever a method invocation occurs, it has to pass through micod, which checks for plugged filters and forwards the call accordingly. This clearly leads to higher overhead during method invocations even if the server object doesn't have any plugged filters. With plugged filters, routing invocations to them results in additional invocation overheads. With choice 3, where mappings are stored on the server-side, plug/unplug overhead is higher than that in choice 2. This overhead increases since sending these beta messages requires obtaining a server object reference and then invoking these beta operations on it. However, with this approach, there is no penalty on method invocations for objects without plugged filters. The method invocation on server objects with plugged filters results in higher overheads because of method routing to filters, which is unavoidable in all the three cases.

From the above discussion, it is clear that choice 1 has comparatively higher overheads than choices 2 and 3. In case of choice 2, though its plug/unplug overheads are low, method invocation overheads are one the higher side. Since method invocations are more frequent than plug/unplug beta messages, an implementation using choice 2 would lead to higher overall timings than choice 3. Hence choice 3 better suits the design considerations and was selected for implementation of the filter object framework.

3   Static Model

The design model includes several modifications to MICO implementation to satisfy the design requirements stated in Section 2.1. In this section, we present the modifications to MICO's static model. Figure 3 shows the class diagram of filter object framework. The modification to the dynamic model are covered in the next section.

3.1   Modifications to MICO

Modifications were introduced into the MICO implementation to satisfy the filtering requirements (Section 2.1). These changes include creating new interfaces and modifying the existing interfaces by including new methods to fulfill additional set of responsibilities. We now discuss each of these.

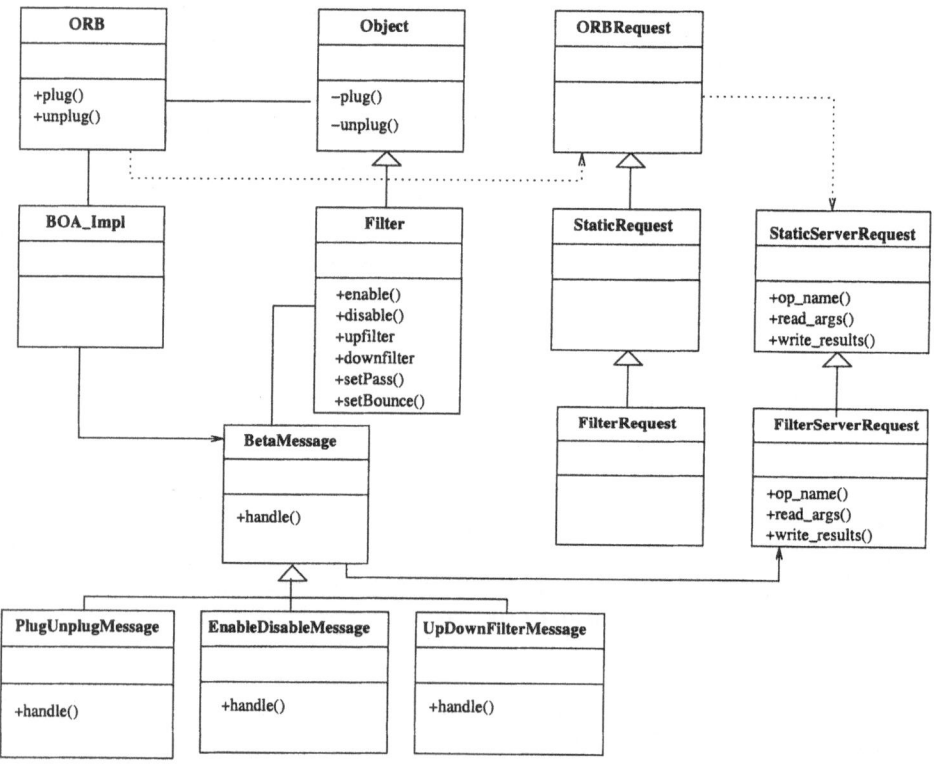

Fig. 3. Filter Framework - Static Model

CORBA::Filter class. The CORBA::Filter class is the common superclass of all *filter objects*. Since all filter objects are CORBA objects, the Filter class inherits from the CORBA::Object class. Filter class gives concrete implementations of the following methods:

- enable: enables a particular filter method, passed as argument.
- disable: disables a particular filter method, passed as argument.
- upfilter: maps a filter method as an *upfilter* to a server method.
- downfilter: maps a filter method as a *downfilter* to a server method.
- setPass: to be used by the filter developer in case of a *pass* action.
- setBounce: to be used by the filter developer in case of a *bounce* action.

CORBA::Object class. The CORBA::Object class is the common superclass of all CORBA objects. This class gets the additional responsibility of maintaining filter-server mappings. The system can access these mappings through private methods.

- plug: Plugs the filter object onto the server object.
- unplug: Unplugs the filter object from the server object.

CORBA::ORB class. The ORB class implements the ORB interface defined by OMG-CORBA standard. For plugging and unplugging filter objects onto the server objects, additional public interfaces are required. These are provided by the ORB class through the plug and unplug methods. The process managing filter objects called the *catalyst* uses this interface for plug/unplug actions on the server object.

Carrying Filter Requests. In the MICO implementation, static invocations are encapsulated into objects of StaticRequest class on the client side, and into objects of StaticServerRequest class on the server side. We specialize these two classes to carry *filter requests*—invocations routed to filter objects. Hence classes FilterRequest and FilterServerRequest inherit StaticRequest and StaticServerRequest classes respectively. Methods op_name, read_args and write_results of the StaticServerRequest class are overridden in the Filter-ServerRequest class for specialized implementation.

Carrying Beta Messages. All the privileged filter messages like plug–unplug, enable–disable and set method mappings (upfilter–downfilter) are handled internally by objects of a specialized handler class called BetaMessage. This class defines a virtual handle function. The concrete handler implementation appears in the following three subclasses of the BetaMessage class.

- The PlugUnplugMessage class: Handles plug and unplug messages.
- The EnableDisableMessage class: Handles enable and disable messages.
- The UpDownFilterMessage class: Handle upfilter and downfilter messages to set upfilter and downfilter mappings at the filter objects.

4   Dynamic Model

In this section, we present a behavioral view of the system. In the following subsections, we discuss modifications to normal method invocation sequence by the filter object framework and persistence of information supporting the framework, starting with beta message handling.

4.1   Beta Message Handling

As discussed in Section 3.1, *beta messages* are special control messages, which must be handled by the filter object framework. Although these are special messages, they follow normal method invocation sequence followed in MICO. All beta messages are handled by BOA in its `invoke` method.

Upfilter/Downfilter beta messages. Each filter object interface consists of *upfilter* and *downfilter* methods. *upfilter* methods filter corresponding client methods whereas *downfilter* methods filter return results. Multiple upfilter and downfilter methods can be associated with single client method. To provide this facility to every filter object, `Filter`, the base class of each filter object maintains mappings between client method and corresponding upfilter and downfilter methods. These mappings can be manipulated by sending *upfilter* or *downfilter* beta messages. Each beta message takes client method name and corresponding upfilter/downfilter method name as arguments. The filter object framework includes *filterconf* utility that facilitates sending these messages to filter objects. We now present the algorithm for sending and handling these messages which is implemented in the `handle` method of the corresponding classes.

Scenario: Sending Up/Down filter message

1. Create `StaticAny` objects representing client and filter method names.
2. Create `StaticRequest` object representing appropriate beta message.
3. Add the arguments and invoke the request.

Scenario: Handling Up/Down filter message

1. Create server side request and read the client and filter method names using it.
2. Check whether filter object contains mapping corresponding to client method.
3. If yes, get the corresponding Up/Down filter methods and add the filter method name if it does not exist.
4. If no, create appropriate mapping in the filter object between received client and filter method.
5. Add the filter method name with *disable* status if it does not exist.

Enable/Disable beta messages. These beta messages control status of individual filter methods. `Filter`, the base class of every filter object maintains filter method names and their status. The filter method status can be changed by sending *enable* or *disable* beta messages. Each beta message takes filter method name as argument. The filter object framework includes *filterconf* utility that facilitates sending these messages to filter objects. We now present the algorithm for sending and handling these messages.

Scenario: Sending Enable/Disable message

1. Create `StaticAny` object representing filter method name.
2. Create `StaticRequest` object representing appropriate beta message.
3. Add the argument and invoke the request.

Scenario: Handling Enable/Disable message

1. Create server side request and read the filter method name using it.
2. If this is an enable message, enable corresponding filter method.
3. Search Up/Down filter methods corresponding to every client method to check if the filter method is part of either Upfilter or Downfilter methods. If yes, change the status of other methods to disabled. This ensures that at most one Up/Down method is enabled for any client method.
4. If this is a disable message, disable corresponding filter method.

Plug/Unplug beta messages. These beta messages allow plugging and unplugging of filters from their clients. `ORB` provides a public interface *plug* and *unplug* for this purpose. This interface in turn makes use of private interface of `Object`, which stores a list of plugged filters. The filter object framework includes *filterconf* utility that facilitates sending these messages to client objects. We now present the algorithm for sending and handling these messages.

Scenario: Sending Plug/Unplug message

1. Convert a filter object reference to string.
2. Create `StaticAny` object representing stringified filter object reference.
3. Create `StaticRequest` object representing appropriate beta message.
4. Add the argument and invoke the request.

Scenario: Handling Plug/Unplug message

1. Create server side request and read the stringified reference using it.
2. Convert the stringified reference to object reference and narrow it to the filter reference.
3. If this is a plug message, add the filter reference to filters list if it does not exist.
4. If this is an unplug message, remove the filter reference from filters list if it exists.

4.2   Filtered Method Invocation

We discuss modifications made to normal MICO method invocation sequence in order to incorporate the filtering functionality. First important modification to invocation sequence is creation of a specialized `FilterServerRequest` instead of `StaticServerRequest` in `make_request()` method. The responsibilities of server-side filter request object include method name translation and performing *upfiltering* and *downfiltering*. To satisfy these responsibilities, it overrides three methods viz. `op_name()`, `read_args()` and `write_results()`.

Method name translation. The translation process is performed by `op_name()` method. This method returns current operation (method) name. In the filter object framework, it performs the translation from intercepted filter client method name to appropriate filter method name. Here, we present algorithm used by the translation process.

Scenario: Method name translation

1. If the current object is not a *filter*, then no translation is needed. Set invocation status to normal and return the actual method name.
2. If this is an intercepted method call from filter client:
   a) If the current filter object doesn't have mappings corresponding to intercepted client method, then set the invocation status as bad filter client invocation and return.
   b) If intercepted method call is *Up* call, search the Up filter methods corresponding to intercepted client method.
   c) If intercepted method call is *Down* call, search the Down filter methods corresponding to intercepted client method.
   d) If one of the Up/Down filter methods is enabled, set the invocation status as normal filter client invocation and return enabled method name.
   e) Otherwise, set the invocation status as bad filter client invocation and return.
3. Else set the invocation status as normal filter method invocation and return the actual method name.

Up filtering. The `read_args()` method performs the work of reading the argument data, which was sent as part of method invocation from client side. This data is then passed on to actual method at server side provided `read_args()` is successful in reading the data. In the filter object framework, `read_args()` method handles additional responsibility of *Up* filtering. Here, we present algorithm used to carry out Up filtering.

Scenario: Up filtering

1. Read the argument data. If unsuccessful, set read status as false and return.
2. Perform Up filtering setting method *pass* status.

   a) If the invocation status is *bad filter client invocation*, set the pass status
      as false.
   b) If there are no filters plugged to current object, set the pass status as
      true.
   c) Else iterate through plugged filters in LIFO order till all filters are tra-
      versed or one of the filters cause method to bounce. For every filter,
      create a filter request and copy the current invocation request's argu-
      ments and return value to it. Treat the copied arguments as of *inout*
      type. Finally, invoke the intercepted filter client method call using newly
      created filter request.
   d) If none of the plugged filters bounce the method, set pass status as true
      else set it as false.
3. If pass status is true, set read status to true and return.
4. Else set read status to false and call `write_results()`.

Down filtering. The `write_results()` method performs the work of communicating return results and *out* argument values to the client side. In the filter
object framework, `write_results()` method handles additional responsibility
of *Down* filtering. Here, we present the algorithm used to carry out Down
filtering.

Scenario: Down filtering

1. Perform Down filtering if method *pass* status is true.
   a) If current method has *void* return type, do nothing.
   b) If the invocation status is *bad filter client invocation*, do nothing.
   c) If there are no filters plugged to current object, do nothing.
   d) Else iterate through plugged filters in FIFO order till all filters are tra-
      versed. For every filter, create a filter request and copy the current invo-
      cation request's return value to it. Add the current invocation request's
      return value to the request as *in* argument. Finally, invoke the inter-
      cepted filter client method call using newly created filter request.
2. Communicate results of current invocation back to client side.
3. If current call is intercepted call at filter object, communicate method pass
   status to filter client.

4.3   Persistence of Framework Related Information

As described in Section 4.1, every filter client maintains a list of plugged filters
and every filter maintains mappings from client method to upfilter/downfilter
methods and status of each of its methods. Any CORBA object providing
a service may *deactivate* itself to save resources if it anticipates period of
inactivity. Deactivation involves stopping the service and freeing all resources.
The object is reactivated whenever the service it offers is requested. Since filter
clients and filters are CORBA objects, they can also choose to be deactivated.

If the framework related information mentioned above is not saved while deactivation, it is lost making the framework ineffective. In this section, we discuss the strategy adopted by us to make the framework related information persistent.

A CORBA object requests its deactivation by calling `shutdown()` on BOA. The shutdown procedure in BOA involves deactivating object implementations. Before deactivation, an object is given an option to save its data by `save_object()` method in BOA. This method calls `_save_object()` on every object, which does actual work of storing object data, usually in a file. On reactivation, object initializes itself using the stored data.

In our approach for making the framework information persistent, we have modified the `save_object()` method of BOA. Before an object saves its data, framework specific information in filter client and filter object is stored in files as appropriate. The information is stored in two files containing client specific data and filter specific data respectively. Creation of these files is not mutually exclusive since a filter client can itself be a filter e.g. in case of multi-level filtering.

On reactivation of the object, saved framework information is not immediately restored since it is required only when a method is to be invoked on that object. The method invocation request is represented at server-side by `FilterServerRequest`. Hence, the framework information is restored only during creation of this server-side request. File names, where the framework information is stored, are made unique for every object by using `_ident()` method of `Object`.

5   Key Features

MICO filter object framework has certain key advantages over existing filter implementations. These are listed below:

1. The existing software can be evolved with minimal change in code and in most cases with no change.
2. All the filtering properties, essential as well as extended, have been implemented.
3. Multiple methods can filter a single server method, though, at a time, at most only one is enabled.
4. Filter methods need not comply to any naming rules, thus giving more flexibility to the filter developer. The methods though need to have a compatible signature.

There are certain limitations of the current implementation. The current implementation is designed for intercepting only static invocations on server objects using the Basic Object Adapter (BOA). It does not intercept dynamic invocations made using the dynamic invocation interface (DII). Since the server-filter mappings are maintained at the server-side, every invocation has go through the server first, before the appropriate filter method is called. Logically, though, the filtering semantics are retained using this strategy, it leads to some overheads. There might be cases where all the filter methods corresponding to a server method are disabled. Even in such case, an invocation of that method is redirected to the filter incurring overheads.

6   Filter Object Development Process

The following sections depict the steps involved in building filter objects using this framework to evolve the existing system.

6.1   Building Filter IDL from Server IDL

Filter IDL can be obtained from the server IDL in two ways:

- By manually writing the code for the IDL satisfying a set of predefined relationship rules mentioned below.
- By using the fidlgen utility.

Relationships between server and filter interfaces:

- For every method in the server interface, there exists at least one *up-filter* method in the filter interface.
- For each *up-filter* method in the filter interface, all the arguments corresponding to those in the server method are inout.
- For every method in the server interface returning non-void value, there exists at least one *down-filter* method.

The fidlgen utility can be used to directly generate the filter IDLs.

6.2   Compiling the Filter IDL

Once filter IDL is obtained, it can be compiled using MICO IDL compiler (idl) to obtain the files defining the filter, the filter stub, and the filter skeleton classes. The current filter framework only intercepts static invocations using the Basic Object Adapter (BOA) on server objects with shared activation policy. Hence idl -no-poa -boa options should be used during compilation.

6.3   Post-processing the Filter Header File

Post-processing of the filter header file can be done in two ways:

- By manually inheriting the filter class (declared in the filter header file) from CORBA::Filter instead of CORBA::Object.
- The above task can also be accomplished by using filtergen utility. Along with the filter header file, we also need to supply the filter class name to the utility. The syntax is as given below:

```
filtergen <filter header file> <filter class>
```

```
/* Filter section with unique key filter */
[ filter ]
{
    [ FilterRepo ] /* contains filter IMR repoid */
    {
        /* Filter id and Tag */
        IDL:AccountFilter:1.0   foobar
    }
    [ Enable ]  /* contains filter method to be enabled. */
    {
        balanceUp
        balanceDown
    }
    [ Mappings ]  /* contains up & down method mappings. */
    {
        Up balance balanceUp
        Down balance balanceDown
    }
}
[ client ]  /* Client section with unique key 'client' */
{
    /* contains client and filter ids to be plugged. */
    [ Plug ]
    {
        [ ClientRepo ]  /* contains client IMR repoids */
        {
            IDL:Account:1.0 foobar
        }
        [ FilterRepo ]  /* contains filter IMR repoids */
        {
            IDL:AccountFilter:1.0    foobar
        }
    }
}
```

Fig. 4. Sample Configuration File

6.4   Implementing Filter Objects

Since filter objects are full-fledged CORBA objects, implementing a filter object is similar to implementing any other CORBA object. Each of the filter method is implemented keeping in mind the server method it is going to up-filter or down-filter.

6.5   The Filterconf Utility and BetaFiles

BetaFiles are configuration files for using filters. Figure 4 is a sample BetaFile. This file can contain multiple sections. Each top level section is identified by unique key. Top level sections may in turn contain subsections. There are two basic kinds of top level sections. First type of section contains information needed by a filter object and second type of section contains information related filter-client (server) object. These two type of top level sections with keys *filter* & *client* sections respectively are described in this file.

Filter section. This section can contain three subsections viz. *Enable, Disable* & *Mappings.* All three subsections need not be present in this section but it must at least contain one of the three subsections. Each subsection requires an *id* of the destination filter. This *id* can be either naming service identifier or implementation repository identifier (*repoid*). The filter id is written in another subsection either *FilterNS* OR *FilterRepo* based on type of id. Possible subsections are *Enable, Disable, Mappings, FilterNS* and *FilterRepo* with no restrictions on their order.

Client Section. This section can contain two subsections viz. *Plug & Unplug.* Both subsections need not be present in this section but it must at least contain one of them. Each subsection contains list of filter-client (server) and filter ids. These ids can be naming service or implementation repository repoids. These ids must be specified in appropriate sub-subsections, i.e., *ClientNS, ClientRepo, FilterNS* and *FilterRepo.* It is possible to plug or unplug one filter to multiple servers and multiple filters to one server.

6.6   Working with Catalysts

Catalysts are processes which manage the filter objects in the system. This involves plugging/unplugging filter objects, mapping filter methods to server methods, and enabling and disabling filter methods selectively. This is achieved using several interfaces provided by the framework.

Toggling with filter objects. Filter objects can be plugged and unplugged from a server object dynamically. This is achieved using the `plug` and `unplug` methods of the `CORBA::ORB` class. Hence before we can plug or unplug filter objects from the system, we need to obtain a local ORB reference. The filter and server object references are passed as parameters.

Mapping method names. Though there are strict rules for filter method signatures with respect to corresponding server method, no such rules exist regarding naming of filter methods. Hence the names of filter methods need to be mapped to the corresponding server methods, they are supposed to filter. The `upfilter` and the `downfilter` methods of the `CORBA::Filter` class map the upfilter and downfilter method names to that of the server class. The mappings are established after a filter object is created. Unless the methods are appropriately mapped, filtering action cannot occur even if the filter has been plugged to the server. In such cases the call continues normally as if no filter exists.

Toggling with filter methods. A filter object can have more than one method mapped to a single server object method. But at the same time at the most only one method can be enabled to act as a filter method for the corresponding server method. The `enable` and `disable` methods of the `CORBA::Filter` class are provided for this purpose. All the filter methods corresponding to a server method being disabled is semantically equivalent to normal invocation of that server method.

7   Applications Using Filters

Distributed object-oriented systems built using MICO can be evolved using transparent filter objects based on inter-class filter relationship. Applications of transparent filter objects include on-line pluggable caches [6] and filter configurations [4] such as loggers, replacers, balancers, routers, monitors etc. Various configurations resulting from the filter relationship along with other meta patterns can be applied to carry out system evolution. It is possible to inject filter objects or a network of filter objects into the system at runtime and satisfy certain kinds of evolutionary requirements without having to bring down an existing system.

8   Performance Evaluation

The performance implications of using the filtered delivery model are discussed in this section. The test setup included Pentium IV machines connected through a 100 Mbps LAN, running MICO version 2.3.4 with integrated filter object framework on Linux.

Table 2 indicates time required to make direct calls to local and remote servers in absence of plugged filters. These timings are used to calculate the overheads of the filter object framework.

Table 3 shows timings for beta messages (control messages) to local and remote servers and filters. Timings for *filtered* method invocation with one filter plugged are shown in Table 4. The table presents the time required to make a filtered call with *Up/Down* filtering enabled and disabled. Time measurements are shown for four configurations of clients and filters: (i) Local Client/Local Filter (ii) Local Client/Remote Filter (iii) Remote Client/Local Filter and (iv) Remote Client/Remote Filter.

Table 2. Direct call

Local server (μs)	660
Remote server (μs)	850

By comparing direct calls (Table 2) and *passed* filtered calls with Up/Down filtering enabled (Table 4), it can be observed that later incurs approximately 2.5 times overheads over direct call. Similarly overheads of *bounced* filtered calls with Up/Down filtering enabled over direct calls are approximately 1.6 times. With Up/Down filtering disabled, overheads are approximately twice that of a

Table 3. Client and filter beta messages

Plug/Unplug	Local server (μs)	Remote server (μs)
	2150	2450
Mappings/Enable /Disable	Local filter (μs)	Remote filter (μs)
	450	530

Table 4. Filtered call

Up/Down		LC/LF	LC/RF	RC/LF	RC/RF
Enabled	Bounce	1090	1300	1160	1190
	Pass	1850	2050	1950	1880
Disabled		1450	1600	1550	1500

direct call. Even with disabled Up/Down filtering, these high overheads can be attributed to filtered method call always consulting plugged filter for its method status, which is controllable at runtime.

Conclusions

A filtering framework was designed and implemented for MICO, an open-source CORBA implementation. The model supports all essential as well as extended filter properties. Filter objects are first class full fledged CORBA objects, which are dynamically pluggable. Filtering framework is supported through modifications to an implementation of MICO version 2.3.4 which is compliant with OMG-CORBA 2.2 standard. Tools have also been developed to support the development process.

References

1. M. Aksit, J. Bosch, L. Bergmans: Abstracting Object Interactions using Composition Filters. Proceedings of the ECOOP'93 Workshop on Object-based Distributed Programming, 1994.
2. Inprise Corp.: Visibroker for JAVA Programmer's Guide, 1999.
3. IONA Technologies PLC.: Orbix Programmer's Guide C++ Edition, 2000.
4. Rushikesh K. Joshi: Filter Configurations for Transparent Interactions in Distributed Object Systems. Journal of Object Oriented Programming. June 2001, pp. 12–17.
5. Rushikesh K. Joshi, Neeraj Agrawal, AspectJ Based Implementation of Dynamically Pluggable Filter Objects in a Distributed Environment, In Proceedings of the 2nd German Workshop on Aspect Oriented Software Development, University of Bonn, Feb. 2002.
6. Rushikesh K. Joshi, N. Vivekananda, D. Janaki Ram: Message Filters for Object-oriented Systems. Software Practice and Experience. June 1997, pp. 677–699.
7. Rushikesh K. Joshi, Maureen R. Mascarenhas: Filter Objects for JAVA, Technical Report, Department of Computer Science and Engineering, Indian Institute of Technology, Bombay, Jan. 2001.

8. P. Narasimhan, L. Moser, P. Melliar-Smith, Using Interceptors to Enhance CORBA, IEEE Computer, July 1999.
9. James Noble, Encapsulators in Self, in ECOOP 1996 Workshop on Prototype Base Object Oriented Programming.
10. Object Management Group (OMG): The Common Object Request Broker: Architecture and Specification 2.4.1, Nov 2000.
11. G. Srirami Reddy and Rushikesh K. Joshi: Filter Objects for Distributed Object Systems. Journal of Object Oriented Programming. Jan 2001, pp. 12–17.
12. Kay Romer, A. Puder and F. Pilhofer, MICO: An Open Source CORBA Implementation. http://www.mico.org.

Design and Performance of a Modular Portable Object Adapter for Distributed, Real-Time, and Embedded CORBA Applications

Raymond Klefstad, Arvind S. Krishna, and Douglas C. Schmidt

Electrical and Computer Engineering Dept.
University of California, Irvine, CA 92697, USA *
{klefstad, krishnaa, schmidt}@uci.edu

Abstract. ZEN is a CORBA ORB designed to support distributed, real-time, and embedded (DRE) applications that have stringent memory constraints. This paper discusses the design and performance of ZENs portable object adapter (POA) which is an important component in a CORBA object request broker (ORB). This paper makes the following three contributions to the study of middleware for memory-constrained DRE applications. First, it presents three alternative designs of the CORBA POA. Second, it explains how design patterns can be applied to improve the quality and performance of POA implementations. Finally, it presents empirical measurements based on the ZEN ORB showing how memory footprint can be reduced significantly while throughput is comparable to a conventional ORB implementation.

Keywords. Distributed Real-time and Embedded Systems, Real-time CORBA, Portable Object Adapter, Real-time Java.

1 Introduction to Distributed, Real-Time, Embedded Systems

Distributed, real-time, and embedded (DRE) systems are becoming increasingly widespread and important. There are many types of DRE systems, but they have one thing in common: *the right answer delivered too late becomes the wrong answer*. Common DRE systems include telecommunication networks (em e.g., wireless phone services), tele-medicine (*e.g.*, remote surgery), manufacturing process automation (*e.g.*, hot rolling mills), and defense applications (*e.g.*, avionics mission computing systems). Over the past decade, distributed object computing (DOC) middleware frameworks, such as CORBA [13], Java RMI [3], and SOAP/.NET [14], have emerged to help reduce the complexity of developing distributed applications.

Real-time CORBA [13] is a rapidly maturing DOC middleware technology standardized by the OMG that can simplify many challenges for DRE applications, just as CORBA has for large-scale business systems. Real-time CORBA

---

* This work was funded in part by ATD, DARPA, SAIC, and Siemens.

R. Meersman, Z. Tari (Eds.): CoopIS/DOA/ODBASE 2002, LNCS 2519, pp. 549–567, 2002.

is designed for applications with hard real-time requirements, such as avionics mission computing It can also handle applications with stringent soft real-time requirements, such as telecommunication call processing and streaming video.

ZEN [17] is an open-source Real-time CORBA object request broker (ORB) implemented in Real-time Java [12]. ZEN is inspired by many of the patterns, techniques, and lessons learned in The ACE ORB (TAO) [18], which is a widely-used, open-source implementation of Real-time CORBA written in C++. A key difference between the design of ZEN and that of earlier CORBA ORBs is its extensive application of the *Virtual Component* pattern [16]. This pattern helps reduce the memory footprint contributed by the middleware by factoring out optional or rarely-used functionality from a specific application of the middleware. Many earlier ORB designs were *monolithic* because they included code that supports all of the possible features, choices, and variants specified in the voluminous CORBA specification [13].

A substantial and significant component of an ORB supporting the style of object-oriented distributed computing is the *portable object adapter* (POA). Unlike its woefully underspecified predecessor, the basic object adapter (BOA), the POA specification is well designed and provides standardized APIs for the POA operations. Some of main functionalities of the POA include: Creating object references with the appropriate policies, Activating and deactivating objects, Etherealizing and Incarnating object implementations (known as *servants* in CORBA terminology) and Demultiplexing requests sent by remote clients to the appropriate servants in the server.[1]

It is important that an ORB's POA implementation be designed and optimized efficiently and predictably since conventional ORBs spend a significant amount of the total server time demultiplexing requests to servants [6]. This paper makes the following contributions to the design of POAs for Real-time CORBA middleware: (1) It describes three alternative designs of the Portable Object Adapter (POA): *monolithic, coarse-grain,* and *fine-grain* architectures. (2) It explains how design patterns [11] can be applied to improve the quality and performance of POA implementations. (3) It presents empirical measurements based on the ZEN ORB showing how memory footprint can be reduced significantly while throughput is comparable to a monolithic/conventional ORB implementation.

The remainder of this paper is organized as follows: Section 2 describes the benefits of a highly-modular architecture and two alternative highly-modular architectures for a POA. Section 3 provides empirical results for the alternative POA designs and compares the performance of ZEN's POA against the performance of JacORB's POA [5]; Section 4 compares our work on POAs with related work; and Section 5 presents concluding remarks and outlines future work.

---

[1] For a detailed description about POAs, POA policies, POA structure and Dynamics, refer to [8]

2   The Design of ZEN's POA

This section details both the goals for ZEN's POA and several alternative POA design that may achieve those goals. Each alternative design is implemented and the benchmark comparisons are presented in Section 3.

2.1   Goals of ZEN's POA Design

Our experience building TAO taught us that to achieve a small middleware footprint, feature subsetting must be planned early in the design stages since it is hard to reduce footprint after an implementation has become tightly coupled. Pluggability of optional components, ease of extension, and footprint reduction are primary design goals for ZEN and the POA. More specifically, we have the following goals for ZEN's POA design:

Minimize footprint. An important goal of ZEN's POA design is to achieve a small memory footprint for the middleware suitable for DRE systems. Each application should only incorporate the sections of middleware code that it actually needs. By decomposing the POA into Virtual Components, the POA requires minimal memory for each application using ZEN.

Ease adaptation to new changes in the CORBA specification. A pluggable, highly-modular POA design applies the core software engineering concept of *separation of concerns*. Each of the Virtual Components in ZEN's POA encapsulates the implementation for a particular POA policy.

Facilitate addition of new custom POA polices. ZEN is a research platform, so it is important to enable experiments with new algorithms, data structures, and capabilities.

2.2   Alternative POA Architectures

This section presents an overview of each of the three alternative POA design architectures we implemented, measured, and compared: *monolithic POA, coarse-grain POA,* and *fine-grain POA.*

Monolithic POA Architecture. In a monolithic POA architecture, the POA is a single large component that contains the semantics needed to implement (1) policies in the OMG's POA specification and (2) ORB-specific policies. The monolithic design can increase the footprint (both code and data size) of the POA considerably since the POA implements the behavior required by the entire set of policies, rather than a minimal subset. Monolithic POA also cannot be easily extended as new polices are added to the CORBA POA specification. Moreover, monolithic POA implementations complicate the addition of ORB-specific policies. Monolithic POA implementations also suffer from inefficiency in terms of redundant checking required to determine the appropriate course of action based on POA policies.

Coarse-grain POA Architecture. In a coarse-grain POA architecture, the POA is still a single, large component, but we apply the Virtual Component pattern treating the entire POA as one component so it can be plugged-in or removed as shown in Figure 1.

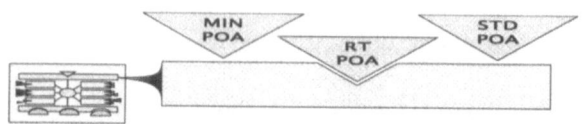

Fig. 1. Pluggable Object Adapters

A coarse-grain POA architecture is useful for pure clients, which need no object adapter and can reduce their footprint by completely removing all POA methods. It also useful for pure servers, which can reduce their footprint and achieve custom functionality by loading the most appropriate POA (*e.g.*, the RootPOA on demand. The coarse-grain pluggable POA design also simplifies the addition of new object adapters as they are standardized by the OMG. This coarse-grained POA architecture has been implemented in TAO [18] using the Component Configurator [11] pattern and dynamic link libraries (DLLs) to load each POA implementation variant.

Fine-grain POA Architecture. In ZEN, we have more aggressively applied the Virtual Component pattern to allow greater subsetting of portions of the POA based on the application's needs. We call this the "fine-grain POA architecture." In this approach, instead of an all-or-nothing loading of the POA, individual components of the POA can be loaded as needed.

Based on our work with TAO [8], we observed it is possible to divide the POA into smaller pieces and make them virtual components. Such a fine-grain level of control can further reduce the footprint of a POA when it is needed by an application. We have found it useful to decompose the POA as dictated by the values of the POA policies. Each of the CORBA POA policies has a set of policy values that specify the behavior of the POA with that policy. By breaking down the policies according to their possible values, it is therefore possible to load only the pieces that the POA needs, based on the list of policies specified at POA creation time. For example, the Figure 2 shows the fine-grain architecture of the ZEN POA, each POA policy is factored out into a separate class hierarchy by applying the Strategy pattern [2], as described next in Section 2.3.

2.3   The Design of ZEN's Fine-Grain POA Architecture

The remainder of this section describes how ZEN's POA is decomposed into modular components in accordance with POA policy values. We then provide an overview of each POA policy and explain how ZEN implements this policy in a highly modular manner using the Virtual Components of ZEN's fine-grain POA architecture.

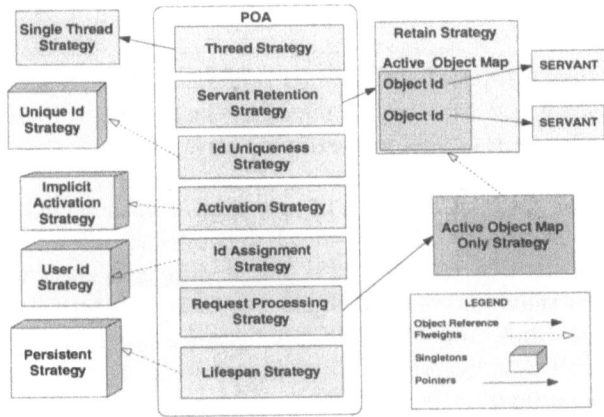

Fig. 2. Fine-grain Architecture of the ZEN POA

Primary POA Components. The four strategies described below are considered to be *primary components* in ZEN, *i.e.*, their behavior does not depend on other components. At POA creation time, these components are created first and hold the smallest amount of state. The following are the primary components of the POA.

ThreadStrategy component. This component implements the *Thread* policy, which is used to specify the threading model used in the POA. The POA can have one of the following threading models: *single thread*, *ORB controlled*, or *main thread*. If the POA is single-threaded, all the requests of the POA are processed sequentially. In a multi-threaded environment, all upcalls to the servant are invoked in a manner that is safe for multi-thread unaware code. In contrast, in the ORB-controlled model, multiple requests may be delivered simultaneously using multiple threads. All requests to a main thread POA are processed sequentially in the thread that runs the `main()` function. All upcalls made by POAs with this policy to servants are made in a manner that is safe for thread-unaware code. If the environment has special requirements that some code must run on a distinguished main thread, servant upcalls will be processed on that thread.

Using the Strategy pattern, the semantics of implementing the *Thread* policy can be strategized into two alternatives: class `SingleThread` and class `ORBContro-1Model`. Each class encapsulates the state and the logic of implementing the behavior specified by the policy. In ZEN,the main thread model strategy and the single thread strategy are equivalent. Figure 3 shows the class diagram for ZEN's `ThreadPolicyStrategy` alternatives.

At POA creation time, a factory method `init()` in the base class `ThreadPo-licyStrategy` creates the appropriate strategy instance based on the POA's policy list. Since the `ORBControl` component does not maintain state specific to a POA, it is implemented using the Flyweight pattern [2]. This pattern uses sharing to support large numbers of fine-grain objects efficiently, which means there is one instance of the `ORBControl` object. Prior to making the upcall on the servant, the POA uses the `ThreadPolicyStrategy`'s `enter()` method. If the `SingleThread` strategy is in place, this method acquires a mutex lock. After the upcall is performed, the `exit()` method releases the lock. This synchronization is not present in the `ORBControlModel` strategy.

LifespanStrategy component. This component implements the *Lifespan* policy, which is used to specify whether the CORBA object references created within a POA are persistent or transient. Persistent object references can outlive the process in which they are created. Unlike persistent object references, transient object references cannot outlive the POA instance in which they were first created. After the POA is deactivated, the use of object references generated from it will result in an `OBJECT_NOT_EXIST` exception.

The mechanism for implementing the POA's *Lifespan* policy has been separated into ZEN's `Persistent` and `Transient` strategies. Figure 4 shows the class diagram of the `LifespanStrategy` component. The responsibilities of the strategy include the creation of object ids for objects registered with the POA and validation of object keys contained in the client requests.

When asked to activate an object, the POA uses the `create()` method to generate an object id for the CORBA object. The object id generated depends on the concrete strategy loaded into the ORB. For example, the object id generated by a transient transient POA has a time stamp. When a client request is received, the `validate()` method of the `LifespanStrategy` determines whether it was this POA that generated the object id. If the POA is transient and the above is not true then a `OBJECT_NOT_EXIST` exception is returned to the client. In the persistent case, the adapter activator of the closest existing ancestor is used to create the POA automatically. In ZEN, the persistent strategy does not maintain state specific to a POA, so it can be implemented as a flyweight `PersistentStrategy` object.

ActivationStrategy component. This component implements the `Activa-tion` policy, which is used to specify whether implicit activation of servants is supported in the POA. If the implicit activation policy is active,

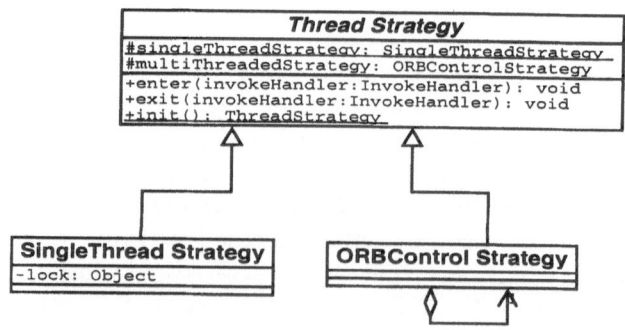

Fig. 3. ZEN's Thread Strategy

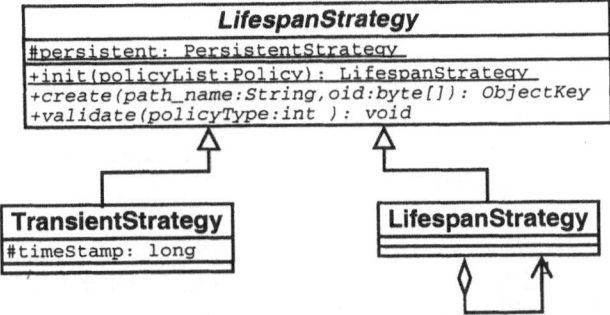

Fig. 4. ZEN's Lifespan Strategy

it causes two things to happen when the servant method _this() is called: (1) The servant is registered with the POA and (2) The object reference for that servant is implicitly created. Without this policy, the server must call either activate_object() or activate_object_with_id() to achieve this effect.

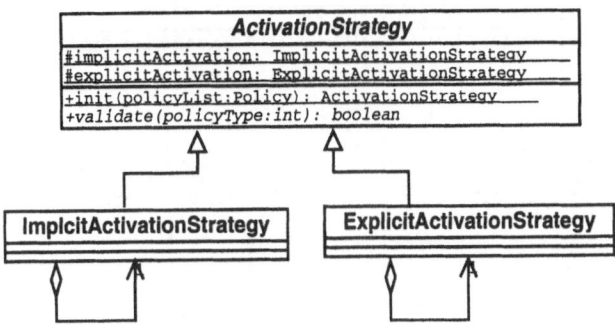

Fig. 5. ZEN's Activation Strategy

ZEN uses the ActivationStrategy shown in Figure 5, to implement the behavior required by the *ImplicitActivation* policy. The validate() method is invoked to check if implicit activation is permitted, on this POA. Depending on the concrete strategy that is plugged into the ORB, the operation returns true or false. For example, the servant_to_id() and servant_to_reference() operations use the method to check if implicit activation is allowed. Both of the following concrete strategies, ImplicitActivationStrategy and ExplicitActivati-onStrategy maintain no state within them and are implemented as flyweights to conserve memory.

Secondary POA Components. The secondary components in ZEN are strategies whose behavior depends on the values of primary strategies. These dependencies can lead to conflicts. When two policies cannot co-exist they are said to be in *conflict*. If the policy list specified at POA creation has conflicts, the strategies would also be in conflict. For example, if the *ImplicitActivation* policy value is IMPLICIT_ACTIVATION, the *IdAssignment* policy value cannot be USER_ID. In ZEN, these conflicts are identified at strategy creation time (that is, *before* processing client requests), and appropriate response can be taken (for instance, raise an exception to the user, apply reflection to automatically select a non-conflicting set of policies, etc).

IdAssignmentStrategy component. This component implements the *IdAssignment* policy, which is used to specify whether object ids in the POA are generated by the application or by the POA. The possible object id assignment policy values are either **User-assigned** or **System-assigned**. Moreover, if the POA has both the SYSTEM_ID *IdAssignment* policy and PERSISTENT *Lifespan* policy enabled, object ids generated must be unique across all instantiations of the same POA. If the POA has the *ImplicitActivation* policy, this policy's value cannot be USER_ID. This subtle interaction between POA policy values is implicit, but must be enforced at POA creation time.

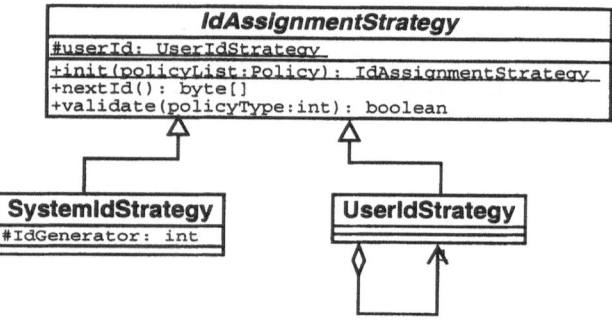

Fig. 6. ZEN's Id Assignment Strategy

In ZEN, the IdAssignmentStrategy class models the behavior required by the Id Assignment policy. The interface of the IdAssignmentStrategy is shown in Figure 6. The init() factory method, that creates the concrete strategy also checks for conflicts and raises the WRONG_POLICY exception if necessary. The only responsibility of this strategy is to generate object ids for registering objects with the POA.

Under certain conditions, POA operations, such as activate_object() and servant_to_id(), can activate servant using POA generated object ids. The nextId() method generates the new object id if the system id policy value is present in the POA. If the user id policy value is present, a WRONG_POLICY exception is raised. The semantics of incorporating the above behavior is present each of the concrete strategies. The UserIdStrategy does not maintain any state specific to a POA, so it is designed as a flyweight.

IdUniquenessStrategy component. This component implements the *IdUniqueness* policy, which is used to specify if the servants activated in the POA must have unique object ids. If the policy value is unique id, servant activated by the POA support exactly one object Id. With the multiple id policy, servants activated by the POA may support multiple object Ids. The use of unique id policy value in conjunction with the *NonRetain* policy is meaningless. The OMG specification allows the ORB not to report an error if this combination is used, in ZEN this is considered to be in conflict and a `WRONG_POLICY` exception is raised.

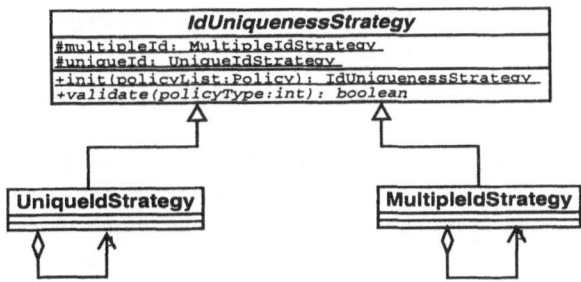

Fig. 7. ZEN's Id-Uniqueness Strategy

The `IdUniquenessStrategy` enforces the behavior required by the policy. Figure 7 shows the class diagram and the concrete strategies that extend the `IdUniquenessStrategy`. The `validate()` method is used by the POA to check for the policy value associated with the POA. For example, `activate_object()` operation before activation of an already existing servant, calls the `validate()` method to check if re-registration is permitted. Both the concrete strategies do not maintain any state within them and hence are designed as flyweight references.

ServantRetentionStrategy component. This component implements the *Servant Retention* policy, which is used to specify if the POA retains the active servants in an active object map. This policy can either have retain or non-retain as the possible policy values. Some combinations of POA policies are not allowed. For example, the *ServantRetention* policy may have a value of `NON_RETAIN` and an *ImplicitActivation* policy may have a value of `IMPLICIT_ACTIVATION`, but they cannot have those values simultaneously since they conflict with one another. Again, these implicit and subtle issues must be enforced at POA creation time.

In ZEN, the `ServantRetentionStrategy` models the behavior required by the *ServantRetention* policy. Figure 8 shows the concrete strategies that extend the `ServantRetentionStrategy`. The `ServantRetentionStrategy` maintains an active object map where the association between the CORBA object and the servant is maintained. If a POA has unique id and retain policies, there

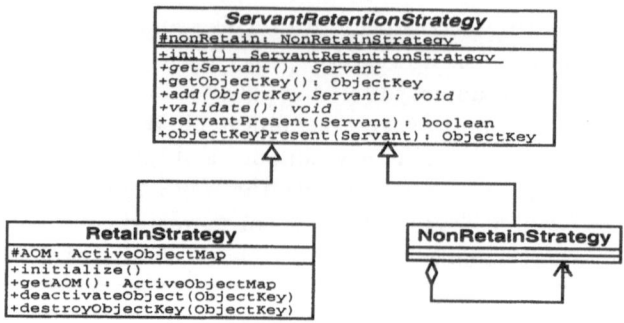

Fig. 8. ZEN's Servant Retention Strategy

exists a one-to-one relationship between the object ids and servants and vice versa. In this case, operations `servant_to_id()` and `servant_to_reference()` support reverse lookups (*e.g.*, given a pointer to a servant, return the object associated with it). To speed up these operations, ZEN uses a reverse map that maps servants to their object ids. Since this reverse map is only needed in certain cases, the active object map is further strategized into Single and Dual Maps .

The optimization describe above further reduces the footprint of the POA when a multiple id policy value is used. In the traditional approach, operations requiring lookups on the active object map would have to be preceded by guard conditions that check if the POA has the retain policy. In ZEN, depending on the concrete strategy in place, these either produce the desired behavior or raise the `WRONG_POLICY` exception. The `NonRetainStrategy` encapsulates the mechanism of enforcing the non-retain policy. This strategy does not maintain any state specific to the POA and is implemented as a flyweight. All POA's having the non-retain policy have references to this flyweight.

RequestProcessingStrategy component. This component implements the *RequestProcessing* policy, which specifies how the POA should process requests. On receipt of a request, the POA based on the request processing policy value can do one of the following.

Consult the active object map only. The POA using the object id searches the map for the associated Servant. It then uses that servant to process the request. If unsuccessful, an exception is returned to the client.

Use a default servant. If the POA has the *Retain* policy and Step 1 is unsuccessful, then a default servant if present is used to service the request. If a default servant has not been associated or the POA does not have the policy an exception is returned to the client.

Use Servant Manager. If the POA has the *UseServantManager* policy, the application supplied manager can be asked to incarnate/activate a servant for the object id. This servant is used by the POA to service the request. Depending on the *ServantRetention* policy, the servant manager can either be a servant activator or a servant locator.

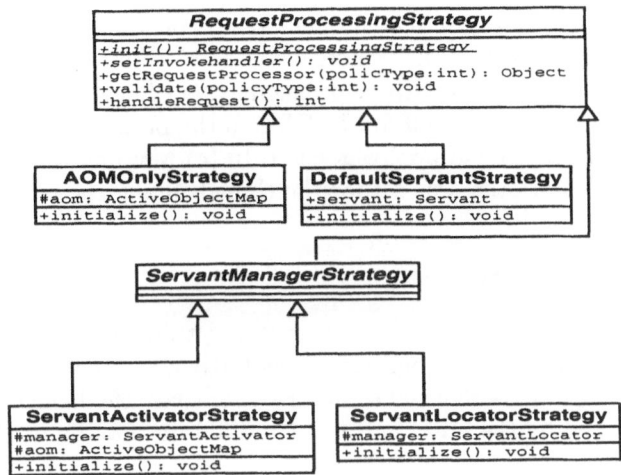

Fig. 9. Request Processing Strategy

The *RequestProcessing* policy is strategized along the three alternate courses of action mentioned above. Figure 9 shows the class diagram for the RequestPro-cessingStrategy. ActiveObjectMapOnlyStrategy encapsulates the logic of request dispatch if the active object map only policy is used. The POA uses the handleRequest() method of the base strategy strategy to service requests.

The DefaultServantStrategy is associated with the POA if the appropriate policy value is used. Depending on the servant retention policy value, this strategy either consults the active object map first for request dispatch, or uses the default servant. If the non-retain policy value is used the POA, the servant is directly used. In either of the cases, if no servant is associated with the POA, an exception is raised.

The ServantManagerStrategy is associated with the POA if the Use Servant Manager policy value is specified. Moreover, depending on the *ServantRetention* policy for the POA, this is strategized into a ServantActivatorStrategy or a ServantLocatorStrategy. Each of these concrete strategies have the semantics necessary for request dispatch. In a traditional POA implementation, each time a POA receives a request it must check the value of the request processing policy. In ZEN, however, the semantics of request processing in each case is present in the concrete strategy for that policy, so the policy value need not be checked at all.

3   Empirical Results

This section presents the results of both blackbox and whitebox benchmark measurements. These measurements were performed on a dual-CPU Intel Xeon 1,700 Mhz processor with 256 KB of main memory. The experiments compare the results obtained from ZEN version 0.8 alpha with that of JacORB version

1.4 beta 4. All tests were conducted on JVM version 1.4.0 running on Linux OS 2.4.18. Further, to eliminate differences in the POA configurations, the following properties were set in both ZEN and JacORB: (1) Logging was turned off (2) POA monitoring was turned off for JacORB in the properties file. (3) The number of threads in the thread pool was set to 10 (4) Maximum queue size was set to 100 and (5) No priority was set for the threads doing the request processing.

3.1 Blackbox Experiments

Blackbox experiments do not instrument the software internals when evaluating the performance tests. In our case, each ORB was benchmarked end-to-end without knowledge of its internal structure. Moreover, the benchmarks used operations published by the ORB interfaces and did not modify or restructure the ORB internals.

Root POA Metrics

Overview. As discussed earlier, the root POA is an integral part of every CORBA server and is always present, whether or not any other child POAs exist. A root POA suffices for many applications, unless the server needs to provide different QoS guarantees, such as object reference persistence. Thus, minimizing the footprint of the root POA is vital to minimizing server footprint.

This test measures the increase in footprint after the root POA has been associated with the ORB. The memory increase prior to and after the call to the `resolve_initial_references()` gives the foot print increase contributed by the root POA.

Results and analysis. Figure 10 illustrates that the footprint of the root POA in ZEN is 61 kbytes, while that of JacORB is 180 kbytes. Thus, ZEN's root

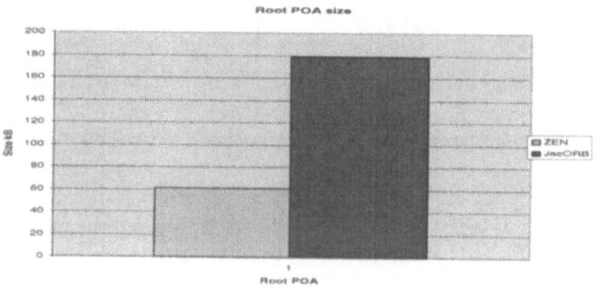

Fig. 10. Root POA Footprint

POA is one third the size of JacORB's root POA. In ZEN, the creation of the root POA results in initialization of all the base abstract strategies and the creation of the appropriate concrete strategies for the root POA policies. The root POA maintains the maximum state among all POAs in ZEN. This small footprint bolsters the micro POA design in the ZEN. Since JacORB is designed monolithically, it suffers from a larger memory footprint.

Child POA Footprint Metrics

Overview. A key design goal of the micro POA architecture is to minimize footprint for DRE systems. This paper would therefore be incomplete without the results for the footprint analysis for the child POAs. A CORBA server creates child POAs for the CORBA objects if the QoS parameters require persistent object reference, memory reduction (*e.g.*, associating multiple objects with a default servant), etc.

This test measures the variation of footprint with the number of POAs created. The increase in footprint prior to and after the call to the `create_POA()` method is measured in each of the case. Each of the POAs created have the following policy values: (1) *NonRetain* policy, (2) *ServantManager* policy, and (3) *UserId* policy. This combination is chosen as since it minimizes the footprint for the ZEN POA.

Results and analysis. Figure 11 shows how memory increases with the number of child POAs. Both JacORB and ZEN, grow linearly. Though ZEN seems to be constant, it rate of growth is very low. The average size of the child POAs in ZEN is 35 kbytes, while that of JacORB is around 300 kbytes. Thus, on average JacORB's POA is larger by a factor of 8.

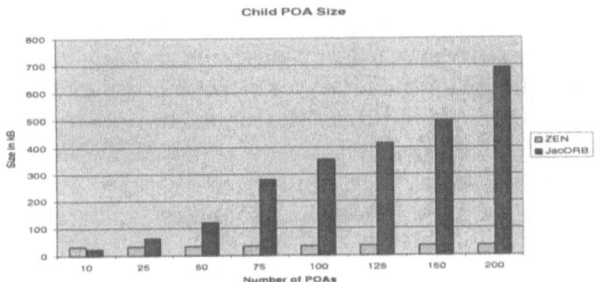

Fig. 11. Child POA Footprint Results

Several factors, other than just the POA, may contribute to the footprint increase. In the case of JacORB, the contribution of these other factors is significant. For example, in JacORB for every POA created, the following additional overhead occurs.

1. A request controller is associated with each POA. The Request controller is a thread pool that manages the request processing for that POA. In ZEN, the thread pool is associated with the ORB and not with each POA. For example, when 100 child POAs are created in JacORB, each POA has its own thread pool and specified channel capacity, adding significantly to the footprint of POA.

2. A POA monitor is initialized with every POA created even if monitoring is disabled in the properties file.

Even if a POA has only default set of policies, however, due to JacORB's monolithic design it still has the semantics for implementing ORB-specific policies, such as bi-directional GIOP. For the reasons mentioned above, the relative difference between the sizes of the POAs for ZEN and JacORB is large. Even with these differences, ZEN's design is more scalable since the footprint increase is minimal with an increase in the number of POAs created.

3.2   Whitebox Experiments

Whitebox benchmarks are a performance evaluation technique where explicit knowledge of software internals is used to select the benchmark data. Unlike blackbox benchmarks, whitebox tests uses instrumentation of software internals to evaluate performance. Below, we present whitebox experiments on POA-related demultiplexing that were conducted using JacORB and ZEN.

A key function of a POA is demultiplexing of requests to servants. Demultiplexing in conventional CORBA implementations is typically inefficient and unpredictable. For instance, [6] show that conventional ORBs spend 17% of the total server time processing demultiplexing requests. Constant time request demultiplexing regardless of organization of the POA hierarchy or number of POAs, servants, or operations, allows an ORB to provide uniform, scalable QoS guarantees to real-time applications.

In the whitebox experiments, a single-threaded client issued IDL operations at the fastest possible rate using a "flooding" model. Timers used internally within the ORB Core measure the *dispatch time* for each client request. Dispatch time was measured as the time taken for request processing from the time when the appropriate POA is found until the time the request was delivered to the servant. This definition of dispatch time eliminated the demarshaling overhead and measured the demultiplexing time required by the POA. The variation of average dispatch time with the depth of the POA hierarchy, breadth of the hierarchy and the number of objects registered with the POA was measured. These metrics underscore the dependency of dispatch time on the aforementioned factors.

POA Demultiplexing

Overview. The first step in the request delivery is to determine which POA will service the request. As explained earlier, the POA hierarchy can be arbitrarily deep and broad. Traditionally, ORBs performed a look up for each level of the POA hierarchy until the "leaf" POA is reached. This linear search strategy is expensive, however, and increases the demultiplexing time greatly. This test measures the variation in the POA demultiplexing time with the increase in the depth, breadth, and number of objects of the POA hierarchy.

Results. Figure 12 compares the effect of the depth of the POA hierarchy on the demultiplexing times for ZEN and JacORB. The latency of ZEN and JacORB both increase with the depth of the POA hierarchy. However, ZEN's degradation

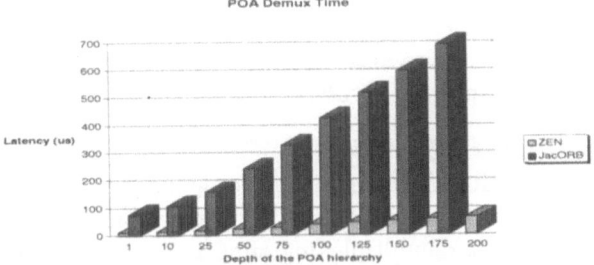

Fig. 12. POA Demux Time v/s Depth of the POA Hierarchy

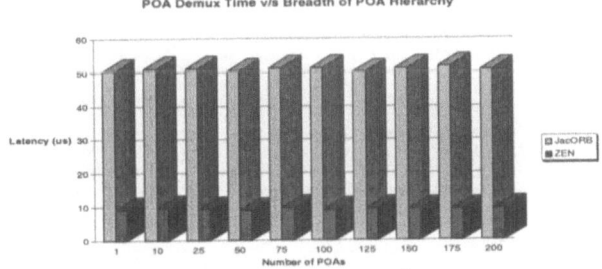

Fig. 13. POA Demux Time v/s Breadth of POA Hierarchy

is more graceful than JacORB's. This behavior stems from the fact that ZEN flattens the POA hierarchy so the appropriate POA servicing the request can be determined in a single lookup.[2] In contrast, JacORB incurs a lookup for ever depth of the POA hierarchy, leading to the steep degradation of its performance as the POA hierarchy deepens.

ZEN stores the complete POA path name (similar to the path name of a directory or URL), along with the POA reference, in a hash table.[3] The linear increase in ZEN is due to the increase in the length of the POA path name with the deepening of the POA hierarchy. This increase in path name contributes to comparison time needed for a successful lookup, though ZEN is still much faster than JacORB. Figure 13 compares the variation in the demultiplexing time with the breadth of the POA hierarchy. This figure shows that the POA demultiplexing time remains constant for both ZEN and JacORB as the breadth and the number of objects in the POA hierarchy are increased. However, the latency in JacORB is much higher than in ZEN, which can be attributed to JacORB's sequential traversal of the POA namespace.

---

[2] If the lookup fails, the POA hierarchy is traversed sequentially and the required POAs are activated using the user-supplied adapter activator.

[3] We are currently using `Hashtable` provided by Java, *i.e.*, `java.util.Hashtable`.

To prevent the linear increase of demultiplexing time with the depth of the POA hierarchy, an *active demultiplexing* strategy (such as the one used in TAO [8]) should be used. Predictability is essential for real-time systems, so we will add active demultiplexing to ZEN before release version 1.0.

Servant Demultiplexing

Overview. Once the ORB Core demultiplexes a client request to the right POA, this POA demultiplexes the request to the corresponding servant. In this test, the variation of servant demultiplexing time is measured with the number of active objects in the POA.

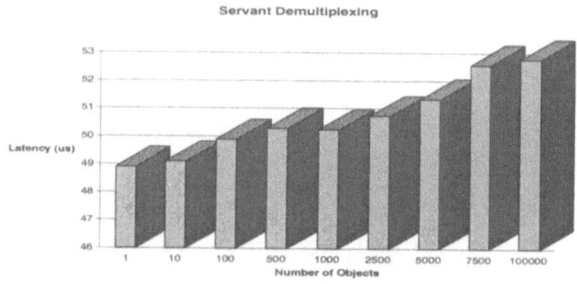

Fig. 14. Servant Demultiplexing Time

Results. Figure 14 shows the variation of servant demultiplexing time with the increase in the number of servant in the active object map. In ZEN, we are are currently using dynamic hashing for this stage of demultiplexing (as before, we use the hash table provided by Java's `java.util.Hashtable`). To locate the appropriate servant, the POA uses the object id part of the object key to look up the servant in the active object map, hence this stage is independent of the POA hierarchy. There are three steps in locating a servant: (1) Parsing the object key (2) Checking if the key is present and (3) Looking up the appropriate hash data structure that contains the servant.

ZEN's servant demultiplexing implementation incurs a significant overhead during hash table lookup operations that contribute to its latency, which stems from the synchronized methods of Java's `java.util.Hashtable` class. Some overhead is also necessary to compute the hash function, which uses the `hash-Code()` method of Java's `String` class. In addition, there is a gradual increase in the latency with the increase in the number of active objects in the POA. As stated above, in the first non-alpha release of ZEN we will also be implementing an active demultiplexing scheme for this stage of demultiplexing.

JacORB does not allow associating multiple objects with a single servant, even with the *Multiple-Id* policy value for the POA, so we are unable to present its results.

Operation Demultiplexing

Overview. The final step at the Object Adapter layer involves demultiplexing a request to the appropriate servant's skeleton. This skeleton then demarshals the request and dispatches the designated operation upcall in the servant. For real-time embedded systems, operation demultiplexing should be efficient, scalable, and predictable. To prevent variations in operation dispatch time with number of methods, we use a Java-variant of GPERF [1] called JPERF, which is an open-source perfect hash function generator. JPERF automatically constructs perfect hash functions from a user-supplied list of keywords. Perfect hashing is predictable and efficient, and outperforms other search techniques, such as binary search and dynamic hashing. JacORB uses dynamic hashing for this stage.[4]

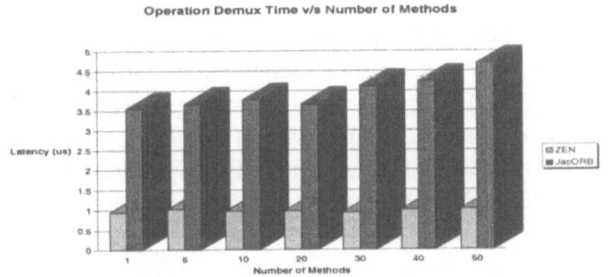

Fig. 15. Operation Demultiplexing Time

Results. Figure 15 illustrates the variation in operation demultiplexing time as the number of methods increases. This figure shows that operation lookup is constant in ZEN and does not vary with the increase in the number of methods. Latency in ZEN is ~1 μsec, while that of JacORB is ~4 μsecs. The higher latency of JacORB stems from its dynamic hashing overhead, which also increases the lookup time as the number of methods increase.

4   Related Work

TAO's Portable Object Adapter. TAO is an open-source, high-performance real-time ORB written in C++. TAO had the first implementation of the POA specification [8]. The design of the POA is based on several design patterns, many of which have been adopted in ZEN. TAO also uses an optimized set of request processing strategies [9], *e.g.*, active demultiplexing and perfect hashing. These strategies allow TAO's POA to provide constant-time lookup of servants

---

[4] For our experiments, we used `java.util.Hashtable` for both ZEN and JacORB.

based on object keys and operation names contained in CORBA requests. In ZEN, we have based our design on several optimizations used in the design of TAO's POA, *e.g.*, perfect hashing for O(1) time servant lookups and flattening the POA hierarchy to prevent a lookup for every level in the POA hierarchy.

JacORB. JacORB [5] is an open-source Java ORB developed at the University of Berlin. Like TAO, JacORB has been widely embraced in the industry. Likewise, JacORB has a monolithic POA design. JacORB also has a POA monitoring GUI that can be used to monitor the operations on the POA and request dispatch. JacORB does not implement some of the request demultiplexing techniques discussed earlier, *e.g.*, perfect hashing or flattening the POA hierarchy that help in bounding lookup times.

Reflective POAs. One other possible solution to fine-grain control over the components of the POA is to apply advanced meta-programming techniques, such as reflection [7,10,15] and aspect-oriented programming [4], These techniques can be used to auto-generate most of the POA in such a way that only a minimal amount of space is used, while still supporting the standard CORBA APIs. Our future research will focus on exploring this alternative.

5   Concluding Remarks and Future Work

ZEN is a long-term research project with well-defined goals targeting distributed, real-time, and embedded (DRE) applications. We learned from our experience with TAO that a small memory footprint must be achieved during the initial design phase. ZEN's POA has been decomposed into a highly-modular, loosely coupled set of Virtual Components that may be loaded either on a fine-grain or a coarse-grain bases - depending on the application developers configuration options. This paper presents empirical results that measure the footprint and performance of three alternative POA designs. The conclusion is that considerable footprint savings can result from the fine-grain highly-modular design, without unduly reducing performance relative to existing Java ORBs.

References

1. Schmidt,D.C : GPERF: A Perfect Hash Function Generator Proceedings of the 2nd C++ Conference USENIX Vol.10, No.10 (1990) 87–102
2. Gamma, E., Helm, R., Johnson, R., Vlisside, J.: Design Patterns: Elements of Reusable Object-Oriented Software Addison-Wesley, Reading, Massachusetts (1995)
3. Wollrath, A., Riggs, R., Wald, J.: A Distributed Object Model for the Java Systems USENIX Computing Systems Vol.9, No.4 (1996)
4. Kiczales, G., Lamping, J., Mendhekar, A.,Maeda,C.,Lopez,C.V,Loingtier,J.,Irwin, J.: Aspect-Oriented Programming Proceedings of the 11th European Conference on Object-Oriented Programming 1997

5. Brose, G: JacORB: Implementation and Design of a Java ORB Proc. DAIS'97, IFIP WG 6.1 International Working Conference on Distributed Aplications and Interoperable Systems, Chapman & Hall (1997) 143–154
6. Gokhale, A., Schmidt, D.C : Measuring and Optimizing CORBA Latency and Scalability Over High-speed Networks, IEEE Transactions on Computing, Vol.47, No.4 (1998)
7. Blair, G.S, Coulson, G., Robin, P., Papathomas, M.: An Architecture for Next Generation Middleware, Distributed Systems Platforms and Open Distributed Processing, Springer-Verlag London, (1998) 191–206
8. Pyarali, I., Schmidt, D.C: An Overview of the CORBA Portable Object Adapter, ACM StandardView, Vol. 6, No.1 (1998)
9. Pyarali, I. O'Ryan, C., Schmidt, D.C, Wang, N., Kachroo V., Gokhale, A.: Applying Optimization Patterns to the Design of Real-time ORBs, Proceedings of the 5th Conference on Object-Oriented Technologies and Systems, USENIX (1999)
10. Costa, F.M, Blair, S: A Reflective Architecture for Middleware: Design and Implementation ECOOP'99, Workshop for PhD Students in Object Oriented Systems (1999)
11. Schmidt, D.C., Stal, M., Rohnert, H., Buschman, F: Pattern-Oriented Software Architecture: Patterns for Concurrent and Networked Objects, Volume 2 Wiley & Sons New York (2000)
12. Bollella, Gosling, Brosgol, Dibble, Furr, Hardin, Turnbul: The Real-Time Specification for Java Addison-Wesley (2000)
13. Object Management Group: The Common Object Request Broker: Architecture and Specification (2001)
14. Snell, J., MacLeo, K.: Programming Web Applications with SOAP O'Reilly (2001)
15. Kon, F., Costa, F., Blair, G., Campbel, R.H: The Case for Reflective Middleware, Cacm, Vol.45, No.6 (2002) 33–38
16. Corsaro, A., Schmidt, D.C, Klefstad, R., O'Ryan, C.: Virtual Component: a Design Pattern for Memory-Constrained Embedded Applications, 9th Annual Conference on the Pattern Languages of Program (2002) (to appear)
17. Klefstad,R., Schmidt, D.C, O'Ryan, C.: Towards Highly Configurable Real-time Object Request Brokers International Symposium on Object-Oriented Real-time Distributed Computing (2002)
18. Center for Distributed Object Computing: The ACE ORB (TAO) www.cs.wustl.edu/~schmidt/TAO.htm Washington University

Design and Performance of Asynchronous Method Handling for CORBA*

Mayur Deshpande, Douglas C. Schmidt, Carlos O'Ryan, and Darrell Brunsch

Department of Electrical and Computer Engineering,
University of California, Irvine, 92612
{deshpanm,schmidt,coryan,brunsch}@uci.edu

Abstract. This paper describes the design and performance of a new mechanism, called asynchronous method handling (AMH), that allows CORBA servers to process client requests asynchronously. AMH decouples the association of an incoming request from the run-time stack that received the request, without incurring the context-switching, synchronization, and data movement overhead of conventional CORBA multi-threading models.

This paper provides two contributions to the study of asynchrony for CORBA servers. First, it describes the design and implementation of AMH in The ACE ORB (TAO), a C++ CORBA ORB. The syntax and semantics of AMH are defined using the CORBA Interface Definition Language (IDL), the forces that guided the design of AMH are described, and the patterns and C++ idioms used to resolve these forces are presented. Second, we empirically compare a middle-tier server implemented using AMH against other CORBA server concurrency models and show the advantages of the AMH mechanism against the other models.

1 Introduction

Problem → scalable servers. For many types of distributed applications, the CORBA asynchronous method invocation (AMI) mechanism can improve concurrency, scalability, and responsiveness significantly [18]. AMI allows clients to invoke multiple two-way requests without waiting synchronously for responses. The time normally spent waiting for replies can therefore be used to perform other useful work.

CORBA AMI is completely transparent to servers, *i.e.*, a server does not know whether a request it received, emanated from a synchronous or asynchronous method invocation. Therefore, while AMI improves throughput in client applications, it does not improve server applications, particularly *middle-tier servers* [19]. In these architectures, one or more intermediate servers are interposed between a source client and a sink server, as shown in Figure 1.

Middle-tier servers can be used for many types of systems, such as (1) a firewall gateway that validates requests from external clients before forwarding

---

* This work was supported in part by ATD, SAIC, and Siemens MED.

R. Meersman, Z. Tari (Eds.): CoopIS/DOA/ODBASE 2002, LNCS 2519, pp. 568–586, 2002.

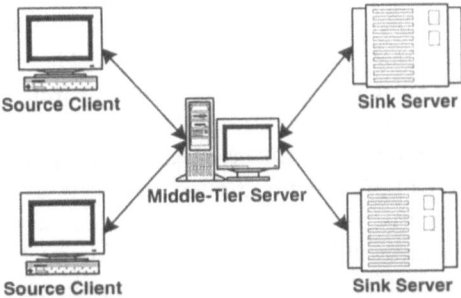

Fig. 1. A Three-tier Client/Server Architecture

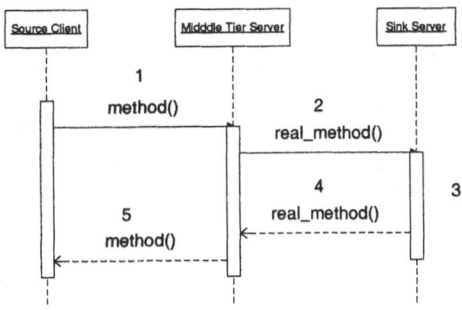

Fig. 2. Conventional CORBA Middle-tier Server Interactions

them to sink server or (2) a load-balancer [20] that distributes access to a group of database servers. In both cases, the middle-tier servers act as *intermediaries* that accept requests from a client and then pass the requests on to another server or external data source. When an intermediary receives a response, it sends its own response back to the source client.

The general behavior of a middle-tier server is summarized in Figure 2, where a middle-tier server blocks awaiting a reply to return from a sink server. The following steps typically occur in this type of server:

1. The source client invokes an operation on the middle-tier server
2. The middle-tier server processes the request and invokes an operation on a sink server
3. The sink server processes the operation
4. The sink server returns the data to the middle-tier server and
5. The middle-tier server returns the data to the client.

Unlike ordinary source clients, middle-tier servers must communicate with multiple source clients and sink servers. They must therefore be highly scalable to avoid becoming a bottleneck. A common way to improve the throughput of a middle-tier server is to multi-thread it using various concurrency models [21], such as thread pool, thread-per-connection, or thread-per-request. In these models, threads can process new incoming client requests even while other threads are blocked waiting to receive a response from a sink server. Due to the cost of thread creation, context switching, synchronization, and data movement, however, it may not be scalable to have many threads in the server. In particular, each of the above concurrency models have the following limitations:

- Thread pool—The number of threads in the pool limits the throughput of the thread pool model. For example, if all threads are blocked waiting for replies from sink servers no new requests can be handled, which can degrade the throughput of busy middle-tier servers.
- Thread-per-request—If each request creates a new thread, this concurrency model may not scale when a high volume of requests spawns an excessive number of threads.
- Thread-per-connection—The server can also run out of threads in this model if a large number of clients connect to the server at once. Moreover, if a server is busy processing a client's request, that client can open a new connection to send a new request. If the server is slow in processing a client request, a single client may create a large number of connections and threads on the server, further slowing it down.

The overhead for threads motivates the need for another way to increase middle-tier server scalability. Unfortunately, these servers cannot leverage the benefits of AMI fully since AMI only provides asynchrony to clients. In a middle-tier server, therefore, outgoing requests can use AMI to return control from the ORB (Object Request Broker) quickly, but the request handler for incoming requests must remain active until a response can be returned to the source client. In particular, each request needs its own activation record, which effectively restricts a request/response pair to a single thread in standard CORBA.

Solution → Asynchronous method handling. Asynchronous method handling (AMH) is a technique that extends the capabilities of AMI from CORBA clients to CORBA servers. AMH is a CORBA-based variant of the *continuation model* [11], which allows a program's run-time system to transfer the control of a method closure from one part of the program to another.

Figure 3 illustrates the sequence of steps involved in handling a request by an AMH-enabled middle-tier server. Each of these steps is described below:

1. The source client invokes an operation on the middle-tier server
2. The middle-tier server uses AMH to store information about the client request in a heap-allocated object called ResponseHandler and returns control to the ORB immediately
3. The sink server processes the request

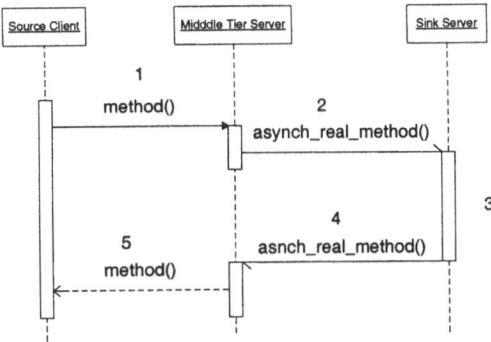

Fig. 3. AMH CORBA Middle-tier Server Interactions

4. The sink server returns the data to the middle-tier server and
5. The middle-tier server fetches the corresponding ResponseHandler and uses it to send the reply data back to the client.

Since the middle-tier server need not block waiting to receive a response, it can handle many requests concurrently using a single thread of control.

Paper outline. The remainder of this paper is organized as follows: Section 2 specifies the AMH capabilities using the CORBA interface definition language (IDL); Section 3 describes the challenges faced while designing and implementing AMH and how we resolved them using patterns and C++ idioms; Section 4 illustrates the inner workings of AMH; Section 5 examines the results of empirically comparing TAO's AMH implementation with other common server concurrency models, such as thread-per-connection and thread pool; Section 6 outlines future research directions related to AMH; Section 7 compares our work on AMH with related research; and Section 8 presents concluding remarks.

2 The Asynchronous Method Handling Specification

This section describes the interface and semantics of AMH. We specify AMH using OMG IDL so that it can be implemented in CORBA-compliant ORBs and mapped to many programming languages. Since AMH is not yet part of the Object Management Group (OMG) CORBA standard [22], an IDL specification provides a common schema for describing AMH.

As with the CORBA AMI specification, we define the semantics of AMH using "implied-IDL." Implied-IDL refers to additional IDL that the IDL compiler "logically" generates based on the standard IDL declarations it parses.[1] The original IDL and the implied IDL are then compiled into stubs and skeletons.

---

[1] In the case of TAO, this is triggered by specifying the -GH option to TAO's IDL compiler.

To focus our discussion, we use the following IDL interface for all our examples:

```
module Stock {
  exception Invalid_Stock_Symbol {};

  interface Quoter {
    long get_quote (in string stock_name)
      raises (Invalid_Stock_Symbol);
  };
};
```

The AMH implied-IDL for the above Stock::Quoter interface is:

```
module Stock
{
  // Forward declarations.
  local interface AMH_QuoterResponseHandler;
  valuetype AMH_QuoterExceptionHolder;

  // The AMH skeleton.
  local interface AMH_Quoter {
    // The AMH operation.
    void get_quote
      (in AMH_QuoterResponseHandler handler,
       in string stock_name);
  };

  // The AMH ResponseHolder.
  local interface AMH_QuoterResponseHandler {
    // Operation to send asynchronous reply
    void get_quote (in long return_value);

    // Operation to asynchronous exception.
    void get_quote_excep
      (in AMH_QuoterExceptionHolder holder);
  };

  // Exception Holder for raising AMH exceptions.
  valuetype AMH_QuoterExceptionHolder {
    void raise_get_quote ()
        raises (Invalid_Stock_Symbol);
  };
};
```

We next describe the rules by which the additional interfaces are generated.[2] The implied-IDL for AMH has three new generated interfaces that we describe below.

The AMH Skeleton. The AMH skeleton (AMH_Quoter) is the AMH version of a normal skeleton. A skeleton demarshals method arguments, invokes an upcall to the designated servant method with these arguments, and marshals any return/out parameters. All operations in an AMH skeleton can return control back to the ORB immediately, *i.e.*, they need not block while the server processes the invocation.

The AMH skeleton interface contains all the operations specified in the original interface. However, the signatures of the AMH skeleton operations (which we refer to as *asynchronous operations*) are different from the original operations in the following ways:

- The in and inout parameters in each operation of the original IDL interface are mapped to in parameters for each asynchronous operation.
- An extra in parameter of type ResponseHandler (described below) is passed as the first argument.
- The asynchronous operation has a void "return" type.
- The out and return arguments are omitted from the asynchronous operation.

The AMH ResponseHandler. The ResponseHandler (AMH_QuoterResponse Handler) object stores the relevant client request information. All operations in the original interface are present in the ResponseHandler interface. Invoking a ResponseHandler operation sends a reply (out/inout/return values) to the client .

The implied-IDL AMH_QuoterResponseHandler interface is related to the Quoter interface as follows:

- The out, inout, or return values for an operation in the original interface are mapped to in parameters in the corresponding method of the ResponseHandler interface.
- The in parameters for an operation in the original interface are omitted in the corresponding operation of the ResponseHandler.
- All ResponseHandler operations have a void "return" type.

All implied-IDL ResponseHandlers are *local interfaces*, *i.e.*, they are always collocated in the address space of the server. Although they appear as regular CORBA objects to server programmers, they cannot be passed or accessed outside of the server's address space. Another special characteristic of a ResponseHandler is that it can be invoked only once. Invoking it more than once raises the BAD_INV_ORDER system exception in the servant.

Any ORB-specific state that is needed to send a reply to the client is stored in a base ResponseHandler class. This state includes the connection on which

---

[2] Though we use the Quoter interface to illustrate the generation of implied-IDL, the rules themselves can be applied to any IDL interface.

the request arrived and the service context of the request. All derived ResponseHandlers (*e.g.*, the AMH_QuoterResponseHandler) can be viewed as deriving from the base ResponseHandler. The base ResponseHandler is not specified by any implied-IDL; in TAO we implement this interface in the concrete class TAO_AMH_ResponseHandler.

The AMH ResponseHandler also contains an *exception operation* (get_quote_excep()) for every operation (get_quote()) in the original IDL interface. The exception operation coordinates with the ExceptionHolder (see next paragraph) and the stored state to return the exception to the client.

The AMH exception holder. The ExceptionHolder (AMH_QuoterExceptionHolder) object is used to store a user- or system-defined exception. It is also used by the exception operation (Section 2) to send an exception to the client. The AMH Exception Holder is generated according to the following rules:

– For every operation (get_quote()) in the original interface, a corresponding *raise operation* (raise_get_quote()) is present in the exception holder.
– The signature of the raises clause of the raise operation matches the raises clause of the corresponding original operation exactly.

3   Resolving AMH Design Challenges

TAO's AMH implementation was designed to resolve the following challenges:

– Providing complete client transparency
– Ensuring AMH servants have the same semantics as non-AMH servants

This section describes how we designed AMH to resolve these challenges.

3.1   Challenge 1: Providing Complete Client Transparency

Problem. AMH is purely a server mechanism. It should therefore be completely transparent to clients, which must not require changes to interact with an AMH server.

Solution. The AMH skeleton (AMH_Quoter) interface is a server-specific interface that is not visible to clients. The AMH skeleton is transparent to the client because it masquerades as the original server (Quoter) interface and receives and handles all the client operation invocations. We use the `Quoter` interface as a concrete example below to demonstrate how the masquerade works.

In the _this() method of AMH_Quoter, we return a `Quoter` object reference instead of an AMH_Quoter object reference, which implies that the AMH_Quoter servant has registered itself to implement the Quoter interface. The _this() code is shown below:

```
class AMH_Quoter
  : public virtual PortableServer::ServantBase
{
public:
  Stock::Quoter *_this ();
};
```

When the object reference exported by this AMH_Quoter servant is narrowed by the client, the resulting reference is a Quoter and not an AMH_Quoter. Whenever the client invokes an operation on the Quoter, the operation parameters are marshaled using the Quoter stub.

On the server, the AMH_Quoter skeleton demarshals the arguments it is passed by the ORB. The logic to demarshal the arguments for an AMH_Quoter that have been marshaled using the Quoter interface are generated automatically by TAO's IDL compiler since the rules to generate the AMH_Quoter implied-IDL from the original Quoter IDL are specified rigorously (Section 2). The client is therefore oblivious to whether its request is handled synchronously or asynchronously. Moreover, the is_a() method of the AMH_Quoter is also changed to return true when the object reference being tested is a Quoter, thereby making the AMH_Quoter completely transparent to the client.

3.2   Challenge 2: Ensuring AMH Servants Have the Same Semantics as Non-AMH Servants

Problem. Server application developers should be able to program AMH servants largely like they do non-AMH servants. For example, the semantics of registering AMH servants with the POA (Portable Object Adapter) and the interaction with the ORB should be the same as with non-AMH servants. Having the same semantics simplifies ease of use and yields faster adoption of the AMH mechanism.

Solution. If the application programming interface between the AMH servant to the ORB and POA is kept the same as a non-AMH servant, the semantics of use of AMH servants is the same as non-AMH servants. AMH servants differ from non-AMH servants in the skeleton classes they derive from. Thus, if all changes required for asynchrony are restricted to AMH skeletons, then we can provide the required guarantee of semantics.

In TAO, the ResponseHandler is created by the AMH skeleton (Section 4). In turn, the ResponseHandler duplicates certain ORB data structures that it needs (Section 4). Thus, by taking on the responsibility for creating the ResponseHandler, the AMH skeleton has made asynchrony transparent to the ORB and the POA, from an application developer perspective.

This design provides maximum flexibility, while requiring minimal changes to existing servant code. For example, AMH servants can be registered in any POA, even along with normal servants. No new POA-Policies need to be defined to make a servant asynchronous. AMH servants can be created and used just as any other servant. Also, the ORB transparency makes AMH orthogonal to the threading model in the server; AMH servants can be used in any multi-threaded server, *e.g.*, thread-per-connection or thread pool, supported by TAO.

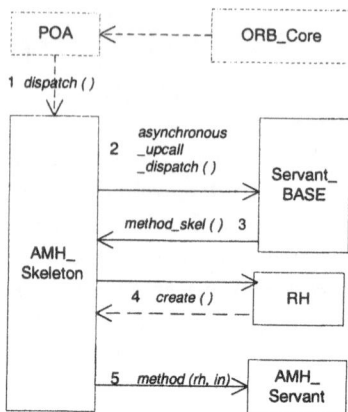

Fig. 4. TAO's AMH Implementation

4   AMH in Action

This section describes how AMH handles a request asynchronously, stores enough state from a request so that the reply can be sent later, and sends exceptions asynchronously.

Asynchronous Request Handling. The stub and skeleton classes generated for each IDL interface by an OMG IDL compiler are used as follows:

- Client applications use stub classes to narrow server references and to marshal/demarshal method arguments (when operations are invoked on the narrowed reference).
- Server applications implement servant classes that derive from skeleton classes and implement the functionality for the interface.

Figure 4 shows how the various components (servant/skeleton/poa/orb) interact to handle an asynchronous request:

1. The client request is received by the server ORB and is dispatched to the POA as usual.
2. The POA locates the servant that handles the request and dispatches the request to it. Until this point, the path taken by the client request is identical to the path of a synchronous request.
3. The servant that is dispatched by the POA is an asynchronous servant (henceforth referred to as *AMH servant*), since it derives from an asynchronous skeleton (henceforth referred to as an *AMH skeleton*). Section 3.1 describes how the AMH servant registers with the POA to handle asynchronous requests.
4. The Servant_Base calls the appropriate method of the derived AMH skeleton.

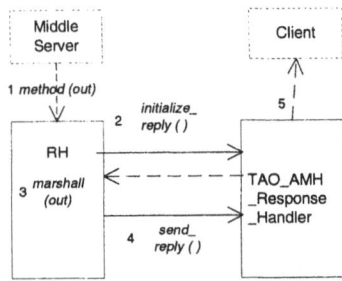

Fig. 5. TAO's Asynchronous Return Implementation

5. The AMH skeleton method first demarshals the in and inout parameters and then creates the ResponseHandler for the request.
6. The ResponseHandler along with the in parameters are then passed to the AMH servant that processes the request.

Interfacing the AMH Skeleton to the ORB-Core: All skeletons (whether synchronous or asynchronous) derive from a base skeleton class called the Servant_Base class. In the case of a synchronous request, this base class dispatches the method in the derived skeleton class and sends the marshaled out, inout, and return parameters back to the client. To implement AMH, we added a new method in the Servant_Base class called asynchronous_upcall_dispatch(), which upcalls the method in the derived AMH skeleton class but does not implement the functionality of sending the return values to the client. This design enables the asynchronous-upcall to return immediately without waiting for the upcall to process the request and marshal the out, inout, and return parameters. By restricting all changes to within the skeleton classes we ensure that asynchronous servants are transparent to both the ORB and the POA. Section 3.2 describes the advantages of this degree of transparency in TAO's AMH design.

Asynchronous Reply. All ResponseHandler classes derive from a base class ResponseHandler called TAO_AMH_ResponseHandler, as described in Section 2. When a server finishes processing an upcall and is ready to send a reply to the client, it invokes the ResponseHandler with the appropriate out, inout, and return parameters. Figure- 5 shows how the ResponseHandler sends the reply back to the client. Each of these steps is described below:

1. The middle-tier server invokes the ResponseHandler (RH) with the appropriate parameters
2. The derived RH invokes a method on its base RH to initialize the ORB parameters needed to send a reply
3. The derived RH marshals the out, inout, and return parameters
4. The derived RH then invokes the base class's send_reply method and
5. This method sends the marshaled parameters to the client.

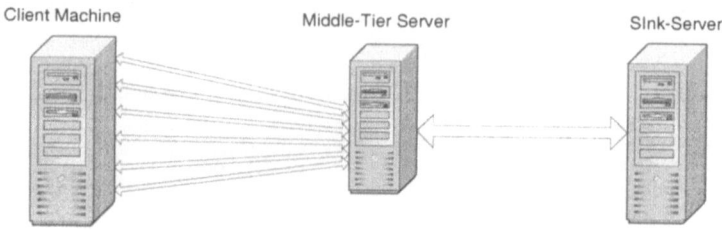

Fig. 6. Benchmarks Testbed

Interfacing the ResponseHandler to the ORB-Core: When the derived RH is first constructed, various ORB parameters are stored in the heap memory by the RH constructor These parameters are subsequently used when the marshaled parameters are sent to the client. The derived RH functionality is limited to only marshaling the parameters, *i.e.*, all ORB-specific functionality is present in the base TAO_AMH_ResponseHandler class.

5   An Empirical Comparison of ORB Concurrency Models

A key goal motivating our work on AMH was to improve the scalability of CORBA servers. To determine whether our design and implementation of AMH in TAO achieved this goal, we benchmarked the throughput of AMH against other common CORBA server models: thread-per-connection, thread pool and single-threaded reactive model. We defined throughput as the total number of replies that the middle-tier server sends to the client divided by the total time the middle-tier server takes to send those replies. The benchmark involved a middle-tier server run using various types of concurrency models. This section describes the benchmark testbed and the results of our experiments.

5.1   Overview of Benchmarking Testbed

Hardware and systems software. The benchmark was performed using three separate machines all interconnected by a 10 Mbps LAN. Figure 6 shows the configuration of the testbed, which is outlined below:

- The *source client machine* was a dual Intel XEON CPU machine with 1GB of RAM and each CPU running at 1,700MHz.
- The *middle-tier server machine* was an Intel single CPU 733 MHz machine with 512KB of RAM.
- The *sink-sever machine* was a dual Intel Pentium III CPU machine with 512 KB of RAM and each CPU running at 733 MHz.

This configuration of the middle-tier server being the most resource constrained machine was chosen so that the middle-tier server machine could be pushed to its maximum capacity and any bottleneck would only exist on the middle-server machine. All machines ran some variant of Linux (kernel 2.2.18 and above) and all TAO code was compiled and linked statically with TAO release 1.2.2. Complete source-code for the benchmark tests are available in the TAO open-source release in $TAO_ROOT/examples/AMH/Middle_Server.

Throughput benchmark test description. The client machine spawns a specified number of clients that then flood the middle-tier server with requests. Each client sends the next request when it receives a reply to the current request. The middle-tier server forwards these requests to a sink server. The sink server can be configured to delay sending response to the middle-tier server by a designated number of milliseconds. The sink server sends the response to the middle-tier server after the predefined delay and the middle-server then returns that response to the client.

Middle-tier server models. We used the following five concurrency models of middle-tier servers in our experiments:

• *Thread-Per-Connection (TPC).* In this server, a new server thread is spawned for each new client and is exclusive to that client. The maximum number of threads that can be spawned is limited only by the number of threads that the OS can spawn.

• *Single-Threaded Reactive (TPR-ST).* In this server, a single thread handles all requests and replies. Since the server is single-threaded, TAO can be configured so that all synchronizers are removed, which increases the throughput of the server. This single thread is dispatched reactively by the ORB so it can handle many different client connections, client requests, and sink server responses.

• *Thread Pool Reactive (TPR-2).* In this server, a predefined number of threads are spawned when the server starts up (in this case, two threads). Since the threads are managed by a reactive ORB, they are not exclusive to any client and thus can be reused to handle requests for multiple clients.

• *Single-Threaded AMH (AMH-ST).* In this server, the ResponseHandler and timestamp for each client request is passed to an AMI servant. The AMI servant stores this value-pair in a hash map and invokes an asynchronous call on the sink server. The AMH servant returns immediately to handle more client requests. When a response from the sink server shows up, the AMI-servant extracts the appropriate ResponseHandler from the hash map using the timestamp (since the sink server returns back the same timestamp) and invokes the method on the ResponseHandler with the timestamp. The ResponseHandler sends the timestamp value to the client.

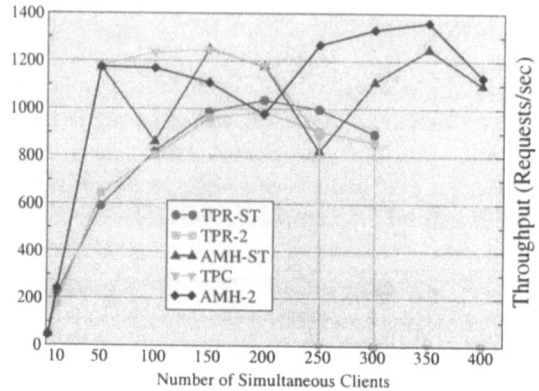

Fig. 7. Throughput of Middle-tier Servers with Increasing Clients

• *Multi-Threaded AMH (AMH-2)*. In this server, we have two threads controlled by a reactive-ORB that do the same work as the ST-AMH server. Except for the spawning of two threads (and hence synchronizers being present in the ORB), this test is the same as the AMH-ST middle-tier server.

5.2   Client Scalability Test

Overview. In this test, the number of clients are steadily increased. Each client makes 1,000 twoway requests to the middle-tier server. The sink server is configured to delay the response by 40 milliseconds. In an ideal middle-tier server we could expect the throughput to increase with the number of clients until the middle-tier server reaches its maximum capacity. Thereafter, the throughput should remain constant, even with further increase in the number of clients.

Empirical results. Figure 7 shows the result of running the benchmark with different middle-tier servers. The test results for each concurrency model are described below.

• *Thread-Per-Connection (TPC)*. In this middle-tier configuration, the middle-tier server could only spawn 250 threads before the context switching overhead surpassed any useful work done. The highest throughput is at 150 clients, after which there is a steady decrease in throughput. This degradation seems to stem from the excessive time the server is spending context-switching between the various threads.

• *Thread Pool Reactive (TPR-2)*. This server has the worst throughput among all the servers, though it is a bit more scalable than TPC, up to 50 clients more. In TPR-2, two threads can handle many simultaneous client requests. Since a new activation record is created for each new client request, however, the threads cannot handle the responses sent by the sink server in any order. Instead, they can unwind the stack only if the current response corresponds to the top of the activation record; otherwise, the thread cannot process the response. This constraint not only decreases the throughput of the server, but when the stack of the thread grows beyond the 2 MB limit on our machine, the server crashes due to unprocessed replies when more client requests arrive. This behavior occurs when more than 300 simultaneous clients are connected to the middle-tier server.

- *Single-Threaded Reactive (TPR-ST)*. The performance of this server closely follows the TPR-2 server. Although there are no synchronizers in this server, the gain in performance by the removal of the locks is offset by having to make a single thread handle all the work.

- *Single-Threaded AMH (AMH-ST)*. The AMH-ST server scales well, handling up to 400 simultaneous clients. We did not test the server with more than 400 clients since at that point the client-machine and the sink server machine were starting to bias the results because the load on them was quite high. With faster and much more powerful client and sink server machines, AMH-ST server would likely have been able to handle even more clients. The throughput of the AMH-ST server, however, tends to dip sharply at certain points (100 and 250 clients). We are investigating what is triggering this errant behavior.

- *Multi-threaded AMH (AMH-2)*. The AMH-2 server performs better than the AMH-ST server under conditions of heavy load (upwards of 250 clients) but with light or moderate load, the AMH-ST server sometimes performs better (150 and 200 clients).

Results synopsis. AMH middle-servers deliver higher throughput than conventional ORB threading models, such as thread-per-connection and thread pool, under conditions of heavy load. Under conditions of light or medium load, the AMH servers are at par or only slightly below par the conventional CORBA servers. Only at one data-point (100 clients) is one of the conventional servers (thread-per-connection) better than either of the AMH servers. For some cases (more than 300 clients), AMH based servers are the only option since only they can cope with that kind of load. Figure 8 compares one server each from each camp (AMH-2 from the AMH camp and TPC from the traditional servers camp). As shown in the figure, AMH-2 lags in performance as compared to TPC in the medium-range of load (from 100 to 200 clients). When the load is heavy, however, the AMH-2 server performs far better. It is also illustrative to see that if it were possible to switch dynamically between middle-server implementations the throughput can be almost constant, across all types of loads, *i.e.*, light, medium or heavy.

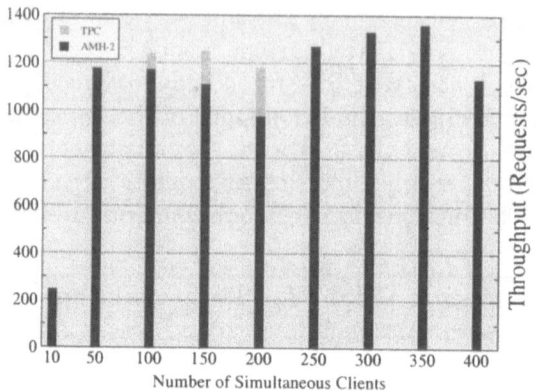

Fig. 8. Comparison Between TPC and AMH wrt Throughput Scalability

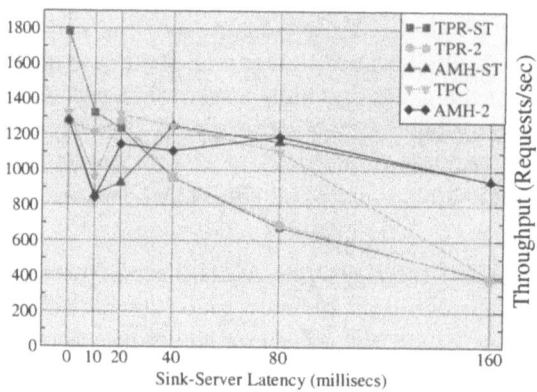

Fig. 9. Throughput of Middle-tier Servers with Increasing Sink Server Latency

5.3   Latency Scalability Test

Overview. In this test, the number of clients is held constant at 150 clients. Each client makes 1,000 requests to the middle-tier server. The sink server delay is then varied by an increasing amount of time.

Empirical results. Figure 9 shows the result of this benchmark. The test results for each concurrency model are described below.

• *Single-Threaded Reactive (TPR-ST).* This server shows the highest throughput when the latency is minimum, delivering up to 500 requests/sec more than any of the other servers at 0 sink server delay. As the sink server latency increases, however, the throughput degrades rapidly in a linear fashion.

- *Thread Pool Reactive (TPR-2)*. The throughput of the thread pool reactive middle-server (TPR-2) is almost constant until ~20 milli-second sink server delay. It also reaches it maximum throughput at this point with 1,281 requests/sec. After this point, there is a rapid and linear decline in throughput.

- *Thread-Per-Connection (TPC)*. This middle-server model does much better, showing an almost consistent throughput around 1,000 requests/sec until the delay from the sink server hits 80 milliseconds. At this point, the throughput suddenly drops. When the delay is high enough (in this case 80 milliseconds), all threads in the middle-tier server are blocked waiting for the sink server replies to arrive. When the replies arrive the middle-tier server suddenly becomes busy in a burst, spending considerable time context switching between the many threads that have suddenly become active to handle the pending client requests and the pending sink server responses.

- *AMH servers (AMH-ST and AMH-2)*. The AMH servers behave quite similarly with respect to each other. Initially, when the latency is low they lag behind in throughput compared to the other servers (TPC and TPR-2). This behavior may occur since the AMH servers allocate ResponseHandlers on the heap, which is costlier than the stack allocation used by the other servers. As the time to allocate on the heap becomes insignificant compared to the blocking time, however, the AMH servers clearly show their ability to scale with respect to sink server delay. At 160 milliseconds delay from the sink server, the AMH servers are very close at achieving the maximum throughput (1,000 requests/sec) at that delay, achieving a throughput of 941 requests/sec and 938 requests/sec for AMH-ST and AMH-2, respectively. The other servers are half that throughput, achieving 381 requests/sec and 396 requests/sec for TPR-2 and TPC, respectively.

Result synopsis. AMH is a clear winner when the blocking time is quite large. Conversely, if it is known that the blocking time will be low and the load on the server will be constantly high, thread pool or thread-per-connection may be a better choice.

6   Research Directions

Allocating requests on the heap raises many dynamic memory management issues, such as heap fragmentation, jitter induced by heap-allocation algorithms, and obtaining and releasing locks during memory management operations. Since AMH is on the critical-path, this overhead could lead to higher jitter, which is undesirable in real-time systems. We are in the process of analyzing and empirically benchmarking if AMH introduces jitter and ways to reduce it.

Many services offered by TAO, such as Load-Balancing and Event-Service, are used in middle-tier servers. Incorporating AMH into these services would improve their efficiency. Future work would include designing and incorporating AMH into these services.

7   Related Work

Distributed systems modeled as entities, such as Actors [1], sending asynchronous messages to each other have been studied theoretically, as well as implemented commercially as Message Oriented Middleware (MOM) (with less stringent semantics [2,3]). Having an explicit asynchronous model offers more flexibility and dynamicity in the system since individual messages can be 'acted-upon', transformed or rerouted easily [4]. However, this flexibility often yields lower performance [5].

CORBA has an explicitly synchronous model based upon the RPC mechanism [6]. Throughput in a synchronous system, though, may degrade dramatically when system resources, such as threads, are wasted while waiting for a long I/O or external events. This degradation becomes easily apparent when a client is blocked waiting for a response from a server that is taking a long time to send a reply. The AMI specification in CORBA was designed specifically to overcome this problem for clients. The same problem exists for servers, however, as described in Section 1. Different server concurrency models have been proposed and implemented [7,8,9] to better utilize system resources for various types of client requests [10]. AMH is specifically aimed at addressing the root of this problem: *explicitly dissociating the request reception from request processing.* An initial inspiration for this approach was the implementation of *continuations* in the MACH kernel, which resulted in significant performance improvements in that OS kernel [11]. Other examples of similar work include Futures [12] and Promises [13], which are language mechanisms that decouple method invocation from method return values passed back to the caller when a method finishes executing.

Other distributed object computing middleware, such as DCOM [14,15], also support asynchronous invocations on the client and the server side. Java RMI [16, 17] does not provide asynchronous functionality on either the client or the server, resulting in performance degradation when servers take a long time to respond to calls. The Java Messaging Service (JMS) [3] tries to alleviate this problem by providing a mechanism for receiving sending and messages asynchronously.

8   Concluding Remarks

The CORBA asynchronous method invocation (AMI) mechanism can significantly improve the scalability and responsiveness of many types of client applications. A similar mechanism for servers to handle method calls asynchronously has not been available until now. Asynchronous server support is useful in many situations, such as building scalable middle-tier servers, improving the scalability of servers that are constrained to be single-threaded, or allowing servers to perform multiple requests in parallel to backend-servers for a single client request.

This paper defines a specification for an asynchronous method handling mechanism (AMH) and describes how it has been designed and implemented in

The ACE ORB (TAO). Empirical benchmarks show how asynchronous servers scale better than other server concurrency models, such as thread-per-connection and thread pool, in terms of the number of concurrent clients and long running server upcalls.

References

1. Agha, G.: A Model of Concurrent Computation in Distributed Systems. MIT Press (1986)
2. IBM: MQSeries Family, http://www-4.ibm.com/software/ts/mqseries/ (1999)
3. SUN: Java Messaging Service Specification, http://jcp.org/aboutJava/community-process/maintenance/JMS/ (2002)
4. Venkatasubramaniam, N., Deshpande, M., Mohapatra, S., Gutierrez-Nolasco, S., Wickramasuriya J.: Design and Implementation of a Composable Reflective Middleware Framework. International Conference on Distributed Computer Systems (ICDCS), IEEE, Phoenix, Arizona, April (2001)
5. Birman, K.P.: Building Secure and Reliable Network Applications. WWCA (1997), 15-28
6. Schmidt, D.C., Vinoski, S.: Standard C++ and the OMG C++ Mapping. C/C++ Users Journal, January (2001)
7. Schmidt, D.C., Vinoski, S.: Comparing Alternative Programming Techniques for Multi-threaded CORBA Servers: Thread-per-Object. C/C++ Report, Vol. 8, No. 7, July (1996)
8. Schmidt, D.C., Vinoski, S.: Comparing Alternative Programming Techniques for Multi-threaded CORBA Servers: Thread-per-Request. C/C++ Report, Vol. 8, No. 2, February (1996)
9. Schmidt, D.C., Vinoski, S.: Comparing Alternative Programming Techniques for Multi-threaded CORBA Servers: Thread Pool. C/C++ Report, Vol. 8, No. 4, April (1996)
10. Hu, J., Pyarali, I., Schmidt, D.C.: The Object-Oriented Design and Performance of JAWS: A High-performance Web Server Optimized for High-speed Networks. Parallel and Distributed Computing Practices Journal, special issue on Distributed Object-Oriented Systems. Vol. 3, No. 1, March (2000)
11. Draves, R.P., Bershad, B.N., Rashid, R.F., Dean, R.W.: Using Continuations to Implement Thread Management and Communication in Operating Systems. ACM, SOSP13, Pacific Grove, CA, October (1991), 122-136
12. Halstead, Jr., Robert H.: Multilisp: A Language for Concurrent Symbolic Computation. toplas, Vol. 7, No. 4, October (1985) 501-538
13. Liskov, B., Shrira, L.: Promises: Linguistic Support for Efficient Asynchronous Procedure Calls in Distributed Systems. Proceedings of the SIGPLAN'88 Conference on Programming Language Design and Implementation. June (1988) 260-267
14. Distributed Component Object Model Protocol (DCOM). Microsoft Corporation, January (1998)
15. Box, D.: Essential COM. Addison-Wesley, Reading, Massachusetts.(1997)
16. SUN: Java Remote Method Invocation (RMI) Specification. http://java.sun.com/products/jdk/1.2/docs/guide/rmi/spec/rmiTOC.doc.html (2002)
17. Wollrath, A., Riggs, R., Waldo, J:. A Distributed Object Model for the Java System. USENIX Computing Systems, MIT Press, Vol. 9, No. 4 (1996)

18. Arulanthu, A.B., O'Ryan, C., Schmidt, D.C., Kircher, M., Parsons, J.: The Design and Performance of a Scalable ORB Architecture for CORBA Asynchronous Messaging. Proceedings of the Middleware 2000 Conference, ACM/IFIP, Pallisades, New York (April 2000)
19. Eckerson, W.W.: Three Tier Client/Server Architecture: Achieving Scalability, Performance and Efficiency in Client Server Applications. Open Information Systems, Vol. 10, No. 1 (1995)
20. Othman, O., O'Ryan, C., Schmidt, D.C.: An Efficient Adaptive Load Balancing Service for CORBA. IEEE Distributed Systems Online, Vol. 2, No. 3 (2000)
21. Schmidt, D.C.: Evaluating Architectures for Multi-threaded CORBA Object Request Brokers. Communications of the ACM special issue on CORBA, Vol. 41 No. 10 (1998)
22. Object Management Group: The Common Object Request Broker: Architecture and Specification. December (2001)

Web Services Interoperability: A Practitioner's Experience

Pradyumna Siddhartha and Shubhashis Sengupta[1]

Software Concept Laboratory
Infosys Technologies Ltd.
Bangalore 561 229, India
Tel: 91 80 852 0261
Fax: 91 80 852 0740
siddhart@stanford.edu, shubhashis_sengupta @infosys.com

Abstract. Web services are hot. To make them workable in practice, however, is not easy. Often, successful implementations of Web services warrant that various applications on heterogeneous platforms participating in a service communicate correctly and effectively. But achieving seamless interoperability among participating entities in a Web service can be tricky. Despite the advances made by standards bodies like Web Services Interoperability Organization, many architectural and implementation level mismatches remain to be tackled. These mismatches stem mainly from the differences in the way various commercial and open-source Web services toolkits implement the core Web services protocols. In this paper, we look at the problems arising for accessing enterprise Java beans exposed through open source Apache SOAP server from Microsoft clients and suggest workarounds to achieve end-to-end interoperability. We demonstrate our approach through a toy application.

1 Introduction

A major selling proposition for Web services is its promise for interoperability. In theory, Web services should allow any client to invoke any service over HTTP and XML wire protocols. This feature sets it apart from many other frameworks for distributed computing such as DCOM, which require a single almost homogeneous environment for successful end-to-end deployment. Though some distributed computing environments like CORBA provide interoperability between different operating systems, languages and implementations, application interoperability over the Web could not be realized with them. Web services envision a "publish-find-bind" scenario where services are published with a broker and the clients discover and bind to the services they need on the fly to create an environment of flexible workflows over the Web regardless of the language in which the services are implemented, and platforms on which they are running. To enable this, members of standard making bodies like W3 consortium and UDDI community have drafted vendor neutral open standards of the core Web services protocols like Simple Object Access Protocol

---

[1] Corresponding author

R. Meersman, Z. Tari (Eds.): CoopIS/DOA/ODBASE 2002, LNCS 2519, pp. 587–601, 2002.
© Springer-Verlag Berlin Heidelberg 2002

(SOAP) [1], Web Services Description Language (WSDL) [2], and Universal Description Discovery and Integration (UDDI) [3]. For the purpose of messaging and service description, these protocols depend on basic schema like XML Schema 1.0 [4].

In reality, however, interoperability is proving to be one of the major stumbling blocks for adopting Web services in the enterprise. The main culprit is the proliferation of "me too" solution stacks and toolkits based on open and non-specific nature of the standards which often result is mutual inconsistent implementations and schema. The proliferation of implementation variations has prompted many vendors to join hands together to float an industry wide body called Web services Interoperability Organization [5] to address this issue at a level above implementation typicality. There are also reports of developer community efforts like SOAPBuilders Interoperability Labs – an organization chartered with identifying interoperability problems, fixing them through consensus, and ensuring vendor compliance through tests. While initiatives by standard bodies and industry are steps in the correct direction, the current state-of-the-art provides too little support for the practitioners to implement Web services using components from multiple platforms and software development toolkits (SDK).

In this paper, we study interoperability issues between two main Web services platforms, namely, SOAP toolkit from Microsoft Web services environment [6] and Apache foundation's open-source SOAP toolkit [7], in which IBM is the main contributor. In particular, we investigate the incompatibility between the XML encoding classes, and inconsistent support for WSDL standard between two platforms. We also study how two applications running in these two disparate platforms can be engaged in a stateful conversation over SOAP. To study these issues, we have built a toy Web services scenario where a minimal set of banking services, running on a Java-based server, are accessed from Microsoft application-based clients. The services are implemented as Enterprise Java beans (EJB) [8] and clients are coded in Visual Basic.

The paper is structured as follows: in Section 2, we introduce a toy banking example, its main components and their composition. In Section 3, we illustrate the building blocks of a basic SOAP service framework. Exposing EJB as SOAP services in Apache toolkit, a non-trivial task, is explained in brief in Section 4. Section 5 describes interoperability issues with Microsoft SOAP. We conclude the article in Section 6 by outlining the key learning from this exercise and future work.

2 Example of a Banking Web Service

Consider a scenario where a large bank is revamping its existing infrastructure. Suppose some of the Automated Teller Machines (ATM) supported by Microsoft platforms now need to be connected to a central server running Java based applications in Unix. Rather than rewriting the client or server applications, it may be cost effective to connect the existing applications as Web services. The minimal and simplified set of services provided to the ATM clients are opening or closing a checking or savings account, inquiring the balance the from checking / savings account, transactions like withdrawal from and deposit into an account and transfer of money between the checking and the savings accounts and vice-versa. The services are implemented as Enterprise Java beans. The operations of creation and deletion of an account and inquiring the balance of an account is handled by *ATMAccount* bean and all other account transactions are handled by *ATMService* bean. Since creation and deletion of an account is one time request-response operation, the *ATMAccount* bean is implemented as a stateless session bean. The *ATMService* bean, on the other hand, is implemented as a stateful session bean due to the types of operations it supports. For example, withdrawal of money from a certain account will involve two round trips to the same bean instance - one for checking the balance in a particular account and the other for actually performing the withdrawal and it is essential to maintain conversational state between the trips both at the client and the server. To implement the banking services, we use open-source JBoss version 3.0 EJB container [9] where the Enterprise beans are developed and deployed. We expose these services as SOAP service through Apache foundation's open-source SOAP toolkit version 2.2 running on a Tomcat version 3.2.2 server. The services run on IBM box running Windows 2000. The same experiment was repeated with server running on Red Hat Linux version 7.1.

The *ATMClient* application is coded in Visual Basic version 6.0 and has corresponding methods for each of the operations. The client application runs as a process in Windows NT (version 4) workstation and communicate with the server through Microsoft SOAP toolkit version 2.02. The versions are chosen such that they represent the latest or most stabilized build releases in respective platforms at the time of implementation.

3   Building Blocks of SOAP Services

A SOAP service framework consists of one or more clients, one or more service classes, and SOAP servers to process and delegate the requests and responses. The principal constituents of a SOAP framework having Apache SOAP server and Microsoft client are

- *Call* object. It is a client-side object used to send SOAP requests to the server via HTTP. The client uses the call object to format the SOAP envelope by supplying the service Universal Resource Indicator (URI), method name, parameters etc. We will not dwell on the anatomy of a SOAP envelope here. This can be obtained from [6] and [7].
- *ServiceManager* object. It provides interfaces for deploying, un-deploying, and accessing SOAP services. It attaches to a *ConfigManager*, which provides the actual mechanisms for storing service information in the form of *DeploymentDescriptor* instances. The *ServiceManager* is queried by the servlet to get service deployment descriptors.
- *RPCRouterServlet* object. It receives the HTTP request from the client, and extracts the Call object from the request object. It then locates the service's

deployment descriptor from *ServiceManager*, creates an instance of the appropriate provider class, and invokes the service.

- *ConfigManager* object. This provides storage for *DeploymentDescriptors* and the servlet context and is accessed via the *ServiceManager*.

- *DeploymentDescriptor* object. It provides information about the specifics of a particular service, including the scope, the service class, the type of class (Java, script, and so on), as well as utilities for parsing from and writing to XML.

- Provider classes including *RPCJavaProvider*, *StatefulEJBProvider*, and others. The Provider interface has two methods - `locate` is used to acquire the correct instance of the service class, and `invoke` is used to execute the service and return a response.

Service administration in Apache SOAP is through the SOAP Admin tool that defines the service by a unique URI and provides a list of method names, as well as a service class. Using the information supplied by the administrator, the SOAP server generates and stores (in the *ConfigManager*) a *DeploymentDescriptor* instance for the service. The Call object is configured by entering the service URI, method name, parameters, and the like, then an HTTP request (with an XML message) is made to the SOAP server. Figure 1 depicts how the appropriate *DeploymentDescriptor* is retrieved based on the URI provided, and is used to create an instance of the desired Provider class, which then services the request.

An actual Web service would of course not be invoked as mere SOAP methods. Rather, it will be exposed in terms of WSDL binding. WSDL ports will be the endpoints of the service and the service will be specified in terms of `<port type>` and `<operation>` tags. The service details need to be discovered from the UDDI registry or through some inspection mechanism. However, to simplify matters, we assume that client knows the service end-points, i.e., the server where the service is hosted, the corresponding methods and the method parameters.

4   Exposing EJB as Services

EJB-based SOAP services require EJBs to be exposed properly as service end-points on the SOAP server. Additionally, both stateless and stateful bean sessions should run flawlessly as services. Unfortunately, both are cumbersome in current version of Apache SOAP server. Presently the EJB services must be deployed as user-defined service Providers (like *StatefulEJBProvider*), rather than having a specific category for deployment. This entails manually providing all the information required to successfully expose the service, including the specific provider class implementation, as well as encoding a series of options, such as *JNDIName*, *FullHomeInterfaceName*, and the like, with the correct key/value pairs. To avoid such a convoluted procedure, we have modified the portions of Apache SOAP server code. As the article focuses mainly on achieving interoperability, we will only mention the modifications done briefly.

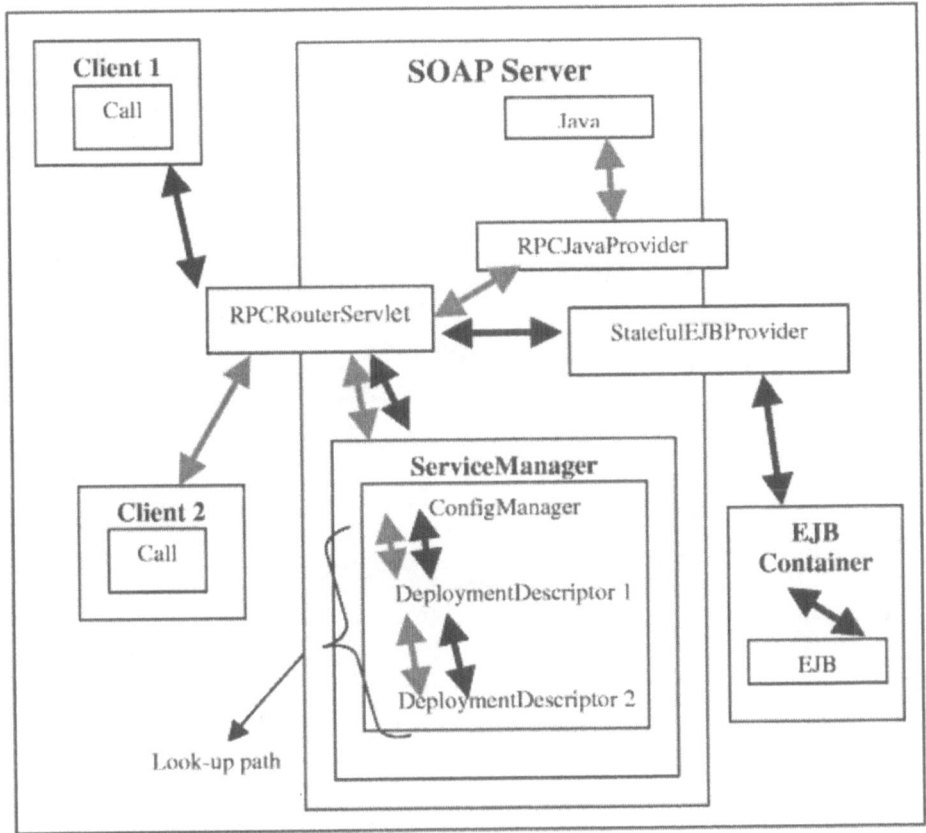

Fig. 1. Two clients look up for different deployment descriptors

Easier deployment of EJBs as SOAP services was effected through three simple steps. First of all, we have modified the *DeploymentDescriptor* class to include provider classes for different types of session and entity beans. This called for adding constants for depicting types of provider classes in the *DeploymentDescriptor* and mapping proper class strings to these constants. Next, we changed the *RPCRouterServlet* class to enable it to select of proper EJB provider classes. Finally, the code of SOAP administrative tool was changed to allow explicit deployment of EJBs.

Maintaining stateful session with the EJB services, however, is trickier. Maintaining states across service calls requires the context information be saved at some point, preferably at the server. In Apache SOAP server the context information is saved in *FullTargetURI* object. In case of EJB, the context object refers to the EJB handle. Any attempt to serialize and deserialize this object for a stateful session bean fails where container is other than IBM Web Sphere (in our case, JBoss). This is because the Apache code, by default, presumes Websphere as EJB container and initializes the context accordingly for each invocation. To avoid losing context information, we implemented a simple workaround. Instead of directly serializing and deserializing the EJB handle to access the service object, we stored the objects in a hash table in the *ServiceManager*, using the serialized handles as keys. From the client's perspective, the process of maintaining a stateful session remains the same. This problem never manifested when running stateless sessions, as there is no requirement for context serialization. Figure 2 traces a SOAP service execution in the Apache SOAP server and highlights the modification done for deployment of EJB and stateful service access.

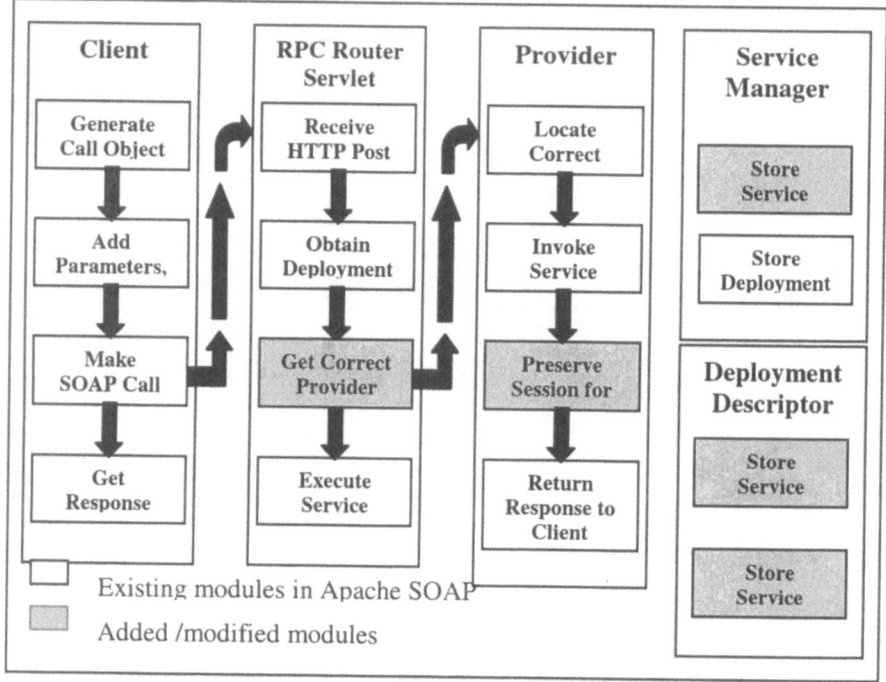

Fig. 2. Changes made to Apache SOAP toolkit

5   Interoperability with Microsoft SOAP 2.0

As both the Microsoft and Apache open-source platforms promise support for SOAP 1.1 protocol, the service invocation should be easy – in theory, at least. For example, to get the balance of a checking account, all the client needs to do is to wrap the GetBalance method (code sample 1) in a SOAP call, send it across to the proper service end-point, which is the GetBalance method of *ATMService* bean instance (code sample 2) and get the response. Unfortunately, even this simple invocation fails. Let us investigate the causes for this failure.

5.1   XML Schema Incompatibility

The first hurdle comes from incompatibility between Microsoft and Apache SOAP encoding schema. The problems of incompatibility range from minor issues involving syntax to more fundamental issues of API design. Microsoft provides two APIs for wrapping a method call in SOAP--a high-level API that provides automation, and a low-level one that it encapsulates. The client-side high-level API consists of *SOAPClient*, which encapsulates a large number of other classes and provides complete functionality as a client to a SOAP service. The client-side low-level API consists of a variety of classes each of which carry out small portions of the service invocation. The most important of these APIs are

- *SOAPConnector*. This provides the actual connection to the server, through which the SOAP message can be transmitted.

- *SOAPSerializer*. An implementation of *HTTPSerializer*, this class allows the client to manually (with a number of helper functions) encode the SOAP XML envelope and then transmit it through the *SOAPConnector* object.

- *SOAPReader*. This parses a SOAP message into a document object model, allowing clients to read specific elements of the message.

```
public class ATMServiceBean implements SessionBean {

  // ATMService bean implementation class
  ...
public long GetBalance(String accountID, String accountType)
throws        RemoteException {

    ATMAccount atmaccount   = (ATMAccount)
accounts.get(accountID);
    if(atmaccount == null) {

        atmaccount = new ATMAccount();
        accounts.put(accountID, atmaccount);
    }
    else {

      if (accountType .equals("savings"))
        return atmaccount.getSavingsBalance();
      else    return atmaccount.getCheckingBalance();
    }
  } ...
}
```

Code sample 1: Java implementation of *ATMServiceBean* class

The SOAP request, by default, does not provide explicit typing information for the variables in the SOAP envelope. Thus, the sample code generates XML (code sample 3) that provides no specific information on how it is to be decoded.

```
Private Function GetBalance(ByVal account As Integer) As Long
                                         'VB Client code

...
     Set Connector = New HttpConnector
     Connector.Property("EndPointURL") =
     "http://blrkec15719:8080/soap/server/rpcrouter"
     Connector.Property("SoapAction") = "uri:GetBalance"
     Connector.Connect
     Set Serializer = New SoapSerializer
     Serializer.Init Connector.InputStream

     Connector.BeginMessage
     Serializer.startEnvelope
     Serializer.startBody
     Serializer.startElement "GetBalance", Method_NS, "m"
     Serializer.startElement "id"
     Serializer.endElement
     Serializer.startElement "account"
     Serializer.endElement
     Serializer.endBody
     Serializer.endEnvelope
     Connector.EndMessage
     Set Reader = New SoapReader
     Reader.Load Connector.OutputStream
     NameSpace = Reader.Body.childNodes.Item(1).namespaceURI
     MsgBox Reader.RPCResult.Text
...
```

Code sample 2: Client side VB function

Apache SOAP, meanwhile, requires explicit typing of all parameters. It is thus necessary to provide this information, as well as the schemas for the variable types. The envelope encoding should reflect this with the appropriate type attributes entered for each variable. This provides the necessary schema information, as well as explicitly typing for each variable. On the other hand, as the server response contained fully typed XML, there is no need to rewrite any of the server code to get the service working. The Apache SOAP server processes the resulting XML without error. The explicit typing of attributes and parameters in the call object are shown in code sample 4. The same problem appears when one uses the high level API. However, there is no way to explicitly enter the variable types into the SOAP envelope using the high level API. The workaround in the case involves editing the WSDL file. If all variable types are set to "xsd:anyType", the Microsoft SOAP client provides the necessary typing information in the envelope. This proves to be fairly convenient in that both the client and server code are entirely unchanged.

```
<!--XML Code Sample 3:-->

<?xml version="1.0" encoding="UTF-8" standalone="no" ?>
<SOAP-ENV:Envelope
```

```
        xmlns:SOAP-
ENV="http://schemas.xmlsoap.org/soap/envelope/">
        <SOAP-ENV:Body>
            <SOAPSDK1:GetBalance
            xmlns:SOAPSDK1="urn:mySoapTest:ATMClient"
            SOAP-
ENV:encodingStyle="http://schemas.xmlsoap.org/soap/encoding/">
                <A>12697J3E</A>
                <B>checking</B>
            </SOAPSDK1:GetBalance>
        </SOAP-ENV:Body>
</SOAP-ENV:Envelope>
```

Code sample 3: SOAP envelope for *ATMClient* using MS SOAP toolkit

```
Private Function GetBalance(ByVal account As Integer) As Long
                                'SOAP wrapper for VB
client
    ...
    Set Connector = New HttpConnector
        Connector.Property("EndPointURL") =
        "http://blrkec15719:8080/soap/server/rpcrouter"
    Connector.Property("SoapAction") = "uri:GetBalance"
    Connector.Connect
    Set Serializer = New SoapSerializer
    Serializer.Init Connector.InputStream

    Connector.BeginMessage
    Serializer.startEnvelope
        Serializer.SoapAttribute "xmlns:xsi", ,
        "http://www.w3.org/1999/XMLSchema-instance", ""
    Serializer.SoapAttribute "xmlns:xsd", ,
    "http://www.w3.org/1999/XMLSchema", ""
    Serializer.startBody
    Serializer.startElement "GetBalance", Method_NS, "STANDARD",
""
    Serializer.startElement "id"
    Serializer.SoapAttribute "xsi:type", , "xsd:string", ""
    Serializer.writeString userID
    Serializer.endElement
    Serializer.startElement "account"
    Serializer.SoapAttribute "xsi:type", , "xsd:string", ""
    Serializer.writeString accnt
    ...
    Connector.EndMessage
    ...
```

Code sample 4: Explicit typing of XML request

5.2   Session Scoping with Microsoft Clients

Now that we have established communication between the Visual Basic client and Apache SOAP server, the next issue to tackle is that of maintaining the service scope. For example, suppose the client wishes to check her account balance and transfer some amount from her saving to checking account. For this the *ATMClient* has to establish a stateful conversation with *ATMService* bean instance. Unfortunately, this experiment also ends abruptly due to lack of inherent support for stateful conversation on part of Microsoft SOAP.

There are three levels of scope/persistence supported by the Apache SOAP toolkit, which can be used to configure the services operating on the server. These are

- *Request.* Every time the client requests the use of a service, a new instance of the service object is generated.
- *Session.* Multiple requests from the same client will be processed by the same instance of the service object. For the purpose of this discussion, a client can be defined as a single *Call* object with a constant target service end-point (in terms of URI). All calls made by this *Call* object will be processed by the same instance of the service object--the SOAP server can process requests from other clients and still maintain the state of any given session-scoped service.
- *Application.* The same instance of the service object will service client requests as long as the server is operational. This means that multiple *Call* objects are possible for the same client application, as well as multiple clients can use the same instance of the service object to process requests. The SOAP server has no means of differentiating between multiple client applications and multiple Call objects within the same client.

For our purpose, the issue of persistence is only considered for session-scoped objects, i.e., a single service instance of *ATMService* bean is instantiated for a "client" session. We aren't examining Request and Application scopes because the implementation is comparatively trivial. Microsoft's APIs have no built-in support for stateful services. Moreover, the Apache SOAP API is somewhat inconsistent in the way it handles persistent service objects, which makes any reasonable client-side implementation of session-scoped objects extremely difficult. We'll first examine the problems posed by the server-side inconsistencies.

The Provider classes contain most of the code that deals with object persistence. The *RPCJavaProvider* maintains the correct instance of the service by storing/loading the object to/from the current *HTTPSession* (for session scope) or the current *ServletContext* (for application scope). This makes the persistence management theoretically largely client-independent. This setup works well when using a Java client, which makes requests using a *Call* object. As long as the address of the *Call* object remains unchanged, the session is maintained, and session-scoped conversations are possible. By contrast, when EJB services are deployed, the *StatefulEJBProvider* does not store and load the service object independently of the client. Rather, the service object stub is serialized, and the serialized string is returned to the client, who can then decide whether or not to maintain the instance of the service object. Of the two, the first requires less code on the part of the client in order to maintain a persistent session. However, the serialization method appears to be the more powerful and versatile of the two, as it allows the client more control over session length, and the like, rather than burying the service objects deep inside the system architecture (in the session/context). Additionally, by serializing the object into the response string, the state is managed almost entirely in XML code, which considerably enhances the interoperability of the system.

```
Set Connector = New HttpConnector

Connector.Property("EndPointURL") = END_POINT_URL
Connector.Property("SoapAction") = "uri:" & Method
Connector.Connect

For i% = 1 To 3
        Set Serializer = New SoapSerializer
        Serializer.Init Connector.InputStream
        Connector.BeginMessage
        ...
        Serializer.startElement Method, Method_NS, "STANDARD", ""
        ...
        Connector.EndMessage
        Set Reader = New SoapReader
        Reader.Load Connector.OutputStream
        Method_NS = Reader.Body.childNodes.Item(1).namespaceURI
Next i%
```

Code sample 5: Session scope setting in client

The next major problem is in the client's layer. The storage mechanism involving referencing the service object from the *HTTPSession* object is useless with Visual Basic clients, as Microsoft's API HTTP tools end the session after every request and there is no way to maintain it. Additionally, there is no support at the high-level for capturing and manipulating the actual SOAP envelope, or for setting the actual target object URI. Thus, it is impossible to maintain a persistent session using the high level API. The low-level API holds considerably more promise in this regard, as it is possible to easily dissect the XML message being returned, and to explicitly set the target object URI. It is thus a reasonably simple matter to set up a session-scoped conversation using the low-level API, using a procedure similar to that used in Java clients (code sample 5). One has to extract the namespace URI from the response envelope and set the next call's method namespace to that value. The *EJBProvider* method of maintaining a copy of the object appears to be a better way of handling the task, especially with a Microsoft client. The level of platform independence it provides is extremely valuable. To provide stateful conversations with a wider variety of SOAP services (Java classes, for example) we modified the RPCJavaProvider by reusing the method of session retrieval used by the *StatefulEJBProvider*. The process used to store and load the service objects is largely the same as with the *EJBProvider*, with the exception of the key used to reference the service objects. Instead of serializing the service class (there is no guarantee that the Java class is serializable), a unique number is generated by the provider instance and this is used to store the object in the service manager's hash table (code sample 6).

```
//Apache ServiceManager code
locate() {
        ...
        fullURI = call.getFullTargetObjectURI();
        objectKey = StatefulEJBProvider.getUniqueId(fullURI);
        if (objectKey!=null) {
                targetObject =
serviceManager.loadObject(objectKey);
                return;
        }
        ...
}
invoke() {
        ...
        String newURI = fullURI;
        if (objectKey==null) {
                uniqueNum++;  objectKey=""+uniqueNum;
                newURI=
TargetObjectURI+StatefulEJBProvider.DELIM_CHAR+objectKey;
        }
        ServiceManager sm;
        sm =
ServerHTTPUtils.getServiceManagerFromContext(context);
        sm.storeObject(objectKey,targetObject);
        try {
                Response resp = RPCRouter.invoke( dd, call,
targetObject,
                reqContext, resContext );
        resp.setFullTargetObjectURI(newURI);
                ...
}
```

Code sample 6: Setting session instance

Figure 3 schematically represents the major modifications done to the SOAP framework to attain the session management. Before modification of the framework, the HTTPSession Object would maintain the correct instance of service object for stateful sessions. Objects were maintained as long as session was not broken. Under this condition, we could not have stateful conversation with VB Clients, as session would get broken after each request. After modification, the server passes back a unique object ID that can be used to retrieve the correct instance of the service object from a hash table in the server. Now, session persistence is controlled through the SOAP message and is thus much more client-independent – VB clients can now hold stateful conversations with the Java server-side objects.

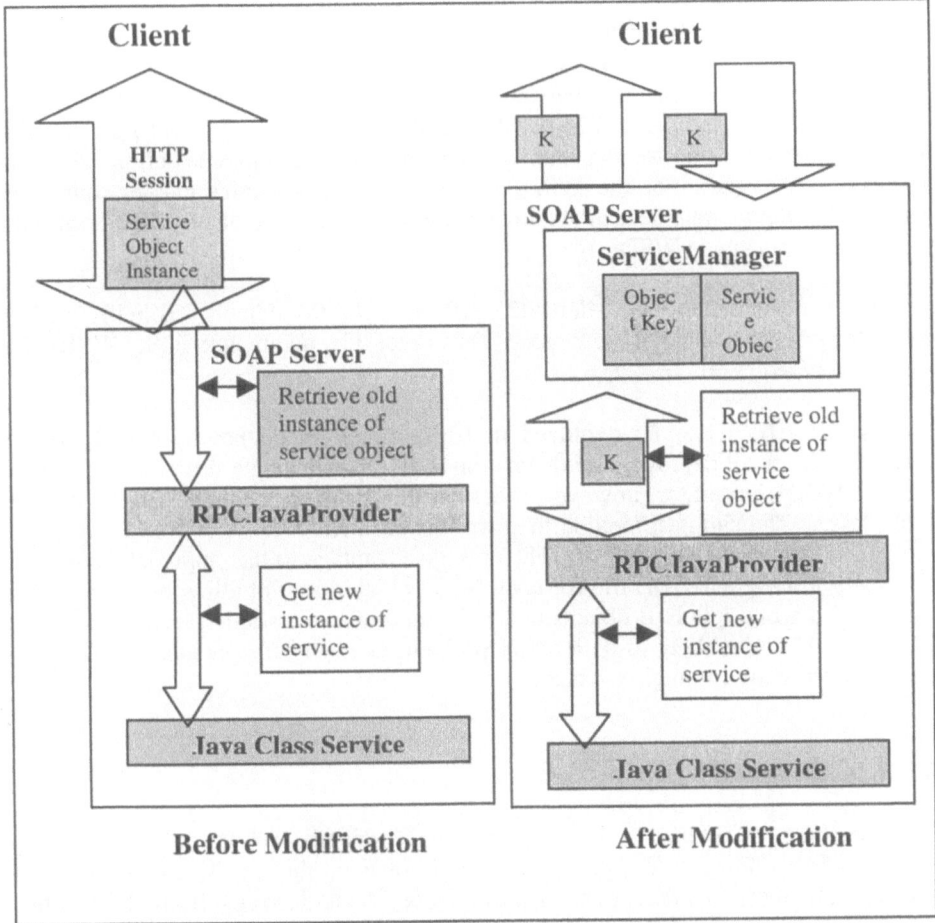

Fig. 3. Attaining session management with Apache SOAP toolkit

5.3 From SOAP Services to Web Services

One of the key features of web services is having service descriptions published in a portable format easily accessible to clients on all platforms. Files written in the Web Service Description Language (WSDL) 1.1 provide this functionality. While the framework discussed so far is sufficient for exposing EJBs as SOAP-accessible services; to fully integrate them as web services effective WSDL-based access is a necessity. In theory, as with any XML-based interface, there should be no problems of interoperability. However, there are compatibility problems that must be overcome in practice.

Microsoft SOAP's high-level API depends on WSDL files to provide the necessary service information to the client. For this purpose, we have used IBM's Web Services Toolkit (WSTK) 2.3 that enables the automatic generation of WSDL files from Java classes, EJB Jars, and the like. This is a useful tool, but there are certain minor problems that must be overcome before the IBM toolkit can be used to deploy services that a Microsoft client can read.

First, there are discrepancies between the numbers and schema of WSDL files generated in two platforms. The IBM toolkit generates two WSDL files (against Microsoft's one) – one for the interface, and one for the implementation. The files reference each other. For the WSDL to work with Microsoft's classes, one must remove the import statement or statements and copy the body of the one file into the other, creating a single WSDL file.

Second, as discussed earlier, Microsoft's API does not (by default) explicitly provide type information in the XML envelope. To correct this, parameters in the WSDL file should be typed "`xsd:anyType`".

Finally, the EJB 1.1 JARs deployed in JBoss container do not by default have a manifest file, as all deployment information is stored in a single descriptor. The IBM Toolkit WSDL generator, however, relies on the manifest when writing WSDL for EJB classes. The simplest method to solve this problem is to write WSDL files as if the EJB classes were Java objects. The only disadvantage to this approach is that it is necessary to have a WSDL file for each bean, which does not allow one to maintain services from multiple EJB objects under the umbrella of a single service name/URI. However, this is unlikely to be a major problem as most services can effectively be encapsulated within a single interface.

6   Conclusion

Interoperability problems in Web services arise mainly due to mismatch in the versions of specification, in the way vendors implement the specifications and in the service semantics. In this paper, we have reported our learning from the practical obstacles to achieve end-to-end interoperability between two different Web services platforms in a toy application example of a bank ATM. The application discussed in this paper is straight forward as it does not require transformation of any complex user-defined schema, nor does it require the advance concepts of transaction management and security. Yet, we find that such a simple invocation across platforms is difficult to achieve. At this point, it becomes clear that while it is possible to maintain conversation between different SOAP implementations, the process involves a great deal of tinkering with the code. Many of these details are counter-intuitive and more importantly, undocumented. These factors pose a significant roadblock to potential web service/SOAP service developers. Given that in this experiment we have only considered two different SOAP implementations, it seems fair to say that the problems would be magnified for a framework of services written on a variety of the dozens of the SOAP packages in the marketplace. Additionally, many of the modifications are specifically designed to help two specific platforms communicate--a principle that requires detail knowledge of specific toolkits. Thus, it is necessary to define a set of standards around which SOAP toolkits can be designed. This way, there is a much higher chance of code written on one SDK working with others. While the specifics of such a standard are not within the scope of this article, they should be specific and comprehensive enough to ensure near-flawless interoperability. It is hoped that the Web services interoperability group will look into this issue at a right level of abstraction.

References

1. D. Box, D. Ehnebuske, G. Kakivaya, A. Layman, N. Mendelsohn, H.F. Neilsen, S. Thatte, D. Winer, *Simple Object Access Protocol (SOAP) 1.1*, World Wide Web consortium (W3C) Note 8th May 2000, http://www.w3.org/TR/SOAP.html
2. E. Christensen, F. Curbera, G. Meredith, S. Weerawarana, *Web Services Definition Language (WSDL) 1.1*, W3C Note 15 March 2001, http://www.w3.org/TR/wsdl.html
3. *Universal Description Discovery and Integration (UDDI) 2.0*, UDDI community specification, http://www.uddi.org/specification.html
4. *XML Schema 1.0*, W3C Recommendation 2nd May 2000, http://www.w3.org/TR/xmlschema-0/
5. *Web Services Interoperability working group's introduction presentation*, http://www.ws-i.org/docs/WS-I_Introduction.pdf
6. *Microsoft SOAP toolkit 2.0*, http://www.msdn.microsoft.com/soap/
7. *SOAP toolkit 2.2 from Apache community*, 30th May 2001, http://xml.apache.org/dist/SOAP/version-2.2/
8. *Java 2 Enterprise Edition 1.3 platform specification*, http://java.sun.com/j2ee/j2ee-1_3-fr-spec.pdf
9. *JBoss 3.0 documentation*, 2nd May 2002, http://www.jboss.org/online-manual/HTML/index.html

Cooking the Web-ERP

A Practical Recipe to Stir-up Monolithic Enterprise Information Systems Using DOC- and XML-Standards

Michael Gillmann, Joachim Hertel, Christoph G. Jung, Günther Kaufmann, and Michael Wolber

infor: business solutions AG,
Hauerstrasse 12, DE-66299 Friedrichsthal, Germany
http://www.infor-business-solutions.com/

Abstract. When it comes to controlling and optimising information- and value flows in manufacturing industry, *Enterprise Resource Planning (ERP)* is still the preferred option. Despite the immense potential, there is currently a particular caution to be observed in the market for ERP systems. One reason is a prevalent uncertainty about the ongoing 'e-revolution' of traditional business processes. Because the standard ERP systems regard themselves as the epicentre of any enterprise architecture, they cause exceeding consequential costs for reengineering a business. The term *ERP-II* has been coined to describe alternative information system architectures in which flexible and customized federations of smaller *business components* interact, even over enterprise and intranet boundaries, by means of a platform-neutral *communication bus*. It is the central challenge for the ERP vendors at the beginning of the new millennium to evolve and migrate their existing logic and customer installations towards this vision. In this paper, we would like to share our experiences in transforming a particular ERP product for mid-sized businesses into an ERP-II platform. To realise the proposed business bus, we chose a modern middleware based on the ubiquitous *eXtended Markup Language*. To realise a suitable, object-oriented runtime environment for business components, we chose the powerful *Java 2 Enterprise Edition™*. Both flavours have been conveniently blended into the notion of *Business Web Services* to cook a new generation of business processes inside the *Web-ERP*.

1 Introduction

1.1 The Demise of Monolithic ERP Systems

In the current age of business globalization and worldwide marketing, midsize companies too are forced to compete against a hoard of competitors from all over the world [1]. It is therefore imperative for them to increase the quality of both their value-added and information flows. With such growing requirements, one is able to observe a corresponding progression of *Enterprise Information Systems* (EIS) from *Inventory Control* (IC) via *Material Requirements Planning* (MRP), *Manufacturing Resource Planning* (MRP II) up to *Enterprise Resource Planning* (ERP) systems [13].

R. Meersman, Z. Tari (Eds.): CoopIS/DOA/ODBASE 2002, LNCS 2519, pp. 602–617, 2002.

When IC systems made the first steps towards the electronic administration of how to satisfy a company's raw material demand, MRP added conception and execution planning to that. Today, ERP optimises enterprise-wide and simultaneous production processes based on metrics such as warehousing costs, capacity utilisation, throughput and adherence to delivery dates. Figure 1 shows the most common architecture of ERP products, such as SAP R/3 [20] and infor:COM [9]. In these products, *business modules*, such as warehousing, scheduling, accounting, purchasing, sales, and operating data, are appended into a fairly complex software package.

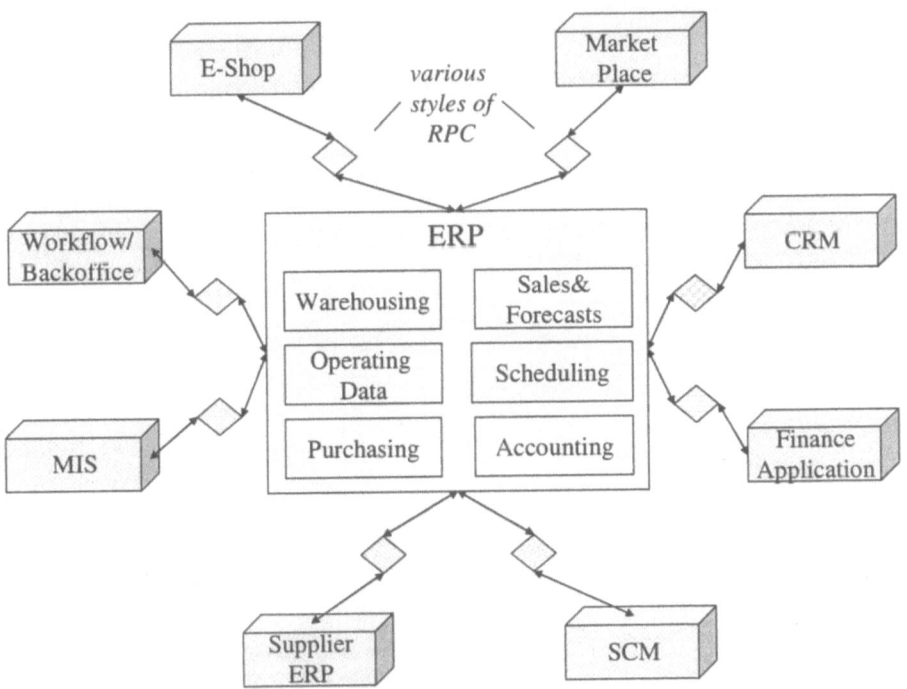

Fig. 1. Monolithic ERP system with extensions

Despite the existing potential especially in the mid-market, ERP sales figures have increased significantly less than analysts expected [15] and threatened the existence of some traditional companies with good reputations, such as Baan [3]. One reason for this phenomenon is the fear of exploding, unmaneagable costs that may occur in conjunction with ERP software projects and their further evolution [21, 22].

Indeed, monolithic ERP systems such as those shown in Figure 1 have serious disadvantages when business processes change regularly [24]. If legacy applications and software of other vendors (e.g. finance applications, backoffice products, e-shops, management information systems, supply chain queues) are to be integrated, the development and the maintenance of dedicated interfaces becomes necessary [23]. Technically, such interfaces often rely on various styles of *Remote Procedure Call* (RPC) [17] and easily degenerate into hardly maintainable 'spaghetti' landscapes centred around the central ERP system.

One side effect is that the resulting conglomerate systems are nearly impossible to interlink with complementary business information systems of customers or suppliers via standardized formats over the Internet. This is urgently needed for, e.g. realising true supply chain automation. Another result is that common ERP systems are not able to be easily downsized. So, the customers buy and install a lot of business logic that they may never need.

Therefore a mismatch between the highly sophisticated economical know-how and an antiquated technical core of the ERP software exists that results in expensive maintenance and limitations.

1.2 ERP-II – The Business Backbone of (Virtual) Enterprises

A new approach to enterprise information systems has been cultivated under the umbrella title Enterprise Application Integration (EAI) [23]. EAI extends the use of engineering techniques such as those known in component-based programming [26] into the area of business logic in order to guarantee the customers a mid- and long-term return on investment [7,18,21].

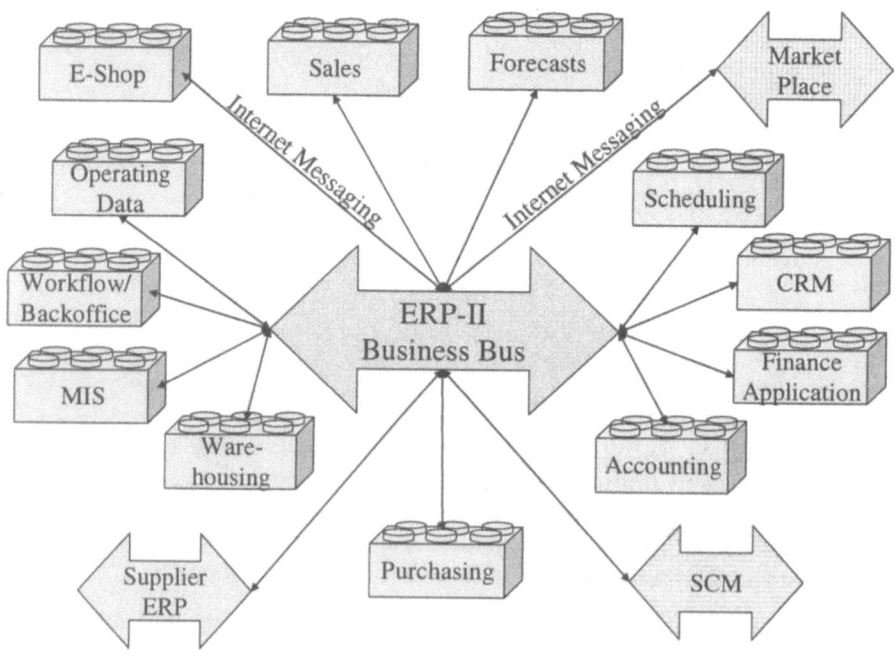

Fig. 2. ERP-II Bus with Business Components

From the perspective that we have depicted in Figure 2, a complex and customized application emerges by the interplay of an upwards and downwards scalable federation of individual software components, each optimally designed for partial functionality [13,24]. These components communicate by means of a universal software bus that is a generalization of the *Distributed Object Computing* (DOC) model, such as pioneered by DCOM and CORBA [19].

The fundamental difference from the 'legacy approach' of Figure 1 is to stop thinking of the ERP system as quasi-middleware, but to dissolve, componentise, and decouple the ERP monolith successively by the middleware [18]. It is only by this approach that modifications in the business processes can be reasonably accommodated and supported by the ERP core. It is only by this approach that specific customer requirements beyond superficial GUI features may be suitably addressed. And it is only by this approach that future business components can be fully integrated into the so-called 'standard logic' to interact in the networked virtual enterprises of the future.

However, if we do not formulate further requirements to the new central notion of the business bus, which we now call *ERP II* [33], then this vision will not be achieved and has already been missed in a vast number of EAI projects [29]:

1. Firstly, it must be ensured that the horizontal view of Figure 2 coincides with the pertaining vertically-tiered architectures [32] to offer a suitable runtime environment for business components.

2. Secondly, such an enterprise bus transporting conceptually rich business messages over the Internet must not build on a connection-oriented communication protocol that is dependent on a particular computing platform. For example, DCOM is tightly bound to the Microsoft™ *Dynamic Network Architecture* and hence to the 32bit versions of the Windows™ operating systems.

3. And thirdly, the business bus must allow a suitable migration strategy from the huge and well established code base written in *4th Generation Languages* (4GLs, such as SAP´s ABAP, Microsoft´s VisualBasic, and infor´s LJ4) into the Distributed Object Computing world. This is certainly a strategy that lies between the two extremes of the 'big bang' and 'legacy' scenarios.

1.3 Contribution and Outline

In this paper, we document the experiences and results of a development project that has been run by infor business solutions AG between 2000 and 2001. In this project, the three aforementioned fundamental requirements on a business bus have been jointly addressed in transforming the existing ERP product infor:COM into a component-oriented ERP-II system that is particularly well-suited for mid-sized manufacturing companies:

1. A three-tier business component runtime environment (Section 2.1) has been based on the object-oriented principles of the *Java 2 Enterprise Edition* (J2EE™) [25]. The runtime core has a small footprint and is easy to extend by additional components.

2. Secondly, business components have been added to by Internet technologies, more specifically XML-based *Web Services* [6]. The resulting 'business federation' is highly suitable for building globally networked applications (Web-ERP, Section 2.2).

3. Thirdly, due to the modularity of J2EE™ and the openness of the Web Service paradigm, we have been able to build a hybrid, albeit integrated product in which state-of-the-art Java components coexist and mutually interact with established 4GL code. In Section 3, we address technical and logical challenges of our ongoing work to incrementally port 4GL modules into coherent ERP-II components.

The presented ERP-II solution including an initial set of migrated and recently developed business components, such as Internationalization, Measures, and Sales Forecasting, is already installed and successfully tested at selected customer sites and will be officially released in 2003. We conclude in Section 4 by a discussion of the suitable (open source) tools that we used.

2 An ERP-II System Based on J2EE™ and Web Services

2.1 Logical Architecture and Runtime Environment

Our architectural blueprint (Figure 3) is based on a traditional three-tier model consisting of *Presentation*, *Application* and *Persistence*. Although the separation of client-side presentation control from server-side application logic goes back to early terminal-based systems, it is today receiving a lot of attention, again, because it enables the simultaneous access by browser-based user interfaces on the one hand and highly-integrated and user-friendly rich clients on the other hand [32].

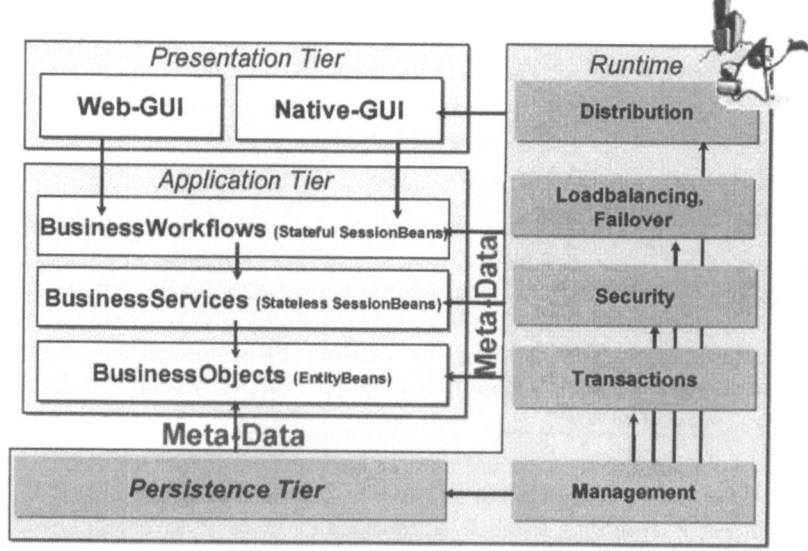

Fig. 3. Declarative Programming in the J2EE™ Model

Similar to other business architectures, such as *San Francisco*™ [2], our application tier is further divided into the *Business Object* (BO), the *Business Service* (BS) and the BusinessWorkflow (BW) tiers. Business objects such as documents, business partners, or sales items represent the persistent entities of an application. Business services such as document administrators or warehouse services implement and publish *Business Methods* to manipulate the BOs. Examples for such business methods are the copying of a document, the retrieval of an archived invoice, or the checking of deliverability. Business methods correspond to individual steps of the *Business Processes*, such as the acceptance a new customer order, that are instantiated by concrete Business Workflows and hence supported by the overall *Business Application Programming Interface* (BAPI).

The visibility between the tiers – BWs can import BSs which can import BOs, but not vice versa – may appear distinctly 'un-OO-ish' at the first sight. However, it follows the well-known *'strategy'* design pattern [31]. Representations that stay constant over a long period of time have to be put into the centre of a software architecture. For example, in the recent, from a business standpoint very turbulent, years, typical business partner contact details have only changed by the addition of an e-mail address and a homepage URL. In contrast, there have been highly mutable parts of the business logic, for example for accomodating business partners in the still evolving e-procurement area. Following the theory, those parts are to be separated into a different service tier of an extensible architecture.

A similar argument holds for the unidirectional dependency from the persistence tier to the BO tier as seen in Figure 3. This means that BOs have no insight into, e.g. database- and transaction-related code packages. Instead, the persistence tier that is a part of the generic runtime environment is able to inspect BOs and to persist BOs state in a relational database with the aim of reinitialising it later 'automagically'. For the sake of performance and simplicity, the impact of this design decision has been neglected in many *object-relational* (OR) persistence frameworks in which the application must include customized database interaction code within the BOs.

The result is a cluttering-up of the business logic with driver programming, particular SQL dialects and error-prone transaction processing. This may be tolerable for small and short-lived applications, but leads to a quick 'death by maintenance' when applied to domains of the size of ERP. Furthermore, due to recent improvements in meta-programming in both Java and C#, building generic persistence frameworks is neither more complicated nor subject to severe performance drawbacks.

The elegant methodology of separating such technically detailed, non-business related and fault critical functionalities (as well as persistence we can also count security, transaction management, distribution, management, caching etc. to these) from the application code and to embody them via flexible code annotations, so-called *'meta-data'*, into the runtime environment is called *Declarative Programming* [14][1] and has been successfully introduced by the *Microsoft Transaction Server* (MTS). Declarative Programming continued to grow into a quite substantial market especially through the *Java 2 Enterprise Edition* (J2EE™) [25].

---

[1] This is, at the first sight, not to confuse with the identical term used in *Logic Programming* (LP). But interestingly, the underlying equation of "Algorithm = Logic + Control" [34] applies to our domain in exactly the same manner.

In J2EE™, business workflows and business services are called (stateful and stateless, respectively) session beans; BOs have a natural counterpart in the so-called entity beans. Because J2EE™ is merely a specification that is to be followed by a number of compliant and differently targetted products (application servers), we could build a small and mostly vendor-independent bridge that allows to run our BO/BS/BW-based ERP logic in various application servers. With the advent of J2EE™ 1.3, the capabilities of server-managed entity bean persistence have been substantially increased and now compete with stand-alone OR products.

For our target market of mid-sized businesses, we currently prefer the highly customizable Open Source application server JBoss [10] to the high-end commercial products, such as BEA WebLogic [30]. This is because we needed to slightly enrich the *Enterprise Java Beans™* (EJB) programming model in two respects. First, object- and component models coincide in EJB™. Secondly, the binary and strongly-typed *Internet Inter-Orb Procotol* of the CORBA specification [19] is proposed as the standard communication language.

We found it initially very hard to assemble a complex ERP-II system from such a finely granular and highly coupled model. We found it even harder to interface the resulting EJB™ logic from windows-based native and web clients. However, as we will describe in more detail in the following section, it is possible to extend these concepts into a suitable business bus architecture.

2.2 Business Components and Web Services

The definition of a *Software Component* in computer science [26] describes a self-contained logical unit that can be individually developed, produced, distributed, installed and run in loose coupling with other components by a suitable runtime environment. In the ERP case, we define a *Business Component* such as sales order processing, rough planning, and warehouse capacity, as a coherent set of business objects, services, workflows and their corresponding meta-data which together form a reasonable partial functionality of the total system (see Figure 4).

Business components are hence considerably smaller than the standard ERP modules such as sales, scheduling or warehousing, whose grandiose amount of logic calls for redundancy-diminishing distribution and flexible decoupling. Business components are, on the other hand, significantly larger than a single and by itself insufficient JavaBean as proposed by the initial EJB™ component specification.

In the J2EE world, a business component has rather a matching concept in terms of an *Enterprise Application,* which is a form of bundling a complete installation in a single ZIP file. Originally, individual applications are isolated from each other, i.e. though they may run within the same virtual machine and shared memory, they may not directly exchange byte code, mutually invoke methods, etc.

As Figure 4 illustrates, our recent additions to the JBoss application server introduce this facility in order to let J2EE applications cluster together with each other, with external components, and also with various user front-ends. Within each of the business components shown (sales order processing, rough planning, and warehouse capacity in Figure 4), we therefore keep up a purely object-oriented view dealing with interfaces, objects and method invocation, e.g. the business services inside the order processing component interact with each other via normal Corba-based method calls.

However, this form of communication cannot be chosen whenever source and target component of such an interaction differ significantly in byte code, class definitions, basic forms of representation (e.g. Java™ versus C#™ classes) or even the runtime environment (e.g. Sun´s JRE™ versus Microsoft´s Common Language Runtime™).

Hence, any interaction either over tier borders, such as the access from a Win32-based administration GUI or a browser-based e-shop, or over component borders, such as calling a deliverability computation inside a warehouse service in order to create a request approval in a sales service or even automatically transmitting a material order to a supplier system via a Biztalk™ B2B Server, has to be mediated through an additional transport layer. For this transport layer, a representation must be found which bridges the different platforms for implementing business logic (compiled versus interpreted, object-oriented versus functional, stateless versus state full) and which enables the 'pluggability' with other software busses, such as needed for B2B supply chain management and electronic marketplaces. As depicted in Figure 4, this is the ideal application of the Simple Object Access Protocol (SOAP) [16].

SOAP is a W3C specification that is based on the eXtended Markup Language (XML) [27] and describes how distributed procedure calls, in our example in Figure 4 a call of the business method reserveItem(Item item, int quantity) in the WareHouse service, are to be encoded independently of their concrete (OO) representations in an XML document which can then be shipped synchronously via the Hypertext Transfer Protocol (HTTP, HTTP/S) or asynchronously via the Simple Mail Transfer Protocol (SMTP).

The choice of HTTP and SMTP as transport protocols has many advantages over dedicated RPC protocols. Because they are standard Internet protocols, there is the possibility to easily tunnel business messages through existing firewall architectures. This would be very difficult to configure for, e.g. CORBA ORBs. Furthermore, due to the messaging character behind HTTP and SMTP, the resulting IP sessions are furthermore very short-lived which saves resources and diminishes the vulnerability of the connections against hostile attacks.

The choice of a tagged XML text format as the basic form of representation also has advantages over, e.g. the typed IIOP byte format. XML is not bound to a particular form of memory structures to be serialized from and deserialized into. XML can encode a rich set of data relationships including inheritance and polymorphism. XML does not require a special-purpose parser; event-based XML parsers are already a part of even the most embedded platforms. XML documents are very modular to synthesize. XML can be easily transformed using the *XML Stylesheet Language* (XSL). And finally, there are a standardized meta-data formats, such as XML Schema (XSD) [8] and the Web Service Description Language (WSDL) [5] which are by themselves bootstrapped through XML.

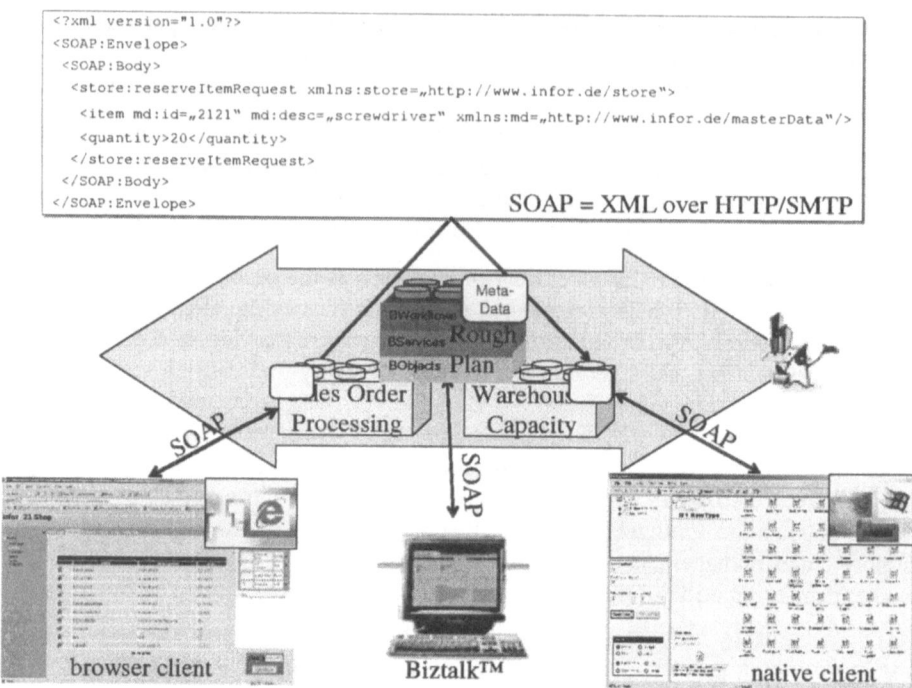

```
<?xml version="1.0"?>
<SOAP:Envelope>
 <SOAP:Body>
  <store:reserveItemRequest xmlns:store="http://www.infor.de/store">
   <item md:id="2121" md:desc="screwdriver" xmlns:md="http://www.infor.de/masterData"/>
   <quantity>20</quantity>
  </store:reserveItemRequest>
 </SOAP:Body>
</SOAP:Envelope>                                    SOAP = XML over HTTP/SMTP
```

Fig. 4. Business Components 'talk SOAP'

In Figure 5, we have demonstrated the application of these meta formats to our ERP-II architecture. Business objects, such as the Item entity bean, expose their data structure in the form of corresponding *XML Types* (<Item/>)defined in XML Schema documents ("Item.xsd"). One could look at an XML Type as obtaining a particular, platform-independent view onto the business object quite like the business object itself operates as a view into the underlying database model.

Business Workflows and Business Services, such as the Warehouse session bean, expose their implemented logic in the form of corresponding *Operations* (<reserveItem/>) defined in WSDL documents ("Warehouse.wsdl"). In a way, WSDL just puts operational semantics on top of XSD because the operations are specified by well-formed request and response messages which themselves build upon the XML schemas of the arguments, return types, and exceptions such as defined "Item.xsd". In WSDL, operations are bundled into so-called *Port Types*, the platform-independent version of Java interfaces, and finally *bound* to particular low-level transports, such as http endpoints located on particular machines in the network.

XSD, SOAP and WSDL currently are part of all the major business platforms ranging from Microsoft .Net or popular scripting languages up to many J2EE™ products. As demonstrated, they therefore establish the platform-independent BAPI that we were looking for in order to specify the representations on the ERP-II software bus. To fully exploit the concept of globally visible *Business Web Services*, we can finally register the meta descriptions with the increasingly common capability of *Universal Description Discovery Integration* (UDDI) registries [28].

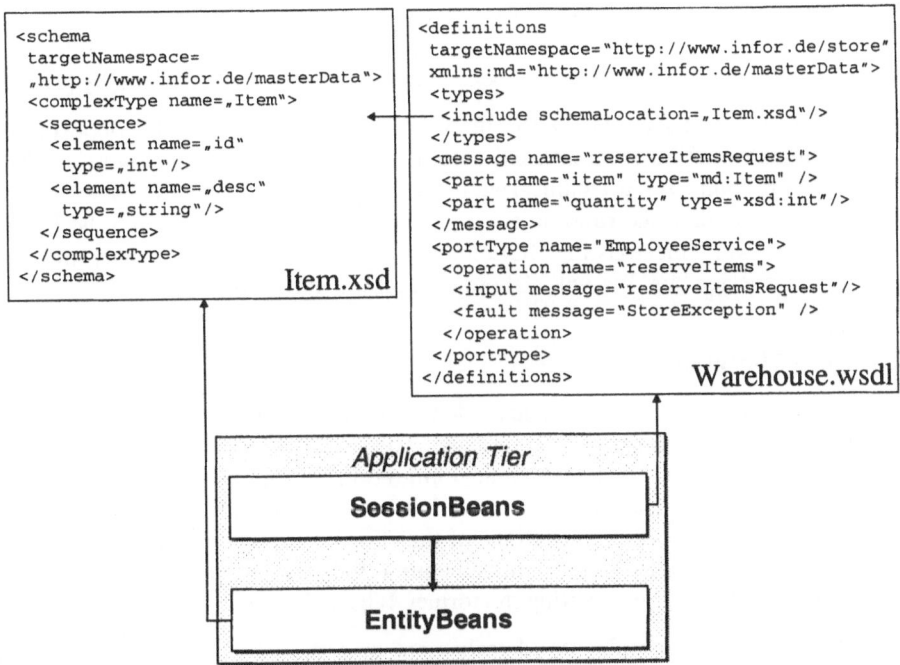

```
<schema
 targetNamespace=
 „http://www.infor.de/masterData">
<complexType name=„Item">
 <sequence>
  <element name=„id"
   type=„int"/>
  <element name=„desc"
   type=„string"/>
 </sequence>
 </complexType>
</schema>                    Item.xsd
```

```
<definitions
 targetNamespace="http://www.infor.de/store"
 xmlns:md="http://www.infor.de/masterData">
 <types>
  <include schemaLocation=„Item.xsd"/>
 </types>
 <message name="reserveItemsRequest">
  <part name="item" type="md:Item" />
  <part name="quantity" type="xsd:int"/>
 </message>
 <portType name="EmployeeService">
  <operation name="reserveItems">
   <input message="reserveItemsRequest"/>
   <fault message="StoreException" />
  </operation>
 </portType>
</definitions>              Warehouse.wsdl
```

Application Tier

SessionBeans

EntityBeans

Fig. 5. WSDL and XSD describe a platform-neutral BAPI on top of J2EE™

In infor:COM, or rather JBoss3.0, the mapping between the JavaBeans and the universal XML structures and registries is another example of the convenient and highly productive declarative programming approach. In the JBoss.net project [11],an existing SOAP messaging product is incorporated to complement the existing CORBA invocation engine with an additional SOAP layer. This layer operates transparently to the application logic and is controlled by additional meta-data annotations in the deployable business components.

3 The Smooth Migration from ERP to ERP-II

We have already sufficiently discussed that the monolithic ERP architecture shown in Figure 1 has serious disadvantages in system extensibility and maintainability [13,24] especially in the current age of Internet technology and global virtual enterprises. So it has to be migrated to the new technological state of the art that we have developed in the Section 2 above. However, a big bang strategy to completely replace the legacy ERP by a brand-new ERP-II approach would significantly increase dangers and result in large (financial) risks, and not only for the ERP vendors.

Typically ERP systems such as infor:COM consist of several million lines of 4GL source code and so it is safe to say that the development of a subsequent product release takes years. Furthermore, long-term customers whose systems have been used for years do not want to trash their experiences and familiar working processes gained in using the ERP software. Further to learn the new system from scratch. What they want is to exchange only those components that require the new functionality [12].

The solution that we have taken with infor:COM in order to resolve this opposition is a smooth transformation from an ERP system to an ERP-II system (Figure 6). This transformation comprises a technical and a logical migration path. Technically it is meant to tightly couple the runtime environments of the ERP system and the ERP-II system, i.e. making the existing 4GL logic a proper part of the freshly installed business web service bus. We will elaborate that issue in Section 3.2.

3.1 Logical Migration

Logically a smooth migration means identifying and publishing service-relevant interfaces from the existing 4GL code base. This is the harder and more resource-intensive task. However, once the technical migration problem is resolved, the logical transformation need not be done at once, but can be done incrementally and on-demand by identifying coherent portions of the ERP business logic, defining suitable replacement interfaces for them, implementing those interfaces by new ERP-II components, and finally deactivating the former 4GL code.

Figure 6 shows, for example, the detachement of a new ERP-II sales forecasting component from the older ERP sales module that we have already successfully performed in infor:COM. Through the business bus, the ERP-II component now looks at the still existing ERP modules as standard, albeit legacy components. The ERP modules interact with the new ERP-II component transparently through technical interface code that replaces the former implementation. This technique can also be be used to extend particular 4GL process logic which should not yet be totally replaced, but needs some temporary upgrade, e.g. to access partner products, perform additional messaging, etc.

The customer is thereby provided with frequent product updates (in our case starting after two initial years of research) of a modern, hybrid product. This ERP-II product is not restricted to a partial functionality of the ERP core as it would have been necessary when building it completely from scratch. In this product, even the 4GL logic not yet migrated gains value through the increased (Internet) business process capabilities of the embedding ERP-II platform as it would not have been possible, if treating the complete ERP as a single, monolithic legacy component. The classical ERP system is therefore slowly dissolved. Its enterprise-critical core functions will smoothly transform into ERP-II components.

3.2 Technical Migration

It must be noted that the success of this migration approach depends highly on the quality of the 4GL code base and the technical measures chosen. Whenever the code base becomes too big , too cluttered or cannot be processed with the help of modern

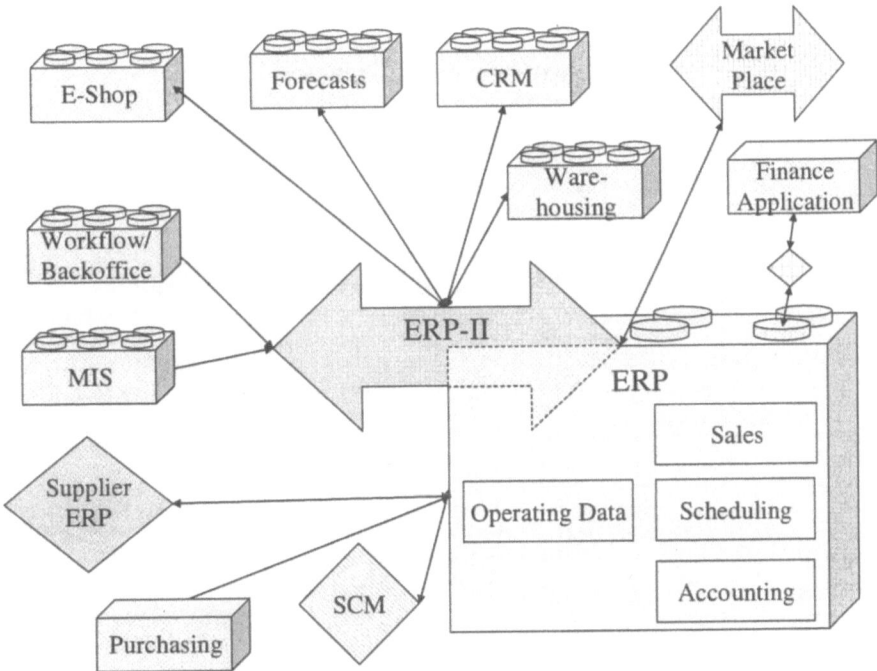

Fig. 6. Coexistence of ERP and ERP-II in a hybrid system

code analysis and cross-compilation tools, even the first step of identifying separable interfaces may fail. In infor:COM, the 4GL language is an in-house development called *LJ4*. Because of our experience with appropriate compiler technology and the size of the product which is targeted to mid-size companies, we are quite confident of the road taken. This has been confirmed by our initial successes in migrating, e.g. the Sales Forecasting logic, within the hybrid product.

However, these successes would not have been possible without carefully preparing a technical 'bed' for the now unified J2EE™ and 4GL runtime environments (Figure 7). When comparing the vertical architectures, we recognise that the modern concepts of BSs, BOs, and the persistence tier have 'outdated' counterparts in the form of LJ4 procedures operating on Vtabs which are implementations of typical relational SQL datasets. But we also recognise that infor:COM stems from a traditional two-tier background in which presentation logic and application logic reside on the same physical computing device.

To enable business processes to freely flow between the two sides, we hence need elaborated technical integration methods for each of the tiers shown (Figure 7). For example, to couple the ERP database with the ERP-II persistence engine, we have employed a distributed transaction manager to synchronize the database operations.

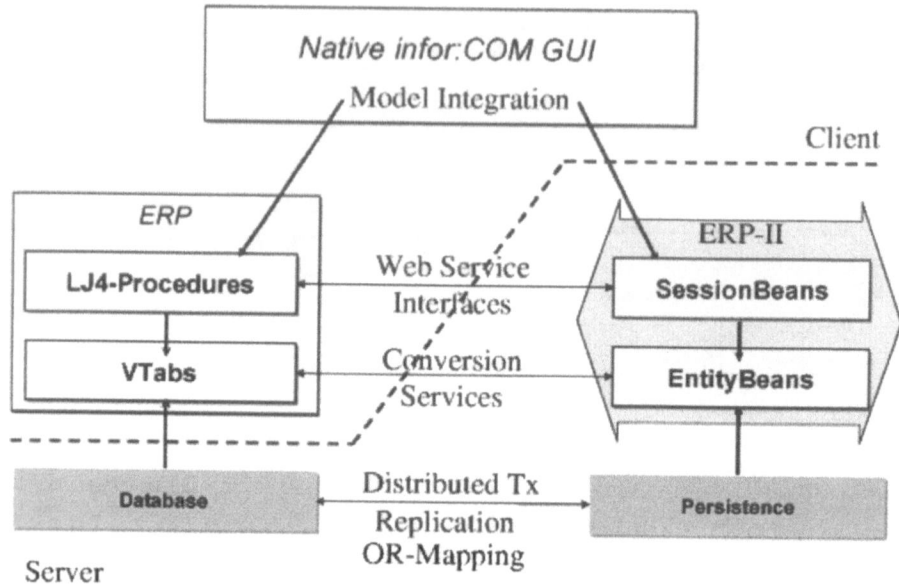

Fig. 7. Methods for Technical Migration

Where data must be present in fundamentally different schemas to feed both the ERP and ERP-II logic, we employ replication techniques. In the easier case, it is possible to map dedicated BOs onto the existing tables in the ERP system.

This is complemented on the next tier by technical services which can convert Vtab memory structures into entity bean structures and vice versa. Using the already described, platform-neutral Web Service layer on the BS and BW tiers already described, it is then possible to exchange method/procedure calls, including the exchange of data, between both platforms.

Finally, we have decided not to build two separate clients, but to retain the existing native application to which a broad community of users has been well accustomed by now and which supports their typical use cases in an optimal manner. For that purpose, we have managed to extend the existing presentation model in order to cope with the new business representations of the Web-ERP platform.

4 Conclusion

In this paper, we have presented the experiences gained while preparing infor business solutions AG's upcoming release of the infor:COM product. infor:COM 6.3 is based on a component-based extensible ERP-II architecture (Web-ERP) with a small system footprint. New and globally networked business components, such as our currently piloted Sales Forecasting component, are built upon a combination of modern DOC- and XML-ingredients. They coexist in a hybrid, albeit technically-integrated environment with established 4GL code, such as for resource planning, which will be incrementally transformed through an ongoing logical migration effort.

The work that we have described has been eased by the consistent use of and contribution to the Open Source community. In the recent past, Open Source software has made quite a progression from operating systems (Linux), via tools and libraries (GNU), web servers (Apache) up to the first business logic environments (OpenEJB, Jonas and JBoss [10]). It is now a viable alternative to costly in-house developments as well as to ready-made, but closed-source commercial middleware.

This way, independent business software vendors can share their development efforts with respect to the application server while still competing at the level of the commercial business logic and development tools. For example, infor has developed an extension to the UML tool TogetherJ™ (Figure 8) which allows the developer to seemlessly specify, architect, implement, assemble and even debug infor:COM business components. Because of standard Java interfaces and the open deployment formats, the corresponding code is even compliant with the strict rules of the Lesser General Public License (LGPL).

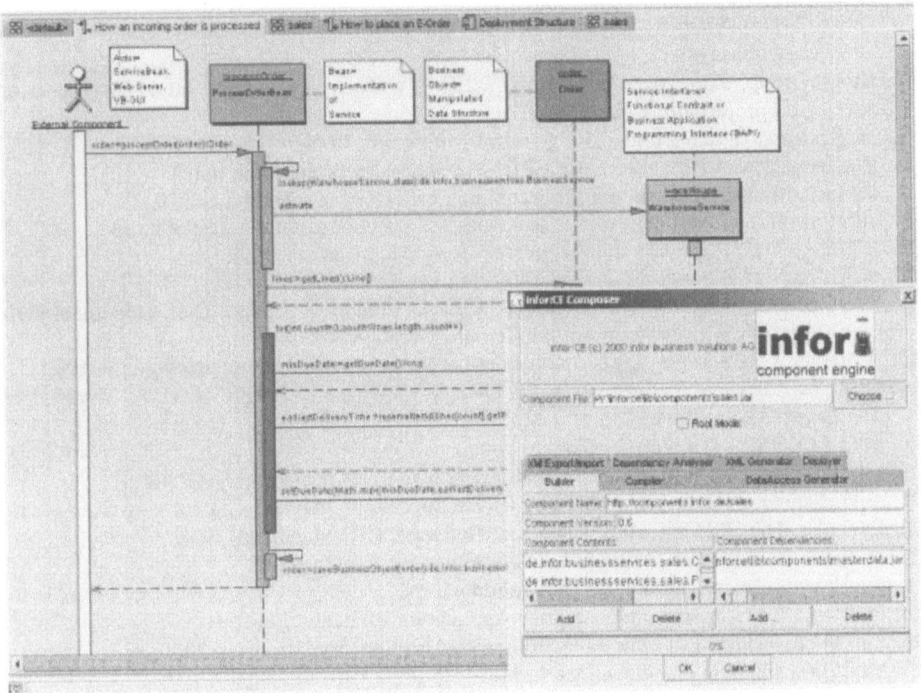

Fig. 8. Developing Business Components with UML

Acknowledgements. We would like to thank Michael Abel, Johannes Beck, Ralf Immer, Georg Röver, Darius Schier and Andreas Schörk for contributing much to the work presented. Most valuable comments to this paper have been given by Colm Stephens and Richard Hunn. Furthermore, we would like to thank the many talented contributors to the JBoss project.

References

1. R. Adhikari, ERP Meets The Middle Market, IndustryWeek, 1999
2. K. A. Bohrer, Architecture of the San Francisco frameworks, IBM Systems Journal, Vol. 37, No. 2, 1998
3. S. Baker, M. Spiro, S Hamm, The Fall of Baan, Business Week International, August 2000
4. Communications of the ACM, Vol. 43, No. 4, 2000
5. E. Christensen, F. Curbera, G. Meredith, S. Weerawarana, Web Service Description Language (WSDL) 1.1, W3C Note, 2001, http://www.w3.org/TR/wsdl
6. E. Cerami, Web Service Essentials, O'Reilly, February 2002
7. T. H. Davenport, Realizing the Promise of Enterprise Systems, Harvard Business School Press, 2000
8. D. Fallside, Xml Schema Part 0: Primer, W3C Recommendation, May 2001
9. infor business solutions AG, A Fitness Boost for your Business, http://www.infor-business-solutions.com/cms/solutions
10. JBoss Group, !Simpler, Cheaper, Better!, The Java App-Server reference implementation, http://www.jboss.org
11. JBoss Group, JBoss.net: Integrating J2EE™ with Web-Services, http://www.jboss.org/developers/projects/jboss/dotnet.jsp
12. M. Kremers, H. van Dissel, ERP Systems Migrations, in [4]
13. K. Kumar, J. van Hilleghersberg, ERP Experiences and Evolution, in [4]
14. J. MasterMann, Transactional Programming, MSDN Magazine, June 2000, http://msdn.microsoft.com/msdnmag/issues/0600/advbasics/advbasics0600.asp
15. J. Menezes, ERP vendors´ bubble bursts, Computing Canada, 1999
16. N. Mitra, SOAP Version 1.2, W3C Working Draft, December 2001
17. The Open Group, CAE Specification, DCE1.1: Remote Procedure Call, Document C706, 1997, http://www.opengroup.org/public/pubs/catalog/c706.htm
18. A. Parker, ERP's future lies in modules rather than monoliths, ComputerWeekly, 1999
19. G. S. Raj, A detailed comparison of CORBA, DCOM, and Java/RMI, OMG Whitepapers, The Object Management Group, 1997
20. SAP AG, SAP R/3 Enterprise, White Paper, http://www.sap.com/solutions/technology/ pdf/SAP_R3_Enterprise_WP.pdf
21. A.W. Scheer, F. Habermann, Making ERP a Success, in [4]
22. D. Slater, The Hidden Cost of Enterprise Software, CIO Magazine, 1998
23. D. Slater, Middleware Demystified, CIO Magazine, 2000, http://www.cio.com/archive/051500_middle.html
24. D. Sprott, Componentizing Enterprise Application Packages, in [4]
25. Sun Microsystems Ltd., The Java 2 Enterprise Edition Specification, 2000, http://java.sun.com/j2ee/download.html
26. C. Szyperski, Component Software Beyond Object-Oriented Programming, Addison-Wesley / ACM Press, 1998
27. T. Bray, J. Paoli, C. M. Sperberg-McQueen, E. Maler, Extensible Markup Language (XML) 1.0 (Second Edition), The World-Wide Web consortium, 2000
28. The UDDI organization, UDDI Executive White Paper, http://uddi.org/pubs/UDDI_Executive_White_Paper.PDF

29. J. Vowler, You cannot afford to ignore integration, ComputerWeekly, 1999
30. Bea Systems, Managing Complexity with Application Infrastructure, Whitepaper, http://contact2.bea.com/bea/www/wli/paper.jsp?PC=WLILG-WLP
31. E. Gamma, R. Helm, R. Johnson, J. Vlissides, Design Patterns: elements of reusable object-oriented software, Addison Wesley, 1995
32. J. Noack, H. Mehmanesh, H. Mehmaneche, A. Zendler, Architectures for Network Computing (in German), Wirtschaftsinformatik, Vol. 42, No. 1, 2000
33. Y. Genovese, B. Bond, B. Zrimseck, N. Frey, The transition to ERP-II: Meeting the Challenges, Gartner Group, R-14-0612, Sep. 2001
34. R. A. Kowalski, Algorithm = Logic + Control, Communications of the ACM, Number 22, Volume 7, pages 424-436, 1979

Web Services and CORBA

Seán Baker

IONA Technologies
Shelbourne Road, Dublin, Ireland

Abstract. Web Services and CORBA complement each other in a number of ways. CORBA offers Web Services a mature platform to implement services. Web Services offer a straightforward path to web-enabling CORBA applications. In addition, Web Services, CORBA, and other middleware platforms can participate in a multi-level Service Oriented Architecture, with Web Services playing the role of middleware-to-middleware integration technology. This paper describes in detail the relationship between CORBA and Web Services. It also argues that different forms of middleware, including Web Services and CORBA, should be used together so that developers and integrators can choose from a well-integrated toolkit of different technologies.

1 Introduction

CORBA and Web Services differ in many ways, including their initial design goals, their support for objects, the methods by which the standards are being agreed, and so on. Nevertheless they are based on the same fundamental distributed systems techniques, especially since both support interface definitions, message passing, operation invocation, and resource naming/location. This paper describes why and how they should be used together. In our view they are more complementary than conflicting, and there are many advantages in using them together.

There are three reasons why the two technologies should be used together:

1. Web Services allow CORBA resources to be leveraged in an internet environment.
2. The CORBA platform is a good choice for implementing a Web Service. This is especially useful for non-Java and non-C# projects, or Java projects that need high flexibility.
3. Many companies use more than one type of middleware. Some of these allow high-level interoperability (CORBA and J2EE, for example), but others are difficult to interoperate. Web Services is a good choice for such middleware-to-middleware interworking.

Briefest Introduction to Web Services

Web Services are used to bridge the boundaries between enterprises, and those between different middlewares within an enterprise. Currently, three initial specifica-

R. Meersman, Z. Tari (Eds.): CoopIS/DOA/ODBASE 2002, LNCS 2519, pp. 618–632, 2002.

tions are in various stages of being specified: SOAP (the protocol to interact with a Web Service), WSDL (the language for specifying the interface to a Web Service) and UDDI (the repository for storing references to Web Services so that clients can find them). Roughly, these correspond respectively to IIOP, IDL, and the Naming/Trading services. (Albeit, the last of these has the least accurate correspondence because UDDI has a much stronger business focus. For example, a company can describe not only a WSDL interface that they provide, but also extensive details about the company itself).

XML is used extensively. WSDL is written in XML (a WSDL interface specification is formatted as an XML document that conforms to an agreed schema); SOAP messages are XML documents; and the interface to UDDI is defined in XML.

2 One Size Doesn't Fit All

The use of just one type of middleware may seem ideal, but this goal is as difficult to achieve as the use of one programming language for all programming needs. Indeed, the use of one middleware is often inappropriate. Different middleware has different advantages, so even projects started at the same time are likely to choose different middleware to suit their own needs. In addition, different types of middleware have been in use for more than two decades, and we can expect new and innovative forms to be introduced in the future.

Although it a little simplified, it is useful to view middleware as being either *platform middleware* or *integration middleware*. Platform middleware helps both in the development of applications (by reducing the amount of code that a developer needs to write to solve complex problems such as object lifecycle, transactions, security, and so on), and in the subsequent interoperability of these applications. Integration middleware helps in the integration of existing applications[1]. CORBA and J2EE are two widely used platform middleware standards. .NET also clearly qualifies as platform middleware. Unfortunately, there has been no standard for integration middleware. Interestingly, Web Services has many of the properties required for this.

It is too difficult for a single middleware standard or product to incorporate all of the advantages of the different types of middleware. Firstly, the numerous approaches to middleware, and the number of techniques built up over the decades, would mean that an „all-inclusive" middleware would be bloated and overly complex. Secondly, some aspects of middleware are mutually exclusive. For example, J2EE uses Java to define interfaces (and this gives ease-of-use for Java programmers), while CORBA uses IDL (which gives easy multi-language support).

As a result, we can identify different advantages for the various middleware choices. We will look at the advantages of CORBA and Web Services because this paper is primarily concerned with these two technologies. The advantages of CORBA are:

---

[1] CORBA and J2EE are wider in their applicability than captured in this simplified view. See [1] for a more extensive discussion. The main point being made in this section is that it is very useful to be able to draw on an extensive toolkit of middleware technology when building and integrating systems.

- It supports multiple programming languages in a straightforward way. In addition, it does this in a way that means that programmers in any particular language need not be aware of the rules appropriate to the other languages, or even that multiple languages are being used in a system. For example, a C++ programmer writing a server needs to do nothing special to allow a Visual Basic client to access its services.

- It is platform middleware and therefore it helps developers to build systems. The components of these systems can be immediately available as components of a „software bus" that spans the internal systems of an enterprise. This gives direct support to the concept of a Service Oriented Architecture (SOA). Software analysts recommend this approach because the alternative way of integrating applications is via a series of point-to-point integrations that result in increased complexity and cost.

- The writers of the CORBA standard, and the implementers of products, have spent considerable effort ensuring that it interoperates with other middleware, in particular with COM and J2EE.

- It is highly flexible because it gives programmers access to many configuration and programming choices. Commonly-used approaches are available as patterns, but programmers can make minor or major changes to these to suit the needs of particular applications, or they can define new patterns to suit their special needs. This flexibility results in very high performance and scalability. It also means that complex tasks can be tackled in straightforward ways. This is in contrast to using a middleware standard that offers a small number of fixed choices that capture some simple usage patterns. That approach can mean that complex tasks that require significant architectural choice can be overly complicated to achieve, because the fixed patterns must be worked around or cheated.

- It supports both the Remote Procedure Call and message-passing paradigms. The former is supported directly by IDL. The latter is supported to some extent by Oneway operations in IDL (but use of this mechanism depends too much on the implementation choices of the CORBA vendor), and much more strongly by the Event, Notification and Log Services, which offer publish-and-subscribe type interactions. In addition, CORBA supports highly efficient parallel communication with many recipients, via its multi-cast protocol.

- Although I have no empirical evidence to back up this claim, I believe that the use of IDL, rather than a programming language, to define interfaces results in higher-level and better-structured interfaces. The fact that an interface cannot be implemented in IDL means that a programmer using it to define an interface will concentrate more on the needs of the clients than the lower-level needs of the programming language that will be used to implement it. In addition, there can be no „accidental interfaces" when using CORBA: either an interface is meant to be exposed as a service to other applications (because it is defined in IDL), or it isn't (because it is defined in the chosen programming language). An existing interface defined in a programming language cannot be exposed without re-defining it in IDL, and this step acts as a simple check of whether or not it makes sense to expose this interface. It also provides an opportunity to improve the interface from the perspective of the clients that must use it.

- Use of IDL also means that interoperability with other forms of middleware is much easier than if interfaces are defined in a programming language. IDL has been specifically designed to make it easy to translate into other languages. As we'll see later, this point is important when considering how Web Services and CORBA can be used together.

- CORBA is very well proven across a set of domains, including banking, telecommunications, utilities, government, defence, utilities, computer animation, astronomy, weather simulation, and so on. In each of these areas there are many examples of highly successful integration and development projects based on CORBA, and of companies whose businesses depend on its reliability.

The advantages of Web Services are:

- Like CORBA, Web Services encourage the SOA approach, and also support of multiple programming languages.

- It has been designed specifically with the Web in mind. From the start it has been layered on HTTP so that requests can pass through firewalls. However, this could be achieved for most protocols, and has already been done for CORBA's IIOP. Therefore, a more important distinction is that Web Services are accepted by the Web community for use in inter-enterprise communication, whereas many other middleware standards, including CORBA, are not. An example of this is that the obvious security risks of HTTP tunnelling (allowing another protocol, in this case SOAP, to get through firewalls because they can sit on top of HTTP) are considered to be a challenge in the context of Web Services. In contrast, they are considered a show-stopper by many in the case of IIOP. Another example is that the SOAP protocol of Web Services has been adopted by important B2B standards such as ebXML and RosettaNet.

- Web Services makes no assumption that the same technology will be at both ends of the connection. A SOAP message processor is required at both ends, but this is a simple piece of technology, and there are many tools (such as XML processors) that make it easy to write.

  However, too much shouldn't be read into this advantage because it will diminish rapidly when Web Services are augmented with „services" such as security, transactions, work-flow and so on. When this happens, the technology at both ends will be very significantly more complex, and it will not be an easy matter to add this support at both end of the connection. This will require a significant investment, either in the form of in-house development or bought-in middleware technology.

  Nevertheless, it will still be possible for Web Services to continue to integrate different technologies, provided full-service toolkits are available for integration with those technologies that do not have native Web Services support. These toolkits are not in place today, but there will be strong motivation for doing this as long as Web Services is the only standard, or at least a primary standard, for integration middleware.[2]

- Web Services uses XML to define interfaces and to format messages. This has the advantage that messages are more „open" than if they were defined in a binary format. At the very least, programmers are more likely to write code to create or understand an XML message. Of course, this advantage shouldn't be over stated. There is a belief that applications can understand XML messages because they are „self-describing." Sometimes this is indeed an advantage, but it must also be remembered that there is no guarantee that two applications will take the same meaning from a „self-describing" XML message. While it is easy to write software that can parse any XML message (it's especially easy since there are tools like DOM and SAX to help do this), most applications can only deal with XML that they have been written to handle. Indeed, in many cases, the message formats that an application needs to handle are fixed, or at least they are fixed for considerable lengths of time. Sometimes, it is possible to write software to handle specific XML, but which can also handle an XML document that contains extra elements. This is often achieved simply by having the software ignore elements that it wasn't expecting. It's difficult to achieve the same approach using CORBA[3].

Overall, even in cases where the formats of messages are quite simple and fixed, use of XML seems to be an important psychological advantage for the acceptance of the Web Services standards.

One of the disadvantages of XML is that messages are larger compared to the more optimized formats used by CORBA. Also, the marshalling of these messages is more complex and therefore more processor intensive. These will not be important concerns for some applications, but they will be critical for others. New Web Services standards may define more optimized protocols (either based on binary-encoding of XML, or not based on XML at all).

---

[2] There is a danger that this will not happen quite as planned. If Web Services fulfils its promise as an important integration middleware, then it may cross over the line and become a platform middleware. (That is, it will be possible to implement services using extensions to the Web Services model.) This would mean that Web Services would have to redefine (or, less likely, to adopt) all of the technology that makes a middleware standard a platform (this would include many of the aspects of CORBA, J2EE and/or .NET). In addition, these extensions to Web Services may well be proprietary, with the associated risks and long-term costs. Nevertheless, such extensions may be a natural implication of competition in the computer industry.

There is also a danger that one or more major players will fear losing out to Web Services, and therefore view it as competitive. One of them might then release a rival standard that does not incorporate Web Services and will not interoperate well with them. Independent companies may define and implement interoperability rules between the two (or more) approaches, but it may be difficult to get industry-wide consensus for these. Such a scenario is of course not just idle speculation; it has happened a number of times before, and it is likely to happen again. The need for interworking is the only thing that remains a constant in the world of middleware. The need for interoperability will be removed only in a (boring) homogeneous world with no competition!

Some people have said that one of the advantages of SOAP messages being formatted in XML is that humans can read them. People will quickly tire of reading XML messages, especially as use of Web Services transitions from the lab to the mainstream. Anyway, programmers that use middleware with binary message formats can use „snooping" utilities to read the contents of messages. Also, most inter-enterprise messages will be encrypted, which means that they will be binary even if they start life as nicely formatted XML.

- Web Services has initial support from a wider set of software vendors than even CORBA, which was the first middleware standard to reach a critical mass of support. CORBA still has significantly more user involvement in the writing of standards and in setting the agenda of what needs to be standardized. Nevertheless, part of the promise of Web Services is the wide vendor support that it has attracted, and the corresponding promise of ubiquity. The true worth of this initial support will become clearer when some companies start to win the battle to be one of the leading Web Services vendors, and of course others begin to lose out.

The remainder of this paper looks in turn at the three reasons, already outlined in the Introduction, that CORBA and Web Services will be used together.[3]

3 CORBA Resources in a Web Environment

Technically it is possible to use CORBA's IIOP protocol to access a CORBA object through a firewall. However, as stated previously, this is not politically acceptable to many people, and especially not to the web community. Therefore, the combination of CORBA and Web Services extends the usefulness of CORBA objects in a way that CORBA itself cannot. Because Web Services is similar to CORBA in many ways, this type of front-ending is easy to achieve. This is very different to exposing a CORBA interface via a web-based portal or user-interface technology, where the CORBA interface would be almost unrecognizable at the web front-end.

You should not read into this that all CORBA interfaces can and should be exposed to the web via Web Services. Some will use IDL datatypes that are hard to translate (for example, the Any datatype). Even more importantly, many IDL interfaces will not offer a service that is suitable for exportation to the web.

If we leave to one side for a moment the question of whether or not a CORBA interface should be exposed via Web Services, the actual exposing of it would mean

---

3 It is interesting to note that most of the observations made in the following sections also apply to how J2EE and Web Services interrelate. J2EE provides servlets and JSPs for use in Web development. However, JSPs are browser-oriented rather than being concerned with application-to-application integration. Although many implementations of Web Services are implemented on top of the Servlets, the standard itself is at too low a level for high-level application-to-application integration (because the interface only deals with receiving a block of data from a caller). Web Services is therefore a powerful way to integrate J2EE applications with the application–to-application integration and business-to-business integration aspects of the web. It is also a good way to allow J2EE applications to interwork with non-Java applications.

that the IDL must be translated into WSDL and a wrapper generated (or a generic one installed) that will accept SOAP messages and forward them to the CORBA objects. In some cases, this wrapper will also have to handle calls in the other direction. Web Service implementations, such as XMLBus[5], provide tools to carry out these steps, so that the WSDL interface and the wrapper code can be generated automatically.

IDL is a good starting point for a Web Service interface definition because IDL has been designed to be easy to translate to other languages. CORBA's object-by-value support and the Any datatype cause difficulties, but all of the other datatypes can be translated easily. Generating a Web Service interface from a programming language interface can be much more difficult, because nearly all programming languages have many datatypes that cause difficulties (see [2] for a discussion of the difficulties in translating Java to other languages). The ease of translating IDL into WSDL comes as no surprise of course, since it has already been translated into languages such as C, C++, Java, Visual Basic, COBOL, Ada, Smalltalk, PL/I, Lisp, Python, Perl, Objective-C, Oberon, Eiffel, Modula 3, Scheme and TCL.

A much higher-level issue is whether or not it is advisable to release a given IDL interface (really an instance, of course) as a Web Service. Some will be suitable, but releasing one that is not suitable will either lead to Web Services that are difficult to use or it will expose the provider of the Web Service to unwanted risks that the interface will be misused by the clients. Most CORBA interfaces are already written with the needs of other applications in mind, so there is a better chance that an IDL interface will be suitable. This contrasts greatly to interfaces written in a programming language. (Some IDL interfaces are written for use within a single application or closed group of applications, and these are either protected using the security service or care is taken not to expose them outside of a closed environment). Nevertheless, many IDL interfaces may be at too low a level of abstraction to be suitable.

A simple example of this is where two operations (of the same or of different interfaces) must be called in a certain order. The applications that use these operations currently may be trusted to obey this rule, but the new applications that need to use them may not be trusted, or it could be an unacceptable burden on these new applications to always ensure that the rule is obeyed. The solution is of course to move to a higher level of abstraction, for example by exposing a single operation that calls the other two in the correct order. If a single operation is exposed, then this could be part of a new interface that has to be written in order to expose an acceptable interface to the new applications. An alternative solution is to adopt a process flow system.[4]

The less control the existing server(s) have over the new applications, the higher the level of abstraction of the interface that should be exposed. Very little of this type of control exists between enterprises, and this explains the high level of abstraction needed of the interfaces between them.

Some IDL interfaces are too „chatty" to be useful in a web environment, where the network latency can be much higher than for internal networks. A „chatty" interface often requires a number of calls to an object in order to achieve some result. Designers of CORBA systems know that they cannot make their interfaces as „chatty" as

---

[4] XMLBus provides a number of alternative ways to increase the level of abstraction. A new interface can be defined and implemented by a developer (perhaps using CORBA or J2EE) and then exposed using Web Services; an *operation flow* can be defined (using a GUI tool) that exposes a high level Web Services operation that calls the two operations in the correct order; or a full process flow system can be used.

they would if their entire system ran inside one process. Hence, for example, they may extend interfaces with operations that return all of the properties of the target object, rather than requiring clients to make multiple calls to operations that return individual properties.

The difference in latency between in-process calls and network calls requires designers of interfaces to be aware of a number of techniques like this. Web-based applications face an even higher network latency, and a subset of Web Services interfaces will have to take this into account (remember that Web Services can also be used on high-performance networks inside an organization). In some cases, interfaces will become very coarse-grained. For example, in a CORBA system that implements a computerized sales system, an interface to order electronic goods may have operations to request what goods are available in a particular category, to check the price and color of a particular model, and so on. These interfaces would be used by other systems inside the enterprise (for example, by a web portal). In some Web Services systems this type of interface may have to be augmented with a very coarse grained one in which a client can request a full brochure (as an XML document), and later purchase an item by calling an operation that accepts full details of the item to be purchased.

Sometimes there is an even higher-level reason why a direct translation of an existing IDL interface might not be suitable for exposing to another enterprise. Many enterprises are members of industry groups that standardize the format of data sent between them. Many of these industry groups will adopt Web Services as the underlying middleware, but they will standardize the format of the XML messages, and in some cases these will be rather complex. Even though an enterprise may have a CORBA server that already implements the service that is to be exposed, a direct translation of the IDL into WSDL would not give the required XML formatting.

Because of all of these reasons, it is our view that in all cases you should plan to increase the level of abstraction above that of the existing CORBA layer, so that the existing interfaces can be improved, combined or otherwise changed in order to bring them to the right level of abstraction for the software boundary to be bridged with the Web Services technology. This increase in abstraction can be achieved using a separately programmed layer, or a productivity tool (such as the XMLBus „operation flow" support) can be used to generate it.

The complexity of this interface layer will depend on the nature of the IDL interfaces being exposed (whether or not they were designed for use by applications over which the provider had little control; what type of network latency was assumed; and so on). In general, there will be less work required when Web Services are used to bridge boundaries inside an enterprise; and more work will be required to offer services on the web.

Where the level of abstraction has to be increased using a separately programmed layer, then CORBA can be used to implement that layer. A valid approach for a CORBA programmer is to design one or more higher-level IDL interfaces, to implement these using the existing interfaces, and to expose the higher-level IDL via the IDL-to-WSDL automatic translation tools.

4 Implementing Web Services Using CORBA

In many cases the best starting point for a Web Service will be a definition of the WSDL interface to the service that is to be exposed. In this case, CORBA is a good choice for implementing the service itself. In contrast, Web Services cannot be used to implement services because it is integration middleware, not platform middleware. There are no rules in the standard for how to write a service – just how to communicate with one.

CORBA is an especially good choice for the platform middleware where the programming language is not Java or C#, or where Java is being used to write a service requires more flexibility than offered by J2EE (more programmer choice, more patterns, more control).

The only difficulty with starting with the Web Services definition (that is, top-down) is that it is very difficult to write WSDL by hand. In particular, the syntax is very error prone and verbose for a human, and there is considerable repetition of important details. One solution may be to start with UML diagrams (perhaps using MDA to model the system independently of the underlying platform). Another approach in the future may be to use a simplified human-oriented language that captures the important aspects of a WSDL interface without repetition (with low-level details, such the Web Service binding information, being provided via a configuration file, perhaps). This language would look much like CORBA IDL (indeed most interface definition languages look similar).

In fact, starting with IDL itself is a valid approach, especially if combined with the automatic translation of this to WSDL. The service provider would have to ensure that the generated WSDL is well formed and readable, but again IDL's simplicity will usually mean that good quality WSDL will be produced. This is in contrast to starting with a programming language, for example Java. There are large differences in the data types supported by different programming languages, even object-oriented ones, and mapping from one to another often results in types that are difficult to use [2].

If WSDL is written without starting with IDL, then it can be translated into IDL so that it can be implemented using CORBA. WSDL, despite its syntactic (XML-based) complexity, at its core defines (XML) messages and combines these into interfaces. Like IDL, it is programming language neutral.

However, there is another major difficulty in starting with WSDL. WSDL uses XML Schema to define data types and this can result in very complex data types that cannot be mapped easily to any other language. (For example, you can define a type that is a string of no more than 8 characters from the range [abcd] that must start with 'd'.) Each interface definition language has some complex data types (those within CORBA are primarily Any and object-by-value), but WSDL has a wide range of these because of the extensive ability to define new types in XML Schema. In our view, the only way to resolve this is to define a subset of types that map easily to other languages, and agree that only this „profile" be used to define WSDL interfaces. (This subsetting will be important where Web services need to be used in conjunction with other middleware — and it's our view that this will be so in the majority of cases.)

5 Middleware-to-Middleware

To coin an acronym, M2M (middleware-to-middleware) is an area of increasing interest. Applications written for each type of middleware can normally interoperate with ease, but the different islands of middleware create a middleware-to-middleware interoperability challenge. Some middleware standards integrate together reasonably easily, for example CORBA and J2EE. CORBA also integrates well (in both directions) with COM. However, CORBA is a special case in the world of middleware because considerable effort has been put into how it integrates with other standards and products. This has not been the case with other middleware, with the result that often they are isolated islands with poor interoperability. Furthermore, many are proprietary, and this creates special difficulties because many of the technology levels (the protocols, for example) are either hidden or protected by copyright or patents.

Gateways (adaptors or connectors) can be used to integrate between middleware islands, but if these are not available off-the-shelf then customers need to be experts in middleware technologies, and their implementation details, in order to construct a gateway. This is an unreasonable requirement for most enterprises, where the preference is to concentrate on higher-level business issues, not low-level technology ones.

[1] explains in more detail why Web Services is a very promising technology for M2M interoperability. Web Services can be viewed as the first standard for high-level integration middleware (in contrast to platform middleware), and many of these properties make it useful for M2M integration.

To date, CORBA has been by far the strongest technology for M2M interoperability, especially given its close association with J2EE (the sharing of many technologies), and its gateway to and from COM. Inside an enterprise, there is no rival for CORBA's interoperability across these high-level boundaries. However, Web Services adds some important support:

- CORBA is the natural choice for integration between certain platform middleware: in particular between COM, J2EE and CORBA. Interoperability with the .NET platform is a special case, where Web Services will be the natural choice.
- Web Services may be the choice for integration between different forms of integration middleware, or between platform and integration middleware. But it should also be remembered that CORBA has out-of-the-box integration with some integration middleware (MQSeries, Tibco, etc.). Large scale, enterprise-wide initiatives to integrate integration-middleware with other middleware are likely to be done with Web Services.
- Across multiple enterprises, Web Services will be a more common choice for inter-enterprise M2M interoperability.

A number of approaches can be used to allow a CORBA application to interact with an application written with middleware that does not provide native support for IIOP. Firstly, the other middleware, or the applications written on top of it, could be augmented to support IIOP. IIOP is not a complex protocol, and the source code of full implementations can easily be obtained, but nevertheless, most projects will not be willing to use this approach.

Secondly, a gateway can be written, or perhaps acquired, to translate between the protocols. Such a gateway could be generated from the interfaces being used; or it could be dynamic in the sense that it can deal with any interface (the CORBA side would use the Dynamic Skeleton Interface (DSI) and Dynamic Invocation Interface (DII)). Of course this means that the CORBA application can interact only with applications written with the middleware that the gateway understands. On the other hand, wrapping a CORBA application with a Web Services layer/gateway has the advantage that it can be called by any application that can call a Web Service, and we believe that this will be a large class of applications

5.1 Multiple SOA Layers

One interesting way to view the use of multiple middleware is to consider multiple Service Oriented Architect (SOA) layers [1]. Some middleware offers high-level support for SOA, which simply means that services are offered on a software bus. These services can be used by any application on the bus, subject to security of course. The alternative is a series of one-to-one integrations, which leads to a spaghetti of integration techniques and ad hoc rules. If another application needs to use the facilities provided by a given application, then another point-to-point integration is required. Use of SOA has therefore become a strong recommendation of industry analysts. Both CORBA and Web Services provide strong SOA support.

The different advantages of various forms of middleware mean that different forms will be used for different roles. The result will not be one SOA layer, but a set of SOA layers that interoperate. When CORBA and Web Services are used together, the usual approach will be to use CORBA for lower level SOA layers, and Web Services for upper levels. This will allow enterprises to benefit from CORBA platform support and its high scalability and performance at the levels where these are all-important. Web Services comes into its own where higher-level software boundaries need to be bridged, in particular those between different enterprises, and between different middleware.

6 History Can't Be Rewritten

This section reinforces the preceding sections by looking at how the history of the development of middleware could have given CORBA a much stronger role in M2M and Internet computing. It is deliberately CORBA-centric in order to emphasize how the Web Services and the CORBA stories augment each other. It starts by looking at M2M and then addresses the Internet boundary.

6.1 Using CORBA for M2M

It could be argued that CORBA has been designed as much for M2M interoperability as application-to-application communication. In fact, this is how both the standards writers and vendors have behaved. If vendor-based politics had not intervened, an extended CORBA could by now be the neutral choice for interoperability at all levels. All platform middleware has already been integrated into it, and the Event/Notification services could have been used as the basis for the first standard for integration middleware. It is programming language independent, and it provides multiple language mappings. It enjoys a strong open standards process.

On a number of occasions CORBA needed only small changes in order to incorporate new technologies, and there aren't any real technical barriers to it being extended to handle inter-enterprise and inter-middleware integration. Using this logic, Web Services are not necessary. All we need is an extended CORBA.

This argument is very appealing to those of us who have adopted CORBA. However, it ignores some political and technical issues. At the political level, we are more likely to introduce new technology to solve a problem, than we are to adopt or extend existing technology. CORBA is also a platform, rather than just integration middleware, which makes it more of a rival to other platforms such as J2EE and COM. For political reasons, therefore, it is difficult if not impossible for a platform middleware to act as the mediator of all middlewares.

At the technical level, CORBA lacks some of the properties required. In particular, it does not provide a standard for how messages can be transformed as they are being transmitted, or how adaptors to off-the-shelf applications should be written.

CORBA must be at both ends of the connection for integration to occur, or gateways between IIOP and other protocols are required. Although it is possible for other systems/middleware to support IIOP, this is a „do it my way attitude." One mitigating factor here is that IIOP is non-proprietary. Another is that there are IIOP implementations that do not require the other parts of CORBA, and these can be „plugged into" other technologies to achieve interoperability. Yet another is that J2EE has adopted IIOP. Nevertheless, IIOP has been adopted by only two middleware standards.

Gateways are a valid way to achieve interoperability, but there are normally limitations put on one or both sides in order to do the necessary translation between type systems and other rules. In addition, while CORBA provides strong support for interoperability with COM and J2EE, it doesn't offer other gateways for widely available technologies and protocols.

6.2 Using CORBA for Integration across the Internet?

CORBA has many of the middleware properties needed for inter-enterprise communication, including programming language independence and an open standards process. Its main protocol, IIOP, has been layered on HTTP, and therefore it is possible to bridge across firewalls. In addition, firewalls have been given special security support, whereby it is possible to specify which objects can be accessed via IIOP from outside of the firewall, by whom, and in what way (that is, which operation calls are permitted). Whatever XML support is required could have been added.

However, these are some of the reasons why this hasn't happened. The web community hasn't accepted CORBA. This is in part because it is a platform middleware; and in part because CORBA didn't lead the way with HTTP and XML support. In addition, CORBA does not support some of the features required for a rich inter-enterprise middleware. One such feature is the passing of documents; another is sup port for process flow.[5] Another is that CORBA must be at both ends of the communication, and this is too restrictive when more than one enterprise is involved in the communication. Interestingly, Web Services does not support all of the required features for inter-enterprise communication, but today the momentum for providing an appropriate inter-enterprise middleware lies with Web Services and not with other middleware standards.

7 The Near-Term Future of Web Services

The Web Service standards are very immature (in fact, they barely have the status of proposed standards at the time this is being written). The only aspects that have any agreement are the protocol (SOAP), interface definition (WSDL), and naming/description/discovery (UDDI). Many other „services" will be required in order to make Web Services a full middleware offering. Looking at the evolution of CORBA over the past decade, it is easy to predict that the following technology areas will be standardized within Web Services:

- Security: there are a number of competing security proposals for Web Services, and Web Services has a long way to go before it can provide a lightweight, easy-to-use standard that makes inter-enterprise communications secure for all intended usages. Some companies provide solutions today, but a standard is needed. Further, this needs to be integrated with whatever form of process flow is standardized (so that the participants in a given process flow can be controlled).
- Publish and subscribe, and other sophisticated messaging facilities: currently there is no Web Service equivalent of the CORBA Event and Notification Service, or the multicast support.
- Transactions: it's currently not clear what form of transaction support the evolving Web Services standard should include. Some very limited subset of intra-enterprise uses may benefit from traditional ACID support, with or without distributed two-phase support. However, most will want to have support for a flexible form of undo or compensating actions, akin to the CORBA Activity Specification.
- Management: of the Web Services implementation layer, of Web Services themselves built on top, and of clients of these Web Services (including the communication channels). Again, some companies provide technology for this today, but there is no standard.

Each of these will have a special Web Services flavor once it is standardized, and won't be directly compatible with the standards used by any other middleware. There

---

[5] Documents can be passed using one of CORBA string types, but this isn't efficient for XML documents. CORBA does specify a useful standard (called DOM/Value) for passing XML documents, but commercial quality implementations aren't available. See [4] for a more detailed discussion of the issues that arise when passing documents between CORBA clients and servers. CORBA also specifies a very powerful standard (the Activity Service) for process flow, that supports long-lived transactions and compensating actions. Again, this is new and hasn't yet been implemented by many vendors.

will then need to be an overarching framework to provide inter-working and inter-management between these systems

Some aspects of CORBA, such as the Portable Object Adapter (POA), and its real-time and persistence support, have little role to play in Web Services, because Web Services does not aim to be a platform.

Today Web Services consists of three specifications (SOAP, WSDL, and UDDI), but before long it will have to grow substantially in order to fulfil the needs of both inter-enterprise and inter-middleware communication.

8 Conclusions

Web Services and CORBA complement each other in a number of ways. In addition, both are based on similar underlying technology (message passing and operation calls; interface definition; naming-description-discovery), which means that there can be a straightforward integration between the two.

The advantage of this combination for CORBA applications is that they can be web-enabled, using a similar but complementary technology. Web enabling CORBA applications using portal and user interface technology is really an inappropriate choice for the high-level nature of CORBA interfaces.

In addition, Web Services give access to CORBA applications across certain high-level software boundaries *within* an enterprise. CORBA itself can be used for integration with other platform middleware such as COM and J2EE. Integration with .NET is best done using Web Services. Integration between a platform middleware and integration middleware, or between two or more integration middlewares, may be best done using Web Services because it is has a higher claim to neutrality, since it is not a platform. In addition, this type of integration is normally done at a high SOA layer (adopting the model of multiple SOA layers, using an appropriate choice of middleware at each). This is close to the SOA layer that is used to bridge between different enterprises, and since Web Services is used for the latter, it is a strong candidate for use in the former.

CORBA offers Web Services a strong, mature and well-proven platform to implement services. It is the natural choice for services written in C++, and it offers higher flexibility and control for a class of Java applications that need more architectural choice than the J2EE platform provides. CORBA also supports a wide range of other languages.

Web Services won't replace CORBA inside the enterprise for a number of reasons, including:

- Web Services is not a platform for building the implementation of services. CORBA is a strong platform for building services, and for integrating systems at a level below that of Web Services.
- Web Services is too slow for some uses: messages are too bulky, because the communication protocol passes verbose text rather a compact binary format. This isn't to say that Web Services won't be used inside an enterprise (they will: for middleware-to-middleware interoperability). In addition, it must be remembered that the speed disadvantage will be lessened over time, as networks increase in speed, and as the Web Services protocols mature. (In addition, the packets can be

compressed, albeit that this trades network bandwidth and latency for processing overhead.)

- CORBA provides support for the construction and interoperability of realtime systems.
- CORBA is often used in a strongly object-oriented manner. It provides support for object identity and typing, including a simple type hierarchy.

On the other hand, Web Services *is* a major threat to traditional integration middleware, or at least it will require that they adhere to the Web Services standards. Although Web Services was initially envisaged to provide the inter-enterprise SOA layer, it will also be used for upper SOA layers *within* an enterprise. Web Services is the first standard for integration middleware, and this is going to have a profound effect on the industry.

We believe that it is very important that the different forms of middleware, including Web Services and CORBA, should be used together. There should be no artificial boundaries created because one middleware is labeled as B2B middleware, another as integration middleware, and so on. Instead, developers and integrators should be able to choose from a well-integrated toolkit of different middleware technologies, so that they can choose the right middleware or mix of middleware for a given problem.

Acknowledgements. Many thanks to John Parodi and Margaret O'Keefe for help with this paper. My understanding of the benefits of CORBA and Web Services have been greatly enhanced through discussions with Michi Henning, Oisin Hurley and Eric Newcomer.

References

1. Seán Baker, „The Role of Web Services in a Multi-layer SOA Structure", The 2002 International Conference on Internet Computing (IC'02), Las Vegas, USA, June, 2002. (An extended version of this paper is available from IONA.)
2. „CORBA EJB Interoperability", IONA White Paper, http://www.iona.com/whitepapers/CORBA-EJB-Interoperability-WP-V00-02.pdf
3. D.C. Schmidt and S. Vinoski. "CORBA and XML, Part 1: Versioning," C/C++ Users Journal C++ Experts Forum, May 2001, www.cuj.com/experts/1905/vinoski.htm
4. D.C. Schmidt and S. Vinoski. "CORBA and XML, Part 2: XML as CORBA Data," C/C++ Users Journal C++ Experts Forum, July 2001, www.cuj.com/experts/1907/vinoski.htm
5. See www.xmlbus.com for details

Composing and Deploying Grid Middleware Web Services Using Model Driven Architecture

Aniruddha Gokhale[1] and Balachandran Natarajan[1]

Institute for Software Integrated Systems, Vanderbilt University,
PO Box 36, Peabody,
Nashville, TN 37221
{a.gokhale, b.natarajan}@vanderbilt.edu

Abstract. Rapid advances in networking, hardware, and middleware technologies are facilitating the development and deployment of complex grid applications, such as large-scale distributed collaborative scientific simulation, analysis of experiments in elementary particle physics, distributed mission training and virtual surgery for medical instruction. These predominantly collaborative applications are characterized by their very high demand for computing, storage and network bandwidth requirements. Grid applications require secure, controlled, reliable, and guaranteed access to different types of resources, such as network bandwidth, computing power, and storage capabilities, available from multiple service providers. Moreover, they demand multiple, simultaneous end-to-end quality of service (QoS) properties, such as delay guarantees, jitter guarantees, security, scalability, reliability and availability guarantees, and bandwidth and throughput guarantees, for their effective operation.

Existing grid infrastructure middleware, such as Globus, ICENI, and Legion, offer simplified application programming interfaces (APIs) for deploying grid applications. However, grid applications using these APIs become tightly coupled to their respective middleware infrastructure creating an impediment to interoperability, portability, maintenance and extensibility. Moreover, existing grid infrastructure middleware offer only the means and not the solutions for reserving and securely accessing resources. Thus, the onus of actually reserving and provisioning these different resources while also ensuring end-to-end QoS still lies on the grid applications. These low-level concerns increase the accidental complexities incurred developing complex grid applications.

A promising solution to remedy these problems is to use the Model-Integrated Computing (MIC) paradigm to model the resource and QoS requirements of grid applications and integrate it with grid component middleware. MIC tools can perform feasibility analysis of the application's resource and QoS requirements and determine the right resource provisioning strategies. The MIC tools can subsequently synthesize, assemble and deploy QoS-enabled grid middleware components configured with the resource reservation and service provisioning strategies tailored to the needs of the grid application, while also delivering end-to-end QoS. Moreover, MIC tools can also be used to expose the deployed grid middleware as a Web service thereby decoupling grid applications from any particular middleware API.

The paper provides three contributions to the study of a model-driven approach to assembling and deploying QoS-enabled grid middleware capable of provisioning resources and delivering QoS end-to-end to grid applications. First, we describe

R. Meersman, Z. Tari (Eds.): CoopIS/DOA/ODBASE 2002, LNCS 2519, pp. 633–649, 2002.
© Springer-Verlag Berlin Heidelberg 2002

our Grid component middleware called GriT, which is based on the Object Management Group's (OMG) CORBA Component Model (CCM). Second, we explain how we are using the OMG Model Driven Architecture (MDA), which is a standardization of the MIC technology, to develop a tool called CoSMIC. CoSMIC is used to simplify composition of semantically compatible components of GriT to provide end-to-end QoS and resource guarantees to grid applications. Third, we show how the CoSMIC tools expose the deployed GriT middleware as a Web service that enables grid applications to use ubiquitous web protocols, such as Session Initiation Protocol (SIP) to create, join, or leave collaborative grid applications.

Keywords: Model-Integrated Computing, Model Driven Architectures, CORBA Component Model, Grid Computing, QoS

1   Introduction

The term *grid applications* applies to a special class of distributed applications that have very high computing and resource requirements, and are often collaborative in nature. Grid computing [1] is an emerging paradigm that seeks to harness the power of the internet and the sophisticated resources spread across it, such as super computers, storage devices, and others to support grid applications.

The grid computing paradigm envisages a distributed hardware infrastructure and a wide range of software infrastructure for services, programming models, tools, programming languages and methodologies capable of providing the massive computational requirements (Petaflops) and massive storage capacities (Petabytes) required by grid applications. Moreover, it is also expected to support high-fidelity, real-time collaboration between geographically distributed *virtual organizations* (VOs) [2], that comprise researchers, scientists, other users, and organizations.

For grid applications to operate effectively, however, they simultaneously require:

- secure and controlled access to many different resources available from multiple resource and service providers, including networking resources (such as bandwidth and buffers), operating system resources (such as threads, CPU and kernel buffers), storage resources (such as high performance databases and RAIDs), computing resources (such as supercomputers), display resources capable of 3-D rendering, and many other specialized types of resources, such as sensors, telescopes, oscilloscopes, and other electronic equipment
- end-to-end multiple (QoS) properties, such as *delay guarantees*, *jitter guarantees*, *security, scalability, high reliability and availability guarantees*, and *bandwidth and throughput guarantees* to grid applications.

The *infrastructure middleware* that hosts grid applications is called a *Computational Grid* or simply a *Grid* [1]. Examples of grid infrastructure middleware include Globus [3], Legion [4] and ICENI [5] among others. The Grid provides dependable, consistent, pervasive and inexpensive access to high-end computational capabilities useful for *distributed super-computing, on-demand computing, high-throughput computing, data-intensive computing* and *collaborative computing*.

Although existing grid infrastructure middleware seems suited to supporting next-generation grid applications, however, developing distributed grid applications using these is fraught with the following challenges.

Challenge 1: Tight coupling with grid infrastructure middleware: Grid applications are developed using one of existing grid infrastructure middleware technologies, such as Globus, Legion, ICENI, and others making them tightly coupled to the underlying middleware. However, with advances and sophistication in grid middleware technologies, it is imperative for grid applications to avail of these advances. This in turn implies that grid applications be seamlessly portable across different middleware without significantly affecting existing applications thereby preserving investments. This proliferation of grid middleware choices has raised the level of accidental complexity by increasing the amount of effort required to interoperate and port applications between grid middleware technologies.

An effective approach to decouple grid applications from the underlying grid middleware is to expose the grid middleware as a Web service [6]. Grid applications can then use *standards*-based ubiquitous web protocols such as *http* and (SIP) to access the underlying grid middleware.

Challenge 2. Accidental complexities in integrating software systems. To reduce lifecycle costs and time-to-market, application developers are attempting to assemble and deploy distributed grid applications by selecting the right set of compatible grid middleware components, which in itself is a daunting task. The problem is further exacerbated by the existence of myriad strategies for configuring and deploying the underlying component middleware to leverage the environment advantages. Moreover, integrating applications using multiple middleware technologies demands multiple skill sets which makes the task even more complicated. Application developers therefore spend non-trivial amounts of time debugging problems associated with the selection of incompatible strategies and components. What is needed is an integrated set of processes and tools that can (1) select and validate a suitable configuration of middleware components and (2) generate optimized Web service configurations automatically.

Challenge 3: Satisfying multiple quality of service requirements simultaneously: As noted earlier, grid applications demand varying degrees and forms of QoS support from their grid middleware. For example, collaborative scientific applications involving geographically dispersed scientists, engineers, and physicists working on real-time experiments and data require the infrastructure to be efficient, predictable, scalable, secure, and fault tolerant. Owing to the complex nature of these QoS requirements, it is not feasible for a single grid infrastructure middleware to provide an end-to-end solution that addresses all these challenges. Instead, highly configurable, flexible, and optimized higher-level, grid middleware components based on *standards*, such as CORBA Component Model (CCM) [7], must be used to assemble and deploy middleware tailored to the needs of the grid application.

Challenge 4: Lack of well-defined patterns for resource reservation: As mentioned earlier, grid applications require simultaneous access to several different types of resources available from multiple resource and service providers that own them. These service providers include internet service providers (ISPs), storage service providers (SSPs), content service providers (CSPs), and others. For example, a distributed virtual surgery application involving geographically dispersed doctors, radiologists, medical professionals, and medical students will require high bandwidth for collaboration, large storage databases to hold patient records and radiology images, expensive display devices for precise 3-D modeling and rendering of images, virtual reality equipment for simulating surgeries, and telephony equipment to maintain multi-leg call sessions.

Applications that require these resources must maintain Service Level Agreements (SLAs) with each individual service provider that provide the resources and services. Moreover, today's grid applications must authenticate themselves with each service provider everytime they access resources owned by the provider.

Conventional grid infrastructure middleware provide only the means to securely access the resources from different service provider. However, the responsibility of reserving and accessing the resources is still the responsibility of the grid applications. A possible solution to address this problem is for the grid middleware to provide a set of generic resource reservation strategies that grid applications can use. However, such a solution fails to serve the needs of all grid applications, each of whom might have differing end-to-end resource and QoS needs. What is therefore needed is an ability to compose patterns-based strategies for multiple resource reservations while assuring the end-to-end QoS requirements of the grid aplications. Moreover, these strategies should be deployed within the grid middleware and made available to the grid applications as a Web service.

Challenge 5: Provisioning and managing resources is hard: As mentioned in challenge 4, grid applications must make reservations for several different resources while ensuring that the end-to-end QoS requirements are met. Even if this problem is resolved by deploying custom resource reservation strategies within the grid middleware as outlined above, provisioning and managing multiple resources from multiple providers is a daunting task that existing grid infrastructure middleware currently do not handle and leave it to the grid application.

What is required is an ability to model the resource and QoS requirements of grid applications using Unified Modeling Language (UML) [8] modeling tools or State-charts [9]. Model analysis tools can be used to determine if provisioning such a system is feasible or not. If it is, then a separate set of tools can synthesize the appropriate resource provisioning and management strategies composed from a library of higher-level QoS-enabled grid middleware components.

A promising way to address the challenges developing grid applications described above is to use *Model-Integrated Computing* technologies [10]. Understanding how to integrate Model-integrated Computing (MIC) and grid component middleware is essential to resolve the configuration, management, and deployment challenges of deploying QoS-enabled grid middleware as Web services. This paper provides the following three contributions toward the successful integration of Model-Integrated Computing and grid component middleware that is essential to develop QoS-enabled Web services to address the challenges presented above:

- We illustrate how the Model-Integrated Computing paradigm can be applied to simplify the development of large-scale grid applications that integrate components of our QoS-enabled reusable component middleware, called Grid TAO (GriT) [11].
- We discuss how emerging standards, such as the Object Management Groups (OMG)'s Model Driven Architecture (MDA) [12] and the CORBA Component Model (CCM) [7] can be used to provide a standards-based approach to assemble and deploy grid middleware Web services.
- We describe how QoS-enabled component middleware enables modeling and synthesis tools to rapidly develop, assemble, and deploy flexible Web services that support heterogeneity, yet can be tailored readily to meet the needs of grid applications with multiple simultaneous QoS requirements.

The rest of the paper is organized as follows: Section 2 presents an overview of the MIC paradigm and MDA, and describes our MDA tool, called CoSMIC; Section 3 explains the GriT component middleware architecture; Section 4 explains how the CoSMIC tools is used to compose, assemble, and deploy GriT middleware components as a Web service that is tailored to the needs of grid applications; Section 5 describes related research; and finally Section 6 provides concluding remarks.

2 Model Integrated Computing and Component Middleware Synthesis: The Key to Developing Next Generation Grid Applications

Model Integrated Computing (MIC) [10] is a paradigm for expressing application functionality and QoS requirements at higher levels of abstraction than is possible using third-generation programming languages, such as Visual Basic, Java, C++, or C#. In the context of grid applications, MIC tools can be applied to

1. **Analyze** different—but interdependent—characteristics of system behavior *e.g.* resource requirements, such as network bandwidth, CPU processing speed, and storage capacity, and QoS requirements, such as scalability, predictability, safety, and security. Tool-specific model interpreters translate the information specified by models into the input format expected by analysis tools. These tools can check whether the requested behavior and properties are feasible given the constraints.
2. **Synthesize** platform-specific code that is customized for specific grid middleware and grid application properties, such as end-to-end timing deadlines, throughput requirements of simulations, and authentication and authorization strategies modeled at a higher level of abstraction.

The Object Management Group (OMG) has recently adopted the Model Driven Architecture (MDA) [12] to standardize the integration of MIC paradigm with component middleware technologies and web services. This section provides an overview of the MIC and MDA technologies. We then describe a tool called CoSMIC [13] we are developing to model grid application resource and QoS requirements.

2.1   Overview of Model-Integrated Computing

Model-Integrated Computing (MIC) [10] is a development paradigm that applies domain-specific modeling languages systematically to engineer computing systems ranging from small-scale real-time embedded systems to large-scale distributed enterprise and grid applications. MIC provides rich, domain-specific modeling environments, including model analysis and model-based program synthesis tools [14]. In the MIC paradigm, application developers model an integrated, end-to-end view of the entire application, including the interdependencies of its components. Rather than focusing on a single, custom application, therefore, MIC models capture the essence of a class of applications. MIC also allows the modeling languages and environments themselves to be modeled by so-called *meta-models* [15], which help to synthesize domain-specific modeling languages that can capture the nuances of domains they are designed to model.

When implemented properly, MIC technologies help to:

- Free application developers from dependencies on particular software APIs, which ensures that the models can be used for a long time, even as existing software APIs become obsolete and replaced by newer ones.
- Provide correctness proofs for various algorithms by analyzing the models automatically and offering refinements to satisfy various constraints.
- Synthesize code that is highly dependable and robust since the tools can be built using provably correct technologies.
- Rapidly prototype new concepts and applications that can be modeled quickly using this paradigm, compared to the effort required to prototype them manually.
- Save organizations significant amounts of time and effort, while also reducing application time-to-market.

Popular examples of MIC tools being used today include the Generic Modeling Environment (GME) [14] and Ptolemy [16] (which are used primarily in the real-time and embedded domain) and UML/XML tools based on the OMG Model Driven Architecture (MDA) [12] (used primarily in the enterprise application domain thus far).

As shown in Figure 1, MIC uses a set of tools to

- Analyze the interdependent features of the system captured in a model and
- Determine the feasibility of supporting different non-functional system aspects, such as QoS requirements, in the context of the specified constraints.

Another set of tools then translates models into executable specifications that capture the platform behavior, constraints, and interactions with the environment. These executable specifications can in turn be used to synthesize application software.

2.2   Overview of the OMG Model Driven Architecture

The OMG MDA [12] defines standard ways to address many of the challenges facing complex applications, such as the grid applications, outlined in Section 1. The MDA builds upon years of research on model-integrated computing [10,9,17] to provide standard modeling notations based on the Unified Modeling Language (UML) [8]. Figure 2 illustrates the structure of the MDA.

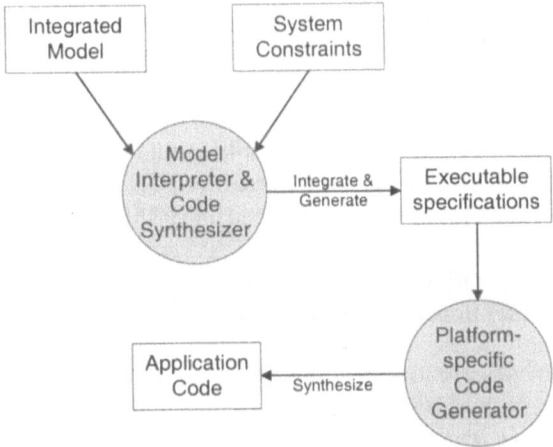

Fig. 1. The Model-Integrated Computing Process

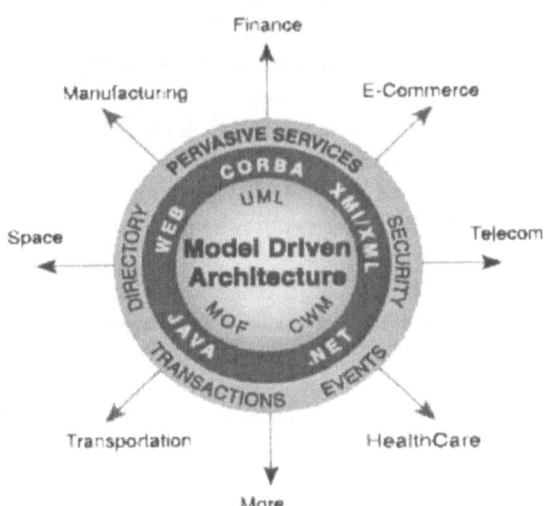

Fig. 2. Overview of the OMG Model Driven Architecture (Copyright OMG, reproduced by permission)

The MDA defines platform-independent models (PIMs) and platform-specific models (PSMs) that streamline platform integration issues and protect investments against the uncertainty of changing platform technology. These two levels of models can be differentiated as follows:

- The PIMs describe at a high-level how applications will be structured and integrated, without concern for the middleware/OS platforms or programming languages, on which they will be deployed. PIMs provide a formal definition of an application's functionality, as well as a representation of the application as a computation-independent business model, grid experiment model or a military strategy, also referred to as a *Domain Model*. For example, resource and QoS requirements of grid applications can be modeled generically using modeling tools based on UML.

- The PSMs are so-called *constrained* formal models since they express platform-specific details. The PIM models are mapped into PSMs via translators. For example, the generic operation that is specified in the PIM could be mapped and refined to the domain-specific operation, such as limits on response time accessing a resource, in the underlying Real-time CORBA platform.

Both PIM and PSM descriptions of applications are formal specifications built using modeling standards, such as UML, which can be used to model application functionality and system interactions. The MDA also defines a platform-independent meta-modeling language that allows platform-specific models to be modeled at an even higher level of abstraction.

2.3   Component Synthesis with Model Integrated Computing (CoSMIC)

Figure 3 illustrates how we are applying the MIC technology to build a MDA-based tool called CoSMIC (which stands for *Component Synthesis with Model Integrated Computing*) suitable for modeling resource and QoS requirements of grid applications. The CoSMIC tool composes grid middleware tailored to grid application requirements from functional building blocks of the Grid TAO (GriT) middleware, which is explained in Section 3. Moreover, CoSMIC tools expose the deployed grid middelware as a web service.

In the CoSMIC approach, higher-level modeling languages, such as UML [8] are used to model grid application QoS and resource requirements. CoSMIC analysis tools then determine the feasibility of the requirements. Once a feasibility analysis is complete, CoSMIC translator tools are used to synthesize pattern-oriented, semantically compatible grid middleware code composed from a set of reusable, QoS-enabled GriT components. The decision on which patterns make most sense are made by the CoSMIC synthesis tools based on the input models and constraints.

3   The Grid TAO (GriT) Middleware Architecture

This section describes our next generation Grid component middleware called Grid TAO (GriT) [11]. GriT enhances the Component Integrated ACE ORB (CIAO) [18,13] middleware, which is our CCM [7] implementation of the *The ACE ORB* (TAO) [19, 20]. TAO is an open-source, high-performance, highly configurable CORBA ORB that implements key patterns [21] to meet the demanding QoS requirements of distributed systems.

Figure 4 illustrates the components of the GriT middleware architecture. Below we explain each component of the architecture in detail.

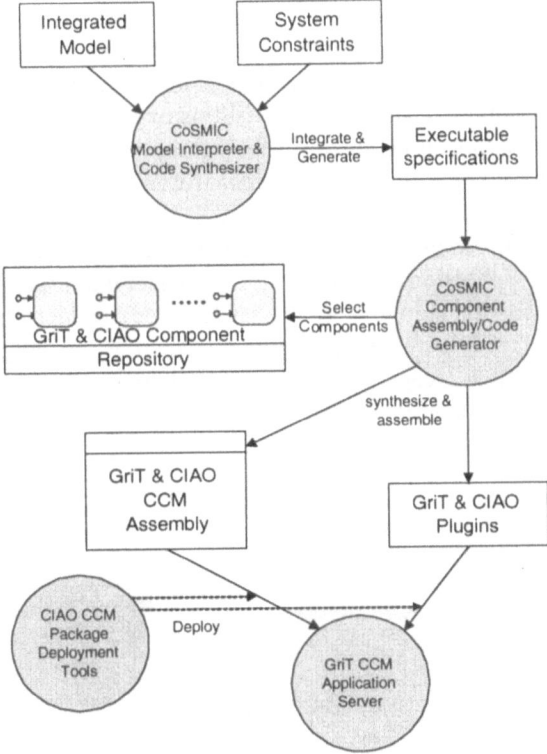

Fig. 3. The CoSMIC MDA Tool

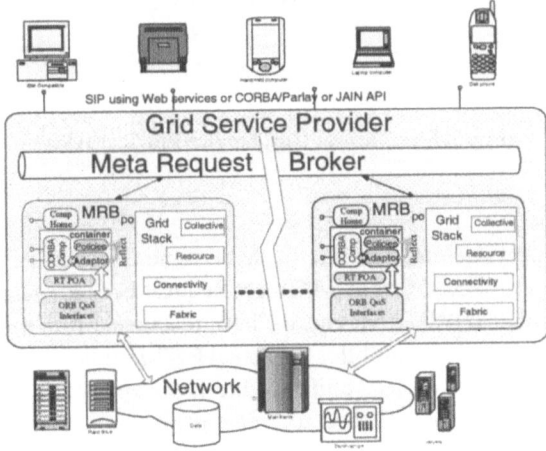

Fig. 4. Grid TAO (GriT) Middleware Architecture

Grid Service Provider (GSP). The GriT middleware comprises the notion of a Grid Service Provider (GSP) similar to other service providers such as ISPs, SSPs, CSPs and other providers providing specialized services such as access to advanced displays, virtual reality equipment, telescopes, oscilloscopes, etc. A fundamental difference between a GSP and other service providers is that a GSP is an abstract notion. The GSP does not actually own resources. The goal of the GSP is to provide a standard, unified view of resources to grid applications thereby eliminating the need for grid applications to require the knowledge and location of individual resource service providers.

Moreover, the GSP provides a *single sign-on* capability for grid applications, which eliminates the need for multiple SLAs and authentication mechanisms with multiple service providers. Applications use the GSP to delegate the responsibility of authenticating themselves with the individual specialized service providers. In addition, the GSP offers its user interface as a standard web service, thereby enabling grid clients to use techniques such as SIP to create, join, or leave collaborative grid applications. Figure 5 illustrates the concept of a GSP.

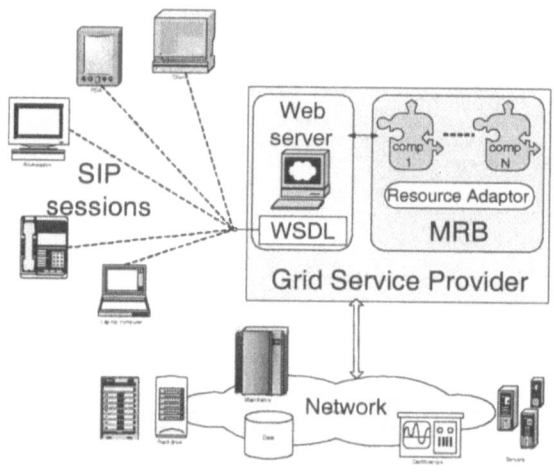

Fig. 5. Overview of Grid Service Provider (GSP)

Meta-Resource Broker Architecture. At the heart of the GSP is a Meta Resource Broker (MRB), which is an enhanced Common Object Request Broker Architecture (CORBA), Object Request Broker (ORB), that encapsulates resources from multiple providers as CORBA objects. The MRB exemplifies the actual GriT middleware. The MRB provides applications with standards-based, uniform interfaces and mechanisms to access and manage the underlying resources, and to create or join new or existing collaborative sessions, respectively.

The MRB is based on the CCM, where components represent the policies to manage the *virtual* resources. The resources are virtual since the GSP does not actually own any resources, but maintains only abstractions of them. These components therefore serve as a resource *proxy* of the actual resources thereby providing a uniform view to client applications. The internal structure of the MRB is illustrated in Figure 6.

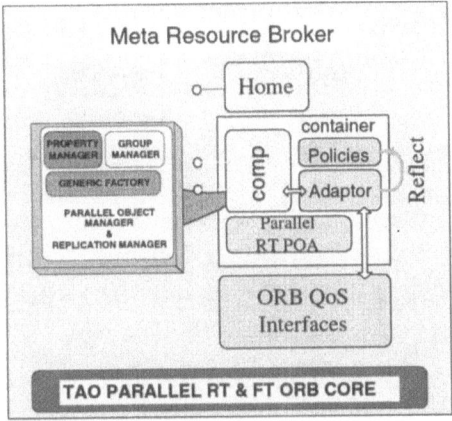

Fig. 6. Meta-Resource Broker Internals

The MRB mediates requests for different services and resources on behalf of grid applications and delivers them with the resources and guaranteed quality of service (QoS). This is accomplished by the MRB delegating the task of looking up individual resources required by the grid applications to MRB *part objects*. Figure 7 illustrates the use of part objects as defined in the Data Parallel CORBA (DP-CORBA) [22] specification.

When a grid application makes a reservation request to the GSP for all the different resources it needs and the QoS guarantees, this request is handed down by the GSP to its underlying MRB parallel object. The MRB parallel object will in turn partition the request using the techniques described in the DP-CORBA specification and the *Data Reorganization Effort* (www.data-re.org), such as *block distribution* or *cyclic distribution*. The partitioned request is then handed over to the MRB part objects. Each MRB part object is responsible to discover the appropriate resources that can meet the application's QoS requirements. This discovery process is performed in parallel thereby providing a highly scalable and predictable solution to determine the feasibility of resources and service provisioning.

The mechanism of resource discovery outlined above is akin to a *nested transaction*. If any one of the *child* transaction *i.e.,* resource discovery undertaken by a part object, is unsuccessful, then the *parent* transaction *i.e.,* the request initiated by the MRB parallel object, is rolled back.

If the request for resources is feasible, then the result of the MRB part object resource discovery operation is a collection of resources required by the application that provide it with the QoS guarantees. This collection of virtual resources is subsequently managed by the MRB as another *parallel object*. It is then upto the grid application to efficiently utilize these resources, although GriT will manage them on behalf of the grid application.

Figure 7 illustrates how the MRB reserves and manages different types of *virtual* resources, which are high-level abstractions of resources, such as network bandwidth, databases, or supercomputers, belonging to different service providers.

[11] provides detail information on the GriT middleware architecture.

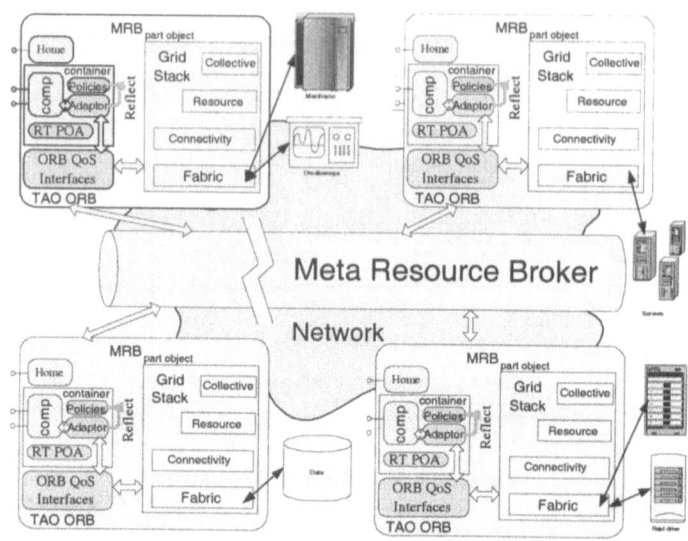

Fig. 7. Meta-Resource Broker Architecture

4 Resolving Grid Application Challenges Using Model Integrated Computing

This section describes how the MDA-based CoSMIC tool can be used to develop, assemble and deploy GriT middleware components as a web service, which is tailored to the needs of complex grid applications. In particular, we show how the application functionality specified as models can be used to synthesize new components that implement the web service, as well as to assemble them with semantically compatible reusable components provided by the GriT middleware.

First we describe how we provision the middleware components with appropriate strategies to reserve and manage the resources. Next we describe how these deployed components are made available as a web service so that grid applications can use it via standard web protocols such as *http* and SIP.

4.1 Model Driven Grid Middleware Deployment

Context. Today's grid applications are built using conventional grid infrastructure middleware, such as Globus or Legion. These middleware provide the APIs required to reserve the resources and securely access them.

Problem. Conventional grid infrastructure middleware make it hard to develop next-generation grid applications for the following reasons outlined in Section 1.

1. tight coupling with grid infrastruture middleware
2. accidental complexities in integrating software systems
3. satisfying multiple quality of service requirements simultaneously

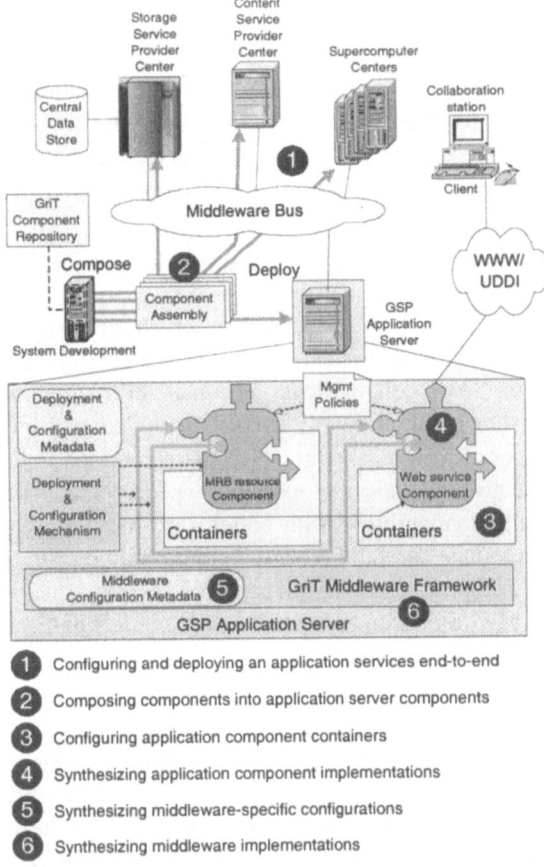

Fig. 8. Composing Grid Middleware from Models

4. lack of well-defined patterns for resource reservation
5. provisioning and managing resources is hard

In order to support next-generation grid applications effectively, there is a need to address these challenges. Our approach of using model integrated computing tools to assemble and deploy grid middleware as web services addresses these challenges.

Solution. Our solution involves using the MDA-based tool, called CoSMIC, to compose resource provisioning and QoS management patterns from building blocks of the GriT component middleware and to deploy them as web services. Our approach is illustrated in Figure 8.

Figure 8 illustrates six points at which Model-Integrated Computing, espoused by the CoSMIC tool, can be integrated into the grid middleware architecture, called GriT. We describe each of these six integration points below.

1. Configuring and deploying application services end-to-end: Assembling and deploying collaborative grid applications with stringent end-to-end QoS and resource guarantees is a daunting task. We are using CoSMIC to configure the right set of services to guarantee the QoS and resource requirement.

2. Composing components into application servers: Integration at this level will help compose the application server, which is responsible for hosting the application. We are using CoSMIC tools to compose grid application servers out of semantically compatible standard middleware components and possibly legacy components available as part of a component library.

3. Configuring application component containers: Application components use containers to interact with the application servers in which they are configured. Containers provide many policies that grid applications can use to fine-tune underlying component middleware behavior. Since grid applications consist of many interacting components, their containers must be configured with consistent and compatible policies.

Due to the number of policies and the intricate interactions among them, it is tedious and error-prone for an application to *manually* specify and maintain its component policies and semantic compatibility with policies of other components. We are using CoSMIC tools to automate the validation and configuration of these container policies by allowing system designers to specify the required system properties as a set of models. Another set of CoSMIC tools can then analyze the models and generate the necessary policies and ensure their consistency.

4. Synthesizing application component implementations: We are using modeling languages and tools to increase the automation in generating and integrating grid application components. The goal is to bridge the gap between specification and implementation via sophisticated aspect weavers and generator tools that can synthesize platform-specific code customized for specific application properties, such as resilience to denial of service attacks, robust behaviour under heavy load, and good performance for normal load.

5. Synthesizing middleware-specific configurations: In this step, the CoSMIC tools generate the deployment descriptors for the grid middleware. The deployment descriptors take into account the application's QoS and resource requirements along with the constraints.

6. Synthesizing middleware implementations: The CoSMIC tools can also be used to generate custom grid middleware implementations. This is a more aggressive use of modeling and synthesis than integration point 5 described above since it affects middleware *implementations*, rather than their configurations.

4.2   Model Driven Grid Web Service Deployment

Context. Both wireless and wireline client applications must be able to participate in collaborative grid applications. This requires *thin* client applications that can use the grid middleware interfaces to share resources.

Problem. As mentioned earlier, programming directly at the grid framework-specific protocols is too low-level and hence tedious and error-prone. Additionally, it ties the application to the underlying middleware API making portability infeasible. Moreover, for small footprint wireless clients and other embedded devices to use the grid framework, standards-based protocols and interfaces must be used.

Solution. The services offered by the GSP will be hosted as a web service as shown in Figure 5. This approach is similar to the ideas proposed in Open Grid Services Architecture (OGSA) [6]. The CoSMIC tools can be used to synthesize a Web Service Description Language (WSDL) description of the GSP's services. Moreover, CoSMIC tools can also help deploy these services and register it with naming services, such as UDDI or a CORBA Trader. Client applications can then access the GSP services via the web.

This web services approach provides grid application developers tremendous benefits when establishing SIP sessions [23]. SIP is designed to enable two or more participants to establish a session consisting of multiple media streams including audio, video, and other internet-based communication mechanisms such as distributed gaming, shared applications, whiteboards, etc. Participants in a collaborative application will use the GSP's interfaces and services to set up SIP-enabled collaborative sessions.

5   Related Work

Our previous work in collaboration with researchers at University of California, Irvine, on a high-performance, real-time CORBA ORB called The ADAPTIVE Communication Environment (ACE) ORB TAO [24] has examined many dimensions of ORB middleware design, including static operation scheduling, event processing, I/O subsystem and pluggable protocol integration, both synchronous and asynchronous ORB Core architectures, IDL compiler features and optimizations, systematic benchmarking of multiple ORBs, patterns for ORB extensibility, high-performance fault-tolerant CORBA, and ORB performance.

The Component Integrated ACE ORB (CIAO) [18,13] is our CCM-enabled version of the TAO ORB. The GriT middleware described in this paper enhanced CIAO by providing grid computing-specific components.

Grid computing is an emerging powerful paradigm to build large-scale, distributed, collaborative applications that require secure, controlled access to different resources from multiple providers. The GriT middleware is a distribution middleware that complements and enhances the low-level grid infrastructure middleware such as Globus [3], Legion [4], and ICENI [5].

Our research is exploring the use of Model-Intergrated Computing (MIC) [10,25, 17] to model and synthesize Grid middleware code for provisioning Grid applications.

Popular examples of MIC technology being used today include Generic Modeling Language (GME) [14] and Ptolemy [16] (which are used primarily in the real-time and embedded domain) and MDA [12] based on UML [8] and Extensible Markup Language (XML) [26] (which is used primarily in the business domain).

6   Conclusions

The key to the success of developing next generation grid applications lies in the integration of Model Integrated Computing and component middleware. This paper describes a MIC tool we are developing, called CoSMIC. We show how CoSMIC can be used to assemble and deploy grid middleware from fundamental building blocks provided by the GriT middleware. Moreover, we show how the same synthesis process can also be used to expose the grid middleware as a Web service, thereby decoupling grid applications from any particular middleware API.

References

1. Ian Foster and Carl Kesselman, *The Grid: Blueprint for a New Computing Infrastructure,* Harper Collins, 1999.
2. Ian Foster, Carl Kesselman, and Steven Tuecke, "The Anatomy of the Grid: Enabling Scalable Virtual Organizations," *International Journal of Supercomputer Applications,* vol. 15, no. 3, pp. 205–220, Apr. 2001.
3. I. Foster and C. Kesselman, "Globus: A metacomputing infrastructure toolkit," *International Journal of Supercomputer Applications,* vol. 11, no. 2, pp. 115–128, 1997.
4. Andrew S. Grimshaw and Wm. A. Wulf et al., "The legion vision of a worldwide virtual computer," *Communications of the ACM,* vol. 40, no. 1, pp. 39–45, Jan. 1997.
5. N. Furmento, A. Mayer, S. Gough, S. Newhouse, T. Field, and J. Darlington, "An integrated grid environment for component applications," in *Proceedings of the Second International Workshop on Grid Computing-Grid 2001, Denver 2001.* 2001, Springer-Verlag LNCS.
6. I. Foster, C. Kesselman, J. Nick, and S. Tuecke, "The physiology of the grid: An open grid services architecture for distributed systems integration," http://www.globus.org/research/papers/ogsa.pdf, Jan. 2002, DRAFT.
7. Object Management Group, *CORBA 3.0 New Components Chapters,* OMG TC Document ptc/2001-11-03 edition, Nov. 2001.
8. Object Management Group, *Unified Modeling Language (UML) v1.4,* OMG Document formal/2001-09-67 edition, Sept. 2001.
9. David Harel and Eran Gery, "Executable Object Modeling with Statecharts," *IEEE Computer,* vol. 30, no. 7, pp. 31–42, July 1997.
10. Janos Sztipanovits and Gabor Karsai, "Model-Integrated Computing," IEEE Computer, vol. 30, no. 4, pp. 110–112, Apr. 1997.
11. Aniruddha Gokhale and Balachandran Natarajan, "GriT: A CORBA Based Grid Middleware Architecture," in *Submitted to Hawaii International Conference on System Sciences, Software Technology Track, Distributed Object and Component-based Software Systems Minitrack, HICSS 2003,* Honolulu, HW, Jan. 2003, HICSS.
12. Object Management Group, *Model Driven Architecture (MDA),* OMG Document ormsc/2001-07-01 edition, July 2001.
13. Nanbor Wang, Douglas C. Schmidt, Aniruddha Gokhale, and Balachandran Natarajan, "Using Model-Integrated Computing to Compose Web Services for Distributed Real-time and Embedded Applications," *Submitted to IEEE Internet Computing Special Issue on Web Services,* May 2003.
14. Akos Ledeczi, Arpad Bakay, Miklos Maroti, Peter Volgysei, Greg Nordstrom, Jonathan Sprinkle, and Gabor Karsai, "Composing Domain-Specific Design Environments," *IEEE Computer,* pp. 44–51, Nov. 2001.

15. Jonathan M. Sprinkle, Gabor Karsai, Akos Ledeczi, and Greg G. Nordstrom, "The New Metamodeling Generation," in *IEEE Engineering of Computer Based Systems,* Washington, DC, Apr. 2001, IEEE, p. 275.

16. J. T. Buck, S. Ha, E. A. Lee, , and D. G. Messerschmitt, "Ptolemy: A Framework for Simulating and Prototyping Heterogeneous Systems," *International Journal of Computer Simulation, Special Issue on Simulation Software Development Component Development Strategies,* vol. 4, Apr. 1994.

17. Man Lin, "Synthesis of Control Software in a Layered Architecture from Hybrid Automata," in *HSCC,* 1999, pp. 152–164.

18. Aniruddha Gokhale, Douglas C. Schmidt, Balachandra Natarajan, and Nanbor Wang, "Applying Model-Integrated Computing to Component Middleware and Enterprise Applications," *The Communications of the ACM special issue on Enterprise Components, Service and Business Rules,* vol. 45, no. 10, Oct. 2002.

19. Douglas C. Schmidt, David L. Levine, and Sumedh Mungee, "The Design and Performance of Real-Time Object Request Brokers," *Computer Communications,* vol. 21, no. 4, pp. 294–324, Apr. 1998.

20. Douglas C. Schmidt et. al, "TAO: A Pattern-Oriented Object Request Broker for Distributed Real-time and Embedded Systems," *IEEE Distributed Systems Online,* vol. 3, no. 2, Feb. 2002.

21. Douglas C. Schmidt, Michael Stal, Hans Rohnert, and Frank Buschmann, *Pattern-Oriented Software Architecture: Patterns for Concurrent and Networked Objects,* Volume 2, Wiley & Sons, New York, 2000.

22. Object Management Group, *Data Parallel CORBA Specification,* ptc/2001-11-09 edition, Nov. 2001.

23. Ubiquity Software Corporation, "White Paper: SIP and SOAP," http://www.sipforum.org/whitepapers/USC-SIPSOAP-WP2.pdf.

24. Center for Distributed Object Computing, "The ACE ORB (TAO)," www.cs.wustl.edu/~schmidt/TAO.html, Washington University.

25. David Harel and Eran Gery, "Executable Object Modeling with Statecharts," in *Proceedings of the 18th International Conference on Software Engineering.* 1996, pp. 246–257, IEEE Computer Society Press.

26. W3C Architecture Domain, "Extensible Markup Language (XML)," http://www.w3c.org/XML.

A Design Pattern for Efficient Retrieval of Large Data Sets from Remote Data Sources

Brad Long

Australian Development Centre,
Oracle Corporation,
Brisbane, Qld. 4000, Australia.
brad.long@oracle.com
and
School of Information Technology and Elec. Eng.,
The University of Queensland,
Brisbane, Qld. 4072, Australia.
brad@itee.uq.edu.au

Abstract. Retrieving large amounts of information over wide area networks, including the Internet, is problematic due to issues arising from latency of response, lack of direct memory access to data serving resources, and fault tolerance. This paper describes a design pattern for solving the issues of handling results from queries that return large amounts of data. Typically these queries would be made by a client process across a wide area network (or Internet), with one or more middle-tiers, to a relational database residing on a remote server. The solution involves implementing a combination of data retrieval strategies, including the use of iterators for traversing data sets and providing an appropriate level of abstraction to the client, double-buffering of data subsets, multi-threaded data retrieval, and query slicing. This design has recently been implemented and incorporated into the framework of a commercial software product developed at Oracle Corporation.

1 Introduction

As computer systems are becoming more distributed in nature and an ever increasing amount of information is being demanded by the public, the requirement for efficient retrieval of large amounts of information over wide area networks is of paramount importance.

Distributed computing inherently adds complexity to computer software. Latency, distributed memory management, heterogeneous networks, fault tolerance and security are some of the issues contributing to this added complexity [7,9]. Specific key challenges concern server reliability, availability, and robustness; bandwidth allocation and sharing; and scalability of web and data servers [8].

Object oriented languages also add extra challenges. Results from a query are usually returned in some form of result set object. When the query is requested against a local data source, the iterator on the result set returned can be a reference to a current database row. That is, the results can be *streamed*. However, a truly robust distributed query is stateless, so does not retain a reference to a row in the remote database. A robust query

R. Meersman, Z. Tari (Eds.): CoopIS/DOA/ODBASE 2002, LNCS 2519, pp. 650–660, 2002.

can only deal with the results transmitted over the network. Now, what if the result contains millions of rows? The client machine may run out of memory whilst trying to deserialize the returned results into a collection of millions of objects. In this case, clearly the performance of the system will also be impacted.

Although performance and efficiency are considered, data caching and database tuning are not included in these considerations.

Five requirements for robust, efficient, distributed retrieval of large data sets are proposed. Specifically, results returned from a query:

1. must conserve resources
2. must respond within a reasonable time
3. must be robust
4. must not be limited to a partial result set
5. must be intuitive to use

Related work is reviewed in Section 2. In Section 3, the five requirements are explored in more detail, and in Section 4 the solution is described and discussed.

2   Related Work

Sun's page-by-page iterator pattern [6] goes some way to solving the issues of retrieving large amounts of data from remote data sources. However, it requires the developer to consider *pages* of information being fetched from the database. The approach presented in this paper abstracts such issues. Sun's page-by-page iterator was specifically designed for cases when:

– the user will be interested in only a portion of the list at any time.
– the entire list will not fit on the client display.
– the entire list will not fit in memory.
– transmitting the entire list at once would take too much time.

Although the last two bullet points are important to consider and are two of the issues our design pattern addresses, we do not require developers to consider the first two bullet points. Although these points may be satisfied in many applications, they are not required to be considered when applying the design patten presented in this paper. In addition, the application developer is not required to think in terms of *pages* as they are with the page-by-page iterator.

It is also important to note that Sun's page-by-page iterator is not a robust iterator. By design, the iterator does not keep its own copy of the list being traversed. Consequently, insertions or removals will interfere with the traversal; the iterator may access a remote item twice or miss it completely. This issue is considered in the section on Query Slicing. We provide the application developer with a robust iterator.

Other similar work has concentrated on using cached objects with enough information to connect back to the server to request more information [3]. However, such solutions require resources to be held open on the server, waiting for client responses.

3 Five Requirements for Robust, Efficient, Distributed Queries

3.1 Requirement 1: Must Conserve Resources

Since there is no restriction on how many rows (or objects) a query may return, resources must clearly be conserved to cater for the potentially unlimited set of results.
Conservation of resources is achieved on the server by never holding onto any database
resources. For example, a local implementation may use an iterator or placeholder to
store the current position in the result set. Remote queries should not do this. Remote
queries should not rely on server resources being held open whilst clients are iterating
over the results. Imagine a user browsing pages of results, one at a time. The user decides
to get a cup of coffee after browsing one of ten pages. The resource is being held open
on the server. Now, imagine hundreds of clients doing this. Consider how inefficient and
unacceptable this strategy is. The application will not scale. In addition, on the client
side, potentially millions of objects need to be created from the serialized data received
from the server before returning the results to the user application. Creating millions of
objects may consume vast amounts of memory. Also, it may take a significant amount
of time, thus violating the Second Requirement.

3.2 Requirement 2: Must Respond in a Reasonable Amount of Time

The query should take about the same time to execute as a local query (i.e. within the
same order of magnitude). That is, it must respond with the first row(s) of information
with the same latency as a local query.

3.3 Requirement 3: Must Be Robust

There are two forms of robustness. The first form of robustness relates to the returned
results. Whilst the client is iterating over the result set, they do not want other users
to interfere with the returned results. The second form of robustness relates to remote
resources. If the network connection is lost for any reason, relying on obscure error
conditions to handle server resource cleanup is undesirable. Therefore, server resources
are not held open across client requests.

3.4 Requirement 4: Must Not Be Limited to a Partial Result Set

This requirement simply states that any method for retrieving information must not limit
the number of rows returned. All rows of query data should be returned from the server.

3.5 Requirement 5: Must Be Intuitive to Use (Regardless of Deployment Mode)

The client developer should find retrieving data similar to or better than current local
query approaches. In addition, the client using the query method should not be required
to make allowances for the fact that it is a remote query. They should be able to use the
same client code for local and remote queries.

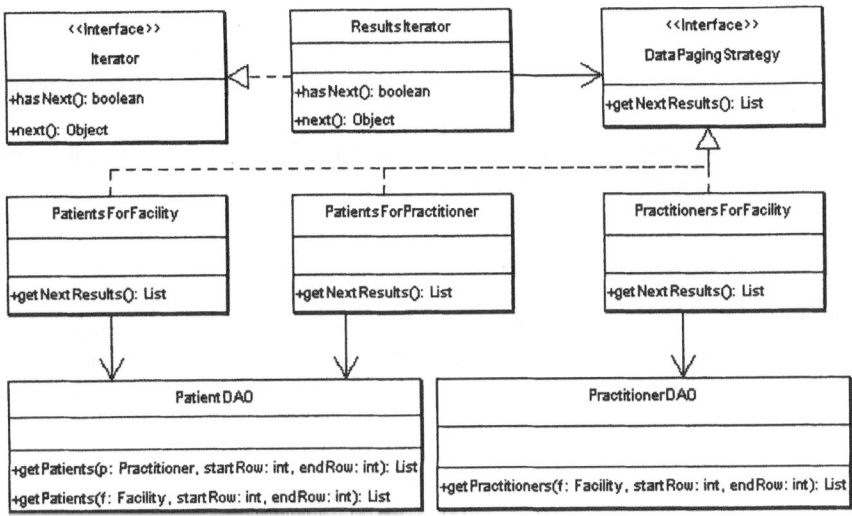

Fig. 1. The design pattern

4   The Design Pattern

Figure 1 illustrates the object model for the design pattern. The classes are now discussed in turn.

The `Iterator` interface is Sun's standard java.util.Iterator. More information on the iterator pattern can be found in [5].

`ResultsIterator` implements the `Iterator` interface. This class includes logic to determine when data pages are required to be fetched from the server. It also includes data page buffer and multi-threaded components for data fetching. The `ResultsIterator` constructor takes a class that implements the `DataPagingStrategy` interface. When extra pages of results are required as determined by `ResultsIterator`, the `getNextResults` method on the class that implements the `DataPagingStrategy` interface is called to fetch the data. For example, `PatientsForPractitioner` is an example of a class that implements the `DataPagingStrategy` interface. When required, `getNextResults` is called to fetch data for patients for a practitioner.

Internally, the class simply delegates to the appropriate `DataAccessObject` (DAO) class. More information on the *Data Access Object* pattern can be found in [1]. Here, consider the `DataAccessObject` to simply connect to a relational database and execute an SQL query. Data access objects may have local or remote implementations depending on the deployment mode of the application. Note that the method calls to these classes have `startRow` and `endRow` parameters. These parameters are used to slice the query into data pages.

Most of the methods in the classes in Figure 1 return objects of type java.util.List. This could actually be any collection class (java.util.Collection) and even an array of typed objects. Furthermore, the objects in the array can be value objects [2]. It is perfectly valid to use an array for passing data pages between the different layers. The important issue is that the array is not exposed to the application developer, only the iterator is accessible.

The following subsections provide further information on the sub-patterns used, and addresses issues involving the five requirements.

4.1   Iterator Pattern

The Iterator pattern [5] is used to provide a familiar level of abstraction to the application developer thus satisfying the Fifth Requirement. It is clear that returning an array of results is not a satisfactory solution. Since an array is of fixed length, it has all the shortcomings associated with deserializing the entire data set into objects before returning them to the client. Although we make use of fixed-length data pages in the transport layer when communicating with the server, the iterator provides an abstraction which allows the client to deal consistently with the entire data set.

```
public interface Iterator {
    public boolean hasNext();
    public Object next();
}
```

Fig. 2. Iterator interface definition

In Java, the application developer is already provided with a java.util.Iterator interface (Figure 2). It is natural to use this as the interface for our design pattern. The usage of the iterator is illustrated in Figure 3.

```
Iterator results = PatientService.getAllPatients();
while (results.hasNext()) {
    Patient p = (Patient) results.next();
    p.doStuff();
}
```

Fig. 3. Example iterator usage

Unlike Sun's page-by-page iterator pattern [6], using the standard Java iterator means that the application developer is not required to think in terms of pages. The application developer uses the iterator to traverse the entire set of returned results using the next() method until the hasNext() method returns false. This is the normal usage of the Iterator pattern. That is, the application developer is not concerned with the deployment mode (local or remote) of the software.

4.2   Data Paging

A *data set* is defined as the set of all results of a query returned from the server. A *data page* is a subset of a data set. Each data set has n disjoint data pages, and corollary, the data set is the union of all n data pages.

Data is required to be passed from the server to the client in data pages to enable us to deal with huge amounts of data. A large data set could easily consist of hundreds and thousands of rows (or more). By setting the maximum number of rows for each data page to a manageable size, for example 1000 rows, it enables us to (a) limit the amount of data being sent across the network at a time, and (b) limit the number of objects that need to be constructed in memory. Eventually all data pages that make up the data set will be received (Fourth Requirement).

This ensures a speedy response to queries by keeping network bandwidth low and only requiring the server process to retrieve, package, and transmit 1000 objects at a time. It also gives the client an immediate response to large queries. This technique solves the speed of response (Second Requirement) and memory resource problems (First Requirement).

The iterator retrieves rows from the returned data page of size m rows. When the iterator reaches the last entry, a query is automatically sent to the server to fetch another m rows. On the server, m rows at a time can be retrieved by employing a technique we call *query slicing*.

4.3   Query Slicing

The following are problems whilst attempting to retrieve large amounts of information from a remote data source to a client application:

- When loading information into a server object for transmission to the client or loading the requested information into a client object, the computer may run out of memory resources.
- Retrieving all rows from the server may require transmission of vast amounts of information that will be slow to transfer over the network.

To retrieve data pages of information from the server, a technique that we call *query slicing* is used.

As an example, consider the single query.

```
SELECT PATIENT_ID, PATIENT_NAME FROM PATIENTS
```

This may potentially return many thousands of rows of information. This query can be sliced by surrounding the single query with a slicing template. Three options are presented: 1) an Oracle specific version, 2) an ANSI SQL version, and 3) a hybrid approach. It should be noted that the ANSI SQL version is extremely slow. Many database vendors provide enhanced SQL language features that allow the developer to select a range of rows based on some artificial row number. It is suggested that the more efficient row selection capability of a particular database is used. In the following examples, slices of 1000 rows are demonstrated.

```
SELECT *
FROM (
          SELECT ROWNUM RNUM, INLINE_VIEW.*
          FROM (
                    SELECT PATIENT_ID, PATIENT_NAME
                    FROM PATIENTS
               ) INLINE_VIEW
     )
WHERE RNUM BETWEEN x AND y;
```

Fig. 4. Oracle specific slicing template

An efficient, but not robust, query slicer. Figure 4 details the SQL for the Oracle specific slicing template. Assuming our slice size is set to 1000, the first time the query is called $x = 1$ and $y = 1000$. After each call, the values of x and y are updated for the next call to the query as follows: $x = y + 1$ and $y = y + 1000$. The next call to retrieve data will use $x = 1001$ and $y = 2000$.

```
SELECT *
FROM (
          SELECT ROWNUM RNUM, PATIENT_ID, PATIENT_NAME
          FROM PATIENTS
     )
WHERE RNUM BETWEEN x AND y;
```

Fig. 5. Oracle specific simplified slicing template

Although the query in Figure 4 can be simplified to the one in Figure 5, it does not require modification to the original SQL. The simplified query requires modification to the SQL, specifically the addition of the rownum field to the original query, whereas the structure used in Figure 4 allows the original unmodified query to be wrapped with the slicing code. This does not degrade query performance. The query returns in under 6 seconds when tested on a table with 1.45 million rows. This performance is consistent irrespective of whether the first data page (i.e. first 1000 rows) or last data page is retrieved.

Note that the query timings have not been taken on high-end systems. The purpose of the timings is to relate the general magnitude of time that the query took to execute. Improving the times further may require higher-end systems, database tuning and caching techniques. These issues are not discussed here.

For tables that are read only, this solution is satisfactory. But it is not robust if data is inserted during retrieval. The problems are described in the following example:

Consider a table of more than 1000 rows (e.g. 10,000).

1. A data page of 1000 rows is retrieved, specifically, rows 1 to 1000.
2. A new row is inserted somewhere into the lower 1000 records in the database table.
3. Then, rows 1001 to 2000 are retrieved. But, since a row has been inserted, row 1001 has already been retrieved. It was row 1000 last time! Hence, the same row has been retrieved twice.

Also, if a row was deleted in step 2, we would actually miss a row of data, since row 1001 would become row 1000, the number of which had already been retrieved.

A robust, but inefficient, query slicer. The solution to the problem of stateless retrieval is not to rely on $rownum$, but to rely on the primary key values of the table being accessed. The ANSI SQL slicing template (Figure 6) is quite different. The value id will begin as some initial low value, for a character column this might be a space character. It is the primary key, in this case patient identifier, of the last row returned from the previous execution of the query. The query returns in several minutes when tested on a table with 1.45 million rows, which is clearly unacceptable performance.

```
SELECT P1.PATIENT_ID, P1.PATIENT_NAME
FROM PATIENTS P1
WHERE P1.PATIENT_ID > id AND
    1000 > (
            SELECT COUNT(*)
            FROM PATIENTS P2
            WHERE P1.PATIENT_ID > P2.PATIENT_ID
              AND P2.PATIENT_ID > id
          )
```

Fig. 6. ANSI SQL slicing template

Again, consider a table of more than 1000 rows (e.g. 10,000).

1. A data page of 1000 rows is retrieved.
2. A new row is inserted somewhere into the lower 1000 records in the database table.
3. Then, the next 1000 rows are retrieved. But, the new row has an id less than the one we are looking for, so it is correctly ignored, and does not throw out our query, that is, the next correct set of rows is retrieved.

Also, if a row was deleted in step 2, we would not miss a row of data, because we are not relying on ordinal position, but primary key value.

This approach is robust but is inefficiently executed by database SQL engines. One reason for this that the join on the patient tables *P1* and *P2* is asymmetric (see the *where* clause P1.PATIENT_ID > P2.PATIENT_ID in Figure 6).

```
SELECT *
FROM (
        SELECT ROWNUM RNUM, INLINE_VIEW.*
        FROM (
                SELECT PATIENT_ID, PATIENT_NAME
                FROM PATIENTS
                WHERE PATIENT_ID > id
            ) INLINE_VIEW
    )
WHERE RNUM < 1001
```

Fig. 7. Hybrid slicing template

An efficient and robust query slicer. By combining the two approaches, we can come up with a robust and efficient approach (Figure 7).

As with the ANSI SQL approach, *id* is the primary key value of the last row retrieved from the previous call.

This query combines both the relatively efficient *rownum* approach with the robust primary key approach, providing us with a solution for using iterators in stateless situations. The query returns in under 3 seconds when tested on a table with 1.45 million rows. As the latter data pages are retrieved the query performs even more efficiently. This is due to the $WHERE$ clause of the inner (wrapped) query causing the return of a diminishing result set as the *id* increases.

For tables with composite keys, instead of *where key > id* use:

- for 2 columns: *where key1 >= id1 and key2 > id2.*
- for 3 columns: *where key1 >= id1 and key2 >= id2 and key3 > id3.*

That is, all comparisons are $>=$ except the final comparison which is $>$.

Using this method the query can be cut into manageable data pages. These examples use data pages with a page size of 1000 rows. Other page sizes may be chosen as appropriate. This solution allows all server database resources to be released between queries, providing a scalable (Second Requirement) and robust (Third Requirement) solution.

4.4   Double-Buffering Data Pages

Double-buffering is a technique used in graphics programming. A double-buffered system is one in which the image in one buffer is displayed while the image in the other buffer is computed [4].

We apply this technique to data pages retrieved from a server. Initially, we retrieve a data page, to load data into one result set. Whilst the first result set is being used by the client we load the second result set. When the client has finished with the first result set, the empty result set is returned to the loader, and the second result set is given to the client.

4.5   Multithreaded Data Fetching

To retrieve the double-buffered pages into memory, we use multithreaded data fetching. When the iterator object is created, the first data page is retrieved. This is called the *primary* data page. A call to next() will return the first row in the query. In addition, for the first call to next() on the primary data page, a thread is spawned to retrieve the secondary data page. The secondary data page is added to a buffer for later use.

When the iterator has traversed all rows in the primary data page, the next call to next() automatically swaps the secondary data page with the primary data page. Now that this is the first call on a new primary page, a thread is spawned to retrieve the secondary data page and the pattern continues. When all data has been retrieved from the server, hasNext() is false.

5   Conclusion

The world's computers are already connected to vast repositories of information and demand for accessing and transporting this information continually increases. To meet this demand we must be able to provide the necessary delivery mechanisms and technologies. In this paper, a design pattern has been presented for retrieving large amounts of information from remote data sources.

The design pattern allows information providers to conserve resources, provide reasonable response times to user requests, and provide robust and full data access in an easy-to-use manner. The design pattern presented in this paper has improved on design patterns that require developers to think in terms of *pages* and other segmented data sets, by providing the developer with a standard iterator interface which abstracts such issues.

The approach satisfies the five requirements proposed for robust, efficient, distributed retrieval of large result sets:

1. must conserve resources
2. must respond within a reasonable time
3. must be robust
4. must not be limited to a partial result set
5. must be intuitive to use

Further work will consist of considering the impact to the design pattern and query slicing technique when retrieving data in a variety of sort orderings other than by primary key. In addition, applying advanced data caching strategies may be worthwhile investigating and incorporating into the design pattern to provide further performance improvements.

Acknowledgements. Thanks to Paul Strooper for comments on an earlier version of this paper.

References

1. D. Alur, J. Crupi, and D. Malks. *Core J2EE Patterns: Best Practices and Design Strategies*, pages 390–407. Prentice Hall, 2001.
2. D. Alur, J. Crupi, and D. Malks. *Core J2EE Patterns: Best Practices and Design Strategies*, pages 261–290. Prentice Hall, 2001.
3. E. Chan and K. Ueda. Efficient query result retrieval over the web. In *Proceedings International Conference on Parallel and Distributed Systems*. IEEE Computer Society, 2000.
4. J.D. Foley, A. van Dam, S.K. Feiner, and J.F. Hughes. *Computer Graphics: Principles and Practice*. Addison Wesley, 1990.
5. E. Gamma, R. Helm, R. Johnson, and J. Vlissides. *Design Patterns: Elements of Reusable Object-Oriented Software*. Addison Wesley, 1999.
6. Sun Microsystems Inc. Page-by-page iterator. Available online at http://java.sun.com/blueprints/patterns/j2ee_patterns/page_by_page_iterator/.
7. B. Long and P. Strooper. A case study in testing distributed systems. In *Proceedings of the 3rd International Symposium on Distributed Objects and Applications*, pages 20–29. IEEE Computer Society, 2001.
8. M.R. Lyu. Guest editor's introduction to the special issue on web technologies. *IEEE Transactions on Knowledge and Data Engineering*, 11(4):505–508, 1991.
9. J. Waldo, G. Wyant, A. Wollrath, and S. Kendall. A note on distributed computing. Technical Report 94-29, Sun Microsystems Laboratories, Inc., California, November 1994.

Replacement Policies for a Distributed Object Caching Service*

Hilla Atzmon, Roy Friedman, and Roman Vitenberg

Computer Science Department, The Technion, Haifa 32000, Israel.
{atzmonh,roy,romanv}@cs.technion.ac.il

Abstract. This paper investigates replacement policies for an object caching service. The replacement policies studied include several previously known schemes, as well as a couple of new schemes that take into account the hierarchical structure of the caching service. Three metrics are used in comparing the replacement policies: cache *hit rate* - the percentage of requests that were answered from the cache, *byte hit rate* - the percentage of bytes in replies that were answered from the cache, and *access time* - average time a client request has to wait for the corresponding reply. Also, unlike most works on cache replacement, this work examines the behavior of the entire system, rather than looking at a single cache at a time.

Keywords: Object Caching, Cache Replacement Policies, CORBA

1 Introduction

One of the main goals of modern middlewares, such as CORBA [15] and .NET [16], is to facilitate the design of interoperable, extensible and portable distributed systems. This is done by standardizing a programming language independent Interface Definition Language (IDL), a large set of useful services, a generic inter Object Request Broker (ORB) communication protocol (GIOP/IIOP in the case of CORBA and SOAP in the case of .NET), and bridges to other common middlewares. Such middlewares combined with the global connectivity of the Internet, create a potential for truly global services that are available for clients anywhere in the world.

However, the long and unpredictable latencies of the Internet as well as its unreliability, complicate the realization of this potential. In particular, the difference in response time for accessing objects spread over the Internet might be dramatic, regardless of the middleware and ORB being used. Moreover, the scalability of such services is likely to be limited by the relatively high communication overhead imposed on servers exporting the services. These can adversely affect the end-user experience, rendering such services unreliable and therefor useless for practical purposes.

* This work was supported by the Israeli Ministry of Science and Technology grant number 1230 and by Technion VPR funds.

R. Meersman, Z. Tari (Eds.): CoopIS/DOA/ODBASE 2002, LNCS 2519, pp. 661–674, 2002.

As in other areas of computer science, caching can be used to improve availability, predictability, and scalability of distributed services offered through middlewares. Specifically, accessing a copy of an object that is cached near the client is much faster than accessing a far away object. Moreover, shorter connections have lower chances of getting congested and fail, and thus accessing a local copy is more likely to succeed and behave in a predictable manner. Finally, if most client requests are handled by caches, fewer requests will reach the server, and thus the system as a whole will be able to handle more concurrent client requests.

Since the cache size might be limited, we may need to use cache replacement, as done in many Web caching systems. Moreover, unlike Web caching, in our case we maintain objects in memory, and thus the cache size is much more limited than when caching HTML documents that are usually kept on disk. As indicated by Web caching studies, the exact cache replacement policy can have a significant effect on the cache performance.

In this paper, we investigate several cache replacement policies for a distributed objects caching service. We compare these policies using three metrics: *hit rate* - the percentage of all requests that are served from the cache; *byte hit rate* - the percentage of bytes in replies that are served from the cache; and *access time* - the average time that a client waits between issuing a request and receiving a reply. Note that byte hit rate is important, since many wide area networks have limited bandwidth. Thus, in such settings, the byte hit rate may be a more significant performance factor than the hit rate. As for access time, this is the bottom line from the client's point of view, since this is what the client notices. As can be seen from the results of this work, having the highest hit rate, or even highest byte hit rate, does not necessarily mean having the shortest access time. This is due to the fact that misses may take longer to serve, based on where in the network they occur.

Some of the policies we consider, including LRU [13], LFU-DA [4], SIZE [20], and GDSF [10], are known from Web caching studies. Additionally, we introduce and explore a couple of new replacement policies, that we nicknamed H-BASED and LFU-H-BASED, which take into account the hierarchical nature of the caching service that we use in this study.

More specifically, all our measurements are conducted on the CASCADE system [11], which is a caching service for active CORBA objects, i.e., objects that include both data and code. CASCADE employs an update-based scheme to synchronize objects. An important aspect of CASCADE is that it dynamically builds a hierarchy for each cached object based on clients' access pattern, as described in Section 2. As described in more detail in Section 3.2, the H-BASED policy takes into account, when deciding which object to evacuate, the position of cached object in its hierarchy, in order to reduce the overall access time. The LFU-H-BASED policy combines the benefits of LFU-DA and H-BASED, and is designed to optimize both the hit rate and access time of the system.

The results of these experiments suggest that for a completely random trace, the SIZE policy performs best when considering hit rate. For traces that were generated by a workload generator, frequency and recency based policies like

LFU-DA and LRU perform best when considering hit rate and byte hit rate. The new policies, H-BASED and LFU-H-BASED, improve the average access time in many cases.

2 CASCADE

This section briefly describes CASCADE, the caching service we use in this work. It appears here for the sake of completeness. More details about CASCADE can be found in [11].

CASCADE is a generic caching service for CORBA objects, supporting caching of active objects, which include both data and code. Caching objects without code either entails using the pre-defined confined set of possible operations or requires the code to be distributed over all the sites that can potentially keep a cached object copy. In the former case, generality is restricted. In the latter case, caching cannot be deployed in large scale dynamic environments. CASCADE allows to distribute object code dynamically upon request. Code caching also enables to preserve the standard CORBA programming model: The application works with the cached copy through the same interface it would have worked with the original object. In addition, all object methods (including updates) can be invoked locally, often eliminating the need to contact the remote object. CASCADE is highly configurable with regard to a broad spectrum of application parameters. It allows client applications to fully control many aspects of object caching, by specifying a variety of policies for cache management, consistency maintenance, persistence, security, etc. CASCADE is specifically designed to operate over the Internet by employing a dynamically built cache hierarchy.

The caching service is provided by a number of servers, each of which is responsible for a specific *logical* domain. In practice, these domains can correspond to geographical areas. The servers are called *Domain Caching Servers (DCSs)*. Cached copies of each object are organized into a hierarchy. A separate hierarchy is dynamically constructed for each object. The hierarchy construction is driven by client requests. The construction mechanism ensures that for each client, client's local DCS (i.e., the DCS responsible for the client's domain) obtains a copy of the object. In addition, this mechanism attempts to guarantee that the object copy is obtained from the nearest DCS having a copy of this object. This feature dramatically reduces response time and contributes to the scalability of the system. Once the local DCS has an object copy, all client requests for object method invocation go to this DCS, so that the client does not have to communicate to a far server.

The DCS that holds an original object becomes the *root* for this object cache hierarchy. It plays a special role in building the hierarchy and in ensuring consistency of the cached copies. Hierarchies corresponding to each object are superimposed on the DCS infrastructure: Different object hierarchies may overlap or be completely disjoint. Also, overlapping object hierarchies do not necessarily have the same root.

The hierarchy construction protocol, as described in [11], guarantees that for each client there is a local DCS that has a cached copy of the object; the local DCS handles the client's requests. It is this fact and the hierarchical architecture of the system that allow to significantly reduce the response time, to distribute the load on DCSs and to render the caching service scalable.

2.1   Cache Management in CASCADE

Cache Manager Module. The cache manager controls insertion/deletion of objects to/from the object cache. There is one manager per DCS. The manager uses a configurable replacement policy in order to decide which object is to be evacuated from the cache, when a cache does not have enough space for a new copy of an object. When the manager is created, the policy to be used is determined. A different policy can be used for each DCS, but once it is determined for a specific DCS, it will not change. Each time an object is to be inserted to a cache, the manager first calculates the object's size, checks whether there is enough space in cache, evacuates objects from cache if necessary, and maintains the structures used for the chosen replacement policy. When evacuating an object from a cache, the manager notifies the object itself, so it can perform some last actions, such as releasing unnecessary memory, and is then evicted.

Object Evacuation and Reconstruction. In CASCADE's model, a client has to explicitly de-register an object from its local DCS. As long as the object was not de-registered, the client is likely to access the object again. Thus, when a DCS decides to evict an object, it does not completely forget about it. Instead, the evicting DCS keeps a small record of the object's identity and hierarchy, and uses it to disseminate requests and replies along that hierarchy. However, the memory that holds the object's state is released.

If some previously evacuated object is required later by a client, it will be acquired again from the parent node transparently to this client. In turn, if the parent node also does not have a copy of the requested object, it will try to acquire it from its parent node. This way the request ascends all the way up along the hierarchy until the DCS that has a copy of the object is reached. In the worst case, the chain reaches the root of the hierarchy. The object copy then descends along the hierarchy back to the request originator.

3   Replacement Policies

3.1   Known Replacement Policies

Below we describe the main policies that were introduced in the past and were used in our study, due to the fact that in the previous Web caching studies they achieved better results than other policies. We then also briefly mention other known replacement policies.

Least Recently Used (LRU) replaces the document in the cache that was not accessed for the longest period of time. The basic premise behind the LRU algorithm is that documents that have been referenced in the recent past will likely be referenced again in the near future. This property is known as *temporal locality*. The LRU algorithm is usually employed in disk block caches. It is justified by the temporal locality that commonly exists in file I/O request streams.

SIZE removes largest files first [20]. It tries to maximize hit rate by replacing one large document instead of many small ones. This naturally reduces the number of future cache misses. In this study we also used the **INVERSE(SIZE)** policy, which removes the smallest file first. The main goal in using this policy is the comparison of SIZE and its inverse policy.

GreedyDual-Size with Frequency (GDSF) is a hybrid policy, that combines in its decisions the recency of accesses, the cost of bringing an object to the cache, the object's size, and the frequency in which it was accessed with some aging mechanism [10]. It improves the basic GreedyDual algorithm [21] that only combined recency and cost, and the GD-Size algorithm that combined recency, cost, and size. The idea is as follows: The mechanism attaches a key to each object, which is updated dynamically, and whenever there is not enough room in the cache, the object with the lowest key is removed. The key of each object is initialized when the object is inserted into the cache as the cost of bringing the object to the cache. Additionally, the mechanism uses an *inflation factor* variable denoted by L, which is initialized to 0. Then, each time an object is accessed, its key is being updated by: $K_i = (C_i/S_i) * F_i + L$ where C_i is the object's cost, S_i is its size, F_i is its frequency. Further, whenever an object with key k is evacuated, L is set to k.

Least Frequently Used with Dynamic Aging (LFU-DA) is an improvement of the basic Least Frequently Used (LFU) policy, which employs an automatic aging mechanism. That is, LFU simply replaces the object that was least accessed. The problem with this is that if there are bursts of accesses to some object, that object builds a very large frequency counter, and is thus never replaced, even if it is no longer being accessed. An aging mechanism periodically reduces the frequency count of each object, thereby avoiding this problem. Similarly to GDSF, instead of a simple frequency count, LFU-DA attaches a key k_i to each object i, and updates this key to $K_i = C_i * F_i + L$ (L is the same inflation factor as in GDSF) whenever the object is accessed.

Other Known Techniques. LRU-MIN and LRU-THOLD are two variants of LRU that were investigated in [2], which also investigated the FIFO policy. $\log_2(SIZE)$ is a variant of SIZE that was introduced in [20]. Frequency Based Replacement (FBR) was proposed in [19]. It is a hybrid replacement policy, which attempts to capture the benefits of both LRU and LFU. Other forms of LFU that were introduced in the past include LFU-Aging, LFU*, and LFU*-Aging [7].

3.2   New Replacement Policies

In the first new policy, called **H-BASED**, replacement decisions are based on the hierarchy construction of the objects. For each object in the hierarchy, the replacement key is the number of direct descendants it has that were evacuated from cache. That is, when the cache is full, the cache manager will evacuate the object with the smallest key. The motivation behind this policy is to reduce access time. When an evacuated object is referenced, the object is reconstructed. Reconstruction is time consuming, since it involves requesting the copy from the parent node. This request can ascend all the way up along the hierarchy, after which the copy will descend down the hierarchy. The more evacuated descendants an object has, the chance that one of them will be referenced is bigger. In order to save access time, it is worthwhile to keep this object in the cache.

An example for a replacement decision of the H-BASED policy is depicted in Figure 1. In this example, there are a couple of subtrees that are part of two larger hierarchies for Objects X and Y. Each node in a subtree is a copy of an object that resides in a different DCS. The shaded nodes represent valid copies. The white nodes represent objects that were evacuated from cache. Assume that the roots of these subtrees reside in the same DCS, and one of them has to be evacuated. Object y has four direct descendants that were evacuated from cache, while object x has two. According to the H-BASED policy, x will be evacuated from cache. It is worthwhile to keep y in the cache since there is more chance that one of the direct descendants of y will ask for a copy from its parent.

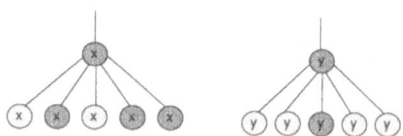

Fig. 1. H-BASED example

The second policy, called LFU-H-BASED, combines the LFU-DA and H-BASED policies, in order to combine the benefits of both. As discussed above, with LFU-DA, each object in the cache is associated with a priority key. When an object is to be removed from cache, the one with the lowest key is removed. If there are several objects whose key is equal to the lowest key, one of them is chosen according to the secondary key. The secondary key in this case is the key used in H-BASED. We used LFU-DA as a primary key in the LFU-H-BASED since LFU-DA performs better than the other policies we investigated.

4   Performance Measurements

4.1   The Environment

We have conducted the experiments using CASCADE, by playing artificially generated client access traces, as described below, on a system consisting of 10

DCSs. The DCSs, as well as the clients, were run on Windows 2000 powered Intel based Dual 1.7 GHz Pentium 4 Xeon with 1G RDRAM. The network connecting the DCSs was a 100 Mbps Fast Switched Ethernet, but we emulated a general Internet topology by inserting artificial delays on invocations between DCSs that are proportional to the size of messages sent.

The traces played on the system consisted of clients issuing the following types of requests: *registration* and *subscription*. A registration request is used to register a new object into one of the DCSs, which also creates a new hierarchy for this object. After registering, the client always performs one read and one write operation on the new object. In a subscription request, the client asks for a reference for an object from a specific DCS. If the DCS is not part of the requested object's hierarchy, it joins the hierarchy at this point. Once the DCS becomes part of the hierarchy, it returns a reference for the object to the client. After receiving the reference, the client always performs one read and one write operation. As the trace proceeds, hierarchies are built and objects are cached.

4.2   Trace Generation

The main parameters for generating a trace are the number of servers, number of original objects, sizes of objects, number of requests, objects popularity, order of requests, and correlation between objects and servers in the request itself. We have generated four traces, one of which is completely random, and the others based on a trace generator, called ProWGen [9], that allows inducing more sophisticated distributions, and correlations between the various emulation parameters. All our traces included 10 servers and 1,000 objects, and start by issuing 1,000 registration requests, one for each object, followed by a total of 20,000 subscription requests distributed among the DCSs and objects.

In the random trace, object sizes, the order of requests to objects, and the correlation between objects and servers are chosen in random using uniform distribution. In the following subsection, we describe the various ProWGen parameters, what was their setting in each of the traces, and how we adapted traces generated by ProWGen to our needs.

ProWGen. ProWGen incorporates five selected workload characteristics, which are *one-time referencing, file popularity, file size distribution, correlation between file size and popularity,* and *temporal locality.* In our experiments, we used 50-70% one-time referencing, which corresponds to results from Web caching studies, a value of $\beta = 0.75$ in the Zipf-like distribution [17] that controls the file popularity [4,3,8,14,18], and zero correlation between file size and popularity. File size distribution is modeled in ProWGen using lognormal distribution with a tail modeled with a *Pareto* distribution [1,5,6,12]. The file size distribution and temporal locality are the main parameters that distinguish among the tests we performed, as outlined below.

Each reference in the workload generated by ProWGen is a two-tuple consisting of a *file id* followed by a *file size*. In order to make the traces applicable for CASCADE, we mapped these generated workloads to a workloads of CAS-CADE requests, as follows: Each distinct file id is mapped to a distinct object name. Each reference in the original workload is translated into a subscription request for that object. The target of the request is chosen randomly from the 10 DCSs initiated for that run. At the beginning of the run, registration requests are initiated for all distinct objects. The target of each registration request is chosen randomly as well.

We used three different ProWGen traces in our experiment. The differences between the traces refer to the amount of one-timers and to the body of the size distribution. In Trace 1, one-timers make 70% of the distinct objects, resulting in 700 one-timers out of 1,000. The range of object sizes is 0-24K, while the log-normal distribution of the sizes has a mean value of 7000 and standard deviation of 11,000, which creates a wide body. In Trace 2, one-timers consist 50% of the distinct objects, resulting in 500 one-timers out of 1,000. The range of sizes is 0-50K, while the lognormal distribution has a mean value of 2,000 and standard deviation of 2,500, meaning many small objects. Trace 3 is the same as Trace 2, except for the lognormal distribution: Trace 3 is generated with mean value of 2,000 and standard deviation of 1,000, meaning many intermediate sized objects.

4.3   Results

Random Trace Results. Figure 2 exhibits the results of all seven replacement policies, for cache sizes ranging from 30 KB through 7680 KB. As can be seen, SIZE outperforms all other policies when considering the hit rate metric. All other policies perform roughly the same, except for INVERSE(SIZE) which is the worse. Since the trace is random, there is no locality effect, and therefore the only differentiating factor is the size of objects.

It can also be seen that no policy outperforms another when considering the byte hit rate metric. Since SIZE prefers to keep in the cache many small objects, the amount of bytes it satisfies in a hit is small. This is the reason that the byte hit rate of SIZE is similar to the other policies, despite that fact that its hit rate is better. INVERSE(SIZE) has the opposite behavior. It has the biggest miss rate, but since it keeps large objects in cache, every hit returns a large amount of data.

The results in Figure 2 indicate that H-BASED has the best access time, which was expected, given the discussion in Section 3.2. INVERSE(SIZE) performs worst, since its hit rate is substantially poorer than the others.

ProWGen Traces Results. Figure 3 shows the average hit rate obtained for the three ProWGen traces. In all of them LFU-DA, LFU-H-BASED and LRU outperform the other policies. In Traces 1 and 3, GDSF is the next best policy. In Trace 2, SIZE is very similar to GDSF. The reason is that in Trace 2 there are many small objects, and SIZE keeps many of them in cache instead of large objects. H-BASED performs worse than GDSF with small caches, but performs the same as GDSF for bigger caches. INVERSE(SIZE) performs worst, as expected.

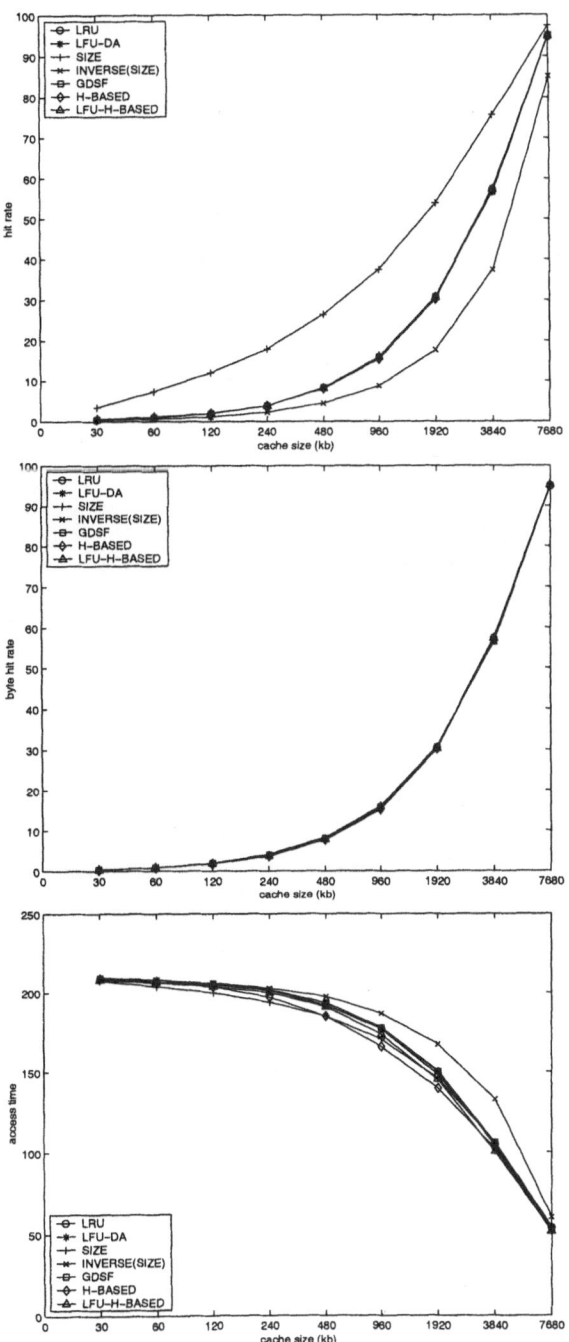

Fig. 2. Random Trace

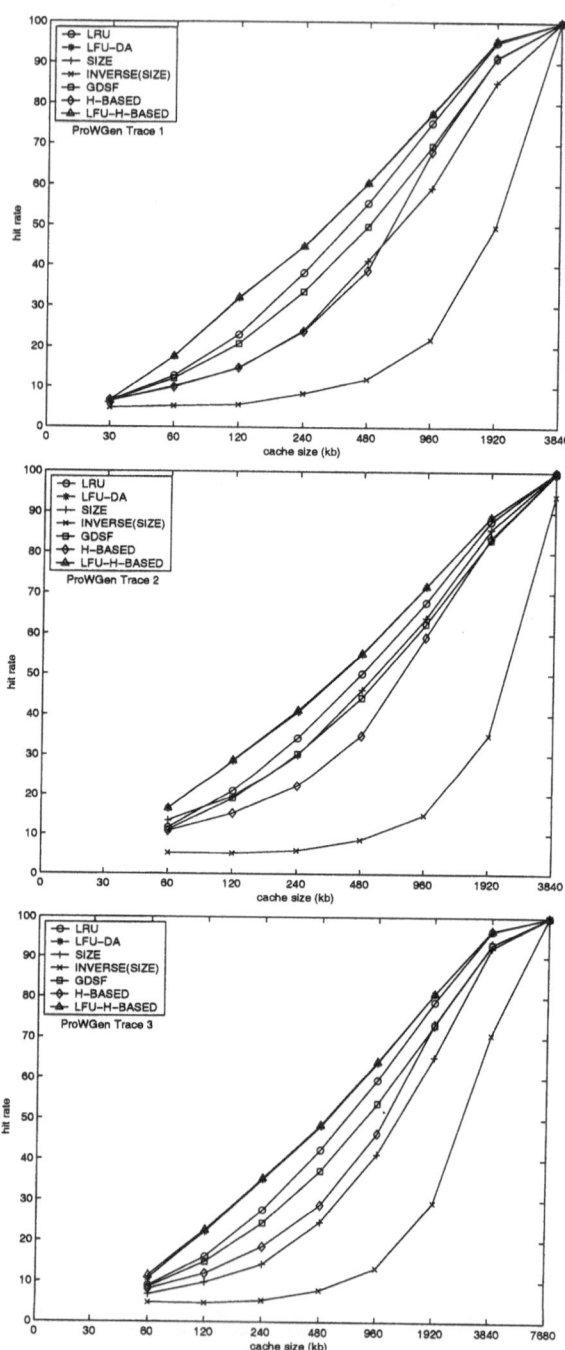

Fig. 3. ProWGen Traces Hit Rate

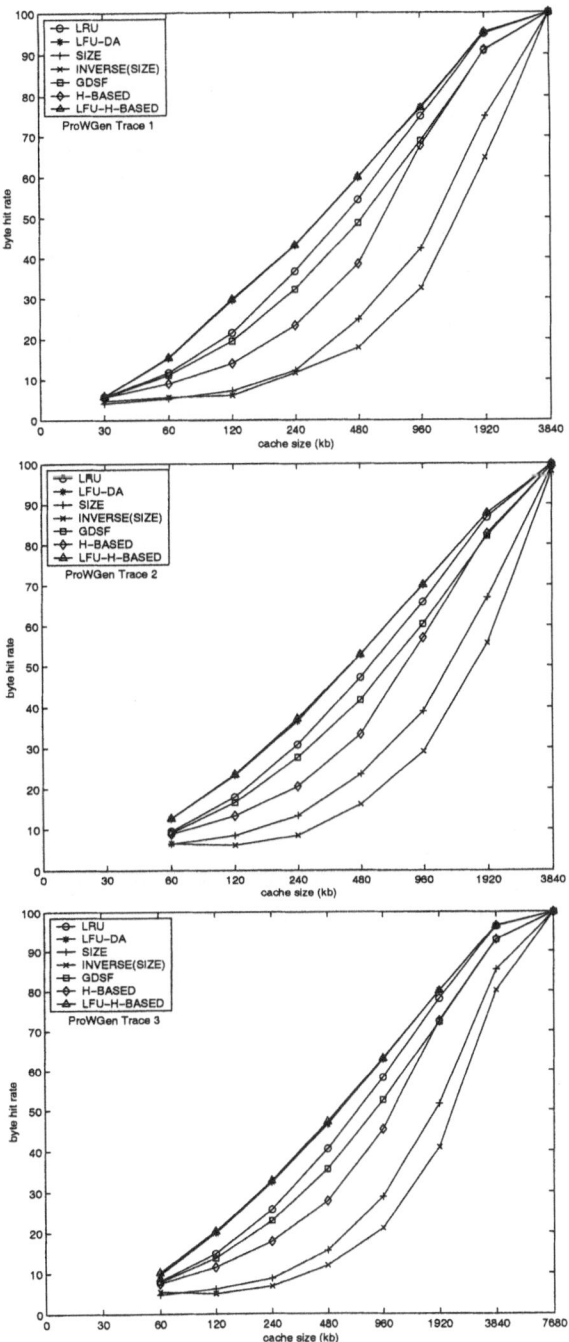

Fig. 4. ProWGen Traces Byte Hit Rate

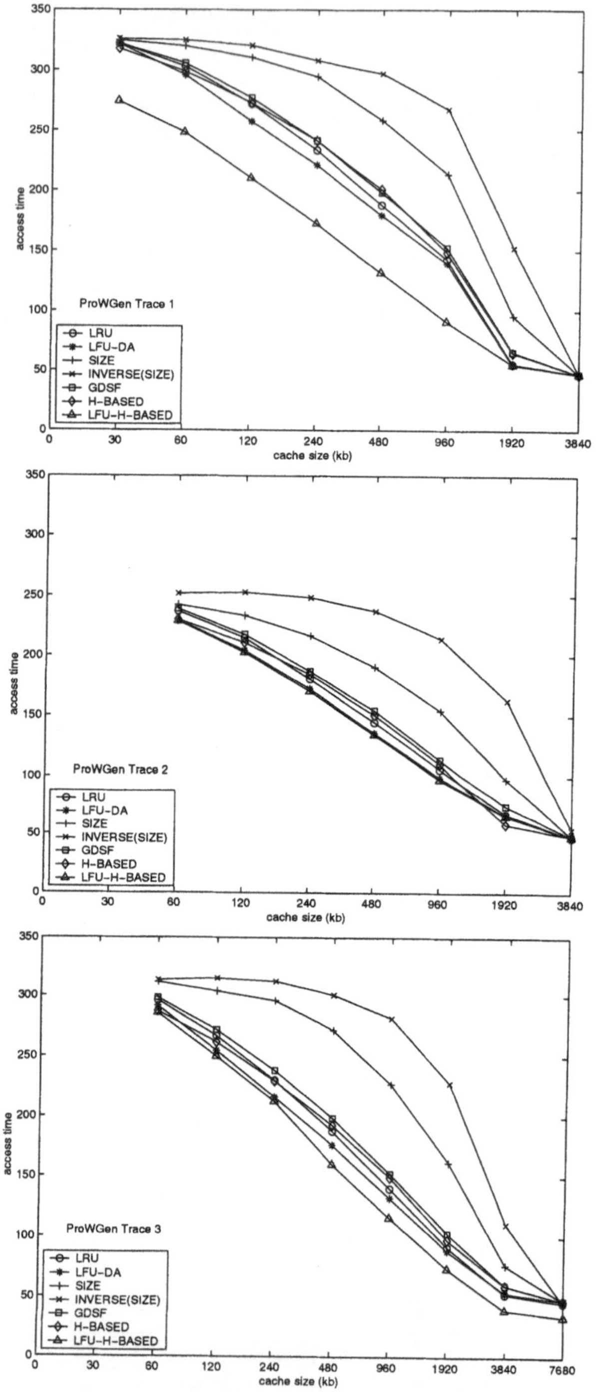

Fig. 5. ProWGen Traces Access Time

Figure 4 shows the average byte hit rate obtained for the three ProWGen traces. In all traces, LFU-DA and LFU-H-BASED outperform the other policies. Next is LRU, GDSF and H-BASED. SIZE and INVERSE(SIZE) perform the worst. The bad performance of SIZE can be explained by the fact that SIZE keeps small objects in cache. Thus, the number of bytes that are found in the cache, when using the SIZE policy, is relatively small.

Figure 5 shows the average access time obtained for the three ProWGen traces. It can be seen that in most cases LFU-H-BASED improves the average access time achieved by LFU-DA. The largest improvement is in Trace 1: up to 35%. In Trace 2 the performance of LFU-H-BASED is the same as of LFU-DA. In Trace 3 there is an improvement of up to 30%. The relative order of performance of the other policies is similar to the order seen by the average byte hit rate. LFU-DA has the lowest access time after LFU-H-BASED, LRU is next, followed by H-BASED and GDSF. SIZE is much worse since its byte hit rate is very low compared to the other policies. Low byte hit rate indicates that many bytes are being transferred through the network, which increases the average access time. INVERSE(SIZE) has the worst average access time, as both its hit rate and byte hit rate are very low.

5   Conclusions

This paper presented a performance study of replacement policies of an object caching service. The work investigated several known policies and a couple of new ones. Emulation of a real Internet wide distributed system was used in order to evaluate the performance of the policies. All experiments used CASCADE, a caching service for CORBA objects. Traces with different characteristics were generated. One trace was generated randomly and three traces were generated with the help of ProWGen, a synthetic workload generator. Our results show that performance of a policy in a specific experiment heavily depends on the trace being used. The results suggest that for a random trace, the SIZE policy performs best when considering hit rate, while all policies perform roughly the same when considering byte hit rate. The results of the traces generated by ProWGen indicate that frequency and recency based policies, like LFU-DA, LFU-H-BASED, and LRU have the best hit rate and byte hit rate. Also, while H-BASED did not achieve as good performance as we hoped, LFU-H-BASED managed to obtain the best average access time, while keeping the same good hit rate and byte hit rate as LFU-DA.

References

1. G. Abdulla, E. Fox, M. Abrams, and S. Williams. WWW proxy traffic characterization with application to caching. Technical Report TR-97-03, Computer Science Department, Virginia Tech., March 1997.
2. M. Abrams, C. Standridge, G. Abdulla, S. Williams, and E. Fox. Caching proxies: Limitations and potentials. In *Proceedings of the Fourth International World Wide Web Conference*, pages 119–133, Boston, USA, December 1995.

3. V. Almeida, M. Cesario, R. Fonseca, W. Meira Jr., and C. Murta. Analysing the behavior of a proxy server in light of regional and cultural issues. In *Proceedings of the Third International WWW Caching Workshop*, Manchester, England, June 1998.

4. M. Arlitt, L. Cherkasova, J. Dilley, R. Friedrich, and T. Jin. Evaluating content management techniques for web proxy caches. *Performance Evaluation Review*, 27(4):3–11, March 2000.

5. M. Arlitt and T. Jin. A workload characterization study of the 1998 world cup web site. *IEEE Network*, 14(3):30–37, May/June 2000.

6. M. Arlitt and C. Williamson. Internet web servers: workload characterization and performance implications. *IEEE/ACM Transactions on Networking*, 5(5):631–645, October 1997.

7. M. Arlitt and C. Williamson. Trace-driven simulation of document caching strategies for internet web servers. *Simulation Journal*, 68(1):23–33, January 1997.

8. L. Breslau, P. Cao, L. Fan, G. Phillips, and S. Shenker. Web caching and Zipf-like distributions: Evidence and implications. In *Proceedings of IEEE INFOCOM 1999*, pages 126–134, New York, NY, March 1999.

9. M. Busary and C. Williamson. On the sensitivity of web proxy cache performance to workload characteristics. In *Proceedings of IEEE INFOCOM 2001*, pages 1225–1234, Anchorage, Alaska USA, April 2001.

10. L. Cherkasova. Improving WWW proxies performance with greedy-dual-size-frequency caching policy. Technical Report HPL-98-69R1, Hewlett-Packard Laboratories, November 1998.

11. G. Chockler, D. Dolev, R. Friedman, and R. Vitenberg. Implementing a caching service for distributed CORBA objects. In *Proceedings of Middleware '00*, pages 1–23, April 2000.

12. B. Duska, D. Marwood, and M. Feeley. The measured access characteristics of world-wide-web client proxy caches. In *Proceedings of the USENIX Symposium on Internet Technologies and Systems*, pages 23–35, December 1997.

13. J. Hennessy and D. Patterson. *Computer Architecture – a Quantitive Approach*. Morgan Kaufmann Publishers, 1990.

14. A. Mahanti, C. Williamson, and D. Eager. Traffic analysis of a web proxy caching hierarchy. *IEEE Network*, 14(3):16–23, May/June 2000.

15. OMG. *The Common Object Request Broker: Architecture and Specification*. OMG, 1995.

16. D. Platt. *Introducing Microsoft^{TM}.NET*. Microsoft^{TM}Press, 2001.

17. References on Zipf's law. Available at http://linkage.rockefeller.edu/wli/zipf/.

18. C. Roadknight, I. Marshall, and D. Vearer. File popularity characterisation. *ACM Sigmetrics Performance Evaluation Review*, 27(4):45–50, March 2000.

19. J.T. Robinson and M.V. Devarakonda. Data cache management using frequency-based replacement. In *Proceedings of the ACM SIGMETRICS Conference on Measurement and Modeling of Computer Systems*, pages 134–142, May 1990.

20. S. Williams, M. Abrams, C.R. Standridge, G. Abdulla, and E.A. Fox. Removal policies in network caches for World-Wide Web documents. In *Proceedings of the ACM SIGCOMM'96 conference*, pages 293–305, Palo Alto, CA USA, August 1996.

21. N. Young. On-line caching as cache size varies. In *Proceedings of the second annual ACM-SIAM symposium on Discrete algorithms*, pages 241–250, San Francisco, CA USA, January 1991.

Design and Performance of a Media Gateway Trader

Hans Ole Rafaelsen[1] and Frank Eliassen[2]

[1] Dept. of Computer Science, University of Tromsø, Norway
hansr@cs.uit.no
[2] Simula Research Laboratory, P.O. Box 134, 1325 Lysaker, Norway
frank@simula.no

Abstract. Multimedia applications of tomorrow face new challenges. As we move towards ubiquitous computing systems, users will require that the multimedia applications adopt to behave well in this new setting. This will require that application developers are equipped with new development tools and abstractions to help construct these new applications. A binding framework which supports heterogeneous participants in multimedia bindings is presented. This framework allows for run-time checking of whether binding participants can meaningfully bind to each other. It also supports *media gateways*. These are services which can be used to automatically resolve incompatibilities between heterogeneous participants in multimedia bindings. Properties of gateways can be described trough a proposed gateway description language (GDL), and it is shown how gateways can be automatically selected at run-time. The design, implementation and a performance evaluation of a media gateway trader prototype is given.

1 Introduction

Next generation computer systems will consist of a large number of different services and devices. This will be the case as we move towards ubiquitous computing [24] and home area networks. Users will access services through devices with highly different capabilities, and each user will have a number of different devices. Services will be built by requiring service from other services, and devices will need to talk to other devices. Multimedia applications in this setting will have to support new patterns of interactions after they have been deployed, as users discover new ways to use the systems using new kinds of devices with capabilities not known of at the time of development of the multimedia application. To ensure interoperability between the various services and devices will be a major challenge for next generation computer systems.

To illustrate the above situation, consider an interactive distance learning system such as the one depicted in figure 1. During a lecture, the lecturer might decide to show a video to illustrate some points. The video is stored in a given media format (also called type) on the personal computer of the lecturer. The video is to be presented on the display wall of the class room for the students that are present there, and on another display wall in another classroom where

R. Meersman, Z. Tari (Eds.): CoopIS/DOA/ODBASE 2002, LNCS 2519, pp. 675–692, 2002.
© Springer-Verlag Berlin Heidelberg 2002

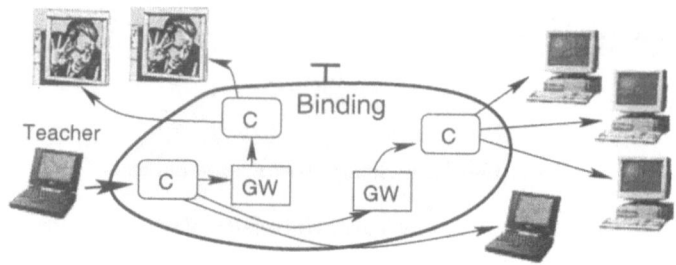

Fig. 1. A distance learning system

some other students are located. In addition the video shall also be viewed by distance students at home. Thus, the computing system should make sure that the display device in the rooms are capable of showing the video, and also that the distance students can view it. We may safely assume that the receivers of the video will have different capabilities with respect to supported video formats, processing, and communication. In general this will require that the supporting infrastructure (such as a middleware system) must be able to insert media gateways into the communication path (i.e. the binding) between the sender and the receivers to transcode between different video formats and/or scale the video streams to match the different capabilities of the receivers. Also, the supporting infrastructure has to be able to make multiple copies of the stream, in order to deliver it to multiple receivers in a cost-effective way. That is, multicast should be supported.

In environments such as the one indicated above, it becomes imperative that the supporting infrastructure is able to detect when data formats and other capabilities are not compatible with output devices, and automatically adapt or scale the content as necessary. Media gateways (hereafter called gateways) provide a mechanism which can be introduced to dynamically resolve incompatibilities between communication end points. The purpose of a gateway is to transform a media stream from one format to another, or to change other properties of the media streams through different forms of scaling.

The binding given in figure 1 contains both gateways and *clones*. Clones are abstractions which provide multicast support. Basically a clone receive a media stream and makes multiple copies of it. The copies are sent to multiple receivers. How a clone achieve this is an issue of the implementation of the clone. In the simplest, and most costly, case it simply makes *n* copies and uses *n* point-to-point connections to send it to the receivers. If multicast facilities are provided within the *technology domain* [8] where the clone is installed, it can be used to achieve cheaper multicast. Supporting efficient insertion of gateways and clones in the bindings to take advantage of the facilities found in various technology domains is an important task of the middleware. How this is achieved is however outside the scope of this paper.

In this paper we present an approach to a method for dynamically selecting and inserting gateways into one-to-one bindings at run-time, to resolve detected

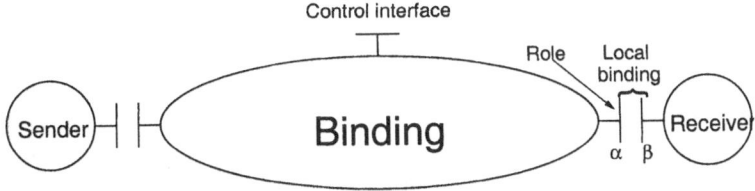

Fig. 2. Point-to-point binding

incompatibilities between multimedia communication end points. We refer to bindings built dynamically during run time as ad-hoc bindings. We propose a language for specifying media gateways, and a trading-based method to search for suitable gateway offers within the run-time environment. The latter approach makes it straight-forward to extend a distributed computing environment with new gateways that can be dynamically selected to resolve new kinds of incompatibilities.

Our approach builds on our earlier work on developing a binding framework for multimedia applications [6] [4] [5] [18]. The binding framework includes languages for specifying bindings and multimedia stream interfaces, and methods for detecting incompatibilities between stream interfaces. The binding framework is based on the concept of open bindings [7]. An open binding is a composite distributed object, used to connect multiple interfaces across a distributed computing environment. An open binding usually has multiple levels of composition, which means that a binding can be composed of lower level bindings. Openness allows adaptation of the binding such as inclusion of gateways.

In the next section we briefly present the binding framework mentioned above. In section 3 we then introduce a the Gateway Definition Language (GDL). A prototype implementation is described and evaluated in section 4. Related work is given in section 5. The last section concludes and give the outline of further work.

2   Open Explicit Bindings

In the reference model for Open Distributed Processing (RM-ODP) [10] stream bindings are explicit. This supports direct client control of the binding during its lifetime. Furthermore, bindings are first class objects and are created, managed and invoked in the same way as other objects [3]. The main rationale for explicit bindings is to support QoS management in terms of QoS specification, monitoring and control [3]. For example, the binding control interface of a stream binding can be used to control and monitor the QoS of ongoing streams. An example of a point-to-point binding is depicted in figure 2.

For the explicit binding and stream abstractions, we have developed a generic model called MBS (Model of Bindings and Streams) [18]. MBS will constitute a part of the foundation for the programming model of an adaptive multimedia ORB called MULTE-ORB [12]. MBS is based on a generic type model for stream flows and associated type checking rules earlier proposed in [6]. This model is open-ended and can in principle support any set of flow parameters. It also includes compatibility rules ensuring the correctness of binding attempts of flow end-points, and conformance rules expressing conditions for substitutability [4]. An implementation of the type model including procedures for determining compatibility and examples of its application are described in [5].

A binding type (or template) defines a particular class of binding objects by identifying the type of interfaces which can participate in the binding, the roles they play, and the way behavior at the various binding interfaces are linked [13]. For example, a multicast video binding would typically support a producer role and a consumer role. In some cases the binding will support operations for adding interfaces to a binding in a named role (e.g. a new multicast receiver), and for removing interfaces from the binding (e.g. remove a multicast receiver from the binding).

Through the local bindings the binding object receives and delivers information for binding participants according to the causality and type of the bound interfaces. Type checking is applied when creating the binding and when adding a new interface to the binding. When creating the binding, type information about the application object interfaces to be initially bound and the corresponding roles they will fulfill in the binding, is provided as parameters of the create method call. Corresponding interfaces with the appropriate roles are as a result added to the binding. If an application object interface β is offered to fulfill a role α, then the type of β must be compatible with the type of α.

In MBS, stream interfaces are specified as a set of alternative behaviors that are supported by the interface. For stream interfaces this refers to the alternative properties of media streams (such as format and QoS characteristics) that may be produced by a source interface or consumed by a sink interface. Formally, this set of alternative behaviors for a given interface α we refer to as the interpretation of α, denoted $I(\alpha)$. Two interfaces are then compatible if their respective interpretations have a non-empty intersection. Otherwise they are incompatible. For further details of the type model the reader is referred to [6] [4] [5].

As part of the work on MBS, the Flow Interface Description Language (FIDL) has been developed . This language enables an application programmer to specify the interface characteristics of stream interfaces as a collection of directional media flow end-points. This is also referred to as the type of the interface. In addition, algorithms were developed to determine if interfaces specified in FIDL are compatible such that they can be meaningfully bound to each other. Media flows are made up of flow entities. The properties of the entities are given by a set of attributes. Attributes have names and values. Values can be a single value, a set of values or ranges of values. The two latter cases reflect the interface's support of alternative behaviors in the corresponding QoS dimension. The language also has a notation of constraints which specifies how elements can be combined in the media flows. That is, constraint expressions specify which constellations of element types are allowed to appear at a flow end-point. They are expressed as logical *and* and *or* expressions between elements.

To enable interoperability, it is required that all participants have the same semantic understanding of the interface descriptions. The structure of interface description, attribute name and semantics have to be standardized. This will enable any participant to determine whether they are compatible with other participants.

Program 1 FIDL description of two interfaces

```
stream IS {
  source flow AVSender {
    video v {
      encoding = "MJPEG";
      samplerate = {20, 25, 30};
    };
    audio a {
      encoding = "AIFF";
      samplerate = (16000..44400);
      channels = {2, 6};
      samplesize = 24;
    };
    constraint (a & v) | a;
  }; // flow
}; // stream

stream IR {
  sink flow AReceiver {
    audio a {
      encoding = "GSM";
      samplerate = 8000.0;
      channels = {1};
      samplesize = {8};
    };
    constraint a;
  }; // flow
}; // stream
```

Program 1 shows an example of two interfaces, specified in FIDL. It specifies two directional media end-points. Stream IS contains a single *source* flow AVSender. The flow has an entity v of generic type *video* and an entity a of generic type *audio*. The properties of entity a are given by its two attributes. Attribute samplerate has three possible attribute values, giving the set of possible behaviors for this particular QoS dimension. The constraint, (a & v) | a, requires that either the audio and video entities are present, or only the audio.

3   Media Gateways

When attempting to bind two application interfaces that are incompatible, a media gateway can be inserted into the binding in order to overcome the incompatibility. A gateway is a component with two stream interfaces. One is the input (sink) interface which the stream producer binds to, and the other is the output (source) interface which the stream consumer binds to. The gateway transcodes and/or scales the media stream from the sender into a stream with properties the receiver is capable of receiving.

3.1   Semantics of Media Gateways

In order to determine whether a gateway might be used between two interfaces, the properties of a gateway has to be specified in such a way that we can algorithmically reason about its suitability. The properties of a gateway is specified by its external behavior, which are the alternative behaviors of its input and output interfaces, and the casual relationship between behavior at those two interfaces. The relationship we refer to as the *dependency* between the two interfaces. This dependency can be expressed as constraints on the behavior between the input and output interface. Since behavior is expressed as attribute values this reduces to attribute constraint relationships between attributes of input and output interface.

Accordingly, the semantics of a gateway can be specified as a 3-tuple $<\text{IF}^{in}$, IF^{out}, $dep>$, where IF^{in} is a sink stream interface, and IF^{out} is a source stream interface and dep is the dependency between the two interfaces. IF^{in} and IF^{out} are specified using FIDL [5].

The dependency part is given as as set of dependency elements $dep = \{d_1, d_2, \ldots, d_n\}$, where each d_i is a triple (a^{in}, a^{out}, d) where a^{in} is an attribute of the input interface, a^{out} is an attribute of the output interface, and d is either a partial, monotonic and continuous function from the domain of a^{in} to the domain of a^{out}, or from the domain of a^{out} to the domain of a^{in}; or a prepositional logic predicate p in which a^{in} and a^{out} occur as variables; or a value constraint between a^{in} and a^{out}. If d is a function $f()$, then the inverse function $f^{-1}()$ must also be provided. Dependencies thus express "computable" relationships between attributes of the input and output interface of the gateway that must always hold.

For a gateway with a given dependency specification and a set of possible input and output interface behaviors, the set of possible behaviors of the interfaces can be computed. This is in practice done for each attribute of the interfaces for which a dependency is defined.

For example, consider the dependency element (a^{in}, a^{out}, d) where d is a function $f()$, from the domain of a^{in} to the domain a^{out}, and the value of a^{in} is specified as a range (l, h). Then the resulting value of $a^{out'}$ can be computed as the range $(f(l), f(h))$. The inverse function $f^{-1}()$ is used to compute $a^{in'}$ from a^{out}. The set of attribute values which holds for the dependency is: $a^{in} \cap a^{in'}$ and $a^{out} \cap a^{out'}$. If on the other hand d is a predicate $p(a^{in}, a^{out})$, then the resulting

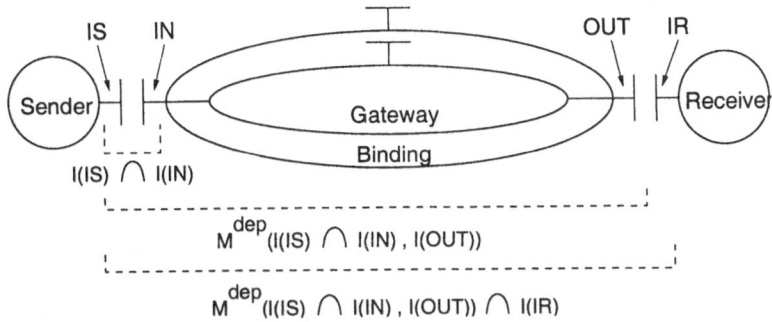

Fig. 3. Gateway within a binding

values of $a^{in'}$ and $a^{out'}$ are those values of a^{in} and a^{out}, which holds under the given predicate.

To denote the derived properties I(OUT') of the output interface OUT of a gateway and the derived properties I(IN') of the input interface IN, which holds the the dependency specification *dep*, we introduce the matching function M^{dep} : $(I(IN), I(OUT)) \rightarrow (I(IN'), I(OUT'))$. Hence M^{dep} computes the possible set of behaviors for the input and output interface of a gateway, which holds for the dependency *dep*.

Armed with the above notions, we may now formulate the conditions for the suitability of a gateway to resolve an incompatibility between two stream interfaces. A gateway with input interface IN, output interface OUT, and dependency *dep* can be used to resolve an incompatibility between a receiver interface IR and a sender interface IS, where I(IR) ∩ I(IS) = ∅, if I(IS) ∩ I(IN) ≠ ∅ and M^{dep}(I(IS) ∩ I(IN), I(OUT)) ∩ I(IR)≠ ∅. This means that first of all, the sender interface and the input interface of the gateway must be compatible. The behavior they have in common is expressed by I(IS) ∩ I(IN). Furthermore, the behavior of the output interface when derived from the common behavior of the sender interface and the input interface of the gateway, must be compatible with the receiver interface (see figure 3).

An interpreter is provided for the evaluation of functions and predicates when selecting gateways. The evaluation process to determine whether a given gateway can be used between two interfaces consists of three stages:

1. Compute the intersection of the interpretations of the sender interface and the input interface of the gateway. For details see [5].
2. Use the dependency matching function M^{dep} of the gateway to compute the constrained interpretation of the input and output interface of the gateway which holds for the dependency *dep*, and the intersection computed in stage 1.
3. Intersect the outcome of stage 2 with the interpretation of the interface of the receiver to calculate the set of possible behaviors the binding might take. If this set is non-empty, the gateway can be used. If it is empty, this gateway can not be used and the next gateway offer stored at the trader is evaluated.

3.2   Gateway Definition Language

The *Gateway Definition Language* (GDL) has been developed as a concrete syntax in order to express the semantics of media gateways. This is a language used to describe meta-information and reason about the behavior of media gateways. It is similar to how CORBA IDL [15] is used for describing the interface of CORBA objects.

GDL uses FIDL to specify the behavior of the input and output interface of a gateway. Additionally it introduces language constructs to express the dependency part of a gateway specification. The dependencies are described as a list of dependency statements. These statements are grouped together using OR and AND constructs. An implicit AND is assumed if no grouping construct is provided. A dependency is either a *value constraint,* a *predicate* or a *function.*

A value constraint statement is given by:

IF <attribute>[values from attribute domain] **THEN**
        <attribute'>[value from attribute' domain];

For example:

IF IN.AIn.a.samplesize[20, 25] **THEN**
        OUT.AOut.a.samplesize[10, 15];

states that when IN.AIn.a.samplesize has values "20" or "25", then OUT.AOut.a.samplesize is required to have values "10" or "15".

A value predicate statement is given by:

IF <attribute>[values from attribute domain] **THEN**
        <comparison operator> <attribute'>[value from attribute'
        domain];

where the *comparison operation* is one of the following: $==, <=, >=, <$, or $>$. For example:

IF IN.AIn.a.samplesize **THEN**
        $>=$ OUT.AOut.a.samplesize;

states that the sample size of the input has to be the same or greater than that of the output.

Functions are allowed to be used in conjunction with predicate statements. They are specified after the attribute the apply to:

IF <attribute>[values from attribute domain] [function value]
    THEN <comparison operator> <attribute'>[value from
            attribute' domain] [function' value'];

The only functions supported are arithmetic operations, $+, -, *, /$. So far our experience is that these functions are sufficient for describing properties of gateways. The framework does however allow for adding additional functions, should later experience show that the current set of functions are insufficient. The only thing required for these functions is that they have the requirements which are proposed for dependency functions. That is, they have to be a partial, monotonic and continuous function from the domain of one of the attributes to the domain of the other attribute. Values used with a function must be from the value domain of that function. Usually the *comparison operation* will be the equality operator $(=)$. For example:

Program 2 A simplified gateway specification

```
gateway audioGW {
  stream IN {
    sink flow AIn {
      audio a {
        encoding = "AIFF";
        samplerate = 16000;
        channels = {2};
        samplesize = {16, 24};
      };
      constraint a;
    }; // flow
  }; // stream

  stream OUT {
    source flow AOut {
      audio a {
        encoding = "GSM";
        samplerate = 8000.0;
        channels = {1};
        samplesize = {8};
      };
      constraint a;
    }; // flow
  }; // stream

  where {
    IF OUT.AOut.a.samplerate THEN = IN.AIn.a.samplerate / 2;
    IF IN.AIn.a.samplesize THEN >= OUT.AOut.a.samplesize;
    IF IN.AIn.a.channels THEN >= OUT.AOut.a.channels;
  }; // dependency
} // gateway
```

```
IF IN.VIn.video.height / 2 THEN
   = OUT.VOut.video.height;
IF IN.VIn.video.width / 2 THEN
   = OUT.VOut.video.width;
```

requires the spatial resolution of the output of the video to be a quarter of the input of the video.

Program 2 shows a simple specification of a gateway that can be injected into a binding to resolve incompatibilities. For example, this gateway can be injected into the binding to bind IS and IR specified in program 1. Computing the intersection of the interpretations of the sender interface and the input interface of the gateway, $I(IS) \cap I(IN)$, yields the stream properties:

```
audio.encoding = ''AIFF'';
audio.samplerate = 16000;
```

```
audio.channels = 2;
audio.samplesize = 24;
```

Computing the constrained stream properties of the output interface of the gateway, M^{dep}(I(IS) ∩ I(IN)) yields:

```
audio.encoding = ''GSM'';
audio.samplerate = 8000;
audio.channels = 1;
audio.samplesize = 8;
```

Computing the set of stream properties of the output interface of the gateway that is also acceptable to the receiver interface, M^{dep}(I(IS) ∩ I(IN)) ∩ I(IR), yields:

```
audio.encoding = ''GSM'';
audio.samplerate = 8000;
audio.channels = 1;
audio.samplesize = 8;
```

In this case it is just a single possible configuration. In the general case, the interpretation of this set might have several possible configurations. This requires some negotiation protocol to select a concrete configuration (see [18] for an example of a negotiation protocol for this purpose).

In order to ease the gateway selection process, dependencies should be described between interfaces in both directions. That is, for each dependency function $f()$ the inverse function $f^{-1}()$ should be defined. For our current set of functions this holds. This makes it possible for both parties to decide the configuration of the binding, supporting both sender oriented binding protocols like ST2[21] and receiver oriented protocols like RSVP[27]. Predicates and attribute constraints work in both directions.

4   Gateway Trader Prototype

To evaluate the soundness of the GDL language, a prototype trader has been designed and implemented. Gateways use GDL to describe the properties of the service they offer. This advertisement is exported to the trader. Clients of the gateway services can locate this service offer by searching the trader. To describe the properties of the service needed, a client uses FIDL to describe the properties of two interface which needs to be bound. Based on these description, the trader searches the service offers to see if some meets the requirements. The prototype is implemented using the Objective Caml programming language [9]. It consists of around 6000 lines of code. The motivation for writing a specialized trader for trading media gateways, instead of using standard trading services like the CORBA trader [16], is that our earlier attempts at using the CORBA trader found it to be insufficient for our particular needs [19]. The main problem we encountered was the inability to specify dependencies between attributes of input and output interfaces.

4.1   Overview of Trader Services

The trader provides services through its `Register` and Lookup interfaces. A service offer is exported using the `Register` interface. Service offers are parsed and checked for ambiguity. If they are found to be sound, they are registered in the trader's repository. If they for some reason are rejected, the offer is discarded, and an error message is returned to the exporter, giving an explanation for the rejection.

When a import is requested from a client using the Lookup interface, the two FIDL descriptions are parsed. It is required that one of the interfaces is a source interface, and that the other is a sink interface. The order of the interfaces determines if the binding will be sender or receiver oriented. If the first interface given is a source, then the binding protocol will be sender oriented. The search process is then started, consisting of the following major stages:

1. Gateway descriptions are retrieved from the repository. For each of these, an intersection is made between the first interface provided by the importer, and the interface from the gateway offer matching the direction of the first interface provided by the importer. That is, the interface with the opposite direction. This result in a new set of attribute values, for their common set of configurations.

2. If the set of common configurations is non-empty, the new capabilities of the gateways other interface is inferred. This is done by evaluating the dependency statements. Statements referring to attributes in the second interface, of the gateway, retrieve their values directly from the interface. For statements referring to attributes in the first interface, values are not retrieved from the interface. Instead they are retrieved from the set of values resulting from the intersection in stage 1.

3. If stage 2 results in a non-empty set of capabilities for the second interface, then an intersection is made between this interface and the second interface provided by the importer.

If the result of stage 3 is an non-empty set of capabilities, then this is a valid offer, and a reference to this gateway can be returned to the importer. Should the result of any of the 3 stages result in an empty set of capabilities, then that particular gateway can not be used. The evaluation is stopped for this offer, and the next gateway offer in the repository is evaluated. This is done until all offers in the repository have been evaluated, or the maximum number of offers, set by the import policy, is reached.

The interface intersection involved in stage 1 and 3 have been previously described in [5], a more detailed description of the considerations which have to be taken in stage 2 is described below. First issues regarding the the GDL interpreter during the gateway offer registering process is discussed. Then a discussion of the role of the GDL interpreter during gateway searches is discussed.

4.2   The GDL Interpreter

The *GDL interpreter* must evaluate gateway specifications in two different situations. The first is when a gateway export its offer, and the other is when a client searches for a particular service offer. These two cases have to be handled a little differently.

Registering Gateways in the Repository. One of the main tasks for the trader when a new service advertisement is exported, is to evaluate the soundness of this. The trader parses the GDL description to create the tables holding the interface descriptions and the intermediate code for the dependency description. Apart from syntax errors in the description, there are other semantic errors which has to be checked for in order to determine if this is a valid description. Also these errors should be caught by the trader when an exporter tries to make an offer. If some given attribute value does not hold for a given dependency, then the service offer is rejected, and the exporter is notified of the reason for the rejection.

4.3   Gateway Lookup

The GDL interpreter is also involved when searching for gateway offers. The interpretation of missing attribute values is however different for searches. While it is considered an error in the specification if a dependency does not hold during gateway offer evaluation, a dependency which does not hold initially is not considered an error during the search phase. The dependency is made true again by changing the conditions which makes if false.

If a dependency statement refers to `attrS[14]`, but there is no value "14" for attribute `attrS`, then this indicates that this configuration have been removed from the set of possible configurations for this attribute as a result of and `intersect()`, between the interface of this attribute and another interface. It is however required that the dependency holds, so in order to make it hold, some attribute values of other attributes involved in this dependency might have to be removed. If the dependency had been for example:

(**IF** attrS[14] **THEN** = attrR);

and "14" was not among the remaining values of `attrS`, then the value "14" has to be removed from the set of remaining attributes of `attrR`.

Similar checks are performed for all dependency statements, and the set of interface capabilities resulting from this evaluation is then used in the next stage of the gateway search.

4.4   Performance Evaluation

For the performance of the trader, the most important part is the execution of queries for clients searching for gateway offers. Registering gateway offers will for most parts be done at start-up time, and a few will be registered or removed during run-time. Clients importing gateway offers will be the main activity for the trader. This takes place during run-time, with users waiting for a fast response. For this reason, only the performance of the trader when doing query() at the Lookup interface have been evaluated. Measurement are all done locally. Thus, communication overhead is not considered. Furthermore, parsing of the source media object and sink media object interface descriptions are not part of the results presented. They are only done once for each search. Their performance were checked, and their contribution to the overall search time was found to be negligible.

The experiment was conducted on a 1GHz Pentium 3 processor ThinkPad T22, having 384MB of RAM. The computer was running the Linux Read Hat 7.1 operating system. The source code was compiled using the Objective Caml high-performance native-code compiler ocamlopt version 3.04 [9].

The evaluation was done by registering gateway offers of different complexity at the trader. Three complexity classes were used. *Simple* gateways consisting of a single element in its audio flow. This element consisted of 5 attributes with their given values. 5 dependency statements described the dependency between attributes of the sink and the source interface. The second class, of *medium* complexity, consisted of a video flow with a single element having 10 attributes, and 10 dependency statements. As the third and most *complex* experiment, these two elements where combined into a flow which offered both audio or video, or only audio. The total number of dependencies where 15. Most of the attributes contained only a few attribute values, e.g: depth = {8, 16, 24, 32} and dependency statements mostly contained a single dependency, e.g: out.depth <= in.depth.

For all experiments the source and sink media objects did not match directly. The gateways used where all suitable to be used between the media objects. The reason for this choice, is that it is more costly to evaluate the usefulness of a gateway which matches, than for one which can not be used. If a gateway offer is determined to be of no use during the first intersection, then the last two stages of the query() are not needed. Thus, populating the trader with such offers, would make the trader seem to perform much better. Thus, we are ensuring that the trader performs all stages during the evaluation.

Figure 4 gives an illustration of the performance of the trader. The trader was populated with between 10 and 200 filters of the three classes described. As can be seen from the figure, the cost of searching through a set of gateways scales linearly to the number of filters. Searching through complex specifications are more costly than for simple gateway specifications. This behavior was expected.

In addition to the above evaluation, more detailed inspection on the relative time spent within the three major stages of the search were also conducted. These evaluations revealed that most of the time is spent in interpreting the dependency statements. Between 90-96% of the time was consumed by this stage. Table 1 shows the relative time spent in each of the three stages, for searches of the three classes of filters.

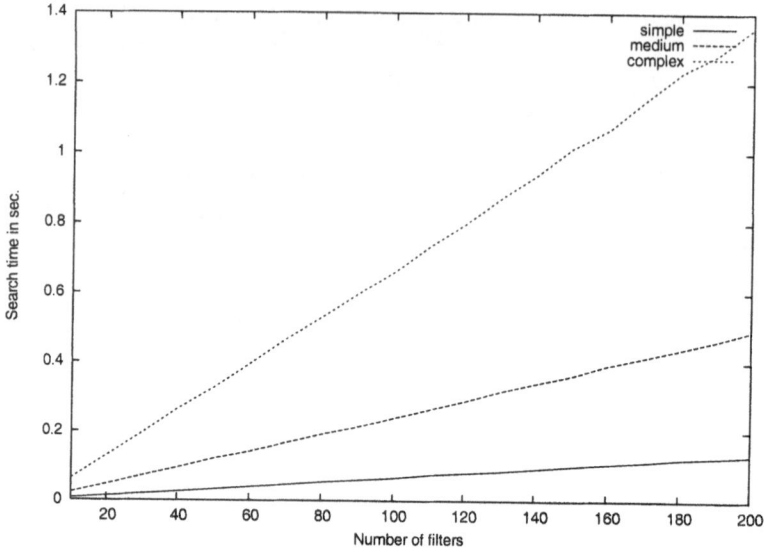

Fig. 4. Time used searching through the trader's filter repository

Table 1. Relative performance of search stages

Complexity	Percentage of time spent in search		
	Intersect 1	Dependency	Intersect 2
Simple	4.34%	91.57%	4.09%
Medium	4.74%	90.98%	4.28%
Complex	1.94%	95.47%	2.59%

4.5   Discussion

Our prototype implementation seems to scale linearly, with complexity $O(n)$. Locating a gateway is a search problem, so ideally it should be $O(log(n))$. Obtaining $O(log(n))$ requires that there is some ordering amongst the elements being searched. This far we have not been able find a way to order the gateway descriptions. Thus, it has to be searched through a list of offers one by one, resulting in a complexity of $O(n)$. Some increased performance might be gained by ensuring that both for intersection of interfaces and evaluation of dependency statements, attributes which are more discriminating that others are always evaluated first. Attribute `encoding` will typically be such an attribute.

It should also be noticed that in the experiments conducted, all searches had matching offers. Matching offers result in that all stages of the search are executed. In the general case a searches will often fail at the first stage, resulting in that the more costly second stage is avoided for this particular gateway offer is avoided.

For a low number of gateway offers the search time of our prototype might be acceptable for certain applications. But if many offers are required and/or the request rate becomes high, then more effort has will have to go into the optimizing the trader in order for it to be useful.

The observation that most of the time is spent interpreting the dependency part of GDL, is an observation which might be useful in order to boost overall performance. If some media stream becomes particular popular, and that format and QoS properties of the stream is different from what is required for most of the receivers, caching techniques might be used to boots performance. In such cases it might be more efficient to store the "new" interface which is inferred from the media source interface and a gateway, among the possible set of configurations of the given media source. This way, computing resources can be considerably reduced on the cost of more storage usage. Which media sources and gateways which will be pre-computed can be decided by some caching policy. So far we have done no work in this direction, but we observe that this might be an option to consider should gateway trading become a bottleneck in the system.

Another approach to optimize the performance of the trader, might be to execute stage 1 and a modified version of stage 3 before stage 2. The modification of stage 3 is that it retrieves its values from the service offer in the similar way as stage 1 does. Stage 2 is only executed if both stage 1 and stage 2 results in a valid set of capabilities. If so this might be a valid offer, and stage 2 is executed to evaluate if the offer is valid. This way non useful offers are removed by executing less costly operations.

The size of a gateway description will typically be in the order of 5 to 15 attributes for each of the entities in the stream. For example, Sun's Java Media Framework [20] uses at most 10 attributes to describe properties of audio and video formats. The size of a gateway supporting both audio and video will thus be in the order of 20-30 attributes. Between 2-10 attribute values for each attribute seem like an reasonable estimate. For most of the attributes, there will be a dependency between the attributes at each interface, so there will be between 20-30 dependency statements in the specification of a typical gateway.

5 Related Work

Supporting media processing within the network has been proposed as a solution for solving the heterogeneity problem. Usage of video gateways are suggested by Turletti and Bolot[22], as an alternative to layered coding, when the receivers have different bandwidth requirements. In [26] Yeadon et. al. creates a set of filters which implements and demonstrate the idea. Amir et. al. [2] design and implements a video gateway to address the problem of heterogeneity, in particular difference in bandwidth.

Work on locating media gateways have been an area of research. In the AGLP control protocol proposed by Ooi and van Renesse [17], programmable Internet servers which process multimedia stream are discovered. The protocol requires clients to upload the media processing gateway program. A multicast extension is proposed, in which several clients can take advantage of the same media gateway. The search criteria when locating a media gateway is its processing capabilities, and placement along the source to sink path. Placement is of interest in order to take advantage of bandwidth reduction as much as possible. The work of Xu et. al. [25] also deals with locating media gateways in the MeGaDip protocol. This protocol takes location and resource situation into account when discovering gateways.

The BMA protocol proposed by Rosenberg and Schulzrinne [11] deals with issues in locating gateways to the public switched telephone network, within the Internet. It is tailored toward voice over IP applications. The Service Location Protocol [23] propose standards for locating services within the Internet.

Microsoft's DirectShow [14] and Sun's Java Media Framework [20] uses the concept of filters. They are components which can be plugged together to process media streams. They are mainly targeted used at the endpoints, as part of the application. Evaluation of the usefulness of a particular filter is done by the application it selves, and not treated as an additional service provided by the binding framework.

Our work differs from the above in that we emphasizes the description of media gateways. In particular we build our work on a type model for describing flow types. The properties of media gateways are taken out of the gateway implementations them selves, and treated as meta-information. This increases the flexibility of the binding framework in that it enables reasoning about the usefulness of gateways without having access to their implementation. Thus, the plan for binding configurations can be created at the meta-level, before the binding protocols start to install/activate the particular components of the binding. Gateways can be inserted anywhere in the distributed computing environment, given that technology domain provides *active service* [1] facilities. Currently our work does not address the issue of resource availability or physical location of gateways.

6   Conclusion and Further Work

A binding framework which supports dynamic creation of bindings have been proposed. The aim is to provide better support to application developers when developing distributed multimedia applications. It provides developers with higher level abstractions. Heterogeneity of participants are solved by the introduction of media gateways. A model for describing gateways and algorithms to evaluate suitability of gateways is presented. Based on this gateway descriptions and algorithms, a prototype gateway trader has been implemented. The performance of the prototype was evaluated. The trader seems to work satisfactory when the number of gateway offers or the number of request of stays low. More work should be done in order to make the trader scale better, but a really good solution to this problem seems hard to find.

Our experience with the framework is that it seems to be a feasible approach to automatically solve incompatibility between participants in distributed multimedia bindings. In further work we plan on investigate how this binding framework can be mapped down to concrete realizations. In particular we are interesting in multi-party bindings spanning multiple *technology domains* [8]. Resource management issues should also be considered for further versions of the framework. For a solution like this to be feasible in a global scale, it is important that the structure and semantics of interface descriptions and gateway descriptions are standardized.

References

1. E. Amir, S. McCanne, and R. Katz. An Active Service Framework and its Application to Real-Time Multimedia Transcoding. In Proceedings of BIBLIOGRAPHY 190 SIGCOMM, September 1998. , 1998.
2. E. Amir, S. McCanne, and H. Zhang. An Application Level Video Gateway. In *ACM Multimedia 95*, pages 255–266, San Francisco, California, November 5-9 1995.
3. G. Blair, G. Coulson, and N. Davies. Adaptive middleware for mobile multimedia applications. In *Proceedings of the 8th International Workshop on Network and Operating System Support for Digital Audio and Video (NOSSDAV)*, pages 259–273, 1997.
4. F. Eliassen. A Conformance Relationship for Stream Interfaces. In *2nd Int'l Conf on Formal Methods in Open Object-based Distributed Systems (FMOODS'97)*, Canterbury, July 1997.
5. F. Eliassen and S. Mehus. Type Checking Stream Flow Endpoints. In *Middleware'98*, pages 305–322, The Lake District, England, September 1998. Chapman & Hall.
6. F. Eliassen and J. R. Nicol. Supporting Interoperation of Continuous Media Objects. *Theory and Practice of Object System*, 2(2):95–117, 1996.
7. T. Fitzpatrick, G. Blair, G. Coulson, N. Davies, and P. Robin. Supporting Adaptive Multimedia Applications through Open Bindings. In *4th International Conference on Configurable Distributed Systems (ICCDS'98)*, Annapolis, Maryland, USA, May 1998.
8. C. Hesselman and H. Eertink. Broadcasting Multimedia Channels in Future Mobile Systems. In *PROMS 2001, LNCS 2213*, pages 35–43, 2001.
9. INRIA. Objective Caml. http://caml.inria.fr/.
10. ISO/IEC. CD 10746-1 — ITU Recomandation X.901, Open Distribted Processing - Reference Model - Part 1: Overview., 1995.
11. J. Rosenberg and H. Schulzrinne. Internet Telephony Gateway Location. In *Proceedings of the Conference on Computer Communications (IEEE Infocom)*, San Francisco, California, USA, March/April 1998.
12. T. Kristensen and T. Plagemann. Enabling Flexible QoS Support in the Object Request Broker COOL. In *Proceedings of International Workshop on Distributed Real-Time Systems (IWDRS 2000), in conjunction with the 20th International Conference on Distributed Computing Systems (ICDCS 2000)*, Taipei, Taiwan, Apr. 2000.
13. D. Lindsey and P. Linington. RIVUS: A Stream Template Language for Capturing Multimedia Requirements. In *Lecture Notes in Computer Science (LNCS 1052)*, pages 259–277. Springer Verlag, 1995.

14. Microsoft Corporation. DirectX 8, DirectShow, 2000.
15. Object Management Group. OMG IDL CORBA/IIOP 2.2 Specification.
16. Object Management Group. CORBAservices: Common Object Service Specification. Technical report, Object Management Group, Framingham, MA, 1997.
17. W. T. Ooi and R. van Renesse. An adaptive protocol for locating programmable media gateways. In *ACM Multimedia 2000*, Los Angeles, California, USA, October/November 2000.
18. H. Rafaelsen and F. Eliassen. Trading and Negotiating Stream Bindings. In *IFIP/ACM International Conference on Distributed Systems Platforms (Middleware'2000)*, New York, USA, April 2000.
19. H. O. Rafaelsen and F. Eliassen. Trading Media Gateways with CORBA Trader. In *International Symposium on Distributed Objects and Applications (DOA'01)*, Rome, Italy, September 2001.
20. Sun Microsystems. Java Media Framework, version 2.1.1, 2001. Sun Microsystems, Inc. 901 San Antonio Road, Palo Alto, California, 9430 3, U.S.A.
21. C. Topolcic. Experimental Internet Stream Protocol, Version 2 (ST-II). Internet RFC 1190, October 1990.
22. T. Turletti and J.-C. Bolot. Issues with multicast video distribution in heterogeneous packet networks. In *Proc. 6th International Workshop on PACKET VIDEO*, pages F3.1–3.4, Portland, Oregon, 26-27 September 1994.
23. J. Veizades, E. Guttman, C. Perkins, and S. Kaplan. *Service Location Protocol.* IETF RFC-2165, June 1997.
24. M. Weiser. The computer for the 21st century. *Scientific American*, pages 94–104, September 1991.
25. D. Xu, K. Nahrstedt, and D. Wichadakul. MeGaDiP: A Wide-Area Media Gateway Discovery Protocol. In *19th IEEE International Performance, Computing, and Communications Conference (IPCCC 2000)*, Phoenix, AZ, USA, February 2000.
26. N. Yeadon, F. Garcia, D. Hutchison, and D. Shepherd. Filters: QoS Support Mechanisms for Mulipeer Communications. *IEEE Journal on Selected Areas in Computing (JSAC) special issue on Distributed Multimedia Systems and Technology*, 14(7):1245–1262, September 1996.
27. L. Zhang, S. Deering, D. Estrin, S. Shenker, and D. Zappala. RSVP: A New Resource ReSerVation Protocol. *IEEE Network*, September 1993.